ESTATE PLANNING AND DRAFTING
Third Edition

By

Regis W. Campfield
Professor of Law & Marilyn Jean Johnson Distinguished Law Faculty Fellow.
Southern Methodist University Dedman School of Law

AMERICAN CASEBOOK SERIES®

THOMSON

WEST

Mat # 15591137

American Casebook Series and West Group are trademarks registered in the U.S. Patent and Trademark Office.

© 2007 Thomson/¢est
    610 Opperman Drive
    P.O. Box 64526
    St. Paul, MN 55164–0526
    1–800–328–9352

ISBN: 978–0–314–23136–9

TEXT IS PRINTED ON 10% POST
CONSUMER RECYCLED PAPER

1st Reprint — 2009

For Mary, Allison (and Mike) and Claire (and John) (and Matthew, Laura, Mary, Jane and the other grandchildren to come) and particularly my father and the memory of my mother who together had the dream, the energy, the will and the love.

r.w.c.

*

Preface

The term "estate planning" is sometimes criticized as being overused, but no other term describes as well the process by which individuals arrange their affairs in an orderly way for management during life and for disposition during life and/or after death. This is a "problems-driven" book, meaning that cases and rulings are included as resource materials for use in solving the problems. The materials are arranged in the fashion that individuals think about wealth transmission, beginning with wills, going on to trusts for non-tax reasons, then to tax planning at death and, finally, to lifetime tax planning. Recognizing that users of these materials will have different objectives and different levels of sophistication, the materials are arranged so that each chapter can be used independently of the chapters which follow or precede it. In each case, the issues are approached transactionally, i.e., in terms of what people want to do and why they want to do it. Thus, users who are new to estate planning may want to concentrate on the non-tax drafting materials and limit attention to tax considerations, such as, perhaps, the marital deduction materials. On the other hand, those well-grounded in fundamental non-tax aspects of wills and trusts will largely ignore these materials and focus on the basic tax-oriented planning materials. Materials range from those on marital deduction, the bypass trust, generation skipping, lifetime gifting (e.g., *Crummy* trusts to § 529 plans, retirement distribution planning, compensation planning, and planning for the person with a small business as well as counseling the client). It is expected that users will customize the materials by selecting those portions of interest to them, utilizing the convenient paragraph numbering system (with the full expectation that the paragraphs selected will stand alone and not be dependent on other portions of the materials). This "pick and choose" feature renders the materials accessible for the sophisticated (the experienced user) and not so sophisticated.

The time available for use of these materials will vary. They are designed to be used in two-, three-, and four-hour courses. While it is thought unlikely that an instructor would assign the entire book for less than a six-hour course, most of it can be profitably covered in four hours. Two-hour seminars in will drafting could easily be accommodated as could two-hour seminars in the basics of estate planning. There is a "Hot Topics" chapter—entitled Discounts, Creditors and Beneficiaries—that itself could almost be the basis of a two-hour seminar. Similarly, Appendix B includes a client fact pattern that is largely the basis for 12 discreet projects that could form the basis of a two-hour seminar or serve as written assignments for students engaged in a more 3 or 4 hour traditional course. All well and good, but most users will probably devote three hours to these materials. The volume itself includes many problems and should be seen as a resource, eclectic use being expected, encouraged, and facilitated by a virtual paragraph numbering system that facilitates assignments of bits and pieces of this 30 chapter volume.

Recommended assignments, depending on the user's objectives and available times, will vary. However, here are some suggestions:

1. For a two-credit-hour course or seminar in the basics of will and trust drafting, Chapters 1–5; 13; 15; and 18 (including, possibly, Projects 1–2);

2. For a two-credit-hour seminar in the basics of estate planning, Chapters 1–2; 13; 15–20; and 23 (including, possibly, or perhaps based around Projects 4–8);

3. For a three-hour basic estate planning course, Chapters 1–2; 6–11; 13–20; and 30 (including, possibly, or perhaps based around Projects 4–8);

4. For a four-credit-hour course, Chapters 1–23; and 30 (including, possibly, or perhaps based round, Projects 3–9 and 11);

5. For advanced seminars (which presuppose experience with the concepts developed in the remainder of the materials), Chapters 12 and 21 (Discounts, Creditors and Beneficiaries) and Chapters 24–30, also supplemented by other materials of the user's choice from the balance of the text (including, possibly, or perhaps based around, Projects 9–12).

While these materials are mainly classroom-oriented, they should also serve to provide a structured introduction to estate planning for professionals who want to approach the subject transactionally. Nonetheless, the materials, while robust in places, are for instructional purposes, i.e., they are teaching materials, project and problem based. They should not be relied upon as the basis of professional advice.

Users are invited to suggest improvements and additions to the text for purposes of future editions.

REGIS W. CAMPFIELD

December, 2006

Acknowledgments to the Third Edition

Every project of this magnitude requires the help and support of many people. One most important person to this project has been Sheridith Yonash of the publisher's editorial staff. Her good spirit and gracious and generous attention to detail was a great contribution.

Kathleen Vaughan, my retired former assistant (who had contributed significantly to the 1st and 2nd editions), came back from retirement as needed and contributed in many ways, at many times, to this 3rd edition, through many drafts, in the most thorough fashion and I am indebted to her for her untiring efforts and her limitless good cheer (which is a significant accomplishment having put up with a seemingly unending string of demanding projects over almost 25 years). Jan Spann, my current assistant, does all that and more and I am most appreciative. Excellent support has been provided by Michelle Oswald, as well. Carolyn Yates gets a special thanks for undertaking much bibliographic detail with special, timely, careful, and greatly appreciated attention.

I thank, too, the many students who labored through earlier editions as well as drafts of these materials and, in so doing, were responsible for many improvements. Moreover, over the years, numerous students provided research assistance. Their efforts are very much appreciated. Notable contributors to the 2nd edition were David Mao, John Fletcher, Brett Enzor, and Kate Warner. Sarah Patel Pacheco contributed to almost every chapter of the 2nd edition and her work was of the highest professional quality, reflecting both maturity of thought and careful analysis. She was extraordinarily helpful. William W. Merrill, an LLM graduate tax student and Dallas attorney made a like contribution in scope and breath, one of extraordinary value, to the 3rd edition. Kathy P. Boyett, also an LLM graduate tax student and Dallas attorney, made a similar contribution to the life insurance chapter. Other law students contributing to this 3rd edition in particularly helpful ways were Glen David Webb (LLM Grad Tax), Melanie Ann Spriggs, Leisa Pulliam (LLM Grad Tax), Frank Lawson, Matt Brown, Jim Stanford, Ryan Sweeney, and Crystal Gobble. Melanie Ann Spriggs also provided exemplary assistance with the Teachers' Manual.

I especially thank Santo (Sandy) Bisignano, a former student from my time at Notre Dame Law School, and now a Dallas, Texas, practitioner, a widely recognized presenter at continuing legal education conferences, and a member of the American College of Trust and Estate Counsel, for his good counsel, friendship, and allowing me to include several short memoranda as part of the student projects in Appendix B.

Dean John B. Attanasio merits a special acknowledgement because of his unfailing confidence in his faculty and the support he has given us all. His generously provided summer research support is especially appreciated and acknowledged.

Similarly, this project could not have begun, let alone concluded, without the help of SMU's law library staff. Particular acknowledgment must be made of the interest, attentiveness, and creativity of Gregory Ivy, Associate Law Librarian, who cheerfully and successfully managed the many library tasks generated by this project (and who was always willing to respond to the next crisis in the most competent manner imaginable).

While errors and shortcomings are mine alone, I acknowledge most helpful comments, suggestions, and inspiration (for this or prior editions or drafts thereof) offered by James Griffin (Dallas) (chapter 28) and Natalie Choate (chapters 29-30).

I have benefitted in countless ways from the counsel of my colleague, Professor Joseph W. McKnight, and from the continuing dialogue I have with the tax teachers here at SMU, my colleagues, Henry Lischer, Jack Mylan, and Christopher Hanna and my new wills and trust colleague, Joshua Tate. So, too, I note the work and friendship of my former Dean and colleague, Charles O'Neill Galvin, whose scholarship in the tax policy field, among others, has long been widely recognized for its significance.

For inspiration I note the special role of Frank S. Berall, a distinguished Connecticut practitioner. His friendship and collaboration on many different projects over thirty years has been of immeasurable personal and professional significance. I salute also my former colleague, Professor Thomas L. Shaffer, whose scholarship and insight have contributed much to helping lawyers understand that communication between lawyer and client is critical to the representational process.

With appreciation I note, too, the support and friendship of my former student, Roger Stanley Johnson, MD, whose generous funding resulted in the establishment of the Marilyn Jeanne Johnson Distinguished Law Faculty Fellowship here at SMU, the fellowship honoring the memory of Roger's spouse. I was genuinely honored by my appointment as the first holder of that fellowship.

For their friendship and the chance to observe their scholarship I thank and applaud the many professionals who take to the continuing education pulpit (particularly those who have presented these past 32 years at the Notre Dame Tax and Estate Planning Institute which I have chaired since inception) to share their insight and experience with their fellow practitioners.

For never ending support, kindly, caringly, and generously given, I thank my wife, Mary, my daughters, Allison and Claire, and particularly my parents. I thank, too, my son-in-law, Dallas lawyer Michael E. Taten, for his kind, caring and generously given, hands on efforts with management, technical and editorial matters.

REGIS W. CAMPFIELD

December, 2006

*

Acknowledgments to the Second Edition

While these materials have been substantially revised for this 3rd edition, particularly worth repeating are these acknowledgments from the 2nd edition.

Chapter 24

Some of the text material in this chapter, particularly that relating expressly to Super Electronics, is an adaptation of an article, Planning for Closely Held Business Interests, prepared by John R. Cohan and Laurence Peters of the Los Angeles firm of Irell & Manella and is used with permission. It appeared in its original version in 3 Notre Dame Est. Plan Inst. 589 (R. Campfield, ed. 1979). The editor takes full responsibility for all modifications, changes, and supplementation made in the original text to adapt it for presentation in these materials.

Chapter 27

In preparing this chapter for the first edition, liberal use was made of materials supplied by Frank S. Berall of the Hartford, Connecticut law firm of Copp & Berall. The original version of Mr. Berall's materials was published as A Comprehensive Guide to Tax Aspects of Charitable Giving, in 5 Notre Dame Est. Plan. Inst. 1131 (R. Campfield ed. 1981) and was used here with permission of Mr. Berall. In addition, the format of some of the tables were based on those which appear in Arthur Andersen & Co., Tax Economics of Charitable Giving (7th ed. 1979).

Chapter 29

The material contained in parts 29-B through 29-C (¶¶ 29,051-29,401) has been updated since its appearance in the first edition. The original materials were excerpted (with editing) or based in part upon an article by Morton Zalutsky, Income and Estate Tax Planning with Qualified Plans, 4 Notre Dame Est. Plan. Inst. 115 (R. Campfield, ed. 1980)

*

Editing Conventions

References to "§" and "Reg §" are references to the Internal Revenue Code of 1986 and its implementing regulations except in a few instances where a different reference is clear from the context. All references to "UPC § _____" are references to the Uniform Probate Code and may be found in Unif. Probate Code (amended 1993), 8 U.L.A. (1998 & Supp. 2006). Uniform Acts may be found at http://www.nccusl.org.

While deletions in reproduced materials are oftentimes shown by asterisks ("***"), particularly when the deletions are material, the effort to indicate deletions has been inconsistent in the sense that it was a function of varying situational objectives. Certainly citations have been freely omitted without so indicating. Moreover, "§" and "Reg. §" have been freely substituted for longer references, e.g., "section of the estate tax regulations", without indication. Case names have been italicized or not italicized throughout in an effort at consistency.

*

Permissions

Excerpted materials have been included with appropriate permissions. In particular, the following permissions are specially noted:

Robert Bandy, Statement of Principles of the Estate Planning Attorney in Texas, 41 Tex. B.J. 169, 169-72, 174 (1978). These excerpts are reprinted with permission of the author and the copyright holder, the State Bar of Texas.

J. Thomas Eubank, The Future for Estate Lawyers, 10 Real Prop., Prob. & Tr. J. 223, 224-27 (1975). The excerpt is reprinted by permission of the author and the Section of Real Property, Probate and Trust Law. Copyright 1975, American Bar Association, Chicago, Illinois.

Harrop A. Freeman, The Role of Lawyers as Counselors, 7 Wm. And Mary L. Rev., 203, 207-208 (1966). Reprinted by permission. Copyright 1966 by the College of William and Mary.

Sussman, Cates, and Smith, Will Making: An Examination of Client and Lawyer Attitudes, 23 U. Fla. L. Rev. 25, 25-29 (1970). The excerpt is reprinted with the permission of the University of Florida Law Review. Copyright 1970.

Thomas L. Shaffer, Models for the "Estate Planning" Counselor, 6 U. Miami Est. Plan. Inst., at ¶ 72-11, 1100-1103 (1972). The excerpt is reprinted with the permission of the author and copyright holder.

*

Summary of Contents

———————

PART VII.   FINANCIAL AND RETIREMENT COMPENSATION PLANNING

Table of Contents

PART III.   TRANSFERS FOR THE BENEFIT
OF THE TRANSFEROR

Table of Cases

The principal cases are in bold type. Cases cited or discussed in the text are roman type. References are to paragraphs. Cases cited in principal cases and within other quoted materials are not included.

*

Table of Statutes

*

Table of Treasury Regulations

Table of Technical Advice Memoranda

*

Table of Revenue Rulings

Table of Revenue Procedures

*

Table of Private Letter Rulings

Table of Internal Revenue Service Notices

---

*

Table of Internal Revenue Service
Actions on Decisions

---

*

ESTATE PLANNING AND DRAFTING

Third Edition

*

Chapter 1

INTRODUCTION

A. OBJECTIVES

[¶ 1001]

This book contains not only an array of problems but also a generous supply of resources for solving these problems. The materials were developed from the perspective that problem orientation is important in teaching advanced law courses. The function of the problems is to focus the user's inquiry on problems commonly experienced by practitioners. The problems are designed to enable the user to develop techniques of analysis, synthesis, and communication, it being toward these goals that lawyers' activities have been traditionally directed. Perhaps it is also appropriate to say that learning is made much more interesting when done in a problem context.

With the exception of the Internal Revenue Code and Treasury Regulations, the basic resource materials necessary to enable the user to perform lawyer-like problem-solving assignments have been included in this volume. For that reason, the materials are also suitable for individual use and for use in courses that do not emphasize problems. In addition, the Appendix B contains assignments that can be the basis for an in class case files experience or alternatively will support research initiatives beyond the casebook. Only by "doing," in conjunction with classwork, will the student appreciate the careful work required of practitioners.

Clients refuse to pay legal fees that are perceived as inflated. Yet advances in technology require major capital investments and new skills on the part of both support staff and professional alike. The pressure to reduce costs is obviously enormous. Since lawyers must search for cost-effective delivery techniques while trying to maintain appropriate standards of care, competitive pressures can lead to "short-cuts" and less than the best work. In the face of these real life demands, ethics instruction alone—even when accompanied by the ever present risk of the malpractice lawsuit—is hardly sufficient to allow maintenance or development of appropriate standards of care in the face of increasingly complex tax statutes and regulations. Only technical competence of the kind that makes solutions to commonly encountered problems almost second nature can insure that appropriate standards of care and craftsmanship prevail. The materials and problems in this book were collected so that the "hard" problems could be considered in the classroom— and understanding and appreciation of the lawyer's obligation would there begin. From these experiences should come the beginnings of the self-confidence and self-esteem necessary to find responsible alternatives when "it can't be done" the way the client wants it to be done.

The scope of this book purports to be more than what is commonly understood to be described by the term *estate planning*. More important, it is more than what is commonly understood by labels such as *taxation of estates, trusts,* and *beneficiaries*. This book is intended to support not only specialized estate planning seminars but also the newer estate planning courses and the new taxation of trusts and estates courses. Basic concepts are developed in a planning context. Yet, at the same time, the reader is expected to explore the policy aspects of the scheme of federal taxation of trusts, estates, and beneficiaries. The opportunity for such exploration is created by asking the reader to examine the commonly used techniques of wealth transfer in the context of developing federal tax policy initiatives, initiatives aimed at protecting the fisc from creative professionals who seemingly are able to find new pathways through the labyrinth. The last 10 years have seen the development of the limited liability company and the family limited partnership while witnessing the effective closing off of estate freezes and generation-skipping trusts. As one avenue closes, another is found. By exploring these techniques, readers will develop skills of analysis, synthesis, communication, and application as they integrate statutes, administrative regulations, and judicial interpretation.

In the estate planning area there is only one fundamental concept or problem. Despite what have been undoubtedly the very best of efforts, no one seems to have found a way to take along all of one's property—or even most of it—on that final journey. The task, then, is disposition, oftentimes in favor of lineal descendants, in a way that is meaningful, perhaps expressing love and affection, or a sense of fairness or justice. In most cases, the prospective decedent will want to so arrange his or her affairs so that the property will be largely intact when received by the beneficiaries of his or her largesse. Professor Thomas L. Shaffer once explained one aspect of client motivation as living on through your property. The estate planner's duty is one, then, of considering the different kinds of property commonly held and proposing alternative dispositive schemes that accomplish the traveler's goals at minimum cost.

An ancillary issue concerns how the testator's exercise of "freedom of disposition" impacts public policy considerations relating to the accumulation of wealth, the need for revenue for governmental purposes, and the social implications of possibly vast accumulations in the hands of a few. While it could be ventured that inability to control the gene pool will solve the vast accumulation problem, there remains the tension between public policy and the goals of the individual taxpayer. Having said that, it still remains to be said that the learning in these materials is about not many problems but about different aspects of the same problem.

¶ 1001

B. MOTIVATIONS

[¶ 1051]

Understanding these materials requires technical competence (which can be acquired from the materials themselves) as well as some feeling for client motivations (which must be acquired from life's experiences using one's own developed sensitivity).

Motivation for wealth planning, for some, means providing an orderly scheme for the transfer of property—and nothing more. For many others, however, the process is more complex. Intending to be provocative, here are some other possible motivations for what people do in wealth planning (which you may want to add to):

1. *Give it away but keep the benefit of it.* This is what everyone wants to do—along with live forever. This suggests that, for many, there is little motivation for wealth-shifting lifetime gifts except tax minimization.

2. *Give it away but keep control of it.* This, too, is what everyone wants to do.

3. *Who knows better than me what's good for thee.* This means that the donor is committed to controlling the enjoyment of the property that he or she gives to others. It is based on the fundamental notion that there are few persons who get pleasure from watching loved ones dissipate property that has been accumulated over time through hard work—and, perhaps, a little luck (the latter being one factor that is conveniently ignored when explaining financial success).

4. *If it feels good, do it.* This is what donors remember their children as having at one time said. Donors commonly have this recollection when thinking about structuring gifts to the children, either by will or by trust.

5. *All I want to do is protect you from the predators of the world— (silently) and the biggest predator of them all is you.* Donors who say this are most likely to create trusts that last for a very, very long time.

6. *Control—without adverse tax consequences.* Everyone wants this. Donors wants this. Donees want this. But to each it means something different. The donor wants to control the donee's enjoyment of the transferred property. The donee wants unrestricted access to the transferred property. Practically speaking, control—be it from different perspectives—is the basis for much of the planning suggested in these materials.

7. *Justice and love.* Clients want to be perceived as being fair. And most love and want to be loved.

Beyond that, keep in mind that there are two kinds of clients: (1) those whose motivation is solely tax planning and (2) those whose motivation is both tax planning and property management. Many times the client does not know into which category he or she fits. There are some advantages to

¶ 1051

professional property management—even in cases where tax planning is not as important or even unimportant. Moreover, some of the alleged drawbacks to professional management may be more myth than reality. Nonetheless, some clients want their beneficiaries to have all the property management responsibilities. The estate planning professional can be of help here in sorting through these alternatives.

Rare is the client who does not care about tax minimization—despite saying things like, "We're gonna spend it all." No one really means this—except those who have little or no alternative. Finally, love is at the root of almost all decision-making. We tend not to give property to those whom we do not love (although fairly often concepts of justice and fairness get mixed into the equation). And, if you have ever watched a check for the life insurance proceeds being delivered to the beneficiary, you know that the hardest of hearts can soften—much as the insured had hoped would happen.

C. ROLE OF ESTATE ("DEATH") TAXATION

[¶ 1061]

The Tucson, Arizona, law firm of Fleming & Curti, P.L.C., as part of its regular postings on the internet, offered the following observations as to tax planning, all in the interest of having its readers develop perspective on the role of taxation in their wealth management decision making:

Fleming & Curti, P.L.C., Estate Tax Concerns No Longer Drive Most Planning Decisions

14 Elder Law Issues No. 5, www.elder-law.com (July 31, 2006).

For decades the principal concern of "estate planning" has been to minimize taxes due at death. In recent years (since the estate tax level began to first creep, and then rush, upward beginning in 1998) tax considerations have become less central to estate planning. Those changes, and the remote possibility that the estate tax exemption level might drop back to $1,000,000 in 2011, have made uncertainty the biggest problem to tackle these days. How can you plan in a shifting estate tax environment?

First determine if you are concerned about estate taxes at all. If not, you can make your plans based on what you want to accomplish—and not spend time, money or energy on planning for a tax that your estate will simply not bear.

If your entire estate—including life insurance and the cash value of your retirement plans—is less than $1,000,000 then you stop worrying about estate taxes. Even if Congress makes no changes, your estate will pay no tax on your death—and Arizona, like most states, effectively repealed its state estate tax by failing to make changes after federal law revisions.

Incidentally, even though your estate may not be taxable it still might be larger than average. Slightly more than 1% of decedents would have to file estate tax returns at the $1,000,000 threshold.

¶ **1051**

If your estate is larger than that, but still less than $2,000,000, you can worry—but not much. You will not be subjected to any estate tax if you die between now and 2011, and virtually no one believes that Congress will let the law drop the estate tax level back below the current exemption level.

If your estate is worth more than $2,000,000, there's some good news mixed in with the bad: you are among the less than 1% of the population who needs to worry about estate taxation. And you are likely to see relief even from the current level of burden, as Congress is discussing lifting the limit to $5,000,000—which would mean that fewer than 3,000 estates each year would pay any tax.

After reviewing the real likelihood of your estate paying any tax, you may still feel like you need to make plans. If you are married, one easy choice is to establish a "credit shelter" trust arrangement—sometimes referred to as a "decedent's trust" or an "A/B" trust division. Even better for most people, you might look into a "disclaimer" trust, allowing the surviving spouse to make decisions about estate taxes after the death of the first spouse. This approach can double the amount that escapes taxation.

Still worried about estate taxes? Consider regular gifts to your children and grandchildren, or charitable bequests (and gifts). Now focus on what you actually want to accomplish with your estate plan.

D. ROLE OF INCOME TAXATION

[¶ 1081]

Income is income until it is taxed to someone as income! Despite the importance of this notion, the "when" and "how" (or "if") are ever important in the estate plan. As for "when", income tax deferral over the lifetime of younger generation beneficiaries, for example, is a really important opportunity when considering the yet-to-be taxed property held in tax qualified retirement plans and IRAs. ¶¶ 30,754–30,841. Similarly, "when" is the issue in structuring so-called "non[tax] qualified" deferred compensation arrangements (e.g., celebrities, athletes, highly paid professionals and executives): Chapter 28. As for "how", are items of income to be taxed at ordinary income tax rates (as high as 35 percent in 2006) or at preferential capital gain rates (generally 15 percent in 2006 but as low as 5 percent) or even excluded from income taxation if used for qualified college expenses as in the case of distributions from § 529 plans. ¶¶ 19,114. Even a lawyer's choice of business entity for his or her law practice can provide income tax management options. See ¶ 24,435. While seemingly the work of compensation specialists, estate planning professionals often play a major role.

E. ORGANIZATION

[¶ 1101]

The materials in this book are organized so that each chapter builds upon the prior chapter. Yet, at the same time, the instructor can assign only as

¶ 1101

many chapters as time considerations permit, and the student will have an integrated experience even though more ideas remain to be considered in the remainder of the book. More important, despite the building-block approach, the instructor may wish to reorder the chapters or to eliminate several of them. In anticipation of this development, to the extent possible, each chapter stands independently of the others. This is possible because each estate planning technique requires consideration of the entire range of income, estate and gift tax issues.

The problems are approached, first, from the standpoint of the donor who wants, in both life and death, to keep control of the property he or she transfers. Sometimes control is in the form of retained enjoyment. In other instances, it is enough if the donor can control the enjoyment by his or her beneficiaries of the property given to them. The problems are also approached from the standpoint of the donee, the beneficiary, who also wants control, i.e., the ability to enjoy the transferred property without restriction. It is the "right" blend of restriction and freedom that makes for a happy beneficiary. "Happiness" in this sense means: (1) the beneficiary has what to him or her is the degree of access necessary to support the beneficiary's lifestyle and (2) the gifted property "bypasses" the beneficiary's estate for tax purposes at death.

At the conclusion of these materials, the student should be prepared to deal with sophisticated problems, having examined many of the estate planning devices commonly used today.

[¶ 1109]

1. LIVING AND DYING

The instructor may want to consider an unorthodox approach to the scheduling of the counseling chapter. While "Counseling the Client" will be found as the second chapter in these materials, it can be argued that legal counseling is effectively undertaken only when the counselor has a substantive law background. This suggests that counseling should be the last topic considered. While nothing that lawyers do is more important than counseling, the premise of these materials is that property law and taxes so impact decision-making in the wealth transmission area that an understanding of how these substantive considerations affect the wealth transmission process is necessary to even consider actually undertaking the counseling function.

Chapter 3 introduces the subject of intestacy and wills and emphasizes the considerations that cause certain provisions to be common to all well-drafted wills. Also noted is the increasing need for and interest in making body parts available after death as support for the medical advances that permit transplantation to be a viable solution for many whose organs have failed.

The focus of Chapter 4 is on living too long, i.e., living beyond the time when we lose either our ability to manage or our interest in managing ourselves and our property. Guardianships are considered as well as advance directives as to health care. Living wills are important in this process. In widespread use is the living trust, the subject of advertised seminars in most areas. The revocable living trust is the centerpiece of many estate plans, serving as the principal wealth transmission device in use today as well as the technique of choice in providing for property management in periods of disability. Powers of attorney are considered.

Chapter 5 is devoted to drafting for successive enjoyment, i.e., drafting for future interests on the assumption that all but the simplest dispositive schemes provide for successive enjoyment of property and, whenever successive enjoyment is provided for, the donor has created a future interest with all of the implications inherent in such an arrangement. The materials on future interests were organized to demonstrate to the reader that the study of future interests is not an outmoded concept but is, in fact, an even greater imperative today than in earlier times.

To those who have more than an adequate background in wills, trusts, and future interests, Chapters 3 through 5 will be at best a review and a reference. In that sense, these chapters should be useful as a supplement to more traditional materials. Of course, where an integrated estate planning course is offered in lieu of the more traditional separate courses in wills and trusts, Chapters 3 through 5 can satisfy the pedagogical requirements of such a course.

[¶ 1117]

2. TAX CONSIDERATIONS

Chapter 6, "Taxable Transfers: An Introduction," permits the reader to begin to develop a sensitivity to the reach of the federal estate and gift taxes. With the brief introduction afforded by Chapter 6 in mind, Chapter 7, "Transfer Tax Computations: Policy and Practice," demonstrates the scheme used to integrate the federal estate and gift taxes. But Chapter 6 also does much, much more. It causes the reader to appreciate that tax planning is motivated by the "bottom line." Rightly or wrongly, for many taxpayers, the determining factor in choosing among alternative dispositive schemes is the net transfer cost of the alternatives presented to them. One counseling function, then, is to remind the client of "people considerations" and that tax considerations must clearly be of secondary importance.

Income taxes are as important as estate and gift taxes when planning wealth shifts. Understanding, particularly, how income taxes impact trusts (and estates) is preliminary to using trusts. Chapter 8 provides an overview of the salient features, emphasizing the general rule that income kept in a trust is taxed to the trust and income distributed to the trust beneficiaries is taxed to the beneficiaries. Warehousing income in a trust has obvious appeal for estate and gift tax purposes but, with the advent of income tax rate compression as applied to trusts (and estates), serious thought must be given to the trust's distribution provisions. While discretionary distributions have much appeal, "mandatory pay" will often yield income tax savings.

The generation-skipping transfer tax is almost a separate subject. It is dauntingly complex—but remarkably effective in accomplishing its purposes.

Chapter 9 provides a detailed review of the basics, a review that the reader ignores at his or her peril. With a flat tax rate equal to the top estate tax rate—46 percent in 2006—the generation-skipping tax bite is deep and lasting.

[¶ 1125]

3. TRANSFERS FOR THE BENEFIT OF THE TRANSFEROR

Chapter 10, "Retained Interests," is devoted to the one of the most appealing of all tax planning suggestions. The suggestion is that "somehow" it is possible to shield property from the estate tax while keeping both the control and enjoyment of the property during life.

Chapter 11 is about forms of concurrent ownership, ranging from joint tenancy with right of survivorship to community property. Outlined are many of the issues encountered in thinking about joint tenancy with right of survivorship and tenancy by the entirety as a form of ownership for spousal property. Clearly, these forms of ownership are enormously popular. Is that popularity deserved or are the so-called advantages of joint property largely a myth? One point is clear. The taxation of joint property has grown increasingly complex as Congress has attempted to create a fair and equitable system for taxing such property.

Joint tenancy is voluntary. Community property is state imposed, a scheme to reflect the partnership seen by some as inherent in the marriage relationship. Planning for community property raises special problems—including problems that are not unique to community property jurisdictions as it becomes more and more common for workers to reside in both community and separate property states over the course of a lifetime. The property that these migrants take with them when locating to a separate property jurisdiction is burdened with community character. Creative solutions prevail in community property jurisdictions, ranging from community property agreements to so-called widow's election wills (wherein the first spouse to die attempts to control both halves of the community property through his or her will). The widow's election was called a taxpayer's utopia in one Fifth Circuit case.

Estate freezing is a popular expression. It seems to mean that the value of the decedent's property has been frozen for estate tax purposes at some value that is lower than the property's value at the death of the decedent. This wonderfully appealing concept has attracted the attention of Congress, which has produced a comprehensive scheme that both attacks value freezing schemes (by imposing a "zero valuation" rule) while expressly carving out narrow safe havens bearing labels such as "qualified personal residence trust" or QPRT (pronounced "Qpert"). Chapter 12 details these complicated rules and considers some other techniques such as self-canceling installment sales (SCINs) and private annuities. While ignorance of the zero valuation rules is perilous, the investigation of these rules requires tenacity.

4. SPOUSAL GIFTS AND DISCLAIMERS

While it is hard to generalize, for many taxpayers, fundamental tax planning consists of causing a portion of the family's property to be taxed at the death of the first spouse to die and the remainder to be taxed at the death of the second spouse. In such cases, tax minimization is frustrated whenever a part of the spouses' combined resources are taxed at the death of both of them. Chapter 13 is concerned with how best to implement this basic tax plan and considers variations appropriate to clients with different circumstances. Primarily, Chapter 13 is concerned with demonstrating the role of the bypass trust in the estate plan as the receptacle for the property which, at the death of the first spouse, is either taxed or sheltered by the estate tax exemption (technically speaking, it is a credit against tax rather than an exemption) available to that spouse.

Since 1981 all transfers between spouses—which satisfy certain specified conditions—are free of federal estate and gift taxation. This concept of tax-free interspousal transfers is given effect by allowing a deduction for such transfers—a marital deduction—in computing the estate and gift tax liability of the donor spouse. While all transfers between spouses can be structured to be tax free, oftentimes the most effective tax-minimization program—particularly when taken in conjunction with family considerations—will call for the donor spouse to give the donee spouse less than the maximum marital deduction, i.e., less than all of the donor spouse's property. For example, many taxpayers will consider structuring gifts to their spouses in such a way that the amount which can pass tax free—because of the exemption equivalent to the credit against tax that is available to each donor, technically, the applicable exclusion amount, § 2010(c)—passes not to their respective spouses but to a bypass trust for the surviving spouse. The bypass trust can be structured so that the surviving spouse will have access to the trust property but the property will not be taxed at the death of the surviving spouse.

Chapter 14 is devoted to how a taxpayer qualifies gifts to a spouse for the marital deduction. Chapter 15 deals with drafting of clauses aimed at most effectively utilizing the marital deduction.

Chapter 16 is concerned with the disclaimer, the postmortem technique commonly employed to save an estate plan where a decedent has not effectively implemented a bypass trust. Chapter 17 is concerned with the circumstances in which it is appropriate to consider making transfers between spouses for reasons other than love and affection.

5. THE BYPASS TRUST AND RELATED GIFT PLANNING

As noted earlier, central to the basic tax plan and tax planning generally is the bypass trust. Normally, the surviving spouse will have an income interest in the property in the bypass trust and, at the death of the surviving spouse, the trust will continue for the benefit of the decedent's children until they reach a certain age or will terminate if they have reached that age at the death of the surviving parent. Chapter 18 is concerned with structuring the bypass trust. Considered are the five decisions that must be made in "growing" any trust. The perspective used is that of a prospective decedent's wanting to give his or her spouse, the principal beneficiary of the trust, total control of the trust, short of having the trust property included in the surviving spouse's estate at the spouse's later death. Considered are powers of appointment as well as income tax considerations and the possible creation of an "Acapulco fund," meaning a fund which the surviving spouse can access at will for any purpose.

Obviously, taxpayers are concerned about providing for their loved ones and, in so doing, are concerned about shrinking the size of their estate for estate tax purposes. Often they are also concerned about deflecting some of their income to those members of the family unit to whom they are obligated to support. Chapter 19 is concerned with gifts to minors and others under disability. Chapter 19 also introduces the ever-popular *Crummey* powers, which strike at the heart of the integrity of the tax structure and threaten to emasculate it. Noted are § 529 plans, the greatest thing sliced bread for gifting for educational purposes.

Chapter 20 includes materials on life insurance choices. Life insurance, an asset common to almost every taxpayer, is uniquely suited to being "flushed" out of the decedent's estate during his or her lifetime, inasmuch as it rarely provides any current enjoyment. Alternatives include transferring the life insurance to the insured's spouse or establishing an irrevocable trust to hold the insurance for the benefit of the insured's spouse and children. If the life insurance trust is established, arguably, the proceeds of the insurance can be made available to the insured's family yet kept out of the estate of both the insured and his or her spouse. The do's and don'ts in structuring such transfers are many, and these transfers raise many important policy issues.

"Growing" a trust involves a interdependent choices. Impacting the decision making are the payout provisions. While "mandatory pay" of income has initial appeal, many trusts are "discretionary pay." While discretionary trusts have many, many advantages—asset protection, responsive to beneficiary "needs", possibly "incentivized" beneficiary behavior, enhanced tax planning—some management problems arise when trusts are discretionary pay—sometimes lack of transparency, potential for unwanted litigation and liability for the fiduciary, and what can be complicated income tax accounting for distributions in kind. These are considered in Chapter 21 as well as the "hot topics" of family limited partnerships (FLPs)—offering both discounted wealth transfer possibilities and creditor protection to beneficiaries—and situs choices to take advantage of laws repealing the Rule Against Perpetuities, community property, states that do not impose income taxes on trusts or their beneficiaries, etc.

Regarding, FLPs, it might be said, with tongue-in-cheek, that you can't get into a decent country club unless you have created a limited family partnership for your children. These limited partnerships have achieved popularity because of the "minority discount" available when valuing a partnership interest for tax purposes. Suppose, for example, that Mom has $3 million of listed securities. She creates a limited partnership with her children and transfers the securities to the partnership. At her death, the securities have a market value of $4 million, but Mom's executor will claim that Mom's interest in the partnership needs to be discounted to reflect her minority interest in the partnership. Typical discounts claimed range from 25 percent to 40 percent. The viability of some of the schemes currently afloat remains untested—although the principle permitting the minority discount has been accepted.

Two sets of rules govern the income taxation of trusts. Under the regular rules, considered in Chapter 8, income is taxed to the trust unless distributed to the trust beneficiaries. By way of contrast, the grantor trust rules, as they are known, are a series of special rules that apply when, practically speaking, the grantor of the trust has dominion and control over the trust. The grantor trust rules, when applicable, as described in Chapter 22, result in the trust income being taxed to the grantor of the trust even though the grantor did not receive the trust income. Sometimes, under these rules, the trust income is taxed to someone other than the grantor even though that other person did not receive that income. This is particularly a risk where the trust beneficiary is also trustee of the trust. Because of these possibilities, the grantor trust rules are seen as both a trap and an opportunity.

Chapter 23 looks at alternatives to the generation-skipping transfer tax. Inasmuch as there are few unintended gaps in the generation-skipping tax, alternatives consist of safe harbors carved out in the legislation. Three of the most popular techniques involve use of the $2 million generation-skipping tax exemption,"layering" gifts, and the fall out from use of the so-called "reverse" QTIP election (when it was an available feature).

Each subject considered in this part of the book is a study in and of itself, but each subject impacts the bypass trust in a significant way. For that reason, the bypass trust is a useful vehicle for teaching about what appear to be disparate subjects.

[¶ 1149]

6. SPECIAL SITUATIONS

Chapter 24 deals with the asset—the closely held business—which often prompts much litigation and at the same time represents a substantial proportion of the estates of more people than we would imagine. Planning for the closely held business is very complicated and involves many different considerations, and the planner must be conscious of all of them and also be well-grounded in the fundamentals of corporate and partnership taxation. The immensely popular limited liability company is considered. So, too, are the zero valuation rules applicable in a business context. These rules are extraordinarily complex but enormously effective in limiting the use of traditional "estate freezes." The traditional "freeze" often involved a recapitalization of the business enterprise with the parent taking back preferred stock and the children getting all of the common. The value of the enterprise would be assigned to the preferred stock, but the appreciation the enterprise was expected to experience would accrue to the common stock given the children.

Inasmuch as most of the value of the enterprise at the time of the recapitalization was assigned to the preferred stock, the common could be given to the children effectively gift tax free.

Charities, too, are important because our society has made a policy determination that it can respond most efficiently to changing goals and needs by encouraging private philanthropy through a tax subsidy, namely, the tax deduction for gifts to charity. Chapters 25 through 27 include materials relating to many of the techniques in widespread use.

[¶ 1157]

7. FINANCIAL AND RETIREMENT COMPENSATION PLANNING

Property held in deferred compensation or retirement plans represents, with life insurance, the bulk of the assets of most taxpayers who are employees. No estate plan can be put together without attention to these benefits.

In Chapter 28, "Nonqualified Deferred Compensation Opportunities," the reader may consider selected forms of these plans, which enjoy special tax treatment because of the talents of the designer in structuring the plan. The critical elements in such plans are often income tax deferral as well as protection of the plan benefits from the obligor's creditors (in anticipation of the obligor encountering financial difficulty).

Chapter 29 is a more ambitious undertaking, attempting to cover qualified retirement plans. Qualified plans are those that enjoy preferential treatment for income, estate and gift tax purposes. While these plans are properly the work of specialists, it is the unusual client who has not taken advantage of one of these plans to defer income tax on a portion of his or her earnings. Chapter 30 engages issues in planning distributions from qualified plans. The assumption always is that the employee will retire and live happily ever after. The flaw in that analysis is that one day the employee will die—sometimes even before retirement. How do the dollars come out of the plan? What are the tax consequences? How do we reconcile the notion held by some taxpayers that the retirement plan is a "capital warehouse" with Congress's feeling that the qualified plan is merely a tax advantaged fund for retirement, a fund that should be exhausted at the death of the both the employee and the employee's spouse—and, to the extent not exhausted, perhaps taxed away!

F. SCHEMATIC ILLUSTRATIONS

[¶ 1201]

Figure 1.1 depicts a dispositive scheme for married taxpayers seeking to minimize death costs. The scheme integrates the unlimited marital deduction and the $2 million applicable exclusion amount (§ 2010(c))—in 2006—by providing for a bypass trust as the receptacle for the credit shelter or tax free amount. (The text material included in the diagram is necessarily general and, for that reason, must be recognized as potentially misleading when applied to some cases.)

In cases where there are minor children but taxation is not a factor in the dispositive scheme, the schematic in Figure 1.1 continues to be recommended *sans* the tax planning.

Figure 1.3 displays, with the briefest recitation of features, some of the principal devices utilized to "shrink" estates for estate tax purposes and to "deflect" income for income tax purposes. (Again, the textual representations as to the features of these devices are at best generalizations and sometimes only speculation as to the results to be achieved by the particular scheme.)

While noting these limitations, the reader may find these schematic illustrations initially intriguing, and ultimately they may prove useful in contributing to an integrated understanding of the dispositive alternatives available to prospective decedents.

¶ 1201

Figure 1.1 MARRIED TAXPAYERS' DISPOSITION OF PROPERTY TO MINIMIZE DEATH COSTS

PLAN FOR [*YOUR NAME*] FAMILY

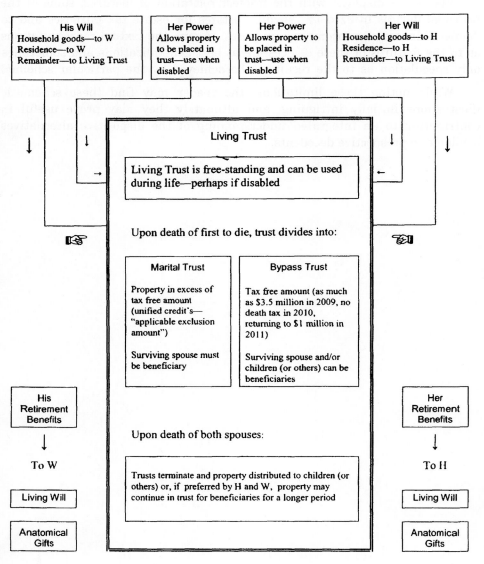

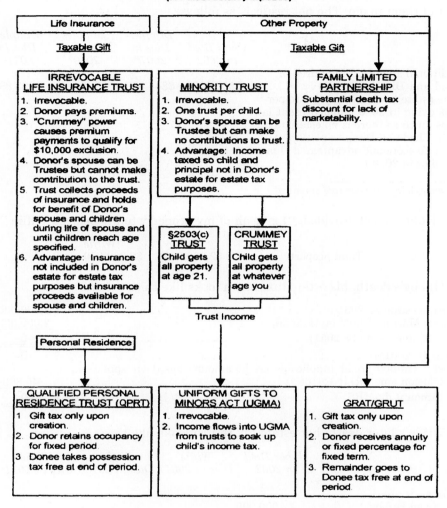

Figure 1.2 LIFETIME GIVING PROGRAM TO SHRINK ESTATE AND DEFLECT INCOME FOR PERSONS WITH TAXABLE ESTATES AND/OR HIGH INCOME TAX BRACKETS

(for discussion purposes)

G. TAX SHELTERING THE TAX–FREE AMOUNT: THE STORY OF HUBBY & WIFFIE AND CHAD & DIMPLES

[¶ 1301]

This is the story of two couples, Hubby and Wiffie and Chad and Dimples. They have equal-sized estates, but their wills are different. As a result, Hubby and Wiffie's children will have less property after paying death taxes than will

¶ 1301

the children of Chad and Dimples. The differences are striking. Chad and Dimples used a bypass trust, but Hubby and Wiffie, wanting to avoid complexity and what they perceived would be a burdensome trust arrangement, used simple wills whereby the survivor took all of the property belonging to the first of them to die. The net result is as follows:

	Chad Died in 2002	Dimples Dies in 2007*	Dimples Dies in 2010*	Dimples Dies in 2011*
Additional amount for children of Chad and Dimples	$550,000	$844,839	-0-	$883,890

(The estate tax is not applied to persons dying in 2010 under present law. In as much as there is no estate tax then, Chad and Dimples plan gives them no economic advantage if Dimples dies in 2010.)

Assumes a 5% after-tax rate of return.

Hubby's will provided: "I give all of my property to my beloved Wiffie."

	Hubby	Wiffie
Total property	$2,000,000	$2,000,000

At Hubby's death, his estate tax return looks like this:

Gross estate [§ 2031(a)]	$ 2,000,000
Less: Marital deduction [§ 2056]	2,000,000
Taxable estate [§ 2051]	$ –0–
Tax [§ 2001(a)]	$ –0–
Less: Unified credit (applicable credit amount based on applicable exclusion amount) [§ 2010(c)]	345,800
Amount due IRS	$ –0–

At Wiffie's later death, her estate tax return looks like this:

	Hubby Died in 2002	Wiffie Dies in 2007*	Wiffie Dies in 2010*	Wiffie Dies in 2011*
Gross estate:				
From Hubby	$2,000,000			
Wiffie's property	2,000,000			
	$4,000,000	$5,105,126	$5,909,822	$6,205,313
Less: Marital deduction	–0–	–0–	–0–	–0–
Taxable estate	$4,000,000	$5,105,126	$5,909,822	$6,205,313
Tax...................	$1,840,800	$2,448,619	–0–	$3,084,382
Less: Unified credit	345,800	$ 780,800	–0–	$ 345,800
Amount due IRS	$1,495,000	$1,667,819	–0–	$2,738,582

Assume a 5% after-tax rate of return.

Chad wasn't content with a simple will. Instead, he opted for a will and a tax planning trust. In brief, Chad's will provided:

¶ 1301

1. Dimples is to receive the smallest amount necessary to eliminate any federal estate tax from Chad's estate. (Whether this gift to Dimples is in trust or in fee, free of trust, is dictated by Chad. In making this determination, Chad should have weighed any preferences he may have for professional property management and "dead hand" control against the advantages of allowing Dimples freedom to access and manage this property without fiduciary responsibilities.)

2. The balance of Chad's property is to go into a trust, perhaps with Dimples as trustee. Dimples will receive all of the trust income and be able to receive principal for her health, education, support and maintenance in her accustomed manner of living (after taking into account the other property available to her for these purposes). (The trust property will "bypass" Dimples's estate for estate tax purposes because she does not have a general power of appointment over the trust.)

	Chad	Dimples
Total property	$2,000,000	$2,000,000

Chad's estate tax return will look like this:

	Died in 2002	2007*	2010*	2011*
Gross estate	$2,000,000			
Less Marital Deduction....	1,000,000			
Taxable estate (goes into bypass trust)	$1,000,000	$1,276,282	$1,477,455	$1,551,328
Tax	$ 345,800			
Less: Unified credit	345,800			
Amount due IRS..........	$0			

This is the value of the property at the indicated dates that was placed in trust at the death of Chad

---

Assumes a 5% after-tax rate of return.

At Dimples's later death, her estate tax return looks like this:

	Chad Died in 2002	Dimples Dies in 2007*	Dimples Dies in 2010*	Dimples Dies in 2011*
Gross estate				
From Chad.............	$1,000,000			
Dimples's property......	2,000,000			
Total	$3,000,000	$3,828,845	$4,432,366	$4,653,985
Tax	$1,290,800	$1,603,780	$0	$2,200,492
Less: Unified credit	345,800	780,800	$0	345,800
Amount due IRS........	$ 945,000	$822,980	$0	$1,854,692
Total taxes imposed on Hubby & Wiffie...........	$1,495,000	$1,667,819	$0	$2,738,582
Total taxes imposed on Chad and Dimples	945,000	822,980	$0	1,854,692
Amount saved by Chad & Dimples.................	$ 550,000	$844,839	$0	$883 890

¶ 1301

	Chad Died in 2002	Dimples Dies in 2007*	Dimples Dies in 2010*	Dimples Dies in 2011*
Amount remaining for the Children:				
Hubby & Wiffie.........	$2,505,000	$3,437,307	$5,909,822	$3,466,731
Chad & Dimples	3,055,000	4,282,146	5,909,822	4,350,621
Additional amount for the children of Chad & Dimples..................	$550,000	$844,839	$0	$883,890

*Assumes a 5% after-tax rate of return

H. BYPASS THE CHILDREN? THE STORY OF BIFF & BUNNY AND FRED & GERTRUDE

[¶ 1401]

Take advantage of the generation skipping tax exemption? Burden your children with a trust? Or give it to them "free of trust, bidding them to 'enjoy'!"? Consider two couples, Biff and Bunny and Fred and Gertrude, each have estates exceeding $2 million. Biff and Bunny had wills that caused $2 million of their property (after taxes) to be placed in trust for their children for life and, at the death of the children, the property then in the trust was to be distributed to their grandchildren. Fred and Gertrude, on the other hand, did not like trusts. Moreover, their children did not like trusts and wanted the flexibility to do as they pleased with whatever property that they inherited from Fred and Gertrude, the children thinking that having the property in trust would restrict their investment opportunities. As a result, Fred and Gertrude's wills did not include trusts; instead, at the death of Fred and Gertrude, all of their property passed free of trust to their children. As can be seen below, the amount of property remaining for the grandchildren of Biff and Bunny is greater than that remaining for the grandchildren of Fred and Gertrude—but only if the repeal of the estate tax in 2010 *does not* become permanent! Note that both couples have two children.

	Dies in 2002	Dies in 2007*	Dies in 2010*	Dies in 2011*
Amount available to grandchildren of Biff and Bunny	$2,000,000	$2,552,563	$2,954,911	$3,102,656
Amount available to grandchildren of Fred and Gertrude...........	2,000,000	2,552,564	2,954,910	2,636,460
Additional amount available to grandchildren of Biff and Bunny	$0	$0	$0	$466,196

*Amount available assuming a 5% after-tax return (compounded annually), no distributions to the children during their lifetimes, and the children all die at the same time (as indicated) after the death of their respective parents, Biff & Bunny and Fred & Gertrude.

No part of the trusts established by Biff and Bunny for their two children, Ricky and Britney, is includable in the taxable estates of the children, the property in the trusts passing tax free to the grandchildren of Biff and Bunny.

Fred and Gertrude had two children, Billy Bob and Sugar Plum. At the death of Billy Bob and Sugar Plum, their respective estates for tax purposes consisted entirely of the $1 million each had received upon the death of Fred and Gertrude (adjusted as shown below according to the interval between the deaths of Fred and Gertrude and the deaths of Billy Bob and Sugar Plum based on an assumed 5% return compounded annually). As a result, the estate taxes and the amounts remaining for the grandchildren of Fred and Gertrude are as follows:

DEATH OF BILLY BOB

	Died in 2002	Dies in 2007*	Dies in 2010*	Dies in 2011*
Taxable estate	$1,000,000	$1,276,282	$1,477,455	$1,551,328
Tax	$345,800	$459,601	$0	$578,898
Less: Unified credit	348,200	780,800	$0	345,800
Amount due IRS	$0	$0	$0	$233,098
Amount available to Billy Bob's children	$1,000,000	$1,276,282	$1,477,455	$466,196

DEATH OF SUGAR PLUM

	Died in 2002	Dies in 2007*	Dies in 2010*	Dies in 2011*
Taxable estate	$1,000,000	$1,276,282	$1,477,455	$1,551,328
Tax	$ 345,800	$ 459,601	$0	$ 578,898
Less: Unified credit	192,800	780,800	$0	345,800
Amount due IRS	$0	$0	$0	$ 233,098
Amount available to Sugar Plum's children	$1,000,000	$1,276,282	$1,628,895	$1,318,230
Combining the amounts available to Sugar Plum's children with the amount available to Billy Bob's children provides the total available to the grandchildren of Fred and Gertrude	$2,000,000	$2,552,564	$2,957,910	$2,636,460

Amount available assuming a 5% after-tax return

Ah, but what if the parents, Biff and Bunny, funded each child's trust with more than $1 million, say $3 million each? In 2002, the generation skipping tax exemption was $1 million per donor (adjusted by inflation, technically it was $1,060,000), meaning that, together, Biff and Bunny had a combined $2 million GST exemption. As a result, $1 million of Ricky's trust and $1 million of Britney's trust is GST tax protected. The remaining, $2 million in each trust (2/3rd's of the trust) is unprotected. As a result, any distribution, for example, in 2007 to a grandchild of Biff or Bunny from either trust, will be subject to a 45% flat rate GST tax on 2/3rds of the distribution. Thus if $30,000 is distributed to Ricky's child, Little Ricky, in 2007 (so that

¶ 1401

Little Ricky might make a world tour), the GST tax on the distribution would be $9,000 (45% x 2/3rd's of $30,000). Disregarding the deadhand control incentives of placing property in trust for loved ones, there well may be circumstances where gifts free of trust are tax advantaged. Would Fred and Gertrude be able to less expensively tax-wise make a gift to a grandchild in 2007 who wanted to go around the world? Probably. However, the story does not end here; this is only the beginning of the planning. There is more, much more. Among the obvious questions is whether generation-skipping transfers in excess of the GST exemption are to be recommended.

¶ 1401

Part I

LIVING AND DYING

Chapter 2

COUNSELING THE CLIENT

A. OBJECTIVES

[¶ 2001]

Lawyers call themselves *counselors* at law and they *do* counsel. However, how effectively and how conscientiously they counsel are questions not often raised either in the study of law or, unfortunately, even later in the practice of law. In fact, many students may obtain a law degree without focusing on the basic question: What is counseling?

This chapter presents a discussion of some of the major issues involved in the role of the estate and trust lawyer as counselor. Following this are excerpts of some of the writings of various lawyers and psychologists (and some combinations of the two). The purpose of this discussion is not to propound a particular point of view but rather to expose the reader to various approaches. The reader is free to draw his or her own definition of counseling: the significant point here is that counseling is an integral, inescapable part of the lawyer's role. It is the most difficult, yet the most gratifying, of the lawyer's tasks.

B. WHAT DO YOU NEED TO KNOW?

[¶ 2051]

1. INTRODUCTION

In its simplest, most fundamental form, counseling in an estate planning context is the process by which the professional determines what it is that the client wants to do with his or her property at deathtime. Some clients will want to make lifetime transfers, but the great majority will want to keep control of their property until death.

Looking towards counseling will-making clients, do you agree that, fundamentally, the counseling objective is to determine the answer to four questions, namely:

    1. To whom does the testator want to give his or her property?

    2. Who is to be executor of the testator's estate?

    3. Who is to be the ''parental guardian'' of the testator's minor children in the event of premature death?

4. Does the testator need tax planning advice?

[¶ 2059]

2. WHO IS THE BENEFICIARY?

For most clients, the beneficiary is "my spouse if my spouse survives me; if not, my children." Such cases, notwithstanding the apparent simplicity of such a wish, inherently involve some significant drafting issues; these issues are more fully discussed in Chapter 3.

In cases where the client expresses a different dispositive scheme, time must be given to "classification" of the client's property.

Example 1. Dove would like to include a provision in her will giving Blackacre to her new spouse, Clint. However, Dove holds Blackacre as joint tenant with right of survivorship with her father, Fred. Accordingly, at Dove's death, her interest in Blackacre will be extinguished and that of her father will expand so that her father would then own all of Blackacre. As a joint tenant, Dove could have disposed of her interest in Blackacre during her lifetime; at her death, however, the survivorship feature inherent in the joint tenancy relationship is superior to any provision in her will. See ¶ 11,067.

Example 2. Bart is a resident of a community property jurisdiction. He holds a deed to some rental property, Whiteacre, which is in his name alone. However, Bart "financed" the acquisition of Whiteacre and the lender secured his loan by taking back a mortgage on Whiteacre. Bart's spouse, Chastity, was jointly and severally liable on the note secured by the mortgage. Accordingly, Whiteacre is the community property of Bart and Chastity. Bart would like to give Whiteacre to his mother, Myrt. If Bart gives Whiteacre to Myrt at his death, he can give her only one-half of the property. However, he can give all of Whiteacre to Myrt during his lifetime so long as such a gift would not be construed to be a fraud on the community. See ¶ 11,089–11,121.

For discussion of classification issues, see ¶ 11,051.

Problem

[¶ 2065]

Consider how to best go about learning about the dispositive scheme the client has chosen. Should you open the interview by asking detailed questions about the client's family and property? Or is the best approach to open the formal conversation by asking simply, "To whom do you want to give your property?" Do you agree that such an open-ended invitation should cause the client to identify the persons whose identity you need to know and give you the opportunity to gather specific information about the persons so identified?

¶ 2065

[¶ 2067]

3. WHO IS TO BE "EXECUTOR" AND WHO IS TO BE "GUARD-IAN"?

Oftentimes the principal motivation for making a will is "to appoint a guardian for our son and daughter in case anything happens to us." Selection of an executor and the problems inherent in guardianships are discussed at ¶ 3601 and 4051, respectively.

In many other cases, the will-making client has not given thought to the identification of a person to be designated guardian or executor. In such cases, there is some risk that the interview will "hang up" on these issues and the will-making will be postponed.

Problem

[¶ 2073]

Consult ¶ 3051 and determine whether the advantages of dying testate—with a will—as opposed to intestate are sufficiently significant that the client should be strongly urged to proceed with the will-making while deferring a decision on either or both the guardian or executor question.

[¶ 2075]

4. IS TAX PLANNING NECESSARY?

a. Death Costs

When the client's objectives have been determined, the starting point in all tax planning is to determine the costs that would be incurred by the death of the client. "Death costs," generally speaking, means death taxes. However, to be accurate, death costs also include expenses of administration. Expenses of administration can often be reduced or kept within manageable proportions if the following steps are taken:

1. Executing a properly drafted will;

2. Considering the use of a revocable trust to hold real property located in jurisdictions other than that in which the client is domiciled; and

3. Giving attention to income tax management during the period of administration of the estate.

Another "death cost" might be liquidation of the client's property at distress prices because of cash requirements that could not be readily met because of illiquidity in the estate of the client. (Illiquidity can sometimes be addressed by life insurance. See discussion in Chapter 20.)

In calculating the costs associated with the death of the client, the procedure is to determine the costs that would be incurred if the client died *today* with his or her present dispositive scheme in place. First, compute the costs that would be incurred if the client's wishes were expressed in the form of a dispositive scheme which is the simplest, most understandable method by which the client's wishes can be given effect. The estate and trust lawyer's burden is then to suggest alternative schemes that might represent some departure from the client's expressed wishes but which would accomplish his or her general intent with lower death costs. In addition, lifetime gifts will have to be considered where death costs are significant. See Chapter 19 for discussion of gift strategies.

Chapter 7 details the computation of the federal estate tax and is a useful beginning point in analyzing alternative dispositive schemes in terms of the tax component of death costs generated by each such alternative.

[¶ 2083]

b. *Valuation*

In order to produce an analysis of death costs, the value of the client's property must be determined. Inasmuch as values change daily, only approximations are necessary to the analysis process.

In cases where the client's property includes business interests and/or real property, valuation becomes much more complicated. For discussion, see ¶ 24,101.

[¶ 2091]

c. *Classification*

"Classification" is also an important part of the process of valuation in those cases where the client owns property in common with others inasmuch as tax consequences depend heavily on classification. As noted earlier, property can be owned in common when it is held by tenants in common, by joint tenants with right of survivorship, by tenants by the entirety, or as community property.

Example 1. Xandra and her brother Larry own Greenbottom as joint tenants with right of survivorship. Xandra paid the full purchase price for Greenbottom from her separate property. However, at Larry's death the full fair market value of Greenbottom will be included in Larry's estate for federal estate tax purposes unless Xandra can prove that she purchased Greenbottom with her property. See § 2040(a); ¶ 11,259. Xandra can claim a new basis (equal to the estate tax value) for income tax purposes on the property. § 1014(b)(6).

Example 2. Miguel and his wife Elena own Starburst as joint tenants with right of survivorship. Elena paid the full purchase price for Starburst from her separate property. However, at Miguel's death, one-half of the full fair market value of Starburst will be included in Miguel's estate for federal estate tax purposes. The rule of inclusion where property is jointly held by husband and wife is absolute, and Elena will not have the opportunity to prove that she purchased the property with her separate property. See § 2040(b); ¶ 11,383. Miguel's one-half will get a new basis for income tax purposes (normally an advantage on subsequent disposi-

¶ 2091

tion). In most cases, the new basis will equal date of death value. § 1014(b)(6).

Example 3. Ming and her husband Biff own Breakwater as their community property. At the death of the first of them to die, only one-half of the fair market value of Breakwater will be included in that first decedent's estate for federal estate tax purposes—but both halves will get a new basis for income tax purposes. See §§ 2033, 1014(b)(6); ¶ 11,137.

Problem

[¶ 2100]

While it may be premature, consider whether you think that there are other fundamental questions, in addition to those outlined in ¶ 2051–2091, that must be answered by the will-making client. Keep these questions in mind as you read on.

C. WHAT ARE YOUR RESPONSIBILITIES?

[¶ 2151]

1. ESTATE PLANNING

It should be obvious from the foregoing that a certain minimum level of sophistication is required to counsel clients in the area of estate planning. This should be particularly apparent as you review the "Legal Tasks" portion of the following excerpt from Robert Bandy's article, Statement of Principles of the Estate Planning Attorney in Texas, 41 Tex. B.J. 169, 169–72 (1978).

What Is Estate Planning?

Estate planning is the process by which the client plans the accumulation, management, conservation, and disposition of his estate so that he and his beneficiaries will derive the maximum benefit during his lifetime and after his death. This process requires coordination and integration of the client's personal, financial and business affairs.

What Are the Specific Skills?

In order for an individual to hold himself out to the public as an estate planner, he must be thoroughly skilled in the law pertaining to wills, trusts, property rights and estates; he must be capable of concise and unambiguous draftsmanship; he must understand the broad trends and the applicable rules of income, estate, inheritance and gift taxation; he should be acquainted with the practices and customs of the professional fiduciaries in his area; he should be schooled in the law of business entities and be prepared to continue, dispose of, or dismember a business; he should be familiar with the essentials pertaining to pension and profit sharing plans and deferred compensation arrangements; he must have knowledge and experience and be familiar with the basic essentials of investments, insurance and accounting, and the sources of specialized advice in these areas; he should have a good understanding of the basic principles of business operations and financing; he should be a counselor with a good understanding of psychology; and finally, he should be willing to cooperate with other members of the estate planning team in the creation and implementation of the estate plan.

The foregoing comprehensive capabilities demonstrate how difficult it is to become a proficient estate planner. In fact, mastery of these essential skills by one person is an enormous undertaking. In their formal education, lawyers have been trained in few of these skills which are not strictly legal but are nevertheless collateral to legal expertness in the art of estate planning. Accordingly, the client is best served by the additional knowledge and experience of other professionals who have this training.

Who Does Estate Planning?

Because of the divergency and complexity of problems encountered in the planning of an estate and its implementation, estate planning is frequently a team effort consisting of several distinct skills: the art of the lawyer charged with the ultimate authority and responsibility, who will draw the will, trust agreements and other documents; the art of the life insurance expert, who can provide for the liquidity of the estate, settlement options and provisions for annuities or other forms of life income and can suggest uses of life insurance that may not have occurred to the lawyer; the art of the accountant, who knows what assets are available and what various objectives or alternatives will cost, and will be helpful in providing an accurate view of the client's financial history; and the art of the trust officer, who provides the knowledge and experience of fiduciary management and a facility with perpetual existence.

The lawyer is responsible for coordinating the work of the other professionals into a unified estate plan because of his broad training and objective position. The lawyer is charged with this primary responsibility for several reasons. First, the sole duty of the lawyer is to render skilled, independent and objective legal advice to his client; second, his remuneration is not contingent on the sale or solicitation of new business; third, the client can communicate freely with his lawyer concerning his personal, financial and business affairs, secure in the knowledge that these communications will remain privileged and confidential and cannot be divulged during the client's life except with the client's consent; and fourth, the lawyer has the judgment and analytical training needed to formulate long-range plans not only to meet the client's present objectives but also to provide for flexibility in the estate plan in the event of changes in the law, economy, personal objectives or family situation. Moreover, the legal profession will have the sole responsibility for conducting any litigation growing out of the estate planning process, whether it involves taxation, construction of documents, or the contest of title to properties.

What Is the Responsibility of the Non–Specialist Practitioner?

A client will continue to go to a lawyer from whom he has customarily obtained legal advice, whether or not he is an estate planning special-

¶ **2151**

ist. He is the lawyer who likely has drawn the client's first will or assisted the client in the purchase of his home. He is perhaps the lawyer with whom the client has formed a lifelong professional association, who knows the family of the client and has watched the development of the client's business interests. The knowledge of these facts acquired through years of professional association is an important element in the formulation of an adequate estate plan. However, it alone will not qualify the lawyer to represent his client competently in planning his estate. Busy with the day-to-day concerns of his client, the family lawyer may not be fully aware of the most recent developments and opportunities in the technical field of estate planning. Having performed various legal tasks for his client through a successful business career, the lawyer is under a duty to his client to continue giving appropriate advice for the protection of the family of the client. Accordingly, the lawyer has the responsibility to maintain a reasonable understanding of the principal elements of estate planning either by himself or by associating himself with another lawyer who is competent in the estate planning field.

* * *

What Legal Tasks Should Be the Lawyer's Responsibility?

* * *

The following is a list of the legal tasks which, where appropriate, should be the responsibility of the lawyer in estate planning:

Legal Tasks

1.   Data Gathering and Determination of Client Objectives:

1.01   Secure from the client information concerning his family, including the identities, ages, and relationships of members of his immediate family and those of collateral relatives to the extent necessary to advise the client concerning his estate plan.

1.02   Secure from the client information concerning legal relationships or unusual family matters which may affect the client's estate plan, including the existence of any prior marriages of the client or his spouse, the existence of property settlement agreements, court orders, or other agreements concerning any prior marriages of the client or his spouse, and the existence of any health problems or other matters affecting particular family members.

1.03   Secure from the client information necessary to determine the identity, location, and approximate value of the client's estate assets.

1.04   Secure from the client information (including actual documents where appropriate) necessary to determine the existing ownership and title arrangements with respect to the client's estate assets, including co-ownership and survivorship arrangements.

1.05   Secure from the client information necessary to determine the community or separate property characterization and information relating to management and control of the client's estate assets, to the extent necessary to advise the client concerning relevant estate planning matters.

1.06   Secure from the client information concerning any joint and mutual will, contracts to will or other legal impediments to dispose freely of the client's estate assets.

1.07   Determine the existence and nature of the client's present estate planning arrangements, including business succession agreements, survivorship arrangements, and beneficiary or other designations with regard to insurance, employee benefits, or other estate assets to the extent disclosed by the client. In reviewing existing estate planning documents, a number of matters should be considered, including: (i) whether existing documents are satisfactory, or are capable of being modified through trust amendment or codicil; (ii) whether they contain any libelous material or matter which would be in poor taste as a public record; (iii) whether existing will and codicils appear to be properly executed and self-proved; (iv) whether the client has advised proposed fiduciaries of their appointment and provided any needed guidelines for exercise of fiduciary discretion; and (v) whether all original executed copies of existing estate planning documents are readily available if needed.

1.08   Determine the existence and nature of the estate plans of other persons, living or deceased, which affect the client's estate plan, including other wills, trust agreements, powers of appointment, and beneficiary designations to the extent disclosed by the client.

1.09   Review the client's current will and other estate planning documents, where available and disclosed by the client, to the extent necessary to secure complete and accurate information concerning the matters set forth in §§ 1.01 through 1.08.

1.10   Determine * * * the client's desires and objectives regarding the disposition of his estate assets, both probate and non-probate, during his lifetime or upon his death.

1.11   Determine * * * the client's desires and objectives regarding the selection of fiduciaries to serve in connection with the administration of his estate and any trusts established in connection with his estate planning, the selection of a guardian for the client's minor children, the choice of custodians, and the safekeeping of the client's estate planning documents.

[¶ 2159]

2. FINANCIAL PLANNING

The role of the estate planning attorney is expanding to yet a broader area—that of financial counseling—as envisioned and detailed by J. Thomas Eubank in The Future for Estate Lawyers, 10 Real Prop., Prob. & Tr. J. 223, 224–27 (1975).

¶ 2159

Many clients who come to a lawyer for a will or estate planning need and want much broader services than those described above as essential legal services for the lawyer to perform. They want someone to tackle virtually every aspect of their present and future financial life. They want someone to visualize the big picture and to paint it for them in detail, present and future, after having analyzed it and formulated recommendations. This service usually is called financial counseling. As far as I can ascertain, no lawyer in this nation is offering his clients financial counseling as a single package, although many doubtless cover many or all aspects in the course of counseling a family. Instead, financial counseling as a package is offered by certain banks, large accounting firms and specialized business enterprises. Life underwriters give similar services, but, in my experience, those services are less encompassing than what I call here financial counseling. In the main, financial counseling thus far has been for corporate business executives, although the market among professionals and closely held business owners is considered to have great potential and is being developed.

A.   *Nature of Financial Counseling*

In the case of a corporate executive, the financial counseling report often includes these matters:

1.   A great deal of information is collected and set forth. This includes family information, personal considerations, a net worth statement and a statement of income and expenses.

2.   The present estate planning documents are analyzed, and various death tax and income tax consequences are set forth, often determined by a computer. The net economic result is also set forth. The documents thus analyzed include the wills for the husband and wife, as well as existing trust instruments, insurance and employee benefit plans, and ownership and beneficiary designations for such plans. Legal and taxation strengths and weaknesses in the documents often are noted.

3.   Having painted in detail the present and the future under the existing plan, the report then proceeds into recommendations for a new, improved plan. Lifetime gifts may be recommended in great detail as to amount, timing, selection of assets, basis problems, gift tax advice, use of trusts and custodianships, and specific details as to the nature and type of trusts. If the lifetime gift is in trust, the specifics may include not only whether it is a * * * present interest trust for minors or a long term family trust with many details about the features of each being recommended. Unless the lawyer exerts his counseling function, he is in this situation just an order-taker, akin to a short-order cook.

4.   Recommended action for all employee benefits and insurance is set forth, with taxation results and family considerations noted. New life insurance may be suggested as to type, ownership, method of paying premiums and beneficiary designations.

¶ 2159

5. A great deal of information about stock options is given, and recommendations are made as to exercise: when, how to obtain the funds, security law aspects, payment of loans obtained and taxation.

6. The new estate plan is also set forth, again with specifics, such as the kind of marital deduction provision and features of the A Trust and B Trust.

7. Then the taxation and net economic results of the new plan are set forth and contrasted with those of the existing plan.

Often the report goes on into many other areas of advice needed by the customer. Does the customer have adequate casualty and liability insurance? Can he afford a new second home or the existing one? Is the family budget being managed well and in conformity with usual patterns? Where is his family spending too much or too little money? Are his bank loans too great or too little? Does he have the right kind of loans? What professional help should he get to manage his investments? What general investment changes should be made; for example, should he shift more to tax-exempt securities? What estate liquidity problems exist? Can he afford the lifestyle he has or wants or the one his wife wants? Will he leave his wife and children with what he wants them to have? Should he get into new tax-sheltered investments and which ones specifically?

Many of the financial counselors also offer some of the recommended services, such as investment management, fiduciary services and placement of tax-sheltered investments.

B.   The Lawyer as Financial Counselor

Obviously financial counseling includes many legal services and many nonlegal services. One immediate question financial counseling raises for lawyers is whether they should and can offer these services. The answer to this is not easy.

The arguments against doing so include these: a lawyer should confine himself to the practice of law; a lawyer does not have the expertise, equipment and staff to enter into many of these nonlegal services; this financial counseling is a flash in the pan and will not continue, and in any event the market and the need are too limited for lawyers to be concerned.

My major concern with financial counseling is that if the lawyer does not engage in it, he will be excluded too much from one of his major, historical roles, namely, counseling the individual client. He can, of course, exercise that function significantly by criticizing the financial counseling report. Is that enough for that role? Aside from counseling by criticism, he may be likened in this situation to an order-taker for documents. With the current development of programmed documents by many lawyers, it may be unrealistic for lawyers to expect substantial fees or high professional standing for simply having an automatic typewriter hammer out a programmed document prescribed by a nonlawyer in a financial counseling report.

¶ 2159

I believe that there is a major public need for financial counseling, broadly speaking, among the rich, the not-so-rich and even people of relatively modest means. The extent of this need is largely unrecognized. I also believe that where there is such a need, someone is going to fill that need, even in the market areas where cost is now prohibitive, because someone is going to figure out a means of mass production for those market areas. My strongest belief on this question is that a lawyer should be in the control room that creates a financial counseling report. Whether he should be in charge of the control room, with others present and participating, I leave to further development, but I do like that idea.

Can lawyers get into financial counseling? It would certainly take a lot of changes by lawyers, but the answer is clearly yes. It would take large investments of capital, and it would require that many experts in fields other than law be employed. Since the largest law firms are not nearly as large as the largest banks and accounting firms which are investing that capital and employing those experts, the effort by lawyers might have to be on some joint or cooperative basis, perhaps through service corporations established by lawyers. Possibly an existing business enterprise could establish the service for subscription thereto by lawyers. Another possibility that could be explored is bringing the individual's lawyer into the existing financial counseling projects to a greater extent, perhaps into the control room between the preliminary and final drafts of the report or perhaps only to the extent of having that lawyer prepare an addendum to the final report.

3. MALPRACTICE

[¶ 2169]

BELT v. OPPENHEIMER

Supreme Court of Texas, 2006.
192 S.W.3d 780.

Chief Justice JEFFERSON delivered the opinion of the Court.

Kristin Terk Belt and Kimberly Terk Murphy (the Terks)—joint, independent executors of their father David Terk's estate—sued several attorneys and their law firm * * * (collectively, the Attorneys) for legal malpractice. The Attorneys moved for summary judgment on the ground that estate planners owe no duty to the personal representatives of a deceased client's estate. The trial court granted the motion, and the court of appeals affirmed the judgment. We hold, to the contrary, that there is no legal bar preventing an estate's personal representative from maintaining a legal malpractice claim on behalf of the estate against the decedent's estate planners. Accordingly, we reverse the court of appeals' judgment and remand to the trial court for further proceedings.

I

BACKGROUND

David Terk hired the Attorneys to prepare his will. After his death, the Terks became the joint, independent executors of their father's estate. As executors, the Terks sued the Attorneys for legal malpractice, alleging that the Attorneys were negligent in drafting their father's will and in advising him on asset management. They claim the estate incurred over $1,500,000 in tax liability that could have been avoided by competent estate planning.

In affirming the trial court's judgment for the Attorneys, the court of appeals cited *Barcelo v. Elliott,* in which we held that beneficiaries cannot maintain a malpractice cause of action against a decedent's estate-planning attorney because the attorney lacks privity with non-client beneficiaries and therefore owes them no duty. 141 S.W.3d 706, 708–09 (citing *Barcelo,* 923 S.W.2d 575 (Tex.1996)). The Terks argue that the *Barcelo* rule bars only claims by beneficiaries suing for their own injuries and does not preclude suits brought by personal representatives on an estate's behalf. We granted the Terks' petition to consider whether personal representatives may bring legal malpractice claims on behalf of a decedent's estate.

II

DISCUSSION

Legal malpractice claims sound in tort. The plaintiff must demonstrate "that (1) the attorney owed the plaintiff a duty, (2) the attorney breached that duty, (3) the breach proximately caused the plaintiff's injuries, and (4) damages occurred." *Peeler v. Hughes & Luce,* 909 S.W.2d 494, 496 (Tex.1995).

While an attorney always owes a duty of care to a client, no such duty is owed to non-client beneficiaries, even if they are damaged by the attorney's malpractice. *See Barcelo,* 923 S.W.2d at 577. In *Barcelo,* we considered whether beneficiaries dissatisfied with the distribution of estate assets may sue an estate-planning attorney for legal malpractice after a client's death. *Id.* at 576. In that case, the intended beneficiaries of a trust, which was declared invalid after the client's death, sued the attorney who drafted the trust agreement. *Id.* We held that the non-client beneficiaries could not maintain a suit against the decedent's estate planner because "the greater good is served by preserving a bright-line privity rule which denies a cause of action to all beneficiaries whom the attorney did not represent." *Id.* at 578.

Several policy considerations supported our *Barcelo* holding. First, the threat of suits by disappointed heirs after a client's death could create conflicts during the estate-planning process and divide the attorney's loyalty between the client and potential beneficiaries, generally compromising the quality of the attorney's representation. *Id.* at 578. We also noted that suits brought by bickering beneficiaries would necessarily require extrinsic evidence to prove how a decedent intended to distribute the estate, creating a "host of difficulties." *Id.* We therefore held that barring a cause of action for estate-planning malpractice by beneficiaries would help ensure that estate planners "zealously represent[ed]" their clients. *Id.* at 578–79.

¶ 2169

Thus, in Texas, a legal malpractice claim in the estate-planning context may be maintained only by the estate planner's client. This is the minority rule in the United States—only eight other states require strict privity in estate-planning malpractice suits. In the majority of states, a beneficiary harmed by a lawyer's negligence in drafting a will or trust may bring a malpractice claim against the attorney, even though the beneficiary was not the attorney's client. *See, e.g., Lucas v. Hamm,* 56 Cal.2d 583, 15 Cal.Rptr. 821, 364 P.2d 685, 689 (1961), *cert. denied,* 368 U.S. 987 (1962); *Schreiner v. Scoville,* 410 N.W.2d 679, 683 (Iowa 1987).

The question in this case, however, is whether the *Barcelo* rule bars suits brought *on behalf of* the decedent client by his estate's personal representatives. Because most states allow beneficiaries to maintain estate-planning malpractice claims, only a handful of jurisdictions have considered this specific issue. We confront this question for the first time today.

Generally, in Texas an estate's personal representative has the capacity to bring a survival action on behalf of a decedent's estate. Therefore, if the Terks' legal malpractice claim is brought on behalf of the decedent's estate and survives the decedent, the Terks may maintain a suit against the Attorneys.

A

* * *

We have never specifically considered whether a legal malpractice claim in the estate-planning context survives a deceased client. A claim that an estate planner's negligence resulted in the improper depletion of a client's estate involves injury to the decedent's property. Moreover, when an attorney's malpractice results in financial loss, the aggrieved client is fully compensated by recovery of that loss; the client may not recover damages for mental anguish or other personal injuries. *See Douglas v. Delp,* 987 S.W.2d 879, 885 (Tex.1999).

Thus, estate-planning malpractice claims seeking recovery for pure economic loss are limited to recovery for property damage. Therefore, in accordance with the long-standing, common-law principle that actions for damage to property survive the death of the injured party, we hold that legal malpractice claims alleging pure economic loss survive in favor of a deceased client's estate, because such claims are necessarily limited to recovery for property damage.

The court of appeals found for the Attorneys after holding that its prior decision in *Estate of Arlitt v. Paterson* controlled. 141 S.W.3d at 708. In *Estate of Arlitt,* the court held that an estate-planning malpractice claim does not accrue during a decedent's lifetime—and therefore does not survive the decedent—because the estate's injuries do not arise until after death. *See Estate of Arlitt v. Paterson,* 995 S.W.2d 713, 720 (Tex.App.—San Antonio 1999, pet. denied). [*Ed.*—In a footnote, the court said "Some states have used similar reasoning in determining that estate planning malpractice claims do not survive, and a few of those courts have held that language in their state's survival statute necessitated such a result. *See McDonald v. Pettus,* 337 Ark. 265, 988 S.W.2d 9, 15 (1999) (personal representative could not bring tort-based malpractice claim on behalf of decedent; Arkansas's survival statute required decedent suffer injury or damages prior to death, but injury or damages caused by estate-planning malpractice did not occur until will took effect after death); *Rutter,* 568 S.E.2d at 695 (no survival action because claim did not "exist" prior to death—as required by Virginia's survival statute— since the client's estate did not suffer damage or injury until after client's death); *see also Brewer v. Davis,* 593 So.2d 67, 68 (Ala.1991) (state's survival statute precluded survival of a tort-based malpractice action that was not filed until after client's death). Other jurisdictions, however, have held such claims do not survive as a matter of common law. *See Deeb,* 566 N.Y.S.2d at 689 (in New York, malpractice claim did not survive because estate did not incur damages until after client's death); *Heyer v. Flaig,* 70 Cal.2d 223, 74 Cal.Rptr. 225, 449 P.2d 161, 165 (1969) (noting that "the executor of an estate has no standing . . . , since in the normal case the estate is not injured by [negligent estate planning] except to the extent of the [attorney's] fees paid").")]

We disapprove *Estate of Arlitt*'s holding that no legal malpractice claim accrues before death when an estate-planning attorney's negligent drafting results in increased estate tax consequences. Even though an estate may suffer significant damages after a client's death, this does not preclude survival of an estate-planning malpractice claim. While the primary damages at issue here—increased tax liability—did not occur until after the decedent's death, the lawyer's alleged negligence occurred while the decedent was alive. If the decedent had discovered this injury prior to his death, he could have brought suit against his estate planners to recover the fees paid to them. In addition, the decedent could have recovered the costs incurred in restructuring his estate to minimize tax liability. Therefore, if the injury occurs during the client's lifetime, a claim for estate-planning malpractice survives the client's death.

B

Because legal malpractice claims survive in favor of the decedent's estate, the estate has a justiciable interest in the controversy sufficient to confer standing. A decedent's estate, however "is not a legal entity and may not properly sue or be sued as such." *Id.* at 849. (citing *Price v. Estate of Anderson,* 522 S.W.2d 690, 691 (Tex.1975)). Rather, certain individuals have the capacity to bring a claim on the estate's behalf. *Id.* Generally, "only the estate's personal representative has the capacity to bring a survival claim." *Id.* at 850–51 (noting that in certain circumstances, heirs may bring suit on behalf of the estate, such as when no administration is pending or necessary).

In this case, it is undisputed that the Terks are the independent executors of their father's estate. Thus, they may bring a claim on behalf of the estate in their capacity as personal representatives. We have previously held that a bankruptcy trustee can maintain a legal malpractice claim on behalf of a debtor's estate, and we see no reason to curtail a personal representative's similar malpractice claim on behalf of a decedent's estate. This holding is in accord with other jurisdictions, which have also recognized that, because the

¶ 2169

estate "stands in the shoes" of a decedent, it is in privity with the decedent's estate-planning attorney and, therefore, the estate's personal representative has the capacity to maintain the malpractice claim on the estate's behalf.

C

In holding for the Attorneys, the court of appeals noted that the policy concerns expressed in *Barcelo* concerning suits against estate planners by intended beneficiaries should also bar suits brought by personal representatives of an estate. As noted above, in *Barcelo* we held that an attorney's ability to represent a client zealously would be compromised if the attorney knew that, after the client's death, he could be second-guessed by the client's disappointed heirs. 923 S.W.2d at 578. Accordingly, we held that estate-planning attorneys owe no professional duty to beneficiaries named in a trust or will. *Id.* at 578–79.

While this concern applies when disappointed heirs seek to dispute the size of their bequest or their omission from an estate plan, it does not apply when an estate's personal representative seeks to recover damages incurred by the estate itself. Cases brought by quarreling beneficiaries would require a court to decide how the decedent intended to apportion the estate, a near-impossible task given the limited, and often conflicting, evidence available to prove such intent. *See id.* at 578 (noting the problems associated with allowing extrinsic evidence to prove testator intent). In cases involving depletion of the decedent's estate due to negligent tax planning, however, the personal representative need not prove how the decedent intended to distribute the estate; rather, the representative need only demonstrate that the decedent intended to minimize tax liability for the estate as a whole.

Additionally, while the interests of the decedent and a potential beneficiary may conflict, a decedent's interests should mirror those of his estate. Thus, the conflicts that concerned us in *Barcelo* are not present in malpractice suits brought on behalf of the estate. *See Nevin v. Union Trust Co.*, 726 A.2d 694, 701 (Me.1999) (holding that the better rule is to allow only personal representatives, not beneficiaries, to sue for estate-planning malpractice, because what may be good for one beneficiary is not necessarily good for the estate as a whole).

We note, however, that beneficiaries often act as the estate's personal representative, and our holding today arguably presents an opportunity for some disappointed beneficiaries to recast a malpractice claim for their own "lost" inheritance, which would be barred by *Barcelo,* as a claim brought on behalf of the estate. The temptation to bring such claims will likely be tempered, however, by the fact that a personal representative who mismanages the performance of his or her duties may be removed from the position. Additionally, even assuming that a beneficiary serving as personal representative could prove, for example, that the deceased client intended to maximize the size of the entire estate by leaving a larger inheritance to the personal representative, he or she would not necessarily recover the lost inheritance should the malpractice claim succeed. Because the claim allowed under our holding today is for injuries suffered by the client's *estate,* any damages

¶ 2169

recovered would be paid to the estate and, only then, distributed in accordance with the decedent's existing estate plan. Thus, the recovery would flow to the disappointed beneficiary only if the estate plan had provided for such a distribution, fulfilling the decedent's wishes. These factors prevent personal representatives who are also beneficiaries from using our holding today as an end run around *Barcelo*.

* * * Limiting * * * the class of potential estate-planning malpractice claimants to the personal representatives of a client's estate will ensure that estate-planning attorneys are not subject to "almost unlimited liability."

Finally, we note that precluding both beneficiaries and personal representatives from bringing suit for estate-planning malpractice would essentially immunize estate-planning attorneys from liability for breaching their duty to their clients. As the *Barcelo* dissent noted, however, allowing estate-planning malpractice suits may help "provide accountability and thus an incentive for lawyers to use greater care in estate planning." 923 S.W.2d at 580 (Cornyn, J., dissenting). Limiting estate-planning malpractice suits to those brought by either the client or the client's personal representative strikes the appropriate balance between providing accountability for attorney negligence and protecting the sanctity of the attorney-client relationship.

III

CONCLUSION

The Terks—in their capacity as personal representatives of their father's estate—may maintain an estate-planning malpractice claim against the Attorneys. We therefore reverse the court of appeals' judgment and remand to the trial court for further proceedings consistent with this opinion.

D. WHY CLIENTS ELECT TO MAKE WILLS

[¶ 2201]

The reasons and expectations of the client in electing to make a will are described in Sussman, Cates, and Smith, Will Making: An Examination of Client and Lawyer Attitudes, 23 U. Fla. L. Rev. 25, 25–29 (1970).

The typical will maker is likely to be a married man in early middle age, and although he is more affluent than the general population, he is not wealthy. The data in this § are based upon the responses of 1,230 survivors. Of these persons, 58 percent (711) had already made a will [hereinafter "testators" or "testate group"], 35 percent (427) said they planned to make a will [hereinafter "planners"]; and only 8 percent (92) had no plans to make a will. * * *

Of the 92 who planned to remain intestate, 52 (57 percent) stated that they did not have enough property to justify a will. Eighteen were simply satisfied with the intestate distribution. There were 22 additional idiosyncratic reasons. The finding that a lack of property was the major reason for intestacy proved to be consistent with the datum of a positive association between property and testacy.

In spite of the overall finding that persons with higher equity were more likely to be testate, the notion of having "enough" property to make a will varied considerably according to the individual. One elderly woman who planned to make a will gave as her reason, "I have a new winter coat. It cost $75. I want to leave it to someone who will appreciate it." A serious consideration of motivations for testacy must account for these highly subjective and individualistic perceptions of worth.

The reasons for making a will fall into two categories: (1) personal circumstances or change in them and (2) the perceived capabilities of a will. These reasons are interrelated, but the degree of connectedness depends upon the individual's situation at any given time.

The possibility of death because of old age, serious illness, or while making an extended trip were motives given far more frequently by the testators than by the planners. Either the experiences of the two groups differ (the testate group is older) or their reactions to similar experiences are different. An impending trip may be the impetus for will making, but only if it is associated with the possibility or heightened probability of death. This association is evident in the following statement: "We were traveling to California. Well, you know, accidents can happen." The notion of imminent death was given relatively infrequently, even by the testate group; 11 percent of the testators offered responses that fell into this category. This response is not surprising, since most individuals express a perceived invincibility regarding the subject of their own death.

Economic wealth was positively associated with testacy for both the decedent sample and survivor population, but the acquisition of property was mentioned by 8 and 6 percent, respectively, of the testators and those who intended to be testate [planners]. The absence of property operated to deter people from making a will, but the presence of property was not paramount in the decision for testacy. Property was a necessary but not sufficient condition for will making.

This group of survivors had recent probate experience and may consequently differ from the general population in their motives for making wills in that their experience may have impressed upon them the importance of having a will. * * *

[MARRIED WITH CHILDREN]

The situations that were by far the most conducive to will making were getting married and having children. The subjective responses of both testators and planners showed the importance given to family responsibilities in making a will. One hundred twenty-eight of the testators (18 percent) and 68 of the planners (16 percent) gave one or both of these reasons as their motivation for testacy.

Related to this emphasis upon familial responsibility was the desire to alter the intestate distribution. One hundred sixty-five of the testators (23 percent) and 158 of the planners (37 percent) said they made or would make wills because they preferred not to have their property distributed in strict accordance with the intestate statutes.

¶ 2201

A sizable number of respondents had the mistaken notion that having a will solves all the cumbersome problems of property distribution and many survivors were surprised at the delays encountered with probate procedures. One hundred fifty-seven (22 percent) of the testators and 130 (30 percent) of the will planners felt that having a will saves time, money, or both. But there are other popular misconceptions about the advantages of a will. One widow remarked, "what good did my husband's will do? I still had to go to court. You shouldn't have to go to court if there is a will." Others, although not holding this misconception, did believe that a will makes things go more quickly or that having a will means that the estate settlement will cost less. They did not have in mind anything so specific as the saving of estate taxes or dispensing with the personal representative's bond. Taxes and the appointment of an executor were categorized separately; they were mentioned by only 13 testators and seven planners. The client was inclined to place little emphasis on facets of the will that could challenge the attorney's skill; the client was seldom interested in tax savings except insofar as he or she misconceived the advantages of testacy. Moreover, the client had given little thought to the selection of an executor. Although he may have realized the position is one of trust, he usually knew little or nothing of the executor's specific duties.

The naming of a guardian of minors and their estates was the most important motive for making a will among the testators (24 percent). The choice of a guardian may be of utmost importance to the client; but the qualities required of a guardian are not adequately defined by law, nor are they necessarily within the lawyer's competence. Among the planners, guardianship ranked equally with marriage and children (both 16 percent) but was far less important than other reasons, such as altering the intestate distribution (37 percent) and saving money or time (30 percent).

E. THE COUNSELING FUNCTION

[¶ 2251]

The chapters in this book are structured so as to provide a basis for accomplishing client objectives at the lowest possible tax cost. However, if you focus exclusively on the technical skills necessary to "save taxes," it is likely that you will ill serve your client.

It is without doubt that your obligation is to help your client, and to help your client it is important to create an environment in which the client can help himself or herself. In order for the client to be able to help himself or herself, the client must be able to communicate with you, and that communication will be possible only if you are a caring person and able to manifest this attitude to your client. Otherwise, the representational process is purely mechanical. In such an atmosphere it is unlikely that you will ever find out what it is the client really wants to do with his or her property.

For those setting themselves up as estate planning professionals, Thomas L. Shaffer in Models for the "Estate Planning" Counselor, 6 U. Miami Est.

¶ 2251

Plan. Inst., at ¶ 72–11, .1100–.1103 (1972), offers a glimpse of typical role models assumed by the practitioner: the companion model, the competition model, and the dependent model.

The companion model for counselors is the dominant model in modern human-relations work—among school counselors, vocational counselors, psychological counselors in industrial personnel relations, and even in education (although rarely in legal education). There is a vast literature about it, and there is coming to be a vast amount of empirical and experimental research to validate it. In the last analysis, though, other counselors, legal counselors and teachers of legal counselors choose the companion model because it sounds like a good way to live and not because it is a result of careful consideration of the research * * * I think it is possible to be a legal counselor and at the same time a companion, a friend. I accept for myself and my students Carl Rogers' aspiration for those who set themselves up as helping professionals: "I will enter into your world of perception as completely as I am able," he says to his client. "I will become, in a sense, another self for you—an alter ego of your own attitudes and feelings—a safe opportunity for you to discern yourself more clearly, to experience yourself more truly and deeply, to choose more significantly."

The companion model for the counselor builds upon the difficult ability to feel what the client is feeling. * * *

"Estate-planning" interviews are often games we lawyers prepare in advance to win. The average prosperous law office suite is an engine of one-upmanship, from opulent decor to copies of *Barrons* and rooms lined with the *English Reports*. Our offices are only a trifle more subtle than the chair Mr. Tutt kept for unwelcome visitors; it had an inch cut off each of the front legs. Lawyers meet people in coat and tie, sit behind massive desks in massive chairs, and barricade themselves with superior demeanors, and yellow pads fourteen inches long, and gadgets like "squawk box" telephones. Our heady language suggests that all communication is what the late Eric Berne would have called from parent to child. Our written product is usually unreadable, but it has a price tag which is a mighty nonverbal claxon saying to clients "SIT UP AND PAY ATTENTION, I'M IN CHARGE HERE."

* * * I, too, have spent time with clients and I think it is possible to level with them, to enjoy their leveling with me, and to work together. It is possible to be a friend. I do not *need* to be either an intimidator or an intimidatee.

But I think we have to level with ourselves first. We are trained in law school to be competitive; in fact we are selected, and we select ourselves for legal education, because of competitive talents. The educational atmosphere I live in and you are nostalgic about is a jungle atmosphere—much more of a jungle, I think, than the practice of law is. Lawyers are people who need to win arguments; we are often people who have only one way to deal with our own internal conflict, our doubt, our hurt—and that way is to slug it out with somebody else.

¶ 2251

And that leads me to think that the milieu of competition will foul up our ability to be companions for our clients *unless* we learn how to deal with ourselves, as a valid and important professional preparation for dealing with clients. What we have to be able to say, verbally and nonverbally, to clients is: "There is no need to compete in this office. I am your friend and I will prove it by being willing to tell you how I feel; I am going to try to take down the barriers that I and my law teachers and my colleagues in the practice have built between me and the people I care about."

Companionship is threatened by competition. It is as seriously threatened from the other direction, from dependence in the client. I cannot regard you as a companion unless I can grant you dignity and self-determination and the freedom to *be who you are*. The threat to a companionship counseling model may be that lawyer treats client as a child, and client treats lawyer as a parent.

Psychiatry calls this the transference phenomenon. The idea is that the client is reliving some emotional relationship from the past and is casting his lawyer in a role. The lawyer is made to stand in for some important person in the client's life—typically, in the Freudian view of things, the client's father. The result is inappropriate dependence on the lawyer—not just the normal dependence we find common in people who think we know a lot, but a focused, emotional dependence, so that critical choices and biases and distortions are likely to come *from the lawyer,* not from the client. The evidence and learned opinion from psychology is that this sort of thing happens all the time, that it happens to lawyers all the time, that decisions apparently made by clients in the law office are in fact being made by lawyers, because clients are *too dependent* on lawyers. It is likely that transference feelings exist in *most* protracted lawyer-client relationships. We are wise papas most of the time, even with people who are old enough to be *our* papas.

My students and I like to try out this possibility with some questions to ourselves:

How does it feel to be dependent, to *not know* what is happening to you (in a dentist's chair, or a used car lot)?

How would it feel to have the person sitting next to you place a blindfold over your eyes, then take your hand and lead you around Miami?

(These are the feelings clients have when they come to see you, and your reaction to them will either deepen the dependence or work toward dissolving it by helping the client to affirm his own dignity, his own ability to choose.)

How does it feel to be depended upon? Do you react to this dependence, when it is clear to you, by accepting the "wise papa" role? Are you annoyed? Bored? Afraid? To put that into four somewhat more specific contexts:

¶ 2251

Case One: Client says he wants a will which makes it impossible for his wife to control his property.

Case Two: Client chooses to nominate as guardian for his children a relative you know to be stupid and cruel.

Case Three: Client wants a will which will cut off his wife and children and give all his money to the Christian Anti–Communist Crusade.

Case Four: Client looks at you with tears in his eyes (or hers) and says, "Forget my relatives. What I really want to do is give all of my money to *you!*"

The lawyer's reaction to these client feelings will either advance or retard the dependence on which the "wise papa" counseling model rests. And the one thing that is not possible in these situations is not to react. Some of us may think we can say, "Okay, whatever you want," but, as a matter of fact, we cannot. I am bound to have feelings in every one of these cases, and the fact that I have feelings is bound to be picked up by the client and to matter to him. The client may not get my feelings accurately, but he will get something. In each of those cases I am likely to feel moral disapproval, or rebellion, or panic, or a lack of control over the situation or a need to protect the client from himself. My feelings, the feelings of the lawyer in these scenes, have everything to do with the way the dependence will be resolved.

If the lawyer reacts in these cases as a parent would react—with fatherly approval or disapproval—he will encourage dependence. Dependence will sometimes be expressed in submission, sometimes in rebellion, but it will be dependence nonetheless—a situation in which the client believes and is being led to believe that he is not old enough, not wise enough, not courageous enough, to act for himself. He has to have a wise papa.

There is an alternative. Part of it is to sort out the feelings involved, to discover with my client where the boundary lies between *his* feelings and attitudes and *my* feelings and attitudes. But to do that I will have to level with him. I will have to tell him how I feel about what he is doing; I cannot leave him guessing. If his attitude toward his wife annoys me, I am going to have to tell him I am annoyed.

Another part of the alternative is to accept his feelings, whatever they are. The idea, put negatively, is that the counselor refuses to be a judge. It says to the client: I hear what you're saying; I accept and understand your feelings, but I refuse to judge them, one way or the other, because it is *you* who are important to me.

It must sound pretty hard to be both open and accepting at the same time, but I think that is what is required if one wants to avoid becoming a wise papa for his clients—if one wants to insist on maintaining his role as a companion rather than a censor. The key to it, in Rogers' phrase, is to enter into the client's world. To feel it as he feels it. It is a subtle and difficult skill; Rogers relates it to empathy. The empathic response to people is acceptance without judging—what Roger calls "unconditional positive regard"—and an affirmation of the client's dignity and ability to choose for himself.

Many lawyers are instinctively good at this—much better at it than people like me who talk about it. But a lot of us are not very good at it. And I fear that the result of our being poor counselors, poor companions, is an immense amount of property disposition which is not representative of our clients' ability to be themselves. There is evidence for that generalization. The prevalence of spendthrift clauses in trust instruments is an example; there cannot be that many clients who think of their loved ones as dim-witted. Another example is the staggering amount of sexism in most wills and trusts—dehumanizing disabilities on widows, assumptions that daughters (but not sons) need trustee protection, biased distinctions between sons-in-law and daughters-in-law. Another set of examples clusters around draftsmanship which facilitates commercial transactions at the expense of the people the instrument is supposed to serve—distributions of tangible personalty outright to minor beneficiaries, for instance, so that the trustee need not be bothered with storing and selling it; protections of third persons who deal with the trustee, at the expense of the beneficiaries; provisions which relieve trustees from a duty of loyalty, or a duty to account, or a duty to observe investment guidelines, or to post surety bonds. We could argue about the abstract merits of clauses of this sort. I am not interested in their merits. I want only to ask you: How often do these significant provisions proceed from the client's own dignified, *affirmed* ability to choose, and how often do they proceed from his inappropriate dependence on his lawyer.

F. CLIENT INTERVIEWS

[¶ 2301]

The importance of employing good interview techniques to establish a successful interrelationship with a client is developed by Harrop A. Freeman in The Role of Lawyers as Counselors, 7 Wm. And Mary L. Rev. 203, 207–208 (1966).

A great deal could be written about techniques and establishing interrelation. We can only sketch the roughest outline. The lawyer should be friendly and informal, but professional. He must be a sympathetic, interested and attentive listener; tolerant and non-judgmental; neutral as to the subject matter, concerned as to the person; empathetic and creating rapport; neither under-or over-involved emotionally; giving the feeling of working "with" rather than "for". The lawyer must put the interviewee at ease and be committed to the interview. But, long before the lawyer has met the interviewee he will have decided many strategy questions: where shall I get the information, from whom; will this interviewee furnish it or show me where I can get it; will the atmosphere be hostile, friendly, intermediate—ambivalent or polarized; should I be "sponsored"; who is the best interviewer, the best place for interview,

¶ 2301

time, setting; how much information shall I try to get in one interview, several; how much existing information shall be shared, etc. Some interviewers use a check list on a given problem. In all events, whatever techniques are used, we are trying to obtain the information wanted, motivate the giving of information, assure the accuracy of the giving, hear and observe fairly, record and evaluate wisely.

It may seem to state the obvious that interviewing is communication, but this can never be stated too often. You want the client's story; words are slippery tools. The client must use words which he thinks will convey his exact meaning (he will not); the interviewer must try to get the same connotations (he will not). Do not hesitate to go back and clarify meaning; watch for one-word or "escape" answers and for Freudian slips. Watch also for "body language"—the nods, smiles, grimaces, stammerings, blushes, shakes, tics, as well as the lighting of cigarettes, crossing of legs, and other nervous acts. Listening is both a receptive ear and an observant eye. And you must watch your own communication—speak to the client, speak slowly, speak clearly, and use language he will understand. Learn facilitators and inhibitors of communication; you may have to find an appropriate way to stop a man who has diarrhea of the mouth or to virtually mine the information from a shy and reticent interviewee. Interviewing is subject to the difficulties lawyers know so well as to witnesses and facts—forgetfulness, chronological inaccuracy, inferential error, faulty observation, inaccuracy or incompleteness of all reports, emotions and conclusions posing as facts. For memory is fickle and recall a thief. And it is the interviewer who must steer the interview past these pitfalls.

Good interviewing is all the things we have mentioned: an art, interpersonal relations, maximizing information flow, communication, questioning, selecting, empathy and sharing confidences, total confidentiality, timing, collecting, verifying, synthesizing, and framing hypotheses. But, in the end, interviewing like other relationships, is being yourself. Studies show that it is not the method, the techniques, the "school" of the interviewer, but whether he seeks the real client and shows his real self which determines success.

G.   GATHERING INFORMATION

[¶ 2351]

Even if you believe that will-making cannot be reduced to the fundamental level described at ¶ 2051, you must agree that the obvious question is "how do you gather the required information?" This is the counseling function. Do you do this in the context of a formal conference with the client or do you send out a questionnaire which raises these questions and directs the client to contact your office once he or she has completed the questionnaire? Alternatively, do you arrange a formal meeting with the client and, after greetings are exchanged, hand the client over to a paralegal who will gather the required information and prepare a memorandum for your review summarizing the information relevant to the preparation of the dispositive instruments?

H.   FEES FOR ESTATE PLANNING SERVICES

[¶ 2401]

The factors to be given significant weight in determining reasonable estate planning attorney's fees for services in the planning of an estate are pointed out by Robert Bandy in Statement of Principles Concerning the Responsibilities of the Estate Planning Attorney in Texas, 41 TEX. B. J. 169, 174 (1978).

> The public is entitled to assurance that the overall cost of the planning of an individual's estate will be fair and reasonable in light of the circumstances of the particular plan, always keeping in mind the variations in the amount of services actually rendered by the estate planning attorney in such cases.

> The fee of the attorney for services in the planning of an individual's estate should bear a reasonable relationship to the value of the *services* actually rendered and the *responsibility* actually assumed by the estate planning attorney involved (even though on occasion it may be difficult to delineate the extent of the services properly to be rendered and the responsibility properly to be assumed by the estate planning attorney, such services and responsibilities are spelled out in detail in this Statement of Principles). The following factors, in particular, should be given significant weight in determining reasonable estate planning attorney's fees for services in the planning of an estate:

> (a) the extent of the responsibilities assumed and the results obtained; and

> (b) the time and labor required, the novelty and difficulty of the questions involved, and the skill requisite to perform the services properly; and

> (c) the sufficiency of assets properly available to pay for the services.

> The estate planning attorney should also advise the client concerning what portion of the legal fees are deductible for income tax purposes under § 212 of the Internal Revenue Code as expenses incurred with respect to tax planning and what portions are non-deductible personal expenses.

[¶ 2403]

LUMAN v. COMMISSIONER

United States Tax Court, 1982.
79 T.C. 846.

SIMPSON, Judge: * * *

On April 19, 1974, the Lumans were visited by two men, Logan Barclay and Frank Carnefix, who were representatives of Educational Scientific Publishers (ESP). Mr. Barclay and Mr. Carnefix sought to persuade the Lumans to establish a family trust, using forms provided by ESP. The Lumans saw this proposal as an opportunity to ensure the "orderly transfer of [their] assets to * * * [their] children when * * * [they] should be gone," and for such reason, the Lumans accepted the ESP proposal. The ESP family trust documents are drawn with a purpose of shifting the incidence of taxation from the grantor to the trust, but the discussions between the Lumans and the representatives of ESP included no discussions about taxes. The Lumans did not consult with an attorney before deciding to accept the ESP proposal because they lacked respect for attorneys as a result of their prior experience with attorneys.

The ESP family trust plan used by the Lumans involved the creation of two trusts: the Robert B. Luman Educational Trust (the educational trust) and the Robert B. Luman Family Estate (A Trust) (the family trust). On April 20, 1974, Robert Luman executed a declaration of trust by which he, as grantor, created the educational trust. The purpose of this trust was to provide the Lumans with information regarding the establishment and operation of the family trust. The trustees of the educational trust were the two representatives of ESP, Mr. Barclay and Mr. Carnefix. The Lumans paid this trust $20,000. The payment was, in effect, the fee charged by ESP for its assistance in establishing the family trust. Such assistance included the furnishing of forms for establishing the trust and advice from a lawyer, Paul Wright, and a CPA concerning the conduct of the trust as it related to the Lumans' business affairs. However, the Lumans received no legal advice in establishing the trust; in fact, they received no legal advice concerning the trust until 1976. The educational trust is no longer in existence.

* * *

[The court held that the trust was ineffective to shift the income tax liability for the trust's income from the petitioner, the Lumans, to the trust.]

[Estate Planning Fees]

The second issue for decision is whether the petitioner is entitled to a deduction for the $20,000 that she and her husband paid to ESP in connection with the creation of the family trust in 1974. She contends that this fee is deductible under § 212. * * * The Commissioner argues that the trust was created solely for personal reasons and that the fee is a nondeductible personal expense. § 262. The petitioner has the burden of proving that she is entitled to the deduction. * * *

Section 212(2) allows a deduction for all the ordinary and necessary expenses paid or incurred during the taxable year for the management, conservation, or maintenance of property held for the production of income. The petitioner contends that the $20,000 payment to ESP was incurred to manage, conserve, or maintain the Lumans' ranch and their securities.

The deduction provided by § 212(2) is limited in application: An expenditure is not deductible under such § if it is incurred with respect to property that is not held for the production of income. Reg. § 1.212–1(h); Contini v. Commissioner, 76 T.C. 447, 452–53 (1981). Also, an expenditure is not deductible under § 212(2) if it is a personal, living, or family expense which is nondeductible pursuant to § 262. Regs. §§ 1.211–1, 1.212–1. In Epp v. Commissioner, 78 T.C. 801 (1982), this Court recently held that the expense of creating a similar family trust was a personal expense not deductible under § 212(2).

In *Epp,* the taxpayer was concerned with protecting her interest in property, some of which may have been income-producing property, and ensuring that such property would pass to her sisters upon her death without diminution by reason of probate and related expenses. She sought to deduct under § 212(2) the cost of the materials and services used to create the trust, including legal and accounting services and tax advice. In determining what a taxpayer must show to qualify for a deduction under § 212(2), we said:

> advice on merely how to rearrange title to income-producing property relates to neither the management nor the conservation of such property within the meaning of § 212. See Schultz v. Commissioner, 50 T.C. 688, 689–700 (1968), affd. per curiam, 420 F.2d 490 (3d Cir. 1970); Bagley v. Commissioner, * * * [8 T.C. 130, 135 (1947).]

> * * *

> We have held that amounts paid for advice with respect to planning one's personal and family affairs, such as establishing trusts for family members or making gifts, are nondeductible personal expenditures within the meaning of § 262. Mathews v. Commissioner, 61 T.C. 12, 27 (1973), revd. on another issue 520 F.2d 323 (5th Cir. 1975); Cobb v. Commissioner, 10 T.C. 380, 383 (1948), affd. 173 F.2d 711 (6th Cir. 1949); Bagley v. Commissioner, supra. * * *

> * * * Moreover, the deduction under § 212(2) applies to expenditures for the protection or preservation of property itself, such as safeguarding or keeping it up, but not to the expenditures for a taxpayer's retention of ownership in it. United States v. Gilmore, 372 U.S. 39, 44 (1963); Reed v. Commissioner, 55 T.C. 32, 42 (1970) * * * [78 T.C. at 805–806; fn. ref. omitted.]

Thus, in *Epp,* we held that an expenditure for rearranging title to income-producing property, for planning one's personal and family affairs (such as establishing trusts for family members or making gifts), or for retaining ownership of property are not deductible under § 212(2) but are nondeductible personal expenditures within the meaning of § 262.

¶ 2403

In Bagley v. Commissioner, 8 T.C. 130, 135 (1947), there was an expenditure for legal advice to review proposed estate plans. The plans proposed a substantial rearrangement and reinvestment of the taxpayer's entire estate of income-producing properties. The proposal included the creation of inter vivos trusts in which the taxpayer retained the income for life and the drafting of testamentary trusts. We analogized the expense to the cost of investment counsel, for which a deduction was, and is, allowable (Reg. § 1.212–1(g)), and we held the expenditure deductible under the predecessor of § 212(2). In the same case, we denied a deduction for the cost of legal advice received by the taxpayer concerning the creation of an inter vivos trust for the benefit of her daughter and the release of the taxpayer's powers of appointment. We said:

> We are unable to see what possible connection the disposition of part of petitioner's income-producing securities by way of gift in trust could have with the production or collection of income; nor do we think that it can properly be said to have a proximate connection with the management, conservation, or maintenance of such property * * * [8 T.C. at 135.]

We believe that *Bagley* supports our holding in *Epp*. The deduction allowed in *Bagley* was generally for legal services in the nature of investment advice for the management of income-producing property; a deduction was expressly denied for advice concerning the advisable methods for making gifts of property. However, to the extent that *Bagley* is inconsistent with our later decision in *Epp, Bagley* will no longer be followed.

Merians v. Commissioner, 60 T.C. 187 (1973), also involved the question of the deductibility of the costs of developing an estate plan. In that case, the petitioners claimed a deduction under § 212(3) for the costs of the tax advice received in developing such plan, but they did not claim a deduction under § 212(2) for the other legal services involved in developing such plan. Although there was a question as to the precise amount allocable to the cost of the tax advice, we were convinced that a significant portion of the payment was allocable to such advice, and hence, we allowed a deduction under § 212(3) for that amount. In *Epp,* the petitioner could not support a claim for a deduction for tax advice under § 212(3), and therefore, there is no inconsistency between our opinions in *Merians* and in *Epp*.

In this case, it is clear that the trust was created to serve the petitioner's purely personal objectives. The Lumans created the family trust in an attempt to retain their ranch in the family for as long as possible and to ensure "an orderly transfer of assets to our children when we should be gone." The Lumans were not influenced by business or tax considerations. They sought to achieve their goal by transferring most of their property, both income-producing and non-income-producing, to the trust. The purpose and effect of the trust are the same as those encountered in *Epp*. Under these circumstances, we hold that the Lumans may not deduct under § 212(2) the cost of the ESP materials and assistance in creating the trust.

Moreover, the petitioner has not met her burden of proving that any portion of the expenditure was attributable to a cost other than the nondeductible cost of creating the trust. Rule 142(a); Welch v. Helvering, *supra*. The petitioner testified that the fee was payment for advice from an attorney and

¶ 2403

a CPA concerning the operation of the family trust as it related to the Lumans' ranching business. She also testified that the fee was paid to provide information regarding the management of the trust. This testimony is the only indication that the $20,000 fee, or any part of it, may have been paid for the management of the Lumans' income-producing property.

The petitioner's testimony concerning what she and her husband purchased with the fee is vague and is patently inconsistent with other evidence of record. It is clear that a portion of the fee must be allocated to nondeductible personal expenditures, such as to the cost of the forms used to create the trust, to the advice needed to complete such forms, and to determining which family members would receive an interest in the ranch and the share of each. Also, the ranch residence and its contents, which may have constituted a significant part of the property transferred to the family trust by the Lumans, were not income-producing property, but were used by the Lumans for personal purposes, and the portion of the fee attributable to the management, conservation, or maintenance of the personal residence is not deductible. Reg. § 1.212–1(h); Contini v. Commissioner, 76 T.C. at 453. Therefore, it is highly questionable whether any substantial amount of the fee is attributable to an expenditure deductible under § 212(2).

In addition, there is no evidence showing whether the information which the Lumans were to receive concerning "trust management" related solely to the creation of the trust or to the management of trust assets. In fact, the Lumans continued to manage their business themselves, as they had prior to the creation of the trust. The petitioner and her husband, in occasional consultation with the daughter, made all investment and business decisions. What is more, they received no legal or accounting advice until 1976, 2 years after they created the trust, and there is no evidence that this advice in any way concerned the management, conservation, or maintenance of the Lumans' income-producing property. In summary, to allow a deduction under § 212(2), it would be necessary to allocate the fee between the portions attributable to income-producing and non-income-producing properties and between the portions attributable to the management of the income-producing property and other portions attributable to other activities, including the creation of the trust. Such an allocation is impossible on the meager evidence in this record.

When a petitioner proves that some part of an expenditure was made for deductible purposes, and when the record contains sufficient evidence for us to make a reasonable allocation, we will do so. Cohan v. Commissioner, 39 F.2d 540 (2d Cir. 1930); Merians v. Commissioner, 60 T.C. at 189–190. In this case, all that the petitioner has shown is that some portion of the payment to ESP conceivably could have been attributable to the management of the Lumans' income-producing property. A deduction cannot stand on so flimsy a foundation. An allocation of any portion of the payment to a § 212(2) purpose would be speculative, amounting to "unguided largesse." Williams v. United States, 245 F.2d 559, 560 (5th Cir. 1957); Epp v. Commissioner, 78 T.C. at 807; see Contini v. Commissioner, 76 T.C. at 454; Schultz v. Commissioner, 50

¶ 2403

T.C. at 700. Consequently, we hold that the petitioner is not entitled to deduct any portion of the $20,000 payment under § 212(2).

[Tax Advice Deductible]

Nor is the petitioner entitled to deduct any portion of the fee under § 212(3). Such section permits a deduction for the ordinary and necessary expenses paid or incurred during the taxable year in connection with the determination, collection, or refund of any tax. Thus, expenses for tax counsel are deductible (Reg. § 1.212–1(1)), and estate planning advice to reduce taxes may be deductible under § 212(3). Epp v. Commissioner, 78 T.C. at 805; Merians v. Commissioner, *supra*. However, the petitioner does not contend that payment of the $20,000 fee entitled the Lumans to receive any tax counsel, and the record contains no evidence indicating that any of the fee was paid for such purpose. Indeed, the petitioner concedes that tax considerations in no way influenced the Lumans' decision to create the family trust. Hence, there is no basis for allowing a deduction under § 212(3). Epp v. Commissioner, supra at 805.

* * *

Reviewed by the Court.

NIMS, J., concurring: While I fully agree with the result reached in this case, I do not fully agree with the route by which it was reached. I regard this case merely as one more routine family trust case, and as such do not view it as an appropriate vehicle for an extended reexamination of the deductibility of estate planning expenses. In particular, I do not agree with the mixed signals we are sending out regarding the continued efficacy of Bagley v. Commissioner, 8 T.C. 130 (1947).

FEATHERSTON, J., agrees with this concurring opinion.

GOFFE, J., concurring in part and dissenting in part: I respectfully dissent as to the second issue. In my view, the majority has failed to heed the admonition of Justice Frankfurter, "The baby is not to be thrown out with the bath." International Salt Co. v. United States, 332 U.S. 392, 405 (1947). I fully recognize that problems that have been created by what the majority describes as "canned" trusts sold by ESP and others. Horvat v. Commissioner, 671 F.2d 990 (7th Cir. 1982), affg. a Memorandum Opinion of this Court. Nevertheless, the instant case does not involve an attempt to tax income from personal services to a trust instead of taxing it to the true earner of the income. In its enthusiasm to deny the deduction for the $20,000 which petitioner and her husband paid for the creation of the trust, the majority has seriously undercut the case law which permits deductions under § 212(2).

I was the trier of fact in this case. I agree with the findings of fact as stated by the majority but I do not agree with some of the inferences which it draws, and I strongly disagree with the manner in which the majority has applied the law.

The majority points out that petitioner received no legal advice regarding the trust until 1976. If this is interpreted to mean that petitioner received no advice from a lawyer until 1976, then it is correct. If, instead, it implies that petitioner and her husband received no advice as to the legal effect of having their property held in trust, then the inference is incorrect. As the majority points out, petitioner and her husband prepared and executed meticulous minutes of the meeting of the trustees. This fact demonstrates that they received considerable instructions on the law, the cost of which should be deductible as part of the cost of management, conservation, or maintenance of property held for the production of income. Petitioner, her husband, and their daughter carefully observed the legal distinctions brought about by the creation of the trust.

I strongly disagree with the legal reasoning of the majority. Its opinion is in conflict with our previous holding in Bagley v. Commissioner, 8 T.C. 130 (1947), as to what constitutes a deduction for estate planning under § 212(2). Indeed, the majority overrules that decision. *Bagley* was not appealed by the Commissioner, nor has it previously been criticized nor limited in its application, although it has been relied upon for a long period of time. In Schultz v. Commissioner, 50 T.C. 688, 700 (1968), we stated the following:

> The record herein furnishes no basis for an allocation. Such being the case, we cannot determine to what extent the services included estate planning of the type which might give rise to a deductible expense under § 212. Nancy Reynolds Bagley, 8 T.C. 130 (1947). * * *

The present case, involving a trust tainted with the pejorative connotations of an ESP trust which was expressly designed to shift income, is an exceedingly poor vehicle for reconsidering the parameters of § 212(2). The vast majority of estate planning expenses are legitimate in all respects. I would not characterize the expenses which we allowed in *Bagley* as "investment advice" as does the majority, but would, instead describe them as estate planning expenses. The expenses incurred by the Lumans were for advice in the establishment and operations of an inter vivos trust, the income from which is deemed retained by them for life. Under the rationale of *Bagley*, the $20,000 fee paid by the Lumans is deductible.

Let us suppose, for example, that an elderly couple owns a large ranch with a large herd of cattle. They want their children to inherit the ranch and, in the meantime, want the ranch to be managed carefully. They consult their attorney, who is a member of a prominent, "silk stocking" law firm, who prepares an inter vivos trust to own the ranch in which the couple retains the income of the trust for life. They approve the trust agreement and appoint the trust department of a large bank as trustee because it has a very competent farm and ranch management department. Under the rationale of the majority in the instant case, the fee which the couple pays to their attorney is not deductible. But doesn't this fee represent services rendered for the management, conservation, or maintenance of property held for the production of income? I think that it does and that such a fee should be deductible. I view the payment in my example, in *Bagley*, and in the instant case as coming within the plain language of § 212(2).

The majority attempts to holster its holding by relying upon Epp v. Commissioner, 78 T.C. 801 (1982). I likewise think *Epp* is a poor vehicle for overruling *Bagley*. I viewed *Epp* when it was filed as merely a case where the taxpayer failed to prove that the property she conveyed to the trust was income-producing property. In the instant case, the majority makes a point of the fact that the residence on the ranch was not income-producing property. The residence on an active, income-producing ranch has been held by us to be a part of the business premises of a ranch, and it follows, therefore, that it is an integral part of the income-producing asset, the ranch. *McDowell v. Commissioner,* T.C. Memo. 1974–72.

Lastly, the suggestion of the majority as to an allocation of such fees is unworkable. If I were an attorney preparing an estate plan, I could not conceive of a way to allocate my fee among the various results of my work in order for some of the fee to be deductible. Any allocation would be nothing more than a fiction.

Problem

[¶ 2411]

Under what circumstances, if any, should a client be advised to claim an income tax deduction for estate planning fees? Does it depend upon whether the services were rendered by lawyers or nonlawyers? Could you, as the provider of such services, structure your billing so as to make the tax deduction more readily available to your client? If so, are you troubled by the potential for improper manipulation of the tax laws? Berall, Deductibility of Legal Fees in Estate Planning and Administration, 33 Est. Plan 19 (2006).

I.   CONFLICT OF INTEREST IN SPOUSAL REPRESENTATION

[¶ 2451]

It is the unusual case when persons married to each other seek separate representation when estate planning. To have both spouses come together to the planning sessions is invariably the experience of those who work in this field. Unfortunately, in many situations, representing both spouses constitutes a conflict of interest for the professional.

Rule 1.7(a) of the American Bar Association Model Rules of Professional Conduct (2003) states that:

> [A] lawyer shall not represent a client if the representation involves a concurrent conflict of interest. A concurrent conflict of interest exists if: (1) the representation of one client will be directly adverse to another client; or (2) there is a significant risk that the representation of one or more clients will be materially limited by the lawyer's responsibilities to another client, a former client or a third person or by a personal interest of the lawyer.

Rule 1.7(b) goes further and states that:

> [A] lawyer may represent a client if: (1) the lawyer reasonably believes that the lawyer will be able to provide competent and diligent representa-

¶ 2403

tion to each affected client; (2) the representation is not prohibited by law; (3) the representation does not involve the assertion of a claim by one client against another client represented by the lawyer in the same litigation or other proceeding before a tribunal; and (4) each affected client gives informed consent, confirmed in writing.

Concurrent representation is the subject of spirited debate. See G. Hazard, Jr., Conflict of Interest in Estate Planning for Husband and Wife, 20 Prob. Law. 1–23 (American College of Trust & Estate Counsel 1994); A. Hilker, It's a Family Affair: Ethical Problems for Estate Planners, Prof'l Law. (Symposium Issue) 66, 69 (1993). Professor Hazard concludes that, contrary to some opinion, there is no "separate track" for estate planners when it comes to the rules of professional conduct. He rejects, too, notions of "family representation," i.e., that somehow the family is an entity for purposes of estate planning. He concludes, however, that the rules of professional conduct sanction concurrent representation so long as there is informed consent. For Professor Hazard, informed consent means, in estate planning for husband and wife, full disclosure to each spouse of the other spouse's expectations concerning the property of both spouses. By way of contrast, he rejects the notion that there can be "separate representation" of husband and wife, i.e., that a lawyer can undertake to represent both husband and wife without disclosure to one spouse of the other spouse's "intentions and purposes * * * that have material significance" with respect to the first spouse's expectations concerning the matter. Professor Hazard urges separate interviews with each spouse to ascertain commonality of interest and identification of conflict.

The concept of "separate representation" has been embraced by a Study Committee of the American Bar Association Section of Real Property, Probate & Trust. See M. Moore & A. Hilker, Representing Both Spouses: The New Section Recommendations, Prob. & Prop., July–Aug. 1993, at 26, 30; Am. Coll. of Trust & Estate Counsel, ACTEC Commentaries on Model Rules of Prof'l Conduct, 63–64, 76–77 (Am. College of Trust and Estate Counsel Found., 4th ed. 2006). Some lawyers with experience in estate planning chose to represent spouses separately on a regular basis. ACTEC Commentaries at 63, 77. It has been suggested that it is enough that the lawyer gives notice to each spouse that the lawyer is also doing estate planning for the other spouse. It has been said, too, that in a "separate representation * * * the lawyer may not disclose information to one spouse that has been obtained in confidence from the other spouse." A. K. Hilker, It's a Family Affair: Ethical Problems for Estate Planners, Prof'l Law. (Symposium Issue) 66, 81–82 (1993). However, the ACTEC Commentaries caution that, "[a] lawyer who is asked to provide separate representation to multiple clients should do so with great care because of the stress it necessarily places on the lawyer's duties of impartiality and loyalty and the extent to which it may limit the lawyer's ability to advise each of the clients adequately." ACTEC Commentaries at 63.

Many attorneys agree to represent husbands and wives parties jointly, even if their individual interests are not identical. Id. at 63. Joint representation will likely be less costly for the client, and may enable the attorney to provide better representation because the attorney has a greater understand-

¶ 2451

ing of all of the concerns facing the married couple and their family. Id. at 76. When the individual clients have different goals, a lawyer that represents the entire family may be in a better position to advise clients and elicit cooperation in order to meet the common goals of the family. Id. In fact, an attorney is presumed to represent multiple related clients jointly, unless there is an agreement to the contrary. Id. at 63.

If the attorney chooses to represent spouses jointly, it is important that the attorney discuss with each spouse the extent to which information may be shared with the other spouse, because significant complications when a spouse desires to keep statements confidential from the other spouse. See id. at 63, 76. Further, the attorney should explain that he or she may be required to withdraw his or her representation if the spouses' interests become so disparate that the attorney could not represent both spouses effectively. Id. at 76. Indeed, an attorney may not represent spouses jointly if there are serious conflicts at the outset of representation that prevent the attorney from effectively representing each spouse's interests. Id. at 77. The ACTEC Commentaries suggest meeting with clients separately before agreeing to joint representation so that they feel comfortable disclosing areas where potential conflicts of interest may arise. Id. at 63, 76. In addition, attorneys should obtain written consent from clients when representing spouses—either jointly or separately—that includes full written disclosure of the implications of joint and separate representation. Id. at 77.

Problems

[¶ 2461]

1. Jack and Jill, newlyweds, come for a will. Jack is 30 and just getting started as a computer programmer after completing, at long last, a correspondence course. Jill is 52 and the mother of three adult children, one of whom, Billy, is capable, at best, of living independently only with a strong support unit at hand. Jack has "no property to speak of" but Jill has an estate of more than $3 million (received upon termination of a trust established by her grandfather). Jack begins the conversation by saying that "we both see marriage as a partnership and, when we married, what was mine became hers and what was hers became mine. If I die first, I want Jill to have everything and, if Jill dies first, Jill wants me to have everything." At this point, Jill smiles, seeming to agree. Can you represent Jack and Jill?

2. Raj is dead. You drafted Raj's will wherein he gives his wife, Lu, the income from a trust for life. The trust terminates at Lu's death. Lu has the express right, by appropriate provision in her will, to select the person or persons who will receive the trust property when the trust terminates. Under the terms of Raj's will, Lu could select even her own estate as the ultimate beneficiary. However, to exercise the power—Lu's right is called a power of appointment—Raj's will insists that Lu's will make express reference to the paragraph in Raj's will that gives Lu the right of selection. In the event Lu fails to effectively exercise the power Raj has

given her over his property, the trust property is to be distributed to Raj's aged mother.

You handled the administration of Raj's estate. It is now completed and Lu comes to you, impressed by your careful and effective work, and asks you to prepare a will for her. She reports that her child from a prior marriage is to be the sole beneficiary of her estate. Lu does not seem to know about her power over Raj's trust, saying only, "I have no control over Raj's trust; it all goes to his mother after I die."

You recall that, at the time Raj's will was being prepared, Raj included Lu's power of appointment only because you had advised him that the presence of such a power resulted in a deferral of estate tax on the trust property until the death of Lu—and that Raj never expected Lu to exercise the power of appointment.

Would you have a conflict of interest in preparing Lu's will? That is, would you have a duty to enlighten Lu as to her power? Would you breach your duty to Raj if you enlightened Lu?

3. Your longtime client, Clarissa, telephones and reports that her aunt, Gert, is hospitalized with a terminal illness—and does not have a will. Clarissa asks that you prepare a will for Gert and send it by messenger to Gert at the hospital. Clarissa tells you that her children, Pedro and Lupe, are to be the sole beneficiaries. The will is prepared and sent on to the hospital where Gert, in the presence of two nurses as witnesses, signs the will— and falls dead immediately thereafter. Afterwards you learn that Clarissa's sister, Marissa, is claiming the will to be invalid since it failed to make mention of her and her children. Clarissa assures you that Gert had no affection for Marissa and her family and did not want them included in the will. Will you sleep well tonight?

¶ 2461

Chapter 3

WILL PLANNING

A. OBJECTIVES

[¶ 3001]

The very least that can be done for a testator is to give the testator a will which is worthy of the name. This is not a nostalgic call for a return to the era of "whereas," "hereinbefore," "said," and "whereof," all of which was aimed at precision in drafting but, in turn, sometimes produced sentences and paragraphs so convoluted that not even other lawyers—let alone the testator—were able to understand what the draftsperson meant. Trachtman, in Maxims for Estate Planners, 11 Prac. Law. 77, 82 (1965), said it well:

> The language of a well-written will is beautiful. The beauty comes not from rich imagery or refined use of shades of meaning or from elegant variations of words. There is beauty in language that is put together in straight lines without embellishment. "Pay to the order of" has the sweet sound of a sonnet.
>
> It is no more tedious to strive for this kind of beauty than to produce dreary, overblown, mechanically used language. Drudgery cannot be avoided, but why not try for the pleasure and pride that comes from writing neat and tidy instruments? With practice, no more time will be consumed in doing so.

How then do you express the testator's wishes in the plain English imperative of today? The trick of it all is as it was years ago. Understandable prose can be written if the draftsperson makes a comprehensive textual outline of the ideas which the instrument must address. The ideas which make up the outline are the wishes of the testator leavened by the scholarship of the draftsperson. This is the counseling function. But the only effective counselor is the informed counselor.

The function of the materials in this chapter is to give the draftsperson insight as to the drafting problems most often encountered and how these issues are typically addressed.

Another function of this chapter is to demystify will drafting and demonstrate that will drafting is hardly more than an enumeration of the wishes of the testator in logical fashion accompanied by some technical enabling language to facilitate administration of the testator's estate.

B. THE NEED FOR A WILL

[¶ 3051]

1. INTESTACY

It is a common law principle that when a person dies without a will, the community should cause the decedent's property to be distributed as the decedent would have wanted had a will been executed. Dunham, The Method, Process and Frequency of Wealth Transmission at Death, 30 U. Chi. L. Rev. 241 (1963). See also Parry, The Law of Succession 158 (2d ed. 1947). This principle has been considered the basis for the rules of intestate succession which exist in the various jurisdictions. Chaffin, A Reappraisal of the Wealth Transmission Process: The Surviving Spouse, Year's Support and Intestate Succession, 10 Ga. L. Rev. 447, 448 (1976). Whether intestate laws adequately accomplish this objective is questionable. For example, in one study it was concluded that the intestate laws distribute property in a manner "seriously contrary to the average expectations of the community." See Dunham, The Method, Process and Frequency of Wealth Transmission at Death, 30 U. Chi. L. Rev. 241, 285 (1963) (Illinois); Intestate Succession in New Jersey, 12 Colum. J. Law & Soc. 253 (1976) (Morris County, New Jersey).

The problem with statutes regarding intestacy is that these laws are designed to distribute a moderately sized estate comprised of ordinary types of property to a number of blood relatives who are friendly toward each other. W. Leach, Cases and Text on the Law of Wills 8 (2d ed. 1960). Moreover, intestacy statutes are designed to account for all decedents' estates and cannot provide for individual circumstances.

Generalization is risky, but it probably can be safely said that descendants are preferred to ancestors, meaning that where an intestate is survived by both parents and children, the children will divide all of the intestate's property and the parents will take nothing. Where there is a surviving spouse, the spouse will typically receive one-third, while the children will divide the remaining two-thirds. Most statutes anticipate that one or more children will have predeceased the intestate and that children of the deceased children, i.e., grandchildren, will have survived the intestate. Normally, the surviving grandchildren will take the share that the deceased child would have taken had he or she survived the intestate. There is disagreement as to how that share is to be divided among the grandchildren in cases where two or more children have predeceased the intestate. Under one view, each grandchild is to take an equal share of the deceased children's shares. Under another view, each deceased child's share is divided among his or her children.

> *Example.* Bud died intestate. His two children, Chip and Clara, predeceased him. Chip was survived only by his son, Duff; Clara by her eight children. Under the first view, Duff and the other grandchildren would each take one-ninth of Bud's property. See Unif. Probate Code § 2–106(b) (amended 1990), 8 U.L.A. 85–86 (1998). Under the other view, Duff would take one-half of Bud's property and Clara's eight children would divide equally the other one-half. See Restatement (Second) of Property § 28.2 (1988).

¶ 3051

Modern statutes will give preference to the surviving spouse. For example, the surviving spouse is to take the intestate's entire estate under UPC § 2–102 if all of the intestate's descendants are also descendants of the surviving spouse and the surviving spouse has no other surviving descendants. Where the intestate is survived not by descendants but by a spouse and one or more parents, the surviving spouse is to take the first $200,000 plus three-fourths of the remaining intestate property. The surviving parent or parents take the balance.

[¶ 3059]

2. THE WILLS PRIVILEGE

Little attention is given to the fairness of the intestate schemes adopted by the several states because individuals who want to make a different disposition of their property may do so by the simple expedient of making a will. By will, a person can dispose of his or her property in whatsoever manner that he or she wishes so long as the disposition does not, in some way, offend public policy. (A devise will offend public policy if it violates the Rule Against Perpetuities (see ¶ 5401). Does a direction to "destroy my dwelling house" offend public policy?)

Whether a will is a privilege or a right can be debated. Is it a constitutionally protected right guaranteed by the Due Process Clause or does it exist only as a matter of legislative grace?

Historically, wills of land were not permitted in England prior to the Statute of Wills in 1540. However, lifetime transfers of real property were permitted by livery of seisin. Accordingly, some persons undertook to make lifetime conveyances which contained a stipulation that the grantee would hold the subject premises for the benefit of the grantor during the grantor's lifetime and, after the grantor's death, would hold the premises for the benefit of other persons, normally the natural objects of the grantor's bounty. This contrivance, called a "use," was the forerunner of the device known today as the "trust." However, it took the courts of equity to create the modern trust. Apparently some grantees of uses (called "feoffees to use") declined to respect their commitments to their respective grantors. They did so on the basis that the courts of law had responsibility for the disposition of real property and, so far as these courts were concerned, the grantees had the fee interest in the property. It was the fee interest which the courts of law considered to be ownership and it was this interest which the law courts would recognize and protect. Not wanting a dispute with the courts of law, the courts of equity, in response to the complaints of the disenfranchised grantors, first recognized that the grantees had the fee interest, but then determined that it was inequitable for the grantees to refuse to hold the property for the benefit of the grantor and the beneficiary the grantor had identified. This determination that the grantee had acted in an inequitable manner caused the court of equity to exercise its *in personam* jurisdiction over the grantee and incarcerate the grantee until such time as the grantee decided to honor the commitments to the grantor.

¶ 3051

In 1536, Parliament passed the Statute of Uses, which effectively terminated all uses (trusts) where the feoffees to use (the trustee) had no duties other than to act as a stakeholder to avoid the ban on wills of land. These uses were deemed "executed" in the sense that the *cestui que* uses (trust beneficiaries) were deemed to have both the equitable and legal interest in the property which was the subject matter of the use. As a result, the executed use was deemed to have ended.

Then, in 1540, the Statute of Wills permitted wills of land. Nonetheless, the creation of the courts of equity, the use, continued to exist in those cases where the trustee had some duties to perform with respect to the trust property (other than to merely act as a stakeholder).

Interestingly, prior to 1540 and the Statute of Wills, wills of personal property (called "testaments," hence the term "Last Will and *Testament*") could be made orally to clergymen, for it was to the clergy that supervision of the process of disposing of personal property at death was committed.

Thus, from that checkered beginning, is it appropriate to conclude that wills are a privilege or a right? Several states have insisted that testators who make wills must *literally* comply with the requirements of the legislation authorizing wills that each state has adopted. Does that suggest that wills are a matter of legislative grace?

The modern wills statutes are all almost copies of the Statute of Wills of 1540. Typically, they provide, as does the Texas Probate Code (in pertinent part):

> Every last will and testament, except where otherwise provided by law, shall be in writing and signed by the testator in person or by another person for him by his direction and in his presence, and shall, if not wholly in the handwriting of the testator, be attested by two or more credible witnesses above the age of fourteen years who shall subscribe their names thereto in their own handwriting in the presence of the testator.

Tex. Prob. Code Ann. § 59(a) (Vernon 2003).

[¶ 3067]

3. CULTURAL BIAS IN FAVOR OF JOINT PROPERTY

Undoubtedly some choose to die intestate, in most cases probably believing that a will is an unneeded luxury. See ¶ 2201. In some cases this belief is based not on plain ignorance but on the assumptions: (1) that all property can be held in joint tenancy with right of survivorship (or, where recognized, in tenancy by the entirety) and (2) that any life insurance can be made payable to a named beneficiary. (Some form of tenancy by the entirety apparently exists in more than 20 states, including Alaska, Arkansas, Delaware, Florida, Indiana, Kentucky, Maryland, Massachusetts, Michigan, Missouri, New Jersey, New York, North Carolina, Oklahoma, Oregon, Pennsylvania, Rhode Island, Tennessee, Vermont, Virginia, Wisconsin, and Wyoming.)

¶ 3067

Because of the popularity of these will substitutes—joint tenancy with right of survivorship and beneficiary designation—it is easily understood that some may view the will as a needless formality. Unfortunately, it is the rare individual who can manage to cause *all* of his or her property to be jointly held. Moreover, it is one thing to hold property jointly with one's spouse. It is another to have taken steps to hold property jointly with beneficiaries other than a spouse. And, of course, there is the ever present risk that both spouses will die within a short time of each other, perhaps in the proverbial common disaster, before property interests can be retitled.

For a detailed discussion of joint tenancy, see Chapter 11.

[¶ 3075]

4. THE MIGRANT CLIENT'S SPECIAL NEED FOR A WILL

a. *Reliance on Joint Ownership*

Relying on joint ownership to avoid making a will becomes even chancier in a mobile society where persons are apt to have lived in multiple states during their lifetimes. In a number of jurisdictions, survivorship rights are not routinely available. In these states any conveyance to two or more persons is construed as a tenancy in common with no rights of survivorship, unless the instrument creating the interest clearly indicates otherwise. For example, an Illinois statute provides in pertinent part: "No estate in joint tenancy in any lands, tenements or hereditaments, * * * shall be held or claimed under any grant, legacy or conveyance * * * unless the premises therein mentioned shall expressly be thereby declared to pass not in tenancy in common but in joint tenancy * * *." 765 Ill. Comp. Stat. Ann. 1005/1 (West 2001). For years this, too, was the rule in Ohio. See Sergeant v. Steinberger, 2 Ohio 305 (1826). However, Ohio currently allows creation of tenancies by the entirety when a deed following the form provided in the statute is executed. See Ohio Rev. Code Ann. § 5302.17 (West 1995, Supp. 2006).

[¶ 3083]

b. *Conflicting Interpretations by State Courts*

Variances in states' laws can result in different distributions of property even where the statutes involved are nearly identical! In Carver v. Gilbert, 387 P.2d 928 (Alaska 1963), the grantor and his wife acquired the disputed property by a warranty deed which described them as husband and wife. The wife died intestate prior to the husband's conveyance of the land to the plaintiff. A question arose as to whether the plaintiff had acquired full title to this property or only a one-fourth interest as a tenant in common with the grantor's son. Resolution of this issue turned on whether the grantor and his wife held the land as tenants by the entirety or as tenants in common. The relevant statute in Alaska at that time, § 22–3–8 A.C.L.A. (1949), provided that a tenancy in common is created unless an express intention to create a tenancy by the entirety is manifest. This statute was nearly identical to a parallel Oregon statute which the Oregon Supreme Court had construed to create a tenancy by the entirety. However, the Alaska Supreme Court concluded that the deed to the grantor and his wife created a tenancy in common, and that to overcome the presumption, the conveyance must expressly declare that the grantees take as tenants of the entirety with rights of survivorship.

Thus, simply taking title to property as husband and wife will not automatically create a joint tenancy with rights of survivorship but may only create a tenancy in common. Indeed, even where a deed specifically referred to a married couple as tenants by the entirety, one court found a tenancy in common. In Fay v. Smiley, 201 Iowa 1290, 207 N.W. 369 (1926), the spouse claimed title to land under a deed from the husband to husband and wife as tenants by the entirety and not as tenants in common. Despite this language, the Iowa Supreme Court ruled that those words were merely descriptive of the parties and not controlling as to the type of estate created. In the absence of greater detail, the court construed the deed to create a tenancy in common.

Even if rights of survivorship exist where a migrant happens to die, some jurisdictions will differentiate between real and personal property. In addition to states which disallow tenancies by the entirety altogether, a number of states, which recognize tenancies by the entirety in real property, will not recognize tenancies by the entirety in personal property or certain kinds of personal property. Michael A. DiSabatino, Annotation, Estates by the Entirety in Personal Property, 22 A.L.R.4th 459 (2002).

[¶ 3091]

c. *Community Property*

Many persons are surprised to learn that, generally, there is no survivorship feature associated with community property. (Community property exists in nine states—Arizona, California, Idaho, Louisiana, Nevada, New Mexico, Texas, Washington, and Wisconsin, the latter having adopted a version of community property referred to as marital property. See ¶ 11,089–11,193.)

Moreover, once community property, always community property, unless the spouses affirmatively undertake to change the character. Thus, once having acquired community property by virtue of a sojourn in a community property jurisdiction, spouses must continue to treat this property as community even if they remove themselves to a noncommunity property jurisdiction. Of course, practically speaking, this issue will present itself only at the death of one of the parties or the dissolution of the marriage and then only if the spouses disagree as to how the community property should be disposed of.

Most common law states have no specific statutory rule for community property owned by a decedent who was domiciled in the common law property jurisdiction. A few states, however, have adopted the Uniform Disposition of Community Property Rights at Death Act, under which the community character of property will be preserved after it has been transplanted to a common law property jurisdiction. Unif. Disposition of Cmty. Prop. Rights at Death Act §§ 1–13, 8A U.L.A. 216–17 (2003); ¶ 11,185. Among the states are: Alaska, Arkansas, Colorado, Connecticut, Florida, Hawaii, Kentucky, Michigan, Montana, New York, North Carolina, Oregon, Virginia, and Wyoming.

¶ 3091

Generally speaking, the community property states provide different dispositive schemes for separate and community property. Texas goes even further and provides dispositive schemes for a deceased spouse's intestate separate property depending on whether the property is real or personal. In Texas, *separate real property* is distributed one-third to the spouse for life with the remainder in that one-third plus the other two-thirds to the children. Tex. Prob. Code Ann. § 38(b) (Vernon 2003). *Separate personal property* is divided one-third to the spouse and two-thirds to the intestate's children. On the other hand, Texas provides that the decedent's one-half *community property* passes to the decedent's children to the exclusion of the surviving spouse unless the spouse is also the parent of the decedent's children. Tex. Prob. Code Ann. § 45 (Vernon 2003).

Perhaps it should be noted, too, that moving to a community property jurisdiction does not cause the spouses' separate property to become community property.

[¶ 3099]

5. SMALL ESTATES

Do surviving spouses automatically gain full ownership of automobiles, household goods, cash and accrued but unpaid wages? The answer depends on state law. Illinois, for example, presumes that a married couple takes title to property as tenants in common with no corresponding rights of survivorship but makes an exception for certain items of personal property such as joint bank deposits, stocks and bonds, U.S. government obligations, and motor vehicles. 765 Comp. Ill. Stat. Ann. 1005/1 (West 2001). Also, exemption statutes and family allowance provisions are used to shelter this property from the intestate statutes in the absence of a will. Every state has such statutes, but most are archaic and provide little relief or protection to the surviving spouse and family. Chaffin, A Reappraisal of the Wealth Transmission Process! The Surviving Spouse, Year's Support and Intestate Succession, 10 Ga. L. Rev. 447, 475 (1976).

[¶ 3107]

6. OTHER CONSIDERATIONS

A client should also be aware of other important considerations in assessing the need for a will. Which portion of the estate will be used to satisfy the burden of federal and state taxes: the residuary estate or will there be apportionment among the takers, including recipients of nonprobate property? Who will be the executor of the estate and what powers will that executor possess? How should the client's estate be divided among his or her descendants—equally or by representation? What happens if the client and spouse are killed simultaneously? Obviously, the client can best answer these questions by expressing his or her wishes in a will. The alternative is to permit the intestacy laws of the state in which the client by chance dies to resolve these important questions.

¶ 3091

For additional discussion of migrant client problems, see Louis A. Mezzullo & Derry W. Swanger, The Migrant Client: Tax, Community Property, & Other Considerations, 803–2d Tax Mgmt (BNA) A–1 to A–61 (2004).

Problem

[¶ 3120]

Consider whether you would be comfortable if you had the attention of everyone at a cocktail party and were asked to defend the proposition, "Everyone needs a will."

C. ORGANIZATIONAL SCHEME FOR THE WILL

[¶ 3151]

While there is nothing magical about the order in which provisions appear in a will, it was, for a long time, customary for the will to begin with a clause directing that the testator's debts be first paid followed by a direction to pay taxes. Thereafter would come the specific bequests ("My grandfather clock to my daughter."); general legacies ("$10,000 to my son."); occasionally a demonstrative gift ("I give $5,000 to my aunt, Dilly, to be paid out of my account at the First National Bank."); and, finally, the residuary gift ("All of the rest and residue of my estate I give to my children share and share alike."). At this point, it was common for many years to name an executor for the will and to give the executor certain powers to assist in executing the will.

The modern trend is toward beginning all wills with a listing of the players. This section is often referred to as the "identification" section. Here the testator names all of the will beneficiaries as well as the executor. Oftentimes, this section of the will also contains definitions of technical terms used in the will.

One argument for the modern approach is that it can reduce the expense of preparing wills. Because many persons adopt the same dispositive schemes, wills can be drafted so as to employ standardized provisions. Standardization should not only improve the quality of the will, it should reduce the expense of preparation because less professional time will be required. But even with standardization, much preparation time goes into assembly of a will. To be sure, the assembly time could be reduced by using what some practitioners refer to as preprints. Preprints are photocopies of standard pages which are to be included in most wills. With the use of preprints (and the modern organizational approach), all that must be done to customize a will for an individual testator is to prepare the list of players to appear at the beginning of the assembled preprints.

Of course, with the advent of modern word processing with its "global search and replace function," it is possible to use standardized pages which appear to be customized because the beneficiaries' names appear throughout the instrument. Perhaps, more importantly, the testator gets a ribbon copy of the will rather than a collection of photocopies.

¶ 3151

Problem

[¶ 3170]

Do you think most clients care whether they have a will which consists of preprints? Do you think that the order in which provisions of the will appear is important to the testator's understanding of and satisfaction with the will?

D. PAYMENT OF DEBTS AND ADMINISTRATION EXPENSES

[¶ 3201]

Creditors of the decedent will have to be paid. So too will those who render services to the decedent's estate such as attorneys and executors of the decedent's estate.

Disposition of a decedent's property is governed by state law, and, in the usual case, state law provides that these claimants (and those who have claims arising out of the disposition of the decedent's remains) will be first satisfied from the decedent's estate. While most wills direct that the testator's funeral expenses, debts, and administration expenses are to be paid, such provisions are meaningless unless they go further and stipulate the source of the funds to be used to discharge these obligations.

Example. Zack has an estate of $100,000 in cash. His will contains the following provisions:

1. Pay my debts.
2. I give $80,000 to Mary Lou.
3. All the rest of my estate I give to my spouse, Alice.

At his death, Zack had an outstanding unsecured indebtedness of $85,000. Would the $85,000 be paid out of the spouse's share of Zack's estate or out of Mary Lou's share?

This dilemma is commonly referred to as the *abatement* problem. Putting the question more directly, in what order should the testator's gifts abate? Should Mary Lou and the spouse have their respective gifts reduced proportionally?

The solution has its roots in antiquity. At early common law it was presumed that the gifts in the will which were most important to the testator were those about which the testator was most specific. The least important were those about which the testator was more general. Accordingly, gifts in a will were deemed to abate in the following order: (1) intestate property; (2) residuary gifts; (3) general legacies; (4) demonstrative gifts; and (5) specific bequests.

Inasmuch as the common practice in modern times is to cause the residuary gift to be the most important ("everything to my spouse"), would you guess that the ancient rule of order of abatement had been modernized? If you said yes, you would have been wrong. See, e.g., UPC § 3–902. Can you

¶ 3170

offer any explanation as to why the rule has not been modernized? Is it because there is no practical alternative? What does this teach, then, to the wills draftsperson?

Problem

[¶ 3230]

Refer to the immediately preceding discussion in the text and indicate how you would draft Mary Lou's gift if Zack told you that the gift to his spouse was most important to him but that he expected to have a $1 million estate and that he wanted Mary Lou, his longtime underpaid secretary, to receive $80,000, an amount he calculated he would have paid her had he been able to afford it. What questions would you ask Zack in order that he might be more specific about his intention?

E. TAX ALLOCATION CLAUSES

[¶ 3251]

Under common law, liability for death taxes is imposed on the decedent's residuary estate. However, in an ever growing number of states, the legislature has changed the common law rule. In these states, in the absence of a contrary intention expressed by the decedent, the federal estate tax burden is apportioned among the recipients of the decedent's property, both testamentary and nontestamentary. In addition to the District of Columbia, among the states that have adopted the doctrine of equitable apportionment in statutory form are Alaska, Arkansas, California, Colorado, Connecticut, Delaware, Hawaii, Idaho, Indiana, Louisiana, Maine, Maryland, Michigan, Mississippi, Minnesota, Montana, Nebraska, Nevada, New Hampshire, New Jersey, New Mexico, New York, North Dakota, Oregon, Rhode Island, South Carolina, South Dakota, Tennessee, Texas, Utah, Vermont, Washington, Virginia, West Virginia, and Wyoming). In several other states, judicial decisions have applied a doctrine of equitable apportionment in order to place the burden of the estate tax on those persons actually receiving the decedent's property, without regard to whether the property is testamentary and nontestamentary. (At one time those states included: Kentucky, Missouri, and Oklahoma. See Donna Litman, Apportionment of the Federal Estate Tax—Effect of Selective Apportionment and Need for Reform, 33 Real Prop. Prob. & Tr. J. 327, 393 (1998)).

By way of illustration, in states following the common law rule, the burden of the estate tax falls upon the residuary estate. Thus, in the absence of an express declaration to the contrary, property which is not part of the testamentary estate will not be burdened by federal estate taxes. This means that life insurance, employee benefit plans, bank accounts with designated beneficiaries—all common methods of transfer today—would pass without bearing any part of the federal estate tax, thus placing a heavy and potentially unfair burden on the beneficiaries of the residue of the estate.

¶ 3251

Federal law provides limited relief. Sections 2206, 2207, and 2207A of the Internal Revenue Code address life insurance proceeds, power of appointment property, and marital deduction property, respectively. If the gross estate includes the proceeds of insurance on the life of the decedent payable to a beneficiary other than the executor, or if the gross estate includes property over which the decedent had a power of appointment, then the executor will be entitled to recover from the recipients of that property the portion of the tax allocable to it.

Section 2207A involves the marital deduction. A problem was created in 1981, when Congress allowed property to qualify for the unlimited marital deduction even though it had passed into a trust over which the surviving spouse did not have a general power of appointment. § 2056(b)(7). Allowing this property to qualify for the marital deduction meant that it was excluded from the estate of the first spouse to die. Naturally, the price of this exclusion was to require the excluded property to be taxed at the death of the surviving spouse. In order to bring about taxation of the excluded property at the later death of the surviving spouse, Congress put forth § 2044, which causes this trust property to be in the gross estate of the surviving spouse. That led to the problem of giving the surviving spouse a source of funds from which to pay the tax attributable to the marital property. In § 2207A, Congress, recognizing that the tax burden was imposed on the surviving spouse, allowed the executor of the surviving spouse's estate to seek reimbursement from the trust in which the marital share had been maintained.

Aside from these exceptions, however, state law is controlling on the issue of apportionment of the tax burden.

Practically speaking, the problem of tax allocation is most effectively addressed by provision in the testator's will. Thus, it becomes necessary to determine the testator's preference regarding the allocation of the tax burden—and to integrate those preferences with helpful statutory provisions. It is far from an easy task. Sometimes the results are far from advantageous. For example, in Estate of Fagan v. Commissioner, 77 T.C.M. (CCH) 1427 (1999), the decedent's will provided that all estate taxes were to be paid from the residuary without apportionment and the residuary estate was left to the decedent's revocable trust. The revocable trust provided that portions paid to charities "shall not be reduced by any taxes chargeable against the Grantor's gross estate." The Tax Court held in favor of the IRS that the will negated the applicable apportionment statute and the charitable portion of the trust would be reduced by its portion of estate taxes thereby increasing the overall tax burden. See also Tech. Adv. Mem. 1999–15–001 (decedent's will waived tax apportionment, but the estate is entitled to reimbursement from revocable trust). In Estate of Miller v. Commissioner, 76 T.C.M. (CCH) 892 (1998) the decedent's will directed that estate taxes were to be paid from the residuary estate thus negating the applicable apportionment statute, Tex. Prob. Code Ann. § 322A(c)-(d) (Vernon 2003, Supp. 2005), which exempted bequests to the surviving spouse that qualified for the marital deduction. As a result, both marital and nonmarital residual beneficiaries bore their portion of estate taxes, the amount available for the marital deduction was reduced, and the estate's tax burden was considerably larger that it would have been had the statute been in effect. See also Stickley v. Stickley, 255 Va. 405, 497 S.E.2d 862 (1998) (holding that excess estate taxes were to be paid from the probate estate because the clause directing estate taxes to be paid from the residuary nullified the statute that would have apportioned excess estate taxes against both the probate and nonprobate assets).

Problem

[¶ 3270]

Carla died domiciled in a state which follows the common law rule and imposes all taxes on the residuary estate except in those cases where a testator expressly directs otherwise in his or her will. Carla's will made no reference to whether she wanted the tax burden imposed on her residuary estate or apportioned among the recipients of her property proportionately. Her husband's executor had claimed the full marital deduction for property placed in trust for Carla (as permitted by § 2056(b)(7)) and, accordingly, that property was included in her estate for estate tax purposes (even though she had no ability to dispose of it at any time). See § 2044. Does the state law (imposing the death tax burden on Carla's residuary estate) preclude Carla's executor from seeking contributions from the trust pursuant to § 2207A for the amount of additional estate taxes paid by Carla's estate because the marital trust was included in her estate? Is the federal remedy one which Carla's executor has discretion to pursue or not pursue as he elects? Draft an appropriate provision to put in Carla's will to avoid this dilemma. In doing so, consider the suitability of the following for this purpose:

> My Executor shall pay all estate, inheritance and succession taxes, both state and federal, including penalties and interest thereon (but not any generation-skipping tax imposed by Section 2601 of the Internal Revenue Code of 1986, nor any additional taxes imposed on my estate by reason of an election made by the executor of my spouse's estate), assessed by reason of my death out of that portion of the residue of my testamentary estate which does not qualify for the marital deduction for federal estate tax purposes, if any, without recovery from any recipient or beneficiary of any property by which such tax is measured, including, but not by way of limitation, the recipients and beneficiaries of property transferred by me during my life, whether in trust or otherwise, the proceeds of insurance upon my life, property passing by right of survivorship, and property over which I had any power of appointment.

F. SPECIFIC BEQUESTS IN GENERAL

[¶ 3301]

1. ADEMPTION BY EXTINCTION

Suppose a testator's will included a specific bequest of "my circa 1790 grandfather clock." If the grandfather clock had been destroyed in a fire prior to the testator's death, the gift would be deemed to have been adeemed by

¶ 3301

extinction. Why? Because there is no practical alternative assumption that the law could make with any assurance that the alternative assumption would not significantly distort the testator's intention.

Accordingly, in cases where a testator wishes to make a specific bequest, it is incumbent upon the draftsperson to anticipate the absence at death of the thing which is the subject matter of the bequest. Probably the only approach the draftsperson can take is to question the testator about his or her wishes should it happen that the thing has been destroyed or is missing at the testator's death. Perhaps the testator will want to substitute other property or direct the executor to go into the marketplace and purchase something which is comparable to the thing which was the subject matter of the bequest. At the very least, perhaps the testator will want any proceeds of any casualty insurance on the *thing* to be distributed to the legatee.

Problem

[¶ 3305]

Draft a provision suitable for use where the testator wants his "circa 1790 grandfather clock to go to * * * [his] grandson, Louie" if the testator still has the clock at death. If the testator no longer has the clock, he wants the boy to have the proceeds of any casualty insurance payable as a result of the clock's destruction (assuming the clock has been destroyed), so long as those proceeds have not been paid to the testator prior to his death.

[¶ 3309]

2. ADEMPTION BY SATISFACTION

Consider the case where the testator has provided for a general legacy of $10,000 to "Ralph, the tech support guy at the computer store," but during the testator's lifetime after the execution of the will, the testator gives Ralph $10,000. Should Ralph get another $10,000 under the decedent's will? Or should the gift in the will be adeemed by satisfaction? These questions obviously depend on what the testator intends. In most cases, the testator's intention will not be clear from the will.

Problem

[¶ 3313]

Would it be appropriate to include in every will the following boilerplate, except in cases where it was clearly contrary to the testator's intention?

Any transfers of real or personal property by me during my lifetime shall not be deemed to be in satisfaction of any gifts I have made in this will.

[¶ 3317]

3. ACCESSIONS

From time to time, testators will make specific bequests of things such as shares of stock. Suppose, for example, that Larry's will contained this provision: "I give to my son my 500 shares of General Industries stock." When Larry died his estate included 1,000 shares of General Industries stock. His executor determined that Larry had received the additional 500 shares as a result of a 2–for–1 stock split. The son claims all 1,000 shares. He claims that the 1,000 shares represent the same proportionate ownership interest in the corporation. Needless to say, there will be those beneficiaries who claim that the son is entitled to only the 500 shares the will provides that he is to receive. They argue that, theoretically speaking, the son's proportionate ownership in the corporation was adeemed by extinction when his father did not increase the bequest to the son upon receipt of the additional shares. They say it is better to take this view than it is to give the son the additional shares since the father limited the gift to 500 shares and that to argue that the father intended the child to have the additional shares is mere speculation.

Problems

[¶ 3335]

1. Draft a provision that will effectively deal with the issues presented in text. Assume first that the testator wants to give the donee whatever increase is experienced by the investment.

2. Are there any circumstances when you would want to leave the instrument silent as to what the testator's wishes were with respect to accessions between the time that the will is executed and the date of the testator's death?

G. TANGIBLE PERSONAL PROPERTY AND PERSONAL RESIDENCE

[¶ 3351]

1. TAX CONSIDERATIONS AND OTHER REDUNDANCIES

Many so-called simple wills contain three provisions which the casual but charitable observer would describe as redundant. These provisions, simply expressed, are:

    1. All of my tangible personal property to my spouse.

    2. All of my interest in any real property which I am occupying as my principal residence at my death to my spouse.

    3. All the rest and residue of my property to my spouse.

Undoubtedly, the less charitable observer would comment that this redundancy is yet another example of the legal profession's inefficiency, if not incompetence. However, this redundancy can be explained as a postmortem income tax planning device and the use of the estate as a tax shelter during the course of the administration of the testator's estate.

The basic rule of income taxation of estates and trusts is that the income of the estate will be taxed to the estate unless it is distributed to the beneficiaries of the estate. I.R.C. § 641(a); ¶ 8001. Of course, to prevent

¶ 3351

taxpayers from stacking income in the estates of decedents in cases where the estate is in a lower income tax bracket than the beneficiaries, Congress adopted the rule that every distribution from an estate or trust carries out the income of the estate or trust to the beneficiary who received the distribution. See § 661. There is one basic exception to this rule. Distributions from an estate or trust in satisfaction of a specific bequest do not carry out the income of the estate or trust. See § 663(a)(1).

Income tax planning for distributions from estates and trusts is considered in Chapters 8 and 21. Suffice it to say at this point, using the rates in effect in 2006, warehousing the first $10,650 in an estate's income in the estate each year rather than distributing it to the estate's beneficiaries can result in an income tax savings of as much as $1,131.50—but only in cases where the estate's beneficiaries are in the top income tax bracket. The amount is less in the case of a trust—$10,050 with an annual income tax savings of $956. ¶ 21,351. This comes about because: (1) the estate and trust each starts out in the lowest income tax bracket and (2) both enjoy a small yearly exemption, $600 in the case of the estate and $100 in the case of the trust. § 642(b). To preserve the tax shelter potential inherent in the estate the executor should plan to avoid distributions from the estate which will carry out its income—but only after comparing the estate's income tax bracket to those of the estate's beneficiaries. Preventing estate income from being carried out to beneficiaries can be done only by having the executor postpone distributions from the estate to the beneficiaries, unless, of course, distributions can be made in satisfaction of specific bequests which will not carry out income. If that is done, the undistributed income earned by the estate during the years that it is open (other than the last year of the estate's administration) will be taxed to the estate and not to the beneficiaries.

Since withholding distributions is often not an acceptable alternative to the estate's beneficiaries, a premium is placed on drafting wills which take full advantage of the specific bequest exception. This is particularly important in the case of items of personal property which the executor is likely to want to distribute early during the administration of the estate so as to avoid the cost and other burdens associated with the storage of these items. Similarly, the decedent's personal residence is often an object of early distribution.

Some readers are undoubtedly surprised to learn that the distribution of the testator's automobile or personal residence pursuant to the testator's will will carry out the income of the estate or trust. Think about it in these terms—and be reminded that these ideas are noted at ¶ 8551 and 8701: Would you look forward to telling the surviving spouse that the automobile of the testator which was distributed to the spouse shortly after the testator's death constituted taxable income to the spouse? It would be little consolation that this result was strictly the consequence of either the executor making a premature distribution or the draftsperson failing to anticipate this problem by including a provision in the testator's will making the automobile the object of a specific bequest.

With this background, consider next the question of where the title to the testator's property is after his or her death.

¶ 3351

In the majority of states, title to real property, and in some states, personal property, vests immediately in the decedent's heirs who are the beneficiaries under the decedent's will. See 6 William J. Bowe & Douglas H. Parker, Page on Wills, § 59.2 (Rev. ed. 2005). This means that even though the executor may collect and hold the assets of the estate, legal title to those assets vests in the indicated beneficiary. Consequently, subsequent confirmation of title in the indicated beneficiary will not result in the income of the estate being taxed to the beneficiary (§ 663) as would happen upon distribution of estate property where title vests in the executor during the course of administration. §§ 661, 662.

Generalization in this area is risky. In Texas, for example, title to both real and personal property vests in the decedent's beneficiaries or heirs, subject, however, to power in the fiduciary to take possession to pay the debts of the estate. Jones v. Whittington, 194 F.2d 812 (10th Cir. 1952).

On the other hand, the UPC intends to give the decedent's personal representative the "broadest possible 'power over title'" when it provides that the personal representative "has the same power over the title to property of the estate that an absolute owner would have." UPC § 3–711. The personal representative's possession is not limited to the case where necessary for purposes of sale to pay debts but seems much broader.

With that in mind, it is fair to conclude that testators domiciled in either a UPC jurisdiction or in Texas at the time of their deaths will be subject to the same rules regarding distributions from their estates during the course of administration. And, if title is determinative of tax consequences, then distributions from the estates of Texas decedents should never carry out income. Needless to say, to state the proposition is to suggest the conclusion. What has happened is that the courts have ignored state law characterizations of title. Apparently, where the fiduciary, under state law (as in Texas) has control over the property and the right to possession, the fiduciary becomes primarily liable for any tax. See Kuldell v. Commissioner, 69 F.2d 739 (5th Cir. 1934) (Texas); Estate of Cohen v. Commissioner, 8 T.C. 784 (1947) (California).

Thus, as a practical matter, distribution of real property and tangible personal property from an estate in Texas or one in California, *inter alia,* is deemed to carry out income from the estate with the resulting loss of the estate as a tax shelter in the year of distribution. Accordingly, it is appropriate to provide for a specific bequest of tangible personal property and real property in the decedent's will in Texas, California, and UPC jurisdictions even if the residuary taker is also the recipient of the tangible personal property and real property. Actually, the planning suggestion is that every will should contain specific bequests of tangible personal property and other items such as real property likely to be distributed early in the administration of a decedent's estate.

Having said all that, to further emphasize the role of taxation in will drafting, consider the recent phenomenon known as rate compression. While rate compression is discussed in detail in chapter 21, suffice it to say that, in 2006, taxable income in excess of $10,050 is taxed at a flat rate of 35 percent. Rev. Proc. 2005–70, 2005–47 I.R.B. 979. (By way of contrast, for tax years

¶ 3351

beginning in 2006, adjusted for inflation, the first $30,650 of income received by an unmarried taxpayer (and the first $61,300 of income received by married taxpayers filing jointly) is taxed at a rate of 15 percent or less (the first $7,550 and $15,100 respectively, at 10 percent), I.R.C. § 1(a), (c), and (i); Rev. Proc. 2005–70, 2005–47 I.R.B. 979.) Most beneficiaries will be in lower income tax brackets, leading to the suggestion that the decedent's personal representative will minimize income taxes each year by distributing estate income to the extent necessary to, at least, equalize the respective tax brackets of estate and beneficiary.

[¶ 3359]

2. INCORPORATION BY REFERENCE

It is relatively common for a testator to wish to specify the recipients of items of personal property, such as jewelry, china, automobiles, and other items having great personal value. And it is equally common for the draftsperson to suggest that a list of these items be made with the beneficiaries indicated and that the list be placed with the executed copy of the will. This is in lieu of "cluttering up" the will with this information.

How effective, then, is such a list? Are the beneficiaries bound by it? Regrettably, no—at least not in the usual case. Understanding wills means understanding that all of the pages to be given effect as part of a will must be together with the page signed by the maker at the time the will is executed. Pages not meeting this test are not part of the will and will not enjoy judicial recognition—except in those cases where a valid "incorporation by reference" has been accomplished.

Incorporation by reference is said, by UPC § 2–510, to be effective if intent to incorporate is manifest in the will and the writing to be incorporated is described sufficiently to permit its identification. According to the common law, a valid incorporation by reference also requires the writing to be incorporated to be described as in existence at the time the will was being executed, it being generally believed that a writing not in existence when the will is executed cannot be validly incorporated by reference. See generally, 2 William J. Bowe & Douglas H. Parker, Page on Wills, §§ 19.18–19.36 (Rev. ed. 2003). For additional consideration of incorporation by reference, see ¶ 4575.

Not only does the UPC liberalize the requirements for an effective incorporation by reference, UPC § 2–513, reflecting a broad policy determination to relax the formalities associated with wills, specifically permits a testator to use a writing that is separate and apart from the will to dispose of tangible personal property other than money so long as reference is made to that writing in the testator's will. The separate writing must be signed by the testator but it can be prepared after the will is executed and it is freely amendable. Using "all my tangible personal property" is a sufficient description of the property to be disposed of by the separate writing.

While the modern view, as expressed in the UPC, is to accept writings separate from the will (when incorporated by reference), historically, at least, some states have refused. See generally 2 William J. Bowe & Douglas H.

Parker, Page on Wills, §§ 19.18–19.36 (Rev. ed. 2003). However, these same states, when confronted with pourovers from a will to a revocable trust, are able to validate those pourovers because the Uniform Testamentary Addition to Trusts Act (amended 1991), 8B U.L.A. 360–66 (2001) has been adopted by the state. For discussion, see ¶ 4575.

Problem

[¶ 3380]

Mei Ling's will included the following provision: "I give all of my household goods and personal effects to my children, to be divided among them as I shall specify in a memorandum which I will prepare and attach to this will." After Mei Ling's death, a typewritten memorandum was found as described in the will. The date on the will and on the memorandum were the same. Mei Ling's oldest child wants the items given her in the memorandum; the other children, however, claim the memorandum is ineffective. Do you agree with the oldest child? Why not?

H. PROPERTY SUBJECT TO INDEBTEDNESS

[¶ 3401]

A specific bequest of a testator's personal residence is a feature common to many wills if, for no other reason, for postmortem income tax planning reasons (discussed at ¶ 3351). Oftentimes the testator's personal residence is subject to an encumbrance which is intended to secure the indebtedness the testator incurred when the premises were purchased. The question which frequently comes up is, "Does the donee of the personal residence take it subject to the encumbrance or free of the encumbrance?" If the donee takes free of the encumbrance, out of which funds is the indebtedness to be discharged so as to eliminate the encumbrance?

At common law, the donee of the gift was presumed to take free of the encumbrance. It was said that the gift was exonerated of the indebtedness and so came into the law the doctrine of exoneration. A number of states by specific legislation have reversed the presumption. So, too, has the UPC, in § 2–607.

Problems

[¶ 3435]

1. A testator wants the gift of a personal residence to the spouse to pass to the spouse subject to any encumbrance thereon at the testator's death, and the law applicable in the jurisdiction in which the testator currently resides follows the UPC rule. Do you think it is necessary to specify in the testator's will that the spouse is to take the property subject to the encumbrance?

2. Draft a provision which will cause the testator's property to pass to the spouse subject to any encumbrance thereon at the death of the testator.

¶ 3435

I. LAPSE AND CLOSE ORDER OF DEATH

[¶ 3451]

1. ANTI-LAPSE STATUTES

Dispositive schemes are often expressed in terms of survivorship. For example, it would be common to express a gift to a child in these terms: "I give my ranch to my child if my child survives me for 30 days."

Suppose the testator made no reference to the child's survivorship and expressed the gift in these terms: "I give my ranch to my child." At common law, if the child does not survive the testator, the gift would lapse. But almost all—if not all—states have so-called anti-lapse statutes. These statutes save the gift to the child for the child's lineal descendants, if any.

Addition of the phrase "if my child survives me" avoids application of the anti-lapse statute in the case where the child predeceases the parent. The survivorship language renders the anti-lapse statute inapplicable by conditioning the gift on the child's surviving the parent. If the child does not survive, the child does not take! The gift then goes to an alternate taker or falls into the residuary (or, if there is no residuary, passes by intestacy).

Why not allow the anti-lapse statute to apply? After all, it may be the decedent's intention! If the decedent intended this result, spell it out in the will. Specify that the gift for the child is conditional upon the child's surviving the decedent, and if the child doesn't survive, designate the child's lineal descendants as alternative takers. Don't assume that the testator will die domiciled in the jurisdiction in which the will is prepared or that *your* anti-lapse statute will apply. Even if it does apply, it may have been changed by the time the testator dies.

[¶ 3459]

2. CLOSE ORDER OF DEATH

Addition of the phrase "for 30 days" avoids issues that arise because of the close order of death of testator and beneficiary. Absent this provision, questions can arise as to the order of death where there is little or no evidence and the claim is made that the testator and beneficiary died "simultaneously."

Example. Dad and Son perish together in a plane crash which has no survivors. Dad's will gives everything to Son, but if Son does not survive Dad, Dad's property passes to his college's scholarship fund. Son's will gives everything to the surviving members of his rock band who, upon hearing the news: (1) exclaim "We're rich! We're rich!"; (2) vote to claim all of Dad's estate; and (3) decide to go into retirement. Dad has millions and Son has a faithful following.

UPC § 2–702 requires a beneficiary to survive the testator by 120 hours unless the testator clearly indicates that the 120–hour survival is not required. The purpose is to keep the same property from passing through two estates and thus being subject to two taxable events. But is 120 hours long enough? Would 30 days be better? What about 60 days? What would be too long?

Most states adopted the Uniform Simultaneous Death Act (USDA) (amended 1993), 8B U.L.A. 147–58 (2001), as originally promulgated in 1940. Since 1991, the USDA has been identical to UPC § 2–702, adopting the 120–hour survival requirement. However, the 1953 amended version of the USDA required a finding of "no sufficient evidence" of the order in which donor and donee died. The 1953 amended version of USDA § 1 provides:

> Where the title to property or the devolution thereof depends upon priority of death and there is no sufficient evidence that the persons have died otherwise than simultaneously, the property of each person shall be disposed of as if he had survived, except as provided otherwise in this Act.

Suppose the decedent and the child are killed in a so-called common disaster and there is no evidence of the order of their deaths. In this case, the USDA causes the parent's property to be distributed as if the child predeceased the parent. In this case, addition of the 30–day survivorship requirement is unnecessary.

Consider another case. Suppose that the decedent and the child are killed in a so-called common disaster but that there is evidence the child survived the parent for approximately 15 minutes. In this case, the USDA is deemed not to apply and the child takes the gift under the will. That is, it passes through the child's estate and is taxed in the child's estate. More importantly, it will be distributed as provided in the child's will and not as provided in the parent's will. The addition of a 30–day survivorship clause will avoid this result. If the child does not survive the parent by 30 days, the child takes nothing and the property passes to the alternate taker under the donor's will.

The 1953 version of the USDA provided only for the contingency of no "sufficient" evidence of the order of deaths. Disputes, naturally, occur as to whether the evidence is, in fact, "sufficient."

Let's consider yet another example. Assume the gift is to the decedent's spouse. Should we condition the spouse's gift on the spouse's surviving the decedent by 30 days? If the marital deduction (provided by § 2056) is important to the decedent's plan, then the survivorship requirement should be eliminated and the draftsperson should insert a provision providing that the spouse is presumed to survive the decedent where there is no evidence of the order of their deaths. Such a clause might read as follows:

> If my spouse and I die under such circumstances that the order of our deaths cannot be established by proof, my spouse shall be deemed to have survived me. Furthermore, the gift to my spouse in this will shall not fail on account of the operation of any rule of law, statutory or otherwise, treating my said spouse who survives me, either in fact for any period of time, or by reason of the preceding sentence, as though my spouse had predeceased me.

This clause will insure the marital deduction, where there is uncertainty as to the order of deaths. See discussion at ¶ 14,201. Passing the same property through two estates will result in additional probate expense, but the avail-

¶ 3459

ability of the marital deduction should outweigh this disadvantage since it gives the testator the opportunity to split the estate with his or her spouse for tax purposes.

Incidentally, would it be appropriate to say, "Not to worry about taxes"? That is, there is a credit against federal estate tax liability available to the beneficiary for taxes paid by the testator on property passing to the beneficiary. See § 2013 and discussion at ¶ 7501. This is to prevent the family fortune from being wiped out by multiple taxable events triggered by close order of deaths. However, while the federal credit is helpful in these cases, the question remains as to whether the states offer similar relief against state death taxes.

Close order of death and jointly owned property is considered at ¶ 11,551.

J. GIFTS TO LINEAL DESCENDANTS

[¶ 3501]

A typical will might include the following language:

All of my estate to my spouse if my spouse survives me for 30 days; otherwise to my then living lineal descendants *per stirpes.*

Why not "children" in place of "lineal descendants"? Isn't that what most testators want? Sure it is. But what if a child dies prematurely, i.e., before the testator? Do you think the testator wants to exclude the grandchildren—the children of the deceased child—simply because the child failed to survive the testator?

What about the word "issue"? Isn't it more commonly used than "lineal descendants"? Unfortunately, "issue" is inappropriate because it could be construed as referring only to children. While there is no general agreement as to the meaning of "issue," in certain statutory contexts "issue" does not mean descendants, but is limited to natural children of the testator. Central Nat. Bank of Cleveland v. Morris, 10 Ohio App.2d 225, 227 N.E.2d 418, 420 (1967). Moreover, the word "issue" as used in a will does not have such a fixed and definite meaning that its meaning cannot vary with the intention of the testator who uses it. Gannett v. Old Colony Trust Co., 155 Me. 248, 153 A.2d 122 (1959); Plainfield Trust Co. v. Hagedorn, 28 N.J. 483, 147 A.2d 254, 257 (1958); In re Collins Estate, 393 Pa. 195, 142 A.2d 178 (1958) ("issue" defined as issue of the body, offspring, natural children, and the word is a description of the person next to take from the testator and not a line of inheritance). Normally the term "issue" will not be deemed to include descendants of living children unless that is the clear intention of the testator. See, e.g., Theopold v. Sears, 357 Mass. 460, 258 N.E.2d 559, 561 (1970); Watson v. Goldthwaite, 345 Mass. 29, 184 N.E.2d 340, 342 (1962). One court preserved a devise from violation of the Rule Against Perpetuities by construing "issue" to mean children and *not* an indefinite succession of lineal descendants. Poindexter v. Wachovia Bank and Trust Co., 258 N.C. 371, 128 S.E.2d 867, 872 (1963).

¶ 3459

Of course, many cases have held that "issue" is synonymous or coextensive with "descendants." See, e.g., In re Palmer's Estate, 237 N.Y.S.2d 524, 526, 38 Misc.2d 553 (1963); In re Moses' Estate, 58 N.J.Super. 67, 155 A.2d 273, 276 (1959); Stewart v. Lafferty, 12 Ill.2d 224, 145 N.E.2d 640, 642 (1957). One court noted the ambiguity of "issue" as encompassing either the first degree or all degrees of offspring, and commented that "in contrast 'descendants' is a word of fixed meaning, or at least less flexible, and is rarely restricted to mean first-degree offspring." In re Gardiner's Will, 191 N.Y.S.2d 520, 527, 20 Misc.2d 722 (1959).

By way of contrast, the words "lineal descendants" are generally construed to mean all those, even to the remotest generation, who by consanguinity trace their lineage to the specified ancestor. Green v. Hussey, 228 Mass. 537, 117 N.E. 798 (1917). Because the words normally connote blood relationship, they do not include more unless a contrary intent of the testator is clear. In re Buell's Estate, 167 Or. 295, 117 P.2d 832, 838 (1941).

While there is some uncertainty as to whether the words "lineal descendants" include adopted children, many jurisdictions include adopted children as "lineal descendants." See, e.g., Denton v. Miller, 110 Kan. 292, 203 P. 693, 694 (1922); Warren v. Prescott, 84 Me. 483, 24 A. 948 (1892); contra, Crawford v. Arends, 351 Mo. 1100, 176 S.W.2d 1 (1943); Appeal of Wildman, 111 Conn. 683, 151 A. 265, 266 (1930) (no presumption where testator was stranger to the adopted child). There is no pattern, however, in the courts' reluctance to uphold a legacy to an adopted child because of the adoptive parent's relationship to the testator.

For purposes of devises to "lineal descendants *per stirpes*," however, there is less likelihood of ambiguity if the testator is the one adopting a child. In such a case, the courts should be more willing to charge the adoptive parent with knowledge of the effect of adoption statutes.

One question remains: Do you agree that the words "lineal descendants" are susceptible of only one meaning if the words are given the meaning normally associated with them? If not, would it help to define the term as follows?

"Descendants" means the immediate and remote lawful, lineal descendants of the person referred to who are in being at the time they must be ascertained in order to give effect to the reference to them, whether they are born before or after my death or the death of any other person.

T. Shaffer & C. Mooney, The Planning And Drafting of Wills And Trusts, 222 (3rd ed. 1991).

K. *PER STIRPES* AND THE ROOT GENERATION CLAUSE

[¶ 3551]

Per stirpes means taking in a representative capacity. It is oftentimes described in terms of taking the share your ancestor would have taken had he or she survived. In the following examples, assume D's wife does not survive him and that D is survived by children, grandchildren, and great grandchildren (and that his will gives "everything" to his "then living lineal descendants *per stirpes*).

Example 1. All of D's lineal descendants (children, grandchildren, and great grandchildren) survive him. Do you agree that the children take equally, to the exclusion of the grandchildren and great grandchildren? Would it make a difference if the gift was *per capita*? What if it were to "then living lineal descendants" without further specification?

Example 2. A, one of D's three children, predeceases D. A's two children, G and H, and D's other two children, B and C, survive D. How is D's estate divided? Easy case. G and H take the share their father, A, would have taken had he survived D. A would have taken one-third of D's estate had he survived and therefore G and H each take one-half of one-third.

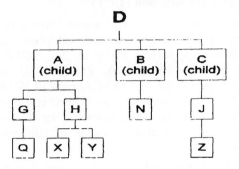

Example 3. All of D's children predecease him, but he is survived by all of his grandchildren, namely, G, H, N, and J. Do G, H, N, and J take equal shares of D's property? Or do N and J each take one-third and G and H split one-third?

Example 4. Let's kill off all of D's children and grandchildren except N.

That means Q, X, Y, N, and Z are claimants. N will get at least one-fourth. Should he get one-third?

Designation of the "root generation" determines the share each lineal descendant takes in Examples 3 and 4. How best can that be accomplished? Would use of the words "to my then living descendants *per stirpes*" be adequate to designate a root generation? More to the point, does the presence of the words "then living" designate a root generation? Certainly, the phrase "then living" indicates that only the living are beneficiaries of D's generosity. It avoids any argument that D intended to benefit deceased lineals. Would this problem be eliminated by the adoption of the definition of "descendants" suggested in ¶ 3501?

If the phrase "then living" is not enough to designate a root, what help does the applicable state property law provide? None! That's right! None of the states appears to have legislation applicable to wills which attempts to express a constructional preference for any particular root. A few states, like Texas, attempt to define *per stirpes* and identify a root generation for purposes of intestate distributions *only:*

When the intestate's children, descendants, brothers, sisters, uncles, aunts, or any other relatives of the deceased standing in the first or same degree alone come into the distribution upon intestacy, they shall take

¶ 3551

per capita, namely: by persons; and when a part of them being dead and a part living, the descendants of those dead shall have right to distribution upon intestacy, such descendants shall inherit only such portion of said property as the parent through whom they inherit would be entitled to if alive.

Tex. Prob. Code Ann. § 43 (Vernon 2003).

UPC § 2–106(b) identifies a root generation, but also only in the intestate context. The UPC provides that whenever a representative taking is called for in the case of intestacy, the intestate's estate is to be:

> [d]ivided into as many shares as there are surviving heirs in the nearest degree of kinship and deceased persons in the same degree who left issue who survive the decedent, each surviving heir in the nearest degree receiving one share and the share of each deceased person in the same degree being divided among his issue in the same manner.

The practical effect of this UPC provision is to provide for what could be called a *per stirpes* distribution with a *per capita* distribution at each generation, meaning that persons with an equal degree of kindred to the decedent are treated equally.

Since the respective legislatures have not addressed this issue, one would think the courts would be likely to have expressed a preference for one construction rather than another. Surprisingly, this is not the case. What has happened is that the courts find "clearly" that the testator intended a certain generation to be the root, oftentimes reaching different conclusions about instruments containing similar language. Thus, "intention" becomes a handy safe harbor when the alternative is to express a constructional preference. L.S. Tellier, Annotation, Taking Per Stirpes or Per Capita Under Will, 13 A.L.R.2d 1023 (2006).

Accordingly, the draftsperson must deal with the root generation identification problem in drafting the will either by specific language or by incorporating the statute by reference.

Problems

[¶ 3591]

1. Try drafting a paragraph defining *per stirpes* for use in your instruments.

2. Would the following language be an acceptable definition of a root generation for inclusion in your instruments?

   The phrase "per stirpes" as used herein shall be construed to mean that the gift referred to is to be divided so that there is: (1) one share for each of the then living lineal descendants of the person referred to in the gift who are in the nearest degree of kinship to that person and (2) one share for each lineal descendant in the same degree who has lineal descendants surviving the person referred to in the gift. Each surviving lineal descendant in the nearest degree is to receive one share, and the share of each deceased lineal descendant in the same degree shall be divided among his or her lineal descendants in the same manner.

¶ 3591

3. In this age of plain English, how could the words *per stirpes* be eliminated from your instruments and the root generation be described in terms which are more understandable to the testator? Would it help to substitute the words "by representation"?

4. Do you think the testator cares which root the will identifies? If no, why should you?

L. SELECTION OF EXECUTOR

[¶ 3601]

1. QUALIFICATIONS

Selection of an executor by a testator is often a highly personal decision, and it is not often that objective criteria are introduced into the process.

The function of the executor is to collect the testator's property and distribute that property at the conclusion of the administration process. The scope of the management responsibilities of the executor during the period of administration is hard to define. In theory, the executor is not seen as a manager but more as a collector and liquidator. To illustrate, occasionally an older person who is appointed as executor will recall serving as an executor for another estate at an earlier time and, as a result of that experience, will want to know when to "begin the process of converting all of the testator's property to cash" in order to facilitate distribution (and to reduce or eliminate any chance of liability being imposed on the executor if the value of the estate properly declines during administration). Despite such perceptions, there is a distinct management responsibility imposed on today's executor which, at the very least, is one of preservation and recordkeeping.

The choices are a natural person or a corporate fiduciary.

[¶ 3609]

2. NONRESIDENTS AS EXECUTORS

Some jurisdictions, as a practical matter, will not appoint a nonresident as executor of a decedent's estate. For example, Wisconsin, while requiring appointment of a resident agent for a nonresident executor, allows courts to refuse appointment or cause removal of an executor solely because of nonresidency. Wis. Stat. Ann. § 856.23 (West 2002). Several states permit a nonresident to be an executor if he appoints a resident agent for service of process. 755 Ill. Comp. Stat. Ann. 5/6–13 (West 1992); Ky. Rev. Stat. Ann. § 395.015 (LexisNexis 1999); N.C. Gen. Stat. § 28A–4–2 (2005); Wis. Stat. Ann. § 856.23 (West 2002); Wyo. Stat. Ann. § 2–11–301 (2005).

However, the federal courts declared unconstitutional the Florida statute permitting appointment of only Florida residents as executors of the estates of Florida decedents. In Fain v. Hall, 463 F.Supp. 661 (D. Fla. 1979), a Florida law (Fla. Stat. Ann. §§ 733.302, 733.304 (West 1976)), which disqualified nonresidents from serving as personal representatives of decedents to whom they were not related, was held to establish an unconstitutional "presumption'' of incompetence merely because of nonresidence which violated due process. The court reasoned that any proper objection could be raised at a hearing before appointment. The Florida Supreme Court had previously held unconstitutional, as a denial of equal protection, the provision of the Florida statute (Fla. Stat. Ann. § 733.302 (West 1976)) that an administrator be a citizen of the United States. Re Estate of Fernandez, 335 So.2d 829 (Fla. 1976).

Jurisdictions, such as Texas, which will appoint a nonresident of the jurisdiction as executor of a testator's estate usually require the nonresident (either a natural person or corporation) to appoint a resident agent to accept service of process in all actions or proceedings and to file such appointment with the court. Tex. Prob. Code Ann. § 78(c) (Vernon 2003); Betts v. Betts, 395 S.W.2d 673 (Tex. Civ. App. 1965). Cf. In re Roots' Estate, 596 S.W.2d 240 (Tex. Civ. App. 1980) (testator's power to select executor cannot be overturned by discretion of court unless appointee is a minor or insane). As an alternative procedure, a testator may prefer to appoint a local bank to act as fiduciary solely or as co-fiduciary with the nonresident. This could be accomplished by designating a bank in the instrument (after consulting the bank) or perhaps by requiring, in the instrument, that the selection of such a bank be made by the nonresident (or by all the beneficiaries or perhaps the then partners of the firm preparing the instrument). For example, in Texas, because a nonresident has the right to be appointed personal representative for a decedent's estate, it appears that the person can also renounce the privilege and designate someone to be appointed in his or her place. Stevens v. Cameron, 100 Tex. 515, 101 S.W. 791 (1907). By way of contrast, it appears that in Texas, a trustee cannot delegate the authority conferred by the governing instrument. West v. Hapgood, 141 Tex. 576, 174 S.W.2d 963 (1943).

[¶ 3617]

3. FIDUCIARY POWERS

Most wills include a recitation of fiduciary powers. Wills drafted in jurisdictions which have adopted the UPC, however, may be silent as to fiduciary powers. The UPC lists extensive powers and duties applicable to all fiduciaries. These powers include the power to retain and receive assets, perform or refuse to perform decedent's contracts, satisfy written charitable pledges, invest liquid assets of the estate, acquire or dispose of an asset, make ordinary or extraordinary repairs or alterations in buildings, subdivide or develop land, etc. UPC § 3–711 (general power same as absolute owners); UPC § 3–715 (enumeration of specific powers).

For similar reasons, wills drawn in states such as Texas, Maryland, and Indiana may not contain language empowering the personal representative. Maryland provides, for example, that a personal representative ''shall use the authority'' given the representative by statute in settling estates, Md. Code Ann., [Est. & Trusts] § 7–101 (LexisNexis 2001), except as validly limited by the will. The representative's powers, in addition to those other than common law or statutory powers, are enumerated in § 7–401, Maryland's version of the comparable UPC provision. Md. Code Ann., [Est. & Trusts] § 7–401 (WL 2001).

Indiana does *not* have a similar enumeration of fiduciary powers that apply without provision in the will, Ind. Code Ann. §§ 29–1–13–1 et seq. (West 1999), which means, for example, that in Indiana a personal representative needs an order of court to compromise an obligation of the estate, § 29–1–13–5, an abandonment of property, § 29–1–13–8, or any contract or conveyance of land not provided for in the will, § 29–1–13–12.

Wills prepared in Texas often contain only a provision designating "an independent executor to serve without bond." It is sometimes argued that such wills, under Texas law, give the executor authority to perform any act with respect to the estate which a court could authorize to be performed if it had supervision of the estate. Tex. Prob. Code Ann. § 145 (Vernon 2003); Etter v. Tuck, 91 S.W.2d 875 (Tex. Civ. App. 1936). Actually, in order to provide for independent administration in Texas, the testator should borrow the words of the applicable statute, specify in the will that no other action be taken in the county court in relation to the settlement of the estate other than the probating and recording of the will, and the return of an inventory, appraisement, and list of claims of the estate. Tex. Prob. Code Ann. § 145(b) (Vernon 2003); Glover v. Coit, 36 Tex.Civ.App. 104, 81 S.W. 136 (1904); cf. In re Dulin's Estate, 244 S.W.2d 242 (Tex. Civ. App. 1951) (not essential to creation of independent administration to use the exact words of statute); Epperson v. Reeves, 35 Tex.Civ.App. 167, 79 S.W. 845 (1904).

Case law suggests that the powers of the independent executor in Texas may even be broader than what could be accomplished under judicial control, including the power to sell securities, Parks v. Purnell, 144 S.W.2d 599 (Tex. Civ. App. 1940); to employ agents, Lang v. Shell Petroleum Corp., 138 Tex. 399, 159 S.W.2d 478 (1942); and to borrow money, Becker v. American Nat'l Bank, 286 S.W. 889 (Tex. Civ. App. 1926). For a general discussion of the powers of an independent executor, see 17 M. Woodward & E. Smith III, Texas Practice: Probate and Decedent's Estates § 489 (1971 & A. Leopold and Gerry W. Beyer Supp. 1994). As a practical matter, in the absence of court action, whether a fiduciary actually enjoys a particular power when dealing with a decedent's estate is determined by the willingness of third parties to respect the fiduciary's claims of authority.

For discussion of problems related to managing the family business in an estate, see ¶ 24,147.

[¶ 3625]

4.   THE BONDING REQUIREMENT

The will should expressly excuse the executor from posting bond. Bond is generally an unnecessary expense and is not guaranteed to prevent mismanagement of the estate. Should it appear during the administration of an estate that the executor is mismanaging the property or has betrayed or is about to betray his or her trust, then the executor may be required to give bond (or be removed in appropriate cases) upon proper proceedings.

Problems

[¶ 3630]

1. Suppose Mr. D died in a jurisdiction other than Texas. His will made no reference to fiduciary powers but did provide that Charles Abel was to be "independent executor" of his estate and "serve without bond." Do you think other jurisdictions would look to Texas law to determine exactly what Mr. D meant by the term "independent executor"? Would the court be more likely to do so if the instrument provided that "administration of my estate shall be governed by the laws of Texas"? What if Mr. D had never been in Texas in his entire life but had simply inserted this language in his will?

2. Suppose Mr. E was a Texas resident at the time he approached you about making a will. Would you include a recitation of fiduciary powers or simply describe his executor as being independent? What if he was a resident of a jurisdiction which had adopted the UPC?

3. How do you determine which fiduciary powers to include in an instrument? (Make this determination only by considering the function of the executor. The executor fund function is twofold: (1) to collect the testator's property and (2) to distribute that property in accordance with the decedent's will. What powers, then, are necessary to accomplish these functions?)

4. Look at the following list of fiduciary powers and consider how they relate to the collection and distribution functions of the executor. Indicate why each of them is necessary or unnecessary to the efficient administration of the testator's estate. Lastly, what would state law applicable in your jurisdiction provide as to authority to do a particular thing if the formal grant of power to do that thing were eliminated from the instrument?

ITEM 6: EXECUTOR'S POWERS, DUTIES, DISCRETIONS, AND IMMUNITIES

6.01.   *In General.* In addition to the powers my Executor shall enjoy as independent Executor, I also authorize my Executor to compromise, adjust, release, subordinate and discharge in such manner as my Executor deems proper all debts and claims owed to me or by me; to sell or exchange at private or public sale, and in such manner and upon such terms of credit or otherwise as my Executor may deem proper, all or any part of my property, real or personal, except property specifically devised or bequeathed herein, regardless of whether such sale shall be necessary for the payment of debts, expenses or administration of my estate, taxes, legacies, or other obligations; to renew or extend any debts owed by me; to borrow money for the purpose of paying estate or inheritance taxes and to secure any such debt by a pledge or mortgage or any part of my property; to retain property originally comprising my estate, and to invest and reinvest funds of my estate, as my Executor, in my Executor's sole discretion, may deem proper, without regard to any restrictions, statutory or otherwise,

¶ 3630

normally incident to executorship, and without greater liability for loss than if such investment were of a class otherwise expressly authorized by law for fiduciaries; to lease real estate for any term and to improve, repair and maintain the same; to grant options to purchase any property comprising my estate; to make distribution in kind of any property comprising my estate without obtaining the consent of any beneficiary; to execute, acknowledge and deliver instruments of conveyance, including deeds in fee simple, notes, mortgages, and agreements of pledge, and all other instruments necessary or incidental to the execution of the foregoing powers; and in general, to do all things necessary or appropriate for the administration of my estate. All powers herein granted to or by law conferred upon my Executor may be exercised by my Executor without order of any court.

6.02.   *Transactions with Executor.* No persons dealing with my Executor shall be bound to inquire concerning the validity of any act of my Executor or be liable for the applications of any money or other consideration paid or loaned by such person to my Executor.

6.03.   *Federal Income and Gift Tax Returns.* I authorize my Executor to file joint federal income tax returns with my spouse, or if my spouse is not living, with the Executor or Administrator of my spouse's estate for any period or periods for which such a return may be permitted following my death; to pay from my estate the full amount of the tax due thereon or any adjustment thereof; and to consent that any gifts made by me or by my spouse prior to my death shall, for gift tax purposes, be considered as having been made one-half by me and one-half by my spouse, and if such consent be given to pay from my estate all gift taxes that may be due because of such gifts, my Executor may assume any liability incident to such taxes.

6.04.   *Tax Elections.* When a choice is available as to whether certain deductions shall be taken as income tax deductions or estate tax deductions, the decision of my Executor in this regard shall be considered final as to all concerned, and no adjustment of income and principal accounts in the estate shall be made as the result of such decision. Furthermore, the choice of my Executor of a method of valuing farmland or closely held business interests in accordance with § 2032A of the Internal Revenue Code of 1986 shall be final.

6.05.   *Claims to Community Property.* I direct that my Executor shall make no claim to any community interest that I may have in any policy of life insurance or employee benefit plan which may become distributable, at my death or at the death of my spouse, to my spouse or to a trustee under any trust that my spouse or I established during our respective lives for the primary benefit of my spouse and/or my lineal descendants. Furthermore, my Executor shall have no duty to seek an accounting from my spouse as to applications of any community property made by my spouse during my lifetime.

6.06. *Trust Code.* In addition, my Executor shall have, in extension of, and not in limitation of, the powers given by law or the terms of this instrument, all of the administrative powers and powers of sale granted to a trustee under any statutory scheme governing trusts which is applicable in the jurisdiction in which my estate is being administered, whether domiciliary or ancillary, such powers to be exercised without court supervision or control.

6.07. *Court Supervision.* I direct that no action be had in the court responsible for the administration of my estate, to the extent permitted by applicable law, with respect to my estate other than to probate this will and to make, return, and record an inventory and appraisement of my estate and list of claims. I specifically request, however, that, if permitted by applicable law, no appraisement of my household goods and furniture be made.

6.08. *Fees.* My executor shall be entitled to reasonable fees commensurate with the duties required and responsibilities assumed, taking into account the value and nature of my estate and the time and work involved.

5. Note the decimal numbering system used in the immediately preceding problem. Do you agree that this scheme for organizing a will facilitates cross-referencing and item location and is much to be preferred over the more conventional organizational scheme of using letters to label paragraphs within numbered articles?

M. CONFLICTS OF LAW

[¶ 3651]

1. VALIDITY OF EXECUTION IN OTHER STATES

Requirements for execution of a valid will are such that, generally speaking, any will valid in the place of execution will be valid in all of the other states. Moreover, many states seem to follow the general rule and accept wills which are valid in the decedent's domicile.

[¶ 3659]

2. JURISDICTION

Obviously, many wills are drafted without regard to the possibility that they will have to be probated in another jurisdiction. Such provincialism is a disservice to clients. Instead, special effort should be made by the draftsperson to avoid tying the will to local law.

[¶ 3667]

3. CHOICE OF LAW ISSUES

Ambiguities in a will which require construction by a court raise the question of which state's law of wills to apply. Unfortunately, there is no single resolution applicable to ambiguities because courts often distinguish rules of choice of law depending upon the nature of the property devised. If it is personal property, then the law of the testator's domicile at death is applied in the absence of any designation of law in the will. Restatement (Second) Conflict of Laws § 264 (1971). If a devise of realty is being construed, the courts usually apply the law of the situs of the realty. Id. § 240. UPC § 2–703 authorizes the testator to choose the law of any state for the construction of the testator's will, but then it attaches the unsettling provision that the testator's choice of law applies unless application would be against the policy of the code limiting a decedent's ability to disinherit his or her surviving spouse.

Even if there is no ambiguity in deciding which state's law to apply, there may still be the question of whether to construe the will in terms of the law in effect at the time the will was executed or at the time of the decedent's death. Most states apply the latter rule. See, e.g., Estate of Stanford v. Reynolds, 49 Cal.2d 120, 315 P.2d 681 (1957); Ford v. Ford, 70 Wis. 19, 33 N.W. 188 (1887). These decisions are based on the presumption that the testator must have known the existing statutes were subject to change and must have intended the statute in effect at the time the gift became operative to be controlling. See, e.g., Lincoln v. Aldrich, 149 Mass. 368, 21 N.E. 671 (1889). Of course, if the legislative intent is clear that a statute is to be retroactive then there is no ambiguity.

A few courts have at least considered the law of the state in which the testator executed the will even if the testator died while later domiciled elsewhere. In re Flagler's Will, 4 Misc.2d 705, 158 N.Y.S.2d 941 (N.Y. Surr. Ct. 1957); Blatt v. Blatt, 79 Colo. 57, 243 P. 1099 (1926). In one case, the court applied the later rule for the additional reason that before the testator had moved to her domicile at death she had become mentally incapacitated, and, therefore, had no effective opportunity to change her will in accordance with the law of her new domicile. Royce v. Estate of Denby, 117 N.H. 893, 379 A.2d 1256 (1977).

N. AVOIDING ANCILLARY ADMINISTRATION

[¶ 3701]

1. REAL PROPERTY

It is not uncommon for a testator to have real property in several states. Inasmuch as the law of the situs controls the disposition of real property, a separate estate administration, known as an ancillary administration, will have to be conducted in each state in which the testator has real property subject to disposition by the testator's will. Ancillary administration is expensive since essentially it means repeating the entire administrative process in each state where the decedent has real property.

The draftsperson should anticipate the need for an ancillary administration by recommending that the testator use either a revocable trust or a joint tenancy with right of survivorship to hold the testator's nondomiciliary property. Taxwise, the U.S. Supreme Court has held that the *only* state which may constitutionally levy an inheritance tax on real property and *tangible* personal property is the state in which such property is located at the owner's death. Treichler v. Wisconsin, 338 U.S. 251 (1949); City Bank Farmers' Trust Co. v. Schnader, 293 U.S. 112 (1934); Frick v. Pennsylvania, 268 U.S. 473 (1975).

[¶ 3709]

2. PERSONAL PROPERTY

Ancillary administration problems do not often arise with respect to personal property since the law of the testator's domicile controls the disposition of personal property owned by the testator.

Interestingly, as to intangibles, the Supreme Court has held that there is no constitutional prohibition to inheritance taxation by both the decedent's domiciliary jurisdiction and any other state or states which furnish "benefit and protection" to such intangible property interests. Curry v. McCanless, 307 U.S. 357 (1939); Greenough v. Tax Assessors, 331 U.S. 486 (1947).

[¶ 3717]

3. DOMICILE

The testator's "permanent home" is the testator's domicile. Domicile is often defined in terms of presence plus no intent to go elsewhere.

It is appropriate to insure that indicia of domicile all point in one direction, e.g., auto registration; voter registration; provisions in a will; where income tax returns filed; where state personal property tax forms filed.

Problem

[¶ 3725]

1. Hobart is survived by his wife, Wilhelmina, and his orphaned nephew, Charlie. Hobart's estate consists of $600,000 of separate property, plus his house and personal effects of limited value. His estate is burdened by $500,000 of separate indebtedness. He has no community property. Hobart's will, brief and to the point, is set forth below:

Will

First: Pay all my debts.

Second: Pay all my taxes.

Third: $100,000 to Charlie.

Fourth: My house to Wilhelmina if she survives me for 30 days.

Fifth: My tangible personal property to Wilhelmina if she survives me for 30 days.

Sixth: The balance to Wilhelmina if she survives me for 30 days; otherwise to my then living lineal descendants *per stirpes*.

¶ 3725

Seventh: Wilhelmina shall be my "independent executor."

/s/ Hobart

Witnesses:
/s/ I. Sawit
/s/ M. E. Tu

(a) Which gift in the will is reduced by the indebtedness? ¶ 3401.

(b) Assume that Hobart's estate has no indebtedness. Which gift in the will is charged with the federal death taxes, which, in this case, total $10,800? ¶ 3251.

(c) Why the redundancy in Hobart's will, as reflected by paragraphs Fourth through Sixth? ¶ 3551.

(d) Why the condition of survivorship in paragraphs Fourth through Sixth? ¶ 3451.

(e) Why the 30 days survivorship requirement in paragraphs Fourth through Sixth? ¶ 3459.

(f) The marital deduction will be available to Hobart's estate to allow all of his estate to escape taxation at his death. Does the 30–day survivorship requirement defeat the marital deduction in the event of simultaneous death? See § 2056. See also discussion at ¶ 14,201.

(g) What does *per stirpes* mean in paragraph Sixth? ¶ 3551.

(h) What is the significance of describing Wilhelmina as independent executor in paragraph Seventh? Would it be preferable to recite that the executor could do with the decedent's property all that the decedent could do if living? ¶ 3601.

(i) Can you offer any criticism of the structure of the gift to Charlie? (For a discussion of the disadvantages of distributing property to a child under age 18, see ¶ 4051.)

O. ANATOMICAL GIFTS

[¶ 3751]

There is a critical scarcity of body parts and organs for transplantation—and an unexplained widespread failure to make such gifts. In 2002, the total number of people on the Organ Procurement and Transplantation Network national patent waiting list was said to number almost 80,000. A 1985 Gallup poll reported that 93 percent of all respondents knew about organ transplantation, 75 percent approved of the concept, but only 27 percent indicated that they would be likely to donate their own organs, with 17 percent having actually completed donor cards. See Unif. Anatomical Gift Act (UAGA) prefatory note (amended 1987), 8A U.L.A. 5 (2003).

While the sale or purchase of body parts is prohibited, donation could not be easier. A simple written statement signed by the donor is all that is required. Unif. Anatomical Gift Act § 2. The gift can be made by will. While

¶ 3725

state law should be reviewed, a possible form of gift, which must be signed by the donor, is as follows:

> Upon my death, I give any needed organs, tissues, or parts for any legally permissible purpose.

Often the back side of a driver's license will set out an organ donation form. And, while, the gift can be made by will, the delay between death and the reading of the will often makes the use of a will for organ transplantation less than the best alternative and it is not recommended. If the decedent has not executed a anatomical gift form, the UAGA permits certain individuals such as a spouse, child, or parent to authorize anatomical gifts if the decedent has not indicated opposition to donating his or her organs.

Section 5 of the UAGA requires hospital administrators to ask new patients who are at least 18 years of age on or before admission if he or she is an organ donor. Furthermore, if there is no record that the patient has made or refused to make a gift, the hospital is encouraged to discuss organ donation with the next of kin, if the patient is at or near death. Unif. Anatomical Gift Act § 5(b). At least 46 states and the District of Columbia have adopted some form of this section. Fred H. Cate, Human Organ Transplantation: The Role of Law, 20 J. Corp. L. 69 (1995). However, the required request statute has been ineffective in practice due to hospitals' lack of enforcement. See Gloria S. Neuwirth, Guidelines for Clients Contemplating Organ Donation, 23 Est. Plan. 345 (1996).

¶ 3751

Chapter 4

POWERS OF ATTORNEY, ADVANCE DIRECTIVES, AND LIVING TRUSTS: DISABILITY PLANNING AND OTHER APPLICATIONS

A. OBJECTIVES

[¶ 4001]

The trust can be an important part of almost every plan for the orderly disposition of property. When the trust is *revocable*—as contrasted with *irrevocable*—the settlor can keep control of the property during life, while not under any legal disability. Moreover, in the event of the settlor's disability, the trust is an infinitely better alternative than a guardianship. Furthermore, the revocable trust offers many advantages not even available with a general power of attorney.

The trust can also be utilized so as to: (1) insure privacy by allowing the decedent's property to avoid probate, i.e., to be omitted from the inventory of the decedent's property that is filed with the probate court; (2) avoid ancillary administration of real property located in other jurisdictions by transferring that property to the trust while the settlor is living (see ¶ 3701); and (3) avoid court supervision of trusts created by a decedent for his or her loved ones which are to continue after the death of the decedent.

The trust most commonly used is structured as a *revocable* life insurance trust, i.e., the trust is named the beneficiary of the settlor's life insurance. In most of these cases life insurance is the sole funding of the trust. Most commonly, ownership of the insurance remains in the insured, and the trust is named either primary or secondary beneficiary of the life insurance. If the trust is secondary beneficiary, the trust could be referred to as a contingent life insurance trust (as it is in ¶ 4441).

The trust envisioned here is commonly known as a *living trust* because it is created by the settlor during life. A particular function of this chapter is to identify some of the issues that must be considered in effectively utilizing such a trust for property management during periods of disability as well as a vehicle to accomplish post-death objectives. Health care management, on the other hand, is considered in terms of the *living will* and the health care power of attorney.

B. GUARDIANSHIP OF INCOMPETENTS

[¶ 4051]

1. INTRODUCTION

Suppose a person becomes incompetent whether for reasons of advancing age, illness, or injury. As an incompetent, the person can take and hold property, but may not manage it. Similarly, children under the age of 18 are deemed to be under legal disability and, as such, are incompetent to manage their own property although they, too, may take and hold property.

Each state addresses this management problem by providing for the appointment of a guardian—sometimes called a conservator—of the estate of the incompetent person. Each state also provides for the appointment of a guardian of the person of an incompetent. However, in many cases where a person is incompetent to manage his or her property, the person is competent to manage his or her person without supervision.

[¶ 4059]

2. KINDS OF GUARDIANSHIPS

Incidentally, for convenience of reference, you should note that guardians of the persons of minor children are sometimes referred to as *parental guardians*. Guardians of the estate are sometimes referred to as the *financial guardians*.

[¶ 4067]

3. NATURE OF GUARDIANSHIPS

For a state to recognize the need to provide for the management of both the person and property of those of its citizens who become incompetent is a critical state function. The guardianship scheme is society's attempt to protect those who are unable to manage their own affairs from themselves and from others who would take advantage of their condition. The procedure commonly adopted is designed to provide not only supervision of person and property but also supervision of the "supervisor" by the probate court having jurisdiction over the person of the incompetent. The supervision imposed upon the guardian of the estate is so complete that the only way to describe the guardian's function is to say that the guardian exercises no *discretionary* authority but performs only *ministerial* functions. (Ministerial functions include safekeeping of the ward's property while discretionary functions include making distributions or sales of the ward's property.)

[¶ 4075]

4. THE NOTICE REQUIREMENT

Appointment of a guardian begins with formal notice, usually by the county sheriff, to the prospective ward to the effect that the ward's competence is being adjudicated and that the prospective ward should appear at the time set for the hearing. Oftentimes a family will delay beginning incompeten-

¶ 4075

cy proceedings out of reluctance to give a loved one—in need of protection—notice that the proceeding is taking place for fear that the prospective ward's health will be jeopardized by the trauma associated with receipt of the notice. Modern statutes require the appointment of an attorney *ad litem* to represent the prospective ward in the competency hearing.

[¶ 4083]

5. THE BONDING REQUIREMENT

Faithful performance by the guardian of his or her duties is, in theory, secured by a bond which must be posted with the court as a condition of the appointment of the guardian. Normally, the bond is in the form of a promise by an insurance company to reconstitute the estate of the ward if the guardian breaches any duties and if the breach causes loss to the ward's estate. The bond premium will be roughly $10 per thousand and bond will have to be posted which is equivalent to twice the value of the ward's personal property. The bond premium is an annual charge against the ward's property.

Some jurisdictions permit bond to be waived. Normally, waiver of bond is permitted only where: (1) the guardian is named in the will of the parent of the ward and the parent's will provides that the guardian shall serve without bond, see, e.g., Tex. Prob. Code Ann. § 702 (Vernon 2003) or (2) the guardian is designated by the ward in a pre-need declaration. See, e.g., Conn. Gen. Stat. Ann. § 45a–645 (West 2004).

[¶ 4091]

6. MANAGEMENT ISSUES

Disbursements for the benefit of the ward must be made only with court approval, although it is common to obtain prior blanket approval for expenditure of a monthly maintenance fee for the ward.

Normally, sales or exchanges of the ward's property can be accomplished only with court approval. Generally, this is an expensive and time-consuming process inasmuch as the court must be satisfied that the proposed sale is in the best interests of the ward. Usually appraisals of the property by independent appraisers are required.

Investment of the ward's property is sometimes restricted to property found on so-called legal lists or other secure investments, meaning investments that have little or no appreciation potential but that are seen as safe in the sense that, if held to maturity, the face value of the investment will be recaptured albeit depreciated in inflationary times.

Questions arise that go to the philosophical heart of the guardianship. Traditionally, the guardian's function has been one of asset preservation. What then should be done when, for example, guaranteed issue options on a life insurance policy become exercisable? Purchase of additional life insurance could be seen as benefitting persons other than the ward—and depleting the ward's property that might be required for the ward's care. See, e.g., E. LeFevre, Annotation, Power of Guardian of Incompetent To Change Beneficiary in Ward's Life Insurance Policy, 21 A.L.R.2d 1191 (1952; Supp. 1982; Supp. 1994).

Modern statutes, of course, address some or all of these issues. For example, UPC § 5–410 says that the court which is supervising the guardianship is to have all the powers that the ward would have if the person were of full capacity. UPC § 5–410. Beneficiaries of the ward's life insurance, for example, can be changed by the conservator and supervising court after notice and hearing. UPC § 5–411.

[¶ 4099]

7. THE ACCOUNTING DUTY

The court discharges its supervisory function largely by requiring an accounting by the guardian on an annual basis. The account normally consists of the following:

1. An itemization of all cash received and all cash disbursed by the guardian since the last account; and

2. An itemization of all sales or exchanges of guardianship property since the last account; and

3. A beginning inventory and an ending inventory of the ward's property.

Normally, the account must be supported by receipts for each and every disbursement.

[¶ 4107]

8. ESTATE PLANNING IMPLICATIONS

a. *Doctrine of Substituted Judgment*

Suppose the ward has been supporting one or more family members. Can that support continue? UPC § 5–427 approves distributions for the benefit of dependents. What about others? While the policy of the UPC is against an overly intrusive exercise of control over property of the protected person, there seems to be no answer.

The UPC does permit the making of gifts by the ward, including gifts to charity, as well as other natural objects of the ward's bounty so long as the amount does not exceed 20 percent of the estates income in a given year. See UPC § 5–427(b); see also R. Wormser, The Doctrine of Substitution of Judgment, 9 U. Miami. Inst. On Est. Plan. ¶ 1500 (1975). The making of tax-motivated gifts is an important power for the guardian to enjoy.

[¶ 4115]

b. *Predesignation of Guardian*

Increasingly, states are coming to recognize the use of a pre-need declaration, wherein a person is designated the declarant's guardian in the event of incapacity. Such declarations may also give the declarant the opportunity to stipulate that certain persons should not be appointed guardian. Not only may such a declaration need to be witnessed, but the witnesses and the declarant may be required to sign a self-proving affidavit modeled after that commonly in use with wills. See, e.g., Tex. Prob. Code Ann. § 679 (Vernon 2003).

[¶ 4123]

c. *Impact of Guardian's Appointment on Power of Attorney*

Sometimes the appointment of a guardian will have the effect of terminating the authority of the person holding the ward's power of attorney. See, e.g., Conn. Gen. Stat. Ann. § 45a–562 (West 2004); Kan. Stat. Ann. § 59–3075(e)(7)(B) (2005); Fla. Stat. Ann. § 709.08(3)(b) (West 2000, Supp. 2006); Tex. Prob. Code Ann. § 485 (2003). Yet, in other states such as South Carolina, a power of attorney may remain in effect along with the appointment of a guardian if it provides accordingly. *"Unless the power of attorney provides otherwise*, appointment of a guardian terminates all or part of the power of attorney that relates to matters within the scope of the guardianship...."* S.C. Code Ann. § 62–5–501(B) (1987, Supp. 2005) (emphasis added). Moreover, appeals courts have been noted as having found error when persons who were nominated in powers of attorney were not appointed guardian. See, e.g., In re Sylvester, 409 Pa.Super. 439, 598 A.2d 76, 83–84 (1991); In re Medsker, 66 Ohio App.3d 219, 583 N.E.2d 1091, 1092–93 (1990).

A previously executed and valid power of attorney will generally forbear the need for a court appointed guardian. See Wilhelm v. Wilhelm, 441 Pa.Super. 230, 657 A.2d 34, 39 (1995) ("If the court finds that the power of attorney signed by [Appellant] was valid, there shall be no need for a guardianship decision ..."). However, nothing prevents an incapacitated person's relatives from petitioning a court to institute guardianship proceedings even in cases where a durable power of attorney is in existence. Smith v. Lynch, 821 So.2d 1197 (Fla. App. 2002) (ward's grand niece and grand nephew sought guardianship although the ward's husband and step-daughter had a durable power of attorney). The *Smith* court stated that the appointment of a guardian is permitted "only when no other lesser intrusion on the privacy of the ward will accomplish the purpose of protecting the ward's property." Id. at 1199. The court held that, under the circumstances, appointing a guardian would "unnecessarily interfere with the family" emphasizing the close and long-term relationship between the ward and her husband. Conversely, the niece and nephew were not as close and played a less significant role in the ward's life. Id.

When selecting a guardian, the decision is primarily at the discretion of the appointing court subject to statutory constraints, and as a general rule, when courts consider appointing a guardian, the "best interests of [the] incompetent are of paramount consideration." Peter G. Guthrie, Annotation, Priority and Preference in Appointment of Conservator or Guardian for an Incompetent, 65 A.L.R.3d 991, 997 (1975 & Supp. 2002).

¶ 4115

Problem

[¶ 4130]

Review the guardianship provisions of your own state to determine whether they are more liberal or stricter than those described here. Consider whether the law of guardianship should be liberalized to reduce the administrative burden and expense imposed on the guardian and, ultimately, the ward.

C. DURABLE POWERS OF ATTORNEY

[¶ 4201]

1. PROPERTY POWERS

a. *Third Party Acceptance*

An area of estate planning that sometimes receives inadequate attention is the preparation for disability or incompetency and durable powers of attorney are an important tool for such a situation. Gerry E. Beyer, The Durable Power of Attorney for Property Management, 59 Tex. B.J. 314 (1996). Every state has enacted legislation which acknowledges the validity of durable powers of attorney—instruments which do not terminate upon the principal's incapacity or incompetency. However, because there is a profound lack of uniformity among the various states, applicable state law must be analyzed in order to determine the authorized uses and formalities required for an effective durable power of attorney. A number of states have adopted the Durable Power of Attorney Act, which appears also as UPC §§ 5–501 through 5–505. Unif. Probate Code §§ 5–501 through 505 (amended 1993), 8 U.L.A. 419–24 (1998).

Durable powers of attorney have some significant limitations. For example, third parties may be reluctant to transact business with an agent authorized under a durable power of attorney. Banks, insurance companies, and stockbrokers often insist that the principal use a company-authorized form and/or that the power must be recently executed. It is not unusual for a company to reject a power that is currently effective under applicable state law because it was not recently executed, i.e., because it is "stale." Good estate planning means re-execution of powers every couple of years to prevent staleness. Sometimes acceptance is enhanced if the power contains a "hold harmless and indemnity" clause.

[¶ 4203]

b. *Gifting Authority of Agents*

An agent's authority is usually limited to those acts expressly conferred in the power. In Estate of Casey v. Commissioner, 948 F.2d 895 (4th Cir. 1991), the court held that because a durable power of attorney did not specifically authorize the making of gifts, the gifts the agent made on behalf of the principal to reduce her estate were revocable transfers under § 2038

¶ 4203

and includible in the principal's estate. The rationale was that a power to make gifts on the principal's behalf could not be inferred from a power that did not specifically authorize such gifts or from the past gifting pattern of the principal. The court stated that such a "bright line" test was necessary to prevent the "temptations for self-dealing" a holder of a power may experience. Id. at 898. Furthermore, Private Letter Ruling 8635007 held that such powers under applicable state law should be strictly construed and a general power to act on a principal's behalf "does not include the power to make gifts." Fortunately, the IRS concluded that the power to make gifts can be specifically granted. Therefore, a person who wishes his agent under a durable power of attorney to continue to make lifetime gifts after he or she becomes incapacitated must specifically so state in the power or all gifts made by the agent are revocable and included in the principal's estate under § 2038.

Since *Casey*, however, several cases have held that where the durable power of attorney did not expressly grant gift-giving authority the transferred property was not includible in the decedent's estate under § 2038 because the gifts were not revocable. See, e.g., Estate of Neff v. Commissioner, 73 T.C.M. (CCH) 2606 (1997); Estate of Ridenour v. Commissioner, 36 F.3d 332 (4th Cir. 1994). The courts in both cases looked at extrinsic evidence to determine if there was intent to authorize the agent to make the gifts. Additionally, Private Letter Ruling 9708004 held that a series of gifts made by the agent were not includible in the decedent's estate although the durable power of attorney did not expressly grant such authority. In that case, the decedent executed a statement subsequent to the durable power of attorney, which made specific reference to the power of attorney, that he intended to make annual gifts through the direction of his agent, some of which he made himself. The IRS reasoned that the decedent made substantial gifts himself and the gifts at issue were made after the letter was dated evidenced his intent to authorize gift giving. The IRS noted that whether one can look at extrinsic evidence will depend on state law.

[¶ 4204]

c. *Amanuensis and not as Agent*

In what capacity did the person sign? As agent under the power of attorney? Or as *amanuensis*, i.e., as merely the instrument of the will of the principal? In Estate of Stephens, 28 Cal.4th 665, 122 Cal.Rptr.2d 358, 49 P.3d 1093 (2002), Austin Stephens, a widower, had executed a durable power of attorney with his daughter, Shirley, as his agent. The power of attorney did not specifically grant the authority to make gifts. Shirley had been caring for him while his health was in decline and his son had moved out of the state. Austin decided to give his house to his daughter and essentially disinherit his son because he felt that his son had moved when he needed him. Austin directed Shirley to sign a deed transferring the house to each of them as joint tenants. She signed the deed in Austin's name in the presence of a notary, but in the absence of Austin. However, Austin confirmed the transfer on many occasions with various people including a person at the County Recorder who had phoned him and inquired about the transfer.

¶ 4203

The California Supreme Court reversed the appeals court and found the transfer valid under the *amanuensis* rule, which operates as an exception of both the Civil and the Probate Code. Under the *amanuensis* rule, when a person signs the grantor's name with the grantor's express authority, she "is not deemed an agent but is instead regarded as a mere instrument or amanuensis of the grantor * * *." Section 2309 of the California Civil Code requires that the agent's authority to execute a deed must be conferred in writing by the principal, and § 4264 of the California Probate Code states that a power of attorney must expressly grant gift giving authority to the agent for a gift to be valid. Cal. [Civ.] Code § 2309 (West 1985); Cal. [Prob.] Code § 4264 (West Supp. 2006). While the lower court was found to have correctly concluded that the power of attorney did not grant the daughter the authority to make gifts, the supreme court decided that "Shirley's signature of Austin's name was a purely ministerial, mechanical act and was not an exercise by Shirley of any authority under the power of attorney * * *." Shirley, the signor, was an interested person and, as such, had to overcome, by a preponderance of the evidence, a presumption that the transfer was invalid. The supreme court concluded that she had done so.

[¶ 4205]

d. *Statutory Powers of Attorney*

Ideally the estate planner will carefully draft a durable power of attorney and include express provisions of all of the powers that the individual intends to authorize. Short of that, some states, such as Texas, provide a default statutory durable power of attorney. The Texas statutory form lists 13 powers that are either to be initialed if accepted or crossed out if rejected and it provides a special optional section for specific gifting powers relating to the annual federal gift tax exclusion. Tex. Prob. Code Ann. § 490 (Vernon 2003). Explanations of the specific rights and powers that accompany each of the 13 powers are described in §§ 491 through 504.

Problem

[¶ 4206]

List the specific powers that you think should be included in a general power of attorney. In preparing your list, try to imagine all of the issues that a person will encounter in managing property.

Could the drafting be simplified by preparing a power which said only that "my attorney may do with my property all those things which I could do if I were competent"?

[¶ 4209]

2. HEALTH POWERS

An important aspect of estate planning is the preparation and use of advance directives in anticipation of the client becoming incapacitated and unable to make health care decisions. The two principal forms of advance directives are the health care durable power of attorney or health care proxy and the living will. Two other advance directives that are used are the pre-hospital do not resuscitate order and the declaration of mental health treatment. Every state has legislation that authorizes the use of either the health care durable power of attorney or the living will as a method for individuals to plan their health care if they become incompetent. See Unif. Health–Care Decisions Act prefatory note, 9 U.L.A. 84 (2005).

Over the years an effort has been made by various states to eliminate weaknesses and inconsistencies in their respective statutes and consolidate them into a single comprehensive law. See, e.g., Ariz. Rev. Stat. Ann. § 36–3201 (2003); Md. Code Ann., [Health–Gen.] § 5–601 (LexisNexis 2005); N.J. Stat. Ann. § 26:2H–53 (West 1996); Tex. [Health & Safety] Code Ann. § 166.001 (Vernon 2001).

Often the decision whether to initiate or continue life-sustaining treatment must be made in the absence of an advance directive. Most states allow family members to make such decisions, but in some states the power of family members is limited, such as in Arizona where a family member does not have the power to remove or refuse artificial nutrition and hydration unless he or she is the patient's guardian or agent as authorized by statute. Ariz. Rev. Stat. Ann. § 36–3231(D) (West 2003). Even so, unaffordable and unnecessary expense as well as mental anguish are the likely result. Consider the plight of Engracia Torregosa Garcia who suffered cardiac arrest. Although she was resuscitated, her brain damage had been damaged and she remained in a vegetative state. Her family wanted to have her feeding tube removed, but the trial court issued a permanent injunction against removing it because she did not have specific language in a living will or power of attorney directing such an action. The appeals court reversed the trial court and ordered the feeding tube removed because there was clear evidence that Ms. Garcia would not want to be kept alive by artificial means. San Juan–Torregosa v. Garcia 80 S.W.3d 539 (Tenn. Ct. App. 2002). The appeals court decision was approximately ten months after Ms. Garcia suffered cardiac arrest.

[¶ 4210]

a. Health Care Durable Power of Attorney a.k.a. Advance Directives

A durable health power of attorney is similar to a property durable power of attorney (as discussed in ¶ 4201) except that health powers are used specifically for health care decisions. Almost all of the states have some form of legislation which allows a patient, the "principal," to appoint another individual, the "agent," to make decisions regarding acceptance or denial of medical treatment for the patient when incapacitated. The ability to appoint someone to make decisions, e.g., whether to be placed on a life support system or when a life-sustaining system should be withdrawn, gives a patient the ability to decide his or her destiny and relieves the physician of making this critical decision when the patient's wishes are not made known to the physician prior to the incapacitation.

Many states require special forms to be used, or particular procedures to be followed, in order for a health care power of attorney to be effective in that particular state. Generally speaking, however, in drafting a durable health power of attorney, the following considerations should be addressed in conjunction with applicable state law:

1. The designated agent should be someone the principal trusts to carry out his or her health care wishes. The agent should be in good health. Use of the principal's health care provider, such as the principal's doctor, is strongly discouraged because of ethical conflicts. A successor or alternative agent should be named to prevent the lapse of the power should the first agent become unavailable or predecease the principal.

2. The power should state when and under what conditions the power is to be effective, and it should provide a standard to determine when the principal is "incapacitated."

3. The power should state the extent of the agent's power to make decisions and any particular limitations the principal wishes to place on the agent.

4. The power should state the right of the principal to revoke the durable health power or the appointed agent's authority to act on the principal's behalf. Providing that the power is to expire as of a specified event or date may result in the power being found to be expired at the moment of need.

Care should be taken to fulfill all the administrative requirements under applicable state law in executing the health power.

[¶ 4217]

b. Living Wills or "Let Me Go" Language

Living wills and health care powers are different. Health care powers empower the powerholder to make health care decisions for another. Living wills consist of a series of directives or instructions to be followed in specified circumstances. Provisions of a living will reflect decisions made by the grantor as to a course of action to be followed if specified conditions prevail. A statutory example of a provision in a living will is as follows: "I do not wish to receive artificially supplied nutrition and hydration, if the effort to sustain life is futile or excessively burdensome to me." Ind. Code Ann. § 16–36–4–10 (West 1997).

As one might expect with such a sensitive subject, serious issues may be encountered when attempting to abide by the instructions in a living will. A typical problem that may occur is the "classic right-to-die" dilemma where the family wishes to discontinue life-sustaining treatment and the physician refuses or the converse where the physician wishes to discontinue life-sustaining treatment, usually due to its futility, in opposition to the family's wishes. Thomas Wm. Mayo, Health Care Law, 53 SMU L. Rev. 1101, 1110 (2000). Texas has addressed this issue by codifying the American Medical Association's resolution procedure, which provides legal protection for the hospital if it follows the statutory process. Tex. [Health & Safety] Code Ann. § 166.045 (Vernon 2001). The process includes a review by an ethics committee; the health care provider is obliged to provide ten days of life-sustaining treatment while the family reviews the ethics committee's decision; and a reasonable attempt to transfer the patient to another health care provider must be made if the family does not agree with the decision. Tex. [Health & Safety] Code Ann. § 166.046 (Vernon 2001, Supp. 2005).

Living wills are statute-based and must conform to those requirements, requirements which vary by state.

D. THE STANDBY REVOCABLE TRUST AND LIMITED-POWERS FOR DISABILITY

[¶ 4251]

1. RELATIONSHIP

Given the limitations of the durable *general* power of attorney, revocable trusts are a popular alternative management device in anticipation of possible incompetence. The trust is structured so that if funds are added to the trust during the lifetime of the creator, the trustee will manage them for the creator's benefit and, when the disability is removed, the creator can revoke the trust.

Obviously the prospective incompetent cannot wait until he or she becomes incompetent to create a trust. The trust needs to be created during a period of competency if it is to be effective. Alternatively, the trust can be created by someone holding a power of attorney—provided the power expressly authorizes creation of a trust for these purposes. Similarly, if the trust has been created but the incompetent's property remains outside the trust, the trust can be funded by the holder of a power of attorney. In cases like this, a *limited* power of attorney is often used, the power being limited to allowing a trust to be created or to allowing an existing trust to be created. General powers are of equal utility, but some clients are reluctant to give anyone a *general* power of attorney.

Usually trusts created in anticipation of disability are revocable. These trusts are commonly known as living trusts (apparently to distinguish them from trusts created by will).

[¶ 4301]

2. LIVING TRUSTS

Living trusts can be revocable or irrevocable, although traditionally the term "living trust" is associated with revocable trusts. See ¶ 4433. Living trusts can be funded or unfunded. *Unfunded trusts* are those in which funding is nothing more than the right to receive the proceeds of insurance on the life of the creator or settlor of the trust. See ¶ 4441; for an example, see ¶ 4511. *Funded trusts* refers to trusts into which the creator of the trust has placed

¶ 4217

property other than life insurance, the property funding the trust having more than nominal value.

[¶ 4351]

3. JOINT TRUSTS

Normally, trusts have only one creator. However, joint trusts are becoming more popular. Joint trusts are trusts having more than one creator or settlor. Joint trusts are popular with spouses, particularly where the spouses have community property. Spouses holding property as joint tenants with right of survivorship also may favor the joint trust.

Typically, the joint trust becomes partially irrevocable at the death of the first of the settlors to die. At that time, the trust property is divided between a newly created irrevocable trust and the continuing revocable trust. Tax considerations drive the creation of these kinds of joint trusts; discussion of tax issues, however, must be put off until later chapters relating to the marital deduction (Chapters 13–15) and concurrent ownership (Chapter 11).

Problem

[¶ 4385]

Alice does not want to establish a revocable trust during her lifetime because of the expense. Could Alice "have her cake and eat it too" by giving her attorney a durable power to create a revocable trust for her if the attorney should ever come to the conclusion that Alice was unable to manage her affairs?

Are there any additional powers that could appropriately be included in a limited durable power of attorney?

E. THE BACKUP TRUST FOR BENEFICIARIES UNDER LEGAL DISABILITY; ALTERNATIVES

[¶ 4401]

1. GUARDIANSHIPS

The dispositive scheme most commonly employed by the careful draftsperson when tax planning is not important is to dispose of the residue of the testator's estate in favor of the testator's "spouse if the spouse survives [the testator] for thirty (30) days; otherwise to [the testator's] then living lineal descendants *per stirpes.*" Such a disposition assumes that the testator's lineal descendants will be under no legal disability at the time they are to receive their share of the testator's property. If any of them are then under legal disability, each such lineal's share will be distributed to a guardian of his or her estate appointed by the local probate court. The guardian will be charged with managing the ward's property until the legal disability is removed.

As noted earlier, guardianships are extremely cumbersome management devices and, in the smaller estates, the expense is disproportionate to the size of the estate. One alternative is a custodianship established under the Uniform Transfers to Minors Act. An even better alternative is the trust.

[¶ 4409]

2. UNIFORM ACTS (UGMA AND UTMA)

Persons under 18 years of age are under legal disability and cannot administer their own property. A guardian of the estate for such persons must be appointed when one of them is the recipient of property. Usually the guardian who is appointed is the ward's parent, if living, but even a parent who is serving as guardian of the estate of a minor child is subject to all of the burdens imposed on guardians.

As an alternative procedure, the various states have adopted either the Uniform Transfers to Minors Act (UTMA), 8C U.L.A. 1–2 (2001), or its predecessor, the Uniform Gifts to Minors Act (UGMA), 8A U.L.A. 420 (1993), as a means by which property can be transferred to persons not yet 18 years of age without going through the formalities of a formal guardianship. UTMA and UGMA are nothing more than legislature authored agreements, the terms of which a donor can adopt simply by having property titled in the name of *"(custodian)* as custodian for *(beneficiary)* under the Uniform Transfers [Gifts] to Minors Act as adopted by (state)." Initially UGMA gifts could be made of only personal property, but a number of states permitted UGMA gifts of real property. UTMA permits gifts of real property. UGMA and UTMA agreements are not trusts (although the custodian is clearly a fiduciary).

Even more importantly, a few states such as Texas permit a testator to establish an UTMA custodianship and make a gift to it in the testator's will. Tex. Prop. Code Ann. § 141.003 (Vernon 1995, Supp. 2005). Allowing a UTMA custodianship to be created by will is an enormously important breakthrough. Now, parents wishing to plan for the possibility that their children will be orphaned can do so without having to incur the expense of creating a contingent revocable trust for the children. The disadvantages of UTMA are that: (1) the property held in the UTMA custodianship will be distributed to the child at age 21 (or 18 in some jurisdictions) and (2) each UTMA custodianship can have only one beneficiary. Limiting the UTMA custodianship to one beneficiary means that the custodian cannot reallocate property among the decedent's children in response to their changing and varied needs. Thus, some parents will still elect to use a trust when planning for the possibility that their children will be orphaned.

Both tax and nontax aspects of UTMA transfers are considered beginning at ¶ 19,251.

[¶ 4417]

3. TRUSTS

A trustee can be freed of many of the burdensome aspects of a guardianship. For example, the settlor or creator of the trust can stipulate that the trustee need not post bond, may sell the beneficiaries' property without court approval, may distribute property from the trust without court approval, and

¶ 4401

may invest as a prudent person would do. Also, the settlor can specify the age at which the beneficiary is to receive the trust property. (Under both the guardianship and the custodianship authorized by UTMA and UGMA, the ward will receive the property at age 21 if the ward is not under any other disability.)

One of the principal advantages of a trust over a guardianship or a custodianship is the ability to provide for beneficiaries with different needs. While most parents provide for equal treatment of their children, Roy and Jimmie Sue's situation is different. They believe that the needs of their children, Clint and Joe Bob, ages 17 and 16, respectively, may be very different from those of Little Miss Afterthought, their child of three months. Obviously, Clint and Joe Bob have been depleting the storehouse for 17 and 16 years, respectively. Little Miss Afterthought needs some time to catch up. In a case like this where the parent's resources are limited, strict equality would work a hardship on the three-month-old. If Roy and Jimmie Sue elect to use a trust, all of their limited resources could be kept together in one fund, with the trustee having discretion to make distributions according to the respective needs of the children.

Problem

[¶ 4423]

How would you structure the above-described trust so that the older children get a share *now?* Or must they wait until Miss Afterthought reaches 18 or some other age?

[¶ 4425]

4. THE TESTAMENTARY TRUST

A testamentary trust is a trust which is provided for in the testator's will. For example, in the case where a parent anticipates the possibility that his or her children may be orphaned, the parent might include a provision similar to the following in a will:

> Notwithstanding the foregoing, if any person who is to receive a distribution from my estate is under legal disability at the time such distribution is to be made, that person's share of my estate shall be distributed to my Trustee to be held, managed, and disposed of by my Trustee as provided [in a later paragraph of the will].

The disadvantage to a testamentary trust is that, in many jurisdictions, testamentary trusts are subject to the continuing judicial supervision of the probate court. What this means, practically speaking, is that the trustee will be required to file an annual or biannual account with the local probate court setting forth much the same information which a guardian is required to provide the court in the guardian's accounts. This one requirement is usually seen as a disadvantage by most persons, and it prompts many of them to elect to create a revocable trust to manage property which becomes distributable to orphaned children under their wills.

In some jurisdictions, a testamentary trust is not subject to judicial supervision. In these jurisdictions, probably the only reason to use a revocable trust is to have it available as a property management device in the event of the creator's subsequent incompetence or in anticipation of the client's departure from the state.

[¶ 4433]

5. THE REVOCABLE TRUST

The "revocable trust" is a trust established during the lifetime of the creator or settlor of the trust which is revocable by the settlor during lifetime. The right of revocation must be expressly reserved to the settlor by the trust instrument inasmuch as the majority of jurisdictions presume that all trusts are irrevocable unless they are expressly revocable. Normally, the revocable trust becomes irrevocable upon the death of the settlor.

Sometimes revocable trusts are referred to as "living trusts" because they are created during the lifetime of the settlor. This is obviously misleading inasmuch as trusts which are irrevocable are also often created during the lifetime of the settlor.

The advantage of the revocable trust over the testamentary trust, primarily, is that the revocable trust is free of judicial supervision in all jurisdictions. This means that the trustee need not file annual or biannual accountings with the local probate court. Practically speaking, it means little else. But this is considered a significant advantage in terms of the privacy afforded the beneficiaries and in terms of the expense. However, it should be noted that while accountings by the trustee for a revocable trust need not be provided the local probate court, the trust instrument (or fiduciary law) will require the trustee to provide accountings to the trust beneficiaries. The difference, of course, is in the manner and form of the accounting. Each probate court usually has its own requirements for the form of the account. Most require that copies of receipts or cancelled checks accompany the account. On the other hand, the trustee of a revocable trust need only satisfy the beneficiaries as to the manner and form of the account the trustee provides them. The flexibility inherent in this arrangement can lead to significant savings in time for the trustee without a necessary increase in abuse.

The reader might wonder about the policy justification for court supervision of testamentary trusts while allowing revocable trusts to be free of such supervision. The difference in treatment can only be explained in these terms. Testamentary trusts are subject to judicial supervision because they are a part of the settlor's will, and wills are subject to continuing judicial supervision until such time as the entire will has been executed or carried out. On the other hand, revocable trusts, like other trusts created outside of wills, historically speaking, only came to the attention of the courts of equity if a beneficiary complained about the trustee's conduct in the discharge of fiduciary duties. And so it is today. Some jurisdictions have recognized that there is little reason to insist upon supervision of testamentary trusts and to ignore other trusts and, in those jurisdictions, court supervision of testamentary trusts has been abolished by statute. Indiana is an example of such a jurisdiction. Normally these statutes provide that the court can reassert jurisdiction over the trust if circumstances warrant.

[¶ 4441]

6. CONTINGENT INSURANCE TRUSTS

The contingent life insurance trust is in widespread use. Typically, such a trust is revocable and, as its name suggests, it is characterized by being designated as the contingent beneficiary of the settlor's life insurance. The trust is the contingent beneficiary in the sense that the trust is the secondary beneficiary after the settlor's spouse, collecting the life insurance proceeds only if the spouse predeceases the settlor.

The contingent life insurance trust is popular with persons of all ages and family status. It is particularly popular with parents who have young children. Practically speaking, those with children under legal disability—as well as many others, parents and nonparents alike—typically have wills giving "everything" to the surviving spouse and, if none, *per stirpes* to the decedent's lineal descendants who survive the decedent. These wills typically continue by providing that if "any one or more" of the decedent's lineals are under a specified age—for example, 21 or 34, or even 55—each such lineal's share— sometimes the decedent's entire estate—is to be distributed to the trustee of a contingent life insurance trust. The contingent life insurance trust can be established inter vivos, i.e., during the settlor's life, in which case it will probably be referred to as a living trust, or it can be testamentary in the sense that it is part of the creator's will.

Life insurance may be the principal, perhaps "only," property owned by a person. Many have a house and a mortgage, personal effects, and vehicles, but nothing of great monetary value—except for the life insurance and possibly retirement plan benefits. But with term life insurance being relatively cheap for young parents, receipt of the proceeds can seem like winning the lottery. What, then, should be done with the proceeds as they are received for the benefit of the children? Guardianship? Trust?

Cost is a driving force in the choice of a trust. Where the children are under age 18, an alternative is a guardianship—but a guardianship is a terribly expensive proposition. Using notions of cost/benefit, it has been suggested that the creation of a contingent life insurance trust for a minor child is akin to a single premium insurance policy, i.e., the single premium is the attorney's fee for providing the advice and preparing the trust documents. J. Corcoran, Jr., The Contingent Insurance Trust—Hidden Bonanza for Minor Children, 55 Ill. B.J. 596 (1967). Offsetting this fee are the annual costs associated with the guardianship during the child's minority—plus the costs resulting from the child receiving the property at age 18, a time when most persons are best spared the burdens of property management.

Costs associated with the guardianship are: (1) attorneys' fees incurred annually in conjunction with the required guardianship accountings to the court; (2) guardianship fees incurred annually throughout the duration of the guardianship; (3) court costs incurred annually as a result of the required guardianship accountings; and (4) bond premiums, also an annual expense (usually $10 per thousand of value of property subject to the guardianship). How much typically are attorneys' fees? Guardianship fees? Make your own judgments as to the value of time, both that of an attorney and a guardian. How many hours will be required to get together all of the cancelled checks supporting the disbursements from the guardianship for a single year? To present that information in a form acceptable to a court? For the attorney to interact with the guardian? Multiply that by the number of children for whom a guardianship has to be established—and multiply that by the number of years that each guardianship must continue, i.e., the number of years until each child attains age 18.

The described expenses are charged against the guardianship property. By way of contrast, with a trust there would, quite possibly, only be a trustee's fee. The trustee's fee would be imposed on property whose value should be increasing if the trust property is invested successfully. The guardian's fee, no less than the trustee's fee, is often imposed on property having a static value because guardians, fearful of loss or constrained by applicable law or court supervision, invest in governmentals or bank accounts rather than stocks likely to appreciate in value.

The UTMA custodianship is limited to those age 18 and under, a drawback to many.

Problem

[¶ 4447]

Contact the local probate court and ascertain the projected annual court costs for a guardianship. Ask the court clerk responsible for guardianship accountings about typical attorneys' fees. Look at local statutes or rules of court to ascertain guardianship fees. Call a bonding company and ask about annual bond premiums. How do these fees in the aggregate compare with the cost of preparing a contingent life insurance trust? Remember, it is unusual for children to be orphaned. Accordingly, only a relatively few children will have need for a contingent life insurance trust. (Of course, there is always the possibility that at the death of an ancestor, property will be given to a child under disability. What can be done in these cases? Consider the alternative set forth in the Uniform Transfers to Minors Act, discussed at ¶ 4409.)

F. NATURE OF A TRUST

[¶ 4449]

A trust is a unique Anglo–American device for the management of property. It had its roots in the creative genius of the early common lawyers and has survived today because it is enormously useful.

Prior to 1540, wills of land were not permitted in England. (Wills of personal property, called testaments, were permitted. These were made orally to members of the ecclesiastical establishment, who had the responsibility for

¶ 4441

disposing of a decedent's personal property.) Since wills of land were not permitted but lifetime conveyances were, prospective decedents made lifetime conveyances to third persons with the understanding that the third person, then called a feoffee to use and now called a trustee, would hold the property for the benefit of the donor, and upon the donor's death, the trustee was to deliver the property to the person or persons chosen by the donor. The courts of law, which had jurisdiction over the disposition of land, would not enforce these early trusts because they concluded that the trustee had what they considered to be ownership, essentially in fee simple. However, the courts of equity were careful not to challenge the basic idea that the trustee had title to the property. They simply concluded that while the trustee had ownership of the property—that which the courts of law would recognize and protect—it was inequitable for the trustee to refuse to honor his or her commitment.

The trust remains unchanged today. It continues to be a creature of equity.

Until recently, only a few states had codified the law of trusts. Texas is one such state—but its codification had come about solely for the purposes of writing down the common law rules and not as a means of law reform. By way of contrast, an aspect of the Uniform Trust Code was law reform. Unif. Trust Code prefatory note (amended 2005), 7C U.L.A. 202 (Supp. 2006).

G. ELEMENTS OF A TRUST

[¶ 4501]

1. ESTABLISHING THE TRUST

How does one establish a trust? A trust is established by the settlor conveying the property to another person, the trustee, subject to the condition that the trustee hold, manage, and dispose of the property in the manner stipulated in the conveyance. More technically speaking, the transfer of the property must be made with the intention to impose on the trustee the legal obligation to hold the property as trustee. The elements, then, are delivery and the requisite donative intent. In addition, the trustee must accept the conveyance subject to burdens imposed upon the trustee by the settlor.

Trusts of real property must be in writing in many states, particularly those which have the Statute of Frauds. Section VII of the English Statute of Frauds requires all trusts of real property to be manifested and proved by a writing. The writing must set forth with reasonable definiteness the trust beneficiary, the trust property, and the trust purpose.

[¶ 4509]

2. THE TRUST RES

The trust res is the trust property. The trust property is the subject matter of the trust and without it there can be no trust. Why not? For historical reasons. The trust grew up as a device for managing property. And it has been property ever since. Trusts for services have never existed and, perhaps, could not, but it is worth making the point that only property can be the subject matter of the trust. If the trust holds no property, there is no trust notwithstanding any written commitment by the trustee to serve as a trustee. This notion becomes important in two cases:

1. Where the trustee has looted the trust, and creditors of the trustee, in his or her individual capacity, as well as the beneficiaries of the trust, are proceeding against the trustee's nontrust property. In such a case, the trust beneficiaries and the creditors stand on an equal footing. In other words, the beneficiaries are not preferred creditors.

2. Where the testator is using the trust as a receptacle for a distribution of property from the will, such as in the case of a contingent trust for minor beneficiaries.

Consider the following case, in which the court discussed the adequacy of the res with which the trust was provided. The issue in the case is, under what circumstances is the contingent right to receive the proceeds of a policy of life insurance an adequate res? The importance of this issue cannot be overstated inasmuch as, without a res, there is no trust.

Consider, too, the following case as a useful model in thinking about the provisions typically found in contingent life insurance trusts. See ¶ 4441. These trusts form the basis of much of modern estate planning.

[¶ 4511]

GORDON v. PORTLAND TRUST BANK

Oregon Supreme Court, 1954.
201 Or. 648, 271 P.2d 653.

LUSK, Justice:

This is an action at law brought by Leotta Belle Gordon as executrix under the last will and testament of Albert Leslie Gordon, deceased, to recover the sum of $526,352.75 from the Portland Trust Bank. * * *

As the complaint discloses, the money involved is the proceeds of fifteen policies of insurance upon the life of Albert Leslie Gordon, deceased, which he delivered to the bank pursuant to the terms of an instrument in writing, executed by Gordon as trustor and the bank as trustee. Gordon caused the bank to be designated beneficiary under the insurance policies, and after his death the bank collected the proceeds of the policies, which it claims the right to hold and to distribute in accordance with the provisions of the trust agreement.

It is the theory of the plaintiff that the trust agreement is actually a "testamentary disposition or Last Will and Testament", and that it was revoked by a will executed by Gordon four days later under which Mrs. Gordon has been appointed executrix.

The trust instrument, a copy of which is made an exhibit to the complaint, is dated August 3, 1942. It recites that the parties, Gordon as trustor and the bank as trustee, have agreed that the bank has been designated beneficiary as trustee under the policies of life insurance enumerated in an attached schedule for the uses and purposes thereinafter stated. The bank agreed:

To hold said insurance policies during the life of the Trustor without any duties of any nature in respect thereto other than the safekeeping thereof; it being expressly agreed that the said Trustee shall not in any event be obliged or required to pay any premium, assessment or other sum that may become due or payable on any of the said policies. In no event is it the intention of the parties hereto that this agreement should restrict the rights of the Trustor under any policy contained in this trust, the Trustor reserving the right to obtain loans under any policy or to surrender any policy for the cash surrender value, or to exercise any other right or option under the said insurance policies, this trust becoming effective only insofar as the said insurance policies are concerned upon the death of the Trustor.

Upon the Trustee receiving proof of the death of the Trustor, it is agreed that it will use its best efforts to collect and receive any and all sums of money payable thereunder, the receipt of said Trustee to be a full and complete release to any insurance company for any and all funds paid to the said Trustee as beneficiary under the said insurance policy or policies which may be hereafter deposited.

Other pertinent provisions follow: After paying the expenses incurred in managing the trust estate and deducting the same from the gross income, the trustee shall distribute the net income of the trust estate in quarterly installments to the trustor's wife, Leotta Belle Gordon, until her death or remarriage, and, upon the happening of either of those events, the trustee shall distribute the corpus equally between the trustor's two daughters, with further provisions for the contingencies of the death of either or both daughters before the death or remarriage of the widow.

The Trustor shall have power at any time during his life by an instrument in writing delivered to the Trustee to modify, alter or terminate this agreement, in whole or in part, provided, however, that the duties, powers and liabilities of the Trustee hereunder shall not be substantially changed without its written consent.

The trustee shall not in any event be obliged or required to pay any premium, assessment or other sum that may become due or payable on any of the said policies; and it shall not be obliged to bring suit to collect the principal amount on any of the policies unless properly indemnified, the sole obligation and liability of the trustee being to receive, manage and dispose of such money as may be paid to it under the said policies:

In the event that the said Trustor shall at any time after having designated said Trustee as beneficiary under said policies, subsequently cause such designation to be changed so that another beneficiary be named or other payment of the proceeds of such policies provided, this trust, and all rights and obligations hereunder, shall as to such policy or policies thereupon become null and void for every purpose, and said

¶ 4511

Trustee shall as to such policy or policies be released from all liability and obligation.

The agreement also contains a section entitled "Open Trust Clause" under which the trustor was authorized to deposit with the trustee securities, personal property and sums of money, and to deed to the trustees real property, which would become part of the trust res, but there is nothing to show that any property of any kind was ever added to the trust res in pursuance of this authority. * * *

It should be noted that life insurance, and its natural concomitant, the insurance trust, did not become popular in the United States until the latter half of the nineteenth century. At that time the doctrine of the third-party beneficiary had not developed as yet and the status of the beneficiary under an insurance policy was defined in several early cases. * * * [T]he important thing in these early cases is that the beneficiary was declared to be the owner. This view is entirely understandable in the light of the provisions of life insurance contracts then written. There were no loan or cash values, no extensive powers of assignment or change of beneficiary.

The older rule which gave a vested interest to the beneficiary does not, of course, square with the modern notions of life policies. In modern times, the real incidents of ownership are indisputably vested in the insured and it was only logical that many courts should take the position that the beneficiary, where he is subject to divestment at the mere whim of the insured, takes only a contingent interest or an expectancy. Thus, today there is considerable authority for the view that the beneficiary gets a vested right only as his expectancy or contingent interest matures on the death of the insured. * * * But the courts are by no means in accord on the issue. Many hold that the beneficiary takes a vested interest subject to divestment upon change of beneficiary in accordance with the *provisions* of the policy. * * * Where this view obtains, there is no problem concerning the testamentary aspect of the transaction, for the vested right of the beneficiary is without doubt a proper subject for a trust. Restatement, Trusts § 57, comment f, p. 178; § 84, comment b. * * *

Under the general view that the beneficiary has no more than an expectancy, it is more difficult to find the necessary res for a present trust. Rather, the transaction appears to be a contract with the trust-beneficiary to create a trust at the insured's death. The courts, however, have not felt constrained to arrive at this conclusion, and the cases are legion which have upheld the usual form of unfunded insurance trust even where the court had previously announced that the beneficiary has no more than a mere expectancy. In some of the earlier cases, the rationale appeared to be that, since a life insurance policy payable to an ordinary third-party beneficiary is not testamentary, then neither is one wherein the third-party beneficiary is also trustee, for in both cases the legal title to the proceeds is in the beneficiary according to the doctrine of the third-party beneficiary as it has developed in the law of contracts. In the insurance trust device, the trustee-beneficiary takes a divided interest in the property, but this is specifically a trust problem and has no bearing on the testamentary character of the device. * * * We

¶ 4511

observe, therefore, that both under the old view, where the beneficiary is considered the owner, and under the new view where he has only an expectancy, the result is the same, for even in the new view, the third-party beneficiary has a present right to fulfillment of the insurer's promise to pay. There is no inconsistency in this position. A right of revocation of the trust deed in the case of any trust cannot really be distinguished from the power reserved by the insured to change the beneficiary. The extent of control reserved to the donor and the insured is the same in both cases, and the vested interest of the beneficiary of the ordinary trust is not open to question, despite the fact that the donor might revoke the trust at his pleasure. * * * A close analogy is found in the so-called "Totten" or tentative savings bank trust, under which complete control is likewise reserved by the donor during his lifetime, but the beneficiary is permitted to take the money on his death. See, Matter of Totten, 179 N.Y. 112, 71 N.E. 748, 70 L.R.A. 711.

This court, having carefully reviewed the cases, is of the opinion that the insurance trust attacked in this case can be sustained without deciding that the beneficiary-trustee has either vested rights or a mere expectancy. We perceive that some courts have taken steps to avoid the pitfalls of this particular aspect of the insurance trust problems. Some have resolved the problem by calling the right of the beneficiary a contingent interest which is something more than a mere expectancy, yet something less than a vested interest. * * * These cases, it should be noted, were decided at a time when the life policies in question had none of the modern features such as cash rights, borrowing, reserves, etc. Our own view is that the ownership of the modern policy is actually divided between the beneficiary and the insured. The various marketing or sales features, such as the loan and cash surrender values, are clearly the property of the insured. On the other hand, the beneficiary is the owner of a promise to pay the proceeds at the death of insured, subject to insured's right of revocation. It seems to us that the right of the beneficiary is actually the primary right under the policy, whereas the insured's rights are secondary and have nothing to do with the basic purpose of life insurance.

[¶ 4517]

3. THE TRUST BENEFICIARIES

By definition a trust must have a beneficiary or it is not a trust. The essence of a trust is the notion of a trustee holding the trust property for the benefit of another, namely the beneficiary. The presence of a beneficiary is critical because it is only the beneficiary of the trust who can invoke the aid of the court of equity in enforcing the terms of the trust. Did you get that? It is only the beneficiary who can enforce the terms of the trust, and not the settlor of the trust unless, of course, the settlor, too, has a beneficial interest in the trust. It can be said that there must always be someone in the position to enforce the terms of the trust. If there comes a time when the trust does not have a beneficiary, then the trust ceases to exist. For a related discussion, see ¶ 4601.

Curiously not all trustees routinely provide accountings to all trust beneficiaries, limiting accountings to those beneficiaries who are eligible to receive current distributions from the trust. The Uniform Trust Code mandates transparency in the form of annual accountings to all beneficiaries, whether distribution eligible or not. See UTC § 813 (amended 2004), 7C U.L.A. 364 (Supp. 2006).

Problem

[¶ 4520]

Jack and Jill, married now two years, are parents to their child, Albert, as well as his Jack's three children from his prior marriages and Jill's two children from her prior marriages, the older five children all being over 21 years of age. In making his will, Jack wants to "give it all to Jill if she survives me, otherwise divide it equally among the six children." The lawyer tells Jack there are and other tax advantages to "putting it all in trust for Jill for life, remainder after Jill's death to the kids." Jack grudgingly agrees only on condition that the children not be in a position to "hamstring" Jill in her use of the money, saying, "she is my wife and what's mine is hers and what's hers is mine and we don't want the children pickin' at the survivor of us over one thing and another. However, I do hate taxes and if this will save taxes, I am all for it." The lawyer replies that he will "fix it" so that Jill will be trustee—and that means she is a fiduciary and as such she must honor the terms of the trust, limiting herself to distributions only as provided in the trust agreement ("all the income and so much of the principal as is necessary for her health, maintenance and support"). However, he tells Jack that the trust agreement will stipulate that so long as Jill is alive and serving as trustee she will not need to provide accountings to the children for her stewardship of the trust in as much as the children are not eligible to receive distributions from the trust during Jill's life. Can the lawyer include such a provision and have it be effective?

[¶ 4525]

4. THE TRUST PURPOSE

The Statute of Uses of 1536 executed passive uses (trusts). Passive uses were those trusts without any purpose or those trusts in which the trustee had no duties except to act as a mere stakeholder. That principle applies to modern trusts—at least formally—in apparently all jurisdictions. Despite the formal recognition of the Statute of Uses, several states—principally Illinois (by judicial decision) and Indiana (by statute)—recognize a device commonly referred to as an Illinois Land Trust. Essentially these are trusts in which the trustee has no real duties of management over the trust property. See Cassidy, The Illinois Land Trust in Indiana Practice, 19 Res Gestae 318 (1975).

The concept of purpose can best be understood in terms of duties imposed on the trustee with respect to the trust property for the benefit of the indicated beneficiaries. The question is not what powers does the trustee have, but what must the trustee do? A conveyance in trust to "hold the property until 2008" without more is a valid trust. The trustee's duty is to hold until 2008. From this duty, the law will imply that the trustee has the requisite powers to manage the property in the interim. See, e.g., Finch v. Honeycutt, 246 N.C. 91, 97 S.E.2d 478 (1957). For a state-by-state review of the duties required of trustees in order for a trust to be recognized as valid, see S. Balbach, Study #15: Validity of Illinois Land Trusts, in American College of Trust & Estate Counsel Studies (1993).

It is not often that the trust instrument will spell out the purpose of the trust. What is more common is for the trust instrument to direct that the trustee *do* certain things with respect to the trust property for the benefit of the beneficiary. These are the duties or purpose of the trust.

[¶ 4533]

5. THE TRUSTEE

It is often said that "every trust must have a trustee, but no trust fails for want of a trustee." Why? Because if there is a vacancy in the trusteeship, the court will appoint a successor trustee if the trust instrument fails to make provision for a successor trustee. What if the duties imposed on a trustee are so special that only *a specific trustee* could execute the terms of the trust? If this was truly the case, then it would not be a trust because it would not be possible for a court to determine, acting upon the complaint of the beneficiary, whether the trustee was or was not in breach of trust. The point is that if the duties of the trustee were unique to a specific trustee, then it could not be a trust because there would not be anyone—such as a court of equity—to stand in judgment of the trustee.

H. POUROVER WILLS

[¶ 4551]

A favorite dispositive scheme consists of a will which, after making disposition of the testator's tangible personal property and the premises the testator and spouse occupy for residential purposes at the testator's death, provides that all of the testator's property is to pass to the trustee of a revocable or living trust to be held, managed, and disposed of as an integral part of that trust. This pourover feature, taken for granted by many, raises a number of legal issues.

[¶ 4559]

1. POLICY OF THE WILLS ACT

The various wills acts, beginning with the Statute of Wills of 1540, have, in substance, provided that:

> Wills must be in writing, signed by the maker in the presence of two disinterested witnesses who sign the instrument in the presence of the maker and in the presence of each other.

¶ 4559

From these simple requirements have come two important ideas:

1. All of the pages of the will must be together at the time of execution with the page that is to be executed and

2. All testamentary dispositions must *literally* comply with these requirements. Traditionally, no exceptions to this policy have been formally recognized (although there are informally recognized exceptions such as Totten Trusts, which are discussed at ¶ 19,151). The reasoning is that by so limiting the devices which are effective to pass property at deathtime, there will be some limitation to the litigation that would otherwise result if any contrivance of a decedent constituted an acceptable dispositive device. (In one particular respect, UPC § 2–503 departs from this tradition, recognizing that a will should not be declared invalid because of "harmless error" in the will's signing. What qualifies as harmless error is to be judicially determined on a case by case basis.)

[¶ 4567]

2. VALIDITY OF THE POUROVER

a. *Independent Legal Significance*

With the foregoing principles in mind, consider what kind of devices might be frustrated by them. Suppose, for example, that the testator's will provided that all of the testator's property was to pass to the trustee of a living trust. Would this dispositive scheme run afoul of the requirement that all of the pages of the will be together with the page to be signed by the testator? Doesn't this separate writing—the trust—complete a disposition which begins in the will and, in that sense, is it not a will? Take note of the doctrine of independent legal significance, the safe harbor exception embraced in *Pinion* below. Note, too, the limitations of the doctrine of incorporation by reference, a sometime safe harbor in these cases. For related discussion, see ¶ 3359.

[¶ 4569]

SECOND BANK–STATE STREET TRUST CO. v. PINION

Massachusetts Supreme Judicial Court, 1960.
341 Mass. 366, 170 N.E.2d 350.

WHITTEMORE, Justice.

Each of the wills of Richard W. Symons and his wife Edna H. executed April 27, 1955, gave the residue to the trustees under a revocable and amendable inter vivos trust established by them under date of "September 13, 1945, as amended." On November 19, 1955, Richard and Edna as settlors, and Richard as one of the trustees, signed and acknowledged an instrument purporting to amend the trust by altering the disposition of the trust property to be made after the death of both settlors. The trust provided for amendment by a written instrument signed and acknowledged by the settlors and the trustees. The other trustee, Second Bank–State Street Trust Company, signed and acknowledged the amending instrument on November 23, 1955. Richard and Edna, also on November 19, 1955, executed codicils to their wills to name a coexecutor and each codicil ratified and confirmed the will in all other respects.

Following the death of Edna on November 20, 1956, and of Richard on March 13, 1958, the bank, as executor, asked to be instructed, under each will, whether the residue passed to the trustees to hold under the trust as amended, or, if not, then subject to the terms of the unamended trust, or, alternatively, how it should be distributed. * * * We hold for reasons stated below that under each will there was, as all the respondents contend, an effective residual gift to the trustees to hold under the trust as amended on November 19, 1955.

It is to be observed at the threshold that the doctrine of incorporation by reference is inapplicable. Any intent to incorporate into the wills the dispositive provisions of the trust and thus to make them dispositive parts of the wills was expressly negatived. Each of the residuary clauses provided that the fund paid to the trustee was "to be held, administered, and distributed solely under the provisions of such indenture, and in no way as trustee under this will nor as a trustee subject to appointment by or jurisdiction of any probate or other court." See Restatement 2d: Trusts, § 54, comment k. It is therefore immaterial that at the time of the execution of the codicils the terms of a proposed, but incompleted, amendment to the trust were set out in writing. * * *

No amendment to the trust existed until November 23, 1955, when the second trustee executed and acknowledged the instrument as required by the trust indenture. * * * If attestation under the statute of wills was required to give effect to the trustee's disposition, under the amended trust, of assets received from the executor, it could not be supplied by the attestation of the codicil prior to the effective execution of the trust amendment. * * * The doctrine of incorporation by reference, even if applicable at all where an intent to incorporate in the usual sense is negatived (* * * Lauritzen, Can a Revocable Trust Be Incorporated by Reference, 45 Ill. L. Rev. 583, 600; Polasky, "Pourover" Wills and the Statutory Blessing, 98 Trusts & Estates 949, 954–55; compare Old Colony Trust Co. v. Cleveland, 291 Mass. 380, 196 N.E. 920; Bolles v. Toledo Trust Co., 144 Ohio St. 195, 58 N.E.2d 381, 157 A.L.R. 1164; Restatement [2d]: Trusts, § 54, comments e-j, 1), could not import the nonexistent amendment.

We agree with the suggestion that such a gift as this "stand[s] on its own merits, to be compared to a gift to a corporation or any other entity, and as such wholly distinguishable from an attempted incorporation into the will of the terms of the trust as to additional property." Annotation, 21 A.L.R.2d 223. * * * Such a gift is no less valid because of the reservation in the settlor of the power to amend or revoke the trust. * * *

We agree with modern legal thought that a subsequent amendment is effective because of the applicability of the established equitable doctrine that subsequent acts of independent significance do not require attestation under

¶ 4569

the statute of wills. Scott, Trusts (2d ed.) § 54.3. McClanahan, Bequests to an Existing Trust, 47 Cal. L. Rev. 267, 287, 292–294, and articles cited note p. 267. Palmer, Testamentary Disposition to the Trustee of an Inter Vivos Trust, 50 Mich. L. Rev. 33, 55–59. * * * This is the view of the Restatement 2d: Trusts, § 54, comment i, and reporter's note. * * *

* * *

Dispositions to persons employed at the testator's death have been held valid in our decisions without reference to the possible objection of action of testamentary significance subsequent to the will. * * * The court in Holmes v. Coates, 159 Mass. 226, 228–229, 34 N.E. 190, sustained a gift of whatever sum should be necessary to add to gifts made by the testator in his lifetime for the benefit of a class of disabled soldiers and seamen to cause the total to equal $500 per year up to his decease despite the contention that the gift was void because dependent upon the contents of books of account not in existence when the will was made. We are unable to distinguish these cases in applicable principle from the cases at bar.

Scott, Trusts (2d ed.) § 54.3, pp. 376–377, observes, "it is true that the testator is thereby enabled to change the testamentary disposition without executing codicils to his will. This is, however, what he does where he bequeaths the contents of a room or of a safe-deposit box, since he can modify the contents from time to time by removing or adding articles. The same thing is true where he bequeaths property to persons in his employ at the time of his death. * * * Indeed, there seems to be no greater objection than there is to the whole doctrine which permits a testator originally to make a disposition by reference to a living trust, the terms of which are not stated in the will. The test is not whether the facts are subject to the control of the testator, but whether they are facts which have significance apart from the disposition of the property bequeathed."

The reasons for adoption of the rule of the Restatement are persuasive. The pourover device is important in modern estate planning. * * * The underlying purpose of the statute of wills against frauds is secured in the formalities attendant upon the execution of trusts and the solemnity of the actual transfer of property to trustees. * * *

* * *

The long established recognition in Massachusetts of the doctrine of independent significance makes unnecessary statutory affirmance of its application to pour-over trusts.

* * * [A] decree is to be entered * * * that the trustee is to administer and distribute the funds received from the executor in accordance with the terms of the amended trust.

So ordered.

¶ 4569

Problems

[¶ 4571]

1. From your reading of the *Pinion* case, it should be clear that a living or revocable trust must have independent legal significance if a pourover to that trust is to be valid. Otherwise, the pourover will run afoul of the argument that the trust is really a disguised will which must fail for want of compliance with the requirements of the applicable statute authorizing wills. With this in mind, Gordon v. Portland Trust Bank, set out at ¶ 4511, takes on added significance. It is more significant because, for example, most contingent trusts for minor children are funded only with life insurance. More importantly, oftentimes the living trust is designated as only the secondary beneficiary in a policy beneficiary designation which might appear, in substance, as follows:

> The proceeds shall be paid to the insured's spouse if the spouse survives the insured for thirty (30) days; otherwise to the insured's then living lineal descendants *per stirpes,* provided, however, that if any one or more of the insured's then living lineal descendants is then under twenty-one (21) years of age, that lineal's share of the insurance proceeds shall be paid over to the trustee of the trust which the insured established on the _____ day of _____ 19___.

Would the foregoing beneficiary designation give the trust an adequate res so that it might qualify as a receptacle for the pourover from the testator's will on the grounds the trust had independent legal significance?

2. In the event the foregoing beneficiary designation is inadequate to cause the trust to have a res (thereby giving it independent legal significance), what other theory could be invoked to validate the pourover? Consider incorporation by reference, discussed in *Pinion* and at ¶ 3359.

3. In lieu of the doctrine of incorporation by reference, would the problem of a res be solved by stapling a ten dollar bill to the trust agreement?

[¶ 4575]

b. *Need for Trust Res*

Traditional analysis suggests that an unfunded trust can be the target of a pourover from the will only if: (1) the target trust is incorporated by reference into the will or (2) the trust has independent legal significance, i.e., that the trust has a res in the sense that it is funded, at a minimum, by being designated contingent beneficiary of a policy of life insurance. See Gordon v. Portland Trust Bank, 201 Or. 648, 271 P.2d 653 (1954), reprinted at ¶ 4511. However, Clymer v. Mayo, which follows, considers the impact of the Uniform Testamentary Additions to Trusts Act (amended 1991), 8B U.L.A. 360–66 (2001), the current version of which is reflected as UPC § 2–511, on this traditional analysis, perhaps compromising it. *Clymer* is important because the target trust is completely unfunded, i.e., the only property it will ever hold is that which it receives as a result of the pourover from the decedent's will.

¶ 4575

Unlike in *Gordon,* the *Clymer* trust is not the designated beneficiary—or even the contingent beneficiary—of the decedent's life insurance.

Clymer is different from *Gordon* in that the question is not "is the trust *up*" but rather "does the trust need to be *up* for it to be an eligible recipient of property pouring over from a will." As a result of the Uniform Act, it appears that the trust need not be "up" for it to be a legitimate target of the pourover from the will. Thus, the presence of the Uniform Act in a jurisdiction may mean that traditional inquiries as whether the target has independent legal significance or whether the target is incorporated by reference into the will are unnecessary.

[¶ 4577]

CLYMER v. MAYO

Massachusetts Supreme Judicial Court, 1985.
393 Mass. 754, 473 N.E.2d 1084.

HENNESSEY, Chief Justice.

At the time of her death in November, 1981, the decedent [Clara A. Mayo], then fifty years of age, was employed by Boston University as a professor of psychology. * * *

Under the terms of the decedent's will, * * * [t]he residue of her estate was to "pour over" into the inter vivos trust she created that same day. * * *

* * * At the time of its creation in 1973, the trust was not funded. Its future assets were to consist solely of * * * property which would pour over under the will's residuary clause. The judge found that the * * * trustee has never received any property or held any funds subsequent to the execution of the trust. * * *

The Weisses [decedent's parents] claim that the judge erred in ruling that the decedent's trust was validly created despite the fact that it was not funded until her death. They rely on the common law rule that a trust can be created only when a trust res exists. * * * Arguing that the trust never came into existence, the Weisses claim they are entitled to the decedent's entire estate as her sole heirs at law.

In upholding the validity of the decedent's pour-over trust, the judge cited the relevant provisions of G.L. c. 203, § 3B, * * * the Commonwealth's version of the Uniform Testamentary Additions to Trusts Act. "A devise or bequest, the validity of which is determinable by the laws of the commonwealth, may be made to the trustee or trustees of a trust established or to be established by the testator * * * including a funded or unfunded life insurance trust, although the trustor has reserved any or all rights of ownership of the insurance contracts, if the trust is identified in the will and the terms of the trust are set forth in a written instrument executed before or concurrently with the execution of the testator's will * * * *regardless of the existence, size or character of the corpus of the trust*" (emphasis added.) The decedent's trust instrument, which was executed in Massachusetts and states that it is to be governed by the laws of the Commonwealth, satisfies these statutory conditions. The trust is identified in the residuary clause of her will and the terms of the trust are set out in a written instrument executed contemporaneously with the will. However, the Weisses claim that G.L. c. 203, § 3B, was not intended to change the common law with respect to the necessity for a trust corpus despite the clear language validating pour-over trusts, "regardless of the existence, size or character of the corpus." The Weisses make no showing of legislative intent that would contradict the plain meaning of these words. * * * Moreover, the development of the common law of this Commonwealth with regard to pour-over trusts demonstrates that G.L. c. 203, § 3B, takes on practical meaning only if the Legislature meant exactly what the statute says concerning the need for a trust corpus.

This court was one of the first courts to validate pour-over devises to a living trust. In Second Bank–State St. Trust Co. v. Pinion, 341 Mass. 366, 371, 170 N.E.2d 350 (1960), decided prior to the adoption of G.L. c. 203, § 3B, we upheld a testamentary gift to a revocable and amendable inter vivos trust established by the testator before the execution of his will and which he amended after the will's execution. * * *

However, in *Pinion,* we were not presented with an unfunded pour-over trust. Nor, prior to G.L. c. 203, § 3B, did other authority exist in this Commonwealth for recognizing testamentary transfers to unfunded trusts. The doctrine of independent significance, upon which we relied in *Pinion,* assumes that "property was included in the purported inter vivos trust, prior to the testator's death." Restatement (Second) of Trusts § 54, comment f (1959). That is why commentators have recognized that G.L. c. 203, § 3B, "[m]akes some * * * modification of the *Pinion* doctrine. The act does not require that the trust res be more than nominal or even existent." E. Slizewski, Legislation: Uniform Testamentary Additions to Trusts Act, 10 Ann. Surv. of Mass. Law § 2.7, 39 (1963). See Osgood, Pour Over Will: Appraisal of Uniform Testamentary Additions to Trusts Act, 104 Trusts 768, 769 (1965) ("The Act * * * eliminates the necessity that there be a trust corpus").

* * * By analogy, in Trosch v. Maryland Nat'l Bank, 32 Md. App. 249, 252, 359 N.E.2d 564 (1976), the court construed Maryland's Testamentary Additions to Trusts Act as "conditionally abrogating the common law rule * * * that a trust must have a corpus to be in existence." Despite minor differences in the relevant language of Maryland's Estates and Trusts Act, § 4–411, and our G.L. c. 203 § 3B, we agree with the court's conclusion that "the statute is not conditioned upon the existence of a trust but upon the existence of a trust *instrument*" (emphasis in original). *Id.* at 253, 359 A.2d 564. * * *

For the foregoing reasons we conclude, in accordance with G.L. c. 203, § 3B, that the decedent established a valid inter vivos trust in 1973 and that its trustee may properly receive the residue of her estate. We affirm the judge's ruling on this issue.

¶ 4577

[¶ 4583]

c. Administrative Provisions

Crucial to the success of any trust are the administrative provisions which are included to facilitate the trustee's administration of the trust. Examples would include provisions authorizing the trustee to retain in the trust unproductive property which the trustee receives from the settlor. (Fiduciary law requires that the trustee make the trust productive.) Another example would be a provision freeing the trustee from any duty to make the trust productive when the trust res consists of cash in an amount of less than $500. (This might be an important provision in a standby or contingent trust which has funding in an amount sufficient only to give it an adequate res so as to qualify it as a receptacle for a pourover will.) Care must be taken to prepare these administrative provisions.

I. THE ILLUSORY TRUST DOCTRINE

[¶ 4601]

Will contests, real and threatened, are part of everyday conversation. Understood, in concept, by all, little is left to the imagination. What about trusts, particularly the so-called ubiquitous "living trust"? How does one "contest" a trust? If the trust is irrevocable, the challenge is probably expressed in terms of: (1) mistake on the part of the creator or (2) fraud, duress, or undue influence. Of course, the challenge can always take the form of an action to construe the trust.

But what about the living trust, commonly viewed as being revocable? Here the challenge is expressed in terms of "no trust," i.e., that the trust is "illusory" in the sense that no enforceable, cognizable interest was created in the trust beneficiaries during the lifetime of the creator of the trust. The argument leads to the conclusion that since there is no trust—because there is no enforceable, cognizable interest given anyone other the creator of the trust—the trust fails, i.e., it is essentially testamentary and must satisfy the requirements of the applicable statute authorizing wills. And it is at that point that the decedent's executor claims the trust property for the benefit of the decedent's probate estate.

The success or failure of the illusory trust challenge may well depend upon whether the claimant hails from a protected class of persons, e.g., a surviving spouse, or from another less sympathetic source. In this regard, compare Farkas v. Williams and Newman v. Dore, both of which appear below.

Remember to turn the question around. That is, remember to think about how to sustain the trust against challenges that it is illusory or suffers from some other fatal flaw. That is the task of the estate planning professional.

[¶ 4603]

FARKAS v. WILLIAMS

Illinois Supreme Court, 1955.
5 Ill.2d 417, 125 N.E.2d 600.

HERSHEY, Justice * * *

The plaintiffs asked the court to declare their legal rights, as coadminis-trators, in four stock certificates issued by Investors Mutual Inc. in the name of "Albert B. Farkas, as trustee for Richard J. Williams" and which were issued pursuant to written declarations of trust. The decree of the circuit court found that said declarations were testamentary in character, and not having been executed with the formalities of a will, were invalid, and directed that the stock be awarded to the plaintiffs as an asset of the estate of said Albert B. Farkas. Upon appeal to the Appellate Court, the decree was affirmed. * * *

Albert B. Farkas died intestate at the age of sixty-seven years, a resident of Chicago, leaving as his only heirs-at-law brothers, sisters, a nephew and a niece. Although retired at the time of his death, he had for many years practiced veterinary medicine and operated a veterinarian establishment in Chicago. During a considerable portion of that time, he employed the defen-dant Williams, who was not related to him.

On four occasions * * * Farkas purchased stock of Investors Mutual, Inc. At the time of each purchase he executed a written application to Investors Mutual, Inc., instructing them to issue the stock in his name "as trustee for Richard J. Williams." Investors Mutual, Inc., by its agent, accepted each of these applications in writing by signature on the face of the application. Coincident with the execution of these applications, Farkas signed separate declarations of trust, all of which were identical except as to dates. The terms of said trust instruments are as follows:

> Declaration of Trust—Revocable. I, the undersigned, having pur-chased or declared my intention to purchase certain shares of capital stock of Investors Mutual, Inc. (the Company), and having directed that the certificate for said stock be issued in my name as trustee for Richard J. Williams as beneficiary, whose address is * * *, under this Declaration of Trust Do Hereby Declare that the terms and conditions upon which I shall hold said stock in trust and any additional stock resulting from reinvestments of cash dividends upon such original or additional shares are as follows:

> (1) During my lifetime all cash dividends are to be paid to me individually for my own personal account and use; provided, however, that any such additional stock purchased under an authorized reinvest-ment of cash dividends shall become a part of and subject to this trust.

> (2) Upon my death the title to any stock subject hereto and the right to any subsequent payments or distributions shall be vested absolutely in the beneficiary. The record date for the payment of dividends, rather than

¶ 4603

the date of declaration of the dividend, shall, with reference to my death, determine whether any particular dividend shall be payable to my estate or to the beneficiary.

(3) During my lifetime I reserve the right, as trustee, to vote, sell, redeem, exchange or otherwise deal in or with the stock subject hereto, but upon any sale or redemption of said stock or any part thereof, the trust hereby declared shall terminate as to the stock sold or redeemed, and I shall be entitled to retain the proceeds of sale or redemption for my own personal account and use.

(4) I reserve the right at any time to change the beneficiary or revoke this trust, but it is understood that no change of beneficiary and no revocation of this trust except by death of the beneficiary, shall be effective as to the Company for any purpose unless and until written notice thereof in such form as the Company shall prescribe is delivered to the Company at Minneapolis, Minnesota. The decease of the beneficiary before my death shall operate as a revocation of this trust.

(5) In the event this trust shall be revoked or otherwise terminated, said stock and all rights and privileges thereunder shall belong to and be exercised by me in my individual capacity.

(6) The Company shall not be liable for the validity or existence of any trust created by me, and any payment or other consideration made or given by the Company to me as trustee or otherwise, in connection with said stock or any cash dividends thereon, or in the event of my death prior to revocation, to the beneficiary, shall to the extent of such payment fully release and discharge the Company from liability with respect to said stock or any cash dividends thereon.

The applications and declarations of trust were delivered to Investors Mutual, Inc., and held by the company until Farkas's death. The stock certificates were issued in the name of Farkas as "trustee for Richard J. Williams" and were discovered in a safety-deposit box of Farkas after his death, along with other securities, some of which were in the name of Williams alone.

The sole question presented on this appeal is whether the instruments entitled "Declaration of Trust—Revocable" and executed by Farkas created valid *inter vivos* trusts of the stock of Investors Mutual, Inc. The plaintiffs contend that said stock is free and clear from any trust or beneficial interest in the defendant Williams, for the reason that said purported trust instruments were attempted testamentary dispositions and invalid for want of compliance with the statute on wills. The defendants, on the other hand, insist that said instruments created valid *inter vivos* trusts and were not testamentary in character.

It is conceded that the instruments were not executed in such a way as to satisfy the requirements of the statute on wills; hence, our inquiry is limited to whether said trust instruments created valid *inter vivos* trusts effective to give the purported beneficiary, Williams, title to the stock in question after the death of the settlor-trustee, Farkas. To make this determination we must

¶ 4603

consider: (1) whether upon execution of the so-called trust instruments defendant Williams acquired an interest in the subject matter of the trusts, the stock of defendant Investors Mutual, Inc., (2) whether Farkas, as settlor-trustee, retained such control over the subject matter of the trusts as to render said trust instruments attempted testamentary dispositions.

First, upon execution of these trust instruments did defendant Williams presently acquire an interest in the subject matter of the intended trusts?

If no interest passed to Williams before the death of Farkas, the intended trusts are testamentary and hence invalid for failure to comply with the statute on wills. * * *

But considering the terms of these instruments we believe Farkas did intend to presently give Williams an interest in the property referred to. For it may be said, at the very least, that upon his executing one of these instruments, he showed an intention to presently part with some of the incidents of ownership in the stock. Immediately after the execution of each of these instruments, he could not deal with the stock therein referred to the same as if he owned the property absolutely, but only in accordance with the terms of the instrument. He purported to set himself up as trustee of the stock for the benefit of Williams, and the stock was registered in his name as trustee for Williams. Thus assuming to act as trustee, he is held to have intended to take on those obligations which are expressly set out in the instrument, as well as those fiduciary obligations implied by law. In addition, he manifested an intention to bind himself to having this property pass upon his death to Williams, unless he changed the beneficiary or revoked the trust, and then such change of beneficiary or revocation was not to be effective as to Investors Mutual, Inc., unless and until written notice thereof in such form as the company prescribed was delivered to them at Minneapolis, Minnesota. An absolute owner can dispose of his property, either in his lifetime or by will, in any way he sees fit without notifying or securing approval from anyone and without being held to the duties of a fiduciary in so doing.

It seems to follow that what incidents of ownership Farkas intended to relinquish, in a sense he intended Williams to acquire. That is, Williams was to be the beneficiary to whom Farkas was to be obligated, and unless Farkas revoked the instrument in the manner therein set out or the instrument was otherwise terminated in a manner therein provided for, upon Farkas's death Williams was to become absolute owner of the trust property. It is difficult to name this interest of Williams, nor is there any reason for so doing so long as it passed to him immediately upon the creation of the trust. As stated in 4 Powell, The Law of Real Property, at page 87: "Interests of beneficiaries of private express trusts run the gamut from valuable-substantialities to evanescent hopes. Such a beneficiary may have any one of an almost infinite variety of the possible aggregates of rights, privileges, powers and immunities."

An additional problem is presented here, however, for it is to be noted that the trust instruments provide: "The decease of the beneficiary before my death shall operate as a revocation of this trust." The plaintiffs argue that the presence of this provision removes the only possible distinction which might have been drawn between these instruments and a will. Being thus conditioned on his surviving, it is argued that the "interest" of Williams until the death of Farkas was a mere expectancy. Conversely, they assert, the interest of Farkas in the securities until his death was precisely the same as that of a testator who bequeaths securities by his will since he had all the rights accruing to an absolute owner.

Admittedly, had this provision been absent the interest of Williams would have been greater, since he would then have had an inheritable interest in the lifetime of Farkas. But to say his interest would have been greater is not to say that he here did not have a beneficial interest, properly so-called, during the lifetime of Farkas. * * *

* * *

Second, did Farkas retain such control over the subject matter of the trust as to render said trust instruments attempted testamentary dispositions?

In each of these trust instruments, Farkas reserved to himself as settlor the following powers: (1) the right to receive during his lifetime all cash dividends; (2) the right at any time to change the beneficiary or revoke the trust; and (3) upon sale or redemption of any portion of the trust property, the right to retain the proceeds therefrom for his own use.

Additionally, Farkas reserved the right to act as sole trustee, and in such capacity, he was accorded the right to vote, sell, redeem, exchange or otherwise deal in the stock which formed the subject matter of the trust.

* * *

It is well established that the retention by the settlor of the power to revoke, even when coupled with the reservation of a life interest in the trust property, does not render the trust inoperative for want of execution as a will. * * *

Only when it is thought that there are additional reservations present of such a substantial nature as to amount to the retention of full ownership is a court likely to invalidate an *inter vivos* trust by reason of its not being executed as a will. * * * (See Restatement of the Law of Trusts, § 57.) In 1 Scott, The Law of Trusts, § 57.1, the author says at pages 336–337: "It is immaterial whether the settlor reserves simply a power to revoke the whole trust at one time or whether he reserves also a power to revoke the trust as to any part of the property from time to time. It is immaterial whether the power to revoke includes a power to revoke by will as well as a power to revoke by a transaction *inter vivos*. It is immaterial that the settlor reserves not only a power to revoke the trust but in addition a power to alter or modify its terms."

However, it is not every so-called additional reservation of power that will be deemed sufficient to invalidate a trust of this nature. In 32 A.L.R.2d 1270, it is stated at pages 1276–1277: "The later cases, as do the earlier ones, justify the general conclusion that many and extensive rights and power may be reserved by a settlor, in addition to a life interest and power of revocation, without defeating the trust. The instrument is likely to be upheld notwithstanding it includes additionally the reservation of power to amend the trust on whole or in part, or extensive powers over investments, management, or administration, or power to appoint or remove trustees or to appoint interests in remainder, or the right to act as trustee or as one of the trustees, or to enjoy limited rights in the principal, or to withdraw part or all of the principal, or to possess, use, or enjoy the trust property, or to sell or mortgage the property or any of it and appropriate the proceeds."

We conclude therefore, in accordance with the great weight of authority, said powers which Farkas reserved to himself as settlor were not such as to render the intended trusts invalid as attempted testamentary dispositions.

A more difficult problem is posed, however, by the fact that Farkas is also trustee, and as such, is empowered to vote, sell, redeem, exchange and otherwise deal in and with the subject matter of the trusts.

That a settlor may create a trust of personal property whereby he names himself as trustee and acts as such for the beneficiary is clear. Restatement of the Law of Trusts, § 17.

Moreover, the later cases indicate that the mere fact that the settlor in addition to making himself sole trustee also reserves a life interest and a power of revocation does not render the trust invalid as testamentary in character. 32 A.L.R.2d 1286. In 1 Scott, The Law of Trusts, it is stated at pages 353–354: "The owner of property may create a trust not only by transferring the property to another person as trustee, but also by declaring himself trustee. Such a declaration of trust, although gratuitous, is valid. * * * Suppose, however, that the settlor reserves not only a beneficial life interest but also a power of revocation. It would seem that such a trust is not necessarily testamentary. The declaration of trust immediately creates an equitable interest in the beneficiaries, although the enjoyment of the interest is postponed until the death of the settlor, and although the interest may be divested by the exercise of the power of revocation. The disposition is not essentially different from that which is made where the settlor transfers the property to another person as trustee. It is true that where the settlor declares himself trustee he controls the administration of the trust. As has been stated, if the settlor transfers property upon trust and reserves not only a power of revocation but also power to control the administration of the trust, the trust is testamentary. There is this difference, however: the power of control which the settlor has as trustee is not an irresponsible power and can be exercised only in accordance with the terms of the trust." See also Restatement of the Law of Trusts, § 57, comment b.

In the instant case the plaintiffs contend that Farkas, as settlor-trustee, retained complete control and dominion over the securities for his own benefit during his lifetime. It is argued that he had the power to deal with the property as he liked so long as he lived and owed no enforceable duties of any kind to Williams as beneficiary. * * *

That the retention of the power by Farkas as trustee to sell or redeem the stock and keep the proceeds for his own use should not render these trust instruments testamentary in character becomes more evident upon analyzing

¶ 4603

the real import and significance of the powers to revoke and to amend the trust, the reservation of which the courts uniformly hold does not invalidate an *inter vivos* trust.

It is obvious that a settlor with the power to revoke and to amend the trust at any time is, for all practical purpose, in a position to exert considerable control over the trustee regarding the administration of the trust. For anything believed to be inimical to his best interests can be thwarted or prevented by simply revoking the trust or amending it in such a way as to conform to his wishes. Indeed, it seems that many of those powers which from time to time have been viewed as "additional powers" are already, in a sense, virtually contained within the overriding power of revocation or the power to amend the trust. Consider, for example, the following: (1) the power to consume the principal; (2) the power to sell or mortgage the trust property and appropriate the proceeds; (3) the power to appoint or remove trustees; (4) the power to supervise and direct investments; and (5) the power to otherwise direct and supervise the trustee in the administration of the trust. Actually, any of the above powers could readily be assumed by a settlor with the reserved power of revocation through the simple expedient of revoking the trust, and then, as absolute owner of the subject matter, doing with the property as he chooses. Even though no actual termination of the trust is effectuated, however, it could hardly be questioned but that the mere existence of this power in the settlor is sufficient to enable his influence to be felt in a practical way in the administration of the trust. * * * In 1 Bogert, Trusts and Trustees, § 104, the author states at pages 484–485: "Often the grantor-settlor holds back for himself the power to manage the property directly and indirectly. He provides that he himself shall have power to sell, lease, mortgage, pay taxes, make investments, and perform other acts of trust administration, or that he shall have authority to direct the trustees how they shall perform these duties. These reservations have not generally been deemed to show that the grantor remains during his life the master of the property to such an extent as to make his gift to the *cestuis* testamentary. So long as the trust continues, the *cestuis* have equitable interests, no matter who acts for them in protecting those interests, whether it be trustee or settlor. If the exercise of these powers by the settlor involves the total or partial destruction of the trust, as where the settlor has power to sell the *res* and keep the proceeds, the power seems to be treated as practically that of revocation of the trust. It leaves an equitable interest in the *cestuis* till revocation. It shows a vested interest, subject to divestment, and not the lack of any interest at all."

In the case at bar, the power of Farkas to vote, sell, redeem, exchange or otherwise deal in the stock was reserved to him as trustee, and it was only upon sale or redemption that he was entitled to keep the proceeds for his own use. Thus, the control reserved is not as great as in those cases where said power is reserved to the owner as settlor. For as trustee he must so conduct himself in accordance with standards applicable to trustees generally. It is not a valid objection to this to say that Williams would never question Farkas's conduct, inasmuch as Farkas could then revoke the trust and destroy what interest Williams has. Such a possibility exists in any case where the settlor

¶ 4603

has the power of revocation. Still, Williams has rights the same as any beneficiary, although it may not be feasible for him to exercise them. Moreover, it is entirely possible that he might in certain situations have a right to hold Farkas's estate liable for breaches of trust committed by Farkas during his lifetime. In this regard, consider what would happen if, without having revoked the trust, Farkas as trustee had given the stock away without receiving any consideration therefor, had pledged the stock improperly for his own personal debt and allowed it to be lost by foreclosure or had exchanged the stock for another security or other worthless property in such manner as to constitute gross impropriety and gross negligence. In such instances, it would seem in accordance with the terms of these instruments that Williams would have had an enforceable claim against Farkas's estate for whatever damage had been suffered. Contrast this with the rights of a legatee or devisee under a will. The testator could waste the property or do anything with it he wished during his lifetime without incurring any liability to those designated by the will to inherit the property. In any event, if Farkas as settlor could reserve the power to sell or otherwise deal with the property and retain the proceeds, which the cases indicate he could, then it necessarily follows that he should have the right to sell or otherwise deal with the property as trustee and retain the proceeds from a sale or redemption without having the instruments rendered invalid as testamentary dispositions.

Another factor often considered in determining whether an *inter vivos* trust is an attempted testamentary disposition is the formality of the transaction. Restatement of the Law of Trusts, § 57, comment g. * * * Historically, the purpose behind the enactment of the statute on wills was the prevention of fraud. The requirement as to witnesses was deemed necessary because a will is ordinarily an expression of the secret wish of the testator, signed out of the presence of all concerned. The possibility of forgery and fraud are ever present in such situations. Here, Farkas executed four separate applications for stock of Investors Mutual, Inc., in which he directed that the stock be issued in his name as trustee for Williams, and he executed four separate declarations of trust in which he declared he was holding said stock in trust for Williams. The stock certificates in question were issued in his name as trustee for Williams. He thus manifested his intention in a solemn and formal manner.

For the reasons stated, we conclude that these trust declarations executed by Farkas constituted valid *inter vivos* trusts and were not attempted testamentary dispositions. It must be conceded that they have, in the words of Mr. Justice Holmes in Bromley v. Mitchell, 155 Mass. 509, 30 N.E. 83, a "testamentary look." Moreover, it must be admitted that the line should be drawn somewhere, but after a study of this case we do not believe that point has here been reached.

Problem

[¶ 4611]

Suppose a revocable trust has been established and the settlor, Sam, has died. The trust is funded with the proceeds of life insurance in, let us say, the amount of $200,000. The trust beneficiaries are Sam's next-door neighbors, who have cared for him in his last years, and Sam's niece and nephew in Australia, who would take Sam's estate if he died intestate. Sam's niece and nephew claim the trust is invalid. They argue that the trust is essentially testamentary and, as a testamentary device, it must comply with the applicable statute of wills. Since it does not, it fails and the property in the trust—the $200,000—flows into the testator's probate estate to be disposed of under his will and, if not effectively disposed of by the will, passes by intestacy to the niece and nephew. On what theories might the niece and nephew proceed?

J. CLAIMS OF THE SURVIVING SPOUSE

[¶ 4651]

1. SPOUSAL PROTECTION STATUTES

All of the separate property jurisdictions and at least one of the community property jurisdictions have some form of spousal protection statute. Generally these statutes give the surviving spouse the right to repudiate the testator's will and claim an intestate share of the testator's *probate* property. *Probate* property for these purposes is property subject to disposition by the testator's will. It does not include property held as joint tenants with right of survivorship nor does it include the proceeds of insurance on the life of the testator if those proceeds are payable to a beneficiary named in the contract of insurance. For related material, see ¶ 21,900.

[¶ 4659]

2. DISINHERITANCE BY REVOCABLE TRUST

Probate property does not include property included in a revocable trust. At least it does not include such property under the more common form of spousal protection statute unless the trust is illusory and therefore testamentary. See discussion at ¶ 4603. Therefore, the testator who wants to disinherit his or her spouse may well be advised to consider transferring all of his or her property to a revocable trust during lifetime. At the testator's death, the spouse would take no part of the property. Even if the spouse did elect to repudiate the testator's will and claim an intestate share of the testator's probate property, oftentimes little such property will remain in the probate estate within the reach of the surviving spouse.

That having been said, consider Newman v. Dore, which follows. The court considered—and rejected—the fraud-on-the-spouse challenge to the revocable trust. However, the court set the trust aside because it was found to be illusory on the facts presented. On the one hand, then, you have the result in *Farkas* (see ¶ 4603), where the trust was sustained against the claim that it was illusory and, on the other hand, the result in Newman v. Dore, setting the trust aside. Could the difference be the identity of the claimant? That is, is the outcome dependent upon whether the claimants are siblings who are the intestate takers or the surviving spouse?

¶ 4611

[¶ 4661]

NEWMAN v. DORE

New York Court of Appeals, 1937.
275 N.Y. 371, 9 N.E.2d 966.

LEHMAN, Judge.

The Decedent Estate Law (Consol. Laws, c. 13, arts. 2, 3) regulates the testamentary disposition and the descent and distribution of the real and personal property of decedents. It does not limit or affect disposition of property inter vivos. In terms and in intent it applies only to decedents' estates. Property which did not belong to a decedent at his death and which does not become part of his estate does not come within its scope. * * * By § 18 of the revised Decedent Estate Law, "a personal right of election is given to the surviving spouse to take his or her share of the estate as in intestacy, subject to the limitations, conditions and exceptions contained in this section." These limitations and exceptions include a case where "the testator has devised or bequeathed in trust an amount equal to or greater than the intestate share, with income thereof payable to the surviving spouse for life." * * *

Ferdinand Straus died on July 1, 1934, leaving a last will and testament dated May 5, 1934, which contained a provision for a trust for his wife for her life of one-third of the decedent's property both real and personal. In such case the statute did not give the wife a right of election to take her share of the estate as in intestacy. She receives the income for life from a trust fund of the amount of the intestate share, but does not take the share. That share is one-third of the decedent's estate. It includes no property which does not form part of the estate at the decedent's death. The testator on June 28, 1934, three days before his death, executed trust agreements by which, in form at least, he transferred to trustees all his real and personal property. If the agreements effectively divested the settlor of title to his property, then the decedent left no estate and the widow takes nothing. The widow has challenged the validity of the transfer to the trustees. The beneficiary named in the trust agreement has brought this action to compel the trustees to carry out its terms. The trial court has found that the "trust agreements were made, executed and delivered by said Ferdinand Straus for the purpose of evading and circumventing the laws of the State of New York, and particularly §§ 18 and 83 of the Decedent Estate Law." Undoubtedly the settlor's purpose was to provide that at his death his property should pass to beneficiaries named in the trust agreement to the exclusion of his wife. Under the provisions of the Decedent Estate Law the decedent could not effect the desired purpose by testamentary disposition of his property. The problem in this case is whether he has accomplished that result by creating a trust during his lifetime.

The validity of the attempted transfer depends upon whether "the laws of the State of New York and particularly §§ 18 and 83 of the Decedent Estate Law" prohibit or permit such transfer. If the statute, in express language or by clear implication, prohibits the transfer, it is illegal; if the laws of the state do not prohibit it, the transfer is legal. * * * Under the laws of the State of New York, and particularly §§ 18 and 83 of the Decedent Estate Law, neither spouse has any immediate interest in the property of the other. The "enlarged property rights" which the Legislature intended to confer is only an expectant interest dependent upon the contingency that the property to which the interest attaches becomes part of a decedent's estate. The contingency does not occur, and the expectant property right does not ripen into a property right in possession, if the owner sells or gives away the property. * * * Defeat of a contingent expectant interest by means available under the law cannot be regarded as an unlawful "evasion" of the law. A duty imperfectly defined by law may at times be evaded or a right imperfectly protected by law may be violated with impunity, but to say that an act, lawful under common-law rules and not prohibited by any express or implied statutory provision, is in itself a "fraud" on the law or an "evasion" of the law, involves a contradiction in terms.

That does not mean, of course, that the law may not place its ban upon an intended result even though the means to effect that result may be lawful. * * * Under the trust agreements executed a few days before the death of the settlor, he reserved the enjoyment of the entire income as long as he should live, and a right to revoke the trust at his will, and in general the powers granted to the trustees were in terms made "subject to the settlor's control during his life," and could be exercised "in such manner only as the settlor shall from time to time direct in writing." Thus, by the trust agreement which transferred to the trustees the settlor's entire property, the settlor reserved substantially the same rights to enjoy and control the disposition of the property as he previously had possessed, and the inference is inescapable that the trust agreements were executed by the settlor, as the court has found, "with the intention and for the purpose of diminishing his estate and thereby to reduce in amount the share" of his wife in his estate upon his death and as a "contrivance to deprive * * * his widow of any rights in and to his property upon his death." They had no other purpose and substantially they had no other effect. Does the statute intend that such a transfer shall be available as a means of defeating the contingent expectant estate of a spouse?

In a few states where a wife has a similar contingent expectant interest or estate in the property of her husband, it has been held that her rights may not be defeated by any transfer made during life with intent to deprive the wife of property, which under the law would otherwise pass to her. * * * In those states it is the intent to defeat the wife's contingent rights which creates the invalidity and it seems that an absolute transfer of all his property by a married man during his life, if made with other purpose and intent than to cut off an unloved wife, is valid even though its effect is to deprive the wife of any share in the property of her husband at his death. * * * The rule has been stated that "while the wife cannot complain of reasonable gifts or advancements by a husband to his children by a former marriage, yet, if the gifts constitute the principal part of the husband's estate and be made without the wife's knowledge, a presumption of fraud arises, and it rests upon the beneficiaries to explain away that presumption." * * *

¶ 4661

Motive or intent is an unsatisfactory test of the validity of a transfer of property. In most jurisdictions it has been rejected, sometimes for the reason that it would cast doubt upon the validity of all transfers made by a married man, outside of the regular course of business; sometimes because it is difficult to find a satisfactory logical foundation for it. Intent may, at times, be relevant in determining whether an act is fraudulent, but there can be no fraud where no right of any person is invaded. * * * Since the law gives the wife only an expectant interest in the property of her husband which becomes part of his estate, and since the law does not restrict transfers of property by the husband during his life, it would seem that the only sound test of the validity of a challenged transfer is whether it is real or illusory. * * * The test has been formulated in different ways, but in most jurisdictions the test applied is essentially the test of whether the husband has in good faith divested himself of ownership of his property or has made an illusory transfer. * * * [C]ourts have sustained the validity of the trusts even where a husband reserved to himself the income for life, power of revocation, and a considerable measure of control. * * * [T]ransfers in trust have been upheld regardless of their purpose where a husband retained a right to enjoy the income during his life. * * * In some of these cases the settlor retained, also, a power of revocation. In no jurisdiction has a transfer in trust been upheld where the conveyance is intended only to cover up the fact that the husband is retaining full control of the property though in form he has parted with it. Though a person may use means lawfully available to him to keep outside of the scope of a statute, a false appearance of legality, however attained, will not avail him. Reality, not appearance, should determine legal rights. * * *

In this case the decedent, as we have said, retained not only the income for life and power to revoke the trust, but also the right to control the trustees. We need not now determine whether such a trust is for any purpose, a valid present trust. It has been said that, "where the settlor transfers property in trust and reserves not only * * * a power to revoke and modify the trust but also such power to control the trustee as to the details of the administration of the trust that the trustee is the agent of the settlor, the disposition so far as it is intended to take effect after his death is testamentary. * * *" American Law Institute, Restatement of the Law of Trusts, § 57, subd. 2. We do not now consider whether the rule so stated is in accord with the law of this state or whether in this case the reserved power of control is so great that the trustee is in fact "the agent of the settlor." We assume, without deciding, that except for the provisions of § 18 of the Decedent Estate Law the trust would be valid. * * * Perhaps "from the technical point of view such a conveyance does not quite take back all that it gives, but practically it does." That is enough to render it an unlawful invasion of the expectant interest of the wife. * * *

Judged by the substance, not by the form, the testator's conveyance is illusory, intended only as a mask for the effective retention by the settlor of the property which in form he had conveyed. We do not attempt now to formulate any general test of how far a settlor must divest himself of his interest in the trust property to render the conveyance more than illusory. Question of whether reservation of the income or of a power of revocation, or

¶ **4661**

both, might even without reservation of the power of control be sufficient to show that the transfer was not intended in good faith to divest the settlor of his property must await decision until such question arises. In this case it is clear that the settlor never intended to divest himself of his property. He was unwilling to do so even when death was near.

The judgment should be affirmed, with costs.

[¶ 4663]

Note

1. Cases collected and discussed as part of the Reporter's Note 4, Comment j to § 9.1 of the Restatement (Third) of Property (Wills and Other Donative Transfers), indicate that there is genuine division among the courts as to elective share claims to property placed in revocable trusts. Rest. (Third) of Prop.: Donative Transfers § 9.1 (2003). Absent a statute making the trust property subject to elective share claims, would you agree that findings similar to those made in Newman v. Dore need to be made to get around the almost universal conclusion that the revocable trust is an effective means to transfer property—as was concluded in *Farkas?* Or should it be enough for a court to say, "The integrity of the spousal protection statute is compromised unless a judicial determination is made here that the forced heirship statute allows a spousal claim to property placed in a revocable trust despite the statute being expressly limited to probate property." Such a conclusion avoids the philosophical conflict between cases like Newman v. Dore and *Farkas*. After all, the results in *Farkas* must be sustained or the whole wealth transfer system built around the revocable or living trust collapses—and the words "estate and trust litigator" will take on a whole new meaning.

2. Revocable trusts established in New York after August 31, 1966, can be reached by the surviving spouse to satisfy the spouse's claim to an elective share of the decedent's property. See McKinney's N.Y. Estate Powers & Trust Law, 5–1.1(b)(1)(E); see also Matter of Reynolds, 87 N.Y.2d 633, 642 N.Y.S.2d 147, 149, 664 N.E.2d 1209 (App.Div. 1996) (surviving spouse can reach the assets of a revocable Medicaid trust as part of his elective share under New York statute because the decedent retained "meaningful control over the trust during her lifetime").

3. Under the long-standing Massachusetts rule, announced in Kerwin v. Donaghy, 317 Mass. 559, 59 N.E.2d 299 (1945), the surviving spouse's forced heirship claim would not reach property transferred to a revocable trust by the deceased prior to death. However, in Sullivan v. Burkin, 390 Mass. 864, 460 N.E.2d 572 (1984), the Massachusetts Supreme Court announced that it was abandoning the *Kerwin* rule. The court indicated that it was persuaded by what has become Restatement (Third) of Prop.: Donative Transfers § 9.1 (2003). Comment j of Section 9.1 of the Restatement says that for purposes of determining the amount of the elective share, "property owned or owned in substance by the decedent immediately before death that passed outside of probate" where the decedent had various powers over the transferred property, "such as the power to revoke, withdraw, invade, or sever, or to appoint the

decedent or the decedent's estate as beneficiary" is to be included in the decedent's estate. In that sense, factors making up "control," as identified in Newman v. Dore for a finding that the trust was illusory, are irrelevant in the Restatement view, the test being whether the transferor had a general power over the property he or she transferred during life. See Chapter 18 for a discussion of general powers of appointment.

[¶ 4667]

3.   THE UNIFORM PROBATE CODE SOLUTION

The draftspersons of the UPC decided that the spousal protection statute that was to be included in the UPC should give the surviving spouse a claim not only against probate property but also against property subject to a revocable trust established by the testator. UPC §§ 2–202 through 2–214 detail the elective share rights of the surviving spouse. These provisions were crafted with the intention of reflecting contemporary views of marriage as an economic partnership. Marriage as an economic partnership is the principle underlying: (1) the community property system and (2) the equitable distribution system applied in both common law and community property jurisdictions in the event of divorce. The goal of the UPC provisions was to "increase the entitlement of a surviving spouses in a long-term marriage in cases in which the marital assets were disproportionately titled in the decedent's name." UPC art. II, pt. 2, gen. cmt.

In sum, if the marriage is of long duration—for example, more than 15 years—the surviving spouse is entitled to 50 percent of the decedent's "augmented estate," a UPC-defined term. The augmented estate consists not only of the decedent's property but also the property transferred by the decedent during life over which the decedent has, at death, some control (whether it be beneficial or only to control the enjoyment of the property by others). The augmented estate includes joint tenancy with right of survivorship property and life insurance on the life of the decedent which was owned by the decedent. It even includes property transferred within two years of death. Thus, in essence, with a few exceptions, the UPC augmented estate concept has been modeled on the federal estate tax.

In addition, the augmented estate is also to include the property owned by the surviving spouse! By this provision the UPC takes account of the economic circumstances of the surviving spouse. Such a view reflects the UPC conclusion that marriage created an economic partnership—and if the surviving spouse has ample provisions relative to the value of the combined estates, the surviving spouse should take no more.

[¶ 4675]

4.   COMMUNITY PROPERTY

a.   In General

In each of the community property jurisdictions, each spouse is deemed to own one-half of the community property acquired by the spouses during the marriage. Generally speaking, the spouses' community property is presumed to be all property acquired by the spouses during the marriage. The presumption can be rebutted by a showing that the property in question is the separate property of one of the spouses. Property will be deemed separate property if it was acquired prior to the marriage or, if acquired during the marriage, it was acquired as a result of a gift, devise, bequest, or inheritance. In a number of jurisdictions (California, for one), income produced during the marriage by the *separate* property of one of the spouses is the *separate* property of the spouse whose separate property produced the income. In other jurisdictions (Texas, for one), income produced during the marriage by the *separate* property of one of the spouses is *community* property. See 3 L. Simpkins, Texas Family Law § 15:39 (Speer's 5th ed. 1976). For additional discussion of community property, see Chapter 11.

Under the community property system, a spouse is free at deathtime to dispose of all of his or her separate property but only his or her one-half of the community property. ¶ 11,105. While a spouse cannot make a deathtime disposition of the surviving spouse's one-half of the community, on rare occasions, a contrivance known as a widow's election is used to tempt the surviving spouse into allowing the deceased spouse to control the disposition of the survivor's property. ¶ 11,901.

Thus, the community property system is seen as inherently equitable. If the marriage was of long duration, there should be much community property, and the surviving spouse would have one-half. If the marriage was of short duration, there would be little community property, and the surviving spouse would have only one-half of this smaller amount.

The community property rule should be contrasted with the forced heirship system in place in non-community property jurisdictions. There, before the advent of the UPC's augmented estate (¶ 4667), whether the marriage be long or short, the surviving spouse had the same claim. This suggests that the community property system is superior, in terms of equity, to the forced heirship system in place in non-UPC jurisdictions. The actual needs of the surviving spouse are not a factor under either system.

For discussion of community property with right of survivorship, see ¶ 11,105.

[¶ 4683]

b. *Quasi-Community Property*

California, Idaho, and at least Washington have created a third class of spousal property. It is called quasi-community property. Quasi-community property is property which the spouses acquired while living in another jurisdiction but "which would have been" community property if it had been acquired while the spouses were living in the state recognizing quasi-community property. See, e.g., Cal. [Prob.] Code § 66 (West 2002); Wash. Rev. Code. Ann. § 26.16.220 (West 2005). A surviving spouse may claim a forced heir's share of the quasi-community property belonging to the deceased spouse. See, e.g., Idaho Code Ann. § 15–2–202 (2001).

¶ 4675

Problems

[¶ 4689]

1. Mr. Mudd is your client. He wants all of his property to pass to his child, Mark, at his death, and he is prepared to make a will to this effect. Under no circumstances does he want anything to pass to his spouse, Gidget. He and Gidget have been married for 36 years and, apparently, for 36 years they have lived in a state of near war. (Gidget is Mr. Mudd's second spouse. His first spouse, Mollie, died when Mark was an infant.) Mr. Mudd and Gidget are planning to relocate to the Sun Belt for their retirement years. They plan to choose either Florida or Texas. Florida is a separate property jurisdiction and Texas is a community property jurisdiction. Should Mr. Mudd's dispositive scheme have any impact on his choice of jurisdictions? See Louis A. Mezzullo & Derry W. Swanger, The Migrant Client: Tax, Community Property, & Other Considerations, 803–2d Tax Mgmt (BNA) A–1 to A–61 (2004).

2. Do you think it is likely that the other community property jurisdictions will ultimately adopt the quasi-community property classification and make a forced heirship claim available to the surviving spouse?

[¶ 4691]

c. **The Revocable Trust**

The revocable trust is as useful in a community property jurisdiction as it is in a separate property jurisdiction.

On occasion one spouse, without the knowledge of the other spouse, will fund a revocable trust with community property. Whether the surviving spouse will have any claim against the community property in the trust will depend, in part, on the jurisdiction in which the issue is raised, inasmuch as each community property jurisdiction has developed its own set of governing principles. However, by way of illustration, consider Texas. In Texas, whether the surviving spouse has any claim will depend on: (1) whether the first spouse was the "manager" of the property which was put into the trust and (2) whether the transfer into the trust was a "fraud" on the community. Under Texas law, the manager of a particular item of community property is the spouse whose effort (or whose property) produced it. Whether a particular transfer is a fraud on the community depends, in part, on whether the transfer was in the best interests of the community and, in part, on whether the surviving spouse was injured by the conveyance. See R. Campfield, Interspousal Transfers, 32 Sw. L.J. 1032, 1115–21 (1979).

Chapter 5

DRAFTING FOR SUCCESSIVE ENJOYMENT

A. OBJECTIVES

[¶ 5001]

Any effective discussion of successive enjoyment must focus on planning for and drafting of future interests. By the same token, any discussion of drafting techniques must focus on future interests. The goal of this chapter is to demystify future interests by putting the subject in a functional context. These materials were organized to raise the more common future interest issues as they *impact drafting* and to create a framework in which the reader can work out solutions to the drafting issues presented.

B. COMMON DISPOSITIVE SCHEME

[¶ 5051]

A not uncommon dispositive scheme calls for the decedent's property to go into trust for the decedent's surviving spouse for life, with remainder to the decedent's then living lineal descendants *per stirpes*. The appeal of this scheme is that it provides property management for the surviving spouse for life and, thus, provides a financial safety net. It also enables the testator to control the ultimate disposition of the property. These considerations may be sufficiently important to the testator that he or she will be inclined to continue the trust beyond the lifetime of his or her spouse, perhaps through children's and grandchildren's generations.

Tax considerations also provide incentive for committing property to a trust. Prior to the advent of the generation-skipping transfer tax (for discussion, see ¶ 9001 et seq.), there were definite estate tax incentives to use trusts to limit the right of successive generations to enjoy a decedent's property. Such a dispositive scheme might include the following provisions:

During the continuance of the trust, the trustee shall pay so much or all of the income and principal of the trust to my spouse and lineal descendants living from time to time as the trustee shall deem necessary for the health, education, maintenance, and support of each such person. The trust will terminate upon the death of the last to die of my great-grandchildren. Upon termination, the remaining trust estate shall be distributed to my then living lineal descendants *per stirpes.*

Before considering the enormous problems of perpetuity inherent in this scheme, note that it may make more sense than a scheme which provides for mandatory distribution of income on a generational basis. Some of the beneficiaries will need the income; some will not. And where there is no need, it may make sense to consider the relative income tax brackets of the trust and the beneficiaries in making distributions. In that regard, there may need to be another sentence added to the above dispositive provision indicating that the trustee can take into account relative income tax brackets in making distribution determinations. For a discussion of the income taxation of trusts, see Chapter 8.

> *Example.* Bank has the discretion to make distributions from Trust. Bank plans to distribute sufficient income to Beneficiary so that Trust's marginal income tax bracket and Beneficiary's income tax bracket are identical.

Furthermore, stacking unneeded income in the surviving spouse's estate (or that of any other family member) means that it will accumulate and be subject to estate tax at his or her death.

Thus, there are both tax and nontax reasons for providing for successive enjoyment of property through the use of future interests. The problem is drafting the gifts of the future interests so as to limit the litigation that is so common whenever future interests are created. The most common reason for a case to go to litigation is the inability of the draftsperson to foresee the circumstances which materialize and to provide for those circumstances in the dispositive instrument. For illustration, see ¶ 21,800.

Thus, it is only fair to end this brief perspective on "why future interests?" by noting that the dispositive provision set forth above violates the common law Rule Against Perpetuities. See ¶ 5401. Before considering why, there are preliminary matters to address.

C. BACKGROUND

[¶ 5101]

Classification of future interests is not within the scope of this chapter. However, some familiarity with the terminology of future interests is necessary to work with these materials. The importance of classification becomes obvious when the reader considers that the fabled Rule Against Perpetuities applies *only* to contingent remainders, executory interests, and vested remainders subject to open.

Generally, future interests can be classified into those which become possessory in the grantor and the grantor's heirs and those which become possessory in persons other than the grantor or the grantor's heirs. Interests which become possessory in the grantor or the grantor's heirs are reversion, the possibility of reverter, and the right of re-entry for condition broken.

Interests which become possessory in persons other than the grantor or the grantor's heirs include remainders and executory interests.

D.   GIFTS TO HEIRS

[¶ 5201]

1.   INTRODUCTION

Gifts to "heirs" should be included in a dispositive instrument only in limited circumstances and only if the draftsperson fully appreciates such principles as the Rule in Shelley's Case and the inter vivos branch of the doctrine of worthier title (sometimes called the conveyor-heir rule).

[¶ 5209]

2.   RULE IN SHELLEY'S CASE

Almost all jurisdictions have abolished the Rule in Shelley's Case. However, *Shelley* continues to be important not only in the jurisdictions in which it has been retained but also in jurisdictions where it has been abolished. It is important in these latter jurisdictions because of its application to interests created *prior* to the legislative enactment abolishing it.

The Rule in Shelley's Case is expressed in these terms: If A is given a life estate in land and a remainder in the heirs or the heirs of a body of A is created by the same instrument of transfer and the life estate and the remainder are of the same quality (both legal or both equitable), then A has a fee simple.

The disposition to which *Shelley* most directly applies is the following:

Life estate to A, followed by a remainder to the heirs of A.

Applying *Shelley* to this disposition means that A will be deemed to have a fee simple. This conclusion is arrived at because *Shelley,* when applied, causes the phrase "remainder to the heirs of A" to be read as "remainder to A and A's heirs." The doctrine of merger takes care of the rest.

Shelley is a rule of law and not construction. Therefore it applies without regard to the donor's intention.

The importance of *Shelley* can be illustrated by the case of Sybert v. Sybert, 152 Tex. 106, 254 S.W.2d 999 (1953), where there were two rival sets of claimants to certain property. One set of claimants prevailed if *Shelley* applied, another set if it did not.

[¶ 5217]

3.   CONVEYOR-HEIR RULE

The conveyor-heir rule is unlike *Shelley* in three notable respects. First, the conveyor-heir rule is a rule of construction and not a rule of law and does not apply if the donor intends for it not to apply. Second, unlike *Shelley,* the conveyor-heir rule survives in many jurisdictions. Third, the conveyor-heir rule applies to both realty and personalty.

¶ 5101

The conveyor-heir rule can be expressed in these terms: In cases where a person transfers a remainder interest in property during life to his or her heirs or next of kin, the remainder interest is null and void and the transferor is deemed to have retained a reversion in the transferee property. The rule applies only if the words "heirs" or "next of kin" are used.

Consider the implications of the conveyor-heir rule in a drafting context. For example, in preparing a trust, it is common to anticipate the possibility—albeit unlikely—that none of the contemplated beneficiaries will be on hand at the termination of the trust. In such cases, it is appropriate to provide an alternative taker, oftentimes heirs of the settlor of the trust.

Problems

[¶ 5240]

1. After provisions for the income to be paid to his son, Claude, for life, Dimitri's trust provided that the trust will terminate upon Claude's death and the property be distributed "to my [Dimitri's] then living lineal descendants *per stirpes* but if none, to my [Dimitri's] heirs at law." Dimitri was survived by his son, Claude, and by his brother, Ben. Dimitri's will gave "all to my brother, Ben." Claude's will gave all to his physician, "Doc," who treated him in his final illness, "to be his forever." Doc claims the balance remaining in the trust. Ben also claims the balance in the trust. Evaluate the claims.

    Would Ben's claim be better if Dimitri had provided that his "heirs-at-law are to be determined as if I [Dimitri] died on the date the trust terminates"?

2. During her lifetime Doris has established an irrevocable trust. Doris is to get all of the income from the trust and, at her death, the trust is to terminate. Upon termination, the trust property is to be distributed "to such persons as I shall select by provision in my will; and in default of effective selection, to my heirs at law." Doris has announced that she wishes to terminate the trust, but the trustee refuses. Can you help Doris? See Stewart v. Merchants Nat'l Bank of Aurora, 3 Ill.App.3d 337, 278 N.E.2d 10 (1972).

E. EXPRESS AND IMPLIED CONDITIONS OF SURVIVORSHIP

[¶ 5251]

Much more common than the problems created by either the Rule in Shelley's Case or the conveyor-heir rule are the problems presented by express and implied conditions of survivorship. For example, take the case where H's will contains the following gift:

> All of my estate in trust for my spouse, W. Upon her death the trust will terminate and be distributed to my then living lineal descendants *per stirpes*.

¶ 5251

Assume H's three children, Bud, Chip, and Daffy, survive H, but Chip dies before his mother, W. Chip's will gave "all to my friend LeRoy," and LeRoy claims Chip's share of the trust. Chip's share is also claimed by his child, Chaps, who was excluded from Chip's will but who claims as an heir of H.

In considering the rules which impact the creation of future interests, remember that the Rule in Shelley's Case and the Rule Against Perpetuities are the most significant rules which are *rules of law* and not *rules of construction*. The other rules, for the most part, give way to the decedent's intention. Such is the case as to the rules regarding express and implied conditions of survivorship. The decedent's intention controls, but if the decedent's intention cannot be determined, the courts will apply certain constructional preferences. These constructional preferences can be expressed in these terms: (1) The law will not imply a condition of survivorship and (2) Whenever an instrument contains an express condition of survivorship, the law will insist that the person or persons whose interest is conditioned on survivorship survive the expiration of all prior estates. These principles can be easily illustrated by the following two cases.

1. Estate of Ferry, 55 Cal.2d 776, 13 Cal.Rptr. 180, 361 P.2d 900, 90 A.L.R.2d 300 (1961), in which J.S. Ferry's will established a trust for the benefit of his son Joseph. The trust was to terminate upon alternative events: either 20 years from the date of J.S.'s death or upon son Joseph's death, whichever occurred first. If Joseph was living at the termination of the trust, he was to receive possession of the residue, but if he died before the 20–year period elapsed, then the residue was to go to Joseph's wife and issue, but if "no wife or issue," then to J.S.'s sister, Mary. Son Joseph and sister Mary survived J.S. Ferry. However, Mary predeceased Joseph. At Joseph's later death, Joseph's will gave "everything to Clarence and Joseph Telles."

The dispute was between Mary's son and daughter and the Telles. Both claimed the balance of the trust property. The court, reasoning that the law will not imply a condition of survivorship, held that Mary's son and daughter were to take the remaining trust property.

2. In re Gautier's Will, 3 N.Y.2d 502, 169 N.Y.S.2d 4, 146 N.E.2d 771 (1957), where the court said:

> The controversy revolves about the term "surviving" as used in paragraph Ninth, subdivision (b), and calls upon us to say whether the essential survivorship refers to survival merely to the death of the testator * * * or * * * to the death of the life beneficiary.

> * * * [At issue was half of the testator's estate, which was to] be divided into eight shares, of which four were to be in trust for his sister Clara Bird for life and, after her death, each of said four shares was to be held as a separate trust for the benefit of her four children, his nephews and nieces, Oliver Bird, Claire Bird Lewis, Dudley Bird and Marie Louise Bird, during the life of each of them. On his or her death, the will continues, "the one share held in trust for the one so dying shall cease and the share of such nephew or niece shall be paid to his or her children, if any, and in the event that the nephew or niece dies leaving no children

the share shall be divided equally amongst his or her brothers and sisters surviving."

The testator's sister Clara, the primary life beneficiary as to four shares, died some years after her brother. Upon her death, trusts were set up for the benefit of each of her children, the named Oliver, Claire, Dudley and Marie Louise. On the death of Oliver and Claire, the corpus of each of the trusts set up for them went to their respective children. Marie Louise died in 1955 leaving no issue and is survived only by Dudley who is still alive.

The court stated, "There just cannot be any question that the testator intended the remainderman, in order to share in the corpus of the trust, outlive the life beneficiary, not himself." Since only Dudley survived the childless Marie Louise, the court held that only Dudley was entitled to the entire corpus of the trust set up for her benefit.

F. CLASS GIFTS

[¶ 5301]

1. INTRODUCTION

Often a donor makes gifts to one or more persons as a group. Sometimes the donor intends to make a gift to each member of the group as individuals and has chosen to group the intended beneficiaries only for convenience of reference. In the case of such groupings, each member of the group would take his or her gift as a tenant in common with the other members of the group in cases where the subject matter of the gift did not lend itself to division. An example of such a gift would be a gift to "Tom, Dick, and Harry."

In the case of a gift by will where one of the individuals included in the group did not survive the testator, the gift to that individual would lapse but would be subject to any applicable anti-lapse statute. For a discussion of lapse and anti-lapse statutes, see ¶ 3451.

Whether a gift in a will to "my children" is a gift to the children living at the date the will is executed or to the children living at the testator's date of death is unclear. It becomes even more unclear when, for example, the testator provides for a life estate to her spouse, followed by a remainder to her brother's children. Does she mean the children of her brother who survive the life tenant or was she referring to the children living at the date the will was signed? Essentially, the question is, was the testator group-minded such that she contemplated that some persons within the group will die before the property was distributed and that additional persons to whom the group language applied would come into being? If this was the case, the testator's gift will be deemed a class gift and a set of rules will apply that are different from those applied if the testator is deemed to have made a gift to individuals and used group language merely as a convenient means of reference.

More often, gifts in which group language is used are not gifts to specific individuals but to one or more classes of persons. In such cases, the issue is to ascertain who are the class members. Obviously, the donor should specify the class boundaries in the dispositive instrument. Unfortunately, the class boundaries often are not clearly established in the instrument, probably because the draftsperson did not foresee all of the possibilities. In such cases, the courts must look for the donor's intention and, if it is unclear, must resort to rules of construction.

Determination of the class boundaries is a function of the following three questions: (1) When does the class open? (2) When is the minimum membership of the class determined? and (3) When does the class close?

[¶ 5309]

2. DRAFTING BY FORMULA

Even the most casual review of a collection of future interest cases will suggest that much drafting is done in stream of consciousness fashion, with the draftsperson attempting to get it all in one paragraph, if not one sentence. This kind of drafting should be a thing of the past with the advent of the word processor. The word processor offers: (1) the ability to quickly and easily number paragraphs and (2) access to the discipline of outlining a dispositive scheme.

Structurally, think in terms of providing separate paragraphs to accomplish the following functions—and strictly adhere to the function of the paragraphs in preparing that paragraph: (1) What?—Establish the trust; (2) Who?—Describe the persons to whom and the circumstances under which income and principal is to be distributed during the continuance of the trust; (3) When?—Have the trust end on the occurrence of one or more conditions; and (4) Who?—Provide for distribution upon the ending of the trust. Thus, in the simplest of terms, think of the paragraphs that begin: (1) "I give the following property to my trustee"; (2) "During the continuance of the trust, the trustee shall pay so much or all of the income and principal to the beneficiary [quarterly] [in the discretion of the trustee] [as needed for the beneficiary's health, education, maintenance, and support]"; (3) "The trust will terminate upon [the death of the beneficiary] [the first to occur of the following events] [the last to occur of the following events]"; and (4) "Upon termination, the property then constituting the trust estate will be distributed *per stirpes* to the then living lineal descendants of [the beneficiary] [some other person]."

The solution to many, many drafting problems is always to: (1) think in terms of gifts to classes of persons, e.g., lineal descendants and (2) remember to find a common denominator, i.e., a common ancestor to whom reference can be made in making the gift to lineal descendants of that ancestor. The outlining function of the word processor provides the necessary discipline to accomplish this kind of structured drafting.

Problem

[¶ 5340]

1. In each of the following cases, (1) from the language included in the disposition, determine the donor's intention and (2) redraft the dispositive

provision so as to eliminate the controversy which developed. Note that often the donor's intention cannot be ascertained from the language used in the dispositive provision. Probably more often than not the donor did not correctly anticipate the configuration of the cast of claimants which prevailed. Perhaps, too, in many cases a donor will have had conflicting and irreconcilable objectives.

(a) First Nat'l Bank v. Evenson, 274 Wis. 459, 80 N.W.2d 408 (1957):

> Third, I give, devise and bequeath to my grandchildren the sum of Fifty Thousand Dollars ($50,000), said sum to be placed in trust by my executor in a trust company or bank exercising trust powers, the income from the principal being allowed to accumulate until said grandchildren shall respectively become of age. After each grandchild becomes of age he is to receive the income which accumulates on his share, said income to be paid to him annually until he reaches the age of thirty years. After each grandchild reaches the age of thirty years he is to be paid his full share of the principal sum of this bequest together with the interest which has accumulated thereon.

At the time of his death, the decedent left six grandchildren, four of whom were born prior to the execution of the will and two of whom were born after the execution. Subsequently, but before the eldest of the six attained the age of 30, three additional grandchildren were born. The court held that these three additional grandchildren were included in the class since the class did not close until one class member actually reached the age of 30.

(b) Crow v. Marshall & Ilsley Bank, 17 Wis.2d 181, 116 N.W.2d 106 (1962):

> The remainder of my estate is then to be held in trust until such time as the youngest of my great nephews and nieces is fifty (50) years old. The interest from it to be divided among them every year. At the time the youngest great-nephew or niece is 50 years old the residue of my estate is to be divided among them all share and share alike.

G. DEATH WITHOUT ISSUE

[¶ 5351]

The draftsperson creates troublesome problems when a disposition is made to a named person, followed by a gift over if such person should "die without issue." This kind of drafting is understandable in that many clients wish to provide gifts over to an alternate taker if the donee dies and the donee's lineal line is extinguished. For example, it is not uncommon for parents to want their property to go to their children, but if any child dies: (1) before the death of the surviving parent and (2) without lineal descendants of the child who predeceases the surviving parent, the parents want the deceased child's share to be distributed to the remaining children.

¶ 5351

Problems

[¶ 5390]

1. Did the immediately preceding sentence in the text seem unduly complex? Could it be simplified for inclusion in a will so that it reads, "but if any child dies without lineal descendants, that child's share will be distributed to the remaining children"? What if a child dies before the parents but is survived by lineals who then die before the surviving parent? Who are the so-called "remaining children"? Is the use of that term ambiguous?

Could the entire disposition be simplified by including the following provision in the will of both parents: "All to my spouse if my spouse survives me for 30 days; otherwise to my then living lineal descendants"?

2. Consider Goldberger v. Goldberger, 34 Del.Ch. 237, 102 A.2d 338 (1954), in which the testator's will provided in pertinent part:

> Second: I give, devise and bequeath all my property and estate of whatsoever nature whether real, personal or mixed and wheresoever situate, unto my two beloved children, Saul Harold Goldberger, and Frances Estelle Shore, absolutely and in fee simple, share and share alike; should either of my said children die leaving issue, then the share of such child so dying shall go to his or her issue; should either of *my* said children die without issue, then the share of the child so dying shall go to the survivor.

Saul and Francis survived the testator and claim that they hold a fee simple as tenants in common in the testator's property. Saul and Francis' children (grandchildren of the testator) also survived the testator and are represented by a guardian ad litem. Satisfy yourself that you understand the basis of the dispute in *Goldberger* and suggest an appropriate restructuring of the dispositive provision which gives rise to the uncertainty so as to eliminate the controversy.

H. THE RULE AGAINST PERPETUITIES

[¶ 5401]

1. INTRODUCTION

The Rule Against Perpetuities is a judicial expression of society's conclusion that the dead should not control for *too long* the enjoyment of the property they leave behind. The Rule is as vital and *as relevant* today as it was during its period of formulation.

The commonly accepted expression of the Rule is that formulated by Professor John Chipman Gray in Rule Against Perpetuities 191 (4th ed. 1942):

> NO INTEREST IS GOOD UNLESS IT MUST VEST, IF AT ALL, NOT LATER THAN TWENTY–ONE YEARS AFTER SOME LIFE IN BEING AT THE CREATION OF THE INTEREST.

The following observations about the Rule should be noted:

¶ **5390**

1. *It applies to possibilities.* An interest which *may* not vest within the period of the Rule is void. That is, the interest is void unless it is absolutely certain that it cannot vest outside the period. The fact that the interest does in fact vest within the period of the Rule is irrelevant. The possibility that the interest might not vest within the period of the Rule is to be determined from the terms of the instrument and the facts which exist at the effective date of the instrument.

2. *It is a rule of law and not a rule of construction.*

3. *The Rule is applied remorselessly without regard to the donor's intentions.*

4. *The Rule is applied with mathematical precision.* Yet many persons find it difficult to apply the Rule. Even the California Supreme Court, in Lucas v. Hamm, 56 Cal.2d 583, 15 Cal.Rptr. 821, 364 P.2d 685 (1961), cert. den., 368 U.S. 987 (1962), concluded that it was *not* malpractice for a draftsperson to unknowingly violate the Rule. Nonetheless, the reason so many of us have difficulty with the Rule is our inability to project creatively into the future to anticipate the possibility that an interest might not vest within the period of the Rule.

5. *The Rule applies to both equitable and legal interests.*

6. *The Rule applies to both real and personal property.*

[¶ 5409]

2. PROCEDURE

In order to apply the Rule Against Perpetuities in a drafting context, the following procedure might be helpful:

1. Determine if the interest being created is a contingent remainder, executory interest, or vested remainder subject to open. If it is, the Rule has possible application.

2. Next, position yourself mentally at the effective date of the instrument creating the interest.

3. Ask yourself whether vesting of the interest is tied expressly to any life or lives. If so, those lives are *postponing lives.* The postponing lives will also be the *measuring lives* if they are all in being at the effective date of the instrument creating the interest.

4. If there are no express lives, look for dependent lives. Ask yourself whether vesting of the interest in one or more persons now in being or who could come into being is postponed by any other life or lives. Consider, for example, the case of a gift of a life estate to B followed by a remainder to "B's children." At present, B has two children, and their interests are vested at the effective date of the instrument. B, however, could always have more children, who would be also included in the class of persons referred to as "B's children." Therefore, using the term "postponed" in its technical Perpetuities sense, vest-

ing of the interest is postponed by the continuation of B's life. Thus, B becomes a postponing life.

5. If there are one or more postponing lives, ask yourself whether all of the postponing lives are in being at the effective date of the instrument which creates the interest.

   a. If the answer is yes, then the postponing lives are *measuring lives* and the interest is valid.

   b. If the answer is no, then there are no *measuring lives* and the interest will be void unless it must vest, if at all, not later than 21 years after the effective date of the instrument creating the interest.

[¶ 5417]

3. CLASS GIFTS

As mentioned earlier, the Rule Against Perpetuities is applied to class gifts, including vested remainders subject to open. The Rule will void an *entire* gift if there is any possibility that the interest could vest in a class member beyond the period of the Rule. Put another way, if either the minimum or maximum membership of the class may not be determined within the period of the Rule, the class gift as a whole is void. Expressed even more simply, the interests of all class members must vest within the period of the Rule or the gift to the entire class is void.

There are two exceptions to this "bad-as-to-one, bad-as-to-all" rule, namely: (1) If separate gifts are provided each member of the class, the interests which timely vest will be valid and (2) Occasionally a settlor will divide a class into subclasses—interests which timely vest in subclasses will be valid.

Consider the following dispositive provision in T's will:

To C for life, remainder to such of C's children who attain age 25.

C is alive and has two children, X and Y. At T's death X is then age 26 and Y is age 25. The class gift is void! C could have a child, Z, after T's death. All the persons living at T's death could die before Z attained four years of age. The gift to Z would not vest in interest until more than 21 years after the death of the last to die of those persons living at T's death.

The class closing rules do not help. The class will not close until C's death. Z will then be in being (or, barring sperm banks, Z will never be in being). Z will be in the class with a vested interest subject to divestment.

The effect is that the gift to X and Y is void.

[¶ 5425]

4. POWERS OF APPOINTMENT

Although seemingly not within the literal language of the Rule Against Perpetuities, powers of appointment also have perpetuity implications. The rules are relatively simple. The first step is to classify powers as either: (1)

¶ 5409

general powers presently exercisable or (2) general testamentary powers and special or limited powers. The second step is to determine whether the power is being tested for: (1) validity at creation or (2) validity at the time of exercise.

[¶ 5433]

a. *General Powers Presently Exercisable*

Dad's will gives Junior the income for life from a trust and the power to withdraw principal in unlimited amounts from the trust during life as well as the power to select the ultimate recipient of the trust property after Junior's death. This is a general power presently exercisable. It can be inspected for validity at the time of Dad's death (validity at creation). The inquiry is as to whether the powerholder will acquire the power within 21 years after some life or lives in being at the creation of the interest. Since Junior is alive at Dad's death, Junior acquires the power at that time for purposes of the rule, and the power is valid.

Suppose Junior exercises the power, say, by will, in favor of his children and grandchildren for life, with the remainder *per stirpes* to those of his lineal descendants who survive the death of the last to die of his children and grandchildren. The power can be inspected for validity at the time of Junior's exercise of the power (validity at exercise). The question is whether there is any possibility that the remainder will vest in a lineal descendant more than 21 years after the death of some person living at Junior's death. Which person? Some person reasonably related to the interest being tested? How about Junior's children and grandchildren? Fine. The children and grandchildren postpone vesting in the lineal descendants—and, thus, could be described as postponing lives. The question is reframed in terms of whether there is any possibility that: (1) one of Junior's grandchildren will come into being after Junior dies and (2) that the afterborn grandchild will outlive, by more than 21 years, all of the children and grandchildren who were living at Junior's death. If the answer is yes, the gift to the lineal descendants is void under the rule against perpetuities.

Suppose, by way of further example, Uncle gives Nephew the income for life from a trust and also gives Nephew the right to withdraw the entire trust property from the trust at any time as well as the right to choose who will receive any trust property remaining in the trust at Nephew's death. Nephew creates a trust for his children for life with the remainder to those of Nephew's grandchildren who are living at the death of the last to die of Nephew's children. The interests created by Nephew are valid since all of Nephew's children will be in being within nine months of Nephew's death (unless Nephew has contributed to a sperm bank).

In summary, the rules as to general powers presently exercisable are as follows:

1. The power is valid at the time of creation if it will be acquired by the powerholder or becomes exercisable not more than 21 years after some life or lives in being at the creation of the power and

2. An interest created by the exercise of a power is valid if the interest will vest, if at all, not later than 21 years after some life or lives in being at the exercise of the power. For these purposes, the "life or lives" are those specified by the powerholder and, if none are specified, the reference will be to lives reasonably related to the interest, meaning lives that postpone vesting of the interest. The interest is valid if all of the postponing lives are in being at the exercise of the power; the interest is void if any of the possible postponing lives are not in being at the exercise of the power.

In conjunction with the exercise of the power by Junior, Junior validates the interests created by his exercise of the power by providing, in his dispositive instrument, a perpetuities savings clause that provides "notwithstanding other provisions of this instrument," the trust for Junior's children and Junior's grandchildren will terminate at the death of the last to die of Junior's children and grandchildren who are living on the date of Junior's death.

[¶ 5441]

b. *General Testamentary Powers and Limited Powers*

i. *Validity at Creation*

Suppose Mom's will creates a trust for her child, Sugar, for life with remainder to such persons as Sugar shall select by provision in her will. This is a general testamentary power and would be valid since Sugar will exercise the power or not exercise the power within her own lifetime—and she is a life in being at the creation of the power.

At the same time, Mom's sister, Aunt, creates a trust in her will. The trust is for Niece for life and then for Niece's children for life, with remainder to such of Niece's lineal descendants as shall be selected by the last to die of Niece's children. This is a special or limited power of appointment and would be void. Not only could the power be exercised by a child of Niece who was not in being at Aunt's death, but it could also be exercised more than 21 years after the death of all of the children of Niece who were in being at Aunt's death. Those two factors, taken together, void the power.

In summary, the rule is that a general testamentary power or a special or limited power is void if there is any possibility that the power will be exercised more than 21 years after some life or lives in being at the creation of the power.

As for Aunt's will, she could have avoided the problem by including a provision in her will that begins with "notwithstanding any other provision of this will," the power given to Niece's children can only be exercised: (1) by a child of Niece who is living at the death the Aunt or (2) by a child of Niece who was not living at the death of Aunt if the afterborn child exercises that power within 21 years after the death of the last to die of those children of Niece who were living at Aunt's death.

¶ 5433

[¶ 5449]

ii. Validity at Exercise

Suppose Mom's child, Sugar, exercises the power to create a trust for her children for life with remainder *per stirpes* to Sugar's then living lineal descendants. At first glance the gift of the remainder is void. All of Sugar's lineal descendants will possibly not be determined until the death of the last to die of Sugar's children. The last to die of Sugar's children could be a child born after Mom's death who outlives Sugar's other children by more than 21 years.

There is relief here in the form of the Second Look doctrine. Final judgment as to the validity of the interests created by Sugar's exercise of the power will be postponed until Sugar's death. At that time, we'll take a second look. If all of Sugar's children were in being at Mom's death, the gift to Sugar's lineal descendants will be valid. However, if one of Sugar's children was born after Mom's death, Sugar's gift to her lineal descendants will be void.

Thus, the rule is that the interest created by the exercise of a general testamentary power and a special or limited power is void if there is any possibility that the interest will vest more than 21 years after some life or lives in being at the time the power was created, not the date the power was exercised. Final judgment, however, will be deferred in these matters until the date the power is exercised. At that time, we'll take a second look, and if all of the lives that could possibly postpone vesting were in being at the creation of the power, the interests created by the exercise of the power will be valid. The key to this analysis is understanding that Sugar, when exercising the power given her by Mom, is filling a gap in Mom's will, i.e., filling a blank that Mom left in her will. Accordingly, Sugar's exercise of the power "relates back" to Mom's death for perpetuities purposes.

Sugar could have solved the problem she created by stipulating in her will that "notwithstanding any other provision of this will," the trust for the benefit of Sugar's children will terminate not later than 21 years after the death of the last to die of those children of Sugar's who were living at the date of Mom's death.

Problems

[¶ 5485]

1. Alonzo's will created a trust for the benefit of his son, Dennis, for life and then for the life of Dennis's spouse, if any, with remainder to Dennis's lineal descendants *per stirpes*. Alonzo was survived by Dennis. Dennis had never married. However, 30 years later, finally freeing himself of Alonzo's domination, Dennis took a bride, Beauty, age 20, and gave rise to nine children. Is the gift to Beauty valid? Is the gift to Dennis's lineals valid?

2. Ten years before her death, Bonnie created an irrevocable trust for the benefit of her child, Renee, for life and after Renee's death, for the benefit

¶ 5485

of Renee's children for life with remainder to such of Renee's lineal descendants "as Renee shall select by provision in her will." Any invalidity here?

3. Fifteen years before her death, Elaine created an irrevocable trust for the benefit of her children, including children born after the creation of the trust. At the time, she had four children. The trust was to continue until the death of the last to die of her children (including afterborns). Upon termination, the trust property was to be distributed to those lineal descendants of Elaine selected by the last to die of her children. If there is any invalidity here, how could it be cured?

[¶ 5525]

5. ALTERNATIVES TO THE COMMON LAW RULE AGAINST PERPETUITY

The common law Rule Against Perpetuities states that no interest is good unless it must vest, if at all, not less than twenty-one years after some life in being at the creation of the interest. Some states have adopted an alternative Rule Against Perpetuities called the Uniform Statutory Rule Against Perpetuities (USRAP) (amended 1990), 8B U.L.A. 236–92 (2001). Promulgated in 1986, the USRAP provides that an interest is valid if it would be valid under the common law Rule or if the interest will either vest or terminate at the end of ninety years. The original version of the USRAP allowed the settlor to create an interest that terminates on the later of the expiration of the common law Rule *or* 90 years. But after the Treasury objected to this ability to elect the longer of two periods, citing its distaste for the possibility of more easily extending the possible length of a trust and thereby the length of time of the exemption from the generation-skipping transfer tax, § 1(e) was added to USRAP in 1990. Section 1(e) disallows this "longer of" approach. If the settlor does elect this approach, section 1(e) invalidates the election and defaults to the common law Rule. But not every USRAP state has adopted section 1(e) and, although the Treasury has stated that it will allow the ninety-year period as the equivalent of the common law Rule, it is uncertain what the Treasury will do if the settlor adopts the "longer of" approach.

The Treasury Regulations have not addressed the *creation* of a "longer of" trust, but they *did* address the *exercise of a special power of appointment* that takes this approach in the 1995 version of Reg. § 26.2652–1(a)(4). If the donee used the "longer of" approach when exercising a special power of appointment to appoint in further trust, the exercise would be treated as a new transfer, and the donee would be subject to federal estate or gift tax if the exercise would "postpone or suspend the vesting, absolute ownership, or power of alienation of an interest in property" beyond the common law perpetuities period. This provision was deleted in 1997 because the Treasury believed that the wording could be misconstrued to allow the initial transferor to avoid the generation skipping tax if the gift was valid under the common law Rule. So there is no longer any guidance regarding the treatment of trusts that take the "longer of" approach. But this is not an issue that the Treasury is likely to allow to remain dormant, particularly in the face of legislation in

¶ 5485

many states eliminating the Rule altogether (see ¶ 5600), and the reader should be aware that there will most likely be another attempt to curb both the "longer of" approach and so-called perpetual dynasty trusts.

Perpetual dynasty trusts concern the Treasury more than those that use the "longer of" approach because of the enormous tax avoidance opportunity that could result from the developing trend of repealing the Rule *altogether* for certain transactions. With no Rule Against Perpetuities, a donor could create a trust that would continue, quite literally, in perpetuity, leveraging the $2 million generation skipping tax exemption—$3.5 million in 2009—far more effectively than Congress ever anticipated.

[¶ 5600]

6. REPEAL OF THE RULE AGAINST PERPETUITY

In 1983, South Dakota became the first state in the United States to repeal the Rule Against Perpetuities, requiring that the trustee have the power to sell the trust assets or that one or more persons in being have unlimited power to terminate the trust. S.D. Codified Laws Ann. §§ 43–5–1, 43–5–8 (2004). Delaware followed suit in 1995, repealing the Rule for personal property held in an irrevocable trust but retaining its 110 year limitation on irrevocable trusts holding real property. Del. Code Ann. tit. 25 § 503(b) (1989, Supp. 2004). And neither of these two states impose an income tax on trusts— a fact that can have a significant effect on the value of these dynasty trusts of potentially infinite duration.

Wisconsin has a rule similar to that of South Dakota, requiring that the trustee have the power to sell the trusts assets or that one or more persons in being have an unlimited power to terminate the interest. Wis. Stat. Ann. § 700.16 (West 2001). Wisconsin trusts are subject to a state income tax. Idaho repealed the Rule for personal property but has retained a modified version of the Rule for real property that has a period of twenty-five years plus some life in being at creation of the interest. Idaho Code Ann. § 55–111 (2003). Idaho trusts are subject to an income tax if three of five factors is satisfied. These factors will generally be met by Idaho residents but are more easily avoided by nonresidents with careful planning, allowing Idaho to generate revenue on the trusts most likely to be created in-state despite the income tax while attracting more out-of-state trust business.

Illinois has promulgated a Rule that is essentially elective. The Rule does not apply to trusts that, by their terms, are not subject to the Rule and that grant the trustee the power to sell, lease or mortgage trust property for any time beyond the period of the Rule. 765 Ill. Comp. Stat. Ann. 305/4 (West 2001). Illinois imposed an income tax on trusts created by residents but no income tax on trusts created by nonresidents. Maryland has a similar elective provision. Md. Code Ann., [Est. & Trusts] § 11–102 (LexisNexis 2001).

In 1997, possibly seeking to establish the state as a center for the situs and administration of trusts, Alaska essentially repealed the Rule, providing that a nonvested property interest is invalid unless the interest is in a trust and all or part of the trust can be distributed, in the discretion of the trustee, to someone living when the trust is created. In 2004, the Alaska Legislature then repealed the 1997 version and passed a new statute that attempts to avert statutory construction problems. Under the new statute, property interests subject to a special power of appointment must vest or terminate within 1,000 years. Alaska Stat. § 34.27.051 (2004). The second part of Alaska's plan to coax foreign trust business is its aggressive scheme to protect debtors from their creditors by allowing debtors to create self-settled asset-protection trusts. ¶¶ 21,300–315. An added bonus is the fact that Alaska trusts are not subject to state income tax. For related material, see ¶¶ 7478, 10,119, 10,209, 11,089, and 21,870.

One practical result of the repeal of the Rule Against Perpetuities is that a person can create a dynasty trust that could potentially provide for future generations indefinitely. Whether many will wish to exercise such dead hand control, to impose their will on successive generations, is yet to be determined. The trade off, though, is the asset protection potential of such trusts for successive generations, generations able, as a result of such trusts, to have the benefit of limited tax liability, the prospect of disappointing creditors, and possibly reduced intensity in property settlement disputes upon marital dissolution.

¶ 5600

Part II

TAX CONSIDERATIONS

Chapter 6

TAXABLE TRANSFERS: AN INTRODUCTION

A. OBJECTIVES

[¶ 6001]

The federal gift tax and the federal estate tax, set forth in Internal Revenue Code Chapters 11 and 12, respectively, are taxes imposed on individuals who exercise their privilege of transferring their property during their life or at their death. More simply, the estate and gift taxes are taxes on *transfers*. Reg. §§ 20.0–2(a), 25.2501–1(a)(1).

Note that the estate and gift taxes are not imposed on gross transfers but on *net transfers*. For gift tax purposes, net transfers are gross transfers reduced by the $12,000 per donee per annum exclusion, as adjusted for inflation ($10,000 for transfers prior to 2003 and $3,000 for transfers prior to 1982) (§ 2503(b)); the gift-splitting provisions (§ 2513); the charitable deduction (§ 2522); and the marital deduction (§ 2523). (For a more complete discussion, see ¶ 7351.) Net transfers for gift tax purposes are referred to as *taxable gifts*. § 2503(a). Thus, it is important to distinguish between *taxable gifts* and *gross gifts* when discussing the federal gift tax because the tax is imposed only on *taxable gifts*. See § 2502(a).

Similarly, the estate tax is not imposed on gross transfers. Gross transfers for estate tax purposes are referred to as the *gross estate* of the decedent. See § 2033. The tax is imposed on the *taxable estate*, which is the gross estate reduced by debts, taxes, and administration expenses (§§ 2053, 2054), and certain policy deductions such as the charitable deduction (§ 2055), and the marital deduction (§ 2056).

Problem

[¶ 6040]

Why does Congress allow a deduction for debts, administration expenses, and taxes in fixing the estate tax base, the so-called taxable estate? Why do we refer to the charitable and marital deductions as policy deductions? *(Hint: Isn't there a parallel scheme in computing the federal income tax base, so-called taxable income?)*

The material which follows in this chapter will focus on creating an awareness of what constitutes a gross transfer for gift tax purposes and what is included in a decedent's gross estate. There are no hard and fast rules but merely principles which, when applied with attention to applicable policy considerations, should yield fairly predictable results in the majority of cases. In the meantime, keep in mind the relationship between *gross transfers* and *taxable gifts* and the *gross estate* and the *taxable estate*.

B. POLICY CONSIDERATIONS

[¶ 6051]

The estate tax is imposed on transferors. So, too, is the gift tax. What possible justification is there for a tax on the exercise of the privilege of transferring property? Could it be said that the estate tax is designed to redistribute wealth? Or is it designed to prevent the concentration of wealth in the hands of a few? Perhaps it should be seen as merely another source of federal revenue. Yet, estate and gift tax collections totaled little more than $27.2 billion in fiscal year 2002, slightly off the high of $29.2 billion in 2000.

What role does the federal gift tax have? Is its role simply one of preventing emasculation of the estate tax by imposing a tax cost on those lifetime transfers which tend to bring about a diminution of the transferor's estate?

On the other hand, could it not be said that the gift tax contributes to maintaining the integrity of the income tax? How? By imposing a tax cost on shifts of property to others for purposes of causing the income from that property to be taxed to the transferee rather than the transferor? Oftentimes the transferor and transferee are within the same family unit and, after the transfer, the transferor continues to have effective control over the transferred property. Thus, but for the gift tax cost, such property shifts for income tax shifting purposes would be relatively painless to the transferor. (Support for this analysis may well be readily found in the 2001 decision by Congress to *disengage* the estate and gift tax exemptions, exemptions that had been in lock-step since 1977. That is, the estate tax exemption—technically the "applicable exclusion amount," § 2010(c)—is scheduled to increase to $3.5 million in 2009 and the estate tax itself is repealed for 2010 (before returning in 2011 with only a $1 million exemption. The gift tax exemption—technically, again, the "applicable exclusion amount", § 2505(a)—is fixed at $1 million *and the gift tax is not ever repealed* under present law, *i.e.*, it continues *forever* (or at least until Congress decides to do something else) with a $1 million exemption.

In 2005, 39,481 estate tax returns were filed (down from 114,000 in 2002), 18,431 of which were nontaxable. Only 760 were estates of more than $20 million, and only 498 were taxable. In 2004, 224,987 gift tax returns were filed (down from 282,600 in 2002), 219,993 of which were non taxable.

¶ 6051

C. FORMULATION OF THE GIFT TAX RULE

[¶ 6101]

While the gift tax is imposed on transfers, other requirements are that a *shift of dominion and control* take place and that the transfer be *complete* during the transferor's life. Reg. §§ 25.2511–1(a) and (g)(1) and 25.2511–2(a) provide:

The gift tax applies to a transfer by way of gift whether the transfer is in trust or otherwise, whether the gift is direct or indirect, and whether the property is real or personal, tangible or intangible. For example, a taxable transfer may be effected by the creation of a trust, the forgiving of a debt, the assignment of a judgment, the assignment of the benefits of an insurance policy, or the transfer of cash, certificates of deposit, or Federal, State or municipal bonds.

* * *

Donative intent on the part of the transferor is not an essential element in the application of the gift tax to the transfer. The application of the tax is based on the objective facts of the transfer and the circumstances under which it is made, rather than on the subjective motives of the donor. However, there are certain types of transfers to which the tax is not applicable. It is applicable only to a transfer of a beneficial interest in property. It is not applicable to a transfer of bare legal title to a trustee. A transfer by a trustee of trust property in which he has no beneficial interest does not constitute a gift by the trustee (but such a transfer may constitute a gift by the creator of the trust, if until the transfer he had the power to change the beneficiaries by amending or revoking the trust). The gift tax is not applicable to a transfer for a full and adequate consideration in money or money's worth, or to ordinary business transactions, described in § 25.2512–8.

* * *

The gift tax is not imposed upon the receipt of the property by the donee, nor is it necessarily determined by the measure of enrichment resulting to the donee from the transfer, nor is it conditioned upon ability to identify the donee at the time of the transfer. On the contrary, the tax is a primary and personal liability of the donor, is an excise upon his act of making the transfer, is measured by the value of the property passing from the donor, and attaches regardless of the fact that the identity of the donee may not then be known or ascertainable.

In Pauley v. United States, 459 F.2d 624 (9th Cir. 1972), the court defined: (1) a completed gift as a donation that is out of the dominion and control of the donor and (2) dominion and control as "the retention by the donor of power to direct the disposition or manner of enjoyment of the subject of the gift." Id. at 626. In Macklem v. United States, 757 F.Supp. 6 (D. Conn. 1991), a taxpayer, Mr. Macklem, claimed a deduction for a $3,500 donation to a church located in the taxpayer's residence, founded by the taxpayer, and of which the taxpayer was the sole member. Mr. Macklem was the sole signatory on the church's bank account in which the donation was deposited. The court held the taxpayer was not entitled to a deduction for the gift because Mr. Macklem "possessed sole signatory authority over the account [and] [b]y retaining such power, he exercised dominion and control over the funds which precludes a finding that there was a charitable gift." Id. at 8.

Jury instructions were considered in Heyen v. United States, 731 F.Supp. 1488 (D. Kan. 1990) (see ¶ 6103), where the court was asked to enter a judgment notwithstanding the verdict or order a new trial. While the opinion was unclear, it appeared that the donor, Jennie Owen, whose death was imminent, had made transfers and claimed that each transfer qualified for the $10,000 per donee per annum gift tax exclusion provided by § 2503(b). However, following the transfer, each recipient then retransferred the property to members of the transferor's family. Apparently the IRS challenged the claimed gift tax exclusions, reasoning that the gifts were to members of the transferor's family and that the intermediate or temporary transferees were never intended to be the actual recipients of the property. The case is noted here for the court's discussion of the applicable standards and the judicial history, particularly the notion that substance over form is controlling.

[¶ 6103]

HEYEN v. UNITED STATES

United States District Court, District of Kansas, 1990.
731 F.Supp. 1488.

CROW, District Judge.

In her present motion, as well as throughout the trial, plaintiff has contended the "regulations clearly say that the motive [of the donor] is not to be considered" in gift tax situations. * * * Plaintiff also offers as support of her position the case of Commissioner v. Wemyss, 324 U.S. 303 (1945). In *Wemyss,* the Supreme Court explained the intent of Congress to use the term "gifts" in its broadest meaning and to dispense with the common-law requirement of proving the elusive element of donative intent. 324 U.S at 306. The Supreme Court agreed with the Tax Court that the taxpayer's transfer of stock in consideration for her marriage was not an arm's length transaction made in the ordinary course of business. *Id.* at 307. The Court also observed Congress' desire to recognize certain limited and well-defined exclusions to the gift tax:

> To reinforce the evident desire of Congress to hit all the protean arrangements which the wit of man can devise that are not business transactions within the meaning of ordinary speech, the Treasury Regulations make clear that no genuine business transaction comes within the purport of the gift tax by excluding "a sale, exchange, or other transfer of property made in the ordinary course of business (a transaction which is bona fide, at arm's length, and free from any *donative intent)*." Treasury Regulations 79 (1936 ed) Art 8.

¶ 6103

324 U.S. at 306 (emphasis supplied). This court firmly believes that the plaintiff misunderstands the regulation and the *Wemyss* decision, and that both of the authorities fully support the court's instructions.

Starting with the language of the regulation itself, it states, in pertinent part:

> Donative intent on the part of the transferor is not an essential element in the application of the gift tax to the transfer. The application of the tax is based on the objective facts of the transfer and the circumstances under which it is made, rather than on the subjective motives of the donor.

Reg. § 25.2511–1(g)(1). Contrary to plaintiff's argued interpretation, the regulation does not bar or preclude the consideration of the transferor's donative intent. It merely allows for an application of the gift tax to a gratuitous transfer without specific proof of donative intent In effect, the regulation presumes a donative intent for purposes of gift tax application whenever a property interest is voluntarily transferred in exchange for nothing or for something less than the adequate and full consideration of the property interest.

The reasonableness of this interpretation of the regulation is strengthened by looking to other regulatory language concerning one of the transactions excluded from the gift tax. As stated in § 25.2511–1(g)(1), the gift tax does not apply to "ordinary business transactions described in § 25.2512–8." This exception is defined and explained as "a sale, exchange or other transfer of property made in the ordinary course of business (a transaction which is bona fide, at arm's length, and free from any donative intent), will be considered as made for an adequate and full consideration in money or money's worth." Reg. § 25.2512–8. Simply put, proof of any donative intent will defeat the gift tax exclusion for ordinary business transactions. It is clear that the regulations themselves do not forbid the consideration of donative intent, and, in fact, they expressly recognize it as a factor relevant when the objective circumstances of a transaction otherwise indicate a nontaxable transfer. * * *

Congress imposed the gift tax to protect and supplement the estate tax and income tax. Dickman v. Commissioner, 465 U.S. 330, 338 (1984). Before the *Wemyss* decision, courts had restricted the federal gift tax to transfers motivated by donative intent, an element of common-law gifts. * * * In furtherance of "the evident desire of Congress to hit [with the gift tax] all the protean arrangements which the wit of man can devise," the Supreme Court lifted the restriction of donative intent from the definition of a gift. *Wemyss*, 324 U.S. at 306–308. As a result, the gift tax was not limited to transfers meeting the definition of a common-law gift, but it was to encompass those transfers within the broader, objective definition of a gift. See Fehrs v. United States, 620 F.2d 255, 260 (Ct.Cl. 1980).

Since the *Wemyss* decision, courts have still looked to donative intent, when evident, in determining whether a gift was made. In Kincaid v. United States, 682 F.2d 1220 (5th Cir. 1982), the Government appealed a jury verdict

¶ 6103

that the taxpayer's transfer of her ranch to a closely held corporation in exchange for 34% of the voting stock of the corporation was a nontaxable exchange performed in the ordinary course of business. The taxpayer and her two sons formed the corporation to own and operate the ranch. The Fifth Circuit reversed the district court's denial of the Government's motion for JNOV concluding that "no businesswoman would have entered into this transaction." 682 F.2d at 1225. Confronted with an intra-family transfer, the Fifth Circuit resorted to the general rule that: "when, as here, 'the moving impulse for the * * * transaction was a desire to pass the family fortune on to others[,] [i]t is impossible to conceive of this as even approaching a transaction in the ordinary course of business.' " 682 F.2d at 1225 (quoting Robinette v. Helvering, 318 U.S. 184, 187–88 (1943)). The Fifth Circuit was convinced the taxpayer only had a donative purpose for accepting less value in return for what she transferred. 682 F.2d at 1226.

In the decision of Fehrs v. United States, the Court of Claims affirmed and adopted the trial court's decision that the taxpayers' transfers of shares in return for annuities were a gift, and not an ordinary business transaction, to the extent of the disparity in value between the interests transferred and received. 620 F.2d at 259–60. The court recognized that the breadth of the gift definition "is plainly sufficient to encompass * * * those transfers which accord with the common law concept of gift." 620 F.2d at 260. As in *Kincaid,* an intra-family transfer was involved triggering a special scrutiny of the transaction. It was concluded:

> A close look at the transaction is, therefore, unavoidable; the disparities in value that we ultimately come to, when taken together with the plaintiffs' full control over both ends of the transaction, are inconsistent with any form of property transfer save that of a gift. To put it another way, *since the visible aspects of the transaction do not negate the existence of donative intent,* there exists no ground upon which to conclude that the transaction was prompted solely by business considerations.

620 F.2d at 260 (emphasis supplied).

Finally, the court directs the plaintiff to the decision of Diedrich v. Commissioner, 457 U.S. 191 (1982), which the court cited to the parties at the time of the jury instruction conference. The Supreme Court there held that the donor realizes taxable income when the donee pays the resulting gift taxes. The following critical language is found in that decision:

> When a donor makes a gift to a donee, a "debt" to the United States for the amount of the gift tax is incurred by the donor. Those taxes are as much the legal obligation of the donor as the donor's income taxes. * * * Similarly, when a donee agrees to discharge an indebtedness in consideration of the gift, the person relieved of the tax liability realizes an economic benefit. * * *

> An examination of the donor's intent does not change the character of this benefit. Although intent is relevant in determining whether a gift has been made, subjective intent has not characteristically been a factor in determining whether an individual has realized income.

¶ 6103

Id. at 197 (footnote omitted). This statement on the relevance of donative intent appears to address the context of gift taxes. Furthermore, plaintiff has not come forward with any authority stating that the general principles governing gifts under federal income tax law are inapplicable to gift tax law.

The court believes instruction 16 fairly and plainly states the substance of the above regulations and authorities. Instruction 16 provides:

> A taxable gift is the voluntary and gratuitous transfer of a property interest in exchange for nothing or for something less than the adequate and full value of the property interest. Though not necessary for its existence, a valid gift commonly features two characteristics or elements. First, intent on the part of the donor to make a gift. Second, the donor does everything reasonably permitted by the nature of the property and the circumstances of the transaction to part with ownership of the property.

> For purposes of gift tax law, the general rule is that the subjective motive or donative intent of the transferor is not an essential element to a taxable gift. The law recognizes that the determination of whether a gift was actually made and completed can be based entirely upon the objective facts and circumstances of the transfer. However, any evidence of the donor's intent concerning the transfer may still be considered by you in making these determinations.

> For the gift of property to be complete, the donor must relinquish dominion and control of it leaving himself or herself without any power to change its disposition. Generally, if a donor delivers a properly endorsed stock certificate to the donee or the donee's agent, the gift is completed for gift tax purposes on the date of delivery. Generally, if the donor delivers the certificate to his bank or broker as his agent, or to the issuing corporation or its transfer agent, for transfer in to the name of the donee, the gift is completed on the date the stock is transferred on the books of the corporation.

> You should always remember that it is the substance of the transaction, rather than its form, which should control your determination of a taxable gift.

Plaintiff's contrary construction of the Treasury Regulation and understanding of *Wemyss*, besides being inconsistent with the broad purpose of gift taxes, is entirely untenable and myopic.

Plaintiff also takes issue with the form over substance language contained in instructions 16 and 17. Plaintiff challenges the Government to cite a single gift tax case supporting the language found in instruction 17. This instruction reads:

> The gift tax also applies to gifts indirectly made. Thus, any transaction in which a property interest is gratuitously passed to another, regardless of the means or device employed, constitutes a taxable gift. It is the substance, not the form, of the transaction which controls. Stated another way, what is critical in evaluating the nature of a transaction is its practical effect.

¶ 6103

The first two sentences essentially quote Reg. § 25.2511–1(c)(1). The remaining portion of instruction 17 is simply a restatement of long and well established federal tax law. "To permit the true nature of a transaction to be disguised by mere formalisms, which exist solely to alter tax liabilities, would seriously impair the effective administration of the tax policies of Congress." Commissioner v. Court Holding Co., 324 U.S 331, 334 (1945). As to plaintiff's challenge, the infrequent use of the substance over form doctrine in the area of gift taxes is explained in part by the fact that resorting to this specialized role of objectivity is unnecessary because its purpose is achieved by the objective focus behind the definition of a gift. Yet, at least one court has stated in a gift tax case that "what is crucial is the practical effect of a given transaction." See Tax Analysts and Advocates v. Shultz, 376 F.Supp. 889, 900 (D.D.C. 1974).

Ample evidence was presented for a reasonable jury to reach the same verdict that was rendered in this case. The testimony of several intermediate donees was that they never knew or actually believed that they owned the stock for some period of time. Both the manner and timing of the stock transfers, as well as the eventual recipients of those transfers, provide substantial evidence of Owen's intent to transfer the stock to her heirs before her imminent death. The testimony of certain bank employees who had temporarily received some of Owen's stock demonstrates that Owen may have never parted with ownership and control of the stock during the first transfer. The jury could reasonably infer that because of Owen's intent similar circumstances surrounded the transfer of stock to the other intermediate donees. The evidence shows that, whether it was out of a friendship or a business relationship, the intermediate donees accepted the stock with the understanding that it was to be then transferred to Owen's intended beneficiaries. The jury was given an adequate factual basis to pierce the formalities of these nominal gifts and to attribute the substantive gifts to the heirs of Jennie Owen.

Problems

[¶ 6105]

1. In the following cases should Dad be deemed to have made a taxable gift to Son?

    a. Dad died at age 80 with a gross estate for federal estate tax purposes of $1,000,000. When Dad was 70, he gave Son $400,000 in order to reduce the size of his estate for estate tax purposes. See Reg. § 25.2511–2.

    b. Suppose that Dad, 33 years before his death, paid Son's tuition and living expenses while Son was in law school. Son began law school at age 22 while he was married and the father of a small child. See § 2503(e).

    c. Dad also paid Son's tuition to a preparatory school which Son attended from the time Son was 10 years old until he began college at age 18. Dad also paid all of Son's tuition and room and board while Son was in college.

¶ 6105

d. Suppose that Dad, 30 years before his death, gave Son a new fuel-efficient automobile called a Miser when Son graduated from law school at age 24. Dad paid $15,000 cash for the automobile.

e. Suppose that Dad, having just paid $15,000 for the Miser, immediately sold it to Son for $2,000. See Reg. § 25.2512–8.

f. Instead, suppose that Dad was driving the Miser to Son's graduation when he had an accident for which he was at fault. Dad carried no collision insurance on the Miser and he, therefore, had to bear the entire risk of loss. The wrecking service truck driver offered Dad $500 for the remains of the Miser and Dad accepted. Actually, the Miser had suffered only $1,000 of damage and its market value was $6,000 after the accident and before the repairs.

2. Assume that you conclude that Dad had gift tax liability in one or more of the foregoing transactions. What if he didn't file gift tax returns prior to his death? Is the Internal Revenue Service time barred from asserting liability for such unpaid gift taxes? See § 6501(c)(3).

Must Dad file gift tax returns if his total gifts over his lifetime have not exhausted the unified credit provided by § 2505? See § 6019(a).

3. Would the following statement constitute a workable formulation of the gift tax rule?

The gift tax applies to transfers of property interest by an individual during his or her lifetime, provided the transferor's dominion and control over the transferred property shifts from the transferor during the transferor's lifetime. Excepted from this rule (and the gift tax) will be transfers made in a bargaining context. Where no bargaining context exists, but the transferee gave something of value to the transferor at the time of the transfer, the transferor shall reduce the value of the gift for tax purposes by the value of the thing received.

Can you think of any cases where the foregoing rule would not accomplish the purpose of the gift tax? Would it be a better rule to state simply that the gift tax is imposed on transfers which proceed from disinterested generosity?

D. FORMULATION OF AN ESTATE TAX RULE

[¶ 6151]

1. COMPLETE TRANSFER RULE

While the estate tax and gift tax are separate and distinct taxes, they use the same tax rate schedule and the operative term for application of both taxes is *transfer*. That is, both taxes are imposed upon the exercise of the privilege of transferring property. §§ 2001(a), 2501(a)(1). In that sense both taxes are classified as excise taxes. However, not only must there be a transfer of property for the estate or gift tax to apply, but the tax does not apply until the *shift of dominion and control* is *complete*. While *transfer* is the operative

¶ 6105

term and appears in the portion of the statute imposing the tax, the term *complete* is judge-given.

> *Example.* Claudia created a trust for the benefit of her young son, Alfonso, expressly reserving the right to revoke the trust at any time. Claudia placed $1 million in the trust. Since Claudia can revoke the trust at any time, the transfer is not complete for gift tax purposes and has no gift tax consequences. Of course, at Claudia's death the gift is *complete* because she no longer has the power to revoke the trust. It is at this point that the estate tax is imposed.

Overlapping estate and gift taxes were considered in Smith v. Shaugnessy, 318 U.S. 176 (1943), with the Court concluding that both taxes applied.

[¶ 6153]

SMITH v. SHAUGHNESSY

United States Supreme Court, 1943.
318 U.S. 176.

BLACK, Associate Justice.

The petitioner, age 72, made an irrevocable transfer in trust of 3,000 shares of stock worth $571,000. The trust income was payable to his wife, age 44, for life; upon her death, the stock was to be returned to the petitioner, if he was living; if he was not living, it was to go to such persons as his wife might designate by will, or in default of a will by her, to her intestate successors under applicable New York law. * * *

Three interests are involved here: the life estate, the remainder, and the reversion. The taxpayer concedes that the life estate is subject to the gift tax. The government concedes that the right of reversion to the donor in case he outlives his wife is an interest having value which can be calculated by an actuarial device, and.that it is immune from the gift tax. The controversy, then, reduces itself to the question of the taxability of the remainder.

The taxpayer's principal argument here is that * * * the value of the remainder will be included in the grantor's gross estate for estate tax purposes; and that in the *Sanford* case [308 U.S. 39 (1939)] we intimated a general policy against allowing the same property to be taxed both as an estate and as a gift.

This view, we think, misunderstands our position in the *Sanford* case. As we said there, the gift and estate tax laws are closely related and the gift tax serves to supplement the estate tax. [In a footnote, the court further observed that the "gift tax was passed not only to prevent estate tax avoidance, but also to prevent income tax avoidance through reducing yearly income and thereby escaping the effect of progressive surtax rates. House Report No. 708. 72d Cong., 1st Seas., p. 28."–*Ed.*] We said that the taxes are not "always mutually exclusive," and called attention to § 322 of the 1924 Act there involved (reenacted with amendments in § 801 of the 1932 Act) which charts the course for granting credits on estate taxes by reason of previous payment of gift taxes on the same property. The scope of that provision we need not

¶ 6153

now determine. It is sufficient to note here that Congress plainly pointed out that "some" of the "total gifts subject to gift taxes * * * may be included for estate tax purposes and some not." House Report No. 708, 72d Cong., 1st Sess., p. 45. Under the statute the gift tax amounts in some instances to a security, a form of down-payment on the estate tax which secures the eventual payment of the latter; it is in no sense double taxation as the taxpayer suggests.

We conclude that under the present statute, Congress has provided as its plan for integrating the estate and gift taxes this system of secured payment on gifts which will later be subject to the estate tax.

Unencumbered by any notion of policy against subjecting this transaction to both estate and gift taxes, we turn to the basic question of whether there was a gift of the remainder. The government argues that for gift tax purposes the taxpayer has abandoned control of the remainder and that it is therefore taxable, while the taxpayer contends that no realistic value can be placed on the contingent remainder and that it therefore should not be classed as a gift.

We cannot accept any suggestion that the complexity of a property interest created by a trust can serve to defeat a tax. For many years Congress has sought vigorously to close tax loopholes against ingenious trust instruments. Even though these concepts of property and value may be slippery and elusive they can not escape taxation so long as they are used in the world of business. The language of the gift tax statute, "property * * * real or personal, tangible or intangible," is broad enough to include property, however conceptual or contingent. * * *

* * *

The Treasury regulations, which we think carry out the Act's purpose, made specific provisions for application of the tax to, and determination of the value of, "a remainder * * * subject to an outstanding life estate."

The essence of a gift by trust is the abandonment of control over the property put in trust. The separable interests transferred are not gifts to the extent that power remains to revoke the trust or recapture the property represented by any of them, * * * or to modify the terms of the arrangement so as to make other disposition of the property, * * * In cases such as this, where the grantor has neither the form nor substance of control and never will have unless he outlives his wife, we must conclude that he has lost all "economic control" and that the gift is complete except for the value of his reversionary interest.

[¶ 6159]

2. OVERLAP OF ESTATE AND GIFT TAXES

In cases such as Smith v. Shaughnessy (¶ 6153), where the same transfer attracts both the estate tax and the gift tax, the overlap is reconciled so as to avoid double taxation by crediting the gift tax paid against the estate tax liability. See § 2001(b).

¶ 6153

Example. Lucy deeded her farm to her nephew, Lucky, expressly reserving to herself "the right to all of the income from the farm during my life and the right to occupy" the farm for life. Lucy has made a transfer to Lucky for gift tax purposes of a future interest, namely the right to possession and enjoyment of the farm after Lucy dies. This transfer is complete for gift tax purposes at the time Lucy delivered the deed to Lucky. The gift to Lucky will be valued actuarially, taking into account Lucy's age at the time of the gift. For example, if the gift was made in February, 2004, at a time when the farm had a fair market value of $1 million and Lucy was 60 years of age, the gift of the future interest to Lucky would have a value of $460,660 (assuming a § 7520 mandated interest rate of 4.2 percent and using Table S provided in Reg. § 20.2031–7(d), as required by Reg. § 25.2512–5(a)). The gift tax on the transfer to Lucky is $142,424 (using the rate tables found in § 2001(c), as required by § 2502(a)), but it can be offset by the $345,800 credit provided Lucy by § 2505 (assuming Lucy had made no prior taxable gifts), $345,800 being the gift tax credit shelter that results from the $1 million "applicable exclusion amount".

While Lucky has neither the possession nor the enjoyment of the farm during Lucy's life, his interest in the farm is a valuable property right, so valuable in fact that, if Lucky predeceases Lucy, Lucky's future interest in the farm will be subject to estate tax at his death (and will pass under his will if he has a will or will pass under the intestate laws if Lucky does not have a will).

At Lucy's death—assuming she died in 2005 when the farm had doubled in value to $2 million—the farm is included in Lucy's estate for estate tax purposes. § 2036(a)(1). The farm is included in Lucy's estate at its fair market value of $2 million. The basis of inclusion is that Lucy retained for her life the use and enjoyment of the farm and the estate tax would be emasculated if the estate tax could be avoided by lifetime transfers such as Lucy has made. Including the farm in Lucy's estate meant a minimum estate tax liability of $780,800 (determined by reference to the tax rate table in § 2001(c)), reduced by the estate tax's applicable credit amount of $555,800 (available in 2005 in 2005 when the applicable exclusion allowance under § 2010(a) was $1.5 million), meaning that Lucy's estate would pay $225,000 in estate taxes. Had any gift taxes been paid by Lucy on the gift to Lucky of the future interest, practically speaking, she would have received a credit against her estate tax liability for that payment. See § 2001(b)(2).

(In passing, it might be useful to note that Lucy's retained interest in the farm would be valued at zero for gift tax purposes if the gift had been made to her child, Lackluster, rather than to her nephew, Lucky. Zero valuation, a subject considered at ¶ 12,051, is required by § 2702 whenever a gift is made to a "member of the transferor's family." For these purposes, a child is a member of the family and a nephew is not. See §§ 2702(e), 2704(c)(2).)

[handwritten margin note: Note: "zero valuation"]

Problems

[¶ 6180]

1. Mom, age 55, deeded her farm, Goodacre (having a fair market value of $1,000,000) to Daughter. Following the granting clause, Mom inserted the following provision in the deed: "subject, however, to the right of the grantor to occupy the premises for her life." Should Mom be deemed to have made a gift for gift tax purposes? Mom died 10 years later. She had occupied the farm until her death. Should any part of Goodacre be included in Mom's gross estate for estate tax purposes? See § 2036(a)(1). Assume that at Mom's death, Goodacre has a value of $2.5 million. Note that Mom never filed any gift tax returns during her lifetime.

2. From the immediately preceding problem, would it be possible to formulate the following general rule for application of the estate tax?

   a. There must be a transfer by this decedent either during her life or at her death, and

   b. The decedent's dominion and control over the transferred property interest must shift from the decedent at death.

   What role should "consideration" play in an estate tax general rule? See § 2043(a). Suppose Mom paid $100,000 to an insurance company in return for their promise to pay her an annuity of a fixed amount each month for the remainder of her life. The insurance company's obligation under the contract was to cease at Mom's death. If Mom died four years later, after receiving only $36,000 from the insurance company, is she deemed to have made a taxable gift? To whom? Is anything included in Mom's gross estate? Should there be? See § 2039(a) and (b).

Chapter 7

TRANSFER TAX COMPUTATIONS: POLICY AND PRACTICE

A. OBJECTIVES

[¶ 7001]

Each taxpayer will have both tax and nontax objectives in developing an estate plan. The taxpayer's tax objectives are, obviously, to minimize the impact of taxation on the choices he or she has made for the disposition of his or her property on the occasion of death. Accordingly, *all* tax planning begins with a demonstration to the taxpayer of the impact of taxation on his or her wealth transmission scheme.

Essentially, four federal taxes—the income tax, the gift tax, the estate tax, and the generation-skipping transfer tax—impact taxpayer decision-making. In addition, many of the states have their own income, estate, gift, and, to a lesser extent, generation-skipping taxes. Some of the states have adopted an inheritance tax in lieu of an estate tax. The principal difference between an estate tax and an inheritance tax is that the estate tax is imposed on the donor's exercise of the privilege to *transfer* property. An inheritance tax is imposed on each donee who *receives* property as the result of a gratuitous conveyance by a decedent. Thus, the estate tax (and the gift tax) are taxes on *transfers,* and the inheritance tax is a tax on property *received* from decedents.

The materials in this chapter are designed, principally, to enable the reader to develop an appreciation of the functional relationship of the federal estate tax and the federal gift tax, but the relationship to the income tax and to the various state death taxes is also considered. The federal estate and gift taxes were unified in 1976 through the use of a complex computational model. Accordingly, the relationship between the two is explained through a demonstration model using hypothetical transactions that require the reader to work through the applicable statutes. Through this exercise, the reader will, in addition, gain some experience with statutory interpretation.

Primarily for reasons of completeness, this chapter also contains a discussion of the credits against the federal estate tax, such as the state death tax credit, which are not functionally involved with the unification of the federal estate and gift taxes. However, the materials on the state death tax credit also serve to put in context the role of state death taxes in estate planning.

Of importance, too, is the opportunity to learn about gifting strategies. These strategies become apparent from experience with the mechanics of the estate and gift tax computational model. Here, the income tax basis rules come into play. That is, the basis of the gifted property in the hands of the donee for purposes of determining gain or loss upon disposition is a factor in developing gifting strategies.

Finally, and perhaps most importantly, this chapter introduces the concept of tax-free interspousal transfers. Since 1948, transfers between spouses have enjoyed preferential treatment for estate and gift tax purposes. And, beginning in 1982, transfers between spouses have been totally free of estate and gift taxation so long as the transfer was outright to the spouse or in a form that was specifically approved by Congress. § 2056(b)(5)-(8).

The "tax-free interspousal transfer" principle is implemented not by simply excluding interspousal transfers from the gift and estate tax computational scheme but by allowing the donor spouse to deduct the value of gifts to the other spouse in computing gift and estate tax liability. This deduction is referred to as the marital deduction. The marital deduction is the subject of Chapters 14 and 15. The marital deduction is also discussed in this chapter because appreciating the complexity of this appealingly simple concept is bound up in the computational model.

B. HISTORICAL PERSPECTIVE

[¶ 7051]

1. 1797 TO 1916

The first federal involvement with an estate tax began in 1797 when Congress enacted a stamp tax on legacies, probates of wills and letters of administration. The stamp tax lasted until 1802 when it was repealed.

As a method of raising revenue to finance the Civil War, Congress enacted an inheritance tax in 1862. Rates ranged up to five percent. The tax was repealed in 1870.

The next federal estate tax was imposed by the War Revenue Act of 1898. Rates ranged to 15 percent and there was an exemption of $10,000. The tax was repealed in 1902.

[¶ 7059]

2. 1916 THROUGH 1976

The Revenue Act of 1916 imposed an estate tax that has remained in force until the present time, although it has been modified in numerous ways since then. Among significant developments between 1916 and 1977 were: (1) adoption of a gift tax in 1932 which continues in force and (2) implementation of the marital deduction in 1948, the purpose of which was generally to equate the tax treatment of decedents owning separate property with that accorded decedents owning community property. The marital deduction as originally adopted was limited to 50 percent of what was, at that time, defined by

¶ 7001

statute as the decedent's adjusted gross estate, i.e., the decedent's gross estate reduced by debts and administration expenses.

[¶ 7067]

3. 1977 TO PRESENT

On September 8, 1976, Congress abruptly restructured the federal estate and gift taxes by causing them to be integrated so as to provide a final accounting at death for all gratuitous transfers by a taxpayer. The changes were effective as to gifts made after 1976 and decedents dying after 1976. Replaced was the existing estate tax which, at the time, provided an exemption of $60,000 and a top marginal estate tax rate of 77 percent on estates in excess of $10 million. Replaced, too, was the existing gift tax, which provided a $30,000 exemption, and tax rates, which were 75 percent of the estate tax rates.

Subsequently, effective beginning in 1982, Congress acted to permit unlimited tax-free transfers between persons married to each other. Also, effective in 1982, the prevailing $3,000 per donee per annum gift exclusion was replaced with an enlarged $10,000 per donee per annum gift tax exclusion. § 2503(b)(1). Adjusted for inflation, the per donee per annum exclusion became $12,000 in 2006. § 2503(b)(2); Rev. Proc. 2005–70, 2005–47 IRB 979.

The first of two additional developments during this period that are arguably the most significant was the adoption of the generation-skipping tax, initially in 1976, followed by repeal in 1986, and finally by replacement by an entirely new statutory scheme also in 1986. The generation-skipping tax appears in §§ 2601–2663; it is discussed in Chapters 9 and 23 of this book.

The second change of significance was the adoption of the zero valuation rules of §§ 2701–2704, discussed principally in Chapters 10, 12, and 24. The zero valuation rules apply to retained interests. That is, the donor who makes a lifetime transfer of only a partial interest in property will sometimes be treated as having given away the entire interest for gift tax purposes—rather than only a partial interest—in those cases where the donee is a member of the donor's family. See § 2702(a); ¶ 6159. The zero valuation rules represented an effort to frustrate a number of value-freezing devices then employed by taxpayers.

C. ESTATE AND GIFT TAXES: AN OVERVIEW

[¶ 7101]

1. THE ESTATE TAX (§§ 2001–2056)

An estate tax return must be filed within nine months after death for each decedent whose estate tax base the applicable exclusion amount established in § 2010(c), e.g., $2 million as to persons dying in 2006. § 6018(a)(1) and (3). The estate tax base consists of several elements, principally the decedent's gross estate and the taxable gifts made by the decedent after 1976. Property is included at its fair market value on the date of death as to property included in the gross estate (§ 2031(a)) and at its fair market value as of the date of the gift in the case of taxable gifts after 1976 (§ 2001(b) (last sentence)).

The estate tax is calculated after deducting the decedent's debts and mortgages, expenses of administering the decedent's estate, the decedent's funeral expenses, losses incurred during administration, gifts to the decedent's spouse (if made in a qualifying way), and gifts to charity. §§ 2051–2056.

The estate tax is traditionally viewed as a progressive tax but the rate scale could be said to begin, for all practical purposes, at 45 percent—with a top rate of 46 percent on estates over $2 million applicable to persons dying in 2006. § 2001(c). The top rate is declining though, and is scheduled to reach a flat 45 percent for persons dying in 2007 through 2009. Total repeal of the estate tax is to take effect as to persons who die in 2010—but the estate tax will automatically be

> *Curious why the estate tax exemption, i.e., the applicable exclusion amount, will be $1 million when the current rules "sunset" in 2011? One might have thought that with the "sunset" of the current rules, the rules in place in 2001 would apply, meaning the exemption would be $675,000 as it was in 2001. The exemption will be $1 million because, under the rules prevailing in 2001, the exemption was scheduled to increase to $1 million in 2006—and since it will be 2011 when the current rates sunset, the $1 million exemption previously scheduled to be available beginning in 2006 will be applicable in 20 11. Got that?*

resurrected effective as to persons dying in 2011 and thereafter (and then offer an exemption of only $1 million and progressive tax rates that top out at 55 percent on estates greater than $3 million) unless Congress acts in the meantime!

[¶ 7109]

2. THE GIFT TAX (§§ 2501–2524)

Gift tax returns must be filed annually. § 6019(a). A gift tax return must be filed whenever total gifts to the same donee, in the same year, exceed § 2503(b)'s $12,000 per donee per annum gift tax exclusion. (Note that gifts to the donor's spouse are an exception and are not required to be reported for gift tax purposes. § 6019(a)(2).) While a gift tax return is required whenever gifts to a single donee in the same year exceed $12,000, the donor will not pay any gift tax until the donor's total lifetime gifts (in excess of the $12,000 per donee per annum exclusion) exceed $1 million. Gifts are valued for gift tax purposes at their fair market value on the date of the gift. § 2512. Gifts to the donor's spouse are tax free if made in a qualifying way—as are gifts to charity. §§ 2522, 2523.

[handwritten margin note: Gifts to Spouses are Gift Tax free]

The scheduled repeal of the estate tax in 2010 does not extend to the gift tax. The exemption remains at $1 million through 2009. However, in 2010, the maximum gift tax rate drops to 35 percent—but in 2011 the higher gift tax rates in effect in 2001 are resurrected (unless Congress acts in the meantime to effect a different rule)!

¶ 7101

[¶ 7117]

3. INTEGRATION OF THE ESTATE AND GIFT TAXES

a. Adjusted Taxable Gifts (§ 2001(b))

The estate and gift tax computational scheme is quite complex, in part because the two separate taxes are to be integrated so as to limit each taxpayer to the equivalent of one lifetime exemption. Additional complication results from the need to integrate the tax rules applicable to gifts made before 1977 with those made after 1976. In sum, the complication results from the fact that gifts made any time by a taxpayer are aggregated to determine the tax rate applicable to the most recent gift. This is important so that the progressivity of the tax system can be maintained. However, in determining the tax rate applicable to property subject to the estate tax, only gifts made after 1976 are aggregated with the property transfers made by the taxpayer at death. These post–1976 gifts are referred to as "adjusted taxable gifts," a term that is important only for estate tax purposes. Integration of estate and gift taxes is expressed graphically in Figure 7.1. (Pre–1977 gifts are not taken into account for estate tax computation purposes.)

post-1976 gifts are "adjustable tax-able gifts."

Thus, gifts made after 1976 which exceed the per donee per annum (PDPA) gift tax exclusion available to the donor under § 2503 constitute adjusted taxable gifts. § 2001(b) (last sentence). (The PDPA was $3,000 until 1982; $10,000, 1982–2002; $11,000, 2003–05; and $12,000, 2006. Rev. Proc. 2005–70, 2005–47 IRB 979.) Moreover, adjusted taxable gifts are included in the donor's estate tax base, i.e., the base used to determine the rate of tax applicable to property subject to the estate tax at the donor's death. § 6018(a)(1) and (3).

This is CW

2006–from 2008: 12,000

2009–2011: $13,000

> *Example 1.* LaVonda died with a gross estate of $700,000 for federal estate tax purposes. However, LaVonda had made gifts after 1976 of $2 million (in excess of the gift tax exclusions available to her to shelter those gifts) prior to her death in 2004. As a consequence, the estate tax rate applicable to the $700,000 includible in LaVonda's estate at her death is 48 percent. § 2001(c)(2)(D). LaVonda's estate was pushed up into the higher rate bracket because it was stacked on top of her adjusted taxable gifts. Had LaVonda's $2 million of gifts been made prior to 1977, LaVonda's $700,000 gross estate would have been subject to a marginal estate tax rate of 37 percent (and no estate tax would have been payable because the estate tax generated by the $700,000 would have been sheltered by the $1.5 million exemption available in 2004).

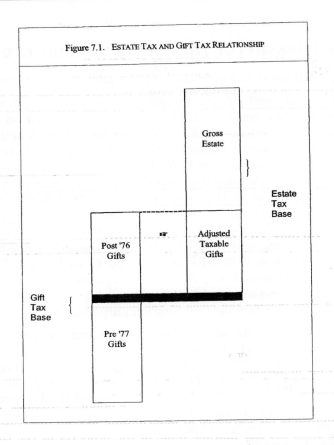

Figure 7.1. ESTATE TAX AND GIFT TAX RELATIONSHIP

Example 2. Melvin made a gift of $100,000 to his son, Jasper, in 1974 and another gift of $210,000 to Jasper in 1987. Melvin died in 2005. He willed all of his property to Jasper. At his death, Melvin's estate was valued at $1.5 million, but the base used in computing his estate tax liability was grossed up to $1.7 million by including the $200,000 of post–1976 gifts. (Note that the gift tax exclusion provided for in § 2503(b) allowed $10,000 to escape classification as an adjusted taxable gift.) Using the rate tables given in § 2001, Melvin's estate tax liability is $645,800 before the unified credit of $555,800 is applied as provided in § 2010(c), and after the credit is taken off, his estate tax liability is $90,000. (While Melvin had no gift tax to pay in 1987 because his $210,000 transfer to Jasper was sheltered by the then $10,000 gift tax per donee per annum exclusion and the $54,800 unified credit, he was obligated to file a gift tax return. See § 6019.) The effect of taking into account the $200,000 of post–1976 gifts is to push Melvin's estate into the 45 percent bracket.

[¶ 7125]

b.   *Valuation Controversy as to Finality of Gift Tax Valuations*

Adjusted taxable gifts are valued at their fair market value on the date of the gift—not the date of the donor's death—for purposes of computing the donor's estate tax base and, in turn, the donor's estate tax liability. See § 2001(b) (last sentence). This value-freezing factor is often cited as one reason favoring lifetime transfers of property likely to appreciate.

Sections 2001(f) and 2504(c) provide that gift tax valuations are binding for purposes of determining the estate tax rate and the gift tax rate applicable to death time transfers and/or subsequent gifts once the statute of limitations has passed for challenging the valuation of that particular gift. Without this "finality", it was possible for the IRS to revisit gift tax valuations when auditing the donor's estate tax return and attempt an upward adjustment of those "adjusted taxable gifts", sometimes thereby pushing the donor's estate into a higher estate tax bracket.

[¶ 7133]

c. Income Tax Basis (§ 1014(b)(6))

Income tax basis considerations play a role in thinking about adjusted taxable gifts, particularly in the development of gifting strategies.

Property included in the decedent's estate for estate tax purposes acquires a new income tax basis at the decedent's death. § 1014(b)(6). That is, to determine gain or loss for income tax purposes on the disposition of property acquired from a decedent, the basis of that property is its fair market value as of the date of the decedent's death. § 1001.

So far as property received by way of gift is concerned, the donor's basis carries over to the donee, i.e., the property in the hands of the donee has the same basis as it did in the hands of the donor. § 1015(a). There is a special rule applicable for purposes of determining loss on disposition. If the basis is greater than the fair market value of the property at the time of the gift, for purposes of determining loss the basis of the property shall be its fair market value at the time of the gift.

These "carryover basis" rules apply to adjusted taxable gifts, i.e., the donor's basis in an adjusted taxable gift carries over to the donee for purposes of determining gain or loss (with the exception noted above as to property sold at a loss).

For additional material, see ¶¶ 8751–8801.

[¶ 7141]

4. UNIFIED CREDIT (§§ 2010, 2505)

In 1976, the $30,000 lifetime gift tax exemption and the $60,000 estate tax exemption were eliminated and a single lifetime "unified credit" against estate and gift tax was substituted. See Table 7.4. The unified credit—$780,800 in 2006 through 2008, increasing to $1,455,800 in 2009 before total repeal of the estate tax in 2010—is best understood when expressed as an "exemption" (or, technically, the "applicable exclusion amount" from which the "applicable credit amount"—or unified credit—can be determined). § 2010(c). In 2006 through 2008, the estate tax "exemption" is $2 million, increasing to $3.5 million in 2009.

The appearance of the unified credit in both the estate tax and gift tax sometimes leads to the mistaken assumption that there are separate credits and that the careful planner can shelter in 2009, for example, a total of $4.5 million from estate ($3.5 million) and gift ($1 million) taxes. That is not the case. Each individual has a single unified credit; if some part is utilized to offset lifetime transfers, only the remaining portion will be available to offset death time transfers.

The unified credit has been gradually increased since its introduction, first effective as to gifts made in 1977. While that, too, complicates estate and gift tax computations, a shift from an exemption to a credit was seen as essential to giving each taxpayer the same dollar benefit, something that is not possible with an exemption where a progressive tax rate system is in effect. Where an exemption is utilized, higher tax bracket taxpayers derive greater benefit from the exemption—which is essentially a deduction—than do lower tax bracket taxpayers. That is, a 1987 decedent in the 55 percent estate tax bracket would have gotten a greater dollar benefit from a $600,000 exemption than would have a decedent in the 37 percent estate tax bracket. But each would have gotten the same dollar benefit from a credit against tax of $192,800, the unified credit in 1987. It comes to mind, though, to ask whether the premises of the unified credit have continuing vitality when the estate tax is a flat rate 45 percent (beginning in 2007).

In light of these developments, why not, then, return to the days of simplicity and offer an understandable "exemption" rather than a system that calls for determination of the "applicable exclusion amount" which leads to determination of the "applicable credit amount"—itself the unified credit? §§ 2010, 2505? Or is it possible that continuity in the computational integrity of the estate tax and, particularly, the gift tax was a particular value in as much as the unified credit system has been in place for roughly 30 years and it is premised on a gross-up-over-life accounting?

Finally, it is appropriate to look at the unified credit in terms of the estate tax return filing requirement. In short, an estate tax return is required to be filed only for those decedents whose estate tax base exceeds the applicable exclusion amount, *i.e.*, the "exemption". §§ 2010(c), 6018(a)(1) and (3).

[¶ 7149]

5. EXCLUSIONS (§ 2503(b) and (e))

The gift tax—but not the estate tax—provides for a $12,000 annual exclusion, adjusted for inflation. § 2503(b)(2); Rev. Proc. 2005–70, 2005–47 IRB 979. That means that an individual could make a gift of $12,000 each year to every person in Wyoming (or New York or wherever) without gift tax consequences and without having to file a gift tax return. To qualify, gifts must be a present interest. Reg. § 25.2503–3. Gifts of a future interest do not qualify. For additional material, see ¶¶ 19,459 (*Crummey*) and 21,212 (*Hackl*).

The gift tax also provides for an exclusion for transfers for educational and medical expenses. § 2503(e).

Exclusion of educational and medical expenses.

¶ 7141

[¶ 7157]

6. TRANSITIONAL RULES

There are several transitional rules in place to take account of changes that took place in 1976 in the structure of the estate and gift taxes.

[¶ 7161]

a. *Credit for Gift Taxes Paid on Pre–1976 Gifts (§ 2012)*

The gift tax rates were 75 percent of the estate tax rates prior to 1977. Some taxpayers currently living will have made gifts prior to 1977 when they were subject to those rules and rates. Some of these taxpayers will enjoy something of a windfall as a result of one of the transition rules. That is, as a means of simplifying current gift tax computations, taxpayers who made pre–1977 gifts are given credit for having paid gift tax at post–1976 rates even though the tax actually paid at the time of the pre–1977 transfer was less than the credit allowed that transferor in determining post–1976 gift tax liability. See § 2502(a). Mechanically speaking, this results because the gift tax on prior gifts is computed using the current rate table rather than the rate table in effect when the gift was made.

[¶ 7169]

b. *Gifts Made Between September 8, 1976 and December 31, 1976 (§§ 2010(b), 2505(b))*

[handwritten: Watch for this.]

Many gifts were made between September 8, 1976 and December 31, 1976, oftentimes solely to utilize the $30,000 gift tax exemption that was scheduled to expire on December 31, 1976 (as part of the transition to an integrated or unified estate and gift tax structure). A special rule applies to some of these taxpayers. Under that rule, taxpayers who utilized the $30,000 exemption during this 1976 "window" suffer a penalty of as much as a $6,000 reduction in the unified credit—$780,800 in 2006 (sheltering $2 million) but scheduled to rise to $1,455,800 (sheltering $3.5 million)—otherwise later available to them to shelter other lifetime and deathtime transfers. The penalty is equal to 20 percent of whatever portion of the $30,000 gift tax exemption that was used between September 8, 1976 and December 31, 1976. §§ 2010(b), 2505(b). *[handwritten: ok]*

> *Example.* Clarice gave $16,000 to a niece in December, 1976, and sheltered that gift by using her $30,000 exemption. As a result, Clarice's unified credit is only $552,600 rather than $555,800. The unified credit is reduced by $3,200 ($16,000 x 20%).

[¶ 7177]

7. TRANSFERS WITHIN THREE YEARS OF DEATH (§ 2035)

a. *Recapture Repealed: In General*

Effective in 1982, with several notable exceptions set out in § 2035, Congress reversed its long-standing rule that transfers within three years of death would be recaptured for estate tax purposes and included in the transferor's gross estate for tax computation purposes. It was explained that recapture was no longer "as significant" as under prior law where there was a separate gift tax with rates that were 75 percent of the estate tax rates, meaning that, with the integration or unification of the estate and gift taxes with a common rate table, there was diminished incentive to make deathbed transfers. Of course, lifetime transfers mean frozen values as of the date of the gift inasmuch as adjusted taxable gifts are taken into account in determining the decedent's estate tax base—but the adjusted taxable gifts are valued as of the date of the gift rather than the date of the transferor's death. § 2001(b) (last sentence).

For discussion of transfers within three years of death for income tax purposes, see ¶ 11,501.

[¶ 7185]

b. *Recapture of Gift Taxes: Tax Exclusive v. Tax Inclusive*

In abolishing the recapture rule for transfers within three years of death, Congress especially excepted gift taxes paid on transfers within three years of death. § 2035(c). That is, the amount of any gift taxes paid on transfers within three years of death will be recaptured and included in the donor's gross estate for estate tax computation purposes. Why? To eliminate one of the very real incentives to make deathbed transfers, that incentive being the opportunity to reduce the transferor's gross estate not only by the value of the property transferred to loved ones but also by the amount of the gift tax that was paid.

Understanding the nature of the gift tax and the nature of the estate tax is important to understanding this point. The gift tax is "tax exclusive" but the estate tax is "tax inclusive"—as is the income tax. The gift tax is tax exclusive in the sense that the gift tax base or the amount upon which the gift tax is determined does not include the amount of the gift tax. On the other hand, the estate tax—and income tax—are tax inclusive in the sense that the estate tax base—and the income tax base—includes the amount that is subsequently determined to be the tax that must be paid. That is, the estate tax is a tax on a tax! The income tax is a tax on a tax! Both the estate tax and the income tax are determined without any reduction for the amount of tax paid.

> **Example.** Verity wants to make a gift of $100,000 to her nephew so that he will be able to "go to college." The gift tax bill is $40,000. By virtue of making the gift, Verity's estate will shrink by $140,000. However, if Verity postpones the gift until her death and the nephew receives the $100,000 as a result of a provision in Verity's will, Verity's estate tax base will include both the $100,000 and the $40,000 with no deduction for the amount of estate tax that must be paid, meaning that the tax cost of giving the nephew $100,000 will be higher if the gift is postponed until Verity's death. (Of course, if Verity dies within three years of making the gift, the $40,000 gift tax will be recaptured for estate tax purposes, thereby neutralizing the tax advantage of the lifetime transfer.)

[¶ 7193]

8. EXAMPLES

The following are somewhat updated examples based upon illustrations included in IRS Publication 448, Federal Estate and Gift Taxes, at 35 and 49 (Rev. August 1992), a publication currently out of print.

Example 1. In 1979 Bill Smith gave his daughter a gift of property valued at $250,000, with the understanding that he could continue using the property until his death. He filed a gift tax return and paid a net gift tax of $32,800 (tentative gift tax, $70,800, minus unified credit, $38,000). He had not made any prior gifts.

Bill Smith died in 2005. Because the gift to his daughter is a transfer with a retained life estate, the value of the gift is included in his gross estate. The estate is valued as of the date of death. The value of the gift on that date is $300,000. The gift taxes paid on the gift are not included in the gross estate because the gift was made more than three years before death. The net estate tax is computed as follows:

Gross estate	$1,907,800
Minus: Debts and administration expenses	107,800
Taxable estate	$1,800,000
Add: Adjusted taxable gifts	–0–
Taxable amount	$1,800,000
Tentative tax	$690,800
Minus: Gift taxes payable	32,800
Gross estate tax	$658,000
Minus: Unified credit	555,800
Estate tax after unified credit	$102,200

Example 2. Assume the same facts as in Example 1, except that Bill did not retain any interest in the property. His gross estate does not include the value of the gift. However, the value of the taxable gift is added to the taxable estate for purposes of determining the gross estate tax. The net estate tax is computed as follows:

Gross estate	$1,607,800
Minus: Debts and administration expenses	107,800
Taxable estate	$1,500,000
Add: Adjusted taxable gifts	250,000
Taxable amount	$1,750,000
Tentative tax	$668,300
Minus: Gift taxes payable	32,800
Gross estate tax	$635,500
Minus: Unified credit	555,800
Estate tax after unified credit	$79,700

The difference in the amount of the net estate tax is due to a combination of changes:

1.   The value of the gift at the date of death ($300,000) is not included in the gross estate.

2. The taxable gift ($250,000) is included in the computation of the gross estate tax as an adjusted taxable gift. The gift is included at this point in the computation because it is not included in the gross estate.

Example 3. In October 1976, George Ash made a gift to his niece, Sally, of property valued at $53,000. On his federal gift tax return, George claimed all of the specific exemption in the amount of $30,000 plus the annual exclusion of $3,000. In 1986, George made a gift of $550,000 to his nephew, Barry. The gift tax before the unified credit was $174,200. The unified credit for 1986 was $155,800; however, because George had claimed the specific exemption for the October 1976 gift, the credit must be reduced by $6,000 (20% x $30,000). Therefore, the allowable unified credit is $149,800. George is liable for a net gift tax of $24,400.

After the 1986 gift, George has used $155,800 of his unified credit. His allowable unified credit for a gift made in 2005 is $400,000 ($555,800—$155,800).

Example 4. Using the same facts as in the preceding example, assume that George Ash made a gift of $550,000 in 1986 and that the only prior taxable gift was the one made in 1976. George computes his gift tax for 1986 as follows:

Total gifts for 1986	$550,000
Minus: Annual exclusion	10,000
Taxable gifts	$540,000
Plus: Prior taxable gifts	20,000
Total taxable gifts	$560,000
Tentative tax on total taxable gifts	$178,000
Minus: Tentative tax on prior taxable gifts (using 1986 tax rates)	3,800
Gift tax before unified credit	$174,200
Minus: Allowable unified credit ($155,800—$6,000)	149,800
Net gift tax	$24,400

In 2005, George made a gift to his niece of property valued at $1,151,000. He computed his gift tax for 2005 as follows:

Total taxable gifts for 2005	$1,151,000
Minus: Annual exclusion	11,000
Taxable gifts	$1,140,000
Plus: Prior taxable gifts	560,000
Total taxable gifts at current rates	$1,700,000
Tentative tax on total taxable gifts	$645,800
Minus: Tentative tax on prior taxable gifts	178,000
Gift tax before unified credit	$467,800
Minus: Allowable unified credit ($345,800—$6,000—$149,800))	190,000
Net gift tax	$277,800

¶ **7193**

Problems

[¶ 7198]

1. Effective in 1982, Congress eliminated the rule requiring the recapture and inclusion in the decedent's gross estate of certain property transferred within three years of death. The rule was retained as to, *inter alia*, life insurance. § 2035(a)(2). Congress also elected to retain the rule requiring inclusion in a decedent's gross estate of any gift tax paid on transfers made within *three* years of death. § 2035(b). Can you offer any plausible explanation for this seemingly inconsistent treatment? Perhaps it would be helpful to your analysis to note that House Committee Report contained the following statement:

> Thus, gifts made within three years of death will not be included in the decedent's gross estate, and the *post-gift appreciation* will not be subject to transfer taxes. Accordingly, such property will not be considered to pass from the decedent, and the step-up basis rules of § 1014 will not apply. (Emphasis supplied.)

By way of explaining Congress's reference to the step-up in basis rules, note that property included in a decedent's gross estate for federal estate tax purposes acquires as its basis for determining gain or loss for income tax purposes on subsequent sale, the value of the property as finally determined for federal estate tax purposes. See § 1014. On the other hand, recipients of lifetime gifts take the donor's basis in the transferred property. See § 1015. With that in mind, is Congress really being generous in allowing so-called *post-gift appreciation* to escape recapture or does the potential for income tax on the gain realized upon sale of the property by the donee raise the spectre of even greater tax revenue?

2. Consider two taxpayers, A and B, both of whom are crossing the street on the way to their broker's office to sell 100 shares of MicroWidget stock. Both taxpayers have a basis of $10 per share in their stock for income tax purposes. Secondly, both taxpayers have: (1) estates in an assumed 50 percent estate tax bracket; (2) incomes that place each of them in an assumed 31 percent income tax bracket; and (3) the maximum tax rate applied to capital gains is an assumed 20 percent. Finally, both taxpayers are killed by the same truck while crossing the street. Taxpayer B is killed on his way to sell the stock and Taxpayer A is killed after he has sold the MicroWidget stock and is returning to his parked car. Taxpayer B's shares are sold the following day by the executor of his estate. The shares of each taxpayer were sold for $200 per share.

   a. Determine the total tax burden imposed on each taxpayer, i.e., total the income taxes and the estate taxes imposed on each taxpayer. Which set of facts would result in the greatest total tax revenue? Would your answer be different if the rate of tax imposed on capital gains was reduced, perhaps halved?

   b. Suppose B had given his shares to his son, Shad, shortly before B died. If Shad sold the 100 shares of MicroWidget after his father died, he would have realized a taxable gain of as much as $19,000 (as did Taxpayer A) which would have resulted in an income tax liability of $3,800. Why? Because Shad assumed his father's income tax basis of $1,000 in the shares.

However, Shad's basis in the shares would be adjusted upward to reflect any gift tax paid by B when the transfer was made to Shad. For example, assume the shares had been given to Shad earlier this year as a birthday present and that B's previous taxable gifts caused him to be in the 50 percent gift tax bracket. Determine: (1) the gift tax liability that B would have incurred at the time of the transfer of the shares to Shad; (2) Shad's income tax basis in the shares he received (according to § 1015(d)(1)(A)); (3) Shad's gain on the sale and his income tax liability (assuming Shad is in the 35 percent income tax bracket). Determine, too, (1) whether the shares will be included in B's estate tax base as part of his gross estate or as an adjusted taxable gift and (2) the value assigned the shares in B's estate for purposes of determining B's estate tax liability.

c. Suppose B had not transferred the shares while he was living. As a result the shares are included in his estate for estate tax purposes. By what amount would the shares have had to appreciate for the federal revenues to be greater than if the shares were transferred by B during life?

[¶ 7201]

9. STRUCTURAL MODEL

The following flow chart illustrates the relationship between the gross estate, the taxable estate, and adjusted taxable gifts:

FIGURE 7.2 ESTATE TAX COMPUTATIONAL MODEL

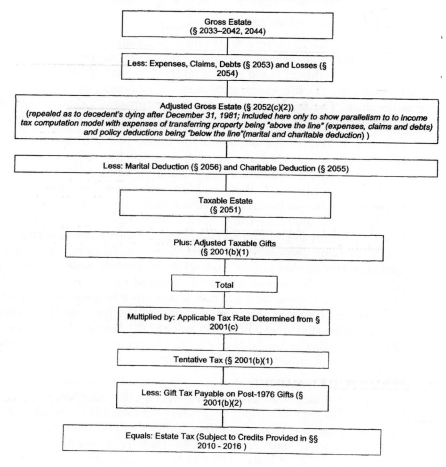

[¶ 7209]

10. VALUATION PRINCIPLES

a. General Rules

Fair market value is used for estate and gift tax purposes. That is, as a general rule, "date of death fair market value" is used in valuing property for federal estate tax purposes. § 2031(a). An alternative valuation date is available in limited circumstances. § 2032(a). So, too, is special use valuation as to farm property. § 2032A. For discussion of special use valuation, see ¶ 24,829.

"Date of gift fair market value" is used in valuing property for federal gift tax purposes. § 2512(a). However, a special "zero valuation rule" is used in certain cases if the donor has retained an interest in the transferred property. §§ 2701–2704; ¶ 12,051.

"Zero valuation rule" in the case of retained interest.

¶ 7209 applicable under what circumstances?

[¶ 7217]

b. *Actuarial Valuations*

Transfers of partial interests are quite common. Examples are annuities, interests for life or a term of years, and remainder or reversionary interests. The fair market value of these partial interests at date of death or date of gift is a function of: (1) life expectancy and (2) interest rates prevailing at the valuation date. The task is to determine the "present value" of the interests being transferred.

Example 1. Harry, age 36, deeds his house to his long-time companion, Louise, subject to his right to occupy it for life. What value should be assigned Louise's future interest? That is, what is the present market value of her interest? That will depend upon how long Harry lives. Suppose the house has a fair market value of $200,000. Would a buyer pay Louise $200,000 for the property while Harry is alive? Unlikely. The buyer will want to pay Louise less than $200,000 since Louise's interest is not at present possessory—and the buyer is forgoing other investment opportunities for his or her cash while everybody waits for Harry to die. In sum, Louise's interest will be discounted by the buyer to reflect rates of interest that could be earned in alternative investments. However, the interest (or "discount") rate is only part of the formula. The other part is Harry's life expectancy. What do you think? Would the IRS use average life expectancies or would Harry's life expectancy somehow be determined for purposes of valuing Louise's interest?

Section 7520 requires that tables of value for different interest rates, reflecting current actuarial data, be provided by the Internal Revenue Service. Section 7520 also provides that the interest rate used is to equal "120 percent of the Federal midterm rate in effect under § 1274(d)(1) for the month in which the valuation date falls." While that is a mouthful—and awfully intimidating—relief is at hand. The so-called "applicable Federal rate" can be found in the Internal Revenue Bulletin several months in advance of the month for which the valuation is to be made.

Learning the applicable interest rate is the easy part. The hard part is finding the correct table. The estate tax and gift tax share tables. The more commonly used tables appear in Reg. § 20.2031–7(d)(7). More exotic tables, e.g., those providing two-life actuarial factors, as well as many one-life factors and term-certain factors not found in the regulations tables, are found in Internal Revenue Service, Actuarial Tables Alpha Volume (Publication 1457, July 1999) (http://www.irs.gov/pub/irs-pdf/p1457.pdf)) and and Internal Revenue Service, Actuarial Values Beta Volume (Publication 1458, July 1999) (http://www.irs.gov/pub/irs-pdf/p1458.pdf).

Example 2. Harry's gift of a remainder interest to Louise has a value of $33,316 (.16658 x $200,000). This is based on an assumed § 7520 rate of 5 percent. The factor provided by Table S or Reg. § 20.2031–7(d)(7) for 36–year-old Harry is .16658. This means that the value of Harry's retained life estate is $166,684 ($200,000—$33,316).

¶ 7217

Interest rates dramatically impact gift planning. For example, in the foregoing example, Harry's gift to Louise would be valued at $15,162 if the § 7520 rate was eight percent but at $45,444 if the § 7520 rate was four percent (as it was in March, 2004).

[¶ 7235]

c. Software

Thanks to the personal computer, most of the actuarial tables (including the more exotic tables) needed to value transfer of partial interests can be found in one or more software programs that are quite easy to use, almost child's play, in fact. Some of the available programs—all of which have been used most satisfactorily in the preparation of these materials—are listed in Appendix A.

D. ESTATE AND GIFT TAX RATE TABLES AND WORKSHEETS

[¶ 7251]

The following worksheets may be useful in illustrating the conceptual relationships that are the basis of the estate and gift tax computational model.

1. WORKSHEETS

The worksheets in Tables 7.1 and 7.2 may be useful in illustrating the conceptual relationships that are the basis of the estate and gift tax computational model.

Table 7.1 Gift Tax Computation Worksheet Annotated*		
A. Amount of current taxable gift[1] . . . . $ _____		
B. Aggregate prior taxable gifts[2] . . . . + _____		
C. Tentative gift tax base (A + B)[3] . . . . $ _____		
D. Tentative Tax #1 on C[4]	$ _____	
E. Tentative Tax #2 on B only[5]	− _____	
F. Gift tax before unified credit (D—E)[6]	$ _____	
G. Unified gift tax credit for current year[7] . . . . $ _____		
H. Unified gift tax credit previously used[8] . . . . − _____		
I. Unified gift tax credit available (G—H)[9]	− _____	
J. Gift tax payable (F—I)[10]	$ _____	

---

* This table is based upon and largely drawn from a similar one that appeared in L. Hodges, Cumulative Transfer Tax Calculations, 117 TR. & EST. 84, 86 (1978). See generally Reg. § 25.2502–1(a).

1. § 2503 defines a post–1976 taxable gift as the fair market value of the gift (§ 2512), less any exclusion (annual, medical or educational) (§ 2503), gift tax marital deduction (§ 2523), and gift tax charitable deduction (§ 2522) allowed with respect to the transfer. Gift-splitting enables a donor and his or her spouse to divide, between themselves for gift tax purposes, taxable gifts made to third parties by one of them (§ 2513).

2. Pre–1977 taxable gifts may have been reduced by use of the $30,000 exemption available to shelter gifts made prior to January 1, 1977 (§ 2521, now repealed). It is the aggregate value of

prior taxable gifts, as determined at the time of the gifts, *after the exemption and exclusions are claimed,* that is taken into account here (§ 2504).

3.   § 2502(a)(1).

4.   The unified rates in § 2001(c) are applied to the tentative gift tax base.

5.   § 2502(a)(2). The § 2001(c) unified rates are to be used in making the tentative tax #2 computation even though pre–1977 taxable gifts were subject to the old gift tax rates. (Normally this will result in a "windfall" to the donor inasmuch as the post–1976 gift tax rates are higher than the pre–1977 rates.)

6.   § 2502(a).

7.   § 2505(b). The unified gift tax credit otherwise available is reduced by 20 percent of any portion of the $30,000 exemption (available to shelter gifts made before January 1, 1977) to the extent used to shelter gifts made after September 8, 1976, and before January 1, 1977. § 2505(c).

8.   § 2505(a)(2).

9.   § 2505(a). The credit allowed against the gift tax may not exceed the tax liability. § 2505(d).

10.   The gift tax payable will later operate as a credit in computing the donor's estate tax. § 2001(b)(2). (The credit against the donor's estate tax liability is the amount of the gift tax which would have been payable had the gift been subject to the rate schedule in effect at the decedent's death.)

Table 7.2 ESTATE TAX COMPUTATION WORKSHEET ANNOTATED*		
A. Amount of the taxable estate[1] ....$_____		
B. Aggregate adjusted taxable gifts[2] ....+ _____		
C. Estate tax computations base (A + B)[3] ....$_____		
D. Tentative estate tax on C[4]		$_____
E. Gift tax on post–1976 gifts[5] ....$_____		
F. Unified estate tax credit[6] .... _____		
G. State death tax credit[7] .... _____		
H. Any other credits allowable[8] ....+ _____		
I. Sum of E, F, G and H[9]		– _____
J. Estate tax payable (D—I)		$_____

* This table is based upon and largely drawn from a similar one that appeared in L. Hodges, Cumulative Transfer Tax Calculations, 117 TR. & EST. 84 (1978).

1.   § 2053 defines the taxable estate as the gross estate less the deductions allowed for: funeral expenses (§ 2053(a)(1)); administration expenses (§ 2053(a)(2)); claims against the estate (§ 2053(a)(3)); unpaid mortgages and other indebtedness against property included in the gross estate (§ 2053(a)(4)); expenses of administering property not subject to claims (§ 2053(b)); state and foreign death taxes on public or charitable bequests (§ 2053(d)); casualty losses during administration (§ 2054); public or charitable bequests (§ 2055); and marital bequests (§ 2056).

2.   § 2001(b) defines adjusted taxable gifts as post–1976 taxable gifts, as determined for gift tax purposes, other than gifts includible in the gross estate. Taxable gifts are the gross amount of gifts, less any annual exclusions (annual, medical or educational), gift tax marital deduction, or gift tax charitable deduction allowed, for these gifts (§ 2503). Taxable gifts for these purposes do not include that one-half of each gift that the donor has elected, pursuant to § 2513, to "split" with his or her spouse. Gift-splitting allows married persons to divide the taxable gifts of a one of them between the donor and his or her spouse for gift tax computation purposes.

3.   § 2001(b)(1).

4.   The unified rates in § 2001(c) are applied to the estate tax computation base.

5.   § 2001(b)(2). The credit for gift tax payable is the amount of gift tax which would have been payable had the gifts been subject to the gift tax rate schedule in effect at the decedent's death. Thus, the gift tax actually paid is disregarded. (This rule is designed to prevent donors who paid gift tax at rates above 55 percent from getting credit for taxes paid at those rates if they die when the rate ceiling is 55 percent.)

6.   § 2010. The unified estate tax credit is available even if the unified gift tax credit was fully used up during life. The credit is reduced, however, by 20 percent of any portion of the long ago

¶ 7251

repealed $30,000 gift tax exemption that was used to shelter gifts made after September 8, 1976 and before January 1, 1977. § 2010(c).

7.   § 2011. To calculate the state death tax credit, the taxable estate must be reduced by $60,000 to get the "adjusted taxable estate," to which the § 2011(b) schedule applies. The state death tax credit is not available to decedents dying after 2004.

8.   These other credits include: the credit for gift taxes paid on pre–1977 gifts included in the gross estate (§ 2012); the credit for tax on prior transfers (§ 2031); the credit for foreign death taxes (§ 2014); and the credit for death taxes on certain remainder and reversionary interests (§ 2015).

9.   The credits, individually and collectively, may not exceed the tentative estate tax. The credits have been listed in the order of their priority. For example, if the credit for post–1976 gift taxes paid and the unified credit completely offset the tentative tax, none of the other credits would be allowed.

[¶ 7259]

2.   TAX RATE TABLES

Tables 7.4 and 7.5 contain the current estate and gift tax rates. Table 7.3 provides the gift tax rates in effect prior to 1977. These pre–1977 rates have current utility in cases where required gift tax returns were not timely filed for pre–1977 gifts. The pre–1977 estate tax rate tables are also provided in Table 7.3 for comparison purposes.

Table 7.3				PRE-1977 ESTATE AND GIFT TAX RATES*			
PRE-1977 ESTATE TAX RATES				**PRE-1977 GIFT TAX RATES**			
(A)	*(B)*	*Tax Before Credits*		*(A)*	*(B)*	*(C)*	*(D)*
Taxable estate over	But not exceeding	*Tax on Amount in Column (A)*	*Rate of Tax on Excess over Amount in Column (A)*	Amount of Taxable Gifts Equal to or More Than —	Amount of Taxable Gifts Less Than —	*Tax on Amount in Column (A)*	*Rate of Tax on Excess over Amount in Column (A)*
			Percent				*Percent*
$	$ 5,000	$	3	$	$ 5,000	$	2 1/4
5,000	10,000	150	7	5,000	10,000	112.50	5 1/4
10,000	20,000	500	11	10,000	20,000	375	8 1/4
20,000	30,000	1,600	14	20,000	30,000	1,200	10 ½
30,000	40,000	3,000	18	30,000	40,000	2,250	13 ½
40,000	50,000	4,800	22	40,000	50,000	3,600	16 ½
50,000	60,000	7,000	25	50,000	60,000	5,250	18 3/4
60,000	100,000	9,500	28	60,000	100,000	7,125	21
100,000	250,000	20,700	30	100,000	250,000	15,525	22 ½
250,000	500,000	65,700	32	250,000	500,000	49,275	24
500,000	750,000	145,700	35	500,000	750,000	109,275	26 1/4
750,000	1,000,000	233,200	37	750,000	1,000,000	174,900	27 3/4
1,000,000	1,250,000	325,700	39	1,000,000	1,250,000	244,275	29 1/4
1,250,000	1,500,000	423,200	42	1,250,000	1,500,000	317,400	31 ½
1,500,000	2,000,000	528,200	45	1,500,000	2,000,000	396,150	33 1/4
2,000,000	2,500,000	753,200	49	2,000,000	2,500,000	564,900	36 3/4
2,500,000	3,000,000	998,200	53	2,500,000	3,000,000	748,650	39 3/4
3,000,000	3,500,000	1,263,200	56	3,000,000	3,500,000	947,400	42
3,500,000	4,000,000	1,543,200	59	3,500,000	4,000,000	1,157,400	44 1/4
4,000,000	5,000,000	1,838,200	63	4,000,000	5,000,000	1,378,650	47 1/4
5,000,000	6,000,000	2,468,200	67	5,000,000	6,000,000	1,851,150	50 1/4
6,000,000	7,000,000	3,138,200	70	6,000,000	7,000,000	2,353,650	52 ½
7,000,000	8,000,000	3,838,200	73	7,000,000	8,000,000	2,878,650	54 3/4
8,000,000	10,000,000	4,568,200	76	8,000,000	10,000,000	3,426,150	57
10,000,000	...	6,088,200	77	10,000,000	...	4,566,150	57 3/4

* Gift tax rates are 75% of estate tax rates

¶ **7259**

[handwritten: Amt. of tax applic. on exclus amt.]

Table 7.4 — UNIFIED TRANSFER TAX RATE SCHEDULE (§ 2001(c)) (For gifts made after and decedents dying after 1977)

(A) Taxable Amount over	(B) Taxable amount not over	(C) Tax on Amount in Column (A)	(D) Rate of Tax on Excess over Amount in Column (A) Percent
$ 0	$ 10,000	$ 0	18
10,000	20,000	1,800	20
20,000	40,000	3,800	22
40,000	60,000	8,200	24
60,000	80,000	13,000	26
80,000	100,000	18,200	28
100,000	150,000	23,800	30
150,000	250,000	38,800	32
250,000	500,000	70,800	34
500,000	750,000	155,800	37
750,000	1,000,000	248,300	39
1,000,000	1,250,000	345,800	41
1,250,000	1,500,000	448,300	43
1,500,000	2,000,000	555,800	45
2,000,000	....	780,800	* 48

* In 2005, the maximum rate is 47 percent; 2006, 46 percent; and in 2007–09, 45 percent.

Table 7.5 — UNIFIED CREDIT (§ 2010(a)) (For gifts made after and decedents dying after 1977)

Year	Applicable credit amount *	Applicable exclusion amount **
1977	$ 30,000	$ 120,666
1978	34,000	134,000
1979	38,000	147,333
1980	42,500	161,563
1981	47,000	175,625
1982	62,800	225,000
1983	79,300	275,000
1984	96,300	325,000
1985	121,800	400,000
1986	155,800	500,000
1987 through 1997 .	192,800	600,000
1998	202,050	625,000
1999	211,300	650,000
2000 and 2001	220,550	675,000
2002 and 2003	345,800	1,000,000
2004 and 2005	*** 555,800	*** 1,500,000
2006, 2007, and 2008	*** 780,800	*** 2,000,000
2009	*** 1,455,800	*** 3,500,000
2010	345,800	† -0-
2011 and after	345,800	1,000,000

* Referred to as the "unified credit" prior to 1998.

** Referred to informally as the "exemption equivalent to the unified credit" prior to 1998.

*** The gift tax *applicable credit amount* and *applicable exclusion amount* are frozen at $345,800 and $1 million , respectively.

† Unlike the estate tax, the gift tax is not repealed in 2010.

*[handwritten, left margin: * Fm 2001–2010 for gift tax purposes exclus. $345,800 (because cld. never gift more than $1.0m).]*

[handwritten, right margin: 555,800 / 780,800 / 1,455,800]

E. DEMONSTRATION MODEL: AN UNMARRIED TAXPAYER

Problem

[¶ 7301]

On October 10, 1976, Daisy, a widow, made gifts of $50,000 to each of her ten grandchildren. Daisy had made no prior gifts.

a. What is the total value of Daisy's taxable gifts in 1976? ¶ 7067.

b. What are the tax consequences if Daisy makes annual gifts of $50,000 to each of her ten grandchildren in both 1977 and 1990? ¶ 7109–7193.

c. Prior to her death, Daisy told you that, in computing her gift tax liability prior to 1977, her accountant advised that she "could claim both the specific exemption and the annual exclusion." Are these "deducts" still available? What is the "specific exemption" and the "annual exclusion"? See §§ 2503(b), 2513, 2521. Can you demonstrate how these "deducts" were used in the gift tax computation scheme?

¶ 7259

d.   Last year, Daisy, by then in poor health, transferred ownership of a $1,000,000 life insurance policy to her son, Clint. Daisy was the insured under the policy. At the time of the transfer to Clint, the policy had a cash surrender value of $190,000. Determine the gift tax consequences of the transfer of the life insurance policy. Reg. §§ 25.2511–1(h)(8), 25.2512–6.

e.   Daisy died this year on January 1. At her death, Daisy's property consisted of a bank account containing $500,000. Determine Daisy's federal estate tax liability.

F. DEMONSTRATION MODEL: A MARRIED TAXPAYER

[¶ 7351]

1. GIFT-SPLITTING

Under § 2513, a spouse may consent to be treated as the donor of one-half of a gift made by the other spouse to a third party. This is referred to as "gift-splitting." The effect, in most cases, is to reduce the total gift tax payable as a result of the gift. Why? Because each spouse can utilize the $12,000 per donee per annum gift tax exclusion, as adjusted for inflation, to shelter a portion of the gift attributed to him or her (unless the exclusion has already been used during that year to shelter a part or all of another gift). See § 2503(b). In addition, splitting the gift may allow the donor to fall back into a lower gift tax bracket. Or perhaps the donor's spouse will be in an even lower gift tax bracket.

[¶ 7359]

2. THE UNLIMITED MARITAL DEDUCTION

Spouses can make transfers one to another totally free of all gift taxes. § 2523(a). Similarly, decedents may make deathtime transfers to their respective spouses totally free of estate taxes. § 2056(a). This privilege is referred to as the "marital deduction" because the amount transferred is treated as a deduction in the computational scheme for both the estate tax and the gift tax. However, transfers to a spouse will be tax free only in limited circumstances. Clearly, a transfer in fee simple to one's spouse will be tax free. Whether transfers in trust are free of estate or gift taxes will depend upon the terms of the trust. For detailed discussion, see ¶ 14,351 and 14,401.

Notes Spouse can make gift to each other free of gift taxes

Problem

[¶ 7363]

Hub, a surgeon, and Wanda (referred to affectionately by Hub as "W") had been married for 35 years when they were divorced last year on February 1.

On February 2 of last year, Hub married his neighbor's nanny, Sybil. Two weeks later Sybil disclosed that she was in the United States illegally.

Outraged, Hub demanded that she "leave", whereupon she returned to her native land.

Hub's divorce from Sybil was final this year on January 15. Immediately thereafter, Hub married Winifred ("Win"). Their marriage continued until Hub's death on May 13. Hub was 60 years old at his death. Win was 55. (Coincidentally, both of them had been born on December 25.) The value of Hub's probate estate is $100,000.

In the process of collecting Hub's property, Hub's executor determined that Hub had made a number of transfers beginning four years ago, none of which had been reported for gift tax purposes. The executor would like your advice as to the tax consequences of those transfers. He reports that each of the transfers was made with the consent of the person who was Hub's spouse at the time of the particular transfer. Moreover, the executor reports that Win, Wanda, and Sybil (who came back and is again the neighbor's nanny), in the words of Sybil, are each willing to "sign a paper" to signify her consent to the gifts made while married to Hub "because that is what Hub would have wanted."

Except as noted (or as suggested by the circumstances), all of the transfers were made from Hub's separate property. Hub's executor has also learned that Win made several gifts to her children and grandchildren this year, both before and after her marriage to Hub, including after his death. These gifts were all made from Win's separate property.

Neither Hub nor any of his spouses had made any gifts heretofore except as noted.

(a) Two years ago, on December 25, Hub and Wanda "joined" in making a gift of $20,000 to their son, Hubcap. § 2513(a).

    (1) Why must Hub file a return? §§ 2503(b), 2513(a), 6019; Reg. § 25.6019–2.

    (2) When must the consent be given by the nondonor spouse? Reg. § 25.2513–2.

(b) Last year, on January 1, Hub and Wanda "joined" in making a gift of $20,000 to their son, Elijah. Found among Hub's papers at his death was a copy of a note to Elijah transmitting the $20,000 gift in which Hub said the gift was "to be used, first, for orthodontia, and second, for educational expenses incurred at State Ag & Tech," where Elijah was then enrolled.

    (1) Education exclusion? § 2503(e)(2)(A).

    (2) Medical exclusion? § 2503(e)(2)(B).

    (3) Annual exclusion? § 2503(b).

    (4) Gift-split? § 2513.

(c) Last year, on February 20, Hub, "joined" by Sybil, made a gift of $250,000 to another of his sons, Grandy. §§ 2503(b), 2513(a)(1); Reg. § 25.2513–1(a).

¶ 7363

(d) Last year, on February 26, Hub gave his daughter, Doozie, $20,000. He made the gift by endorsing over to Doozie a check that he had received for a surgical procedure he had performed earlier that week. (What if the fee was community property? ¶ 11,089.)

(e) Last year, also on February 26, Hub gave his other daughter, Lulu, $36,000. This gift, too, was made by Hub endorsing a fee-for-services check over to Lulu. (What if the fee was community property? ¶ 11,089.)

(f) This year, on January 25, Hub gave Win $10,000 in securities. §§ 2523, 6019(a).

(g) This year, on February 12, Hub handed Win a deed to Blackacre, an undeveloped tract of land. At the time of the conveyance, the property had a value of $300,000. (What if it was community property? ¶ 11,089.)

(h) This year, on February 22, Hub established a trust for Win's benefit. Hub funded the trust with securities having a value of $200,000. The trustee was obligated to distribute all of the trust income to Win annually or more often. The trust is to terminate at Win's death, whereupon the trust principal is to be distributed to Vaughan, Hub's son from an earlier marriage. Does Win's gift qualify for the marital deduction? Has Hub made a gift to Vaughan? § 2523(f).

(i) In addition, this year on February 12, Hub established an irrevocable trust and funded it with $100,000. His secretary, Kathleen, age 55, is to receive all of the income for life. At Kathleen's death the trust was to terminate, whereupon the trust principal is to be distributed to Billie Bob, another of Hub's sons from an earlier marriage.

    (1) Is the donee's identity of any relevance? §§ 2503(b) and (e), 2522, 2523.

    (2) What is Kathleen's interest? § 7520; Reg. §§ 20.2031–7(d)(6), 25.2512–5(a), 25.7520–1(c); ¶ 6151.

    (3) What is Billie Bob's interest?

    (4) Is gift-splitting available? § 2013(a).

    (5) Does Billie Bob's interest qualify for the annual exclusion? § 2503(b).

    (6) What is a future interest? Reg. § 25.2503–3.

(j) This year, on March 15, Hub gave another son, Ned, $25,000. §§ 2503(b), 2513.

(k) This year, on March 16, Win gave $30,000 to her grandson, Lott. §§ 2503(b), 2513.

(l) This year, on March 16, Win also gave $4,000 to Win's grandson, Lug. §§ 2503(b), 2513.

¶ 7363

3. COMMUNITY PROPERTY

The unlimited marital deduction is available for transfers of both separate and community property that are made after 1981. Both lifetime and deathtime gifts of community property qualify.

G. CREDITS AGAINST THE ESTATE TAX

[¶ 7451]

After computing the tentative estate tax, the available credits are subtracted. The Internal Revenue Code provides <u>six principal credits</u>, in the following order of priority:

1. A credit for post–1976 gift taxes paid attributable to adjusted taxable gifts (§ 2001(b)(2)), discussed at ¶ 7117;

2. A unified estate tax credit (§§ 2010, 2505), discussed at ¶ 7141;

3. A credit for state death taxes (§ 2011), discussed at ¶ 7459;

4. A credit for the amount of gift taxes paid by the decedent on transfers of property before January 1, 1977, which are included in the gross estate (§ 2012), discussed at ¶ 7493;

5. A credit for federal estate tax on prior transfers to the decedent (§ 2013), discussed at ¶ 7501; and

6. A credit for foreign death taxes paid (§ 2014), discussed at ¶ 7509.

[¶ 7459]

1. STATE DEATH TAXES

a. *Federal Credit for State Death Taxes Paid (§ 2011)*

Persons dying in 2005 and thereafter no longer enjoy a credit against their estate tax bill for state death taxes. Instead, § 2058 provides a deduction for state death taxes paid. However § 2058 "sunsets" and the federal credit for state death taxes is revived effective as to decedents dying in 2011—unless Congress acts, in the meantime, to make repeal permanent.

i. *Historical Perspective*

The federal credit for state death taxes paid originated in 1926 at a time when Congress considered eliminating the federal estate tax. The Coolidge Administration conceived of the scheme whereby the federal government would rebate to the states 80 percent of the federal estate tax collected. However, in order to participate in this early form of revenue-sharing, a state had to have a death tax. This prompted all states except Nevada to adopt death taxes. A number of states adopted taxes that were exactly equal to the federal credit.

Later, the federal government decided to get back into the death tax business. However, because so many states had keyed their revenue expectations to the continued presence of the federal credit, Congress felt that the federal credit for state death taxes paid could not be repealed. Instead, Congress raised the rates and otherwise restructured the federal estate tax but always kept the federal credit exactly equal to the credit that was made available to the states in 1926 when the federal credit was first introduced into the federal estate tax.

In 2001, Congress got over its inhibitions and repealed the federal credit for state death taxes paid, phasing it out gradually through 2004.

Note that while some states have gift taxes, at no time has there been a federal credit for gift taxes paid.

[¶ 7467]

ii. Computation of the Credit

The federal credit for state death taxes paid was equal to the *lesser* of:

1. The total of the state death taxes *actually* paid or

2. The amount determined from the state death tax credit table that appears in § 2011(b);

3. Reduced by the applicable percentage for the year of death found in § 2011(b)(2)(B).

Critical to the use of the state death tax credit table is the concept of *"adjusted taxable estate,"* a term which has no other place in the Internal Revenue Code. The adjusted taxable estate is the decedent's "taxable estate" *less* $60,000. See § 2011(b) (last sentence).

Problem

[¶ 7473]

While the federal credit for state death taxes paid ended in 2004, it is restored automatically to decedents dying in 2011 and thereafter, absent Congressional action. Restoration will provide a immediate revenue surge to states whose death tax was linked to the federal credit (and who found themselves with a revenue loss when the credit ended in 2004.) Thus, for a quick look at how the federal credit was determined when it was available, using Table 7.6, determine the maximum credit for state death taxes paid available to the estate of Rachel (assuming she dies in 2011). Rachel's taxable estate was $5,128,500.

Table 7.6
STATE DEATH TAX CREDIT TABLE*
(For estates of persons dying after 1976)

(A) At least	(B) But less than	(C) Credit =	+ %	(D) Of Excess Over	(E) At least	(F) But less than	(G) Credit =	(H) + %	(I) Of Excess Over
$ 0	$ 40,000	0	0.0	$ 0	2,540,000	3,040,000	146,800	8.8	2,540,000
40,000	90,000	0	0.8	40,000	3,040,000	3,540,000	190,800	9.6	3,040,000
90,000	140,000	400	1.6	90,000	3,540,000	4,040,000	238,800	10.4	3,540,000
140,000	240,000	1,200	2.4	140,000	4,040,000	5,040,000	290,800	11.2	4,040,000
240,000	440,000	3,600	3.2	240,000	5,040,000	6,040,000	402,800	12.0	5,040,000
440,000	640,000	10,000	4.0	440,000	6,040,000	7,040,000	522,800	12.8	6,040,000
640,000	840,000	18,000	4.8	640,000	7,040,000	8,040,000	650,800	13.6	7,040,000
840,000	1,040,000	27,600	5.6	840,000	8,040,000	9,040,000	786,800	14.4	8,040,000
1,040,000	1,540,000	38,800	6.4	1,040,000	9,040,000	10,040,000	930,800	15.2	9,040,000
1,540,000	2,040,000	70,800	7.2	1,540,000	10,040,000	....	1,082,800	16.0	10,040,000
2,040,000	2,540,000	106,800	8.0	2,040,000					

* "Adjusted taxable estate" equals taxable estate minus $60,000. § 2011(b)(last sentence)

[¶ 7475]

b. State Death Tax Systems

The death tax systems in a few states are patterned after the federal estate tax. Many states, however, have another form of death tax commonly referred to as an inheritance tax. An inheritance tax differs from an estate tax in the sense that the available exemption and the applicable tax rates are determined by the relationship of the decedent and the beneficiaries of the decedent's estate. That is, property passing to a surviving spouse will be subject to lower rates and enjoy a higher exemption than property passing from the decedent to a nonrelative.

In recent years, many states abandoned their formal inheritance tax systems and substituted what is variously referred to as a "soak-up tax" or a "pick-up tax". That is, these states imposed an inheritance tax exactly equal to the maximum federal credit available when computing the estate tax liability of the decedent for state death taxes paid by that decedent. Obviously, the administrative problems were greatly reduced by such a system. Despite the apparent simplicity of the soak-up tax alternative, a number of states resisted it out of concerns that its application would produce less tax in some estates than the state's independent inheritance tax system.

[¶ 7478]

c. Decoupling and Choice of Law

In retrospect those states that maintained an inheritance tax independent of the maximum federal credit, i.e., those states whose inheritance was "decoupled" from the federal credit were prescient. With the repeal of the federal credit effective as to those decedents dying after 2004, states that coupled their inheritance tax to the federal credit find that the state inheritance tax has been effectively repealed. Faced with this prospect, state legislatures are confronted with either finding other sources to make up the loss of revenue or reintroducing an independent inheritance tax to an electorate acculturated to the notion that a decedent's property should not be subject to a "death tax". The results vary from state to state. Some states were fortunate in having legislated the pick-up tax less than artfully and the result is that the pick-up tax endures despite the repeal of the federal credit.

The resulting hodge podge of legislation means that, ever more so, domiciliary choice is important to how much tax is paid at death. Some states, such as Texas which does not have a state income tax and whose pick up inheritance tax has been effectively repealed, have become especially attractive as a possible domicile. Other states have become less attractive because they offer an independent inheritance tax that is on top of the federal estate tax—usually with an income tax to top it off.

For related material, see ¶¶ 11,089; 15,281; 21,870.

[¶ 7483]

d. Inheritance Tax Administration Problems

An inheritance tax does not work very well when applied to future interests. In most instances, until the future interest becomes possessory, the ultimate recipient of the property is uncertain. Since the applicable inheritance tax rate and exemption is determined by reference to the relationship of the donor and donee, computation of the final inheritance tax liability for gifts of future interests must often be deferred until the interest becomes possessory and the ultimate taker is ascertained. In the meantime, it is common to collect inheritance tax from the decedent's estate on the assumption that the property will pass to the beneficiary whose relationship to the donee will enable the state to collect the most tax. Tax is then paid under a "temporary" court order pending determination of the actual recipient of the future interest which may occur many years later. When the ultimate taker is finally identified, he or she can then petition for a refund of the inheritance tax paid under the "temporary" court order.

Payment of inheritance tax under the "temporary" order procedure means not only that for many years the decedent's beneficiaries may not have the use of property held by the court under the "temporary" order, but also, it creates problems with the administration of the federal estate tax.

[¶ 7485]

ESTATE OF WEISSBERGER v. COMMISSIONER

United States Tax Court, 1957.
29 T.C. 217, acq., 1958–2 C.B. 8.

FORRESTER, Judge. * * *

Petitioner paid to the State of Ohio the amount of $6,710.41 on account of the inheritance tax imposed by that State. Of that amount, $3,677.22 was paid under permanent order, pursuant to one provision of the State law, and the remaining $3,033.19 was paid under temporary order, pursuant to another provision thereof.

Under Ohio law, the tax rate may vary depending upon the nature of actual succession to the decedent's estate. Where such succession is subject to conditions or contingencies a tax is imposed at the highest rate possible under any resolution thereof. If succession as ultimately determined warrants a lower tax, a refund may be made of the excess. Ohio Rev. Code Ann. § 5731.28 (page 1954).

* * *

Respondent has determined that no part of the amount paid under temporary order qualifies for the credit against the basic estate tax as set forth in [1986 Code § 2011(d)]. We believe that determination erroneous.

Respondent's argument, based upon the possibility of a refund in the future, is unsound. A refund of any tax paid is always possible, at least until barred by an applicable period of limitation. A tax paid may have to be refunded in whole or in part for any one of an infinite variety of reasons. To deny the credit claimed here simply because a future refund is possible is to judicially repeal [1986 Code § 2011(d)].

Furthermore, Congress has recognized the possibility of such refunds and has made express provision therefore. [1986 Code § 2016] The normal period of limitation will not bar respondent from collecting any additional estate tax due as a result of the refund of a part of the amount paid under temporary order.

* * *

[The court took special note of the fact that] the amount in question was in fact paid and not merely deposited, and was paid in respect of property included in the gross estate [in concluding that the credit was available].

Problem

[¶ 7487]

What is the basic estate tax referred to in § 2011(d) and in the *Weissberger* case? Does it have any relevance for the administration of the federal estate tax? Perhaps it has relevance only because it facilitates the administration of the several state death tax schemes? See, e.g., Ohio Rev. Code Ann. § 5731.18 (Page 1973).

[¶ 7489]

Note

Payment of state inheritance taxes under temporary order made necessary § 2015, "Credit for Death Taxes on Remainders," and § 2016, "Recovery of Taxes Claimed as Credit."

¶ 7485

[¶ 7493]

2. CREDIT FOR GIFT TAX ON PRE–1977 TRANSFERS (§ 2012)

Gift taxes paid on pre–1977 transfers are treated differently than gift taxes paid or deemed payable on post–1976 transfers. Section 2012 applies to gift taxes paid on pre–1977 transfers while § 2001(b)(1) applies to post–1976 transfers.

General Explanation of the Tax Reform Act of 1976, prepared by the Staff of the Joint Committee on Taxation, part II, 530 (1976) states:

> The special credit against estate tax for gift tax payable with respect to lifetime transfers which are included in a decedent's gross estate (§ 2012) is not to apply to gifts made after December 31, 1976. For these gifts, the computation of the gross estate payable will reflect the credit for gift tax paid on lifetime transfers included in the gross estate. Thus, the special gift tax credit provision is not necessary under a unified transfer tax approach.

The § 2012 credit is available only in those cases where property which was transferred prior to 1977 is subsequently included in the donor's gross estate for estate tax purposes. Property transferred prior to 1977 will only be included in the transferor's gross estate for estate tax purposes if the transferor had an interest in the transferred property at death.

Example 1. Henry transferred Blackacre to his child, Mark, but retained the right to occupy Blackacre for the balance of his life. Henry was 80 at the time of the transfer in 1975 and Blackacre then had a value of $100,000. Henry will be deemed to have transferred a remainder interest to Mark. The remainder can be valued actuarially for gift tax purposes. Since Henry was 80 at the time of the conveyance, his life estate would be deemed to have a value of $27,098 ($100,000 x .27098 (Reg. § 20.2031–10, Table A–1)). Accordingly, Mark received a gift of $72,902.

Henry was required to file a gift tax return for the gift to Mark but the annual exclusion would not be available to Henry. § 2503(b). However, if Henry was married at the time of the gift, he could split the gift with his spouse. § 2013. Or if Blackacre was community property his wife would be deemed to have made one-half of the gift.

Assuming that Henry was not married at the time of the gift and that he had made no taxable gifts prior to the conveyance of Blackacre to Mark, Henry would have $5,438.44 of gift tax liability in 1975 as a result of the gift to Mark. His tax would have been determined as follows:

Value of remainder interest	$72,902.00
Less: Specific exemption	(30,000.00)
Taxable gifts	$42,902.00
Tax	$ 5,438.44

Example 2. Henry died in 2004. You can assume that Blackacre had a value of $300,000 in 2004. Accordingly, at Henry's death Blackacre would

be included in Henry's estate at its date of death value of $300,000. His executor could then claim a credit for the $5,438.44 of gift tax that was paid in 1975 on the property.

In determining the availability of the credit for gift tax on pre–1977 transfers it is relevant to know how the property came to be included in the decedent's estate.

> *Example 3.* Suppose Bob had given Whiteacre to his son, Tad, in 1975, and paid gift tax on the transfer. Assume that Tad died in 2000 leaving a will giving Whiteacre back to Bob. At Bob's death in 2004 his estate would not be entitled to a credit for the gift tax Bob paid in 1975 on the original transfer of Whiteacre. See Rev. Rul. 74–363, 1974–2 C.B. 290.

The credit for gift taxes paid on pre–1977 transfers is limited to (a) the *estate tax* attributable to the includible gifts or (b) the *gift tax* attributable to the includible gifts.

The effect of these limitations is to sometimes deny the transferor's estate a dollar-for-dollar credit for the gift tax paid on pre–1976 transfers. Dollar-for-dollar credit may be denied a transferor's estate, for example, if the property which gave rise to the particular gift tax has depreciated between the date of the gift and the date of the donor's death. See § 2012. For purposes of both limitations, the tax attributable to the gifted property is the proportionate share of the total tax and not the tax at the top marginal rates.

Return preparers do not often encounter an opportunity to utilize the credit for gift taxes paid on transfers made prior to 1977. However, in a case where it applies it would be a significant oversight not to claim it.

[¶ 7501]

3. CREDIT FOR TAX ON PRIOR TRANSFERS (§ 2013)

A decedent's estate often includes property transferred to the decedent as a result of the death of another person. If that person died less than 10 years before or two years after the decedent, a credit may be allowed under § 2013 against the federal estate tax for the tax paid on the property transferred to the decedent. The closer in time the decedent died to the transferor, the larger the credit. (This credit is sometimes referred to as the PPT, or property previously taxed, credit.)

It is interesting to note that neither the Internal Revenue Code nor the Regulations require that the transferred property be included or identified in the decedent's estate when applying for a prior transfer tax credit. Rev. Rul. 59–9, 1959–1 C.B. 232. In fact, the property need not even be in existence on the date of the decedent's death. Reg. § 20.2013–1(a). To establish the estate's right to a credit, an executor must establish that:

1. The decedent in fact received the property and that it was subjected to estate tax in the estate of the transferor. Reg. § 20.2013–1(a);

2. The decedent owned more than bare legal title to the property, such as that of a trustee. Reg. § 20.2013–5(a); and

3. The transferred property was capable of valuation by recognized valuation principles on the date of the transferor's death. Rev. Rul. 67–33, 1967–1 C.B. 62.

[¶ 7509]

4.   CREDIT FOR FOREIGN DEATH TAXES (§ 2014)

A credit is allowed against the federal estate tax for death taxes paid to foreign countries on the value of property included in the decedent's gross estate. § 2014. This credit is deducted only *after* deducting all other estate tax credits allowable. In the case of a resident alien, the credit is allowed only if the country of which the decedent was a national allows a similar credit in the case of a citizen of the United States resident in such country at the time of death. § 2014(h).

The credit is allowed only with respect to property which is: (1) subjected to the death tax of a foreign country, (2) situated in such foreign country, and (3) included in the decedent's *gross estate* for federal estate tax purposes. § 2014(a). Furthermore, the foreign death tax credit is allowed on an amount which is equal to the lesser of (1) the foreign tax attributable to the property and (2) the estate tax attributable to the property. The tax attributable to the property is a proportionate amount of the total tax, not the tax at the highest marginal rates.

H.   GIFT STRATEGIES

[¶ 7601]

Experience with the estate tax and gift tax computational model suggests certain strategies when making gifts. For example, donors are always advantaged by transfers that are sheltered by the $12,000 per donee per annum exclusion provided by § 2503(b). Such transfers are particularly attractive on the deathbed. Yet, by way of contrast, deathbed transfers that generate gift tax liability have little appeal because the gift tax paid on transfers within three years of death will be recaptured and included in the donor's gross estate for estate tax purposes. For discussion, see ¶ 7185. Moreover, deathbed transfers of appreciated property are particularly to be avoided because of the carryover basis rules which result in the donee's assuming the donor's basis in the transferred property. For discussion, see ¶ 7133. If the same property is held until death, the property will possibly receive a tax-free step-up in basis free of income tax. § 1014(b)(6).

Problem

[¶ 7612]

Outline a gifting strategy for Jane. Jane's will causes all of her property to be divided in varying proportions among her cousins and her nephews and nieces. Her estate is substantial and includes cash, securities listed on the New York and other stock exchanges, mineral interests, and rental real property. Should Jane be encouraged to make $12,000 gifts to each of her beneficiaries? Would she be advantaged to give away property likely to appreciate? Depreciate? Property with a high basis relative to current fair market value? A low basis? Should she pay gift tax or should she limit herself to gifts that can be sheltered by the unified credit? Would your strategy be different if Jane were on her deathbed?

Chapter 8

INCOME TAXATION OF ESTATES AND TRUSTS

A. OBJECTIVES

[¶ 8001]

While the provisions of the Internal Revenue Code dealing with the income taxation of trusts and estates are complicated, they are based on two simple principles.

First is the "conduit" or "passthrough" principle. As a general rule, income earned by a trust will be taxed to either the trust or the beneficiary to whom the income is distributed, *but not to both of them*. Mechanically speaking, this principle is given effect by allowing the trust to deduct from its taxable income distributions made to beneficiaries and requiring the recipients to report the distribution as taxable income. When a trust accumulates income, it will pay a tax on the income in the year of accumulation. When that income is distributed to the beneficiary in a later year, the beneficiary will be income tax free.

The second principle is that "trust distributions always carry out income first." If the trust income is available for distribution in a given year—referred to as distributable net income (DNI) (see ¶ 8351)—all trust distributions will be deemed to be from income until DNI has been exhausted. After that, all distributions will be deemed to come from corpus and will pass to the distributees tax free.

"distributable net income"

The rule that trust distributions carry out income first is virtually absolute. It does not matter that the trustee of the trust says that the distribution is coming from corpus rather than income. It does not matter that the trust books state that a particular distribution was charged to corpus. It does not even matter that the trust instrument forbids the distribution of income to the person who received the distribution (so long as the distribution made to this recipient was authorized by the instrument). If the distribution was made while there was still DNI to be distributed, it will be deemed an income distribution and the beneficiary will be taxed as having received income.

So far as estates are concerned, the references in these materials are largely to trusts, but the principles developed apply equally to estates, except as noted.

Understanding how the income of trusts and estates is taxed is of obvious importance in structuring property transfers. The materials in this chapter provide a review of the fundamentals.

B. TAX POLICY DETERMINATIONS

[¶ 8051]

Congress appears to be absolutely committed to eliminating the trust as an income tax shelter. To that end, the income tax rules applicable to trusts (and estates, as well) have been made so restrictive that some of the rules can be seen as almost punitive. These special rules are referred to in the following terms:

1. *Rate compression* (see ¶ 21,351), meaning that the income tax rates applicable to trusts and estates are "compressed" relative to the income tax rates applicable to individuals, e.g., for 2006, taxable income of trusts and estates in excess of $10,050 is taxed at 35 percent, while the first $61,300 of taxable income for married persons filing jointly is taxed at 15 percent; only when the taxable income of married persons filing jointly, unmarried persons, or heads of households exceeds $336,550 will the excess be taxed at 35 percent.

2. *The trust consolidation rules* (see ¶ 21,520), meaning that some trusts having the same grantor and the same beneficiaries will be consolidated for income tax purposes; and

3. *The grantor trust rules* (see Chapter 22), which specify, among other things, that the income of certain trusts will be taxed to persons other than the persons who actually received that income.

C. WHAT IS INCOME?

[¶ 8101]

Receipts that constitute gross income when received by an individual will constitute gross income when received by a trust. Thus, the traditional exclusions apply. For example, transfers of property to the trust ordinarily will not constitute gross income. § 102(a). But if the subject of a transfer is the right to income from property, the income when earned will be taxable to the recipient—in this case, the trust. § 102(b)(2); Irwin v. Gavit, 268 U.S. 161 (1925).

In addition, a further distinction is made between income in a *trust* accounting sense and income in a *tax* accounting sense. The former is determined according to state law and the provisions of the governing instrument. Reg. § 1.643(b)–1. The latter is as defined by the Internal Revenue Code. See § 641(b), which provides that the taxable income of an estate or trust is to be computed in the same manner as for an individual, subject to certain exceptions. See also § 63(b), which defines taxable income for an individual.

¶ 8001

Example. State law or the governing instrument may direct that gains from the sale of trust property be allocated to the principal of the trust rather than to the income beneficiary. Such an allocation, however, will not change the federal tax consequences of the sale. To the extent gain is realized on the sale or exchange (Reg. § 1.61–6(a); § 1001), the gain will be recognized (§§ 61(a)(3), 1002) as gross income except to the extent the gain qualifies for nonrecognition pursuant to one of several provisions (Reg. § 1.61–6(b)) developed by Congress to cover instances where Congress felt that imposition of a tax would contravene social policy.

D. WHO IS THE TAXPAYER?

[¶ 8151]

1. TRUSTS DISTINGUISHED FROM CORPORATIONS

Trusts, unlike corporations, lack most of the attributes of separate juristic existence. See 1 Austin Wakeman Scott, et al., Scott & Ascher on Trusts § 2.1.4 (5th ed. 2006). This is because, conceptually, a trust is a relationship rather than an entity. Title to property transferred in trust is held by the trustee (and not the trust) subject, of course, to the duties of the beneficiary of the trust. See Restatement (Third) of Trusts § 2 (1992). For federal tax purposes, however, the trust is treated as a taxpaying entity. § 641(a). It is distinguished from a corporation, however, in the sense that the trust is allowed a deduction in computing its taxable income for amounts of income distributed to its beneficiaries. §§ 651(a), 661(a). Correspondingly, the recipient of the distribution must include the income received in his gross income. § 61(a)(15). A corporation, on the other hand, cannot deduct the dividends it pays to its shareholders in computing its taxable income. The obvious incentive to operate a business in trust form, however, is limited by the Internal Revenue Service's power to tax trusts as corporations where the trust has been created for the conduct of a business for profit. See Morrissey v. Commissioner, 296 U.S. 344 (1935). Trustlike tax treatment is limited to arrangements vesting in trustees "responsibility for the protection and conservation of property for beneficiaries." Reg. § 301.7701–4(a). However, the IRS has been unsuccessful in a number of cases where it attempted to tax trusts as corporations. For example, in Bedell v. Commissioner, 86 T.C. 1207 (1986), the court concluded that a testamentary trust for the decedent's surviving spouse and children was not "an association taxable as a corporation" because the beneficiaries were not "associates and their trust is not an association." Id. at 1222. Despite its conclusion, the court observed that the case "should not be regarded as authority for the conclusion that no testamentary trust can be classified as an association."

Problem

[¶ 8155]

Consider the following provision for possible inclusion in a trust. Would such a provision be effective to prevent claims by the IRS that the trust should be taxed like a corporation, i.e., so that the trust income is taxed at the trust level and again at the beneficiary level (without any deduction at the trust level for distributions of that income)?

Engaging in business. Notwithstanding any other provision in this instrument, the Trustee is specifically prohibited from engaging in any business enterprise or operating any business if such activity would constitute carrying on a business as that notion is understood under Reg. § 301.7701–2. Settlor's objective in granting broad administrative powers to the Trustee is to facilitate the Trustee in holding and conserving the property of the trust and not to permit the Trustee to carry on a business that results in the sharing of gains as would be commonly expected when persons are engaged in the conduct of a business.

[¶ 8160]

2.   DISTRIBUTIONS CARRY OUT INCOME

Is the income taxed to the trust? To the beneficiary? The rule might be stated this way: income retained by the trust will be taxed to the trust; income distributed to a beneficiary of a trust will be taxed to the beneficiary. A necessary corollary is the following rule: subject to certain limitations, every distribution from a trust to a beneficiary eligible to receive an income distribution carries out income from the trust to the beneficiary to the extent income is available for distribution. The purpose is to avoid manipulation of income tax consequences by trustee decisions to distribute or not to distribute. §§ 651(b), 661(a); ¶ 8351, 8701.

Example. Newt was the beneficiary of a trust that required all income to be distributed to Newt. The trust terminated at Newt's death, and Rupert was the designated remainderman. That year, the trust had dividend income of $20 and realized a gain of $8 when it sold its shares of MicroMagic, Inc. for $10. The trust's basis in the shares sold was $2. While the trust had $28 of gross income, the amount available for distribution was limited to $20 inasmuch as the $8 gain is allocated to principal under generally accepted trust accounting principles. See ¶ 8651. As a result, Newt is entitled to a distribution this year of, at most, $20. (The amount available to Newt might be further reduced by expenses incurred by the trust.)

E.   WHEN IS TRUST INCOME TAXABLE?

[¶ 8201]

Trusts and estates are required to report their income on an annual basis like other taxpayers. § 441(a). Trusts must report their income on a calendar year basis (§ 645(a)), but estates may use a fiscal year for income tax reporting purposes. § 441(b)(2).

An estate's ability to elect a fiscal year for tax purposes provides a distinct income tax planning device for distributions from the estate to a

¶ 8155

beneficiary. That is, income distributed to a beneficiary will only be recognized as such in the taxable year of the beneficiary in which falls the last month of the estate's taxable year.

> *Example.* The Jones estate elects a January 31st fiscal year (beginning February 1, 2006, and ending January 31, 2007). Assume further that on February 1, 2006, the estate distributes income to a beneficiary. Assuming that the beneficiary is a calendar year taxpayer, such income will be taxed to the beneficiary in 2007; the tax attributable to that income will not be payable until April 15, 2008 (although quarterly estimated payments may be required of the beneficiary during 2007). Thus, the beneficiary has the tax-free use of the 2006 distribution for two years.

> This deferral opportunity is permitted because the estate will be unable to calculate the income it has available for distribution—its distributable net income (DNI)—until the end of the estate's fiscal year (January 31, 2007); accordingly, the distribution on February 1, 2006 cannot be characterized as income or principal before January 31, 2007.

F. REQUIRED TAX RETURN

[¶ 8251]

An executor must file Form 1041, U.S. Fiduciary Income Tax Return, for the estate if the estate has gross income for its taxable year of $600 or more. § 6012(a)(3).

A trustee must file Form 1041 for the trust for each year in which the trust has "any taxable income" or if the trust has "gross income of $600 or over, regardless of the amount of taxable income." § 6012(a)(4). However, a special rule applies if the trust is revocable and the grantor is trustee. In that instance, the trust income need only be reported on the grantor's personal income tax return, using Form 1040. Reg. § 1.671–4(b).

G. THE COMPUTATIONAL SCHEME

[¶ 8301]

With modifications, taxable income is computed for trusts in the same manner as for individuals. § 641(b). For individuals, gross income is reduced by the cost of producing that income to determine adjusted gross income, and adjusted gross income, in turn, is reduced by certain other deductions specifically authorized by Congress for policy reasons. § 63. This results in taxable income against which is applied the tax table or rate schedule, whichever applies. See § 1. The amount is further reduced by credits specifically allowed by law. §§ 31–53.

When these concepts are applied to trust income taxation, items which will be gross income to an individual will be gross income to the trust. Reg. § 1.641(a)–2. Similarly, costs of producing the income, such as court costs, attorney and fiduciary fees (Reg. § 1.212–1(i)), taxes (§ 164), etc., will be deductible by the trust. See Reg. § 1.641(b)–1.

The rules for taxing the income from trusts and estates include these modifications:

1. *Exemption.* Trusts which must distribute all of their income currently—sometimes misleadingly referred to as simple trusts, see ¶ 8501—are entitled to a deduction for a personal exemption of $300. § 642(b). For all other trusts, the personal deduction is limited to $100. Estates get a $600 exemption.

2. *Distribution Deduction.* As a general rule, distributions made to beneficiaries are required to be deducted by both trusts and estates in determining taxable income, but only to the extent that the trust or estate has "distributable net income" (DNI) as determined under § 643(b). ¶ 8351. For exceptions, see ¶ 8701.

3. *Charitable Deduction.* While the charitable deduction (§ 170) is not available to trusts, amounts "paid" pursuant to the terms of the governing instrument for public charitable purposes are deductible by both estates and trusts, and amounts "permanently set aside" are deductible by estates and certain (not all) trusts. § 642(c).

4. *Income in Respect of a Decedent.* Trusts and estates are entitled to deduct federal estate taxes attributable to income in respect of a decedent (IRD) when such income is realized by the trust or estate. § 691(c)(1)(B). Examples of IRD, which are subject to both federal estate tax as well as federal income tax (upon receipt in the latter case), include:

   a. Accrued interest on United States Series E and EE savings bonds;

   b. Lump-sum or periodic distributions from pension and profit-sharing plans of previously untaxed amounts;

   c. Payments received as a result of an installment sale contract made by the decedent during life, such as periodic payments required by a land sale contract;

   d. Salary or other compensation owed the decedent at the time of death, the payment of which was not required prior to the death of the decedent, such as a bonus payable at year-end to a salesperson who died at midyear but met certain sales goals prior to death; and

   e. Renewal commissions payable to a deceased life insurance salesperson which are payable only when and if the policies sold by that salesperson are renewed by the purchaser. The availability of the deduction for federal estate taxes attributable to items of IRD means that the portion of the income in respect of the decedent which will theoretically be used to discharge the burden of the estate tax attributed to such income will not also be subject to income tax.

5. *Miscellaneous Itemized Deductions.* Estates and trusts may deduct "miscellaneous itemized deductions" to the extent that such deduc-

tions exceed 2 percent of the estate's or trust's adjusted gross income. § 67(a). While the adjusted gross income of an estate or trust is "computed in the same manner as in the case of an individual," an estate or trust, in arriving at adjusted gross income, is entitled to a deduction for 100 percent of the "costs which are paid or incurred in connection with the administration of the estate or trust," so long as those costs "would not have been incurred if the property were not held in such trust or estate." § 67(e). Four cases of note have been reported. In dispute, in each case, was the full deductibility of the fees incurred for investment advisory services provided the fiduciary whose task, typically, is to make the trust property productive. The argument is that these fees are subject to the 2 percent "haircut". The first decision, William J. O'Neill, Jr., Irrevocable Trust v. Commissioner, 994 F.2d 302 (6th Cir. 1993), nonacq. 1994–38 IRB 4, concluded that investment counsel fees were not subject to 2 percent floor. The later decisions, Scott v. United States, 328 F.3d 132 (4th Cir.2003); Mellon Bank, N.A. v. United States, 265 F.3d 1275 (Fed. Cir.2001); and Rudkin Testamentary Trust v. Commissioner, 124 T.C. 304 (2005) concluded otherwise. Certainly there was agreement in *O'Neill* and *Mellon Bank* that trustee fees were not subject to the 2 percent "haircut" and were fully deductible. (*Query*: Whether the dispute could be avoided if the trustee increased his or her fees by an amount sufficient to cover the investment advisory fees incurred by the trust and, on the trustee's personal income tax return, claimed a business expense deduction for the fees paid to the investment advisor. Or are there ethical implications—and, possibly, legal—implications for such a strategy?) Finally, it is fair to say, that all the courts would agree that the personal exemption deduction available to trusts and estates under § 642(b) and the distribution deduction under §§ 651 and 661, respectively, for amounts distributed to beneficiaries are fully deductible and not subject to the 2–percent "haircut."

The scheme for taxing trust income, then, is as follows (tracking here for convenience of reference, the U.S. Fiduciary Income Tax Return—Form 1041, assuming a discretionary trust with $1,000 of dividend income, $100 of attorney fees, and a distribution of $200 to a beneficiary):

Gross income	$1,000
Less: Cost of producing income (interest, taxes, etc.)	(100)
Adjusted total (adjusted gross) income	$ 900
Less: Deduction for distributions to beneficiaries......................	(200)
Federal estate tax attributable to income in respect of a decedent	–0–
Exemption	(100)
Taxable income	$ 600
Tax	$ 90
Less: Credits..	–0–
Tax liability	$ 90

¶ 8301

H. DISTRIBUTABLE NET INCOME (DNI)

[¶ 8351]

As noted earlier, a trust is essentially a conduit. To the extent income is retained by the trust, it is taxed to the trust. To the extent it is distributed by the trust, it will be taxed to the beneficiary. However, to limit the role of taxation in motivating distribution decisions, Congress established the principle that, with certain exceptions, every distribution to a beneficiary would constitute taxable income to the extent of the trust's distributable net income (DNI). Mechanically speaking, the trust is entitled to a deduction in computing its taxable income to the extent of the lesser of: (1) the amounts actually distributed or (2) distributable net income. §§ 651(b), 661(a). The amount constituting the distribution deduction allowable to the trust will correspondingly constitute gross income to those recipients who receive the distribution. §§ 652(a), 662(a).

The distributable net income concept (§ 643(a)) is designed to insure that the trust distribution deduction is limited to that amount of *income actually available for distribution.*

> *Example.* Recall the capital gains example noted in ¶ 8101. In that case, the governing instrument or state law may mandate that such gains be held in trust as a part of principal, thus rendering them unavailable for immediate distribution. Nonetheless, the gain continues to be recognized for federal income tax purposes by the trust (see Reg. § 1.641(a)–2; § 61(a)(3)), and, *but for the limitation of DNI* (see Reg. § 1.643(a)–3), the distribution to the beneficiary, which would otherwise be principal, would be taxed as income to the beneficiary.

Distributable net income is determined by adding to "adjusted gross income" the tax-exempt interest received by the trust and then reducing such "adjusted gross income" by the amount of capital gains, extraordinary dividends, and taxable stock dividends which are allocated to the principal of the trust pursuant to state law or the governing instrument and which, accordingly, are not available for distribution to the beneficiaries.

Strictly speaking, the statute approaches distributable net income from the standpoint of the "taxable income of the estate or trust computed with" certain indicated modifications. § 643(a). This approach is confusing in that the trust's taxable income cannot be determined until the trust's distribution deduction is determined. It is easiest to start with the "adjusted gross income" of the trust and then make the appropriate modifications to determine exactly how much is available for distribution. In fact, the Fiduciary Income Tax Return (Form 1041) begins with "adjusted gross income" (without describing it as such, choosing instead to describe it as "adjusted total income") in directing the determination of DNI.

¶ 8351

I. DISTRIBUTION DEDUCTIONS

[¶ 8401]

A trust is entitled to a deduction for amounts distributed to its beneficiaries to the extent of the nonexempt portion of the trust's DNI (§§ 651(a), 661(a)), provided such distributions are not merely distributions of specific property or payments of a sum of money (in not more than three installments) which were required by the governing instrument. § 663(a)(1). *Thus, it will not be uncommon for a distribution of corpus to be eligible for the distribution deduction and, thereby, constitute taxable income in the hands of the recipient.* That could happen, for instance, where a trustee elects to make a distribution to a beneficiary eligible for distributions of corpus *only,* makes no other distributions that tax year, and the trust has distributable net income. Reg. § 1.661(a)–2(c).

> *Comment.* While the distribution described illustrates the basic proposition, it is possible that in an actual case the separate share rule of § 663(c) will prevent the corpus distribution from carrying out the available DNI to the recipient of the corpus distribution. Section 663(c) provides: "For the sole purpose of determining the amount of distributable net income in the application of §§ 661 and 662, in the case of a single trust having more than one beneficiary, substantially separate and independent shares of different beneficiaries in the trust shall be treated as separate trusts." Conversely, distributions from whatever source in excess of DNI will not be deductible by the trust or taxable to the distributee.

J. CHARACTER OF DISTRIBUTION IN BENEFICIARIES' HANDS

[¶ 8451]

The conduit concept of taxing trust income requires that trust income which is distributed to the beneficiary have the same character in his or her hands as it would have if it had been retained by the trust. See §§ 652(b), 662(b).

Income retains its "character"

> *Example.* Capital gains or exempt interest when distributed to the beneficiary must be treated as capital gains and exempt interest for purposes of the beneficiary's income tax return. To do otherwise would impair the integrity of the conduit principle that governs trust income taxation.

K. SIMPLE TRUSTS

[¶ 8501]

Subpart 13 (§§ 651 and 652) of Subchapter J deals with what are called "simple" trusts. To qualify as a simple trust, the trust instrument or local law must require that all of the trust income be distributed in the year of receipt.

All income must be distributed in the year of receipt

¶ 8501

Further, there must be no charitable contributions for the taxable year and no distributions of amounts other than income. Note that a trust may qualify as a simple trust one year and as a complex trust the next year, when a distribution from corpus is made. A trust is never a simple trust in the year of its termination (because of the corpus distribution upon termination), and an estate is never a simple trust.

If a trust qualifies as a simple trust, the allocation of taxable income between the trust and the beneficiaries is relatively uncomplicated. Section 651 allows the trust a deduction for the amount required to be distributed currently, up to DNI (less any items not included in the trust's gross income). Section 652 provides for the inclusion in the beneficiary's gross income of all amounts required to be distributed currently by the trust, whether actually distributed or not, up to DNI. If there is more than one beneficiary, each includes the amount required to be distributed to him or her, and, if total distributions exceed DNI, each beneficiary includes a portion of DNI proportionate to the percentage of the income he or she received.

Deductions are allocated among the items of income. Any direct expenses are allocated first to the item of income to which the expense is attributable. Other indirect expenses are allocated pro rata among all the items of income.

L.   COMPLEX TRUSTS

[¶ 8551]

Complex trusts and estates are governed by the same set of distribution rules. These rules are set out in §§ 661 and 662.

Complex trusts cannot be effectively defined. At best they can be described. Probably the most accurate description of a complex trust is that it is a trust which is not a simple trust. While that statement, at best, could be described as "not helpful," perhaps the following examples of complex trusts will illustrate the problem inherent in finding a definition:

1. Trusts which make distributions of *both* income and corpus in the same tax year are complex trusts.

2. Trusts which are not required to make distributions and, in fact, do not make any distributions during a tax year are also complex trusts.

Trusts which are required to distribute all of the trust's income annually enjoy a $300 exemption for federal income tax purposes. § 642(b). Trusts which are not required to distribute all of the trust's income annually enjoy only a $100 exemption. (Estates enjoy a $600 exemption.)

There is a tendency to say that trusts entitled to a $300 exemption are "simple" trusts and that trusts not entitled to the $300 exemption are "complex" trusts. Such labels are misleading. A trust required by the governing instrument to distribute all of its income is entitled to the $300 exemption, even in years when it is classified as a complex trust because corpus was distributed from the trust in that particular year. See Reg. § 1.642(b)–1; § 651 (last sentence). Classification as a complex trust means that the rules

¶ 8501

set out in §§ 661–662 apply to the trust rather than those set out in §§ 651–652.

The principal distinction between complex and simple trusts is related to the problem of determining whether the property distributed by the trust constitutes taxable income to the beneficiary or represents a tax-free distribution of corpus. This problem is not present in the case of simple trusts because in such trusts the entire distribution constitutes taxable income to the distributees. By definition, a trust would not be a simple trust if amounts were distributed in excess of the trust's income. § 651(a) (last sentence).

Practically speaking, the complex trust rules have, as probably their most important function, the task of allocating the trust's DNI whenever trust distributions are made to more than one beneficiary in a particular year.

Where more than one distributee receives amounts from the trust, DNI is normally apportioned between them ratably, regardless of the nature of the assets actually distributed to each or to the trust accounting source of the payment (that is, without regard to whether, for trust accounting purposes, the distribution is deemed to come from corpus rather than income). There are three exceptions to this rule which are important from a planning standpoint:

1. *The Specific Bequest Rule.* Satisfaction of a gift of specific property or payment of a specific sum of money payable in not more than three installments is treated as a gift of property rather than income. § 663(a)(1). Therefore, in keeping with the principle that gifts or bequests are not income (see § 102(a) and Irwin v. Gavit, 268 U.S. 161 (1925)), such amounts simply fall outside the distribution rules completely, and satisfaction of such gifts and bequests does not carry out income to the legatee.

2. *The Separate Share Rule.* If separate shares are set aside solely for the benefit of designated beneficiaries without power in the fiduciary to invade either principal or income for the benefit of other beneficiaries, the DNI of one such separate share will not be deemed distributed to another beneficiary. § 663(c).

3. *The Tier System.* Priority in DNI payments is accorded to mandatory "income" distributees and annuitants (to the extent the latter are actually paid out of "income"). Other distributees are deemed to receive DNI only to the extent that it exceeds so-called "first tier" payments to such distributees. § 662(a)(1) and (2).

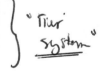

M.   THE TIER SYSTEM OF PRIORITIES

[¶ 8601]

The so-called tier system of allocating DNI among multiple distributees from the same trust refers to the mandatory allocation of DNI whenever there are: (1) both mandatory and discretionary income recipients and/or (2) multiple recipients of mandatory payments and/or discretionary payments.

The "first tier" recipients are those who have a legally enforceable right to a current distribution of income from the trust. §§ 652(a), 662(a)(1). The available DNI will be prorated among these beneficiaries, with each beneficiary taking his pro rata share of dividends, capital gain, and tax-exempt income, as well as other income included in the DNI of the trust.

The "second tier" distributees are all others who receive distributions but have no legally enforceable right to a distribution of income. § 662(a)(2). Distributions to second tier beneficiaries will constitute taxable income only to the extent that the first tier beneficiaries did not exhaust the available DNI. The DNI remaining after the allocation to the first tier beneficiaries is prorated among the second tier beneficiaries with each one taking a proportionate share of dividend income, capital gain, tax-exempt interest, etc. § 662(a)(2)(B).

> *Example.* Dad's trust provides that Mom is to receive all income for life. The trustee is also authorized to distribute principal to Son. This year the trust has $10 of income, distributes $10 to Mom, and distributes $4 to Son. The $10 distributed to Mom is taxable income to Mom, while the $4 distributed to Son is a nontaxable distribution.

The statute speaks in terms of second tier distributions being "properly paid, credited, or required to be distributed to all beneficiaries." §§ 661(a)(2), 662(a)(2). Each of those words is important in determining the distribution deduction of the trust and the taxable income of the beneficiaries inasmuch as distributions which are "properly paid, credited, or required to be distributed" carry out the trust's income to the recipient of the distribution.

Determination of whether or not the payments are "proper" turns on applicable local law and the governing instrument. See, e.g., Kennedy v. Commissioner, 38 B.T.A. 1307 (1938) (distribution deductible by trust in computing income only if the payment is proper); Buckmaster v. United States, 984 F.2d 379 (10th Cir.1993) (distributions not improper because made prior to court approval where court approval later obtained).

For an amount to be determined "paid" or "credited," an actual payment or specific credit to the beneficiary must occur. In determining whether an amount has been "paid," neither accrual notions nor the idea of constructive receipt is utilized. See McCauley v. United States, 61–1 USTC ¶ 9108 (E.D.Ark.1960), (not considered "paid" where the executrix, as sole beneficiary of the estate, deposited estate funds to her own bank account, intending thereby merely to repay herself for advances to the estate). However, there will be a payment within the meaning of the statute when the trustee uses trust funds to discharge a legal obligation of the beneficiary. See Old Colony Trust Co. v. Commissioner, 279 U.S. 716 (1929). In such cases, the beneficiary is deemed to have taxable income to the extent that his legal obligation is discharged. Rev. Rul. 58–69, 1958–1 C.B. 254.

When an amount is "credited" to a beneficiary, actual payment need not be made. A mere bookkeeping entry is not sufficient, however, because the amount must be subject to immediate enjoyment by the beneficiary. This

¶ 8601

becomes a question of fact for the courts. See Harris v. United States, 370 F.2d 887 (4th Cir.1966).

N. DNI v. FIDUCIARY ACCOUNTING INCOME

[¶ 8651]

Distributable net income is a federal tax concept created in the Internal Revenue Code, whereas fiduciary accounting income is the concept used to establish the competing rights of income beneficiaries and remaindermen. This latter concept is determined by the governing instrument and applicable local law. Essentially, wherever the term "income" appears in Subchapter J and is not preceded by words such as "taxable," "distributable net," "undistributed net," or "gross," it refers to fiduciary accounting income. This is defined by the statute to be the amount of income of the estate or trust for the taxable year determined "under the terms of the governing instrument and applicable local law." § 643(b). This deference to state law is a keystone of federal taxing policy. Thus, exercise of discretion by a fiduciary in allocating between principal and income will be binding if the fiduciary acts in good faith. Thornton v. Commissioner, 5 T.C. 1177 (1945), acq., 1946–2 C.B. 4. Where a trustee abused his discretion and allocated ordinary dividends to principal, the Service refused to be bound. Doty v. Commissioner, 148 F.2d 503 (1st Cir.1945). The only limitation on this deference to state law and the governing instrument is that the federal courts reserve the right to make an independent determination of what state law will be in a particular case in those instances in which the highest court of the state has not yet ruled on the issue. Commissioner v. Bosch, 387 U.S. 456 (1967); Case v. Commissioner, 8 T.C. 343 (1947), acq., 1947–1 C.B. 1.

The distinction between DNI and fiduciary accounting income is an important one for understanding Subchapter J. For example, the tier system of allocating DNI among distributees of the same trust is pegged to fiduciary accounting income. Thus, first tier beneficiaries are those who have a claim to income as that income is determined for fiduciary accounting purposes. §§ 662(a)(1), 643(b).

O. NONDEDUCTIBLE DISTRIBUTIONS

[¶ 8701]

There are several circumstances in which distributions from a trust (or an estate) will not be deductible in computing the trust's taxable income. §§ 651(b), 661(a). Specifically:

1. Distributions in excess of DNI will not be deductible by the trust (or estate) or taxable to the recipient. §§ 652(a), 662(a).

2. Distributions which meet the specific bequest rule of § 663(a)(1) are disengaged from the distribution rules. These distributions are specifically denied deduction by the trust (or estate) and are not included in

the income of the distributee. Distribution to a beneficiary in satisfaction of a specific bequest of "my grandfather clock" would satisfy § 663(a)(1). For related discussion, see ¶ 3351, 8551.

P.   BASIS OF PROPERTY HELD IN TRUST

[¶ 8751]

1.   INTRODUCTION

When it comes to basis, trusts and estates are treated like any other taxpayer. More specifically, property purchased by the trustee has its cost as its basis. § 1012. Property acquired from the settlor or creator of the trust has for its basis the grantor's basis if the trust was created inter vivos, § 1015, or, if testamentary, the estate tax value at date of death or at alternate valuation date. § 1014(a).

Technically speaking, property included in the estate of a decedent has, for its basis in the hands of a donee, its estate tax value at the decedent's date of death or at alternate valuation date. Thus, in cases where property was transferred to a trust during the life of the transferor and is subsequently included in the transferor's gross estate for estate tax purposes, that property will have as its basis in the hands of the trustee its estate tax value at the death of the transferor.

[¶ 8755]

2.   CARRY OVER BASIS

In 2010, carry over basis is scheduled to replace the new-basis-at-death rule. § 1022. The basis of property acquired from decedents dying in 2010 will, in principle, carry over to the recipient of that property. However, the new-basis-at-death rule will automatically be revived as to decedents dying in 2011 and subsequent years—unless Congress acts to bring about a different result in the meantime.

As for that carry over basis year—2010—a number of exceptions and modifications will apply in determining basis in the hands of recipients. First, basis in the hands of the recipient will be the *lower* of the decedent's basis or fair market value of the transferred property at the decedent's death. § 1022(a). Second, a $1.3 million aggregate basis increase is available to be allocated among the different items of property included in the decedent's estate. § 1022(b). Third, an additional $3 million aggregate basis increase is available to be allocated among items acquired by a surviving spouse from the decedent. § 1022(c) The $3 million spousal basis increase is available for qualified terminable interest property held in trust. § 1022(c)(3)(B). Notwithstanding the foregoing, worth noting, is that resulting basis in the hands of recipients cannot exceed the date of death value of that property. § 1022(d)(2).

¶ 8701

[¶ 8765]

3. ADJUSTMENTS TO BASIS OF TRUST AND ESTATE PROPERTY

Depreciation deductions are allowable to both estates and trusts with respect to income-producing or business property (§ 167(a)(1) and (2)) held by the estate or trust. However, the depreciation deduction will be shared with the beneficiaries in proportion to the income distributed to the beneficiaries and the income retained by the estate or trust. §§ 642(e) and 167(h); Reg. § 1.167(h)–1. Furthermore, regardless of the allocation of the depreciation deduction, the basis of property in the hands of the fiduciary is required to be adjusted downward to take account of depreciation.

Q. BENEFICIARY'S BASIS

[¶ 8801]

The beneficiary's basis in distributed property is the trust's (or estate's) basis immediately prior to distribution (see § 1015(a)), except in cases where gain or loss has been recognized by the trust (or estate) as a result of the distribution in kind. See § 643(e). For discussion, see ¶ 21,400–417. A distribution in kind will constitute gross income to a beneficiary only if the distribution is not within the "specific gift or bequest" rule of § 663 and either: (a) the trust has DNI and the only distribution during that tax year is one in kind (i.e., no cash is distributed) or (b) if cash is distributed, along with property, the DNI exceeds the cash. Reg. § 1.661(a)–2(f)(3). To the extent the cash distribution does not soak up the available DNI, the DNI will be allocated to the distribution in kind, causing that portion of the distribution in kind to be gross income to the recipient.

Problems

[¶ 8820]

1. Mollie is to get all of the income produced by a trust each year. In addition, she is to receive from the principal of the trust whatever additional amount is necessary for her health, education, maintenance, and support. In Year 4, the trust, with a corpus of $200,000, produced $9,000 of dividend income and $1,000 of capital gain realized on the sale of securities held by the trust. The trustee, T, distributed $10,000 to Mollie during Year 4. What are the income tax consequences to the trust? To Mollie? Assume that the capital gain was attributed to Mollie. (Remember that amounts distributed to beneficiaries are to have the same character in the hands of the recipients as they would have had had those amounts been retained by the entity. §§ 652(b), 662(b). That is, tax-exempt interest income is to be tax-exempt interest income to the distributee. Capital gains are to be capital gains in the hands of the distributee. You say, so what? It may mean a great deal taxwise to the recipient. Can you explain why?)

2. Refer to the facts in the preceding problem and assume $12,000 was distributed to Mollie in Year 4. Assume that the capital gains were attributed to the trust.

¶ 8820

3.   Refer to the preceding problem and assume that in Year 4, Mollie's child, Chad, was also eligible to receive distributions of principal for his maintenance, care, and support and that the trustee distributed $3,000 to Chad (in addition to $12,000 to Mollie). Assume that the capital gain is attributed to the beneficiaries. (Remember that where there are two or more beneficiaries, DNI is to be allocated among the distributees according to their respective eligibility for distributions of income. See § 662(a).)

Chapter 9

GENERATION–SKIPPING TAX BASICS

A. OBJECTIVES

[¶ 9001]

Chapter 13 of the Internal Revenue Code imposes an excise tax on generation-skipping transfers. Although mastery of the subtleties of this so-called generation-skipping tax ("GST") requires considerable study, a general understanding of the workings of the tax and its underlying concepts is essential to effective tax planning.

In order to understand the tax, ask the "who, what, when" questions familiar to tax planners. First, the tax applies only to transfers of property to transferees who are at least two generations younger than the transferor—and who are called "skip persons" in Chapter 13 of the Internal Revenue Code.

Example. H's will establishes a trust which provides that the trustee may make distributions for the benefit of W and the lineal descendants of H. At H's death, H has a child, C, and a grandchild, X (a "skip person"). The trust is to terminate at W's death, and the remaining trust property is to be distributed to H's then living lineal descendants *per stirpes*.

The trust is a generation-skipping trust because its beneficiaries include X—and X's generation assignment is two generations younger than that of H, the transferor. However, whether the tax applies depends on whether a "taxable termination," a "taxable distribution," or a "direct skip" occurs. A taxable distribution will occur if the trustee makes a distribution to X during C's lifetime, C being a "non-skip person." A taxable termination will occur if C predeceases W and the trustee distributes the trust property to X at W's death. A direct skip would occur if, in the creation of the trust, H provided that X was the sole beneficiary of the trust.

Comment: Gifts to skip persons attract both the generation-skipping tax and either the estate or the gift tax. This is a powerfully important point that needs specific emphasis.

Who pays the tax? The trustee is liable for the tax in the event of a taxable termination or a direct skip from a trust. In the event of a taxable distribution, the beneficiary receiving the distribution is liable. The transferor is liable for the tax on a direct skip which is not from a trust.

How is the tax determined? <u>First, the amount of property subject to the tax is determined</u>. This amount is then <u>multiplied by the applicable rate, which is found by determining the "inclusion ratio" and multiplying it by the *maximum* federal estate tax rate</u>.

Not to be overlooked is the $2 million generation-skipping tax exemption. Each taxpayer has a $2 million exemption that can be used to shelter his or her generation-skipping transfers from the generation-skipping tax. That means, for example, that a taxpayer could create a $2 million trust by will for the benefit of his or her children, grandchildren, great-grandchildren and so on, limited only by the rule against perpetuities (to the extent applicable), and distributions from the trust over the years to skip persons, namely grandchildren and great-grandchildren, etc., <u>will be completely free of the generation-skipping tax</u>. The distributions will be completely free of the tax even though the total distributions (and the value of the trust) greatly exceed $2 million. <u>The critical determination as to whether the trust is exempt from the generation-skipping tax is made at the time that the $2 million is placed in the trust.</u> Once exempt, always exempt (so long as modifications or additions are not made to the trust).

Despite this engagingly simplistic description of the generation-skipping tax, even the most sophisticated of observers view the operative provisions of Chapter 13 of the Internal Revenue Code as <u>daunting-</u>

> *While the GST exemption and the estate tax exemption—both $2 million in 2006 through 2008—are each scheduled to increase $3.5 million in 2009, the gift tax per donee per annum exclusion—$12,000 in 2006—is adjusted by the IRS for inflation as warranted.*

ly complex. Moreover, because of the risk that even because of the risk that even simple arrangements may generate a generation-skipping transfer and trigger the tax, the tax cannot be ignored. As quick but stunning examples of the kinds of arrangements that are subject to the tax, note that a gift of more than $12,000 to a grandchild in 2006 used up a portion of the donor's $2 million exemption and that a gift of $12,000 or less to a single trust for the benefit of both of the donor's children and grandchildren used up to $12,000 of the donor's $2 million exemption (<u>despite both gifts possibly being sheltered from the gift tax by the annual $10,000—$12,000 in 2006, adjusted for inflation—per donee per annum gift tax exclusion provided by § 2503(b)</u>). See § 2642(c), discussed at ¶ 9309, 9357–9365, 23,251.

In addition to detailing the operation of the generation-skipping tax (and defining the many terms whose meaning is essential to understanding the tax), these materials will highlight some of the generation-skipping tax pitfalls awaiting unwary tax planners and, in some instances, suggest how they can be avoided. The chapter will also include suggestions as to how to take advantage of some of the planning opportunities inherent in the generation-skipping tax scheme.

¶ 9001

Perhaps the best beginning would be to turn to the summary at the end of this chapter (¶ 9501) so as to identify the targets of your inquiry as you proceed through the materials.

B.   HISTORICAL PERSPECTIVE

[¶ 9051]

1.   INTRODUCTION

The easiest way to begin to understand the operation of Chapter 13 is to understand its purpose. The generation-skipping tax is designed to operate in conjunction with the estate and gift transfer taxes to ensure the once-a-generation taxation of wealth. This is known as the "periodic" aspect of transfer taxation; it has been one of the central goals of federal taxation since the enactment of the first federal estate tax.

Were there no federal or state taxes on the transfer of property between generations, it may well be that most property would pass outright (*i.e.*, free of trust) from one generation to the next. That is, absent tax considerations, most persons survived only by children would have wills that cause their property to pass to the children free of trust. When property passes in this manner, wealth is enjoyed by each successive generation, and anything remaining at the death of a member of one generation will pass, via his or her will or by intestacy, to the decedent's loved ones in the next generation. (Counter to this notion is the situation involving beneficiaries needing protection, in the thinking of the donor, from the predators of the world, the biggest predator sometimes being the beneficiaries themselves.)

However, so long as there is an estate tax, many taxpayers will look for techniques that make it possible for the taxpayer to enjoy the benefits from or control the enjoyment of property during life, while escaping tax on that property at death. It was the reaction of Congress to these tax-avoidance schemes that led to the amendment of the estate tax laws in 1976 and their integration with the federal gift tax system in a manner which reduced (but did not eliminate entirely) the incentive to make lifetime transfers for tax-avoidance purposes. See § 2001(b); ¶ 7117.

Problem

[¶ 9057]

If the estate tax and gift tax rates are the same, why is there an incentive to make lifetime gifts? After all, adjusted taxable gifts are added back into a decedent's gross estate at the decedent's death. What is not added back? See §§ 2001(b)(1)(B); 2035(b).

[¶ 9059]

2.   ESTATE TAX–AVOIDANCE

Notwithstanding Congress's efforts, certain tax-avoidance techniques utilized by taxpayers over the years defeated (particularly until 1976) the periodicity of the federal estate tax, *i.e.*, the tax-once-a-generation principle. For example, the concept basic to the estate tax is that the estate tax is imposed on the transferor of the property. This notion prevented "life interests," *i.e.*, interests which terminated at the life tenant's death, from being included in the life tenant's gross estate (except in cases where the deceased life tenant had been the initial transferor of the property in which he or she held the life estate at death). Read § 2036, which makes life estates includible in the life tenant's gross estate only if "retained" by the life tenant following a lifetime transfer. From your reading of § 2036, you will probably agree with the conclusion that much property undoubtedly passes free of the estate tax because the decedent—in this example, the life tenant—was not a "transferor" of the property since, with limited exceptions, the estate tax applies only to property "transferred" by the decedent.

[¶ 9067]

3. THE GENERATION–SKIPPING BYPASS TRUST

The failure of the estate tax to subject a life estate to tax at the death of the life tenant gave estate planners a powerful tool for reducing the efficiency of the estate tax. Although a transfer tax—the gift tax—would have to be paid on the initial transfer of property for the benefit of another for life, interests in the property could be split in a fashion that would allow one or more generations to enjoy the property while incurring no estate tax liability at death. (The proverbial case being "life estate to the children, followed by a life estate to the grandchildren, followed by a life estate to the great-grandchildren," subject only to the rule against perpetuities, where applicable.) As a result of such interest-splitting, estate tax liability was easily limited to every other generation, or even less frequently. This can be illustrated by the following example.

Example. If there were no estate tax, Grandmother Smith (a widow) would be likely to leave all of her property outright at death to her two sons, Clem and Zeke. When Clem and Zeke die, each would likely leave his share of his mother's property to his children (after likely providing for any surviving spouse by giving the spouse a life estate in the property).

Instead, prior to 1976, because of the estate tax, Grandmother Smith would likely have been well-advised to provide in her will that her property was to be divided into two shares, each of which would be used to fund a trust. Each trust would provide income for life to one of her sons; on the death of that child, the remainder would pass to his descendants free of trust. (Interestingly, it would be uncommon to find that Grandmother Smith had made provision for the spouses of her children.)

Although estate tax would have to be paid at Grandmother Smith's death on her transfer of the property into trust, no part of her estate would be included in the estates of Clem or Zeke when they died. Their life "income interests" would terminate at death, and the trust property would "bypass" their estates for estate tax purposes. Thus, one estate tax would be skipped, and Clem and Zeke would be able to enjoy their respective shares of their mother's estate in a manner substantially identical to their enjoyment had the property been given to them free of trust.

Prior to the enactment of the generation-skipping tax, as noted above parenthetically, the Rule Against Perpetuities provided the only limitation on the period in which estate taxation could be avoided by a string of successive life interests such as that contemplated by Grandmother Smith's single-generation skip.

[¶ 9075]

4. MOVE FOR REFORM

Both Congress and the Department of the Treasury became increasingly aware that generation-skipping transfers were being used for tax avoidance. A 1969 study of estate and gift tax returns from 1957 and 1959 caused the IRS to conclude that more than 25 percent of the value of property transferred in those years, by decedents whose gross estates equalled or exceeded $1.5 million, passed by way of untaxed generation-skipping transfers. As a result of these and other findings, the Treasury Department, and then Congress, became convinced that some means had to be devised to stop this perceived leakage of the transfer tax base.

[¶ 9083]

5. THE 1976 AND 1986 GST SCHEMES

The first generation-skipping taxation scheme was enacted by Congress in 1976. It basically provided that only those arrangements allowing persons to enjoy the benefits of property without including it in their gross estates would be subject to the generation-skipping tax. This scheme was expressed in terms of "no benefit/no tax."

The 1976 version of the statute, however, proved to be so very complex in comprehension and computation that Congress, in the Tax Reform Act of 1986 at the suggestion of the Treasury Department, completely revised Chapter 13, keeping the same objectives but intending the provisions to be much simpler in application and understanding. In the process, Congress completely repealed the original version of Chapter 13 retroactively and provided for the substituted statute to become effective, generally, with respect to generation-skipping transfers made after October 22, 1986 (the date of enactment of the legislation).

6. "GRANDFATHERED" ARRANGEMENTS

When the present GST was implemented in the Tax Reform Act of 1986, the Treasury enacted Temporary Reg. § 26.2601–1(b)(1)(v)(A) in order to protect taxpayers who had legitimately made trust and estate provisions that made sense prior to enactment of the 1986 GST but which were no longer advantageous. The regulation provided that the GST will not apply to "any generation-skipping transfer under a trust which was irrevocable on September 25, 1985, but only to the extent that such transfer is not made out of *corpus added to the trust* after September 25, 1985 (emphasis added)." While that sounds simple enough, beware the *constructive addition*. In Peterson Marital Trust v. Commissioner, 78 F.3d 795 (2d Cir.1996), the court found that the surviving spouse had made a constructive addition to a grandfathered pre–1985 trust when she allowed her general testamentary power over the corpus of the trust to lapse, resulting in the property passing to the contingent beneficiary, a trust for the benefit of her grandchildren. As a consequence, Mrs. Peterson's estate had to pay both estate tax and GST on the property subject to the lapsed power despite the fact that the trust itself was created and became irrevocable prior to 1985. (Technically speaking, as you will see later in this chapter, using GST-speak, a "direct skip" to "skip persons" occurred because the beneficiaries were all grandchildren of Mrs. Peterson.)

C. STRUCTURAL ELEMENTS

[¶ 9101]

1. USE OF TERMS

Many commonly used legal terms have special meanings when used to effect the generation-skipping tax. The Chapter 13 definition of a term may be far broader, or narrower, than the traditional definition, or it may have been given an unexpected meaning. For example, Chapter 13 considers certain persons "transferors" who do not fall within the traditional trust law definition of that term. Becoming familiar with the meanings of the various special terms will make it easier to understand the operation of Chapter 13's taxation scheme.

Initial contact with Chapter 13's definitional system is a frustrating experience, reminiscent of opening one door, only to find another, and another, and another. The chapter's key terms are defined by reference to other terms, which are often defined by reference to yet other terms.

One of the easier methods of mastering the meaning of Chapter 13's key definitional terms involves scanning the definition of a key term, learning the meanings of its component parts, and integrating that knowledge back into the original definition. The first key term examined in this manner is "generation-skipping transfer." Read § 2611(a). Read it again and try to keep the general structure of what it says in mind when reading the definitions of other terms.

[¶ 9117]

2. GENERATION-SKIPPING TRANSFER—THE CODE DEFINITION

Section 2611(a) defines a "generation-skipping transfer" as any one of three events: "(1) a taxable distribution, (2) a taxable termination, and (3) a direct skip." Each of these involves a transfer of income or corpus to at least one beneficiary who is two or more generations younger than the transferor. The tax is imposed whenever one of these three events occurs, whether the transfer was in trust, pursuant to an arrangement having substantially the same effect as a trust, or outright.

3. SKIP PERSON

The events triggering the tax refer to a "skip person" in their definitions, so it will be easier to understand the tax if the term "skip person" is first clarified. The generation-skipping tax is imposed only on transfers to a skip person. Basically, a skip person is a recipient of the transferred property who meets certain requirements.

"Skip person" is defined in § 2613. If the transferee is a natural person, the transferee is a skip person if his or her "generation assignment" makes the transferee two or more generations younger than the transferor. The "generation assignment" rules are discussed at ¶ 9173.

If the transferee is a trust, the trust may be a skip person in two situations. First, a trust is a skip person if only individuals who are skip persons, determined by the above rule, hold interests in the trust. The second situation in which a trust is a skip person is when no person holds a present interest in the trust and no distributions may be made from the trust to non-skip persons after the date of transfer, including distributions on termination of the trust. Cases in which a trust is a skip person are discussed at ¶ 9157 and require an understanding of the meaning of "interest" as described in Chapter 13. See ¶ 9133 for a discussion of the meaning of an "interest."

Thus, "skip persons" can be either certain types of trusts or persons in the grandchildrens' generation and in generations younger than grandchildren. A "non-skip person" is defined in § 2613(b) as a person who is not a skip person. See § 2651 for rules in determining to which generation a person is assigned.

4. INTEREST

a. Introduction

The skip person must have an "interest" in the transferred property in order for a generation-skipping transfer to occur. This conclusion comes from the definitions of the three taxable events (taxable terminations, taxable distributions and direct skips), all of which are discussed below. For example, a taxable termination is defined as the "termination * * * of an interest in property held in trust." § 2612(a)(1). Similarly, the definitions of direct skip and taxable termination require that the skip person receive an interest in the transferred property. See § 2612. Therefore, it is necessary to understand the meaning of an "interest" in property for Chapter 13 purposes.

The "person" who may have an interest in the trust property includes individuals, other trusts, estates, partnerships, associations, or corporations.

GEN
"skip" person
must have
an "interest"

Additionally, a claimed interest will be disregarded if it was created *primarily* to postpone or avoid the generation-skipping tax. § 2652(c)(2). Regulations go further and provide that an interest will be disregarded "if a significant purpose for the creation of the interest is to postpone or avoid" the generation-skipping tax. Reg. § 26.2612–1(e)(2)(ii). To illustrate, where income or principal of a trust can, but is not required to, be used to discharge a parent's support obligations, the parent will not be considered to have an interest in the trust. § 2652(c)(3). See ¶ 9149.

[¶ 9141]

b. *Transfers in Trust*

A generation-skipping transfer that is not made to a trust (i.e., it is made to a "natural person") is always considered a transfer of an "interest" in the transferred property. Where the property is transferred to a trust, however, the rules become more complicated. Section 2652(c)(1) defines persons having an "interest" in trust property to include only those persons with a present right to the income or corpus of the trust, or persons who are "permissible current recipient[s] of income or corpus from the trust." Since future interests are thus excluded from the definition of "interest" for Chapter 13 purposes, to determine at what time the skip person must have a "present interest" or be a "permissible current recipient" of the property, reference to the type of generation-skipping transfer must be made. Therefore, for taxable distributions and direct skips (discussed at ¶ 9221 and 9253), this means that a person has an interest in a trust if the terms of the trust allow distributions (including discretionary distributions) of income or corpus to him or her at the creation of the trust. For taxable terminations (discussed at ¶ 9245), the skip person must have the right to receive the income or corpus of the trust at the time a taxable termination occurs. These explanations may be somewhat confusing at this point, but will become clearer after consideration of the materials that follow.

[handwritten margin note: need to have "current right" to distrib.]

[¶ 9149]

c. *Legal Obligation*

A person also has an interest in trust property if the trust property can be used to satisfy a legal obligation of that person. ¶ 9133. However, § 2652(c)(3) excludes situations in which the property is only available for use to satisfy a legal obligation at the discretion of a fiduciary or pursuant to the Uniform Gifts to Minors Act or the Uniform Transfers to Minors Act. Reg. § 26.2612–1(e)(2)(i). Consdier whether this means that a person will be found to have an interest if a nonfiduciary has discretion to satisfy the person's legal obligations.

[handwritten margin note: satisfy legal oblig.]

Problems

[¶ 9155]

1. Jim transferred property to a trust with instructions that the trustee is to pay income to Jim's child Betty until Betty dies, the remainder to Betty's

children if they survive Betty, otherwise to Betty's sister, Belle. Any tax consequences at Betty's death? Who has an interest for purposes of the generation-skipping tax? See § 2652(c)(1).

2. Jennifer placed property in trust with the income to be paid at the trustee's discretion to her grandchild, Mark, until Mark's death, with the remainder to Sam, Jennifer's child, if Sam survives Mark, otherwise to Jennifer's sister, Sarah. Sam died before Mark. Any tax consequences at Sam's death? See §§ 2652(c)(1) and 2612(a).

[¶ 9157]

5. TRUSTS AND DEEMED TRUSTS (GENERATION–SKIPPING TRUST EQUIVALENTS)

A generation-skipping transfer may be made both to a trust and from a trust. Where the transfer is made to a trust, the trust may be a skip person in two situations: (1) if all the interests in the trust property are held by skip persons or (2) if no one holds a present interest in the trust property, and future distributions or terminations may be made only to skip persons. § 2613. Therefore, where non-skip persons have a present interest in the trust or a future interest in distributions or terminations, the trust will not be a skip person even though skip persons also have present or future interests.

For purposes of the generation-skipping tax, the term "trust" includes both the traditional trust and certain nontrust arrangements called "deemed trusts" or "trust equivalents." The traditional, or explicit, trust has been defined as "an arrangement created by a will or by an inter vivos declaration whereby trustees take title to property for the purpose of protecting or conserving it for the beneficiaries under the ordinary rule applied in chancery or probate courts." Reg. § 301.7701–4(a).

The drafters of Chapter 13, aware that some nontrust arrangements could be utilized to yield the same tax avoidance as would have been achieved through use of an explicit trust, chose to include those nontrust devices within the purview of the Chapter 13 taxation scheme. Denominated "deemed trusts" or "generation-skipping trust equivalents," these devices are identified by function, rather than format. That is, the definition of "trust" is expanded to include "any arrangement (other than an estate) which, although not a trust, has substantially the same effect as a trust." § 2652(b)(1). Therefore, if the arrangement allows a beneficiary to enjoy substantial benefits from property while his or her interest continues, yet pay no tax on the termination of that interest, the property arrangement is a deemed trust.

Section 2652(b)(3) provides a partial listing of the types of interests that may be components of a "deemed trust." These include terms for years, life estates, insurance and annuity interests, remainders and other split interests. Insurance, for example, could be utilized as a deemed trust.

Example. Grantor purchases an insurance policy on his own life, instructing the insurance company to hold the proceeds payable under the policy until the death of Grantor's son, then distribute the proceeds to Grantor's grandsons. During the son's lifetime, he is to receive any interest accruing to the proceeds in the hands of the insurance company. Although not formally a trust, this arrangement serves the functions of a generation-skipping trust. The son is enjoying the income from the insurance fund during the period he survives his father but will have nothing of the proceeds in his taxable estate when he dies. The insurance company is serving as a quasi-trustee, holding and distributing the proceeds in accordance with the original instructions of the grantor/insured.

Problems

[¶ 9163]

1. Grantor's will gives a life estate in Blackacre to his grandson, and upon his grandson's death, Blackacre is to pass to Grantor's lineal descendants *per stirpes*. Would the grandson's life estate be a deemed trust? Why or why not? See Reg. § 26.2652–1(b). (*Hint:* See the definition of a direct skip (§ 2612(c)) and the discussion at ¶ 9253.)

2. Grantor's will gives $100,000 to his child, C, provided C survives Grantor by six months, otherwise to Grantor's grandchild, GC. C dies three months after Grantor's death. Is the bequest a transfer in trust? See Reg. § 26.2652–1(b)(2), Example 2. Is it a generation-skipping transfer? See § 2612(c).

3. Same facts except Grantor's will requires C to survive him by two years to receive the bequest. Is the bequest a transfer in trust? See Reg. § 26.2652–1(b)(2), Example 3. Is it a generation-skipping transfer? See § 2612(a).

[¶ 9165]

6. THE CONCEPT OF "TRANSFEROR" (AND GIFT–SPLITTING)

The definition of "transferor" is found in § 2652(a). The term is defined according to what taxes are imposed on the transferred property. Generally, a transferor will be either a decedent (where transferred property is subject to estate tax) or a donor (where transferred property is subject to gift tax). However, there are a number of instances in which nontransferors are treated as transferors, a possibility that has tax planning significance. For example, note the special rule that allows a married person to split a gift with his or her spouse. § 2513. In such cases, each spouse will be considered the transferor of one-half of the entire gift (resulting in a benefit to taxpayers that comes from a virtual doubling of the $10,000 ($12,000 in 2006, adjusted for inflation) per donee per annum gift tax exclusion). § 2503(b).

[¶ 9173]

7. "GENERATION" ASSIGNMENT

a. *Family Members*

The concept of generation assignment is critical to the functioning of Chapter 13. No generation-skipping tax can be imposed unless skip persons are first found to exist who are assigned to two (or more) different generations younger than that of the grantor. Section 2651 establishes rules for ascertaining the generation assignment of an individual. Read it.

All generation assignments are made with reference to the grantor. To be a skip person, for example, an individual must be a beneficiary assigned to a generation at least one generation younger than that of the grantor. Generations are determined by two different methods; the method used depends on the closeness of the blood relationship, if any, between the grantor and the beneficiary.

Predictably, actual family generation assignments are used whenever a grantor is closely related to a beneficiary. Section 2651(b)(1) provides for the use of "family tree" generation assignments for all individuals who are lineal descendants of the grantor's grandparents. This encompasses most, if not all, of the blood relatives who would be expected to be natural objects of a grantor's bounty. Cousins and their descendants are included in this group, as well as the grantor, his brothers and sisters, and their descendants. Spouses are deemed to belong to the same generation as the person they are (or have at one time been) married to, if that person received his generation assignment by virtue of blood relationship to the grantor. § 2651(c). Lineal descendants of the grantor's spouse's grandparents are also included in the "family tree" under § 2651(b)(2), with their generation assignment determined in relation to the generation of the spouse. Adopted children and persons related to the grantor by "half-blood" are considered related by whole blood. § 2651(b)(3).

Note: Spouses are deemed to belong to the same generation as the person they are married to.

Problem

[¶ 9179]

To what generation (relative to the transferor) would the following individuals be assigned?

(a) Transferor's great-grandson.

(b) Transferor's daughter-in-law.

(c) The ex-spouse of Transferor's first cousin.

(d) Transferor's second cousin. (*Hint:* Check the scope of "family tree" generation assignments. What happens when a person is too distantly related?)

(e) Transferor's brother's grandson.

(f) Transferor's 29–year-old wife (Transferor is 82).

[¶ 9181]

b. *Nonfamily Members*

When the transferor is not closely related to a beneficiary, generation assignment is the result of a mathematical test, based on 25–year generations. § 2651(d). A person whose age is between zero and 12 1/2 years younger than that of the transferor is a member of the transferor's generation. The first generation below that of the transferor consists of those persons who are between 12 1/2 and 37 1/2 years younger than the transferor. Every 25–year group thereafter constitutes another generation younger than the transferor.

This rule can have serious consequences for the unwary. For example, a transferor's will gave a life estate in some property to a friend who was 40 years younger than the transferor, with the remainder to the transferor's daughter. The IRS found that a direct skip had occurred and the entire value of the property was subject to the tax. Priv. Ltr. Rul. 9105006. Why? The friend was a skip person under § 2651(d), and a "deemed trust" had been created under § 2652(b). Since only present interests in income or corpus are looked at in determining a generation-skipping trust interest, only the friend's interest was considered in determining the property subject to the tax, since the daughter had a future interest in the remainder. Therefore, a direct skip occurred, and the entire value of the property was subject to the tax under § 2623.

Problem

[¶ 9187]

To what generation are the following persons assigned? Assume that the Transferor is 87 years old.

(a) Transferor's 81–year-old second cousin.

(b) Transferor's 27–year-old second cousin, raised by Transferor and legally adopted as Transferor's son. See § 2651(b).

(c) Transferor's trusted friend, age 76.

(d) The wife of Transferor's trusted friend, age 35.

(e) The daughter of Transferor's trusted friend, age 10.

[¶ 9189]

c. *Multiple Generation Membership*

In those rare situations in which a person could be assigned to two different generations, *e.g.*, Grandfather adopts Grandchild after the death of the youngster's parents, the beneficiary will be assigned to the youngest generation to which he or she could belong. § 2651. Therefore, Grandchild would be assigned to the grandchildren's generation despite his or her adoption by Grandfather.

[¶ 9197]

d. *Gifts to Entities and "Veil Piercing"*

When a beneficiary is an entity, rather than a person, "piercing the veil" of the entity is mandatory. See § 2651(f)(2). All persons who have interests in the entity will be deemed beneficiaries of the trust and receive generation assignments according to their age or relationship to the trust grantor. For example, if a grantor establishes a trust for the benefit of his nephew's sole-proprietorship business, the nephew will be deemed a beneficiary of the trust.

The nephew's generation assignment will be the children's generation. If the nephew later brought his son and his son's best friend into the business as a partner, they would also be deemed beneficiaries. The son, grantor's great-nephew, would be classed in the grandchildren's generation, and the friend would be classed according to his age in relation to the grantor's age.

[¶ 9205]

8. ILLUSTRATION

Some of the ideas that have been discussed so far can be illustrated by the following hypothetical:

George "Grantor" Smoot died at the age of 95. Half of his estate he left outright to his second wife, Eleanor "Binkie" Smoot, 35. The remainder of his estate passed to a "bypass trust," which is to provide life income benefits for each of George's children, with the remainder passing *per stirpes* to George's then living lineal descendants.

At the time of George's death, he was survived by three children: Belinda, 68; Phoebe, 65; and Scott, 12. Belinda has a daughter, Simone, 36, and a granddaughter, Mabel, 15. Two children, George, Jr. and Delia, predeceased George. George, Jr. never married and had no children. Delia left an adopted daughter, Sophia, 39.

The generation assignments and interests of George's family in the trust are as follows:

1. *Binkie.* She has received a possible interest in the corpus of the bypass trust, but it is not a present interest for Chapter 13 purposes. See § 2652(c)(1). The outright gift of half of George's estate is not relevant for Chapter 13 purposes, since it is not a transfer in trust or a "deemed trust." § 2652(b). Since she is George's widow (despite a 60–year age difference), she is assigned to George's generation.

2. *Belinda, Phoebe, and Scott.* They are beneficiaries of the trust because they have the right to receive income from the trust established by George's will. They are all assigned to the first generation younger than George because they are his children.

3. *Sophie and Simone.* They are beneficiaries, although their interest in the trust at the present time is but a contingent future interest. They must survive until the last of George's children dies and the trust proceeds are distributed if they are to receive anything. Since adopted children are treated the same as blood children for Chapter 13 purposes, Sophie and Simone are both grandchildren and are assigned to the second generation younger than George. Upon the termination of the bypass trust, they will have a present right to the income and corpus of the trust, and will therefore have an interest for Chapter 13 purposes at that time.

4. *Mabel.* Her situation is the same as Sophie and Simone, except that she is assigned to the third generation younger than George.

¶ 9205

D. TAX-TRIGGERING EVENTS

[¶ 9213]

1. INTRODUCTION

The mere existence of a generation-skipping trust will not give rise to Chapter 13 liability. Some further event must occur. Congress, in drafting Chapter 13, divided these "triggering" events into three categories: "taxable distributions," "taxable terminations,"and "direct skips."

[¶ 9221]

2. TAXABLE DISTRIBUTIONS

"Inc. or corpus"

If distrib. s.t. estate or gift tax then not "taxable trans." for GST.

A taxable distribution occurs when there is a distribution of income or corpus from a trust to a skip person (from a trust in which both skip and non-skip persons had or have a present interest) other than by way of a termination of the trust or a direct skip. § 2612(b). However, in cases where the distribution is subject to estate or gift tax, it will not be considered a taxable distribution for generation-skipping tax purposes. (A transfer is considered subject to gift tax *if* by its terms § 2051(a) imposes the gift tax even though, because of exemptions, exclusions, deductions or credits, no gift tax is actually payable. For example, a transfer would be considered subject to the gift tax for these purposes even if no gift tax were actually payable because the transfer had a value of less than or equal to the § 2503(b) annual gift tax exclusion ($12,000 in 2006, adjusted for inflation). Similarly, if the transferred property is includible in the transferor's gross estate under §§ 2031 or 2103, the property is considered subject to estate tax. Reg. § 26.2652–1(a)(2).)

[¶ 9229]

a. *Illustration of a Taxable Distribution*

Grantor establishes a trust, instructing the trustee to pay out income from the trust (in the trustee's sole discretion) to a class of beneficiaries consisting of the grantor's then living lineal descendants. The grantor had two living children, four living grandchildren, and one great-grandchild. The trustee distributed $12,000 from the trust corpus to one of the grandchildren. This is a taxable distribution, because it is a payment out of trust corpus to a skip person.

[¶ 9237]

b. *Dangers of Having More Than One Generation of Permissible Recipients*

If it does little else, the above example should demonstrate the hazards associated with establishing classes of permissible recipients of trust corpus that cross generational lines. As soon as an individual is listed in a class of permissible recipients of trust corpus, he or she acquires a *present* interest in the trust for Chapter 13 purposes. From that moment forward, any distribution out of trust corpus to a beneficiary who is a skip person will be deemed a "taxable distribution." For example, Grantor establishes a trust for the benefit of her Law School Alumni Association. The trustee is instructed to pay out income from the trust to the member of the Association who has, in the trustee's sole discretion, performed the greatest amount of pro bono work in the preceding year. Each member of the Association will have a present interest in the trust as a permissible recipient of the trust income and will be assigned to a generation according to his or her age in relation to Grantor's age. Each time the recipient of the trust income is a skip person due to the generation assignment, a taxable distribution will occur. Therefore, the generation-skipping tax could be due on a yearly basis because of the terms of the trust.

Problem

[¶ 9243]

Does a "taxable distribution" occur in the following situations?

(a) Grantor's will creates a trust providing for payment of income to her husband until his death, then to pay income to her then living children and grandchildren, and at the death of the last to die of her children, remainder to the grantor's then living lineal descendants *per stirpes*. The trustee pays $110,000 to the grantor's husband during his lifetime. After his death, the trustee distributes $10,000 to each of the grantor's two children and four grandchildren. See § 2612(b).

(b) Same facts as (a), but no child survived the death of the grantor's husband and distributions were thereafter made only to the grandchildren. See § 2612(c).

(c) Grantor creates a trust for the benefit of his children and grandchildren. The trustee is directed to pay income on a discretionary basis to the children and grandchildren until the death of the last to die of the children, at which time the trust terminates and the corpus of the trust is to be distributed among the then living grandchildren. The trustee distributes $10,000 to each of the children during their lifetime, but makes no distributions to the grandchildren until the last child dies. After the death of the last child, the trustee distributes $20,000 to each grandchild. See § 2612(a).

(d) Grantor creates a trust under which income is payable to his child, C, during his life and C's child, GC, is to receive one-half of the principal of the trust when GC reaches 35. The remaining one-half of the principal is to be distributed to GC on C's death. C dies when GC is 50. Reg. § 26.2612–1(f), Example 12.

[¶ 9245]

3. TAXABLE TERMINATIONS

A taxable termination means the termination of an interest in a trust (whether by reason of death, passage of time, or cessation of a power) as a result of which trust property (or income) is distributed to a skip person.

¶ 9245

§ 2612(a). (This assumes that the initial transfer of the property to the trust did not constitute a direct skip, a direct skip being itself subject to the generation-skipping tax.) An example of such a taxable termination would involve a trust established by a parent to provide life income for a child, and then, upon the child's death, to distribute the corpus free of trust to the child's children; the taxable termination would occur upon the child's death. However, a taxable termination does not occur if the transferred property is subject to estate or gift tax. Reg. § 26.2612–1(b)(1)(i). That means, for example, that if the child had a general power of appointment over the trust property which caused the trust property to be included in the child's estate under § 2041, no taxable termination would occur at the child's death.

[margin note:] no "tax. term." if transfr s.t. estate or gift tax.

Furthermore, no taxable termination occurs if, immediately after the termination of the interest in the trust property, a non-skip person has an interest in the property or if no distribution (including distributions made because of the termination) may be made to a skip person. § 2612(a). For example, no "taxable termination" would occur if the beneficiaries of the trust described above were both the child's children and the parent's church or if, after the child's death, the entire corpus of the trust was to be distributed to the parent's church. Where a termination results from a single event, such as the death of the transferor's child, only one taxable termination occurs, even if the transferred property is distributed upon termination to skip persons of more than one generation. Reg. § 26.2612–1(f), Example 10. For example, suppose a trust is created to pay income to the transferor's spouse and child until the death of the child and then to distribute all trust property to the grandchild. If the child dies while the spouse is living, only one taxable termination will be deemed to have occurred, despite termination of both the spouse's and the child's interests.

When a taxable termination occurs, the value of all property subject to the terminated interest or power is subject to generation-skipping tax. Thus, when Son dies and his life interest in Blackacre expires, the entire value of Blackacre is subject to tax because Son had the right to use Blackacre in its entirety. If Son had been given a life interest in only half of Blackacre, only half would be taxed on the termination of his interest. See § 2612(a)(2).

Problem

[¶ 9251]

In each of the following situations determine: (1) whether a taxable termination has taken place and (2) if there has been a taxable termination, state the amount that will be subject to generation-skipping tax as a result of the termination.

(a) Grantor left $1.5 million in trust. During the life of Grantor's son, the son was to receive the income from the trust. At the death of the son, the remainder in the trust was to be distributed to Grantor's then living lineal descendants *per stirpes*. The son died, and the entire trust was distributed to Grantor's two grandchildren (who were offspring of the son). See § 2612(a).

¶ 9245

(b) Same facts as (a), except that the trust proceeds were distributed to Grantor's one surviving grandchild and two great-grandchildren (the offspring of a deceased grandchild). See Reg. § 26.2612–1(f), Example 10. (*Note:* After you have determined whether the son's death resulted in a taxable termination, decide whether the death of the grandchild was also a taxable termination.)

(c) Same facts as (a), except that the trust proceeds were distributed half to Grantor's daughter (sister of the deceased son) and half to the son's two children. See § 2612(a)(2).

(d) Grantor left $2 million in trust. The income from the trust was to be paid to Grantor's grandchildren for their lives, with the remainder passing on the death of the last surviving grandchild to Grantor's then living lineal descendants *per stirpes*. The trustee was authorized to invade the trust corpus on behalf of, and make payments to, Grantor's son, subject to an ascertainable standard. It was never necessary to invade the trust corpus for the son. Son dies. Taxable termination? Last grandchild dies. Taxable termination?

(e) Grantor's will left $1.5 million in trust, income to be paid to his widow for life, then to his son for life, with the remainder to be paid over at the son's death to Grantor's then living lineal descendants. Grantor's son died while his mother was still living.

(f) Same facts as (e), except that trustee had discretionary power to make payments to the son from trust income during the life of Grantor's widow. No payments were ever actually made.

(g) Grantor left $1.5 million in trust, income to be paid to his widow for life, then to his grandchildren for their lives. On the death of the last surviving grandchild, the remainder in trust was to be distributed to Grantor's then living lineal descendants *per stirpes*. Grantor's son was given a lifetime special power of appointment, beginning upon the death of Grantor's widow, to appoint up to one-half of the trust corpus to a class of beneficiaries consisting of various charities and friends of Grantor. Grantor's widow died, followed by Grantor's son. Is the death of the son a taxable termination? Will the death of the last grandchild be a taxable termination? See Reg. § 26.2612–1(b)(1)(i).

(h) Same facts as (g), except that the son predeceased Grantor's widow.

[¶ 9253]

4. DIRECT SKIPS

A transfer that is <u>subject to either the estate or gift tax and that gives an interest in the transferred property to a skip person</u> is a direct skip. § 2612(c). <u>This includes a transfer in trust, subject to the estate or gift tax, where no one has an interest in the property other than a skip person.</u> Id. Even if the transfer skips more than one generation (*e.g.*, a transfer is made to a great-grandchild), <u>only one direct skip will be found to have occurred.</u> Reg. § 26.2612–1(a)(2).

s.t. estate tax
or gift tax and
gives interest to a
"skip person"

¶ **9253**

Note: "predeceased child rule".

A simple example of this would be a transfer of property outright to a grandchild. However, if the grandchild's parents are dead at the time of the transfer, the tax will not apply. This is due to the "predeceased child rule," which treats the grandchild as the transferor's child in determining whether the transfer is a direct skip. § 2651(e)(1). See ¶ 9325 for additional discussion of the predeceased child rule. Another case would be where a transfer in trust constituted a direct skip because none of the trust beneficiaries were non-skip persons. In such a case, distributions from the trust would not constitute either taxable distributions or taxable terminations, all such distributions being free of the generation-skipping tax.

Transfer to trust= direct skip where none of benficiaries are non-skip persons.

Tax paid at formation

Problem

[¶ 9258]

Determine whether a direct skip has occurred in the following situations:

(a) Grantor creates a trust which provides for income to be distributed to his grandchildren during their lifetimes, remainder to his then living lineal descendants *per stirpes*. Trustee makes an annual distribution of $10,000 to each grandchild during his or her lifetime. See § 2612(c).

(b) Same facts as (a). After the death of the last grandchild, the trustee distributes the remainder of the trust to Grantor's then living lineal descendants *per stirpes*. See § 2611(b)(2).

[¶ 9261]

5. DETERMINING WHICH TYPE OF EVENT HAS OCCURRED

The determination of whether a taxable termination, taxable distribution or direct skip has occurred will affect both the method of computing the tax and who is liable for the tax. Seemingly, the definition of a taxable distribution—"any distribution from a trust to a skip person (*other than a taxable termination or a direct skip*)"—precludes a finding that a taxable termination or a direct skip has occurred. § 2612(b) (emphasis added). Therefore, a transfer that could be considered either a taxable termination or a taxable distribution will be deemed to be a taxable termination. § 2612(b). For example, suppose a parent creates a trust giving a child a life estate in the trust and, upon the child's death, giving the corpus to or his or her grandchildren; at the child's death there is a taxable termination of the child's income interest in the trust and a taxable distribution to the grandchildren. Under § 2612(b), the child's death is treated as a taxable termination.

OK

Where a transfer meets the statutory definition of both a taxable termination and a direct skip, the regulations provide that certain transfers will be treated as direct skips rather than as taxable terminations. Reg. § 26.2612–1(b)(1)(i). The statutory definitions of direct skips and taxable terminations would seem to be mutually exclusive since, in a taxable termination, the transferred property must not be subject to estate or gift tax and the transferred property in a direct skip *is* subject to estate or gift tax. For

Note this

¶ 9253

example, if a trust is established for the transferor's child's life, remainder to the transferor's grandchildren, a taxable termination occurs on the child's death since the trust property is not subject to the estate or gift tax.

E.   COMPUTING AND PAYING THE GENERATION–SKIPPING TAX

[¶ 9277]

1.   COMPUTING THE TAX: ACHIEVING A FRAME OF REFERENCE

After it has been determined that an event has occurred that generates liability under the generation-skipping transfer tax provisions, two further items must be ascertained: (1) the amount of the tax and (2) when the tax is due.

Determination of the amount of tax imposed by Chapter 13 on a particular generation-skipping transfer is a function of the amount of property subject to the tax (the "taxable amount"), its value at the appropriate time of valuation, and the rate at which the tax is to be assessed ("applicable rate"). Although the issue of how much property is subject to the tax has already been discussed, questions of valuation and marginal rate remain to be considered.

[¶ 9281]

a.   *Valuation: When the Property's Value Is Determined*

The value of property passing as a result of a generation-skipping tax is generally determined as of the time of the transfer. § 2624(a). This means that for taxable distributions, the value of the property received by the transferee is determined as of the date of distribution. The value of the property with respect to which a taxable termination occurs is determined on the date of the termination. If a taxable termination occurs as the result of death, however, the transferee may elect to value the property in accordance with § 2032 (providing for an alternate valuation date six months after the taxable termination). § 2624(c).

In the case of a direct skip, the value of the property passing by the direct skip is its value on the date the skip person receives the property. § 2624. However, if the property passing to the skip person in a direct skip is included in the gross estate of the grantor, the value of the property is the same as its estate tax value. § 2624(b).

[¶ 9285]

b.   *The Taxable Amount: What Property Is Subject to the Tax?*

The amount subject to the generation-skipping tax varies according to whether a taxable termination, taxable distribution, or a direct skip has occurred. See §§ 2621–2623. Generally, only the property which actually passes to the transferee is subject to the tax, with some special exceptions discussed below.

In a direct skip, the taxable amount is equal to the value of the property received by the skip person. § 2623. The amount of the tax is not included in the taxable amount of the direct skip, i.e., the tax is imposed on a tax-exclusive basis.

In a taxable distribution, the amount subject to the tax is the value of the property received by the transferee, less any expense incurred by the transferee in connection with the determination of the generation-skipping tax on the transfer. § 2621. Inasmuch as the generation-skipping tax is imposed on the transferee, the amount subject to the tax will include the tax itself, i.e., the tax is imposed on a tax inclusive basis. And the statute makes it clear that, if the tax is paid by the trust upon the distribution, the tax so paid will be treated as a part of the taxable distribution. § 2621(b).

The taxable amount in a taxable termination is the fair market value of the property distributed as a result of the taxable termination, decreased by expenses, debts and taxes attributable to the property and similar to the deductions allowable under § 2053 of the estate tax statute. § 2622. This amount will include the amount of the generation-skipping tax itself, as in the case of taxable distributions, i.e., the tax is imposed on a tax inclusive basis. If the termination occurs as to an interest in income only, however, the taxable amount will not be only the value of the income. Rather, the value of the entire amount of the corpus which generated the terminated income will be subject to the tax, even if the transferee never actually received any income. For example, if the trust provided for discretionary distributions of income to a skip person for life, but no distributions were actually made, the entire corpus would probably be subject to the tax upon the termination of the income interest.

The value of transferred property under any of the three methods is reduced by the amount of any consideration furnished by the transferee. § 2624(d). This does not mean the payment of the generation-skipping tax by the transferee, but instead, actual consideration paid. For example, where the transferor gives the transferee a car worth $20,000 in return for $1,000, the value of the transfer is $19,000.

Problems

[¶ 9291]

1. A transferor transfers property to a discretionary trust for the benefit of his lineal descendants until the death of his child. During the child's life, $1.5 million is distributed to the transferor's grandchild and $1,000 is paid to an attorney to determine the amount of the generation-skipping tax. Disregarding any exemptions or exclusions, what is the taxable amount? See § 2621.

2. A Transferor transfers $1.5 million to a trust to pay the income to the transferor's child until the child's death, with the remainder to the transferor's grandchildren. Upon the child's death, the trustee pays himself a fee of $50,000. What is the taxable amount? See § 2622.

3. A transferor gives $4 million to his grandchild. The grandchild's parent is living at the time of the transfer. What is the taxable amount? See § 2623.

¶ 9285

[¶ 9293]

2. WHO IS LIABLE FOR GST TAX?

Section 2603 sets out the liability for the tax as follows. The transferee is liable for the tax imposed on a taxable distribution. § 2603(a)(1). In a taxable termination, the trustee is liable for the tax. § 2603(a)(2). A direct skip imposes liability on either the trustee (if it is a direct skip from a trust) or the transferor (in any nontrust direct skip). § 2603(a)(2) and (3).

[handwritten margin notes: Tax Dist. = Transferee / Tax Term. = Trustee / Direct Skip = Trustee / Transferor]

[¶ 9301]

3. APPORTIONMENT

Once it is known who is liable for the tax, the question is, "Where is the person liable for the tax to get the money to pay the tax?" Under § 2603(b), the generation-skipping tax is charged to the property being transferred unless there is a specific reference to the generation-skipping tax in the instrument creating the transfer which directs that the tax be paid from a different source. An example of such a provision is as follows:

> My Executor shall pay all estate, inheritance and succession taxes, both state and federal, including all penalties and interest thereon (including any generation-skipping tax imposed by § 2601 of the Internal Revenue Code of 1986), assessed by reason of my death out of that portion of the residue of my testamentary estate which does not qualify for the marital deduction for federal estate tax purposes, if any, without recovery from any recipient or beneficiary of any property by which such tax is measured.

When the liability provisions of § 2603(a) are read with subsection (b), the general rule is that the transferee of the property will be required to pay the tax from the property received. However, this rule does not apply to inter vivos direct skips of nontrust property. In that situation, the tax is paid by the transferor from separate property, notwithstanding the language of § 2603(b). For example, John, during his life, gives his grandson $1.5 million. John is liable for the tax and must pay it out of separate property. (This example ignores the $2 million GST exemption available in 2006. ¶ 9309.) If, however, John's will provided that $1.5 million is to be divided equally between his child, John, Jr., and his grandchild, John III, and no mention is made of the generation-skipping tax in the will, John, Jr. will receive $500,000, but John III will receive less since his share is subject to the tax and no provision was made for another source (such as the residuary estate) to bear the burden of paying the tax.

[handwritten margin note: ? Should be 750,000?]

F.   GST EXEMPTION

[¶ 9309]

1. THE $2 MILLION EXEMPTION

Every person is currently allowed an exemption from the generation-skipping tax. In 2006 through 2008 the GST exemption is $2 million; it rises to $3.5 million in 2009. The GST tax itself disappears in 2010 only to reappear in 2011 but with an exemption of only $1million! (For generation-skipping transfers after 2003, the exemption amount is equal to the estate tax applicable exclusion amount which, for 2006 through 2008, is $2 million. §§ 2010(c), 2631(c).

The GST exemption that may be allocated to both lifetime and deathtime property transfers. Any such allocation is irrevocable. § 2631(b).

two-thirds?

The effect of the GST exemption is profound. For example, if a transferor creates a trust in 2006 containing $3 million, the transferor may allocate the entire $2 million exemption to the trust, and one-third of each distribution from the trust will thereafter always be exempt from the generation-skipping tax no matter the ultimate size of the trust. Similarly, if the original trust was for $2 million and the transferor allocated the entire $2 million exemption to it, the entire trust would always be exempt from the tax, no matter how much over $2 million the trust eventually grows to contain.

The planning imperative inherent in the $2 million GST exemption is very real. Recall Grandmother Smith? ¶ 9067. Lets pick up the conversation at her table in the dining room of the assisted living center, where Grandmother Smith, known to her dining companions as "Myrtle", her given name, is telling of her meeting with her lawyer that afternoon in the parlor.

"They got a new tax." No one says anything. A bit later, Myrtle says, again, "They got a new tax!" Finally Albert stirs and says, "What kind of tax?" "A special tax on gifts I make to the grandchildren," says Myrtle. "My lawyer calls it the GST and says it is both a blessing and curse (pause) but I think its just a way for her to charge me more." "How's that?" Albert inquires. Myrtle describes the trusts that she created for her sons, Clem and Zeke, and says, "The lawyer says I must do more; now I have to change the trust so that it lasts forever—something about almost in perpetuity—so that not only my children but my grandchildren and their children and so on can benefit. It all seems so complicated and my grandchildren are not even out of high school yet." Gertrude, her other dining companion, joins in and says, "Why do it if you don't like it?" Myrtle replies, "The lawyer says its almost malpractice for her not to suggest it to me and *crazy* of me not to do it because the tax benefits—the blessing—are so great. She says I can put $2 million in trust at my death—maybe more depending on when I die—and when the trust finally ends, say, when my great grandchildren die, and the trust then has a value of, say, $30 million, all $30 million can go to my great *great* grandchildren free of all taxes. She said it would be like creating a *dynasty*, that is, that it was a *real deal*!" Gertrude commented, "But you don't even know your great *great* grandchildren, do you?" Albert looks up and says, "Do it. Beats the government out of the money."

Obviously, if Grandmother Smith does not create the $2 million *dynasty* trust for her descendants "that will last forever", the $2 million will be subject to estate tax at each generation. All that estate tax is spared by the creation of the trust which is designed to make effective use of the $2 million GST exemption. Is this, then, to say, that the advice of Grandmother Smith's

¶ 9309

lawyer should be followed by every taxpayer if at all practical, i.e., taking into consideration the trust maintenance costs? "After all," so it could be argued, "the trust will be protected at least from the claims of creditors of future generations, something that can't be said of the property is held by descendants free of trust." Are there societal implications to this kind of thinking?

[¶ 9311]

2. VOLUNTARY ALLOCATION

The exemption may be allocated by the transferor during life or after death by his or her executor. Reg. § 26.2632–1(b)(2) and (d)(1). The allocation may be made at any time from the date of the transfer to the date on which the transferor's federal estate tax return is due. Reg. § 26.2632–1(a). The allocation may be made during the transferor's lifetime on a timely filed federal gift tax return. Allocations after death may be made on or before the date for filing the transferor's federal estate tax return (including any extensions actually granted). The allocation is irrevocable after the due date (plus extensions granted) of the estate or gift tax return. Reg. § 26.2632–1(b)(2) and (d)(2).

If the amount of the exemption allocated to a transfer is greater than the amount necessary to bring the inclusion ratio to zero, the excess amount allocated is void as to the transfer and can be allocated to other transfers. Reg. § 26.2632–1(b)(2)(i). An allocation is also void if the allocation is made with respect to a trust that has no generation-skipping transfer potential, with respect to the transferor making the allocation, at the time of the allocation. For this purpose, a trust has generation-skipping transfer potential even if the possibility of a generation-skipping transfer is so remote as to be negligible. Reg. § 26.2632–1(b)(2)(i).

The allocation may be made by formula (e.g., "the amount necessary to produce an inclusion ratio of zero"). If the transferred property is held in trust, the allocation is to the entire trust, not to specific property held in the trust. Reg. § 26.2632–1(a). The transferor cannot allocate the exemption to only a portion of the trust.

[¶ 9313]

3. AUTOMATIC ALLOCATION RULES

If the transferor makes either a direct skip or an "indirect skip" (one that is made to a GST trust and subject to gift tax) during his or her lifetime, there is a deemed allocation of the transferor's unused GST exemption amount to the property transferred, to the extent necessary to make the inclusion ratio zero. § 2632(b)(1) and (c)(1). However, the transferor may elect, on a timely filed gift tax return for the calendar year in which the transfer was made, not to have the automatic exemption allocation made to the skip. § 2632(b)(3) and (c)(5).

If the exemption has not been allocated by the decedent's executor on or before the due date for filing the estate tax return, the unused exemption is automatically allocated pro rata first to direct skips and then to trusts which may experience either a taxable termination or a taxable distribution. However, certain exceptions to the automatic allocation are provided which prevent waste of the exemption. The automatic allocation is not made in two situations: (1) if the trust will have a new transferor before a generation-skipping transfer occurs, e.g., where a QTIP election (provided for in § 2056(b)(7)) is made as to the transferred property, thereby treating the grantor's spouse as the transferor or (2) if no generation-skipping transfer occurs with respect to a trust within nine months of the death of the transferor and no generation-skipping transfer can occur thereafter. Reg. § 26.2632–1(d)(2). Any allocation, including automatic allocation to direct skips or election out of the automatic allocation to direct skips, is irrevocable after the due date of the federal estate tax return. Reg. § 26.2632–1(d)(2).

While a gift-splitting election under § 2513 gives married couples the benefit of a $4 generation-skipping transfer exemption in 2006 through 2008 (and $7 million in 2009), see § 2652(a)(2), one spouse may not directly transfer his or her exemption to the other spouse. See ¶ 23,151.

million (?)

[¶ 9325]

NB

4. THE PREDECEASED CHILD RULE

A transfer made to a grandchild of the transferor, or to the grandchild's spouse or former spouse, is not considered a direct skip if, at the time of the transfer, the grandchild's parent is dead and the parent was a lineal descendent of either the transferor or the transferor's spouse or former spouse. § 2651(e)(1). This is a result of the "predeceased child rule." If a transfer to a trust is not a direct skip because of the predeceased child rule, the grandchild is treated as though he or she is the transferor's child (i.e., his or her generation assignment is moved up one level), and the grandchild's children move up to the grandchild's generation, the grandchild's grandchildren move up to the grandchild's children's generation, etc., for purposes of determining whether future transfers of the property involved in the direct skip are generation-skipping transfers. § 2651(e)(1). Note, however, that the predeceased child rule will not apply if a non-skip person has an interest in the trust, as there is no direct skip.

Note where rule does not apply

> *Example.* T transfers $100,000 to a trust for the benefit of GC, his grandchild, with the remainder to his lineal descendants *per stirpes*. At the time of the transfer, GC's parents, C1 and C2, are dead, and GC has two children, GGC1 and GGC2. Under the predeceased child rule, GC is treated as T's child, and GGC1 and GGC2 are treated as T's grandchildren for generation-skipping tax purposes. Thus, no direct skip occurs on GC's death, as GC is a non-skip person, but a taxable termination occurs at that time. If, however, the original transfer was for the benefit of both GC and S, T's spouse, with remainder to T's lineal descendants *per stirpes,* the predeceased child rule would not apply since no direct skip would occur because S is a non-skip person with a present interest in the trust. Therefore, taxable distributions would occur when trust income or corpus was distributed to GC, and a taxable termination would occur on the death of the last to die of S and GC.

¶ 9313

G. GST EXCLUSIONS

[¶ 9341]

1. ANNUAL, MEDICAL, AND EDUCATIONAL EXCLUSIONS

Generally speaking, inter vivos transfers which are exempt from federal gift tax are exempt from the generation-skipping tax if they derive their gift tax exemption by virtue of: (1) an exclusion for certain medical or tuition expenses provided in § 2503(e) (§ 2611(b), as noted in ¶ 9349) or (2) the $10,000—$12,000 in 2006, as adjusted for inflation—per donee per annum gift tax exclusion for inter vivos transfers provided in § 2503(b). See § 2642(c), as noted in ¶ 9357.

[¶ 9349]

a. The Tuition and Medical Expense Exclusion

The generation-skipping tax does not apply to lifetime transfers (including transfers from a trust) made directly to pay for tuition or medical expenses which, if made during the transferor's lifetime, would not have been a taxable gift under § 2503(e) (relating to certain transfers for tuition or medical expenses). §§ 2611(b); 2642(c)(3)(B).

[¶ 9357]

b. The $12,000 Per Donee Per Annum Nontaxable Transfer Exclusion

i. Gifts Free of Trust

Direct skips to natural persons that are nontaxable gifts are free of the generation-skipping tax. § 2642(c)(1). A nontaxable gift is defined in § 2642(c)(3) as "any transfer of property to the extent that such transfer is not treated as a taxable gift" under § 2503(b) (the $10,000—$12,000 in 2006, as adjusted for inflation—per donee per annum gift tax exclusion) or § 2503(e) (dealing with gifts for educational or medical expenses).

[¶ 9365]

ii. Gifts in Trust

A direct skip will result from a transfer to a trust that has no nonskip beneficiaries—and GST will be immediately payable unless (1) the predeceased child exemption comes into play, ¶ 9325; (2) some part or all of the donor's GST exemption ($2 million in 2006 through 2008) is allocated to the trust, ¶ 9309; or (3) the transfer qualifies for the $10,000—$12,000 in 2006, as adjusted for inflation—GST per donee per annum exclusion. § 2642(c)(2).

To qualify for the GST per donee per annum exclusion, the person identified as the donee when the annual exclusion is claimed must be the sole beneficiary of the trust. More specifically, the GST annual exclusion is

donee must be the sole beneficiary of the trust.

¶ 9365

available only in cases where (1) during the lifetime of the person identified as the donee when the gift tax annual exclusion was claimed, distributions from the trust can be made only to that person, and (2) if the person identified as the donee when the gift tax annual exclusion was claimed dies before the trust terminates, the property in the trust at that person's death will be included in the gross estate of such person for federal estate tax purposes. See the discussion at ¶ 23,151 on using *Crummey* trusts for transfers.

It is worth noting that a transfer in trust might well qualify for the *gift* tax $10,000—$12,000 in 2006, as adjusted for inflation—per donee annual exclusion but not qualify for the GST annual exclusion. (And that, where there are nonskip beneficiaries, there is no direct skip.)

Problem

[¶ 9371]

What exemptions and/or exclusions could the grantor allocate to the following transfers:

(a) Grantor establishes a trust worth $5,000,000 that provides for income distributions to his spouse, remainder to his grandchildren.

(b) Grantor, during his life, gives his grandchild $11,000 outright.

(c) Grantor, during his life, creates a trust worth $1,500,000 for the benefit of his grandchild. The trustee is instructed to pay income to the grandchild until her 21st birthday, at which time the trust is terminated and the corpus of the trust is to be distributed to the grandchild.

(d) Grantor's will creates a trust providing for distributions of income to his grandchildren to pay for their college educations. Assume this would not be a taxable gift under § 2503(e).

(e) Grantor's will creates a trust containing $3,000,000. The trustee is directed to pay income to the grantor's spouse during her lifetime, remainder to his then living lineal descendants *per stirpes*. Grantor's will also gives $11,000 as specific bequests to each of his grandchildren. At the time of his death, Grantor is survived by his wife, two children, and five grandchildren. One grandchild's parents died in 2000.

[¶ 9373]

2. OTHER EXCLUDED TRANSFERS

Certain transfers are excluded from the definition of generation-skipping transfers under § 2611(b). Among the excluded transfers are those in which (1) the transferred property was previously subject to the generation-skipping tax; (2) the current transferee and the transferee of the prior transfer are deemed to be in either the same generation or the prior transferee is in a lower generation than the current transferee; and (3) the generation-skipping tax is not avoided as a result of the transfer. § 2611(b)(2).

Problem

[¶ 9375]

John creates a trust which provides for the trustee to make income distributions to Mary, his wife, during her lifetime, then to Jeff, John's grandson, during his lifetime, remainder to Ann, John's granddaughter, after Jeff's death. Jeff and Ann are skip persons in the same generation. See § 2651. Would the transfer of the property from Jeff to Ann be a generation-skipping transfer? Why or why not? See § 2611(b).

H. COMPUTING GST TAX: WORKING WITH THE NUMBERS

[¶ 9381]

1. THE APPLICABLE RATE

The generation-skipping tax imposed by § 2601 is calculated by multiplying the taxable amount by the applicable rate. § 2602. This seemingly simple formula quickly becomes complicated. While the "taxable amount" is fairly straight forward (as shown in ¶ 9281), determining the "applicable rate" requires additional computations.

Finding the applicable rate requires the determination of both "the maximum Federal estate tax rate" and "the inclusion ratio with respect to the transfer." § 2641.

[¶ 9389]

a. The Maximum Federal Estate Tax Rate

The maximum federal estate tax rate is determined under § 2001 at the time of the generation-skipping transfer. § 2641(b). This means that the maximum estate tax rate in effect in the year in which the taxable distribution, taxable termination, or direct skip occurs will be used to determine the applicable rate for those generation-skipping transfers.

[¶ 9397]

b. The Inclusion Ratio

The definition of the inclusion ratio is found in § 2642. It is determined by subtracting the applicable fraction from 1; in turn, the applicable fraction is made up of a numerator consisting of the generation-skipping exemption allocated to the trust or the direct skip and a denominator that is the value of the property placed in trust or the property subject to the direct skip, reduced by any estate tax attributable to the property in trust and any charitable gift involved. For example, where the transferor places $500,000 in trust and allocates $100,000 of his exemption to the trust, the applicable fraction is $100,000/$500,000 or 1/5, which is subtracted from 1 to give an inclusion ratio of 4/5. The general purpose of the inclusion ratio is to eliminate from the flat-rate tax the portion of the transfer that is covered by the allocated exemption.

c. Application

Once both the maximum federal estate tax rate and the inclusion ratio are known, they are multiplied and the result is the applicable rate. § 2641. Thus, if the inclusion ratio is 1, the applicable rate is equal to the maximum estate tax rate. If the inclusion ratio is less than 1 but greater than zero, the applicable rate will be less than the maximum estate tax rate. If the inclusion ratio is zero, the applicable rate will be zero (zero multiplied by the applicable estate tax rate which, in 2006, is 46 percent (45 percent beginning in 2007), § 2001(c)(2)(B)), and the generation-skipping tax will be zero. In order to get an inclusion ratio of zero, the applicable fraction must be 1, which occurs when the allocated exemption is the same as the value of the property transferred (*e.g.*, the exemption is $2 million and the property's value is $2 million, thus producing an applicable fraction of $2,000,000/$2,000,000, or 1, which is then subtracted from 1 to result in an inclusion ratio of zero). On the other hand, if the applicable fraction is zero (resulting when either no exemption is allowed or the property has no value), the inclusion ratio will be 1 and the entire transfer is subject to the maximum estate tax rate.

2. THE FORMULA

The applicable rate, once known, is multiplied by the taxable amount. Thus, the steps in determining the generation-skipping tax are as follows:

Step 1. Inclusion ratio = 1 − allocated exemption/property value when placed in trust

Step 2. Applicable rate = maximum estate tax rate x inclusion ratio

Step 3. Taxable amount:

(a) Taxable termination = full market value of property − expenses, debts, and taxes

(b) Taxable distribution = value of property received − transferee's expenses in determining tax

(c) Direct skip = amount received by transferee

Step 4. Generation-skipping tax = taxable amount x applicable rate

3. AN ILLUSTRATION

An example of how the generation-skipping tax is determined would be the establishment of a trust in a parent's will to provide income to the child for life and upon the child's death to the grandchild outright. The trust is funded with $4,500,000 from the parent's estate after the payment of all death taxes. The child subsequently dies when the trust has a value of $5,000,000 and the maximum estate tax rate is 45 percent. The parent had not used any part of his or her then available $1,500,000 exemption prior to his or her death in 2004, and the decedent's executor allowed the automatic allocation to apply to cause an <u>allocation of the $1,500,000 exemption to the trust</u>. § 2632(e)(1). At the child's death, there is a taxable termination, and the taxable amount will be the <u>$5,000,000</u> value of the trust property at that time. The trustee must pay the <u>generation-skipping</u> tax out of the trust assets, and the taxable amount will include <u>that tax.</u> The inclusion ratio will be 1 minus a fraction with a numerator of $2 million (the allocated exemption) and a denominator of $4.5 million (<u>the value of the property placed in trust</u>); this results in an inclusion ratio or fraction of 2/3. Thus, 2/3 times 45 percent (the maximum estate tax rate) times $5,000,000 is the generation-skipping transfer tax payable after the child's death out of the trust property; the tax is $2 million.

Mistake!
should be
$1.5 mill?

Problem

[¶ 9427]

What are the inclusion ratio and applicable rate in the following situations?

(a) Grantor gives his granddaughter a boat worth $150,000. Grantor allocates none of his exemption to the transfer.

(b) Grantor creates a trust worth $11 million for the benefit of his grandchildren. The entire $2 million exemption is allocated to the trust.

(c) Grantor's will creates a trust worth $900,000 for the benefit of his children and grandchildren. Grantor's executor allocates $500,000 of the $2 million to the trust.

I. EFFECT OF GST TAX ON BASIS

[¶ 9429]

The gift tax and estate tax rules play a role in determining the basis of the transferred property. <u>When a generation-skipping transfer occurs during the transferor's lifetime, the basis of the property transferred increases up to the fair market value of the property.</u> Under § 2654(a)(1), the increase in basis is equal to the amount of the generation-skipping tax which is attributable to appreciation of the property. Appreciation, in turn, is determined by using the basis adjustments made under § 1015 for any gift tax paid on the transfer.

Where the generation-skipping transfer is a taxable termination at death, the basis adjustment will be "in a manner similar to the manner provided under § 1014(a)." § 2654(a)(2). Section 1014(a) provides for a "fresh start" basis equal to the fair market value of the property at the time of death. Thus, the basis adjustment in a taxable termination is generally more favorable than in taxable distributions or direct skips. If the inclusion ratio of the property transferred in a taxable termination at death is less than 1, however, the basis adjustment is limited as it is multiplied by the inclusion ratio to produce the increase or decrease in basis. Section 2654(a)(2).

Problem

[¶ 9450]

Describe how the generation-skipping tax would apply to the following situations, classifying the respective beneficiaries in each scenario as either "skip persons" or "non-skip persons" (§ 2613); indicating when and if a taxable termination, a taxable distribution, or direct skip will occur (§ 2612); and determining how the property subject to the generation-skipping tax will be valued at the time of the taxable event (§§ 2621–2624), the amount of the inclusion ratio (§ 2642(a)), the rate of tax that will be applied (§ 2641), and the exemption (§ 2631).

(a) Sam Smith's will devises Blackacre to his wife, Ann, for life, then to his son, John, for his life, then to his grandson, Bob, for his life, and then to Bob's issue in fee.

(b) Harry left by will one-half of his adjusted gross estate outright to his wife, and the residue he left in trust to the Farmer Trust Company to distribute the income among his wife and children in accordance with their best interests and to accumulate the balance of the income and upon the death of the last survivor of his wife and children to distribute the remaining corpus among his issue then living per stirpes.

(c) Ann created a trust with a $5,500,000 corpus, providing for the payment of income to her grandchild for life and upon his death to the grandchildren's children outright. Would it make any difference for tax purposes if the transfer of the $5,500,000 were made to the grandchild directly and not subject to the trust? Would it be relevant to the tax determination if the grandchild were an orphan at the time of the transfer?

(d) Randy's will leaves his property in trust for his wife's life with the income currently payable to his wife for her life; upon her death the income to be payable to their son, Mark; and upon Mark's death, to divide the corpus among Mark's issue then living. Randy died in 2000, Mark died in 2001, Randy's widow died this year. Mark's only issue living at the time of the widow's death was a son, Mark, Jr.

(e) Susan, placed $2,500,000 into an irrevocable trust for granddaughter, Mary, the trust to continue until Mary attains age 55 or dies. During the continuance of the trust, Mary is to receive all of the trust income and such amounts of the principal as are needed for her health, education, maintenance and support. Upon termination of the trust, the property is to be distributed to Mary, if living, otherwise to the lineal descendants of Susan. Jane, the mother of Mary, is the trustee. Assume that this year the trustee distributes $22,000 from the principal of the trust to Mary to enable Mary to pay her tuition to law school. Determine whether the distribution for tuition is a generation-skipping transfer and, if so, the amount of the tax.

J. SUMMARY

[¶ 9501]

The good news is that there is a $2 million exemption for generation-skipping tax purposes—and it is scheduled to increase. §§ 2631(c); 2001(c)(2)(B).

The bad news is the generation-skipping tax is a flat rate tax, the tax rate being the maximum federal estate tax rate. Equally bad news is that the generation-skipping tax applies to all gifts, in trust or free of trust, to grandchildren and grandchildren equivalents unless these so-called direct skips are sheltered by the $10,000 ($12,000, in 2006, adjusted for inflation) per donee per annum generation-skipping tax exclusion or an allocation of a part or all of the donor's generation-skipping tax $2 million exemption is made to shelter the direct skip. Putting it more simply, a gift to a trust whose beneficiaries are only grandchildren or grandchildren equivalents (or even younger generation beneficiaries) is a *direct skip*, a tax triggering event for purposes of the GST.

The generation-skipping tax also applies to *taxable distributions* to skip persons and *taxable terminations* to *skip persons* from trusts which have *non-skip beneficiaries* (or higher generation skip person beneficiaries), skip persons being grandchildren and grandchildren equivalents (or even younger generation beneficiaries) and non-skip persons being children and children equivalents. The generation-skipping tax will apply to such trusts to the extent the trust is not sheltered from the generation-skipping tax by an allocation of part or all of the transferor's $2 million generation-skipping tax exemption.

Who is the *transferor*? The *transferor* is the last person who is or was subject to the gift or estate tax with respect to the property.

*

Part III

TRANSFERS FOR THE BENEFIT
OF THE TRANSFEROR

Chapter 10

RETAINED INTERESTS

A. OBJECTIVES

[¶ 10,001]

Every taxpayer would be delighted if it were possible for the taxpayer to give property away during life, keep the benefit of it until the taxpayer dies, *and* have it excluded from the taxpayer's estate for estate tax purposes! This utopian proposition is the subject of § 2036, which is titled, appropriately enough, "Transfers with Retained Life Estate."

Generally speaking, § 2036 speaks to lifetime transfers in which the transferor has retained an interest until death. The classic example is the case in which the transferor deeds Blackacre to a child but retains the right to occupy the property for lifetime. If § 2036 did not reach such cases, the estate tax avoidance potential of a lifetime transfer would be enormous.

Much litigation has been generated by efforts of the IRS to apply § 2036. Such litigation continues as new applications of the section are constantly being tested. Clearly, an in-depth understanding of the present applications of § 2036 is the basis for almost all tax planning.

This chapter is concerned only with § 2036(a)(1), which relates to cases in which the transferor has retained *for his or her own benefit* the economic enjoyment of the transferred property. Several commonly encountered situations illustrate the application of § 2036(a)(1). One of the most common is the case in which the transferor deeds residential premises to a child and continues to occupy the premises even though the transferor has not expressly retained the right to such occupancy in the deed of transfer.

Another case is the one in which the transferor puts property into an irrevocable trust with a third party as trustee. Suppose the transferor is the beneficiary of the trust for life. Upon the transferor's death, the trust is to terminate and the undistributed trust property is to be distributed to then living lineal descendants. Suppose further that the agreement expressly provides that all distributions from the trust of income and principal are at the sole discretion of the trustee, the trustee being subject only to the requirement that the trustee act in good faith and not arbitrarily. The question, then, becomes one of determining whether any portion of the trust property should be included in the transferor's gross estate for federal estate tax purposes. If the answer is that no part of the trust estate will be included in the transferor's gross estate, for some taxpayers, this device would probably have some attraction.

These are only a few of the possible applications of § 2036(a)(1).

Section 2036(a)(2), which relates to cases in which the transferor has retained the right to control the enjoyment *by others* of property which the transferor has transferred during life, is an integral part of Chapter 19, "Making Gifts To Loved Ones."

B.   THE RIGHT TO INCOME CASES

[¶ 10,051]

ESTATE OF McNICHOL v. COMMISSIONER

United States Court of Appeals, Third Circuit, 1959.
265 F.2d 667, cert. denied, 361 U.S. 829.

STEEL, District Judge.

More than nine years before his death, the decedent purported to convey certain income-producing real estate to his children. Thereafter, pursuant to an oral understanding with his children, the decedent continued to receive the rents from the properties until his death. The Tax Court held that the properties were includable in the decedent's gross estate.

* * *

Between 1939 and 1942 the decedent, a Pennsylvania resident, executed general warranty deeds to his children for income-producing real estate, together with the rentals therefrom, which he owned in Pennsylvania. The deeds were recorded. They reserved no interest in the realty or rents to the decedent, and the decedent received no consideration in connection with the transaction. * * *

Contemporaneously with and subsequent to the execution of the deeds, it was orally understood between the decedent and his children that the decedent should retain for his lifetime the income from the real estate. In accordance with this understanding the decedent actually received all of such income from the dates of the deeds to the time of his death.

In his federal income tax returns for 1948 to 1950, inclusive, and for the period from January 1, 1951 to the time of his death on June 17, 1951 the decedent reported the rents as his personal income. In the same returns the decedent claimed as deductions depreciation, taxes and water rent applicable to the properties.

The petitioners contended before the Tax Court that under Pennsylvania law the deeds conferred upon the children a fee simple title, that the Pennsylvania statute of frauds barred the grantor from enforcing his oral understanding against his children, and that the grantor therefore had retained no "right" to the income "under" the transfer within the meaning of the statute. The Tax Court rejected this argument and held that Pennsylvania law was immaterial, and that the test of gross estate includability under § 811(c)(1)(B) [1986 Code § 2036(a)(1)] was a factual one; i.e., whether a decedent in reality had retained possession or enjoyment of the property. Finding that the collection of the rents by decedent pursuant to his understanding with his children constituted a factual enjoyment of the properties under the transfer, the Tax Court held that the properties were properly included in decedent's gross estate.

Petitioners argue that § 811(c)(1)(B) [1986 Code § 2036(a)(1)] is inapplicable to a transfer with a retained income interest unless that interest is reserved in the instrument of transfer. This argument is based upon the statutory provision that the income must be retained *"under"* the transfer. This is too constricted an interpretation to place on the statute. The statute means only that the life interest must be retained in connection with or as an incident to the transfer.

Next, petitioners point out that the statute speaks of the retention of "the right to the income". Emphasizing the word "right", petitioners argue that Congress has decreed that § 811(c)(1)(B) [1986 Code § 2036(a)(1)] is applicable only if a transferor reserves to himself an enforceable claim to the income. Since, according to petitioners, the statute of frauds of Pennsylvania would foreclose judicial enforcement of the oral understanding between the decedent and his children, petitioners conclude that the decedent had no "right" to the income from the property.

It is not necessary for us to delve into Pennsylvania law, for the question is not one of local law. Rather, it is whether Congress intended that § 811(c)(1)(B) [1986 Code § 2036(a)(1)] should subject to an estate tax property conveyed under circumstances which here prevail. While state law creates legal interests and rights, it is the federal law which designates which of these interests and rights shall be taxed. Morgan v. Commissioner, 1940, 309 U.S. 78, 80–81, * * * Helvering v. Stuart, 1942, 317 U.S. 154, 162 * * *.

In seeking to discover the type of transfers at which § 811(c)(1)(B) [1986 Code § 2036(a)(1)] is aimed, the words "right to the income" are not entitled to undue emphasis. Section 811(c)(1)(B) states that property which has been transferred *inter vivos* is includable in the gross estate of a decedent when the decedent "has retained for his life * * * the possession or enjoyment of, or the right to the income from the property * * *". Thus, the statute deals with two things: retention of "possession or enjoyment" and retention of "the right to the income".

The history of the statute discloses that "the right to the income" clause was not intended to limit the scope of the "possession or enjoyment" clause used in § 811(c)(1)(B) [1986 Code § 2036(a)(1)]. Section 811(c)(1)(B) derives directly from § 302(c) of the Act of 1926, as amended in 1931 and 1932, 26 U.S.C.A. Int.Rev.Acts, pages 227, 228. The amendment of 1931 included for the first time express language taxing property which had been transferred *inter vivos* with a lifetime retention of "the possession or enjoyment of, or the income from" the property. This amendment said nothing about the "right to" income. The words "right to" were inserted for the first time by the 1932 amendment, and the language of the 1932 amendment was carried over into

§ 811(c) of the I.R.C. of 1939 [1986 Code § 2036]. This insertion was to make clear that Congress intended that the statute should apply to cases where a decedent was entitled to income even though he did not actually receive it. H.R.Rep. No. 708, 72d Cong.; 1st Sess. pp. 46–7 (C.B. 1939–1, Part 2, pp. 490–1); Sen.Rep. No. 665, 72d Cong.; 1st Sess. pp. 49–50 (C.B. 1939–1, Part 2, p. 532). [In referring to the changes made by the 1932 Act to the Joint Resolution of March 3, 1931, H.R.Rep. No. 708 states:

> (3) The insertion of the words "the right to the income" in place of the words "the income" is designed to reach a case where decedent had the right to the income, though he did not actually receive it. This is also a clarifying change.

Sen. Rep. No. 665 says the same thing.] Hence, the "right to income" clause, instead of circumscribing the "possession or enjoyment" clause in its application to retained income, broadened its sweep.

[Substantial Present Economic Benefit]

The conclusion is irresistible that the petitioners' decedent "enjoyed" the properties until he died. If, as was said in Commissioner v. Estate of Church [335 U.S. 632, 645 (1949)], * * * the most valuable property attribute of stocks is their income, it is no less true that one of the most valuable incidents of income-producing real estate is the rent which it yields. He who receives the rent in fact enjoys the property. Enjoyment as used in the death tax statute is not a term of art, but is synonymous with substantial present economic benefit. Commissioner v. Estate of Holmes, 1945, 326 U.S. 480, 486, * * * Under this realistic point of view the enjoyment of the properties which the decedent conveyed to his children was continued in decedent by prearrangement and ended only when he died. The transfers were clearly of a kind which Congress intended that § 811(c)(1)(B) [1986 Code § 2036(a)(1)] should reach.

This conclusion, petitioners insist, is irreconcilable with * * * Nichols v. Coolidge, 1927, 274 U.S. 531 * * *

There, the grantor without consideration had conveyed the fee of her residences to her children, with a contemporaneous lease back for a nominal consideration. It was understood that the lease would be renewed so long as the grantor desired. Four years later the grantor died. The Commissioner included the realty in the decedent's gross estate * * * on the ground that the transfer was "intended to take effect in possession or enjoyment at or after his death". The District Court held that the Commissioner's action was unauthorized. It reasoned that the grantor had no "valid agreement" for the renewal of the lease, that the conveyance gave the grantees full possession and enjoyment of the properties, and that the transaction vested in the grantees "complete title". The Supreme Court affirmed upon the basis of the District Court decision.

The present-day importance of Nichols v. Coolidge can be understood only when it is viewed in its historical setting. The statute under which it was decided provided that property transferred *inter vivos* should be included in the gross estate of a decedent when the transfer was

¶ 10,051

* * * in contemplation of or intended to take effect in possession or enjoyment at or after his death.

Interpreting this same statutory language four years later, the Court held in May v. Heiner, 1930, 281 U.S. 238, * * * that property which had been irrevocably transferred under a formal agreement of trust reserving to the settlor an interest in the income terminable at his death was not includable in the gross estate of the settlor since the title had vested in the transferee at the time of transfer. Although May v. Heiner made no reference to Nichols v. Coolidge, both decisions turned upon the fact that legal title had been technically transferred prior to death, and hence the transfer was not "intended to take effect in possession or enjoyment at or after his death". This dispositive principle was reaffirmed on March 2, 1931 in Burnet v. Northern Trust Co., 1931, 283 U.S. 782 * * *; Morsman v. Burnet, 1931, 283 U.S. 783, and McCormick v. Burnet, 1931, 283 U.S. 784, * * * by *per curiam* decisions based upon May v. Heiner. These decisions upset the long-standing Treasury interpretation of the "intended to take effect in possession or enjoyment" clause which had been in the Revenue Act since 1916, 39 Stat. 777.

The following day Congress, in order to close the obvious tax loophole which the decisions had opened, adopted the Joint Resolution of March 3, 1931. This resolution redefined the phrase "intended to take effect in possession and enjoyment at or after his death" so that it would include a transfer under which the transferor "retained for his life * * * the possession or enjoyment of, or the income from" the transferred property. This provision and its substantial embodiment in later amendments to the Revenue Act made taxable property which had been transferred *inter vivos* under a formal declaration of trust with a life estate reserved to the settlor. That was its purpose. By this resolution Congress rejected the view of May v. Heiner and its progeny that estate tax includability depended upon whether or not title had technically passed. Cf. Hassett v. Welch, 1938, 303 U.S. 303, 309–310, * * * The premise of Nichols v. Coolidge was precisely the same as that of May v. Heiner; hence, the effect of the Joint Resolution was to undo Nichols v. Coolidge as well. Since Congress barred resort to formal trust agreements with reserved life estates as a means of circumventing the payment of death taxes, it is unreasonable to conclude that it intended to permit the accomplishment of the same result by an oral agreement having an identical effect.

* * *

[The Church Case]

What we have said finds substantiation in the basic philosophy of Commissioner v. Estate of Church, supra, which expressly repudiated May v. Heiner. The Church opinion emphasizes that the criterion for determining whether property transferred *inter vivos* is subject to a death tax is the effect of the transfer, and states that whenever in fact the ultimate possession or enjoyment of property is held in suspense until the death of the transferor, the property is swept into the decedent's gross estate by the statute. Substance and not form is made the touchstone of taxability. The Court holds that an estate tax cannot be avoided by a gift unless it is (335 U.S. at 645):

¶ 10,051

* * * a bona fide transfer in which the settlor, absolutely, unequivocally, irrevocably, and without possible reservations, parts with all of his title and all of his possession and all of his enjoyment of the transferred property. * * *

It is true that the *Church* opinion refers to "a property right" in the income, "the right to the income", the "right to possess or to enjoy the property" and other expressions which may be pointed to as imputing legal collectability of the income. The *Church* language was, of course, patterned to fit the situation with which the Court was dealing, i.e., a transfer of property under a formal trust agreement in which the trustor retained an enforceable right to the income. But as we read the decision its bite goes deeper; and the opinion constitutes a sweeping and forthright declaration that technical concepts pertaining to the law of conveyancing cannot be used as a shield against the impact of death taxes when in fact possession or enjoyment of the property by the transferor—and more particularly his enjoyment of the income from the property—ceases only with his death.

* * *

The decision of the Tax Court will be affirmed.

C. THE USE, POSSESSION, ENJOYMENT CASES

As seen in *McNichol* the presence of a mere oral agreement is sufficient to trigger inclusion in the gross estate under § 2036(a)(1) of property in which the transferor is said to have retained an interest. So too can it said that even absent a finding of an express agreement, the requisite agreement can be implied from the facts and circumstances. This is the teaching of *Estate of Maxwell v. Commissioner*, 3 F.3d 591 (2d Cir. 1993), reprinted at ¶ 12,804, where the facts are classic, classic in the sense of a taxpayer attempting to avoid the reach of the statute by papering the transaction with all the bells and whistles that could come to mind that would suggest a transfer without a retained life estate. This is tax planning at its best—or worst, depending upon whether you believe that the transaction was form over substance or vice versa (in which case the taxpayer experienced an unjust outcome).

[¶ 10,101]

1. RESIDENTIAL PROPERTY

ESTATE OF GUTCHESS v. COMMISSIONER

United States Tax Court, 1967.
46 T.C. 554, acq., 1967–1 C.B. 2.

MULRONEY, Judge:

* * *

On or about September 8, 1949, the decedent quit-claimed the title to his residence property, known as 2311 Evergreen Road, Ottawa Hills, Toledo,

Ohio, to his wife Julia B. Gutchess who at all times after September 9, 1949, and up to and subsequent to decedent's death, was the record owner of the property. No consideration was paid to decedent for the conveyance. Decedent paid taxes on the residence after the transfer and also on other property Julia owned.

* * *

It is respondent's position that the residence involved in this proceeding is includable in the gross estate of decedent under § 2036. We have set forth the pertinent portion of said statute in the margin.

In order for the statute to apply with respect to an inter vivos transfer of property there must be a retention of "the possession or enjoyment" of the property by the transferor. There is some indication in respondent's brief that he is arguing that the mere fact the husband continued to live in the residence after the transfer and until he died is sufficient to make the property includable in the husband's estate under the above statute.

Some statements in some of the decided cases in this area offer support for the conclusion that express or implied retention of rights to use or enjoy the property is not necessary where there was actual use and enjoyment by the transferor after the transfer.

[The court discussed the facts in the *McNichol* case (reproduced at ¶ 10,051) and the *Skinner* case (reproduced at ¶ 10,133) and concluded that:]

In all of the above cases there are statements that could be said to mean no right of retention would be necessary if there was actual retention of use and enjoyment by the transferor after the transfer. However, in all of these cases involving transfers of income-producing property the courts were able to find agreements or prearrangements with respect to retention that were express or implied on which to base the transferor's right of retention. Where post-transfer *income* is actually retained without any objection by the transferee, it is reasonable to conclude that some pretransfer agreement or arrangement for such retention existed.

[Facts and Circumstances]

Respondent argues here that there was retained possession because there was post-transfer occupancy and therefore there must have been an understanding or implied agreement between decedent and his wife that decedent would continue to occupy the residence. But the spouses' joint occupancy of a home after an inter spouse transfer of the residence is insufficient in and of itself to indicate the existence of an agreement for retained enjoyment. In such a case there is not such a withholding of use from the transferee as is present when the transferor actually retains income from property he has transferred. The transferor husband's use of the property by occupancy after the transfer is a natural use which does not diminish transferee wife's enjoyment and possession and which grows out of a congenial and happy family relationship. Such post-transfer use is insufficient to indicate any prior agreement or prearrangement for retention of use by the transferor.

¶ 10,101

Respondent makes some argument that there was an express agreement for the husband's post-transfer occupancy. The agreement is based upon that portion of Julia's testimony where she said at the time the residence was purchased in 1932 she and her husband decided to make it their family home. This fragment of testimony is construed by respondent on brief as showing an agreement between them for joint occupancy that was never changed. There is no merit in this argument. Julia's testimony with respect to any express retention by decedent is very clear. When she was asked, if at the time of the transfer there was any written or oral agreement with respect to his right to continue to reside in the residence, her answer was a firm: "Not a word."

Respondent also makes some argument that under Ohio law (Ohio Rev. § 3103.04) one spouse cannot be excluded from residence in the other's dwelling except by decree of court, and no such decree was obtained here. It is difficult to see how that would have any bearing here. If decedent had some residence rights granted by Ohio law that would not mean retention of use and enjoyment *"under"* a transfer as required by the statute that is here involved.

[Legal Obligation]

Respondent makes some argument that the transfer of his residence was a partial fulfillment of decedent's legal obligation to support his family, citing his regulation, § 20.2036–1(b)(2). There is nothing in the instrument of transfer and no evidence at all that the transfer was in satisfaction of decedent's obligation to support his wife. There is nothing here to indicate decedent's duty to support his wife was discharged in any manner by the gift. A husband can certainly make a gift to his wife of the family home without affecting his duty to support her.

We hold for petitioner on the issue presented. * * *

[¶ 10,109]

REVENUE RULING 78–409

1978–2 C.B. 70.

ISSUE

Whether, under the circumstances described below, any portion of the value of a residence transferred by a decedent to his son and daughter-in-law is includible in decedent's gross estate under § 2036.

FACTS

The decedent was the owner of a residence in State *X*. In 1965, after the death of the decedent's spouse, the decedent's child *A*, and *A's* spouse, moved into the residence and lived with the decedent. In 1970, the decedent gratuitously conveyed the residence to *A* in fee simple. At the time of the transfer it was assumed by the decedent and *A*, although not expressly agreed, that the decedent would continue to live in the residence. After the conveyance, *A* paid for the upkeep of the property. <u>The decedent died in 1975 while still occupying the residence.</u>

Under the law of State *X, A* was the absolute owner of the residence at the time of the decedent's death. The decedent had not retained any interest in the property that was recognized by state law.

LAW AND ANALYSIS

* * *

[Implied Agreement]

<u>An interest retained pursuant to an understanding or arrangement comes within § 2036.</u> *Skinner v. United States,* 316 F.2d 517 (3d Cir. 1963). The arrangement may be express, or it may be implied from the circumstances surrounding the transfer. Estate of Linderme v. Commissioner, 52 T.C. 305 (1969); Estate of Kerdolff v. Commissioner, 57 T.C. 643 (1972); Rev. Rul. 70–155, 1970–1 C.B. 189.

In the present case, the evidence supports a conclusion that the decedent retained a right pursuant to an implied understanding with *A,* to share possession and enjoyment of the residence for life. Consequently, whatever portion of the residence was subject to this retained interest <u>is now includible in the decedent's gross estate.</u>

In Diehl v. United States, Civil No. C–67–74 (W.D. Tenn., Oct. 18, 1967), the decedent transferred his home to his son and daughter-in-law. Prior to the transfer the decedent had an addition constructed onto the house, wherein he resided after the transfer. After the transfer, the decedent contributed toward the household expenses and utilities, while the son paid the taxes on the residence. The court concluded under these facts that there was no "understanding" between transferor and transferee that the decedent would live at the residence although it was "assumed" by both transferor and transferee that the transferor would continue to reside there after the transfer.

The Internal Revenue Service will not follow Diehl v. United States because the court erred in concluding that there was no implied agreement or "understanding" that the decedent would continue to reside there. The fact that a special addition was constructed onto the house and the fact that the court found that it was assumed that the decedent would reside in the home, clearly shows that after the transfer, the decedent retained an interest in the home.

[Facts and Circumstances]

Under the principal facts, the extent of the decedent's interest will not be considered limited for purposes of § 2036 solely because the residence was shared with *A* and *A's* spouse until the decedent's death. * * *

HOLDING

Here, it was assumed by both the decedent and *A* that the decedent would reside at the home after the transfer. No evidence exists that the decedent's enjoyment of the residence was restricted in any manner. Under these circumstances, where the decedent's possession and enjoyment of the residence continue without limitation, the retained rights extend to all the property.

Accordingly, the entire value of the residence is includible in the decedent's gross estate under § 2036(a)(1).

[¶ 10,115]

2. LEGAL OBLIGATIONS

Most startling to some is the prospect that a donor will have included, in his or her estate, transferred property which is used to discharge the donor's legal obligations. Reg. § 20.2036–1(b)(2). The creative use of this concept reflected in *Sullivan,* which follows, is particularly interesting.

[¶ 10,117]

ESTATE OF SULLIVAN v. COMMISSIONER

United States Tax Court, 1993.
66 T.C.M. (CCH) 1329, T.C.M. (RIA) ¶ 93,531.

GERBER, Judge: * * * The issue for our consideration is whether within the meaning of § 2036(a), Virgil C. Sullivan (decedent) retained the possession or enjoyment of, or the right to the income from, transferred trust assets. In resolving these questions we consider: (1) Whether decedent retained a right to use the income of the trust to discharge a legal obligation to support his wife, and (2) whether decedent retained an interest in the trust corpus.

FINDINGS OF FACT

* * *

Virgil C. Sullivan, a resident of the State of Minnesota, died on December 20, 1986, survived by his widow, Christine Sullivan (Christine), three sons from his prior marriage, and three grandchildren. At the time of his death decedent was 82 years of age and Christine was 79 years of age. * * *

Decedent created an irrevocable trust (the Trust) under agreement dated December 29, 1967, by and between decedent as settlor, and decedent and Robert Don (Don) as trustees. Don and decedent were close friends. * * *

Article I(A) of the Trust provides as follows:

During the lifetime of Christine Sullivan, wife of the Settlor, the Trustees shall pay to said Christine Sullivan the entire net income from the Trust Estate in quarterly or more frequent installments so long as she shall live, and in addition to such payments of net income, the Trustees shall pay to or expend for the benefit of said Christine Sullivan such sum or sums from the principal of the Trust Estate as the Trustees, in the exercise of their discretion, may deem necessary or advisable from time to time to provide for her proper care, support, maintenance and health, taking into consideration her needs and the other sources of financial assistance, if any, which may be or may become available for such purposes.

Article I(B) provides that upon Christine's death all principal and undistributed income is to be distributed in equal shares to decedent's sons or their survivors.

Article II provides:

The Settlor having been fully advised in respect thereto, hereby expressly surrenders all right and power to amend, modify or revoke this trust in whole or in part, and does hereby irrevocably divest himself of all interests of whatever nature in and to any estate therein.

Article III provides in pertinent part:

The Trustees shall have the sole legal and equitable title to all properties at any time held, acquired or received by them under the terms of this agreement, subject to the conditions and provisions hereof.

The Trustees shall have and exercise the exclusive management and control of the Trust Estate, and without limiting the generality of the foregoing, they are vested with the following additional powers and discretions:

(K) To make payment of any funds by the terms hereof payable to or for the benefit of any minor or person determined by the Trustees to be unable to manage and care for his personal business affairs, at the sole discretion of the Trustees exercised from time to time in any one or more of the following ways: (1) directly for the support, maintenance, education and general welfare of such beneficiary, or (2) to the legal or natural guardian of such beneficiary, or (3) to any relative or friend of such beneficiary who shall have custody and care of the person of such beneficiary, or (4) directly to such beneficiary. * * *

Article IV of the Trust agreement provides that as long as the settlor is a cotrustee he has the exclusive right to exercise the powers and discretions granted to the trustees under the terms of article III. The Trust agreement provides that the Trust is to be construed under the laws of the State of Minnesota.

From the time the Trust was created through decedent's death, Don neither requested nor was provided any documentation indicating how the Trust assets were invested. * * * Decedent, with the assistance of professional advisers, handled all administrative matters of the Trust, including purchase and sale of investments, record keeping, and accounting matters. Don did not participate in any of these matters. At no time did Don discuss or question decedent about the amounts that were paid to Christine out of the Trust, nor was he provided with any information or documentation in this regard. From its creation in 1967 through decedent's death, Don did not receive any trustee fees from the Trust.

The Trust assets consisting of cash and marketable securities had a value at the time of decedent's death of $1,032,184.72. * * *

¶ 10,117

OPINION

* * * The purpose of § 2036 is to impose the estate tax on property which was transferred during the decedent's life but in which the transferor retained until his death the right to economic benefit. * * * Section 2036(a) reflects a "legislative policy of subjecting to tax all property which has been the subject of an incomplete *inter vivos* transfer." United States v. O'Malley, 383 U.S. 627, 631 (1966).

Respondent's position is that decedent retained the right to use both trust income and corpus to discharge his legal support obligations within the meaning of Reg. § 20.2036–1(b)(2). Respondent contends that this retained right constitutes "possession and enjoyment", and therefore, trust income and corpus are includable in the gross estate under § 2036(a)(1). Petitioner maintains that decedent retained no rights in trust income and further argues that § 2036(a)(1) does not apply to retained interests in the corpus of income-producing property.

1.   The Application of § 2036—Trust Income

The trust income would be considered as retained by the decedent under § 2036 if it could be applied toward discharging decedent's legal obligation to support his spouse during his lifetime. Reg. § 20.2036–1(b)(2).

Respondent maintains that under article III(K) of the Trust decedent retained the right to make payments directly for the support and maintenance of his wife in the event of her incapacity. Petitioner argues that article I of the Trust grants outright all income from the Trust to Christine and that article III(K) is merely to facilitate payment of article I.

Respondent agrees that article I(A) provides for an income interest that is not limited to decedent's wife's support and maintenance, but contends that decedent reserved an enforceable right to have the income applied toward his wife's support under article III(X). * * *

It is well established that one spouse may make a gift to the other spouse without affecting their duty of support, and there is no presumption that such a gift is in discharge of the donor's marital duty. Colonial–American National Bank v. United States, 243 F.2d 312, 314 (4th Cir. 1957). However, where it is clear from the trust document that the trust property is to be applied to discharge a support obligation, the trust property is includable in the decedent's gross estate. Commissioner v. Dwight's Estate, 205 F.2d 298 (2d Cir. 1953), revg. 17 T.C. 1317 (1952). Inclusion is also warranted when trust income may be applied at the settlor's discretion to discharge a legal obligation by virtue of the settlor's powers as trustee. Estate of Pardee v. Commissioner, supra at 148–149; Estate of McTighe v. Commissioner, T.C. Memo. 1977–410. Inclusion is also appropriate where it may be inferred from the circumstances attendant upon the transfer and the manner in which the transferred property is used that decedent retained "possession or enjoyment of, or the right to income from, the property." * * *

While State law determines the legal interests and rights created by a trust instrument, Federal law determines the Federal tax consequences of those interests and rights. Morgan v. Commissioner, 309 U.S. 78, 80 (1940),

¶ 10,117

amended on denial of rehearing 309 U.S. 626 (1940); Estate of Vissering v. Commissioner, 96 T.C. 749, 755–756 (1991), revd. and remanded on other grounds, 990 F.2d 578 (10th Cir. 1993); Estate of Little v. Commissioner, 87 T.C. 599, 601 (1986). Here, in accord with the Trust agreement, Minnesota law governs the construction of the interests created. * * * In construing trust instruments, "One of the court's highest duties is to give effect to the donor's dominant intention as gathered from the instrument as a whole." Id. * * * In determining the donor's intent the court first looks to the language used in the trust instrument. * * * The donor's intent, as expressed in the language of the trust, dominates construction; if there is no ambiguity in language when read in light of the surrounding circumstances, extrinsic evidence of a trustor's intent is not allowed. * * *

The circumstances here lead us to conclude that the Trust was not designed to discharge or relieve the decedent of his legal obligation to support his wife. The disposition clause of article I in clear and unambiguous language directs the trustee to pay the income to the wife. It is an unconditional gift and is not limited for support. A grantor is not deemed to have retained a right to trust income where, as here, it is payable to a wife or child without any restriction that it be used for the beneficiary's support or applied toward the discharge of a legal obligation of the grantor. * * *

[Facility of Payment Clause]

Article II of the Trust instrument also supports the conclusion that the donor did not reserve a right to direct that the income be applied to his wife's support or restricted for that purpose. Article III is more logically interpreted as an administrative provision due to its relative position within the Trust instrument; i.e., following the dispositive provisions of trust income in articles I and II. This interpretation is supported by the fact that the Minnesota Trustees' Powers Act in enumerating the administrative powers of a trustee provides a provision similar to article III(K) to facilitate payment. Minn. Stat. § 501B.81(25) (1989).

Respondent also relies on Rev. Rul. 85–35, 1985–1 C.B. 329, in arguing that article III would restrict the trustees from using the income for any purpose other than her support in the event of Christine's incapacity. That ruling considered a payment clause similar to the one here, but in the context of § 2056(b)(5), which provides for a marital deduction when a surviving spouse receives a lifetime income interest coupled with a general testamentary power to appoint the trust corpus and no other person has the power to appoint any part of the property to any person other than the surviving spouse. Respondent concluded in the ruling that the requirements of § 2056(b)(5) were satisfied stating:

> The purpose of the state statute and facility of payment clause is to make certain that the beneficiary has the beneficial ownership of the trust income and to provide protection and assistance to the beneficiary if the beneficiary becomes legally disabled. The trust income is payable to A or, if A becomes legally disabled, to or for the benefit of A. The fiduciary standards imposed by State X and general principles of trust law prevent

the abuse of the powers of the trustee, and constrain the conduct of any third party distributee, thus ensuring that all trust income will be expended for A's benefit. No amount of trust income may be paid for the benefit of a third person. * * * [Rev. Rul. 85–35, 1985–1 C.B. 329.]

Respondent contends that under article III(K) decedent, as the sole trustee, would have been required to apply the funds directly to Christine's support and maintenance and would be precluded from distributing funds to third parties as Christine would have been free to do if she were capable. Respondent asserts that it is precisely for this reason that the facility of payment provision in Rev. Rul. 85–35, 1985–1 C.B. 329, satisfies § 2056(b)(5). However, the requirements of § 2056(b)(5) are met in the revenue ruling not because the income is restricted to the "support" of the surviving spouse, but because the facility of payment provision ensures that the income be expended for her benefit. Similarly, article III(K) makes certain that, as the income beneficiary, Christine, in the event of her incapacity, continues to enjoy the beneficial ownership of the Trust income.

Accordingly, we disagree with respondent and hold that decedent did not retain enjoyment of the Trust income for purposes of § 2036(a)(1).

2.   The Application of § 2036—Trust Corpus

Petitioner contends that the wording of § 2036(a)(1) limits the section's application to non-income-producing property or income from income-producing property. It is petitioner's position that § 2036(a)(1) is inapplicable to income-producing property even if decedent retained the right to satisfy his support obligations from principal. Petitioner contends the statute does not apply to interests in the principal of income-producing property in trust. Respondent argues that petitioner's interpretation is too narrow and that if decedent retained possession or enjoyment of income-producing property then the property is includable in the gross estate under § 2036(a)(1). We agree with respondent.

Section 2036(a)(1) contains three descriptions under which an interest in property will be included in the gross estate: "(1) if the decedent retains the 'possession' of the property transferred or (2) 'enjoyment' of the property or (3) the 'right to the income' from the property." Skinner's Estate v. United States, 197 F.Supp. 726, 728 (E.D. Pa. 1961), affd. 316 F.2d 517 (3d Cir. 1963). These statutory standards for inclusion are stated in the alternative and have not been read in a manner which would preclude retained interests in income-producing properties. See Estate of McCabe v. United States, 201 Ct. Cl. 243, 475 F.2d 1142 (1973) (inclusion based on retained right to use income-producing trust corpus); Estate of McNichol v. Commissioner, 29 T.C. 1179, 1183 (1958), affd. 265 F.2d 667, 671 (3d Cir. 1959) (interpreting § 811(c)(1)(B), the forerunner of present § 2036(a)(1), right to income does not limit scope of the alternative possession and enjoyment provision).

In Commissioner v. Estate of Church, 335 U.S. 632 (1949), the Supreme Court * * * stated that "The basic 'settled principle' now * * * is that where a trust agreement reserves the settlor's possession or enjoyment of part or all of the trust property until death, the value of the trust should be included in the settlor's gross estate. ⁽⁵⁾ Commissioner v. Estate of Church, supra at 651 n.11.

This Court in Estate of Linderme v. Commissioner, 52 T.C. 305, 309 (1969), relying upon Commissioner v. Estate of Church, supra, stated that "We take our cue from this mandate for a broad inclusion within the gross estate pursuant to § 2036(a)(1)." In distinguishing those cases where inclusion under § 2036(a) was upheld from those in which it was not, we stated:

> The presence of income from the property was simply a useful ancillary tool for decision rather than a limiting principle imposed as a matter of law. The retention of income was thus only an example, albeit a very clear one, of "possession or enjoyment." * * * [Estate of Linderme v. Commissioner, supra at 309.]

[Support Obligations]

Having concluded that § 2036(a) applies to a retained interest in income-producing property, we proceed to consider whether decedent retained the power to use trust corpus to discharge his duty of support. Petitioner contends that the Trust was not a support trust and the principal of the Trust was not to be so applied. Petitioner asserts that the Trust agreement requires the trustees to consider other resources available to Christine and that decedent's status as cotrustee precluded him from unilaterally exercising control over the Trust corpus. Should we find that a portion of the Trust is includable in the gross estate, petitioner also contends that the amount includable is limited to the portion needed to discharge decedent's support obligation. Respondent counters that where a possibility of corpus invasion exists, inclusion of the entire interest is warranted. Respondent contends that remoteness and improbability of the exercise of the right does not preclude the application of § 2036(a)(1). Finally, respondent asserts that decedent's status as a cotrustee does not affect the applicability of § 2036(a)(1).

Petitioner's argument that distributions in discharge of decedent's support obligations were effectively precluded because the trustees were required to consider Christine's other resources is misplaced. The trustees' ability to consider other sources of funds is not a bar to the exercise of discretion. Instead, it is a consideration or guideline in the exercise of that discretionary authority. Williams v. United States, 180 Ct. Cl. 417, 378 F.2d 693, 695–696 (1967). Under the principles of local law, a Minnesota court will not substitute its discretion for that of the trustee except when necessary to prevent the abuse of discretion. * * *

The likelihood that decedent would actually use the trust funds to satisfy his support obligations is irrelevant. If the decedent, as trustee, has the power to discharge his legal obligations, that power triggers the applicability of § 2036(a)(1). * * * Section 2036(a)(1) does not require that the transferor pull the "string" or even intend to pull the string on the transferred property; all that is required is that the string exist. * * *

* * * Petitioner argues that distributions from principal required joint action by decedent and Don, thus depriving decedent of unfettered control over the Trust assets. Petitioner contends that absent specific statutory

¶ 10,117

language such as that found in §§ 2036(a)(2) and 2038(a), joint power does not give the transferor sufficient dominion over the property to warrant inclusion. We cannot agree with petitioner, either as a matter of fact or law, that decedent lacked the requisite dominion and control over the Trust corpus to avoid inclusion.

While petitioner is correct that § 2036(a)(1), unlike §§ 2036(a)(2) and 2038(a), does not contain the "in conjunction with any other person" language, this does not adequately address the question. The question of whether decedent retained the right to invade corpus is a factual one. * * *

While recognizing that the basis for this factual determination is not limited to the construction, either express or implied, of the words of the instrument of transfer, * * * we note that the Trust agreement, as it pertains to principal, does not contain an outright grant to Christine. Under the Trust, the trustees have discretion to invade principal for Christine's "proper care, support, maintenance and health". Unlike Trust income, the Trust principal could only be used for Christine's support. Upon Christine's death, principal and undistributed income were to be distributed to decedent's sons or survivors.

Decedent's status as cotrustee does not preclude application of § 2036(a)(1). Inclusion under this § has been found applicable where the facts demonstrated that a cotrustee "for all intents and purposes in actual practice was the sole trustee." Estate of Paxton v. Commissioner, 86 T.C. 785, 813 (1986); Estate of Wedum v. Commissioner, T.C. Memo. 1989–184. See also Estate of McCabe v. United States, 201 Ct. Cl. 243, 475 F.2d 1142, 1147 (1973) (inference of prearrangement that decedent who was not a trustee was to retain control warranted inclusion); Estate of Klauber v. Commissioner, 34 T.C. 968, 973 (1960) (power of settlor/cotrustee to invade principal was reversionary interest within § 2037 based on settlor's ability to dominate the nominal holder of the power).

The facts of this case demonstrate that decedent was for all intents and purposes the sole trustee. The express language of article IV of the Trust agreement reflects decedent's intent to exercise exclusively the powers and discretions granted to the trustees under article III. Don was a nominal trustee; decedent at all times acted as sole trustee without consulting Don, who neither participated in nor was informed about the administration or activity of the Trust.

Having held that § 2036(a)(1) is applicable, we must consider what portion of the assets are properly includable. Petitioner contends that inclusion is limited to that portion of trust assets necessary to satisfy decedent's support obligation. Respondent argues that the entire trust corpus is includable.

Petitioner relies upon Estate of Pardee v. Commissioner, supra, wherein we stated:

> the right retained "for any period which does not in fact end before his death" under § 2036(a)(1) was the right to satisfy his legal obligation of $500 per month for the two children under 18, and so much of the corpus

¶ **10,117**

necessary to generate this amount is includable in his gross estate. [49 T.C. at 150.]

Respondent seeks to distinguish *Pardee* because of her concession in *Pardee* that the full amount was not includable. Respondent also points out that in *Pardee* less than the total corpus was required to produce enough income to fulfill the taxpayer's support obligations. Respondent also relies upon Estate of Toeller v. Commissioner, 6 T.C. 832 (1946), affd. 165 F.2d 665 (7th Cir. 1948). After determining that the taxpayer/grantor had an enforceable right to have the corpus invaded for his benefit, the Court addressed the question of the value of the interest reserved by the taxpayer. The Court in rejecting any limitation on the value of the interest to be included, stated that the term " 'sickness or misfortune' used in the trust instrument is so broad in scope as to cover any conceivable form of calamity, physical, mental, or even economic, to which humanity is subject." Id. at 839.

In this case there is a qualification with respect to the amount of corpus invasion. Decedent, as trustee, had the power to use corpus for his wife's support, but only after considering her needs and her other sources of "financial assistance". Here, Christine's needs and her other sources of income have been shown with sufficient clarity to permit a valuation of the terms set forth in the trust for purposes of the inclusion of a discrete amount in decedent's gross estate. In addition, the Minnesota case law and statutes provide guidance as to the parameters for decedent's support obligation. Minn. Stat. Ann. §§ 518.552, 519.05 (West 1990); Meagher v. Hennepin County Welf. Bd., 300 Minn. 446, 221 N.W.2d 140 (1974), Bergh v. Warner, 47 Minn. 250, 50 N.W. 77 (1891).

Decedent and Christine had 1986 after-tax joint income of about $190,000 and for 1987, Christine had an after-tax income of $115,969. The living expenses for 1986 (jointly) and 1987 (Christine only) were $41,404 and $26,589, respectively, without considering decedent's gifts to charity or family. Christine's fixed sources of income are the Social Security payments and her pension of $6,090 and $1,439, respectively. The facts here are somewhat unique because it has been shown that the decedent and Christine lived most conservatively and well within their means. Additionally, their living expenditures have been shown to be consistent and unusually predictable. These factors aid in our ability to find that decedent's net obligation to support Christine under the terms of the trust would not exceed about $20,000 annually.

Referring to Reg. § 20.2031–7, as in effect at the time of decedent's death, we use a 10–percent interest factor to reach the conclusion that $200,000 of the corpus would be necessary to fund decedent's $20,000 annual obligation to support Christine. Accordingly, $200,000 of the trust corpus is includable in decedent's gross estate.

[¶ 10,119]

3. CREDITOR-FREE DISCRETIONARY PAY TRUSTS

Give special attention to the trust payout provisions in *Estate of Sullivan.* Those terms are about as common as can be found, yet the inclusion of these provisions in the Sullivan trust resulted in quite unexpected estate tax consequences. The trust provided for the "mandatory pay" of trust income and the "discretionary pay subject to a standard" of the trust principal—all quite common. The following cases, *Uhl* and *Skinner,* are discretionary pay cases both as to income and principal. Are the results in these cases reconcilable with the result in *Estate of Sullivan?* With each other?

Consider whether significance should be attached to the ability of the transferor's creditors to reach the trust property in satisfaction of the transferor's obligations. For example, while the *Uhl* court was satisfied to conclude that a discretionary pay trust was free of claims by the Indiana-based transferor's creditors, such a conclusion is contrary to the general rule that a transferor's creditors can reach property held in a discretionary pay trust. Even so, the implication is that a transferor shall be deemed to have retained a life estate in property transferred to a discretionary pay trust in those instances where the transferor's creditors can reach the trust property.

Uhl and *Skinner* considered trusts that would, today, be referred to as "self-settled *irrevocable* discretionary pay trusts". Such trusts are aspirationally if not optimistically viewed by practitioners and clients alike as a possible form of asset protection, i.e., a trust whose property is shielded from the client's creditors. "And", says Wogmoppet, the Alaska estate planning lawyer, "even better if the trust is free of estate tax at the death of the transferor." Wogmoppet beams as he points to Alaska's statute barring creditors of the trust's settler from reaching trust property in those instances where the trust is found to be an Alaska trust and distributions are at the discretion of an Alaska-based trustee (other than the settlor of the trust).

Alaska has triggered a lemming-like rush among the states to free self-settled *irrevocable* discretionary pay trusts from the claims of creditors. The obvious effect is to enable local trustees to compete for the trust business traditionally attracted to offshore venues which claim to provide creditor protection. A byproduct (possibly) is the estate tax benefit that is claimed to be offered by the Alaska legislation. As Wogmoppet was heard to say, "Man, you got to be *crazee* not to want one of my trusts."

For additional material, see ¶¶ 5600; 7478; 10,209; 21,315; and 21,870.

What does the IRS have to say about all this? Consider Priv. Ltr. Ruls. 9646021, 9837007, and 9917001.

[¶ 10,125]

ESTATE OF UHL v. COMMISSIONER

United States Court of Appeals, Seventh Circuit, 1957.
241 F.2d 867.

LINDLEY, Circuit Judge.

The deceased, Edgar M. Uhl, died testate March 7, 1951. On March 2, 1938, he transferred, by an irrevocable trust indenture to an Indiana bank, personal property consisting principally of Government bonds but including

¶ 10,125

also some stocks. Under this instrument, he reserved $100.00 monthly from the income from the corpus vested in the trustee, but retained no control over the property. Upon termination of the trust, by his death, the property was to be divided equally between a nephew and two nieces.

The controversy presented is whether the value of the entire trust estate, $84,217.42, is subject to a federal estate tax as a part of the decedent's gross estate. * * * The petitioner admitted then and admits now that that part of the estate necessary to produce the income of $100 a month was properly included in the settlor's gross estate. This amount was $50,218.85, or 59.63% of the corpus. Though agreeing that a federal estate tax was due upon this amount, he denies that the rest of the trust property could properly be included in the settlor's estate at the time of his death. The Tax Court held that the entire corpus should be included in the decedent's estate and approved a deficiency in the sum of $9,265.99 as the additional tax due as a result of inclusion of the questioned amount of 40.37%. In its decision the Tax Court relied upon a provision of the trust agreement that: "The trustee may in his discretion * * * pay a greater sum than $100.00 a month if it shall deem advisable."

The Tax Court did not find that the settlor had retained for his own use and in his own right more than $100.00 a month, but held that, in view of the fact that, as it thought, at the time the trust agreement was executed, the Indiana law was such that creditors of the settlor, if any there were, or if any had come into existence, might have successfully brought suit to reach all the income from the trust, saying: "As the decedent's creditors could have reached the income which was distributable to him in the trustee's discretion, the decedent could have obtained the enjoyment and economic benefit of such income by the simple expedient of borrowing money or otherwise becoming indebted, and then relegating the creditor to the trust income for reimbursement," and holding that therefore, the trust contained sufficient retention of the settlor's right to all the income to satisfy the requirements of § 811(c)(1)(B) [1986 Code § 2036(a)(1)] and thereby make the entire corpus includable in the decedent's gross estate.

The pertinent sections of the Revenue Act, § 811(c)(1)(B), [1986 Code § 2036(a)(1)], provide that, the value of the decedent's gross estate shall include any interest of which he has made a transfer, under which he has retained for his life or for any period not ascertainable with reference to his death, or for any period which does not in fact end before his death, "the possession or enjoyment of or the right to income from the property." It seems obvious that, under this section, by the retention of $100.00 a month the settlor reserved a right to the income from the property to that extent, and that, so far as retention of other interest by him was concerned, the balance of the trust estate was removed from his dominion or control, so that in the absence of any other factors affecting the result, the only part of the trust estate which should have been included in his gross estate at the time of his death was that part which represented the income to the receipt of which he retained the right, and that the amount of the estate irrevocably conveyed to the trustee and eventually to beneficiaries was a completed gift which thereafter remained no part of his estate. While no cases under the federal estate tax law have dealt with this precise question, both parties seem to admit that the gift tax law is in *pari materia* with that governing estate taxes. The Supreme Court has so indicated in Sanford's Estate v. Commissioner, 308 U.S. 39. * * * Consequently, we look to the precedents under the gift tax law.

[Completed Gift Where Discretionary Pay]

In Herzog v. Commissioner, 2 Cir., 116 F.2d 591, 593, the grantor had executed an irrevocable trust which gave to the trustee the choice, in its discretion, of paying the income either to the settlor or his wife. The question presented was whether this discretionary power of the trustee amounted to a reversion in the settlor of the right to enjoyment of the income or whether the title had vested in the trustee exclusive of any such right. The court said: "It was only by virtue of the trustee's direction, which on this record must be regarded as entirely voluntary, that the donor received any of the income; and this direction might be terminated whenever the trustee deemed it proper that the wife should receive the income. Such a hope or passive expectancy is not a right. It is not enough to lessen the value of the property transferred." In Rheinstrom v. Commissioner, 8 Cir., 105 F.2d 642, 648, * * * the taxpayer had executed a trust irrevocably transferring property for the benefit of taxpayer and her four children. The taxpayer retained a life interest in 40% of the net income. 50% was to be paid to the beneficiaries, and the remaining 10% was to be held by the trustees with discretion to pay to taxpayer such part thereof as to the trustees might seem best. The court held that the taxpayer had retained no legal interest in the 10%, saying: "Whether she would ever receive any of this reserve fund depended entirely upon the trustees, over whose acts she retained no control. The fact that the record shows that they have paid it to her or used it for her benefit, we do not consider of importance. By the terms of the trust instrument, they might distribute all or part of the reserve fund to her during her lifetime, or they might withhold all of it." It added that no one could compute the value of the taxpayer's hoped for expectation that her trustees would ever pay over to her an amount in addition to the enjoyment which she reserved. The Tax Court itself, in the Estate of Ben F. Hazelton, Jr., v. Commissioner, Memorandum Decision, § 40,425, relying upon both Rheinstrom and Herzog, followed the same rule, saying: "Whether he would enjoy any of the income of the trust depended entirely upon the uncontrolled discretion of the Advisory Committee. His hope or expectancy that such committee might, in the language of the trust instrument, deem payment to him to be necessary for his suitable comfort and support and conducive to his general welfare, is not a right."

We conclude, therefore, that no part of the trust estate, the income from which was not reserved to the grantor, should have been included in the gross estate, in view of the fact that the settlor reserved no right to compel the trustee to pay him any sums other than $100.00 a month, and the trustee was under no duty to pay him more than that.

[Creditor Claims]

The Tax Court did not hold otherwise, but based its decision upon the theory that the settlor's creditors, by proper litigation, might have reached all of the corpus of the estate including that over which the taxpayer had retained no control, saying: "While the decedent may not have been able to force the trustee to distribute the income to him, nevertheless he could have reached the full amount of the trust income through his creditors." It reasoned that, though it had found no Indiana case in point, that state would probably hold that the corpus could be reached by the settlor's creditors, and that such a possibility constituted retention of the right to all the income on the part of the settlor. Of course, such a right, if it existed, was the right of the creditors, not that of the grantor.

The Indiana Statute, Burns' Indiana Statutes Annotated, § 33–409, provides that all deeds of gift "made in trust for the use of the person making the same" shall be void as against creditors existing or subsequent. This provision is a part of the Indiana Statute of Frauds, enacted in 1852. It is entitled "An act for the prevention of frauds and perjuries," and requires certain contracts to be in writing and declares certain conveyances void. Section 21 provides that the question of fraudulent intent in all cases arising under the act shall be deemed a question of fact. The legislative purpose, as disclosed by the title and the statute itself, was to prevent debtors from intentionally defrauding creditors by the fraudulent conveyance of property.

* * * Here, that part of the estate the income from which the settlor did not enjoy was not held for his use. Therefore, it was not within the statute of Indiana * * * a trust where the enjoyment of all the trust property was retained in the settlor. In the present case that part of the estate other than the part necessary to produce the $100.00 a month income was not put in trust for the benefit, use or enjoyment of the settlor. He parted with dominion over it forever. Even granting that, under the Indiana authorities, that part of the estate which produced his $100.00 a month might have been reached by his creditors, the statute itself does not apply, under its express terms, to property or the income therefrom over which the settlor retained no dominion and no control. All that part of the corpus of the estate was, after the creation of the trust, the property of the beneficiaries, subject only to an uncontrolled discretion in the trustee to divert to the settlor something the settlor could not have compelled the trustee to give him. Consequently, on the face of the record, the Indiana Statute has no application. It should be observed also that, in Indiana, in order to avoid a transfer, fraud must be proved as a fact. Here there is not the slightest inference to be drawn from the record that any part of the corpus of the estate was conveyed for the purpose of defeating creditors.

We conclude that the Commissioner properly levied a deficiency estate tax for that part of the corpus necessary to produce the $100.00 a month. But the remainder of the corpus, over which the control of the settlor had ended, subject only to an uncontrolled discretion in the trustee, did not remain his property until his death but passed to the grantee at the time of the creation of the trust without hindrance or suspicion of any fraudulent intent. The decision is reversed and the cause remanded with directions to proceed in conformity with the announcements of this opinion.

¶ 10,125

[¶ 10,133]

ESTATE OF SKINNER v. UNITED STATES

United States District Court, Eastern District, Pennsylvania, 1961.
197 F.Supp. 726 , aff'd, 316 F.2d 517 (3d Cir.1963)

LAYTON, District Judge.

* * * On March 5, 1936, Maria M. Coxe Skinner (the decedent herein) executed an irrevocable trust to conserve certain interests and property "for the benefit of herself", her surviving issue, a brother, and next of kin. Plaintiff, Girard Trust Corn Exchange Bank (suing as executor here) and Marcel A. Viti were named corporate and individual trustees, respectively. The pertinent part of the Trust instrument provided that the trustees were to pay the decedent settlor " * * * the net income of the said estate, or so much thereof as trustees, may, *in their sole and absolute discretion,* deem proper under all the circumstances for the comfortable support, and maintenance of the [settlor], and after making such payment from income for her, *or in the exercise of their discretion as aforesaid, without making such payments for her,* to pay the net income, or the balance thereof, to [her lawful issue and other relatives]."

Shortly after the establishment of the 1936 Trust, the settlor filed a gift tax return for the year 1936 and attempted to exclude from a schedule of assets transferred by the Trust the value of her retained life estate. In January, 1938, the Commissioner assessed a gift tax deficiency based on disallowing exclusion of this alleged life interest in the income. The settlor was advised by the Commissioner as follows:

> * * * In view of the absolute discretionary power vested in the trustees, it is considered that you did not reserve a life estate in the trust, and the amount of the income that may be paid to you by the trustees is not susceptible of an accurate determination. Accordingly, no deduction is allowed for the life estate claimed.

An agreement was reached whereby an additional gift tax of $3,905.05 was paid.

The settlor died on January 12, 1953. During her life she had in fact received all the income from the Trust. * * *

The only issue here is the correctness of the Commissioner's inclusion of the 1936 Trust corpus in the gross estate of the decedent settlor. * * *

[Right to Income]

Defendant urges that the absence of a "right" to the income is fatal despite its uninterrupted receipt by the settlor during her life. But this argument, and all the cases cited to demonstrate the lack of an enforceable legal "right" to income under applicable state law, overlooks the alternative structure of § 811(c)(1)(B)(i) [1986 Code § 2036(a)(1)]. By the plain terms of the statute, the Trust corpus must still be included in the settlor's gross estate if she retained "enjoyment" of the property for a period which did not in fact end before her death, even though she did not retain a "right to the income" from the property. The scope of our inquiry is therefore narrowed to asking whether receipt of all the income from trust property is equivalent to "enjoyment * * * of the property."

* * *

Except for the presence of the unenforceable oral agreement between the settlor and his children, [Estate of McNichol v. Commissioner, 265 F.2d 667 (3d Cir.1959), cert. denied, 361 U.S. 829 (1959)] is flat authority for the proposition that the actual fact of uninterrupted receipt of all income, arising from the trust property amounts to a retention of "enjoyment" within the meaning of the statute. But the *McNichol* court apparently had doubts whether the receipt of all income from the property alone is sufficient, without the oral agreement, to satisfy the "enjoyment" clause. The court said:

> We intimate no opinion as to whether we would have followed these decisions if, in the case before us, the decedent had received the rents following the transfer without an agreement with his children that he might do so. 265 F.2d at page 671, Note 6.

[Lack of Oral Agreement]

In the case at bar, there is no direct evidence of an oral agreement between trustee and settlor. This Court shares doubts intimated by the Court of Appeals whether such an oral agreement is necessary before there can be "enjoyment" within the meaning of the statute. Section 811(c)(1)(B)(i) [1986 Code § 2036(a)(1)] says that enjoyment must be "retained" by the settlor. The word "retained" implies that the settlor has not given something away at the time he signed the trust agreement. To "retain" enjoyment does not necessarily mean retention of a legally enforceable "right" to income, but it does suggest the need for prearrangement, or informal agreement comparable to the oral agreement in the *McNichol* case, and not just receipt of the income alone.

[Prearrangement Inferred]

However, the court believes that the necessary prearrangement between settlor and trustee can be inferred from the evidence in this case. It will be recalled that in 1936, the settlor filed a gift tax return attempting to exclude from a schedule of assets transferred by the Trust the value of her retained life interest. Thus, in 1936, the settlor thought she had a life interest in the income from the Trust. In actual fact, the settlor did receive the income for life. These two circumstances coupled together create a strong inference that there existed an understanding between the settlor and the trustee that the trustee's so-called "discretion" would be exercised exclusively in favor of the settlor for her life. The court, therefore, infers that an informal prearrangement comparable to that made in the *McNichol* case was made, and that settlor "enjoyed" the property within the meaning of the statute. Consequently, the Trust corpus must be included in the decedent settlor's estate according to law.

¶ 10,133

[Burden on Taxpayer]

The court is aware that the holding in this case places a heavy burden upon the estate of a settlor of a discretionary trust to avoid the inference of secret prearrangements with the trustee when the settlor has in fact received all income during his life. However, any other holding would permit easy evasion of the estate tax. Most settlors would have no trouble finding a trustee friendly to his interests who could be counted on to honor informal prearrangements to exercise "absolute discretion" over income payments in favor of the settlor during his life. The existence of such prearrangements is difficult at best for the government to prove. Therefore, the court must go beyond the form in which the agreement is drawn, * * * and, looking to the substance of the matter, draw reasonable inferences from the evidence that such a prearrangement did exist.

The holding here does not necessarily cover facts where, in the exercise of the trustee's "discretion", the settlor has received the entire income for life but there is no evidence from which any prearrangement can be inferred; or where the settlor has received only a part of the income from the trust property, and at irregular intervals and in irregular amounts; or under any other circumstances in which the election of the trustee to pay income regularly to the settlor apparently was not foreordained at the time of the execution of the trust. However, the fair conclusion in the case at bar is that the settlor "retained the enjoyment" of the property within the meaning of § 811(c)(1)(B)(i) [1986 Code § 2036(a)(1)]. * * *

While some of the language in In re Uhl's Estate, 7 Cir., 1957, 241 F.2d 867, arguably may conflict with the conclusion here reached, it should be borne in mind that the facts were quite different in that case. True, the Trust instrument gave absolute discretion to the trustee over income payments in excess of $100 monthly. But the trustee apparently exercised his discretion in favor of the settlor in only two out of the eight years of the Trust's duration, and during these two years the discretionary payments were irregular and were never paid directly to the settlor, but indirectly, for medical expenses. * * *

Problem

[¶ 10,135]

Suppose David reports to you that trusts established for his benefit many years ago by his father and grandfather provide him with sufficient income to maintain a handsome lifestyle. As a consequence, David would like to make gifts of all of his property during his lifetime so as to avoid tax on the transferred property at his death, his intended beneficiaries being his niece, Alberta, and his nephews, Butch and Charlie. However, during the course of your interview, David tells you that, notwithstanding his comfortable circumstances, he has always suffered insecurity in his personal relationships and that this insecurity has infected his sense of his financial well-being. For that reason, David would like to give his property away "in such a way that he could get it back or, at least, have the benefit of it if he needed it."

¶ 10,135

Can you help David realize his objectives? Suppose David puts all of this property into an irrevocable trust during his life. Would it make any difference if the trust income was:

    1.   Required to be paid out to David annually (a "mandatory pay" feature); or

    2.   To be paid out only when the trustee deemed it appropriate (a "discretionary pay" feature); or

    3.   To be paid out only when the trustee deemed it necessary for David's maintenance, care, support and education (a "discretionary pay subject to a standard" feature)?

Will it make any difference who is the trustee of the trust? For example, could David be the trustee?

D. INADVERTENT TRANSFERORS

[¶ 10,137]

Private Letter Ruling 200340015 concluded that the trustees, who were also beneficiaries of a trust (as well as husband and wife), had, in fact, become *transferors* relative to the trust by virtue of having paid the trust's income tax liability from personal rather than trust funds. The payments were made unintentionally because the trustees erroneously believed that they were taxable personally on the trust's income (and reported it on their personal income tax return). While no distributions had ever been made from the trust to the beneficiaries, distributions were permitted but those distributions were limited by a recognized safe harbor, *i.e.*, an ascertainable standard, in this case, "maintenance, support, health and education." (The trust barred distributions for purposes of discharging the trustees' legal obligations to support their children although, as is common in these cases, distributions were permitted to the trustees children as required by the ascertainable standard.)

The trustees also made interest free loans and below market loans to the trust. While the principal of the loans had been repaid, no interest was ever paid by the trust. The amount of the foregone interest was also considered in the ruling to constitute a *transfer* to the trust by the trustees.

The trustees were authorized to pay themselves a fee for fiduciary services provided the trust but none was ever charged or collected. The ruling said these foregone fees did not constitute tainting transfers to the trust by the trustees.

E. ATTRIBUTION: MORE ON BECOMING A TRANSFEROR

[¶ 10,138]

While Wife wants to shrink her estate by getting property off to the children, she cannot bear the thought of not "having it in case I need it."

After pondering for what seems forever, she brightens and joyously exclaims to Lawyer, "If I can't set up a trust for myself and avoid taxes, Husband and I will set up trusts for each other. I'll be beneficiary of his trust, and he'll be beneficiary of my trust." Wife outlines the plan. Wife will create a trust for Husband's benefit for life, with remainder to the children, and, that same day, Husband will create a trust for Wife's benefit for life, with remainder to the children. Lawyer, who finally understands what Wife is suggesting, says, "Stop! What you propose are reciprocal or 'crossed' trusts." He goes on to explain that, at Wife's death, for example, the trusts will likely be uncrossed, and Wife will be treated as having created the trust Husband created for her benefit. The result is that Wife will be treated, for estate tax purposes, as being the transferor of the property Husband put into the trust for her benefit. In this context, transferor-like status is attributed to Wife. Since Wife has a beneficial interest in the trust, it will be included in her estate as a transfer subject to a retained life estate (depending, of course, upon the nature of the interest she has in the trust for her benefit, i.e., whether it is mandatory pay, discretionary pay, or discretionary subject to a standard). See United States v. Estate of Grace, 395 U.S. 316 (1969) (trusts uncrossed where trusts are interrelated and settlors' economic position remains the same as before trusts uncrossed); Rev. Rul. 74–533, 1974–2 C.B. 293 (value included in estate where trusts uncrossed). Cf. Estate of Levy v. Commissioner, 46 T.C.M. (CCH) 910, T.C.M. (P–H) ¶ 83,453 (1983) (reciprocal trusts not uncrossed where substantially different because wife had special power of appointment over "her" trust and husband had no such power over "his" trust).

F. TRANSFERS TAKING EFFECT AT DEATH

[¶ 10,143]

Reversions happen—and are included in the transferor's gross estate under § 2033 because reversions are probate property, passing under the transferor's will. Relatively uncommon, however, are reversionary interests that come into being only because a donee did not survive the donor. Here we are speaking of mere possibilities—but possibilities also have value and are sometimes subject to transfer taxes. Reversionary interests that are mere possibilities, i.e., reversionary interests that have not ripened into possession, is the subject of § 2037. Section 2037 bears the compelling label "transfers taking effect at death" and works its magic by including in the transferor's estate property interests the enjoyment of which can only be obtained by surviving the transferor.

Section 2037 is aimed at reversionary interests that the transferor may never come to enjoy or possess but which are notable because the donee will only enjoy or possess the interest if he or she survives the transferor. Often the transferor may not even recall that he or she has such an interest. Yet it is not uncommon for a transferor to retain such a reversionary interest in anticipation of a gap occurring in the beneficial ownership of the transferred property.

¶ **10,143**

Example. Mr. Thacher created an irrevocable trust for the benefit of his wife Catherine for life. At Catherine's death, the trust was to terminate, and the property then included in the trust was to be distributed to Mr. Thacher's then living lineal descendants *per stirpes.* However, in the event Mr. Thacher and Catherine divorced or legally separated, the trust was to terminate, and the trust property was to be paid over to Mr. Thacher. If Catherine survived Mr. Thacher and they had not divorced or separated prior to his death, the trust would continue for her benefit until she died or remarried. Under these facts, the court held that the transfer to Catherine was a transfer "intended to take effect in possession or enjoyment at or after the decedent's death" and, therefore, the value of Catherine's estate was included in Mr. Thacher's gross estate for estate tax purposes. Thacher v. Commissioner, 20 T.C. 474 (1953). The court reasoned that Catherine "acquired a life estate, absolute and unconditional, except in the event of her remarriage, *upon her survival*" of Mr. Thacher.

There is little or no planning potential here. There are mostly traps for the unwary. The saving feature is that § 2037 is triggered only when three very unique conditions all occur:

  1. The beneficiary can only possess or enjoy the transferred property by surviving the transferor;

  2. The transferor has kept a reversionary interest in the transferred property; and

  3. The value of the reversionary interest, actuarially determined, immediately before the death of the transferor is more than 5 percent of the value of the entire property.

Suppose that Husband's employer is contractually obligated to pay a death benefit to Wife if Wife survives Husband but, if Husband survives Wife, the death benefit is payable to Husband's estate. Husband will have retained a reversionary interest in the death benefit if the value of the reversionary interest in the death benefit the moment before Husband's death was more than 5 percent of the death benefit payment. Moreover, all three conditions will have been met, and the death benefit will be included in Husband's estate. § 2037.

By way of contrast, nothing will be included in Dad's estate under § 2037 based on the following facts. Dad created a trust for Mom for life, with remainder to those of their children who survive Mom. In the event none of the children survive Mom, the trust property will be distributed to Dad upon Mom's death. Section 2037 will not apply because each beneficiary can enjoy the property without surviving Dad. However, even though the entire trust property will not be included in Dad's estate, the value of Dad's reversionary interest will be included.

Suppose Dad's trust for Mom had provided that the trust property was distributable to Dad if he survived Mom, unless one or more children also survived Mom. In the case where the children survived Mom, Dad was to take nothing, and all of the trust property was to be distributed to the children.

Since the children were only to take if they survived Dad, Dad's reversion possibility, as well as the value of the children's future interest, will be included in Dad's estate (assuming that Mom died before Dad).

G. INCOME TAX CONSIDERATIONS

[¶ 10,151]

An important income tax consideration in every transfer is the transferor's basis in the transferred property. The basis of the property in the hands of the donee will generally be the transferor's basis in the transferred property. See § 1015(a). By way of contrast, property received from a decedent will enjoy a new basis, generally one that is equal to the fair market value of the transferred property on the date of the transferor's death. See § 1014(a). For related material, see ¶¶ 7133; 8751–8801.

Taxation of trust income is another important consideration where transfers for the benefit of the transferor are made in trust. There are two sets of rules and one will apply. The general rules, expressed in §§ 641–667 and discussed in Chapter 8, provide generally that trust income will be taxed to the trust if retained by the trust but taxed to the beneficiaries to the extent the trust income is distributed to the beneficiaries. The special rules, expressed in §§ 671–678 and discussed in Chapter 22, describe the circumstances under which trust income will be taxed to someone other than the recipient of the income. The underlying rationale for taxing trust income to someone other than the recipient of the trust income is that income should be taxed to those who have dominion and control over it. While "dominion and control" is expressly not the test currently in use, it remains a rationalizing principle. See § 671 (last sentence). While a detailed discussion of the grantor trust rules is more appropriately deferred to Chapter 22, consider the problem which follows.

Problem

[¶ 10,180]

Refer to ¶ 10,135 and consider whether the income from David's trust will be taxed to him under each of the proposed "payout" options he is considering. David is hopeful that the trust income can be taxed to the trust rather than to him, except, of course, in those cases where the income is actually distributed to him. Needless to say, David is realistic enough to recognize that he who receives income should be taxed on it. What delights David, however, is the prospect of using the trust as an income tax shelter. Will David's scheme work? See § 677. For additional discussion, see ¶ 22,451.

H. GIFT TAX CONSIDERATIONS

[¶ 10,201]

1. TRANSFERS THAT CONSTITUTE COMPLETED GIFTS

As was suggested in ¶ 6159, Lucy's deed of her farm to Lucky, subject to Lucy's right of occupancy for life, has gift tax consequences. Lucy has made a legally effective transfer of the future enjoyment of the premises and given up her right to make a different disposition of the property. Lazarus v. Commissioner, 58 T.C. 854 (1972). Lucy has given up her right to commit waste on the premises, i.e., Lucy has given up her "right to cut down the trees," although she can harvest the trees (to the extent they constitute a crop).

Reg. § 25.2511–1(a) provides, in a most effective summary, that the federal gift tax applies:

> [W]hether the transfer is in trust or otherwise, whether the gift is direct or indirect, and whether the property is real or personal, tangible or intangible. For example, a taxable transfer may be effected by the creation of a trust, the forgiving of a debt, the assignment of a judgment, the assignment of the benefits of an insurance policy, or the transfer of cash, certificates of deposit, or Federal, State or municipal bonds.

Donative intent is not an element. That is, a transfer may very well be subject to the federal gift tax without any finding that the transferor had a donative intent. Reg. § 25.2511–1(g)(1) says that the "application of the tax is based on the objective facts of the transfer and the circumstances under which it is made, rather than on the subjective motives of the transferor."

The gift tax applies only to transfers of the beneficial interest in property. It is not applicable to a transfer of bare legal title to a trustee. Thus, a transfer by a trustee of trust property in which the trustee has no beneficial interest does not constitute a gift by the trustee. Moreover, "the gift tax is not applicable to a transfer for a full and adequate consideration in money or money's worth, or to ordinary business transactions." Reg. § 25.2511–1(g)(1).

Looking back to Lucy's transfer, suppose the transfer had been in trust with the trust to terminate at Lucy's death and, "upon termination, the trust property is to be distributed to Lucy's then living lineal descendants *per stirpes*." Clearly the ultimate takers in this situation will not be determined until Lucy's death—but there will be no question that a gift was made at the time of Lucy's initial transfer in trust (inasmuch as Lucy can now deal with the trust property only as a fiduciary as compared with her unrestricted right to enjoy the property as she saw fit before the transfer).

There is no need to be able to identify the donee at the time of the transfer for gift tax purposes. Generally speaking, the identity of the donee is not important in determining whether a gift is made; the identity of the donee becomes important primarily for determining eligibility for the various exclusions and deductions that are available to shelter transfers that would otherwise be subject to the gift tax (such as the $12,000 per donee per annum gift tax exclusion provided in § 2503(b), adjusted for inflation, and the unlimited gift tax charitable deduction and unlimited marital deduction provided, respectively, in §§ 2523 and 2525). Thus, the gift tax is: (1) the personal liability of the transferor; (2) an excise tax upon the transferor's act of making the transfer; (3) measured by the value of the property passing from the transferor; and (4) applied regardless of the fact that the identity of the donee may not then be known or ascertainable.

The gift tax applies when the gift is "complete," "complete" being the standard for determining application of the gift tax to property transfers. See Reg. § 25.2511–2(a). In the case of Lucy's transfer, as noted above, Lucy has made a legally effective transfer of the future enjoyment of the property, the value of which can be actuarially determined. In this sense, the gift is complete.

Whether a gift is complete has been variously expressed in terms of whether the transferor has retained control over the donated property. Illustrative is Estate of Sanford v. Commissioner, 308 U.S. 39 (1939), where the taxpayer had created a trust in which he had retained a right to revoke the trust and also a right to modify the trust by designating new beneficiaries (other than himself). In one year—before the adoption of the federal gift tax— he gave up the right to revoke the trust and, in another year—after the adoption of the federal gift tax—he gave up the right to designate new beneficiaries of the trust. The Supreme Court held that the gift was not complete until the transferor gave up his power to designate new beneficiaries of the trust. The Court found that the tax laws are more concerned with "actual command over the property," 308 U.S. at 43, and not so much with the concept of title. "[Any] retention of control over disposition of trust property * * * renders the gift incomplete until the power is relinquished whether in life or at death." In reaching its decision, the Court expressly ruled that a gift is not complete so long as the transferor has no power to make himself a beneficiary). If the transfer fell short of being a completed gift, so that no gift tax was imposed, the transferred property would be included in the transferor's taxable estate at death, subject to estate tax.

Clearly, the transferor must relinquish economic control of the property in order to make a completed gift. Once economic control has been relinquished and the transferor has relinquished all other dominion and control over the transferred property, the gift is complete for gift tax purposes.

[¶ 10,209]

2. DISCRETIONARY PAY TRUSTS

If a transferor places property in trust and gives the trustee absolute discretion in making distributions to the beneficiary, the transferor has relinquished dominion and control over the trust property, thus making a completed gift for tax purposes. If, however, the transferor limits the trustee's discretion by specifying distributions to the beneficiary for either support and maintenance or another ascertainable standard, and if the transferor is the beneficiary, the transferor has retained an indirect interest in the trust property. The transferor has made a completed gift only of the amount of the trust corpus in excess of the value of the transferor beneficiary's right to support according to the ascertainable standard.

Example 1. Decedent created a trust with cash and property, with the income payable to decedent for life and then to his wife for life if she survived him. The trust agreement also allowed the trustee to invade the corpus for the welfare, comfort, support, hospitalization or other emergency needs of decedent or his wife. In Estate of Holtz v. Commissioner, 38 T.C. 37, 43–44 (1962), the Tax Court held that, under these circumstances, no completed gift has been made because it was reasonably possible that the trust corpus could be depleted by distributions to the transferor. The words in the trust agreement were found to have created an ascertainable standard that a court would enforce, thereby preventing the transferor from having given up dominion and control over the transferred property as required for a completed gift. If there were no enforceable standard, however, and the trustee had complete discretion to invade the principal, the transferor would have had only an expectancy that would not render the gift incomplete.

Example 2. The grantor conveyed property to an irrevocable inter vivos trust that required the trustee to accumulate the income and add it to the principal during the grantor's life. At the grantor's death, the trust was to terminate with the property being distributed to the grantor's spouse and children. The trust agreement allowed the trustee, in the trustee's absolute and uncontrolled discretion, to invade the trust corpus for the grantor's benefit. Applicable state law made the trustee's decision to invade strictly voluntary. Since the grantor had not retained an interest in the trust corpus and the trustee could not be compelled to invade the corpus for the grantor's benefit, a completed gift had been made and the transfer was subject to gift tax. The grantor had only an expectancy in the corpus and this alone would not render the gift incomplete. Also, the grantor could not utilize the trust assets by directing that they be paid over to his creditors to satisfy debts, further evidencing the grantor's lack of dominion and control over the trust corpus. See Rev. Rul. 77–378, 1977–2 C.B. 347.

The *Holtz* case and Revenue Ruling 77–378 can be reconciled on the basis that the latter deals with a discretionary pay trust, while the former is concerned with a trust in which the discretionary payments are subject to a standard. If the trustee's discretion is complete, as the *Holtz* court points out, "the settlor retains a mere expectancy which does not make the gift of corpus incomplete." 38 T.C. at 42. Thus, so long as there is no understanding between the trustee and the beneficiary so as to limit the trustee's exercise of the discretion given the trustee, the transfer will be complete for gift tax purposes. By way of contrast, the existence of an external, legally enforceable standard, however, gives the income beneficiary the right to demand that payments be made in accordance with the standard. If such payments could conceivably exhaust the corpus, there is no certainty that any gift will ultimately be made—and the transfer is incomplete for gift tax purposes.

A transfer is only complete for federal estate and gift tax purposes once it is no longer subject to the claims of the transferor's creditors. Rev. Rul. 76–103, 1976–1 C.B 293. The reason for this is that the transferor could make

The rule:

an alleged completed gift and later simply run up excessive debt, leaving his creditors to go after the trust assets, reserving the ability to indirectly reach all of the trust assets for his own benefit. Most states do not protect trust assets from creditors if the trustee has discretion to make distributions to the settlor. Therefore, it is usually impossible to create these self-settled trusts as a completed gift. But Alaska and Delaware, in addition to many foreign jurisdictions, allow transferors to create self-settled trusts that are not subject to creditor claims. As a result, these trust not only provide protection from creditor claims, they are completed transfers for federal estate and gift tax purposes. For additional material, see ¶¶ 5600, 7478, 10,119, 21,315, and 21,870.

For the estate planner, asset protection trusts that effectively cut off claims by creditors of the settler remedy another problem that has plagued traditional self-settled trusts, whether they are completed gifts for federal estate and gift tax purposes. The IRS position is that a transfer is only complete for federal estate and gift tax purposes when it is no longer subject to claims of the transferor's creditors. Since traditional self-settled trusts were subject to the claims of the transferor's creditors, they were not completed transfers and were therefore not subject to "value-freezing" for federal estate and gift tax purposes. Since offshore trusts and the new domestic asset protection trusts are arguably not subject to the claims of creditors, such transfers should be complete for federal estate and gift tax purposes while allowing the settler to remain a permissible trust beneficiary—the trustee having discretion to make distributions to the settler—in the unlikely event the settler "needs" the trust property. Such a conclusion will allow many a settler to significantly reduce federal estate exposure while effectively protecting his or her assets from creditors. Worthy of note, thought But a word of caution is warranted. Although it is well established that offshore trusts remove the assets from the settlors estate, the IRS recently refused to rule on the effect on domestic asset protection trusts in avoiding inclusion for estate tax purposes. Priv. Ltr. Rul. 9837007.

Estate of Vak v. Commissioner, 973 F.2d 1409 (8th Cir.1992), considered the complete gift rule in the context of a grantor giving up the right to remove the trustee.

[¶ 10,217]

3. VALUATION OF THE GIFT

a. Gifts to Nonfamily Members

Section 2512 provides that the value of the transferred property on the date of the gift is its value for gift tax purposes. Where the gift is of a future interest, i.e., one to take effect in possession and enjoyment in the future, actuarial computations as described in Reg. § 25.2512–5 are used. See ¶ 6159.

[¶ 10,225]

b. Gifts to Family Members

Gifts to family members and nonfamily members alike are valued identically except in cases where the transferor has retained an interest in the transferred property. Where the gift subject to the retained interest is to a family member (Lucy's child Lackluster is a family member), special valuation rules apply, ¶ 6159. Those rules, expressed in § 2702 (which defines "member of the family"), stipulate that the value of the life estate retained, for example, by Lucy shall be zero for purposes of determining the value of the transfer of the future interest to child Lackluster. That means that if the fair market value of the farm at the time of the transfer to Lackluster is $1 million, Lucy is deemed to have made a taxable gift to Lackluster of $1 million, even though Lackluster cannot enjoy the property until Lucy's death.

And, note this: At Lucy's subsequent death, the full fair market value of the residence will be included in Lucy's estate for estate tax purposes at its date of death value. See § 2036(a)(1). Of course, Lucy's estate will get credit, against Lucy's estate tax liability, for any gift tax paid or payable as a result of the gift tax liability incurred. See § 2001(b)(2).

The zero valuation rules are discussed in greater detail in Chapter 12. Suffice it to note, at this juncture, that had Lucy transferred only her residence to Lackluster, it is possible that the transfer could have been structured differently so that the zero valuation rule would not have applied. Such a restructuring would have meant use of a Personal Residence Trust (PRT) or a Qualified Personal Residence Trust (QPRT)—and that might mean that Lucy would need to plan to vacate the premises if she lived beyond a specified period and, at that time, deliver enjoyment to Lackluster! (Lackluster says that there are "some really lovely nursing homes" in Lucy's community "where Lucy wouldn't be too far from those of her friends who are still living at that time.") Barring use of a PRT or a QPRT, the zero valuation rules apply to Lucy's transfer to Lackluster. For discussion of PRT and QPRT, see ¶ 12,059.

There is another alternative worth noting by those who wish to escape the zero valuation rule. Reg. § 25.2702–1(c)(6) says that the zero valuation rule does not apply if the transferor has retained only the right to receive distributions of income at the sole discretion of an independent trustee, independent trustee being defined as in § 674(c). See ¶ 22,392 for discussion of independent trustee.

> *Example.* Lazlo transferred property to an irrevocable trust. Independent Bank & Trust Company was trustee. Lazlo had no right to remove the trustee. All distributions from the trust were at the sole discretion of the trustee. Lazlo was eligible to receive income distributions only. The zero valuation rule would not apply. Instead, looking to Revenue Ruling 77–378, 1977–2 C.B. 347, discussed at ¶ 10,209, Lazlo would be deemed to have made a completed gift of the entire property.

Problems

[¶ 10,250]

1. Refer to ¶ 10,135 and determine what steps should be taken to value David's gifts to his nieces and nephews and suggest the value of those gifts.

¶ 10,225

2. Refer to the preceding problem and determine what steps should be taken to value David's gifts if David had married before establishing the trust and his bride (rather than his niece and nephews) was to receive the trust property in the event of David's death.

Chapter 11

JOINT TENANCY AND OTHER FORMS OF CONCURRENT OWNERSHIP

A. OBJECTIVES

[¶ 11,001]

Joint tenancy with right of survivorship is an enormously popular method of co-ownership. Almost without exception, taxpayers will suggest joint tenancy as the form in which they wish to "own" property. The reasons are, undoubtedly, varied. In most cases, however, the notion of "partnership" reflected by the joint ownership is probably an influential factor in the decision for joint ownership. Probably of equal importance is the thought that joint tenancy will facilitate transfer of the property at the death of the first joint tenant to die.

What then is the reality? Is joint ownership advisable? And what are the consequences when the joint tenants want to anticipate disability by creating a revocable trust funded with the joint property? See ¶ 11,751.

B. CO-OWNERSHIP: STATE LAW

[¶ 11,051]

1. FORMS OF CO-OWNERSHIP

There are four popular forms of co-ownership: tenancy in common; joint tenancy with right of survivorship; tenancy by the entirety; and community property. When the terms "joint tenancy," "jointly held property" or "joint tenancy with right of survivorship" are used, the reference includes tenancy by the entirety except where specifically noted otherwise. For a discussion of the characteristics of joint tenancies, tenancies by the entirety and tenancies in common, see 1 J. Mertens, The Law of Federal Gift and Estate Taxation §§ 11.03 and 11.04 (1959) [hereinafter Mertens]; see also Rich, Joint Ownership of Property and Joint Wills, 15 Inst. Of Taxation 825 (1957); R. Powell, 7 Powell on Real Property §§ 49–53 (M. Wolf, ed. 2005) [hereinafter Powell]. For a thorough discussion of the disjointed approaches to joint tenancy taken by various jurisdictions, see Dominic J. Campisi, Joint Tenancy Accounts [An Un–Uniform Law], 30 Real Prop. Prob. & Trust L.J. 399 (1995), where the author explores the expectations of laymen and the evidentiary hurdles encountered.

[¶ 11,059]

2. TENANCY IN COMMON

Tenancy in common is a type of co-ownership of real or personal property in which each of the co-tenants has a distinct and separate interest in the property but each tenant is entitled to possession and enjoyment of the entire property subject to the same right in the other co-tenants. Sheldon F. Kurtz, Moynihan's Introduction to the Law of Real Property 281–82 (4th ed. 2005) [hereinafter Kurtz]. More importantly, each tenant in common has the unfettered right to dispose of his or her interest by will; see Powell, *supra* ¶ 11,051, at § 50.02[9]. If a tenant fails to do so, it will pass at that tenant's death under the controlling intestate statute. During that tenant's lifetime, that tenant may transfer his or her interest or encumber it without the consent of the other tenant in common. Moreover, any transferee will be admitted to all the rights and privileges enjoyed by the transferring tenant in common. Id. See also A. J. Casner & J. N. Pennell, 2 Estate Planning § 10.1 (6th ed. 1995 & Supp. 2004).

[¶ 11,067]

3. JOINT TENANCY WITH RIGHT OF SURVIVORSHIP

A joint tenancy with right of survivorship is distinguished from a tenancy in common essentially only in respect to the survivorship feature. There are some other technical differences, the practical consequences of which vary from state to state. For example, the joint tenancy relationship is described as the fictional unity of persons as co-owners. This unity is usually expressed in terms of unity of interest, unity of title, unity of time, and unity of possession. In common law, this concept of unity of persons required co-owners to acquire their interest at the same time and by the same instrument. In some jurisdictions, this remains the rule and a husband, for example, cannot create a joint tenancy with his wife without deeding the property to a strawman and having the "straw" deed it back to husband and wife as joint tenants with right of survivorship. Kurtz, *supra* ¶ 11,059, at 273–81; Powell, *supra* ¶ 11,051, at § 51.02[3].

A co-tenant in property held as joint tenants with right of survivorship may alienate or transfer his or her fractional interest in the jointly held property at any time during life. Such a transfer, however, converts the joint tenancy into a tenancy in common. If there were originally more than one joint tenant, the remaining original joint tenants continue to hold their interests as joint tenants with right of survivorship but the transferee tenant holds as a tenant in common. "The transfer destroys the unities of title and of time since the transferee ... acquires his interest by a different title and at a different time ..." Kurtz, *supra* ¶ 11,059, at 278. *[handwritten margin note: transfer converts to t.i.c.]*

At death, however, the joint tenant loses control over the property. The survivorship feature causes the deceased co-tenant's fractional interest to expire and the surviving co-tenant's interest to expand to include the entire interest in the property. See Powell, *supra* ¶ 11,051, at § 51.03[3].

The advantages of <u>joint tenancy with right of survivorship</u> include the following:

1. *Jointly held property is free from the claims of creditors of either spouse.* For example, in some states if the property is held by the spouses as tenants by the entirety the property can be removed from the reach of the separate creditors of the husband and wife and from the reach of prior spouses. See Lewis v. United States, 485 F.2d 606 (Cl.Ct.1973) (tenancy by the entirety used "to thwart significant third-party claims." Id. at 612). Nevertheless, this so-called advantage has appeal only in those cases where a decedent's probate property is inadequate to satisfy creditors' claims. Even where claims exceed probate property, this incident of joint ownership will offer little real protection. For example, it is an unusual case for a lender to make a loan to one spouse without securing the other spouse's personal guaranty. And if the joint tenants are not married to one another, the existence of the joint property will be disclosed on the borrower's financial data summary provided the lender, and the lender, no doubt, will take steps to make this collateral available to secure the deal.

2. *Joint property expresses the idea of partnership in a marriage and reinforces family security and harmony.* This kind of argument is hard to combat, and it cannot be dismissed as trivial.

The following advantages also have appeal, <u>but a revocable trust will accomplish the same results</u> (where the property is not jointly held) with greater predictability as to tax consequences and with significant non-tax planning opportunities. For a discussion of the revocable trust, see ¶ 4433.

3. *Joint property reduces administration costs.* This is true in the sense that the estate's executor or administrator cannot include jointly held property in the base used in computing the fiduciary's fees. However, in computing the attorney's fee, the presence of joint property will reduce the time required to accomplish title transfers but will not affect the amount of time required to prepare the necessary estate and inheritance tax returns.

4. *Joint property avoids probate delays.* Generally speaking, jointly held property is available to the survivor immediately after death (subject, oftentimes, to liens for payment of death taxes). See, e.g., § 6324. Distribution of property, however, is often delayed: (1) by the time required to accomplish probate of the will and appointment of an executor or an administrator of the estate; (2) by the statutorily established period for the filing of creditor claims; and (3) until receipt of federal estate and state inheritance tax closing letters, a delay prompted by concerns of the executor or administrator that additional taxes will be determined to be payable.

¶ 11,067

5. *Joint property avoids publicity.* It is common in some communities for the newspapers to regularly publish the probate contents of a decedent's estate as reported to the court having jurisdiction over estates. However, the decedent's joint property will only appear on the tax returns filed for the decedent's estate. In theory, at least, those returns are confidential and not available for inspection by the public.

6. *Joint property is convenient.* While it is perhaps commonly believed that either joint tenant is free to manage the joint property without the consent of the other joint tenant, practically speaking, that is probably not the case. Certainly as to property held as tenants by the entirety, the consent of both spouses is required to effect a transfer of that property. And, if held as joint tenants with right of survivorship, in most cases each joint tenant is limited to being able to dispose of his or her fractional interest.

7. *Joint property avoids fragmentation of ownership.* Intestate distribution of a decedent's property sometimes fragments ownership. The survivorship feature of the joint tenancy avoids that result, but an ordinary will can be drafted which will have the same effect.

8. *Jointly held property enjoys preferential treatment for state death tax purposes.* Any state death tax advantage enjoyed by joint tenants is, as a practical matter, largely a myth. While it is difficult to generalize about the different state death tax systems, it could be reasonably concluded that the various states follow the federal rule expressed in § 2040(a) and tax all joint property at the death of the first joint tenant to die except to the extent the survivor can prove contribution. See, e.g., Ind. Code Ann. § 6–4.1–2–5 (West 2006). And, as the federal system does in § 2040(b), the states apply different rules to property held as joint tenants by persons married to each other. Like the federal system, some states exempt from state death taxation one-half of all joint property where the joint tenants are husband and wife. See, e.g., Ohio Rev. Code Ann. § 5731.10(B) (West 2002). (This is an advantage where the first spouse to die has provided all the consideration for the joint property. It is hardly an advantage where the noncontributing spouse dies first.) Other states exempt only real property held by the husband and wife as tenants by the entirety. See, e.g., 72 Pa. Cons. Stat. Ann. § 9111(m) (West 2000 & Supp. 2006).

The advent of the unlimited marital deduction for interspousal transfers in 1981 provided by § 2056 caused many states to copy, in effect, the federal statute and eliminate the death taxes that would otherwise have applied, at the state level, to interspousal transfers. See, e.g., Ind. Code Ann. § 6–4.1–3–7 (West 2006). In addition, many states chose to simplify their state death tax structure so that the state death tax burden was decreed to be equal to the federal credit for state death taxes paid allowed under § 2011 for federal estate tax purposes, the effect being to eliminate the need for a set of rules for determining the state death tax. See, e.g., Ariz. Rev. Stat. Ann.

¶ 11,067

§ 42–4051 (2006); Fla. Stat. Ann. § 198.02 (West 2005). As a result of these developments, any advantage enjoyed by joint tenants who are married to each other has been as a practical matter, effectively eliminated inasmuch as spouses can easily arrange their affairs to take advantage of the unlimited marital deduction.

[¶ 11,073]

4. TENANCY BY THE ENTIRETY

A tenancy by the entirety (which also has a survivorship feature) is distinguished from a joint tenancy in several respects: (1) it may be created only between husband and wife, see Powell, *supra* ¶ 11,059, at § 52.02[1]; (2) neither spouse can alienate or transfer his or her interest in the subject premises without the consent of the other tenant by the entirety; (3) not all states recognize tenancy by the entirety; and (4) of those states recognizing tenancy by the entirety, many restrict it to real property. Powell, *supra* ¶ 11,059, at § 52.01[1], [3]; Kurtz, *supra* ¶ 11,059, at 286–92. In a few jurisdictions, including New York and New Jersey, it has been held that each tenant by the entirety may dispose of his or her interest in the tenancy by the entirety without the consent of the other tenant. However, even in those jurisdictions, the conveyance will not defeat the right of survivorship or the right to possession of the tenant who has not conveyed his or her interest. Powell, *supra* ¶ 11,059, at § 52.01[3]; Kurtz, *supra* ¶ 11,059, at 291.

Generally speaking, (1) each tenant by the entirety has an equal right to the income from the entirety property and (2) creditors of one tenant by the entirety may not subject the entirety property to their claims. Powell, *supra* ¶ 11,059, at § 52.03[2], [3]. In other words, the survivorship feature is superior to the right of a creditor of one of the tenants to subject the entirety property to his or her claims. See Powell, *supra* ¶ 11,059, at § 52.03[3].

When title is taken by husband and wife as tenants by the entirety, each of them will be deemed to have a vested present (but undivided) fractional interest in the tenancy. This is a state law determination made without regard to the respective contributions of the spouses to the purchase price. See Kurtz, *supra* ¶ 11,059, at 291–92.

In cases where the contributions of the spouses are not equal, it would seem appropriate to conclude that the spouse contributing the greater amount has made a gift for state law purposes to the other spouse of the amount by which such contribution exceeds the value of the interest in the tenancy given to the spouse by state law.

[¶ 11,081]

5. BANK ACCOUNTS

In many cases there is often genuine concern—and real litigation—over whether a deceased joint tenant who has contributed to a joint bank account intended his or her contribution to become the sole property of the surviving joint tenant at the deceased tenant's death. While each tenant is presumed to have an equal undivided fractional interest in the joint bank account, the

¶ 11,067

courts are increasingly willing to take evidence directed toward overcoming this presumption. See, e.g., Frey v. Wubbena, 26 Ill.2d 62, 185 N.E.2d 850 (1962); G. Spivey, Annotation., Creation of Joint Savings Account or Savings Certificate as Gift to Survivor, 43 A.L.R. 3d 971 (1972).

[¶ 11,089]

6. COMMUNITY PROPERTY

a. *What Is It?*

Generalizing about community property is virtually impossible because no two states have adopted identical rules for each situation. With that caveat in mind, it can be said that ten states have adopted the concept of community property. The states are Washington, California, Nevada, Arizona, New Mexico, Texas, Louisiana, Idaho, Wisconsin and, beginning in 1998, Alaska (but Alaska made it elective). In those states, except for Alaska, property acquired by married persons *after marriage* other than by gift, devise, bequest, or inheritance is community property. All other property owned by married persons is separate property.

In simpler terms, property that represents the fruit of person's labor expended during marriage is community property. In addition, in Texas, Louisiana and Idaho, income from separate property is also community. See R.W. Campfield, Interspousal Transfers, 32 Sw. L.J.1091, 1094 (1979). Alaska has what might be termed a hybrid statute as you will see below. But in California and the other western community property states, income from separate property is separate property.

The Alaska Community Property Act, passed in 1998, does not mandate but rather allows spousal election of community property treatment of the marital estate. Both spouses must sign a community property agreement in compliance with the statute. They are given great latitude in choosing which property to add to the community and which to keep separate. Property that is owned by a spouse prior to marriage is not community property except to the extent that the community property agreement provides otherwise. And property received by gift or disposition at death, as well as income from separate property, is also separate property unless otherwise expressly provided in the community property agreement or comingled with community property. See Alaska Stat. §§ 34.77.010 et seq. (2004).

An additional twist to the Alaska statute is that it allows the creation of a community property trust, in which persons domiciled in a non-community property state can place their funds and receive community property treatment. Alaska's legislature enacted this provision, along with those repealing the Rule Against Perpetuities and those allowing self-settled spendthrift trusts, in order to attract increased trust business from other states. See ¶ 5600; Alaska Stat.§§ 34.27.051, 34.77.010 et seq. (2004). In order to create a valid community property trust, one of the trustees must have basic maintenance powers over the trust and be either an individual who is a permanent resident of Alaska or a trust company that has its principal place of business in Alaska. Alaska Stat. § 34.77.100 (2004). The significance of this provision

¶ 11,089

is that the § 1014 new-basis-at-death rule applies not just to the half of the marital estate held by the decedent, but also to that of the surviving spouse— a benefit that has long been available in community property jurisdictions. This increase in basis results in a windfall reduction in tax that would not otherwise be available to the surviving spouse in a non-community property jurisdiction. See § 1014(b)(6).

[¶ 11,097]

b.   What Does It Mean?

Each spouse is deemed to own one-half of the community property acquired during his or her marriage.

[¶ 11,105]

i.   At Death?

At death, each spouse can make a will disposing of his or her one-half of the community property. Normally, there is no survivorship feature to community property. As a result, there is no certainty that the surviving spouse will receive the deceased spouse's one-half interest in the community. Instead, the property will be disposed of as the first spouse to die provides in his or her will. That might be in favor of the surviving spouse, but it could be to a stranger.

In the absence of an effective will, the decedent's one-half of the community will pass by intestacy statutes. Generally, intestate community property passes to the surviving spouse. However, the community property systems are known more by their differences than by their similarities. The rule in Texas is illustrative. Intestate community property passes to the surviving spouse only if the surviving spouse is the parent of the decedent's children. Tex. Prob. Code Ann. § 45(a)(2) (Vernon 2003). Otherwise, the decedent's spouse takes one-half of the intestate community property and the other one-half passes to the decedent's children. Tex. Prob. Code Ann. § 45(b) (Vernon 2003).

And, while traditionally there was no survivorship associated with community property, the majority of community property states now provide a hybrid form called community property with right of survivorship or CPWROS. See, e.g., Tex. Prob. Code Ann. § 451 (Vernon 2003); Idaho Code Ann. § 15–6–201 (2001); Ariz. Rev. Stat. Ann. § 14–1201(28) (2005), and § 33–431(C) (2000); Nev. Rev. Stat. § 111.064(2) (2005); N.M. Stat. §§ 40–3–8(B), 45–2–805(A) (1978); Wash. Rev. Code Ann. § 64.28.040(1) (West 2005). Addition of the right of survivorship by contract does not convert community property to joint property with right of survivorship. This distinction is important to emphasize because of the differing treatment given joint property and community property in determining basis for income tax purposes. For discussion, see ¶ 11,407.

Intestate separate property, on the other hand, generally speaking, is distributed by the community states in the manner and proportions similar to the distribution schemes utilized in noncommunity property states. See, e.g., Tex. Prob. Code Ann. § 38(b) (Vernon 2003). However, a spouse is free to dispose of his or her separate property by will to whomever he or she wishes. Traditionally, the community property states have seen no need for the clumsy restrictions imposed by the separate property jurisdictions on the right of a spouse to dispose of his or her separate property. They reason that if the spouses have had a long marriage, there will be much community property reflecting the contributions each has made to the success of the community. If the marriage is of short duration, they question why the separate property states authorize the surviving spouse, out of spousal protection concerns, to claim up to one-half of the decedent's separate property notwithstanding a contrary provision in his or her will. See ¶ 4651. For consideration of spousal property brought from a separate property state to a community property state—commonly referred to as quasi-community property—see ¶ 4683.

[¶ 11,113]

ii.   During Life?

Management is the issue. Texas, for example, in Texas Family Code § 3.102 (Vernon 2006), has adopted a split management scheme which is as follows:

1.   Each spouse is responsible for the management of that community property which is produced by his or her labor or his or her separate property.

2.   Property that is "mixed" as to source will be subject to joint management.

What is the nature and extent of this "management" right? It means simply, at least in Texas, that the manager of the community property can do whatever he or she wishes to do with that property so long as the transaction does not work a fraud on the community. What is a "fraud on the community"? That can only be determined by a trier of fact, and few generalizations are possible. See J. W. McKnight & W. A. Reppy, Jr., Tex. Matrimonial Prop. L., 173–197 (1998). However, by way of illustration, it may be useful to note that the fact that a spouse gives away more than one-half of the community property does not necessarily mean that it is a fraud on the community. Horlock v. Horlock, 533 S.W.2d 52 (Tex.Civ.App.—Houston [14th Dist.] 1975, writ dism'd).

In California and other community property states, the general rule is that community property is subject to joint management. See W. A. Reppy, Jr. & C. A. Samuel, Community Property in the United States, 14–4 to 14–5, 15–1 (3d ed. 1991) [hereinafter Reppy & Samuel].

[¶ 11,121]

iii.   At Divorce?

Theoretically, community property is divided equally at the time of divorce. However, courts are authorized to make an *equitable division* of the

¶ 11,121

community property. See, e.g., Ariz. Rev. Stat. Ann. § 25–318 (2000 & Supp. 2005).

[¶ 11,129]

c.   How Is It Taxed?

i.   Estate and Gift Taxation

Only one-half of the community property is included in the estate of the first spouse to die (inasmuch as each spouse can dispose of only his or her one-half of the community at death). See ¶ 17,107. Similarly, when a gift is made of community property, each spouse is deemed to have transferred only one-half of the property for gift tax purposes. Cf. Reg. § 25.2511–1(h)(9).

[¶ 11,137]

ii.   Income Taxation

For income tax purposes, both halves of the community receive a new basis at the death of the first spouse to die. § 1014(b)(6).

For related material as to Alaska, see ¶ 11,089.

[¶ 11,145]

iii.   Division of Community Property

Disproportionate divisions of community assets have not been treated as constituting a taxable sale or exchange. Carrieres v. Commissioner, 64 T.C. 959 (1975), aff'd, 552 F.2d 1350 (9th Cir. 1977), acq., 1976–2 C.B. 1; Rev. Rul. 76–883, 1976–1 C.B. 213. In 1984, Congress removed all doubt as to the proper treatment of such divisions by adding § 1041 to provide that "[n]o gain or loss shall be recognized on a transfer of property from an individual to (or in trust for the benefit of) * * * a spouse." However, where neither gain nor loss is recognized, the transferee assumes the transferor's basis. § 1041(b)(2).

With the advent of the unlimited marital deduction under §§ 2056 and 2523, there should be no gift tax consequences to a division of community property.

[¶ 11,153]

7.   COMMUNITY PROPERTY AND THE MIGRANT CLIENT

a.   Separate Property

Separate property remains separate property when taken into a community property state. Restatement (Second) of Conflicts of Law § 259 (1969).

¶ 11,121

[¶ 11,161]

b. *Community Property*

i.   *In the Courts*

Community *realty* in the community property state is not altered by reason of the migration to a common law state. Succession of Packwood, 43 Am. Dec. 237 (La.1845); In re Warburg's Estate, 38 Misc.2d 997, 237 N.Y.S.2d 557 (Sur.1963). An attempt to alter a spouse's interest merely because of a change of domicile violates due process under the Fourteenth Amendment. In re Thornton's Estate, 1 Cal.2d 1, 33 P.2d 1 (1934); see also Addison v. Addison, 62 Cal.2d 558, 43 Cal.Rptr. 97, 399 P.2d 897 (1965) (California "quasi-community property" statute allows separate property from common law state to be divided in equitable manner with reliance on the courts to insure due process).

Similarly, although the situs is changed, the vested rights of the spouses in community *personalty* should not be altered by migration to a common law state. Wallack v. Wallack, 211 Ga. 745, 88 S.E.2d 154 (1955); In re Majot's Estate, 199 N.Y. 29, 92 N.E. 402 (1910). Restatement (Second) of Conflicts § 259 (1969) provides that moveables held by spouses in community continue to be held in community when taken into a state which is not a community property state. However, whether community character will be recognized depends, naturally, on whether it is pleaded and proven. Wallack v. Wallack, *supra*.

In Travelers Insurance Co. v. Walden, 160 F.Supp. 845 (M.D.Ala.1958), a California domiciliary who had paid premiums for many years on his life insurance while a resident of California and then moved to Alabama, divorced his wife and changed the beneficiary of the policy. Following his death, the wife claimed she was entitled to half of the proceeds of the policy, on the grounds that it was California community property. Since there was no valuable consideration given by the insured to change the beneficiary to his sister without his wife's consent, this change, under California law (which the court applied here) did not operate to divest the wife of her community property interest in half of the proceeds; nothing has been done by either party to dissolve the community status of the property.

Similarly, in Crichton's Will, 49 Misc.2d 405, 267 N.Y.S.2d 706 (Sur.), aff'd mem., 26 A.D.2d 639, 272 N.Y.S.2d 987 (1966), the New York Surrogate Court refused to apply Louisiana community property laws to intangible moveables located in Louisiana but owned by a deceased New York resident. New York was the state of the matrimonial domicile, and the New Yorker had never resided in Louisiana. Accordingly, the court held that the survivor had never acquired any community property rights in the decedent's personal property. The court reached this result despite the fact that Article 2400 of the Louisiana Civil Code provides that all property acquired in Louisiana by nonresident married persons, regardless of which spouse has title or if it is in joint names, shall be subject to the same provisions of law which regulate citizens of Louisiana. The court said New York will not give effect to, or be bound by, Louisiana's attempt to apply its community property laws to personal property of non-domiciliaries of Louisiana.

Even if community property, as such, is not recognized in the common law state, the vested rights of the spouses are recognized and protected in different ways. For example, if one spouse holds title in his or her own name, he or she may be deemed to be a trustee of a constructive or resulting trust for the other spouse as to one-half. See Goodrich, Conflict of Laws, 122 (3d ed. 1949); Edwards v. Edwards, 108 Okla. 93, 233 P. 477 (1924); Depas v. Mayo, 11 Mo. 314, 49 Am. Dec. 88 (1848); Quintant v. Ordono, 195 So.2d 577 (Fla.App. 3 Dist.), cert. dismissed, 202 So.2d 178 (Fla.1967). Alternatively, if title is in both names, the spouses may be treated as tenants in common. See, e.g., In re Kessler's Estate, 177 Ohio St. 136, 203 N.E.2d 221 (1964).

Practically speaking, however, treating community property as a tenancy in common will typically have the effect of either enlarging or diminishing the right or burdens of the spouses, respectively. Moreover, even where the courts claim to have recognized that the property is community, it is often mere lip service. For example, in *Kessler's Estate,* which, in effect, recognized the community property interest of each spouse, the court imposed a full Ohio inheritance tax on the transfer from husband to wife at the death of the husband on the theory that something had "passed" to the wife upon the husband's death, since the husband had been the manager of the community during his life. In making this analysis, clearly, the court reflected a lack of understanding of community property. While one spouse may have the management of the community (or a portion of it), that spouse's right of management is limited in two significant respects:

1. Each spouse's management must be for the benefit of the community and may not constitute a fraud on the community. What constitutes fraud is a question of fact.

2. The so-called manager of the community does not have the right to make a deathtime disposition of the community which he or she manages. Moreover, the other spouse has the right to dispose of one-half of the community at death without regard to any rights of management the surviving spouse had while both spouses were alive.

The analysis used in *Kessler* would have limited applicability currently. The notion that the husband is the manager of the community has given way to notions of equal management of the community. However, the notion of management by one spouse still has vitality with respect to community property acquired in a state such as Texas which provides for three kinds of community property: his, hers, and theirs. In Texas, each spouse has the right to manage (a) that portion of the community which is produced by his or her labor and (b) that community which is the fruit of his or her separate property. This property could be referred to as sole management or separate management community. (Recall that in Texas, Idaho, and Louisiana, income from separate property is community.) Community property which is not attributable to the labor or separate property of either spouse is deemed joint management community.

¶ 11,161

Montana has also recognized, in In re Hunter's Estate, 125 Mont. 315, 236 P.2d 94 (1951), that property purchased with community property brought from California remains community property. However, like the Ohio court in *Kessler*, the Montana court concluded that, under California community property law, the wife's half was not really vested and that it did not become so until the husband's managerial powers ceased because of his death. For that reason the court taxed all of the property in the husband's estate.

Citing *Hunter,* a Virginia court assessed a gift tax on 100 percent, rather than 50 percent, of the value of a home purchased with community funds and placed in the name of the wife. Virginia v. Terjen, 197 Va. 596, 90 S.E.2d 801 (1956). The *Terjen* result appears to be an incorrect application of theory of California community property law. By way of contrast, North Carolina reached the correct result in finding that only a gift as to 50 percent had taken place. See Op. Atty. General, Feb. 23, 1954 (N.C.). Similarly, in Colorado v. Bejarano, 145 Colo. 304, 358 P.2d 866 (1961), a widow's interest in a pension plan was excludable for Colorado State inheritance tax purposes.

A good treatment of this subject can be found in 40 Op. Atty. General 526 (Maryland 1955), in which Maryland's Attorney General recognized the community interest of a former Texas couple who came to Maryland and held that as to anything not recorded, Maryland inheritance tax would only be assessed against one-half thereof. However, where record title to property was in the name of only one spouse, Maryland inheritance tax would be imposed upon everything so held on the grounds that the Register of Wills did not have the power to make a determination contrary to the record title.

[¶ 11,169]

ii.   Action of the Parties

Subsequent dealings with the property after moving to the common law state may alter the character of the property and the rights of the parties, such as a partition with each spouse taking one-half the separate property or conversion to a form of joint ownership recognized in the common law jurisdiction or by placing the property entirely in the name of the spouse.

Similarly, the general rule is that spouses can transmute separate property into community property.

[¶ 11,177]

iii.   Sale and Purchase of a Residence

Suppose a migrant sells his home in the community property state and reinvests the proceeds in a new home in a common law state. Taking title as tenants in common or as joint tenants with right of survivorship (if the survivorship feature is desired) would probably destroy community character resulting in loss of "fresh-start" income tax basis for both halves of the property at the death of one of the spouses (§ 1014(b)(6)) (unless the spouses have entered into an agreement which states that, despite the titling of real

? What?
↓
See bottom

¶ 11,177   P. 304

property, they still regard it as community property). It is clear that no gift has occurred as a result of this titling, however, and that only one-half of the property would be included in the estate of the first to die.

[¶ 11,185]

c. *Uniform Disposition of Community Property Rights at Death Act*

The Uniform Disposition of Community Property Rights at Death Act has been adopted by New York and, at least, 13 other states. 8A U.L.A. 213 (2003). It provides in § 3:

1. One-half of the property belongs to the surviving spouse and is not subject to testamentary disposition by the decedent.

2. The surviving spouse has no right to elect against the will as to the decedent's one-half and has no dower or curtesy right in it.

3. One-half of the property is subject to testamentary disposition and will pass by intestacy if there is no will.

[¶ 11,193]

d. *Maintaining Community or Separate Character*

Special planning and record keeping is required to keep separate property segregated from community property. Although classification and segregation of these properties may not always be necessary—as in the case where the surviving spouse is sole beneficiary of the deceased spouse's estate—it can be of paramount importance in other circumstances. Detailed records can be used to provide an equitable division of property during a divorce action or in planning for estate tax minimization. See Gerald B. Treacy, Jr., Planning to Preserve the Advantages of Community Property, 23 Estate Planning 24 (1996).

If an individual is currently married or anticipates marriage sometime in his or her lifetime, accurate and detailed records will enable each spouse to maintain property as separate or community throughout the marriage. This is especially important if the spouses have lived in both community property jurisdictions and separate property jurisdictions during the course of the marriage. In planning for the migrating client, steps should be taken to assure that separate property can be identified and segregated from other property acquired during marriage. These steps include the following:

1. At the time the marriage is entered into, each spouse should generate a list of all property acquired prior to the marriage that he or she wishes to remain separate property.

2. If the couple moves from a community property state to a separate property state or vice versa, an inventory should be taken and each item classified as: (a) the husband's separate property; (b) the wife's separate property; or (c) the husband and wife's community property.

¶ 11,177

3. During the marriage separate property should not be commingled with community property. Liquid assets, such as currency and brokerage accounts, are especially susceptible to loss of separate property status due to commingling with community property. Consider these steps:

    a. *Bank Accounts*. Each spouse should maintain a separate bank account to segregate separate funds, and a joint community account should be maintained to deposit community funds. If the couple lives in a community property jurisdiction in which the interest earned on separate property is deemed to be community, the interest should be withdrawn or rolled over to the community property account to avoid commingling of the different assets.

    b. *Brokerage Accounts*. Each spouse should maintain a separate brokerage account to be used to hold and trade the separate securities of each spouse. However, if the dividends received on these accounts are deemed to be community property, the dividends should not be deposited in the separate account but rolled over to the couple's community brokerage account or bank account.

4. For assets acquired during the marriage with separate funds, a detailed account of the purchase of each asset should be subscribed. If separate property is used to purchase the asset, the asset acquired will also be characterized as separate property. An accurate record of such purchases accompanied by the bills of sale and canceled checks showing the source of funds will provide persuasive evidence as to the separate character of the property.

[¶ 11,201]

e. *Pre-and Postnuptial Agreements*

Contracts between persons about to marry are becoming more common. The goal of many of these contracts—sometimes called marriage contracts or prenuptial or antenuptial agreements—is to preserve the character of the property each spouse brings to the marriage and to permit each spouse to dispose of his or her separate property free of any claims against that property granted by state law to the surviving spouse. One feature wanted by some couples is a provision rejecting the community property system and allowing each spouse to treat, as his or her separate property, property acquired during marriage that would otherwise be community property. It appears that all states allow such agreements. See Reppy & Samuel, *supra* ¶ 11–113, at 3–1. Postnuptial agreements, too, are allowed. For related material as to Alaska, see ¶ 11,089.

While there is an enormous amount of litigation involving the validity of pre-and postnuptial agreements, the only tests that have any rational basis involve determinations of whether the parties understood the nature and effect of the agreement. See, e.g., Rosenberg v. Lipnick, 377 Mass. 666, 389 N.E.2d 385 (1979). Inasmuch as the parties contemplating marriage—as well as those already married—are in a confidential relationship one to another, they owe each other the highest duty of loyalty and care. That duty means full disclosure of the nature and extent of the property of each spouse so that the other spouse knows what it is that he or she is bargaining about. Unif. Premarital Agreement Act § 6(a), 96 U.L.A. 48–49 (2001); Casteel, Guidelines for Planning & Drafting Effective Premarital Agreements, 33 Est. Plan. 14 (2006); for related discussion, see ¶ 21,900.

[¶ 11,209]

8. JOINT PROPERTY AND COMMUNITY PROPERTY

Texas and California courts have consistently held that community property cannot be held as joint tenants with right of survivorship without first terminating the community character of the property. See Williams v. McKnight, 402 S.W.2d 505 (Tex.1966); Hilley v. Hilley, 161 Tex. 569, 342 S.W.2d 565 (1961); Reppy & Samuel, *supra* ¶ 11–113, at 3–3. However, some states allow a right of survivorship to be added to community property without impairing its character as community. See ¶ 11,105.

C. NONSPOUSAL JOINT PROPERTY TAXATION

[¶ 11,251]

1. INTRODUCTION

Except in the case of bank accounts, brokerage accounts and the like, when speaking of joint property, title appears determinative of the ownership question without regard to the respective contributions of the co-owners. Thus, applying the old bromide that federal taxing statutes follow state property law determinations, Commissioner v. Estate of Bosch, 387 U.S. 456 (1966); see also R. Stephens, G. Maxfield & S. Lind, Federal Estate & Gift Taxation ¶ 4.05–.06 (7th ed. 1996) [hereinafter Stephens], it would seem logical that each co-owner would have included in his or her gross estate for federal death tax purposes the fair market value of the fractional interest state law believes the co-owner to have. Needless to say, such is not always the case.

[¶ 11,259]

2. CONSIDERATION-FURNISHED TEST

Section 2040(a) sets forth the general rule that, as to co-owners not married to each other, all jointly held property is included in the estate of the first of the joint tenants to die except to the extent the survivor can prove contribution. There are two exceptions to this general rule. Excepted are qualified joint interests, i.e., joint interests between husband and wife, as described in § 2040(b) and joint interests created by gift, devise, bequest or inheritance.

Note: The term "property held jointly" is defined in Reg. § 20.2040–1(b). The term includes both real and personal property held in a joint tenancy, a tenancy by the entirety, or a joint bank account payable to the survivor. Id. Property held in a tenancy in common is specifically excluded from jointly held property. Id.

Under the so-called "consideration-furnished rule," the amount excluded from the estate of the first joint tenant to die is not the amount contributed by the survivor but that portion of the value of the joint property which is proportionate to the survivor's contribution. See Stephens, *supra* ¶ 11,251, at ¶ 4.12[5]. As might be suspected, there is considerable litigation with respect to what constitutes the survivor's contribution. See 2 Mertens, *supra* ¶ 11,051, at §§ 15.05–15.06 (1959 and Supp. 1975).

More important to an understanding of the consideration-furnished rule are the following observations:

1. The consideration-furnished rule emphasizes contribution without regard to state law determinations of the respective ownership interests and

2. Payment of federal gift tax by the joint tenant who made the larger contribution at the time the property becomes jointly held does not avoid application of the federal estate tax to such jointly held property at the death of the first joint tenant to die.

Example. Larry took title to property as joint tenants with right of survivorship with his son, Dud. Larry paid the full purchase price from his separate property. He also paid gift tax on the transfer. At Larry's death the full fair market value of the property is included in Larry's estate. § 2040(a).

It is significant that § 2040(a) expressly contemplates "tracing." This means that the source of the contributions made by the surviving joint tenant is always at issue. If the surviving joint tenant's contribution is made from resources provided by the decedent, the value of the jointly held property proportionate to these resources will be included in the decedent's gross estate. See Reg. § 20.2040–1(c)(4). It is an efficient mechanical rule that puts the burden of proof on the surviving joint tenant. Thus, the survivor cannot claim as his or her contribution a gift he or she received from the decedent. Cf. Estate of E.T. Kelley v. Commissioner, 22 B.T.A. 421 (1931), acq., 1931–2 C.B. 37.

The tracing principle represents a reasonable attempt to emphasize substance over form. A taxpayer should not be able to defeat the death tax on jointly held property by funneling a portion of the consideration for such property through the other joint tenant. There is, however, a surprising limitation to this notion where income-producing property is involved. Reg. § 20.2040–1(c)(5) provides:

If the decedent, before the acquisition of the property by himself and the other joint owner, transferred to the latter for less than an adequate and full consideration in money or money's worth other income-producing property, the income from which belonged to and became the other joint owner's entire contribution to the purchase price, then the value of the jointly held property less that portion attributable to the income which the other joint owner did furnish is included in the decedent's gross estate.

In Revenue Ruling 79–372, 1979–2 C.B. 330, decedent gave money to his child, money that was subsequently invested by the child in income-producing property. The child subsequently sold the property and deposited the proceeds in a joint account with himself and decedent as joint tenants. The Service ruled that the amount to be included in decedent's gross estate is the amount of money originally given to the child. And, in Revenue Ruling 78–418, 1978–2 C.B. 236, the decedent and his spouse used community funds to acquire property which they took as joint tenants. They later moved to a common law property state, sold the property, and used the proceeds to acquire other property which they took as joint tenants. The Service ruled that one-half the value of the property should be included in the husband's estate.

[¶ 11,267]

3. FRACTIONAL INTEREST RULE

Section 2040(a) contains an important exception to the consideration-furnished test for jointly held property acquired by gift, devise, or bequest. Where property is thus acquired, the proportionate contributions of the joint tenants are determined by the interests which the tenants take under local law. Reg. § 20.2040–1(a)(1).

[¶ 11,275]

4. FEDERAL GIFT TAXES

Given the estate tax disregard for state law notions of "ownership," it is surprising, then, to note that the federal tax on gifts—lifetime transfers for less than adequate and full consideration in money or money's worth in other than a business context (see §§ 2501, 2511, 2512; Reg. § 25.2512–8; see generally 5 Mertens, *supra* ¶ 11,051, at §§ 36.06–36.07)—follows state law determinations. If state law declares that a co-owner took a greater interest in property than his or her contribution would entitle the co-owner to, the other co-owner is deemed to have made a taxable gift to the extent the fair market value of the interest taken by the other co-owner exceeds his or her contribution. See Reg. § 25.2511–1(h)(5).

> *Example.* Bill purchased Blackacre with $100,000 of his separate property. He took title in his name and that of his daughter, Daisy, as joint tenants with right of survivorship. Bill will be deemed to have made a gift of $50,000 to Daisy for gift tax purposes less the $12,000 annual gift tax exclusion offered by § 2503(b).

The Treasury Regulations are silent with respect to the gift tax consequences of creating tenancies in common, but it seems clear that a taxable gift will occur where the fractional interests received by the tenants in common are disproportionate to their contributions to the purchase price of the property. Stephens, *supra* ¶ 11,251, at ¶ 10.01[3][f].

[¶ 11,283]

5. BANK ACCOUNTS

In the case of joint bank accounts, federal law follows state law. Since under state law, the interest of each co-owner in a joint bank account is limited, practically speaking, so too, under federal law, no gift is made until a co-owner withdraws an amount in excess of his or her contribution to the account. Reg. § 25.2511–1(h)(4) provides:

> If A creates a joint bank account for himself and B (or a similar type of ownership by which A can regain the entire fund without B's consent), there is a gift to B when B draws upon the account for his own benefit, to the extent of the amount drawn without any obligation to account for a part of the proceeds to A. Similarly, if A purchases a United States savings bond, registered as payable to "A or B," there is a gift to B when B surrenders the bond for cash without any obligation to account for a part of the proceeds to A.

There is speculation about the situation where, under local law, the donor-spouse does not have the right to regain the entire fund. Presumably, if under some peculiar doctrine of local law, or some contractual arrangement, when a person deposited money in a joint bank account this created a joint tenancy with respect to the money so that the depositor lost title to half of the money at the time the deposit was made, and the depositor could not withdraw half of the account so that the transfer of that half was complete and irrevocable, this would be a gift of half of the account to the other depositor at the time the deposit was made. Stephens, *supra* ¶ 11,251, at ¶ 10.01[5][c].

[¶ 11,291]

6. UNITED STATES SAVINGS BONDS

Where a United States savings bond is acquired by one person from separate property and is payable either to that person or another person, there is no completed gift unless (1) the noncontributing co-owner cashes the bond or (2) the bond is reissued in the name of the noncontributing co-owner alone. Rev. Rul. 55–278, 1955–1 C.B. 471, 472; see also Stephens, *supra* ¶ 11,251, at ¶ 10.01[5][c].

Following the same reasoning, the Supreme Court in United States v. Chandler, 410 U.S. 257 (1973) (per curiam), held that even though the decedent had made a valid gift of savings bonds under state law, the bonds were includable in the decedent's estate under § 2040 because the federal regulations require that the bonds be reissued in order to change ownership. See also Estate of Curry v. United States, 409 F.2d 671 (6th Cir.1969); Elliott v. Commissioner, 57 T.C. 152 (1971), aff'd, 474 F.2d 1008 (5th Cir.1973) (upholding the Service's position). The Treasury Savings Bond Regulations are at 31 C.F.R. § 315. See generally Rev. Rul. 68–269, 1968–1 C.B. 399 (Situations 2–5, 7—gift tax payable on savings bonds in various factual situations).

¶ 11,291

[¶ 11,299]

7. JOINT BROKERAGE ACCOUNTS

Joint brokerage accounts where the contributing co-owner could withdraw all of the funds are also treated like joint bank accounts. See Rev. Rul. 69–148, 1969–1 C.B. 226.

D. SPOUSAL JOINT PROPERTY: TAXATION

[¶ 11,351]

1. INTRODUCTION

Congress has had difficulty developing a satisfactory scheme for the estate and gift taxation of property held by husband and wife as joint tenants with right of survivorship or as tenants by the entirety. Generally speaking, Congress has singled out such property for special tax treatment.

[¶ 11,359]

2. GIFT TAX TREATMENT OF SPOUSAL JOINTLY HELD PROPERTY

a. Real Property

In 1954 Congress added § 2515 to the Internal Revenue Code. Section 2515 provided that when husband and wife took title to real property as joint tenants with right of survivorship (or as tenants by the entirety) they had the option of reporting or not reporting the transaction for federal gift tax purposes. Section 2515 was repealed and is not applicable to interspousal gifts made after 1981.

The one-time presence of § 2515 makes for a crazy quilt. While it existed, spouses could use it to shelter their gifts to one another. Otherwise, the general rule is that the creation of a joint tenancy in real property results in a gift, unless the respective joint tenants contribute consideration to the acquisition of the joint property which is proportionate to the interest state law gives the respective joint tenants. Of course, the § 2523 unlimited marital deduction makes creation of a joint tenancy a tax-free event where the joint tenants are married to each other.

[¶ 11,367]

b. Personal Property

For gift tax purposes, spousal jointly held *personal* property and nonspousal jointly held *personal* property have always been treated identically. Creation of the joint tenancy results in a gift unless the respective joint tenants contribute consideration to the acquisition of the joint property which is proportionate to the interest state law gives the respective joint tenants. Here again, of course, the unlimited marital deduction makes such a transfer a tax-free event.

[¶ 11,375]

3. ESTATE TAX TREATMENT OF SPOUSAL JOINTLY HELD PROPERTY

As a general rule, 50 percent of jointly held property is included in the estate of the first spouse to die. § 2040(b). The relative contribution by each spouse to the cost of acquiring the jointly held property is ignored. (However, as a result of the decision in Gallenstein v. United States, 975 F.2d 286 (6th Cir.1992), the consideration-furnished test provided by § 2040(a) applies to all spousal joint property acquired before 1977. This is advantageous in cases where the first spouse to die has contributed more the property's acquisition cost and it has, in the meantime, appreciated. The surviving spouse will enjoy a higher basis in such cases for purposes of determining gain on disposition.)

Table 11.1 describes the estate and gift tax treatment of jointly held property according to the date the joint interest was created and the type of property.

[handwritten margin note: Wait! Marital deduction not reflected]

Table 11.1 ESTATE AND GIFT TAX TREATMENT OF JOINTLY HELD PROPERTY*			
Date Joint Interest Created	Real Property	Personal Property	Bank Accounts
Pre-'55	Gift tax at creation	Gift tax at creation	Gift tax only when withdrawn
	Estate tax: consideration furnished test[1] applies	Estate tax consideration furnished test applies	Estate tax: consideration furnished test applies
Post-'54	Gift tax but if joint tenants married to each other, gift tax only if *election* made	Gift tax at creation	Gift tax only when withdrawn
	Estate tax: consideration furnished test applies	Estate tax: consideration furnished test applies	Estate tax: consideration furnished test applies
Post-'76	Gift tax but if joint tenants married to each other, gift tax only if *election* made	Gift tax at creation	Gift tax only when withdrawn
	Estate tax: consideration furnished test applies unless joint tenants married to each other and make QJI[2] *election*	Estate tax: consideration furnished test applies but if joint tenants are married to each other, QJI treatment is mandatory.	Estate tax: consideration furnished test applies
Post-'81	Gift tax at creation	Gift tax at creation	Gift tax only when withdrawn
	Estate tax: consideration furnished test applies but if joint tenants are married to each other, QJI treatment is mandatory.[3]	Estate tax: consideration furnished test applies but if joint tenants are married to each other, QJI treatment is mandatory.[3]	Estate tax consideration furnished test applies but if joint tenants are married to each other, QJI treatment is mandatory.[3]

---

* The limited marital deduction became available in 1948 for gift tax purposes (§ 2523) and estate tax purposes (§ 2056). The unlimited marital deduction became available in 1982. The effect of the marital deduction on the tax consequences suggested is not reflected in Table 11.1.
[1] The term "consideration furnished test" refers to the rule provided in § 2040(a) which, generally stated, provides that all jointly held property will be included in the estate of the first of the joint tenants to die except to the extent the survivor can establish the consideration he or she contributed to the acquisition of the jointly held property.
[2] The term "QJI", refers to jointly held property interests which are deemed qualified joint interests by § 2040(b), which was added to the Internal Revenue Code in 1976.
[3] § 2040(b). Qualified Joint Interest (QJI) treatment became *mandatory* after 1981 as to all property held jointly by husband and wife.

[¶ 11,383]

4. INCOME TAX BASIS

a. *General Rule*

The basis of joint tenancy property in the hands of the surviving spouse is the most critical dilemma presented by the 1981 adoption of the Qualified Joint Interest rule as expressed in § 2040(b). Under § 1014(b)(9), the basis of property acquired from a decedent through rights of survivorship will be stepped up (or down) to its estate tax value only to the extent that the property is required to be included in valuing the decedent's gross estate. After 1981, only 50 percent of Qualified Joint Interest property is required to be included in valuing the gross estate of the first spouse to die. Thus, the step-up (or down) in basis to estate tax value will apply only to the 50 percent statutory interest of the decedent. The 50 percent excluded under § 2040(b) will retain its predeath basis in the hands of the survivor.

Example. Assume that Horatio and Winkie acquire jointly held real estate at a cost of $100,000; their basis is $100,000. At Horatio's death in 1995, the real estate has a value of $250,000. One-half of the date-of-death value ($125,000) must be included in the value of his estate. Winkie will then have a basis of $175,000 (one-half of the original basis plus one-half of the stepped-up basis). A sale of the property by Winkie will result in a realized gain of $75,000.

If death had occurred in 1981, assuming the full value of the real estate was includible in Horatio's estate, Winkie would have had a basis of $250,000 and no gain would result if she sold the property at that price.

(The decision in Gallenstein v. United States, 975 F.2d 286 (6th Cir.1992), noted in ¶ 11,375, finding that the consideration-furnished test provided by § 2040(a) applies to all spousal joint property acquired before 1977, sometimes provides an income tax advantage. Where the first spouse to die has contributed more the property's acquisition cost and the property has, in the meantime, appreciated, the surviving spouse will enjoy a higher basis in such cases for purposes of determining gain on disposition.)

[¶ 11,391]

b. *Planning Implications*

In some cases the income tax detriment created by a reduced basis may not be significant. For example, consider the case where the jointly held property is residential real estate. Under § 121, married taxpayers filing joint returns can exclude $500,000 of gain on the sale of a principal residence if they meet certain conditions.

Similarly, a reduced income tax basis may not be disadvantageous where the joint tenancy property is not likely to be sold until the death of the surviving spouse. Although the survivor would receive a new basis as to only a part of the property at the death of the first spouse, the full value of the property would get a new basis equal to fair market value at the survivor's death. Sale at the later time to pay taxes would generally result in no taxable gain because of the new basis.

[¶ 11,399]

c. *Inflating Values for Estate Tax Purposes*

In situations where there is likely to be no death tax at the death of either spouse, due to § 2056's unlimited marital deduction at the first death and the availability of the unified credit at the second death, income tax basis planning, not estate tax avoidance planning, has priority. In furtherance of this objective, the elimination of joint tenancies in contemplation of the death of the first spouse may be indicated. This would allow the survivor a full basis step-up for appreciated property held in the decedent's sole name.

> *Example.* If Hotspur and Winglet own nonresidential real estate which has greatly appreciated in value, it may be Winglet's desire to sell the real estate at Hotspur's death, particularly where Hotspur had managed the real estate and Winglet is inexperienced in the operation. If the real estate were in Hotspur's sole name, and his will devised the real estate to Winglet, the full value of the real estate would be included in Hotspur's estate. Accordingly, Winglet could sell the real estate virtually tax free immediately after Hotspur's death. Winglet's basis would equal the full value, and the sale price would equal the basis. No gain would be recognized on the sale.

The rule of § 1014(b)(9) applies as long as the joint tenancy is required to be included in the decedent's estate for federal estate tax purposes. See Reg. § 1.1014–2(b)(2) (second sentence). Whether or not there is estate tax liability or the necessity of filing an estate tax return is irrelevant to the basis issue.

Section 2040 is somewhat vague about who has the burden of proof with respect to contribution to jointly held property, but the regulations clearly impose that burden on the decedent's executor. Reg. § 20.2040–1(a)(2) even implies that the matter of proof of contribution is committed to the executor and if he or she declines, the IRS could not usurp this function:

> The entire value of jointly held property is included in a decedent's gross estate unless the executor submits facts sufficient to show that property was not acquired entirely with consideration furnished by the decedent.* * *

However, cases suggest that inflated values for estate tax purposes are to be disregarded for income tax basis purposes. For example, in Madden v. Commissioner, 52 T.C. 845 (1969), aff'd per curiam, 440 F.2d 784 (7th Cir.1971), it

¶ 11,399

was held that, for purposes of the basis rules of § 1014, the decedent's executor has the burden of proving that jointly held property was *required to be included* in the estate of the deceased joint tenant. In *Madden,* the surviving spouse argued that the jointly held property had acquired as its basis for income tax purposes that value at which it was included in the estate of the deceased joint tenant. Noting that the estate tax rules for jointly held property have been on the books since 1916, the court said:

> However, we cannot believe that Congress contemplated that the term "required" should be construed so as to give survivors an option to decrease income tax by increasing estate tax, or to shift to the respondent, in income tax controversies, the burden of proving that less property was required to be included in the gross estate than was actually included. There is no indication that Congress contemplated that it was conferring upon a surviving joint tenant the privilege of paying more estate tax than was necessary so as to reduce his income tax liability on the subsequent sale of the property. It seems more likely that when the term "required" was used, it was assumed that the executor or other interested person would attempt to secure the maximum exclusion of the jointly owned property from the estate; only to the extent that the executor was unable to show that the property was not excludable was it required to be included in the gross estate. Such an interpretation of "required" is consistent with the practice that existed in 1954 and has the effect of imposing the burden upon the person who has the information most readily available.

In considering *Madden,* it may be appropriate to note that the government had declined to allow inclusion in the decedent's estate of the property in question. The basis step-up was not allowed, and the property was excluded from the gross estate. The court seemed to find this significant. It said, "We are not concerned with a situation in which there has been a final determination of the amount includible in the gross estate; the estate tax return involved herein was not accepted by the respondent."

Finally, not to be overlooked is the penalty imposed by § 6662(e) in the event of an underpayment of income tax due to a valuation understatement of valuation misstatement. Penalty determination is a complicated undertaking but, suffice it to say, that the penalty will be a minimum 20 percent of the underpayment. See § 6662(a); ¶ 24,131.

Underpayment of estate and gift taxes will also result in a similar penalty if it results from a valuation understatement. § 6662(a) and (g); ¶ 24,131.

[¶ 11,407]

d.   *Contrast with Community Property*

Contrast the income tax basis rules applicable to Qualified Joint Interests with those applicable to community property. Section 1014(b)(6) provides that both halves of the community get a new basis at death, while only one-half of the jointly held property gets a new basis at death. More importantly, if spouses hold all of their property as joint tenants with right of survivorship, they will lose the opportunity to use a bypass trust to shelter the credit equivalent provided by § 2010. ¶ 13,059.

E. TRANSFERS WITHIN THREE YEARS OF DEATH FOR ESTATE TAX PURPOSES

[¶ 11,451]

Section 2035 requires certain transfers made within three years of death to be recaptured and included in the transferor's gross estate. Jointly held property is conspicuously absent from the list of interests to which the three-year recapture rule applies. Accordingly, it is appropriate to conclude that joint tenancies which are terminated within three years of death will not be subject to any of the § 2040 rules. Thus, taxpayers who find § 2040 onerous for any reason can avoid its reach by terminating their joint tenancies in contemplation of death.

Again, doesn't this have tax implicati

Problem

[¶ 11,490]

Terminations of joint interests should be free of federal gift tax consequences except in the case where the jointly held property is a bank account. See Reg. § 25.2511–1(h)(4). Why is there an exception for bank accounts? Would it make a difference to your conclusion if the joint tenants were husband and wife?

F. TRANSFERS WITHIN THREE YEARS OF DEATH FOR INCOME TAX PURPOSES

[¶ 11,501]

The unlimited marital deduction of § 2056 and the expanded unified credit of § 2010, taken together, or taken separately, undoubtedly free many estates from federal estate tax liability. For many such taxpayers, planning consists of efforts to reduce the income tax burden. Effective utilization of the "fresh start" basis rules provided in § 1014 is important. Section 1014, generally speaking, provides that "the basis of property in the hands of a person acquiring the property from a decedent * * * shall * * * be the fair market value of the property at the date of the decedent's death.* * * "

In cases where death is imminent and the prospective decedent has a nontaxable estate (for estate tax purposes), the prospective surviving spouse has every incentive to "load up" the prospective decedent's estate through gifts of low basis appreciated property. The gifts can be made tax free because of the unlimited marital deduction available for gifts between spouses and, once in the prospective decedent's estate, the basis step-up rules of § 1014 will be applicable at the donee's death to give the appreciated property a tax-free new basis in the hands of the persons who take the appreciated property at the death of the donee.

Unlimited Gift Tax exclusion between Spouses.

¶ 11,501

"one year" claw back

To minimize the extent of this "laundering operation," Congress added § 1014(e) to the Internal Revenue Code. Section 1014(e) provides that if a decedent-donee dies within one year after the date of a gift to him or her of appreciated property and the donor reacquires the gift property from decedent's estate, the donor-beneficiary's basis for the property will be the same as the decedent's basis immediately before death. In such a situation, the donor's basis in the "comeback" property will be essentially the same as its basis, in the donor's hands, before the gift was made.

Applies to spouses and other taxpayers.

Section 1014(e) applies to transfers between spouses as well as between other taxpayers. The intent of the rule is to prevent the transfer of appreciated property to an individual whose death is imminent, anticipating at the time of the transfer that the donor will reacquire the property by devise or inheritance. The donor's intention in making the transfer of property to the decedent-donee is irrelevant in determining the application of § 1014(e).

> *Example.* Consider Frank and his son, Chip. As Frank advanced in years he arranged to title property in his name and that of Chip as joint tenants with right of survivorship. Unfortunately Chip was killed within the year and the property came back to Frank. Even though the "comeback" property was included in Chip's estate for federal estate tax purposes (and even though estate tax was paid by Chip's estate on the "comeback" property), the jointly held property in Frank's hands after Chip's death retains the basis it had in Frank's hands before the property was titled in his name and that of Chip as joint tenants with right of survivorship. Moreover, it would appear that Frank would not enjoy an increase in the property's basis to reflect the estate tax paid by Chip's estate.

Whether § 1014(e) will apply upon the termination of joint tenancies within one year of the death of one of the spouses depends upon how the words "acquired * * * by gift" are interpreted. These words are found in § 1014(e)(1)(A) which provides, in pertinent part, that appreciated property "acquired by the decedent by gift during the one-year period ending on the date of the decedent's death" shall retain the basis it had in the hands of the donor-beneficiary and will not acquire a new basis simply because it was included in the estate of the decedent-donee.

With the advent of the unlimited marital deduction it is easy to conceive of the situation in which a joint tenancy is terminated and the spouse whose death is imminent takes title to all of the jointly held property. More commonly, spouses might "equalize" their respective estates by terminating joint tenancies in contemplation of the death of one of them in order to be able to utilize a bypass trust to shelter the credit equivalent at the death of the first joint tenant to die. For discussion of the bypass trust concept, see Chapter 18. State property law dictates that, with respect to property other than bank accounts, each spouse will be deemed to own an undivided one-half interest in the jointly held property from the date the joint tenancy was originally established. See discussion at ¶ 11,051. Accordingly, there clearly will be no gift from a state property law standpoint at the time the joint tenancy is terminated so long as the joint tenants divide the property proportionately to the interests state law determines them to have in the jointly held property. Thus, in the case where the jointly held property is evenly divided between the joint tenants, for state law purposes, no gift will be deemed made. But where one of the joint tenants ends up with all of the property, a gift to that joint tenant will have occurred.

Example. Herb and Wilda own common stock in Belchfire Motors as joint tenants with right of survivorship. Herb bought the stock with his separate property. Although he never filed gift tax returns to reflect the transaction (and his estate may be liable for delinquent gift taxes), Herb clearly made a gift to Wilda of one-half of the value of the shares at the time title to the shares was taken as joint tenants with right of survivorship. See Reg. § 25.2511–1(h)(5). Of course, the transfer qualifies for the unlimited marital deduction. § 2523.

1. If Wilda transfers her interest in the stock to Herb within one year of his death, her one-half of the stock will be denied a new basis at his death if, for example, it comes back to her pursuant to his will. Why? Because Wilda's one-half of the stock will clearly have been acquired by Herb by "gift" for both federal and state law purposes.

2. What to do? If it is important to Herb and Wilda to have a new basis for both halves of the jointly held property at Herb's death, Wilda could reconvey to Herb in anticipation of Herb's death and he could give what would otherwise be "comeback" property to another beneficiary. Section 1014(e) will not apply because the stock was not reacquired by Wilda, the donor.

On the other hand, what if one of the spouses had furnished all of the consideration for the acquisition of the jointly held property but had never reported the establishment of the joint tenancy for federal gift tax purposes? Whether or not the gift was reported for federal gift tax purposes is irrelevant for purposes of imposing gift tax liability. If liability has arisen, failure to file the necessary returns means simply that the donor is delinquent.

But what of the case where the donor was not required to file a gift tax return? For example a gift tax return might not have been required because the value of the gift to the other joint tenant was less than the amount of the annual exclusion. Alternatively, the joint tenancy may have been established in real property and, during the period 1955–1981, § 2515 gave spouses the option of reporting or not reporting, for gift tax purposes, the establishment of joint tenancies in real property. Furthermore, since 1981, § 6019 has provided that "transfer by gift" between spouses need not be reported for gift tax purposes.

In such cases, it is arguable that § 1014(e) should apply to deny a new basis to the contributor's one-half of the appreciated property in cases where the noncontributor dies first and the appreciated property comes back to the person who originally provided the consideration for the acquisition of the jointly held property. This argument is based on the assumption that "gift" in § 1014(e) means "gift for state property law purposes."

¶ 11,501

Problem

[¶ 11,540]

Consider the case of Hubert and Wendy. Hubert provided all of the consideration to acquire Blackacre, which they held as joint tenants with right of survivorship. Blackacre was purchased for $30,000 and has a current value of $180,000.

(a) Assume, first, that Hubert's death is imminent and that the value of his estate is much below the $2,000,000 credit equivalent available to persons dying in 2006. § 2010. Wendy proposes to reconvey all of her interest in Blackacre to Hubert so that it will all be included in his estate at his death and, thereby, enjoy a basis step-up at his death. Has Wendy made a "gift" to Hubert of her one-half interest in Blackacre for purposes of § 1014(e)? Should the answer be different depending on whether the acquisition of Blackacre was reported, or was required to be reported, for federal gift tax purposes? For example, assume that the property was acquired in 1982 and, that while a gift of one-half the value of the jointly held property was made to Wendy, the gift did not have to be reported for federal gift tax purposes because of the unlimited marital deduction. § 6019.

(b) Alternatively, suppose the property was acquired in 1974 but Hubert elected not to report, for federal gift tax purposes, the gift to Wendy of one-half the value of the jointly held property. It would seem that it could be argued that when Congress used the term "gift" in § 1014(e), it meant gift for tax purposes and not gift for state law purposes. Using this approach could possibly mean that both Hubert's one-half and Wendy's one-half of the jointly held property would both enjoy a basis step-up at Hubert's death. Why?

(c) On the other hand, suppose Wendy's death were imminent and the spouses terminated the joint tenancy in anticipation of her death and equally divided the jointly held property between themselves. Would Wendy's one-half of the property enjoy a basis step-up?

(d) Which approach is most likely to prevail?

G. CLOSE ORDER OF DEATH

[¶ 11,551]

Section 3 of the Uniform Simultaneous Death Act (USDA) of 1940, 8B ULA 160 (2001) adopted in 34 states and the District of Columbia, provides that where there is no evidence that two joint tenants died otherwise than simultaneously, the jointly held property "shall be distributed one-half as if one had survived and one-half as if the other had survived."

USDA was revised in 1991 and 1993, 8B ULA 141 (2001), and, while freestanding, it is also a part of the Uniform Probate Code. The 1993 version has been adopted by 18 states thus far. 8B ULA 20 (Supp. 2006). As revised,

USDA now provides that where there is no clear and convincing evidence that one co-owner survived the other by more than <u>120</u> hours, one-half of the jointly owned property will be distributed as if the one had survived by 120 hours and the other one-half shall be distributed as if the other had survived by 120 hours. UPC § 2–702(c).

Revenue Ruling 76–303, 1976–2 C.B. 266, set forth the position of the IRS with respect to cases in which USDA § 3 is applicable. The Service took the position that all of the jointly held property was included in the estate of the spouse who furnished all of the consideration for the jointly held property. The Service reasoned that the consideration furnished test of § 2040(a) would be applicable because USDA § 3 provides that the jointly held property is to be distributed as if each joint tenant "had survived."

The Service also concluded that one-half of the jointly held property would be included in the estate of the noncontributor because the noncontributor has an ownership interest in one-half of the jointly held property which will be disposed of under the noncontributor's will or, if there is no will, by virtue of the intestate statute applicable to the noncontributor's estate.

[I]n order for any of the value of jointly held property * * * to be includible in a decedent's gross estate under § 2040 * * *, the decedent must be survived by a joint tenant. * * * Under * * * [USDA § 3], the husband and wife are each considered to have *survived* with respect to one-half of the property. Thus, *§ 2040 will be applicable for determining the includibility of the value of one-half of the property in each of their gross estates.* Since there is no evidence to indicate the wife furnished any consideration for the property, the value of one-half of the property *with respect to which the wife is considered to have survived* is includible in the husband's gross estate under § 2040.* * *

In addition, since each is considered to have survived as to one-half of the property, each is considered to have acquired an absolute, sole ownership interest in one-half of the property before death. Thus, the value of one-half of the property is includible in each of their gross estates under § 2033.

Revenue Ruling 76–303 should continue to have applicability to nonspousal jointly held property, the effect being to produce a rule of 150 percent includibility, i.e., a penalty.

Example. Consider Bob and Barney, father and son, who hold Blackacre, a property valued at $100,000, as joint tenants with rights of survivorship. Bob provided all of the consideration for the acquisition of Blackacre. In the event that when they die there is no evidence of the order of their deaths, Bob will have included $100,000 in his estate for estate tax purposes and Barney will have included $50,000. However, § 2013, which provides a credit for tax on prior transfers, should be available to mitigate the harshness of this result.

Problems

[¶ 11,590]

1. Does Revenue Ruling 76–303 have continued applicability after the adoption of the Qualified Joint Interest rule of § 2040(b)? Consider the case of Hip and Wilda, who were killed simultaneously. At the time of their death, they owned Greenfields as joint tenants with right of survivorship. The property had a value of $100,000 at their respective deaths. Describe the estate tax consequences to Hip and Wilda.

2. Bob and Twinkie are both retired police officers. The total value of their combined estate is, by conservative estimate, $2.1 million, consisting of cash in the amount of approximately $95,000 and their personal residence which by coincidence sits at the intersection of two interstate highways in an upper middle class suburban neighborhood of a major metropolitan area. The dwelling is situated on two acres of land, surrounded by newly constructed office and retail space. Bob and Twinkie acquired the property in 1950 when it was considered rural agricultural property, long before the interstate highway systems were even on the drawing boards. The basis in the residence property for income tax purposes is $22,500.

The residence is considered the community property of Bob and Twinkie under local law. Bob does not have a will and has recently learned that if he dies the property will not pass automatically to Twinkie. Instead, it would go to Ned, his son by his first marriage to Carla. Bob has not seen Ned in 30 years and was horrified at the prospect of Ned receiving one-half of his property at the expense of Twinkie. Bob wants you to prepare a will for him whereby he gives it "all to Twinkie." And, "for insurance," Bob is going to convert the residence to separate property and have it titled in his name and that of Twinkie as "joint tenants with right of survivorship."

Bob says that "when the price gets right" he and Twinkie plan to "sell the homeplace and cash in." Bob's health has begun to deteriorate, and he wonders if there isn't "something seriously wrong." He says that "if something happens to me, Twinkie would immediately sell the homeplace." In these circumstances, what is the most important reason why Bob and Twinkie should not take steps to own their home as joint tenants with right of survivorship?

Would your answer be any different if the residence property were of a more modest value? Alternatively, would your answer be any different if Twinkie were determined to remain in the "homeplace" until she dies?

Does the exclusion provided in § 121 have any bearing on your conclusion?

3. Both Muffy and Doug have wills containing the following provisions:

> I give (1) to my spouse the smallest amount of my estate necessary to eliminate all federal estate tax at my death and (2) to Accumulation National Bank, as trustee, the balance of my estate. During the continuance of the trust the trustee shall distribute all of the trust

income to my spouse. The trust shall terminate upon the death of my spouse. Upon termination, the undistributed trust property shall be distributed to my then living lineal descendants *per stirpes.*

Muffy died in 2006. She was survived by Doug. Muffy's property consisted entirely of cash and real estate, all of which she held with Doug as "joint tenants with right of survivorship." The total value of the property was $2,200,000.

How much of Muffy's property was allocated to the trust maintained at Accumulation National Bank for Doug's benefit?

4. Are you able to generalize and suggest whether spouses should be counseled to cause their property to be held as joint tenants with right of survivorship? Clearly, most spouses would be inclined to hold their property as joint tenants. With that in mind, detail the advantages and disadvantages of joint tenancy.

5. Do you agree or disagree with the assertion that the Qualified Joint Interest rule of § 2040(b) has little or no utility and, in fact, constitutes one of the principal drawbacks to spouses holding property as joint tenants?

H. DISCLAIMER

[¶ 11,601]

1. INTRODUCTION

Jointly held property creates special problems when a disclaimer of an interest in that property is attempted under § 2518. Prior to 1998, the regulations generally required a disclaimer of a survivorship interest to be made within nine months of the contributions that created the interest in a nonseverable joint tenancy or a tenancy by the entirety. D. Llewellyn et al., Disclaimers by a Surviving Spouse: The Trend of Increased Opportunities for Post Mortem Tax Planning Continues, 35 Real Prop. Prob. & Tr. J. 1, 11 (2000); Reg. § 25.2518–2(c)(4)(i) (prior to 1997 amendment). The current regulations provide that a disclaimer of a property interest held in joint tenancy with right of survivorship or tenancy by the entirety (except for joint bank, brokerage, and other investment accounts) must be made within nine months of the transfer creating the tenancy regardless of whether it is unilaterally severable; or if it is a survivorship interest succeeding by operation of law, the qualified disclaimer "must be made no later than [nine] months after the death of the first joint tenant to die regardless of whether such interest can be unilaterally severed under local law." Reg. § 25.2518–2(c)(4)(i). However, with respect to property held in joint tenancy with right of survivorship, the seminal issue is whether the deceased joint tenant's interest in the property passing under the right of survivorship is created at the death of the deceased joint tenant or at the time the joint tenancy is itself established.

[¶ 11,609]

2. JOINT TENANCIES WITH RIGHT OF SURVIVORSHIP

Leading up to the IRS's decision to change the regulations, a series of court decisions and letter rulings held that a surviving joint tenant may disclaim or refuse to accept the interest passing from the deceased joint tenant up to nine months after the death of the first-to-die of the joint tenants. In McDonald v. Commissioner, 853 F.2d 1494 (8th Cir.1988), the court held that a joint tenant with a right of survivorship could effectively disclaim up to nine months after the death of the first joint tenant. The court's rationale was that the interest being disclaimed was created at the death of the first joint tenant to die because, prior to death, the deceased joint tenant could unilaterally sever the joint tenancy under state law and divest the surviving joint tenant of the survivorship rights to the decedent's interest in the property. Accord, Kennedy v. Commissioner, 804 F.2d 1332 (7th Cir.1986); Estate of Dancy v. Commissioner, 872 F.2d 84 (4th Cir.1989); Priv. Ltr. Rul. 9135043. Although at the time, the ability of the deceased joint tenant to cut off the survivorship right by unilaterally severing or partitioning the joint tenancy during life was critical to these rulings, as mentioned above, the regulations now provide that whether the interest can be unilaterally severed is irrelevant. Reg. § 25.2518–2(c)(4)(i). However, if the creation of a joint tenancy is considered a gift and it is not unilaterally severable, the nine-month period to disclaim begins when the tenancy is created. J. Bae & D. Maloney, Disclaimers: The Last Line of Defense When Wrestling with Estate Planning Problems, Tr. & Est., Dec. 2000, at 40, 50.

It must be noted, by way of clarification, that no disclaimer will be effective as to the surviving joint tenant's interest in the property. The disclaimer is only effective as to the interest coming from the deceased joint tenant. This conclusion is explainable by the state law rule that each joint tenant has a proportionate ownership interest in the jointly held property upon creation of the joint tenancy. That is, under state law, when Bill and Hillary buy 100 shares of GM stock, taking title as joint tenants with right of survivorship, Bill has a 50 percent interest that he can unilaterally transfer even if Hillary provided 100 percent of the purchase price.

For related material, see ¶ 16,209.

[¶ 11,617]

3. TENANCY BY THE ENTIRETY

Even prior to the 1997 amendments, the rationale in *McDonald* had been expanded to a tenancy by the entirety. If a tenancy by the entirety could be severed under applicable state law prior to the death of a co-tenant, the property interest passing to one co-tenant as a result of the other co-tenant's death can be disclaimed up to nine months after the death of the first joint tenant to die. Priv. Ltr. Rul. 9208003; cf. Reg. § 25.2518–2(c)(4)(i). Whether an interest can be unilaterally severed is determined under applicable state law. Therefore, in Priv. Ltr. Rul. 9208003, it was concluded that if a co-tenant could not unilaterally sever his interest in a joint tenancy under state law while alive, then the disclaimer of the interest must be made within nine months after the tenancy by the entirety is created.

[¶ 11,625]

4. JOINT BANK AND BROKERAGE ACCOUNTS

The Regulations recognize that the survivorship interest in a joint bank account is created upon the death of the first joint tenant to die where that joint tenant funded the bank account. Reg. § 25.2518–2(c)(5), Example 9. That means that if Bill and Hillary have a joint bank account funded entirely by Hillary's earnings, Bill can disclaim 100 percent of the account at Hillary's death. See ¶ 11,081 and 11,283. The requirements for a qualified disclaimer of an interest in a joint bank or investment account differ from other property interests. Under Reg. § 25.2518–2(c)(4)(iii), if the transferor "may unilaterally regain [her] own contributions to the account without the consent of the other cotenant, such that the transfer is not a completed gift * * * the transfer creating the survivor's interest in the decedent's share of the account occurs on the death of the deceased cotenant. Accordingly,* * * the disclaimer must be made within [nine] months of the cotenant's death." The surviving joint tenant may only disclaim the portion of the joint account attributable to consideration furnished by the transferor. Id.

Correspondingly, in relation to spousal joint property, it is important to note that a disclaimer can increase the basis in appreciated joint property when it otherwise would not have occurred, but for the disclaimer. Basically, half of the joint property included in a decedent's estate under § 2040 and all of the property included under § 2033 will receive a stepped-up basis according to § 1014. P. Schneider, The New Regulations on Qualified Disclaimers of Joint Property Interest 5 (July 1998) (unpublished manuscript, on file with author). According to Reg. § 25.2518–2(c)(5), Example 14, the disclaimed portion of joint property (bank account) is to be included in the decedent's gross estate under § 2033; however, the portion not disclaimed retains its joint property character and thus is included in the decedent's gross estate under § 2040(b). Therefore, under certain circumstances, a surviving spouse can disclaim his interest in a joint brokerage account, still receive it through a residuary clause in the decedent's will, and the entire account will receive a stepped-up basis because of its full inclusion in the decedent's gross estate. See Reg. § 25.2518–2(c)(5), Example 14. Of course, this will increase the overall taxes imposed upon the decedent's estate, therefore a careful consideration must be made—whether the increased basis reduces the tax liability on that property to a greater extent than the potential increase in overall death taxes imposed upon the estate.

I. TERMINATION OF NONSPOUSAL JOINT INTERESTS DURING LIFE

[¶ 11,651]

1. JOINT TENANCIES WITH RIGHT OF SURVIVORSHIP

Termination of a joint tenancy with right of survivorship or a tenancy by the entirety *due to the death of one of the tenants* is not treated as a termination because any transfer which occurs at that time is testamentary in nature and is subject to the federal estate tax and not the gift tax. See Reg. § 25.2515–1(b). However, a termination is deemed to have occurred when the tenancy *ends in any other way unless* the property subject to the tenancy is converted in whole or in part into other property held under an identical tenancy. Reg. § 25.2515–1(d)(2)(ii). In the ordinary case there will be no gift tax consequences upon termination of a joint tenancy arrangement provided each joint tenant receives property having a value equal to the value of the interest state law gives him or her in the jointly held property. The termination will not change the fact that gift tax may still be owing from the time when the joint tenancy was created.

Analytically speaking, each joint tenant will be deemed to have acquired an undivided one-half interest in the property when the joint tenancy was created. This is implicit in Reg. § 25.2511–1(h)(5). The respective contributions of the joint tenants are irrelevant to this determination. Federal law, in this respect, is merely recognizing the fact that under state law either joint tenant may sever the joint tenancy and transfer his one-half interest without the consent of the other tenant. See Reg. § 25.2515–2(b)(1); ¶ 11,067 and 11,275. (*Note:* If the respective interests of the joint tenants in the property at the time of acquisition were not proportional to their respective contributions to the purchase price, gift tax returns should have been filed to reflect the fact that one tenant made a gift to the other.) Therefore, if upon termination, each joint tenant receives one-half of the property, there will be no gift tax consequences. See Reg. § 25.2515–4(b). If either joint tenant receives more or less, a taxable gift will have been made by the tenant receiving less than one-half.

Termination of a joint tenancy does not constitute a sale or exchange under § 1001. Revenue Ruling 56–437, 1956–2 C.B. 507, concludes that a partition of jointly owned property is not a sale or exchange because the co-owners of the joint property sever their joint interests but do not acquire a new or additional interest as a result.

[¶ 11,659]

2. JOINT BANK ACCOUNTS

Where the property being divided is a joint bank account, different rules will be employed. At the time the account was established, the interests of the respective co-owners for federal gift tax purposes are deemed to be proportionate to their contributions. See Reg. § 25.2511–1(h)(4).

A gift from one co-owner to the other is recognized only when a co-owner draws from the account an amount in excess of his contribution. Stephens, et al., *supra* ¶ 11,241, at ¶ 10.01[5][c]. Moreover, there is a taxable gift only if a direct payment of the amount withdrawn would have been a gift. Thus, where a dependent withdraws funds from the joint account to apply against necessaries there would be no gift. Rudick, Federal Tax Problems Relating to Property Owned in Joint Tenancy and Tenancy by the Entirety, 4 Tax L. Rev. 3, 21 (1948).

Summarizing, any division of the joint account other than in proportion to the respective contributions of the co-owners results in the imposition of the federal gift tax on the amount by which each co-owner's distribution exceeds the portion of the account attributable to his contribution.

J. TERMINATION OF SPOUSAL JOINT INTERESTS DURING LIFE

[¶ 11,701]

Termination of spousal joint interest during the lifetime of the spouses are free of gift tax consequences because of the unlimited marital deduction available under § 2523 for transfers between spouses.

K. JOINT TENANCIES AND TRUSTS

[¶ 11,751]

1. INTRODUCTION

Trusts are employed in almost every estate plan for both tax and nontax reasons. In planning for jointly held property, however, the trust has limited utility so long as the property remains in joint ownership. The only reason for employing trusts to hold jointly owned property would be for purposes of providing property management during the joint lives of the co-owners. Moreover, such trusts should have appeal only in those cases where the co-owners are reluctant to bring about a lifetime split of the property and insist upon retention of joint beneficial interests in the property.

Property management can be an important consideration. Increasing longevity heightens fears of senility and other mental or physical disability. Where these considerations are present, a trust is clearly preferable to an agency or custody account because the trust may provide for the ultimate disposition of the property and provide protection against incompetency, as well as provide current professional management. For discussion, see ¶ 4251.

Nothing about jointly held property makes an irrevocable trust a particularly attractive or a particularly unattractive receptacle for such property. See ¶ 11,759 and 11,767. However, use of the more common revocable trust to hold jointly held property may sometimes provide a tax advantage (in addition to yielding the other benefits associated with revocable trusts), the tax advantage comes because at least one court has concluded that placing jointly held property in a revocable trust will frustrate the consideration furnished test of § 2040. See ¶ 11,783. Some would say that the revocable trust must become partially irrevocable at the death of the first joint tenant to die in order to realize the full potential inherent in the planning possibilities. See ¶ 11,815. The portion that becomes irrevocable would be held for the benefit of the survivor for life, and, under a properly drafted agreement, the property subject to the irrevocable portion of the trust would be excluded from the survivor's gross estate.

[¶ 11,759]

2. THE IRREVOCABLE TRUST: ESTATE TAX CONSEQUENCES

Generally speaking, while there are many reasons why a taxpayer would want to establish an irrevocable trust, the fact that he or she has jointly held property is a neutral factor.

Where jointly held property is transferred to an irrevocable trust and the transferors retain joint life estates in the trust, one-half of the trust property will be included in the estate of the first of the joint owners to die. See Rev. Rul. 69–577, 1969–2 C.B. 173; cf. United States v. Heasty, 370 F.2d 525 (10th Cir.1966) (transfer of joint tenancy with right of survivorship property to children and grandchildren subject to retained life estate); Glaser v. United States, 306 F.2d 57 (7th Cir.1962) (transfer of tenancy by the entirety property to children subject to retained life estate). The Tenth Circuit explained in *Heasty* at 528–529:

> [S]ection 2040 has no application to a case like this because after the husband and wife took the property as joint tenants there was another transfer.* * * Each spouse individually conveyed some interest to their [sic] children and grandchildren. Whatever law we apply to this case, we cannot say that the wife had no interest to convey because she did have; and she did convey it. She transferred a one-half "interest" in the property. The husband cannot be said to have transferred that "interest." They cannot both own it.* * * The "interest" contemplated by § 2036 must, in a case like the one at bar, be determined according to the state law.

All efforts by the IRS to include all the property that was once jointly held in the estate of the co-owner who had provided all of the consideration for the property were rejected. Both the Tenth and Seventh Circuits reasoned that § 2040 was limited in application to property held jointly *at the time of death* and that it would not otherwise be applied.

The fact that the first joint tenant to die made no contribution to the jointly held property has been deemed irrelevant. See Miller v. United States, 325 F.Supp. 1287 (E.D.Pa.1971). This result can be explained on the grounds that each joint tenant has an interest in the property under state law, and it is that interest which has been conveyed in trust subject to retained joint life estates. From the taxpayer's standpoint this result was preferable to having all of the jointly held property included in the estate of the first of the joint tenants to die, which would have been the result, under the rule applicable at the time these cases were decided, if the transfers in trust had not been made. Thus, escape from the consideration furnished test of § 2040(a) is easily realized through an irrevocable trust. However, escaping § 2040 is an unlikely goal of married joint tenants inasmuch as their jointly held property will be treated as Qualified Joint Interests pursuant to § 2040(b). Such treatment will produce the same estate tax treatment as transfer to an irrevocable trust. However, it may be comforting to note that abandoning Qualified Joint Interest treatment by transferring the jointly held property to an irrevocable trust will be estate tax neutral.

[¶ 11,767]

3. THE IRREVOCABLE TRUST: GIFT TAX CONSEQUENCES

While it is relatively easy to generalize about the estate tax consequences of establishing an irrevocable trust for jointly held property, similar generalization is not possible with respect to federal gift tax consequences. These can only be considered in terms of the kinds of property subject to the gift and when the property was acquired.

Assume, for example, that Bert and Barbara, longtime companions, established an irrevocable trust which provides that they are each to have equal rights in the trust income for their joint lives and that, after the death of one of them, the survivor is to receive all the trust income. The trust is to terminate at the death of the survivor of Bert and Barbara and the trust property is to be distributed to Barbara's child, Chloe. Assume Bert and Barbara are ages 50 and 47, respectively, at the time the trust was established.

Example 1. Bert contributed all the funds to purchase common stock in ABC corporation which is now worth $20,000 and is held by Bert and Barbara as *joint tenants with right of survivorship*. The stock is transferred to Bert and Barbara's irrevocable trust at the time it is established.

1. In this case Bert will be deemed to have made a taxable gift of one-half of the property less the actuarially determined value of the life estate that he has retained in the property.

2. Bert's gift is to Chloe, who gets the remainder interest, and to Barbara, who gets a contingent interest in Bert's half of the income if Bert predeceases Barbara.

3. Barbara will be deemed to have made a similar gift to Bert and Chloe except that the actuarial values used in determining the value of her retained life estate may be different from Bert's.

4. Interestingly, the gifts from Bert to Barbara and Barbara to Bert can be netted against each other so that only one will actually pay gift tax. See Rev. Rul. 69–505, 1969–2 C.B. 179; Rev. Rul. 76–157, 1976–1 C.B. 306. This netting actually provides a "tax break" for the transferor-spouses by reducing their total gift tax liability (and it will not increase their estate tax liability). Revenue Ruling 69–505, 1969–2 C.B. 179, is illustrative. Modifying the ruling only by substituting "Bert" and "Barbara" for "A" and "B" (the terms which appeared in the ruling), the computations in the ruling are presented in Table 11.2.

¶ 11,767

Table 11.2. Illustration Based on Rev. Rul. 69–505

Donor Bert:	
One-half value of property	$10,000.00
Less retained rights ($10,000.00 x factor 0.51970)	5,197.00
. . . .	$4,803.00
Property transferred:	
(a) to Barbara—$10,000 x factor 0.11731	$1,173.10
(b) to Chloe—$10,000 x factor 0.36299	3,629.90
. . . .	$4,803.00
Donor Barbara:	
One-half value of property	$10,000.00
Less retained rights ($10,000 x factor 0.55436)	5,543.60
. . . .	$4,456.40
Property transferred:	
(a) to Bert—$10,000 x factor 0.08265	$826.50
(b) to Chloe—$10,000 x factor 0.36299	3,629.90
. . . .	$4,456.40

RECAPITULATION

	Donor Bert	Donor Barbara
Transfer to Chloe	$3,629.90	$3,629.00
Net transfer to other joint tenant	346.60	–0–
Total gifts made by parties	$3,976.50	$3,629.90

Explanatory Notes:

1. The .51970 factor for Bert and the .55436 factor for Barbara are the entries for ages 50 and 47, respectively, in Reg. § 25.2512–5A(b), Table I, column 3 (which is based on a factor of 3 ½ %) applicable to transfers before January 1, 1971. Reg. § 25.2511–1(f) directed the use of this table at the time Revenue Ruling 69–505 was issued. Reg. § 25.2512–5 has been amended a number of times in the intervening years to reflect different interest rate and mortality assumptions. If Revenue Ruling 69–505 was being prepared currently, the applicable actuarial factors would be found in Reg. § 20.2031–7(d)(7), based on the interest rate found in Reg. § 20.7520–1(b)(1) for the transfer date.

2. The .36299 factor is the present value of $1.000 under the 3 ½ tables that Chloe will receive in the future after Bert and Barbara are both expected to be dead. This factor is taken from the tables showing the present worth of $1 due at the death of the survivor of two persons which are published by the IRS in Publication 11 (5/59), "Actuarial Value for Estate and Gift Tax." Reg. § 20.2031–7(d)(1) and (2)(iii).

3. The .11731 factor is the present worth under the 3 ½ tables of the right to receive the income from $1.00 for the period of time that Barbara is expected to survive Bert. The .11731 factor used in determining Bert's gift to Barbara is developed by subtracting the value of Bert's retained interest (.51970) and the value of Bert's gift to Chloe (.36299) from 1 (1.00—(.51970 + .36299)). The .08265 factor is determined in the same manner. Under the rationale of Revenue Ruling 69–505, Bert is deemed to have transferred to Barbara an interest in property valued at $1,173.10 and Barbara has transferred to Bert an interest valued at $826.50. Since the gift by Barbara is less than the gift by Bert, Bert is deemed to have made a gift to Barbara of the difference in the amount of $346.60. This gift qualifies for the $10,000 per donee per annum exclusion. § 2503(b).

4. The gift to Chloe will not qualify for the $10,000 annual exclusion since not a present interest. Reg. § 25.2503–3(a).

5. The gift to Barbara may qualify for the gift tax marital deduction as a QTIP, if Bert and Barbara are married to one another. See § 2523(e).

6. The taxpayer may be in the unfortunate situation of paying a second gift tax. If Bert's contingent life estate were smaller than Barbara's (so there would be a gift from Barbara to Bert) and Bert originally put up all of the funds and paid the gift tax, then when the trust is set up, Barbara will have to pay a gift tax for the privilege of giving Bert's property back to him. See Reg. § 25.2515–4(b).

¶ 11,767

Problem

[¶ 11,771]

How would the conclusions suggested by the foregoing illustration involving Bert and Barbara apply in the following cases:

(a) Assume Bert and Barbara are husband and wife and that they transfer the following kinds of property held as *joint tenants with right of survivorship* (and not as tenants by the entirety) to an irrevocable trust:

> (1) Personal property, some acquired in 1954 and some in 1973 (except bank accounts and United States Savings Bonds).

> (2) All real property acquired before 1955 and after 1981.

> (3) Real property acquired after 1954 but before 1982 for which gift tax returns were filed to report the gift of one-half interest from Bert to Barbara.

Example 2. Bert provided all of the consideration to purchase Neuteracre; the title was taken by Bert and Barbara, who are husband and wife, for purposes of this example, as *tenants by the entirety.* Neuteracre is transferred to Bert and Barbara's irrevocable trust at the time the trust is established. At that time Neuteracre has a value of $20,000.

1. Because neither Bert nor Barbara can unilaterally terminate the tenancy by entirety, the valuation of their interests must take into account the life expectancies of Bert and Barbara. The first step is to calculate the value of the respective interests of Bert and Barbara in the trust using Table IX (tenancy by the entirety) from IRS Publication 11, "Actuarial Tables for Estate & Gift Tax," which are based on the 3 1/2% interest assumptions for a spouse 50 years old:

Value of property transferred	$20,000
Less: Value of Bert's interest ($20,000 x 46207)	9,241
Value of Barbara's interest	$10,759

2. Bert will then be deemed to have made a taxable gift of $9,241 (rather than one-half of the corpus as in the previous example) to Barbara and Chloe less the actuarially determined value of the life estate he retained in the $9,241. Reg. § 25.2512–9 (applicable to transfers between December 31, 1971 and December 1, 1983). Barbara's taxable gift to Bert and Chloe will be deemed to be $10,759 less the actuarially determined value of her retained life estate in the $10,759.

Problem

[¶ 11,772]

Describe the tax consequences in cases where the following kinds of property held as *tenants by the entirety* are transferred to an irrevocable trust:

(a) Personal property, some acquired in 1953 and some in 1974.

(b) Real property, some acquired before 1955 and some after 1981.

(c) Real property acquired in 1957 for which gift tax returns were filed reporting the gift from Bert to Barbara when the property was taken as tenants by the entirety.

Example 3. Bert and Barbara, who are *not* married to each other, have $20,000 in a bank account which they own as joint tenants with right of survivorship. Bert made the entire deposit from his separate property, and neither tenant had made any withdrawals from the account. No gift tax return has been filed to cover the establishment of the account. The funds in the account were transferred to Bert and Barbara's irrevocable trust when it was established.

1. Bert would be deemed to have made a taxable gift of the full $20,000 to Barbara and Chloe less the actuarially determined value of his retained life estate in one-half of the transferred property. See Reg. § 25.2511–1(h)(4).

2. However, the gift to Barbara may qualify as a QTIP in the case where Bert and Barbara are married to each other. See § 2523(e).

3. Barbara would incur no gift tax liability.

Problems

[¶ 11,773]

1. What principles are applicable where the following kinds of property are transferred to an irrevocable trust:

(a) Bank accounts or United States Savings Bonds held as joint tenants with right of survivorship.

(b) Real property acquired after 1954, for which no gift tax return was filed, which is held either as joint tenants with right of survivorship, or tenants by the entirety.

2. Despite the obvious complexities involved in determining the federal gift tax consequences of establishing an irrevocable trust for jointly held property—and despite some uncertainty as to specific points—do you agree that the gift tax considerations, in and of themselves, do *not* argue against the irrevocable trust for jointly held property?

[¶ 11,775]

4. THE REVOCABLE TRUST: INTRODUCTION

The revocable trust is an appealing management concept. The creator of such a trust parts with no real dominion over the property, yet by a judicious selection of a trustee, the creator can obtain professional property management. See Chapter 2.

[¶ 11,783]

5. *ESTATE OF HORNOR* CONTRASTED WITH *BLACK*

Where *nonspousal* jointly held property is made the subject of a revocable trust, the estate tax consequences are somewhat unpredictable and definitely less appealing than those associated with an irrevocable trust. (It is assumed that the trust will continue to be revocable until both joint tenants are dead.) An analysis of several cases will suggest this conclusion and also focus on the underlying policy consideration.

In Estate of Hornor v. Commissioner, 130 F.2d 649 (3d Cir.1942), aff'g 44 B.T.A. 1136 (1941), accord, Estate of Derby v. Commissioner, 20 T.C. 164 (1953), the trust was expressly revocable but only with the consent of both joint tenants. Neither could revoke the trust acting alone. By its terms the trust became irrevocable upon the death of the first to die of the joint tenants. The court included the full value of the property in the estate of decedent, who was the first of the joint tenants to die, because the decedent was found to have provided all the consideration. (This result was reached by application of § 302(e) of the Revenue Act of 1926, the forerunner of § 2040(a). It was decided before the advent of § 2040(b), the special rule applicable to joint property held by persons married to each other.) The court based its conclusion on the ground that the trust lacked substance because it was revocable.

The *Black* case, reprinted below, is of significance for several reasons. On one hand, the court's decision could be said to emphasize form over substance (in holding that the simple act of transferring joint property to a trust puts the joint property beyond the reach of § 2040). On the other hand, focus must be on the joint trust scheme used by the spouses. The revocable trust was part of an effort to provide not only for the ultimate disposition of their property (including their joint property) using a tax-advantaged plan based on the unlimited marital deduction offered by § 2056 but also to provide a vehicle for lifetime management of that property. Obviously, the scheme implemented was based on one-size-fits-all, but it was not intended to be in any way abusive of the tax system. Consider, then, whether the Black trust would be appropriate for most taxpayers (inasmuch as many taxpayers have property arrangements similar to those of the Blacks).

¶ 11,783

[¶ 11,785]

BLACK v. COMMISSIONER

United States Court of Appeals, Ninth Circuit, 1985.
765 F.2d 862.

CANBY, C.J.: * * * The issue is whether the entire value of the assets formerly held in joint tenancy by the decedent and his spouse, less the contribution of the surviving spouse, should be included in the gross estate under § 2040, even though the assets were transferred shortly before the decedent's death into a revocable trust that modified the surviving spouse's right of survivorship. We hold that the creation of the trust severed the joint tenancy and placed the surviving spouse's share of the trust assets beyond the reach of § 2040. To that extent we reverse the Tax Court judgment.

The Blacks lived in Sun City, Arizona.* * * Among their assets they held a number of securities as joint tenants.

On June 10, 1977, Mr. and Mrs. Black created the Black Revocable Trust. The trust agreement named the Blacks as trustees. Under the agreement, the trust corpus consisted of "all property listed in Schedule A, Husband's Separate Property and Schedule B, Wife's Separate Property, attached to this agreement.* * *" During their joint lives, the Blacks retained unrestricted rights to all trust principal and income. They also reserved a joint power to amend or revoke the trust.

The trust agreement provided that, upon the death of the first spouse to die, the trust assets would be divided into two separate trusts, the "Survivor's Trust" and the "Decedent's Trust." The agreement allocated to the Survivor's Trust the "Surviving Trustor's separate property and the Surviving Trustor's interest in community property," plus the amount necessary to obtain the maximum marital deduction. The remainder of the assets was allocated to the Decedent's Trust.

With respect to the Survivor's Trust, the surviving spouse was given an unfettered right to all principal and income, and a general power of appointment. She also could amend or revoke the trust. With respect to the Decedent's Trust, however, the surviving spouse had fewer rights. The surviving spouse and the Black's daughter. Dorothy Gayle Standish, were co-beneficiaries entitled to discretionary distributions of principal and income. The trust agreement provided that the trustee "shall consider the respective needs of the beneficiaries" in determining whether to make distributions from the Decedent's Trust, and limited the power to invade principal to those amounts necessary for the health, education, and reasonable support of the beneficiaries. Although the agreement designated the surviving spouse as trustee, it prohibited her from "participat(ing) in any decision to invade principal for * * * her benefit." The decision to invade principal was vested in a co-trustee or successor trustee other than the surviving trustor. The surviving spouse had a special power of appointment over the remaining principal and accumulated income.

¶ 11,785

Four days after the creation of the Black Revocable Trust, the Blacks took their jointly held securities to a bank and had the securities reissued to them as trustees. On the same day, they executed the two schedules to which the trust agreement referred, entitled "Schedule A—Husband's Separate Property" and "Schedule B—Wife's Separate Property." Each of the two schedules listed approximately half of the jointly owned securities. On Schedule A, the Blacks in their capacity as trustees acknowledged the receipt of "the above described assets of RICHARD H. BLACK." On Schedule B, the Blacks in their capacity as trustees acknowledged the receipt of "the above described assets of PHYLLIS M. BLACK."

Mr. Black died on August 2, 1977. On that date, the trust contained the securities listed on Schedule A and Schedule B without any additions or subtractions. On the estate tax return filed on Mr. Black's behalf, Schedule G—"Transfers During Decedent's Life"—included only the assets listed on Schedule A of the Black Revocable Trust as Mr. Black's separate property. The assets listed on Schedule B as Mrs. Black's separate property were not reported on the return. In his notice of deficiency, the Commissioner determined that the Blacks held both the Schedule A assets and the Schedule B assets as joint tenants on the date of Mr. Black's death. Accordingly, he included the entire value of the trust assets, less the contribution of the surviving spouse, in the gross estate pursuant to § 2040.

[The Tax Court] * * * concluded that the transfer of the securities to the trust "was ineffective, for Federal estate tax purposes, to sever the joint tenancy." *Id.* at 17. Nowhere did the court refer to general common-law joint tenancy principles or the Arizona law of joint tenancy. * * *

* * * Here we must interpret § 2040 to determine whether the assets held by Mr. and Mrs. Black in the Black Revocable Trust constitute "interest(s) * * * held as joint tenants with right of survivorship by the decedent and any other person." State law—in this instance the law of Arizona— defines the powers that the Blacks could exercise over the trust property. Arizona law, however, does not control our ultimate determination. If the statutory language expresses a Congressional purpose to tax the decedent's interest, that interest is includable in the decedent's gross estate regardless of whether state law would label it a "joint tenancy" interest. * * *

Although Arizona law does not tell us what Congress meant in referring to joint tenancy, general joint tenancy principles guide our interpretation of the statutory language.* * * The common law has firmly established the meaning of the term "joint tenants with right of survivorship." Among the rules defining the term are those which determine how a joint tenancy is severed or destroyed. Those rules are the same in Arizona as elsewhere. We believe that the tax court erred when it construed § 2040 in contradiction of those rules.

The common law governing severance of joint tenancies is relatively simple. Joint tenants can end a joint tenancy by express agreement. They can also sever the estate by implication if they enter into a contract the terms of which are inconsistent with the continued existence of the joint tenancy. Since the distinguishing feature of a joint tenancy is the right of survivorship, a contract which modifies the right of survivorship severs the joint tenancy relationship.* * *

According to these rules, the creation of the Black Revocable Trust severed the joint tenancy in the trust assets. Arguably the express terms of the trust agreement were sufficient to destroy the joint tenancy, since the Blacks listed the securities that they contributed to the trust as their respective separate property. But even if the Blacks did not sever their joint tenancy holdings merely by dividing them and labeling them "separate," they clearly did so by mutually agreeing to alter the right of survivorship. Under the trust agreement, the surviving spouse shares with her daughter the income interest in the one-half of the securities allocated to the Decedent's Trust. She may not invade the principal of the Decedent's Trust except at the discretion of an independent trustee. Upon her death, she may exercise only a special power of appointment over the remaining trust principal and accumulated income. These provisions substantially diminish the undisputed right of ownership that the surviving spouse would otherwise have acquired at the death of her husband. By including them in the trust agreement, the Blacks created a property interest that the common law would not characterize as a joint tenancy.

The Commissioner suggests that the decedent's interest in the trust assets so closely resembled a joint tenancy that Congress must have intended to tax it as if it were in fact a joint tenancy. But we have previously rejected the notion that Congress intended § 2040 to apply where joint tenants have severed a joint tenancy under state law and taken the property in another form of joint ownership. In Sullivan's Estate v. Commissioner, 175 F.2d 657 (9th Cir. 1949), two joint tenants had agreed to terminate their joint tenancy ownership and to hold their property as tenants in common. Even though each co-owner retained substantial rights in the property, including unlimited lifetime rights of management and control and the undisputed right to direct the disposition of half of the property at death, we summarily rejected the idea that the predecessor of § 2040 justified the inclusion of the entire value of the property in a co-owner's gross estate. We reasoned that "the joint tenancy was terminated (by the agreement to sever) before the husband's death. Hence, as to the joint tenancy, the deceased had no "interest therein * * * at the time of his death." *Id.* at 660.

Sullivan applied the established rules of joint tenancy severance even though Congress had specifically provided that an analogous transfer of an outright ownership interest would not have removed the transferred property from the decedent's gross estate. The decedent in *Sullivan* terminated the joint tenancy in contemplation of his death. *Id.* At that time, the gross estate included property "to the extent of any interest therein of which the decedent has at any time made a transfer" in contemplation of death. But we refused to hold that the severance of the joint tenancy constituted a taxable "transfer," even though the effect of the severance was to reduce the decedent's estate at his death by one-half of the value of the property. We stated that "(t)here was no compulsion on the co-tenants to continue the joint tenancy so that (a) taxable event would occur." *Id.* at 659.

¶ 11,785

Other federal appellate courts have similarly declined to hold that Congress intended to create a federal concept of joint tenancy where a decedent has severed a joint tenancy and acquired a different property interest with similar characteristics.* * *

The Commissioner argues that the *Sullivan* line of cases should be distinguished on the ground that none of them involved a revocable trust like the one that the decedent here established. The Commissioner contends, and the tax court held, that the revocation clause in the trust agreement makes the trust assets includable under § 2040. Hornor's Estate v. Commissioner, 44 B.T.A. 1136 (1941), aff'd 130 F.2d 649 (3d Cir. 1942), and Estate of Derby v. Commissioner, 20 T.C. 164 (1953), support that position. In *Hornor*, the decedent and his wife owned a large number of parcels of land as tenants by the entirety. The spouses conveyed their jointly held property to a trust, naming themselves and their son as trustees. The trust provided that the co-owners would manage the property as an investment and pay the net income to the spouses "jointly" during their joint lives and then to the survivor. The spouses retained a joint power of revocation, but the trust became irrevocable upon the death of either spouse. A distribution of property among the couple's beneficiaries, upon the death of the surviving spouse, was specified in the trust agreement. The Tax Court held that the entire value of the trust property was includable in the decedent's gross estate, even though his wife survived him. On appeal, the Third Circuit affirmed on the ground that "the transfer to the trustees * * * was squarely within the provisions of [the predecessor of § 2040]," without further explanation. 130 F.2d at 651. *Derby* followed *Hornor* on very similar facts.

Neither the logic of the Commissioner's position nor the above authority on which he relies is persuasive. In the first place, if "revocability" distinguished taxable transfers of joint tenancy property from non-taxable ones, § 2040 would apply whenever joint tenants sever their joint tenancy and take a tenancy in common or some other form of joint ownership. Owners of jointly held property can always change the form of ownership of the property by agreement among themselves.* * * Thus former joint tenants who hold as tenants in common can "revoke" the severance at any time and resume the joint tenancy. In light of *Sullivan*, we cannot read the statute so broadly that it would tax this kind of "revocable" tenancy in common.

Furthermore, the Board of Tax Appeals in *Hornor*, in reaching the conclusion that a revocable transfer of joint tenancy property does not remove the transferred property from the gross estate, used reasoning that *Sullivan* subsequently rejected. Under § 2038, the gross estate includes the value of property "to the extent of any interest therein of which the decedent has at any time made a (revocable) transfer." *Hornor* permits the government to disregard a revocable transfer of joint tenancy property to a trust because § 2038 would prevent an individual property owner from avoiding the estate tax by making a similar transfer. *Sullivan*, however, does not allow the government to ignore the severance of a joint tenancy on the ground that the decedent accomplished the severance in contemplation of his death.* * * We would create a square conflict with those precedents were we to hold that a revocable transfer of joint tenancy property does not sever the joint tenancy for purposes of federal tax law, and that § 2040 therefore includes the entire value of the property in the gross estate.

We conclude that the trust agreement, as given effect by Arizona law, placed severe limits on the right of the surviving spouse to exercise control over the trust property. This modification of the right of survivorship, which the common law regards as a severance of the joint tenancy, removed the trust property from the reach of § 2040, for the Blacks did not hold the property as "joint tenants with right of survivorship" within the meaning of that statute. The Tax Court therefore erred in including the entire property, minus the survivor's contributions, in the decedent's estate. Only the decedent's interest under the trust agreement should have been included.

REVERSED.

[¶ 11,791]

6.   *ESTATE OF JULIA CRAWFORD HORNOR*

The Hornor trust generated more litigation when Mrs. Hornor died some years later. The trust had become irrevocable upon Mr. Hornor's death and continued by its terms for Mrs. Hornor's life. The court held in Estate of J.C. Hornor v. Commissioner, 305 F.2d 769 (3d Cir.1962), aff'g 36 T.C. 337 (1961), acq. 1969–2 C.B. XXIV, that one-half value of the trust should be included in Julia's estate on the grounds that she had retained a life estate in the trust property. Here, the case was not one of disregarding the trust but recognizing it and applying § 811(c) of the 1939 Code, the forerunner of § 2036.

Problem

[¶ 11,796]

Is it possible to find a basis on which to reconcile the court's position in Mrs. Hornor's case with the position taken in her husband's case?

[¶ 11,799]

7.   THE REVOCABLE TRUST: GIFT TAX CONSEQUENCES

Establishment of a trust which remains revocable until the death of both joint tenants has no federal gift tax consequences. See Reg. § 25.2511–2(b) and (c).

[¶ 11,807]

8.   THE REVOCABLE TRUST: INCOME TAX CONSEQUENCES

The federal income tax disregards revocable trusts and imputes the income from such a trust to the settlor. See § 676; Rev. Rul. 66–283, 1966–2 C.B. 297; Rev. Rul. 66–159, 1966–1 C.B. 162.

[¶ 11,815]

9. THE PARTIALLY REVOCABLE TRUST

The plan utilized in *Black,* ¶ 11,785, is that of a taxpayer who does not want to split jointly held property while both joint tenants are living but wants to do some tax planning and also seeks professional management for the joint property. The *Black* plan called for the establishment of a revocable trust to which the jointly held property was transferred. The trust agreement contained special provisions that made the trust become partially irrevocable on the death of the first to die of the joint tenants. The portion of the trust that became irrevocable was that portion of the trust which was in excess of the amount of the trust property necessary to eliminate any federal estate tax from the estate of the first to die. For a discussion, see R. Campfield, Estate Planning for Joint Tenancy, 1974 Duke L.J. 669.

L. COMMUNITY PROPERTY AND TRUSTS

[¶ 11,851]

The joint trust as used in *Black* has been said to be a staple of planning for community property. See R. Covitt, A. Fink, N. Howard, & C. Larson, Drafting California Revocable Living Trusts (J. Cohan ed., 2d ed. 1984).

M. WIDOW'S ELECTION RULES

[¶ 11,901]

1. INTRODUCTION

Widow's election wills are a device whose use has largely been confined to community property jurisdictions. The device, particularly when referred to by its common name of "widow's election," both by name and design, is a reflection of the male chauvinism of an earlier time.

To understand the widow's election device, you must remember that each spouse is deemed to own one-half of the community property that has come into being during the marriage. As owner, each spouse has the right to dispose of his or her own one-half of the community property at deathtime. (Disposition of community property during the lifetime of the spouses is complicated by issues involving rights of management and is beyond the scope of this chapter.) Thus, for example, the husband, H, can only dispose of his one-half of the community property at his death. Much as he might like to dispose of, or at least control the disposition of, his spouse's one-half, he cannot do so *directly!* See ¶ 11,113. Can he then do *indirectly* that which he can't do *directly?* The widow's election device gives him that opportunity.

Suppose H wishes to take advantage of the widow's election device. In that case, H will include a provision in his will (or perhaps in a so-called living or revocable trust) offering his spouse, W, a life estate in his one-half of the community property if W, in return, will transfer her one-half of the community property to another trust which H has created in his will (or revocable trust during his lifetime) to receive W's one-half of the community property. This way, H controls the disposition of W's one-half of the community property. If W declines H's offer, H's will or revocable trust might provide that she is to take no part of his one-half of the community property. The nontax advantages of this scheme to H are obvious. The tax advantages will be explored below. Suffice it to say that Judge Wisdom has described the widow's election device as a "taxpayer's utopia." Estate of L.B. Vardell v. Commissioner, 307 F.2d 688, 694–700 (5th Cir.1962). But that was before Congress provided for the unlimited marital deduction, thereby making all interspousal transfers tax free. (As a result, you will want to consider whether the widow's election device has lost its tax appeal.)

Widow's election wills are described as either "forced" or "voluntary." The forced election was described in the preceding paragraph. The voluntary widow's election consists of only an invitation to the surviving spouse to transfer her one-half of the community property to the decedent's trust. Unlike the forced election, the voluntary election is not accompanied by a penalty provision.

[¶ 11,909]

2. THE FORCED WIDOW'S ELECTION WILL

a. Dispositive Scheme

In a typical situation, one of the spouses, who will be referred to as H for purposes of this illustration, devises his interest in the family residence and tangible personal property to his spouse, W, free of any election. This is to insure that the surviving spouse will have the family residence and furniture and automobile, even if circumstances require her to refuse the widow's election. H's will then provides for disposition of the entire balance of the community estate in the following manner:

First, H's one-half community share (after taxes and administration expenses) is to be held in trust (the B trust) for W with the remainder to the children. W is to get all the income, and the trustee may be given invasion powers exercisable only in favor of W. W can also be given a special or limited power of appointment, but not a general power of appointment. (The tax objective here is to avoid inclusion of H's one-half of the community property in W's estate and possible double taxation. See § 2041.)

Then, W's one-half of the community property is directed into another trust (the A trust) which gives her the income for life with remainder to the children. No invasion powers over the corpus or testamentary power of appointment, either general or special, can be given to W or to the trustee. See Estate of Steinman v. Commissioner, 69 T.C. 804 (1978). The benefits of the widow's election will can be obtained only if W can truly be said to have relinquished her rights to that property.

[¶ 11,917]

b. Forced Election

H's will goes on to require that W must make an election either to claim her one-half of the community property under the applicable law of the community property jurisdiction or to allow her property to pass under H's will. If W declines to elect to allow her property to pass under H's will, H's will stipulates that she forfeits the life estate in the B trust.

[¶ 11,925]

3. GIFT TAX CONSEQUENCES TO SPOUSE

The widow's election by W to relinquish her one-half of the community property for a life estate in H's one-half of the community property constitutes an immediate taxable gift in cases where the value of the remainder interest given up by W in her one-half of the community property exceeds the value of the life estate H provided for W in his one-half of the community property. However, where the life estate provided for W exceeds the value of the remainder interest W gives to the children, there will be no gift tax consequences.

What is happening is that W is making a transfer for consideration. Her transfer will be deemed to be a gift only to the extent to which the value of the remainder interest that she transfers exceeds the value of the life estate, i.e., the consideration that W received in return. See § 2512.

The values of the life estate and the remainder interest are computed by using actuarial tables provided in Reg. § 20.2031–7(d).

Example. For discussion purposes, assume that the gross value of the community estate subject to the election will is $2 million; that W's share is $1 million; that H's share (after reduction for taxes and administration expenses of $25,000) is $975,000; and that W is 50 years old at the time of H's death and W's election to take under the will. Under Table S of Reg. § 20.2031–7(d)(6), assuming the "applicable federal rate" is 6 percent, the factor for valuing a life estate held by a 50–year-old woman is .77491. Reg. § 20.2031–7(d)(2)(iii). The value of the life estate is calculated by multiplying this factor by the trust corpus. The factor for valuing the remainder interest following a life estate held by a 50–year-old woman is .22509. The remainder interest is then calculated by multiplying this factor (.22509) by the value of the corpus. (These computations can also be made with Steve Leimberg's Financial Calculator. See Appendix A.)

Using the actuarial valuation for the property transferred, W's gift of the remainder interest in the A trust is valued at $225,090 ($1,000,000 x .22509). However, W is entitled to a "consideration offset" for the value of the life estate in the B trust that she received in exchange for making the transfer of her remainder interest in her one-half of the community property. See § 2512(b). In the example given, W's life estate in the B trust is valued at $755,537 ($975,000 x .77491). Since the life estate ($755,537) W received in the B trust is greater than the $225,090 remainder interest she transferred, there is no gift tax because of the consideration offset.

Problem

[¶ 11,930]

In its traditional form, the widow's election requires the surviving spouse to transfer all of his or her half of the community property to the trust provided for by the deceased spouse. In this form, the deceased spouse can be seen as wanting not only the tax advantages that are said to flow from the widow's election, but also to control the disposition of both halves of the community. Clearly, there will be some spouses who consider the widow's election solely for the tax advantages. In such a case, would it be appropriate to insist that the surviving spouse contribute to the trust provided for by the deceased spouse only that amount necessary to maximize the tax advantages of the widow's election? Refer to the example of H and W in text and consider the tax consequences if H's will contained the following widow's election formula provision:

> The value of the property to be placed in the A trust shall be equal in value to the value, at the date of my death, of the income from the B trust (including so much of the community property interest of W as is included therein) for the life expectancy of W, based on the life expectancy tables in use by the Commissioner of the Internal Revenue Service on the date of my death.

Would the necessary computation be relatively easy or relatively hard to make? Look to Reg. § 20.2031–7(d)(2)(iii).

4. ESTATE TAX CONSEQUENCES TO THE SURVIVING SPOUSE

[¶ 11,933]

ESTATE OF VARDELL v. COMMISSIONER

United States Court of Appeals, Fifth Circuit, 1962.
307 F.2d 688.

GRIFFIN B. BELL, Circuit Judge.

This is an estate tax case. It is an appeal by the taxpayer from an adverse decision of the Tax Court. 35 T.C. 50.

Lela Barry Vardell died on September 12, 1955. Her husband, T.W. Vardell, died testate on February 27, 1934. They were domiciled in Texas and all of his property was community property. He put his wife, the decedent here, to an election under his will, either to retain her community one-half interest and receive no part of his estate, or to allow her community one-half interest to be governed by the terms of his will and to receive specified benefits thereunder.

In the latter event, the husband, by Item Two of his will, bequeathed to his wife all of the community property, which, of course, was only his one-half therein "for the term of her life, and so long as she shall remain a widow, she to have, during such time, full and absolute authority to handle, manage, sell, and in any manner dispose of said properties, or any part thereof, and to invest and reinvest any proceeds received from the sale of any part of said properties.* * * "

* * *

Legal title to the remainder interest in the whole of the community passed under the will to Trustees. The beneficiaries under the trust were the two daughters of Mr. and Mrs. Vardell and their lineal descendants.

Decedent elected to take under the will of her husband. A gift tax return was filed by her on the contribution made as a result of the election, and taxes in the amount of $6,617.50 were paid. At the conclusion of the administration of the estate of the husband in 1935 all of the community assets were turned over to decedent and she managed these assets during her lifetime, receiving all of the income therefrom.* * * At her death the remaining community assets passed to the trust under the terms of the will of her husband. At the date decedent elected to take under the will the total value of the whole of the community was $2,304,564.68, attributable, because of taxes and other expenses allocable to the estate of the husband at his death, 53.8 percent to her interest in the community assets, and 46.16 percent to the interest of her husband.

The value of the whole of the community property remaining undisposed of at the time of the death of the widow, valued as of a date one year thereafter, was $3,972,582.99, of which $2,138,838.68 (53.84%) was attributable to the share of Mrs. Vardell. None of the value of this property was included in the Federal estate tax return filed as being in her gross estate. The Commissioner, in determining the deficiency in estate tax, included the community of Mrs. Vardell in her gross estate and the Tax Court affirmed this action, holding that it was included under § 2036, stating that the transfer by her to the remaindermen was not completed until her death. It would also have been includible under § 2038.* * * We would reach the same point taxwise under either or both.

Petitioner took the position before the Tax Court that none of the interest of Mrs. Vardell in the community property was includible because its transfer under the election to which decedent was put constituted a bona fide sale for an adequate and full consideration in money or money's worth within the meaning of § 2036. Alternatively, if there was less than a full consideration, it was urged that decedent was entitled to a credit under § 2043(a) * * * which in effect allows a credit for the amount of the consideration for a transfer, where it is less than full consideration. The gross estate under this section includes only the excess of the fair market value of the property over the value of the consideration received therefor by a decedent where a transfer has been made under §§ 2035 to 2038, inclusive, and § 2041.

The Tax Court disposed of the case by holding the transfer by Mrs. Vardell of her one-half interest in the community to have been incomplete until her death, and that her community was includible in her gross estate under § 2036. This holding was based on the power of disposition vested in Mrs. Vardell by the terms of the will which rendered the remainder contingent as to property. The law of Texas dictates the type of property interest

¶ 11,933

involved, here a life estate * * * and this transaction falls squarely within the terms of § 2036. The Tax Court missed the mark however in failing to apply § 2043(a).

The government concedes that this property, if not includible under § 2033, and we have held that it is not, is includible under § 2036. And we hold, contrary to the contention of the taxpayer, that the transfer was not for a full consideration under § 2036. We put aside any question as to gift tax since it is admitted by the government that the gift tax collected was not due. Nor are we concerned with a valuation of the property transferred by Mrs. Vardell since the very purpose of § 2036 and the related sections is to include all of such property in her gross estate subject to such credits, if any, as may be due.

This brings us to the remaining questions presented. They are: first, whether the transfer was for a consideration within the meaning of § 2043(a); and if so, then second, how the credit is to be computed.

The question regarding consideration under § 2043(a) is of first impression. However, such an exchange has been held to be for a consideration under the gift tax statute. § 1002 of the 1939 Revenue Code [1986 Code § 2512(b)].* * * Section 1002 uses consideration in the same sense as it is used in § 2043(a).* * * We hold that the life estate received by the widow constituted consideration within the purview of § 2043(a).

* * *

Having determined that there is consideration as contemplated by § 2043(a), we come to the method and possibility of computation. The Regulation, § 20.2043–1, provides that the consideration must be reducible to a money value. And the consideration received is to be valued at the time of the transfer, i.e., the date of election. Ithaca Trust Company v. United States, 1929, 279 U.S. 151. Once valued, it is to be credited against the value of the property of the widow at the time of her death. The net is what is to be included in the gross estate.

* * *

The interest that was here transferred by decedent during her lifetime for less than a full consideration was of the § 2036 type to which § 2043(a) applies, as distinguished from being an interest owned at the time of her death under § 2033 to which it does not apply. Our application of § 2043(a) to permit credit for what she received in consideration of the transfer of the remainder in her community as against the value at her death of the property transferred accords with what we deem to be the intent of the applicable statutes, i.e., single taxation and not double taxation as would result if the estate was not credited for the value of the property transferred. Her estate is in no wise depleted for estate tax purposes. Under the computation of the credit what she gave is equal to what she received.* * *

[¶ 11,941]

Note on Computation of Consideration Offset

If the widow's election is used, when W dies, the entire corpus of the A trust will be included in her gross estate as she has made a transfer in trust with a retained life estate. § 2036(a). However, under § 2043(a), W's estate is allowed a deduction for the consideration which she received, i.e., the value of the life estate in her husband's half of the community property, in exchange for making the election-transfer in trust. Thus, in the example given at ¶ 11,925, we can compute the amount ultimately to be included in W's gross estate. Assuming that the corpus of the A trust is valued at the same $1 million at W's death, the computation is as follows:

Trust A included under § 2036	$1,000,000
Less: Consideration offset under § 2043	755,537
Net inclusion in W's gross estate	$244,463

We can see that the use of the widow's election resulted in substantial estate tax savings.

The value assigned the consideration offset in the above example ($755,537) is the result of the decision in Gradow v. United States, 897 F.2d 516 (Fed.Cir.1990), aff'g 87–1 USTC ¶ 13,711, 11 Cl.Ct. 808 (Cl.Ct.1987), which considered similar facts. *Gradow* is important because it demands a bifurcated analysis of the impact of the widow's election device on the estate tax consequences at the death of the surviving spouse. That is, the surviving spouse (W) is deemed to have retained a life estate for purposes of § 2036(a)(1) in the property she transferred to the A trust at the death of the deceased spouse. As a result, as required by § 2036(a)(1), W's estate will include the full fair market value of the property transferred by W, market value to be determined at the death of W. On the other hand, under the rationale of *Gradow,* the consideration offset received by W will be frozen in time, i.e., valued as of the death of the deceased spouse, to wit, at $755,537.

In *Gradow,* the court rejected the taxpayer's argument that no part of the wife's one-half of the community property should be included in her estate at her death because the wife's transfer was for "adequate and full consideration" as provided in § 2043. Referring to the example used above, the taxpayer's rejected argument was that the wife had transferred a remainder interest having a value of $225,090 in return for a life estate in the deceased husband's property of $755,537, an amount which far exceeded that which W had given up—and, thus, the transfer had been made for more than "adequate and full consideration" and no part of the wife's one-half of the community should be included in the wife's estate. As stated above, the judges of the Federal Circuit Court saw the facts differently, concluding that the wife had transferred not merely a remainder interest ($225,090) but the full value of one-half of the community ($1 million)—in which she had retained a life estate.

¶ 11,941

The Third Circuit, on different facts, adopted the thinking of the taxpayer in *Gradow*, holding that if the actuarial value of the life estate received equals or exceeds the value of the remainder interest given up, then the transfer has been made for "adequate and full consideration" and therefore should not be included in the decedent's gross estate. *D'Ambrosio v. Commissioner*, 101 F.3d 309 (3d Cir.1996). While *D'Ambrosio* dealt with the sale of a remainder, the court did not distinguish widow's election cases. Furthermore, the Ninth Circuit rejected *Gradow* and applied *D'Ambrosio* on facts analytically indistinguishable from a widow's election. *Magnin v. Commissioner*, 184 F.3d 1074 (9th Cir.1999). If the D'Ambrosio ruling is applied to the facts given in the immediately preceding example, at W's death the value of the A trust will *not* be included in her gross estate and, accordingly will not have zero estate tax consequences at her death. In sum, before *D'Ambrosio* the widow's election offered the promise of significant estate tax savings; afterwards, it well may be truly "a taxpayer's utopia" as Judge Wisdom suggested. See *Estate of L.B. Vardell v. Commissioner*, 307 F.2d 688, 699 (5th Cir.1962).

[¶ 11,949]

5. INCOME TAX CONSEQUENCES

The following case is noteworthy not only for its determination of the income tax consequences of the widow's election but also for its thorough treatment of the history and policy surrounding the issue.

[¶ 11,951]

KUHN v. UNITED STATES

United States District Court, Southern District, Texas, 1975.
392 F.Supp. 1229.

CARL O. BUE, JR., District Judge.

I. INTRODUCTION

The case presents one legal question: may a taxpayer-surviving spouse who with the decedent spouse transferred all community property to a trust in exchange for receipt of a life estate payable from the trust commencing after the decedent spouse's death amortize the cost basis of the life estate payments over the surviving spouse's life expectancy?* * *

After thorough consideration, and for the reasons stated herein, this Court concludes that the taxpayer is entitled to amortize the cost basis of life estate payments that she received from the trust established in this case. Accordingly, she is entitled to the refund previously stipulated to by the parties.

* * *

On February 25, 1959, taxpayer's husband died leaving a will which he had executed in 1958. Reference was made in this instrument to a trust

¶ 11,941

created between taxpayer and her husband in 1942. This trust agreement established a trust consisting of all the property owned by the spouses.

In 1959, taxpayer transferred her interest in the community property belonging to herself and her husband to the trust and received a life estate in all of said property.* * * Gift tax liability arose as the result of this transfer, * * * and the taxpayer paid a gift tax on $113,496.12, representing the excess of the value of her community property interest transferred to the trust ($156,266.12) over the value of her actuarially computed right to the life estate (15 year life expectancy) in the entire trust ($42,770).* * *

III. INTERPRETATION OF THE TAX CODE

A. *Determining the Proper Statute*

The Court must first determine which Code provision properly applies in this case. The taxpayer correctly points to § 167(h), * * * as the Code provision authorizing amortization deductions to reduce a life tenant's taxable income from the life estate. But the wording of § 273, * * * suggests to the Court that its application takes precedence in determining whether, in the first instance, the taxpayer as life tenant is entitled to an amortization deduction. As will be seen, it is the interpretation of § 273 around which this decision actually turns.

B. *Legislative History of § 273*

The legislative history of § 273 is of only limited assistance.* * * The 1921 committee reports indicate that § 273 was enacted to prohibit the amortization of the gift value of a life estate. Id. But § 273 does not prevent the amortization of a beneficiary's own investment in such a life estate.* * *

C. *Supreme Court Interpretation of § 273*

The United States Supreme Court has held that the Congress intended to incorporate into § 273 terms in common usage in other tax statutes. Lyeth v. Hoey, 305 U.S. 188, 194–5 (1938). As the Supreme Court saw it, § 273 was designed to prevent amortization of income by a taxpayer who had received the life estate income without cost and therefore without tax consequences— i.e., when received by virtue of a gift, bequest or inheritance.

In *Lyeth,* an heir contested his grandmother's will. As a result of the compromise of that contest, the heir received property which would not have been received if the will had gone uncontested. The Court would not permit the taxpayer to reduce by deduction income thus received which was not subject to tax liability. 305 U.S. at 195–97. Instead, the Court established as a standard the need of a taxpayer seeking to amortize to demonstrate the presence of adequate consideration. For example, merely labelling a will agreement as a "contract" and implying the presence of an "offer" and an "acceptance" would not establish the presence of consideration. Implicit in the Court's decision was the premise that a taxpayer wishing to amortize a life estate must demonstrate consideration based on ordinary concepts of the exchanging of rights to property.

¶ 11,951

D. Fifth Circuit Interpretation of § 273

1. The Case of Early v. Commissioner

Lyeth demands that courts closely scrutinize the amortization deduction claims of life estate recipients to verify the underlying foundation of their entitlement to the amortized property. The United States Court of Appeals for the Fifth Circuit has exhibited such scrutiny. In Early v. Commissioner, *supra*, 445 F.2d 166, taxpayers entered into an agreement whereby they compromised a will contest and surrendered stock securities in exchange for a joint life interest. The Court of Appeals held that the life interest had been acquired as the result of a compromise of a disputed right to stock and that the taxpayers were to be deemed as donees. Accordingly, the appellate court interpreted § 273 as precluding amortization of the cost basis of this life interest.

In *Early,* the Court of Appeals adopted the Supreme Court's reasoning in Lyeth v. Hoey and went on to note that *Lyeth* even governs circumstances in which a sale or exchange of property has occurred. As the appellate court saw it, amortization is permissible only when the surrounding circumstances of the transaction fairly demonstrate the taxpayer's possession of an underlying right to exchanged property. When this possibility is excluded, the exchange is, in reality, a compromise of an underlying and controverted claim—such as one of gift, bequest or inheritance, 445 F.2d at 170—and § 273 precludes amortization.

2. Fifth Circuit Analysis of the Gist Case

To illustrate situations of permissible amortization and to distinguish those from the situation before it in *Early,* the Court of Appeals cited the case of Gist v. United States, 296 F.Supp. 526 (S.D.Cal.1968), aff'd, 423 F.2d 1118 (9th Cir. 1970). In *Gist,* the trial and appellate courts were confronted with the identical factual setting and legal question presented in the instant case. Both courts concluded that a wife is eligible to be a purchaser of her husband's life estate for value as she would be if she purchased another's life estate for cash, and that she is therefore eligible to amortize the cost basis of such a life estate. 296 F.Supp. at 528.

The district court enumerated a four-part analysis to support its finding that amortization deductions were permissible under § 273: (1) an election to take under the will not based on tax avoidance motives; (2) possession by the taxpayer, under community property law, of a present, existing and equal interest in the community property before the death of the decedent; (3) an election by the surviving spouse resulting in total relinquishment of that spouse's rights to the remainder interest in his or her one-half share of the community property; and (4) relinquishment of the interest as a condition to receiving a life estate in the decedent's one-half interest in community property, resulting in the transfer of a life estate in the entire property to the survivor. 296 F.Supp. at 529. The United States Court of Appeals for the Ninth Circuit approved the rationale and analysis which yielded this four-part test and affirmed as well the district court's application of the test to conclude legally that a widow's acquisition of a life estate in the decedent spouse's community property interest was a "purchase" for income tax purposes. 423 F.2d at 1120.

The United States Court of Appeals for the Fifth Circuit in *Early* examined the *Gist* transaction for purposes of § 273 analysis and found no dispute which the exchange was said to have compromised. 445 F.2d at 170. That is, the widow's right to property which she exchanged was found not to be in controversy. The *Early* court concluded by stating that "the undisputed and vested character of the wife's community interest, which was exchanged for the life interest", established the permissible amortization of a life estate so purchased. Id.

E.   Impact of Early v. Commissioner

Judge Godbold's language in *Early* foreshadows, if not requires, the permitting of amortization in this case. To this Court, the spirit, if not the command, of *Early* and *Lyeth* is to permit the amortization of a life estate by one who exchanges valuable property in consideration for receiving such a life estate where the right to possession of the property exchanged is undisputed.* * *

IV.   THE *BUTTERWORTH* CASE

[This case, relied on by the Government, was distinguished from the present case in that the widow in *Butterworth* gave up her dower rights (which had no value prior to her husband's death) to take a life estate. Here, the widow gave up her own property.]

V.   IN-DEPTH ANALYSIS OF § 273

Being especially wary of adjudicating a tax question without first consulting all available authorities, the Court independently has sought out scholarly commentary on the legal question presented in this case.* * *

A.   The Case Against Permitting Amortization

Those opposing amortization of the cost basis of life estate payments received as the result of a widow's election focus their opposition primarily upon two factors: the resulting effect of the election on the family estate; and the absence of ordinary notions of a profit motive in the widow's election exchange. Professor Johanson critically points out that under an exchange such as the one effected in the instant case, the wife (as the surviving spouse) receives all of the income from the entire community estate for her lifetime, is taxed on only one-half of the value of the estate and obtains a reduction in the amount of her estate tax. He further contends that the election by the taxpayer to take under the decedent's will is not motivated by the type of economic considerations with which the income tax is concerned. Presumably, neither the taxpayer nor her husband has a profit motive. See Johanson, [Revocable Trusts, Widow's Election Wills, and Community Property: The Tax Problems], 47 Texas L. Rev. [1247,] at 1296–98 [(1969)].

Professor Morrison contends that when the taxpayer elects to take under the will, she does so as a beneficiary of the trust, and nothing is sold, for

¶ 11,951

income tax purposes, when the election is made. Whether there was a "consideration" offset when the transfer was made merely presents a gift tax transfer question, not an income tax question. See Morrison, [The Widow's Election and Its Alternatives, 1971 Texas Tech Tax Inst. 142,] at 148–51 (1971).

In the taxation of trusts, according to Professor Morrison, the issue is *attribution* in determining who receives taxable income: the grantor, the trustee or the beneficiary. In essence, for the wife (taxpayer) to amortize her life estate, it would have to be said that she sold her property to the trustee as purchaser; otherwise, she becomes a beneficiary of the trust. If a sale has occurred and is so treated by the trustee, he should be taxed on all income from the property as property that he has acquired. However, if the trustee treats the receipt of property as a disbursement of income, the taxpayer (wife) is a beneficiary and not a purchaser of a life estate who would be eligible for amortization.

In an exchange involving the husband and wife such as this one, according to Professor Morrison, the husband wants the wife to have the benefits of the trust and not to be treated as an independent purchaser. The gist of trust income allocation is "attribution"—i.e., identifying the source of the income-producing property. For income tax purposes, the taxpayer cannot be viewed as the vendor of property which is transferred to the trustee and which is then paid directly back to the taxpayer in annual installments. Otherwise, the taxpayer is in the position of allegedly having exchanged land while still receiving the income from that land, paying income tax on it and being able to amortize it as her own. See Morrison, [The Widow's Election and Its Alternatives, 1971 Texas Tech Tax Inst. 142 (1971)]; Morrison, [The Widow's Election: The Issue of Consideration,] 44 Texas L. Rev. 223 [(1965)].

The Case for Permitting Amortization

Those favoring amortization of the cost basis of life estate payments received as the result of a widow's election contend that one who utilizes the widow's election device sometimes does not realize all of the tax advantages hypothesized by those who oppose permitting amortization deductions. *Schwartz & Liker* contend that a decedent spouse's income may be snared in a hidden tax trap in the year of death by utilizing the widow's election mechanism. [Schwartz & Liker, 1967 U. MIAMI U. Miami Est. Plan. Inst. 67.1031, 10–21 and 10–22 (1967).] By receiving a remainder interest from the survivor's trust in exchange for transferring an income interest in his (decedent's) trust, the decedent (or his estate) may be deemed to have anticipated the receipt of ordinary income under Hort v. Commissioner, 313 U.S. 28 (1941), and Commissioner v. Lake, 356 U.S. 260 (1958). According to *Schwartz & Liker,* a bunching of ordinary income in the year in which the transfer is made could result. Further, if the value of the remainder interest transferred by the surviving spouse is less than the value of the income interest received by her, she might be held to have realized a capital gain. *Schwartz & Liker, supra,* at 10–21 to –22.

¶ 11,951

Brawerman notes additional disadvantages with the widow's election life estate. See Brawerman, [Disposition of Community Property: Should One Spouse Receive a Life Estate in Other's Half?,] 40 J. TAXATION 116–17. He focuses primarily on the loss of control over the ultimate disposition of the property which the wife, as surviving spouse, must acknowledge in order to be able to amortize her life estate. A surviving spouse cannot simultaneously retain control over disposition of an entire estate and amortize ratable deductions from life estate income. Were she to attempt to retain some control by receiving a general power to appoint principal of her half of the community property and a limited power to appoint principal in the husband's half of the property (to be able to take into account events occurring after the husband's death which may influence the manner of disposition), the wife would not transfer an interest in her half when electing and would pay nothing for her life estate in the husband's half. She would therefore acquire the life estate in the husband's one-half interest by gift rather than purchase, would have no cost for the life estate and would therefore not be entitled to amortize.

Brawerman additionally notes that estate tax consequences attend the wife's election. Her half of the community property will be included in her estate at her later death because she has transferred her half of the property in trust and has retained a life estate. Even though the wife will be able to reduce the amount includable in her estate by the value of the husband's life estate in his half of the property at the date of election, her gross estate will still include income received from the husband's half of the property after his death. *Brawerman, supra,* 40 J. TAXATION at 117.

VI. TAX ANALYSIS IN THIS CASE

The income, estate and gift tax laws are not in pari materia. They were enacted under different circumstances and are generally designed to address different situations. "Consideration" is a term which has been utilized to depict concepts the meaning of which can diverge when applied under the estate and gift tax laws as compared with the income tax laws. *Compare* § 2043 *with* § 1014. However, concepts utilized in one sphere may be applicable in another sphere. The real subject of the estate tax, for example, is not property but the shifting economic benefits of property.* * *

Elections to take under a will have long been recognized as transactions in which the property surrendered is viewed as the consideration for the offer made in the will and accepted at the time of the execution of the will in a contemporaneous instrument or thereafter.* * *

Section 273 applies to an income interest in a trust. Maxfield, Capital Gains and Losses, 25 Tax L. Rev. 565, 577–78 (1970). Therefore, the property surrendered is a consideration for that which is accepted, and a binding contract occurs upon such acceptance.* * * In Vardell v. Commissioner, [307 F.2d 688 (5th Cir. 1962)], a widow elected under her husband's will to receive a life estate in his property with the right to dispose of it at her death, the remainder interest passing to the descendant-trustees. The U.S. Court of Appeals for the Fifth Circuit there held that for purposes of the estate tax, the life estate received by the widow constituted consideration which was valued at the time of transfer.* * *

VII.   CONCLUSION

To this Court, the better result is to permit amortization. In a situation involving the widow's election where the taxpayer exchanges the remainder interest in her community property for a life interest in her husband's community property, what actually occurs can be characterized as part gratuitous disposition—part sale or exchange. Where the wife receives property worth more than the value of the property she transfers, the property received in excess should be viewed as a "bequest" from the husband which is not amortizable. But where the wife transfers property worth more than the value of that which she receives, she purchases property equivalent to the value of the "received" property and is deemed to have made a gift to the beneficiaries of the estate of, and should pay a gift tax on, the excess. That is what the taxpayer did in this case.

The widow exchanges the remainder interest in her community property for the life interest in her husband's share of the community property. The widow may therefore amortize the income received from her husband's segment of the life estate. She remains fully taxable on income received from her own reserved life estate. Gist v. United States, *supra*; Smith, [The Draftsman Vis-a-Vis the Widow's Election and Its Tax Consequences], 21 S.W.L.J. [591, 601–603].

The better result aside, this Court is persuaded by the available authorities that amortization should be permitted. This is so because the language of § 273 as applied by the Supreme Court in Lyeth v. Hoey permits it; because the analytical approach to § 273 utilized by the United States Court of Appeals for the Fifth Circuit in the *Early* case foreshadows such permission; and because the taxpayer here has satisfied the four-part *Gist* test adopted by the Ninth Circuit.

In the first instance, it is the language of a statute as written which must be construed.* * * Interpreting § 273 to prohibit amortization in a case such as this one could only occur by permitting form to conquer substance. The instant taxpayer does not receive income from the subject life estate as the result of a "gift, bequest or inheritance". She has acquired the life estate after exchanging valuable property, the right to which was undisputedly hers at the time of the exchange. She therefore will be permitted to amortize the cost basis of life estate payments received and reduce her taxable income by ratable annual deductions, pursuant to § 167(h).

Judgment is hereby granted in favor of the taxpayer.

[¶ 11,959]

Note on Amortization of "Purchased" Life Estates

Under the rationale of *Kuhn*, a surviving spouse may be entitled to an income tax deduction as a result of allowing his or her half of the community property to be disposed of by the will of a deceased spouse. Where the interest in property transferred by the surviving spouse exceeds the value of the interest given the surviving spouse in the will of a deceased spouse, the excess—the so-called purchase price—can be amortized over the life expectancy of the surviving spouse and deducted for income tax purposes by the surviving spouse over that same period. However, where the value of that received under the will of the deceased spouse exceeds that given up by the surviving spouse, no amortization deduction is available. Looking back to the example of H and W at ¶ 11,925, no amortization deduction would be available to W inasmuch as the value that she gave up (a remainder interest having a value of $225,090) is less than the value she received under the will of H (a life estate having a value of $755,537). However, assuming that the "applicable federal rate" was 6 percent, as in the illustration at ¶ 11,925, and W had been 72 years old at H's death, an amortization deduction would have been available to W because the value of the life estate she received ($482,469 ($975,000 x .49484)) would have been less than the value of the remainder that she gave up ($505,160).

Another issue relates to the income tax consequences to the estate of the deceased spouse. Arguably, since W is deemed to have "purchased" the life estate in the B trust, H's estate must have sold it. If the estate sold the life estate, it ought to recognize gain or loss on the sale or exchange. The gain (or loss) to be recognized would be the value of the remainder interest in the A trust ($225,090) reduced by the estate's basis in the life estate "sold" to W.

Problem

[¶ 11,965]

What is the estate's basis in the life estate which was "sold" in the example in the preceding text? See § 1001(e). Is any gain to be recognized as ordinary income or is it capital gain entitled to preferential income tax treatment? Could it be argued that it is ordinary income because it represents the anticipatory assignment of income? Are the possible income tax implications of this "sale" so onerous that use of the widow's election device is only for the foolhardy?

[¶ 11,967]

6. ESTATE TAX CONSEQUENCES AT DEATH OF FIRST SPOUSE TO DIE

Congress has declared that all lifetime and deathtime interspousal transfers of both community and separate property made *after* 1981 could be free of federal estate taxes. Previously, interspousal transfers of community property were subject to federal gift tax and, except in very limited circumstances, were subject to federal estate tax without any marital deduction. See discussion at ¶ 13,051. Moreover, Congress allowed the marital deduction for property passing into a new kind of trust, commonly referred to as a QTIP. To qualify, all that the decedent must do is make certain that the spouse gets all of the income from the trust for life and that no one other than the spouse is eligible for distributions from the trust. § 2056(b)(7). Moreover, the decedent—

through use of a QTIP trust—can control, without loss of the marital deduction, how the trust property will be distributed after the surviving spouse dies. See § 2056(b)(7).

Problem

[¶ 11,968]

With these principles in mind, has the widow's election device become even more attractive for decedents dying after 1981? That is, is the marital deduction available as to the decedent's one-half of the community property which flows into the trust for the surviving spouse in return for her transfer of her community one-half interest into another trust? Or does the *Stapf* case, which follows, prevent this result?

[¶ 11,969]

UNITED STATES v. STAPF

Supreme Court of the United States, 1963.
375 U.S. 118.

Mr. Justice GOLDBERG delivered the opinion of the court.

* * *

Lowell H. Stapf died testate on July 29, 1953, a resident and domiciliary of Texas, a community property jurisdiction. At the time of his death he owned, in addition to his separate estate, a substantial amount of property in community with his wife. His will required that his widow elect either to retain her one-half interest in the community or to take under the will and allow its terms to govern the disposition of her community interest. If Mrs. Stapf were to elect to take under the will, she would be given, after specific bequests to others, one-third of the community property and one-third of her husband's separate estate. By accepting this bequest she would allow her one-half interest in the community to pass, in accordance with the will, into a trust for the benefit of the children. It was further provided that if she chose to take under the will the executors were to pay "all and not merely one-half" of the community debts and administration expenses.

The relevant facts and computations are not in dispute. The decedent's separate property was valued at $65,100 and the community property at $258,105. The only debts were community debts totalling $32,368. The administration expenses, including attorneys' fees, were $4,073. If Mrs. Stapf had not elected to take under the will, she would have retained her fully vested one-half interest in the community property ($129,052) which would have been charged with one-half of the community debts ($16,184) and 35 percent of the administration expenses ($1,426). Thus, as the parties agree, she would have received a net of $111,443.

In fact Mrs. Stapf elected to take under the will. She received, after specific bequests to others, one-third of the combined separate and community property, a devise valued at $106,268, which was $5,175 less than she would have received had she retained her community property and refused to take under the will.

In computing the net taxable estate, the executors claimed a marital deduction under § 812(e)(1) of the Internal Revenue Code of 1939 [1986 Code § 2056(a)] for the full value of the one-third of decedent's separate estate ($22,367) which passed to his wife under the will.* * * The Commissioner of Internal Revenue disallowed the marital deduction.* * *

I. THE MARITAL DEDUCTION

By electing to take under the will, Mrs. Stapf, in effect, agreed to accept the property devised to her and, in turn, to surrender property of greater value to the trust for the benefit of the children. This raises the question of whether a decedent's estate is allowed a marital deduction under § 812(e)(1)(E)(ii) of the 1939 Code [1986 Code § 2056(b)(4)(B)] where the bequest to the surviving spouse is on the condition that she convey property of equivalent or greater value to her children. The Government contends that, for purposes of a marital deduction, "the value of the interest passing to the wife is the value of the property given her less the value of the property she is required to give another as a condition to receiving it." On this view, since the widow had no net benefit from the exercise of her election, the estate would be entitled to no marital deduction. Respondents reject this net benefit approach and argue that the plain meaning of the statute makes detriment to the surviving spouse immaterial.

Section 812(e)(1)(A) provides that "in general" the marital deduction is for "the value of any interest in property which passes * * * from the decedent to his surviving spouse." Subparagraph (E) [1986 Code § 2056(b)(4)] then deals specifically with the question of valuation:

(E) Valuation Of Interest Passing To Surviving Spouse.—In determining for the purposes of subparagraph (A) the value of any interest in property passing to the surviving spouse for which a deduction is allowed by this subsection—

(ii) where such interest or property is incumbered in any manner, or where the surviving spouse incurs any obligation imposed by the decedent with respect to the passing of such interest, such incumbrance or obligation shall be taken into account in the same manner as if the amount of a gift to such spouse of such interest were being determined.

The disputed deduction turns upon the interpretation of (1) the introductory phrase "any obligation imposed by the decedent with respect to the passing of such interest," and (2) the concluding provision that "such * * * obligation shall be taken into account in the same manner as if the amount of a gift to such spouse of such interest were being determined."

* * *

[The Court denied the marital deduction to Mrs. Stapf's estate and explained:]

¶ 11,969

Our conclusion concerning the congressionally intended result under § 812(e)(1) [1986 Code § 2056(a)] with the general purpose of Congress in creating the marital deduction. The 1948 tax amendments were intended to equalize the effect of the estate taxes in community property and common-law jurisdictions. Under a community property system, such as that in Texas, the spouse receives outright ownership of one-half of the community property and only the other one-half is included in the decedent's estate. To equalize the incidence of progressively scaled estate taxes and to adhere to the patterns of state law, the marital deduction permits a deceased spouse, subject to certain requirements, to transfer free of taxes one-half of the non-community property to the surviving spouse. Although applicable to separately held property in a community property state, the primary thrust of this is to extend to taxpayers in common-law States the advantages of "estate splitting" otherwise available only in community property States. The purpose, however, is only to permit a married couple's property to be taxed in two stages and not to allow a tax-exempt transfer of wealth into succeeding generations. Thus the marital deduction is generally restricted to the transfer of property interests that will be includible in the surviving spouse's gross estate. Respondents' construction of § 812(e)(1) [1986 Code § 2056(a)] would, nevertheless, permit one-half of a spouse's wealth to pass from one generation to another without being subject either to gift or estate taxes. We do not believe that this result, squarely contrary to the concept of the marital deduction, can be justified by the language of § 812(e)(1) [1986 Code § 2056(a)]. Furthermore, since in a community property jurisdiction one-half of the community normally vests in the wife, approval of the claimed deduction would create an opportunity for tax reduction that, as a practical matter, would be more readily available to couples in community property jurisdictions than to couples in common-law jurisdictions. Such a result, again, would be unnecessarily inconsistent with a basic purpose of the statute.

* * * We conclude that, for estate tax purposes, the value of a conditional bequest to a widow should be the value of the property given to her less the value of the property she is required to give to another. In this case the value of the property transferred to Mrs. Stapf ($106,268) must be reduced by the value of the community property she was required to relinquish ($111,443). Since she received no net benefit, the estate is entitled to no marital deduction.

Problem

[¶ 11,973]

Ben Slurry and his wife, Muffy, both of whom were born in 1940, have $4,000,000 of community property. Muffy has consulted you about making a will. She claims Ben is a spendthrift and, but for her careful money management, would have long since dissipated all of their community property. (Apparently both Muffy and Ben are born salespersons, and, together, they have accumulated a tidy sum from their commissions. What do they sell? They sell microcomputers for the home market.) Muffy wants to put her one-half of their community property into a trust for Ben's benefit for life and, after his

¶ 11,969

death, to distribute the property to each of their two children, Biff and Chip, when that child reaches maturity. She thinks maturity comes sometime after age 55, but she is willing to settle for distribution at age 55. Muffy also wants to tie up Ben's one-half of the community property so that if she dies first, there will be something left for their children after Ben dies. Would the widow's election device be of some help in planning Muffy's estate? Analyze the economic consequences to Muffy and Ben of using the widow's election device. In doing so, you'll want to keep in mind that Muffy will want to take advantage of the marital deduction if it is available to her in conjunction with the widow's election device. In thinking about the availability of the marital deduction, you will undoubtedly be concerned about the application of the *Stapf* case.

Assume for the moment, at least, that the *Stapf* case bars the marital deduction for that portion of Muffy's property which is used as the "bait" to cause Ben to transfer his one-half of the community property to a trust set up by Muffy. If that is so, and Muffy wants the marital deduction to the extent necessary to avoid any estate tax at her death, would it be possible to use a modified widow's election device where the "bait" was limited to the applicable exclusion amount available at Muffy's death? See § 2010.

For example, suppose Muffy dies in 2006 when 2010(c)'s applicable exclusion amount is $2 million. Her will calls for the least amount necessary to eliminate any estate tax at her death to flow into a QTIP trust for Ben. See § 2056(b)(7).

The balance of her property she directs to a bypass trust. Ben is to get the income for life from the bypass trust on condition that he transfer his one-half of their community property into another trust (in which he is to have the income for life). Would this scheme effectively utilize the unlimited marital deduction at Muffy's death and, at the same time, give Ben enough "bait" to put his property into the hands of a professional manager, the trustee?

[¶ 11,977]

7. SEPARATE PROPERTY APPLICATION

It seems that the benefits provided under the widow's election will are available for separate property. A "voluntary" widow's election, which proposes to offer the same tax benefits as the present widow's election to any husband and wife regardless of ownership of the property holdings, has been suggested. See Miller and Martin, Voluntary Widow's Election: Nationwide Planning for the Million Dollar Estate, 1 Cal. W. L. Rev. 63–96 (1965). The proposal is that H transfer half of his separate property to a marital deduction trust and half to a bypass trust. W is then given the power to exchange all or part of her remainder interest in the marital trust for an income interest of equal value in the residuary trust. Id. at 86. This assumes that the marital deduction property will be considered the surviving spouse's property. Id. at 92. There remain many unanswered questions about such a plan, such as, the value of the property the surviving spouse transfers and the income tax treatment of the exchange.

Chapter 12

VALUE FREEZING FOR NONBUSINESS INTERESTS

A. OBJECTIVES

[¶ 12,001]

Split-interest property ownership arrangements have become popular as a means of value shifting. That is, property owners seem willing to experiment with property ownership arrangements that result in their having the enjoyment of the property for life or for a period of years after which loved ones succeed them in having the enjoyment of the property. The impetus for this experimentation is the promise or hope that the scheme will result in reduced federal estate and gift tax costs.

The classic illustration is Lucy's deed of the farm to her child, Lackluster, described in Chapters 6 and 10 (see ¶ 6159 and 10,201), subject to Lucy's right to retain enjoyment of the property for life. Of course, this is a failed strategy—for both estate and gift tax reasons as described in Chapter 10. More sophisticated arrangements are the subject of this chapter. Most of these arrangements require valuations that can be easily made using computer software. Offering the greatest number of applications pertinent to the materials in this chapter is NumberCruncher. Also very useful is Estate Planning Assistant and Tiger Tables. See Appendix A for program descriptions.

"I know, I know," acknowledges Ted. "Having Mom deed the house to us and continuing to live there will cause it to be included in her estate for estate tax purposes. But Good Friend Snavely, our lawyer, says there is an alternative. Suppose Mom puts the house in trust for a period of years, say five years, and at the end of five years the trust terminates and the house becomes ours. At that time, Mom can go to the 'Home.' She'll need the care anyway by then."

Alice chimes in with, "What's the advantage?"

Friend Snavely, the lawyer, responds, "We get the appreciation out of Mom's estate for estate tax purposes—if she lives out the five years."

"How's that?" Alice purrs.

"Look at it this way," says Snavely. "You are all betting that the house will increase in value, right?" Ted and Alice nod in agreement and Snavely continues, "Suppose the house is worth $400,000 but that it appreciates to $900,000 over the next five years. Avoiding estate tax on the $500,000 of appreciation at Mom's death has got to be a real high."

Any discussion of split ownership arrangements begins with § 2702, the attempt by Congress to maintain the integrity of the estate and gift tax system in the face of these sophisticated split ownership arrangements. The result, of course, was the zero valuation rules of § 2702, making gifts that are subject to § 2702 particularly expensive from a gift tax standpoint. The materials in this chapter describe and/or illustrate some of the more commonly used arrangements and suggest how those ownership arrangements need to be structured if § 2702 is to be avoided.

B. ZERO VALUATION RULE

[¶ 12,051]

Section 2702 requires a retained interest, which is not a qualified interest under § 2702(b), to be valued at zero. That is, by valuing the retained interest at zero, the transfer tax cost imposed on a donor is based on 100 percent of the fair market value of the transferred property as of the date of the gift of the future interest without any reduction for the value of the interest retained by the donor. However, if the retained interest is a qualified interest under § 2702(b), the retained interest will be valued under § 7520, which will reduce the value of the gift and reduce the transferor's gift tax liability. Interests that qualify for tax-favored treatment include grantor retained annuity trusts (GRATs), grantor retained unitrusts (GRUTs) and qualified remainder interests. See ¶ 12,101–12,301 for discussion. Transfers of a personal residence also qualify for tax-favored treatment under specified conditions. ¶ 12,059.

Section 2702 applies only to a transfer of an interest in trust to or for the benefit of a member of the transferor's family in which the transferor or an applicable family member has retained an interest in the trust. For purposes of § 2702, "member of the family" is limited to the following:

1. The spouse of the transferor;

2. An ancestor or lineal descendant of the transferor or transferor's spouse;

3. A sibling of the transferor; and

4. A spouse of such an ancestor, descendant, or sibling.

Therefore, a transfer to a trust where the transferor retains an income interest and the transferor's niece is to receive the remainder interest is not valued under § 2702 because the transferor's niece is not considered a "family member" for purposes of § 2702. But Lucy's decision to deed the farm to her child, Lackluster, subject to Lucy's right to occupy the farm for life, will mean that Lucy will pay gift tax on 100 percent of the value of the farm on the date of the gift, without any reduction for the value of the life estate she retained. Not only would Lucy pay gift tax at the time of the transfer but the farm will be included in Lucy's estate at Lucy's subsequent death, valued at its fair market value at the date of Lucy's death. § 2036(a)(1).

The term "applicable family member," defined by § 2702(a)(1) by reference to § 2701(e)(2), refers to (1) the transferor's spouse, (2) an ancestor of the transferor or the transferor's spouse, and (3) a spouse of any such ancestor. Based on this definition, a transfer into a trust where the transferor's brother retains an income interest is not to be valued under § 2702 because the brother of the transferor is not within the scope of the term "applicable family member."

Section 2702 has several exceptions. First, it does not apply to incomplete transfers, which are defined in Reg. § 25.2702–1(c)(1) as "[a] transfer no portion of which would be treated as a completed gift without regard to any consideration received by the transferor." For gift tax purposes, the IRS takes the position that a transfer by a taxpayer to a trust for his own benefit will constitute a completed gift if distributions from the trust for the benefit of the taxpayer are to be made "dependent, entirely on the uncontrolled discretion of the trustee." See Rev. Rul. 77–378, 1977–2 C.B. 347; ¶ 10,209. A transfer that is wholly incomplete as to an undivided fractional share of a trust is treated as an incomplete transfer as to that share. Therefore, if the transferor retains a power over the principal of a trust, then the entire transfer is incomplete. However, if the trust is divided into fractional shares and the transferor only retains a power as to one share, the gift of the other shares is deemed to be complete and is subject to § 2702.

A second exception appears in § 2702(a)(3)(A)(ii), which provides that § 2702 does not apply to a trust funded solely with premises which are to be used as a personal residence by the holders of the term interest in the trust. This presents an opportunity to use a grantor retained income trust (GRIT). See ¶ 12,059.

C. GRANTOR RETAINED INCOME TRUST (GRIT)

[¶ 12,101]

1. GENERAL RULE

In a grantor retained income trust (GRIT), the grantor creates an irrevocable trust and retains the right to all the trust income for a specified term, or the first to expire of the specified term and the death of the grantor. If the grantor survives the specified term, the trust principal passes to the grantor's descendants or beneficiaries free of estate taxes. However, since § 2702 requires the gift of the future interest to be valued a zero, the use of a GRIT is essentially the same, for gift tax purposes, as making an outright gift of the trust principal when the gift is to a family member.

Example. Josh owns 3,000 acres of land worth $800 per acre for a total value of $2,400,000. He creates a trust, transfers the land to the trust, and retains a right to the income for a term of 15 years. The trust is irrevocable. Following the expiration of the term, the property will either continue to be held in trust for the benefit of his children or will pass outright to them. The gift tax will apply to the full $2,400,000 at the time of the transfer to the trust. Reg. § 25.2702–2(d), Example 1.

"I hate taxes! Why would I ever do such a thing?" asks Josh. The answer is, "You probably wouldn't—but it would get the property out of your estate if you lived out the 15–year term while giving you the use of it during the intervening years and freezing the value for transfer tax purposes at its gift tax value."

[¶ 12,109]

2. PERSONAL RESIDENCE TRUST (§ 2702(a)(3)(A)(ii))

a. Overview

Would you believe it? There are two kinds of personal residence trusts that qualify for tax-favored treatment. The first, sanctioned by § 2702(a)(3)(A)(ii) as an exception to the zero valuation rule, is referred to simply as the "Personal Residence Trust (PRT)" by the regulations and practitioners alike. Reg. § 25.2702–5(b). The second, sanctioned by Reg. § 25.2702–5(c), bears the label "Qualified Personal Residence Trust (QPRT)" and is deemed a PRT within the meaning of § 2702(a)(3)(A)(ii). Reg. § 25.2702–2(a).

What's the difference between a PRT and QPRT? PRTs are not used much because the PRT must (1) ban sale of the residence during the term of the PRT and (2) prohibit holding any asset other than the residence. Reg. § 25.2702–5(b). QPRTs are more flexible. Reg. § 25.2702–2(c)(5).

"QPRTs sound cute—but why do we even want a QPRT?" interjects Alice.

"Yeah. Why?" asks Ted.

"Like I told you," says Snavely, "if your Mom lives out the term, no part of the house will be in her estate for estate tax purposes, and the gift tax cost of transferring the house to the trust is significantly reduced because Mom keeps the right to occupy the house for the duration of the trust."

"Yes, yes—but I still want to know where Mom is going to live after our cute little QPRT is over," chuckles Alice, bemused by her own humor.

"Let's see," says Snavely, who proceeds to tell Ted and Alice that they must remember that a QPRT is a trust and that the trust is governed by a written trust agreement that tracks the requirements set out in Reg. § 25.2702–5(c). A QPRT can hold only one residence—it can be the primary or vacation residence of the grantor—along with appurtenant structures, plus casualty insurance and enough cash to pay trust expenses—but no more than required for these purposes. Reg. § 25.2702–2(c)(2) and (5). Sale proceeds, as well as insurance and involuntary conversion proceeds, can also be held. All trust income must be distributed annually. The requirements imposed by the regulations are detailed, and compliance is important if QPRT status is to be maintained. Accordingly, it would be useful to allow the trustee to modify the terms of the QPRT if necessary to comply with subsequent interpretations of the requirements.

[¶ 12,117]

b. Estate and Gift Tax Considerations

If the grantor dies during the life of the QPRT, the QPRT property will be included in the grantor's estate for estate tax purposes as a retained life estate. § 2036(a)(1). But if the grantor survives the QPRT term—say it's 15 years—no part of the QPRT property will be included in the grantor's estate for tax purposes. Of course, the initial transfer to the QPRT constitutes a taxable gift—and its value will be an adjusted taxable gift for estate tax computation purposes. § 2001(b)(last sentence). However, the value of the 15–year term interest retained by the grantor at the time of the transfer to the trust will reduce the value of the gift for tax purposes. Moreover, it is commonplace for the grantor to retain a contingent reversion in the residence, meaning that the QPRT will provide that if the grantor dies before the QPRT ends, the residence will revert to the grantor's estate and pass under the grantor's will. The contingent reversion is valued under § 7520 to reduce the value of the gift made by the grantor of the remainder interest in the QPRT. Priv. Ltr. Rul. 9151046 (Sept. 25, 1991).

[¶ 12,125]

c. Income Tax Considerations

The QPRT remaindermen—likely the children—take the grantor's basis in the QPRT property. That is, there is no basis step-up since the property is not included in the estate of the grantor for estate tax purposes. See § 1014(a). Accordingly, in evaluating the estate tax benefits of the QPRT, the capital gain that will be realized when the property is ultimately sold by the remaindermen needs to be considered. It needs to be balanced against the alternative strategy of "doing nothing" and allowing Mom to continue to both own and occupy the residence until her death, even though it means having the property included in Mom's estate for estate tax purposes at her death.

It is important that the QPRT be a grantor trust, i.e., the provisions of the QPRT must be such as to cause all trust income to be taxed to the grantor under the grantor trust rules set out in §§ 671–678. Usually the grantor's retained reversionary interest will have a value greater than five percent of the value of the QPRT property and that will be sufficient to attract the grantor trust rules. See § 673(a).

Having the QPRT treated as a grantor trust means that the grantor retains the income tax advantages of residence ownership. Those advantages include allowing the grantor to deduct mortgage interest payments as specified in § 163(h)(3). Priv. Ltr. Rul. 9249014. It also means that the grantor can exclude any gain recognized from the sale or exchange of the residence within the limitations specified in § 121. Also of importance is the ability of the grantor to repurchase the residence from the QPRT during its term without

(handwritten margin note: No step up in basis as not included in estate.)

the QPRT recognizing as taxable gain the property's appreciation in value. Rev. Rul. 85–13, 1985–1 C.B. 184.

[¶ 12,133]

d. The QPRT Term

Choosing the term of the QPRT is critical. The tax benefits of the QPRT are lost if the grantor does not survive the term. Larger benefits are available if the term is longer. The longer the term, the smaller the taxable gift.

[¶ 12,141]

e. When the QPRT Ends

While it is fun to speculate about finding a bridge for the grantor to live under once the QPRT terms ends, as a practical matter, the grantor can lease the residence from the transferee. See Priv. Ltr. Rul. 9249014. However, the lease arrangement should not be entered into at the creation of the QPRT but only at the end of the QPRT.

Lease at the end.)
the QPRT.

[¶ 12,149]

f. Converting the QPRT to a GRAT

Suppose the grantor ceases to use the QPRT property as his or her personal residence during the QPRT. Reg. § 25.2702–5(c)(7)(i). Or suppose the residential premises are sold during the QPRT. Reg. § 25.2702–5(c)(7)(ii). In each of those cases, as well as in others (Reg. § 25.2702–5(c)(7)(iii)), the QPRT property must be distributed free of tax to the grantor or converted and held as a qualified annuity—a GRAT—for the balance of the term of the QPRT. Reg. § 25.2702–5(c)(8). For this conversion to be accomplished, the QPRT must contain all of the provisions required by Reg. § 25.2702–3. See ¶ 12,201.

[¶ 12,157]

a. Example

Ralph, age 60, transferred his $1 million residence to a five-year QPRT in which he retained a contingent reversion in the event of his death before the end of the QPRT. Assuming 6.0% to be the applicable § 7520 rate, Ralph's made a taxable gift of $747,258 (but only a $417,265 gift if the QPRT was for a term of 15 years). The $747,258 gift value was determined by subtracting from $1 million the value of Ralph's retained income interest and the value of Ralph's contingent reversion. Both interests are valued by reference to the Actuarial Factors, Alpha Volume, provided by the IRS for use in making determinations of this nature.

The entire gift is sheltered by the $1 million dollar gift tax exemption amount. See § 2505. Furthermore, if Ralph dies shortly after the QPRT ends, he will have successfully removed the appreciation of the residence from his estate, thereby reducing his exposure to estate tax.

Problems

[¶ 12,190]

1. Lemuel transfers his 60–acre dairy farm and all of his farm equipment to a 20–year irrevocable trust. Does the trust qualify as a QPRT? Reg. § 25.2702–5(d), Example 3.

2. Sonju wants to create a five-year QPRT. Is there any reason why Sonju cannot be trustee?

D. GRANTOR RETAINED ANNUITY TRUST (GRAT) (§ 2702(b)(1))

[¶ 12,201]

In a grantor retained annuity trust (GRAT), the grantor creates an irrevocable trust and retains the right to receive, for a specified term, an annuity based on a specified sum or a fixed percentage of the value of the property transferred to the trust. The amount or percentage must be paid to the grantor at least annually and may be paid after the end of the taxable year but must be made prior to the due date for filing the return. The trust must prohibit both commutation of the term interest and payment of the qualified amount to any person other than the transferor or the applicable family member prior to the termination of the specified term.

In addition, the payout or percentage payout must be the same for each year of the term. However, if the payout is not the same percentage or dollar amount each year, the lowest payout will be considered the qualified amount for every year during the specified term. The amount in excess of the minimum payout will be excluded from the calculation of the value of the retained interest. In addition, the trust provisions must provide that additional contributions to the trust are prohibited. Reg. § 25.2702–3(b)(4).

Additional contributions prohibited.

The grantor may retain a reversionary interest in the event he or she dies within the term of the trust. However, unlike a QPRT, this reversionary interest cannot be valued under § 7520 and therefore does not reduce the value of the gift. Reg. § 25.2702–3(e), Example 1.

Example. Chun transfers $2,400,000 to a trust and retains a right to receive annual annuity payments of 10 percent of the amount contributed for a term of 15 years. After the 15–year term, the trust property will pass to the children. Chun also retains a reversionary interest if he dies before the 15–year term expires. Assume that the discount rate is 6.0 percent.

Chun will receive $240,000 per year from the trust. The factor for valuing the retained annuity interest is .5827; therefore, the total value of the retained annuity interest is $1,398,564 (.5827 x $2,400,000), and the remainder interest is $1,001,436 (.4173 x $2,400,000). The gift tax only applies to the value of the remainder interest. By retaining an annuity interest, Chun's gift was reduced by the present value of the annuity.

However, the annuity payments to Chun will be taxed to Chun as income under the grantor trust rules. §§ 671–678; Chapter 22. In addition, any excess accumulated interest will also be taxed to Chun as income.

If Chun dies before the expiration of the 15–year term, under § 2036(a)(1), the entire value of the trust property will be included in Chun's estate.

If a GRAT has a remainder interest equal to zero, it is called a "zeroed out" GRAT. Since the valuation of both the retained interest and the remainder interest is performed at the time of the transfer, the transferor, in a zeroed out GRAT, hopes that during the specified term of the annuity, the property in the trust will appreciate by more than the discount factor provided for by § 7520. If this occurs, the excess appreciation will go to the beneficiary free of gift taxes because the valuation of the remainder at the time of the transfer was zero. The problem with the zeroed out GRAT is that the grantor may die before the expiration of the specified term, causing the trust property to revert back to the grantor's estate. This risk can be reduced by creating zeroed out two-year GRATs. By using these short-term GRATs, the probability of the grantor dying within the specified term is reduced, and the grantor can use the proceeds from the existing short-term GRATs to create new short-term GRATs as the old GRATs expire. In addition, the use of multiple short-term GRATs reduces investment risks because, due to the short duration of the trust, the results of a bad year's investment will not adversely affect too many good investment years. This creates a better opportunity for excess appreciation to accumulate within the GRAT and to eventually pass to the beneficiary free of gift taxes.

Problem

[¶ 12,240]

George transfers property to an irrevocable trust retaining the right to receive annually an amount equal to eight percent of the initial fair market value of the trust property for 10 years. Upon expiration of the 10–year term, the trust is to terminate and the entire trust corpus is to be paid to George's child, Winston. If George dies within the 10–year term, the trust corpus is to be paid to George's estate. Is George's interest a qualified annuity interest if the governing instrument also contains the following features?

    (a) All income in excess of the annuity amount is to be paid to George's child, Winston.

    (b) All income in excess of the annuity amount is to be paid to George.

E.   GRANTOR RETAINED UNITRUST (GRUT) (§ 2702(b)(2))

[¶ 12,251]

In a grantor retained unitrust (GRUT), the grantor creates an irrevocable trust and retains, for a specified term, an annual right to receive a fixed percentage of the net fair market value (FMV) of the trust property. Reg. § 25.2702–3(c)(1). The interest is only qualified to the extent that the percentage is the same each year. However, as with the GRAT, the interest does not fail simply because there is a difference in the percentage to be paid out from year to year. If the percentage changes from year to year, the qualified percentage will be the lowest percentage paid out during the specified term.

In addition, the percentage must be paid to the grantor at least annually and may be paid after the end of the taxable year but must be paid prior to the due date for filing the return. Reg. § 25.2702–3(c)(4). Like the GRAT, the GRUT must prohibit both commutation of the term interest and payment of the qualified amount to any person other than the transferor or the applicable family member prior to the termination of the specified term. Reg. § 25.2702–3(d)(4) and (3).

The grantor of a GRUT is also entitled to retain a contingent reversion in the event the grantor dies within the specified term. Reg. § 25.2702–3(e), Example 1. As with a GRAT, this reversionary interest will not be included in the § 7520 calculation of the remainder interest.

F. QUALIFIED REMAINDER INTERESTS
(§ 2702(b)(3))

[¶ 12,301]

A qualified remainder interest is an interest that is a qualified remainder interest in every respect, and all the interests in the trust, other than non-contingent remainder interests, are qualified annuity interests or qualified unitrust interests. § 2702(b)(3). This requires the governing instrument to prohibit payment of income in excess of the annuity or unitrust amount to the termholder. Reg. § 25.2702–3(f)(1)(iv). A remainder interest must be a right to receive all or a fractional share of the trust property upon termination. Reg. § 25.2702–3(f)(2). Therefore, appreciation in the value of the trust corpus (or the fractional share) and any accumulated income must not pass to anyone other than the transferor. In addition, the remainder interest must be noncontingent, i.e., payable to the remainder beneficiary or the beneficiary's estate in all events.

Example 1. Alicia transfers property to an irrevocable trust. Miguel, Alicia's child, is to receive the income from the trust for life. Upon Miguel's death, the trust terminates and the trust corpus is to be paid to Alicia. Alicia's remainder interest is not a qualified remainder because Miguel's interest was neither a GRAT nor a GRUT. See Reg. § 25.2702–3(f)(3), Example 1.

Example 2. Lester transfers property to an irrevocable trust. The trust is to provide a qualified annuity interest to Soume, Lester's spouse, for 10 years. Upon the expiration of the specified term, Lester is to receive half of the trust corpus and Gary, Lester's grandson, is to receive the other half. Lester's interest is not qualified because someone other than Lester may receive the appreciation in the trust corpus. See Reg. § 25.2702–3(f)(1)(iii).

Example 3. Roger transfers property to an irrevocable trust. The trust provides a qualified annuity to Roger's son for a period of 10 years. Upon expiration of the specified term, the trust corpus is to be paid to Roger if he survives the specified term. If Roger is not living, then the trust corpus is to be paid to Roger's child. Roger's interest is not qualified because it is contingent on his survival. See Reg. § 25.2702–3(f)(3), Example 4.

G. JOINT PURCHASES

[¶ 12,351]

Prior to § 2702, the intrafamily joint or split purchase of property was a common technique for estate planning. At the time of purchase, the parent would purchase a life estate, and a child would purchase the remainder interest in the property. If done correctly, the parent would receive the income from the property for life, and upon the death of the parent, the child would receive the remainder free of estate and gift taxes because the child had paid for his or her interest in the property and therefore nothing was transferred to the child.

Section 2702 diminished the benefits of a joint purchase. If two or more members of the same family acquire interests in property where there is at least one term interest, § 2702(c)(2) deems the person acquiring the term interest as purchasing the entire property and then transferring the remaining interest to the others in exchange for any consideration provided by the other persons. Essentially, § 2702 treats a joint purchase as a transfer of the term interest (e.g., life estate or term of years) to a trust. The term interest is then valued under § 2702 to determine whether a gift has occurred. However, the amount to be deemed transferred to the trust is limited to the amount of the total consideration furnished by the person acquiring the life estate. In addition, the consideration furnished by the person acquiring the term interest will include any funds provided by this person either directly or indirectly through a gift or loan to the other purchasers for the purchase of the remainder interest.

Example. A father and son purchase a residence for $1,000,000. The father pays $400,000 and is entitled to use the residence for his life. The son pays the remaining $600,000 and will receive the residence upon his father's death.

For purposes of § 2702, the father is deemed to have purchased the entire property for $1,000,000 and then sold the remainder interest to his son for $600,000. In addition, if the father's life estate has a value of less than $400,000 using the § 2702 valuation rules, then the difference between the consideration paid by the father and the value of the father's life estate will be considered a gift subject to gift taxation. However, if the father's life estate has a value greater than $400,000, then there are no gift taxes. In this example, the father's interest is not a qualified interest under § 2702(b). Therefore, the father's retained interest is valued at zero and the value of his gift to his son is valued at $400,000.

However, the gift tax liability can be reduced by making the retained interest a right to receive a fixed annuity.

H. ANNUITIES

[¶ 12,451]

1. INTRODUCTION

Two primary objectives of tax planning for many taxpayers are income deflection, i.e., taxing income to someone else within the family unit, and estate shrinkage. By estate shrinkage, we mean the process by which a taxpayer causes property to be made available to his loved ones after his death, but at the same time, is able to keep that property out of his gross estate for federal estate tax purposes.

While much of the tax planning literature emphasizes these two objectives, for many taxpayers, a more important objective is their own financial security. Annuities can be an important part of any financial plan because they are expressly designed to provide the annuitant the security one can derive from an endless stream of cash payments. Probably the most common form of annuity is one characterized by a large initial payment to an insurance company in return for the company's promise to pay a fixed sum on a regular basis over a period of time, often the life of the annuitant. The advantage to the annuitant is that the promise of the insurance company to provide the annuity takes the risk out of the annuitant living too long, i.e., outliving his resources. Of course, with inflation, there is substantial risk that an annuity fixed in amount will be inadequate to maintain the annuitant in future years.

Annuities can be immediate in the sense that payments to the annuitant begin immediately after the annuity is purchased. More common are deferred annuities or annuities that provide that payment to the annuitant will be postponed until some future date. Deferred annuities have appeal because the earnings on the amount invested in the annuity build up tax free during the deferral period. That is, the earnings on the annuity are free of income tax until paid out to the annuitant.

Annuities provided by life insurance companies are described as commercial annuities. Private annuities are annuities provided by individuals, usually members of the annuitant's family in return for the transfer of property by the annuitant to the annuity payer. A private annuity has appeal in the case where the prospective annuitant owns unique property such as land or a closely held business. In such a case, the prospective annuitant could convey the property to a loved one who was the natural successor as owner and manager in return for the transferee's promise to provide the transferor an annuity.

Commercial annuities are of two types, namely "fixed" or "variable." Fixed annuities earn rates of interest that are fixed or "guaranteed" for one or more years. Variable annuities contemplate an investment of the annuity funds in one or more mutual funds, with the annuity payment being a function of the investment results realized.

Commercial annuity distributions—typically to living persons on a periodic basis, perhaps over the lifetime of the annuitant—totaled $211.5 billion in 2001. (This is, indeed, a very big business.)

When choosing a commercial annuity, the issuer's financial health needs to be investigated. The issuer's financial health is important because the annuitant is a general creditor of the issuer and does not have an interest in the underlying assets of the issuer. Ratings are available from A. M. Best Co., Standard & Poor's Corp., Moody's Investors Service, Inc., and Duff & Phelps Inc. Also, the interest rate on fixed annuities varies widely as do the expense charges imposed on variable annuities. Sometimes the interest rate applicable in the initial years to a fixed annuity will differ markedly from the interest paid by the issuer in later years.

Annuities are relatively illiquid investments because earnings withdrawn prior to the date when the annuitant attains age 59 1/2 are subject to a 10–percent penalty tax (as well as the regular income tax). § 72(q). While there are no limits on the amount an individual can contribute to an annuity, most annuities impose "surrender charges" when amounts are withdrawn from the annuity within the first seven years after the annuity has been purchased. In the case of most annuities, distributions can be taken in the form of a lump sum, in the form of periodic payments, perhaps over a 20–year period, or in the form of an income stream based on the annuitant's life expectancy.

The tax treatment of annuities depends on whether the annuity is "qualified" or "nonqualified." Qualified annuities are those annuities which Congress has determined are entitled to preferential tax treatment. Providing preferential tax treatment to these annuities grew out of Congress's determination that many workers did not plan adequately for their retirement years. Rather than put the entire burden of providing retirement income upon the social security system, Congress believed that individual employers would contribute to funding the retirement income needs of their employees if adequate incentives were provided. Qualified annuities are the subject matter of Chapters 29 and 30.

The estate tax treatment of nonqualified annuities is the subject matter of § 2039(a) and (b). Section 72 speaks to the income tax treatment of annuities.

[¶ 12,459]

2. INCOME TAX CONSEQUENCES

Each annuity payment consists of two parts. One part is considered a return to the annuitant of the investment in the annuity contract. This is the nontaxable portion of each annuity payment.

The other part of each annuity payment is treated as taxable income.

The portion of each payment which is treated as nontaxable return of capital is determined by an exclusion ratio. § 72. The numerator is the investment in the contract by the annuitant. The denominator is the expected return based upon life expectancy factors found in tables provided in Reg. § 1.72–9.

Because a portion of each annuity payment is nontaxable, persons planning to utilize annuities as a means of support will find that smaller annuity payments will provide amounts of spendable income which are comparable to that generated by larger amounts of taxable income.

[¶ 12,467]

3. ESTATE TAX CONSEQUENCES

a. *General Rule*

Section 2039 speaks to the estate tax treatment of annuities.

Annuities can take many forms. Common varieties are those which have refund features and those without refund features. In the case of nonrefund annuities, the insurance company's obligation terminates upon the death of the annuitant. Accordingly, there is nothing to include in the gross estate of the annuitant inasmuch as no property passes to survivors at death as a result of the annuity.

On the other hand, the presence of a refund feature means that if the annuitant does not survive for a specified term, the insurance company is obligated to pay to his or her survivors either a lump sum or a fixed number of payments. Annuities with refund features are characterized by smaller annuity payments than nonrefund annuities inasmuch as the insurance company is obligated to make payments whether or not the annuitant is living.

For estate tax purposes, the present value of the benefits to be paid to the annuitant's survivors is includible in the estate of the annuitant to the extent the post-death payments are attributable to contributions to the purchase price of the annuity which were made by the deceased annuitant. If the annuitant had paid only a part of the cost of the annuity, then only a corresponding part of the survivor benefits will be included in the annuitant's gross estate. See § 2039(b).

[¶ 12,475]

b. *Amount Included*

The value of the annuity included in the annuitant's gross estate is the cost of replacement, i.e., the cost of purchasing a single premium annuity on the same terms and conditions for the person or persons for whom benefits are to continue after the annuitant's death. The amount actually included is determined as follows:

$$\frac{\text{Decedent's contribution}}{\text{Purchase price of the original annuity}} \times \text{Value of the annuity for the survivor} = \text{Amount included}$$

¶ 12,459

Thus, if the decedent contributed nothing, nothing is included in the decedent's estate even if annuity continues for the life of another. This, then, is the mechanical test that should be applied to every annuity in which a decedent has an interest to determine whether any portion of the annuity is in the gross estate. The attractiveness of the formula is the fact that it functions to automatically exclude annuities in which the decedent is only a beneficiary and not a contributor, i.e., a transferor for federal estate tax purposes.

Problem

[¶ 12,481]

What if the annuity has a refund feature payable at death of the annuitant to his estate? Under what provision of the Internal Revenue Code, if any, is the amount refunded included in the annuitant's gross estate.

[¶ 12,483]

4. Gift Tax Consequences

When a person purchases a commercial annuity for his or her own life only, there is no transfer under the gift tax. However, if one purchases a commercial annuity and gives another non-cancellable rights, such as to another as survivor under a joint and survivor annuity, then the actuarial value of that interest is a transfer under the gift tax.

Sometimes the creation of a private annuity has gift tax consequences. See discussion at ¶ 12,517.

I. PRIVATE ANNUITIES

[¶ 12,501]

1. DISTINGUISHED FROM COMMERCIAL ANNUITIES

A private annuity is different from an ordinary commercial annuity in the sense that the transferee is not in the business of selling annuities. It is different, too, in the respect that the transaction has both sale and annuity elements. It has an annuity element to the extent the transferee is contractually obligated to the annuitant to provide a stream of income. But it has sale aspects in the sense that the annuitant is exchanging property which usually has a low income tax basis for the transferee's promise to provide the stream of income. The transaction can even have gift aspects if the transferee's promise to pay is worth less on a present value basis than the value of the property received from the annuitant.

None of these conditions exist in the ordinary commercial annuity context. There the annuitant provides cash and the insurance company determines actuarially the benefits that it will provide.

¶ 12,501

[¶ 12,509]

2. WHY USE A PRIVATE ANNUITY?

Usually a private annuity is only considered when the proposed annuitant has a unique property, such as a closely held business, that the annuitant wants to keep within the family unit. The transfer of that property to a successor owner/manager in return for the transferee's promise of an annuity offers several advantages. If structured properly, it can remove the property from the annuitant's gross estate without gift tax consequences. While such a transfer will be considered a sale or exchange for income tax purposes, the tax consequences of a sale in exchange for an annuity rather than an outright sale for immediate cash are frequently a decidedly better alternative. Such a sale is attractive because the gain realized by the annuitant on low basis property will be recognized over the annuitant's lifetime rather than in the year of sale. This deferral opportunity is often the most attractive feature of the private annuity.

[¶ 12,517]

3. TAX CONSEQUENCES OF A PRIVATE ANNUITY

Private annuities may be most easily understood by consideration of a comprehensive example. Assume, that in June 2002, Dad deeded his lake cabin to his son, Junior. Dad's adjusted basis in the cabin was $100,000. On the day of transfer, the market value of the cabin was $250,000. The transfer was accomplished under a private annuity agreement. The agreement required Junior to pay $15,000 annually to Dad for the rest of Dad's life. At the time of transfer Dad was 55 years old.

[¶ 12,525]

a. *Transferor's Income Tax Consequences*

Determining Dad's income tax consequences requires consideration of three elements: (1) the exclusion allowed under § 72(b), (2) any capital gain, and (3) ordinary annuity income.

The exclusion ratio is determined under § 72(b). Section 72 states that gross income does not include the amount equal to the ratio of the "investment in the contract" to the "expected return." The two numbers to be determined are: (1) the investment in the contract, which is equal to the adjusted basis of $100,000 and (2) the expected return, which is equal to the life expectancy of the transfer, 28.6 years, under Reg. § 1.72–9, Table V, multiplied by the annual payment of $15,000. Therefore, the annual exclusion ratio is:

$$\frac{\$1,000,000}{\$15,000 \times 28.6} = \frac{\$1,000,000}{\$429,000} = 23.31\%$$

Therefore, for the next 28.6 years, 23.31% of the $15,000, or $3,496.50, will be excluded from Dad's gross income. However, if Dad outlives his life expectancy, the exclusion ratio will be eliminated from the computation. § 72(b)(2). In year 29, the $3,496.50 will be included in Dad's ordinary income because Dad will have fully recovered his "investment in contract" ($3,496.50 x 28.6 = $100,000).

The capital gain to Dad is determined by computing the "amount received" less the adjusted basis in the property. The "amount received" is equal to the present value of the annuity, determined under Reg. § 20.2031–7(d)(7), Table S, as directed by Reg. § 25.2512–5(d)(2)(iv). Thus, the initial gain received can be computed as: ($15,000 x 11.8458)—$100,000 = $77,688. This is deemed to be a capital gain under § 1221.

To determine the portion of the annuity payment that is attributable to the capital gain, divide the total capital gain by the same life expectancy for Dad of 28.6 years. Reg. § 1.72–6(d)(3), Table V:

$$\$77,688/28.6 \text{ years} = \$2,716$$

Therefore, $1,411.28 will be taxed at the long-term capital gain rate for the current taxable year.

The remaining payment will be considered ordinary annuity income under § 72(a). The breakdown of Dad's annuity payment is:

Excludable Income	+	Capital Gain	+	Annuity Income	=	Total
$3,496.50		$2,716		$8,787.50		$15,000

Beginning in Dad's 29th year of annuity payments, the total annual payment of $15,000 will be taxable as ordinary annuity income (and none of it will be excluded or will qualify for special tax treatment).

The above computations are contingent on Dad's having an unsecured right to payment by Junior. If Dad's annuity is secured by a promissory note, the note is subject to immediate taxation. See Estate of Lloyd G. Bell v. Commissioner, 60 T.C. 469 (1973). That is, the entire $77,688 would be taxable in 2002 as a capital gain. Then Dad's "investment in the contract" will be $177,688 and the annual exclusion ratio would be:

$$\frac{\$177,688}{\$15,000 \times 28.6 \text{ yrs.}} = 41\%$$

or $6,213 (15,000 x 41%). In this scenario Dad's income would consist of two elements: (1) the excludable amount of $6,213 and (2) annuity income of $8,787.

A final point worth noting is that if Dad dies before he recovers his total "investment in contract" (in this case his adjusted basis), he may take the "unrecovered investment" as a deduction on his last income tax return. § 72(b)(3). For example, if Dad dies after receiving 15 payments, a deduction of $47,552.40 would be allowed on his last income tax return ([28.6—15] x $3,496.50 = $47,552.40).

¶ **12,525**

[¶ 12,533]

b. Transferee's Income Tax Consequences

The income tax consequences to Junior are determined when he disposes of the property. Junior's basis is increasing yearly with each annuity payment that he makes. The basis upon disposition of the property depends on whether: (1) Junior disposes of the property during Dad's life or (2) Junior disposes of the property after Dad dies.

[¶ 12,541]

i. Disposition During Dad's Life

Assume Junior sells the cabin for $250,000 directly after paying Dad the tenth annuity payment. Furthermore, assume Dad is living when Junior sells the cabin. To determine Junior's income tax consequences, it must first be determined whether the cabin was sold at a gain or a loss. Junior should compute two figures: (1) the transferee's basis for determining gain and (2) the transferee's basis for determining loss.

The basis for gain is (a) the total annuity payment at the date of disposition plus (b) the present value of the remaining annuity payment. The total annuity payments are $15,000 multiplied by 10, which yields a total of $150,000. Compute the present value of the remaining annuity payments by using the factors in Reg. § 20.2031–7(d). If Dad is 65 when the property is sold, and the applicable interest rate assumption is the same as it was when Dad was 55, the factor is 9.7152, which should be multiplied by the annual annuity payment of $15,000. Therefore, Junior's basis for determining gain is computed as follows:

Payments to date	+	Present value of remaining payments	=	Basis
$150,000 ($15,000 × 10)		$145,728.00 ($15,000 × 9.7152)		$295,728

The basis for determining a loss is simply the total annuity payments made to date of $150,000 ($15,000 x 10). Therefore, in the year of disposition Junior will not have a gain because the sale price is less than the basis for determining gain, nor will he have a loss because the sale price is greater than the basis for determining loss.

The second date of importance with regard to the disposition of private annuity properties is the date when total annuity payments to date exceed the selling price. For example, assuming the above facts, in the year Junior makes the 17th payment to Dad, Junior will be able to recognize a loss equal to the excess of the adjusted basis of the disposed property less the sale price:

Payments to date	−	Sale price	=	Loss taken
$255,000 ($15,000 × 17)		$250,000		$5,000

Finally, the last date worth noting is the date of the annuitant's death. Any gains subsequent to the initial disposition will be determined on the day of the original transferor's death. If Dad died after receiving the 15th

¶ 12,533

payment, Junior would have a recognizable gain of $25,000. Junior's gain can be computed as follows:

$$\underset{\$250,000}{\underline{\text{Sales price}}} - \underset{\$225,000\ (\$15,000\ \times\ 15)}{\underline{\text{Total payments to date}}} = \underset{\$25,000}{\underline{\text{Gain recognized on disposition}}}$$

[¶ 12,549]

ii. Disposition After Dad's Death

This is the simplest scenario to compute. The transferee's basis is equal to the total annuity payments under the contract. Therefore, if Dad died directly after receiving the tenth payment, Junior's basis would be equal to $150,000 ($15,000 x 10). If Junior subsequently sells the property for $100,000, Junior will recognize a $50,000 loss. However, if Junior subsequently sells the property for $200,000, Junior will recognize a $50,000 gain.

[¶ 12,557]

c. Transferor's Gift Tax Consequences

Dad will have gift tax consequences if the fair market value of the property on the date of transfer is greater than the present value of the annuity received. The present value is again determined by multiplying the factor in Reg. § 20.2031–7(d) by the annual annuity payment. This figure is computes as:

$$\underset{\$15,000}{\underline{\text{Annual payment}}} \times \underset{11.8458}{\underline{\text{Factor}}} = \underset{\$177,688}{\underline{\text{Present value of annuity}}}$$

Therefore, Dad's current gift tax consequences would be equal to:

Fair market value on the date of transfer	$250,000
Less: Present value of annuity	177,688
Amount of gift	$72,312
Less: Exclusion allowed in 2002 (§ 2503(b))	10,000
Taxable gift value	$ 62,312

[¶ 12,565]

d. Transferee's Gift Tax Consequences

The gift tax consequences to Junior are not as relevant because the tax on gift transfers is imposed on the transferor of the property and not the transferee. However, if the annuity transfer involved a gift, the transferee's basis is the greater of: (1) the amount paid by the transferee or (2) the transferor's adjusted basis in the property at the time of transfer. Reg. § 1.1015–4.

[¶ 12,573]

e. Transferor's Estate Tax Consequences

There are two primary estate tax consequences which may effect Dad. First, the gift tax consequences will be included in the "adjustable taxable gifts" and may "gross up" Dad's estate. § 2001(b)(1)(B). Therefore, the $61,312 will be included in Dad's estate tax return.

Second, if Dad has any "strings" or retained interest in the transferred property, the value of the interest may be included in Dad's estate. § 2036. For example, any "security interest" retained by Dad will be included in Dad's estate for estate tax purposes under § 2036. Thus, if Dad had taken back a mortgage with a value on the date of death of $50,000, the entire $50,000 would be included in Dad's estate. However, as in our example, if Junior is only to pay Dad the $15,000 for Dad's life, Dad's only estate tax consequence will be the amount of the gift, which will "gross up" Dad's estate as an "adjustable taxable gift." § 2001(b)(1)(B); ¶ 7117.

[¶ 12,581]

f. Transferee's Estate Tax Consequences

If Junior dies prior to Dad's death, Junior's estate will continue to be obligated to pay the annual annuity payments of $15,000. Junior's estate will be allowed a deduction under § 2053(a)(3) for the present value of the annuity.For example, if Junior died directly after making the tenth payment to Dad, Junior's estate must pay Dad $15,000 per year, but it would be entitled to a deduction equal to the present value of the remaining payments. Reg. § 20.2031–7(d). This would be computed as follows:

$$\underset{\$15{,}000}{\underline{\text{Payment amounts}}} \times \underset{9.7152}{\underline{\text{Life expectancy factor}}} = \underset{\$145{,}728}{\underline{\text{Deduction}}}$$

However, if Dad predeceased Junior, Junior has no continuing obligation to make the annuity payments. At this point, Junior's adjusted basis in the property will be fixed.

Problems

[¶ 12,590]

1. What are the economic and tax disadvantages of a private annuity to the transferee?

2. The principal disadvantage of a private annuity to the annuitant is the possibility that the transferee will not honor the commitments the transferee made to the annuitant at the time of the transfer. How can the annuitant protect himself? Could the annuitant retain a security interest in the transferred property?

3. What impact should the annuitant's health have on the valuation of the transferee's promise to pay? For example, suppose Mr. A, age 50, was terminally ill. Could he reduce the size of his estate for estate tax purposes by transferring his closely held business to his son, Chip, age 25, for Chip's promise to pay an amount based on the life expectancy of a healthy Mr. A? See Reg. §§ 20.7520–3(b)(3), Example 1, and 25.7520–3(b)(4) (where there is a terminal illness, actual life expectancy must be used in valuing a transfer).

J. USE OF INSTALLMENT SALES AND SELF–CANCELING INSTALLMENT NOTES (SCINS)

[¶ 12,601]

1. REPORTING OF INSTALLMENT SALES

Generally, an installment note is a note between a seller (creditor) and a buyer (debtor) that provides for a stated interest rate and repayment over a fixed period of years. It may be secured or unsecured, and the buyer receives a basis at the time of purchase.

An "installment sale" is a method of property disposition in which the seller receives a portion of the sale proceeds in a year other than the year of sale. § 453(b)(1). Installment sale reporting is assumed by § 453(d) unless the taxpayer makes a timely election to treat the disposition as a noninstallment sale.

The ability of the seller to match the payment of taxes on any gain with the payment inflows from the sale is the significant advantage of installment sale reporting. A taxpayer selling property under the installment sale method of § 453 may annually report the percentage of gain attributable to the payments received in that particular year. Reg. § 15A.453–1(b)(2)(i). The regulations define a payment as any amount that is actually or constructively received during the taxable year.

In structuring an installment sale it is important to remember that not all assets may be sold under the installment sale method provided in § 453. Personal property sold under a revolving credit plan, publicly traded stocks and public securities cannot be reported under the installment sale method. § 453(k)(2). Additionally, the regulations provide further guidance on the applicability of the installment sale reporting in other situations. See Reg. § 15A.453–1.

[¶ 12,609]

2. ESTATE PLANNING CONSEQUENCES OF INSTALLMENT SALES

Because installment sales involve a disposition of property over more than one taxable year, the notes will ordinarily be subject to estate tax at the time of the holder's death. Section 2033 requires the gross estate to include the value of all property in which the decedent had an interest at the time of death. However, the estate tax consequences will depend upon whether the installment note is a regular installment note or a self-canceling installment note (SCIN).

[¶ 12,617]

3. REGULAR INSTALLMENT SALES

A regular installment note requires repayment over a fixed period of years. If either the seller or the buyer dies before the note is fully paid, the estate of the decedent will be affected. If the buyer dies, the buyer's estate is responsible for making the remaining payments. If the seller dies, the note is transferred upon the death of the seller/holder to a new holder either under the will or by intestacy. The obligee will continue to make the payments required under the original agreement to the new holder or to the seller's estate, and the seller's gross estate will include the value of the note as required by § 2033.

[¶ 12,625]

4. SELF-CANCELING INSTALLMENT NOTES (SCINS)

A self-canceling installment note (SCIN) is similar to a regular installment note except that if the seller dies before the note is fully paid, under the terms of the note, the remaining balance is canceled. The SCIN will include a provision which provides for the cancellation or extinguishment of the note, as if the note were fully paid, if the holder dies before the note is fully paid. As consideration for the seller's risk of early cancellation, the SCIN must provide for a "risk premium." This risk premium may be either an increase in the sales price or a higher interest rate.

5. SCIN FREE OF ESTATE TAXES

[¶ 12,633]

ESTATE OF MOSS v. COMMISSIONER

United States Tax Court, 1980.
74 T.C. 1239, acq. in result.

IRWIN, Judge: * * *

The issues presented for our consideration are: (1) Whether promissory notes held by decedent but which were extinguished upon his death are includable in his gross estate; * * *.

John A. Moss (hereafter decedent) died on February 24, 1974. He was survived only by his wife, Dorothy.

Prior to his death, decedent was * * * engaged in the funeral home services business. As of September 11, 1972, decedent owned 231 shares of the 586 issued and outstanding shares of Moss Funeral Home. He also owned property (known as the North Fort Harrison property and parking areas) which was rented by Moss Funeral Home for use as one of its funeral homes.

All of the remaining stock of Moss Funeral Home was held by its employees who had either purchased the stock or been given shares as gifts from decedent over the years. All of the employee-shareholders were part of an agreement that upon their retirement or resignation from the corporation they would sell their shares of stock in Moss Funeral Home either to the corporation or pro rata to the remaining shareholders at a per-share value which approximated the per-share book value attributable to the corporation's capital account.

On September 11, 1972, a special meeting of the stockholders and directors of Moss Funeral Home was held to consider decedent's offer to sell the corporation his 231 shares of Moss Funeral Home and the North Fort Harrison property and parking areas. The decedent offered to sell the stock for $184,800 and the North Fort Harrison property and parking area for $290,000, each to be paid by the issuance of a note by the corporation to the decedent.

* * *

* * * The sale of the 231 shares of Moss Funeral Home, Inc., stock and the North Fort Harrison Chapel and parking areas was a bona fide sale for adequate and full consideration.

The notes issued for the purchase of the stock (hereafter Note B) and for the purchase of the North Fort Harrison property (hereafter Note C) * * * contained the following clause: "Unless sooner paid, all sums, whether principal or interest, shall be deemed cancelled and extinguished as though paid upon death of J.A. Moss."

* * *

On September 11, 1972, the physical and mental condition of decedent was average for a man of 72 years of age. There was nothing to indicate that his life expectancy would be shorter than the approximate 10 years of life expectancy which was indicated by generally accepted mortality tables. Decedent was admitted to the hospital on May 10, 1973, at which time it was discovered that he had cancer of the lymph nodes. * * *

Decedent timely received each payment due under the notes from October 1972 until his death. At that time, there remained unpaid balances of * * * $161,575.50 on Note B, and $253,554.52 on Note C. No payments were made on Notes B and C subsequent to decedent's death.

* * *

* * * The parties have stipulated that decedent's sale of stock for which the notes were issued was a bona fide sale for adequate and full consideration. The cancellation provision was part of the bargained for consideration provided by decedent for the purchase price of the stock. As such, it was an integral provision of the note. We do not have a situation, therefore, where the payee provided in his will or endorses or attaches a statement to a note stating that the payor is to be given a gift by the cancellation of his obligation on the payee's death.

We believe there are significant differences between the situation in which a note contains a cancellation provision as part of the terms agreed upon for its issue and where a debt is canceled in a will. The most significant difference for purposes of the estate tax is, as petitioner points out, that a person can unilaterally revoke a will during his lifetime, and, therefore, direct the transfer of his property, at his death. All interest that decedent had in the notes lapsed at his death.

¶ **12,633**

Respondent * * * contends that the cancellation provision can be considered an assignment of the notes by the decedent to his employees to become effective upon his death. We believe that this is simply a variation of his argument that the cancellation provision is similar to a bequest in a will, and we reject it for the same reasons that we rejected that argument.

* * * [T]he situation here is analogous to that of an annuity or an interest or estate limited for decedent's life. Since there is no interest remaining in decedent at his death, we hold that the notes are not includable in his gross estate.

[Annuity Distinguished]

Respondent * * * relies on Stewart v. United States, 158 F.Supp. 25 (N.D. Cal. 1957), affd. in part and revd. in part 270 F.2d 894 (9th Cir. 1959), cert. denied 361 U.S. 960 (1960), as presenting an analogous situation. In that case, the decedent purchased annuities providing for the payment of monthly sums to her for life, beginning when she reached a designated age. The policies also provided that in the event the decedent died before payment of any annuities or before the amount paid in had been returned, payment was to be made to certain named beneficiaries. A few months prior to her death, the decedent exercised an option in the policy under which the companies would pay her a designated sum for 240 months, and decedent relinquished her right to make payment contingent on her life. In the event of her death prior to the expiration of the 240 months, payment was to be made to her grandchildren. The decedent, either solely or with her husband, had the right to change the beneficiaries. The Court held that the annuities were includable in the decedent's estate under § 811(a) [1986 Code § 2033]:

> Stewart is obviously distinguishable. In that case, the decedent had the right to receive 240 monthly payments. If she died prior to receiving all the payments, the payments continued to be paid to named third parties. The payor was obligated, therefore, to continue making payments under the contract. Moreover, the decedent retained the right to designate the beneficiaries under the contract.

[Unsecured Promise to Pay]

Even should we consider the payments to decedent as an "annuity" the value of the notes would still not be includable in his gross estate. In Estate of Bergan v. Commissioner, 1 T.C. 543 (1943), the decedent had made an inter vivos transfer to her sister of her interest in an estate in exchange for her sister's promise to care for and support the decedent for the remainder of the decedent's life. We held therein that the decedent did not retain a life interest in the income from the transferred property under the predecessor of § 2036 because no trust was created to secure the "annuity" nor did the decedent reserve to herself the right to the income from the transferred property. * * * The decedent merely contracted with her sister for her support and her share of the estate was transferred as the consideration for such contract. Similarly, in the present case, decedent transferred his stock and the North Fort Harrison property as full consideration for Note B and Note C. While the

¶ 12,633

notes were secured by a stock pledge agreement, this fact, alone, is insufficient to include the value of the notes in decedent's gross estate. * * *

[¶ 12,641]

6. INCOME TAX CONSEQUENCES TO SELLER

FRANE v. COMMISSIONER

United States Court of Appeals, Eighth Circuit, 1993.
998 F.2d 567.

GIBSON, Circuit Judge:

In this case we examine the income tax consequences of an estate planning device known as the "death-terminating installment note." Janet Frane and the estate of Robert Frane, her late husband, appeal from a Tax Court decision holding that they were required to report income resulting from the cancellation of notes from the Franes' children upon Robert Frane's death. On appeal the Franes argue that no one should have to recognize income from the cancellation of the notes or, in the alternative, that if anyone does, it should be the estate and not Mr. Frane himself. We affirm the judgment of the Tax Court in part and reverse in part.

At the age of fifty-three, Robert Frane sold stock in his company, the Sherwood Grove Co., to his four children by four separate stock purchase agreements. Each child signed a note for the appraised value of the stock payable in annual installments over twenty years for a total principal amount of $141,050. Key to this litigation is the self-cancellation clause in the stock purchase agreements, which required the notes to provide "that in the event of [Robert Frane's] death prior to the final payment of principal and interest under said note, the unpaid principal and interest of such note shall be deemed cancelled and extinguished as though paid upon the death of [Robert Frane]." * * * The notes so provided, and the Franes contend they also included an above-market interest rate (twelve percent) meant to compensate Robert Frane for assuming the risk that he would die before twenty years passed and thus not receive full payment on the notes. At the time of the sale, Frane's life expectancy (as determined from United States Department of Commerce statistics) exceeded the twenty year term of the promissory notes. * * *

Frane lived to receive two of the installments, recognizing income on each installment according to the ratio between Frane's basis in the stock and the amount he would receive under the contracts if he lived the full twenty years. * * * After Frane died in 1984, his children made no further payments. * * * In 1986, Sherwood liquidated its assets. * * * Two of the children reported a capital loss from the transaction, claiming as their basis in the stock only the amount they actually paid for it (rather than the face amount of the note). The two other children did not report a gain or a loss.

Neither Frane's last income tax return nor the estate's income tax return reported any income resulting from the self-cancellation of the notes. * * * The Commissioner issued a notice of deficiency * * *. The Tax Court upheld

¶ 12,641

the Commissioner's position that gain was recognized upon Frane's death and the cancellation of the notes, but concluded that the gain was taxable to Frane himself, rather than to the estate. * * *

[Meaning of "Cancelled"]

The Franes' principal argument is that the automatic cancellation of the note upon Frane's death did not generate taxable income. This is an uphill battle, since the Internal Revenue Code specifically provides that "if any installment obligation is canceled or otherwise becomes unenforceable," and the obligee and obligor are related persons, it shall cause the obligee to recognize income equal to the difference between the basis of the obligation and its face value [1986 Code § 453B(a), (f)]. A similar provision applies to estates, requiring "cancellation" of an installment obligation to be treated as a transfer of the obligation, which causes the estate to recognize income in respect of a decedent in the face amount of the obligation less its basis in the hands of the decedent [1986 Code § 691(a)(2)].

The Franes argue that the automatic self-cancellation of the notes is not the sort of "cancellation" covered by §§ 453B and 691(a)(5). The Franes first argue that the word "cancellation" does not, in ordinary usage, cover their death-terminating installment note, and second, they argue that since the code sections were drafted to prevent abuses that occur when an obligation is cancelled by an act subsequent and extraneous to the contract, they were not meant to apply to cancellation resulting from an integral term of the contract itself.

The Franes contend that the word "cancellation" describes an action occurring "after the original transaction and independently from it." While we agree with the Franes that there is a distinction to be made between cancellation by act subsequent to the contract and cancellation upon a contingency pursuant to the contract's terms, the term "cancellation" can be used to describe both situations. To establish this we need go no further than point to the commonly used name for the very estate planning device used here: "self-cancelling installment notes" * * *. Most telling, however, is the use of the words "cancelled and extinguished" in the Franes' notes. The Franes' argument is answered by the very words the Franes used.

[Legislative History]

As for Congressional intent, §§ 453B(f) and 691(a)(5) were indeed drafted to prevent an abuse involving after the fact cancellations. In Miller v. Usry, 160 F.Supp. 368 (W.D. La. 1958), a father transferred property to his son in exchange for an installment note payable in twenty annual installments. The father had a low basis in the property and the note was for a much higher amount. *Id.* at 369. The father later cancelled the note. *Id.* The government collected income tax from the father on the difference between his basis and the unpaid balance on the note, but the court held that the father could only be taxed on the amount he actually realized from the sale. *Id.* at 370–72. The unstated result of the *Miller* case was that the appreciation of the property could never be taxed at all, since the son's basis in the property was the face amount of the note, even though the son had not had to pay the note. Thus, the father avoided recognizing income on the property and the son obtained a stepped-up basis in the property without paying for it.

To close this loophole, Congress enacted §§ 453B(f), which provides that when an installment loan between family members is canceled the obligee recognizes as income the difference between his basis in the obligation and the face amount of the note. The legislative history makes it clear that this is the purpose of § 453B(f):

* * *

Under present law, some have argued that the install[ment] obligation disposition rules can be avoided by making gift cancellations of the obligation or the installments as they come due. In other words, by making an installment sale and then cancelling the obligation or a number of installment payments, it is argued that the seller will incur no income tax liability, but possibly some gift taxes, and the buyer will have a cost basis in the property sold although no income tax cost will have been incurred on the transaction. If a direct gift is made, the donee's basis is generally the same as the donor's basis rather than a "cost" basis which reflects future payments which will never be made.

* * *

Reasons for change

The committee believes that present law should be clarified to make it clear that the installment obligation disposition rules cannot be circumvented by cancelling the obligation.

Explanation of provision

The bill makes it clear that the cancellation of an installment obligation is treated as a disposition of the obligation. In the case where the obligor is a related party, the amount taken into account as a disposition triggering recognition of unreported gain atributable (sic) to the obligation is not to be less than the face amount of the installment obligation.

S. Rep. No. 1000, 96th Cong., 2d Sess., at 25–26 (1980), *reprinted in* 1980 U.S.C.C.A.N. 4696, 4720–21. The legislative history gives a similar explanation for § 691(a)(5). See *id.* at 26–27.

[Basis]

The Franes argue that §§ 453B(f) and 691(a)(5) were not meant to apply to death-terminating installment notes because in such notes the actual price depends on when the obligee dies and the obligor's basis in the property acquired is thus the amount he actually paid on the note, not its face value. The Franes claim that the abuse addressed by the statutes is not possible with death-terminating installment notes, because there is no step-up in the obligor's basis in the property; consequently, there is no reason to adjust the basis on the obligee's side, as there would be in a gratuitous cancellation.

¶ **12,641**

In addressing "Death Terminating Installment Sales," the IRS General Counsel acknowledges that generally a taxpayer may not increase its basis in property "to reflect obligations it assumed in acquiring the property which are contingent or indefinite." IRS Gen. Couns. Mem. 39,503. This reasoning would lead to the conclusion that the Frane childrens' basis in the property is the principal they actually paid. However, the memorandum concludes that the obligor of a self-cancelling installment note has a basis in property purchased with the note equal to the note's face value. Interestingly, the General Counsel's reasoning is that since § 453B will tax the obligee on the amount of appreciation, the obligor should get the benefit of an increased basis. This argument is, of course, circular in our case, for the Franes have tried to establish that § 453B cannot tax the obligee because the obligor will not receive the benefit of an increased basis. The General Counsel's reasoning is nevertheless instructive, because the injustice the Franes complain of only occurs if the treatments accorded the obligor and obligee are inconsistent. The General Counsel's memorandum shows that the plain language of §§ 453B and 691(a)(5) can be applied to make the obligee recognize gain, a consistent treatment can be afforded the obligor, and no injustice results.

Therefore, the Franes lose their uphill battle to adopt a specialized meaning for the word "canceled" in §§ 453B and 691(a)(5), and we affirm the Tax Court's result.

[Income Taxed to Estate]

Next, we must decide whether the income should be taxed to Robert Frane individually or to his estate. The Code provides that income in respect of a decedent which is not properly included in the decedent's last tax return shall be taxed to his estate. § 691(a)(1). "Transfer" of the right to receive such income by the estate would be a taxable event for the estate under § 691(a)(2). Section 691(a)(5)(iii) provides that "any cancellation of [an installment] obligation occurring at the death of the decedent shall be treated as a transfer by the estate of the decedent."

The Tax Court reasoned that the cancellation constituted a "disposition," which 453B(f) provides is taxed to the individual under 453B, rather than a "transmission of installment obligations at death," which § 453B(c) provides is covered under § 691 and thus taxed to the estate. * * *

This reasoning appears to us quite nebulous in comparison with the unambiguous language in § 691(a)(5)(iii) that cancellation occurring at the death of obligee shall be treated as a transfer by the estate, taxable under § 691(a)(2). This language covers the case before us. * * *

We affirm the Tax Court's decision that income was recognized on Robert Frane's death [equal to the amount of the remaining unreported gain, i.e., equal to the difference between the face amount of the note and Frane's basis in the note], but reverse the holding that the income was recognizable by Frane himself and hold that instead the estate was responsible for it.

Problems

[¶ 12,647]

1. Do you believe that every taxpayer should attempt to utilize a SCIN to reduce or eliminate estate tax on his or her property while retaining the enjoyment of the property until death? What are the negative aspects of SCINs? Does the recognition of SCINs in *Moss* mean that § 2036(a)(1) has been effectively emasculated?

2. Mrs. Belletower's personal residence was recently reassessed by the county of her residence to "100 percent of value" for local property tax purposes. The property was assigned a value of $400,000. Despite the local publicity given the validity of the reassessment process, Mrs. Belletower believes her property has a market value of $1 million. She wants to continue to occupy her residence until her death. However, her estate will be in the top estate tax bracket, and she is therefore hoping that you'll be able to suggest how she can remain in her residence while freezing its value for estate tax purposes at the $400,000 assessed valuation. Can you make a recommendation to Mrs. Belletower?

[¶ 12,657]

7.   SCIN AS A TAX PLANNING DEVICE

A SCIN may be a valuable estate planning device if the applicable income tax rates are significantly lower than the applicable estate tax rates. If the seller dies before the note is fully paid, the seller's gross estate will not include the value of the property sold or the SCIN. ¶ 12,633. However, the remaining deferred taxable gain will be recognized in the income tax return of the seller's estate. ¶ 12,641. Nonetheless, if, as in 2006, the maximum income tax rate is 35 percent and the maximum estate tax rate is 46 percent, the tax saving can be significant. Furthermore, § 2053(a)(3) allows the seller's estate an estate tax deduction for the income taxes payable on the decedent's final federal income tax return, the effect being a reduction in the seller's taxable estate at the highest marginal rate.

[¶ 12,665]

8.   SCIN COMPARED TO PRIVATE ANNUITIES

Although private annuities and SCIN transactions are relatively similar, the taxation of these for estate, gift and income tax purposes can differ significantly.

[¶ 12,673]

a.   Estate Tax Consequences

One-life private annuities and SCINs are not included in the decedent's estate under either § 2033 or § 2036. ¶¶ 12,467, 12,633. Therefore, there are no estate tax consequences because the decedent does not have an interest at death.

¶ 12,673

[¶ 12,681]

b. Gift Tax Consequences

As illustrated in ¶ 12,557, the taxpayer transferring property in exchange for a private annuity will be subject to gift tax if the present value of the annuity is less than the fair market value of the property transferred at the time of sale. SCINs, however, do not subject the seller to potential gift tax liability if the selling price and the term of the repayment is reasonable. Furthermore, including a risk premium usually prevents a SCIN from being considered a disguised gift.

[¶ 12,689]

c. Income Tax Consequences

The greatest disparity between a private annuity and a SCIN is in the income tax consequences. As seen in ¶ 12,525, § 72 provides for the taxation of private annuities. The gain realized is determined by computing the present value of the annuity less the seller's basis in the property. This gain is recognized over the seller's life expectancy as determined in Table V of Reg. § 1.72–9. Each payment consists of three parts: (1) capital gain; (2) return of capital; and (3) ordinary income. If the seller outlives his or her life expectancy, the remaining payments will be ordinary income. If the seller does not live to the end of his or her determined life expectancy, the remaining unrecognized gain is extinguished and nothing remains to be reported on the decedent's final income tax return. As seen in ¶ 12,533, because the decedent's gain may be extinguished, the buyer's basis is never finally determined until the death of the seller.

Section 453 governs the income taxation of SCINs. SCINs are also divided into three parts: (1) capital gain; (2) return of capital; and (3) interest income. The first calculation necessary to determine the amount of "annual reportable gain" is the gross profit percentage. Gross profit is equal to the selling price less the property's adjusted basis. Reg. § 15A.453–1(b)(2)(v). This equates to the total gain that will be recognized over the term of the installment sale. The annual reportable gain for the year is simply computed by dividing the gross profit by the total sale price and then multiplying this percentage by the annual installment sale payment. This can be expressed as follows:

$$\frac{\text{Selling price} - \text{Adjusted basis}}{\text{Selling price}} \times \text{Annual payment} = \text{Reportable gain}$$

Second, the amount of return of capital can be computed by dividing the seller's adjusted basis by the selling price as follows:

$$\frac{\text{Adjusted basis}}{\text{Selling price}} \times \text{Annual payment} = \text{Return of capital}$$

Finally, because all SCINs must have a stated interest rate, the interest paid under this provision will be reported as interest income to the seller.

Example. Edith sold her farm to Gertrude. Under the terms of the SCIN, Gertrude will make 10 annual payments of $10,000 to Edith plus interest

¶ 12,681

at an annual rate of 10 percent on the outstanding balance. Edith's adjusted basis in the property is $50,000 on the date of sale. This can be computed as follows:

$$\frac{\$100,000 - \$50,000}{\$100,000} = 50\% \times \$10,000 = \$5,000 \text{ reportable gain}$$

Edith's gross profit percentage is 50 percent under the term of the agreement. Each year Edith will receive a nontaxable return of capital of $50,000 and report capital gain income of $5,000 and interest income of 10 percent of the outstanding balance.

If the seller dies before the end of the term of the note, the remaining realized gain is recognized on the decedent's income tax return filed for the seller's estate. Any income tax paid may be deductible by the estate under § 2053(a)(3). If the seller outlives the note's term, the note terminates and the gain is fully recognized; nothing remains to be included on the seller's final income tax return or on the income tax return for the seller's estate. Frane v. Commissioner, 998 F.2d 567 (8th Cir.1993); ¶ 12,641.

K. SALE LEASEBACK OR GIFT LEASEBACK WITH DEBT FORGIVENESS

[¶ 12,801]

The $12,000 per donee per annum gift tax exclusion (adjusted for inflation) provided by § 2503(b) is the focus of much of the gift planning that takes place. Where cash is available, the $12,000 annual gift tax exclusion makes it almost effortless to bring about a significant tax-free reduction in the size of a taxable estate. But where cash or other property readily divisible or easily partitioned is not available, wealth shifts can be more difficult.

Take, for example, Grandpa, who has a large parcel of land. He could have it appraised annually and gift to each of his grandchildren a fractional interest having a value of $12,000. See Rev. Rul. 83–180, 1983–2 C.B. 169. Obviously, that is somewhat complicated, as well as expensive, in terms of appraisal fees and attorney fees to get the transaction together.

As an alternative, Grandpa proposes that he sell the land to his grandchildren, taking back a series of promissory notes, each in the amount of $12,000, aggregating in value the appraised value of the land. Grandpa says, "to make it all legal, each note will be secured by a vendor's lien on the property sold to the grandkids." Grandpa proposes to make a gift of $12,000 to each of the grandchildren in the following years by canceling the notes. Thus, if there are 20 grandchildren, he will cancel 20 notes totaling $240,000, allowing Grandpa to shift $240,000 each year gift tax free.

In Haygood v. Commissioner, 42 T.C. 936 (1964), on facts similar to Grandpa's, the IRS claimed that the vendor had no intention to enforce payment of the notes and, therefore, a gift of the property's entire value was made in the year in which the property was "sold" to the so-called "purchasers." The court rejected this argument, pointing to the vendor's ability to enforce the notes and the validity of the liens. At no time were the purchasers financially able to make the payments required by the notes, but the court said that this was "academic."

The IRS refuses to follow *Haygood*, saying in Revenue Ruling 77–299, 1977–2 C.B. 343, that, in cases like Grandpa's, such a transfer is "merely a disguised gift rather than a bona fide sale." According to the IRS, "whether the transfer of property was a sale or a gift depends upon whether, as part of a prearranged plan" the so-called "seller" "intended to forgive the notes that were received" when the property was initially transferred to the purchasers.

"Say, why don't we have Mom sell us the house, and we'll lease it back to her so that she'll have some place to live," says Huey.

"Oh, I get it, we'll get it out of her estate for tax purposes, but Mom won't have to get out of the house—and she'll get some money," says Dewey.

"I'll go you one better," says Louie. "Why not have Mom just give us the house and we'll rent it back to her—and we'll get some money! Maybe that way, too, Mom'll qualify for Medicaid."

Huey then says, "That wraps it up. I don't know about the Medicaid part, but let's tell Mom the good news."

[¶ 12,804]

ESTATE OF MAXWELL v. COMMISSIONER

United States Court of Appeals, Second Circuit, 1993.
3 F.3d 591

LASKER, Senior District Judge:

* * * The petitioner, the Estate of Lydia G. Maxwell, contends that the tax court erred in holding that the transaction at issue (a) was a transfer with retained life estate within the meaning of § 2036 and (b) was not a bona fide sale for adequate and full consideration under that statute.

The decision of the tax court is affirmed.

I.

On March 14, 1984, Lydia G. Maxwell (the "decedent") conveyed her personal residence, which she had lived in since 1957, to her son Winslow Maxwell, her only heir, and his wife Margaret Jane Maxwell (the "Maxwells"). Following the transfer, the decedent continued to reside in the house until her death on July 30, 1986. At the time of the transfer, she was eighty-two years old and was suffering from cancer.

The transaction was structured as follows:

1) The residence was sold by the decedent to the Maxwells for $270,000 [for purposes of the litigation the fair market value of the property on the date of the purported sale was stipulated to be $280,000—ed.];

¶ 12,801

2) Simultaneously with the sale, the decedent forgave $20,000 of the purchase price (which was equal in amount to the annual gift tax exclusion to which she was entitled);

3) The Maxwells executed a $250,000 mortgage note in favor of decedent;

4) The Maxwells leased the premises to her for five years at the monthly rental of $1800; and

5) The Maxwells were obligated to pay and did pay certain expenses associated with the property following the transfer, including property taxes, insurance costs, and unspecified "other expenses."

While the decedent paid the Maxwells rent totalling $16,200 in 1984, $22,183 in 1985 and $12,600 in 1986, the Maxwells paid the decedent interest on the mortgage totalling $16,875 in 1984, $21,150 in 1985, and $11,475 in 1986. As can be observed, the rent paid by the decedent to the Maxwells came remarkably close to matching the mortgage interest which they paid to her. In 1984, she paid the Maxwells only $675 less than they paid her; in 1985, she paid them only $1,033 more than they paid her, and in 1986 she paid the Maxwells only $1,125 more than they paid her.

Not only did the rent functionally cancel out the interest payments made by the Maxwells, but the Maxwells were at no time called upon to pay any of the principal on the $250,000 mortgage debt; it was forgiven in its entirety. As petitioner's counsel admitted at oral argument, although the Maxwells had executed the mortgage note, "there was an intention by and large that it not be paid." Pursuant to this intention, in each of the following years preceding her death, the decedent forgave $20,000 of the mortgage principal, and, by a provision of her will executed on March 16, 1984 (that is, just two days after the transfer), she forgave the remaining indebtedness.

The decedent reported the sale of her residence on her 1984 federal income tax return but did not pay any tax on the sale because she elected to use the once-in-a-lifetime exclusion on the sale or exchange of a principal residence provided for by § 121.

She continued to occupy the house by herself until her death. At no time during her occupancy did the Maxwells attempt to sell the house to anyone else, but, on September 22, 1986, shortly after the decedent's death, they did sell the house for $550,000.

Under § 2036(a), where property is disposed of by a decedent during her lifetime but the decedent retains "possession or enjoyment" of it until her death, that property is taxable as part of the decedent's gross estate, unless the transfer was a bona fide sale for an "adequate and full" consideration.

* * *

There are two questions before us: Did the decedent retain possession or enjoyment of the property following the transfer. And if she did, was the transfer a bona fide sale for an adequate and full consideration in money or money's worth.

¶ 12,804

II.

* * * In the case of real property, the terms "possession" and "enjoyment" have been interpreted to mean "the lifetime use of the property." United States v. Byrum, 408 U.S. 125 (1972).

In numerous cases, the tax court has held, where an aged family member transferred her home to a relative and continued to reside there until her death, that the decedent-transferor had retained "possession or enjoyment" of the property within the meaning of § 2036. As stated in Rapelje v. Commissioner, 73 T.C. 82 (1979):

> Possession or enjoyment of gifted property is retained [by the transferor] when there is an express or implied understanding to that effect among the parties at the time of transfer. * * *

Id. at 86. As the *Rapelje* opinion indicates by its citation of earlier decisions, courts have held that § 2036(a) requires that the fair market value of such property be included in the decedent's estate

> if he retained the actual possession or enjoyment thereof, even though he may have had no enforceable right to do so. * * *

Id. In such cases, the burden is on the decedent's estate to disprove the existence of any adverse implied agreement or understanding and

> that burden is particularly onerous when intrafamily arrangements are involved.

Id.

As indicated above, the tax court found as a fact that the decedent had transferred her home to the Maxwells "with the understanding, at least implied, that she would continue to reside in her home until her death." This finding was based upon the decedent's advanced age, her medical condition, and the overall result of the sale and lease. The lease was, in the tax court's words, "merely window dressing"—it had no substance.

* * * We agree with the tax court's finding that the decedent transferred her home to the Maxwells "with the understanding, at least implied, that she would continue to reside in her home until her death," and certainly do not find it to be clearly erroneous. The decedent did, in fact, live at her residence until she died, and she had sole possession of the residence during the period between the day she sold her home to the Maxwells and the day she died. There is no evidence that the Maxwells ever intended to occupy the house themselves, or to sell or lease it to anyone else during the decedent's lifetime. Moreover, the Maxwells' failure to demand payment by the estate, as they were entitled to do under the lease, of the rent due for the months following decedent's death and preceding their sale of the property, also supports the tax court's finding.

The petitioner argues * * * that the decedent's status was no more than that of a tenant, and that such a status was insufficient to cause the property to be includible in her estate or to qualify as "possession or enjoyment" under § 2036(a). However, the petitioner misapprehends the tax court's ruling. That court held, on the basis of all the facts described above, that the decedent's

¶ 12,804

use of the house following the transfer depended not on the lease but rather on an implied agreement between the parties that the decedent could and would continue to reside in the house until her death, as she actually did. It found that the lease "represented nothing more than an attempt to add color to the characterization of the transaction as a bona fide sale." The tax court did not rely on the tenancy alone to establish "possession or enjoyment."

Just as petitioner argues that the decedent's tenancy alone does not justify inclusion of the residence in her estate, so it argues that the decedent's payment of rent sanctifies the transaction and renders it legitimate. Both arguments ignore the realities of the rent being offset by mortgage interest, the forgiveness of the entire mortgage debt either by gift or testamentary disposition, and the fact that the decedent was eighty-two at the time of the transfer and actually continued to live in the residence until her death which, at the time of the transfer, she had reason to believe would occur soon in view of her poor health.

The Estate relies primarily on Barlow v. Commissioner, 55 T.C. 666 (1971). In that case, the father transferred a farm to his children and simultaneously leased the right to continue to farm the property. The tax court held that the father did not retain "possession or enjoyment," stating that

> "one of the most valuable incidents of income-producing real estate is the rent which it yields. He who receives the rent in fact enjoys the property."

Barlow, 55 T.C. at 671 (quoting McNichol's v. Commissioner, 265 F.2d 667, 671 (3d Cir.), cert. denied, 361 U.S. 829 (1959)). However, *Barlow* is clearly distinguishable on its facts: In that case, there was evidence that the rent paid was fair and customary and, equally importantly, the rent paid was not offset by the decedent's receipt of interest from the family lessor.

Nor is there any merit to petitioner's contention that the "decedent's status as a tenant" exempts her from § 2036(a) "as a matter of law." *Barlow* itself recognized that where a transferor "by agreement" "reserves the right of occupancy as an incident to the transfer," § 2036(a) applies. *Barlow*, 55 T.C. at 670. The court there simply reached a different conclusion on its facts:

> [The] substance-versus-form argument, while theoretically plausible, depends upon the facts, and we do not think the record as a whole contains the facts required to give it life. . . .

Id. at 670 (emphasis added).

For the reasons stated above, we conclude that the decedent did retain possession or enjoyment of the property for life and turn to the question of whether the transfer constituted "a bona fide sale for adequate and full consideration in money or money's worth."

III.

Section 2036(a) provides that even if possession or enjoyment of transferred property is retained by the decedent until her death, if the transfer was a bona fide sale for adequate and full consideration in money or money's worth, the property is not includible in the estate. Petitioner contends that the Maxwells paid an "adequate and full consideration" for the decedent's residence, $270,000 total, consisting of the $250,000 mortgage note given by the Maxwells to the decedent, and the $20,000 the decedent forgave simultaneously with the conveyance.

The tax court held that neither the Maxwells' mortgage note nor the decedent's $20,000 forgiveness constituted consideration within the meaning of the statute.

$250,000 Mortgage Note

As to the $250,000 mortgage note, the tax court held that:

> Regardless of whether the $250,000 mortgage note might otherwise qualify as "adequate and full consideration in money or money's worth" for a $270,000 or $280,000 house, the mortgage note here had no value at all if there was no intention that it would ever be paid.

> The conduct of decedent and the Maxwells strongly suggest that neither party intended the Maxwells to pay any part of the principal of either the original note or any successor note.

There is no question that the mortgage note here is a fully secured, legally enforceable obligation on its face. The question is whether it is actually what it purports to be—a bona fide instrument of indebtedness—or whether it is a facade. The petitioner argues not only that an allegedly unenforceable intention to forgive indebtedness does not deprive the indebtedness of its status as "consideration in money or money's worth" but also that "[t]his is true even if there was an implied agreement exactly as found by the Tax Court."

We agree with the tax court that where, as here, there is an implied agreement between the parties that the grantee would never be called upon to make any payment to the grantor, as, in fact, actually occurred, the note given by the grantee had "no value at all." We emphatically disagree with the petitioner's view of the law as it applies to the facts of this case. As the Supreme Court has remarked,

> the family relationship often makes it possible for one to shift tax incidence by surface changes of ownership without disturbing in the least his dominion and control over the subject of the gift or the purposes for which the income from the property is used.

Commissioner v. Culbertson, 337 U.S. 733, 746 (1949). There can be no doubt that intent is a relevant inquiry in determining whether a transaction is "bona fide". As another panel of this Court held recently, construing a parallel provision of the Internal Revenue Code, in a case involving an intrafamily transfer:

> when the bona fides of promissory notes is at issue, the taxpayer must demonstrate affirmatively that "there existed at the time of the transaction a real expectation of repayment and an intent to enforce the collection of the indebtedness." * * *

Flandreau v. Commissioner, 994 F.2d 91, 93 (2d Cir.1993) (case involving I.R.C. § 2053(c)(1)). In language strikingly apposite to the situation here, the court stated:

> it is appropriate to look beyond the form of the transactions and to determine, as the tax court did here, that the gifts and loans back to decedent were "component parts of single transactions."

Id. (citation omitted).

The tax court concluded that the evidence "viewed as a whole" left the "unmistakable impression" that

> regardless of how long decedent lived following the transfer of her house, the entire principal balance of the mortgage note would be forgiven, and the Maxwells would not be required to pay any of such principal.

Id.

The petitioner's reliance on Haygood v. Commissioner, 42 T.C. 936 (1964), not followed by Rev.Rul. 77–299, 1977–2 C.B. 343 (1977), Kelley v. Commissioner, 63 T.C. 321 (1974), not followed by Rev.Rul. 77–299, 1977–2 C.B. 343 (1977), and Wilson v. Commissioner, 64 T.C.M. (CCH) 583 (1992), is misplaced. Those cases held only that intent to forgive notes in the future does not per se disqualify such notes from constituting valid consideration. In contrast, in the case at hand, the decedent did far more than merely "indicate[ ] an intent to forgive the indebtedness in the future." *Wilson*, 64 T.C.M. (CCH) 583, 584 (1992).

In *Haygood, Kelley*, and *Wilson*, the question was whether transfers of property by petitioners to their children or grandchildren in exchange for notes were completed gifts within the meaning of the Internal Revenue Code. None of the notes was actually paid by the grantees; instead the notes were either forgiven by petitioners at or about the time they became due (*Haygood* and *Kelley*) or the petitioner died prior to the date when the note was due (*Wilson*). In those circumstances, the tax court held that the notes received by petitioners, secured by valid vendor's liens or by deeds of trust on the property, constituted valuable consideration for the transfer of the property.

The *Kelley* court made no finding as to intent to forgive the notes. In *Haygood*, although the court did find that the "petitioner had no intention of collecting the debts but did intend to forgive each payment as it became due," it also found that the transfer of the property to the children had been a mistake. ["The court stated that it was 'eminently clear from the testimony that it was petitioner's intent to give only a $3,000 interest [in the property] to each of her sons' that year but her lawyer accidentally structured the transaction to give the entire property to the petitioner's sons." 42 T.C. 936, 942, footnote 5] And, the *Wilson* court found that:

> The uncontradicted testimony in this case establishes that petitioner and her children intended that the children would sell the property and pay the note with the proceeds.

Wilson, 64 T.C.M. (CCH) at 584.

By contrast, in the case at hand, the tax court found that, at the time the note was executed, there was "an understanding" between the Maxwells and the decedent that the note would be forgiven.

In our judgment, the conduct of decedent and the Maxwells with respect to the principal balance of the note, when viewed in connection with the initial "forgiveness" of $20,000 of the purported purchase price, strongly suggests the existence of an understanding between decedent and the Maxwells that decedent would forgive $20,000 each year thereafter until her death, when the balance would be forgiven by decedent's will.

* * * Even *Kelley* stated that notes "in proper legal form and regular on their face" are only "prima facie" what they purport to be. *Kelley*, 63 T.C. at 324–25.

$20,000 Initial Forgiveness

We also agree with the tax court that, as to the $20,000 which was forgiven simultaneously with the conveyance,

In the absence of any clear and direct evidence that there existed an obligation or indebtedness capable of being forgiven . . .

the $20,000 item had "no economic substance."

To conclude, we hold that the conveyance was not a bona fide sale for an adequate and full consideration in money or money's worth.

* * *

Section 2043

The petitioner argues finally that the tax court should be reversed because, under § 2043, if there was any consideration in money or money's worth paid to the decedent, even if the payment was inadequate, the Estate is at least entitled to an exclusion pro tanto. The argument has no merit in the circumstances of this case. The tax court held, and we do also, that the transfer was without any consideration. Section 2043 applies only where the court finds that some consideration was given.

The decision of the tax court is affirmed.

WALKER, Circuit Judge, dissenting:

Nearly 60 years ago, in words as true today as they were then, Judge Learned Hand wrote that "[a]ny one may so arrange his affairs that his taxes shall be as low as possible; he is not bound to choose that pattern which will best pay the Treasury; there is not even a patriotic duty to increase one's taxes." Helvering v. Gregory, 69 F.2d 809, 810 (2d Cir.1934), aff'd, 293 U.S. 465 (1935). Thus, "when a taxpayer chooses to conduct his business in a certain form, 'the tax collector may not deprive him of the incidental tax benefits flowing therefrom, unless it first be found to be but a fiction or a sham.' " W. Braun Co. v. Commissioner, 396 F.2d 264, 267 (2d Cir.1968) * * *.

* * *

¶ 12,804

There is no doubt that the decedent and the Maxwells structured the transaction at issue here to maximize tax benefits. However, it is far from clear that the transaction was a sham, and thus could be ignored for tax purposes by the IRS.

In erroneously upholding the Tax Court's determination * * * the majority ignores the settled law of this Circuit and misconstrues Tax Court case law.

I. *The Decedent's "Possession" of the Property*

The majority correctly states that, under § 2036(a)(1), an individual may retain possession or enjoyment of a property, following a legal transfer of ownership, pursuant to an express agreement or an implied understanding to that effect among the parties at the time of transfer. However, physical occupation of a property is not necessarily equivalent to possession or enjoyment of it. Rather, the statute looks to whether an individual gratuitously resides on a property following a sale until her death, thereby effectively retaining an ownership interest in the land.

The majority makes much of the Tax Court's factual finding that the Maxwells intended to permit the decedent to remain living on the property beyond the lease term, if she survived it. The majority also emphasizes that "[t]he decedent did, in fact, live at her residence until she died.... " However, I believe the crucial question under § 2036(a)(1) is not whether the Maxwells intended the decedent to remain on the property, or indeed whether she physically occupied the house until her death. Rather, it is whether she retained incidents of ownership of the land until her death.

In this case, the stipulated facts establish that the decedent remained on the land not as an owner, but as a tenant who fulfilled her duties under a lease by paying a rent of $1,800 per month. After the sale, the Maxwells assumed the burdens and costs of ownership, including insurance and property tax payments that were not off-set by the decedent's rents.

Tax Court case law makes clear that a rent-paying tenant does not retain possession or ownership of property. In *Estate of Barlow*, the decedent parents gave farmland to their children who leased the property back. Focusing on the terms of the lease, the court held that the children were in possession of the property because of their right to receive rental payments:

> One of the most valuable incidents of income-producing real estate is the rent which it yields. He who receives the rent in fact enjoys the property. The record contains no evidence whatever of a contemporaneous agreement, oral or written, expressed or implied, qualifying in any way the terms of the deed and lease.

55 T.C. at 671 (citation omitted). In this case, there is no evidence of an agreement qualifying the Maxwells' right to receive rents under the lease. Indeed, the decedent made rental payments until her death. The majority seeks to distinguish *Estate of Barlow* on ground that the decedent's rental payments approximated the Maxwells' mortgage payments. However, the fact that the payments approximated each other does not obviate the economic significance of the lease, transforming it into a mere "facade." It is reasonable

to expect that a market rent would approximate, if not exceed, the carrying costs of the property.

The proper result here might be different if the Tax Court found that the decedent paid an inflated, above-market rent for the use of the property as a means of subsidizing the Maxwells' mortgage payments. However, the Tax Court did not consider the market-rental value of the property—let alone make findings on the issue. The majority's reliance on the Maxwells' decision not to demand rent from the estate after the decedent's death is misplaced. In *Estate of Barlow*, a delay in the payment of rents for four years did not obviate the economic significance of the lease. See 55 T.C. at 668.

The majority's reasoning is also contrary to our treatment of rental payments in *Rosenfeld* [Rosenfeld v. Commissioner, 706 F.2d 1277, 1281 (2d Cir.1983)]. In that case, a physician gave an ownership interest in his medical office property to an independent trust administered on behalf of his children. In connection with the transfer of the property, the physician retained the right to lease the property at a market rent for use as his office. The Commissioner disallowed the physician's deductions of the rental payments as business expenses on the theory that the gift/leaseback was a sham. As in the case at bar, the Commissioner argued that "nothing changed [following the transfer of the property] because [the taxpayer] was occupying the same premises as a lessee which he previously used as an owner." 706 F.2d at 1282–83. We rejected the Commissioner's argument as "disingenuous," reasoning that the taxpayer "could have given the property to his children in trust and leased property from a third person for an amount equally fair and reasonable for his medical office. It is clear . . . that a rent deduction would have been entirely proper in such a case." Id. at 1283.

Our reasoning in *Rosenfeld* applies equally here. The economic reality of the situation would have been the same if the Maxwells had rented the property to a third party under similar lease terms, and utilized the rental income to satisfy the mortgages. Under Tax Court precedents and the law of this Circuit, the fact that the Maxwells rented the property to the decedent instead of a third party did not make the lease agreement a facade to mask the decedent's continued ownership.

II. *The "Sham" Purchase*

The majority holds that the Maxwells proffered no consideration in connection with their purchase of the property from the decedent and, thus, that there was not a bona fide sale within the meaning of § 2036(a). However, in examining the economic results of the transaction, the majority misconstrues both Tax Court case law and the stipulated facts in the record.

The majority endorses the Tax Court's conclusion that "the mortgage note here had no value at all [for purposes of § 2036(a)] if there was no intention that it would ever be paid." This construction of the statute is flatly contrary to prior Tax Court cases concerning similar transactions upon which the Maxwells apparently relied.

* * *

In a line of cases beginning nearly 30 years ago, the Tax Court has stated that where "property is transferred in exchange for a valid, enforceable, and secured legal obligation to pay full value, there is no gift for Federal tax purposes." Wilson v. Commissioner, 64 Tax Ct.Mem.Dec. (CCH) 583, 584 (1992) * * *. "This is true even if the parties are related and the seller/obligee indicates an intent to forgive the indebtedness in the future." *Wilson*, Tax Ct.Mem.Dec. (CCH) at 584 (emphasis added) * * *. * * * While the Commissioner has consistently expressed disagreement with the reasoning of and refused to acquiesce in the Tax Court's reasoning in these cases, see, e.g., Rev.Rul. 77–299, 1977–2 C.B. 343 (1977), the Commissioner's disagreement does not impair their precedential value. Neither does the Commissioner's nonacquiescence affect the reasonableness of taxpayer reliance upon the Tax Court precedents.

The majority suggests that *Haygood*, *Estate of Kelley* and *Wilson* only stand for the proposition that an "intent to forgive notes in the future does not per se disqualify such notes from constituting valid indebtedness." However, I read these cases to state that the inquiry ends in the taxpayer's favor upon a finding that the payee received a legally enforceable note or other instrument of indebtedness in return for a property.

In *Haygood*, the question before the Tax Court was whether a taxpayer transferred properties to her son for good and adequate consideration, and thus could avoid paying gift tax on the entire value of the properties. In return for the properties, the son gave his mother notes secured by the properties. The mother never intended to collect on the notes, and forgave payments on them as they came due. Indeed, unlike the Maxwells, the son in *Haygood* never made a single payment on the notes. However, the court did not focus upon the failure to enforce the payment obligations. Rather, in ruling for the taxpayer, the court relied on the validity of the obligations created by the notes, stating: "the evidence certainly supports the fact that the notes did create enforceable indebtedness even though petitioner had no intention of collecting the debts but did intend to forgive each payment as it became due." 42 T.C. at 946.

The Tax Court upheld a similar transaction in *Estate of Kelley* by, once again, focusing upon the legal obligations created by the notes:

> There is nothing in the trial record to support a finding that the notes and vendor's liens, both in proper legal form and regular on their face, were not valid and enforceable. Nor is there any evidence of any agreement between petitioners and the donees qualifying the rights of petitioners under either the liens or the notes. There is no solid evidence indicating that petitioners did not purposely and consciously reserve all rights given to them under the liens and notes until they actually forgave the notes. 63 T.C. at 324–25 (emphasis added).

The purposes of the transactions at issue in *Haygood* and *Estate of Kelley* and the transaction in this case were the same: to remove properties from estates without paying taxes by selling them to close relatives in exchange for secured notes. And the notes at issue here were legally valid, like the notes at issue in the earlier Tax Court cases. Yet, in *Haygood* and *Estate of Kelley*, the

Tax Court found such sales bona fide, while, in this case, the Tax Court found that the mortgage notes were without substance.

In attempting to distinguish *Haygood* and *Estate of Kelley*, the majority distorts them. For example, the majority suggests that the Tax Court's finding that the decedent and the Maxwells had an "understanding" that the mortgage would eventually be forgiven at the time the property was transferred makes this case unique. However, the payee in *Haygood* also intended to forgive the notes executed in her favor from the time she received them. See 42 T.C. at 946. And, while the majority correctly states that the *Estate of Kelley* court never explicitly found that the payee had formulated the intent to forgive the notes on the day she received them, the majority fails to note that the *Estate of Kelley* opinion focussed upon the enforceability of the notes—the fact that they could be enforced—and quoted approvingly language in *Haygood* stating that an intent to forgive would not defeat the economic substance of a transaction. See 63 T.C. at 324–25.

* * *

The economic substance of the mortgages is established not only by the lack of evidence contradicting their validity and enforceability, but also by the actions of the parties. The majority states that the Maxwells were never called upon to make payments upon the notes. It is unclear whether the majority means that the Maxwells made no interest or no principal payments. In fact, they made both.

First, as I've discussed, the Maxwells made monthly interest payments on the notes until the decedent's death. The unremarkable fact that the mortgage payments approximated the decedent's rent, which the majority relies upon in considering whether the decedent retained possession of the property, does not in itself vitiate the economic substance of the rents.

Second, the decedent forgave annually $20,000 of the principal amounts the Maxwells owed on the mortgages, starting with an initial forgiveness at the time of the conveyance of the property to the Maxwells. The amounts forgiven corresponded to the decedent's $10,000 per donee exclusion from the gift tax. See § 2503. Thus, each time the decedent forgave a portion of the amounts owed on the mortgages, she effectively made a gift to the Maxwells by reducing their mortgage obligations. The substance of these transactions would have been exactly the same had the decedent made annual cash gifts totalling $20,000 to the Maxwells and the Maxwells then independently chose to use those or other monies to make principal payments on the mortgages. The fact that the decedent chose to benefit the Maxwells by reducing their obligations directly rather than by sending them a check and receiving another check in return does not make the Maxwells' satisfaction of portions of the principal amounts any less genuine.

CONCLUSION

I am convinced that the Tax Court misconstrued its own precedents and disregarded our cases in concluding that the decedent retained possession and enjoyment of the property absent a determination that the rents were an above-market rate subsidy for the Maxwells' mortgage payments. * * *

* * * Were we writing on a clean slate, we might not construe § 2036(a) to uphold the validity for tax purposes of a decedent's sale of a property to a close family member with the intent to forgive mortgage obligations. However, *Haygood*, *Estate of Kelley* and their progeny make it plain that no legal significance attaches to the intent not to collect on such obligations. * * *

I respectfully dissent.

Problem

[¶ 12,857]

Based on *Maxwell* and such other investigation as is warranted, suggest a structure for Mom to utilize in gifting the Homeplace to the Junior while continuing to occupy the Homeplace "for the rest of her days" while preserving as much as possible if not all of her gift tax exemption. Assume the Homeplace—beachfront property in Malibu—has a value of $2 million. Mom is 38 and Junior, Dad's child from his prior marriage, is 50. (Dad is deceased.) Would a QPRT be best? See ¶ 12,109. What about a sale-leaseback with annual debt forgiveness of the installment obligations as they come due (perhaps with provisions in Mom's will for foregiveness of any outstanding obligation on the sale)? Is a SCIN the answer? See ¶ 12,625.

L. GIFT AND LEASEBACK OF BUSINESS PROPERTY

[¶ 12,901]

The tax advantages of gift and leaseback techniques have been described in Kabaker, Gift and Leaseback Techniques, 3 Notre Dame Est. Plan. Inst. 407, at 408–409 (1979), as follows

> The gift and leaseback technique is usually considered for an individual who is in a very high income tax bracket as compared with one or more other members of his or her family. The greater the disparity in marginal rates, the more desirable the redirection of income becomes. This individual should derive all or the great majority of his or her income through the rendition of personal services. Where substantial income is obtained by other assets, alternative devices, such as outright gifts, corporate fringe benefits, etc. are available to the estate planner. Ideally, our hypothetical client should do business out of a building owned by him or her in whole or in part. Partial ownership might be as a tenant in common. This property interest will be the subject of the gift and leaseback.

> *Advantages of Gift and Leaseback Technique*

> Ideally, the gift and leaseback should work in the following manner: Having given the property, in trust or otherwise, to one or more members

of his or her family who are in substantially lower income tax brackets, the donor then leases the property back from the donees and continues to do business in the premises. The rental payments made to the donees are deducted by the donor on his or her income tax return under § 162(a)(3) and are reported by the donees at their lower marginal income tax rates. This has the effect of shifting income from the donor to the donees. As a further attribute, the gift and leaseback should be timed to occur after the donor has already obtained the benefit of a large part of the depreciation deduction, perhaps by having used an accelerated depreciation system. Depreciation accruing after the gift will be taken by the donee.

Internal Revenue Service's Position on Gift and Leaseback

* * * The taxpayer's claim of a deduction for rental payments under the gift and leaseback techniques is one of the prime issues which Revenue agents are instructed to look for in the audit of income tax returns.

In many situations, tax planners devise a plan for a client on the premise that even if the perceived tax advantages are not derived, the client will be in no worse position than if the plan had not been attempted. This is *not* the case here. If the gift and leaseback is attempted and that attempt is found wanting, the client may be in a significantly worse position than if the effort had not been made. The ultimate response by the Internal Revenue Service to the use of the gift and leaseback technique might consist of denial of the deduction for rent paid plus any one or more of the following: (1) requiring rental income to be reported (even if no deduction for rent is allowed); (2) loss of depreciation deduction to the donor; (3) completed gift for gift tax purposes. For these reasons, extreme care should be exercised in using the gift and leaseback technique.

[¶ 12,915]

QUINLIVAN v. COMMISSIONER

United States Tax Court, 1978.
37 T.C.M. (CCH) 346, T.C.M. (P–H) ¶ 78,070, aff'd, 599 F.2d 269 (8th Cir.1979), cert. denied, 444 U.S. 996, 100 S.Ct. 531 (1979).

FAY, Judge:

* * *

Due to concessions, the remaining issue for decision is whether in computing petitioner's share of income from their law practice, a rental expense deduction under § 162(a)(3), should be allowed for payments made for the use of property which petitioners had previously transferred to two short-term trusts.

* * *

In 1962 petitioners were engaged in the active practice of law. In that year, they began construction of a building designed for general purpose office space. Richard and Roger each owned as undivided one-half interest in the building which, upon its completion, contained some 3,275 square feet of

¶ 12,901

office space. In April 1963 the law firm of which petitioners are members became the sole occupant of the building.

On January 2, 1964, Richard and Roger each executed, as grantors, a 10–year 6–month irrevocable Trust Agreement creating two trusts for the benefit of their respective children. Richard and Roger each retained a reversionary interest in their respective trusts. [For many years ending in 1986, tax advantaged income shifting was possible by transferring income producing property to a 10 year or longer trust—a so-called "short-term trust"—despite the fact that, at the end of the trust term, the trust property reverted to the grantor. See ¶ 22,301 for currently permissible alternatives–*Ed.*]

On that same day, Richard and Roger, as grantors, together with their wives, conveyed the realty to the Northwestern National Bank of Minneapolis trustee. After the creation of the trusts, the law firm, as lessee, and the trustee, as lessor, entered into a lease of the realty held by the trusts. The initial lease was for a three-year term and was dated January 2, 1964. At the end of the three-year term, the lessee had the option of renewing the lease "at a rental and terms to be agreed upon."

Throughout the existence of the trusts, the law firm remained as the sole tenant of the building. During the years in issue, the rent paid by the law firm was reasonable in amount and represented the fair rental value of the office space. After the termination of the trusts on July 2, 1974, the law firm leased the office space from petitioners for an amount which was not less than the highest rent paid to the trustee during the period it held the property.

* * *

In Mathews v. Commissioner, * * * 61 T.C. 12 (1973), revd. * * * 520 F. 2d 323 (5th Cir. 1975), cert. denied, 424 U.S. 967 (1976), we set forth our view as to the appropriate test for deductibility of rental payments by the grantor in a gift and leaseback arrangement. In so doing, we held that such payments are deductible if the following requirements are met: (1) "The grantor must not retain 'substantially the same control over the property that he had before' he made the gift." (2) "The leaseback should normally be in writing and must require payment of a reasonable rental." (3) "The leaseback (as distinguished from the gift) must have a bona fide business purpose." (4) In addition, the taxpayer must not possess a disqualifying "equity" in the property within the meaning of the statute.

Based on a careful examination of the facts as presented, we find these requirements have been met.

First, a fundamental prerequisite to the deductibility of rental payments in a gift and leaseback arrangement is the relinquishment by the grantor of a quantum of control over the property which is not insignificant in comparison to the control that he enjoyed prior to making the gift. In this regard, we stated in *Mathews* that this requirement "is usually met through a transfer to an independent trustee who has the right and the opportunity to negotiate regarding the leaseback and who acts for the primary benefit of the beneficiaries, rather than the grantor."

¶ **12,915**

In the instant case, it is undisputed that the trusts were valid and irrevocable under Minnesota law. The trustee was a corporate entity in which the petitioners were not in any way connected as a shareholder, director, officer, depositor, or employee. Nor was the leaseback prearranged. Coupling these factors with the fiduciary obligations imposed under local law, we conclude that the trustee acted independently of the petitioners-grantors. Moreover, under the terms of the trusts, the trustee had broad powers and, of particular import, it had the unfettered power to "sell, lease, exchange or otherwise dispose of the property" held in the trusts, including the building. We believe the evidence sufficient to infer that the trustee carried out its fiduciary duties in accordance with these broad powers granted to it under the trust agreements. Nor does respondent seriously dispute this. Furthermore, as in *Mathews,* the trustee periodically renegotiated the lease of the property which was renewable only under mutually agreeable terms. Specifically, for each of the years in issue, the trustee negotiated a one-year written lease of the office building in what we, based on the evidence, believe were arm's-length transactions. In addition to negotiating renewals, the trustee collected the rents due under the lease and applied the net income of the trusts for the benefit of the income beneficiaries. In light of these facts, we cannot say that the trustee's functions and independence were illusory. See Penn v. Commissioner, * * * 51 T.C. 144 (1968); Van Zandt v. Commissioner, * * * 40 T.C. 824 (1963), affd. * * * 341 F.2d 440 (5th Cir. 1965), cert. denied 382 U.S. 814 (1965). Thus, we hold that petitioners relinquished sufficient control over the realty to satisfy the first requirement in *Mathews.*

As to the second requirement, the lease in question was in writing, and the parties have agreed that the rent thereunder was reasonable for the property.

Petitioners likewise satisfy the third requirement: a business purpose for the lease. [In a footnote, the court specifically rejected the government's argument that "that there must be a business purpose for the gift as well as the leaseback".—*Ed.*]

Petitioners' continued use of the realty was essential to their law practice. After the petitioners conveyed the realty to the trustee, their continued possession of the premises was wholly conditioned upon the payment of rent. Under such circumstances, the execution of the lease was a matter of business necessity. * * *

With respect to the fourth requirement in *Mathews* we cannot agree with respondent's contention that petitioners possessed an equitable interest or "equity" in the realty within the meaning of § 162(a)(3). Briefly stated, petitioners' reversionary interest was not derived from the lease or the lessor and would only become possessory after the termination of the trusts. Therefore, such interest is not within the prohibition of § 162(a)(3). * * *

Accordingly, on the basis of the particular facts and circumstances involved herein, we hold the rental payments in question are deductible as ordinary and necessary business expenses.

¶ 12,915

[¶ 12,920]

ROSENFELD v. COMMISSIONER

United States Court of Appeals, Second Circuit, 1983.
706 F.2d 1277.

[*Note:* In *Rosenfeld* the Second Circuit joined the Third, Seventh, Eighth and Ninth Circuits (declining to follow the view of the Fourth and Fifth Circuits), and upheld a gift-leaseback. In so doing the court rejected the business purpose test.]

KAUFMAN, Circuit Judge:

* * *

The Commissioner also claims, as we have indicated, that the entire transaction, and not merely the leaseback must be imbued with a valid business purpose. But we are of the view that such a requirement is too harsh for it would lead inevitably to a denial of the rent deduction, despite its clear business purpose, because the gift of the land was not *ipso facto* a business transaction. The Commissioner's argument calls for a test which is overly stringent, particularly in the circumstances here. Many financial decisions are motivated by the prospect of legitimate tax savings, rather than business concerns, and we have already expressed our agreement with Judge Learned Hand's view that a transaction which is otherwise legitimate, is not unlawful merely because an individual seeks to minimize the tax consequences of his activities. * * *

* * *

* * * [W]e decline appellant's invitation to adopt a business purpose standard of review. Rather, we believe our inquiry should focus on whether there has been a change in the economic interests of the relevant parties. If their legal rights and beneficial interests have changed, there is no basis for labeling a transaction a "sham" and ignoring it for tax purposes. Indeed, our prior decisions have indicated that this is the relevant inquiry. * * *

It is readily apparent here that there has been a real change in the legal rights and interests of the parties. As we noted, the trustees were granted broad powers over the corpus of the trust, which necessarily reduced Rosenfeld's authority. Moreover, during the years in issue, Rosenfeld had no present or future interest in the property. When he deeded his reversion in 1973, he retained no legal or equitable right to the trust property. * * * In addition, Rosenfeld was legally obligated to pay rent. The trustees were required to collect a fixed rent which the Commissioner concedes is fair, and also to discharge their fiduciary duties to the trust beneficiaries. Although the lease was initially coterminous with the trust, the lease amendments required renegotiation on an annual basis if Rosenfeld was to continue to occupy the building, and there is nothing presented to us to cause us to believe that this bargaining would not be carried out at arm's length.

¶ 12,920

In addition to these substantial changes in the economic positions of the parties, there were legitimate non-tax motives for the creation of the trust and the leaseback. Rosenfeld understandably wanted to guarantee his children's financial well-being, and the trust helped assure realization of this objective. * * * The leaseback was also clearly motivated by concerns other than tax savings and was a business necessity. Rosenfeld required an office to practice medicine, and the rental payments were a condition of continued occupancy.

While recognizing these factors, the Commissioner asserts, nonetheless, that nothing changed because Rosenfeld was occupying the same premises as a lessee which he previously used as the owner. This argument is disingenuous. Rosenfeld could have given the property to his children in trust and leased property from a third party for an amount equally fair and reasonable for his medical office. It is clear, and indeed, counsel conceded at oral argument, that a rent deduction would have been entirely proper in such a case. In real terms, there is little difference between this hypothetical case and the events the Commissioner challenges. In both cases Rosenfeld would have voluntarily relinquished his right to occupy his offices rent-free, and created the need to lease other premises. It can hardly be a matter of concern for the Commissioner, whether Rosenfeld rents from the trust rather than from some third party. In either situation he would be required to pay rent, and the trust could receive rental income from the property it owned.

* * *

In sum, we believe the gift-leaseback transaction substantially altered Rosenfeld's economic and beneficial rights, and accordingly, the arrangement, which was otherwise proper under * * * § 162(a)(3), was not rendered objectionable merely because Rosenfeld's rent payments were made to a trust which he established for the benefit of his children. The Tax Court properly concluded that Rosenfeld had a right to deduct his rent expenses pursuant to § 162(a)(3).

Part IV

SPOUSAL GIFTS AND DISCLAIMERS

Chapter 13

FUNDAMENTALS OF SPOUSAL
TAX PLANNING

A. OBJECTIVES

[¶ 13,001]

Section 2010(a) provides each decedent with a tax-free exclusion for federal estate tax purposes. While expressed as a credit against federal estate tax liability, in practical terms it means each decedent has an exclusion for federal estate tax purposes of $2 million in 2006, 2007, and 2008, an exclusion that is scheduled to increase to $3.5 million in 2009. The estate tax is scheduled to be repealed as to persons dying in 2010—but return with a vengeance in 2011 in the form of *only* a $1 million dollar exclusion (and a higher maximum tax rate). One consequence is that *estate tax planning* has been rendered unnecessary for many persons dying in the 2006–2010 period. (Dark humor includes suggestions about use of respirators to "keep prospective decedents going" until 2010. That same dark humor suggests that 2010 might be a particularly dangerous time for some "prospective decedents.") And, despite the apparent tax appeal of death in 2010—when the estate tax will not apply to anyone—there are income tax incentives to death in 2009 for those with estates of $3.5 million or less. These incentives are in the form of new-basis-at-death (read "step up basis") rather than "carry-over basis" that applies only as to decedents dying in 2010. See ¶¶ 8751–8755.

Furthermore, transfers between spouses (persons married to one another) can be made free of both estate and gift taxes. § 2056. This feature is commonly referred to as the unlimited marital deduction (UMD) or the tax-free interspousal transfer rule. However, despite the apparent simplicity of this "tax break," the complexity of *contemporary tax planning* has not been reduced for many taxpayers. Planning remains complicated—and, perhaps, has become more stressful—for persons who wish to make provision for not only their spouses but also for their children and other lineal descendants. With the advent of the UMD, the testator can choose between giving it all to his or her spouse—tax-free—or splitting the property between spouse and children (and paying estate tax on the portion passing to the children to the extent the children's share exceeds the estate tax exclusion).

In deference to those persons who seek to further refine or balance the interests of spouse and children, § 2056(b)(7) permits a testator to take advantage of the UMD *even when* a gift to a spouse is placed in trust, *provided* the spouse is entitled to all of the trust income during the spouse's life and *provided* that "no person" can direct any part of the property away from the spouse during the spouse's lifetime. The remainder interest can be earmarked by the testator for someone other than the spouse. The obvious disadvantage of this scheme is that while the children will be assured of ultimately getting the trust property, the surviving spouse may survive for many years and outlive several generations of the decedent's lineal descendants, a likely possibility in the case of multiple marriages where there is a significant difference in age between the decedent and the surviving spouse.

Nonetheless, the testator—at least at first glance—has the option of deferring—at a price—all of the estate tax liability until the death of the surviving spouse. Whether the testator, in fact, has that option will depend upon four factors:

1. The nature and extent of the state death taxes imposed upon the testator's estate;

2. The amount of the testator's adjusted taxable gifts (see ¶ 7117);

3. The amount of the testator's testamentary gifts to persons other than his or her spouse; and

4. Whether and to what extent the testator's estate includes property interests which do not qualify for the marital deduction.

Each of these points will be developed in the next several chapters. Suffice it to say at this point that careful tax planning can produce enormous tax savings through the use of at least one trust, commonly referred to as the "B" or bypass trust. Sometimes the plan calls for the use of a second trust, commonly referred to as the "A" or marital trust—or, alternatively, a gift to the spouse free of trust. The tax savings potential of the basic plan will be considered in this chapter.

B. SAVING THE SECOND TAX

[¶ 13,051]

1. THE BYPASS, OR CREDIT SHELTER, TRUST

At first glance, tax planning for persons married to each other is relatively uncomplicated. At a fundamental level, tax planning for married persons consists of saving the second tax, i.e., making certain that the $2 million tax-free amount is not taxed a second time at the death of the surviving spouse. One technique to accomplish this objective is for the first spouse who dies to make a gift of the $2 million tax-free amount to loved ones other than the surviving spouse. Except in what might be described as very large estates— "very large" being a relative term—this alternative has little appeal because most spouses believe that: (1) the survivor will need all the "available" property for support and (2) the survivor should, at least, have access to the property accumulated during the marriage.

The technique of choice is the bypass trust, or credit shelter trust, as it is sometimes called. Under a bypass trust, the first spouse to die directs the $2 million tax-free amount to a trust for the benefit of the surviving spouse. The trust is structured so as to provide the best of all possibilities. On one hand, the surviving spouse is given access to the trust using one of several techniques, the choice being determined by other choices that need to be made as to trustee selection and requirements of the surviving spouse. On the other hand, the surviving spouse's access to the trust is limited so as to prevent the trust property—the $2 million tax-free amount—from being included in the estate of the surviving spouse at the spouse's subsequent death.

prevent access to keep out of) spouse's estate.

Structuring the bypass trust is not an art form. Instead, it requires an informed mixing and matching of provisions to take into account the requirements of the surviving spouse and a statutory provision—§ 2041—that is calculated to snag the trust property in those instances where the spouse has too much control over the trust.

need to ensure that spouse doesn't have "too much control".

Accordingly, the bypass or credit shelter trust plays an important role in planning. It will be the source of funds needed by the settlor's children and, perhaps, spouse. The bypass trust also serves its traditional function of saving the second tax. Remember, the amount qualifying for the marital deduction will not be taxed at the testator's death, but it will be taxed at the death of the surviving spouse. The amount flowing into the bypass trust will *not* be taxed at the death of either spouse, so long as that amount does not exceed the *available* tax-free amount—technically speaking, the applicable exclusion amount. § 2010(c).

[¶ 13,059]

2. ILLUSTRATION OF THE BYPASS TRUST

Assume H had $4 million of separate property, no community property, and W had no separate property. H's will provided "all to W." Assuming H dies in 2006 and that W does not remarry, the tax consequences are:

	H's Death	W's Subsequent Death
Gross Estate	$4,000,000	$4,000,000
Less: Marital deduction	($4,000,000)	–0–
Taxable estate	–0–	$4,000,000
Tentative Tax	–0–	$1,700,800
Unified credit	($780,800)	($780,800)
Amount due	–0–	$920,000

While the marital deduction reduces the tax at H's death, it does nothing to reduce the tax at W's subsequent death. So as to reduce taxes at W's subsequent death, the marital deduction plan of choice can be expressed in these terms (where one spouse is "propertied"): the spouse with the larger estate (H) is to have a will that includes a formula clause that provides for the surviving spouse (W) to receive the smallest portion—an amount or a fraction—necessary to eliminate federal estate tax at the death of the richer spouse, with the balance going into a bypass trust for the surviving spouse (thereby "saving the second tax"). Generally, the bypass trust will provide that the surviving spouse is to receive all the income for life from the trust with the remainder to the decedent's then living lineal descendants *per stirpes*. In this case no part of the bypass trust property will be included in the gross estate of the surviving spouse. Why? Because the federal estate tax applies only to transfers (§ 2001), and, in this case, the surviving spouse is not a transferor of the trust property. A properly drafted bypass trust would avoid giving the surviving spouse any powers under § 2041, which causes some nontransferors to be treated as transferors. See discussion at ¶ 18,151.

The bypass trust could be established in H's will (a testamentary trust) or it could be part of a trust created by H during H's lifetime (a free-standing trust, which often offers certain advantages not available with a testamentary trust, see ¶ 4341). Structurally speaking, the use of a free-standing trust contemplates a will executed by H that directs all of H's property (except specific bequests) after payment of debts, taxes, and administration expenses, to the trustee of the free-standing trust (you might say it "pours over to the living trust"). For discussion, see ¶ 4501. The trust agreement will require the trustee to collect the property pouring into the trust and divide the property collected so that a portion is allocated to the marital share and the balance to the bypass trust.

Assume that H has $4 million of separate property, no community property, and that W has no separate property. With the will and bypass trust described above, the tax consequences are:

	H's Death	W's Subsequent Death
Gross Estate	$4,000,000	$2,000,000
Less: Marital deduction	($2,000,000)	–0–
Taxable estate	$2,000,000	$2,000,000
Tentative Tax	$780,800	$780,800
Unified credit	($780,800)	($780,800)
Amount due	–0–	–0–

[¶ 13,067]

3. CONSEQUENCES WHEN SPOUSE WITH SMALLER ESTATE DIES FIRST

Marital deduction planning with a bypass trust feature is ineffective, however, if the spouse with the smaller estate (the "poorer" spouse) dies first. To illustrate, consider the consequences if W in the preceding illustration was to die first:

W Dies First		H's Subsequent Death	
Gross estate	–0–	Gross Estate	$4,000,000
		Less: Marital deduction	–0–
		Taxable estate	$4,000,000
		Tentative Tax	$1,700,800
		Unified credit	($780,800)
		Amount due	$920,000

¶ 13,067

Because the order of spouses' deaths cannot be predicted, at a minimum it is incumbent upon the taxpayer with separate property who relies on the marital deduction, and upon dying first, to have a will that includes a presumption that the richer spouse is deemed to have survived the poorer spouse if there is any uncertainty about the order of deaths. See Reg. § 20.2056(c)–2(e); ¶ 14,201. Otherwise, statutes in the respective states will presume that the donee spouse predeceased the donor spouse under these circumstances and the marital deduction would be lost to the richer spouse. See ¶ 14,201.

Another approach is for the spouse with the larger estate to begin a series of gifts to the other spouse in an effort to equalize their respective estates. These gifts can be made tax-free. Interspousal gifts are the subject matter of Chapter 17.

A third alternative is based on Priv. Ltr. Rul. 200403094, below. The techniques is described in Len Cason, IRS Ruling Approves 'Poorer Spouse Funding Technique', 31 Est. Plan. 234 (2004). This technique contemplates a reluctance to make lifetime gifts to the poorer spouse. Instead it relies on "laundering" the tax-free amount through the estate of the poorer spouse—assuming the poorer spouse, in fact, dies first—by giving the poorer spouse a general power of appointment over the tax-free amount exerciseable by will and by will alone. Application of the § 2041(a)(2) will result in the "power property", *i.e.,* the tax-free amount, being included in the estate of the poorer spouse for estate tax purposes. Important to the success of the plan are the following: (1) inclusion of a default provision in the instrument of gift—a revocable trust is recommended—a default provision that causes any property not effectively appointed by the poorer spouse to flow into a bypass trust for the surviving spouse (where it will not be taxed at his death so long as he does not have a power or appointment over the bypass trust at his death); and (2) that the surviving spouse not effectively exercise the power of appointment given the poorer spouse (by the richer spouse over the property of the richer spouse).

It is the risk that the poorer spouse might do "something crazy" like exercise the general power in favor of, say, the pizza delivery person or worse, "cable guy", that argues against this latter technique. Instead, one might argue that consideration should be given to use of the tax-free interspousal gift technique coupled with a trust to hold the gifted property, a trust that can be qualified for the UMD by the inclusion of provisions specified in § 2523(f) and the making of the so-called QTIP election provided for in § 2523(f)(4). See ¶ 17,067. Special to this QTIP trust is the absence of any requirement that the poorer spouse be given a general power of appointment—and, thus, there is no risk that the poorer spouse will do "something crazy".

alternative w/ QTIP {

In the meantime, consider the model structure of Priv. Ltr. Rul. 200403094.

¶ 13,067

[¶ 13,070]

PRIVATE LETTER RULING 200403094

January 16, 2004.

The facts submitted and representations made are as follows. Husband will execute Trust and fund it with his own assets.

Under the terms of Trust, Article 3 provides that Husband reserves "personal rights," including the right to amend or revoke Trust and to withdraw income or principal. Husband's personal rights will be suspended while Husband is absent for reasons specified in Trust or while he is incompetent as determined under procedures specified in Trust.

If these personal rights are suspended, the trustees are authorized to make gifts from Trust to Wife and descendants or to trusts primarily for their benefit, but not in excess of the exclusion amounts under § 2503. If an individual eligible to receive gifts is acting as trustee, the aggregate gifts to that individual in any calendar year cannot exceed the greater of $5,000 or 5% of the aggregate value of the trust estate.

During Husband's life, the trustees will pay to Husband any income or principal they deem necessary or advisable for his best interests. If Husband's personal rights are suspended, the trustees will also pay any income or principal the trustees deem necessary or advisable for the health, education, support, and maintenance of Husband's descendants and of Wife.

Article 4.5 provides:

At my wife's death, if I am still living, I give to my wife a testamentary general power of appointment, exercisable alone and in all events to appoint part of the assets of the Trust Estate, having a value equal to (i) the amount of my wife's remaining applicable exclusion amount less (ii) the value of my wife's taxable estate determined by excluding the amount of those assets subject to this power, free of trust to my deceased wife's estate or to or for the benefit of one or more persons or entities, in such proportions, outright, in trust, or otherwise as my wife may direct in her Will.

The trust assets distributed in satisfaction of Wife's exercise of this power will be selected by the trustee and valued as of Wife's date of death.

Trust further provides that, at Husband's death, if Wife survives Husband, after the payment of taxes, administration expenses, and other costs, the trustees will distribute to Wife as the "marital gift" a fraction (determined under a formula) of the residue of Trust. The balance of the residue will be held as Husband's Family Trust. Any portion of the marital gift that Wife disclaims will be held as part of Husband's Family Trust. If Wife does not survive Husband, the entire residue will be held as Husband's Family Trust.

During Wife's life, Wife will receive any of the income and principal of Husband's Family Trust that the trustees in their discretion deem necessary or advisable for her health, education, support, and maintenance. The trus-

¶ 13,070

tees may also pay any income and principal they deem necessary or advisable for the health, education, support, and maintenance of Husband's descendants. If Husband's Family Trust holds Husband's residence, Wife will have the exclusive use of that residence for life or until the trustees determine that the residence is no longer needed for such purpose. No rent or other costs will be charged to Wife, and the trustees will pay all of the expenses of maintaining the residence. The trustees may not sell the residence without Wife's consent unless she is disabled. If the residence is sold, the trustees may purchase or build a replacement residence which will be subject to the provisions applicable to the residence that was sold.

Wife is granted a testamentary special power to appoint the assets of Husband's Family Trust remaining at Wife's death to any of Husband's descendants. Upon the death of the survivor of Wife and Husband, any assets of Husband's Family Trust that Wife does not appoint will be distributed to Husband's then living descendants, per stirpes, or one-half to Wife's heirs and one-half to Husband's heirs determined under State law as if Wife and Husband had each died on that date as residents of State.

Husband is named as the trustee of all trusts to be established under Trust until his death or disability with two individuals named as successors.

Wife plans to execute Will. Article 2.1 of Will makes gifts of Wife's tangible personalty.

Article 2.2 of Will provides:

> I exercise in favor of my estate the power of appointment given to me by Section 4.5 of the Trust created by [Husband] dated [___], and direct that assets having a value equal to (i) the amount of my remaining applicable exclusion amount less (ii) the value of my taxable estate, determined by excluding the amount of those assets subject to this power, be distributed to my estate as soon after my death as possible.

Article 2.3 of Will provides that if Husband survives Wife, Husband will receive a fraction of Wife's residuary estate, after the payment of estate taxes, debts, and expenses, determined as follows:

> The numerator of the fraction will be the smallest pecuniary amount that, if given outright to [Husband], would eliminate or reduce to the lowest possible sum the state and federal estate tax liability of [Wife's] estate. This amount will be calculated by taking into account [Wife's] applicable exclusion amount and all other tax credits, deductions, and other preferences allowed to [Wife's] estate. The balance of the residuary estate will be held as a separate trust (Wife's Family Trust). If Husband does not survive Wife, the entire residuary estate will be held as the Family Trust. Under Article 3 of Will, any part of the gift to Husband that he disclaims will become part of Wife's Family Trust.

Article 4.1 of Will provides that, during Husband's life, Husband will receive any of the income and principal of Wife's Family Trust that the trustees deem necessary or advisable for his health, education, support, and maintenance. The trustees may also pay any income and principal they deem necessary or advisable for the health, education, support, and maintenance of

Husband's descendants. If Wife's Family Trust holds Wife's residence, Husband will have the exclusive use of that residence for life or until the trustees determine that the residence is no longer needed for such purpose. No rent or other costs will be charged to Husband, and the trustees will pay all of the expenses of maintaining the residence. The trustees may not sell the residence without Husband's consent unless he is disabled. If the residence is sold, the trustees may purchase or build a replacement residence to which the provisions of article 4.1 will apply.

Under article 4.1(d), Husband is granted a testamentary special power to appoint the assets of Wife's Family Trust remaining at his death to any of his descendants.

Under article 4.2, upon the death of the survivor of Wife and Husband, any assets of Wife's Family Trust that Husband does not appoint will be distributed to Wife's then living descendants, per stirpes, or one-half to Wife's heirs and one-half to Husband's heirs determined under State law as if Wife and Husband had each died on that date as residents of State.

Husband is named as the trustee of all trusts to be established under Will with two individuals named as successors.

You have requested the following rulings:

    1. On the death of Wife during Husband's lifetime, if Wife exercises the power of appointment granted her under article 4.5 of Trust, Husband will be treated as making a gift that qualifies for the federal gift tax marital deduction to Wife with respect to that portion of Trust appointed by Wife.

    2. If Wife predeceases Husband, of the assets in Trust, the value of Trust assets over which Wife holds a power of appointment under article 4.5 of Trust will be included in Wife's gross estate.

    3. Any assets that originated in Trust and that pass to or from Wife's Family Trust established under Will will not constitute a gift from Husband to the other beneficiaries of Wife's Family Trust.

    4. Any assets that originated in Trust and that pass to Wife's Family Trust established under Will will not be included in Husband's gross estate.

LAW AND ANALYSIS

* * *

[Relevant are §§ 2036(a) (retained life estates), 2038(a) (revocable transfers), 2041(a)(2) (general powers of appointment).–*Ed.*]

Section 2041(b)(1) provides that the term "general power of appointment" means a power that is exercisable in favor of the decedent, the decedent's estate, the decedent's creditors, or the creditors of the decedent's estate, except that a power to consume property for the benefit of the decedent that is limited by an ascertainable standard relating to health, education, support, or maintenance of the decedent is not deemed a general power of appointment.

¶ **13,070**

Section 20.2041–1(b)(2) of the Estate Tax Regulations provides that the term power of appointment does not include powers reserved by the decedent to himself within the concepts of §§ 2036 to 2038.

Section 20.2041–1(c)(1) provides that a power of appointment is not a general power if by its terms it is either (a) exercisable only in favor of one or more designated persons or classes other than the decedent or his creditors, or the decedent's estate or the creditors of his estate, or (b) expressly not exercisable in favor of the decedent or his creditors, or the decedent's estate, or the creditors of his estate.

* * *

Section 25.2511–2(b) of the Gift Tax Regulations provides that as to any property, or part therein, of which the donor has so parted with dominion and control as to leave in him no power to change its disposition, whether for his own benefit or for the benefit of another, the gift is complete. Section 25.2511–2(c) provides that a gift is incomplete in every instance in which a donor reserves the power to revest the beneficial title to the property to himself or herself.

Section 2523 provides that where a donor transfers during the calendar year by gift an interest in property to a donee who at the time of the gift is the donor's spouse, there shall be allowed as a deduction in computing taxable gifts for the calendar year an amount with respect to such interest equal to its value.

Rulings #1 and #2:

Husband proposes to execute Trust and transfer to it property held in Husband's separate name. Husband will retain the power to amend or revoke Trust and to withdraw assets from Trust (unless these powers are suspended due to Husband's incapacity or absence under limited circumstances) until his death. Thus, under § 25.2511–1(c), Husband's initial contribution of assets to Trust will not be a completed gift, because he will retain the right to withdraw assets and to revoke his transfer and revest title in himself.

Under article 4.5 of Trust, if Wife predeceases Husband, at her death Wife will possess a testamentary general power to appoint to Wife's estate or to or for the benefit of one or more persons or entities, Trust assets equal in value to Wife's remaining applicable exclusion amount less the value of Wife's taxable estate determined as if she did not possess this power. Accordingly, we conclude that, if Wife predeceases Husband, the value of Trust assets over which Wife holds a power of appointment under article 4.5 of Trust will be included in Wife's gross estate.

Further, on the death of Wife during Husband's lifetime, if Wife exercises that power of appointment, Husband is treated as relinquishing his dominion and control over the property subject to that power of appointment. Accordingly, on the death of Wife during Husband's lifetime, if Wife exercises the power of appointment granted her under article 4.5 of Trust, Husband will make a completed gift under § 2501. Husband's gift will qualify for the federal gift tax marital deduction under § 2523.

[handwritten margin note: Assets over which wife has power of appointment will be included in wife's gross estate.]

¶ 13,070

Rulings #3 and #4:

Wife plans to execute Will, in which, if she predeceases Husband, she will exercise to the fullest extent the power granted under article 4.5 of Trust. Under the terms of Will, if Husband survives Wife, he will receive an outright payment of a fractional share of her residuary estate. The balance of the residuary estate will be held in Wife's Family Trust. The trustee will pay to Husband and to Husband's descendants any amount of income and principal of Wife's Family Trust that the trustees deem necessary or advisable for the health, education, support, and maintenance of Husband and his descendants. Further, if the trust holds Wife's residence, during his life, Husband will have the exclusive use of that residence, and Wife's Family Trust will pay all costs associated with that use. Husband is named as the initial trustee of Wife's Family Trust. Husband will have a testamentary special power to appoint the assets of Wife's Family Trust among his then living descendants. Any assets that he fails to appoint will be distributed to Wife's then living descendants, per stirpes, or one-half to Wife's heirs and one-half to Husband's heirs determined under State law as if Wife and Husband had each died on that date as residents of State.

Husband will be treated as making a completed gift to Wife of that portion of Trust appointed by Wife, if Wife predeceases Husband. Thus, at her death, Wife will be treated as the owner of the Trust assets she appoints. Under article 2.2 of Will, the Trust assets Wife appoints will be distributed to Wife's estate and will pass under Will. Under the terms of Will, those assets may be among the assets in Wife's residuary estate used to fund Wife's Family Trust. Accordingly, we conclude that any assets that originated in Trust and that pass to or from Wife's Family Trust established under Will will not constitute a gift from Husband to the other beneficiaries of Wife's Family Trust.

Under the terms of Wife's Family Trust, in his role as either a beneficiary or a trustee, Husband will not have a general power under § 2041, because distributions of income and principal from Wife's Family Trust are subject to an ascertainable standard. Further, any interest Husband might have under Wife's Family Trust in a residence in which he may have had an ownership interest would not cause that residence to be includible in his gross estate under § 2036. Accordingly, we conclude that any assets that originated in Trust and that pass to Wife's Family Trust established under Will will not be included in Husband's gross estate.

[¶ 13,075]

4. CONSEQUENCES WHERE BOTH SPOUSES ARE PROPERTIED

Typically, where both spouses have property, the spouses will have reciprocal wills. Each will, patterned after that of the richer spouse described at ¶ 13,059, will include a formula clause giving the surviving spouse the smallest portion necessary to eliminate tax at the death of the first of them to die, with the balance of the decedent's property going to a bypass trust of the benefit of the survivor.

¶ 13,075

The same scheme will be used where there is community property. In such cases, of course, the first spouse to die will be able to dispose of only 50 percent of the community property (barring use of some artful planning, such as is reflected in a scheme known as the "widow's election," described at ¶ 11,901).

[¶ 13,076]

5. NON TAX CONSEQUENCES OF THE INCREASING ESTATE TAX EXCLUSION

The increasing estate tax applicable exclusion allowance provided by § 2010(c)—$2 million in 2006, 2007, and 2008, increasing to $3.5 million in 2009—may mean "too much of a good thing!" While it means that the first spouse to die can tax shelter as much as $3.5 million in the bypass trust, that is not to say that doing so will be consistent with the goals or best interests of the either or both spouses. Taking full advantage of the sheltering possibility in cases where the richer spouse dies first may well mean that no property is available to the surviving spouse free of trust. Undoubtedly there would be some who would be taken aback, if not worse, by that prospect, an equally good argument could be made that having the property in trust protects the surviving spouse from the predators of the world—and provides the opportunity for professional management of the trusteed property.

Problem

[¶ 13,077]

What arguments, if any, can be made for "insisting" that the richer spouse give "at least some property" to the poorer spouse free of trust?

[¶ 13,083]

6. FORMULA CLAUSES

To avoid either overqualifying or underqualifying marital deduction gifts, it is common to use a formula marital deduction clause. Such clauses are either:

1. A pecuniary formula that usually begins: "I give to my spouse the smallest amount necessary to eliminate the federal estate tax" or

2. A fractional formula that usually begins: "I give to my spouse the smallest fraction of my estate that is necessary to eliminate the federal estate tax."

Choosing between the clauses is a complicated process; it is discussed in Chapter 15.

Problem

[¶ 13,089]

During her lifetime, Ruth made adjusted taxable gifts of $450,000. What is the maximum amount that could flow tax-free under a bypass trust at her death?

[¶ 13,091]

7. DEFERRAL AND STACKING v. EQUALIZATION

There was a time when one could speculate about the advantages of "paying some tax" at the death of the first spouse to die. No longer is that the case.

The argument was that in some circumstances payment of estate tax at the death of the first spouse to die accompanied by the benefit of a tax sheltering bypass trust could mean total death taxes would be reduced. The argument was that deferring tax at the death of the first spouse by use of the marital deduction could result in too much property being stacked in the estate of the surviving spouse in the sense that the tax bracket rates applicable at the death of the surviving spouse would result in a larger total death tax bill for the property being transferred by the spouses.

With the scheduled repeal of the Federal estate tax in 2010—albeit for only one year—no one could seriously urge payment of taxes *now*, taxes that will never need to be paid if the estate tax repeal is made permanent. There is every prospect that Congress will act on this question long before 2010. In the meantime, "uncertainty" is the watchword in estate planning.

C. PLANNING FOR A COMMUNITY ESTATE

[¶ 13,151]

An estate that is comprised of all community property makes death tax planning much easier. In these situations, there is no richer spouse and no poorer spouse and, thus, no premium on order of death. Each spouse owns one-half and each spouse can dispose of his or her one-half by will in favor of a person or persons of his or her own choosing. Thus, the spouse first to die can utilize fully the estate tax exclusion and tax shelter his or her one-half of the community in the bypass trust. As for the surviving spouse, he or she will enjoy his or her one-half free of trust. No complaint here about "all of our property being in *that trust!*"

Where the estate of the first to die exceeds the estate tax exclusion, again, there are certain advantages. For example, consider Bunny. Assume that she dies with $7 million of community property, $3.5 million of which is to be included in her estate and is subject to disposition by her will. Assuming that Bunny dies when the applicable estate tax exclusion provided by § 2010(c) is $2 million, and that her then spouse, Waldo, is the father of her children. Bunny begins her planning by placing $2 million in the bypass trust for the benefit of her children. As for the other $1.5 million, she can place this property in a trust that qualifies for the unlimited marital deduction, *i.e.,* one that can only benefit Waldo. Even though Bunny's children must wait until their father dies to enjoy any part of the marital trust property, their father can take care of them to the extent he deems appropriate from his one-half of the community which is outside of the trust (and the children can participate in or be the exclusive beneficiaries of the bypass trust funded with Bunny's $2 applicable exclusion amount.) If Waldo becomes incompetent, the children could invoke the doctrine of substituted judgment and go against his one-half of the community if it is excessive for his needs. Cf., e.g., City Bank Farmers Trust Co. v. McGowan, 323 U.S. 594 (1945) (substantial portion of income of incompetent paid to descendants during lifetime of incompetent where income was excessive for needs of incompetent). Alternatively, a person holding a durable power of appointment given by Waldo which authorizes gifts could make them to the children from Waldo's one-half of the community. For discussion of powers of attorney, see ¶ 4201. (At this point, the reader may wonder aloud that "The $2 million in the bypass trust should be enough for any beneficiary." The response, obviously, is that it's all relative! One beneficiary's wealth threshold is another beneficiary's poverty threshold.)

D. ESTATES *LESS* THAN ESTATE TAX EXCLUSION

[¶ 13,201]

1. SIMPLE WILL v. BYPASS TRUST

The estate tax exclusion is scheduled to increase to $3.5 million in 2009, followed by repeal of the estate tax as to persons dying in 2010, and a return, with a vengeance, of the estate tax in 2011 and thereafter with an exclusion limited to $1 million. The uncertainty makes planning nightmarish—and gives rise to mawkish cartoons that picture Son pushing Dad's wheelchair (and Dad) over the cliff in 2010. There is virtually universal agreement that Congress will act to clarify this situation sometime before 2010. In the meantime, what should the green eye shaded planner do?

Again, there is virtual agreement that the estate tax exclusion will never be less than $2 million, the exemption in 2006–08—and that Congress at some point will make at least this minimum exclusion amount a reality. Planning for estates currently under $2 million requires some careful balancing of possibilities. On the one hand, for example, the testator will probably want to keep it simple, and what seems simplest is a will giving everything to the testator's spouse. On the other hand, where inflationary trends are present, the testator may soon have an estate with a value in excess of $2 million. But even if the testator does find that inflation (or other causes) has produced a larger estate, estate tax liability will not result if the testator's will gives "all" to the testator's spouse. Yet by giving everything to the spouse, the testator has lost the value of the $2 million estate tax applicable exclusion amount which could have been sheltered in a bypass trust and thus kept out of the surviving spouse's estate. Moreover, by use of a bypass trust, the testator could be sure his or her children would be protected against the surviving parent's remarriage and, perhaps, after acquired family. Of course, not being able to shelter the applicable exclusion amount at the death of the first spouse to die will be irrelevant tax wise if the combined property of the testator and spouse never exceeds the exemption equivalent of $2 million—unless Congress does not act and the estate tax applicable exclusion amount reverts to $1 million in 2011 and thereafter, the result under present law. See ¶ 7101.

Finally, not to be overlooked is the possibility that the testator may create a trust for property management reasons without giving any thought to taxes.

Problem

[¶ 13,207]

Are there any factors that impact this analysis and either confirm or contradict the conclusions reached?

[¶ 13,209]

2. BASIS CONSIDERATIONS

Assuming that the testator's property has appreciated, probably the minimum planning that ought to be done for estates under $2 million is to take steps to underline equalize the spouses respective estates so that at least some of the family's property will enjoy a step-up in basis for federal income tax purposes at the death of the first spouse to die (and, hopefully, not a "step-down" in basis because of values at date of death are below the decedent's cost). § 1014(b) (new basis-at-death rule). See Chapter 17 for discussion of when to make spousal transfers. If the spouses' property is all community, equalization has already been accomplished.

Note that while equalization is, in theory, desirable to accomplish step-up of basis of some of the property at the death of the first spouse to die, practically speaking, spouses with less than $2 million of property usually have cash, personal effects and homes and little appreciating property. (The appreciation on the residence can be sheltered under the § 121 exclusion for gains on property sold by persons over 55 years of age.)

[¶ 13,217]

3. GIFT STRATEGY → (property)

It is sometimes said that it is better to die with community property than for equalization of estates to have been brought about by inter vivos conveyance. Why? Because at the death of the first spouse to die, 100 percent of the community receives a new basis (not just the decedent's one-half), while only the separate property owned by the decedent at death gets a new basis. For example, since only 50 percent of the property held by the spouses as joint tenants with right of survivorship or as tenants by the entirety is included in the estate of the first spouse to die, only that amount steps up in basis. See § 2040(b). Accordingly, jointly held property is a much less attractive asset. (It is important to note, however, that separate property is an important asset in an estate because it facilitates lifetime giving. For discussion, see Chapters 11 and 19. It's only at death time that community property is preferable.)

50% held by spouses rule.

¶ 13,217

E. ESTATES *GREATER* THAN ESTATE TAX EXCLUSION

[¶ 13,301]

Planning for estates that exceed the estate tax exclusion is complicated. Tax considerations suggest that the basic plan take advantage of the unlimited marital deduction after setting aside an amount equal to the exemption equivalent in a bypass trust. However, once having come to this conclusion, nontax considerations impact the decisional process significantly. There are two principal nontax considerations:

1. Whether the marital share should be in trust and, if it is to be in trust, what features *should* the trust have (and what features *can* the trust have without impairing the availability of the marital deduction); and

2. Whether the amount in the applicable exclusion trust—the credit shelter or by-pass trust—is adequate to provide for the testator's lineal descendants and others that may look to the testator for support, and, if it is not, what kind of planning can be done during the testator's lifetime to insure that adequate funding is available for this purpose. If such planning is not done, the testator is confronted with having to forgo full utilization of the unlimited marital deduction so as to be able to deliver property to other persons in addition to his or her spouse.

The options available to the testator in structuring the marital gift is the subject of Chapter 14. Chapter 15 looks at drafting the dispositive provisions to allocate the testator's property between the marital share and the credit shelter trust and also focuses on the fact that in many cases involving larger estates, the credit shelter trust will "disappear" or be "wiped out" because the testator made adjusted taxable gifts during lifetime, or because in the will the testator has made specific bequests and general legacies to persons other than his or her spouse. Then, there is always the possibility that state death taxes which are not deductible for federal estate tax purposes will be charged against the nonmarital share. For these reasons, the testator will be forced to consider making inter vivos transfers if the testator is to make tax-free provision for objects of his or her bounty other than or in addition to his or her spouse. Gifts, then, will assume an *even more important* role in estate planning. For related discussion of intergenerational gifts, see Chapters 19 and 22.

F. GROUPING CLIENTS BY OBJECTIVES

[¶ 13,401]

Estate planning clients fit into two groups. Some want property management as well as tax planning for the property passing to their loved ones. Others want only tax planning and would prefer to avoid the use of trusts.

Clients falling into the latter group need only a nonmarital or bypass trust and it is, at best, inattention, in such cases, to routinely direct the marital share into a marital trust. (Gifts in trust for a surviving spouse qualify for the marital deduction only in the limited circumstances discussed at ¶ 14,401.) On the other hand, the client who also wants property management to accompany his or her tax planning should have the benefit of both a bypass trust and a marital trust, the latter being the trust into which property for which the marital deduction is claimed is funneled (rather than being delivered to the spouse free of trust).

In addition, when the client's estate is relatively modest, but large enough to warrant tax planning, the formula for allocation of the client's assets between the marital and nonmarital share should be determined by whether the client wants only tax planning or tax planning coupled with professional management for the property passing to loved ones. For example, if the client dies with an estate of $2.5 million of separate property (and the surviving spouse has no property), $2 million should be directed to the nonmarital or bypass trust if the client wants both property management and tax planning. But if the client wants tax planning only, only $500,000 should be directed to the credit shelter or bypass trust with the balance, $2 million, directed to the surviving spouse in fee simple to be taxed to the spouse at his or her death to the extent not consumed or disposed of in the meantime.

Drafting such dispositive instruments is not easy. (Why? Because a modified formula clause must be used in anticipation of the applicable exclusion amount being other than $2 million, e.g., "to my spouse smallest amount necessary to eliminate federal estate tax but not less than the applicable exclusion amount available at my death.") Despite the drafting intricacies, clients who do not want the bulk of their property tied up in trust should not be thrust into that kind of arrangement when it is unnecessary.

I like this.

Problems

[¶ 13,420]

1. Caspar has an estate of $4 million. He has not given estate planning much thought but his spouse has finally prevailed upon him to make a will. In response to your question, "what do you want to do with your property," Caspar responded, "I guess I want it all to go to my wife. After she dies, give it to the kids." Caspar's children, Uno, Zippo and Zero, are all adults and under no legal disability. At this time, his daughter, Uno, has a child; Zippo and Zero have no children. Recommend to Caspar the dispositive scheme that you think is most appropriate to his circumstances.

2. You have back-to-back estate planning appointments with two unrelated married couples, John and Mary and Ted and Carol. Their dispositive schemes are the same. Each spouse wants all his or her property to pass to the surviving spouse; the survivor is to be free to dispose of the property as he or she sees fit. Both couples have adult children. After both spouses are deceased, each couple's adult children are to receive that couple's property. What planning recommendations would you make to each couple in the following circumstances?

(a) Ted's estate has a value of $3.5 million, including the personal residence he shares with Carol (market value, $800,000) and a vacation condominium (value, $180,000) in another state. The remainder, after $40,000 of personal effects, consists of cash and marketable securities. Carol has been a homemaker/volunteer/coach/carpool driver and has no property of her own.

(b) Mary's estate has a value of $5 million, including the personal residence she shares with John (market value, $900,000), a beach condominium (value, $270,000) and a ski condominium (value, $180,000). Both vacation properties are in other states. The remainder, after $50,000 of personal effects, consists of cash and marketable securities. John has been a sometime politician/maker of toys for fun and profit in his garage/master outdoor barbecue cook/carpool driver and has no property of his own.

(c) Suppose both couples' property is community property rather than the separate property of the indicated spouse. For discussion, see Chapter 11.

(d) Suppose both couples' property is held by them as joint tenants with right of survivorship rather than solely in the name of the indicated spouse. For discussion, see Chapter 11.

(e) Consider, too, whether you can represent them as couples. Are there any conflicts of interest? For discussion, see ¶ 2451.

Chapter 14

QUALIFYING FOR THE MARITAL DEDUCTION

A. OBJECTIVES

[¶ 14,001]

Originally, the marital deduction was available only as to separate property and was limited as to amount. But in 1981, Congress decided to allow decedents dying *after* 1981 an *unlimited* marital deduction. The unlimited marital deduction was also made available to those lifetime gifts made after 1981 from one spouse to the other. And, in a somewhat radical change (made necessary by the adoption of the unlimited marital deduction as to separate property), the unlimited marital deduction was made available to both separate and community property. Thus, beginning in 1982, properly structured interspousal transfers became free of transfer taxes, both estate and gift.

The study of the marital deduction is divided into three parts. The first part, the subject of this chapter, concentrates on the statutory requirements and the types of gifts that qualify for the marital deduction. The second part, also addressed in this chapter, focuses on drafting restrictions to be placed on the gift to the surviving spouse, giving the surviving spouse only that control necessary to enable the gift to qualify for the marital deduction. The third part is concerned with the drafting required to most effectively integrate the $2 million applicable exclusion amount (§ 2010(c))—the tax-free amount—with the marital deduction. The latter materials are presented in Chapter 15.

B. THE LIMITED MARITAL DEDUCTION

[¶ 14,051]

1. HISTORICAL PERSPECTIVE

For gifts made before January 1, 1982, and decedents dying before January 1, 1982, the marital deduction was severely restricted. For discussion purposes, consideration of the marital deduction must be divided into four discrete periods:

(1) The period before 1948, when no marital deduction was allowed;

(2) The period between 1948 and 1977, when the maximum marital deduction was limited to a decedent's separate property and further limited to fifty percent of his or her adjusted gross estate;

(3) The period between 1976 and 1982, when the marital deduction was extended (a) to community property subject to severe restrictions and (b) to allow a minimum marital deduction of $250,000; and

(4) The period after 1981, when transfers between spouses became free of estate and gift taxes (if made in a qualifying way) without regard to whether the property is separate or community.

Problem

[¶ 14,057]

Why did Congress deny the limited marital deduction to community property in 1948 while making it available to separate property? Is the better question, why did Congress originally decide to create the marital deduction? Could Congress's action be explained by the fact that only one-half of a decedent's community property is included in the gross estate for estate tax purposes while all of the decedent's separate property is so included?

[¶ 14,059]

2. WILLS AND REVOCABLE TRUSTS EXECUTED BEFORE SEPTEMBER 12, 1981

a. Marital Deduction Between 1948 and 1982

Between 1948 and 1977, the estate tax marital deduction was limited to 50 percent of the decedent's adjusted gross estate. Adjusted gross estate, for purposes of the marital deduction, was defined as the decedent's gross estate reduced by debts, taxes, administration expenses, and losses incurred during administration. § 2056(c)(2), repealed as to decedents dying after 1981.

During the same period, the gift tax marital deduction was limited to 50 percent of the value of the property transferred by one spouse to the other spouse.

There was also a short period from 1977 through 1981 during which Congress allowed an unlimited marital deduction for amounts up to $250,000 under specified circumstances. Mention is made here of this special period principally to facilitate the reading of cases and rulings from that period which make reference to this unusual provision.

[¶ 14,067]

b. "Grandfather" Provisions

Understanding the pre–1982 law with respect to the marital deduction is important because Congress "grand fathered" those wills and trusts executed prior to September 12, 1981, which contain a formula providing for the "maximum * * * marital deduction." As a result, the pre–1982 rules with respect to the marital deduction will be deemed applicable to these so-called old formula clause wills and trusts (wills and trusts executed prior to September 12, 1981). Thus, several future generations of lawyers will be concerned with the marital deduction rules which prevailed prior to 1982. In some cases, decedents will have made a conscious decision to leave old wills unchanged. In other cases old wills will go unchanged because of neglect or, in some cases, because the testator became incompetent before he or she had the opportunity to modify dispositive instruments to take advantage of the unlimited marital deduction.

Interestingly, "adjusted gross estate" is a term with little present meaning for estate tax purposes. Until 1982, however, it was the reference point in determining the maximum marital deduction allowed a decedent. Currently, the term has significance *only* for purposes of § 6166 relating to extensions of time for payment of estate taxes. It no longer has significance for marital deduction computation purposes.

C. CONDITIONS FOR ALLOWANCE OF MARITAL DEDUCTION

[¶ 14,101]

The conditions under which the marital deduction is allowed a decedent's estate can be more easily grasped by remembering that originally the marital deduction represented Congress's effort to provide similar tax treatment for community and separate property. The premise of the marital deduction was that property passing from a decedent to the spouse at death would escape taxation at the decedent's death on condition that it would be taxed in the estate of the surviving spouse upon the spouse's subsequent death unless the spouse consumed it or disposed of it during lifetime (or it depreciated). While this generalization was subject to severe limitations, the marital deduction roughly approximated the tax treatment of community property in the sense that only one-half of the decedent's community property was (and is) included in the estate of the first spouse to die. The marital deduction had a similar effect by, in principle, excluding up to one-half of a decedent's property from tax at the decedent's death to the extent it passed to the spouse in such a way as to be taxable at the spouse's death.

While the marital deduction is *now* unlimited and applies to both separate and community property, the basic conditions for allowance of the marital deduction have not changed. They are:

1. The *decedent* must have been *a citizen or resident* of the United States at the time of death. § 2001; Reg. § 20.2056(a)–1(a).

2. The *decedent must have been survived by the spouse*. § 2056(a).

3. The *surviving spouse* must be a *citizen* of the United States. (Relief provisions are in place so as to allow the marital deduction for gifts to noncitizen surviving spouses under specified conditions. §§ 2056(d), 2056A.)

4. The marital deduction will be allowed only as to *"interests"* in property which *pass* from the decedent to the spouse. § 2056(a).

5. The interest in property which passes from the decedent to the spouse:

    a.   *must not be a nondeductible terminable interest* (§ 2056(b)); and

    b.   *must be included in the decedent's gross estate.*

D. THE "CITIZEN OR RESIDENT" REQUIREMENT

[¶ 14,151]

The marital deduction is available only to the estates of those decedents who are citizens or residents of the United States. Considered in ¶ 14,201 is the requirement that the surviving spouse be a citizen; it is not enough that the surviving spouse is resident in the United States.

E. THE "SURVIVING SPOUSE" REQUIREMENT

[¶ 14,201]

To qualify for the marital deduction, the decedent must be married to the donee and the donee must survive the decedent. The test is whether the decedent was married at the moment of death. This test is satisfied even if the spouse survives for only a moment.

What if the decedent is legally separated from the spouse at death? The marital relationship has not been terminated and, therefore, the gift to the spouse qualifies for the marital deduction.

Common disaster? The Service will recognize a presumption (whether supplied by the decedent's will, local law, or otherwise) that the decedent's spouse survived the decedent in those cases where the order of death cannot be determined. See Reg. § 20.2056(c)–2(e).

Statutes in many states provide that a decedent shall be presumed to have survived his or her spouse where the order of their deaths cannot be determined. The Uniform Probate Code goes even further. It provides that a decedent shall be presumed to have survived his or her spouse unless the spouse survives for a period of 120 hours. For discussion see ¶ 3459. Consequently, it is imperative to reverse these presumptions by some writing in order to be eligible for the marital deduction in cases where the order of deaths cannot be determined (or where the spouse survives for less than 120 hours).

But, you say, that means that the same property will pass through two estates simultaneously with all the attendant expense and burden!

Let's see! Take a client, H, with a $4 million gross estate. In 2006, he and his wife, W, die in such a way that it is impossible to determine the order of deaths. W has absolutely no property of her own. H's will stipulated that W was to receive the "smallest amount necessary to eliminate federal estate tax" at his death. Since it was impossible to determine the order of deaths, applicable state law will cause W to be deemed to have predeceased H for purposes of the provisions in H's will. As a result, H's estate will not be entitled to any marital deduction and his estate tax liability will be $920,000.

However, if H had included a clause in his will which declared that, in such circumstances, W was deemed to survive him, his estate tax liability would be significantly reduced, as the following illustration indicates:

	H's Estate	W's Estate
Gross estate	$4,000,000	$2,000,000
Less: Marital deduction	2,000,000	
Taxable estate	$2,000,000	$2,000,000
Tentative tax	$780,800	$780,800
Less: Unified credit	780,800	780,800
Tax	–0–	–0–

The other half of H's gross estate is assumed to have passed to someone other than W and will not be included in W's gross estate.

Of course, H could have given W his entire estate. Had he done so, H's estate would have qualified for the unlimited marital deduction (provided H's will included a presumption of survivorship clause) and H's estate would have had no estate tax liability. However, W's estate would be $3 million and her estate tax liability would be $920,000!

The results of these alternatives can be summarized as follows:

	Use of Unlimited Martial Deduction	Equalization	Assuming W Predeceased H
H's tax bill	–0–	–0–	$920,000
W's tax bill	$920,000	–0–	–0–
	$920,000	–0–	$920,000

Problems

[¶ 14,240]

1. Use the marital deduction whenever you can? Is this always true? Yes and No. What if the surviving spouse has an estate of his or her own?

2. Does the following statement serve as an appropriate means to overcome the presumption of the Uniform Simultaneous Death Act and the 120–hour rule of the Uniform Probate Code?

In the event that H and W die under circumstances in which there is no sufficient evidence as to which one of them died first or the order of their deaths cannot be established conclusively, it shall be conclusively presumed that W survived H, notwithstanding any presumption of law to the contrary. For the purposes of this trust, a person other than W shall not be deemed to survive H's death, nor to survive another if such person dies within thirty (30) days of the death of the other.

F. "SPOUSE MUST BE CITIZEN" REQUIREMENT; QUALIFIED DOMESTIC TRUSTS

[¶ 14,251]

Except in limited circumstances, the decedent's spouse must be a United States citizen if the marital deduction is to be allowed for property passing from the decedent to the surviving spouse; i.e., under § 2056(d), enacted in 1988, property passing to a surviving spouse who is not a United States citizen does not qualify for the marital deduction. An exception exists, however, for property passing to the noncitizen spouse in the form of a "Qualified Domestic Trust." § 2056(d)(2)(A). A Qualified Domestic Trust, defined in § 2056A(a), requires that at least one trustee be a United States citizen or domestic corporation and that no distribution be made from the trust without the approval of that trustee (except in cases where the U.S. trustee has the authority to withhold estate tax generated by the distribution). The trust must meet the requirements of regulations prescribed to ensure the collection of estate tax imposed on the trust. Qualified Domestic Trust treatment must be elected by the decedent's executor. The general rule of § 2056(d)(1) does not apply if the surviving spouse becomes a citizen of the United States before the date for filing the estate tax return and the surviving spouse was a United States resident at all times after the decedent's death and before becoming a United States citizen. § 2056(d)(4).

The marital deduction is denied in cases where the decedent's surviving spouse is not a citizen so as to insure collection of the estate tax that was avoided when the decedent's estate claimed the marital deduction for the property passing to the surviving spouse. Congress apparently believed that there were too many instances where estate taxes were not being collected because noncitizen surviving spouses were leaving the United States—and dying elsewhere—with property for which a marital deduction had been claimed. While there was nothing illegal about the actions of such surviving spouses, the loss of the revenue opportunity to the United States as a result of such movements must have been too much for Congress to accept.

Example. Marie, a United States citizen and resident, died in 1987 survived by her husband, Pierre, a Canadian citizen but a resident of the United States at the time of Marie's death. As a result of Marie's will, Pierre received all of Marie's $3 million estate. No estate taxes were paid at Marie's death, her executor having claimed the marital deduction for the $3 million that passed to Pierre. Upon receipt of the $3 million, Pierre returned permanently to Canada, where he died in 2004. Since Pierre was a noncitizen nonresident of the United States at his death, no United States estate tax was ever paid on the $3 million.

The Qualified Domestic Trust authorized in § 2056(d) provides a means by which the marital deduction may be made available if the decedent's surviving spouse is not a citizen. At the death of the surviving spouse, all of the property then in the trust will be subject to estate tax as if it had been taxed to the deceased spouse at the earlier death of the deceased spouse. The rate of tax is determined by reference to the estate of the decedent rather than to the estate of the surviving spouse. § 2056A(b). Furthermore, any distributions from the Qualified Domestic Trust to the surviving spouse during the lifetime of the surviving spouse in excess of the trust income (or for reasons other than hardship or reimbursement of the spouse for federal income tax on undistributed trust income) are subjected to the federal estate tax as if they were a part of the estate of the deceased spouse (at the marginal rate of tax applicable to the deceased spouse). The federal estate tax on such distributions is due on April 15th of the year following the date of the taxable distribution. The trustee of the Qualified Domestic Trust is personally liable for both the estate tax on the Qualified Domestic Trust and the distributions from it. § 2056A(b)(6).

There will be cases where property passes free of trust from a deceased citizen to a noncitizen surviving spouse with the resulting payment of estate taxes at the death of the citizen spouse. If the noncitizen surviving spouse does the unexpected and remains a resident of the United States until his or her death, the property that the surviving spouse received from the decedent will be subject to estate tax at the death of the surviving spouse to the extent that the surviving spouse had not consumed it or disposed of it. To avoid this harsh result, a credit is available to the surviving spouse for the estate tax paid at the death of the first spouse to die. § 2056(d)(3).

Also, property passing to a noncitizen surviving spouse free of trust could be placed in a Qualified Domestic Trust by the surviving spouse. § 2056(d)(2)(B). Moreover, nothing prevents a surviving spouse from creating a Qualified Domestic Trust for this purpose (in cases where the deceased spouse had not provided for such a trust). Furthermore, a nonqualifying trust can be reformed to qualify as a Qualified Domestic Trust. § 2056(d)(5).

G.   THE "PASSING" REQUIREMENT

[¶ 14,301]

1.   INTERESTS IN PROPERTY

It is important to distinguish between property and an interest in property. "The term 'property' refers to the underlying property in which various interests exist." Reg. § 20.2056(b)–1(e)(2). A chunk of property (Blackacre) frequently supports several different interests, e.g., the *interest* of the life tenant and the *interest* of the remainderman in the same *property*. See ¶ 14,359.

[¶ 14,309]

2.   "PASSING" FROM THE DECEDENT TO SURVIVING SPOUSE

a.   *Beneficial Ownership*

The statute defines "passing" very broadly (§ 2056(c)), but it roughly boils down to this: If the surviving spouse receives *as beneficial owner* any interest in property from the decedent which is included in the decedent's gross estate, that interest in property is deemed "to have passed to the surviving spouse from the decedent" for marital deduction purposes, provided it is not a nondeductible terminal interest. Put more plainly, in principle (but not literally), an interest in property passing from a decedent to the surviving spouse escapes taxation in the decedent's estate on condition that it will be included in the surviving spouse's estate for federal estate tax purposes at the spouse's death unless the spouse consumes it or otherwise disposes of it during lifetime.

Interests in property that the surviving spouse acquires by way of bequest, devise or inheritance are deemed to "pass" to the surviving spouse. In addition, there are a variety of other situations in which interests in property "pass" to the surviving spouse. See, e.g., Reg. § 20.2056(c)–2(b). The relevant questions are, first, whether the particular interest in property was included in the decedent's estate and, second, whether the interest passed to the surviving spouse as beneficial owner. Do life insurance proceeds payable to the surviving spouse qualify? Clearly, yes. Does joint and survivorship property in which the surviving spouse is the survivor qualify? Of course. Does property passing to the surviving spouse as trustee for the benefit of a third person? Obviously, no.

[¶ 14,312]

b. *Legally Enforceable*

An interesting example of what it means for an interest to "pass" to the surviving spouse for marital deduction purposes is provided by a case involving Estee Lauder, the cosmetics entrepreneur, where an $8.4 million enhancement in the value of her stock in the family business at the death of her husband was considered to have passed to her even though she was not a beneficiary of his will. *Estate of Lauder* v. *Commissioner*, 68 T.C.M. (CCH) 985, T.C.M. (RIA) ¶ 94,527 (1994), discussed at ¶ 24,117. By way of contrast, the IRS has concluded, in Tech. Adv. Mem. 9610004, that property passing to the surviving spouse (by intestacy) as a result of a court approved decision by the family not to probate the deceased husband's will does not satisfy the "passing" requirement. The IRS looked to Reg. § 20.2056(c)–2(d)(2) which says that an interest will be deemed to have passed to the surviving spouse for marital deduction purposes only if the assignment of the interest to the spouse was a bona fide recognition of enforceable rights of the surviving spouse. Here there was no allegation that the agreement not to probate resulted from the settlement of any dispute that grew out of any legally enforceable claim.

[¶ 14,317]

c. *Undistributed Marital Gift*

What about the case where the surviving spouse fails to claim the property given the spouse in the decedent's will? Does the spouse's acquiescence to an under funding of the spousal gift by the decedent's executor mean that the decedent's gift did not "pass" to the spouse for purposes of the marital deduction?

¶ 14,309

To illustrate, suppose that the decedent's will includes a gift to the spouse of $200,000 and the marital deduction is claimed on the decedent's federal estate tax return for the gift of the $200,000—and the $200,000 marital deduction is allowed by the Internal Revenue Service. Subsequently, at the instigation of the decedent's executor, the local probate court enters an order closing the estate and ordering distribution to the surviving spouse of only $160,000 rather than the $200,000 given the surviving spouse in the will. The surviving spouse neither objects nor appeals the order of the probate court and the order becomes final. These were the facts considered in Revenue Ruling 84–105, 1984–2 C.B. 197. The obvious benefit to the surviving spouse is that the undistributed $40,000 escapes taxation not only at the death of the deceased spouse but also at the death of the surviving spouse. In these circumstances, the Service concluded that the marital gift "passed" to the surviving spouse for purpose of the marital deduction, but that the surviving spouse made a taxable gift to the extent of the $40,000 under funding done with her acquiescence.

H.   THE NONDEDUCTIBLE TERMINABLE INTEREST RULE

[¶ 14,351]

1.   OVERVIEW

An interest in property qualifying for the marital deduction escapes taxation at the death of the first spouse to die on the theory it will be taxed at the death of the other spouse. A "terminable interest" is one that will not be included in the surviving spouse's estate at death and, therefore, in two cases (subject to five exceptions), interests in property that are terminable do not qualify for the marital deduction in the estate of the first spouse to die.

Technically speaking, a terminable interest is an interest in property that will terminate or fail due to: (1) lapse of time or (2) the occurrence or nonoccurrence of some event or contingency. For example, suppose a decedent gives the surviving spouse a life estate in all of the decedent's property with a remainder to the decedent's children. Does the life estate qualify for the marital deduction? No. The interest is terminable; it terminates on the surviving spouse's death. More importantly, the life estate will *not* be subject to federal estate taxes in the surviving spouse's estate at death. (Why is the life estate not included in the surviving spouse's estate at death? Because the federal estate tax is a tax on the privilege of transferring property at death, and if the surviving spouse takes only a life estate from the decedent, the surviving spouse has nothing to transfer at death. The surviving spouse's right to enjoy the property expired at death and the surviving spouse did not have the privilege of deciding who got it next. For discussion, see Chapter 7.)

Note, however, that not all terminable interests are nondeductible. Only in the following two cases are terminable interests nondeductible:

1. Where an interest in the same property in which the spouse takes a terminable interest also passes (for less than adequate and full

consideration in money or money's worth) from the decedent to some third person by virtue of which the third person <u>may possess or enjoy the property after the termination of the surviving spouse's interest.</u> The best example (again): H gives W a life estate in certain property with a <u>remainder in the same property to his children.</u> *(Note:* It is immaterial whether interests in the same property passed to the decedent's spouse and the third person at the same time or under the same instrument. Reg. § 20.2056(b)–1(e)(1).)

2. When the terminable interest is to be acquired for the surviving spouse by the decedent's executor pursuant to the decedent's instruction. For example, where H by his will directs his executor to purchase a $100,000 annuity for W, the annuity will be a nondeductible terminable interest. On the other hand, in Example 3 of Reg. § 20.2056(b)–1(g), the Treasury gives the following example of a nondeductible terminable interest:

    H during his lifetime purchased an annuity contract providing for payments to himself for life and then to W for life if she should survive him. Upon the death of the survivor of H and W, the excess, if any, of the cost of the contract over the annuity payments theretofore made was to be refunded to A. <u>The interest which passed from H to W is a nondeductible interest since A may possess or enjoy a part of the property following the termination of the interest to W</u>. If, however, the contract provided for no refund upon the death of the survivor of H and W, or provided that any refund was to go to the estate of the survivor, then the interest which passed from H to W is (to the extent it is included in H's gross estate) <u>a deductible interest</u>.

The first condition would bar all life estates or conditional interests to the spouse in property in which others are given a remainder interest by the decedent that may be enjoyed after the spouse's interest ceases. The second condition strikes down all terminable interests that the decedent directs his or her executor or a trustee to acquire for the surviving spouse, such as the purchase of a life estate or an annuity, without regard to whether interests in the property are held by others.

[¶ 14,367]

2. ESTATE TRUST

At one time the income tax rates applied to trusts were incentives to accumulate income in the trust (rather than to distribute the income to the trust beneficiaries). During that period, the estate trust had appeal because income could be accumulated in an estate trust without disqualifying the trust for the marital deduction. That is, the estate trust was valued because it permitted income to be accumulated without being considered a nondeductible terminable interest. See Reg. § 20.2056(c)–2(b)(1)(iii).

[¶ 14,369]

REVENUE RULING 68–554

1968–2 C.B. 412.

* * *

A decedent had bequeathed one-half of his adjusted gross estate in trust. The trustee was directed to pay any portion of the income *deemed desirable* to decedent's surviving spouse during her lifetime. The trustee was also authorized to retain any unproductive property received as part of the trust corpus. Upon the death of the surviving spouse the corpus and any accumulated income is to be paid to her estate.

* * *

The interest bequeathed to the surviving spouse in the instant case is an interest passing from the decedent within the meaning of § 2056(e). It is not a nondeductible terminable interest within the meaning of § 2056(b)(1) because no interest in such property passes from the decedent to any person other than the surviving spouse or her estate. Accordingly, it is held that the bequest in trust qualifies for the marital deduction under § 2056(a) , even though the trustee may accumulate the income during the surviving spouse's lifetime and retain unproductive property as part of the trust corpus, since the corpus and any accumulated income is to be paid to the estate of the surviving spouse upon her death.

[¶ 14,371]

Note

1.   The income generated by property included in an estate trust will be taxed to the estate trust to the extent that it is not distributed to the surviving spouse. § 641(a). Taxing the trust income to the trust rather than to the spouse results in an income tax savings to the extent that the income tax bracket of the trust is lower than that of the spouse. However, the income tax rates applied to trusts (and estates) have been compressed and, in 2006, for example, the maximum savings that resulted from having income taxed to the trust (rather than being distributed to the trust beneficiary) was $956. § 1(e). For discussion, see ¶ 21,351. Nonetheless, each year the trustee can defer deciding whether to shelter the income in the trust or to distribute it to the surviving spouse for 65 days after the close of the tax year. See § 663(b).

2.   An estate trust can receive and retain unproductive property (something that is not permitted if the trust is to qualify as a life estate power of appointment trust (LEPA) or a qualified terminable interest property trust (QTIP) under §§ 2056(b)(5) or (7), respectively (discussed at ¶ 14,499)).

3.   In drafting an estate trust, be aware of the interpretation given the instrument by state law. For example, the jurisdictions that follow the Rule in Shelley's Case might find that a grant to the surviving spouse and then to her estate gives the spouse a fee simple, thus destroying the whole trust scheme.

See 1978 Est. Plan. Rev. (CCH) (Special Report), at 5. Other local laws similarly may affect the interpretation of the instrument.

4. Exceptions to the terminable interest rule are few and specific. As is illustrated by Revenue Ruling 75–128, at ¶ 14,373, it is not a good idea to deviate much from the standard language of provisions that fall within those exceptions. An attempt to get "the best of both worlds" may result in loss of the marital deduction altogether.

5. For consideration of *lifetime mutual* estate trusts, i.e., where each spouse, while living, creates an estate trust for the other spouse and funds it with an immediate transfer of property, all in the interests of income tax basis step up at death, see ¶ 17,067. (Use of this technique enhances the utility of the estate trust.)

[¶ 14,373]

REVENUE RULING 75–128

1975–1 C.B. 308.

The decedent bequeathed the residue of his estate in trust. Under the provisions of the trust, his surviving spouse is to receive, for her life, so much of the income as the trustee deems necessary. Any income not distributed to the surviving spouse is to be accumulated in the trust. At the death of the surviving spouse, the entire corpus, including any accumulated income, "shall be distributed to the executor or administrator of her estate to the extent necessary to pay costs of administration of her estate or arising by reason of her death, the trustee in his sole and exclusive discretion to determine the necessity for the amount of such distribution, and the remaining balance shall be distributed to the person or persons designated in her will to receive and enjoy such property." In the event the above power of appointment is not exercised, the remaining corpus is to be paid over to the surviving spouse's estate.

* * *

[Estate Trust Exception]

Section 2056(e) defines interests in property that shall be considered as passing from the decedent to any person. Reg. § 20.2056(c)–2(b)(1)(iii) and (iv) provides that a property interest bequeathed in trust by the decedent will be considered as having passed from him to his surviving spouse if the trust income is to be accumulated for a term of years or for the life of the surviving spouse and the augmented fund paid to her or her estate or the terms of the transfer satisfy the requirements of Reg. § 20.2056(b)–5. Reg. § 20.2056(e)–3 provides that if the decedent creates a power of appointment over a property interest the possible appointees are considered to be persons other than the surviving spouse to whom an interest in the property subject to the power passes.

* * *

The testamentary trust in this case does not satisfy the requirements of § 2056. It is true that the portion of the trust corpus which is to be distributed to the executor or administrator meets the conditions of a qualified estate trust as set out in Reg. § 20.2056(c)–2(b)(1)(iii). See Rev. Rul. 68–534, 1968–2 C.B. 412. However, at the date of the decedent's death there is no means by which the amount that will be distributed to the estate of his surviving spouse for the payment of administrative expenses can be determined. This being true, no deduction is allowed with respect to that portion of the trust corpus. Since the possible appointees under the surviving spouse's power of appointment are considered to be persons other than the surviving spouse to whom an interest in property passes from the decedent, the remaining portion of the trust corpus is a nondeductible terminable interest within the meaning of § 2056(b)(1). Since the surviving spouse is not entitled to all the income for her life payable annually, the requirements set out in § 2056(b)(5) for the life estate power of appointment trust exception to the terminable interest rule are not satisfied.

* * *

This case is distinguishable from Rev. Rul. 72–333, 1972–2 C.B. 530, where the entire trust income was to be distributed to the surviving spouse during her lifetime.

Problems

[¶ 14,377]

1. After reading Revenue Ruling 75–128, consider how you would draft an estate trust to avoid the result reached in that ruling.

2. Try your hand at drafting the income and principal distribution provisions for inclusion in an estate trust.

3. Detail the circumstances in which an estate trust might be useful. See ¶ 17,067.

I. EXCEPTIONS TO NONDEDUCTIBLE TERMINABLE INTEREST RULE

[¶ 14,401]

There are five cases in which a terminable interest that would be nondeductible under the above rules will not be classified as a nondeductible terminable interest. These cases, referred to as exceptions to the general rule, are as follows:

1. The survivorship exception (§ 2056(b)(3));

2. The life estate/power of appointment exception (§ 2056(b)(5));

3. The insurance exception (§ 2056(b)(6));

4. The qualified terminable interest property exception (§ 2056(b)(7)); and

[handwritten margin note: 5 cases where nondeductible term. int. will be permitted.]

[handwritten note: QTIP]

¶ 14,401

5. The charitable remainder trust exception (§ 2056(b)(8)) discussed at ¶ 14,629 and 25,117.

Why the exceptions? Theoretically the tax laws should be neutral and not affect day-to-day decisions. This is obviously a practical impossibility, but, by carving out exceptions to the nondeductible terminable interest rule, Congress has provided some freedom to structure spousal gifts and still qualify for the marital deduction. The alternative is to limit the marital deduction to gifts passing to the surviving spouse free of trust. It is important to note that these exceptions allow the deduction only for property that will be included in the estate of the surviving spouse if not consumed or given away by the surviving spouse prior to death. Remember this principle. It gives coherence to the exceptions.

[¶ 14,409]

1. THE SURVIVORSHIP EXCEPTION

A frequently used provision in pre–1948 wills was a clause designed to avoid multiple administration of estates upon the death of the beneficiary "hard upon the heels" of the testator. Thereunder, a beneficiary dying in a common accident with the testator or within a period of, say, six months of the death of the testator would be considered as having predeceased the testator and thus would not take the gift provided in the will. Inasmuch as such a clause, when applied to the surviving spouse, would result in a nondeductible terminable interest, whether or not the actual deaths occurred as feared, Congress desired to permit the free use of such a clause. Accordingly, § 2056(b)(3) provides that an interest designed to fail if the surviving spouse dies within six months of the decedent's death or with the decedent in a common disaster will not be considered a terminable interest, provided that the deaths do not occur.

[¶ 14,417]

a. Spousal Awards

Common to many states are statutes exempting from creditor claims certain items of the decedent's property or, alternatively, a fixed dollar amount. As part of this scheme of spousal (and sometimes family) protection, most states provide cash allowances from the decedent's estate to support the surviving spouse (and sometimes surviving children) for a period of time after the decedent's death. The amount awarded for the support of the family will depend on the property available for such purposes as well as the needs and standard of living of the family. Often, these support allowances can be substantial. Accordingly, the question has arisen as to whether these support allowances qualify for the marital deduction. A similar question has arisen whether dower interests qualify for the marital deduction. These questions are considered in the *Jackson* case, which follows. *Jackson* is included here not only because of the substantive issues involved but also to demonstrate the kinds of interests which are arguably nondeductible terminable interests.

¶ 14,401

The *Jackson* case is also significant because it is a timing case. That is, it raises the issue of when the amount of the marital deduction must be determined. Is it sufficient to be vested in interest or must the surviving spouse be vested in amount for a gift to the spouse to qualify for the marital deduction? More important, when must this requisite vesting be accomplished? At the date of the decedent's death? At the date fixed by § 2032 as the alternate valuation date? Upon the date for filing the federal estate tax return? Some other date?

[¶ 14,419]

JACKSON v. UNITED STATES

Supreme Court of the United States, 1964.
376 U.S. 503.

MR. JUSTICE WHITE delivered the opinion of the Court.

Since 1948 § 812(e)(1)(A) of the Internal Revenue Code of 1939 [1986 Code § 2056] has allowed a "marital deduction" from a decedent's gross taxable estate for the value of interests in property passing from the decedent to his surviving spouse. Sub§ (B) adds the qualification, however, that interests defined therein as "terminable" shall not qualify as an interest in property to which the marital deduction applies. The question raised by this case is whether the allowance provided by California law for the support of a widow during the settlement of her husband's estate is a terminable interest.

Petitioners are the widow-executrix and testamentary trustee under the will of George Richards who died a resident of California on May 27, 1951. Acting under the Probate Code of California, the state court, on June 30, 1952, allowed Mrs. Richards the sum of $3,000 per month from the corpus of the estate for her support and maintenance, beginning as of May 27, 1951, and continuing for a period of 24 months from that date. Under the terms of the order, an allowance of $42,000 had accrued during the 14 months since her husband's death. This amount, plus an additional $3,000 per month for the remainder of the two-year period, making a total of $72,000, was in fact paid to Mrs. Richards as widow's allowance.

On the federal estate tax return filed on behalf of the estate, the full $72,000 was claimed as a marital deduction. * * * The deduction was disallowed * * *. The District Court granted summary judgment for the United States, holding, * * * that the allowance to the widow was a terminable interest and not deductible under the marital provision of the Internal Revenue Code. The Court of Appeals affirmed. * * * For the reasons given below, we affirm the decision of the Court of Appeals.

* * *

The issue * * * is whether the interest in property passing to Mrs. Richards as widow's allowance would "terminate or fail" upon the "lapse of time, upon the occurrence of an event or contingency, or upon the failure of an event or contingency to occur."

¶ 14,419

We accept the Court of Appeals' description of the nature and characteristics of the widow's allowance under California law. In that State, the right to a widow's allowance is not a vested right and nothing accrues before the order granting it. The right to an allowance is lost when the one for whom it is asked has lost the status upon which the right depends. If a widow dies or remarries prior to securing an order for a widow's allowance, the right does not survive such death or remarriage. The amount of the widow's allowance which has accrued and is unpaid at the date of death of the widow is payable to her estate but the right to future payments abates upon her death. The remarriage of a widow subsequent to an order for an allowance likewise abates her right to future payments.

In light of these characteristics of the California widow's allowance, Mrs. Richards did not have an indefeasible interest in property at the moment of her husband's death since either her death or remarriage would defeat it. If the order for support allowance had been entered on the day of her husband's death, her death or remarriage at any time within two years thereafter would terminate that portion of the interest allocable to the remainder of the two-year period. As of the date of Mr. Richards' death, therefore, the allowance was subject to failure or termination "upon the occurrence of an event or contingency." That the support order was entered in this case 14 months later does not, in our opinion, change the defeasible nature of the interest.

[Timing of Determination]

Petitioners ask us to judge the terminability of the widow's interest in property represented by her allowance as of the date of the Probate Court's order rather than as of the date of her husband's death. The court's order, they argue, unconditionally entitled the widow to $42,000 in accrued allowance of which she could not be deprived by either her death or remarriage. It is true that some courts have followed this path, but it is difficult to accept an approach which would allow a deduction of $42,000 on the facts of this case, a deduction of $72,000 if the order had been entered at the end of two years from Mr. Richards' death and none at all if the order had been entered immediately upon his death. Moreover, judging deductibility as of the date of the Probate Court's order ignores the Senate Committee's admonition that in considering terminability of an interest for purposes of a marital deduction "the situation is viewed as at the date of the decedent's death." S. Rep. No. 1013, Part 2, 80th Cong., 2d Sess., p. 10. We * * * [believe] the date of death of the testator to be the correct point of time from which to judge the nature of a widow's allowance for the purpose of deciding terminability and deductibility under § 812(e)(1) [1986 Code § 2056(a)]. This is in accord with the rule uniformly followed with regard to interests other than the widow's allowance, that qualification for the marital deduction must be determined as of the time of death.

Our conclusion is confirmed by § 812(e)(1)(D) [1986 Code § 2056(b)(3)], which saves from the operation of the terminable-interest rule interests which by their terms may (but do not in fact) terminate only upon failure of the widow to survive her husband for a period not in excess of six months. The premise of this provision is that an interest passing to a widow is normally to be judged as of the time of the testator's death rather than at a later time when the condition imposed may be satisfied; hence the necessity to provide an exception to the rule in the case of a six months' survivorship contingency in a will. A gift conditioned upon eight months' survivorship, rather than six, is a nondeductible terminable interest for reasons which also disqualify the statutory widow's allowance in California where the widow must survive and remain unmarried at least to the date of an allowance order to become indefeasibly entitled to any widow's allowance at all.

[Purpose of Terminable Interest Rule]

Petitioners contend, however, that the sole purpose of the terminable interest provisions is to assure that interests deducted from the estate of the deceased spouse will not also escape taxation in the estate of the survivor. This argument leads to the conclusion that since it is now clear that unless consumed or given away during Mrs. Richards' life, the entire $72,000 will be taxed to her estate, it should not be included in her husband's. But as we have already seen, there is no provision in the Code for deducting all terminable interests which become nonterminable at a later date and therefore taxable in the estate of the surviving spouse if not consumed or transferred. The examples cited in the legislative history make it clear that the determinative factor is not taxability to the surviving spouse but terminability as defined by the statute. Under the view advanced by petitioners all cash allowances actually paid would fall outside § 812(e)(1)(B) [1986 Code § 2056(b)(1)]; on two different occasions the Senate has refused to give its approval to House-passed amendments to the 1954 Code which would have made the terminable-interest rule inapplicable to all widow's allowances actually paid within specified periods of time.

We are mindful that the general goal of the marital deduction provisions was to achieve uniformity of federal estate tax impact between those States with community property laws and those without them. But the device of the marital deduction which Congress chose to achieve uniformity was knowingly hedged with limitations, including the terminable-interest rule. These provisions may be imperfect devices to achieve the desired end, but they are the means which Congress chose. To the extent it was thought desirable to modify the rigors of the terminable-interest rule, exceptions to the rule were written into the Code. Courts should hesitate to provide still another exception by straying so far from the statutory language as to allow a marital deduction for the widow's allowance provided by the California statute. The achievement of the purposes of the marital deduction is dependent to a great degree upon the careful drafting of wills; we have no fear that our decision today will prevent either the full utilization of the marital deduction or the proper support of widows during the pendency of an estate proceeding.

Affirmed.

[¶ 14,425]

Note

1. Under *Jackson*, the spousal award or allowance provided by the laws of most states will be disallowed as a marital deduction because of the

contingency of remarriage or death. Similarly, where the state statute is designed to provide support to the surviving spouse for the period of administration, as is the usual case, a major change in the circumstances of the surviving spouse, such as subsequent remarriage or death, would affect the amount or the continuance of the payments, thus constituting a terminable interest. However, the marital deduction has been allowed for the spousal allowance in several cases. See, e.g., Estate of Green v. United States, 441 F.2d 303 (6th Cir.1971); Estate of Watson v. Commissioner, 94 T.C. 262 (1990). In both cases, under applicable state law (Michigan and Mississippi, respectively), the spousal allowance could have been lost if the spouse had failed to petition the court for the allowance. Moreover, the amount of the allowance was not fixed, the court having authority to set the amount of the allowance in each case. Both courts rejected the argument that the allowances awarded to the respective spouses were terminable interests. Judge Hamblen of the Tax Court explained in *Watson:*

> * * * We agree with the Sixth Circuit that "To hold that an interest is terminable only because legal procedures are invoked to enforce an interest which is otherwise vested at the date of the husband's death, is to hold that all elective rights, such as the widow's allowance and the statutory interest in lieu of dower, are disqualified as marital deductions." Estate of Green v. United States, 441 F.2d at 308. Without a clear expression of intent from Congress that all rights such as the Mississippi widow's allowance should be considered terminable interests, we will not treat the necessity of invoking legal procedures as a condition or contingency making the Mississippi widow's allowance a terminable interest for purposes of § 2056. Accordingly, we hold that the requirement under Mississippi law that the chancellor make a final determination of the amount of the allowance and the possibility that the widow may lose her right to the allowance by failing to take some action to request the allowance are not conditions or contingencies that make the Mississippi widow's allowance a terminable interest. Consequently, we hold that the widow's allowance paid to the decedent's widow qualifies for the marital deduction provided in § 2056(a).

2. The United States Court of Appeals for the Fourth Circuit held in First National Exchange Bank of Roanoke v. United States, 335 F.2d 91 (4th Cir.1964), that a widow's election of her dower rights is not a nondeductible terminable interest and thus qualifies for the marital deduction. When the decedent's widow renounced her husband's will, becoming entitled to half of her husband's net personal estate and a life estate in one-third of his realty, the county court in Virginia found that her dower interest in the realty could not be conveniently assigned to her in kind. The court ordered a sale of the land, and the widow was paid the value of her dower interest in cash.

The Fourth Circuit reasoned that because the life estate in one-third of her husband's realty could not be assigned to her in kind, the widow actually had no right to the life estate (which would have been a terminable interest). What she had was a right to the commuted value of the life estate. Her dower interest was a right to receive cash, a right which was absolute and nonterminable.

The court distinguished *Jackson* on two grounds: First, the widow's allowance in *Jackson* was not a right vested upon the husband's death, whereas the widow's dower right *is* vested upon the husband's death. Second, the widow's death or remarriage within two years of her husband's death in *Jackson* would have terminated a portion of the allowance. In *First National Exchange Bank,* the widow's right to the money was absolute and nonterminable.

3.   In Estate of C.R. Tompkins v. Commissioner, 68 T.C. 912 (1977), the decedent's will gave the surviving spouse a life estate in a trust, but a codicil to the will provided that the spouse could instead elect, by written statement to the executor within 60 days of his qualification as executor, to take $40,000 outright. The codicil further provided that if the election were made, the trust provision would be null and void. The spouse made a timely election and the estate claimed a $40,000 marital deduction.

The Tax Court held that the surviving spouse's right to use $40,000 was nonterminable despite the fact that the interest would fail were an election not timely made. The court found that it is "well established" that a "mere procedural requirement of a personal election" is not a contingency for purposes of § 2056(b)(1). The marital deduction was therefore allowed.

4.   Does the *Jackson* case have implications as to the vesting of the surviving spouse's interest that are broader than the spousal award? For example, if the executor has the power to vary the size of the spouse's bequest through electing the alternate valuation date under § 2032 or by taking administration expenses as deductions for income tax purposes rather than on the estate tax return under § 642(g), will such power make the spouse's bequest so contingent as to prevent it from qualifying under the *Jackson* rule as to vesting at death? Rev. Rul. 85–100 (¶ 14,427). Or does this carry the vesting rule too far?

[¶ 14,427]

b.   *Annuity Payments and Other Contingencies*

REVENUE RULING 85–100
1985–2 C.B. 200.

ISSUE

Does an employee death benefit annuity qualify for the marital deduction * * * if another person's contingent interest therein will be extinguished before the alternate valuation date of § 2032 ?

FACTS

Decedent, *D* died on February 1, 1983, survived by a spouse, *S,* and a minor child, *C*. Prior to *D*'s death, *D* had the right to receive annuity payments for life. Under the terms of the annuity contract, at D's death the payments would continue to S for life. If S died leaving minor children, the payments would continue to the minor children until the last surviving child of D and S reached age 18, at which time any remaining excess of the cost of the contract over the annuity payments already made would be refunded to the surviving children. If S died leaving no surviving minor children, the excess, if any, was to be refunded to S's estate. C reached age 18 on June 5, 1983. Thus, had S died prior to June 5, 1983, C would have been entitled to payments on the annuity (and refund of the excess of the contract cost over the annuity payments). Because S survived until June 5, 1983, S became entitled to receive all of the payments of the annuity until S's death and to have the excess of the cost of the contract over the sum of the annuity payments distributed to S's estate.

The executor timely filed the estate tax return on November 1, 1983, and elected to value all the property included in D's gross estate as of August 1, 1983, the alternate valuation date. * * *

Law and Analysis

Section 2032(a) states that the value of a decedent's gross estate may be determined, if the executor so elects, by valuing all the property included in the gross estate as of the date six months after the decedent's death * * * (commonly referred to as the "alternate valuation date"). * * *

* * *

Whether a property interest meets the requirements of § 2056(b) must be determined in light of events at the time of the decedent's death. * * * An election to value all property included in the gross estate as of the alternate valuation date under § 2032 does not affect the determination of whether a property interest meets the requirements of § 2056(b). * * * With respect to the marital deduction, Senate Report No. 1013 (Part 2), 80th Cong., 2d Sess. 10 (1948), 1948–1 C.B. 338, states:

> The election of the executor to determine the value of the gross estate as of a date subsequent to the decedent's death, as provided in § 811(j) [1986 Code § 2032], does not extend to such later date the time for determining the character of the interest passing to the surviving spouse and its deductibility under [§ 812(e)(1)(B) of the 1939 Code, the predecessor to § 2056(b) of the 1986 Code]. Section 811(j) relates only to valuation and applies only with respect to interests at the date of the decedent's death. * * *

In this case, the annuity received by S at D's death constituted a terminable interest. Moreover, at the date of D's death, C had a contingent right to the annuity payments if S, the surviving spouse, should die before C reached 18 years of age. Because C received an interest in the annuity at D's death and could enjoy the interest after the termination of S's interest, at D's death S's interest is a nondeductible terminable interest as described in § 2056(b).

¶ 14,427

Therefore, as of the date of D's death, the value of the annuity passing to S (to the extent includible in D's gross estate) does not qualify for the marital deduction under § 2056(a).

If D had died after C had reached age 18, the value of the annuity which passed to S would have been a deductible terminable interest under § 2056(a) because no other person would have had a right to possess or enjoy the property after the termination of S's interest.

HOLDING

The value of the annuity does not qualify for the marital deduction under § 2056 , even though another person's contingent interest will be extinguished before the alternate valuation date under § 2032, as elected by the decedent's estate.

[¶ 14,433]

c. *Contingent Dispositions*

Survivorship clauses can result in loss of the marital deduction. In Technical Advice Memorandum 8834002 , a clause providing that a decedent's wife was to receive property only if she survived distribution of the estate was ruled to be a contingent interest that did not qualify for the marital deduction. Reg. § 20.2056(b)–3(d), Example (4).

Similarly, in Estate of Shepherd v. Commissioner, 58 T.C.M. (CCH) 671, T.C.M. (P–H) ¶ 89,610 (1989), the marital deduction was denied because the surviving spouse was required to survive until the decedent's will was "admitted to probate." The spouse did, in fact, survive until the will was probated, but the marital deduction was denied because:

> the possibility existed at the time of the decedent's death that the will might have been admitted to probate beyond the 6–month exception to the terminable interest rule contained in § 2056(b)(3) and that the surviving spouse's interest might have terminated and passed to someone else at a point in time thereafter.

The court said that "the probate of a will has substantive significance and cannot be considered as merely a ministerial act or a method of perfecting title." And, in Revenue Ruling 88–90, 1988–2 C.B. 335, the IRS denied the marital deduction where the spouse was required to survive until a trust provided for in the will was funded. The IRS said that, "due to the requirements of local probate law, the possibility exists at the time of the decedent's death that the funding may occur more than 6 months after the decedent's death."

By way of contrast, in Private Letter Ruling 8809003, the marital deduction was allowed where the surviving spouse was required to survive "for a sufficient length of time to receive" the decedent's property. The IRS explained that the "surviving spouse was competent to serve as Independent Executrix upon the decedent's death, and did in fact assume the position" and for this reason, the surviving spouse:

had the unqualified right to initiate and complete probate proceedings immediately under local law without the need for the probate court to respond or take any further action with respect to the acts of the surviving spouse.

Important to the IRS's determination was the freedom from court supervision that an independent executor enjoyed under state law after probating the will and filing the inventory and list of claims in cases such as this where the decedent's will specifically states that no further action is needed in the probate court.

[¶ 14,441]

d. "Cutback" Clauses

A testamentary gift to a surviving spouse may be expressly conditioned on the spouse surviving the decedent for a period of up to six months. If the spouse predeceases the decedent or fails to survive the decedent by six months, the spouse takes nothing and the marital deduction is not available to the decedent's estate. § 2056(b)(3).

Problems

[¶ 14,443]

1. Howard and his wife, Martha, each have estates of $5 million. For discussion purposes, assume that Howard dies first. Clearly estate tax will be generated at Howard's death unless he makes a gift to Martha that qualifies for the marital deduction. If Martha survives Howard by many years, it is arguable that the estate tax saved at Howard's death will generate enough income over the years which, coupled with hoped for appreciation and a maximum estate tax rate of 45 percent, will mean that deferral of the estate tax through the marital deduction makes economic sense. However, if Martha survives Howard by only six months, deferring the estate tax on Howard's estate until the death of Martha will mean only that Martha's estate is pushed into a higher estate tax bracket. Accordingly, the total estate tax costs imposed on this family unit will be greater than they would have been had Howard not provided for the marital deduction. At this point you should make the necessary computations to either prove or disprove this conclusion. For discussion, see ¶ 13,091. After making these computations, reflect on whether the savings to be realized warrant the expenditure of time to make the analysis and communicate the results of the analysis to Howard and Martha in terms understandable to nonprofessionals.

How could Howard's dispositive scheme be expressed so that Martha could receive all of Howard's estate in a form which qualified for the marital deduction if she survives Howard by more than six months but take nothing if she survives him for less than six months? Try your hand at drafting. In doing so, do you find the following provision helpful?

> I give to my spouse the smallest amount necessary to eliminate all federal estate tax from my estate but this gift to my spouse shall be

¶ 14,433

canceled if my spouse dies within six months of me and her estate is greater than mine.

2. Refer to the preceding problem and note that the proposed clause speaks in terms of a six-month survivorship requirement. Section 2056(b)(3) speaks in terms of alternatives, the alternatives being "6 months" or "common disaster." What would be the implications if the words "six months" were deleted from the proposed clause and the words "common disaster" were substituted? Isn't it true that the words "common disaster" should *never* appear in a will or trust? Why? See Reg. § 20.2056(b)–3(c).

3. Why not simply provide that the "cutback" be effective if the surviving spouse does not survive until distribution of the testator's probate estate? (*Hint:* See ¶ 14,433.)

4. Does § 2056(b)(3) require that the gift to the surviving spouse actually be received by the surviving spouse? Must she receive it within the six-month period? Or is it enough that it merely vest in interest at that time? Or must it vest in both interest and amount? See ¶ 14,317 and 14,419.

5. Should § 2056(b)(3) be construed to mean that to claim the marital deduction for a gift to the surviving spouse, the decedent's executor must be able to position himself or herself at the decedent's death and say with absolute certainty that the gift to the surviving spouse will either vest or not vest in the surviving spouse within six months of the decedent's death? In other words, is it important to be able to say, with absolute certainty, that within six months of the moment of the decedent's death, all conditions precedent to the surviving spouse's taking will be resolved? The question here then would be analogous to that asked in testing interests for perpetuities violations. See ¶ 5401.

6. Refer to Problem 1 and consider whether the suggested "cut back" provision would be appropriate for inclusion in the wills of both Howard and Martha if Howard's estate had a value of $200,000 and Martha's $3,000,000. How would their property be distributed if the order of their deaths could not be ascertained?

7. Refer to Problem 1 and consider whether there are nontax disadvantages to Howard's using the marital deduction (by making a gift to Martha of all of his property) in a case where Martha survives Howard for only a short period of time. (*Hint:* Martha refused to allow Howard to read her will.)

[¶ 14,445]

e. Equalization Clauses (or "Watching the Bouncing Ball")

It is conventional wisdom, balancing all of the factors, that the optimum estate plan will eliminate all estate taxes at the death of the first spouse to die—utilizing the marital deduction—while tax sheltering, in a so-called bypass trust, the applicable exclusion amount ($2 million in 2006–08, but scheduled to rise to $3.5 million in 2009 with repeal of the estate tax scheduled for 2010 followed by return of the $1 million applicable exclusion amount as to persons dying in 2011 and thereafter, baring Congressional action to change all or some of these items). There was a time, though, when optimum planning also included testing the hypothesis that paying some tax at the death of the first spouse to die was advantageous. Even today, perhaps this makes sense when part of a process of attempting to equalize the estates of the respective spouses where they die within a short time of each other. But long term, with the advent, for example, in 2007, of a $2 million applicable exclusion amount and a flat rate 45 percent estate tax, such a strategy makes little sense.

In the near term, though, equalization could be desirable where the surviving spouse dies within a short time after the other spouse. Note, though, that equalization clauses risk challenge as converting the marital gift to a nondeductible terminable interest ineligible for the marital deduction. *Smith,* which follows, is an illustration both of the position that the IRS has taken and the drafting technique. Scrupulous attention needs to be given its parameters. Variation in the particulars is not for the faint of heart. Cause for this concern comes from the literalist point of view of the IRS—and the possibility that it will take a similar position in like cases. (That is the importance of the *Smith* opinion. It emphasizes that the ball always bounces. Sometimes it is the taxpayer who is literal. Sometimes it is the IRS. The lesson for the draftsperson is to literally track the safe harbors in all cases where a particular tax result is to be effected. The lesson lost in *Smith* is that respecting tax policy should produce challenge free documents—but as the text of *Smith* shows, not always!)

[¶ 14,449]

ESTATE OF SMITH v. COMMISSIONER

United States Court of Appeals, Seventh Circuit, 1977.
565 F.2d 455.

PER CURIAM.

* * *

The stipulated facts may be summarized as follows: Charles W. Smith (decedent), a Michigan resident, died in 1970. In 1967, he had established a revocable *inter vivos* trust with the Northern Trust Company of Chicago as Trustee. His federal estate tax return reported a gross estate of about $3,500,000. The assets of the trust amounted to approximately $3,300,000.

On decedent's death, Article IV of the trust divided the trust assets into a "Marital Portion" and a "Residual Portion." The Marital Portion was to be held as a Marital Trust designed to qualify for the marital deduction * * * Under the terms of the Marital Trust, decedent's surviving spouse was to receive all the net income for her lifetime, with a special power of appointment over corpus exercisable by deed and a general power of appointment exercisable by will. Decedent's wife, Alice M. Smith, died shortly more than one year after her husband. The critical provision of Article IV of the trust is the "equalization clause." Its purpose was to equalize the size of the estates of

Mr. and Mrs. Smith in order to minimize the total combined federal estate taxes on both estates.

Article IV of the trust, dealing with distribution upon decedent's death, provided for allocating to the Residual Portion any assets with respect to which the marital deduction would not be allowed if allocated to the Marital Portion. Article IV then provided:

> (b) There shall then [after allocation of the Residual Portion] be allocated to the Marital Portion that percentage interest in the balance of the assets constituting the trust estate which shall when taken together with all other interests and property that qualify for the marital deduction and that pass or shall have passed to Settlor's said wife under other provisions of this trust or otherwise, obtain for Settlor's estate a marital deduction which would result in the lowest Federal estate taxes in Settlor's estate and Settlor's wife's estate, *on the assumption Settlor's wife died after him, but on the date of his death and that her estate were valued as of the date on (and in the manner in) which Settlor's estate is valued for Federal estate tax purposes;* Settlor's purpose is to equalize, insofar as possible, his estate and her estate for Federal estate tax purposes, based upon said assumptions. (Emphasis added.)

The equalization clause contained in Article IV(b) is the only one at issue.

Decedent's estate tax return claimed a marital deduction of $1,521,245.86, representing the value of the Marital Trust as determined by the estate, plus the value of certain other property interests passing to Mrs. Smith outside of the trust. The estate determined that had Mrs. Smith died after decedent, but on the same day, her individual gross estate, including all assets received from decedent outside the trust, would have had a value of $667,331.47 on the date of decedent's death. Under this assumed fact situation, the value of Mrs. Smith's gross estate would have been $813,630.17 one year from the date of her husband's death, the alternate valuation date. * * * On that date, the values of both decedent's estate and the assumed estate of his wife were higher than the date-of-death values. Consequently, in accordance with the terms of the trust, the estate utilized date-of-death values for federal estate tax purposes and for computing the value of the assets in the marital trust.

The Commissioner took the position that the property interest passing from decedent to his wife under the trust was a terminable interest under § 2056(b)(1) * * * and therefore determined an estate tax deficiency in the amount of $646,700.50. * * *

First of all, the Commissioner admits that the equalization clause is not a tax avoidance measure, for estate taxes will still be collected from the estate of each spouse and none of the funds will escape taxation. The clause does have the effect of minimizing the total combined federal estate taxes on both estates by treating the assets of each spouse as if it [they] were pure community property. Such a clause is frequently used in estate planning. * * * Government counsel candidly admitted at the oral argument that there

¶ 14,449

are no policy grounds for vitiating such a clause. This litigation was brought ostensibly because supposedly required by the literal language of § 2056(b).

As taxpayer has put it, * * * if decedent's estate had a value of $2,000,000 on the selected valuation date and Mrs. Smith's "estate" then had a value of $400,000, the amount passing to her under the equalization clause would be $800,000. [The court explained in a footnote that "$800,000 is one half the amount by which the value of the decedent's estate exceeds the value of Mrs. Smith's 'estate.'"–*Ed.*] The agreed reason for using such a clause is that

> under the graduated estate tax rate structure, a smaller aggregate estate tax in the estates of husband and wife will be due [the total will be due after the second death] if both estates are in the same estate tax rate bracket than if the estates are in disparate brackets as a result of the deferral of the maximum estate tax from the death of the first spouse, through use of the maximum marital deduction, to the death of the surviving spouse (Taxpayer's Br. 5).

Since Mrs. Smith had an independent estate in Michigan, a non-community property state, this equalization clause was to achieve a "pure" community property result. This accorded with the purpose of the marital deduction, which was to put residents of non-community and community property states on an equal footing for estate tax purposes. * * * This equalization clause would determine the amount of property to be received by Mrs. Smith under the trust. That amount was meant by decedent to qualify for the marital deduction in his estate and to be taxed in full in his spouse's estate.

The Commissioner contends that because of the remote possibility that Mrs. Smith would receive nothing from the equalization clause bequest, the terminable interest rule of § 2056(b)(1) applies * * *. At the same time, he admits that a formula fractional share bequest "does qualify for the marital deduction" * * * even though the precise fraction and the value of the fractional share cannot be known until the estate makes its choice of valuation dates and the wife there too can theoretically take nothing. To distinguish the formula fractional marital bequest from Mrs. Smith's interest, the Commissioner asserts that there is an additional factor outside decedent's estate that his trustee had to consider, namely, the valuation of Mrs. Smith's "estate" at the alternate valuation date. But, as Judge Drennen responded, "The only possible effect on the spouse's [Mrs. Smith's] interest from [that] 'additional factor' * * * relates to the *value* of that interest. And even that effect is limited solely to the amount of market fluctuation in the value of the assets in the spouse's 'estate.'" * * * Therefore, the Tax Court rightly concluded that both a formula fractional share bequest and an equalization clause bequest should qualify for the marital deduction.

The hidebound position taken by the Commissioner is illustrated by his representative's statement at oral argument that even if this equalization clause had a rider providing that if Mrs. Smith's "estate" were greater, she would still receive $100 from decedent, the terminable interest rule would nevertheless govern. In his brief, the Commissioner stresses that under this equalization clause, the trustee might have to allocate nothing to the marital deduction so that Mrs. Smith's interest would be zero. But, as Judge Drennen noted, in that event the entire value of the trust would be taxed in decedent's estate. There would be no marital trust to tax in Mrs. Smith's estate, and decedent's estate would have no marital deduction entirely independent of § 2056(b)(1). (66 T.C. at 429.)

As the Tax Court explained, the purpose of the terminable interest rule in § 2056(b)(1) forbidding a marital deduction is "to limit the marital deduction to the value of interests in property passing from the decedent to his surviving spouse which were interests of such a character that, unless consumed or disposed of prior to the surviving spouse's death, would be taxable in the surviving spouse's estate at her death" (66 T.C. at 423). That purpose is fully satisfied because Mrs. Smith's equalization clause share was taxable in her estate when she died in 1971. Because the purpose of § 2056(b)(1) has been met, the Commissioner's dependence on any literal statutory language arguably contrary should not prevail, for in such an instance, form may not be elevated over substance. * * * Since there was no possibility of Mrs. Smith's interest in decedent's property passing to others without the payment of an estate or gift tax, the rationale of the terminable interest rule has been fully satisfied. See S.Rep. No. 1013, Part 2, 80th Cong., 2d Sess. (1948–1 Cum. Bull. 332 *et seq.*).

There being no possibility that the interest passing to Mrs. Smith might escape taxation altogether, the Tax Court properly refused to apply the terminable interest rule. Whether or not the value of the property left to Mrs. Smith might change under the equalization clause, the "interest passing" to her (§ 2056(b)(1)) would not terminate, so that even literally the terminable interest rule does not apply. On decedent's death, the corpus was to "be divided into two portions, one of which shall be called the Marital Portion and the other of which shall be called the Residual Portion" (opening clause of Article IV). Thus on his death in 1970, the former interest passed to and was vested in Mrs. Smith, thereby falling outside the language of the terminable interest rule. Under the statute, as the Tax Court realized, the criterion is not the possible termination of value, * * * but the possible termination of "interest" (66 T.C. at 430). Since Mrs. Smith's interest was not terminable, the Tax Court correctly held that this exception to the marital deduction was inapplicable.

Jackson v. United States, 376 U.S. 503, which held that an allowance provided by California law for the support of a widow during the settlement of her husband's estate was a terminable interest * * * is not to the contrary. Because the widow's allowance in that case was a creature of state law, the state courts already had considered the issue of whether the allowance was vested at the time of the husband's death and had held that it did not vest. * * * Both the Court of Appeals and the Supreme Court, apparently based on that state determination, quickly accepted the fact that the interest involved was not vested and focused instead on the taxpayer's position that the terminability of her interest should be judged as of the date of the Probate Court's order rather than as of the date of her husband's death. It was in this context that Justice White used the language * * * that "there is no provision

¶ 14,449

in the Code for deducting all terminable interests which become nonterminable at a later date and therefore taxable in the estate of the surviving spouse if not consumed or transferred." 376 U.S. at 509–510.

* * * Focusing on the issue of terminability at the time of the spouse's death, and guided on that issue not by *Jackson* but instead by the policies declared in Northeastern Pennsylvania Bank & Trust Co. v. United States [387 U.S. 213 (1967)], which construed another subsection of § 2056 and emphasized "Congress' intent to afford a liberal 'estate-splitting' possibility to married couples," 387 U.S. at 221, * * * we have determined that the Marital Portion was non-terminable at the date of the husband's death. * * *

JUDGMENT AFFIRMED.

[¶ 14,451]

Note

1. In Revenue Ruling 82–23, 1982–1 C.B. 139, the IRS announced that it would follow the decision in *Smith* and will allow a marital deduction "for property passing under an 'estate equalization clause' in which the executor has an option to value the spouse's estate, for equalization purposes, on the alternate valuation date, if that is elected for the valuation of the decedent's estate."

2. Given the possible IRS challenge to an equalization clause that is claimed not to have been properly drafted, does it make sense to utilize such clauses? Using the following data (based on death of both spouses in 2004 when the applicable exclusion amount provided in § 2010(c) was $1.5 million), evaluate the risk of faulty drafting that leads to IRS challenge as in *Estate of Smith*.

Taxable Estate		Estate Tax Liability		
Richer Spouse (dies first)	Poorer Spouse	Without Equalization	With Equalization	Savings
$3,000,000	$2,000,000	$945,000	$930,000	$15,000
$3,500,000	$0	$225,000	$225,000	$0
$5,000,000	$1,000,000	$1,425,000	$1,400,000	$25,000

[¶ 14,459]

2. THE LIFE ESTATE/POWER OF APPOINTMENT (LEPA) EXCEPTION

a. *The Requirements: In General*

In adopting the life estate/power of appointment exception to the nondeductible terminable interest rule, Congress saw fit to allow gifts in trust to qualify for the marital deduction. The requirements are stringent and qualification requires sophisticated drafting.

The regulations set forth five conditions that must be met to qualify an interest in property for the marital deduction under the life estate/power of appointment exception (Reg. § 20.2056(b)–5):

¶ 14,449

1. The surviving spouse must be entitled for life to all of the income from the entire interest or a specific portion of the entire interest, or to a specific portion of all the income from the entire interest.

2. The income payable to the surviving spouse must be payable annually or at more frequent intervals.

3. The surviving spouse must have the power to appoint the entire interest or the specific portion pursuant to which the property can be given to the surviving spouse or the spouse's estate.

4. The power in the surviving spouse must be exercisable by the spouse alone and (whether exercisable by will or during life) must be exercisable in all events.

5. The entire interest or the specific portion must not be subject to a power in any other person to appoint any part to any person other than the surviving spouse.

Notes

[¶ 14,467]

b. *Planning Commentary*

Testators commonly create both a bypass trust (the "B" trust) and a marital share trust (an "A" trust). As noted at ¶ 13,059, the bypass trust will make it possible to eliminate all federal estate tax on the amount of property equal to the exemption equivalent to the unified credit by using the bypass trust to keep such property out of the estate of the surviving spouse.

While the bypass trust is most often created for tax reasons, there are times when it is created for nontax reasons. However, the marital share trust is created *only* for nontax reasons, such as a belief that the surviving spouse needs to have the benefit of professional management for the property passing to the surviving spouse from the decedent. There is little or no other justification for creating a marital trust. Unfortunately, it is not uncommon for a marital trust to be created routinely and without conscious deliberation as to whether such a choice is desirable.

Having determined that the only basis for using a marital share trust is property management, it would seem that the testator would want to limit the surviving spouse's control over the marital share trust to that minimum necessary to qualify the gift to the trustee for the marital deduction. That is, it would seem likely that a testator electing to create a marital trust for the surviving spouse (rather than a gift to the spouse that is free of trust) would insist that the spouse's access to the trust be especially limited so as to accomplish the trust's purpose. You would not expect to find, for example, that the surviving spouse would be permitted to freely withdraw from the trust.

The goal then, when the marital gift is in trust for the surviving spouse, is to structure the trust so that it (1) qualifies for the marital deduction but (2) does not give the surviving spouse more access to the trust than the deceased spouse wants the survivor to enjoy. The materials that follow should be explored for purposes of determining the permissible limitations that can be placed on the surviving spouse's enjoyment of the marital gift while preserving the marital deduction.

[¶ 14,475]

c. The "Income" Requirement

The first requirement to be satisfied in creating a marital share trust that qualifies for the marital deduction under the life estate/power of appointment exception is that the surviving spouse must be entitled for life to all of the income from the property interest for which the marital deduction has been claimed. § 2056(b)(5); Reg. § 20.2056(b)–5(a)(1). The meaning to be given to this income requirement is detailed in Reg. § 20.2056(b)–5(f), where a number of examples are given.

[¶ 14,483]

i. Decedent's Intention

The spouse is deemed to have the requisite income interest if the spouse has "substantially that degree of beneficial enjoyment" of the property for which the marital deduction is claimed that the "law of trusts accord to a person who is unqualifiedly designated as the life beneficiary." Whether the trust satisfies this test depends upon whether the terms of the trust evidence an intention that the surviving spouse is to have the requisite income interest.

[¶ 14,485]

WISELY v. UNITED STATES

United States Court of Appeals, Fourth Circuit, 1990.
893 F.2d 660.

FOX, District Judge:

* * * The principal question for our determination is whether the district court properly granted summary judgment for the government in holding that the deceased's will, as drafted, failed to qualify the marital trust for the marital estate tax deduction under § 2056(b)(5). Having concluded that the district court's disposition was proper, we affirm.

* * *

The decedent, William H. Wisely, died testate on November 9, 1982, leaving his Last Will and Testament * * *.

The will contained provisions for the creation of two trusts, the William H. Wisely Family Trust created under Article V, and the marital trust created under Article VI. The portion of the will which is pertinent to this appeal concerns the payment of income from the marital trust and is found in paragraph 2 of Article VI, which states:

> My trustees shall pay to my said wife so much, or all, of the net income of the said trust as my Trustees shall, in their sole discretion,

¶ 14,467

deem necessary to provide for her care and support in the style and manner of living to which she has been accustomed, and to provide for her medical or other emergency needs. Any income not so used shall be accumulated and added to the corpus. Such payments may also be made from the corpus at any time or times in the event of any illness of my said wife or any other emergency, physical or financial.

The will also granted Mrs. Wisely a general testamentary power of appointment over the marital trust corpus. * * *

* * *

* * * Section 2056(b) * * * limits marital deductions of "terminable interests." * * * Included in such "terminable interests" is property transferred as a life estate to the surviving spouse. § 2056(a), Reg. § 20.2056(b)–1(b).

An exception to the general rule barring a marital deduction for a terminable interest is contained in § 2056(b)(5). In order to fall within this exception, the bequest must meet the five separate requirements set forth in Reg. § 20.2056(b)–5(a):

* * *

Under § 20.2056(b)–5(a)(1), the value of the life estate passing to the surviving spouse with a general power of appointment qualifies for the marital deduction if the surviving spouse is entitled for life either: (1) to all of the income from the entire interest; (2) to all of the income from a specific portion of the entire interest; or (3) to a specific portion of all of the income from the entire interest.

The district court concluded that the terms of the marital trust, as found in Article VI, paragraph 2 of the will, did not meet any of these three requirements because the will failed to expressly state that Mrs. Wisely was entitled to either all the income outright or to some lesser specific portion expressed as a "fractional or percentile share" of the marital trust income. We agree with the district court's conclusion.

Under Article VI paragraph 2 of the will, the trustees may, in their *sole discretion,* decide to accumulate any income they do not deem necessary for Mrs. Wisely's support, medical, or emergency expenses. Moreover, Mrs. Wisely is not entitled, under the terms of the trust, to demand that the trustees distribute income to her. On the contrary, the trustees' affirmative action is required in order for the trust to distribute income to Mrs. Wisely. In short, the consent of persons other than Mrs. Wisely is required as a condition precedent to distribution of the marital trust income. Likewise, it is within the discretion of persons other than Mrs. Wisely to accumulate the trust income rather than to pay it to her, if they should determine that the income is not necessary to maintain her standard of living. We agree with the district court's reasoning that the "sole discretion" language in the trust does not entitle Mrs. Wisely to all of the income from the entire interest for life. Furthermore, we affirm the district court's finding that the language of the trust fails to satisfy the second or third conditions of § 20.2056(b)–5(a)(1). We

¶ **14,485**

rely on the district court's reasoning that the language allowing the trustees to pay Mrs. Wisely income in their "sole discretion" fails to designate either a specific portion of the entire interest or a specific portion of all of the income from the entire interest.

Accordingly, we conclude that the district court did not err in finding that the marital trust failed to meet the requirement of § 20.2056(b)–5(a)(1).

* * *

The Estate argues that the district court erred in concluding that the marital trust did not qualify for the marital deduction under §§ 20.2056(b)–5(a)(1) & (2) because the district court failed to refer to extrinsic evidence in construing the terms of the will.

The Estate contends that the two-trust structure of the will (*i.e.,* Family Trust and Marital Trust) when juxtaposed with the discretionary income standard used in the marital trust, creates an ambiguity in the will itself requiring reference to extrinsic evidence of the decedent's intent to qualify the marital trust for the marital deduction.

* * * While the intention of the testator is the "polar star" of construction, intention must be found in the testator's expressed words. The meaning of the words as used by the testator are the equivalent of his legal intention— the intention which the law recognizes as dispositive. A court may not speculate upon what the testator may have intended to do, but rather must give strict effect to the testator's words. Consequently, the true inquiry is not what the testator meant to express, but what the words he has used do actually express. * * *

Here, the Estate's contention that "[t]he decedent's use of a two-trust structure is tantamount to a flat declaration by the decedent that he intended * * * [the Marital Trust to be construed so as to qualify for the marital deduction]" is conjectural. The Estate has not pointed to any language in the will from which it can be concluded that the testator's paramount intention was to qualify the marital trust for a marital deduction, particularly where it requires the court to disregard the decedent's expressed intention that the trustees should use their sole discretion to determine the amount of marital trust income necessary for his wife's support. Because words are not to be rejected unless they manifestly conflict with the plain intention of the testator, there is nothing in the law that would permit reformation of the will to overcome the specific language used in Article VI, paragraph 2, bequeathing marital trust income to decedent's wife in amounts that "the trustees in their sole discretion, deem necessary."

Indeed, the sole discretion vested in decedent's trustees with respect to the marital trust income is likewise vested in the trustees with respect to the Family Trust income, thereby confirming that the decedent intended his words expressed in both Articles V and VI, paragraphs 2.

Here, the decedent did not bequeath the appropriate property interest in the marital trust to his wife to qualify for the marital deduction. Deductions are a matter of legislative grace, and the taxpayer seeking the benefit of a deduction must show that every condition which Congress has seen fit to impose has been fully satisfied. The taxpayer may not haggle with Congress; he either fits squarely within the statute in every particular or the deduction is unavailable. We know of no rule by which the foregoing doctrine is any less applicable to the estate tax than to the income tax. We decline to rewrite Article VI, paragraph 2, to give effect to what the estate contends, based on the will's structure to have been the decedent's intent, when to do so would require ignoring decedent's *express* intention, stated in two separate places in the will, of granting his trustees sole discretion in determining the amount of income necessary for his wife's support.

* * *

[¶ 14,491]

ii. Forbidden Administrative Powers

Qualification for the life estate/power of appointment exception to the nondeductible terminable interest rule depends on the absence of so-called forbidden powers. Forbidden powers are those powers that, if held by a person other than the spouse, could be exercised so as to effectively deny the surviving spouse all of the income from the property for which the marital deduction is claimed or in some way limit the exercise of the general power of appointment the surviving spouse must receive. Reg. § 20.2056(b)–5(f)(8). A prime example is a spendthrift clause. The IRS claims that the marital deduction cannot be allowed where the governing instrument "requires the trustee to accumulate all income of the trust during the period of any attachment, assignment, etc., to or by any creditor rather than pay the income to the surviving spouse." Priv. Ltr. Rul. 8248008. Under these circumstances, the IRS believes, "the surviving spouse is not entitled for life to all the income," as is required for allowance of the marital deduction under the life estate/power of appointment exception.

By way of contrast, purely administrative powers held by a trustee will not disqualify a trust for the marital deduction under the life estate/power of appointment exception. Examples of permitted powers include the ability to apportion items of income and expense between successive beneficial interests where applicable state law requires the trustee's determination to be made fairly so as to balance the interests of the successive beneficiaries; the ability to treat capital gain dividends received from mutual funds as principal; the right to maintain reasonable reserves for depreciation; and the right to charge fiduciary and professional fees to either income or principal, to make distributions in cash or in kind at current values and to make reasonable determinations as to current values. Rev. Rul. 69–56, 1969–1 C.B. 224.

A power allowing income to be accumulated in the discretion of someone other than the surviving spouse will disqualify the trust for the marital deduction. Reg. § 20.2056(b)–5(f)(7). However, the income right is satisfied if the spouse has the "right exercisable annually * * * to require distribution" of the trust income. Reg. § 20.2056(b)–5(f)(8).

¶ 14,491

While the foregoing enumeration is only partial, it is indicative of the range of possibilities available in drafting the marital trust—and the ease with which one can inadvertently disqualify a trust for the marital deduction. As a result, it is commonplace to include language in the trust declaring an intention to qualify the trust for the marital deduction and expressly renouncing any intention that any disqualifying power ever have any application to the marital trust. Despite these declarations, however, the enumeration suggests that limitations have a beneficial effect as in the case where the surviving spouse is mentally incompetent and the distribution of income to that spouse would mean payment to a court-appointed guardian with the fees and burdens associated therewith. In such a case, the trust income can be warehoused in the trust so long as the spouse has the right to call for that income at least annually.

[¶ 14,499]

iii. Unproductive Property

The power to retain assets passing to the trust will not disqualify an income interest for the marital deduction unless the grant of powers evidences an intention to deprive the spouse of the required beneficial enjoyment. Reg. § 20.2056(b)–5(f)(4). However, if the trustee can retain unproductive property in the trust, the surviving spouse must be able to require that the trustee make the property productive or convert it within a reasonable time to productive property. On the other hand, a power to retain a residence or other property for the personal use of the spouse will not disqualify the trust property for the marital deduction.

The following Technical Advice Memorandum illustrates how an option to purchase property at less than fair market value may disqualify the property for the marital deduction.

[¶ 14,501]

TECHNICAL ADVICE MEMORANDUM 9147065
July 12, 1991.

ISSUE

If a trust for the benefit of the surviving spouse is required to be funded, in part, with closely-held stock ["Company stock"] subject to specified restrictions and purchase options described below, does that portion of the trust qualify for the marital deduction under § 2056(b)(5)?

* * *

During her lifetime, the surviving spouse will be paid all income from the trust at least quarterly. * * * The surviving spouse has the power to appoint by will, to any person including her estate, the trust assets remaining at her death. * * *

* * *

¶ 14,491

* * * [A]lthough the will contains a *general* provision to the effect that nonproductive property cannot be held in the spouse's trust for more than a reasonable time, the will *specifically* precludes the trustee from disposing of the (nonproductive) Company stock at any time unless directed by the son authorized to dispose of the Company stock. Under ordinary rules of construction, subsequent and specific directions prevail over preceding and general directions in a will.

Immediately following the provision prohibiting the trustee from selling the Company stock, the will provides, "[n]otwithstanding anything in the above to the contrary * * *" each of the decedent's sons is granted an option to purchase from the executor or the trustee a specified percentage (totaling 100 percent) of the total Company shares at a specified price of $1,000 per share. * * *

* * *

In the present case, no marital deduction can be allowed with respect to the portion of the spouse's trust that is required to be funded with the Company stock.

First, by giving his sons an option to purchase the Company stock at $1,000 a share, the decedent effectively divided the value of the stock between his sons and the spouse's trust. At the decedent's death, the fair market value of the stock was $11,000 per share. This was nearly 11 times the option price. * * * Thus, *viewed as of the decedent's death,* each son held a right, exercisable during the spouse's life, to make a bargain purchase of the Company stock. The effect of the bargain purchase would be to substantially deplete the value of the trust corpus.

[Power of Appointment Given Child]

Each son's option right is, effectively, a right to appoint to himself the excess of the fair market value of a share on the option exercise date over the option price. The sons' rights to purchase Company stock confers upon them a power to withdraw property with a substantial value from the spouse's trust for less than adequate and full consideration. This right is a "power in any other person to appoint any part of the interest, or such specific portion, to any person other than the surviving spouse" as that phrase is used in § 2056(b)(5). Because of this power, the amount of the marital deduction for the property passing to the spouse's trust must be reduced by the value of the stock passing to the trust.

* * *

[Income Right Impaired]

Under the will, unproductive property generally cannot be held for more than a reasonable time during the spouse's life without her written consent. However, the will expressly prohibits the trustee from selling the Company stock, unless so directed by the son authorized to sell it (except if a son exercises his option). Thus, effectively, neither the spouse nor the trustee have any legal right to establish an adequate income flow for the spouse from

¶ 14,501

the Company stock. Consequently, under Reg. § 20.2056(b)–5(f)(4), the spouse is not entitled to "all the income for life" from the stock.

Problem

[¶ 14,505]

Could a defective life estate/power of appointment trust such as that found in *Wisely* and TAM 9147065 be cured of its defect by the inclusion of the following provision?

> All provisions of this instrument shall be construed and applied so that the Marital Share qualifies for the marital deduction in the Settlor's estate if the Settlor's spouse survives or is presumed to survive the Settlor. Any provision of this instrument that cannot be so construed shall not apply to the Marital Share. The Trustee shall take such action and have such powers as are necessary to cause the Marital Share to qualify for the marital deduction and shall take no action and shall have no power that will impair the marital deduction.

The IRS, in Revenue Ruling 65–144, 1965–1 C.B. 442, said that the following provision in a trust instrument "constitutes a mere attempt to impose a condition subsequent with respect to certain powers otherwise granted to the trustees therein named which is wholly void and ineffective in law because of being contrary to public policy":

> If, as a result of any Treasury Ruling or provisions of the Internal Revenue Code or the Regulations promulgated thereunder, the powers, authorities or discretions vested in the trustees herein are construed or considered to render the charitable remainder provided herein as nonseverable or not subject to specific ascertainment, the powers, authorities, and discretions of the trustees are hereby revoked to the extent necessary to make them consistent and conform to said rulings, Code provisions, or Regulations to the end that the charitable remainder provided herein shall be deductible for federal tax purposes.

Can the tainted provision from Revenue Ruling 65–144 be reconciled with the provision proposed here for inclusion in *Wisely* and TAM 9147065? See Rev. Rul. 75–440, 1975–2 C.B. 372; ¶ 19,559.

[¶ 14,507]

d.   The "Payable Annually" Requirement

The income must be payable at least annually. While the income is specifically required to be payable to the spouse "annually or at more frequent intervals," Reg. § 20.2056(b)–5(e) suggests that silence in the will or trust as to the time for payment is not a failure to meet the statute unless local law permits periodic payments to be delayed more than a year.

[¶ 14,515]

e.   The "Power of Appointment" Requirement

A broad power of appointment must be given to the surviving spouse. The surviving spouse must have a power of appointment over the property (or a specific portion thereof) pursuant to which the property can be given to the surviving spouse or to the surviving spouse's estate. However, the necessary power is not defined in terms of a general power of appointment taxable under § 2041; rather, § 2056(b)(5) is explicit as to the requirements that will lead to the allowance of the marital deduction. As a result, there are instances where a trust may not qualify for the marital deduction, even though the gross estate of the surviving spouse may include the trust property because the surviving spouse has a general power of appointment over the trust property as described in § 2041. See, e.g., Reg. § 20.2056(b)–5(g); Estate of Pipe v. Commissioner, 241 F.2d 210 (2d Cir.1957). In *Pipe*, the marital deduction was denied despite the spouse's power during life to use, enjoy, sell or dispose of the trust property "for such purposes or in such manner, as she in her uncontrolled discretion may choose, it being [decedent's] * * * desire to place no restraint on her in any respect concerning the absolute right of full disposition and use * * * [of the trust property] except that she shall have no power over the disposition of such part thereof as remains unexpended at the time of her death."

[¶ 14,517]

f. The "Exercisable Alone and in All Events" Test

i. Permissible Limitations

Another requirement for a marital share trust is that "the power in the surviving spouse must be exercisable by the surviving spouse alone and (whether exercisable by will or during life) must be exercisable in all events" Reg. § 20.2056(b)–5(a)(4). Thus, the requirement is not satisfied if the remarriage of the surviving spouse cancels the power.

The power of appointment held by the surviving spouse must be exercisable in favor of "whomsoever [the surviving spouse] pleases." Reg. § 20.2056(b)–5(g)(2). Thus, the condition would not be satisfied if the surviving spouse entered into a binding agreement with the decedent to exercise the power in favor of their lineal descendants. However, the deceased spouse who created the power is free to specify takers in default if the surviving spouse fails to exercise the power. This right to specify takers in default is a planning possibility for the deceased spouse wanting control. So, too, is another permissible limitation identified in the regulations. Reg. § 20.2056(b)–5(g)(4) says that the surviving spouse's testamentary power may be limited so long as the spouse has an unlimited power to withdraw the marital property during life. Similarly, limitations of a formal nature will not disqualify a power. The most important example of a permissible formal limitation is the rule allowing the deceased spouse to insist that the surviving spouse exercise the power exclusively by will and only by specific reference to the paragraph of the will creating the power. Reg. § 20.2056(b)–5(g)(4). The control possibilities inherent in such a limitation are obvious.

[¶ 14,525]

ii. Incompetency

Suppose that the spouse's right to withdraw from the trust terminates in the event of the spouse's incompetency. The decedent's will in Starrett v. Commissioner, 223 F.2d 163 (1st Cir.1955), created a trust in favor of his wife, who survived him. The trustee was directed to pay her, in quarterly installments, all the net income from the trust for life. The will further provided that the trustee:

> shall, at any time or from time to time, upon the request in writing of my said wife, transfer, convey and pay over to her any part or parts or the whole of said first share free from trust for her absolute use, provided that such right of my wife to call for the transfer or conveyance to her of any part or parts or the whole of the principal of said first share shall cease in case of her legal incapacity from any cause or upon the appointment of a guardian, conservator, or other custodian of her person or estate. * * *

The court disallowed the marital deduction, stating that the surviving spouse's power to invade the corpus was not exercisable by her "in all events," in view of the terminating condition set forth above.

[¶ 14,533]

iii. Distribution Standards

Suppose that the surviving spouse is limited in accessing the trust property to those instances where access is necessary for the surviving spouse's health, education, maintenance, and support. Would the trust be disqualified for the marital deduction under the LEPA exception of § 2056(b)(5)? In Piatt v. Gray, 321 F.2d 79 (6th Cir.1963), the testator's will gave his wife a legal life estate in the residue of his personal property with remainder over to the testator's sister. The testator's wife was given:

> the power, right and authority whenever, in her opinion, it shall be necessary for her maintenance, comfort or well-being to expend all or any part of the principal of my said personal property without being required to account therefore, and she shall have the further right, power and authority to sell, lease, encumber or otherwise dispose of any and all items of personal property belonging to me and to give any purchaser a good fee simple title thereto.

Relying on Reg. § 20.2056(b)–5(g)(3), the court held that although a legal life estate, as well as a trust, may qualify for the marital deduction, the testator's surviving spouse did not possess such an unlimited power to invade the corpus of the estate that she was able to appoint herself "in all events" as an unqualified owner. The regulation states that a power is not exercisable in all events if it is exercisable only for the spouse's support, or only for her limited use, or if the surviving spouse does not have the power to dispose of the property by gift. Yet the testator's wife was empowered to dispose of the property only when she believed it was necessary for her maintenance, comfort or well-being to do so. Further, she was authorized to give good title to "any purchaser" but was not granted authority to give good title to a donee.

Problems

[¶ 14,539]

1. Will the presence of any of the following provisions in a trust cause the trust property to fail to qualify for the life estate/power of appointment exception? Consult Reg. § 20.2056(b)–5(f).

   (a) "During the lifetime of the surviving spouse, the Trustee shall pay to or apply for the benefit of the surviving spouse so much or all of the income of the trust estate as the Trustee shall determine to be in the best interests of the surviving spouse. Any income which is not so distributed may be withdrawn by the surviving spouse from the trust estate at any time or times during the lifetime of the surviving spouse by written demand made upon the Trustee." Is it not true that this provision is preferable (from an administrative point of view) to a provision that calls for the payment of all of the income annually? Why? In anticipation of the surviving spouse's possible future incompetency! How's that? Suppose the surviving spouse becomes incompetent. To whom will the income payments be made under a mandatory "pay income annually" provision? Her court-appointed guardian? To what disadvantage? See ¶ 4051.

   (b) "The Trustee shall allocate receipts, gains, losses and expenditures to income and principal in accordance with generally accepted principles of trust accounting and applicable law governing the trust estate as the same may exist from time to time; *but* the Trustee is directed to allocate to principal all distributions representing capital gains and losses received from the sale of securities held by regulated investment companies, real estate investment trusts, or mutual funds as well as all other realized capital gains and losses, and to allocate to income all current expenses and amortize out of income premiums paid on bonds, debentures or other money obligations."

   (c) "No beneficiary of this trust shall have the right or power to anticipate, by assignment or otherwise, any income or principal given to such beneficiary by this trust, nor in advance of actually receiving the same, have the right or power to sell, transfer, encumber or anywise charge same; nor shall such income or principal, or any portion of the same, be subject to any execution, garnishment, attachment, insolvency, bankruptcy, or legal proceeding of any character, or legal sequestration, levy or sale, or in any event or manner be applicable or subject, voluntarily or involuntarily, to the payment of such beneficiary's estate."

(d) "Any property transferred to the Marital Share shall constitute a proper trust investment. The Trustee shall have no obligation to dispose of or convert to other form any such property; provided, however, that the spouse shall have the power to require the Trustee to make all or part of the principal of the Marital Share productive or to convert promptly any unproductive part into productive property."

2. Why is it important to include the following provision in each life estate/power of appointment trust?

Upon the death of the surviving spouse, the Trustee shall pay over to the spouse's estate any accrued and undistributed income from the trust.

3. Refer to the proposed language in Problem 1, paragraph (a) above and determine whether the trust income that is not distributed to the surviving spouse will be taxed to the trustee or to the surviving spouse. See § 678.

Would capital gains realized by the marital trust (but not distributed to the surviving spouse) be taxed to the surviving spouse or to the trustee if the instrument contained the following language:

In addition to the payment of all the net income, the Trustee shall pay to Settlor's spouse such sums of principal as Settlor's spouse, during life, requests by written instrument delivered to the Trustee.

4. Does the following language satisfy the "exercisable alone and in all events" test? Doesn't this language frustrate Congress's intent to cause community and separate property to be treated alike for tax purposes? (Isn't Congress's intent frustrated because the testator is able to place hurdles in front of the surviving spouse in his or her effort to exercise the general power that Congress insists that the spouse be given.)

If not earlier terminated by distribution of the entire trust estate under the foregoing provisions, the Marital Share Trust shall terminate upon the death of the spouse. At that time, the Trustee shall distribute the then remaining assets of the Marital Share to such one or more persons and entities, including the estate, the creditors, or the creditors of the estate of the spouse, in such proportions and upon such terms and conditions, either outright or in trust, as the spouse shall appoint by a will or a codicil that refers specifically to this power of appointment and expresses the intention to exercise it. To the extent that the spouse does not effectively exercise this testamentary general power of appointment over the Marital Share, then, on the death of the spouse, such remaining assets shall be transferred to the Bypass Trust to be held, managed, and disposed of as though originally a part of the property allocated to the Bypass Trust. Until there is exhibited to the Trustee within 6 months of the death of the surviving spouse, a copy of an instrument admitted to probate in any jurisdiction as the last will of a beneficiary possessing a power of appointment hereunder in which such power is validly exercised (and the Trustee shall be protected in relying on such instrument), the Trustee may hold, manage and distribute the trust (with respect to both principal and income) as though such beneficiary had died without exercising such power, and the Trustee shall not be liable for so doing. This paragraph shall not be construed as a limitation on the right to exercise a power of appointment and shall be without prejudice to the right of any appointee to recover the distributed property from any person receiving such property.

[¶ 14,541]

g. *Policy Issues*

The life estate/power of appointment exception to the nondeductible terminable interest rule is one clear example of a case where Congress seems to have lost sight of its basic goal in adopting the marital deduction. If its basic goal was to put both separate and community property on the same tax footing, allowing the life estate/power of appointment exception gives testators control over the enjoyment of their separate property, a feature not available to testators with community property. Testators owning community property control only one-half of the community and there is no way for the first spouse to die to get control of the survivor's 50 percent of the community (except through a widow's election or other election device, see ¶ 11,901). The testator with separate property can control his or her spouse's enjoyment of the decedent's property through the bypass trust and the marital share trust and still obtain the tax savings benefits of the marital deduction, although the widow's election scheme may make available to the decedent's estate even more attractive tax and control benefits, even though such benefits are not expressly sanctioned by Congress.

Why, then, did Congress allow the marital deduction for gifts in trust? Could it be argued that it was the custom of the time for the male spouse to insist that property passing to his spouse at his death be professionally managed and that it was impolitic to force the male spouse to choose between making a gift in fee simple that would qualify for the marital deduction or one in trust which would not? Or can the life estate/power of appointment exception be justified on the grounds that the required general power causes the power property to be included in the gross estate of the surviving spouse? However, if that were the case, congressional intent has been freely frustrated by the Internal Revenue Service with the blessings of the courts in the many cases where property passing to the wife is found not to qualify for the marital deduction but is included in the surviving spouse's estate at death on the grounds that the spouse has a general power of appointment over the trust property for purposes of § 2041 but the power does not satisfy the requirements of § 2056(b)(5). See ¶ 14,517.

[¶ 14,549]

3. THE INSURANCE EXCEPTION

The "insurance" exception very closely parallels the life estate/power of appointment exception as evidenced by the following five conditions set forth in Reg. § 20.2056(b)–6:

1. The proceeds, or a specific portion of the proceeds, must be held by the insurer subject to an agreement either to pay the entire proceeds or a specific portion thereof in installments, or to pay interest thereon, and all or a specific portion of the installments or interest payable during the life of the surviving spouse must be payable only to the spouse.

2. The installments or interest payable to the surviving spouse must be payable annually, or more frequently, commencing no later than 13 months after the decedent's death.

3. The surviving spouse must have the power to appoint all or a specific portion of the amounts so held by the insurer so as to result in the property being distributed to the spouse or to the spouse's estate.

4. The power in the surviving spouse must be exercisable by the spouse alone and (whether exercisable by will or during life) must be exercisable in all events.

5. The amounts or the specific portion of the amounts payable under such contract must not be subject to a power that allows any other person to appoint any part thereof to anyone other than the surviving spouse.

[¶ 14,557]

4. QUALIFIED TERMINABLE INTEREST PROPERTY (QTIP)

The QTIP exception, like LEPA, must be viewed as a planning opportunity. QTIPs are much more popular than LEPAs. Both are used whenever the marital gift is made in trust (rather than free of trust) so as to limit the surviving spouse's access to the marital gift property. See ¶ 14,467. Look at the following materials in terms of the minimum access to the marital gift property that must be given to the surviving spouse so as to qualify for the marital deduction. Think about how the QTIP can be drafted to accomplish the "control" goals of the deceased spouse without jeopardizing the marital deduction. In sum, walk along the rim of the canyon but do not stumble; IRS challenge waits at the bottom for the careless.

[¶ 14,561]

a. The Requirements: In General

In 1981, Congress *qualitatively* expanded the marital deduction to recognize "qualified terminable interest property" (QTIP) and allow it to qualify for the marital deduction. § 2056(b)(7). For property to qualify as QTIP:

1. The surviving spouse must be entitled to all of the income from the property for life;

2. *No person* may have a power *exercisable during the lifetime of the surviving spouse* to appoint any part of the property to any person other than the surviving spouse; and

¶ 14,549

3. The decedent's executor must elect to claim the marital deduction for the QTIP property on the decedent's federal estate tax return. <u>Once made, the election is irrevocable.</u>

Reg. § 20.2056(b)–7 is almost required reading for anyone seeking to claim the benefits of QTIP treatment.

[¶ 14,565]

b. *Tax Consequences*

QTIP escapes tax at the death of the first spouse to die on the condition it will later be subject to transfer taxes. Accordingly, QTIP will be subject to transfer taxes at the earlier of (1) the date on which the surviving spouse disposes (either by gift, sale, or otherwise) of all *or part* of the qualifying income interest (§ 2519) or (2) the date of the surviving spouse's death (§ 2044). If the property is subject to tax as a result of the surviving spouse's lifetime transfer of QTIP, the entire value of the property, less amounts received by the surviving spouse upon disposition, will be treated as a taxable gift by the surviving spouse. § 2519.

Suppose <u>Wife is given a life estate in a trust by Husband with remainder to Children. Husband makes the QTIP election for the trust.</u> Subsequently, Wife transfers her life estate to Children by deed. At the time of the transfer, Wife's life estate has a value of $100,000 and the remainder interest has a value of $200,000, for an aggregate value of $300,000. Under these circumstances, Wife will be deemed to have made two taxable gifts: (1) a gift of $200,000 under § 2519 and (2) a gift of $100,000 under § 2511(a) of her QTIP-qualifying income interest in the trust. Reg. § 25.2519–1(g), Example 1.

If the property subject to the qualifying income interest is not disposed of prior to the death of the surviving spouse, the fair market value of the property subject to the qualifying income interest determined as of the date of the surviving spouse's death (or the alternate valuation date provided in § 2032, if so elected) will be included in the surviving spouse's gross estate under § 2044 and taxed at the top marginal rate applicable to the surviving spouse's estate.

[¶ 14,573]

c. *The "Income" Requirement*

Reg. § 20.2056(b)–7(d)(2) states that all the principles expressed in Reg. § 20.2056(b)–5(f) (as to the life estate/power of appointment (LEPA) exception to the nondeductible terminable interest rule) apply to the QTIP income entitlement requirement.

i. Decedent's Intention

[¶ 14,575]

ESTATE OF NICHOLSON v. COMMISSIONER

United States Tax Court, 1990.
94 T.C. 666

GERBER, Judge:

* * *

The decedent died testate in 1983. His will provided that his share of community property was to be distributed to an existing inter vivos trust. The trustees were directed to pay the income of the trust to the decedent's surviving spouse "as * * * [she] may from time to time require to maintain * * * [her] usual and customary standard of living * * *." Additionally, "in this regard the Trustees may also invade the corpus of the Trust for these purposes." The decedent further granted the trustees "full and complete independent authority to invest, sell, assign, transfer, trade, mortgage, lease or otherwise deal with the property of this Trust as they may deem to be in the best interests of Dorothy Nell Nicholson. * * *"

In 1984, the trustees and beneficiary of the trust sought and obtained an "Order of Modification" from a Texas State court. Pursuant to that order, the trust instrument was changed to provide that, at the decedent's death, the trustees were to "pay the net income of the Trust estate to * * * [decedent's wife] in quarterly or more frequent installments."

We must decide whether, at the time of the decedent's death, his wife's interest in the trust qualified for an estate tax marital deduction as * * * "qualified terminable interest property," or "QTIP" interests. QTIP interests are those in which a decedent passes to the surviving spouse a "qualifying income interest for life." Generally, when the surviving spouse has a "qualifying income interest for life" she is entitled to "all the income from the property, payable annually or at more frequent intervals," and, while she is alive, no one else can appoint any part of the property to anyone but her. § 2056(b)(7)(B).

[Legislative History]

The legislative history underlying the QTIP provisions indicates that a QTIP interest must meet the requirements of Reg. § 20.2056(b)–5(f). See H. Rept. 97–201 (1981), 1981–2 C.B. 352, 378. Under that regulation, a surviving spouse is entitled to "all the income from the property" if she has the equivalent "beneficial enjoyment" of the trust estate as one who is "unqualifiedly designated as the life beneficiary * * *" Generally, absent indications to the contrary, the "designation of the spouse as sole income beneficiary for life * * * will be sufficient * * *" Reg. § 20.2056(b)–5(f)(1).

[State Law]

A determination of the nature of the interest which passes to the surviving spouse is made under the law of the jurisdiction under which the

¶ 14,575

interest passes. Here, we look to the law of Texas. Under that law, the issue of whether a beneficiary is entitled to a particular interest in the trust estate depends upon the intention of the settlor. The settlor's intention as it existed at the time the trust was created is determinative. * * *

* * *

While we will look to local law in order to determine the nature of the interests provided under a trust document, we are not bound to give effect to a local court order which modifies that document after respondent has acquired rights to tax revenues under its terms. "[N]ot even judicial reformation can operate to change the federal tax consequences of a completed transaction." Van Den Wymelenberg v. United States 397 F.2d 443, 445 (7th Cir. 1968), cert. denied 393 U.S. 953 (1968). The reformation of an instrument has retroactive effect as between the parties to the instrument, but not as to third parties who previously acquired rights under the instrument. As the Court of Appeals explained in Van Den Wymelenberg v. United States, supra at 445—

> As to the parties to the reformed instrument the reformation relates back to the date of the original instrument, but it does not affect the rights acquired by non-parties, including the Government. Were the law otherwise there would exist considerable opportunity for "collusive" state court actions having the sole purpose of reducing federal tax liabilities. Furthermore, federal tax liabilities would remain unsettled for years after their assessment if state courts and private persons were empowered to retroactively affect the tax consequences of completed transactions and completed tax years.

[Trust Terms]

Under the terms of the trust at issue, the decedent's wife is not "entitled to all the income from the property, payable annually or at more frequent intervals" as is required by § 2056(b)(7). Instead, the unambiguous language of the trust only allows her "so much of the net income * * * as * * * [she] may from time to time require to maintain * * * [her] usual and customary standard of living. * * *"

In the context of the trust instrument at issue, the provision for "so much of the net income * * * as * * * [she] may from time to time require" gives Mrs. Nicholson only such income as she may reasonably *need*, but not necessarily all the income that she may *demand*. The trust instrument reveals clearly the decedent's intention that his children, as trustees, were to determine, and provide, the amounts Mrs. Nicholson required to maintain her "usual and customary" standard of living. As long as they carried out their duties, Mrs. Nicholson had neither the obligation, nor the right, to demand "all the income," or any particular amount of income, from the trust.

Consideration of the trust document as a whole reveals no internal inconsistencies with limiting Mrs. Nicholson's income to that which she "may from time to time require." To be sure, nowhere in that document did the decedent make specific provision for the disposition of income in excess of his

¶ 14,575

wife's requirements. That failure, however, does not establish his intention that there would be no excess income. Instead, the trust instrument provides that, when both the decedent and his wife have died, "this irrevocable Trust shall then terminate, and the Trustee or Trustees shall then distribute the Trust estate to SALLY LYNN NICHOLSON MILLER and WILLIAM B. NICHOLSON, equally, share and share alike. * * * " This bequest of the remainder interest, unlike the support bequest for Mrs. Nicholson, makes no distinction between trust corpus and trust income. It is therefore clear that the decedent intended a gift of both the corpus component and the undistributed income component of "the Trust estate" to his children after his wife died.

We are aware that respondent's regulations provide a broad scope for interpreting a trust instrument. Those provisions, however, do not permit us to rewrite the trust instrument. The instrument here, as executed by the decedent, and as in existence at the time of his death, fails to establish that Mrs. Nicholson is "unqualifiedly designated as the life beneficiary * * *." Nor does it otherwise designate her as "sole income beneficiary for life." Reg. § 20.2056(b)–5(f). It instead limits Mrs. Nicholson's trust income to amounts she would "require." Any excess would go to the remaindermen. Plainly, then, under the trust instrument at issue, Mrs. Nicholson is not "entitled to all the income" from the property within the meaning of § 2056(b)(7)(B)(ii), and her interest in the trust fails to qualify for the marital deduction.

[Sources for Ascertaining Testator's Intention]

Petitioner, however, urges that the language of the trust document is ambiguous. It is contended that we must therefore look to the circumstances surrounding the establishment of the trust to determine the decedent's intent. Petitioner then points to the decedent's awareness that the trust assets, at the date of his death, would not generate sufficient income to support Mrs. Nicholson in the manner to which she was accustomed. Petitioner concludes that the decedent must have intended that his wife would receive "all the income" from the trust, plus some amount from the invasion of the corpus. In support of these contentions, petitioner relies heavily upon the Court of Appeals' decision in Estate of Mittleman v. Commissioner 522 F.2d 132 (D.C. Cir. 1975). * * *

Even if petitioner were correct, and we were permitted to look at the circumstances surrounding the execution of the trust, those circumstances do not compel a finding that the decedent "entitled" his wife to all the income from the trust. The extrinsic evidence shows instead that the decedent wished only to provide support to his wife in the manner to which she was accustomed. He especially wished to spare her the concerns of providing for herself, because she was not familiar with business operations. A bequest of all the potential trust income would have been inconsistent with this intention.

* * *

Moreover, Mrs. Nicholson was entitled to only so much of the trust's income as she may "from time to time" require to maintain her usual and customary standard of living. The implication of this language is that Mrs.

Nicholson's requirements for income from the trust were to be evaluated in light of income from other sources * * *.

The extrinsic evidence further shows that the trustees, consistent with the settlor's intent, might well have managed the trust in a way that would generate more income than the sole beneficiary needed to maintain her standard of living. Reinvestment in income-producing property was a very real possibility. * * *

Accordingly, even a consideration of the extrinsic evidence fails to show that the decedent intended that his wife be "entitled to all the income" from the trust.

[Mittleman Distinguished Factually]

The opinion of the Court of Appeals in Estate of Mittleman v. Commissioner, 522 F.2d at 133 n.1, upon which petitioner relies, is not inconsistent with our opinion here. In that case, a decedent left his residuary estate to a trust for the following purposes:

a. To provide for the proper support, maintenance, welfare and comfort of my beloved wife, HENRIETTA MITTLEMAN, for her entire lifetime.

b. To invade the corpus of the trust estate from time to time in the sole and exclusive discretion of the Trustees and to use all or any portion of the said corpus for the proper support, maintenance and welfare of my wife, HENRIETTA MITTLEMAN.

* * *

Respondent argued that the above language failed to provide that "all of the income" of the trust be payable "annually or at more frequent intervals" to the surviving spouse, for purposes of § 2056(b)(5) * * *

* * * [T]he Court of Appeals noted that the Mittleman will made no mention of income from the trust. To the court, the will placed no restriction—either "expressly" or "impliedly"—on the amount of income to be spent on behalf of the beneficiary. The only limitation upon trust expenditures were those restricting expenditures from the corpus to those expenditures made in the "sole and exclusive discretion of the [t]rustees." From this, the Court of Appeals concluded that the "compelling inference" was that the decedent intended to make an unqualified disposition of the income to the wife. The court rejected the notion that the decedent's specific provisions for "the proper support, maintenance, welfare and comfort" of his wife established any limit upon the amount of income she would receive. To the Court of Appeals, that language was "a mere declaration of the purpose of the trust. * * * *" Estate of Mittleman v. Commissioner, 522 F.2d at 138. The court further found the language as to the disposition of income "ambiguous," thus justifying an examination of "surrounding circumstances." The court determined that these surrounding circumstances supported its conclusion that the wife was "entitled to all of the income." It pointed out that the corpus of the trust was "not large" and that the anticipated income, without invasions of the trust, would produce yields "far short of the family income before Mr.

Mittleman died." Estate of Mittleman v. Commissioner, 522 F.2d at 139. The court also took into account the decedent's explicit wish that his estate be able to claim the marital deduction.

This case is factually distinguishable. The trust at issue here, unlike the trust in *Mittleman,* contains explicit language limiting the amount of income that would be paid to the surviving wife. Here, the trustees are directed to pay only "so much of the net income" of the trust to the decedent's surviving spouse "as * * * [she] may from time to time require to maintain * * * [her] usual and customary standard of living. * * *" That language is not ambiguous, and no examination of "surrounding circumstances" is indicated. Were the situation otherwise, however, this case is still not *Mittleman.* The "surrounding circumstances" here show that the estate was capable of yielding income in excess of that needed to maintain the beneficiary in her accustomed standard of living. Accordingly, she was not necessarily entitled to "all the income." Moreover, here the decedent specifically did not draft his trust with an intention to maximize the marital deduction. There is, accordingly, no reason for us to contort the language he used in order to achieve that result.

[Reformation of Trust]

Finally, we do not believe that the modification to the trust instrument made in 1984, after the decedent's death, affects the result we have reached. We have not been provided with the evidence presented to the Texas court; we have only the decree allowing the modification. The new language in that modification provides specifically that the trustees "shall pay the net income of the Trust estate to Dorothy Nell Nicholson in quarterly or more frequent installments." The modified trust instrument appears to meet the requirements for the marital deduction set forth in § 2056(b)(7). As indicated above, however, we have found that respondent is entitled to estate taxes on the basis of the trust provisions that existed at the time of the decedent's death. The attempt to claim an estate tax deduction by means of a post-mortem modification to the trust instrument therefore fails. We will not give effect to a local court order or decree that alters or modifies a trust instrument after respondent has acquired rights to tax revenues under its provisions.

Petitioner, in fact, does not now claim that the language of the 1984 modification is controlling. It is instead urged that the 1984 modification is merely a "clarification" of the decedent's original intention that all the trust income be distributed to his wife at least annually. We do not agree that the 1984 modification serves only to clarify the original instrument. * * * The 1984 modification is * * * a substantial change in the trust instrument made after respondent had secured rights under the original instrument. As such, we will not give it effect.

We are mindful of the statement of the Texas State court that its modification of the 1984 trust instrument "would be in keeping with the intent of the settlors when the Trust was created * * *" That statement, however, does not affect our opinion here. "Although this reformation may comply with the original intentions of the grantor as disclosed by * * * evidence at the hearing in that proceeding, it is not an interpretation of the original instrument * * * " M.T. Straight Trust v. Commissioner, 24 T.C. at 74. Moreover and as we have found, decedent was not concerned with obtaining the maximum estate deduction. He was concerned with taking care of his wife's needs.

We are not unsympathetic to the contention that the decedent herein would have wished to establish a QTIP trust, but the fact is that he did not do so. * * *

* * * For estate taxes, as for income taxes, "Deductions are a matter of legislative grace, and a taxpayer seeking the benefit of a deduction must show that every condition which Congress has seen fit to impose has been fully satisfied."

[¶ 14,581]

Note

In Ellingson v. Commissioner, 964 F.2d 959 (9th Cir.1992), the marital deduction was allowed, based on a QTIP election, in a case where the trustee was expressly allowed to accumulate the trust income if (1) the trust income exceeded the amount which the trustee deemed to be necessary for the "needs, best interests and welfare" of the surviving spouse and (2) the trustee deemed such an accumulation "advisable." The court concluded:

> The Commissioner argues that it would make bad law to read a trust agreement as creating an interest which qualifies for a QTIP deduction solely because the settlor expressly declared in the trust that he intended that effect. We agree. However, this case does not implicate the Commissioner's concern. Certainly, the Trust Agreement could have been more clearly drafted. Nevertheless, the choice for this court is between two plausible readings of the agreement, only one of which effectuates the settlors' clearly manifested intent. If the Accumulation Proviso could plausibly be read only as granting the trustee unlimited discretion, the QTIP deduction would be lost. That is not the case here, however.

[¶ 14,583]

ii.   Default Rules Under State Law

The governing instrument in *Ellingson*, ¶ 14,581, was laced with references to the decedent's intention that the spousal gift qualify for the marital deduction. Such references were not present in Estate of Davis v. Commissioner, 394 F.3d 1294 (9th Cir.2005), where the marital deduction was denied. A significant feature in *Davis* was a California's statute aimed at curing drafting deficiencies. That statute, California Probate Code § 21552, at the time provided as follows:

If an instrument contains a marital deduction gift:

(a) The provisions of the instrument, including any power, duty, or discretionary authority given to a fiduciary, shall be construed to comply with the marital deduction provisions of the Internal Revenue Code.

(b) The fiduciary shall not take any action or have any power that impairs the deduction as applied to the marital deduction gift.

(c) The marital deduction gift may be satisfied only with property that qualifies for the marital deduction.

That statute might well have saved the marital deduction in *Davis* but the decedent did not expressly state that his gift to his spouse was to qualify for the marital deduction. In fact, the marital deduction was not mentioned. While reference to the marital deduction is not a condition of eligibility, such reference is helpful in cases where the language of the marital gift fails to satisfying the statutory requirements for qualification for the marital deduction. In *Davis*, the disqualifying language was as follows:

> [T]he trustee shall pay to or apply for the benefit of the surviving spouse, in quarter annual or more frequent installments, all of the net income from the trust estate as the trustee, in the trustee's reasonable discretion, shall determine to be proper for the health, education, or support, maintenance, comfort and welfare of grantor's surviving spouse in accordance with the surviving spouse's accustomed manner of living.

Davis is consistent with Estate of Walsh v. Commissioner, 110 T.C. 393 (1998), where the testator's expressed intent—to qualify for the marital deduction—was said to be insufficient to overcome the words found in the testator's will that limited the surviving spouse's control over the marital deduction property in the event of incompetency, a possibility that ran afoul of the "all events" requirement for allowance of the marital deduction under § 2056(b)(5), the life estate/power of appointment safe harbor.

[¶ 14,589]

d. *QTIP Not in Trust*

Although it is likely—and prudent—that all QTIP be placed in trust, a trust is not required. (Can you think of any cases in which a legal life estate is preferable to a trust?)

It would seem that a qualifying life income interest *not in trust* must provide the spouse with rights to income that are sufficient to satisfy the rules applicable to legal life estates and marital deduction trusts under present law. With that in mind, the question is whether the QTIP must be income producing. For example, would a gift of a personal residence for life qualify for the unlimited marital deduction as QTIP? Apparently, the answer is yes. See § 2056(b)(7)(B)(ii); Reg. § 20.2056(b)–7(d)(2) and (h), Example 1.

[¶ 14,597]

e. *The Distribution Limitation*

QTIP treatment will be denied if distributions from the trust can be made to a person other than the surviving spouse before the death of the surviving spouse. § 2056(b)(7)(B)(ii)(II). While taxpayer compliance with this requirement so as to insure the marital deduction would seem relatively easy to accomplish, all too frequently it results in the loss of the marital deduction by the innocent, the uninformed, and the well intentioned. In Estate of Bowling v. Commissioner, 93 T.C. 286 (1989), the marital deduction was denied because the will allowed the trustee to invade the trust "for any emergency needs which effect [sic] the support, maintenance and health needs of any beneficiary" of the trust. The surviving spouse was to receive the income for life and, after the death of the wife, the income was to be distributed to the decedent's son, who was institutionalized because of his mental retardation. The court denied the marital deduction after concluding that, during the lifetime of the spouse, the trustee could make distributions for the emergency needs of the institutionalized child. The court rejected the argument that the "emergency needs" authorization was limited to the needs of the current income beneficiary, namely, the surviving spouse during her lifetime. The court pointed to the severely disabled condition of the child as the reason why it was unlikely that the decedent would have intended to prohibit distributions to the son to meet emergency needs. See also Estate of Manscill v. Commissioner, 98 T.C. 413 (1992) (trustee's power to distribute corpus to the child of the surviving spouse invalidated QTIP election).

[¶ 14,599]

TECHNICAL ADVICE MEMORANDUM 8943005

July 9, 1989.

Is the Decedent's estate entitled to a marital deduction under § 2056(b)(7) even though the Spouse, in her individual capacity, was given a general power to annually appoint up to $5,000 or 5 percent of the trust corpus annually?

The Decedent died testate on December 20, 1985. On the Decedent's estate tax return the estate elected to claim a marital deduction for qualified terminable interest property passing to a residuary trust for the benefit of the surviving spouse.

Paragraph FOURTH: (c) of Decedent's will provides in part:

My wife, during her lifetime, is hereby given a general power to appoint from the principal of this trust to whomsoever she may designate, including herself, during each taxable year of the trust, an amount or amounts not exceeding Five Thousand Dollars ($5,000.00) in the aggregate, and, in addition, * * * an amount, if any, by which Five Percent (5%) of the then fair market value of the net principal of this trust, * * * exceeds the amount or amounts previously appointed by my wife for such year. * * *

* * *

Section 2056(b)(7) provides a deduction for qualified terminable interest property (QTIP). * * *

¶ 14,599

The issue presented in this case is whether the Spouse's power to appoint property "to whomsoever she may designate" violates § 2056(b)(7)(B)-(ii)(II), in that the Spouse has a power to appoint part of the property to a person other than the surviving spouse.

Since enactment of the marital deduction provisions in 1948, the philosophy behind this deduction has evolved from an attempt to equate community property with noncommunity property states towards recognition of the marital unit as a single taxpayer. Thus, the Code currently provides fewer restrictions on the availability of the deduction for interspousal transfers. However, one aspect of the deduction that has remained constant over the years is that no deduction is available unless a transfer tax will be imposed when the property is transferred outside the marital unit. The restriction imposed by the terminable interest rule of § 2056(b)(1) was enacted in recognition of the fact that many terminable interest arrangements will not be subject to tax when the surviving spouse's interest, in fact, terminates. In general, the exceptions to the terminable interest rule (such as § 2056(b)(7)) are available to taxpayers only in those cases where the nature of the interest passing to the spouse is such that any enjoyment by any person other than the surviving spouse will result in estate or gift tax liability with respect to the surviving spouse.

The legislative history underlying § 2056(b)(7) states, in part:

> * * * [T]here must be no power in any person (including the spouse) to appoint any part of the property subject to the qualifying income interest to any person other than the spouse during the spouse's life. This rule will * * * insure that the value of the property not consumed by the spouse is subject to tax upon the spouse's death (*or earlier disposition*) * * * [Emphasis added.]

H.R. Rep. No. 201, 97th Cong., 1st Sess., 161 (1981), 1981–2 C.B. 352 at 378.

While it is true that the first parenthetical phrase in the committee report literally precludes a power in the surviving spouse exercisable in favor of any person other than the surviving spouse, we believe such a reading would be unnecessarily restrictive, and, as a practical matter, meaningless. It is axiomatic that a power to appoint exclusively to oneself includes the power to exercise such dominion and control over the property that one may give it to whomsoever one wishes. Thus, it is reasonable to believe that Congress intended that a spouse would be able to give the property away, especially in view of the second (emphasized) parenthetical.

Consistent with this understanding of legislative history, and recognizing that the philosophy of § 2056 requires the imposition of the transfer tax only once during the lives of a husband and wife, we believe the better reading of the legislative history would preclude a spousal power of appointment only where the exercise of the power would not be subject to transfer taxation; i.e., where the power is not a general power of appointment as defined in § 2514.

An interpretation requiring that a spouse must first take physical possession of the property prior to a transfer to a third party would focus too much attention on the form of the transaction. It is sufficient that the exercise of the power by the spouse in favor of a third party would be subject to transfer taxation.

CONCLUSION

Because the power held by the Spouse in this case is a general power of appointment as defined in § 2514, we conclude that the Decedent's estate is entitled to a marital deduction under § 2056(b)(7).

[¶ 14,605]

f. *Election by Executor*

Even if property passes into a QTIP trust, it will not qualify for the unlimited marital deduction unless the decedent's executor makes an election to so qualify the gift. § 2056(b)(7). The election is made on the decedent's federal estate tax return and, *once made,* is irrevocable. Reg. § 20.2056(b)–7(b)(4)(ii).

The election is available for separate properties as well as for specific portions of property. The election is also available to the donor spouse in the case of gifts made to the other spouse while both spouses are living. § 2523(f)(4).

With the availability of the QTIP, the decedent's will need not provide any broad taxable power of appointment in the surviving spouse, so long as no one has the power to appoint the property to anyone else during the spouse's life. This feature, in conjunction with the flexibility of election after death as to the amount of property to be deducted, makes the QTIP an extremely useful tool for the estate planner.

Inasmuch as the QTIP would not be includible in the gross estate of the surviving spouse upon the surviving spouse's subsequent death because the spouse has only a life estate and no taxable power, a special provision, § 2044, brings the QTIP property into the gross estate of the surviving spouse. This is to satisfy the premise on which the marital deduction is based, i.e., that the amount deducted in the first estate will eventually be taxed in the second estate.

[¶ 14,609]

g. *Duty of Consistency (the Shelfer Shuffle)*

Estate of Shelfer v. Commissioner, 86 F.3d 1045 (11th Cir.1996), is illustrative of what appears to be a recurring practice. The QTIP election is made and the marital deduction is allowed in the estate of the first spouse to die. At the subsequent death of the surviving spouse, his or her executor claims that allowance of the marital deduction in the estate of the first spouse to die was improper—because in *Shelfer's* case the surviving spouse was not entitled to the "stub" income, *i.e.*, the income earned prior to the death of the surviving spouse but which is unpaid at the surviving spouse's death. The court rejected the taxpayer's argument. *Accord, Cavanaugh v. Commissioner,* 51 F.3d 597 (5th Cir.1995). In Tech. Adv. Mem. 9548002, the IRS claimed that a duty of consistency required that the property for which the marital deduction was allowed under claim of QTIP should be included in the estate of the surviving spouse—even if the initial allowance of the marital deduction was improper. Lending support to the IRS "duty of consistency" argument is Estate of Letts v. Commissioner, 109 T.C. 290 (1997), where the court carefully worked through the elements of the duty of consistency argument, including the claimed lack of privity between the first and second decedent's estates, and concluded that the duty of consistency mandated inclusion in the estate of the second spouse to die of the property for which the marital deduction was allowed at the death of the first spouse to die. See Joint Committee on Taxation, *Description of Revenue Provisions Contained in the President's Fiscal Year 1999 Budget Proposal* (JCS–4–98), February 24, 1998, at 184–85 (where marital deduction is allowed for QTIP property, inclusion in estate of surviving spouse is proposed to be mandatory).

[¶ 14,611]

h. *Valuation Discount (the Bonner Benefit)*

As a rule-of-thumb, fractionalizing ownership in property not susceptible of ready division is to be avoided. Sometimes, though, it can be advantageous. One such instance is in use of a QTIP for property that might otherwise go free of trust to the surviving spouse. Estate of Bonner v. United States, 84 F.3d 196 (5th Cir.1996) is illustrative. In *Bonner*, a trust created by Mrs. Bonner's will for the benefit of Louis, her husband, owned 37.5% of "the ranch" and 50% of "the New Mexico property" and 50% of a $30,000 boat. Louis Bonner owned the other portions free of trust. Mrs. Bonner's trust was included in Louis' estate under § 2044 because the QTIP election had been made for the trust at Mrs. Bonner's death. Effectively, thus, 100% of each of the three properties were included in Louis' estate for tax purposes at his death. Nonetheless, the court determined that Louis' estate was entitled to a fractional interest discount in valuing each of the parcels for estate tax purposes. (The estate claimed a discount of 45%.) The court explained (84 F.3d at 198):

> In *Estate of Bright v. United States,* [658 F.2d 999 (5th Cir.1981), reprinted at ¶ 24,121] * * *, this Court, sitting *en banc,* rejected a similar argument, there termed the "doctrine of family attribution." In that case, Bright held a 27 ½% interest in an asset as executor of his deceased wife's estate, while simultaneously holding an additional 27 ½% interest in the same asset in his individual capacity. This Court rejected the government's contention that Bright's interests for estate tax purposes should be treated as one 55% interest in the asset.

> * * *

The question before us is controlled by the holding in *Bright*. Although § 2044 contemplates that the QTIP property will be treated as having passed from Bonner for estate tax purposes, the statute does not require, nor logically contemplate that in so passing, the QTIP assets would merge with other assets. The assets in the QTIP trust could have been left to any recipient of Mrs. Bonner's choosing, and neither Bonner nor the estate had any control over their ultimate disposition. We are precluded from considering evidence submitted by the government regarding who actually received the assets. An estate tax is an excise tax on the transfer of property at death and accordingly the valuation is made as of the moment of death and must be measured by the interest that passes, as contrasted with the interest held by the decedent before death or the interest held by the legatee after death. *Bright*, 658 F.2d at 1006.

In addition to arguing that § 2044 mandates merging of the Bonners' fractional interests in the assets, the government also argues that public policy dictates that the Bonners not use the QTIP device to avoid paying taxes on the unified value of the property. In fact, public policy mitigates in favor of the estate's position in this litigation. The estate of each decedent should be required to pay taxes on those assets whose disposition that decedent directs and controls, in spite of the labyrinth of federal tax fictions. In this case, Mrs. Bonner controlled the disposition of her assets, first into a trust with a life interest for Bonner and later to the objects of her largesse. The assets, although taxed as if they passed through Bonner's estate, in fact were controlled at every step by Mrs. Bonner, which a tax valuation with a fractional interest discount would reflect. At the time of Bonner's death, his estate did not have control over Mrs. Bonner's interests in the assets such that it could act as a hypothetical seller negotiating with willing buyers free of the handicaps associated with fractional undivided interests. The valuation of the assets should reflect that reality.

A similar benefit was realized in a slightly different context in Estate of Mellinger v. Commissioner, 112 T.C. 26 (1999). Harriett Mellinger's executor valued each of her shares in Frederick's of Hollywood (FOH) at $4.79 on her estate tax return when filed. The IRS objected, claiming each share had a value of $8.46. The IRS valuation reflected its aggregation of Harriett's 27.8671 percent of FOH with the 27.8671 percent of the shares that her husband, Frederick, had placed in trust for her benefit at the time of his earlier death. Not only did the court reject this aggregation theory—and resulting control premium the IRS placed on the shares—it also allowed Harriett's shares a 25–percent discount for lack of marketability. The effect was to reduce the value of Harriett's FOH shares for estate tax purposes by $8 million. The IRS subsequently agreed with the *Mellinger* decision, its agreement reflected in AOD 1999–006, 1935–35 IRB 314.

For additional planning, see ¶ 15,517.

[¶ 14,613]

i. *Partial QTIP Election (Using Clayton Trigger)*

Can the executor elect to claim the unlimited marital deduction as to only a portion of the property passing to the QTIP trust? The IRS, in Reg. § 20.2056(b)–7(b)(2), expressly sanctions so-called partial elections so long as the election relates to "a fractional or percentage share of the property so that the elective portion reflects its proportionate share of the increase or decrease in value of the entire property."

¶ 14,613

What happens to the fraction of the QTIP trust for which the marital deduction is not elected? Could the testator specify that this portion of the trust shall be automatically diverted from the QTIP trust to a bypass trust for the benefit of, say, the testator's sister? The answer is "yes". Reg. § 20.2056(b)–7(d)(3)(ii) currently provides that an otherwise qualifying income interest that is contingent on an executor's election will not be precluded from QTIP status under the requirements of § 2056(b)(7). Originally, in an earlier regulation (since withdrawn), the IRS claimed that such a provision resulted in the denial of the marital deduction for the QTIP trust because the "drop-back" provision tainted the entire QTIP trust and thereby disqualified even that portion that remains in the QTIP trust. However, the Fifth and Eighth Circuits took a different approach, concluding that the marital deduction is not lost where the spousal gift is contingent on the QTIP election being made. See Estate of Clayton v. Commissioner, 976 F.2d 1486 (5th Cir.1992); Estate of Robertson v. Commissioner, 15 F.3d 779 (8th Cir.1994). The *Clayton* court reasoned that the making of the QTIP election is an essential part of the statutory definition of what constitutes the qualified terminable interest property. That is, the court concluded that "property" in the statutory definition means that property which the executor identified by making the QTIP election, noting that "nothing has been cited to us" or produced by "our independent research" that supports the Commissioner's view. The court then said that evaluation of whether the interest qualifies for the marital deduction begins only after the QTIP election is made. As for the original position of the IRS, the court said to disallow the QTIP election in these cases because the "circular reasoning advanced by the Commissioner" defies "logic, common sense, and the purpose for which QTIP was designed and implemented." 976 F.2d at 1501.

These so-called *Clayton* QTIPs can be an important planning technique.

Partial elections are further considered in Chapter 16 beginning at ¶ 16,401.

Problem

[¶ 14,618]

What special provisions, if any, should be included in the testator's will in anticipation of his need to make the QTIP election for federal estate tax purposes?

    (a) Should the executor be given standards to consider in making the election? What about including exculpatory language in the instrument which requires the executor's election?

    (b) Can the decedent bind his executor to elect the unlimited marital deduction for property passing into a QTIP trust?

[¶ 14,621]

j. QTIP Compared to Life Estate/Power of Appointment

Section 2056(b)(7), providing for Qualified Terminable Interest Property (QTIP), is probably the most important exception, from a planning perspective, to the nondeductible terminable interest rule. The QTIP differs from the life estate/power of appointment exception in two principal respects. First, the decedent's executor has the option whether to elect to claim the marital deduction for the QTIP property or allow the QTIP property to be taxed at the death of the deceased spouse (while the marital deduction is mandatory as to property qualifying for the life estate/power of appointment exception). Second, the marital deduction is available as to the QTIP property even though the surviving spouse has no right to control the disposition of the QTIP property at the subsequent death of the surviving spouse (as contrasted with the life estate/power of appointment exception, the core of which is the general power of appointment which the surviving spouse must have as one of the conditions for qualification for the life estate/power of appointment exception). Thus, as a result of the QTIP exception, a prospective decedent can defer estate taxes until the death of his or her spouse, allow the spouse to enjoy the property during life, while all the while controlling the ultimate disposition of the property.

The QTIP provisions allow the executor to elect to deduct any property passing from the decedent provided: (1) the income is payable to the surviving spouse for life and (2) no one has any power during the life of the surviving spouse to appoint any part of the property to anyone other than the surviving spouse. Moreover, the election has the added flexibility, comparable to what has been observed with regard to the disclaimer provision under § 2518 (see Chapter 16), of being applicable to all or "a specific portion of property," thus permitting an accurate and careful computation of the tax upon the death of the first to die with a better appraisal of the possible tax upon the estate of the survivor.

[¶ 14,629]

5. SPLIT GIFTS

A marital deduction is also available for the value of an income interest payable to the surviving spouse under a qualified charitable remainder trust as defined under § 664. See § 2056(b)(8). Thereunder, if the surviving spouse is the only noncharitable beneficiary of a charitable remainder annuity trust or unitrust, the value of the annuity or fixed payment payable to the surviving spouse is allowable as a marital deduction. And, of course, the value of the remainder interest destined to go to the charitable organization is deductible under § 2055(e)(2)(A). See ¶ 25,167.

[¶ 14,637]

6. SPECIFIC PORTION

A fractional or percentile interest in a property may qualify for the marital deduction. § 2056(b)(10). That is, a partial interest in a property is treated as a "specific portion" within the meaning of § 2056(b)(5) (LEPA) and (7)(B)(iv) (QTIP) for purposes of allowing the marital deduction for that partial interest so long as the surviving spouse's partial interest in the property constitutes a fractional or percentage share of the entire property interest. That means that the surviving spouse's partial interest must share, proportionally, in "the increase or decrease in the value of the entire property." Reg. §§ 20.2056(b)–5(c)(2), 20.2056(b)–7(b)(2).

Problem

[¶ 14,690]

Gloria's will provided that her spouse, Pedro, was to receive $300 per month for life from the trust that Gloria provided for him in her will. If the trust income was insufficient, corpus could be invaded to make the trust payments. Consider whether Pedro has a qualifying income interest in a specific portion of the property for purposes of § 2056(b)(5) and (7). See Reg. § 20.2056(b)–5(c)(2) through (5). Cf. Northeastern Pa. Nat'l Bank & Trust Co. v. United States, 387 U.S. 213 (1967).

J. INTERESTS IN UNIDENTIFIED ASSETS

[¶ 14,701]

Suppose that a will provides a gift to the surviving spouse of an amount equal to the maximum marital deduction allowable to the decedent's estate. Suppose, further, that the decedent's estate contains a nondeductible terminable interest in property that, if bequeathed directly to the surviving spouse, would not qualify for the marital deduction. Suppose, finally, that the decedent's executor could satisfy the marital deduction gift to the surviving spouse out of any of the assets of the decedent's general estate, including the nondeductible terminable interest. (Let's make it even easier. Assume that H dies intestate and W takes one-half of H's net probate estate under the controlling intestacy statute and that H's estate contains a nondeductible terminable interest.)

In this case, since it is possible that the marital deduction gift could be satisfied by a nondeductible terminable interest in property, § 2056(b)(2) requires the marital deduction to be reduced by the value of the nondeductible terminable interest.

What is the result to the decedent's estate? Perhaps payment of some federal estate tax!

How can this result be avoided? By a provision in the decedent's will that only interests in property qualifying for the marital deduction may be used to satisfy the marital gift.

You might ask how could H's estate contain a nondeductible terminable interest? Consider the following example.

Example. Assume that the decedent during his life created a trust reserving the income for himself. The trust was to terminate upon the death of the survivor of himself and his wife, at which time the corpus was to be paid to his children. In addition, the trustee was authorized to make corpus distributions to the decedent's children during the life of the decedent and his wife. The decedent died survived by his wife. The property constituting the trust was included in the decedent's estate for estate tax purposes as required by § 2036(a)(1). The decedent bequeathed one-half of the residue to his surviving spouse. The amount of the marital deduction for the value of one-half of the residue is to be decreased by the value at the time of the decedent's death of such income interest in the trust (and for any other terminable interest included in such residue for which the marital deduction would not be allowed if specifically bequeathed and devised to the decedent's surviving spouse).

Not all is lost! Every cloud has a silver lining. If § 2056(b)(2) applies to a particular estate, consider, if appropriate under local law, allocating the terminable interest to the surviving spouse. Inasmuch as the marital deduction is already reduced or lost, it may be advantageous to fund the spouse's estate with assets which may be consumed or expire prior to the spouse's death. The purpose of such an allocation would be to reduce the spouse's estate at death.

K.   VALUATION OF MARITAL DEDUCTION GIFT

[¶ 14,751]

Section 2056(b)(4) is concerned with the effect of (1) encumbered property, (2) death taxes (both state and federal), and (3) the surviving spouse's right to income during administration of the estate on the amount of property the surviving spouse actually receives. Put another way, the marital deduction is limited to that property which would be in the surviving spouse's estate at the surviving spouse's death. If the property the surviving spouse actually receives is reduced by death taxes on the decedent's estate or if the property at the decedent's death is in any way subject to an encumbrance, the net value to the surviving spouse of that property is reduced accordingly.

Section 2056(b)(4)(B) expressly provides that only the "net value" of the property passing to the surviving spouse qualifies for the marital deduction.

[¶ 14,759]

1. ENCUMBERED PROPERTY

A number of practical problems can develop in estates which include encumbered property where the marital deduction is claimed. See Reg. §§ 20.2056(a)–2(b)(2), 20.2056(b)–4(b).

[¶ 14,761]

WACHOVIA BANK & TRUST CO., EXR.

United States Court of Claims, 1958.
143 Ct.Cl. 376, 163 F.Supp. 832.

JONES, Chief Judge * * *

In 1929, decedent and her husband acquired the property in question to which they took title as tenants by entirety. Each spouse furnished one-half of the purchase price and one-half of the costs of improving the realty. The money was obtained partly from their individual funds and partly from a loan of $250,000 upon their joint note secured by a deed of trust on the property. When the decedent passed away in 1949, one-half of the market value of this realty equaled $252,500. One-half of the obligation remaining on the joint note secured by the deed of trust equaled $51,517.64. Under applicable state law, decedent's estate was liable to pay this latter sum and the decedent had directed in her will that the executors pay or provide for payment of "all debts, taxes, and other charges" against the estate. The executors did pay this sum from the decedent's separate general estate to the holder of the note.

On its estate tax return, the executors of the estate included the full market value of the decedent's one-half interest in the realty, i.e., $252,500, in determining the gross estate. In determining the net estate, plaintiff then deducted the amount of the obligation which the estate owed on the joint note secured by the deed of trust as an "indebtedness" of the estate in respect to property under § 812(b)(4) [1986 Code § 2053(a)(4)]. Plaintiff then deducted (still in the computation of the net estate) the entire value of decedent's one-half interest in the realty, i.e., $252,500, as a marital deduction under § 812(e)(1)(E)(ii) [1986 Code § 2056(b)(4)(B)]. The Commissioner of Internal Revenue reduced the amount of this latter deduction by the amount of the incumbrance on the property passing to the surviving spouse for which the estate had previously taken a deduction as an indebtedness under § 812(b)(4) [1986 Code § 2053(a)(4)].

* * * The sole issue is whether the Commissioner was correct in reducing the marital deduction by the amount of the incumbrance on the property under these circumstances. We think that he was not.

It is the plaintiff's position that if one makes a gift to another of property subject to an incumbrance, the value of the gift is merely the difference between the full value of the property and the amount of the incumbrance. But if the donor, at the same time he makes such a gift, discharges the incumbrance, the value of the gift is the full value of the property, that is, the value is unreduced by the incumbrance which has been discharged by the donor. This analysis would appear to be substantially correct and has authoritative support. * * *

The plaintiff then argues that since § 812(e)(1)(E)(ii) [1986 Code § 2056(b)(4)(B)] has adopted the standard of the gift taxation for the purpose of determining the value of the marital deduction with respect to encumbered property passing to the surviving spouse, the deduction, in the present case, must be the full value of the property (unreduced by the incumbrance) since the estate of the decedent was obligated to, and actually did, discharge the incumbrance, thereby increasing the value of the property received by the surviving spouse. In support of this position, plaintiff refers us to the following passage from the report of the Senate Committee on Finance which accompanied the Revenue Act of 1948 which act contained the present marital deduction provisions:

> Clause (ii) of such subparagraph (E) [1986 Code § 2056(b)(4)(B)] directs that in determining the value of any interest passing from the

decedent to the surviving spouse, encumbrances or obligations shall be taken into account in the same manner as if the value of a gift to the spouse of the interest passing were being determined. * * * If the decedent by his will leaves to his surviving spouse real estate subject to a mortgage (whether or not such mortgage was a personal liability of the decedent) the value of the interest passing to the surviving spouse does not under this § include the mortgage. If, however, the decedent by his will directs the executor to pay off the mortgage, *such payment constitutes an additional interest passing to the surviving spouse.* [Emphasis supplied.]

* * *

[Rejection of "Double Deduction" Argument]

The actual value of the property which was received by the surviving spouse was $252,500 in the instant case. Yet the Government would permit a deduction of only $200,982.36 for this property because, it says, the difference has already been deducted once under § 812(b)(4) [1986 Code § 2053(a)(4)]. But the Government's argument fails to recognize that the deductions under § 812(b) [1986 Code § 2053(a)] and under § 812(e) [1986 Code § 2056(a)] serve two different functions and are not necessarily related. The deduction under § 812(b) [1986 Code § 2053(a)] is allowed to determine the actual value of the property which *is included in the decedent's estate*. The estate is equally entitled to deduct thereafter under § 812(e) [1986 Code § 2056(a)] the actual value of the property which *passes out of the estate* to the surviving spouse. To say that the latter deduction, in the circumstances of the instant case, is in any way equal to, or the same thing as, the former, simply defeats the purpose of the marital deduction as the following examples will illustrate.

If a decedent leaves property subject to an incumbrance, but makes a bequest to the surviving spouse of an amount of money equal to the incumbrance, where is the difference between that case and the present one insofar as the estate tax is concerned? In reality, there is none. In our example, the estate would be entitled to include the full value of the property in the gross estate. It would then equally be entitled to deduct the amount of the incumbrance on the property under § 812(b)(4) [1986 Code § 2053(a)(4)] as an unpaid mortgage upon property (the value of the decedent's interest therein having been included in the gross estate undiminished by such mortgage). Under § 812(e) [1986 Code § 2056(a)], the estate could then deduct the value of the property received by the surviving spouse, which value would be reduced by the amount of the undischarged incumbrance under § 812(e)(1)(E)(ii) [1986 Code § 2056(b)(4)(B)]. As a final step, the estate clearly could deduct the amount of money which equals the amount of the incumbrance as a "bequest" to the surviving spouse under § 812(e)(3)(A) [1986 Code § 2056(c)(1)].

There has been no more a "double deduction" in our example than there is in the present case. An amount equal to the unpaid mortgage has been deducted twice, once under § 812(b)(4) [1986 Code § 2056(a)(4)] and again as a bequest to the surviving spouse, yet we can hardly imagine the Government urging denial of the deduction of the bequest because an equal sum has been previously deducted in determining the actual value of the estate under § 812(b)(4) [1986 Code § 2056(a)(4)].

[¶ 14,767]

2. ALLOCATION OF DEATH TAX BURDEN AND THE INTERDEPENDENT VARIABLE PROBLEM

a. *Interdependent Variable*

Section 2056(b)(4)(A) provides that "there shall be taken into account the effect" of death taxes "on the net value" of the property passing to the surviving spouse for which the marital deduction is claimed. Consider this example. H dies intestate when the estate tax exclusion is $1.5 million. He is survived by his wife, W, and one son, S. The applicable intestate statute provides that W shall take 50 percent of H's estate and that S shall take the other half.

At first glance, H's federal estate tax return, assuming that H did not make any adjusted taxable gifts, should look like this:

H's gross estate	$4,000,000
Less: Debts and administrative expenses	–0–
Marital deduction (property passing to the surviving spouse)	(2,000,000)
H's taxable estate	$2,000,000
Tentative tax	$780,800
Unified credit	(555,800)
Tax	$225,000

But wait! H's jurisdiction requires each recipient of a portion of H's estate to bear his or her proportionate share of the death taxes (federal estate and state inheritance) assessed against H's estate.

Will the share of H's estate passing to W be called upon to bear its proportionate share of the $225,000 federal estate tax shown in the above example? (If so, the amount passing to W will be reduced accordingly!) See Reg. § 20.2056(b)–4(c)(4).

You answer no, reasoning that the share of H's estate passing to W escapes taxation in H's estate by virtue of the marital deduction. You are both right and wrong! True, the share passing to W escapes taxation at H's death. Nonetheless some state legislatures, in attempting to approximate the wishes of the typical decedent, have enacted statutes requiring each share of a decedent's estate to bear its proportionate part of the total death taxes levied against the decedent's estate. The state statutes do not take notice of the fact that property qualifying for the federal marital deduction escapes taxation in H's estate.

Applying such a death tax apportionment statute to H's estate, the share W takes ($2 million) will be reduced by $112,500 (one-half the total death tax bill of $225,000) to $1,887,500 ($2 million less $112,500).

But wait! The marital deduction is limited to that property actually passing to W. (Only that amount, theoretically, will be available to be included in her estate at her death. Note that the federal estate tax is a tax upon a tax! The tax is levied on the decedent's gross estate—all that he owned at death. Out of the property actually taxed, comes the tax. Think about it.)

How much property actually passes to W? $1,887,500. How much is shown in the above tax schedule as passing to the wife? $2 million. That must be wrong! It is! Let's redo the schedule using a marital deduction of $1,887,500.

H's gross estate	$4,000,000
Less: Debts and administrative expenses	–0–
Less: Marital deduction (property passing to the surviving spouse)	(1,887,500)
H's taxable estate	$2,112,500
Tentative tax	$833,675
Less: Unified credit	(555,800)
ax	$277,875

The tax has increased! Must we go back to the drawing board and recompute the marital deduction and ultimately the tax? That approach would lead us to recompute the tax again, and therefore, the marital deduction again, and so forth and so forth. Thus, you have *the case of the interdependent variable:* the marital deduction and the federal estate tax. Sometimes this phenomenon is described as a "tax-on-a-tax" or in terms of requiring a "circular" computation, truly a daunting undertaking. Fortunately, electronic tax planning programs such as those identified in Appendix A effortlessly make the required calculations. (*Comment.* As a result, only "old-timers" can claim first hand experience with these circular calculations. While never an art (and, therefore, not a "lost art"), the circular calculation is gradually becoming a "missed" experience—and, in that sense, the result might be that newcomers might not plan as aggressively to avoid the calculation.)

Does the IRS know about this? Yes. At one time, the IRS provided lengthy supplemental instructions to the Federal Estate Tax Return to facilitate this computation, instructions based largely on performing "trial-and-error" calculations much as described above. Unfortunately, that publication appears no longer to be generally available (perhaps because of the widespread availability of electronic spreadsheets where a simple formula will yield the correct marital deduction and correct tax.) The IRS instructions were known as the "Interrelated Computations for Estate and Gift Taxes (Publication 904, Rev. May 1985)."

How about pre-death planning? Can we do anything to avoid the problem of the interdependent variable? Sure. Make a will and provide that all death taxes shall be paid out of that portion of the decedent's property *not* passing to the surviving spouse. However, as seen in *Martin* which follows, sometimes the decedent's financial facts frustrate the planning—and calculation of the tax-on-a-tax becomes necessary. (*Comment.* Might the financial facts in *Mar-*

¶ **14,767**

tin have been anticipated during pre death planning and steps be taken to avoid those consequences?)

[¶ 14,777]

MARTIN v. UNITED STATES

United States Court of Appeals, Seventh Circuit, 1991.
923 F.2d 504.

EASTERBROOK, Circuit Judge.

The author of a will may specify which bequests pay the taxes and costs of administering the estate. A will may provide, for example, that 50% of the gross assets go to the testator's spouse and the rest to the children, whose portion will be tapped for all taxes and costs. Apportionment may cut down on taxes. Bequests to one's spouse are excluded from the taxable estate. § 2056(a). * * * Esther S. Martin tried to give exactly half of her adjusted gross estate to her husband. In order to minimize taxes, she specified that this bequest could not be charged with costs or taxes. Federal and state law alike honor such requests. Riggs v. del Drago, 317 U.S. 95 (1942); Estate of Reno v. CIR, 916 F.2d 955 (4th Cir. 1990); Ind. Code § 29–2–12–7 (1980). We must decide what happens when the property remaining in the estate after honoring such a request is insufficient to meet acknowledged taxes and expenses.

Esther Martin died in 1981, before the amendment to the Code removing the 50% cap on the marital deduction. Her assets, including insurance proceeds, came to about $14,400; of this only $3,254 was in the estate admitted to probate. She was the life tenant of a trust in which her husband Ross held the remainder interest. The trust was worth $781,764 on the date of her death. During the three years preceding her death Esther had given away another $852,060. The Code treats as part of the estate all property in which the decedent held a life estate and all property transferred during the three years before death. §§ 2035(a), 2036. Esther's gross estate was therefore $1,648,250, of which Ross was to receive the remainder interest in the trust, plus everything else Esther possessed at death up to half of the gross estate. Lee Martin, their son and the executor of Esther's estate, computed the marital deduction as $796,190, a little less than half of the gross. Because the bulk of the lifetime gifts went to charity and was therefore deductible, Lee calculated a total estate tax of $43,815.18, which the estate paid in January 1982. The estate reported expenses of $27,013 and state taxes of $2,024.

The difficulty is that the estate did not *have* $72,852 to cover the state and federal taxes plus the costs of administration. It had only a tad more than $3,000. The rest of the property passes outside the estate—through the trust, through inter vivos gifts, through life insurance, through joint interests in property. Although the estate wrote out the checks, the Commissioner of Internal Revenue thought that the money must have come from the trust. None of Esther's lifetime bequests could be charged with the taxes and administrative expenses, for they were beyond her control at the time of her death. The trust instrument required the trustee (Lee) to "pay from the trust estate all of the legal obligations of her estate and all inheritance and estate taxes becoming due because of [Esther's] death." If it paid the taxes and expenses, Ross necessarily received less. Under § 2056(b)(4) the estate may deduct only the net amounts the spouse actually receives * * *. So the Commissioner reduced the deduction by the $69,000 difference between the probate property and the taxes and expenses concededly due. Because this reduction exposed the estate to further taxes, he made an "interrelated calculation" of tax and deduction (bureaucratic jargon for the calculus). The upshot was a conclusion that Ross received only $700,358, and that the estate owed an extra $22,972 in taxes, plus interest. Lee paid and sued for a refund. We held in Martin v. United States, 833 F.2d 655 (7th Cir. 1987), that the request for a refund of the tax paid in 1982 was untimely. Now we must decide whether the estate gets back the $22,972 paid in 1985 and 1986 plus interest. (The amounts paid in 1982 are no longer in issue.)

The estate relies on the principle that the testator may designate the source of taxes and administrative expenses. If the named sources are insufficient, other bequests will abate in order to supply the necessary cash. * * * No one doubts that Esther wanted to leave half of her *gross* estate to her husband to maximize the marital deduction. The will contains a formula bequest: "I give to my husband a pecuniary amount equal to the maximum marital deduction allowable to my estate for Federal estate tax purposes". It follows, Lee submits, that the estate obtains the full $796,190 deduction. The district court agreed, 1990 WL 208731, 1990 U.S. Dist. LEXIS 3190 (N.D. Ind.), and thought this so clear that it ordered the United States to pay the estate's legal expenses under § 7430, 1990 U.S. Dist. LEXIS 11597.

With the legal principles underlying the district court's decision we have no dispute. Whether a will may make such a formula bequest is a question of state law, see *Riggs,* and Indiana allows such bequests. Yet this is unimportant unless there are other bequests to abate * * * Here there are none. Under the formula of the will, *all* of Esther's remaining property went to her husband. No other bequests could be abated to satisfy taxes. The estate could not retrieve the lifetime gifts (and if it could would be no better off, for recoupment would reduce the charitable deduction and yield the same taxes as the reduction in the marital deduction did). Ross's bequest, via the trust, was the only fund available to satisfy taxes and expenses. Because § 2056(b)(4) allows the deduction only for the amount the spouse actually receives, the unavailability of other sources leaves no alternative to the Commissioner's calculation. It is telling that the estate did not proffer evidence that the initial $43,815 for taxes and $27,013 for administration came from a source other than the corpus of the trust. Indeed the estate has not even *asserted* that there was another source. At oral argument in this court, the estate insisted that the actual source is irrelevant. Given § 2056(b)(4), that cannot be.

Lee observes that never in the history of the estate tax has a court reduced the marital share in the teeth of a maximum formula bequest. Perhaps so, but we could not find another case in which the decedent gave away more than half of the estate during life, leaving behind nothing but the marital bequest. Because giving every remaining penny to Ross did not produce a 50% marital share, the estate was charged with some taxes; because these could be satisfied only out of the marital bequest, a further reduction (the "interrelated computation") was essential. Had Esther been less generous during her life, and the estate larger on her death, the taxes would have been smaller. What might have happened did not happen; the Commissioner computed the tax properly given the estate's actual contents.

Reversed.

Note

[¶ 14,778]

Pitfalls are many when it comes to all-important tax payment clauses common to virtually every will—particularly tax planning wills—and "doing it right" is not the easiest of assignments, albeit its importance. In Patterson v. United States, 181 F.3d 927 (8th Cir.1999), the QTIP election was compromised by the intersection of tax payment provisions commonly found where there is both a will and a (often revocable) so-called "living trust", i.e., a free standing trust as contrasted with a testamentary trust, one found in the will itself. Typically, the plan call for the will to "pour over" to the trust. Sometimes the trust has been funded during the Settlor's life, possibly in anticipation of, or because of, the settlor's feared or actual inability to manage his or her own affairs due to deteriorating health.

Mr. Patterson had executed both a will and a trust. The will provided that the residue of his probate estate—the property passing under his will—was to be added to the trust, as is common. The will included a relatively common tax allocation clause, calling on the executor to pay all death taxes from Mr. Patterson's residuary probate estate. But, again, as is relatively common, the will also provided that all or part of Mr. Patterson's death taxes could, at the discretion of the trustee, be paid from the trust. For its part, the trust authorized the trustee to pay death taxes from the trust if the trustee believed such payment to be "expedient and in the best interests" of the trust beneficiaries. The death taxes were, in fact, paid from the trust.

The dispute in *Patterson* related to the amount of the marital deduction allowable for estate tax purposes. The trust provided that ten percent of the trust estate "computed before any reduction for ... death taxes" would be set aside in a separate trust that would qualify for the QTIP election. The executors made the QTIP election. The IRS then did its arithmetic and concluded that payment of the death taxes—more than $4 million—from the probate estate *rather than from the trust estate* would, under the terms of the will and trust taken together, require the payment of additional death taxes. (Why? Using this assumption, the marital deduction would be less than claimed by the taxpayer because the death taxes would be subtracted before applying the ten percent.) The IRS relied on Jackson v. United States, 376 U.S. 503 (1964), which appears at ¶ 14,419, for the proposition that the value of the probate estate must be fixed at the date of death and not when, as in *Patterson*, the trustee exercises his discretion to pay the death taxes or not pay them (thus leaving that task to the executor who would be obligated to pay the death taxes from the probate estate). It was this discretion that the IRS claimed to be an impermissible power of appointment, impermissible in the sense that its exercise could either bring about, post mortem, either an increase or a decease in the marital deduction. Rejecting the IRS claim, and finding for the taxpayer, the court first looked approvingly to Estate of Clayton v. Commissioner, 976 F.2d 1486 (5th Cir.1992), discussed at ¶ 14,613; and then borrowed the words "counter-intuitive and against common sense" from Estate of Spencer v. Commissioner 43 F.3d 226 (6th Cir.1995), where the facts were similar to those in *Clayton*, and used them inferentially to describe the IRS position in *Patterson*.

Problem

[¶ 14,779]

1. Determine the marital deduction available to Bud's estate. Bud died in 2005 with an estate, after § 2053 and 2054 deductions, of $5,000,000 upon which was levied $700,000 of state death taxes. His will gave everything to his wife.

2. It is common place for the will to provide, in principle, "pay all estate taxes from that part of my testamentary estate that does not passing to my spouse or qualify for the marital deduction and if the my testamentary estate is inadequate for this purposes, my executor is to call upon the trustee of my living trust to make such payments" and for the living trust, as in *Patterson*, to authorized those payments at the discretion of the trustee. Is this language bullet-proof?

[¶ 14,780]

b. Source of Estate Taxes

Section 2207A provides that a decedent's estate can recover estate taxes paid on QTIP included in the decedent's estate. While that sounds simple enough, it does not answer the question of how the decedent's estate will allocate the burden of the estate taxes among the estate's beneficiaries. Death tax allocation is a function of state law—and state law looks first to the decedent's will and if the will is silent, it looks to state statute to allocate the death tax burden among the beneficiaries (and to the common law if no statute has addressed the issue). See *Estate of Vahlteich v. Commissioner*, 69 F.3d 537 (6th Cir.1995). Many states have legislation aimed at preventing inadvertent exoneration.

The surviving spouse's will in *Vahlteich* included what has come to be seen as boiler plate, directing nonspecifically that "all" death taxes be paid from the surviving spouse's residuary estate. The IRS claimed that this meant that the taxes on QTIP included in the decedent's estate were to be paid from the residuary estate and not from the QTIP. (The increased taxes charged against the residuary estate effected a $1.9 million diminution in the value of the residuary estate, all of which passed to two universities.) The court rejected the IRS argument and said that the taxes on the QTIP were to paid out of the QTIP and not out of the surviving spouse's other property passing under the survivor's residuary estate. The court concluded that the so-called tax allocation clause in the survivor's will did not exonerate the QTIP from the tax burden imposed by federal and state law. Exoneration, in the opinion of the court, construing state law, required, in addition, explicit reference to § 2044 or to the QTIP if exoneration was to be effective. The court noted state policy caused the applicable statutory provision to be adopted as a means of preventing inadvertent exoneration.

Note that failure to recover estate taxes from the QTIP constitutes a gift from the surviving spouse where the burden of those taxes falls on the QTIP under applicable law.

Problem

[¶ 14,781]

Kwame's will included a paragraph directing that "all transfer, estate, or inheritance taxes imposed by any taxing authority upon or in relation to any trust, gift, insurance, joint property or transfer included as part of my taxable estate shall be paid as an expense out of my residuary estate without apportionment among the beneficiaries thereof." He wants to know whether the taxes imposed on the QTIP trust created by his deceased spouse will be paid out of the QTIP. What would he need to do to achieve that result if he died domiciled in a state which had specific legislation aimed at preventing inadvertent exoneration by requiring testators to specifically direct exoneration?

[¶ 14,900]

3. INCOME DURING ADMINISTRATION OF THE ESTATE

a. *Year Following Death*

Ordinarily a legatee under a will is not entitled to interest on his legacy during the first year of the estate's administration. On the other hand, the marital deduction is available only as to the net amount (actual amount) passing to the surviving spouse. That leads to the notion that the value of a legacy to the surviving spouse should be reduced for marital deduction purposes to reflect the fact that the surviving spouse did not have the income from the property for the first year following the death of the spouse. Reg. § 20.2056(b)–4(a). To avoid this result, it is common place to provide that all of the income earned by the estate from and after the decedent's death is to be paid to the surviving spouse (in those instances where the gift to the surviving spouse is to qualify for the marital deduction).

[¶ 14,920]

b. *Stub Income: LEPA Contrasted With QTIP*

There remains the "stub" income problem, i.e., the income from the marital property that is earned between the last distribution date and the death of the surviving spouse. Estate of Howard v. Commissioner, 910 F.2d 633 (9th Cir.1990), the so-called stub income case, is a reminder of the careful attention that must be given to statutory requirements when the marital deduction is the object. It also emphasizes the differences between the QTIP exception to the nondeductible terminable interest rule (§ 2056(b)(7); ¶ 14,557) and the life estate/power of appointment exception to that rule (§ 2056(b)(5); ¶ 14,459). *Howard* presented an unusual fact situation that turned on a particular provision in the trust established in the will of the decedent. The IRS had concluded that the trust qualified for the marital deduction, but the decedent's estate argued that the trust did not qualify! The provision in question specified that all trust income should be distributed to the surviving spouse at quarterly intervals for life but that any trust income accrued between the date of the death of the surviving spouse and the immediately preceding quarterly payment date was to be distributed not to the spouse's estate but to the remaindermen, i.e., to those who were to enjoy the trust property after the death of the surviving spouse. The dispute related to this "stub income" and presented the question of whether the trust qualified as a QTIP, since the surviving spouse was not entitled to all trust income for life. The court held that the trust was eligible for QTIP treatment, finding congressional intent by looking to legislative history (which was silent as to stub income) and by contrasting the provisions in § 2056(b)(7) relating to QTIPs with those in § 2056(b)(5) applicable to cases where the marital deduction is claimed on the ground that the surviving spouse has a life estate and a general power of appointment over the property for which the marital deduction is claimed. The life estate/power of appointment provision of § 2056(b)(5) is construed as requiring the stub income to be paid to the surviving spouse's estate. Reg. § 20.2056(b)–5(f)(8). In contrast, the court pointed to then-proposed Reg. § 20.2056(b)–7(c)(ii) (now Reg. § 20.2056(b)–7(d)(4)), relating to QTIPs, which specifically concluded that a trust was eligible for the marital deduction as a QTIP even though the surviving spouse was not entitled to the stub income. See Reg. §§ 20.2056(b)–5(f)(8) (life estate/power of appointment) and 20.2056(b)–7(d)(4) (QTIP).

It should be noted that Reg. § 20.2044–1(d)(2) provides that the stub income is included in the gross estate of the surviving spouse for estate tax purposes even if not distributed to the spouse or to the spouse's estate.

Chapter 15

DRAFTING MARITAL DEDUCTION CLAUSES

A. OBJECTIVES

[¶ 15,001]

Taking advantage of the marital deduction provides one obvious noncontrovertible benefit to a taxpayer and those who are the beneficiaries of the taxpayer's estate: It makes it possible for the decedent's estate to defer paying federal estate tax on the portion of the decedent's property which passes to the surviving spouse at the decedent's death. As indicated in Chapter 14, this deferral is conditional. In order to claim it, the property passing from the decedent to the decedent's spouse must pass to the spouse in such a way that it will be included in the spouse's estate at his or her later death unless the spouse consumes it during life or otherwise disposes of it prior to death.

The purpose of this chapter is to raise the issues encountered in drafting dispositive provisions which produce not only the best tax consequences but which also take account of and reflect the testator's dispositive scheme.

Clearly, the simplest thing that the testator could do is to "give everything" to his or her spouse. That will minimize the death tax cost at the testator's death. It could, however, substantially increase the estate tax cost at the spouse's subsequent death. Why? Because the testator, by giving "everything" to the spouse, is unable to shelter the exemption equivalent to the unified credit from taxation at the spouse's subsequent death.

Example. Suppose Albert dies in 2004 and his spouse in 2005. At his death, his estate has a value of $3 million. If he gives everything to his spouse, he will pay no federal estate tax at his death, but at her death, her estate tax liability will be $695,000 (assuming she still has the $3 million and assuming she made no adjusted taxable gifts during her lifetime and has no other property). Had Albert elected to put $1.5 million of his estate—an amount equal to the applicable exclusion amount provided in § 2010(c)—into a credit shelter trust (referred to for convenience as a bypass trust) for his wife's benefit for life, he could have kept it out of her estate for estate tax purposes but given her the benefit of the property. For discussion, see ¶ 18,151. If the property was not in her estate, she would have no estate tax liability at her subsequent death.

The use of the credit shelter trust means that the savings on the total transfer tax cost at the death of both spouses would be $695,000.

Thus, if the testator chooses "deferral" but has tax minimization as one objective and has decided on the unlimited marital deduction, a decision must be made as to how best to shelter the exemption equivalent to the unified credit. The testator might express his or her intention this way:

> I want $1.5 million to go into the bypass trust, and the balance of my property is to go to my spouse in a form which qualifies for the unlimited marital deduction.

Whether the foregoing formulation is adequate to accomplish the most appropriate split of an estate between a credit shelter (or bypass) trust and the marital share will be developed in this chapter. (One obvious criticism is that fixing the spousal gift at $1.5 million does not take account of the scheduled increases in the applicable exclusion amount.) For now, it is enough to say that the foregoing clause is an example of a nonformula "reverse" pecuniary marital deduction clause. It is called a "reverse pecuniary" because it is more common to have the marital deduction gift appear first in the instrument, with the balance passing to the bypass trust.

Generally speaking, marital deduction clauses can be grouped into pecuniary clauses and fractional share clauses as shown in Table 15.1. They can be further subdivided into formula and nonformula clauses. Formula clauses were designed by sophisticated lawyers to produce the ideal tax result. Examples of several of the formula clauses are set forth in Table 15.2. (For purposes of these materials, no useful purpose would be served by discussing hybrid clauses, particularly given the relative tax uncertainty associated with such clauses.)

The building block approach is used in these materials. Each drafting possibility is considered beginning with the simplest to the most complex. Disadvantages of each are noted by way of explaining why the next most complex type of clause was created by enterprising practitioners in an effort to overcome the disadvantages of the clause discussed in the preceding paragraphs.

Table 15.1 COMMON MARITAL DEDUCTION CLAUSES

Amount of marital deduction shown on federal estate tax return will be exactly the same under either a pecuniary formula clause or a fractional formula clause shown here. Choice of clause is a function of problems expected at the time administration is completed and the estate distributed.

	Pecuniary	Fractional
Nonformula	"$X to my spouse."	"one-half my estate to my spouse..." — *Problem:* No definition of what is included in "estate"; no consideration of nonprobate property
Formula	"to my spouse the smallest amount necessary to eliminate federal estate tax at my death..." — *Problem:* Used most advantageously when estate has large cash reserves; *Problem:* Requires second valuation; size of estate may change	"to my spouse the fraction of my estate that is necessary to eliminate federal estate tax at my death..." — *Problem:* Gives spouse a fractional share in each asset. Could testator provide for non-pro rata distribution? What other technique could be used to avoid fractionalizing ownership of each asset in the estate of the decedent?

Pecuniary Formula — valuation methods:

Standard	Tax Value	Fairly Representative	Minimum Worth
Each asset valued at date of distribution. Distribution in kind constitutes sale or exchange for income tax purposes	Results in denial of marital deduction after Rev. Proc. 64-19 because executor allowed to manipulate tax consequences of distribution	Property given to surviving spouse shall be fairly representative of appreciation or depreciation experienced by estate during period of administration	Assets on date of distribution are to have fair market value of no less than the amount of the bequest.
		Both expressly sanctioned by Rev. Proc. 64-19.	

Fractional Formula:

Simple	Complex
Numerator is maximum estate tax deduction (federal) less any nonprobate property passing to the surviving spouse which qualifies for the marital deduction. *Problem:* Denominator not specified in instrument	Numerator is same as in simple fractional formula clause. Denominator specified in instrument and is that amount to which fraction is applied

Does distribution in kind constitute a sale or exchange for income tax purposes?

Under which clauses is the distributable net income (DNI) of the estate deemed to be carried out to the surviving spouse when the marital share is distributed to the surviving spouse?

B. MARITAL DEDUCTION CLAUSES: IN GENERAL

[¶ 15,051]

Pecuniary marital deduction clauses are those expressed in terms of a dollar amount. A *nonformula* pecuniary clause would be written in terms of a fixed dollar amount.

¶ 15,001

Example 1. I give my spouse $300,000.

A *formula* pecuniary clause would be expressed in terms of a self-adjusting mechanism.

Example 2. I give my spouse that amount which will qualify for the federal estate tax marital deduction and which will cause the least possible federal estate tax to be payable by reason of my death, but in no event shall the amount passing to my spouse be greater than that necessary to eliminate all such federal estate tax liability.

A variation on the foregoing example would be the following:

Example 3. I give my spouse the smallest amount necessary to eliminate federal estate taxes at my death.

Fractional share clauses are those expressed in terms of a fraction of the decedent's estate. A *nonformula* fractional share clause might be expressed as follows:

Example 4. I give to my spouse one-half of my estate.

A *formula* fractional share clause could be identical to the formula pecuniary clause except that the words "fraction of my estate" will be substituted for the word "amount" in the formula pecuniary clause.

Problem

[¶ 15,090]

In what way are the foregoing examples of formula clauses deficient? What is the missing variable in the formula? Reflect on this issue as you read on.

C. NONFORMULA PECUNIARY CLAUSES

[¶ 15,101]

Nonformula pecuniary clauses, under which the surviving spouse gets a fixed monetary bequest (e.g., "$300,000 to my spouse"), have the advantage of simplicity.

This advantage is more than outweighed, however, by the disadvantages. Such a clause fails to anticipate that the value of the testator's estate may change before death. The result is a lack of precision that will almost certainly cause either an underqualification or an overqualification for the marital deduction. "Underqualification" means that the surviving spouse will receive less than the amount necessary to eliminate federal estate tax from the testator's estate at death. "Overqualification" means that the surviving spouse will receive more than is necessary to eliminate federal estate tax from the testator's estate. As a result, the excess will be stacked in the surviving spouse's estate and be subject to estate tax at the spouse's later death. For discussion, see ¶ 16,409.

¶ 15,101

Problem

[¶ 15,140]

Are there cases where the credit shelter trust should be created by simply reversing the nonformula pecuniary gift language so as to provide a gift of "$600,000 to the bypass trust" for the benefit of the testator's children, with the balance passing to the surviving spouse? For example, should this approach be recommended to Henri who has a probate estate of $1,200,000. During his lifetime, Henri has made adjusted taxable gifts of $250,000.

D. NONFORMULA FRACTIONAL SHARE CLAUSES

[¶ 15,151]

Between 1948 and 1982, when the marital deduction was limited (as noted in ¶ 14,051), some practitioners chose to express a *nonformula* fractional share gift in terms of "one-half" of the decedent's estate. The apparent simplicity of this phrase was misleading. One problem inherent in such a gift was defining the base against which was applied the fraction. Was it the decedent's estate before or after deduction of expenses of administration? Perhaps before satisfaction of specific bequests and devises?

There was an additional difficulty with such a clause. It failed to take into consideration nonprobate property which was both included in the decedent's gross estate and which also qualified for the marital deduction. Common examples included life insurance proceeds payable to the surviving spouse and property held as joint tenants with right of survivorship. Often the consequences of such clauses were to either overqualify or underqualify the gift to the surviving spouse for the marital deduction.

Problem

[¶ 15,157]

Suppose Bill's gross estate was equal to $1,200,000 and that the expenses of administering his estate were $40,000. His will contained only the following words: "one-half of my estate to my wife, the balance to my children." Would the wife receive $600,000 or only $580,000?

[¶ 15,159]

Note

Because of its crudeness, it is unlikely that a taxpayer wanting to avoid both overmaritalization and undermaritalization would use a nonformula fractional gift provision. But taxpayers who elect not to adopt the unlimited marital deduction might be tempted to use (or allow to remain in place in an existing will or trust) a nonformula fractional gift.

¶ 15,140

E. FORMULA CLAUSES: IN GENERAL

[¶ 15,201]

1. LIMITED OR UNLIMITED MARITAL DEDUCTION

a. Simple Wills

As noted at ¶ 15,001, drafting for the unlimited marital deduction could take the form of a will giving everything to the surviving spouse. However, that would mean overmaritalization and, thus, loss of the opportunity to shelter the exemption equivalent to the unified credit in a credit shelter or bypass trust at the death of the first spouse to die. Accordingly, few taxpayers with taxable estates will elect to utilize a simple will once they understand the tax advantages of limiting the gift to the surviving spouse.

[¶ 15,209]

b. Formula Clauses

To avoid overmaritalization, and, thus, the loss of the opportunity to shelter the exemption equivalent to the unified credit in a credit shelter or bypass trust at the death of the first spouse to die, most married taxpayers elect to limit their gifts to their surviving spouse—by making the gift to the spouse equal to the smallest *amount* or *fraction* necessary to eliminate federal estate tax at the death of the first spouse to die. Of course, the effect of providing for only the limited marital deduction is that some part of the decedent's property will be distributed either to persons other than the surviving spouse or to a trust (of which the surviving spouse may be a beneficiary).

Most taxpayers will be satisfied to limit gifts to persons other than their spouses to the amount that can be sheltered by the unified credit. However, some taxpayers will conclude that limiting gifts to persons other than their spouse to the exemption equivalent to the unified credit—technically, the applicable exclusion allowance, § 2010(c)—will not be sufficient to accomplish their dispositive objectives. For example, taxpayers wanting to make a greater provision for children of this or another union may choose to increase the nonmarital gift to the point that it exceeds the $2 million tax-free amount. In such a case, of course, the marital deduction will be similarly limited—and death taxes will be payable. See ¶ 14,309.

Whatever the reason for limiting the marital gift, in most cases, "formula" clauses will be the means chosen to accomplish these limited gifts to the testator's spouse. Thus, even with the advent of the unlimited marital deduction after 1981, most tax wise testators will not take full advantage of this opportunity to give "everything" to the spouse tax free. In this sense, current planning is no different than it was during the years between 1948 and 1982. During that period when only the limited marital deduction was available, the objective to be realized by the use of formula marital deduction clauses was to determine the ideal amount *taxwise* to be excluded from the estate of the first spouse to die (and, accordingly, be taxed at the death of the second spouse to die). That continues to be an objective in planning estates despite the availability of the unlimited marital deduction.

[¶ 15,217]

c. *Wills Executed Prior to September 12, 1981*

Wills and trusts executed prior to September 12, 1981, which contain a "formula" referring to the maximum marital deduction will, as general rule, enjoy only the *limited* marital deduction and not the *unlimited* marital deduction. For discussion, see ¶ 14,067.

[¶ 15,225]

2. ESTATE TAX DEDUCTION IDENTICAL

Any consideration of *formula* clauses must be prefaced with an important generalization. No matter which of the formula clauses shown on Table 15.1 that a testator chooses to include in his or her dispositive instrument, the amount of the marital deduction shown on that testator's federal estate tax return will be the same! Why? Because the consequences of choosing a *pecuniary* formula or a *fractional* formula clause do not relate to the amount of the marital deduction to be reflected on the federal estate tax return. For example, the choice of one clause over another is a function of deciding:

1. Which clause will make administration of the testator's estate easier;

2. Which clause will cause the surviving spouse to receive those items of the testator's property which the testator wants him or her to receive; and

3. Which clause will produce the most advantageous income tax consequences during administration of the testator's estate.

The following observations, in summary form, can be made about the two kinds of clauses:

1. Use of a *pecuniary formula clause* means that the surviving spouse is entitled to a dollar amount. If the estate does not have adequate amounts of cash on hand, it means other property must be sold or distributed in kind to the surviving spouse. If appreciated property is sold, the estate will be forced to recognize the gain on the property as taxable income (eligible for capital gain treatment). If the property is distributed in kind, it means that not only must the property be valued at the time of distribution (a second valuation), but also any appreciation in the property will be recognized as taxable income (capital gain) by the estate.

2. Use of the *fractional formula clause* means that the surviving spouse is entitled to a fraction of every asset in the estate (or the fund against which the fraction is applied). This is allegedly a disadvantage, but perhaps it can be overcome by providing for a non-pro rata distribution. Fractionalization can also be avoided by defining the fund against which the fraction is applied so as to exclude the property that should not be fractionalized.

[¶ 15,233]

3. COMMON PROVISIONS

Table 15.2 sets out examples of the principal marital deduction formula clauses commonly used to implement the *limited* marital deduction. As you read them, keep in mind that the amount of the testator's estate which does not flow to the surviving spouse pursuant to the particular marital deduction clause that you are reading will flow to a bypass trust for the benefit (normally) of the testator's spouse and children. See Chapters 13 and 18. Also, ask yourself whether these clauses need to be changed in any way to implement those plans which call for claiming the unlimited marital deduction for all of a testator's property except the amount which qualifies for the exemption equivalent, i.e., the amount that will be sheltered in a bypass trust.

However, before considering the differences between these clauses, focus on the provisions which are common to all of them.

Table 15.2 EXAMPLES OF PRINCIPAL FORMULA CLAUSES*

Straight Pecuniary

If my spouse survives me, I devise and bequeath to the Trustee, to be held, managed and distributed so as to create a separate trust (called the "Marital Trust"), *a pecuniary amount equal to the maximum marital deduction allowable to my estate for federal estate tax purposes* *** less the value, as finally allowed as a marital deduction, of all property which passes to my spouse either under other provisions of this will or otherwise than under this will. Notwithstanding the foregoing provisions of this paragraph, if after taking into consideration such maximum marital deduction, any charitable deductions and all estate tax credits to which my estate is entitled, my estate would incur no federal estate tax, then such devise and bequest shall be reduced by the largest amount by which such maximum marital deduction could be reduced without my estate incurring any federal or *** [state death taxes], it being my intention to utilize fully the unified credit, any charitable deductions and all other federal estate tax credits before utilizing such maximum marital deduction; provided, however, the Executor shall not be required to make any tax election or determination solely to achieve the maximum marital deduction for any purpose of this paragraph. Satisfaction of such devise and bequest shall be in assets which are allowable to my estate as a part of the marital deduction, and *each such asset shall be valued for such purpose at the date of its distribution.*

Fractional

If my spouse survives me, I devise and bequeath to the Trustee, to be held, managed and distributed so as to create a separate trust (called the "Marital Trust"), *a fraction of my residuary estate of which the numerator is equal to the maximum marital deduction allowable to my estate for federal estate tax purposes* *** less the value, as finally allowed as a marital deduction, of all property which passes to my spouse either under other provisions of this will or otherwise than under this will, *and the denominator is the value, as finally determined for federal estate tax purposes, of all property in my estate at the date of distribution which qualified for the marital deduction plus the cost of any property (including cash) acquired after my death and on hand at the date of distribution.* Notwithstanding the foregoing provision of this paragraph, if after taking into consideration *such fraction of my residuary estate,* the value of all other property finally allowed as a marital deduction, any charitable deductions and all estate tax credits to which my estate is entitled, my estate would incur no federal estate tax, *then such numerator shall be reduced by the largest amount by which such numerator could be reduced without my estate incurring any federal or* *** *[state death taxes],* it being my intention to utilize fully the unified credit, any charitable deductions and all other federal estate tax credits before utilizing the maximum marital deduction; provided, however, the Executor shall not be required to make any tax election or determination solely to achieve the maximum marital deduction for any purpose of this paragraph.

Rev. Proc. 64–19

If my spouse survives me, I devise and bequeath to the Trustee *a portion of my residuary estate* to be held, managed and distributed as a separate trust (called the "Marital

¶ 15,233

Trust"), equal in value to the maximum marital deduction allowable to my estate for federal estate tax purposes ***, less the aggregate amount of the marital deduction allowable to my estate for such purposes for any property passing either under other provisions of this will or otherwise than under this will. Notwithstanding the foregoing provisions of this paragraph, if after taking into consideration such maximum marital deduction, any charitable deductions and all estate tax credits to which my estate is entitled, my estate would incur no federal estate tax, then such devise and bequest shall be reduced by the largest amount by which such maximum marital deduction could be reduced without my estate incurring any federal or * * * [state death taxes], it being my intention to utilize fully the unified credit, any charitable deductions and all other federal estate tax credits before utilizing such maximum marital deduction; provided, however, the Executor shall not be required to make any tax election or determination solely to achieve the maximum marital deduction for any purpose of this paragraph. *For the purpose of this paragraph, including distribution, all values shall be those finally determined for federal estate tax purposes, except that property purchased after my death shall be valued at its cost. However the assets, including cash, so distributed (a) shall be fairly representative of the appreciation or depreciation in the value, to the date or dates of distribution, of all property available for distribution in satisfaction of such devise and bequest and (b) shall consist exclusively of assets allowable to my estate as a part of the marital deduction.*

Minimum Worth

If my spouse survives me, I devise and bequeath to the Trustee *a portion of my residuary estate* to be held, managed and distributed as a separate trust (called the "Marital Trust"), equal in value to the maximum marital deduction allowable to my estate for federal estate tax purposes *** less the aggregate amount of the marital deduction allowable to my estate for such purposes for any property

passing either under other provisions of this will or otherwise than under this will. Notwithstanding the foregoing provisions of this paragraph, if after taking into consideration such maximum marital deduction, any charitable deductions and all estate tax credits to which my estate is entitled, my estate would incur no federal estate tax, then such devise and bequest shall be reduced by the largest amount by which such maximum marital deduction could be reduced without my estate incurring any federal or *** [state death taxes], it being my intention to utilize fully the unified credit, any charitable deductions and all other federal estate tax credits before utilizing such maximum marital deduction; provided, however, the Executor shall not be required to make any tax election or determination solely to achieve the maximum marital deduction for any purpose of this paragraph. *For the purpose of distribution, the value of each asset shall be the lower of (a) the value finally determined for federal estate tax purposes (or cost, if it was purchased after my death) or (b) the value on the date of distribution.* However, the assets, including cash, so distributed shall consist exclusively of assets allowable to my estate as a part of the marital deduction.[1]

* Source: Table 15.2 examples prepared by Donald M. Schindel, *Drafting and Funding Marital Trusts After Recent Tax Acts*, 4 Notre Dame Est. Plan. Inst. 469, 502–503 (R. Campfield ed. 1980).

[1] If an aggregate approach is desired, change the last two sentences to read, "For the purposes of this paragraph, including distribution, all values shall be those finally determined for federal estate tax purposes, except that property purchased after my death shall be valued at its cost. However, the assets, including cash, so distributed (a) shall have an aggregate fair market value on the date or dates of distribution amounting to no less than the amount of this devise and bequest and (b) shall consist exclusively of assets allowable to my estate as part of the marital deduction."

[¶ 15,241]

a. Expressing Marital Deduction Formula Clauses

i. Cut–Back or Reduce-to-Zero Clauses

As noted earlier, marital deduction formula clauses are either of the "pecuniary" formula or "fractional" formula *types.* However, certain provisions are common to both. Look to Table 15.2 and note that all of the formulas have a "cut-back" or "reduce-to-zero" clause. That is, each formula begins with a gift that is referenced to the "maximum marital deduction."

¶ 15,233

Immediately following the maximum marital deduction gift appears a sentence that reduces the gift to the surviving spouse to the extent that the marital deduction is not needed to save federal estate tax because of the availability of the unified credit, any charitable deductions, etc.

> *Example 1.* Jim's estate is $30 million. If he died when the estate tax exclusion was $1.5 million, a marital deduction gift of $28,500,000 would have eliminated all federal estate tax from his estate ($30 million less $1.5 million exclusion). Accordingly, in Jim's case, a cut-back clause could have been effectively utilized to limit Jim's gift to his wife to $28,500,000, thereby allowing the $1.5 million exclusion to flow to a bypass trust where it could be sheltered from estate taxation at the death of his spouse.

> *Example 2.* Katherine's estate is $2 million. If she died when the estate tax exclusion was $1.5 million, a marital deduction gift of $500,000 would eliminate all federal estate tax from her estate ($2 million less $1.5 million exclusion). Accordingly, in Katherine's case, a cut-back clause could be effectively utilized to limit Katherine's gift to her husband to $500,000, thereby allowing the $1.5 million exclusion to flow to a bypass trust where it can be sheltered from estate taxation at the death of Katherine's spouse.

[¶ 15,249]

ii.   *Alternatives*

Using cut-back language as part of the marital deduction formula means that the draftsman has approached the marital deduction in what appears to be a less than straightforward manner. The argument against such an approach is that there is little possibility that the testator will understand it. Moreover, there is the very real risk that even professionals who have little or no experience with the marital deduction will have initial difficulty understanding the operation of the cut-back language. Do you agree?

Would it help to think in these terms? The very word "formula" suggests complexity. And so it is when formulas are used to determine the value of the property that is to pass under a will to a surviving spouse. What appears at first glance to be a maze becomes understandable if the reader remembers that a formula is merely a series of directions to follow literally in determining the amount of the gift to the surviving spouse.

Nonetheless, would it be simpler to express the marital gift in the following terms?

> I give to my spouse the smallest (amount) (fraction) of my estate necessary to eliminate all federal estate tax from my estate at my death.

Or do you think that this reference to "smallest" would create anxieties in the prospective surviving spouse who might have difficulty conceptualizing the operation of such a clause? Even if you do agree, perhaps you also believe that the spouse's anxieties would be well founded in the case of the smaller estate such as Katherine's described above. However, keep in mind that the objective in using a limited marital deduction is to take advantage of the exemption equivalent to the unified credit available to each decedent by sheltering this amount in a bypass trust. Whether this is consistent with the wishes of the testator needs to be explored before the testator's death, rather than after the will "matures."

Problems

[¶ 15,254]

1. Why would use of the maximum marital deduction in the examples in the text have resulted in the payment of unnecessary federal estate tax?

2. The effect of the cut-back clause (described in the text) in estates which are less than the exemption equivalent is that *nothing* will pass to the surviving spouse! All of the decedent's property will flow into the bypass trust! Do you think that many testators will be happy with that result? What about their surviving spouses? Could *indiscriminate* use of this cut-back language lead to some malpractice claims against the attorney who thoughtlessly included this language in every will or trust?

3. The preceding problem suggests that an unintended disposition of a testator's property can result from the indiscriminate use of published marital deduction formula clauses. With that in mind, how could you restructure the formula clauses set forth in Table 15.2 for use in smaller estates? Would the addition of the following language at the end of each cut-back clause in the suggested provisions in Table 15.2 be responsive?

   * * * provided, however, in no event shall the amount passing to my spouse which, when added to the other property included in my gross estate for federal estate tax purposes which passes to my spouse at my death, be less than 50 percent of my adjusted gross estate as finally determined for federal estate tax purposes.

   Could it be said that the foregoing language is fatally defective because it makes reference to the testator's adjusted gross estate? (The Economic Recovery Act of 1981 eliminated § 2056(c)(2) which defined "adjusted gross estate.") Could you suggest a simpler way of expressing these ideas, perhaps in language which would be understandable by the testator?

4. Refer back to the preceding problem and consider whether you would want to include the suggested addendum to the cut-back clause if the testator's estate consisted entirely of community property? In such a case, couldn't it be said that the surviving spouse would have 50 percent of the community property without this provision?

[¶ 15,257]

b. Tax Elections

i. Introduction

The forms in Table 15.2 all provide that "the Executor shall not be required to make any tax election or determination solely to achieve the maximum marital deduction." While this permissive approach is designed to provide maximum flexibility during post-mortem planning, it also can (1) present significant conflicts of interests in cases where the surviving spouse is the executor but not the beneficiary of the bypass trust, and (2) create a dilemma for the executor who is disinterested. The questions of whether to use the alternate valuation date and where to claim the deduction for expenses incurred in administering the decedent's estate will illustrate the problem.

[¶ 15,265]

ii.   Income Tax or Estate Tax Deduction?

Expenses incurred during administration of a decedent's estate are deductible for estate tax purposes pursuant to § 2053(a)(2). Alternatively, such expenses are deductible for income tax purposes by the decedent's estate pursuant to § 642(g). The same expenses may not be claimed as deductions for purposes of both taxes. As a result, the decedent's executor has a dilemma and, possibly, a conflict of interest if the executor is the surviving spouse but not the beneficiary of the bypass trust.

Should the expenses incurred during administration be claimed as deductions for estate tax purposes or for income tax purposes? The solution to that dilemma may sometimes be resolved by determining where use of the deduction will be most effective. For example, if the estate tax bracket is 45 percent and the estate's income tax bracket is 35 percent, at first glance, it would appear that there would be little advantage to claiming the administration expenses as deductions on the estate's income tax return rather than on the estate tax return. However, as should be apparent from the following example, such an election may result in inflating the marital gift at the expense of the other beneficiaries of the decedent's estate while possibly producing a significant tax savings.

Example. Mary died in 2005 with an $2 million estate. Her will provided her husband, Joseph, with the "smallest amount necessary to eliminate federal estate tax at my death." The balance of her property was to be placed in a bypass trust for her children, Dick and Jane, who were born to her during a former marriage.   *amounts passing.*

Mary's executor paid $100,000 in fees and expenses of administration— but the estate had $110,000 of income from dividends and interest during administration. If the executor claims the fees and expenses as deductions on the federal estate tax return pursuant to § 2053(a)(2), the marital gift to Joseph will be $400,000, determined as follows:

Gross estate	$2,000,000
Less: Expenses of administration	(100,000)
Marital deduction	(400,000)
Taxable estate	$1,500,000
Federal estate tax	$555,800
Less: Unified credit	(555,800)
Tax liability	$ –0–

¶ 15,265

On the other hand, if Mary's executor chooses to claim the expenses of administering Mary's estate as deductions on the estate's income tax return, then the marital gift to Joseph will be $500,000 rather than $400,000, determined as follows:

Gross estate	$2,000,000
Less: Expenses of administration	–0–
Marital deduction	(500,000)
Taxable estate	$1,500,000
Federal estate tax	$555,800
Less: Unified credit	(555,800)
Tax liability	$ –0–

However, by claiming the administration expenses as deductions for income tax purposes, the estate, in theory, will save $35,000 (35% x $100,000) in income tax without any increase in the estate tax liability!

Hard to resist? For husband Joseph, it means that he gets $500,000 rather than the $400,000 that he would receive if the administration expenses were claimed as a deduction on the estate tax return. No complaint here. How about the children, Dick and Jane? Well, the trust for their benefit gets $65,000 less—$1,507,355, rather than $1,572,355—if the administration expenses are claimed as a deduction on the income tax return. This, they don't like—despite the $35,000 income tax savings. All of this is summarized in Table 15.3.

Table 15.3 PECUNIARY FORMULA CLAUSE: IMPACT OF CLAIMING EXPENSES AS (1) INCOME TAX DEDUCTIONS AND (2) ESTATE TAX DEDUCTIONS

			Income Tax Deduction		Estate Tax Deduction	
			Joseph	Bypass for Children	Joseph	Bypass for Children
Gross estate		$2,000,000		$2,000,000		$2,000,000
Marital deduction—to husband Joseph			$500,000	(500,000)	$400,000	(400,000)
	Deduction on—					
	Income Tax Return	Estate Tax Return				
Income earned during administration	$ 110,000	$ 110,000		110,000		110,000
Less: administration expenses	(100,000)			(100,000)		(100,000)
	$ 10,000	$110,000				
Income taxes	$ 2,645	$ 37,645		(-2645)		(37,645)
Total available to Bypass Trust beneficiaries				$ 1,507,355		$ 1,572,355
Total distributed to Joseph			$500,000	500,000	$400,000	400,000
Total available to beneficiaries (all)				$ 2,007,355		$ 1,972,355

Perhaps Dick and Jane would be more accepting of the idea of claiming the administration expenses on the income tax return if the $500,000 passing to Mary's husband, Joseph, would flow to Joseph in trust for his life, with the remainder to Dick and Jane. However, as matters stand, serving as executor and making this "call" would not be enviable.

Incidentally, this illustration was premised on the gift to Joseph being classified as "pecuniary" (rather than "fractional"), meaning that Joseph will not share in the income earned by the estate during administration nor will he share in any appreciation or depreciation experience by the estate during administration. Suppose the gift were fractional, i.e., that Joseph were to receive the "smallest fraction" of Mary's estate necessary to eliminate estate tax at Mary's death (instead of the "smallest amount"). In that event, Joseph would share in the income—but it would make no practical difference in the economics of the transaction.

Further complicating the decision as to whether administration expenses are claimed as deductions on the estate tax return or on the estate's income tax return is Reg. § 20.2056(b)-4(d) which followed hard on the heels of the Supreme Court's decision in Commissioner v. Estate of Hubert, 520 U.S. 93 (1997). *[Hubert case cite.]*

Post-*Hubert*, the IRS insists that administration expenses be classified either as "estate transmission expenses" or "estate management expenses". *["estate transmission expenses" v. "estate mangmt expenses".]* Reg. § 20.2056(b)-4(d)(1). Then, in Reg. § 20.2056(b)-4(d)(2), it insists that the estate tax marital deduction is to be "reduced by the amount of the estate transmission expenses paid from the marital share." (Estate transmission expenses, in the view of the IRS, are those expenses that would not have been incurred but for the death of the decedent and the resulting need for collecting and distributing the decedent's property. Reg. § 20.2056(b)-4(d)(1)(ii). Examples include attorney fees, court costs—and "any administration expense that is not a management expense." Reg. § 20.2056(b)-4(d)(1)(ii).) "Marital share" is defined as the property for which the marital deduction is allowed for estate tax purposes under § 2056(a) and is further defined as including the income produced by that property during *[Made into regs.]* the period of administration. Reg. § 20.2056(b)-4(d)(1)(iii).

The IRS position is illustrated in a series of examples given in Regulation § 20.2056(b)-4(d)(5), the conclusion from which is that the governing instrument—the will or trust—or applicable state law must impose the burden of the estate transmission expenses on the portion of the decedent's property *not* passing to the surviving spouse. This is the crucial point and it bears emphasis. The governing instrument or applicable state law must impose the actual burden of the estate transmission expenses on the share of the decedent's property passing to others than the surviving spouse. To the extent that these expenses are imposed on the share passing to the surviving spouse, the marital deduction will be reduced. In the latter case, unless the estate transmission expenses are claimed as a deduction of the estate tax return, the estate will not be "zeroed out" for estate tax purposes—and estate tax may well be payable! (Whether estate tax is actually payable depends on whether § 2010(c)'s applicable exclusion amount ($1.5 million in 2004 and 2005; $2 million in 2006) is available to shelter the taxable estate that is thus determined by this process.)

¶ **15,265**

Hubert considered an earlier version of Reg. § 20.2056(b)–4(a) which, at the time, stated that, in "determining the value of the interest in property passing to the spouse, account must be taken of the effect of any material limitations upon her right to income from the property." An example given in the regulation of a "material limitation" was the use of income from property bequeathed to a spouse to pay administration expenses from the time of death until distribution.

Hubert was a plurality decision of the Supreme Court—there was no majority for any one view. At best, perhaps, it can be said that the Supreme Court held in *Hubert* that it was not a "material limitation" (as contemplated by Reg. § 20.2056(b)–4(a)) on the right of the surviving spouse to the income from the marital gift for the personal representative to charge $1.5 million of estate administration expenses (38 percent of the income earned during administration) against the share of the estate passing to the surviving spouse for which the marital deduction was claimed. Beyond knowing that siphoning off 38 percent of the income attributable to the marital share is not a "material limitation" so as to compromise the availability of the marital deduction, not much else can be said about *Hubert* (except, perhaps, to speculate that the Court, given the disparate opinions expressed by the Justices, probably wished *Hubert* had never been accepted for review).

The IRS response to its defeat in *Hubert* was to abandon the "material limitation" standard litigated in *Hubert* and substitute its current rule requiring that estate administration expenses be classified as either an estate transmission expense or an estate management expense. Practically speaking the IRS abandoned the "material limitation" standard and introduced a black-and-white rule, namely that estate transmission expenses reduce the marital share! *And that's final!* Or at least the IRS would appear to hope. What the IRS has done, in abandoning the "material limitation" standard of its earlier regulation, is attempt to prevent courts from deciding, on a case-by-case basis, whether the marital deduction gift should be reduced when so-called estate transmission expenses are claimed on the estate's income tax return.

Among the remaining questions is whether the use of income to pay interest on unpaid estate taxes would impose a "material limitation" on the surviving spouse's right to income from the property for which the marital deduction was claimed. Almost surprisingly—after its aggressive prosecution of its case in *Hubert*—it is the IRS, expressed in Rev. Rul. 93–48, 93–2 C.B. 270, that interest on unpaid estate taxes taken as a deduction on the fiduciary income tax return does not reduce the estate tax marital deduction! The IRS view, expressed in Rev. Rul. 93–48, is in accord with a number of judicial decisions. The court, in one of those decisions, Estate of Richardson v. Commissioner, 89 T.C. 1193 (1987), explained that it found a material difference between administrative expenses which accrue at death and interest on unpaid taxes which accrue after death. The *Richardson* court, in explaining the difference in treatment (and finding that the marital deduction was not reduced by interest on unpaid estate taxes taken as a deduction of the fiduciary income tax return), said that to insist upon a reduction in the marital deduction would be to "reduce the principal of the estate as it existed at the time of decedent's death by interest that has accrued since decedent's death." It concluded that to pay the interest on the deferred taxes out of income of the estate would neither increase nor decrease the principal of the estate as it was at the time of the decedent's death (and, therefore, the marital deduction should not be affected).

How did the Supreme Court feel about interest paid on unpaid taxes (and the impact of such payments on the marital deduction)? Several of the Justices (O'Connor and Scalia) in opinions in *Hubert* mentioned Rev. Rul. 93–48 but could not agree as to the effect to be given it in the *Hubert* context.

Problem

[¶ 15,271]

Suggest a strategy to be followed when drafting a will relative to the deduction for administration expenses. Could the problem be solved by a provision in the will directing that administration expenses be paid out of the share of the decedent's property not passing to the surviving spouse?

[¶ 15,273]

iii. Alternate Valuation Date

Another opportunity for postmortem planning is presented by the option given the decedent's executor to value the decedent's property as of the date of the decedent's death or as of another date, referred to in § 2032 as the "alternate valuation date." With respect to property held by the estate six months after death, such property may be valued for estate tax purposes as of that date. With respect to property disposed of by the executor or distributed to beneficiaries in the meantime, such property is to be valued as of the date of disposition if the alternate valuation date is selected. If the alternate valuation date is selected as to some of the decedent's property, it must be selected as to all of his or her property. The executor may not "pick and choose" which property is to be valued as of a particular date.

An executor might be motivated to choose the alternate valuation date because the decedent's property has depreciated between the date of death and the alternate valuation date and the depreciation results in a reduction in the decedent's estate tax liability. However, in cases where the value of the decedent's property has appreciated after his or her death, § 2032(c) prohibits the use of the alternate valuation date.

Example. The value of Stan's estate appreciated from $2 million to $2.4 million between the date of his death and the alternate valuation date. His will provided that his wife, Sophie, was to receive the "smallest amount necessary to eliminate any federal estate tax liability" from his estate at his death with the balance going to a bypass trust for his mother for her life, remainder to his children. Section 2032(c) prohibits Sophie from electing the alternate valuation date despite Stan's estate having

¶ 15,273

appreciated in value after his death. (Sophie wanted to make this election because it would have given Stan's property a higher basis for income tax purposes.) Furthermore, had Sophie been able to elect alternate valuation, the value of Stan's marital gift to Sophie would have increased from $500,000 to $900,000. Thus, Sophie would have been entitled to receive cash or property having an aggregate value of $900,000 at the time Stan's estate was distributed. (Without the election, the post death appreciation will go to the bypass trust (for the benefit of Stan's mother and not Sophie).)

Problems

[¶ 15,278]

1. As a result of § 2032(c), the alternate valuation date is available only in very limited circumstances. However, after reviewing § 2032(c), would you agree that a taxpayer would *always* be advantaged to elect alternate valuation if eligible to do so? Couldn't such a conclusion be easily supported by comparing the effective minimum estate tax rate of 45 percent (§ 2001) with the effective maximum tax of 15 percent (§ 1(h)) on capital gains?

2. Do you agree with the assertion that where the testator has provided for the unlimited marital deduction, all those expenses that are deductible on either the federal estate tax return or on the estate's income tax return should be deducted on the income tax return? Couldn't this claim be explained by the fact that the unlimited marital deduction eliminates all the federal estate tax at the testator's death and, therefore, to claim these deductions on the estate tax return is to effectively waste them? What limitations are there to this strategy?

[¶ 15,281]

c. *State Death Taxes Paid*

It is common place to see wills that contain the following language as part of a formula unlimited marital deduction clauses:

> In no event shall the state death tax credit be taken into account in computing the gift to the surviving spouse if the effect is to increase the state death tax payable as a result of my death.

With the repeal of § 2011, the credit for state death taxes paid, these provisions are of no value—but do no harm. (See ¶¶ 7451–7483 regarding possible revival of § 2011 in 2011!)

Remaining—but beyond the scope of these materials—is the question of using formula clauses for domiciliaries of states which have "decoupled", i.e., continue to impose a state death tax. See ¶ 7478. It must be understood that the formula clauses noted here that purport to eliminate federal estate tax would not be effective, without modification, to eliminate state death tax in a decoupled state.

¶ 15,273

[¶ 15,297]

d. Income in Respect of a Decedent (IRD)

Virtually every decedent has income which was earned prior to death but which is uncollected at death. If the taxpayer could have collected the income before death *but chose not to,* that income will be reported on the taxpayer's final federal income tax return on the grounds that the taxpayer has *constructively* received it. In addition, that income will be included in the gross estate of that taxpayer for federal estate tax purposes. § 2033.

Sometimes the earned but uncollected income of a taxpayer at death is not collectible prior to the taxpayer's death. That income is referred to as income in respect of a decedent (IRD).

While § 691 prescribes the tax treatment of IRD, nowhere is IRD defined. However, the regulations give several examples. The following are two of those examples given in Reg. § 1.691(a)–2(b):

Example (2). A widow acquired, by bequest from her husband, the right to receive renewal commissions on life insurance sold by him in his lifetime, which commissions were payable over a period of years. The widow died before having received all of such commissions, and her son inherited the right to receive the rest of the commissions. The commissions received by the widow were includible in her gross income. The commissions received by the son were not includible in the widow's gross income but must be included in the gross income of the son.

Example (3). The decedent owned a Series E United States savings bond, with his wife as co-owner or beneficiary, but died before the payment of such bond. The entire amount of interest accruing on the bond and not includible in income by the decedent, not just the amount accruing after the death of the decedent, would be treated as income to his wife when the bond is paid.

Even post-death payments to beneficiaries from employee benefit plans—commonly referred to as pension plans or profit-sharing plans—are under certain circumstances treated as IRD.

[¶ 15,300]

i. Funding Marital Gift with IRD

IRD is a difficult concept. Even more difficult is the tax accounting required whenever IRD is present in an estate. Tax accounting for IRD is complicated because § 691(c) provides an income tax deduction to the recipient of the IRD for the amount of the estate tax attributable to the inclusion of the IRD in the decedent's gross estate for federal estate tax purposes.

In cases where the decedent takes advantage of the marital deduction to eliminate all estate tax at his death, there would obviously not be a § 691(c) deduction to claim since there would not be any estate tax paid at the decedent's death. However, even in such cases, proper planning may suggest

¶ 15,300

that if the decedent plans to have the § 691 income pass to the surviving spouse, the decedent's will should include a specific bequest of that income. It should not be allowed to pass to the spouse pursuant to a formula marital deduction gift. Why? Because distribution of the § 691 income by the decedent's estate will cause the IRD to become taxable income to the estate. See § 691(a)(2). Conversely, satisfaction of a specific bequest of the IRD will not trigger income recognition by the decedent's estate.

> Thus, if the executor uses an installment receivable or a contractual employee death benefit to fund a straight pecuniary marital bequest, the estate should realize present taxable income equal to the present value of the future payments, less their basis, if any. The acceleration of § 691 income may be a reason for requiring the allocation of § 691 income to the residuary [bypass] trust; on the other hand, a specific bequest of the interest in the § 691 income * * * to the marital trust would prevent the acceleration and reduce the value of the marital trust tax in the surviving spouse's estate by the amount of the income tax on the § 691 income. Donald Schindel, Drafting and Funding Marital Trusts After Recent Tax Acts, 4 Notre Dame Est. Plan. Inst. 469, 483 (R. Campfield, ed. 1980).

It is sometimes suggested that IRD should be directed away from the formula marital gift on the grounds that somehow its availability to be used to fund the marital gift will cause the loss of or reduction in the amount of the § 691(c) deduction. This is not the case. Where the decedent's estate will generate federal estate tax liability, that fact alone should have no effect on whether the decedent should make a specific bequest of the IRD. Furthermore the fact that the decedent's estate will generate estate tax liability should not be cause for the decedent to earmark the IRD away from the marital gift.

[¶ 15,303]

ii.   Funding Bypass Trust with IRD

Funding the bypass trust with IRD means underutilization of the applicable amount provided by § 2010(c). The exclusion amount, $2 million in 2006, is underutilized because the IRD counts against the exclusion at face value but, as a practical matter, is effectively reduced by the claim for the unpaid income taxes on the IRD. While not always possible, the estate tax shelter resulting from the availability of the estate tax exclusion is better utilized if IRD is directed away from the bypass trust.

> *Example.* Rachel's bypass trust (for benefit of her children) was the designated beneficiary of the $500,000 of tax-qualified retirement plan benefits unpaid at Rachel's death in 2005 (when the applicable exclusion amount was $1.5 million). Other property having an aggregate value of $1 million was allocated to the trust, with the balance of Rachel's property passing free of trust to her husband, Zack (as a result of Rachel's will giving Zack "the smallest amount necessary to eliminate federal estate tax at my death"). The $500,000 is taxable income to the bypass trust when received because income tax was deferred on (1) the income used to

initially fund Rachel's tax-qualified retirement and (2) the "inside build-up" in value in Rachel's account in the plan. Assuming the trust is in the 35 percent income tax bracket, the value of the property in the bypass trust is $1,325,000 ($1.5 million—$175,000).

Problem

[¶ 15,304]

Implicit in the discussion of the unlimited marital deduction is the notion that through its use testators can free their estates from all federal estate tax liability. And, if that is the case, then the question of how to treat § 691 income in respect of a decedent becomes moot because there will be no federal estate tax to be concerned with. But is it really valid to assume that the unlimited marital deduction has eliminated all estate tax for those testators who avail themselves of its benefits? Consider the case where the testator has made adjusted taxable gifts during his lifetime of $700,000. Or consider the case where the testator has made specific bequests in his will to persons other than his spouse. Those gifts would not qualify for the marital deduction and would soak up the testator's estate tax applicable exclusion amount provided by § 2010(c).

With these points in mind, refer to the text and consider how the possible presence of § 691 income in an estate should impact drafting for the unlimited marital deduction. Can you explain your conclusion?

[¶ 15,305]

e. *Foreign Death Tax Credit*

Foreign assets subject to foreign death taxes should be allocated away from the marital gift in order to avoid loss of the federal estate tax credit for foreign death taxes paid provided for in § 2014.

F. FORMULA PECUNIARY MARITAL DEDUCTION CLAUSES

[¶ 15,351]

1. STANDARD (STRAIGHT) PECUNIARY FORMULA CLAUSES

a. *Introduction*

A *formula* pecuniary marital deduction clause is distinguishable, as noted earlier, from a *nonformula* pecuniary marital deduction clause. Instead of a gift to the surviving spouse of a fixed amount ("I give $300,000 to my spouse"), a formula clause is recognizable because it is expressed in terms of a gift to the spouse of "an amount" or "the smallest amount" which is to be determined after the death of the testator. For an illustration, see Table 15.1.

¶ 15,351

[¶ 15,359]

b. *Advantages*

i. *"Pick and Choose"*

Pecuniary formula marital deduction clauses have both advantages and disadvantages when compared to fractional formula clauses. The principal advantage of a pecuniary formula clause is that the decedent's executor can "pick and choose" the assets with which to fund the marital gift. The availability of this pick and choose feature means, for example, that the executor can allocate property likely to experience significant appreciation to the bypass trust where that appreciation will be sheltered from estate tax at the death of the surviving spouse. Conversely, the executor can allocate to the surviving spouse in satisfaction of a marital gift, property that is least likely to appreciate, thereby "freezing" the value of the estate for federal estate tax purposes on the occasion of the surviving spouse's subsequent death.

[¶ 15,367]

ii. *Simplicity*

Pecuniary formula clauses have the advantage of simplicity. The formula is executed at the time the federal estate tax return is prepared and, from that time forward, the amount to be delivered to the surviving spouse is fixed to the amount shown on the federal estate tax return as the marital deduction. Having the amount to be distributed to the surviving spouse fixed early in the administration will undoubtedly relieve the spouse's anxieties which, incidentally, are not unnatural.

[¶ 15,375]

c. *Disadvantages*

i. *Gain Recognition*

The principal disadvantage of the straight pecuniary formula clause is that capital gains are realized by the estate if the marital gift is funded with property which has appreciated after the date of the testator's death. Why? Because funding the gift to the spouse is deemed to constitute a sale or exchange for income tax purposes. Such funding is a sale or exchange because a fixed dollar obligation is being satisfied by the distribution of the appreciated property to the surviving spouse. See Reg. § 1.1014–4(a)(3); Suisman v. Eaton, 15 F.Supp. 113 (D.Conn.1935), aff'd per curiam, 83 F.2d 1019 (2d Cir. 1936), cert. den., 299 U.S. 573 (1936). (*Note:* § 1223(11) effectively provides that any gain recognized by the estate on the disposition of any of the property which it acquires from the decedent will be long-term capital gain. The maximum tax on long-term capital gain is limited to 15 percent of the gain realized. § 1(h).)

¶ 15,359

Because of these funding problems, the pecuniary formula marital gift is best suited to estates which have large amounts of cash available to satisfy the spouse's claim.

[¶ 15,383]

ii. Second Valuation

Even in cases where the estate's property has not undergone significant appreciation during the course of administration, the amount of appreciation can only be determined by again valuing—this time as of the date of the proposed distribution—the property that has been proposed for distribution to the surviving spouse in satisfaction of the spouse's claim. In the case of readily marketable securities, this second valuation is not difficult. But in the case of unique property—such as stock in a closely held business or real property—not only is the second valuation difficult, it will undoubtedly be expensive. Also, there is always the risk that the beneficiaries will object to the value assigned to the properties and litigation will result.

[¶ 15,391]

iii. Decline in Value

Furthermore, if the estate experiences a significant decline in the value of its property during the course of administration, it is possible that the entire estate will be exhausted in satisfying the spouse's claim and no property will remain in the estate to be allocated to the bypass trust.

On the other hand, all the appreciation experienced during the course of administration of the estate accrues for the benefit of the persons who are the beneficiaries of the bypass trust.

[¶ 15,399]

iv. Loss of Estate as an Income Tax Shelter

Because of the funding problems encountered with pecuniary formula clauses, the executor charged with the administration of a pecuniary formula marital gift may be well advised to fund the marital gift early in the administration of the estate. The advantage of early funding is that such distributions do carry out the income of the estate to be taxed to the surviving spouse instead of being warehoused in the estate and taxed there. See §§ 661, 663. Typically, distributing the income to the spouse will result in a smaller income tax bill, as few spouses will be in the top income tax bracket (while the estate reaches the top bracket with taxable income, for example, of $10,050 in 2006). §§ 1(e); 1(i)); ¶ 21,351.

Comment: Income received by an estate during administration will be taxed to that estate unless it is distributed to the estate's beneficiaries. If it is so distributed, the distributed income will be taxed to the beneficiaries. However, to prevent an executor from claiming that a particular distribution was a distribution of principal and not a distribution of income, Congress adopted an efficient mechanical rule to be used in determining whether a particular distribution is a distribution of income or principal. That rule requires the executor to use Congressionally mandated rules for determining the estate's income which is available for distribution. The amount so determined is known as distributable net income (DNI). Thereafter, the rule is truly mechanical. Every distribution from the estate is deemed to carry out to the beneficiary the estate's income to the extent of the estate's DNI unless the distribution is in satisfaction of a specific bequest as described in § 663(a)(1). See ¶ 3351 and Chapter 8.

[¶ 15,407]

v. Conclusion

While the disadvantages of the pecuniary formula marital deduction clause cannot be ignored it is probably safe to say that the pecuniary formula clause is probably the most widely used of the various alternatives.

[¶ 15,415]

2. TAX VALUE PECUNIARY CLAUSES

The unarticulated issue in the foregoing discussions of the disadvantages of the straight pecuniary formula clause is the valuation date used for property distributed in kind. The general rule is that property distributed in kind in satisfaction of a pecuniary gift is valued as of the date of distribution.

The problem can be analyzed in these terms. If the gift is construed to be a pecuniary gift, the donee has a claim to a fixed number of dollars. The easy solution is for the decedent's executor to simply deliver cash to the donee. If the estate is short of cash, often the executor has a choice. The executor can either sell property to raise cash, or, if the governing instrument (will or trust) permits, the executor can satisfy the bequest by making a distribution of property. If the executor has the option of distributing property in lieu of cash, the issue becomes one of valuing the property. Is it to be valued as of the date of the decedent's death, the alternate valuation date, or the date of distribution (or some other date)? Most wills and trusts and, alternatively, applicable state law, provide for valuation as of date of distribution. However, as indicated in the preceding paragraphs, there are two significant disadvantages to using date of distribution values. Those are the difficulties of a second valuation of the same property and the possibility of income tax consequences when a claim to a specific number of dollars is satisfied by appreciated property. See ¶¶ 21,400–440 for discussion.

Given those problems, the "tax value" clause became popular. It provided that the values placed on property for estate tax purposes at the decedent's death should be used to value property distributed in kind. For an illustration, see Table 15.1. The appeal was obvious. The surviving spouse's gift could be funded with depreciated property. Suppose, for example, that the marital deduction had been allowed in the amount of $300,000 and that the estate consisted of two parcels of real estate on the date chosen by the executor to fund the spouse's gift. Parcel A had a date of death value of $300,000 but a date of distribution value of only $100,000. Parcel B had a date of death value of $100,000 but a date of distribution value of $300,000. Funding the spouse's gift with Parcel B would mean the estate would recognize income of $200,000, equal to the appreciation experienced by Parcel B. Funding the spouse's gift with Parcel A, if a tax value clause were in place, would mean that the estate would have no income tax consequences and that the spouse would receive property having a value of only $100,000. From a tax planning standpoint, this was terrific strategy because it meant that $300,000 escaped taxation at the death of the first spouse to die (because of the marital deduction), but only $100,000 would be taxed in the estate of the surviving spouse (assuming that Parcel A did not appreciate in the hands of the spouse and that Parcel A was not disposed of by the surviving spouse after receipt).

The abuse potential resulted in publication of Revenue Procedure 64–19, 1964–1 C.B. 682, where the Service said that it would deny the marital deduction in many of the cases where a tax value clause was used.

[¶ 15,423]

3. IMPACT OF REVENUE PROCEDURE 64–19

a. Introduction

To the unsophisticated reader, Revenue Procedure 64–19, 1964–1 C.B. 682, will have little meaning. Yet it remains one of the most well known of all the Treasury's published rulings because of its impact on pecuniary formula funding questions. In summary, Revenue Procedure 64–19 had the effect of outlawing the use of tax value clauses and introduced two new concepts which gave names to new pecuniary formula marital deduction clauses. The new clauses that are rooted in Revenue Procedure 64–19 are the "fairly representative" and the "no less than" or "minimum worth," all of which are illustrated in Table 15.2.

[¶ 15,425]

REVENUE PROCEDURE 64–19

1964–1 C.B. 682.

§ 1. PURPOSE

The purpose of this Revenue Procedure is to state the position of the Internal Revenue Service relative to allowance of the marital deduction in cases where there is some uncertainty as to the ultimate distribution to be made in payment of a pecuniary bequest or transfer in trust where the governing instrument provides that the executor or trustee may satisfy bequests in kind with assets at their value as finally determined for Federal estate tax purposes.

§ 2. BACKGROUND

.01 The Internal Revenue Service has received inquiries concerning the amount of the marital deduction which should be allowed for a pecuniary bequest in a will or for a transfer in trust of a pecuniary amount where the governing instrument not only provides that the executor or trustee may, or is required to, select assets in kind to satisfy the bequest or transfer, but also provides that any assets distributed in kind shall be valued at their values as finally determined for Federal estate tax purposes. The question is the same whether the amount of the bequest or transfer is determined by a formula fixing it by reference to the adjusted gross estate of the decedent as finally determined for Federal estate tax purposes, or its amount is determined in some other fashion by which a fixed dollar amount distributable to the surviving spouse can be computed. Any bequest or transfer in trust described in sub§ 2.01 is hereinafter referred to as a "pecuniary bequest or transfer" for purposes of this Revenue Procedure.

.02 Where, by virtue of the duties imposed on the fiduciary either by applicable state law or by the express or implied provisions of the instrument, it is clear that the fiduciary, in order to implement such a bequest or transfer, must distribute assets, including cash, having an aggregate fair market value at the date, or dates, of distribution amounting to no less than the amount of the pecuniary bequest or transfer, as finally determined for Federal estate tax purposes, the marital deduction may be allowed in the full amount of the pecuniary bequest or transfer in trust. Alternatively, where, by virtue of such duties, it is clear that the fiduciary must distribute assets, including cash, fairly representative of appreciation or depreciation in the value of all property thus available for distribution in satisfaction of such pecuniary bequest or transfer, the marital deduction is equally determinable and may be allowed in the full amount of the pecuniary bequest or transfer in trust passing to the surviving spouse.

.03 In many instances, however, by virtue of the provisions of the will or trust, or by virtue of applicable state law (or because of an absence of applicable state decisions), it may not be clear that the discretion of the fiduciary would be limited in this respect, and it cannot be determined that he would be required to make distribution in conformance with one or the other of the above requirements or that one rather than the other is applicable. In such a case, the interest in property passing from the decedent to his surviving spouse would not be ascertainable as of the date of death, if the property available for distribution included assets which might fluctuate in value.

* * *

§ 4. SCOPE

.01 The problem here considered is restricted to the situation involving bequests and transfers in trust described in §§ 1 and 2.01. It does not arise in other cases, for example:

(1) In a bequest or transfer in trust of a fractional share of the estate, under which each beneficiary shares proportionately in the appreciation or depreciation in the value of assets to the date, or dates, of distribution.

(2) In a bequest or transfer in trust of specific assets.

(3) In a pecuniary bequest or transfer in trust, whether in a stated amount or an amount computed by the use of a formula, if:

    (a) The fiduciary must satisfy the pecuniary bequest or transfer in trust solely in cash, or

    (b) The fiduciary has no discretion in the selection of the assets to be distributed in kind, or

    (c) Assets selected by the fiduciary to be distributed in kind in satisfaction of the bequest or transfer in trust are required to be valued at their respective values on the date, or dates, of their distribution.

.02 This Revenue Procedure does not relate to any issue arising under the income tax provisions of the Internal Revenue Code.

[¶ 15,430]

b. Analysis

The position taken by the IRS in Revenue Procedure 64–19 is that the full marital deduction will be allowed in cases where a pecuniary bequest could be satisfied by a distribution in kind only if the fiduciary must distribute property in satisfaction of the pecuniary amount which (1) has "an aggregate fair market value at the date, or dates, of distribution amounting to *no less than the amount of the pecuniary bequest or transfer, as finally determined for Federal estate tax purposes*" or (2) is *"fairly representative of appreciation or depreciation in the value of all property"* (emphasis added) that is available for distribution in satisfaction of the pecuniary bequest.

Revenue Procedure 64–19, by its terms, is not to apply in a number of cases expressly identified in § 4 of the Revenue Procedure, some of which are popular alternatives to kinds of clauses expressly sanctioned by Revenue Procedure 64–19. Of particular note are references to fractional formula clauses and pecuniary formula clauses providing for the use of date-of-distribution values when making distributions in kind.

As a result of Revenue Procedure 64–19, wills and trusts that provide for pecuniary bequests commonly include a stipulation specifying the valuation procedure to be followed in satisfying pecuniary bequests in kind. The governing instrument will either provide that property distributed in kind will be valued using date of distribution values or any property distributed in kind in satisfaction of the pecuniary bequest *shall have a value of not less than* the pecuniary bequest or that the property *shall have an aggregate value that is fairly representative* of the appreciation and depreciation experienced by the estate during administration.

[¶ 15,435]

c. Fairly Representative

The "fairly representative" variation is sometimes referred to as the "64–19 formula." Its advantages include allowing the executor to "pick and choose" (¶ 15,359), thereby allowing the executor to do some postmortem tax planning by allocating to the surviving spouse those assets least likely further to appreciate while allocating to the bypass trust (or other beneficiaries) the assets most likely to experience further appreciation. One drawback to the fairly representative variation is the need for a second valuation, ¶ 15,383.

[¶ 15,440]

d. Minimum Worth or "No Less Than"

The "no less than" or "minimum worth" formula calls for the distribution in kind to be valued using the lower of federal estate tax values or date of distribution values. There are two variations of the minimum worth approach, both of which are illustrated in Table 15.2. One, the aggregate variation, is specifically mentioned in Revenue Procedure 64–19. The other, the individual asset variation, while not mentioned in Revenue Procedure 64–19, should qualify. If federal estate tax values are lower, tax values will be used in valuing all of the property distributed to the surviving spouse. And if date of distribution values are lower, more of the decedent's property will need to be distributed to the surviving spouse in order to satisfy the pecuniary formula amount.

[¶ 15,445]

DONALD SCHINDEL, DRAFTING AND FUNDING MARITAL TRUSTS AFTER RECENT TAX ACTS

4 Notre Dame Est. Plan. Inst. 469, 488–490 (R. Campfield ed. 1980).

The minimum worth formula has the advantage of permitting the greatest flexibility in funding the marital trust.

Example. Assume an estate with a marital bequest of $1,000,000 and only two assets: ABC stock with a federal estate tax value of $1,000,000 and a current value of $1,000,000 and XYZ stock with a federal estate tax value of $1,000,000 and a current value of $2,000,000. In such a case, if the marital trust receives the ABC stock, the residuary trust would receive the XYZ stock worth twice as much.

There would be a problem if the ABC stock had fallen in value to $500,000. In such a case, if all of the ABC stock were distributed to the marital trust, one-half of the XYZ stock would also have to be distributed to the marital trust, resulting in $1,500,000 going to the marital trust and only $1,000,000 going to the residuary trust. The result would not be improved if the XYZ stock ($2,000,000) were distributed to the marital trust at $1,000,000 federal estate tax values, because then the residuary trust would have only the ABC stock worth $500,000. In this case, with stock which has depreciated, the value of the marital trust could be held down by selling stock and distributing cash, but perhaps at a cost of realizing capital gains (if the appreciated XYZ stock is sold).

Like the 64–19 clause, the minimum worth formula avoids capital gains on funding * * * The funding of the individual asset variation could produce a capital loss. This would not be true in the funding of the aggregate variation, although depreciated assets could be sold at a loss, and the funding made in cash.

While the minimum worth formula involves a great deal of leverage and, as the above example shows, in a bull market can be quite advantageous, it can also be quite risky, as is also shown in the above example. In a falling market, a minimum worth formula can bankrupt the residuary trust or overinflate the marital trust. Another problem involves the interpretation of the minimum worth clause when the marital trust is funded with depreciable real estate because it is uncertain whether depreciation is to be taken into account as an adjustment to federal estate tax values.

While the minimum worth formula permits the greatest flexibility in funding, it may be subject to abuse, particularly in second marriage situations. There is also the expense of revaluation, as in the other pecuniary formulas, but detailed reappraisals may not be necessary for appreciated assets under a minimum worth formula. Because of the great flexibility which the executor has in allocating assets to the marital trust, a minimum worth clause should not be used where a charitable deduction is carved out of the residue. The charitable deduction may fail because the amount is unascertainable. It has been contended that the same problem occurs with the 64–19 and straight pecuniary formulas and that the only safe formula where there is a charitable remainder is the fractional formula.

G. FRACTIONAL FORMULA MARITAL DEDUCTION CLAUSES

[¶ 15,501]

1. INTRODUCTION

Like pecuniary marital deduction clauses, fractional marital deduction clauses are divided into formula and nonformula clauses. A nonformula fractional clause would perhaps read: "I give one-half of my estate to my spouse." By way of contrast, a fractional formula clause might provide as follows:

I give to my spouse a fraction of my estate. The numerator of the fraction shall be the smallest amount. * * * The denominator of the fraction shall be. * * *

[¶ 15,509]

2. ADVANTAGES

The principal advantage of the fractional formula clause is that capital gains are not realized upon funding the gift to the surviving spouse. In addition, there is no need to have a second valuation of the property included in the decedent's estate as is the case where property is to be distributed in kind pursuant to a pecuniary formula clause.

[¶ 15,517]

3. DISADVANTAGES

a. *Apparent Simplicity*

On its face a fractional formula clause appears simpler than a pecuniary clause because, in principle, the surviving spouse is entitled to a fraction of every asset in the residuary estate. However, even the required fractionalization itself may prove to be less than desirable if the estate property cannot be easily partitioned and the surviving spouse and the trustees of the bypass trust find themselves in the position of co-owners of fractional interests in the same property.

Estate of Bonner v. United States, 84 F.3d 196 (5th Cir.1996) can be looked to as an argument for fractionalizing the ownership of property not easily partitionable. Louis Bonner's wife created a trust for his benefit in her will and the trust was funded with fractional interests in property not readily divisible. Louis owned remaining interests in the property free of trust. In as much as the QTIP election was made for Mrs. Bonner's trust, all of the trust property was included in Louis' estate for estate tax purposes. Louis' estate claimed and was held to be entitled to a discount in valuing the fractional interests held by him free of trust at the time of his death (in as much as the inability to readily effect a partition of the property renders it less marketable, *i.e.,* that the value of the parts is less than the value of the whole). The court said that the identity of the ultimate recipient of the property held in Mrs. Bonner's trust was irrelevant to the determination. For related discussion, see ¶ 14,611; ¶ 24,117.

[¶ 15,525]

b. *Liquidation*

The fractional ownership of estate property after completion of the estate administration can be avoided in one of several ways. First, such property could be sold and the proceeds of sale distributed to the beneficiaries in accordance with their respective fractional interests.

[¶ 15,533]

c. *Limiting the Residue*

The residue against which the fraction is applied can be defined so as to exclude property which cannot be easily partitioned. Similarly, property which the testator does not think should be partitioned—interests in closely held businesses, for example—can also be the subject of a specific bequest so as to prevent that property from falling into the residue of the testator's estate against which the fraction is to be applied.

[¶ 15,541]

d. Non–Pro Rata Distributions

The testator's will or trust can authorize non-pro rata distributions so as to allow the testator's executor to allocate one asset to the surviving spouse while allocating another asset of equivalent value to the bypass trust. In the absence of explicit authority in the will or trust authorizing such non-pro rata distributions, there is authority that such distributions will constitute a sale or exchange for income tax purposes, thereby possibly generating capital gains to the estate to the extent the property has appreciated in value from the value assigned the property for federal estate tax purposes. See Rev. Rul. 69–486, 1969–2 C.B. 159.

[handwritten margin note: Non-pro rata Distribute Clause eliminates the "Fractional interest" problem.]

[¶ 15,549]

e. Adjusting the Fraction

Probably the most serious objection to the use of a fractional formula marital deduction clause results from the required adjustment in the fraction each time a distribution or payment is made from the share allocated to the bypass trust but not the share allocated to the surviving spouse pursuant to the fraction. For example, take the case where the governing instrument (will or trust) stipulates that the federal estate tax generated by the decedent's estate is to be paid out of the share of the residuary estate not passing to the surviving spouse.

> *Note:* As noted at ¶ 14,767, the marital share cannot be burdened with any part of the estate tax liability imposed upon the estate without causing the loss of a part of the marital deduction because of the interdependent variable problem. That is, unless death taxes are charged against the nonmarital share, the amount of the marital deduction will be dependent upon the amount of the federal estate tax liability and the federal estate tax liability will be dependent upon the amount of the marital deduction. Why? Because the marital deduction is only available as to property passing to the surviving spouse. The marital deduction cannot be claimed for property paid over to the IRS in the form of death taxes. Therefore, any allocation of taxes to the marital share reduces the marital deduction.

In the case where the federal estate tax is to be paid out of the nonmarital share, payment of the tax reduces the nonmarital share which is included in the residuary estate. Thereafter, a greater portion of the income earned on the property included in the residuary estate is attributed to the property which has been allocated to the marital share inasmuch as a greater proportion of the residuary estate consists of the property constituting the marital share. Accordingly, the respective interests of the spouse and the bypass trust must be adjusted—a new fraction determined to take account of these new realities for purposes of dividing the residuary estate (other than the assets on hand at date of death).

Example. Suzie's estate had a value of $900,000 when she died in January, 2005. Her will gave her husband, Wallace, "one-half of the residue of my estate" with the balance passing to a bypass trust for the benefit of her children. Suzie's will provided that "all taxes were to be paid out of that portion of her estate not passing to her husband, if any." Suzie's federal estate tax liability was finally determined to be $42,500, which her executor timely paid on October 1, 2005.

Payment of the federal estate tax liability was the first payment or distribution from Suzie's estate since her death. Thereafter, pending a final determination of the estate's federal estate tax liability, the estate remained open. During this period, the estate's property continued to be income producing.

On August, 15, 2006, the executor received notice from the Internal Revenue Service that the estate tax return had been accepted as filed. Thereupon, the executor set about planning the distribution of Suzie's estate. The executor determined that during the period between Suzie's death and the date on which the federal estate tax was paid, her "all cash" estate earned $33,000 in interest. During the remainder of 2005, after the tax was paid, the estate earned $17,000 in interest. In 2006, the estate earned $20,000 in interest in the period beginning January 1st and ending April 15th (for a total of $37,500), and another $22,000 between April 15th and August 15th. In addition, on April 15, 2006, the executor paid federal income taxes of $12,800 for the period ending December 31, 2005, and in August, 2006, administration expenses of $30,000, all of which he claimed as deductions on the estate's final income tax return.

The foregoing transactions can be scheduled as follows:

	Receipts	Disbursements
Income, 1/1/05–10/1/05	$ 33,000	
Federal estate taxes, 10/1/05		$ 42,500
Income, 10/1/05–12/31/05	17,000	
Income, 1/1/06–4/15/06	20,000	
Income, 4/15/06–8/15/06	22,000	
Income taxes paid, 4/15/06		12,800
Administration expenses paid, 8/15/06	30,000	30,000

The required allocations were as follows:

	Income		Principal	
	Marital Share	Bypass Trust	Marital Share	Bypass Trust
Initial division of estate			$450,000	$450,000
Income allocation (50%–50%) through date of payment of federal estate tax liability	$ 16,500	$ 16,500		
Payment of federal estate tax				(42,500)
Totals	$ 16,500	$ 16,500	$450,000	$407,500

New fractional interests in the residue of the estate for the period 10–1–05 to 12–31–05

¶ 15,549

Spouse:
(450,000 + 16,500)
 —————————— 52.4%
    890,500
Bypass trust:
(407,500 + 16,500)
 —————————— 47.6%
    890,500
Income allocation (52.4% and 47.6%) for
period 10–1–05 to 4–15–06:
     52.4% × $37,000 .... $ 19,388
     7.6% × $37,000 .... $ 17,612

Problems

[¶ 15,590]

1. Refer to the preceding illustration in the text and suggest the allocation that needs to be made for the federal income taxes paid on April 15, 2006 and the $30,000 of administration expenses paid on August 15, 2006. How is the fractional interest of the spouse impacted by the payment of those taxes?

2. As you reflect on the foregoing discussion keep in mind the most common objective of marital deduction planning. That objective is to shelter in the bypass trust precisely the maximum amount of property that can pass free of estate tax (to someone other than the testator's spouse) at the death of the testator. Generally speaking, that means that an amount equal to the estate tax applicable exclusion amount (§ 2010(c)) available to the decedent at his or her death should flow to the bypass trust, there to be sheltered from the estate tax at the death of the surviving spouse. In such a scheme, the balance of the decedent's property would flow to the surviving spouse in a form which would qualify for the marital deduction.

    If the amount to be sheltered in the bypass trust is to be maximized, it becomes necessary for most persons who have taxable estates to use a formula marital deduction clause which will take into account the ever increasing estate tax exclusion—§ 2010(c)—the inability of most persons to predict accurately the year of their death.

    Mr. Shark has an estate of $3 million. He is contemplating executing a will, prepared by himself, which contains the following language: "I give to my spouse the smallest amount necessary to eliminate all federal estate tax from my estate. The balance, to my Bypass Trust." Would you agree that Mr. Shark's proposed marital deduction provision is every bit as good and perhaps better than those proposed in the immediately preceding discussion in text? Clearly Mr. Shark's provision appears simpler and will be more understandable to both lawyer and nonlawyer readers. However, could you argue that the provision will be less than acceptable to the testator's surviving spouse because it gives the surviving spouse "the smallest amount" rather than "an amount equal to the maximum marital deduction"? Even though the amount received by the spouse may be the same under either provision, the less sophisticated reader may feel the "smallest amount" provision might be taken to reflect a miserliness or reluctance to make the gift to the spouse. It is doubtful whether a testator would want his or her spouse to be left with that impression after the testator's death. See also ¶ 15,249.

Furthermore, in light of the discussion in text, do you find any technical problems with Mr. Shark's provisions?

H. "UP–FRONT" CREDIT SHELTER CLAUSES

[¶ 15,601]

Most of the foregoing discussion focuses on preparing either a pecuniary formula marital deduction clause (PMD) or a fractional formula marital deduction clause (FMD). Consider whether it might be more appropriate to use a pecuniary formula exemption equivalent clause (PEE) or a fractional formula exemption equivalent clause (FEE), sometimes called "up-front" credit shelter clauses or "reverse" pecuniary clauses. For example, such a clause might read as follows:

> I give to the Trustee of my Bypass Trust an amount equal to the exemption equivalent to the unified credit available to my estate for federal estate tax purposes. The balance of my property I give to my spouse.

(Use of a pecuniary exemption equivalent clause would mean that the residuary clause would be the marital deduction clause.)

Problem

[¶ 15,640]

Consider what modifications would have to be made, if any, in the up-front credit shelter clause proposed in text to make it suitable for use by your new client, Mr. Belchfire. At first glance, Mr. Belchfire declared that the clause "appealed" to him. He liked the idea of $1.5 million (or whatever is then the estate tax applicable exclusion amount (§ 2010(c)) (flowing to the bypass trust where it would be available on a "needs" basis to his children from his prior marriages. He was also happy with the prospect of the balance of his property flowing to his spouse. Mr. Belchfire has an estate of $3 million and his recent bride, Bunny, also has an estate of $3 million. Mr. Belchfire's estate consists entirely of cash. He has made adjusted taxable gifts of $400,000. The Belchfires are currently domiciled in a state which imposes a flat 5 percent tax on deathtime transfers from a decedent to his spouse and a flat 10 percent tax on deathtime transfers from a decedent to a bypass trust. If the suggested pecuniary exemption equivalent clause was a part of Mr. Belchfire's will and he died today, survived by Bunny, how much of his estate would be allocated to the bypass; how much to Bunny's trust; how much would be paid in state death taxes; and how much, if any, would be paid in federal estate taxes? Assume administration expenses incurred by Mr. Belchfire's estate would be $100,000 and that his will contained the following provision:

¶ 15,590

Pay all of my debts and all of the taxes imposed on my estate by reason of my death from the residue of my estate.

In determining the state death tax burden, consider the implications of the discussion at ¶ 14,767 and 15,281.

If you conclude that Mr. Belchfire's estate will be subject to federal estate tax, restructure the proposed pecuniary exemption equivalent clause and the other provisions of Mr. Belchfire's will so as to eliminate all federal estate tax at his death.

On reflection, do you think that the pecuniary formula exemption equivalent clause (PEE) is simpler or more complex to use than a pecuniary formula marital deduction clause (PMD)?

Would your choice of a PEE clause or a PMD clause for Mr. Belchfire be different if he had an estate of $6 million which consisted almost entirely of various parcels of real property which he was holding for investment purposes.

Chapter 16

DISCLAIMER: THE POSTMORTEM SOLUTION

A. OBJECTIVES

[¶ 16,001]

Disclaimers are viewed by many commentators as an increasingly important, if not popular, planning technique. Disclaimers are important because, through the medium of the disclaimer, lack of planning or defects in the original plan can be remedied.

Example. Edith's property had a value of $1.2 million. Her lawyer proposed that she create a bypass trust of an amount equal to the exemption equivalent to the unified credit (i.e., applicable exclusion amount provided by § 2010(c)) for federal estate tax purposes. Her husband, Charlie, was the proposed life income beneficiary of the trust with the remainder going to their "then living lineal descendants."

Edith rejected her lawyer's suggestion, insisting that she wanted a will that she could "understand" and that was "simple." Accordingly, the lawyer prepared and Edith signed a will whereby Edith gave "all of my property to my beloved husband, Charlie, and if he doesn't survive me, all to my beloved child, Milton."

After Edith's death, Charlie concluded that his resources were adequate to his needs and that he "didn't need much, if any, of Edith's property." Accordingly, Charlie decided to refuse to accept, or to "disclaim," the unwanted portion of Edith's property.

The effect of such a disclaimer is to cause the disclaimed property to pass to Edith's child, Milton, as if Charlie had predeceased Edith. Had Edith not named Milton as "taker in default" in the will, then the disclaimed property would have passed by intestacy. Under the prevailing intestate law in Edith's jurisdiction, Milton and Charlie would equally divide Edith's intestate property. In such a case, in order for Charlie's disclaimer to be *completely* effective, he would also need to refuse to accept or disclaim his intestate share of Edith's property. However, not all states permit disclaimer of intestate property. Therefore, whether Charlie's disclaimer of his share of Edith's intestate property would be effective would depend upon the jurisdiction in which Edith died domiciled.

Inasmuch as most people never have "enough" property, Charlie's action in the foregoing illustration may appear to be inexplicable. One possible explanation is that Charlie did not want to "stack" Edith's property on top of his own for estate tax purposes when he could "shelter" that property under the exemption equivalent to the unified credit available to Edith's estate for federal estate tax purposes. See § 2010(c). For textual discussion, see ¶ 13,091.

The tax issue presented by an alleged disclaimer is whether the disclaimant has "refused to accept" the gift or whether he or she has "accepted" the gift and the disclaimer is nothing more than another transfer under the "cover" of disclaimer. If the "refusal to accept" qualifies as a disclaimer, there are no gift tax consequences to the disclaimant. See §§ 2046, 2518. On the other hand, if the "refusal to accept" does not qualify as a disclaimer, then the putative disclaimant is deemed to have made a taxable gift.

[handwritten margin note: "disclaim" gives rise to no gift tax consequences.]

However, when considering the use of a qualified disclaimer in estate planning, it is imperative to understand all of the potential ramifications which may result. D. Thompson & C. Buchanan, The Law of Unintended Consequences Applied to Disclaimers, 12 Prob. Prac. Rep. 1 (Mar. 2000). For example, in certain situations a surviving spouse's disclaimer will affect the calculation of the marital deduction and thereby increase the estate tax burden. See Estate of DiSanto v. Commissioner, 78 T.C.M. (CCH) 1220 (1999); Estate of Nix v. Commissioner, 78 T.C.M. (CCH) 157 (1999).

The materials in this chapter focus briefly on the state law issues affecting disclaimers but concentrate on the federal tax consequences of disclaimers. Generally speaking, two sets of rules govern the federal tax consequences of disclaimers. Which rules apply depends upon the effective date of the instrument creating the interest which is to be disclaimed. If the instrument was effective after 1976, the disclaimer is governed by § 2518. If the donative instrument was effective before 1977, another set of rules applies. Unfortunately, the pre–1977 rules were not clearly developed (perhaps leading to the adoption of §§ 2046 and 2518 in 1976).

B.   STATE LAW IMPLICATIONS

[¶ 16,051]

Disclaimers have state law implications. While all states explicitly or implicitly permit disclaimers of testamentary gifts, some of them do not permit disclaimers of intestate property. The rationale for this seemingly inconsistent treatment is that testamentary gifts, like all gifts, involve the element of *acceptance* as that term is used in the context of the familiar expression "delivery, donative intent, and *acceptance*." In the case of intestate property, *acceptance* is not an element because the property is not deemed to have been acquired by gift but by operation of law. See Coomes v. Finegan, 233 Ia. 448, 7 N.W.2d 729 (1943); Howe, Renunciation by the Heir, Devisee or

Legatee, 42 Ky. L. Rev. 605 (1953) (criticizing the common law rules that permit beneficiaries under wills to disclaim but deny this same opportunity to intestate takers). This approach to intestate property may be explainable in part because society is seen as having an interest in the orderly disposition of a decedent's property. Actually, the notion probably goes back to feudal times and is a carryover from the time when wills of land were not permitted, because the King had to be certain of the identity of the persons to whom he looked for troops and money.

C. DISCLAIMERS OF PRE–1977 INTERESTS

[¶ 16,101]

Section 2518 covers all disclaimers of interests created by instruments which are effective after 1976. Accordingly, there will be few cases involving the pre–1977 rules. Moreover, each such case will probably involve the issue of the effective date of the gift which is sought to be disclaimed.

> *Example.* At his death in 1936, Sylvester established a trust for his daughter, Janis, for life, with remainder to his nephew, David. Janis died this year, whereupon David first learned about the existence of the trust. After some reflection, David has decided he "doesn't want the trust property." As a result of David's refusal to accept the remainder interest, the trust property will be distributed to Bennie, another of Sylvester's nephews. Will David's refusal to accept qualify as a disclaimer for gift tax purposes or will David be deemed to have made a gift to Bennie? Consider this question in light of the material which follows.

In two notable decisions by the United States Supreme Court which involved interests that were created before 1977 but were disclaimed after 1977. In both instances, the Court, in finding that the purported disclaimers were ineffective, made it clear that it is no friend of disclaimers that result in elimination of gift taxes otherwise payable. The cases are important in the sense of illustrating the importance of literal compliance with the requirements for a valid disclaimer that is effective for federal gift tax purposes–and that the court system is largely unsympathetic to technical arguments that, if accepted, mean gift tax avoidance.

In the first case, Jewett v. Commissioner, 455 U.S. 305 (1982), the Court, after providing an excellent summary of the development of the concepts underlying the federal gift tax, concluded that the disclaimer was ineffective because the disclaimant had not acted to disclaim, as required by Reg. § 25.2511–1(c)(2), "within a reasonable time after knowledge of the existence of the transfer" was acquired by the disclaimant. The disclaimer was attempted 33 years after the disclaimed interest was created but at a time when the disclaimed interest remained contingent. The dispute turned on whether the term "transfer" refers to the date the interest was created or to the date the contingency was removed and the interest vested or became possessory in the disclaimant. The Court was certain that "transfer" referred to the creation of the interest and that, as a result, the attempted disclaimer was too late (meaning that the disclaimant made a taxable gift of a future interest as a result of the untimely disclaimer). Perhaps the Court gave away its true intention when it said:

> Since the practical effect of petitioner's disclaimer was to reduce the expected size of his taxable estate and to confer a gratuitous benefit upon the natural objects of his bounty, the treatment of the disclaimers as taxable gifts is fully consistent with the basic purpose of the statutory scheme.

455 U.S. at 310.

The second case, United States v. Irvine, 511 U.S. 224 (1994), also involved a late disclaimer of a pre–1977 interest, but the taxpayers attempted to distinguish their situation from that considered in *Jewett*. The basis of the claimed distinction was that the interest being disclaimed was created in 1917, before the enactment of the federal gift tax in 1932. The Court rejected this argument, concluding that the purported disclaimer constituted a taxable gift and, in the process, turned conventional disclaimer analysis on its head. The Court said that the relation back theory of disclaimer is a state law created legal fiction that has no bearing on congressional determination to tax transfers of interests in property. The Court said:

> [P]ost-enactment transfers are all that happened on the occasion of Mrs. Irvine's disclaimer. The critical events, the transfers of fractional portions of Mrs. Irvine's remainder to her children, occurred after enactment of the gift tax, though the interests transferred were created before that date. To argue otherwise, that the transfer to be taxed antedated the Act, would be to cling to the legal fiction that the disclaimer related back to the moment in 1917 when Lucius P. Ordway established the trust. This fiction may be indulged under state law as a device to regulate creditors' rights, but the *Jewett* Court clearly held that Congress enacted no such fantasy.

511 U.S. at 241. The Court went on to state:

> The determination of the amount of "reasonable time" that remained after Mrs. Irvine learned of the interest and reached majority status must be based upon the gift tax's purpose to curb avoidance of the estate tax.* * *

* * *

Cases like *Jewett* and this one illustrate as well as any why it is that state property transfer rules do not translate into federal taxation rules. Under state property rules, an effective disclaimer of a testamentary gift is generally treated as relating back to the moment of the original transfer of the interest being disclaimed, having the effect of canceling the transfer to the disclaimant *ab initio* and substituting a single transfer from the original donor to the beneficiary of the disclaimer.* * * Although a state-law right to disclaim with such consequences might be thought to follow from the common-law principle that a gift is a bilateral transaction, requiring not only a donor's intent to give, but also a donee's acceptance,* * * state-law tolerance for delay in disclaiming reflects a less theoretical concern. An important consequence of treating a disclaimer as an *ab initio* defeasance is that the disclaimant's creditors are barred from reaching the disclaimed property.* * * The *ab initio* disclaimer thus operates as a legal fiction obviating a more straightforward rule defeating the claims of a disclaimant's creditors in the property disclaimed.

Id. at 234, 239–240.

D. AFTER 1976: QUALIFIED DISCLAIMERS

[¶ 16,151]

1. INTRODUCTION

In 1976, Congress added § 2518 to the Internal Revenue Code which provided for the "qualified disclaimer". The purpose of § 2518 was to provide uniform and definitive rules for disclaimers for gift and estate purposes. As a result, in order to achieve the desired uniformity from state-to-state, disclaimers which are not effective under local law will be allowed for federal tax purposes if, "under applicable local law, the disclaimed interest in property is, in fact, *transferred*, as a result of attempting the disclaimer, *to another person* without any direction on the part of the disclaimant." Reg. § 25.2518–1(c)(1) (emphasis added). Such a transfer might well be effected where the state disclaimer statute provides that an untimely disclaimer is treated as an assignment of the interest disclaimed to those persons who would have taken had the disclaimer been valid. Reg. § 25.2518–1(c)(3), *Example (1)*. However, the regulations provide that an interest in property will not be considered to be transferred without any direction on the part of the disclaimant if, under applicable local law, the disclaimant has any discretion (whether or not such discretion is exercised) to determine who will receive such interest. Moreover actions by the disclaimant which are required under local law merely to divest ownership of the property from the disclaimant and vest ownership in another person will not disqualify the disclaimer for federal tax purposes.

The effect of a qualified disclaimer is that the transfer will not be subject to any federal gift tax consequences. Reg. § 25.2518–1(b) provides:

[T]he disclaimed interest in property is treated as if it had never been transferred to the person making the qualified disclaimer. Instead, it is considered as passing directly from the transferor of the property to the person entitled to receive the property as a result of the disclaimer. Accordingly, a person making a qualified disclaimer is not treated as making a gift. Similarly, the value of a decedent's gross estate for purposes of the Federal estate tax does not include the value of property with respect to which the decedent, or the decedent's executor or administrator on behalf of the decedent, has made a qualified disclaimer. If the disclaimer is not a qualified disclaimer, for the purposes of the Federal estate, gift, and generation-skipping transfer tax provisions, the disclaimer is disregarded and the disclaimant is treated as having received the interest.

In general, a disclaimer must be an irrevocable and unqualified refusal to accept an interest in property. § 2518(b). "Irrevocable and unqualified" has been defined as "a relinquishment of a legal right that is incapable of being retracted or revoked by the disclaimant and is not modified by reservations or restrictions that limit its enforceability." Estate of Monroe v. Commissioner, 124 F.3d 699, 708 (5th Cir.1997). Furthermore, a qualified disclaimer must be (1) in writing, (2) received within nine months of the creation of the interest in property or within nine months of the disclaimant turning twenty-one years of age, (3) the disclaimant must not have accepted the property or its benefits, and (4) the disclaimed property must pass "without any direction" by the disclaimant. § 2518(b).

[handwritten margin note: Elements of a "qualified disclaimer"]

[¶ 16,159]

2. THE WRITING REQUIREMENT

A disclaimer must be in writing. Reg. § 25.2518–2(b)(1) requires the writing (1) to describe the interest in the property being disclaimed and (2) to be signed by the disclaimant or the disclaimant's legal representative. Little guidance is given as to the contents of the required writing.

[¶ 16,167]

3. THE TIMING REQUIREMENT

Section 2518(b)(2) and Reg. § 25.2518–2(a)(3) and (c) are specific as to the timing requirements for an effective qualified disclaimer. Section 2518(b)(2)(A) generally provides that the nine-month period to disclaim begins when a taxable transfer occurs. Transfers can be grouped for discussion as either (1) testamentary transfers, (2) inter vivos transfers, or (3) joint property. Furthermore, a disclaimer must be delivered to the transferor of the property, his or her legal representative, the legal titleholder to the property, or the person in possession of the property. Reg. § 25.2518–2(b)(2). In addition, state law may require the disclaimer to be filed with a court in the case of a guardianship or estate.

[¶ 16,175]

a. *Testamentary Transfers*

The general rule applicable to testamentary transfers is that all interests must be disclaimed within nine months of the death of the transferor. The date the will is admitted to probate is irrelevant for qualified disclaimer purposes. Estate of Fleming v. Commissioner, 974 F.2d 894 (7th Cir.1992).

[¶ 16,183]

b. *Inter Vivos Transfers*

Reg. § 25.2518–2(c)(3) provides that a taxable transfer "occurs when there is a completed gift for federal gift tax purposes regardless of whether a gift tax is imposed on the completed gift." Such an interest, whether vested or contingent, must be disclaimed nine months from the time such interest is created. Consider the following examples from Reg. § 25.2518–2(c)(5):

> *Example (3).* F creates a trust on April 1, 1978, in which F's child G is to receive the income from the trust for life. Upon G's death, the corpus of the trust is to pass to G's child H. If either G or H wishes to make a qualified disclaimer, it must be made no later than 9 months after April 1, 1978.

> *Example (4).* A creates a trust on February 15, 1978, in which B is named the income beneficiary for life. The trust further provides that upon B's death the proceeds of the trust are to pass to C, if then living. If C predeceases D, the proceeds shall pass to D or D's estate. To have timely disclaimers for purposes of section 2518, B, C, and D must disclaim their respective interests no later than 9 months after February 15, 1978.

In the case of revocable transfers, such as the creation of a revocable trust, the donees must disclaim within nine months after the trust becomes irrevocable.

[¶ 16,191]

c. *Joint Property*

Joint tenancies with right of survivorship between spouses and tenancies by the entirety create special disclaimer problems. The general rule is that a disclaimer of a joint interest must be made within nine months of the creation of the tenancy, or in the case of a survivorship interest, nine months of the death of the first joint tenant to die regardless of whether the interest is unilaterally severable under local law. Reg. § 25.2518–2(c)(4)(i). Disclaimer of joint tenancy interests are specifically considered beginning at ¶ 11,601.

[¶ 16,201]

d. *Tolling Disclaimer Period for Those Not 21*

Section 2518(b)(2)(B) allows persons under the age of 21 to postpone disclaiming an interest until they have reached the age of 21. This is the case even if the beneficiary accepts some of the benefits of the property before he or she reaches the age of 21. Reg. § 25.2518–2(d)(3). Therefore, if a child has a right to all of the income from a particular trust—and actually receives that income—the child may still make a qualified disclaimer under § 2518 of the life estate on his or her 21st birthday. See Reg. § 25.2518–2(d)(4), Examples (1)-(11).

[¶ 16,209]

4. ACCEPTANCE OF BENEFITS

For a disclaimer to be qualified means that the disclaimant did not accept any of the benefits of the property prior to the disclaimer. § 2518(b)(3). The regulations define an acceptance as "an affirmative act which is consistent with ownership of the interest in property." Reg. § 25.2518–2(d)(1). Additionally, the regulation clearly indicates that if any consideration is paid for the disclaimer, it will be deemed an acceptance of the disclaimed property. However, in Lute II v. United States, 19 F.Supp.2d 1047 (D.Neb.1998), a father's renunciation of his interest in his deceased son's estate, which then passed to his son's wife, was a qualified disclaimer although a land trade was a condition to the renunciation. The court found that the land exchange was "on a dollar for dollar basis using appraised values" therefore the father did not receive consideration for the renunciation. Id. at 1056. Moreover, the mere expectation or implied promise of consideration is not sufficient to invalidate a disclaimer. See Estate of Monroe v. Commissioner, 124 F.3d 699 (5th Cir.1997). In the case of a joint tenancy, a disclaimer of the interest passing by right of survivorship will not be considered an acceptance of the joint interest even if the surviving co-tenant resided on the property prior to the disclaimer. Moreover, in Private Letter Ruling 9135044, the IRS concluded that a surviving spouse's disclaimer of the undivided one-half interest in a personal residence passing from the deceased spouse under a right of survivorship agreement was valid, even though the surviving spouse occupied the property before the disclaimer and *continued to do so after the disclaimer*. Of course, any acceptance of benefits by a disclaimant prior to his or her 21st birthday will not disqualify the disclaimer. § 2518(b)(2)(B); Reg. § 25.2518–2(d)(3).

[¶ 16,217]

5. DISCLAIMANT CANNOT DIRECT DISCLAIMED INTEREST

The "redirection" prohibition presents special problems. Section 2518(b)(4) says that the disclaimed property must pass "without any direction on the part of" the disclaimant. Complicating that restriction is an almost unrelated exception that applies when the spouse is the disclaimant. As a result of this exception, spouses may make an effective disclaimer, even though as a result of that disclaimer, the disclaimed property passes to the surviving spouse without any direction on the part of the disclaiming spouse. Reg. § 25.2518–2(e)(2) and § 2518(b)(4)(A).

By way of contrast, a disclaimant other than the spouse may not have an interest, either beneficially or in a fiduciary capacity, in the disclaimed property after the disclaimer. However, even here there is an exception. Where the disclaimant has an interest in a fiduciary capacity, the disclaimer will be effective so long as exercise of the power held by the disclaimant is subject to an ascertainable standard, so long as the power can never be exercised in favor of the disclaimant. Reg. § 25.2518–2(e)(1).

Sound complicated? It is. There are really two rules here, one applicable when the donor's spouse is making the disclaimer and the other applicable when the disclaimer is made by someone other than the donor's spouse. Where the spouse is the disclaimant, the spouse can make an effective disclaimer despite having, after the disclaimer, (1) a beneficial interest in the disclaimed property and (2) the power to accelerate or postpone enjoyment and pick and choose among a group of beneficiaries that includes the spouse— so long as the power is subject to an ascertainable standard and was not created by the disclaiming spouse. Where the disclaimant is someone other than the donor's spouse, the disclaimant cannot be a possible beneficiary of the disclaimed property—although such a disclaimant is allowed power to pick and choose among other beneficiaries, so long as the power is limited by an ascertainable standard.

Table 16.1 describes the effectiveness of disclaimers when the disclaimant is the spouse and when the disclaimant is someone other than the spouse.

Table 16.1 WHEN DISCLAIMERS ARE EFFECTIVE

Disclaimer is effective where:	Spouse as Disclaimant	Disclaimant Other Than Spouse
Disclaimed property must pass without any direction on part of disclaimant	Yes	Yes
Disclaimant has beneficial enjoyment in disclaimed property	Yes	No
Disclaimant has fiduciary power limited by ascertainable standard over disclaimed property	Yes	Yes
Disclaimant has fiduciary power *exercisable in favor of disclaimant* so long as limited by ascertainable standard	Yes	No

[¶ 16,225]

a. Disclaimants Who Are Not Spouses of Donor

The general rule is that a disclaimer will be ineffective if, as a result of such disclaimer, the disclaimed property passes to or for the benefit of the disclaimant. § 2518(b)(4)(B). There is one exception. A disclaimer will not be ineffective solely because the disclaimant, after the disclaimer, has a "fiduciary power to distribute to designated beneficiaries" so long as the power is limited by an ascertainable standard and the disclaimant is not one of the permissible distributees. Reg. § 25.2518–2(e)(1).

Reg. § 25.2518–2(e)(5), Examples (11) and (12) illustrate the aforementioned principle. Note that, in these examples, the disclaimant is not the surviving spouse of the transferor.

Example (11). G creates an irrevocable trust on February 16, 1983, naming H, I and J as the income beneficiaries for life and F as the remainderman. F is also named the trustee and as trustee has the discretionary power to invade the corpus and make discretionary distributions to H, I or J during their lives. F disclaims the remainder interest on August 8, 1983, but retains his discretionary power to invade the corpus.

F has not made a qualified disclaimer because F retains the power to direct enjoyment of the corpus and the retained fiduciary power is not limited by an ascertainable standard.

Example (12). Assume the same facts as in example (11) except that F may only invade the corpus to make distributions for the health, maintenance or support of H, I or J during their lives. If the other requirements of section 2518(b) are met, F has made a qualified disclaimer of the remainder interest because the retained fiduciary power is limited by an ascertainable standard.

[¶ 16,233]

b. *Donor's Spouse as Disclaimant: Retained Interests*

A special rule applies when the disclaimant is the spouse of the donor. § 2518(b)(4)(A). A disclaimer by the donor's spouse is effective even if, as a result of the disclaimer: (1) the disclaimed interest passes to or for the benefit of the spouse without any direction on the part of the spouse and (2) the spouse has the right to direct the beneficial enjoyment of the disclaimed property—perhaps even in favor of the disclaiming spouse—so long as the spouse's power is limited by an ascertainable standard. Reg. § 25.2518–2(e)(2).

An example of an ascertainable standard is the power to distribute the corpus of the trust only for the health, maintenance or support of the children. Consider the following examples from Reg. § 25.2518–2(e)(5):

Example (4). B died testate on February 13, 1980. B's will established both a marital trust and a nonmarital trust. The decedent's surviving spouse, A, is an income beneficiary of the marital trust and has a testamentary general power of appointment over its assets [meaning that A can exercise the power in his or her own favor]. A is also an income beneficiary of the nonmarital trust, but has no power to appoint or invade the corpus. The provisions of the will specify that any portion of the marital trust disclaimed is to be added to the nonmarital trust. A disclaimed 30 percent of the marital trust.* * *Pursuant to the will, this portion of the marital trust property was transferred to the nonmarital trust without any direction on the part of A. This disclaimer by A satisfies section 2518(b)(4).

Example (5). Assume the same facts as in example (4) except that A, the surviving spouse, has both an income interest in the nonmarital trust and a testamentary nongeneral power to appoint among designated beneficiaries [meaning that A has the right to direct the trust property to persons other than himself or herself]. This power is not limited by an ascertainable standard. The requirements of section 2518(b)(4) are not satisfied unless A also disclaims the nongeneral power to appoint the portion of the trust corpus that is attributable to the property that passed to the nonmarital trust as a result of A's disclaimer. Assuming that the fair market value of the disclaimed property on the date of the disclaimer is $250,000 and that the fair market value of the nonmarital trust (including the disclaimed property) immediately after the disclaimer is $750,000, A must disclaim the power to appoint one-third of the nonmarital trust's corpus. The result is the same regardless of whether the nongeneral power is testamentary or inter vivos.

Example (6). Assume the same facts as in example (4) except that A has both an income interest in the nonmarital trust and a power to invade corpus if needed for A's health or maintenance. In addition, an independent trustee has power to distribute to A any portion of the corpus which the trustee determines to be desirable for A's happiness. Assuming the other requirements of section 2518 are satisfied, A may make a qualified disclaimer of interests in the marital trust without disclaiming any of A's interests in the nonmarital trust.

Problems

[¶ 16,240]

1. Wife is the trustee of Marital Trust and Bypass Trust, both created by Husband's will. Wife is to receive all of the income from Marital Trust and is given a general power of appointment over Marital Trust (exercisable in favor of herself or any other person). Husband's will provides that if Wife disclaims Marital Trust, the disclaimed property is added to Bypass Trust. As trustee of Bypass Trust, Wife has discretion to distribute income and principal to herself and to Husband's and her children in amounts and at times necessary for their health, education, maintenance and support. Under the following circumstances, has Wife made a qualified disclaimer for purposes of § 2518?

    (a) Six months after Husband's death, appearing before a Notary Public, Wife executes a statement wherein she refuses to accept the power of appointment given her over Marital Trust. Her statement is recorded in Deed Records.

    (b) Six months after Husband's death, appearing before a Notary Public, Wife executes a statement wherein she refuses to accept not only the power of appointment given her over Marital Trust but any beneficial interest (including income) from Marital Trust. Her statement is recorded in Deed Records.

2. Sister is the trustee of Education Trust and Bypass Trust, both created by Brother's will. Sister is to receive all of the income from Education Trust and is given a general power of appointment over Education Trust (exercisable in favor of herself or any other person). Will provides that if Sister disclaims Education Trust, the disclaimed property is added to Bypass Trust. As trustee of Bypass Trust, Sister has discretion to distribute income and principal to herself and to Sister's children in amounts and at times necessary for their health, education, maintenance and support. Under the following circumstances, has Sister made a qualified disclaimer for purposes of § 2518?

    (a) Six months after Brother's death, appearing before a Notary Public, Sister executes a statement wherein she refuses to accept power of

¶ 16,233

appointment given her over Education Trust. Her statement is recorded in Deed Records.

(b) Six months after Brother's death, appearing before a Notary Public, Sister executes statement wherein she refuses to accept not only the power of appointment given her over Education Trust but any beneficial interest (including income) from Education Trust. Her statement is recorded in Deed Records.

[¶ 16,241]

c. *Intestate Property*

In order for the disclaimer to be qualified, the disclaimant must not be entitled to receive the property after the disclaimer. Therefore, an heir at law must look at applicable state law to determine whether the disclaimed property will pass to or "come back" to the disclaimant under applicable state intestate law or if the disclaimant will be deemed to have predeceased the donor of the interest. In addition, if a disclaimant is a residuary beneficiary, the disclaimant must disclaim not only the gift provided by the testator but also any interest passing under the residuary clause to the disclaimant.

E. TYPES OF INTERESTS

[¶ 16,301]

1. INTRODUCTION

An understanding of what is considered an "interest" is necessary. Under the proposed regulations, all interests in income were treated as one separate interest and all interests in the corpus were another separate interest. T.D. 8095, 1986–2 C.B. 161. However, the final regulations describe a separate interest as "each interest in property that is separately created by the transferor." That seems to imply that any separately created identifiable interest is disclaimable, so long as all the requirements in § 2518 are complied with.

There is an exception to the "separately created" principle stated above. Reg. § 25.2518–3(a)(1) states that when "local law merges interests separately created by the transferor, a qualified disclaimer will only be allowed if there is a disclaimer of the entire merged interest or an undivided portion of such merged interest." For example, a beneficiary is given both a life estate and the remainder interest in a property. If local law merges the two interests to give the beneficiary a fee simple, the beneficiary must disclaim the entire merged interest or an undivided portion of the merged interest in order to make a qualified disclaimer. See Reg. § 25.2518–3(d), Example (12).

The four basic types of interests subject to disclaimer are: (1) interests in income, (2) interests in the corpus, (3) powers of appointment, and (4) interests in trusts.

Four interests subject to disclaimer.

¶ 16,301

[¶ 16,309]

2. INTERESTS IN INCOME

A beneficiary may disclaim an interest in income if the transferor of the interest separately creates it. See Reg. § 25.2518–3(a)(1)(i) (supplying an example in which an interest in a security is given to A for life, then to B for life, with a remainder interest to A's estate. A can make a qualified disclaimer of either the life estate or the remainder).

[¶ 16,317]

3. INTERESTS IN CORPUS

As with the interest in income, a beneficiary may disclaim the interest in the corpus of a property provided that the transferor separately creates the interest. For example, X receives stock in ABC Company but the transferor did not create separate interests in the income interest and the corpus. If X receives and cashes a dividend check of ABC stock, X may not subsequently make a qualified disclaimer of the interest in the corpus of the shares of stock. See Reg. § 25.2518–2(d)(1). Therefore, any potential disclaimant should be careful not to accept an income distribution from an interest in corpus which may eventually be disclaimed or the entire disclaimer will not be a qualified disclaimer under § 2518.

[¶ 16,325]

4. POWERS OF APPOINTMENT

Disclaimers of powers of appointment merit special attention as to when the power may be disclaimed and its effect on potential objects of the power. Reg. § 25.2518–2(c)(3) distinguishes general powers of appointment from nongeneral powers of appointment regarding when the nine-month period begins to run. The donee of a general power of appointment—the powerholder—has nine months from the day the power was created in order to disclaim. A potential beneficiary—someone in whose favor the general power could be exercised—has nine months from the time of exercise or lapse of the power to disclaim such interests. However, in a situation involving a nongeneral power of appointment, both the donee and any potential takers under the power must disclaim within nine months of the creation of the power.

[¶ 16,333]

5. INTERESTS IN TRUSTS

In general, disclaimers of specific properties held in trust are barred. Reg. § 25.2518–3(a)(2) states:

> A disclaimer is not a qualified disclaimer under section 2518 if the beneficiary disclaims income derived from specific property transferred in trust while continuing to accept income derived from the remaining properties in the same trust unless the disclaimer results in such property being removed from the trust and passing, without any direction on the

part of the disclaimant, to persons other than the disclaimant or to the spouse of the decedent.

[¶ 16,341]

6. FRACTIONAL OR PERCENTILE SHARE DISCLAIMED

A disclaimer that does not involve "specific property" but is a disclaimer of an undivided portion of an interest in trust may be a qualified disclaimer. An undivided portion must be a fraction or percentage of the interest and must extend over the entire term of the disclaimant's interest. Reg. § 25.2518–3(b). The following examples from Reg. § 25.2518–3(d) illustrate this point:

Example (5). E died on September 13, 1978. Under the provisions of E's will, E's shares of stock in X, Y, and Z corporations were to be transferred to a trust. The trust provides that all income is to be distributed currently to F and G in equal parts until F attains the age of 45 years. At that time the corpus of the trust is to be divided equally between F and G. F disclaimed the income arising from the shares of X stock. G disclaimed 20 percent of G's interest in the trust. F's disclaimer is not a qualified disclaimer because the X stock remains in the trust. If the remaining requirements of section 2518(b) are met, G's disclaimer is a qualified disclaimer.

Example (6). Assume the same facts as in example (5) except that F disclaimed both the income interest and the remainder interest in the shares of X stock. F's disclaimer results in the X stock being transferred out of the trust to G without any direction on F's part. F's disclaimer is a qualified disclaimer under section 2518(b).

Example (7). Assume the same facts as in example (5) except that F is only an income beneficiary of the trust. The X stock remains in the trust after F's disclaimer of the income arising from the shares of X stock. F's disclaimer is not a qualified disclaimer under section 2518.

Example (8). Assume the same facts as in example (5) except that F disclaimed the entire income interest in the trust while retaining the interest F has in corpus. Alternatively, assume that G disclaimed G's entire corpus interest while retaining G's interest in the income from the trust. If the remaining requirements of section 2518(b) are met, either disclaimer will be a qualified disclaimer.

F. USING DISCLAIMERS AND PARTIAL QTIP ELECTIONS

[¶ 16,401]

1. INTRODUCTION

Disclaimers become very important in both premortem as well as post-mortem tax planning. That is, disclaimers are extremely useful both as "fix-ups" and as an integral part of the premortem planning process. In the premortem planning context, the disclaimer can be utilized as a "poor man's marital deduction." In the postmortem context, disclaimers are useful to avoid both "overmaritalization" and "undermaritalization."

[¶ 16,409]

2. OVERMARITALIZATION OR "THE POOR MAN'S MARITAL DE-DUCTION"

Consider Henry and Win. One child, Chip, was born to Win during her marriage to Henry. At his death, Henry left an estate having a value of $1.2 million, all cash. Henry's will provides as follows, in pertinent part:

> I give all of my property to Accumulation National Bank as Trustee to be held, managed and disposed of as follows:
>
> a.   During the continuance of the trust the Trustee shall distribute the trust income to my beloved wife, Win. In addition, the Trustee shall distribute to Win so much of the principal of the trust as shall be required for her health, education, maintenance, and support.
>
> b.   The trust shall terminate upon the death of Win. Upon termination, the trust property shall be distributed to my then living lineal descendants *per stirpes*.

Henry's gift to the trustee for the benefit of Win qualifies for the marital deduction for federal estate tax purposes under the Qualified Terminable Interest Property (QTIP) exception. See § 2056(b)(7) and discussion at ¶ 14,557. However, QTIP treatment is not mandatory. It must be elected by Henry's executor on the federal estate tax return filed for Henry's estate. Reg. § 20.2056(b)–7(b)(4).

The obvious disadvantage of claiming the marital deduction for the entire trust is that, while the trust will be "excused" from Henry's estate for tax purposes, it will be "stacked" in Win's estate at her subsequent death. See § 2044. The result is that Henry's estate is deprived of the use of § 2010(c)'s applicable exclusion amount as a tax shelter. Had he given Win a lesser amount, limited, perhaps, to the "smallest amount necessary to eliminate any federal estate tax" from his estate, Henry could have directed the balance of his property to a bypass trust where it could have been made available to Win but kept out of her estate for federal estate tax purposes. See ¶ 18,151 for discussion of the bypass trust.

However, with Henry dead, the only alternative is the "fix-up." One form of fix-up is for Win to disclaim or refuse to accept a portion of the trust for her benefit. (Of course, she would also be required to disclaim her intestate share of Henry's estate if her purpose was to allow the disclaimed property to "skip" her estate and pass directly to their son, Chip.) This procedure has been expressly approved where the entire interest was disclaimed except for an amount equal to a formula marital deduction (e.g., "smallest fraction necessary to eliminate any federal estate tax"). Priv. Ltr. Ruls. 8502084; 7913119. The disclaimed property would then pass to someone other than the surviving spouse and the formula amount would pass to the surviving spouse and qualify for the marital deduction.

¶ 16,401

Alternatively, as another form of fix-up, Henry's executor could elect to claim the marital deduction for only a part of Win's trust, so long as the partial election is fractional or percentile in nature. See Reg. §§ 20.2056(b)–7(b)(2)(i); 20.2056(b)–7(h), Examples (7) and (8); Priv. Ltr. Rul. 8301050 (which follows).

[¶ 16,411]

Private Letter Ruling 8301050
September 20, 1982

This is in reference to your letter requesting rulings concerning the federal estate tax consequences of a proposed election under § 2056(b)(7)(B)(v). More specifically, you request rulings that: 1) the fractional share of the property subject to the proposed election will constitute qualified terminable property, and 2) the value of the decedent's taxable estate shall be determined, in part, by deducting from the gross estate an amount equal to the value of the fractional share of the property subject to the proposed election.

Your proposed election states as follows: that specific portion, represented by a fractional share up to 100% of all trust property, that is required to reduce the federal estate tax on [the decedent's] estate to zero based on finally determined federal estate tax values, after taking into consideration all other items deducted on the federal estate tax return, the allowable state death tax credit (to the extent it does not increase the amount of death taxes payable to any state) and unified credit.

The submitted information indicates that the decedent died testate after December 31, 1981, survived by a wife and two children. The decedent had previously executed a will in which he bequeathed to his wife an amount equal to 50 percent of his adjusted gross estate as finally determined for federal estate tax purposes, less property which passed to her either by specific bequest or outside the will and which qualifies for the marital deduction. The remainder of his estate passed to an inter-vivos family trust of which the decedent was the grantor. All state and federal estate taxes and levies, expenses of administration, specific bequests, and other proper charges of the estate are to be paid by the trust upon the decedent's death. The trust provided that, upon the decedent's death, * * * 1) The trustee is to pay all the income of the trust to the wife during her life, at least annually. Any undistributed net income upon the wife's death would be distributed to her estate. 2) The trustee has discretion to pay to the wife all or part of the corpus in order to maintain her in her usual manner and style of living or for illness or other emergency. 3) Upon the death of the wife, the balance of the trust corpus will be divided into separate trusts for the benefit of the decedent's children.

* * *

Section 2056(b)(7)(B) defines qualified terminable interest property as property which passes from the decedent, in which the surviving spouse has a qualifying income interest for life, and as to which an election has been made. In order for the income interest to qualify under § 2056(b)(7)(B), the surviving spouse must be entitled to all the income from the property, payable at least annually, and no person may have the power to appoint any part of the property to any person other than the surviving spouse during the spouse's life. In addition, an irrevocable election must be made by the executor on the estate tax return with respect to such property. Section 2056(b)(7)(B)(iv) provides that a specific portion of property shall be treated as separate property.

The trust, as amended, provides that all the income is paid solely to the wife for her life, at least annually, and that no person other than the wife has an interest in the trust corpus during her life. You intend to elect for treatment as qualifying terminable interest property, a fractional share of the trust property defined by means of a formula and computed in a manner necessary to reduce the decedent's federal estate tax liability to zero. The temporary regulation, § 22.2056–1, provides that such a partial election is valid. The fractional share will be determined in the following manner. The numerator of the fraction will be the smallest amount of the deduction under § 2056(b)(7) that will, after taking into account the allowable unified credit and any other allowable credits and deductions, result in no federal estate tax being imposed on the decedent's estate. The denominator of the fraction will be the value of the trust corpus as finally determined for federal estate tax purposes less any amounts paid out of the trust fund (such as specific bequests, estate taxes, inheritance taxes, any other debts of the estate, decedent, or beneficiaries that are paid out of the trust fund).

The proposed election of the interest of the trust passing to the surviving spouse will result in determination of a specific portion, after final valuation of the decedent's gross estate and taking into account all allowable deductions and credits. Since the surviving spouse has a qualifying income interest in the trust for life, payable at least annually, no other person has an interest in the trust during the spouse's life, and no one has the power to appoint any part of the trust to anyone other than the spouse, the requirements of § 2056(b)(7) are satisfied as to the fractional share subject to the election. Accordingly, the fractional share subject to the election will be treated as qualifying terminable interest property described in § 2056(b)(7) for which a marital deduction will be allowable under § 2056(a).

The value of the decedent's taxable estate shall be determined, in part, by deducting from the value of the gross estate an amount equal to the value of the specific portion (fractional share) of the trust property subject to the election. That same fractional share of the trust will be taxable to the surviving spouse or the surviving spouse's estate under §§ 2519 or 2044, as the case may be.

If all property included in the decedent's gross estate which does not qualify for the marital deduction, excluding the family trust, does not exceed all allowable credits and other deductions, the fractional share of the trust treated as qualified terminable interest property as described above will reduce the decedent's federal estate tax to zero.

¶ 16,411

[¶ 16,413]

Note on Partial Election as an Alternative to Disclaimer

The executor has a considerably longer period of *time to decide* on how much to retain as QTIP than is permitted a disclaiming spouse. An estate tax QTIP election is made on the estate tax return, and a six-month extension to file the return can be obtained under § 6081. See Reg. § 20.6081–1. Under § 2518(b)(2), a disclaimer must be made within nine months (unless the spouse is under 21 years of age). Cf. Rev. Rul. 83–26, 1983–1 C.B. 234 (QTIP election does not bar later disclaimer which was otherwise timely).

[¶ 16,421]

3. UNDERMARITALIZATION

Disclaimers are also important in cases of "undermaritalization." Consider Jeff and Barbara. Jeff's will contained the following bequest for the benefit of Barbara:

I give all of my property to Granite National Bank as Trustee to be held, managed and disposed of as follows:

a.   During the continuance of the trust the Trustee shall distribute the trust income to my beloved wife, Barbara. In addition, the Trustee shall distribute to Barbara so much of the principal of the trust as shall be required for her health, education, maintenance, and support. Finally, the Trustee shall also distribute to such of my children as Barbara shall select such amounts as she shall determine of the principal of the trust estate.

[handwritten:] Busts the QTIP.

b.   The trust shall terminate upon the death of Barbara. Upon termination, the trust property shall be distributed to my then living lineal descendants *per stirpes*.

The trust does not qualify for the marital deduction as a QTIP because Barbara has the power to cause a distribution to be made from the trust to someone other than herself during her lifetime. See § 2056(b)(7)(B)(ii)(II) ("The surviving spouse has a qualifying income interest for life if—* * * no person has a power to appoint any part of the property to any person other than the surviving spouse."). Accordingly, the marital deduction will be available to Jeff's estate only if: (1) Barbara elects to take against Jeff's will (if such election is available under state law); (2) all of Jeff's children make a qualified disclaimer of their interests in the trust; or (3) Barbara disclaims the tainting special power of appointment that appears in Jeff's will (in which case the trust will qualify for QTIP treatment). See Reg. § 25.2518–3(a)(1)(i); Priv. Ltr. Rul. 8935024.

[handwritten: Cool! If Barbara "disclaims" the power of appointment the QTIP is saved.]

[¶ 16,429]

4. DISCLAIMERS BY THIRD PARTIES

Disclaimers by persons other than the surviving spouse are sometimes the only means by which the gift to the surviving spouse can be qualified for the marital deduction. Suppose, for example, that Mom's will provides for a trust for Dad and their three children, with income to be distributed quarter-annually to Dad and the three children. The trust will qualify for the marital deduction only if the children are able to disclaim their interests in the trust and Dad remains as the sole income beneficiary—because of the requirements of § 2056(b)(7) for Qualified Terminable Interest Property. The children may retain any remainder interest they have in the trust if the children's remainder interest was separately created by the transferor.

[¶ 16,431]

Private Letter Ruling 9003007

October 6, 1989

Does D's wife have a qualifying income interest for life in the property described below, within the meaning of § 2056(b)(7)(B)(ii)?

FACTS

D, the decedent, died in 1987. Article Four of D's will provided for the establishment of a trust for the benefit of D's wife and children. Section A–1 of Article Four of the will provided for the distribution of trust income as follows:

> The Trustees shall pay such amount of the income of said trust as they, in their discretion, deem appropriate to my wife * * * for life in monthly or other convenient installments, not less frequently than annually. The remainder of said income, after such payment to my said wife, shall be equally divided between my children * * * and * * *, if living, and their descendants, per stirpes, if not.

Under Article Six, section D of the will, the trustee of any trust administered under the will may encroach upon the corpus of the trust "for the benefit of the income beneficiary thereof to the extent the trustee deems necessary."

Within nine months of D's death, D's children and adult grandchildren filed qualified disclaimers regarding their income rights in the trust. Specifically, each disclaimed "any beneficial interest in whatever capacity in the income of the trust." A guardian ad litem filed similar disclaimers on behalf of the minor grandchildren and the unborn and unascertained contingent beneficiaries. For purposes of this technical advice we assume the disclaimers were qualified disclaimers under § 2518.

LAW AND ANALYSIS

* * *

Section 2056(b)(7)(B)(ii) provides that the surviving spouse has a qualifying income interest for life if the surviving spouse is entitled to all the income from the property, payable annually or at more frequent intervals, and no person has a power during the spouse's lifetime to appoint any part of the property to anyone other than the surviving spouse.

* * *

Under the terms of D's will, the trustees were required to distribute all of the income of the trust currently. The amount payable to D's wife was whatever the trustees in their discretion found appropriate. In the event that not all of the income of the trust was paid to D's wife in any given year, the remaining income would have been required to be distributed to D's children or their descendants.

D's children and adult grandchildren have executed disclaimers of their right to receive income from the trust. Additional disclaimers have been executed on behalf of D's minor grandchildren and the unborn and unascertained contingent beneficiaries. Under applicable state law, an interest disclaimed passes as if the disclaimant had predeceased the decedent. Thus, as a result of these disclaimers, D's wife is now the only person to whom the trustees are authorized to pay any income of the trust during her lifetime.

A literal reading of the will suggests that the trustees may still be empowered to pay something less than all of the income of the trust to D's wife. However, we note that it was D's clearly stated intention that all the income be distributed currently, and the will contains no implication that income may be accumulated under any circumstances. Therefore, in view of the execution of the disclaimers by or on behalf of all other possible income beneficiaries, D's wife is now entitled to all the income from the trust, payable annually or at more frequent intervals.

Further, as a result of the disclaimers, the trustees power to invade corpus under Article Six, section D was limited to invasion for the benefit of D's spouse. As noted above, the trustees could only invade corpus for the benefit of the trust's "income beneficiary." As a result of the disclaimers, D's spouse was the sole income beneficiary of the Article Four trust. Accordingly, the trustees could invade corpus only for the benefit of D's spouse.

* * *

D's wife has a qualifying income interest for life in the property described above, within the meaning of § 2056(b)(7)(B)(ii).

G. MANNER IN WHICH DISCLAIMED PROPERTY PASSES

[¶ 16,501]

Although most state disclaimer statutes provide that disclaimed property will pass as if the disclaimant had predeceased the decedent, such statutes generally provide that this happens only if the decedent has not otherwise made provision in the instrument under which the disclaimed interest passes as to how property passes. If, as is usually the case, the QTIP trust is prefaced by words conditioning the bequest on the survivorship of the spouse, does a disclaimer by the surviving spouse of, say, one-half of the QTIP trust result in having the disclaimed property pass (i) to the remaindermen of the QTIP trust or (ii) to the persons who would have inherited the property under the provisions of the governing instrument that control the disposition of the estate if the surviving spouse predeceases the decedent? Obviously, where the remaindermen of the QTIP trust are identical to the persons designated to take the estate in the event the surviving spouse predeceases, the issue may be moot. However, even then, there may be a difference in the time of vesting of the disclaimed portion, depending upon whether or not the disclaimer of the interest in the QTIP trust accelerates the remainder interest.

In order to avoid these types of questions, the draftsman should be careful to preface the nonmarital trust (or other trust that is to serve as the recipient of disclaimed property) with language clearly identifying that trust as the intended recipient of the nonelective property.

> *Example.* "I give the residue of my estate, [including all property which may be disclaimed by my wife,] * * * to my trustees.* * * "

Problem

[¶ 16,510]

1. For the majority of wills, clients tell their lawyers that "I want it all to go to my spouse, and if my spouse does not survive me, I want it all to go to the kids." What drawbacks, if any, are there to the following strategy: Lawyer prepares a will in which (1) Client's entire estate passes to Spouse or to the children if Spouse does not survive Client (technically the gift will be *"per stirpes"* to Client's "lineal descendants who survive" Client) and (2) if Spouse survives Client but disclaims the estate, the disclaimed property is to pass to Spouse, as trustee, to be held, managed and disposed of for the benefit of Spouse and Client's lineals, Spouse's discretion to make distributions being limited by an ascertainable standard, i.e., being limited to those amounts necessary for the health, education, maintenance, and support of Spouse and Client's lineals?

2. Section 2010(c)'s applicable exclusion amount is scheduled to increase to $ 3.5 million in 2009 from $2 million in 2006 (and outright repeal in 2010). Even with the scheduled return to a $1 million applicable exclusion amount in 2011, might not clients with less than $3.5 million in property be willing to "gamble" and sign the will proposed in the preceding problem rather than "spend the money" for a more sophisticated document that anticipates the return of the $1 million applicable exclusion amount in 2011, the "betting" being that it "will never happen"?

Chapter 17

WHEN TO MAKE INTERSPOUSAL TRANSFERS

A. OBJECTIVES

[¶ 17,001]

Under what circumstances should one spouse undertake to make *lifetime transfers to the other spouse?* Obviously, love and affection is the prime motivation for such transfers. But oftentimes it seems that such transfers (other than those associated with commemorative occasions) tend to be deferred unless tax considerations provide the catalyst. The focus of the materials in this chapter will be on the tax considerations underlying death-time and lifetime transfers.

B. SEPARATE PROPERTY

[¶ 17,051]

1. BASIS CONSIDERATIONS

a. *If the Donor Spouse Dies First*

Suppose H gives W Greenacre at a time when it has a value of $200,000. With the availability of the unlimited marital deduction for transfers between spouses (as provided under § 2523) the transfer will have no federal gift tax consequences. Moreover, W will take H's basis in the property for federal income tax purposes. See § 1015. That means that when W later sells the property her gain or loss on the sale will be determined by reference to H's basis in the property. If H's basis in the property is $10,000 and W sells it for $225,000, she will have a gain of $215,000 for income tax purposes.

Next, assume that H held on to Greenacre until his death. His will provided that "everything goes to W." Thus, W ultimately gets Greenacre. And she gets it at no estate tax cost because of the unlimited marital deduction for estate tax purposes. However, since it was included in H's gross estate for estate tax purposes, the basis of Greenacre in W's hands is its fair market value at H's death (or its fair market value on the alternate valuation date if that election is available to H's estate (§ 2032)). Thus, if the fair market value of Greenacre for federal estate tax purposes is $225,000 and W

[handwritten margin note: Trnsfr @ deth = basis is FMV.]

sells the property for $225,000, she will have no gain for federal income tax purposes.

From the foregoing, it appears that the potential for a stepped-up basis is an important incentive for H to postpone gifts to W until his death. Notwithstanding the obvious appeal of the step-up potential, there are several other considerations which impact the decisional process.

[¶ 17,059]

b. If the Donee Spouse Dies First

Suppose W dies before H. Her will provided that "everything goes to H." If H had completed the gift to W before her death, Greenacre would come back to him with a stepped-up basis because it was subject to estate tax at W's death (even though no tax was paid because of the unlimited marital deduction). If Greenacre had a fair market value of $225,000 at W's death and H sold it for $225,000, he would realize no taxable gain.

Does that suggest that the best plan is for H to hold on to the property until he has some indication of whether he or W will die first? If he believes W will die first, couldn't he then make the gift to W and have it come back to him with a stepped-up basis? Yes and no! § 1014(e) provides that, in such a case, H would not enjoy a step-up in basis if W died within one year of H's transfer to her. However, if W survived the transfer for a period of more than one year, then the property could flow back to H with a stepped-up basis.

[handwritten margin note: C7 / No refund / step up if / death w/i / 1 year.]

[¶ 17,067]

2. POTENTIAL LOSS OF TAX SHELTER

If one spouse has little or no property, the possibility that the poorer spouse may die first is often incentive enough for the richer spouse to make transfers of property to the poorer spouse. Such gifts appeal to the richer spouse for several reasons. First, they give the richer spouse an opportunity to have the basis of the gifted property stepped-up for income tax purposes. Second, the property owned by the poorer spouse at death can be sheltered from later estate taxation at the death of the richer spouse if the poorer spouse puts it into a bypass trust. See ¶ 13,059. Once in the bypass trust, it can be made available to the richer spouse and, to the extent not needed by him or her, can pass to the poorer spouse's lineal descendants (or others as he or she may choose) free of estate tax. For discussion of the bypass trust, see Chapter 18.

Moreover, unless such gifts are made, the poorer spouse's estate either will not utilize or will underutilize the estate tax applicable exclusion allowance available to him or her. § 2010(c). For example, if the poorer spouse had died in 2004, the decedent would have had available to his or her estate an exclusion allowance of $1.5 million. If the poorer spouse died with less than $1.5 million of property, the family unit lost forever the opportunity to permanently shelter $1.5 million from all estate tax.

[¶ 17,070]

3. LIFETIME QTIPS

a. Unlimited Marital Deduction

Augmenting the estate of the poorer spouse in contemplation of the poorer spouse dying first can be accomplished relatively painlessly by making the gift to the poorer spouse in the form of a trust for the benefit of the poorer spouse for life with remainder to the beneficiaries selected by the richer spouse. The gift in trust will qualify for the unlimited marital deduction as Qualified Terminable Interest Property (QTIP) as a result of § 2523(f) so long as: (1) the poorer spouse is entitled to all of the income for life; (2) distributions from the trust to anyone other than the poorer spouse are barred so long as the poorer spouse lives; and (3) the richer spouse makes an express election to qualify the trust for the marital deduction.

A lifetime QTIP has the advantage of qualifying a gift for the marital deduction while allowing the donor spouse to control the ultimate enjoyment of the gifted property. At the death of the donee spouse, § 2044 required inclusion of the QTIP property in the estate of the donee spouse. Any lifetime disposition by the donee spouse of all or part of the donee spouse's qualifying income interest triggers gift taxation. § 2519(a).

[¶ 17,071]

b. Exclusion of QTIP From Estate of Donee Spouse

While there is way to know the real intentions of the surviving spouse, the scheme described in Revenue Ruling 98–8, 1998–1 C.B. 541, could be viewed as a cleaver attempt to circumvent the inclusion rule of § 2044 when applied to QTIP property. There, the surviving spouse acquired the remainder interest in the QTIP trust in exchange for a promissory note equal in value to the actuarially determined value of the remainder interest. Thereafter, the trustee distributed to the surviving spouse all of the QTIP trust property (and terminated the QTIP trust) whereupon the surviving spouse discharged the promissory note by making payment from the QTIP trust property that she received from the QTIP trustee. The end result? At the death of the surviving spouse whatever remained of the QTIP trust property would be included in the spouse's estate for estate tax purposes. However, had the remainderman not transferred the remainder interest to the surviving spouse, § 2044 would have required all of the QTIP trust property would have been included in the estate of the surviving spouse. Thus, the surviving spouse was able to "flush" the remainder from the surviving spouse's estate at its actuarially determined value at the time of the conveyance of the remainder, a date possibly long before the spouse's life estate "caved in" (upon the spouse's death). At the later date, of course, the full fair market value of the QTIP trust would have been included in the estate of the surviving spouse as required by § 2044. Remaining is the question as to the tax consequences to the surviving spouse at the time the surviving spouse acquired the remainder interest. This proved to be "the rub". The IRS, in Revenue Ruling 98–8, concluded that the surviving spouse made a gift at the time the remainder interest was transferred to the surviving spouse. The IRS valued the gift as "equal to the greater of the (i) the value of the remainder interest (pursuant to § 2519), or (ii) the value of the property or cash transferred to the holder of the remainder interest (pursuant to §§ 2511 and 2512)."

Several points were crucial to the IRS analysis in Revenue Ruling 98–8 and their explication is most interesting. Of particular interest is the manner in which the IRS disposed of the taxpayer's adequate and full consideration argument. The IRS reasoned that since the surviving spouse, when acquiring the remainder interest, was acquiring an asset already subject to inclusion in that spouse's gross estate (as a result of § 2044), the acquisition did not constitute adequate and full consideration for estate and gift tax purposes for purposes of offsetting the value of the promissory note given by the surviving spouse (the giving of the note having the effect of depleting the surviving spouse's estate). Accordingly, the giving of the promissory note constituted a gift from the surviving spouse to the remainderman. As explained by the IRS, "any other result would subvert the legislative intent and statutory scheme underlying § 2056(b)(7)."

The other point relied upon by the IRS in 98–8 was rooted in § 2519 which provides that "any disposition of all or part of a qualifying income interest" by the surviving spouse is "treated as a transfer of all interests in such property other than the qualifying income interest." The court concluded that there is "little distinction" between acquisition by the surviving spouse of the remainder interest as described and "sale and commutation transactions treated as dispositions in the regulations." In all these cases "the spouse receives outright ownership of property having a net value equal to the value of the spouse's income interest"—and as was the case on the facts described in Revenue Ruling 98–8.

[¶ 17,073]

c. *Exclusion of 'Comeback QTIP' From Estate of Donor Spouse*

Several Letter Rulings suggest how to structure lifetime QTIPs without subjecting the richer spouse to a retained interest which may cause the property to be included in the richer spouse's estate. Private Letter Ruling 9007015 concluded that if a QTIP trust was created by the donor spouse and the QTIP election was made at the time the trust was created, the trust will be includible in the estate of the surviving spouse, and not the donor spouse, even if the donee spouse died first and the trust was thereafter administered for the benefit of the donor spouse (after the death of the donee spouse). If the donee spouse dies first, the donor spouse's interest is treated as being *created* by the donee spouse rather than *retained* by the donor spouse.

A special or limited power of appointment may be used in conjunction with a lifetime QTIP trust in order to control the disposition of the property by the donee spouse. Private Letter Ruling 8944009 states that the donor spouse may give the donee spouse a testamentary power of attorney to appoint the trust assets to his or her creditors. The donor spouse was held not to have a retained life estate because of the power of the donee spouse to appoint the corpus to their creditors. A donor spouse may also create a special or limited power in the trust agreement that only allows the donee spouse to appoint the trust to the donor or the donor's issue. In Pvt. Ltr. Rul. 9140069, the Service held such a trust would qualify for lifetime QTIP treatment and the donor spouse could take a gift tax marital deduction. Furthermore, it was again concluded that, if the trust corpus is included in the taxable estate of the donee spouse, any reversionary interest to the donor spouse is not considered a "retained interest" subject to taxation under §§ 2036 and 2038.

[¶ 17,080]

4. LIFETIME CREATION OF MUTUAL ESTATE TRUSTS

One strategy calls for spouses to make roughly equalizing transfers of property between themselves so as to cause all the affected property to get a new basis for income tax purposes at the death of the first of them to do, to take the risk out of the chance that the poorer spouse will die first (with little property to have the benefit of the tax free basis step up at death rule of § 1014(b)(6). Spoken about by David Handler, a Chicago lawyer, this technique contemplates lifetime creation of estate trusts—and is not free of complexity or risk of misstep.

Estate trusts created at the death of the first spouse to die were considered at ¶ 14,367. In sum, an estate trust does not run afoul of the nondeductible terminable interest rule and qualifies for the marital deduction. One of its essential feature is a requirement, among several others noted in the materials at ¶¶ 14,347 through 14,377, that the trust property, at the death of the trust beneficiary—by definition, the surviving spouse—be distributed to the estate of the surviving spouse to be distributed under the will of the surviving spouse (or to the surviving spouse's intestate takers if the surviving spouse has no effective will as to the trust property).

There is little current tax incentive to use the estate trust device when the first spouse dies. In fact it may be disadvantageous from an income tax standpoint because, by definition, an estate trust contemplates warehousing of the trust income in the trust—and the taxation of the income to the trust (rather than to the trust beneficiary). Taxing the trust income to the trust rather than to the beneficiary is likely to result in a greater income tax bill than having the trust income distributed to the trust beneficiary and taxed to the trust beneficiary in the year it is earned by the trust. Why? Because of "rate compression", the technique Congress settled on to discourage warehousing trust income in a trust. § 1(f); ¶ 21,351. With rate compression, trust income in excess of $10,000 is taxed at the top income tax bracket. By way of contrast, individual nontrust income taxpayers do not reach the top bracket until their income is more than $300,000. In as much as few beneficiaries are in the top income tax bracket, normally there is income tax incentive to distribute the trust income to the beneficiary so it can be taxed at the lower income tax rates rather than the higher trust income tax rates.

That noted, lifetime estate trusts—as contrasted with a deathtime created estate trust—are said to offer an important advantage, to wit, the opportunity to get a tax free new basis—hopefully, a higher basis—in the trust property in both trusts at the death of the first spouse to die! Such a result would mean

¶ **17,080**

that spousal property—the property of both spouses, not just that of the deceased spouse—could be sold with little or no gain recognition shortly after the death of the first spouse to die.

In the ordinary case, where the estate trust is established at the death of the first spouse to die, only that person's property gets a tax free basis step up at his or her death. The lifetime estate trust technique contemplates that each spouse will establish, while they both live, an estate trust for the other spouse. Each spouse would retain, so long as he or she was living, a § 2038 power to amend the trust to alter the rules governing distributions from the trust to the other spouse.

Example. When H dies, for example, *first,* W's trust for his benefit would be distributed to his executor for distribution under his will—and the trust property would all get a new income tax basis under § 1014(b)(6). In the meantime, the property held in the estate trust H created for W will be included in his estate under § 2038 because of his retained power. That will result in the trust property in second trust getting a new basis at the death of the first spouse to die as well. Neither grantor can be trustee of either trust.

[¶ 17,085]

5. IMPACT OF STATE GIFT AND DEATH TAXES

Few states have gift taxes—and, for that reason, lifetime interspousal transfers can generally be said to be free of state gift taxes. Similarly, few, if any, states have state death taxes that are a factor in planning interspousal transfers. For additional discussion of state death systems, see ¶ 7475.

C. COMMUNITY PROPERTY

[¶ 17,101]

1. BASIS CONSIDERATIONS

For basis purposes, community property will oftentimes enjoy a distinct advantage over separate property. At the death of the first spouse to die, both halves of the community property—his 50 percent and her 50 percent—receive a new basis. See § 1014(b)(6). Thus, the basis of community property in the hands of the beneficiaries is not affected by the order of the spouses' deaths.

In the ordinary case, lifetime gifts of community property from one spouse to the other spouse have distinct disadvantages. Most importantly, such gifts cause the property to lose its character as community property and to become the separate property of the recipient spouse. Once it becomes separate property, the tax analysis appearing at ¶ 17,051 as to separate property must be applied. A quick review will demonstrate plainly, that insofar as basis is concerned, it is better to retain property as community property until the death of the first spouse to die rather than to convert it to the separate property of one of the spouses. Once it is converted, then much basis planning depends upon the order in which the spouses die (and this, much to the chagrin of the tax planner, is somewhat difficult to predict, let alone control). All too often the predicted order of deaths does not materialize and the poorer spouse dies first with the resulting loss of the opportunity for basis step-up.

[¶ 17,109]

2. TAX SHELTER IMPACT

One reason given for lifetime gifts of property from the richer spouse to the poorer spouse was to make certain that the poorer spouse had sufficient property to soak up his or her unified credit in the event the poorer spouse died first. Accordingly, it makes little sense to make lifetime gifts of community property from one spouse to another. Community means equal ownership by the spouses and the effective elimination of any concern about a poorer spouse underutilizing the unified credit.

[¶ 17,117]

3. STATE DEATH TAXES

As in the case of separate property (see discussion at ¶ 17,075), state death taxes generally are not imposed on transfers at death of community property from one spouse to the other. See ¶ 7475. Therefore, given the disadvantages of lifetime transfers of community property, taxpayers should forgo the opportunity to transfer community property from one spouse to the other free of *state* gift tax (as they may do in most states). See ¶ 17,085.

D. RELIEF FOR TRANSFERS WITHIN THREE YEARS OF DEATH

[¶ 17,201]

For many years, Congress insisted that transfers within three years of death be recaptured for estate tax purposes. Beginning in 1982 as to persons dying that year, the requirement was largely eliminated. The rule was retained, however, for purposes of determining eligibility for the three special interest relief provisions, to wit, § 303, redemptions of closely held stock to pay death taxes; § 2032A, special use valuation for real property used in a closely held business; and § 6166, extension of time to pay estate tax on stock in a closely held business. In each case, eligibility depends upon whether the closely held business interest constitutes a specified percentage of the decedent's estate. § 2035(c).

As a result of § 2035(c)(1) and (2), taxpayers who inadvertently restructure their estates immediately preceding death—perhaps by taking advantage of the unlimited marital deduction—can still avail themselves of these relief provisions. For discussion of these relief provisions, see ¶¶ 24,801–24,877.

By way of special emphasis, note that the special treatment described in the preceding paragraph does not require the transferred property to be

¶ 17,201

included in the decedent's gross estate for estate tax purposes. It only requires that the transferred property be included in the computation that must be made to determine eligibility for these relief provisions.

Problem

[¶ 17,210]

Chatsworth, age 28, and Belle, age 60, were recently married. Belle has learned that she has an incurable condition that will likely prevent her from living out her normal life expectancy. Chatsworth has a $2 million estate as a result of gifts from his father. The property consists of shares of Microsoft, an actively traded security, that were transferred to Chatsworth when he was a child, the shares having been acquired by the father at the time of the initial public offering of the stock. The stock's basis in Chatsworth's hands is significantly below its current market value. Chatsworth and Belle also own a condominium that they use as a personal residence. It is heavily mortgaged and they are jointly liable on the debt. What planning might be attractive to Chatsworth and Belle under the foregoing circumstances?

Part V

THE BYPASS TRUST AND RELATED GIFT PLANNING

Chapter 18

POWERS OF APPOINTMENT: DRAFTING THE BYPASS TRUST

A. OBJECTIVES

[¶ 18,001]

Trusts are often said to have been created to provide the beneficiaries with professional property management. Practically speaking, however, claiming to use a trust so as to obtain professional property management is an excuse to "cover" the more fundamental decision that the trust beneficiaries need protection from predators who lurk about. (In some instances, the most feared predators are the trust beneficiaries themselves.) Clearly, a trust is not necessary to accomplish professional property management. Any property owner is free to secure whatever property management that he or she thinks appropriate to the circumstances.

Planning for successive enjoyment is also a reason for creating a trust. In the typical case, the spouse is to enjoy for a time, and then the children, and then perhaps the grandchildren, before the property finally comes to rest in more remote descendants. Again, practically speaking, providing for successive enjoyment is, for some donors, an acceptable means for describing their need for control, i.e., an acceptable means for donors to say to the trust beneficiaries, "Who knows better than me what's good for thee," a means of living on through property and control over the enjoyment of that property. Providing for successive enjoyment is the stuff of future interests, an indispensable part of all will and trust drafting. Successive enjoyment is nontax in nature and is the subject of Chapter 5.

Tax planning is another reason often given for wanting to create a trust. It is hard to argue with the appeal of placing property in trust for successive generations of beneficiaries where it can be enjoyed by those beneficiaries without being burdened by taxes at the death of the respective beneficiaries. These trusts, which bypass the trust beneficiaries for death tax purposes, are appropriately referred to as "bypass trusts." While unmarried persons can and do frequently make gifts in trust designed to bypass the beneficiaries' estates for death tax purposes, probably the most common situation involves married persons who couple together: (1) a gift in trust for the surviving spouse that will qualify for the marital deduction offered by § 2056 and (2) a bypass trust, sometimes referred to as the credit shelter trust, which is funded with the "tax-free amount," i.e., the amount which can pass free of estate tax at death because of the availability of § 2010(c)'s applicable exclusion amount ($2 million in 2006 but scheduled to increase to $3.5 million in 2009).

Example. H died in 2005. His will contained the following provision: "All my property to my beloved wife, W." H had made no lifetime gifts and his federal estate tax returns reflected an adjusted gross estate of $3 million. All of this property passed to W tax free pursuant to the unlimited marital deduction. § 2056(a). At W's death in 2006, assuming no debts or administration expenses and no appreciation or depreciation in the value of the property, the $3 million will generate a federal estate tax liability of $450,000 (estate tax of $1,230,800 less unified credit of $780,800). § 2001.

At his death, H could have created a trust for that portion of his property which was equal to the exemption equivalent to the unified credit available at the time of his death, meaning that $1.5 million would have flowed into the trust (which might have been called a bypass trust or a credit shelter trust). If the trust was structured properly, no part of the trust property would be taxed at W's death even though she enjoyed the benefit of the trust property. The balance of H's property, also $1.5 million, would have flowed free of trust to W and would qualify for the marital deduction (or could have been placed in trust for W for life so long as the trust was structured to satisfy the requirements of § 2056(b) for allowance of the marital deduction).

The obvious advantage to use of the bypass trust causes it to be the cornerstone of modern estate planning. Chapter 14 was dedicated to determining the circumstances in which property passing in trust for the benefit of the surviving spouse would qualify for the marital deduction. (As noted in previous chapters, such trusts are commonly referred to as "marital" trusts, or "A" trusts.) In this and succeeding chapters, the focus will shift to the bypass trust (commonly referred to as the "B" trust) and the powers over the income and corpus of that trust which can be enjoyed by a surviving spouse (and other beneficiaries of the trust) while still avoiding inclusion of trust property in the estate of the surviving spouse (or in the estates of other beneficiaries).

As noted above, taxpayers use trusts for either or both of the following reasons: tax planning and/or property management. See ¶ 13,401. In the cases where property management is not an issue and the bypass trust is created only for tax reasons, it is appropriate, then, to give the surviving spouse maximum control over the bypass trust without causing its inclusion in the surviving spouse's estate. This chapter will look at some of the "control devices" that can be given a surviving spouse short of causing the bypass trust to be taxed in the surviving spouse's estate. Particular emphasis will be placed on the special power of appointment.

The basic bypass trust can be refined. Methods for enabling the trustee of the bypass trust to deal efficiently with problems relating to the distribution and taxation of trust income are considered beginning at ¶ 21,400. Drafting

¶ 18,001

techniques that will minimize the impact of the generation-skipping transfer tax on the bypass trust scheme are considered in Chapters 9 and 23. Although the end-product of these techniques may appear complicated to those un-schooled in the bypass concept, the final bypass trust scheme will be nothing more than the natural step-by-step application of the simple concepts and goals that are developed in these chapters.

B. POWERS OF APPOINTMENT IN GENERAL

[¶ 18,051]

At many places in this chapter, reference will be made to "powers of appointment" and the tax results that flow from the characterization of a power held by the trustee or beneficiary of a bypass trust as a "general power of appointment." What follows is but a general discussion on the subject of powers of appointment; more detailed information is available in a wealth of sources. See, e.g., P. Haskell and T. Bergin, Preface to Estates in Land and Future Interests, 149–177 (2d ed. 1984).

A power of appointment consists of the right, exercisable during life or by will, to designate the recipients of income or corpus from a fund subject to the power. The specific terms of the power of appointment—(1) how it is to be exercised; (2) when it is able to be exercised; (3) who are the permissible recipients of appointed funds (appointees); and (4) what funds are subject to the power—are established by the donor of the power. The donor can create the power by will or by inter vivos instrument (such as a trust). The power can be presently exercisable, or limited to exercise on some future date or upon the occurrence of some particular event.

[¶ 18,059]

1. HISTORY OF POWERS OF APPOINTMENT

Powers of appointment had their roots in England. A property owner, who we will refer to as the settlor (S), wanting to make a will at a time when wills were not permitted, might convey his property to another person, who we will refer to as the trustee (T), with a direction to hold the property for S's life and at S's death to dispose of the property as S directs in a separate writing. S would be described as the *donor* of a power of appointment. In this example, S would also be the *donee* of the power, but if the example is changed and S's wife, W, is given the power to dispose of the property at S's death by direction given to T, W would become the *donee* of the power.

[¶ 18,067]

2. TAXABILITY OF POWERS OF APPOINTMENT

Sections 2041 and 2514 deal with the estate and gift tax consequences that flow from the holding and the exercise of powers of appointment. As a general rule, powers of appointment are divided into two categories for purposes of assigning tax consequences. If a donee of a power can exercise the power in favor of self, creditors, estate, or the creditors of the estate, the donee is deemed to have a "general power of appointment." If the donee cannot exercise the power in favor of any of the four above-mentioned classes of appointees, the donee is considered to have a "special power of appointment."

If a donee dies holding a general power of appointment, all property subject to that power will be included in the donee's gross estate. § 2041(a). If, during the donee's lifetime, the donee *exercises* the general power of appointment in favor of some appointee other than himself or herself, that exercise will be a taxable gift by the donee/powerholder to the appointee. § 2514(a) and (b). If the donee *releases* his general power of appointment, the release will, in most instances, be considered a taxable gift from the donee/powerholder to the "taker in default." Id. The taker in default is the person who will receive the property subject to the general power of appointment if the power is never exercised by the powerholder. The instrument creating the power of appointment usually identifies the taker in default.

There are several exceptions to the basic rule that a power of appointment exercisable in favor of oneself is included in that person's gross estate at death. If the power is limited by an "ascertainable standard relating to the health, education, support, or maintenance of the decedent," it will not be included in the powerholder's gross estate. § 2041(b)(1)(A). See ¶ 18,239.

The adverse party exception exempts powers from the powerholder's gross estate in cases where the power can be exercised only in conjunction with the donor of the power or an individual who has an interest in the trust funds that is adverse to that of the powerholder. § 2041(b)(1)(C). Finally, if a powerholder is able to withdraw an amount not exceeding the greater of $5,000 or 5 percent of the value of trust assets in a given year, and the power is noncumulative, the existence of this lifetime withdrawal power will not result in the inclusion of any trust property in the gross estate of the powerholder (except in the year of death). § 2041(b)(2); Reg. § 20.2041–3(d)(3).

Similarly, there are several exceptions to the basic rule that the exercise or release of a power of appointment exercisable in favor of oneself, one's creditors, one's estate or the creditors of the estate is a taxable transfer for gift tax purposes. If the exercise or release can be made only in conjunction with the donor of the power or someone whose interest in the trust fund is adverse to that of the powerholder, the power shall not be deemed a general power of appointment. § 2514(c)(3). Moreover, if the holder of a power of withdrawal allows it to "lapse," that lapse will be considered a taxable release only insofar as the amount lapsed in a given year exceeds the greater of $5,000 or 5 percent of trust assets. § 2514(e).

The exercise or release of a special power during the lifetime of the powerholder *generally* is not subject to the federal gift tax.

If a person dies holding a special power of appointment, generally speaking, there will be *no inclusion in that person's gross estate* of the trusts assets subject to the power. One exception to this rule, *inter alia,* relates to special powers exercised so as to create another power of appointment the exercise of which, under state law, will not be subject to the Rule Against Perpetuities vesting requirements. The exercise of the special power creating the power will be a taxable event. §§ 2041(a)(3); 2514(d). (Apparently, Delaware, for one, may allow a special power to be exercised in this fashion. See James P. Spied, A Practical Look at Springing the Delaware Tax Trap to Avert Generation Skipping Transfer Tax, 41 R. Prop. Prob. & Trust J. 165 (2006).)

Another exception should be noted, although it is more properly the subject of Chapter 19 inasmuch as it regards the power of a transferor to affect enjoyment of the transferred property after the transfer has been accomplished (see ¶ 19,299). For example, suppose Hannah declares herself trustee of an irrevocable trust for her son, Jimmy, to last until Jimmy reaches age 21. Hannah reserves the right to distribute the trust property to Jimmy before age 21. While Hannah's right to accelerate Jimmy's enjoyment of the trust property is a special power of appointment (i.e., it cannot be exercised in favor of Hannah, her estate, her creditors, or the creditors of her estate), the power property will be included in Hannah's estate if she dies before making a complete distribution to Jimmy of the trust property. § 2038. By way of contrast, the materials in this chapter relate to the case where someone other than the transferor, i.e., someone other than Hannah, has the right to affect enjoyment of the transferred property. Described are the circumstances in which the existence of a general power of appointment, as distinguished from a special power, will cause the power property or the income therefrom to be taxed to the powerholder, it being suggested that special powers, except as noted, are generally free of tax consequences when held by nontransferors. It is this ability to hold a special power in specified situations and be free of adverse tax consequences that is the cornerstone of much of the planning to give trust beneficiaries some control over trust property.

Persons holding general powers of appointment are viewed for federal transfer tax purposes as actually having the property subject to the power. The rationale underlying this view is that the powerholder is able to reduce the property to his or her possession or apply it for his or her benefit simply by exercising the power in favor of self, creditors, estate, or the creditors of the estate. If the powerholder chooses to cause the property to flow to another, by exercising or releasing the power, or by allowing it to lapse, the powerholder is deemed to have chosen to make a gift of something "owned."

If a person has no desire to exercise a general power of appointment, either in favor of himself or herself or others, there is one method by which the person can dispose of the power. Section 2518, relating to disclaimers, allows the power recipient to refuse, in writing, to accept the power no later than nine months after the date the transfer was made (or nine months after the powerholder reaches age 21). See ¶ 16,325. If a proper § 2518 disclaimer is not made, the recipient is "stuck" with the general power of appointment for estate and gift tax purposes.

¶ 18,067

Problems

[¶ 18,077]

1. Who would the taker in default be if the instrument creating the power named no one as such?

2. Suppose W has the right to all of the income from the H Family Trust. In addition, W has the right to appoint so much or all of the trust property to any one or more of W's children. The trust agreement expressly states that W can exercise the power by will or by written notice to Trustee during W's lifetime. Upon receipt of such written notice during W's lifetime, Trustee is obligated to pay over to the indicated child or children the amount specified by W. If W gives Trustee written direction to deliver $100,000 of trust principal to W's child, Claude, has W made a taxable gift? Of what? See Reg. § 25.2514–1(b)(2).

3. In light of the foregoing analysis, would it be appropriate to describe § 2041 as an attribution provision? That is, § 2041 requires property subject of a general power of appointment to be included in the power-holder's gross estate for estate tax purposes. The effect is to cause a nontransferor, the powerholder, to have included in his or her estate the power property. Rhetorically speaking, would this not be inconsistent with the notion that the federal estate tax is imposed on the exercise by an individual of that individual's privilege to transfer property? See Chapter 6. Could it be explained that § 2041 is an *attribution* section in that it treats a *nontransferor* as a *transferor so as to cause the federal estate tax to apply?*

   Are there any other so-called attribution provisions in the federal estate tax? That is, are there any other provisions which cause property to be included in the gross estate of a nontransferor? See § 2044.

[¶ 18,079]

PRIVATE LETTER RULING 7903055
(October 18, 1978).

* * * [Y]ou ask about the includibility in the gross estate [of B] of a power of appointment created by [H's] trust.

* * * The trustees are to pay;

[T]he net dividends and income to [B] * * * for and during the term of her natural life. Upon her death the principal is given either outright or upon further trust, to her heirs-at-law and next of kin, in such manner, interests and proportions as she shall in and by her Last Will and Testament in that behalf direct, limit and appoint and in default of such appointment or insofar as the same shall fail effectually to dispose of said fund then unto the issue of [B]. * * *

* * * In exercising the power of appointment, [B, in her] * * * will provided that the principal of the trust was to pass outright to her four children in equal shares.

¶ 18,079

Section 2041(a)(2) provides that the value of the gross estate shall include the value of all property with respect to which the decedent had, at the time of her death, a general power of appointment. Section 2041(b)(1) defines general power of appointment as a power which is exercisable in favor of the decedent, her estate, her creditors or the creditors of her estate.

[Special Power Only]

[B] * * * possessed the testamentary power to appoint the principal of the trust only to her heirs-at-law or next of kin. She could not exercise the power in favor of herself, her estate, her creditors, or the creditors of her estate. Thus, at death, [B] * * * did not have a general power of appointment over the principal. * * * The principal will not be includible in her gross estate under § 2041 * * *.

[¶ 18,081]

REVENUE RULING 69–342

1969–1 C.B. 221.

* * *

The decedent's husband, who died in 1950, devised and bequeathed the residue of his estate to his wife for her life "with power to mortgage, sell, assign, and convey the same, and use and dispose of the proceeds thereof to all intents and purposes as if she were the absolute owner thereof." Upon her death, the unconsumed portion of the husband's estate, if any, was to be distributed in fee to their daughter. The decedent died in 1968. Under the laws of the state in which the decedent's husband's will was probated the quoted language is not construed to include a power to dispose of the property by gift.

Under the state law applicable to the administration of the deceased wife's estate, an absolute power of disposition given to the owner of a particular estate for life creates a life estate absolute in respect to the rights of creditors and purchasers, but subject to any future estate provided by the grantor.

Section 2041(a)(2) provides that the value of the gross estate shall include the value of all property with respect to which the decedent has at the time of his death a general power of appointment created after October 21, 1942. A power of appointment created by will is, except as provided by § 2041(b)(3), considered to have been created on the date of testator's death.

Section 2041(b) defines the term "general power of appointment" as a power that is exercisable in favor of the decedent, his estate, his creditors, or the creditors of his estate. An exception is provided where a power to consume, invade, or appropriate property for the benefit of the decedent is limited by an ascertainable standard relating to the health, education, support, or maintenance of the decedent.

Reg. § 20.2041–1(b) provides that the term "power of appointment" includes all powers which are in substance and effect powers of appointment regardless of the nomenclature used in creating the powers and regardless of local property law connotations.

The language of the husband's will giving his wife the power to mortgage, sell, assign, and convey the property and use and dispose of the proceeds as if she were the absolute owner thereof clearly manifests his intention that his wife was to have the unlimited right to consume and dispose of the estate (except by gift) without reference to her needs or to any other standard. The interests of the remainderman are entirely subordinate to the desires of the wife, the husband having provided only that the remainderman receive the balance of the estate, if any, at his wife's death.

A power possessed by a lifetime beneficiary to consume, invade, or appropriate the estate for his own benefit, which power is not limited by an ascertainable standard, is within the statutory definition of a general power of appointment for purposes of the estate tax, notwithstanding the beneficiary's lack of power to exercise testamentary control over any unconsumed portion of the estate. * * *

Accordingly, it is held that the deceased wife possessed a general power of appointment, notwithstanding her lack of power to exercise testamentary control over the unconsumed portion of her predeceased husband's estate and notwithstanding that she did not possess the power during her lifetime to dispose of the property by gift. The value of the remaining property of her husband's estate is includible in her gross estate under § 2041.

[¶ 18,083]

Note

In Gaskill v. United States, 561 F.Supp. 73 (D.Kan.1983), aff'd per curiam, 787 F.2d 1446 (10th Cir.1986), on facts relatively identical to those found in Revenue Ruling 69–342, the district court found that the surviving spouse did not have a general power of appointment. In reaching its conclusion in favor of the taxpayer, the court distinguished a number of cases reaching contrary results on the ground that the *Gaskill* will stipulated that "all of the remainder of my estate" was to be distributed to the decedent's children after the death of the surviving spouse, whereas the dispositive provisions found in the cases reaching contrary results indicated that the respective decedents:

> explicitly recognized the possibility that the property held by the life tenants would diminish in quantity and value before that property found its way into the hands of the remaindermen by the use of language such as "the remainder of such residue remaining," "such of my estate as shall remain," and "whatever of my said property, if any * * *" The Gaskill will, in strong contrast, unambiguously directs that all of the life estate property shall go to the remaindermen at the life tenant's death.

Contrast the use of the word "all" in *Gaskill* and the conclusion reached by the court with the operative words described in Revenue Ruling 69–342. Note that in Revenue Ruling 69–342, the IRS concludes that the "interests of the remainderman are entirely subordinate to the desires of the wife." The court in *Gaskill,* on the other hand, says that while the surviving spouse "had unlimited powers to dispose of the life estate property," state law "imposed a correlative duty on her to make any such dispositions for full consideration and to hold the proceeds as a quasi-trustee for the remaindermen."

Problem

[¶ 18,085]

As a practical matter, there is enormous uncertainty as to how to do the tax and nontax accounting for life estates. Moreover, the life estate as a management device is clumsy. For example, suppose that the life tenant becomes incompetent. Rhetorically speaking, under what circumstances can the remaindermen assume responsibility for the property in which the life tenancy exists? Can they sell the homestead in those cases where Dad has been institutionalized and has no realistic prospect of returning to the homestead even though he insists that he "will return"? These practical considerations argue strongly for using a trust in every case where beneficial enjoyment of property is split between two or more persons. With a trust, title (and management) is in the hands of the trustee who is obligated to manage the property for the benefit of both the life tenant and the remaindermen. If circumstances dictate that the property be sold, the trustee can do so without obtaining the approval of either the life tenant or the remaindermen.

Nonetheless, there will be circumstances where a life tenancy can be useful. One such case may be with respect to the decedent's "homeplace." Consider the following provisions which create a life estate. Ask yourself whether all of the issues that come to your mind have been addressed. More importantly, in an effort to provide flexibility, has the draftsperson, perhaps inadvertently, given the surviving spouse a general power of appointment over the "homeplace"? Furthermore, consider whether the life estate qualifies for the marital deduction as qualified terminable interest property. Reg. § 20.2056(b)–7(h), Example (1); ¶ 14,589.

4.1. *Grant of Life Estate.* I give and devise to my spouse, during life, the right to the use and occupancy, rent-free, of any real property which is used by us as our principal residence, together with all improvements thereon (the "Homestead") at the time of my death. The term "Homestead" as used in this Item shall mean the original Homestead or any other Homestead acquired in lieu thereof. In the event the Homestead shall be community property, "Homestead" shall be construed to refer to only my individual one-half interest in these premises. My spouse shall be entitled to full possession and use of the Homestead without the requirement of giving any bond or other security, and my spouse shall not be liable for waste or depreciation. My spouse, during life, shall keep the Homestead adequately insured against loss or damage, shall pay all insurance premiums, all taxes and assessments, and shall maintain and keep the Homestead in good condition and repair.

4.2. *Sales, Lease, or Release of Life Estate.* My spouse shall have the right to sell, exchange, rent, or lease all or any part of the Homestead upon such terms and conditions as my spouse shall deem advisable. Any rental income received from leasing the Homestead shall be paid to my spouse. In the event my spouse elects to sell the Homestead, my spouse's deed alone shall be sufficient to convey the complete title without any obligation on the part of the purchaser to look to the application of the proceeds. Should my spouse no longer desire to retain the life estate provided for in paragraph 4.1, my spouse may release all or any portion of the life estate by an instrument in writing duly acknowledged and filed in the deed records in the county in which the Homestead is located. If, in the opinion of the Trustee of my living Trust, my spouse is unable to occupy the Homestead, the Trustee may exercise the foregoing power to release my spouse's life estate in the Homestead.

4.3. *Termination of Life Estate.* Upon the death of my spouse, or upon the prior release of my spouse's life estate, or upon the sale of the Homestead to the extent the proceeds are not reinvested in another Homestead within one year from the date of sale, my interest in the Homestead or the proceeds thereof not so reinvested shall be delivered to the Trustee of my living Trust, to be held, managed, and disposed as though an integral part of the trust estate. If my spouse fails to survive me, my spouse's life estate shall lapse and my interest in the Homestead shall be added to residue of my estate.

[¶ 18,087]

3. NONTAX DRAFTING AND PLANNING CONSIDERATIONS

a. When to Create

Holding a general power of appointment (GPA) at death will cause the property subject to the power to be included in the powerholder's gross estate for federal estate tax purpose. See § 2041(a); ¶ 18,067. On the other hand, holding a special power will not cause the property to be included in the powerholder's gross estate (unless the powerholder is also the person who created the power). See § 2038. From this it is safe to conclude that GPAs should be created only when no other dispositive device is available to the donor.

With these considerations in mind, under what circumstances would a person have no alternative but to create a GPA? Think about it for a few minutes. Do you find it hard to imagine when a special power would not do all that the donor wanted? Think about it in these terms. A GPA is equivalent to ownership. (Otherwise the property subject to the GPA would not be included in the powerholder's gross estate for federal estate tax purposes.) If the donor of the power wanted the powerholder to have "ownership" of the property subject to the power, the donor would have given it to the powerholder in fee simple absolute! (Do you agree with this conclusion?) By electing to subject the power property to a trust, the donor has essentially made a determination to maintain control over the power property. If the donor wants control, why give it up by creating a GPA?

From the foregoing analysis, could you reasonably conclude that GPAs are created *only* for tax reasons? How's that? Could it be said that GPAs are created only when the donor wants some tax benefit that would otherwise be denied the donor if the donee of the property did not have a GPA over the property? This leads to the question, when do you create GPAs? Practically speaking, isn't it fair to conclude that you create GPAs only in two cases? The obvious first case is in conjunction with a taxpayer's efforts to provide for the marital deduction through the use of the life estate/general power of appointment exception to the nondeductible terminable interest rule. See § 2056(b)(5) and discussion at ¶ 14,459.

The second case? Only one comes to mind. That is, in conjunction with an effort to provide for the annual exclusion for gift tax purposes though the use of a *Crummey* trust. For discussion, see ¶ 19,451.

Can you think of any other cases where you would use a GPA? Keep this question in mind as you go through the balance of these materials.

Thus, there is a certain anomaly here. On the one hand, taxpayers shy away from creating GPAs because they will have estate and gift tax consequences for the powerholder. On the other hand, taxpayers are induced to create GPAs to claim certain tax benefits.

[¶ 18,091]

b. Donor's Burden: Preventing Inadvertent Exercise

Once you assume that GPAs are created only to gain tax benefits, is it not logical to assume that the donor of the power would prefer that the powerholder not exercise the power?

How does the donor prevent exercise? Prevention is impossible if the power is worthy of being described as a GPA. However, there is no reason why the donor cannot insist that the powerholder satisfy certain conditions as a prerequisite to effective exercise of the power. Such conditions might include requiring the powerholder to exercise the GPA only by a provision in the powerholder's will and by further requiring the powerholder to make specific reference to the power if the exercise is to be effective. This has the advantage of preventing inadvertent exercise of a power by a "blind" reference clause. A blind reference clause might provide that "I exercise all powers of appointment that I may have whether known to me or not." See, e.g., Estate of Smith, 41 Colo.App. 366, 585 P.2d 319 (1978).

[¶ 18,099]

c. Donee's Burden: Effective Exercise

Should the powerholder exercise GPAs? Generally, the answer would seem to be yes. Consider the case of Mr. Poor. Mr. Poor was given a GPA over a trust created by his grandfather. The trust provides Mr. Poor with income for life with the remainder as Mr. Poor "shall appoint by will." Mr. Poor, a man of modest circumstances, has become dependent on the income he receives from the trust. He is now about to make a will giving "everything" to his beloved spouse, to whom he has been married for 38 years. Under the circumstances, it is difficult to believe that Mr. Poor would not want to capture the property subject to the power and direct it to his spouse. However, perhaps you can think of circumstances where Mr. Poor would not want to control the power property.

C. THE BYPASS TRUST

[¶ 18,151]

The bypass trust has enormous utility in solving both tax and nontax problems in arranging an orderly property disposition.

Example. Janet Smith consults you regarding an estate plan. She is 35 years old, is married to Geoffrey Dorset, age 37, and has two children, ages five and three. She has not been married previously.

Janet is worth about $3 million, most of which she has earned through skillful real estate investments. Like many of your clients, she has two primary estate planning objectives: (1) she wants to assure that Geoffrey and the children will be well taken care of, in the event that she predeceases them, and (2) she wants to minimize federal taxes on her estate as much as possible.

Geoffrey Dorset is no money-manager. Janet has confided to you that Geoffrey, a not-too-successful painter, is subject to "manic" periods when his financial judgment is totally lacking. She would like Geoffrey to enjoy the benefits of her accumulated wealth, but fears the results of having Geoffrey gain control over the money.

Janet could provide that all of her property is to go to Geoffrey in trust. The trust could be structured as a Qualified Terminable Interest Property (QTIP) Trust to qualify for the unlimited marital deduction (§ 2056(b)(7); for discussion, see ¶ 14,557), and, as so structured, would give Geoffrey the lifetime benefit of Janet's wealth and protect the funds from the dissipation that might occur if Geoffrey received the property outright.

The principal disadvantage to creating a QTIP trust for all of Janet's property is that the children may not receive benefits from the QTIP during Geoffrey's lifetime. For Janet, like many parents, this feature makes a QTIP trust an impossible alternative. Janet insists that at least part of her property must be available to her children during Geoffrey's life notwithstanding the estate tax consequences.

One possibility would be for Janet to leave what remained of her estate, after the transfer of a portion of her property to a QTIP trust for Geoffrey, to her children outright. While the funds would still be included in Janet's estate, they would avoid Geoffrey's estate by passing directly to the children. But Janet worries that if Geoffrey were beset by extraordinary expenses, the QTIP trust could be exhausted and Geoffrey would be destitute without an additional income source. Similarly, Janet worries that if the children are under 18 when she dies, a guardianship will be required for the property she has given them.

These problems make an outright transfer to the children unacceptable to Janet. For that reason, although outright gifts to the children are an attractive alternative from a tax-saving perspective, such a scheme does not meet Janet's nontax goals. She wants the property to be available to Geoffrey if a genuine need arises, and she also wants to assure that the property will be completely preserved and managed—something that the children could not do if they received the property outright while still very young.

A second alternative would involve using that part of Janet's estate remaining after the funding of the QTIP trust to fund a second trust. The trustee of this second trust would have discretionary authority to distribute income from the trust to Geoffrey if needed for his health, education, support, or maintenance. The trust would terminate on Geoffrey's death and the remaining trust property would be distributed outright to Janet's then living lineal descendants.

This trust takes care of only a part of Janet's concerns. It gives Geoffrey a "back-up" fund from which he can obtain money for necessities, but it fails to provide money management in the event that Geoffrey dies while the children are short of adulthood. If Geoffrey dies "early," a burdensome and costly financial guardianship will be necessary to take care of the money that has passed outright to the children. See ¶ 4051–4691. This problem can be addressed by modifying the termination provision such that the trust will not terminate until the later of Geoffrey's death or the eighteenth birthday of the youngest child. (Most parents choose an age later than 18. What practical and not-so-practical reasons can you give for this? Do you agree with this philosophy?) In the event that the trust does continue after Geoffrey's death, the trustee can be authorized to distribute trust income to the person with whom the children reside, also named in the trust instrument, for their health, education, support, and maintenance, until the trust terminates.

The most important characteristic of this second trust (from a tax planning perspective) is that it will not be included in Geoffrey's estate when he dies; instead, it will "bypass" Geoffrey's estate and pass to the next generation tax free.

Drafting a bypass trust need not be a difficult or confusing process; it can be done by asking (and answering) six basic questions, namely, (1) who is to be trustee; (2) what are the income distribution provisions; (3) what are the principal distribution provisions; (4) should a right of withdrawal be included; (5) should a special power of appointment be included; and (6) when does the trust terminate.

[¶ 18,159]

1. WHO SHALL BE TRUSTEE?

There are three possible choices for trustee of the bypass trust: the surviving spouse, another individual, or a corporate fiduciary. As mentioned earlier, taxpayers use trusts for tax planning and/or property management. Selection of a trustee will depend on the primary purpose served by the trust.

Property management is the dominant purpose served by the bypass trust developed for Janet Smith in the previous example. Janet wishes to prevent Geoffrey from obtaining unfettered control over the proceeds of her estate. In a situation such as this, it would defeat the purpose of the trust to make Geoffrey trustee of the bypass trust.

Assume, however, that Geoffrey is an able and skillful money-manager. How might this change the character of Janet's estate plan? For one thing, the QTIP trust may not be necessary, because Janet can be reasonably confident that Geoffrey will not dissipate any property he receives outright in satisfaction of a marital deduction bequest. The bypass trust, however, will continue to be necessary as a matter of tax planning, rather than property management. While Janet may have no qualms about leaving everything outright to a responsible Geoffrey when she dies, she nevertheless wants to avoid the "double inclusion" of any part of her property in both her and Geoffrey's estates. Since Geoffrey is a responsible money-manager, however, Janet sees little reason to hire a corporate fiduciary or other individual to serve as trustee of the "B" or bypass trust. Can Janet make Geoffrey trustee?

Problem

[¶ 18,165]

Is there a situation in which making Geoffrey trustee will cause the trust assets to be included in Geoffrey's estate when he dies? Think about the rules, stated in §§ 2033–2041 and 2044, for determining what will be included in a person's gross estate. Only pursuant to §§ 2041 and 2044 will property be included in a person's gross estate, even though that person never actually had beneficial ownership of those funds. Review § 2041, then answer the following question: If Geoffrey is the trustee, and he has discretion (not subject to any ascertainable standard relating to his health, education, support, or maintenance) to make payments to himself out of trust income, will he be deemed to have a taxable general power of appointment over the trust assets? Are there any circumstances when Geoffrey can be the trustee of the trust and also a beneficiary without having the trust property included in his estate at his subsequent death?

———

Whether a spouse should be named as trustee depends on two factors: (1) whether the trust has been established for the purposes of property management, i.e., to prevent the spouse from having control of trust property and (2) the kind of powers the trustee will have over distribution of trust income and principal to the surviving spouse.

If the spouse is not trustee, there remain available to the settlor the two additional choices mentioned earlier, namely, an individual other than the spouse or a corporate fiduciary. Each of these choices has its peculiar advantages and disadvantages. A corporate fiduciary will know what to expect in terms of the workload involved in administering the trust and, therefore, should be more efficient. On the other hand, the corporate fiduciary not only may be more expensive than an individual (who may serve out of friendship or a sense of "family duty") but also may be less sensitive to the needs of the individual beneficiaries. An individual trustee will usually be more familiar with the testator's desires and the needs of the beneficiaries, but the job of trustee may turn out to be far more burdensome than contemplated by either settlor or trustee. There is also the risk that, as the years pass, the trustee will lose track of the settlor's goals and begin to unconsciously substitute his or her value system (for that of the settlor) when exercising the trust's discretionary authority. Thus, as a practical matter, it is usually unwise to recruit an individual trustee unless that person can be made fully aware of what the responsibilities will be and is capable of discharging them. Sometimes a "trust committee" can be empowered by the settlor in the governing instrument to act to remove the trustee (as a safeguard against trustee excess or neglect).

[¶ 18,167]

2. WHAT ABOUT INCOME?

a. *Mandatory Pay*

The trustee can be empowered to deal with trust income in three different ways. First, the trustee can be instructed to distribute all trust income currently ("mandatory pay") to the person or persons designated as income beneficiaries. Each beneficiary's share of the income may be fixed or the trustee may have discretion to allocate among them. (What purpose would such a "spray" provision serve?)

It should be noted that the beneficiaries of the bypass trust will instinctively, at least initially, prefer that the instrument creating a bypass trust instruct the trustee to distribute all trust income to them currently. This is, in fact, what is done most of the time, but it is sometimes not the most effective course of action from the standpoint of tax minimization.

[¶ 18,175]

b. *Discretionary Pay Subject to a Standard*

The trustee could be authorized to distribute trust income to beneficiaries according to some ascertainable standard relating to the health, education, support, or maintenance of the trust beneficiaries. This would give the trustee the opportunity to accumulate income when it was not needed, while giving the beneficiaries a legally enforceable right to income when they could prove need. (Furthermore, should a grantor make suits by beneficiaries against the trustee easier or more difficult to prosecute? The answer would appear to depend on whose discretion the grantor trusted more—that of the trustee or that of the beneficiary. If the grantor has faith in the decisions made by the trustee, the grantor may shy away from subjecting the trustee's discretion to any kind of standard, unless imposition of such a standard was necessary for tax minimizing purposes.)

[¶ 18,183]

c. *Discretionary Pay*

The trustee could be given unfettered discretion over the distribution of trust income ("discretionary pay"). For example, among the possibilities, the trustee may have (1) discretion to "spray" the income among several persons, i.e., to pick and choose among a group of persons; or (2) discretion as to "timing," i.e., the ability to accelerate or withhold distributions. The instrument might empower the trustee to make decisions with some dominant purpose or purposes in mind, such as tax avoidance or being extrasensitive to the needs and desires of the beneficiaries.

Problem

[¶ 18,189]

Would guidelines for exercise of a trustee's powers give an unhappy beneficiary a toehold in prosecuting an abuse of discretion suit against the trustee? Does this make use of such guidelines questionable for the grantor/testator who wishes the trustee to act as freely as possible? In the absence of any expressed standards, what standards should govern the trustee's exercise of discretion? Would exculpatory language preclude any review of a trustee's conduct? Is such language in an instrument desirable? See Halbach, Problems of Discretion in Discretionary Trusts. 61 Colum. L. Rev. 1425 (1961); Restatement (Second) of Trusts § 187, Comment j, p. 408 (1959).

[¶ 18,191]

d. *Loss of Trust as a Tax Shelter*

Remember that the income from a bypass trust is a secondary source of income to the surviving spouse in an "A/B" trust scheme. The surviving spouse will have access to all the income from the "A," or marital, trust, which may be considerable, while mandatory distributions of income from the "B," or bypass, trust may have the undesirable effect of causing the distributed income to be taxed to the surviving spouse at rates higher than those that would have been paid by the trust had the income been accumulated. However, as a practical matter, given rate compression as applied to trust income (¶ 21,351), it is unlikely that the spouse will be in a higher tax bracket. Nonetheless, suppose that the spouse doesn't spend the income. It will stack up in the spouse's estate and be taxed at the spouse's death, at which time it probably will pass to the same persons who would have received it had it been retained in the bypass trust. Less may pass to these beneficiaries, however, because of unnecessary transfer taxation or possibly even as a result of the unlikely exposure of the income to excess income taxation in the hands of the distributees. Given these facts, it may be preferable for the trustee to distribute income subject to an ascertainable standard relating to beneficiary need, or subject to no standard other than the trustee's discretion.

[¶ 18,199]

e. Selection of Trustee

Selection of the surviving spouse as trustee for the bypass trust automatically eliminates one of the choices regarding income distribution. A spouse/trustee cannot be given unlimited discretion in deciding whether to make income distributions to himself of herself or to accumulate income. Giving a spouse/trustee such discretion is tantamount to giving the spouse a general power of appointment over income, and would cause the inclusion of likely all the bypass trust in the spouse's gross estate. § 2041(a)(2).

Whether a spouse/trustee can avoid having the trust income taxed to him or her in cases where distribution of that income is limited by an ascertainable standard is determined by application of § 678(a)(1). See ¶ 18,257–18,279.

[¶ 18,207]

f. Basis Opportunities and Hazards

As was suggested in ¶ 18,191, critical tax-minimizing opportunities may be forfeited when a trustee is deprived of the discretion to decide whether income will be distributed to the surviving spouse or accumulated. When the trustee is deprived of this discretion, the trustee does not have the opportunity to compare the relative tax brackets of the trust and surviving spouse in determining whether a distribution is advisable from a tax-saving perspective in a given year. See ¶¶ 8101–8801 for discussion of the rules applicable in determining the income taxation of trusts and estates.

An additional argument for causing the bypass trust to be made a discretionary pay trust is the potential to manage more effectively the trust's income tax liability whenever a distribution in kind is contemplated. These issues are addressed beginning at ¶ 21,400.

[¶ 18,215]

g. Requirement to Exhaust Other Property

In theory, the trustee should be prohibited from making distributions from the bypass trust until the surviving spouse has exhausted other available property. Why? Because the property in the bypass trust will escape taxation at the death of the surviving spouse, but the spouse's other property (such as the property in any marital trust) will be included in the surviving spouse's estate at the spouse's later death.

[¶ 18,223]

h. Conclusion

The surviving spouse can serve as trustee and still possess some discretion over whether to make income distributions to himself or herself or accumulate trust income. This is possible when the trust instrument authorizes the trustee to make distributions to himself or herself according to "an

¶ 18,199

ascertainable standard relating to [his or her] health, education, support, or maintenance." § 2041(b)(1)(A). Such a power would not be deemed a general power of appointment for purposes of being included in the surviving spouse's gross estate at death.

[¶ 18,231]

3. WHEN SHALL THE TRUSTEE INVADE PRINCIPAL?

a. *Nontax Considerations*

When estate planning, always "expect the unexpected." While an "A/B" trust scheme may provide income beneficiaries with a more-than-adequate flow of funds from trust income under normal circumstances, extraordinary events may place demands on a beneficiary that go beyond available resources. Most likely the person creating the trust would wish to see the property in the bypass trust made available to the "needy" beneficiary in the event of such an "emergency" and would want the trustee to be empowered to distribute property to the beneficiary from the trust principal.

Two critical questions must be answered in drafting the provisions of the trust instrument that set forth the trustee's "invasion" powers: (1) for whose benefit may the trustee invade corpus? and (2) what limits, if any, should be placed on the trustee's discretion in deciding whether to invade corpus for a "needy" beneficiary?

Most will favor the inclusion of a limited invasion power on behalf of the surviving spouse. No one wants a surviving spouse to be rendered destitute by extraordinary expenses and yet not be able to look to the bypass trust for assistance. Similar concerns cause use of an invasion power exercisable on behalf of children. After all, the children and their descendants are the eventual recipients of the bypass trust, and their financial crises should not go unrelieved simply because the surviving spouse is still alive and using the bypass trust as a "backup" source.

Theoretically, invasion powers come in two forms. In the first, the trustee has unlimited discretion to determine whether or not the needs of the beneficiary warrant invasion. In the second, the decision of the trustee is limited to determining whether the needs of the beneficiary meet an ascertainable standard set forth in the trust instrument.

Invasion powers subject to ascertainable standards are easier to discuss in the abstract than they are to draft. Because the circumstances that might give rise to an invasion of corpus are both unusual and varied, it is impossible as a practical matter to come up with an enumeration of the types of events that will give rise to a duty in the trustee to invade the corpus. On the other hand, the use of general terms like "emergency" or "extraordinary need" provides a standard for the trustee that is so vague as to be no better than the absence of a standard. Use of a vague standard may cause a court to rule that what the testator intended as a power "subject to an ascertainable standard" is, in reality, a power subject to no standard other than the trustee's discretion.

Moreover, leaving the invasion power out of the bypass trust instrument may not be as harmful to the interests of the surviving spouse as it initially appears. If the "A" or marital trust is substantial, chances are that the surviving spouse would never need to look to the principal of the "B" trust. Settlors may nevertheless be unwilling to make any part of their estate inaccessible to their surviving spouse's potential needs.

If ready "invadability" of the corpus of the "B" trust for the benefit of the surviving spouse is among a settlor's primary goals, it is advisable to have someone other than the surviving spouse serve as trustee and give that person an invasion power free of any ascertainable standard. This will allow the trustee maximum flexibility in determining when invasion is and is not warranted.

To the extent that such invasion powers are actually exercised, any tax planning functions served by the trust may be compromised. For example, if a surviving spouse obtains property from the bypass trust principal while substantial property remains in the marital trust, the invasion will have the effect of adding taxable dollars to the surviving spouse's gross estate. These dollars will be taxed at the highest marginal estate tax rate, whereas if they had not been diverted from the "B" trust, they would have avoided inclusion in the spouse's estate altogether.

For these reasons, it is arguable that an invasion power should be made exercisable by a trustee only when the trustee determines that the beneficiary has genuine "needs."

[¶ 18,239]

b. Estate and Gift Tax Considerations

Invasion powers can be a problem in situations in which the surviving spouse is the trustee and the invasion power is exercisable on the surviving spouse's behalf. In such cases, it is not enough that the standard be "ascertainable" for state law purposes. The invasion power must satisfy the additional test of § 2041(b)(1)(A) in that distributions must be prohibited unless limited to those necessary for the "health, education, support, or maintenance" of the beneficiary (also called the HEMS standard). If the invasion power is adjudged not to be bound by the HEMS standard, the surviving spouse will be deemed to have a general power of appointment over the trust property, and that property will be included in his or her gross estate. § 2041(a) and (b)(1)(A). Powers which satisfy the HEMS standard are described in Reg. § 20.2041–1(c)(2). Nonetheless, much litigation occurs over whether invasion rights do or do not satisfy the HEMS standard. Compare Tucker v. United States, 74–2 USTC ¶ 13,026 (S.D.Cal.1974) ("reasonable care, comfort and support" satisfies HEMS standard) and Estate of Sowell v. Commissioner, 708 F.2d 1564 (10th Cir.1983) (ability to invade corpus for "emergency or illness" satisfies HEMS standard) with Rev. Rul. 77–60, 1977–1 C.B. 282 (ability to invade corpus "to continue donee's accustomed standard of living" was not limited by an ascertainable standard) and Priv. Ltr. Rul. 7826004 (the power to sell property for a widow's "support, personal care or medical attention" was not limited by an ascertainable standard and, thus, constituted a general power of appointment).

Problems

[¶ 18,245]

1. Try to draft an invasion power, exercisable by a surviving spouse/trustee on his or her own behalf, which would be deemed "subject to an ascertainable standard" for purposes of § 2041(b)(1)(A). Then try to imagine an emergency that would give rise to a need for money on the part of the surviving spouse, but that would not be included within the parameters of the standard drafted. Finally, test the standard for vagueness. List a series of events and try to explain, using the standard, why they do or do not qualify as triggering events for the invasion power.

2. From what you have read so far, is it practical to structure the bypass so as to permit the surviving spouse to be the trustee of the bypass even if the surviving spouse is its beneficiary? Keep in mind that many taxpayers create trusts only for tax-saving reasons and, but for these considerations, would be happiest if the surviving spouse received all of the decedent's property in fee simple. For these taxpayers, the planner's burden is to structure the bypass so that the surviving spouse has maximum control of the trust property short of having it included in his or her estate for estate tax purposes at death.

3. Sole Beneficiary is serving as sole Trustee of Trust. Trust permits distribution of income and principal for health, education, maintenance, and support. Trustee determines that: (1) Beneficiary has no need for a distribution; (2) a distribution would inflate Beneficiary's estate for estate tax purposes (because Beneficiary would warehouse the distribution); and (3) Beneficiary's income tax bracket is lower than that of Trust.

   (a) Would it be proper for Trustee to distribute income to Beneficiary solely for purposes of effecting the income tax savings?

   (b) Suppose Trust provided that distributions were permissible to effect income tax savings. Would such a provision cause Trust to be included in Beneficiary's estate if Beneficiary was sole Trustee?

[¶ 18,247]

4. SHALL THE BENEFICIARIES BE GIVEN A RIGHT TO WITHDRAW FROM THE BYPASS TRUST?

a. Introduction

Many settlors, wanting to give their surviving spouse and/or children maximum enjoyment of the "B" trust, will request inclusion of a provision in the trust instrument that allows certain beneficiaries to withdraw a limited amount from the trust principal each year, free of the trustee's discretion. Many nontax factors impact the decision to create such withdrawal powers, not the least of which is the potential for abuse by the powerholder.

Similarly, there are many tax considerations which impact the decision to include such withdrawal powers in the "B" trust. Most important is that rights of withdrawal which can be exercised in favor of the powerholder are general powers of appointment. As a result, the powerholder will suffer a variety of estate, gift, and income tax consequences after deciding to exercise or not to exercise a right of withdrawal. However, there are at least two special cases in which a power of withdrawal will not result in such an inclusion. First, if the power of withdrawal is limited by an "ascertainable standard relating to the health, education, support, or maintenance" of the powerholder, no inclusion will occur. § 2041(b)(1)(A). Second, except as to amounts which remain eligible for withdrawal at the moment of death, no inclusion will occur when the power held exists only during the lifetime of the beneficiary and consists of a noncumulative right to withdraw a sum not exceeding $5,000 or 5 percent of the trust assets, whichever is greater. § 2041(b)(2). These "five-and-five" powers can be thought of in the following terms:

1. Either the *exercise* (in favor of someone other than the powerholder) or the *release* of a general power triggers the application of the federal gift tax. See § 2514(b).

2. The *lapse* of a general power constitutes a *release* to the extent that the value of the property subject to the lapsed power exceeds the greater of "$5,000 or 5 percent of the aggregate value of the assets out of which, or the proceeds of which, the exercise of the lapsed power would have been satisfied." § 2514(e).

Thus, the burden on the draftsperson is to appreciate the tax consequences of rights of withdrawal and to draft around any unwanted tax consequences. (As an example of good intentions gone awry, note Estate of Kurz v. Commissioner, 68 F.3d 1027 (7th Cir.1995), where the surviving spouse had an unrestricted right to withdraw from marital trust by merely giving notice. The surviving spouse also had right to withdraw five percent of bypass trust at the time his death—but the withdrawal right was exercisable only if the marital trust had first been exhausted. Nonetheless, the court held five percent of bypass trust (as well as all the marital trust) was included in estate of surviving spouse even though surviving spouse had not exhausted the marital trust.)

[¶ 18,255]

b. *Estate and Gift Tax Consequences*

Problem

[¶ 18,256]

What does the *Horner* case, which follows, suggest about the estate tax consequences to the holder of a five-and-five power who does not exercise his or her right of withdrawal?

¶ 18,247

[¶ 18,257]

HORNER v. UNITED STATES

United States Court of Claims, 1973.
202 Ct.Cl. 649, 485 F.2d 596.

KASHIWA, Judge:

* * *

Dorothy M. Horner, the decedent, (sometimes hereinafter referred to as Dorothy), was born on October 24, 1890, and died on September 14, 1969. In about 1920, she married Louis J. Horner (sometimes hereinafter referred to as Louis), and they had two sons, Stephen and Martin. Louis died testate on May 18, 1928. * * * Stephen and Martin each were * * * bequeathed a one-sixth share of Louis' residuary estate. * * * Dorothy was given a life estate in the remaining four-sixths of Louis' residuary estate, with the remainder at her death to pass in equal shares to Stephen and Martin, their heirs and assigns forever.

* * *

Dorothy, Stephen and Martin executed a trust agreement by which each transferred his entire remaining interest under Louis' will to the National Newark and Essex Banking Company of Newark, New Jersey, as trustee. Under the terms of that agreement, the trustee was empowered as follows:

D.   To pay to Dorothy McGregor Horner for the term of her natural life the sum of Five Hundred Dollars ($500.00) monthly providing said principal produces said income and to pay the Federal income taxes of Dorothy McGregor Horner attributable to all the income providing there is sufficient income available for such purposes and to pay the balance of any annual income to Dorothy McGregor Horner at her written request and such annual income as shall not be requested by Dorothy McGregor Horner during the year it is collected shall be added to the principal of the fund; and upon the death of Dorothy McGregor Horner, to pay, deliver and transfer the principal and undistributed income if any to Stephen Horner and Martin McGregor Horner, their heirs and assigns forever in equal shares.

The trust fund was administered according to the terms of the February 28, 1950, agreement until Dorothy's death in 1969. It distributed to Dorothy $500 each month during that time but did not distribute to her anything in excess of that amount unless she requested such distribution in writing. During that time, the amount of income which was earned by the trust fund but not distributed to Dorothy was $170,809.13. It is accepted as true, for the purposes of the motions, that on numerous occasions, decedent actually made oral requests for additional income, which requests, not being in writing, were refused.

* * *

¶ 18,257

As stated above, Dorothy's failure to make written requests for the excess over her $500 monthly payment caused, during the existence of the inter-vivos trust, a total of $170,809.13 to fall into the principal of the fund. Plaintiffs, as executors of the estate of Dorothy M. Horner, included said $170,809.13 as part of her gross estate and concurrently with the filing of the return and payment of $20,056 in estate taxes attributable to the $170,809.13 inclusion, filed a claim for refund for the $20,056 together with the interest paid in the amount of $702.

The court is faced with the question of whether Dorothy's failure to make written requests for amounts in excess of $500 per month, which failure automatically caused such amounts to fall into principal, constituted "transfers" of property to a trust under which she retained the right to income for life. The question must be answered in the affirmative for the Government to prevail under § 2036.

* * *

Certainly, the formal requirement that to receive more than $500 per month a written request had to be made does not mean that Dorothy had surrendered her life estate in the testamentary trust established after her husband's death.

The 1950 transaction, however, did, in effect, set up a system whereby amounts, otherwise due Dorothy, could, by her failure to make written requests, be automatically transferred to principal. The crucial point, in the context of § 2036, was that the transfer to principal was not absolute. Dorothy's right to receive the income from the augmented trust continued until her death. Dorothy thus transferred away, but with a retained life interest, $170,809.13 of the trust income which was produced by the trust between 1950 and 1969. These are the "transfers" which are relevant to our § 2036 inquiry. Economically, we see no difference between a "transfer" by means of failure to request as compared with a hypothetical case in which Dorothy requested the money and then transferred it to the principal, retaining an income interest. The latter case would be a textbook example of the operation of § 2036(a)(1). We find that there is no fundamental difference between that case and what actually occurred.

The plaintiff would have us adopt a formal and overly technical view of the "transfer" requirement. We choose instead to adopt a liberal understanding of the term "transfer." When Dorothy failed to make a written demand for the income otherwise due her and amounts were automatically added to principal, she made a transfer as fully as she would have by requesting the money and later transferring it to principal. From an economic point of view, the loophole resulting from plaintiffs' view is clear. Had Dorothy not transferred the $170,809.13 to the trust corpus, but instead had received and kept it, it would have been includible in her gross estate by virtue of § 2033. The constructive transfer to the trust, under plaintiffs' view, would result in removing the $170,809.13 from her gross estate, even though she retained the lifetime right to reap the economic benefits of that amount; that is, the income therefrom.

¶ 18,257

The case law fully supports the Government's position. In United States v. O'Malley, 383 U.S. 627 (1966), it is evident that the Supreme Court did not view the "transfer" requirement in a technical or formalistic way. In *O'Malley,* the decedent was one of three trustees of trusts which he had created. As trustee he had power to pay income to the beneficiary or accumulate the income, in which case it became part of principal. Thus, the issue for resolution was whether that trust income which over the years was added to principal was includible in the decedent's gross estate as having been transferred by him but with a retained lifetime power to designate who should enjoy the income therefrom. In holding that such income was includible in the decedent's gross estate, the Supreme Court said:

> The dispute in this case relates to the second condition to the applicability of § 811(c)(1)(B)(ii) [the predecessor of 1986 Code § 2036(a)(2)]—whether Fabrice [the decedent] had ever "transferred" the income additions to the trust principal. Contrary to the judgment of the Court of Appeals, we are sure that he had. * * * With respect to each addition to trust principal from accumulated income, Fabrice had clearly made a "transfer" as required by § 811(c)(1)(B)(ii). Under that section, the power over income retained by Fabrice is sufficient to require the inclusion of the original corpus of the trust in his gross estate. *The accumulated income added to the principal is subject to the same power and is likewise includable.* [383 U.S. at 632–633] [Emphasis supplied.]

Although *O'Malley* involved what is now § 2036(a)(2), while the instant case involves § 2036(a)(1), this difference provides no basis for distinguishing the two cases. Both involve transfers of property, which are incomplete because of a retained lifetime right—be it the right to designate the persons who shall enjoy the income under § 2036(a)(2) or the right to income under § 2036(a)(1).

[Only Accumulated Income Recaptured]

Finally, the fact that Dorothy, unlike the decedent in *O'Malley,* was not the original owner of the trust corpus is immaterial. The Government does not contend that Dorothy's life estate under the trust created pursuant to her husband's will is includible in her gross estate. The Government argues that the income which, had it been accepted and retained by her, would have been includible under § 2033 is includible under § 2036(a)(1) because of income rights retained despite the transfers.

In Estate of Kinney, 39 T.C. 728 (1963), the fact pattern was very similar to the case at bar. There the decedent was, for nearly fifty years, the life income beneficiary of a trust. The remainder was to pass to her heirs at law. During the period of the trust, the trustees received stock dividends, which they held in trust during the decedent's life. The will, under which the trust was created, contained no provision regarding whether such stock dividends were to be allocated to principal or income.

When the Commissioner of Internal Revenue attempted to include the stock dividends in the decedent's gross estate, the estate argued that the dividends were received and held by the trust and that the decedent never transferred the shares to the trust as required by § 2036. The Commissioner, on the other hand, argued that since the decedent was entitled to the shares as a matter of law, she made a transfer to the trust when she permitted the shares to become part of the trust corpus. In prior litigation, the local surrogate's court had determined that the decedent had elected to add the shares to the corpus of the trust. The Tax Court, in addressing itself to the question of whether a "transfer" had been made, held:

> The Supreme Court's opinion in Estate of Sanford v. Commissioner, 308 U.S. 39, 42, 43 (1939), is equally applicable here: "When the gift tax was enacted Congress was aware that the essence of a transfer is the passage of control over the economic benefits of property rather than any technical changes in its title." Here it is clear that decedent deliberately passed control over the stock dividends in question to the trust for the benefit of the remaindermen, retaining only a life interest in the income. We find that this is a "transfer" within the meaning of § 2036, I.R.C. 1954. [39 T.C. at 733.]

Likewise, in the instant case, the decedent had a right to the entire income—$500 per month automatically and the surplus by the mere making of a written request. The Tax Court in *Kinney* held that the stock dividends were includible under § 2036 because the decedent had transferred them to the principal of a trust fund in which she had the income interest for her lifetime and thereby had reserved to herself the income, for life, of the property she transferred. This is effectively the situation in the instant case. In each year that Dorothy elected to leave a portion of the income in the trust, she thereby elected to, and did, irrevocably transfer that sum to the principal of the trust of which she was the lifetime beneficiary. Each of those transfers, therefore, was a transfer with a retained life interest, within the meaning of § 2036(a)(1).

[Relinquishment Constitutes Transfer]

Reason and precedent make it clear that, for estate tax purposes, a "transfer" can be made by relinquishment of a right to property which has never actually been received. In Cerf v. Commissioner of Internal Revenue, 141 F.2d 564 (3d Cir.1944), a gift tax case, the taxpayer was the life income beneficiary of four trusts established by her husband. The trustees were to pay the net income to her during her life

> * * * if she shall accept it, (the right to accept such income or any part thereof to continue in Camelia I. H. Cerf during the term of her natural life, notwithstanding one or more refusals thereof) * * * [141 F.2d at 565.]

The taxpayer later relinquished her right to income in favor of her husband and contended that no transfer had been made because the income was not hers to transfer until, and unless she accepted it. But the court held that, in spite of the taxpayer's argument that she had only received an option to accept income, in reality the trust deeds vested in the taxpayer the right to receive the income. The effect of the relinquishment of this right was characterized as follows:

¶ **18,257**

* * * By completely abandoning her control over her income rights in the trusts during Louis Cerf's lifetime, Camelia Cerf effected a transfer thereof. * * * [141 F.2d at 566.]

The analogy to the instant case is clear. Dorothy had the right to all the income produced by the trust—a portion automatically, the rest by a mere written request. By her periodic relinquishments of the amounts which required written request, Dorothy effected "transfers" to the trust principal.

Still another case in which the relinquishment of a right has been held a "transfer" is Sexton v. United States, 300 F.2d 490 (7th Cir. 1962), cert. denied, 371 U.S. 820 (1962). In *Sexton*, the decedent had been one of seven income beneficiaries of a trust established by her father and was also to share in the corpus upon termination of that trust in 1940. Just prior to the termination date, she and other beneficiaries validly extended the life of the trust. The issue was whether this action constituted a transfer by her of her share of the trust corpus with a retained right to income. The court held that it did.

* * * Since the postponement prevented the beneficiaries from receiving their respective shares of the corpus we conclude that the action of postponement participated in by the decedent was a relinquishment of her property right.

* * *

Once it is determined that decedent relinquished a property interest, there can be do doubt that the value of decedent's equitable share in the trust corpus is taxable at least under § 2036(a)(1). Decedent affirmatively relinquished her right to receive her share in the corpus and thereby is considered to have made a transfer of her property interest in the corpus. The transfer was with a retained interest—an interest in the income of the trust for her life. This is sufficient to make the transfer includible in decedent's gross estate under § 2036. [300 F.2d at 493.]

Plaintiffs suggest that alcoholism " * * * frequently prevented decedent [Dorothy] from prudently managing her own affairs * * * " and that this factor distinguishes the cases discussed, *supra,* in which the decedents could knowledgeably and expressly relinquish or waive rights. We find this argument futile for several reasons. In the first place, the plaintiffs have never gone so far as to allege that Dorothy was legally incompetent. In fact * * * some written requests were actually made for amounts in excess of the $500 per month automatically provided. Secondly, even if it were established that decedent had been adjudicated an incompetent, her rights would have vested in a guardian. For federal estate tax purposes, the fact that her right to income was in a guardian's hands, or that her guardian transferred a portion of the income while retaining her right to the income therefrom, would produce the same result as if she were competent and acting for herself. See City Bank Farmers Trust Co. v. McGowan, 323 U.S. 594 (1945) * * *

Assuming still another possibility, that the decedent might have been incompetent and not been so adjudicated, there would still be no change in result. This was the very argument of the estate in the case of Hurd v.

Commissioner, 160 F.2d 610 (1st Cir. 1947). The court in *Hurd* disagreed with the estate's argument that the fact of decedent's incompetency extinguished the powers which would in the typical case cause the trust property to be included in the gross estate. The court stated:

> * * * The statute is not concerned with the *manner* in which the power is exercised, but rather with the existence of the power. The decedent may have been limited in his method by his incapacity, but it is not open to question that the power existed in his behalf, either by the trust instrument itself, or by the general law of Massachusetts; and he could have been removed * * * [160 F.2d at 613.] [Emphasis in original.]

For the foregoing reasons, we hold that decedent's failure during the nearly 20–year period to make all the written requests possible for her to make for income in excess of $500 per month produced by the inter-vivos trust constituted "transfers" to the principal of the trust. Since she retained for her life the right to income, the amounts so falling into the principal are includible in decedent's gross estate pursuant to the provisions of § 2036(a)(1). Defendant's motion for judgment on the pleading is granted, plaintiffs' motion for summary judgment is denied, and the petition is therefore dismissed.

Problems

[¶ 18,259]

1. Bob died in 1974. His will contained the following provision:

    > I give and bequeath to my wife Flora all of my property for the duration of her natural life. In the use and enjoyment of the life estate herein created, she shall have the right to demand, collect and receive all of the rents, revenues, earnings and dividends derived from my estate and to use such funds for her exclusive benefit so long as she may live.

    After Bob's death, Flora's other resources were more than adequate to meet her needs. Flora was executor of Bob's estate and, at the recommendation of her professional advisors, she claimed no part of the income generated by the property given her by Bob. Instead, that income was accumulated in Bob's estate and, again on the advice of her professional advisors, the income was reported on the income tax return filed for Bob's estate. (Bob's estate was kept open solely for purposes of accounting for the income generated by Bob's property during Flora's lifetime.)

    Flora died this year. At the time of her death, $400,000 of income had been accumulated in Bob's estate as a result of her decision not to claim that income.

    (a) Should the accumulated income be reported on Flora's estate tax return?

    (b) Would your answer be different if Bob's will had contained the following provision:

¶ 18,257

Any income earned during any calendar year by my estate, which is not used by my wife, shall be added to and become a part of the principal or corpus of my estate. My wife Flora shall have complete authority to determine whether, and what part of any receipts from my estate shall constitute corpus or income.

2. Refer to the facts in the immediately preceding problem and assume, additionally, that (a) at Flora's death, Bob's estate had a value of $2,000,000 and (b) the following provision also appears in Bob's will. What impact, if any will it have on the amount includible in Flora's gross estate? See ¶ 18,239.

> I further provide that my wife Flora shall have the right to take, use, and expend during her lifetime as much of the principal of my estate as may be necessary for her to maintain the standard of living to which she was accustomed during our marriage, or to meet any expenses incurred by illness, accident, or invalidism and shall not be required to account for any part of the principal or corpus of my estate so used or expended.

[¶ 18,263]

c. *Income Tax Consequences*

i. *Grantor Trust Rules*

The general rule expressed in §§ 641–667 of Subchapter J is that trust income is to be taxed to the trust unless distributions have been made to the trust beneficiaries and those distributions are "deemed" to have carried out the trust income to those beneficiaries as a result of the application of either § 651 or 652. However, to limit the opportunity of taxpayers to use the trust income tax rules to manipulate their income tax liability, Congress adopted the rules expressed in §§ 671–677. These rules, commonly referred to as the "grantor trust rules" or "Clifford rules," are more fully developed in Chapter 22. Suffice it to say that these rules specify the circumstances in which trust income will be taxed to the person who established the trust without regard to whether that person actually received the trust income. In this sense, the effect is to "disengage" the general rules applicable to the taxation of trust income.

The person to whom the income is to be taxed under the grantor trust rules is referred to as the "owner of the trust." § 671.

Practically speaking, if the grantor trust rules apply, it is correct to say that, to the extent of such application, the trust (or portion thereof) is disregarded as an income tax paying entity and all of the trust income (and authorized deductions) attributable to that portion is to be reported on the grantor's personal income tax return as if the trust did not exist. Reg. § 1.671–4.

Example 1. Hodding established a trust with the Georgia Bank & Trust as trustee, delivering to the trustee $100,000. Hodding reserved the right to revoke the trust at any time. As a result, all of the trust's income was taxable to Hodding in the year that it was earned by the trust even though that income was not distributed to him. See § 676.

Concurrent with the adoption of the grantor trust rules and as a part thereof, Congress also specified certain circumstances in which trust income would be taxed to *a person other than the grantor of the trust*—a nongrantor—without regard to whether that person actually received the trust income. See § 678. While Congress expressly rejected any test of tax liability tied to concepts like "dominion and control over the income," it was undoubtedly reasoned that where the nongrantor had dominion and control over the trust income, he or she should be taxed on that income. See § 671 (last sentence). Thus, § 678(a)(1) implements this principle by providing that a nongrantor "shall be treated as the owner of any portion of a trust with respect to which * * * such person has a power exercisable solely by himself to vest the corpus or the income therefrom in himself."

> *Example 2.* Mary Grace was trustee of a trust established for her by her father in his will. The trust provided, in pertinent part, that Mary Grace could "distribute to herself so much or all of the income of the trust as she wants." The trust had $1,000 of income this year, but Mary Grace decided not to withdraw it from the trust. Even though Mary Grace did not claim the trust income, it is taxable to her and the trust is disregarded as an income tax entity as a result of the grantor trust rules. See §§ 671, 678(a)(1).

Problem

[¶ 18,269]

Would the result in the foregoing example be any different if Mary Grace's power of distribution was limited by an ascertainable standard such as "health, education, or support"?

Mechanically speaking, the grantor trust rules are first applied to each trust to determine whether any part of the trust income should be taxed to someone other than the trust itself or the person or persons who actually received the trust income. If the grantor trust rules prove to be inapplicable, the general rules governing the income taxation of trusts apply. In some cases, a portion of the trust income will be subject to the general rules set forth in §§ 641–667.

Where a portion of a trust is subject to the grantor trust rules, "a pro rata share of each item of income, deduction, and credit is normally allocated to the portion." Reg. § 1.671–3(a)(3). Reg. § 1.671–3(a)(3) goes on to provide:

> [W]here the portion owned consists of an interest in or a right to an amount of corpus only, a fraction of each item (including items allocated to corpus, such as capital gains) is attributed to the portion. The numerator of this fraction is the amount which is subject to the control of the grantor or other person and the denominator is normally the fair market value of the trust corpus at the beginning of the taxable year in question.

¶ 18,263

[¶ 18,271]

ii. *Five-and-Five Powers and § 678(a)(1)*

To the surprise of many, the presence in a trust instrument of a noncumulative power to withdraw the greater of "$5,000 or 5 percent of the aggregate value" of the trust estate at the end of each year means that the powerholder will be subject to income tax on a portion of the trust income whether or not the power is ever exercised. § 678(a)(1). The fact that the failure to exercise the power does not constitute a release of the power for gift tax purposes because of the lapse exclusion provided by § 2514(e) is irrelevant for purposes of determining the application of § 678(a)(1). Accordingly, the holder of a five-and-five power is taxed on 5 percent of the trust income even though that income may be distributable to other persons. Priv. Ltr. Rul. 8308033.

What if the powerholder exercises his or her power of withdrawal? Does that affect the foregoing conclusions? Not at all. In such a case, the powerholder is also taxed on 5 percent of the trust income.

> *Example.* Joe had the right to annual withdrawals of $5,000 from the trust established for him by his deceased wife, Anne. In 2006, he withdrew $5,000 from the trust. At the beginning of 2006, the trust had a value of $100,000 and, during 2006, the trust generated $8,000 of income. Accordingly, Joe will report the receipt of $400 ($8,000 x 5%) of income for income tax purposes in 2006.

The trustee will file an income tax return indicating that a portion of the trust—5 percent—is subject to the grantor trust rules. The income tax return will include only 95 percent of the items of income and expense of the trust. Attached to the return—and supplied to Joe—will be a list setting forth 5 percent of the items of income and expenses of the trust. This 5 percent list will then be reflected by Joe on his personal income tax return for 2000.

Thus, 95 percent of the trust income will be taxable to the trust under the general rules governing the taxation of trust income set forth in §§ 641–667.

[¶ 18,279]

iii. *Five-and-Five Powers and § 678(a)(2)*

In the event of nonexercise of a five-and-five power, the income tax consequences to the powerholder are far from clear. The uncertainty is the result of § 678(a)(2), which provides that a nongrantor shall be treated as the "owner of any portion of a trust with respect to which":

> such person has previously partially released or otherwise modified such a power and after the release or modification retains such control as would, within the principles of §§ 671 to 677, inclusive, subject a grantor of a trust to treatment as the owner thereof.

The haunting question is whether the failure to exercise a five-and-five withdrawal right is a partial release in the contemplation of § 678(a)(2) or whether the failure to exercise is sheltered by the § 2514(e) gift tax lapse exclusion and thus does not constitute a release for income tax purposes. One commentator has observed:

> [I]t is arguable that [the powerholder] becomes the grantor to the extent of the portion of principal permitted to remain in the trust. In future years, if he has thereby become a grantor to part of the trust his right to withdraw would relate partly to the grantor portion and partly to the nongrantor portion and if he never exercises the power he would, under this approach, become an owner of an ever increasing portion of the trust.

Costello, Capital Gains Realized by Trusts: Taxation to Persons Other Than the Trustee, 22 Tax Law. 495, 522 n. 93 (1969).

> *Example.* Sally died four years ago and by her will established a trust for her husband, Fritz. The will gave Fritz the right to withdraw $5,000 each year from the trust for his own use. Fritz never exercised his right of withdrawal. The trust has had a constant value of $100,000 from inception. This year the trust had $10,000 of income. Accordingly, the accountant Fritz regularly employs says that, in his judgment, $2,000 of the trust income is taxable to Fritz in this year even though there have been no distributions from the trust. He reasons that Fritz could have withdrawn 5 percent of the trust assets each year for a period of four years. The accountant reasons that, by his failure to exercise his power of withdrawal over the years, Fritz was an owner of 15 percent (5 percent for 3 years) of the trust at the beginning of this year as a result of § 678(a)(2). When coupled with § 678(a)(1), which caused Fritz to be deemed the owner of 5 percent of the trust income in this year, Fritz became taxable on 20 percent of the trust's income realized in this year.

Problems

[¶ 18,285]

1. Suppose, in the foregoing example, Fritz was the trustee of the trust created by Sally. As trustee, Fritz was authorized to distribute income and principal to himself if it was necessary for his support. The first question is whether Fritz's power over the trust would result in the trust property being included in his estate at his death. To this question, there is an easy answer: Fritz's power is limited by an ascertainable standard, and therefore is not a taxable general power of appointment. § 2041(b)(1)(A).

The second question relates to the trust income. Suppose Fritz does not need the income and, accordingly, claims none of it. Will § 678(a)(1) cause the income to be taxed to Fritz or will the ascertainable standard allow the income to be taxed to the trust? (Note that Fritz's power to make distributions to himself for "support" is a power to control beneficial enjoyment under § 674, which would cause all the trust income to be taxable to him if the trust were subject to the grantor trust rules and he were deemed to be the owner of the trust.) However, would you not agree

¶ 18,279

that Fritz's right "to vest the corpus or the income therefrom in himself" (§ 678(a)(1)) is limited to amounts necessary for his support? And, if no distributions are necessary, then he does not have a § 678(a)(1) power! Do you agree? Does this mean that there is an unstated "ascertainable standard" exception to § 678(a)(1)?

2. Gavin has been convinced that he needs to shelter at least the exemption equivalent to the unified credit (§ 2010(c)'s applicable exclusion amount) in a bypass trust. However, he is undertaking to use a trust most reluctantly and only with the assurance that everything will be done to give his spouse (W) maximum control over the trust property and the enjoyment thereof, while at the same time providing for his children. In putting together the bypass trust, Gavin must select from among the following options:

Feature A: W will be the trustee.

Feature B: A corporate fiduciary will be used.

Feature C: All of the income will be paid to W at least annually.

Feature D: Income will be paid out to W and the children as needed for their health, maintenance, support, and education.

Feature E: Income will be paid out to W and the children in such amounts and at such times as the trustee deems appropriate.

Feature F: Principal will be paid out to W and the children as needed for their health, maintenance, support, and education.

Feature G: Principal will be paid out to W and the children in such amounts and at such times as the trustee deems appropriate.

Feature H: W may withdraw $40,000 from the trust annually upon notice to the trustee. This power is noncumulative and will lapse to the extent not exercised by December 31 of each year.

Feature I: W may withdraw annually the greater of $5,000 or 5 percent of the aggregate value of the trust corpus determined on December 31 of each year. This power is noncumulative and will lapse to the extent not exercised by December 31 of each year.

In deciding upon an appropriate grouping of powers, consider this scenario: In year 3 of the trust, the trust includes property having a value of $600,000, which produces $60,000 of income. If the trust contains the following features, what are the income, estate, and gift tax consequences in year 3?

     (a) Features A, D, F, and H

     (b) Features A, C, F, and H

     (c) Features B, E, G, and I

What are the income, estate, and gift tax consequences if the features are grouped as indicated and W died in year 4, when the trust has appreciated to $720,000 and produced income of $70,000?

3. Draft a five-and-five power and describe the legal and practical issues to which your draft attempts to respond. Consider these questions: At what

point in time during the year should the power be exercisable? Does it make practical sense to say that the power can be exercised only on the last day of the calendar year? How is the trust property to be valued for purposes of determining the fraction which can be withdrawn? What should be done about property which does not have a readily determinable market value?

[¶ 18,287]

5. SHOULD ANYONE BE GIVEN A SPECIAL POWER OF APPOINTMENT OVER THE BYPASS TRUST PROPERTY?

It is not uncommon for one spouse to outlive the other for many years. As a result, a bypass trust for the benefit of the surviving spouse may remain in existence for several decades. The longer the period that the bypass trust remains in existence, the more inevitable it will become that the circumstances that gave rise to the drafting of the original remainder provision will have changed. The tax laws will change, the size and "demographics" of the class known as "then living lineal descendants" will change, and certain members of that class may develop special needs that would make specialized treatment of such members in the trust instrument advisable.

Despite these facts, the death of the settlor will usually be the trigger that causes the bypass trust instrument to become irrevocable. Faced with this situation, the settlor has two basic choices, other than doing nothing and hoping that the estate plan will not be too out-of-date when the surviving spouse dies. First, the settlor can authorize the trustee to amend the trust instrument in a manner that will further some stated purpose of the testator, such as tax minimization. (A proposed provision appears at ¶ 19,562.) See Early, The Irrevocable Trust that Can Be Amended, 18 Inst. On Est. Plan. 17–1 (1984). Second, the testator can grant the surviving spouse (or other trusted person) a special power of appointment over the bypass trust assets.

In reality, both of these alternatives are "special powers of appointment," since that term describes a remarkable variety of arrangements. "Special powers of appointment" share only two characteristics:

1. The powerholder cannot appoint assets which are subject to the power to himself or herself, to the powerholder's creditors or estate, or to the creditors of the powerholder's estate; and

2. The powerholder has the ability to affect beneficial enjoyment of the property subject to the power by selecting beneficiaries and/or varying the amount of property passing to those beneficiaries.

A special power of appointment can be given to a person subject to restrictions as to when it can be exercised, who the permissible appointees will be, and the amounts that will be allowed to pass to those individuals. The special power can also be granted subject to no restrictions at all, or to mere precatory guidelines. How many and what kind of restrictions a settlor will place on the powerholder will depend on the degree to which the settlor has confidence in the initiative, skill, and fidelity of the powerholder. If the settlor believes that the powerholder is well aware of the settlor's wishes, and will be able and willing to alter the distribution scheme as necessary to carry out those wishes, no restrictions may be necessary. One possible recipient of a special power of appointment would be the surviving spouse. Because the power is not a "general power," giving the surviving spouse a special power does not cause the inclusion of the bypass trust assets in that person's gross estate. Moreover, the surviving spouse, by virtue of a close relationship with the testator, is also most likely to be aware of the testator's goals and concerns and will probably share them. Furthermore, even in cases where the surviving spouse is not considered reliable or prudent enough to serve as trustee of the bypass trust, it may be appropriate to give that person a "special power of appointment" over trust assets.

There is at least one risk associated with giving a surviving spouse a special power of appointment over trust assets. As time passes after the death of the decedent, the interests of the surviving spouse may diverge from those of the decedent, particularly if the surviving spouse remarries. Unless the terms of the special power of appointment specifically forbid the appointment of bypass trust assets, by will or by inter vivos transfer, to a subsequent spouse, the surviving spouse may divert funds to the new spouse. This may frustrate a key grantor goal of passing the bypass trust to the grantor's descendants.

A special power of appointment can be structured to be exercisable either inter vivos or by will. Making the special power exercisable by will has the advantage of postponing the drafting of the final distribution plan until the surviving spouse makes his or her last will. Thus, for example, if a testator dies in 1992 and the surviving spouse redraws his or her will in 2006, 2007, and 2012 the making of each will presents an opportunity to update the distribution plan for the remainder of the bypass trust.

[¶ 18,295]

6. HOW SHALL THE BYPASS TRUST TERMINATE?

Drafting the termination provisions for a bypass trust involves the making of two important decisions by the testator. First, it must be determined what event will trigger the termination of the trust. Second, it must be determined which persons will be the remaindermen of the trust when the termination distribution takes place.

Deciding when to terminate by bypass trust is a matter of ascertaining when the purposes of the trust will have been fully served. No trust should continue to exist after its reason for existence has come to an end. If the purpose of the trust was to manage property, the trust should terminate when the property no longer needs to be managed by a trustee. If the purpose of the trust is tax minimization, the trust should terminate when the tax-minimizing goal has been achieved.

One of the purposes of most bypass trusts is to provide a "backup" source of income to the surviving spouse while that person is still alive. Consequently, any bypass trust serving such a purpose should not terminate until the surviving spouse has died. Other bypass trusts, however, may serve an additional purpose, that of managing trust property for children of the testator who have yet to come of age. If this purpose is being served, the trust should continue until the youngest child has attained an age at which he or she can responsibly take possession of the trust assets. What age this should be is a matter for the testator to decide. It does not matter whether the "age of responsibility" is set at 18 or 80. If the trust exists to provide both a backup source of income to the surviving spouse and money management of the bypass trust funds on behalf of both spouse and children, then the trust should not terminate until the surviving spouse has died *and* the children have come of age.

Having decided when the trust will terminate, a decision must be made as to the identity of the trust remaindermen. Since the basic idea behind the bypass trust is to bypass the estate of the surviving spouse, it would be foolish to pour the trust proceeds into the surviving spouse's estate. It is far more likely that the proceeds will be distributed among the descendants, with primary emphasis on distributions to any surviving children of the testator. In Chapter 23, dealing with generation-skipping transfers, modifications will be discussed that could make it possible for a portion of the bypass trust to remain in trust during the life of the testator's children and bypass their estates as well, up to a maximum of $2 million (in 2006) adjusted for inflation (assuming the testator's $2 million generation-skipping exemption is available to be allocated and is, in fact, allocated to the bypass trust). For the present, assume that the bypass trust will distribute all of its proceeds outright to the testator's then living lineal descendants when the trust has completed serving the purpose for which it was created. Note, however, that any trust funds passing to a descendant of the testator who is not of age should be routed into appropriate trusts. See ¶¶ 4051–4099 and 4301–4441.

Chapter 19

MAKING GIFTS TO LOVED ONES

A. OBJECTIVES

[¶ 19,001]

The most important reason for making gifts is love and affection. Any other advantages of giving are lost if the donor's money or property ends up in the hands of a person to whom he or she otherwise would not want it to go. Other than the donor's spouse, therefore, the most obvious beneficiaries of lifetime gifts are his or her children. The materials in this chapter detail the most commonly used gift forms available to the donor wanting to make lifetime gifts to his or her children.

In addition, tax considerations—perhaps selfish ones, at that—suggest that donors will sometimes be advantaged to make "upstream gifts," that is, gifts to ancestors! This, too, is part of the materials in this chapter.

B. WHY MAKE LIFETIME GIFTS?

[¶ 19,051]

Besides love and affection, the other major reason for lifetime giving is the potential for substantial tax reduction or elimination.

[¶ 19,059]

1. ESTATE AND GIFT TAX CONSEQUENCES

For those with sizable estates, lifetime giving can reduce the amount of property that will be in the estate at death, thus reducing the estate tax burden. One way to do this is to utilize § 2503(b)'s annual exclusion for gifts of a present interest in property. (In 2006, the exclusion was $12,000, reflecting an adjustment for inflation. § 2503(b)(2); Rev. Proc. 2005–70, 2005–47 IRB 979.) Under § 2503(b), in 2006, gifts of up to $12,000 per year per donee could be made free of gift tax consequences. Such gifts will then be gone forever from the donor's estate. Because there is no *taxable* gift, the provision in § 2001(b), which requires a decedent's estate to take into account "adjusted taxable gifts," does not apply to a transfer that does not exceed the annual exclusion. Thus, a taxpayer with three children can give each of them $12,000 in 2006 (for a total of $36,000) per year, without gift or estate tax consequences. If this is done for 10 years, $300,000 has been eliminated from the taxpayer's estate, tax free. If the taxpayer is married and the spouse agrees to having one-half of the gift attributed to himself or herself (pursuant to the gift-splitting provisions of § 2513), the value of the property that can be transferred tax free will double. (It should be noted, however, that a gift tax return must be filed in order to make the gift-splitting election. Reg. § 25.2513–2(b)(1).)

Even if transfers exceed the annual exclusion and thus are taken into account as adjusted taxable gifts in computing the transferor's estate tax liability, there may still be a tax advantage in making transfers during life. Such lifetime gifts can be used to freeze the value of appreciating property for estate tax purposes. See ¶ 7601; § 2001(b)(1)(B). Of course, the consequence of freezing values through gifting is that, generally, the donee acquires the donor's income tax basis for the gifted property. § 1015(a).

For a discussion of estate and gift tax liability computation and gift-splitting, see ¶ 7351.

Note, too, that deathbed transfers can be particularly advantageous, especially gifts that are sheltered by the $12,000 per donee per annum gift tax exclusion. Caution here is important. Whether a deathbed transfer will have the desired effect depends upon the kind of property being transferred. Some kinds of property are snagged by § 2035(a), which has the effect of recapturing for estate tax purposes certain kinds of transfers made within three years of death. Recapture property is property "which would have been included in the decedent's gross estate under § 2036, 2037, 2038, or 2042 if such transferred interest or relinquished power had been retained by the decedent on the date of his death." That having been said, score one for obfuscation! In the meantime, it can be said that deathbed transfers of life insurance will be recaptured under this rule. But it can also be said that transfers of cash and other property will be free of the recapture rule so long as the transferor does not retain an interest in or power over the transferred property, i.e., a § 2036, 2037, or 2038 interest in or power over the transferred property.

Also worth noting is the rule requiring recapture of any gift tax paid by a donor within three years of his or her death. § 2035(b); ¶ 7185.

[¶ 19,067]

2. INCOME TAX BASIS CONSIDERATIONS

The choice to transfer property during life rather than at death can affect the donee's basis in the property. Generally, a donee's basis in property acquired by gift is "the same as it would be in the hands of the donor." § 1015(a). However, if at the time of the gift the fair market value is less than the donor's basis and the donee subsequently disposes of the property at a loss, the basis of the property is equal to the fair market value of the property for purposes of computing the loss.

> *Example.* In 2006 Harry gifts to his son, Junior, property having an adjusted basis of $12,000 and a fair market value of $6,000. Junior subsequently sells the property for $5,000. Junior will be allowed a

¶ 19,059

deductible loss of $1,000. This is computed by using the fair market value of $6,000 less the $5,000 received from the sale of the property. If Junior sells the property for $15,000, he will report a gain of $5,000, computed by deducting the adjusted basis of $12,000 from the amount realized of $15,000. Finally, if Junior sells the property for $8,000, he will not recognize either a gain or a loss on the sale because the amount realized is greater than the fair market value at the time of the gift but less than the adjusted basis.

On the other hand, the basis of property acquired at death is the fair market value of the property at the decedent's death or the alternate valuation date, if elected. § 1014(a). Consequently, the general rule is that any property in the decedent's estate at the time of his or her death receives a "new" adjusted basis equal to the fair market value at the time of death. Therefore, a donor should consider such factors as current market conditions and the size of his or her estate when deciding whether to make a gift during lifetime with a carryover basis for the donee or to transfer the property at death with a new basis equal to the fair market value.

[¶ 19,075]

3. INCOME TAX DEFLECTION POTENTIAL

a. *Use of Trusts*

One major reason for lifetime giving is the potential for shifting income from a high to a low bracket taxpayer by creating a new taxpayer in the form of a trust. For example, a taxpayer whose income is taxed at the highest marginal rate may want to transfer property to his or her child who, if the child has no other income, will be taxed on the income from the property, perhaps at much lower rates. Furthermore, if the property is placed in trust for the child, the trust can be structured so as to cause the child to be taxed *only* on the income distributed to the child with the trust being taxed on the remainder. See ¶ 8001. This "income-splitting" may result in a greater portion of the income being taxed at the lower marginal rates.

[¶ 19,078]

b. *"Kiddie Tax"*

Complicating this analysis is the so-called "kiddie tax." § 1(g) provides that, as a general rule, the unearned income of a child under the age of 18 will be taxed to the child as if it had been received by the child's parent and included on the parent's income tax return. The kiddie tax is imposed on the child's "net unearned income" without regard to the source of the property which produced the income. The tax is determined by stacking the child's net unearned income on top of the parent's income for income tax purposes and allocating to the child his or her share of additional tax thus determined. The child's net unearned income involves a complex determination. Generally speaking, in 2006, the child's net unearned income will be all of the child's unearned income which exceeds $1,700. § 1(g)(4). Rev. Proc. 2005–70, 2005–47 IRB 979. Thus, each child under age 18 can shelter $1,700 of unearned income from the kiddie tax. (Earned income of a child under age 18 is not subject to the kiddie tax.) Technically, the child will enjoy a standard deduction of $850; the second $850 will be taxed to the child at the child's income tax rates (rather than to the child at the parent's income tax rates, likely to be much higher).

As an additional means of limiting the benefits of shifting unearned income to a child, children (of any age) eligible to be claimed as dependents on their parents' income tax return may use only $300 of the $5,150 standard deduction available in 2006 to unmarried taxpayers as a means of sheltering unearned income from the income tax. §§ 63(c)(5)(A); 151. (The full standard deduction—$5,150 in 2006—is available to dependent children to offset earned income.)

Additional details that explain the precise relationship between the kiddie tax and the limitation on the use of the standard deduction by dependents are beyond the scope of these materials (which are devoted to planning property transfers). Suffice it to note that Congress seeks to limit income-shifting opportunities within the family unit that are designed to take advantage of income tax rate differentials that apply to different members of the family unit. Not to despair, however, as even a limited exemption from the kiddie tax and a limited standard deduction will allow some income tax savings to be realized from income-shifting transfers (as well as sought-after estate tax savings resulting from a shrunken estate). Moreover, the kiddie tax does not apply to income warehoused in trusts for the benefit of children under the age of 18. Of course, the compressed income tax rates applicable to income accumulated in trust are onerous, beginning at 35 percent on income in excess of $10,050 in 2006. § 1(e). See Rev. Proc. 2005–70, 2005–47 IRB 979; ¶ 21,051.

[¶ 19,083]

4. RETENTION OF CONTROL BY DONOR

Tax considerations can offer a great incentive to transfer property before death. The major disadvantage of gift-giving, however, is that the donor will lose the use of the transferred property. This problem can sometimes be mitigated by structuring the gift so that the donor retains some sort of control. In many cases, however, *any* control over the property will be enough to prevent the gift from qualifying for the annual exclusion. For example, in Estate of Dillingham v. Commissioner, 903 F.2d 760 (10th Cir.1990), checks received in December of 1980 but cashed in January of 1981 did not qualify for the annual gift tax exclusion allowed under § 2503(b). The court held that the donor did not part with dominion and control until the checks were cashed in the following year. Reg. § 25.2511–2(b) defines a completed gift as a gift which "the donor has so parted with dominion and control as to leave in [the donor] no power to change its disposition." The court determined that the donor did not part with the requisite dominion and control because the donor could have stopped payment of the checks under applicable state law up to the time they were cashed.

¶ 19,078

5. GIFTS TO ANCESTORS

Many an ancestor will die with an unused or only partially used unified credit. Rather than have that partially used unified credit die with the ancestor, good planning may well contemplate gifts to one's ancestors so as to fully utilize the ancestor's unified credit, assuming, of course, that the ancestor can be counted on to create a bypass trust for the benefit of the younger lineal descendant. Consider Brittney. Despite grinding poverty in her childhood trailer home, she struck it rich as an entertainer. Now she wants the best of both worlds. Clearly she will provide for her children (aspiring that one day they will "graduate high school") by a stream of gifts that will make them financially independent (and, thus, able to afford the best of the private high schools to which they might aspire). In addition, she is making gifts to her parents, inflating their estates (to the extent of the applicable exclusion amount provided by the § 2010(c), the tax free amount at their respective deaths) because each of them promised her that at their respective deaths, each would create a bypass trust for Brittney's benefit so long as she lives and thereafter for the benefit of her children. As Brittney sees it, the trusts will be free of estate tax at the parent's respective deaths and also free of estate tax at her death (and also free of the generation skipping tax). Meantime, she can access those trusts as beneficiary in accordance with the terms of the trusts without concern that her creditors or spouses can reach the trust property. Of course, the trusts must be irrevocable after her parents' respective deaths to offer these advantages. For discussion of the bypass trust, see Chapter 18.

C. SECTION 529 QUALIFIED TUITION PLANS

1. TAX FREE MONEY

What is a § 529 plan? In its simplest and most common form, it is a tax-qualified college savings program (QTP) established by a state, usually with a mutual fund company, to satisfy the requirements of § 529 of the Internal Revenue Code. Investments in the plan grow income tax free, and qualified distributions pass tax-free to the beneficiary. Qualified distributions include tuition, books, student fees and room and board. § 529(e)(3). Any one can participate in a § 529 plan, including setting up a plan for oneself. See § 529(e). There are no age or income limits, and the funds may be used for undergraduate and post-graduate studies, as well as many vocational schools. See § 529(e)(5).

2. TAX CONSEQUENCES

a. Income Tax

Contributions made to a § 529 plan are made with after-tax dollars, so the donor may not take a deduction on his or her income tax return. See

§ 529(c)(1). However, a number of states do allow residents a deduction for that state's income tax when the resident participate in their own state's plan. "Qualified" distributions are free of income tax.

> *Example.* Dad establishes a § 529 plan for Junior at birth. If Dad contributes $11,000 per year to the account and we assume an 8% annual rate of return, Junior will have over $486,000 for college, all (federal) income tax free if used for qualified educational expenses.

[¶ 19,116]

b. Gift Tax

Contributions to a § 529 plan qualify for § 2503(b)'s per donee per annum exclusion from gift tax of $12,000. See § 529(c)(2). (Contrary to the rule that normally would apply, contributions to a § 529 plan are not considered gifts of a future interest, a disqualifier for the per donee per annum gift tax exclusion. § 2503(b)(1).) Also, a donor may accelerate his exclusion in order to provide the beneficiary with a one-time $60,000 gift that prospectively qualifies for the $12,000 per annum spread over 5 years.

> *Example.* Junior is thirteen when Dad establishes his § 529 plan. Rather than contribute $12,000 annually, Dad makes a one-time gift of $60,000. Dad incurs no gift tax liability, and Junior benefits by reaping the rewards of the full investment from day one.

However, should the donor die within the five-year window that the gift applies to, the unallocated amount of the gift will be recaptured and included in his estate for estate tax purposes. § 529(c)(4)(c).

[¶ 19,120]

c. Estate Tax

Contributions to a § 529 plan remove the assets from the donor's estate. See § 529(c)(4). However, the value of the property in the plan at the death of the plan beneficiary would be included in the estate of the beneficiary at the beneficiary's death for estate tax purposes.

[¶ 19,122]

3. RECAPTURING THE GIFT

What makes § 529 plans so very special is that the donor can recapture the gifted property at any time by simply paying the income tax on the appreciation, as well as a 10% penalty on the earnings. See Code Sec. 529(c)(3).

> *Example.* Dad contributes $12,000 per year to a § 529 plan for Junior for 18 years. On Junior's thirty-third birthday, Dad concludes that Junior is "not college material." Assuming an 8% annual return, the account is now worth $1.5 million. If Dad is in the 28% tax bracket, he can withdraw $1.05 million after taxes and penalties (and never need give anything to or for the benefit of the child).

¶ 19,114

Example. Same as above, but instead of simply withdrawing the money, Dad decides to retire and go back to school for his Ph.D. He can use the assets for his own education tax free, and so long as he attends school at least half time he can also use the funds to pay his living expenses.

[¶ 19,124]

4. DRAWBACKS

There are few drawbacks to a § 529 plan. Careful plan selection— comparison shopping—can minimize many if not all of them. For example, § 529 plans are said to have higher fees than a comparable mutual fund investment. The mutual fund company charges a slightly higher management fee, some plans charge a set-up fee, and the sponsoring state usually receives a small fee as well. Also, your investment choices may be limited to age-based investment portfolios, depending on the plan. Many plans also set a time limit for when the funds can be used, and all plans set a cap of the amount of money that can be invested. See § 529(b)(6).

D. CLOVERDALE EDUCATION SAVINGS ACCOUNTS

[¶ 19,130]

Coverdell Education Savings Accounts, formerly known as Education IRAs, are another vehicle that can be used to fund a child's education expenses while avoiding tax liability. Unlike a § 529 plan, though, these accounts can be used for elementary and secondary education as well as college. Contributions up to $2,000 per year may be deducted from the donor's gross income, subject to certain income limitations. See § 530(c). Like a § 529 plan, capital gains and income from the investment are tax deferred, and qualified distributions may be made without any income tax liability. For higher education uses, the account may also be used to pay for room and board. Estate and gift tax consequences are similar to a § 529 plan. See § 530(d)(3). Since contributions are made with pre-tax dollars, the entire corpus of the account will be subject to income tax for non-qualified distributions.

E. JOBS FOR CHILDREN

[¶ 19,135]

While unpaid internships are the vogue, actual work is sometimes an attractive alternative, particularly where parents can employ children in the family enterprise. Not only are there the traditional benefits associated with a job, e.g., learning how to work and play with others, but also opportunities to learn the business (as part of succession planning) and enjoy the tax advantages of "earned income" (as distinguished from "unearned income" which is subject to the kiddie tax, see ¶ 19,078).

¶ 19,135

Example. In 2006, Pops, a business owner in the 35% tax bracket, hires Susie, his 17–year-old daughter, to help with office work full-time during the summer and part-time into the fall. She earns $5,150 during the year (and doesn't have earnings from other sources). Susie's wages are totally sheltered by the $5,150 standard deduction available to her in 2006. § 63(c)(2). (The kiddie tax § 1(g), does not apply to earned income.) Pops, of course, gets an income tax deduction of $5,150 and thus saves $1,803 (35% of $5,150) in income taxes for the wages paid to Susie. Moreover, because Susie is his child and under 18, neither Susie (nor Pops as the employer) are obligated to pay FICA taxes (Social Security and Medicare) on her wages and, if Susie is under 21, her wages are exempt from FUTA taxes (Federal Unemployment taxes). Thus, Susie picks up at least $5,150 of after-tax spending money and it costs Pops only $3,347 out-of-pocket to get these funds to her (and, meanwhile, he has the benefit of her productivity at the job site). Moreover, if Susie's wages exceed the standard deduction, Susie possibly could make a tax deductible contribution—up to $4,000 (§ 219(b)(5))—to her own Individual Retirement Account (IRA) and Pops can save an additional $1,400 (35% of $4,000) in income taxes. As to Susie's earned income in excess of $4,000, she is a low bracket income tax payer, the beginning bracket applied to her is 10 percent (while Pops is getting his income tax deduction at the 35 percent bracket). Thus, Susie could get at least $9,150 of tax free income and Pops would enjoy an income tax savings of $3,202—and Susie would be on the way to retirement with her own IRA. (It is likely that Pops would need to withhold federal income taxes on Susie's earning but, in the above example, that amount would be recovered when Susie files her income tax return.)

F. THE SAVINGS ACCOUNT TRUST

[¶ 19,151]

At first glance, the savings account trust, sometimes called a Totten trust, might appear to be a simple method for a donor to make a gift and still retain control over the transferred property. Establishment of such a trust consists of the donor making a deposit in a savings account in his or her own name, "in trust for" the donee. Its use has been held by a number of jurisdictions to be a valid means of disposing of sums of money without a will.

[¶ 19,159]

1. NATURE OF THE TRANSFER

Problems arise from the use of the savings account trust, however, because it is not in fact a "trust," and legal rules that apply to trusts are often inapplicable in the savings account trust context.

The modern development of the rules applicable to savings account trusts began with Matter of Totten, 179 N.Y. 112, 71 N.E. 748, 752 (1904), which characterized a savings account trust as a "tentative trust":

¶ 19,135

A deposit by one person of his own money in his own name as trustee for another, standing alone, does not establish an irrevocable trust during the lifetime of the depositor. It is a tentative trust merely, revocable at will, until the depositor dies or completes the gift in his lifetime by some unequivocal act of declaration, such as delivery of the passbook or notice to the beneficiary. In case the depositor dies before the beneficiary without revocation, or some decisive act of declaration or disaffirmance, the presumption arises that an absolute trust was created as to the balance on hand at the death of the depositor.

This concept of the "tentative trust" seems most descriptive of the actual operation of a savings account trust. However, courts outside of New York persist in attempts to classify the savings account trust under traditional trust concepts as either an irrevocable trust or a revocable trust in which each withdrawal constitutes partial revocation. See Note, Savings Account Trusts: A Critical Examination, 49 Notre Dame Law. 686, 691 (1974).

[¶ 19,167]

2. TAX CONSEQUENCES

a. *Income Tax*

Because the trustee is the depositor, all of the income from the savings account trust will be taxed to him or her under the grantor trust rules. See §§ 674–677. For a discussion of these rules, see Chapter 22. Except in jurisdictions where the savings account trust is considered irrevocable and where the donor's estate is charged with any withdrawals, the depositor as trustee will have the power of beneficial enjoyment and the power of revocation, as well as certain forbidden administrative powers. Therefore, no shifting of income from the donor to the donee occurs, and there are no income tax advantages.

[¶ 19,175]

b. *Estate Tax*

Nor does a savings account trust offer any estate tax advantages. Under the Totten trust theory and the revocable trust theory, the transfer to the savings account is revocable by the donor at any time by withdrawal, and the property is therefore included in the donor's estate, at its date-of-death value, under § 2038(a)(1). Furthermore, even under the irrevocable trust theory, the donee must survive the donor in order to receive the money in the savings account. The date-of-death value of the property may thus be included in the donor's estate as a transfer taking place at death, depending upon the value of the donor's reversionary interest before his death. See § 2037(a).

[¶ 19,177]

ESTATE OF SULOVICH v. COMMISSIONER

United States Court of Appeals, Sixth Circuit, 1978.
587 F.2d 845.

PHILLIPS, Chief Judge.

The issue on this appeal is whether the decedent, at his death, possessed sufficient powers over certain savings accounts to require the sums in those accounts to be included in his gross estate under §§ 2036 and 2038 of the Internal Revenue Code. The decedent, Semo A. Sulovich, a Yugoslavian immigrant, was the co-owner and operator of a restaurant in downtown Dallas for approximately thirty years. At his death, most of Sulovich's assets were held in accounts at various Dallas banks. Some of those accounts he held jointly with his niece, Helen Unkovich. Certain other accounts were held by Sulovich as trustee for his niece and each of her four children.* * *

The United States Tax Court held that decedent had made a completed gift of the accounts and they were, therefore, not includible in the decedent's gross estate.* * *

We reverse.

I

On March 2, 1959, the decedent opened five savings accounts at Dallas Federal Savings and Loan Association (Dallas Federal) in his name as trustee for his niece and each of her four children. In connection with the establishment of each of these accounts, decedent executed a signature card, which reserved in him the right, during his lifetime, to assign, transfer, sell or withdraw the funds in each account. The signature cards also authorized the bank to act without further inquiry in accordance with writings bearing decedent's signature. Each of the signature cards contained the following language:

> It is expressly understood that Semo Sulovich shall have the exclusive right during his lifetime, to assign, transfer, and sell the Share Account to be issued under the application on the reverse side hereof, and to withdraw the repurchase value of the said share account. In the event of death or incapacity to act of Semo Sulovich then and in that event the beneficiary, whether a minor or an adult, shall have the right to withdraw the repurchase value of said account to be so issued.

On December 21, 1965, decedent wrote a letter to his niece in which he stated his intention that she use the money in the trust accounts for the needs of her family. Decedent further indicated that he was going to send the niece the five trust account passbooks after the first of the year. Thereafter, decedent sent the five account books to his niece. After his restaurant was robbed in 1967, decedent required duplicate passbooks from the bank, mistakenly believing the originals were stolen in the robbery. He forwarded these duplicate passbooks to his niece.

¶ 19,177

Dallas Federal obtained the social security numbers of decedent's niece and her four children for the trust accounts. Annual statements from the bank indicating the interest attributable to each account were sent to the niece. She reported the interest attributable to the account held in trust for her on her Federal income tax return. No withdrawals were made from the trust accounts during decedent's life. Except under rare circumstances, Dallas Federal would not permit withdrawals without a passbook.

The signature card contracts were in effect at decedent's death and he could have withdrawn the money from the accounts, as trustee, so long as he was in possession of the account passbooks. Furthermore, decedent had full control over the beneficiaries' access to the funds in the trust accounts by the terms of the signature cards, even though the decedent's niece was in possession of the passbooks. At all times it was necessary for decedent to authorize any withdrawal from the trust accounts and, without such permission, no funds could be paid to the beneficiaries.

II

The Commissioner contends that decedent retained sufficient power over the five savings accounts to require their inclusion in his gross estate under §§ 2036 and 2038. Section 2036(a)(2) requires that the value of property transferred in trust be included in the settlor's gross estate where at the time of his death the settlor retains the discretionary right, either alone or in conjunction with another, to designate the person who will possess or enjoy the property. This power to designate includes the power to deny the trust beneficiaries the privilege of immediate enjoyment and to condition their enjoyment upon their surviving the termination of the trust.* * * Section 2038(a)(1) requires inclusion of the value of property transferred in trust in the settlor's gross estate where at the time of his death he retains the discretionary power to terminate the trust and distribute the proceeds to the beneficiaries. The settlor's power to terminate contingencies upon which the beneficiaries' rights to enjoyment of the trust depend has been considered a power to "alter, amend, revoke or terminate" within the meaning of § 2038(a)(1). Lober v. United States, 346 U.S. 335 *[sic]* (1953).* * *

The Tax Court found the savings account trusts valid revocable trusts at their inception.* * * The court recognized that the signature card contracts between the decedent and Dallas Federal delineated decedent's control over the accounts and allowed him to deal with the accounts as his own property, which included making gifts of the accounts.

The Tax Court further held that when the decedent delivered the passbooks to his niece, he intended to make a present gift of the accounts to the trust beneficiaries. The court noted that to make a valid inter vivos gift of a savings account held by the depositor as trustee for another the donor must intend to transfer all dominion and control over the property to the donee and there must be some delivery of the property.* * * The court found strong evidence of decedent's intent by his demonstrated affection for his niece and her children, by the decedent's apparent intention never to disturb the funds in the trusts, by the fact that he never made any withdrawals from the trust accounts, and by decedent's letter to his niece in December 1965 followed by his delivery of the passbooks to her. The Tax Court concluded that since decedent made a completed gift, which necessarily requires the transferring of all dominion and control over the property to the donee, decedent retained no power over the accounts which would require them to be included in his gross estate for Federal estate tax purposes.

III

The ultimate finding of fact by the Tax Court—that the decedent did not possess dominion and control over the savings accounts at the time of his death, within the contemplation of §§ 2036 and 2038, because he had made completed inter vivos gifts thereof—we conclude to be clearly erroneous under the record in this case.* * * The conclusion of the Tax Court is contradicted not only by the express language of the signature cards, but also by the testimony of the officer of Dallas Federal, who advised decedent in the establishment of the trust accounts. William C. H. Jackson, retired Secretary and Treasurer of Dallas Federal, who had known decedent ever since he opened his first account with Dallas Federal in 1948, testified that under the practice of the Association with respect to the restrictions contained in the language of the signature cards, a beneficiary could have withdrawn funds from the accounts only on the authority of Sulovich. Mr. Jackson said: "[H]e would have to withdraw it, but he would have to endorse it * * * as Trustee." This witness further testified that the beneficiaries could have withdrawn funds from the accounts before the death of Sulovich " * * * only through him. If they were ready to go to college and *he wanted them to have it,* he could withdraw it as Trustee* * * " (Emphasis added.)

The record discloses an expressed intention on the part of the decedent that the funds in the accounts be used only for the education and necessities of the beneficiaries. By the exercise of frugality the decedent had built up a substantial estate. The Dallas Federal officer described Sulovich as "tight" and "conservative." It is inconceivable, on the record before us, that Sulovich would have permitted any withdrawals by any beneficiary for any purpose which he considered to be extravagant or unwise. Under the terms of the signature cards, the *unrestricted* right to use the funds in the accounts was not conferred upon the beneficiaries.

A literal reading of §§ 2036 and 2038 mandates that any property transferred by a decedent be included in his gross estate where the decedent retains any power of control.* * * This principle applies even though the transfer takes the form of an ostensibly completed gift. In Kasishke v. United States, 426 F.2d 429, 434 (10th Cir. 1970), the court stated with respect to the application of § 2036:

> All sorts of complicating circumstances may be resorted to, but once the substance of the transaction is determined to meet these requisites, mere form will not avail. And even though it may appear that a position partakes of substance, if its recognition would be defeating to the very purposes of the Act it is not readily to be accepted.* * *

¶ 19,177

The facts in this case present a situation where the substance of the transfer, and not the form, must control. Although decedent delivered the bank account passbooks to his niece, he retained significant powers over those accounts, in accordance with the terms of the enforceable signature card contracts. The mere delivery of the trust account passbooks from decedent to his niece did not nullify the enforceability of the provision of the signature cards. Therefore, the characterization of the transfer from the decedent to the niece of the passbooks as a gift can not be dispositive of federal estate tax liability.

* * *

Even after the decedent delivered the bank account passbooks to his niece, he retained the power to terminate the trusts and distribute their proceeds to the respective beneficiaries. By the terms of the signature card contract, decedent at all times prior to his death had absolute discretionary authority over the immediate access to and enjoyment of the funds in the accounts by the beneficiaries. In effect, the decedent retained both the power to accelerate the beneficiaries' enjoyment of the trust accounts and the power to veto any request by the beneficiaries to immediate enjoyment of the trusts. The powers retained by the decedent through the continued validity of the signature card contracts fall squarely within the scope of §§ 2036 and 2038.

Under the circumstances, it is immaterial how the transfer of the passbook from the decedent to his niece is characterized, or whether decedent's power could be exercised only in favor of the beneficiaries of the trust accounts. "[A] donor who keeps so strong a hold over the actual and immediate enjoyment of what he puts beyond his own power to retake has not divested himself of that degree of control" necessary to avoid federal estate taxes under §§ 2036 and 2038.* * * Nor is it relevant whether decedent had the intent to exercise any of the retained powers enumerated in §§ 2036 and 2038; the determining question is whether the settlor reserved any of those powers.* * *

In Estate of Curry v. United States, 409 F.2d 671 (6th Cir. 1969), we held that for federal estate tax purposes an estate created in United States Series E bonds was a matter of contract. To like effect, see United States v. Chandler, 410 U.S. 257 (1973). In the present case we hold that the issue of estate tax liability is controlled by §§ 2036 and 2038 and the *contract* between the decedent and Dallas Federal, as expressed by the language of the signature cards.

We conclude that the decedent retained sufficient power and control over the five trust savings accounts to require their inclusion in his gross estate, in accordance with §§ 2036 and 2038. Accordingly, the decision of the Tax Court is reversed. No costs are taxed. The parties will bear their own costs on this appeal.

[¶ 19,183]

c. *Gift Tax*

There are no gift tax consequences on transferring funds to a savings account trust. Because the donor has the power to reclaim any deposits made, the gift will be considered incomplete. See Reg. § 25.2511–2(c). If, however, a jurisdiction treats such trusts as irrevocable, there may be a gift of the deposit decreased by the value of the donor's reversionary interest, measured by the likelihood that the donor will survive the donee.

[¶ 19,191]

3. NONTAX DISADVANTAGES

a. *Rights of Others*

Generally, a Totten trust can be reached to pay the depositor's debts as well as any funeral or administrative expenses. Under the revocable trust theory, though, the transfer to the trust is deemed to have been made at the time of the deposit in the savings account. Thus, the notion that the transfer to the Totten trust is a fraud on creditors has been rejected by at least one state (Maryland), holding that creditors may not reach the savings account trust proceeds. See Note, Savings Account Trusts: A Critical Examination, 49 Notre Dame Law. 686, 695 (1974).

The existence of a Totten trust cannot be used to deprive a spouse of the spouse's elective share of the estate, because such a result would violate public policy. See Restatement (Second) of Trusts § 58, Cmt. e (1959).

[¶ 19,199]

b. *Administrative Problems*

The usual trust theories do not apply to savings account trusts, because they are not really trusts. There is no guidance as to what property actually constitutes the trust—either as to specific provisions of the trust such as the termination date—or as to the purpose of the trust. If any such questions arise during the administration of the "trust," there will be no ready answer because this is not a real trust so much as a judicial exception to the Statute of Wills.

[¶ 19,207]

c. *Estate Planning Considerations*

One of the major advantages claimed by the savings account trust is that it allows the donor to pass money to a beneficiary without probate. This advantage becomes less important when one considers that probate will still be necessary for the estate if the donor has any other property that will pass by will or intestacy. Moreover, in many states, a Totten trust can be defeated by a will provision. Although a "rest and residue" clause would probably not be specific enough to defeat the trust, it is possible that a more specific bequest could inadvertently destroy the Totten trust beneficiary's interest.

Finally, there is a possibility of undesirable results if the donor dies unexpectedly. If, for example, the Totten trust is established with the depositor's minor child as the beneficiary, and if the depositor dies while the child is still very young, the proceeds of the account vest in the child. This leaves the depositor's spouse without access to the funds, a result which the depositor probably may not have intended.

[¶ 19,215]

4. CONCLUSION

On the whole, savings account trusts are worthless. There are absolutely no tax advantages to their establishment, and the uncertainty involved in this judicial creation far outweighs any slim benefit gained by avoidance of probate for the property in the account.

Problem

[¶ 19,249]

Albert, a school teacher of modest reputation, was the father of six children, all of whom were less than 18 years of age. Albert's estate was modest by any standard, consisting of his modest heavily mortgaged personal residence having a value of $80,000, a modest savings account containing several thousand dollars, and a modest $100,000 life insurance policy. In addition, Albert, not generally considered to be a proud man, had succeeded in establishing savings accounts for each of his children, the fact of which gave him a great deal of pride. Each account had been opened in his name "as Trustee for" one of the children. He is particularly pleased by his ability to tax-plan "just like the big boys" without the aid of legal counsel. In his mind, his tax planning consists of putting each child's social security number on the bank account bearing the child's name. This, in Albert's mind, causes the interest earned on the account balances to be taxed to the child and not to him.

Albert would like you to prepare a will for him in which he gives everything to his dutiful spouse, the mother of his children. He wants to keep the will modest, in keeping with his lifestyle. Moreover, he can afford only a modest fee.

If "something happens" to Albert, he wants his dutiful spouse to succeed him as trustee of the children's bank accounts and the management of the accounts to continue as though he was alive. His current management scheme is to load up the account bearing the oldest child's name. When she reaches college age, he expects the funds in her account to be used for her college education and, to the extent those funds are not needed for that purpose, he plans to collapse the account balance downward, loading up the account of the next oldest child, and so on. At present, the total value of all six accounts is $98,000.

In your judgment, would it be necessary to make any provision in Albert's will for the savings accounts in the event Albert dies?

¶ 19,249

G. GIFTS TO MINORS

[¶ 19,251]

1. UNIQUE CHARACTER OF DONEE

Any variety of gift techniques can be used when the donor wishes to transfer property to his or her minor children. However, the *form of the gift* assumes enormous significance when the donee is a minor. Minor children (those under age 18) are under legal disability. While they have the capacity to take and hold property, they do not have the legal capacity to administer their property. As a result, a guardian must be appointed to hold or manage property for minor donees. When that happens, many of the advantages of gift-giving may be outweighed by the costs and bother involved in using a legal guardian, who must report to the court for all transactions on behalf of the ward. See ¶ 4099.

[¶ 19,259]

2. UNIFORM ACTS (UGMA AND UTMA)

The Uniform Gifts to Minors Act (UGMA), 8A Unif. Laws Ann. 367 (1993), or its successor, the Uniform Transfers to Minors Act (UTMA), 8B Unif. Laws Ann. 497 (1993), adopted in some form in every state, solves some of the problems of giving property to minors. UGMA replaces the legal guardian with a custodian and allows for discretionary management of the property in the custodianship.

[¶ 19,267]

a. *Qualifying for UGMA and UTMA*

Any adult person may make a gift to a minor under both UGMA and UTMA by transferring property, to himself or herself or to another adult as custodian for the child, in the manner prescribed by UGMA or UTMA as adopted in his or her state. The manner of transfer will usually vary with the type of gift. Each gift may be made to only one minor, and only one person may serve as custodian. The type of property that may be transferred under UGMA depends upon the particular state, but usually includes securities, money, life insurance policies, and annuity contracts; some states, particularly those adopting UTMA, also permit the transfer of real property in this manner. The custodian has discretion to manage and disburse the custodianship property for the minor's benefit, but all of the custodianship property must be distributed to the minor when the minor attains legal majority (or age 21 in jurisdictions where UGMA is exempt from the general statute lowering the age of majority).

[¶ 19,275]

b. *The Custodian*

i. *Powers*

Custodianship under both UGMA and UTMA is much simpler than the common law guardianship. The custodian receives the property on behalf of the minor, and thereafter has the discretion to pay any or all of the income or principal to or for the "support, maintenance, general use, and benefit of the minor." The custodian can act without court supervision or oversight and need make an accounting only on petition of the minor, the minor's legal representative, an adult member of the minor's family, or a donor or the donor's legal representative. Finally, the income from the custodianship property is taxed directly to the minor, so the custodian need not file a fiduciary income tax return. See ¶ 19,291.

Cocktail party conversation is awash with unconfirmed word-of-mouth reports of custodians announcing that, while the beneficiary may now be 18 or 21, "no way" is the custodianship property going to be distributed to the beneficiary, the goal being to "spare" the beneficiary the "burdens" of property management while he or she is viewed, as it may be kindly put, as "being of tender years." *Weiss* v. *Weiss*, 1996 WL 91641 (S.D.N.Y.1996), an unpublished, lengthy magistrate's opinion, presents those facts—and more. The beneficiary, Son, has sued the custodian, Dad, for all manner of wrongdoing including under the Racketeer Influenced and Corrupt Practices Act (RICO). Clearly Dad provided more than generously for Son as he was growing up—and when he was 'all growed up', Dad reimbursed himself from the funds Dad had originally placed in the custodianship for Son's benefit. The discussion of legal obligation of support is superb.

[¶ 19,283]

ii. *Identity*

Eligibility to serve as a custodian varies according to state and to the type of property transferred to the custodian. In most instances, the donor can be the custodian, as can another adult person or trust company. Some states also permit an adult member of the minor's family or a guardian of the minor to serve as custodian.

If a successor custodian is needed, the present custodian can choose from among those eligible to be custodians. Under amendments adopted by some states, if a gift is made by will or trust distributions and no custodian is named (or the designated custodian is unwilling or unable to serve), the executor or trustee can designate a custodian, whereas the successor custodian is appointed by the court.

[¶ 19,291]

c. *Tax Consequences*

i. *Income Tax*

Because gifts under both UGMA and UTMA are irrevocable transfers to the child, all the income is taxed directly to the child (except to the extent income is used to discharge the parents' legal obligation of support, see ¶ 19,381). See Rev. Rul. 56–484, 1956–2 C.B. 23. Thus, the classic benefits of income shifting are accomplished: the income from the custodianship property is taxed to the child, who will have his or her own personal exemption and who will commonly be taxed at a much lower rate than his or her parent (subject, of course, to the kiddie tax imposed by § 1(g), as described in ¶ 19,078).

ii. *Estate and Gift Taxes*

[¶ 19,299]

LOBER v. UNITED STATES

Supreme Court of the United States, 1953.
346 U.S. 335.

Mr. Justice BLACK delivered the opinion of the Court.

This is an action for an estate tax refund brought by the executors of the estate of Morris Lober. In 1924 he signed an instrument conveying to himself as trustee money and stocks for the benefit of his young son. In 1929 he executed two other instruments, one for the benefit of a daughter, the other for a second son. The terms of these three instruments were the same. Lober was to handle the funds, invest and reinvest them as he deemed proper. He could accumulate and reinvest the income with the same freedom until his children reached twenty-one years of age. When twenty-one they were to be paid the accumulated income. Lober could hold the principal of each trust until the beneficiary reached twenty-five. In case he died his wife was to be trustee with the same broad powers Lober had conveyed to himself. The trusts were declared to be irrevocable, and as the case reaches us we may assume that the trust instruments gave Lober's children a "vested interest" under state law, so that if they had died after creation of the trusts their interests would have passed to their estates. A crucial term of the trust instruments was that Lober could at any time he saw fit turn all or any part of the principal of the trusts over to his children. Thus he could at will reduce the principal or pay it all to the beneficiaries, thereby terminating any trusteeship over it.

Lober died in 1942. By that time the trust property was valued at more than $125,000. The Internal Revenue Commissioner treated this as Lober's property and included it in his gross estate. That inclusion brought this lawsuit. The Commissioner relied on § 811(d)(2) of the Internal Revenue

Code, § 811 (1946 ed.) [1986 Code § 2038]. That section, so far as material here, required inclusion in a decedent's gross estate of the value of all property that the decedent had previously transferred by trust "where the enjoyment thereof was subject at the date of his death to any change through the exercise of a power * * * to alter, amend, or revoke.* * *'" In Commissioner v. Holmes, 326 U.S. 480, we held that power to terminate was the equivalent of power to "alter, amend, or revoke" it, and we approved taxation of the Holmes estate on that basis. Relying on the *Holmes* case, the Court of Claims upheld inclusion of these trust properties in Lober's estate.* * * This was done despite the assumption that the trust conveyances gave the Lober children an indefeasible "vested interest" in the properties conveyed.* * *

Petitioners stress a factual difference between this and the *Holmes* case. The *Holmes* trust instrument provided that if a beneficiary died before expiration of the trust his children succeeded to his interest, but if he died without children, his interest would pass to his brothers or their children. Thus the trustee had power to eliminate a contingency that might have prevented passage of a beneficiary's interest to his heirs. Here we assume that upon death of the Lober beneficiaries their part in the trust estate would, under New York law, pass to their heirs. But we cannot agree that this difference should change the *Holmes* result.

We pointed out in the *Holmes* case that § 811(d)(2) [1986 Code § 2038] was more concerned with "present economic benefit" than with "technical vesting of title or estates." And the Lober beneficiaries, like the Holmes beneficiaries, were granted no "present right to immediate enjoyment of either income or principal." The trust instrument here gave none of Lober's children full "enjoyment" of the trust property, whether it "vested" in them or not. To get this full enjoyment they had to wait until they reached the age of twenty-five unless their father sooner gave them the money and stocks by terminating the trust under the power of change he kept to the very date of his death. This father could have given property to his children without reserving in himself any power to change the terms as to the date his gift would be wholly effective, but he did not. What we said in the *Holmes* case fits this situation too: "A donor who keeps so strong a hold over the actual and immediate enjoyment of what he puts beyond his own power to retake has not divested himself of that degree of control which § 811(d)(2) [1986 Code § 2038] requires in order to avoid the tax." Commissioner v. Holmes, supra, at 487.

Affirmed.

Mr. Justice DOUGLAS and Mr. Justice JACKSON dissent.

[¶ 19,301]

REVENUE RULING 59–357

1959–2 C.B. 212.

* * *

Uniform laws have been adopted in many states to facilitate gifts to minors. Generally, these laws eliminate the usual requirement that a guardian be appointed or a trust set up when a minor is to be the donee of a gift.* * * The Uniform Gifts to Minors Act provides that money as well as securities may be the subject of a gift to a minor and that a bank, trust company, or any adult may act as custodian. When a gift is made pursuant to the * * * uniform act the property vests absolutely in the minor. The custodian is authorized to apply as much of the income or principal held by him for the benefit of the minor as he may deem advisable in is sole discretion. Income and principal not so applied are to be delivered to the donee when he reaches the age of 21 or, in event of his prior death, to his estate.

* * *

[A] transfer of property to a minor under statutes patterned after * * * the Uniform Gifts to Minors Act constitutes a completed gift for Federal gift tax purposes to the extent of the full fair market value of the property transferred. Such a gift qualifies for the annual gift tax exclusion authorized by § 2503(b) of the Code. See Rev. Rul. 56–86, C.B. 1956–1, 449, and § 25.2511–2(d) of the Gift Tax Regulations. No taxable gift occurs for Federal gift tax purposes by reason of a subsequent resignation of the custodian or termination of the custodianship.

Income derived from property so transferred which is used in the discharge or satisfaction, in whole or in part, of a legal obligation of any person to support or maintain a minor is taxable to such person to the extent so used, but is otherwise taxable to the minor donee. See Rev. Rul. 56–484, C.B. 1956–2, 23.

The value of property so transferred is includible in the gross estate of the donor for Federal estate tax purpose if * * * the donor appoints himself custodian and dies while serving in that capacity. See Rev. Rul. 57–366, C.B. 1957–2, 618; and § 20.2038–1(a) of the Estate Tax Regulations. In all other circumstances custodial property is includible only in the gross estate of the donee.

To the extent provided by § 2012, any Federal gift tax paid by reason of the earlier transfer to the custodianship will be credited against any Federal estate tax resulting from the inclusion of the custodianship property in the donor's gross estate.

[¶ 19,303]

REVENUE RULING 70–348

1970–2 C.B. 193.

* * *

The donor transferred securities to his wife as custodian for their minor children under the Uniform Gifts to Minors Act. After serving in this capacity for several years, the wife resigned and the donor was appointed successor custodian. He was serving in that capacity at the time of his death.

[Power Need Not Be Retained]

Section 2038 provides that the gross estate shall include the value of all property transferred by the decedent, in trust or otherwise, over which he holds at the date of his death, either alone or in conjunction with any other person, the power to alter, amend, revoke, or terminate the enjoyment of the beneficial interest. It is immaterial in what capacity the power is exercisable or when or from what source the decedent acquired such power.

Revenue Ruling 59–357, C.B. 1959–2, 212, at 214, holds that the value of property transferred to a minor under the Uniform Gifts to Minors Act, or other similar legislation, is includible in the gross estate of the donor for Federal estate tax purposes if the donor appoints himself custodian and dies while serving in that capacity and before the donee attains the age of 21 years.* * * However, it is not necessary that the power to alter, amend, revoke, or terminate the enjoyment of the beneficial interests be *retained* by the donor *at the time of the transfer.* The mere *possession* thereof by the donor *at the time of death* is the factor that results in the inclusion of the value of the transferred property in his gross estate. Section 20.2038–1(a) of the Estate Tax Regulations.

[¶ 19,307]

Note

1. It is worth noting that a transfer may be sheltered from the gift tax by the $12,000 per donee per annum gift tax exclusion provided by § 2503(b) yet be included in the estate of the transferor for estate tax purposes. A gift under UGMA or UTMA where the donor is serving as custodian at death is the obvious example. Stuit v. Commissioner, 452 F.2d 190 (7th Cir.1971).

2. Notable, too, is the conclusion in Revenue Ruling 59–357 that resignation of the custodian is not a taxable gift where the donor is serving as custodian.

3. Similarly notable is the conclusion in Revenue Ruling 70–348 that § 2038 applies to interests *possessed* at death without regard to whether the interest was *retained* at the time of initial transfer.

[¶ 19,315]

d. *Nontax Considerations*

i. *Advantages*

The major advantage of the UGMA and UTMA scheme is simplicity. The custodianship can easily be set up by a donor without legal help, and the administration of the custodianship is much less costly and complicated than a common law guardianship. Furthermore, because it is not a trust, it escapes the complexities of the Subchapter J rules governing complex trusts. See ¶ 8551.

¶ 19,315

[¶ 19,323]

ii.   Disadvantages

The major drawback to the UGMA and UTMA scheme is the requirement that all the custodianship property be distributed to the minor when the minor reaches legal majority as defined in each state's version of the uniform act. In the great majority of states, distribution will be made when the child attains 18 years of age. If the amount is substantial, it is probably unwise from a planning perspective to give the property outright to someone who is likely to be incapable of managing it properly.

Another major disadvantage of UGMA and UTMA gifts is that the property will be in the child's estate and will pass by will or intestacy, usually right back to his or her parents. This frustrates the tax planning purpose of the gift.

Finally, a custodianship must have only one minor beneficiary. Therefore, custodianships cannot be established to provide for afterborn children.

[¶ 19,331]

e.   Conclusion

The method established by both UGMA and UTMA is an uncomplicated and helpful means of transferring property to minors, especially in instances where the total amount of property in question is not great enough to warrant the expense and formality of a trust. The UGMA and UTMA schemes are certainly an improvement over guardianships in getting around the legal disabilities of minors.

Because of the above-mentioned drawbacks, however, it may not be the ideal means of transfer when greater sums of money are involved and when distribution at the age of 18 is not desirable.

[¶ 19,339]

3.   § 2503(c) TRUSTS

As previously mentioned, the provisions of both UGMA and UTMA are parallel to those of § 2503(c). Section 2503(c) provides that a gift in trust for the benefit of a minor can be made to qualify for the $12,000 per donee per annum exclusion for gifts of a present interest, even though all the trust income may be accumulated. The present interest exclusion is permitted if the trust provides that the trust property and income "may be expended by, or for the benefit of, the donee" before the donee is age 21 and that the remainder will be distributed to the donee when the donee reaches age 21. If the donee dies before reaching age 21, the property is to be payable to the donee's estate or as the donee shall appoint.

[¶ 19,347]

a. Tax Consequences

The tax considerations for a § 2503(c) trust are essentially the same as for UGMA and UTMA gifts. The primary attraction of the trust is that gifts to it qualify for the annual gift tax exclusion, so that a program of gift-giving can remove dollars from the donor's estate permanently and shift income-producing property to perhaps a lower bracket taxpayer, all without gift tax cost. Moreover, the trust, like the UGMA and UTMA custodianship, may accumulate all the income so that property need not be given outright to a minor.

[¶ 19,355]

b. Nontax Considerations

i. Distribution at Age 21

As with the UGMA and UTMA scheme, one of the major disadvantages of the § 2503(c) trust is that it requires distribution of the trust property to the beneficiary when he or she reaches age 21. However, as a result of Revenue Ruling 74–43, 1974–1 C.B. 285, it may be possible to continue the trust beyond the beneficiary's 21st birthday. In that ruling, the Service set forth two circumstances under which a § 2503(c) trust could continue after the beneficiary turned 21 while still satisfying the requirements of § 2503(c). The donee must have, "upon reaching age 21, either (1) a continuing right to compel immediate distribution of the trust corpus by giving written notice to the trustee, or to permit the trust to continue by its own terms or (2) a right during a limited period to compel immediate distribution of the trust corpus by giving written notice to the trustee which if not exercised will permit the trust to continue by its own terms."

Thus, for example, where the donee, after his or her 21st birthday, must make a demand for distribution of all the trust property, the trust can continue until the donee is 25 (or another age) if the donee never makes the demand. See Heidrich v. Commissioner, 55 T.C. 746 (1971), acq., 1974–1 C.B. 1. Thus, it seems that distribution at age 21 is not mandatory, so long as the donee has the power to require distribution.

[¶ 19,363]

ii. Restrictions on Discretionary Distribution

One of the requirements of §§ 2503(c) is that the donee "may" receive distributions of income and corpus before reaching age 21. If substantial restrictions are placed on the discretion of the trustee to make such distributions, the "present interest" status of the trust may be jeopardized. See Reg. § 25.2503–4(b)(1).

¶ 19,363

[¶ 19,365]

ILLINOIS NATIONAL BANK OF SPRINGFIELD
v. UNITED STATES

United States District Court, Central District, Illinois, 1991.
756 F.Supp. 1117.

MILLS, Judge:

The basic issue before us is whether the trust funds that the decedent set up for her grand nieces and nephews are subject to a "substantial restriction," as that term is used in treasury regulation 25.2503–4(b)(1), making them non-excludable gifts.

Decedent set up trust accounts for twelve of her grand nieces and nephews. The ages of the beneficiaries of these trusts ranged one month to eight years old. Paragraph 1 of each trust instrument provided:

1. Until termination, the income and principal may be paid to or expended for the benefit of the beneficiary in such amounts as the Trustee deems advisable:

   a.) For college preparatory school, college, university, graduate school of technical school education of the beneficiary.

   b.) In the event of an accident, illness or disability affecting the beneficiary, or, in the event of the death or disability of either or both of the beneficiary's parents, for the care, support, health and education of the beneficiary.

   As to educational expenditures hereunder the Trustee shall consult with beneficiary's father, [father's name], or in the event of his death, with his mother, [mother's name].

Each trust account was established with an initial contribution of $12,000. Additional contributions of $12,000 each were made to eleven of the accounts before decedent's death on April 20, 1987.

In its audit of decedent's estate tax returns, the Internal Revenue Service (IRS) determined the twenty-three transfers of $12,000 each were not excludable taxable gifts. As a result, additional taxes and interest were assessed in the amount of $153,826.42. The estate paid for the assessed amount and filed a claim for a refund, which the IRS disallowed. The estate then filed suit in the Court for a refund.

III. STATUTES AND REGULATIONS

Under § 2001 * * * the computation of the estate tax due from a decedent includes the amount of "adjusted taxable gifts" under § 2503 [which defines the term "taxable gifts" in § 2503(a) before excepting certain transfers in § 2503(c) as follows:]

* * *

(c) Transfer for the benefit of minor.—No part of a gift to an individual who has not attained the age of 21 years on the date of such transfer shall be considered a gift of a future interest in property for purposes of sub§ (b) if the property and the income therefrom—

(1) may be expended by, or for the benefit of, the donee before his attaining the age of 21 years, and

(2) will to the extent not so expended—

(A) pass to the donee on his attaining the age of 21 years, and

(B) in the event the donee dies before attaining the age of 21 years, be payable to the estate of the donee or as he may appoint under a general power of appointment as defined in § 2514(c).

Section 2503(c) is parsimoniously interpreted by treasury regulation 25.2503–4(b)(1), which provides:

[A] a transfer does not fail to satisfy the conditions of § 2503(c) by reason of the mere fact that (1) there is left open to the discretion of a trustee the determination of the amounts, if any, of the income or property to be expended for the benefit of the minors and the purposes for which the expenditure is to be made, *provided there are no substantial restrictions* under the terms of the trust instrument of the exercise of such discretion. (Emphasis added.)

IV. ARGUMENTS

Defendant argues that both paragraph 1(a) and 1(b) of the trust instruments impose a "substantial restriction" and that Defendant is therefore entitled to summary judgment. Paragraph 1(a) is argued to be a gift of a future interest because the trusts were established when the beneficiaries were young and their attendance at any of the [prescribed] schools was many years off and "highly contingent." Similarly, paragraph 1(b) is argued to be a gift of a future interest because the possibility that a parent of any given beneficiary would die or suffer an accident, illness or disability is speculative and highly contingent.

Plaintiff argues that it is the power to expend trust funds, not the probability of trusts funds being expended that matters. Plaintiff suggests that paragraph 1(b) does not contain a "substantial restriction" because the "disability" of the parent should be interpreted to include financial disability. Plaintiff therefore contends that the trustee in this case has more discretion to expend trust funds for the beneficiary's benefit than a guardian under state law, and that it is therefore entitled to summary judgment.

* * *

VI. ANALYSIS

Initially, it must be noted that whether an interest in property is one of a present or future interest for federal gift tax purposes hinges on when the donee's possession or enjoyment of the interest commences, and *not,* as in property law, on when the donee's interest or title vests.* * *

¶ 19,365

Prior to the enactment of § 2503(c), it was possible to argue that any gift to a minor was a gift of a future interest due to the legal disability of a minor and state guardianship laws. Before the enactment of § 2503(c), the Seventh Circuit held that a gift to a minor or an incompetent that would otherwise be a present interest is not transformed into a future interest by the restrictions and contingencies imposed on such persons by state law. Kieckhefer v. Commissioner, 189 F.2d 118, 122 (7th Cir. 1951). Congress substantially adopted this position in 1954 when it enacted § 2503(c).

Surprisingly, our research has revealed no opinions in the Seventh Circuit on what constitutes a "substantial restriction" under treasury regulation 25.2503–4(b)(1). Almost all of the opinions addressing the "substantial restriction" issue have based the determination of whether a restriction was substantial on a comparison with the restrictions imposed on a guardian by state law. One opinion explicitly interpreted the "may be extended" language of § 2503(c) to mean "may be expended within the limitations imposed on guardians by state law." Ross v. United States, 348 F.2d 577, 579 (5th Cir. 1965).

Provisions in trust instruments providing that trust funds may be expended "as may be necessary" or if the minor's needs are "not otherwise adequately provided for" have been held not to constitute substantial restrictions because the restrictions imposed on a guardian under state law were at least as great. See, respectively, Heidrich v. Commissioner, 55 T.C. 746 (1971); Williams v. United States, 378 F.2d 693, 180 Ct.Cl. 417 (1967). Similarly, a trust provision that provided that "no income or principal shall be paid * * * for support of maintenance which the Settlors * * * are legally obligated to provide a Beneficiary" did not constitute a "substantial restriction" since the provision merely insured that [increases in] the minor beneficiaries' present interest would be used to "supplement and not duplicate rights already held by the minors" under state law. Upjohn v. United States, 72–2 U.S. Tax. Cas. (CCH) ¶ 12,888, 30 A.F.T.R.2d (P–H) 72–5918 (1972).

Directives on the use of available funds have been held not to be "substantial restrictions" because the trustee had discretion to determine whether money was "available." For example, in Duncan v. United States, 368 F.2d 98 (5th Cir. 1966), a directive in the trust agreement that the trustee "apply any and all available funds and assets of this trust toward the payment of any premiums due on life insurance policies * * * comprising any portion of the trust corpus" was held not to be a "substantial restriction" since the determination of whether any funds were "available" for this purpose was entirely within the trustee's discretion.

In all of the cases finding no "substantial restriction," the purposes for which the funds could be expended were broad and the controversy surrounded a restriction on expenditures for those broad purposes. For example, in Duncan v. United States, 368 F.2d 98 (5th Cir. 1966), the trustee was authorized to expend trust funds "for the benefit of" the beneficiary. More typical are authorizations for expending funds for the beneficiary's "education, welfare and support" or "maintenance, education, medical care, support and general welfare." See, respectively, Heidrich v. Commissioner, 55

T.C. 746 (1971); Williams v. United States, 378 F.2d 693, 180 Ct.Cl. 417 (1967).

In contrast, when the purposes for which trust funds could be expended [have] been restricted, a "substantial restriction" has been found. In Pettus v. Commissioner, 54 T.C. 112, 117 (1970), a "substantial restriction" was found where the trust instrument provided that the principal of each trust could only be expended if the beneficiary needed funds because of "illness, infirmity or disability, either mental or physical". A similar restriction providing that income from a trust could be used only to provide "for accident, illness or other emergency affecting the beneficiary" was held to constitute a "substantial restriction" in Faber v. United States, 309 F.Supp. 818 (S.D. Ohio 1969), aff'd, 439 F.2d 1189 (6th Cir. 1971).

In this case, the purposes for which the any beneficiary's trust funds may be expended are limited to providing for the education of the beneficiary or, "in the event of an accident, illness or disability affecting the beneficiary, or in the event of the death or disability of either or both of the beneficiary's parents, for the care, support, health and education of the beneficiary".

It is apparent from reading paragraph one of the trust instrument that the principal intent of the settlor of these trusts was to provide for the education of the beneficiaries. This specific wish of the settlor would not constitute a "substantial restriction" so long as the trustee still had as much discretion to expend trust funds for the beneficiary's benefit as a guardian would have under Illinois law.

Under Illinois law, a guardian has a duty to manage a ward's estate frugally and to expend income and principal of the estate "so far as necessary for the comfort and suitable support and education of the ward, his children [and relatives] who are dependent upon or entitled to support from him" and as the court otherwise determines to be in the best interest of the ward. Ill. Rev. Stat. ch. 110 1/2, ¶ 11–13(b).

Although courts have sometimes considered the remoteness of the possibility of a restriction being met to determine that a restriction was substantial, the question is more one of power than of likelihood. In this case, the trustee has less power to expend the trust funds for the benefit of the minor beneficiary than would a guardian under state Illinois law. Plaintiff's suggestion that the "disability of either or both of the beneficiary's parents" includes "financial disability", thus transforming the restrictions in paragraph 1(b) into an authorization to expend funds "as may be needed" or if a parent is killed or physically or mentally disabled, whether or not there is need, is unpersuasive. Plaintiff does not argue that the phrase "disability affecting the beneficiary" which occurs in the same sentence should be interpreted to include financial disability. And there is no indication that the settlor intended "disability" to mean something different in relation to the parents than in relation to the beneficiary or that "disability" was intended to have anything but its commonly understood meaning.

Because the trustee of these trusts may only expend trust funds for the education of the beneficiary or "in the event of an accident, illness or

¶ 19,365

disability affecting the beneficiary, or in the event of the death or disability of either or both of the beneficiary's parents, for the care, support, health and education of the beneficiary", the trustee has less discretion than under Illinois law.

All twelve trusts in this case are therefore subject to a "substantial restriction."

Ergo, Government's motion for summary judgment is ALLOWED; Executor's motion for summary judgment is DENIED.

[¶ 19,381]

iii. Legal Obligations of Support

If the proceeds of a trust of which a minor is the beneficiary are used to discharge the parents' legal obligation to support the child, the income so used is taxable to the parent instead of the child. See § 677(b) (if parent is grantor), § 678(c) (if parent is trustee), and Reg. § 1.662(a)–4 (if parent is neither grantor nor trustee). Such a result would frustrate one of the main purposes of lifetime giving, i.e., the shifting of income from a high-to a low-bracket taxpayer. The only way to avoid this attribution of income to the parent is to be sure that no trust income is used for that portion of the child's support that the parent is legally obligated to provide or for any other legal obligation of the parent.

For additional discussion of legal obligation, see ¶ 10,115 and 22,501–22,509.

[¶ 19,383]

ESTATE OF GOKEY v. COMMISSIONER
United States Tax Court, 1979.
72 T.C. 721.

WILES, Judge:

* * *

The first issue is whether decedent retained the possession or enjoyment of, or the right to the income from, property transferred by him to irrevocable trusts for the benefit of Gretchen and Patrick. If so, the value of the property in those trusts is properly includable in decedent's gross estate under § 2036. The resolution of this issue depends upon whether, within the meaning of § 20.2036–1(b)(2), Estate Tax Regs., the income or property of the trusts was to be applied toward the discharge of the decedent's legal obligation to support Gretchen and Patrick during his lifetime.

Respondent contends that under Illinois law, decedent was under a legal duty to support his minor children, Gretchen and Patrick; that the terms of the children's trusts clearly require the trustees to use the trusts' income and property for their support; and that, therefore, the value of the trust property is includable in decedent's gross estate.

¶ 19,365

Petitioners do not dispute decedent's obligation to support Gretchen and Patrick under Illinois law; however, they contend that the use of the property or income therefrom for the children's support was within the unrestricted discretion of the trustees; that even if trusts did not give the trustees any discretion in this matter, the decedent nevertheless intended to grant them this discretion; that the use of the term "welfare" in the trusts creates an unascertainable standard which, even if ascertainable, is much broader than the standard for support; and that, therefore, the value of the trust property is not includable in decedent's gross estate. We agree with respondent on this issue.

Respondent relies upon Reg. § 20.2036–1(b)(2), which states that the use, possession, right to the income, or other enjoyment of the transferred property is considered as having been retained by or reserved to the decedent within the meaning of § 2036(a)(1) to the extent that the use, possession, right to the income, or other enjoyment *is to be applied* toward the discharge of a legal obligation of decedent which includes an obligation to support a dependent. "Is to be applied" is not to be read as "may be applied," which exists where an independent trustee is vested with discretion over distributions.* * * This creates a factual question as to whether the income from the trust property must be restricted or confined to fulfilling the settlor's obligation to support his dependents.* * *

We believe the language of the children's trusts found in § 2 of the 1961 trust agreement which relates "shall use such part or all of the net income * * * for the support, care, welfare, and education of the beneficiary" clearly manifests decedent's intent to require the trustees to apply the income for the stated purpose. In our view, it is impossible to construe the instrument as one which gives the trustees discretion as to whether or not income shall be used for "support, care, welfare, and education." That standard completely controls the application of the trusts' funds. If those needs exceed the trusts' income, principal may be utilized. If those needs do not absorb all the trusts' income, the remaining income is accumulated and added to principal. Moreover, the § 2 phrase "payments from such net income to be made to such beneficiary or in such other manner as the Trustee deems to be in the best interest of the beneficiary" does not alter our interpretation. Clearly, this phrase only grants the trustee discretion in the method of payment adopted. Since we find decedent's intent clearly expressed in the trust instrument, we need not look beyond the four corners of the instrument to determine intent.

Petitioners next argue that the use of the word "welfare" within the phrase "the Trustee shall use such part or all of the net income of his or her trust for the support, care, welfare, and education of the beneficiary thereof" in § 2 of the 1961 trust instrument, gives the trustee authority to make nonsupport expenditures which, in turn, violates the "is to be applied" language of Reg. § 20.2036–1(b)(2). They support this theory by arguing that the standard "support, care, welfare, and education" is not ascertainable under, among others, §§ 2036(a)(2) and 2041; and even if ascertainable, "welfare" is broader than "support" under Illinois law.

In determining whether "support, care, welfare, and education" is subject to an ascertainable external standard, we must rely upon Illinois law. Estate of Budd v. Commissioner, 49 T.C. 468, 474 (1968); Estate of Pardee v. Commissioner, 49 T.C. 140, 144 (1967). In Estate of Wood v. Commissioner, 39 T.C. 919, 923–924 (1963), we held that the phrase "support, maintenance, welfare, and comfort" was subject to an ascertainable standard:

> We think that these four somewhat overlapping nouns were intended in the aggregate to describe the life beneficiary's standard of living in all its aspects.* * *

> Admittedly, the words "support," and "maintenance" are regarded as referable to a standard of living, and the addition of the naked words "comfort" and "welfare" in the context of the instrument before us merely rounds out the standard of living concept.

In Estate of Bell v. Commissioner, 66 T.C. 729, 734–735 (1976), we found that the phrase "well being and maintenance in health and comfort" was subject to an ascertainable standard in Illinois:

> Although providing a modicum of discretion to the trustees, this language created a standard enforceable in a court of equity. Under Illinois law, a court of equity would look to the beneficiary's accustomed living standard in compelling compliance by the trustees, either to require income distributions for the stated purposes or to restrain distributions for unauthorized purposes. In Re Whitman, 22 Ill. 511 (1859) ("support, education, and maintenance"); French v. Northern Trust Co., 197 Ill. 30, 64 N.E. 105, 106 (1902) ("properly maintained and comfortably provided for out of such property"); Burke v. Burke, 259 Ill. 262, 102 N.E. 293, 294 (1913) ("the comforts and necessities of life").

We similarly believe that under Illinois law, a court of equity would look to Gretchen's and Patrick's accustomed living standard in compelling compliance by the trustee to require income distributions for the stated purposes. As a result, we find that the terms "support, care, welfare, and education," when viewed in the aggregate, were intended to describe the children's standard of living and are, therefore, subject to an external ascertainable standard.* * * Having found that the phrase in the aggregate created an ascertainable standard requiring the trustee to make expenditures for the children's accustomed living standard, we must reject petitioners' argument that the term "welfare" in the phrase allows the trustee to make nonsupport payments because "welfare" is broader than "support" under Illinois law.

Thus, it only remains for us to decide whether, under Illinois law, support is synonymous, for this purpose, with accustomed standard of living. In Rock Island Bank & Trust Co. v. Rhoads, 353 Ill. 131, 187 N.E. 139, 144 (1933), the Illinois Supreme Court stated: "The word 'comfort' must be construed as relating to her *support* and ease.* * * Had this clause provided only for her comfort, it cannot be doubted that such would be a limitation * * * to maintain her in the *station in life to which she was accustomed.*" (Emphasis added.)

¶ 19,383

We view this language as indicative that, under Illinois law, support is equivalent to accustomed standard of living. We are satisfied that the instrument before us provides an ascertainable standard under Illinois law. Accordingly, we find that decedent's gross estate includes the value of Gretchen's and Patrick's trusts since we find them to be support trusts within the meaning of § 2036(a)(1) and Reg. § 20.2036–1(b)(2).

Problems

[¶ 19,385]

1. Would the inclusion of the following language in a trust avoid the risk that trust distributions for the benefit of a minor will be deemed to discharge the parents' legal obligation of support:

    > Under no circumstances shall distributions be made from this trust in satisfaction of the legal obligation of support owed by a parent to a child.

    Assuming this provision would be effective to insulate trust distributions from being treated as satisfying a support obligation, what disadvantage do you see to inclusion of this provision in the instrument?

2. Assume the prohibition proposed in the preceding problem were included in a trust. Would the rule in *Illinois National Bank* (¶ 19,365) preclude the trust from qualifying as a § 2503(c) trust? Note that in Upjohn v. United States, 72–2 USTC ¶ 12,888 (W.D.Mich.1972), a clause prohibiting distributions that discharge a grantor's legal obligation of support was held not to constitute a "substantial restriction" for purposes of § 2503(c).

3. Assume Grandfather established a § 2503(c) trust for Grandson with Parent as Trustee. If Parent dies while serving as Trustee during Grandson's minority, could it be argued that the trust property should be included in Parent's gross estate for federal estate tax purposes? Such an argument would be based on the fact that, as Trustee, Parent could apply the trust income and principal to discharge his or her legal obligation of support. See Reg. § 20.2041–1(c). In Revenue Ruling 77–460, 1977–2 C.B. 323, the parent had died, and under consideration was the notion that § 2041 required inclusion of the custodianship property in the parent's estate. Noting that while § 4(c) of the Uniform Gifts to Minors Act gives a parent the right to petition a court to compel the custodian to distribute such part or all of the custodial property that is "necessary for the minor's support, maintenance or education," the IRS concluded that the parent does not have the equivalent of a general power of appointment over the custodial property as a result of this right to petition.

[¶ 19,389]

iv. *Other Considerations*

A § 2503(c) trust is not as easily created or administered as a gift under UGMA or UTMA. The trust requires a written trust instrument, which will involve attorneys' fees. Furthermore, it will be a complex trust within the meaning of Subchapter J, and there probably will be accountants' fees to pay. See ¶ 8551.

On the other hand, there is the possibility that the trust could continue beyond the beneficiary's 21st birthday, and this may represent a distinct improvement over the UGMA rules. See discussion at ¶ 19,355.

H.   THE CRUMMEY TRUST

[¶ 19,451]

1.   INTRODUCTION

There will often be donors who wish to place property in trust for the donee but want the trust to accumulate the income for a period of time before distribution. This is especially true where the trust beneficiaries are minors who would be unable to manage property given to them outright without a guardian. If a trust is established without a provision for current distributions of income or corpus, however, the beneficiary has only a future interest in the trust. Gifts to the trust, therefore, are not gifts of a present interest and thus do not qualify for the § 2503(b) annual exclusion from the gift tax. Property, and the income therefrom, is still shifted from the donor to the trust, but the shift is at the expense of paying gift tax on the transfer.

Where the beneficiary of the trust is a minor, § 2503(c) provides an exception in certain circumstances to the § 2503(b) requirement that the gift be one of a present interest. See discussion at ¶ 19,339. This exception, however, is not always helpful because it requires distribution of the corpus and accumulated income to the beneficiary when he or she reaches the age of 21. Furthermore, § 2503(c) applies only when the trust beneficiary is a minor; its provisions are inapplicable when a donor wishes the trust to accumulate income for an adult child or for any other adult.

[¶ 19,459]

2.   THE CRUMMEY CASE

CRUMMEY v. COMMISSIONER

United States Court of Appeals, Ninth Circuit, 1968.
397 F.2d 82.

BYRNE, District Judge:* * *

On February 12, 1962, the petitioners executed, as grantors, an irrevocable living trust for the benefit of their four children. The beneficiaries and their ages at relevant times are as follows:

	Age 12/31/62	Age 12/31/63
John Knowles Crummey	22	23
Janet Sheldon Crummey	20	21
David Clarke Crummey	15	16

¶ 19,389

Mark Clifford Crummey............................   11   12

Originally the sum of $50 was contributed to the trust. Thereafter, additional contributions were made by each of the petitioners in the following amounts and on the following dates:

$4,267.77	6/20/62
49,550.00	12/15/62
12,797.81	12/19/63

The dispute revolves around the tax years of 1962 and 1963. Each of the petitioners filed a gift tax return for each year. Each petitioner claimed a $3,000 per beneficiary tax exclusion under the provisions of 2503(b). The total claimed exclusions were as follows:

D. C. Crummey...................	1962–$12,000	1963–$12,000
E. E. Crummey...................	1962–$12,000	1963–$12,000

The Commissioner of Internal Revenue determined that each of the petitioners was entitled to only one $3,000 exclusion for each year. This determination was based upon the Commissioner's belief that the portion of the gifts in trust for the children under the age of 21 were "future interests" which are disallowed under § 2503(b).* * *

The key provision of the trust agreement is the "demand" provision which states:

> THREE. *Additions.* The Trustee may receive any other real or personal property from the Trustors (or either of them) or from any other person or persons, by lifetime gift, under a Will or Trust or from any other source. Such property will be held by the Trustee subject to the terms of this Agreement. A donor may designate or allocate all of his gift to one or more Trusts, or in stated amounts to different Trusts. If the donor does not specifically designate what amount of his gift is to augment each Trust, the Trustee shall divide such gift equally between the Trusts then existing, established by this Agreement. The Trustee agrees, if he accepts such additions, to hold and manage such additions in trust for the uses and in the manner set forth herein. *With respect to such additions, each child of the Trustors may demand at any time (up to and including December 31 of the year in which a transfer to his or her Trust has been made) the sum of Four Thousand Dollars ($4,000) or the amount of the transfer from each donor, whichever is less, payable in cash immediately upon receipt by the Trustee of the demand in writing and in any event, not later than December 31 in the year in which such transfer was made. Such payment shall be made from the gift of that donor for that year. If a child is a minor at the time of such gift of that donor for that year, or fails in legal capacity for any reason, the child's guardian may make such demand on behalf of the child. The property received pursuant to the demand shall be held by the guardian for the benefit and use of the child.* (Emphasis supplied.)

The whole question on this appeal is whether or not a present interest was given by the petitioners to their minor children so as to qualify as an exclusion under § 2503(b).* * *

It was stipulated before the Tax Court in regard to the trust and the parties thereto that at all times relevant all the minor children lived with the petitioners and no legal guardian had been appointed for them. In addition, it was agreed that all the *children* were supported by petitioners and none of them had made a demand against the trust funds or received any distribution from them.

The tax regulations define a "future interest" for the purposes of § 2503(b) as follows:

> "Future interests" is a legal term, and includes reversions, remainder, and other interests or estates, whether vested or contingent, and whether or not supported by a particular interest or estate, which are limited to commence in use, possession or enjoyment at some future date or time. Treasury Regulations of Gift Tax, § 25.2503–3.

This definition has been adopted by the Supreme Court. Fondren v. Commissioner of Internal Revenue 324 U.S. 18 (1945); Commissioner v. Disston 325 U.S. 442 (1945). In *Fondren* the court stated that the important question is when enjoyment begins. There the court held that gifts to an irrevocable trust for the grantor's minor grandchildren were "future interests" where income was to be accumulated and the corpus and the accumulations were not to be paid until designated times commencing with each grandchild's 25th birthday. The trustee was authorized to spend the income or invade the corpus during the minority of the beneficiaries only if need were shown. The facts demonstrated that need had not occurred and was not likely to occur.

Neither of the parties nor the Tax Court has any disagreement with the above summarization of the basic tests. The dispute comes in attempting to narrow the definition of a future interest down to a more specific and useful form.

The Commissioner and the Tax Court both placed primary reliance on the case of Stifel v. Commissioner 197 F.2d 107 (2nd Cir. 1952). In that case an irrevocable trust was involved which provided that the beneficiary, a minor, could demand any part of the funds not expended by the Trustee and, subject to such demand, the Trustee was to accumulate. The trust also provided that it could be terminated by the beneficiary or by her guardian during minority. The court held that gifts to this trust were gifts of "future interests". They relied upon *Fondren* for the proposition that they could look at circumstances as well as the trust agreement and under such circumstances it was clear that the minor could not make the demand and that no guardian had ever been appointed who could make such a demand.

The leading case relied upon by the petitioners is Kieckhefer v. Commissioner 189 F.2d 118 (7th Cir. 1951). In that case the donor set up a trust with his newly born grandson as the beneficiary. The trustee was to hold the funds unless the beneficiary or his legally appointed guardian demanded that the trust be terminated. The Commissioner urged that the grandson could not effectively make such a demand and that no guardian had been appointed. The court disregarded these factors and held that where any restrictions on use were caused by disabilities of a minor rather than by the terms of the trust, the gift was a "present interest". The court further stated that the important thing was the right to enjoy rather than the actual enjoyment of the property.

The *Kieckhefer* case has been followed in several decisions. In Gilmore v. Commissioner of Internal Revenue 213 F.2d 520 (6th Cir. 1954) there was an irrevocable trust for minors. It provided that all principal and accumulated income would be paid on demand of the beneficiary. The trust was to terminate on the beneficiary's death. Anything remaining in the trust at the time of death would go to the beneficiary's estate.

The Tax Court stated that the demand provision would have made the advancements "present interests" but for spendthrift provisions and the authority of the Trustee to invest in nonincome producing properties. The Circuit agreed that the demand provision made the advancements "present interests" and further held that the other provisions did not change that character. Reliance was placed on the "right to enjoy" language of *Kieckhefer*.

In U.S. v. Baker 236 F.2d 317 (4th Cir. 1956) the court followed the *Kieckhefer* case in holding that advances were "present interests" where:

> The trust agreements with which we are concerned here created no barriers to the present enjoyment by the infants of the trust property beyond those which are established by the laws of North Carolina.

That case involved a trust for minors where income and principal were to be used for the support, education and benefit of the beneficiaries according to the discretion of the trustee who was to act as if he were a guardian. What was not expended went to the beneficiary on his 21st birthday.

A final case of interest is Trust No. 3 v. Commissioner 285 F.2d 102 (7th Cir. 1960). This involved the question of whether certain income was taxable to a trust or to the beneficiaries. The court held the income was taxable to the beneficiaries where they had the right to terminate the trust or take any part of it on demand. The beneficiaries were minors, and no guardian had been appointed. The Commissioner urged that no one was ever qualified to make the demand and thus that the beneficiaries could not have taken any property from the trust in the tax year. The court relying on *Kieckhefer* said:

> This distinction is unconvincing in view of the fact that the appointment of a guardian for a minor under a state law is a matter of routine in which the federal government has no concern.

Although there are certainly factual distinctions between the *Stifel* and *Kieckhefer* cases, it seems clear that the two courts took opposing positions on the way the problem of defining "future interests" should be resolved. As we read the *Stifel* case, it says that the court should look at the trust instrument, the law as to minors, and the financial and other circumstances of the parties. From this examination it is up to the court to determine whether it is likely that the minor beneficiary is to receive any present enjoyment of the property. If it is not likely, then the gift is a "future interest". At the other extreme is the holding in *Kieckhefer* which says that a gift to a minor is not a "future interest" if the only reason for a delay in enjoyment is the minority status of the donee and his consequent disabilities. The *Kieckhefer* court noted that under the terms there present, a gift to an adult would have qualified for the exclusion and they refused to discriminate against a minor. The court equated a present interest with a present right to possess, use or enjoy. The facts of the case and the court's reasoning, however, indicate that it was really equating a present interest with a present right to possess, use or enjoy except for the fact that the beneficiary was a minor. In between these two positions there is a third possibility. That possibility is that the court should determine whether the donee is legally and technically capable of immediately enjoying the property. Basically this is the test relied on by the petitioners. Under this theory, the question would be whether the donee could possibly gain immediate enjoyment and the emphasis would be on the trust instrument and the laws of the jurisdiction as to minors. It was primarily on this basis that the Tax Court decided the present case, although some examination of surrounding circumstances was apparently made. This theory appears to be the basis of the decision in George W. Perkins, 27 T.C. 601 (1956). There the Tax Court stated that where the parents were capable of making the demand and there was no showing that the demand could be resisted, the gift was of a present interest. This approach also seems to be the basis of the "right to enjoy" language in both *Kieckhefer* and *Gilmore*.

Under the provisions of this trust the income is to be accumulated and added to the corpus until each minor reaches the age of 21, unless the trustee feels in his discretion that distributions should be made to a needy beneficiary. From 21 to 35 all income is distributed to the beneficiary. After 35 the trustee again has discretion as to both income and corpus, and may distribute whatever is necessary up to the whole thereof. Aside from the actions of the trustee, the only way any beneficiary may get at the property is through the "demand" provision, quoted above.

One question raised in these proceedings is whether or not the trust prohibits a minor child from making a demand on the yearly additions to the trust. The key language from paragraph three is as follows:

> If a child is a minor at the time of such gift of that donor for that year, or fails in legal capacity for any reason, the child's guardian may make such demand on behalf of the child.

The Tax Court interpreted this provision in favor of the taxpayers by saying that "may" is permissive and thus that the minor child can make the demand if allowed by law, or, if not permitted by law, the guardian may do it. Although, as the Commissioner suggests, this strains the language somewhat, it does seem consistent with the obvious intent in drafting this provision. Surely, this provision was intended to give the minor beneficiary the broadest demand power available so that the gift tax exclusion would be applicable.

There is very little dispute between the parties as to the rights and disabilities of a minor accorded by the California statutes and cases. The problem comes in attempting to ascertain from these rights and disabilities

¶ 19,459

the answer to the question of whether a minor may make a demand upon the trustee for a portion of the trust as provided in the trust instrument.

It is agreed that a minor in California may own property.* * * He may receive a gift.* * * A minor may demand his own funds from a bank (Cal. Fin. Code, §§ 850 & 853), a savings institution (Cal. Fin. Code, §§ 7600 & 7606), or a corporation (Cal. Corp. Code, §§ 2221 & 2413). A minor of the age of 14 or over has the right to secure the appointment of a guardian and one will be appointed if the court finds it "necessary or convenient". Cal. Prob. Code, § 1406; Guardianship of Kentera, 41 Cal. 2d 639, 262 P.2d 317 (1953).

It is further agreed that a minor cannot sue in his own name (Cal. Civ. Code, § 42) and cannot appoint an agent. (Cal. Civ. Code, § 33). With certain exceptions a minor can disaffirm contracts made by him during his minority. Cal. Civ. Code, § 35. A minor under the age of 18 cannot make contracts relating to real property or personal property not in his possession or control. Cal. Civ. Code, § 33.

The parent of a child may be its natural guardian, but such a guardianship is of the person of the child and not of his estate.* * *

After examining the same rights and disabilities, the petitioners, the Commissioner, and the Tax Court each arrived at a different solution to our problem. The Tax Court concentrated on the disabilities and concluded that David and Mark could not make an effective demand because they could not sue in their own name, nor appoint an agent and could disaffirm contracts. The court, however, concluded that Janet could make an effective demand because Cal. Civ. Code, § 33 indirectly states that she could make contracts with regard to real and personal property.

The Commissioner concentrated on the inability to sue or appoint an agent and concluded that none of the minors had anything more than paper rights because he or she lacked the capacity to enforce the demand.

The petitioners urge that the right to acquire and hold property is the key. In the alternative they argue that the parent as a natural guardian could make the demand although it would be necessary to appoint a legal guardian to receive the property. Finally, they urge that all the minors over 14 could make a demand since they could request the appointment of a legal guardian.

The position taken by the Tax Court seems clearly untenable. The distinction drawn between David and Mark on the one hand, and Janet on the other, makes no sense. The mere fact that Janet can make certain additional contracts does not have any relevance to the question of whether she is capable of making an effective demand upon the trustee. We cannot agree with the position of the Commissioner because we do not feel that a lawsuit or the appointment of an agent is a necessary prelude to the making of a demand upon the trustee. As we visualize the hypothetical situation, the child would inform the trustee that he demanded his share of the additions up to $4,000. The trustee would petition the court for the appointment of a legal guardian and then turn the funds over to the guardian. It would also seem possible for the parent to make the demand as natural guardian. This would involve the acquisition of property for the child rather than the management of the property. It would then be necessary for a legal guardian to be appointed to take charge of the funds. The only time when the disability to sue would come into play, would be if the trustee disregarded the demand and committed a breach of trust. That would not, however, vitiate the demand.

All this is admittedly speculative since it is highly unlikely that a demand will ever be made or that if one is made, it would be made in this fashion. However, as a technical matter, we think a minor could make the demand.

Given the trust, the California law, and the circumstances in our case, it can be seen that very different results may well be achieved, depending upon the test used. Under a strict interpretation of the *Stifel* test of examining everything and determining whether there is any likelihood of present enjoyment, the gifts to minors in our case would seem to be "future interests". Although under our interpretation neither the trust nor the law technically forbid a demand by the minor, the practical difficulties of a child going through the procedures seem substantial. In addition, the surrounding facts indicate the children were well cared for and the obvious intention of the trustors was to create a long term trust. No guardian had been appointed and, except for the tax difficulties, probably never would be appointed. As a practical matter, it is likely that some, if not all, of the beneficiaries did not even know that they had any right to demand funds from the trust. They probably did not know when contributions were made to the trust or in what amounts. Even had they known, the substantial contributions were made toward the end of the year so that the time to make a demand was severely limited. Nobody had made a demand under the provision, and no distributions had been made. We think it unlikely that any demand ever would have been made.

All exclusions should be allowed under the *Perkins* test or the "right to enjoy" test in *Gilmore*. Under *Perkins,* all that is necessary is to find that the demand could not be resisted. We interpret that to mean legally resisted and, going on that basis, we do not think the trustee would have any choice but to have a guardian appointed to take the property demanded.

Under the general language of *Kieckhefer* which talked of the "right to enjoy", all exclusions in our case would seem to be allowable. The broader *Kieckhefer* rule which we have discussed is inapplicable on the facts of this case. That rule, as we interpret it, is that postponed enjoyment is not equivalent to a "future interest" if the postponement is solely caused by the minority of the beneficiary. In *Kieckhefer,* the income was accumulated and added to the corpus until the beneficiary reached the age of 21. At that time everything was to be turned over to him. This is all that happened unless a demand was made. In our case, on the contrary, if no demand is made in any particular year, the additions are forever removed from the uncontrolled reach of the beneficiary since, with the exception of the yearly demand provision, the only way the corpus can ever be tapped by a beneficiary, is through a distribution at the discretion of the trustee.

We decline to follow a strict reading of the *Stifel* case in our situation because we feel that the solution suggested by that case is inconsistent and unfair. It becomes arbitrary for the I.R.S. to step in and decide who is likely to make an effective demand. Under the circumstances suggested in our case, it is doubtful that any demands will be made against the trust—yet the Commissioner always allowed the exclusion as to adult beneficiaries. There is nothing to indicate that it is any more likely that John will demand funds than that any other beneficiary will do so. The only distinction is that it might be easier for him to make such a demand. Since we conclude that the demand can be made by the others, it follows that the exclusion should also apply to them. In another case we might follow the broader *Kieckhefer* rule, since it seems least arbitrary and establishes a clear standard. However, if the minors have no way of making the demand in our case, then there is more than just a postponement involved, since John could demand his share of yearly additions while the others would never have the opportunity at their shares of those additions but would be limited to taking part of any additions added subsequent to their 21st birthdays.

We conclude that the result under the *Perkins* or "right to enjoy" tests is preferable in our case. The petitioners should be allowed all of the exclusions claimed for the two year period.

* * *

[¶ 19,467]

3. THE INTERNAL REVENUE SERVICE'S POSITION

In Revenue Ruling 73–405, 1973–2 C.B. 321, the Service acquiesced in the *Crummey* decision and decided that "a gift in trust for the benefit of a minor should not be classified as a future interest merely because no guardian was in fact appointed."

Since that time, the Service has published a number of Revenue Rulings and Letter Rulings that have focused on the requirements for a valid *Crummey* power. None of the letter rulings cited can be used as precedent, but they are instructive as indications of what the author of the ruling, an IRS employee, considers a present, effective right of withdrawal. Following are some of the major factors to consider in drafting a *Crummey* power so that gifts to the trust will qualify for the annual exclusion.

[¶ 19,475]

a. *Present Right to Get Property*

The first requirement of a valid *Crummey* power is that the recipient of the power must have the right to receive something of value immediately at the time of the gift; the right to receive the property cannot be deferred. Therefore, no exclusion was allowed where there was no demand right and the trustee had the power to "sprinkle" the trust income among all, some, or none of several different classes of beneficiaries (see Priv. Ltr. Rul. 7817095) or where the beneficiary had a right to receive a "balloon" payment at the end of a six-year period and the value of the payment would not be ascertainable until that time (see Priv. Ltr. Rul. 7830145).

¶ 19,475

The power will not be considered a present right to receive property if its exercise is subject to some contingency or to the will of some other person. However, the mere fact that the beneficiary must demand the property in order to receive payment will not be considered a contingency. This is true even if the beneficiary must make his demand in the form of an act, unless the act is one of independent significance, where the receipt of payments from the trust is but a collateral consequence of the act. For example, where payments to a beneficiary were to commence when the beneficiary was no longer in school, the fact that he could "demand" payments by leaving school did not qualify the gift to the trust as a gift of a present interest. See Rev. Rul. 75–415, 1975–2 C.B. 374.

The determination of whether a gift is one of a present interest is made at the time of the gift, so the right to receive the property must exist at that time. Therefore, a gift to an as-yet unborn child is not a gift of a present interest, even with a withdrawal right, because the beneficiary must be alive at the time of the transfer. See Priv. Ltr. Rul. 8015133.

The IRS has indicated that it will not recognize a valid *Crummy* power where a nominal beneficiary enjoys only "discretionary income interests, contingent rights to the remainder, or no rights whatsoever in the income or remainder, their non-exercise of the withdrawal rights indicates that there was some kind of prearranged understanding with the donor that these rights were not meant to be exercised or that their exercise would result in undesirable consequences, or both." See Action on Decision 1992–009; TAM 9731004.

In *Estate of Kohlsaat v. Commissioner,* 73 T.C.M 2732 (1997), the Tax Court rejected the IRS's contention that inference of a prearrangement could be found in the absence of the beneficiaries having current or vested rights where the provisions of the trust allowed contingent beneficiaries to have unrestricted rights to legally demand immediate distribution to them of the trust property for a 30–day period following the transfer of property. In *Kohlsaat,* the IRS claimed that understandings existed between the decedent and the contingent beneficiaries to the effect that the beneficiaries would not exercise their rights to demand distributions of trust property, that these understandings negated the decedent's donative intent, and that the substance-over-form doctrine should apply to deny the annual gift tax exclusions with regard to the interests held by the contingent beneficiaries. The Court, however, refused to infer any implication that there was a prearranged agreement between the beneficiaries and the settlor simply because none of the beneficiaries had exercised their rights or because none of the beneficiaries had requested notification of future transfers of property to the trust.

Finally, the beneficiary's present interest must be clear and unambiguous; if the clause purporting to create a present interest is too vague, too confusing, or conflicts with other trust provisions, there is a danger than *no present interest will be found.* For this reason, "savings clauses" which provide that a trustee's discretion is limited in such a way that the trustee will not be allowed to forfeit the annual exclusion are usually ineffective where the trustee's discretion is otherwise complete. The clause's language

¶ 19,475

conflicts with other expressions of the trustee's authority, and the IRS considers such a clause too vague to convert future interests to present interests. See Priv. Ltr. Rul. 7905088.

In sum, the clause in the trust creating the demand power should clearly state that the beneficiary has a present interest in the transferred property, and the power should be in effect at the time the gift to the trust is made.

[¶ 19,483]

b. Property Subject to the Demand Right

A second requirement that must be met to qualify for the exclusion is that it must be possible for the beneficiary to actually receive the property over which he or she has a demand right. The donor may get an exclusion only to the extent that there is cash, or assets reducible to cash, in the trust sufficient to satisfy the beneficiary's demand rights. See Priv. Ltr. Rul. 8103074. There is no tracing to see whether the demand right is satisfied from the actual gift for which the exclusion is claimed, so long as it is possible to satisfy the demand from the trust assets as a whole. Thus, there is an exclusion for the transfer of premium payments on group term insurance—a trust asset—where the demand right may be satisfied from any trust asset. See Priv. Ltr. Rul. 8006019. If, however, property is expressly not made available to the beneficiary through the use of his demand right, then the exclusion is available only to the extent of unrestricted gifts, out of which the demand right can be satisfied. For example, if a trust instrument allows the donor to specify, at the time of the gift, whether it is to be subject to the beneficiary's demand right, the exclusion is available only for his unrestricted contributions. See Priv. Ltr. Ruls. 8103074 and 8103069.

In sum, the clause creating the *Crummey* power should provide that the demand for distribution may be satisfied with cash or with property, or the trust should give the trustee the power to sell or otherwise convert the trust assets or to borrow money, so that there will always be a possibility that the beneficiary's demand can be satisfied.

[¶ 19,491]

c. Guardianship

If the beneficiary of the trust is a minor and is disabled under local law from making an effective demand for the permitted amount, the beneficiary will nevertheless be deemed to have a present interest in the trust if a guardian can make the demand in the beneficiary's behalf. The trust instrument need not provide for the appointment of a guardian, but it is a good idea to provide in the instrument that a guardian may be appointed to make the demand for the minor. Many of the demand powers approved by the Service as constituting a present interest included a provision that the rights of minors may be exercised by a guardian. See, e.g., Priv. Ltr. Ruls. 8103074; 8030085; 8015133; 8014078; 8008040; 8007080; 8006048; 8004172; 8003033.

The trust, however, should offer no impediment to appointment of a guardian, nor should there be any impediments under local law. For example, where a minor beneficiary had to make his demand after additions were made to the trust but before the end of the year and the local law required a three-day waiting period for the appointment of a guardian, then a gift to the trust on December 30 would not qualify for the annual exclusion because the beneficiary could not make an effective demand for the property. See Priv. Ltr. Rul. 7922107. Time should be allowed for the guardian to be appointed and for the guardian to become familiar with the terms of the trust. See Priv. Ltr. Rul. 8022048.

Therefore, the trust should contain an express provision allowing the demand right of a minor beneficiary to be exercised for the beneficiary by a legal or natural guardian or other such fiduciary. But see Priv. Ltr. Rul. 8330005 (withdrawal power was illusory if *only* a parent could exercise the power and parent was the only contributor to the trust). Furthermore, a minimum time period should be allowed during which the beneficiary's right can be exercised, and this time period should exceed any impediments to guardian appointment under local law.

[¶ 19,499]

d. *Notice*

It seems clear that a demand right must be known to the beneficiary to be effective. Thus, the beneficiary should be informed of the existence of the right at the time of the trust's formation. The IRS has held that, for an adult beneficiary to have an effective demand right, he must have notice of the demand right. See, e.g., Rev. Rul. 81–7, 1981–1 C.B. 474; Priv. Ltr. Ruls. 7946007; 7947066. Moreover, in several cases, the Service has implied that notice may be necessary even for minor beneficiaries. See Priv. Ltr. Ruls. 8019038 (exclusion for daughter's demand right allowed provided that, *inter alia,* she be given notice of the right); 8014078 (IRS specifically approved the fact that donor's children were given notice of the right); 8008040 (parents were natural guardians for the children, and they knew of demand right). In any case, many of the *Crummey* clauses approved by the Service included notice of the right, and often notice of each subsequent addition to the trust to which the demand right applies, to the beneficiary. See, e.g., Priv. Ltr. Ruls. 8103074; 8103069; 8051128; 8030085; 8015133; 8008040; 8007080; 8004172; 7947066.

The policy of the IRS regarding notification to the beneficiary of additions to the trust seems to be tied to the concept that in order for the gift to be one of a present interest, "the question is not when the title vests, but when the enjoyment begins." Priv. Ltr. Rul. 9625031. Given this emphasis, it would appear that the IRS requires immediate notice to the beneficiary in order for the annual gift tax exclusion to apply.

In sum, the clause must provide that each beneficiary be given notice of the power, at least at the creation of the trust and perhaps at each subsequent addition, to which the demand power applies.

¶ 19,491

[¶ 19,507]

e. Reasonable Time to Exercise Power

A demand right may be deemed to be ineffective where the allowed time in which to exercise it is inadequate. The IRS has not drawn a clear line to separate reasonable from unreasonable time limitations, but *Crummey* powers which are limited in time to as little as 30 days after an addition to the trust have been deemed effective in many cases. See, e.g., Priv. Ltr. Ruls. 9625031; 9532001; 9232013; 8813019; 8103074; 8006048; 8004172. Additionally, the IRS has indicated that where a minor's right to withdrawal must be exercised by a legal guardian, there must be sufficient time to (1) have a guardian appointed and (2) for the guardian to exercise the withdrawal right. Priv. Ltr. Rul. 8022048.

[¶ 19,515]

f. Beneficial Interest: The Cristofani Case

In addition to the requirement that the beneficiary have a present interest in the property, what interest must the beneficiary have in the property before the donor is entitled to the annual gift tax deduction? Suppose that the donor's children, Abel and Kane, are to have beneficial enjoyment of the trust property but that the butcher, baker, candlestick maker, and others—16 in number—are given *Crummey* withdrawal rights which lapse if not exercised. Is the donor entitled to 18 gift tax exclusions?

In Estate of Cristofani v. Commissioner, 97 T.C. 74 (1991), the Tax Court held that the withdrawal rights of contingent beneficiaries were sufficient to create a valid *Crummey* power. In *Cristofani,* the donor executed an irrevocable trust for the benefit of her two children and five grandchildren. The two children were the primary beneficiaries of the trust and were to receive all the trust income until the donor's death. The five grandchildren were contingent beneficiaries of the trust and their rights to receive the benefits of the trust vested only if their respective parent predeceased the donor. However, the trust provided that each child and each grandchild possessed an "unrestricted right to withdraw an amount not to exceed the amount specified for the gift tax exclusion under § 2503(b)" for a period of 15 days from the time the donor contributed property to the trust. 97 T.C. 74. Furthermore, the donor claimed seven annual exclusions of $12,000, one for each child and each grandchild, and excluded a total of $70,000 in transfers on her federal gift tax return.

The issue before court was whether the five grandchildren possessed a "present interest" in the trust property required by § 2503(b). The court held that the correct test for determining whether a present interest was received is not "the likelihood that the beneficiary will actually receive the present enjoyment of the property" but rather the court "must examine the ability of the beneficiaries, in a legal sense, to exercise their right to withdraw trust corpus, and the trustee's rights to legally resist a beneficiary's demand for payment." 97 T.C. at 83. Therefore, the donor was allowed a deduction for each child and grandchild based on the ability of all seven to exercise their withdrawal rights up to the amount of the annual gift tax exclusion regardless of whether their interest in the corpus was a vested or contingent remainder.

The IRS acquiesced only in result to the holding in *Cristofani* and stated (1992–1 C.B. 1):

> The Service does not contest annual gift tax exclusions for *Crummey* powers held by current income beneficiaries and persons with vested remainder interests. However the Service will deny exclusions for powers held by individuals who either have no property interests in the trust except for *Crummey* powers, or hold only contingent remainder interests.

Cristofani has become one of those cases whose names roll off the tongues of experienced estate planning attorneys as easily as "Dallas Cowboys" when talking about "America's Team". Could it be said, though, that the IRS retreated from *Cristofani* and *Crummey* in its publication of TAM 9628004 which follows. The fact pattern is easily recognizable—and that perhaps makes the position taken in this TAM even more important (keeping in mind that § 6110(j)(3) bars use or citation of a TAM as precedent). TAM 9628004 should be read, however, in conjunction with *Estate of Kohlsaat* v. *Commissioner*, 73 T.C.M. (CCH) 2732, T.C.M. (RIA) ¶ 97,212 (1997), and *Estate of Holland* v. *Commissioner*, 73 T.C.M. (CCH) 3236, T.C.M. (RIA) ¶ 97,302 (1997), where the Tax Court rejected IRS claims that failure of remote beneficiaries to exercise their withdrawal powers was not, in and of itself, evidence of an understanding with the donor that those powers would not be exercised. Whether the Tax Court's continuing rebuke of the IRS' efforts by decisions such as *Kohlsaat* and *Holland* will mean final acquiescence by the IRS to naked *Crummey* powers is by no means clear.

TECHNICAL ADVICE MEMORANDUM 9628004
April 1, 1996.

Whether transfers of lapsing powers to withdraw trust corpus constitute gifts of present interests, entitling the donor to annual gift tax exclusions under § 2503(b) for tax years ending December 1990, December 1991, December 1992, and December 1993.

Facts:

Donor, who has three children, seven grandchildren, and two great-grandchildren, created three irrevocable trusts. Trust #1 was established on * * *. Donor's children, A, B, and C, are the trustees of the trust. The trustees may either accumulate the net income of the trust or distribute all or part of the net income as they may determine to A, B, C, and their issue. No trustee may participate in the exercise of a discretionary power affecting distributions of income or principal to himself or herself, or to his or her minor children, nor may the income or principal be utilized to discharge the legal support obligations of the parents of any minor children so long as they are otherwise financially capable of doing so. Any income not distributed is to be accumulated and added to principal.

Donor's children, A, B, and C, their spouses, and Donor's seven grandchildren each have the right to withdraw before December 31, 1990 from

¶ 19,515

principal, and in each succeeding year, that amount that will enable Donor to obtain an annual gift tax exclusion in the maximum amount available under the Internal Revenue Code. The withdrawal rights are non-cumulative. The provisions of Trust #1 do not require that the individuals granted withdrawal rights be given notice of the their right to withdraw, nor do the provisions require notice of additions to the trust.

Upon Donor's death the trust will terminate and the undistributed principal and income is to be distributed 50 percent to A, if living, or if he is deceased, to his living issue, per stirpes, and 50 percent to the trustees of Trust #2 to be held and distributed in accordance with the terms thereof.

On December 31, 1990, Donor's attorney faxed a letter on behalf of Donor to Bank #1 authorizing Bank #1 to transfer $130,000 from Donor's personal account at Bank #1 to the account being established for Trust #1. According to Bank #1, Donor's personal account was debited by $130,000 on December 31, 1990; however, the actual funding of Trust #1 occurred on January 2, 1991, because a Bank #1 rule prevents funding of an account on the day the account is established.

Donor's attorney provided copies of letters dated December 27, 1990, to 12 of the individuals having withdrawal powers in Trust #1, advising those individuals of their right to withdraw. It is represented that all 13 individuals having withdrawal rights were sent a letter of notification.

On Donor's 1990 Form 709, Donor reported $130,000 in gifts for calendar year 1990 and claimed 13 annual exclusions totaling $130,000. In January 1991, Donor transferred an additional $130,000 to Trust #1. This amount was reported on Donor's 1991 Form 709. Donor claimed 13 annual exclusions on her 1991 Form 709. Donor's 1992 and 1993 Forms 709 also reported transfers of $130,000 to Trust #1 and claimed 13 annual gift tax exclusions in each of those years.

Donor established Trust #2 on * * * with A, B, and C as trustees. The trustees in their sole discretion may either accumulate the net income of the trust or distribute all or part of the net income to B and her issue. In addition, principal may be distributed to B for expenses that are the result of accident or illness and to maintain her accustomed standard of living. B cannot participate in the exercise of discretionary power affecting distributions of income or principal to herself or her minor children. Neither may income or principal be utilized by B to discharge her legal support obligations to her minor children, so long as she is otherwise financially capable of doing so. Income that is not distributed is to be accumulated and added to principal.

Upon the death of Donor, 50 percent of the undistributed principal and accumulated income is to be paid to A, if living, or if he is deceased, to his living issue, per stirpes. Upon the death of Donor and B, the undistributed principal and income is to be distributed as B shall direct by her will to her spouse and issue, or any of them. In default of the exercise of this power, the trust estate is to be paid to B's living issue, per stirpes.

No individuals held withdrawal powers in Trust #2 and no annual exclusions were claimed for transfers to Trust #2.

¶ **19,515**

Trust #3 was established on * * * with A, B, and C as trustees. The trustees are authorized to either accumulate the net income or distribute it among B and her issue. Any income that is not distributed is to be accumulated and added to principal. The trustees may also pay so much of the principal as may be necessary for expenses of accident or illness of B, and to maintain her in her accustomed standard of living. B may not participate in the exercise of any discretionary power affecting distributions of income or principal to herself or her minor children, nor may B utilize trust income or principal to discharge her legal support obligations to her minor children, so long as she is otherwise financially capable of doing so.

Four spouses of Donor's grandchildren and Donor's two great-grandchildren each have the right to withdraw before December 31, 1991 from principal, and in each succeeding year, an amount equal to the annual gift tax exclusion. The withdrawal rights of the Donors great-grandchildren may be exercised by the Donor's grandchildren who are the parents of the great-grandchildren. The withdrawal rights are non-cumulative. The provisions of Trust #3 do not require that the individuals granted withdrawal rights be given notice of their right to withdraw, nor do the provisions require notice of additions to the trust.

Upon the death of Donor, the trust will terminate and 50 percent of the principal and accumulated income is to be distributed to B, if living, or if deceased, to her living issue, per stirpes. The other 50 percent is to be distributed to A, if living, or if he is deceased, to A's living issue, per stirpes.

On December 31, 1991, a check dated December 26, 1991, that was drawn on Bank #2 to the order of Trust #3, was deposited by Donor in Bank #1. The check was not processed by Bank #1 until January 2, 1992.

Donor's attorney provided copies of letters dated December 10, 1991, to five individuals having withdrawal rights, advising those individuals of their rights of withdrawal from the trust. It is represented that all six individuals having withdrawal rights were sent a letter of notification.

On each of Donor's 1991, 1992, and 1993 Forms 709, Donor reported transfers to Trust #3 of $60,000 and claimed six annual exclusions in the total amount of $60,000 for each year.

LAW AND ANALYSIS:

* * *

Section 2503(b) provides that, in the case of gifts (other than gifts of future interests in property) made to any person by the donor during the calendar year, the first $10,000 of such gifts to such person shall not be included in the total amount of gifts made during such year. The annual exclusion is only available for gifts of present interests in property.

Section 25.2503–3(a) provides that the term "future interest" includes reversions, remainders, and other interests or estates, whether vested or contingent, and whether or not supported by a particular interest or estate, which are limited to commence in use, possession, or enjoyment at some future date or time. Conversely, an unrestricted right to the immediate use, possession, or enjoyment of property or the income from property (such as a life estate or term certain) is a present interest in property. Section 25.2503–3(b); Fondren v. Commissioner, 324 U.S. 18, 20 (1945).

When a trust instrument gives a beneficiary the unrestricted right to demand immediate possession and enjoyment of trust corpus or income, the beneficiary has received a present interest in property. Crummey v. Commissioner, 397 F.2d 82 (9th Cir.1968); Estate of Cristofani v. Commissioner, 97 T.C. 74 (1991). However, where the facts and circumstances of a particular case show that there was a prearranged understanding that the withdrawal right (*Crummey* power) would not be exercised and/or that doing so would result in undesirable consequences, there is no bona fide unrestricted gift of a present interest in property. See Rev. Rul. 85–24, 1985–1 C.B. 329; Rev. Rul. 81–7, 1981–1 C.B. 474.

It is well settled that the "legal right of a taxpayer to decrease the amount of what otherwise would be his taxes, or altogether avoid them, by means which the law permits, cannot be doubted." Gregory v. Helvering, 293 U.S. 465, 469 (1935). A tax avoidance motive is irrelevant so long as the taxpayer actually did what he purported to do and what he did was "the thing which the statute intended." Id. However, where the transaction is designed to conform to the statute but the normal consequences which would flow from such transaction do not occur and were never intended to occur, the formal appearance of the transaction cannot prevail over what is, in substance, a tax avoidance scheme. Compare *Gregory*, supra, with Perkins v. Commissioner, 27 T.C. 601 (1956).

In *Gregory*, the taxpayer purported to effectuate a corporate reorganization. A new and valid corporation was organized under the laws of Delaware, and every requirement of the relevant reorganization statute was satisfied. In the "reorganization," shares of stock were transferred to the taxpayer who sold them for her individual profit, thereby substantially reducing the amount of tax which would have resulted from a direct transfer by way of dividend. No other business was ever transacted by the new corporation.

The Commissioner determined that the reorganization was without substance. The Court found that the taxpayer never intended that the new corporation transact any business, that the whole transaction was—a mere device which put on the form of a corporate reorganization as a disguise for concealing its real character, and the sole object and accomplishment of which was the consummation of a preconceived plan, not to reorganize a business or any part of a business, but to transfer a parcel of corporate shares to the petitioner. 293 U.S. at 469.

In Heyen v. United States, 945 F.2d 359 (10th Cir.1991), and Deal v. Commissioner, 29 T.C. 730 (1958), the courts found that the transactions at issue were not in substance what they purported to be in form and denied the tax benefits claimed by the taxpayers.

In *Heyen*, the decedent, 9 months before her death, purportedly gifted blocks of stock, each individually valued at less than $10,000, to 29 recipients. Shortly thereafter, 27 of the recipients signed blank stock certificates and the stock was reissued to members of the decedent's family. Claiming 29 annual exclusions, the decedent's estate did not pay a gift tax on the transfers. The Tenth Circuit applied a substance over form analysis and "pierced the veil" of the initial transfers to the 29 recipients. The court concluded that the substance of the undertaking was the decedent's intent to transfer the stock to members of her family and to use the 29 recipients merely to create gift tax exclusions and avoid payment of the gift tax. Because the decedent intended her family to be the ultimate beneficiaries of the stock, the fact that two of the original recipients retained their stock did not change the tax treatment for the other 27 stock transfers. The court ignored those transfers and denied the 27 annual exclusions.

In *Deal*, the taxpayer purportedly sold an interest in property in a bargain sale to her four daughters in exchange for a series of demand notes with a total value of $41,000: three notes per daughter in the amount of $3,000 each, and one note per daughter in the amount of $1,250. The day after the transaction, the taxpayer forgave four of the $3,000 notes. She forgave four more $3,000 notes in each of the succeeding years. She forgave the $1,250 notes in the fourth year.

The taxpayer reported total gifts of $42,000 in the first year, including $30,000 that represented the bargain sale element of the property transferred and $12,000 that represented the forgiven notes. After claiming $12,000 in annual exclusions and the specific exemption of $30,000, the taxpayer reported no gift tax liability for the year. In the following years, the taxpayer reported the forgiveness of the notes and claimed annual exclusions to fully offset the amount of the notes. The Service disallowed all of the annual exclusions claimed by the taxpayer in each of the four years, contending that the notes were never intended to be enforced and that the entire value of the interest in the land was a taxable gift as of the date of the purported sale.

The Tax Court agreed with the Service. The court reasoned: "After carefully considering the record we think that the notes executed by the daughters were not intended to be enforced and were not intended as consideration for the transfer by the [taxpayer], and that, in substance, the transfer of the property was by gift. There is no evidence that the [taxpayer] intended to sell the property to her daughters. On the contrary, a donative intent is evidenced ... Conversely, these facts lend considerable substance to the [Service's] argument that the making and canceling of the notes were a mere device to enable the [taxpayer] to avoid gift tax and to claim exclusions of $3,000 each upon cancellation of the notes ... As we have already stated, we do not regard the notes which [the taxpayer's] four daughters executed to her at the time of the gift as having any effect to reduce amount of the gift. We have found, and held, that these notes were not given as part of the purchase price of the property which [the taxpayer] conveyed to the trust and did not serve to reduce the amount of the gift. Therefore, even if we assume, as [the taxpayer] argues, that the daughters were legally liable on the notes to [the taxpayer], that fact has no effect on the question we have here to decide." 29 T.C. at 736–37.

¶ 19,515

The *Gregory*, *Heyen*, and *Deal* cases show that in determining the substance of the transaction, the intention of the taxpayer is a relevant consideration. While donative intent is not necessary to a finding that a transfer is a gift for gift tax purposes, donative intent does suggest that a transfer is a gift. Heyen, 945 F.2d at 362; Rev. Rul. 81–7.

The facts and circumstances of the instant case indicate that Donor did not intend gifts of present interests by granting the *Crummey* powers in Trust #1 and Trust #3.

With respect to Trust #1, notification was sent to the 13 beneficiaries on Thursday, December 27, 1990. The trust instrument states that the beneficiaries have the "right to withdraw *before* December 31, 1990 from the principal of the trust [the annual exclusion amount]." [Emphasis added.] On December 31, 1990, the trust was not yet funded.

With respect to Trust #3, notification was sent to the six beneficiaries on * * *. The trust instrument states that the beneficiaries have the "right to withdraw *before* December 31, 1991 from the principal of the trust [the annual exclusion amount]." [Emphasis added.] The check which initially funded the trust was not deposited by Donor until December 31, 1991, and was not processed until January 2, 1992.

With respect to the initial funding of both trusts, the Donor's conduct severely restricted the time during which the beneficiaries could exercise their rights and is indicative of the fact that the Donor never intended these rights as bona fide gifts.

The provisions of Trusts #1 and #3 do not require that the individuals granted withdrawal rights be given notice of their right to withdraw, nor do the provisions require notice of additions to the trust. None of the 13 power holders of Trust #1 exercised his or her right in 1990, 1991, 1992, or 1993. None of the six power holders of Trust #3 exercised his or her right in 1991, 1992, or 1993.

Of the 13 *Crummey* beneficiaries of Trust #1, three individuals, the spouses of A, B, and C, have no other interest in the trust aside from their withdrawal right. A, B, and C and the donor's seven grandchildren have discretionary income interests in the trust during the donor's lifetime. However, neither trustee may distribute income to herself or her minor children or himself or his minor children.

At Donor's death, 50 percent of the corpus of Trust #1 will be distributed outright to A, if he is living, or to his issue, per stirpes. A has a vested remainder interest in Trust #1, and his two children have contingent remainders.

At Donor's death, the other 50 percent of the corpus of Trust #1 will be distributed to Trust #2, which is a trust for the benefit of A and B and their issue. B and her issue have discretionary income interests in Trust #2. Although B is a trustee of Trust #2 (together with A and C), she cannot distribute income to herself or her minor children. B has a testamentary special power of appointment over the corpus of Trust #2. A and his issue have no income interests in Trust #2; however, at the Donor's death, 50

¶ 19,515

percent of the corpus of Trust #2 will be distributed outright to A, if he is living, or to his issue, per stirpes.

C and her three children have no income or remainder interests in Trust #1, except for a discretionary income interest. However, C cannot distribute income to herself or her minor children.

None of the six *Crummey* beneficiaries of Trust #3 has any other interest whatsoever in either the trust income or corpus, aside from the withdrawal right.

The Service generally does not contest annual gift tax exclusions for *Crummey* powers held by current income beneficiaries and persons with vested remainder interests. These individuals have current or long term economic interests in the trust and in the value of the corpus. It is understandable that in weighing these interests, they decide not to exercise their withdrawal rights. However, where nominal beneficiaries enjoy only discretionary income interests, remote contingent rights to the remainder, or no rights whatsoever in the income or remainder, their non-exercise indicates that there was some kind of prearranged understanding with the donor that these rights were not meant to be exercised or that their exercise would result in undesirable consequences, or both.

In the instant case, A had a vested remainder interest in Trust #1. All of the holders of withdrawal rights in Trust #1 were given 4 (or fewer) days in the first year of the trust within which to exercise their rights. This leads to the conclusion that no bona fide withdrawal rights were ever created in Trust #1.

The facts of the present case are comparable to those in *Gregory, Heyen*, and *Deal* in important respects. In these cases, the taxpayers purported to do something within the statutory provision at issue and set about satisfying all the requirements to ensure the benefit that particular statute afforded. In *Gregory*, the taxpayer organized a de jure corporation; in *Heyen*, stock certificates were transferred over to 29 individuals; in *Deal*, the taxpayer held notes on which her daughters were legally liable; in the present case, 19 people have, on paper, the right to demand trust corpus from the trustees.

The Courts in the three cases found that the taxpayers intended to do in substance something other than what they purported to do in form. In *Heyen*, the form was so unassailable that two of the recipients kept their "gifts."

The facts of the instant case also indicate that what the Donor did was not "the thing which the statute intended." Gregory, 293 U.S. at 469. See also Knetsch v. United States, 364 U.S. 361 (1960).

Congressional intent in enacting the predecessor to § 2503(b) was, in part, to avoid the necessity of reporting small gifts and, in part, to fix the amount sufficiently large to cover, in most cases, wedding and Christmas gifts and other occasional gifts. H. Rep. No. 708, 72d Cong., 1st Sess. 29 (1939), 1939–1 (Pt. 2) C.B. 457, 478.

In 1941, the Supreme Court addressed the question whether there should be an annual exclusion for each beneficiary when a gift is made in trust for

¶ 19,515

several beneficiaries. Helvering v. Hutchings, 312 U.S. 393 (1941). In that case, the taxpayer had established a single trust for the benefit of his children. The Court held that in speaking of "gifts ... made to any person," the person the statute referred to was not the trustee but the individual beneficiaries for whose benefit the property was transferred. The Court reasoned that if a separate annual exclusion would apply for each of several donees who received a gift of property outright, so should a separate annual exclusion apply for each of several beneficiaries when a gift is made in trust. Moreover, a holding otherwise could be avoided simply by creating as many trusts as there were beneficiaries.

As the Court read Congressional intent, in the case of a gift in trust, a separate annual exclusion applies for each beneficiary of a trust. This rule is perfectly reasonable where a donor who wishes to benefit a certain number of individuals could accomplish this purpose by creating a separate trust for each person or by giving each one a pro rata share of property outright. For wealthy donors, an annual gift of $10,000 to the objects of their bounty incurs no gift tax liability and removes that much money from their gross estates. When these donors intend to benefit the objects of their bounty and choose a tax-free means of doing so, they are actually doing what they are purporting to do and what they are doing is what the statute intended.

In the instant case, Donor intended that, at her death, 50 percent of the corpus of each of the three trusts be transferred outright to A. Trusts #2 and 3 were obviously intended to benefit B and her issue, as well. In creating Trust #1, Donor did not intend to benefit directly the spouses of A, B, or C. Neither does it appear that C or her issue were intended beneficiaries of that particular trust. Therefore, Donor could not have achieved her purpose of benefitting A and B and B's issue if she created 13 separate trusts, one for each *Crummey* beneficiary, or if she had transferred $10,000 outright to each one of them.

In creating Trust #3, Donor did not intend to benefit directly the four spouses of her grandchildren and her two great-grandchildren. Therefore, she could not have achieved her purpose of benefitting A and B by creating, instead, 6 separate trusts for the four spouses of her grandchildren and her two great-grandchildren or by transferring $10,000 to each of them.

It is highly doubtful that Congress could have intended that § 2503(b) apply to situations like the present case where the Donor could not achieve her intended purpose in creating Trusts #1, #2, and #3 by creating 19 separate trusts or making 19 outright gifts of $10,000 each.

We have considered the facts and circumstances surrounding the creation, initial funding, and purpose of each trust. We conclude that Donor did not intend at the creation of the trusts to make bona fide gifts of present interests to any of the trusts' beneficiaries. There is no logical reason for her intent to have changed in the following years. We note that while the $130,000 transfers for 1991 and 1993 were made early in those years, the $130,000 transfer to Trust #1 for 1992 was made on December 30, 1992. The $60,000 transfer to Trust #3 for 1993 was made early in that year, while the $60,000 transfer for 1992 was made on December 30, 1992.

¶ **19,515**

We also considered the fact that none of the rights were ever exercised, even by those who had no other interests in the trusts, and conclude that as part of a prearranged understanding, all of the beneficiaries knew that their rights were paper rights only, or that exercising them would result in unfavorable consequences. There is no other logical reason why these individuals would choose not to withdraw $10,000 a year as a gift which would not be includible in their income or subject the Donor to the gift tax.

CONCLUSION:

Transfers by the Donor of 13 lapsing powers to withdraw trust corpus from Trust #1 are not gifts of present interests in property, and the Donor is not entitled to 13 annual gift tax exclusions under § 2503(b) for transfers to Trust #1 in tax years ending December 1990, December 1991, December 1992, and December 1993.

Transfers by the Donor of six lapsing powers to withdraw trust corpus from Trust #3 are not gifts of present interests in property, and the Donor is not entitled to six annual gift tax exclusions under § 2503(b) for transfers to Trust #3 in tax years ending December 1991, December 1992, and December 1993.

[¶ 19,531]

4. DONEE'S EXERCISE OF CRUMMEY POWER

a. *Estate and Gift Tax Consequences*

There will be no gift or estate tax consequences to the donee who exercises a right to withdraw from a trust.

[¶ 19,539]

b. *Income Tax Consequences*

Section 678(a)(1) makes the donee subject to income tax on "his proportionate share" of the trust income for each year in which the donee could make a withdrawal from the trust whether or not the right of withdrawal is exercised. What this means is that the donee is treated as co-owner of the trust because of the ability to control a portion of the principal of the trust. What portion does the donee control? The donee controls the portion which is represented by a fraction, the numerator of which is the amount which the donee could withdraw. The denominator of the fraction is the value of the entire trust. See ¶ 18,257 for additional discussion of this issue.

Problem

[¶ 19,545]

From the time she was an infant, Brooke Bucks has had the right to withdraw the lesser of $12,000 or the value of each addition made to the Brooke Bucks Minority Trust. This year Calvin Bucks added $12,000 to Brooke's trust and Brooke, now age 18, exercised her right of withdrawal for the first time. She demanded and received the full $12,000 from the trustee. The value of the trust assets at the time Brooke exercised her right of withdrawal was $100,000. This year the trust had taxable income of $9,000. No other distributions were made from the trust this year. What are the income tax consequences to Brooke as a result of her exercise of her right of withdrawal this year?

[¶ 19,547]

5.   DONEE'S FAILURE TO EXERCISE CRUMMEY POWER

Implicit in every gift to a *Crummey* trust is the notion that the person having the right of withdrawal will not exercise that right of withdrawal. Failure to exercise the right of withdrawal means that the gift to the trust will continue in trust for the beneficiaries until the time established by the settlor for termination of the trust (unless, of course, the trustee makes an earlier distribution pursuant to authority given him or her in the instrument).

[¶ 19,555]

a.   *Estate and Gift Tax Consequences*

Two characteristics are common to all *Crummey* trusts. First, in each trust, some person or persons are given the right to withdraw some part or all of each addition to the trust, including the initial contribution. These rights of withdrawal are given out because those who contribute to the *Crummey* trust want their gift to qualify for the annual exclusion for gift tax purposes (either to preserve their § 2505 unified credit or, in the case of those who have exhausted their unified credit through prior transfers, to avoid paying gift tax on the transfer to the *Crummey* trust).

The second characteristic common to *Crummey* trusts is limitations on the exercise of the right of withdrawal. The person or persons having the right of withdrawal are commonly limited as to the time and the amount of property which they can withdraw from the trust. These limitations as to *time* and *amount* are a function of two considerations. First, the donor will either (a) want to control the trust property or (b) believe that the trust beneficiaries are not capable of managing the trust property. Aside from these nontax considerations, the donor will not want to impose estate and gift tax burdens on the persons who are given the rights of withdrawal.

Persons with a right of withdrawal may be burdened by estate and gift tax concerns because the right to withdraw an amount from a trust, commonly referred to as a *Crummey* power, is in reality a *general* power of appointment. (It is a general power because it can be exercised in favor of the powerholder.) Accordingly, the estate and gift tax rules set out in §§ 2041 and 2514 applicable to powers of appointment are applicable to *Crummey* powers.

Failure to exercise a general power of appointment constitutes a release of the power *and* a release of a general power is a taxable event for both estate and gift tax purposes. See §§ 2514(b), 2041(a)(2). However, the *lapse* of a general power is distinguished from the *release* of a general power. A lapse will constitute a release only to the extent the amount "which could have

¶ 19,555

been appointed by exercise of such lapsed powers exceeds in value the greater of the following amounts:

(1) $5,000 or

(2) 5 percent of the aggregate value of the assets out of which, or the proceeds of which, the exercise of the lapsed powers could have been satisfied." § 2514(e).

With those considerations in mind, it is customary for each person who creates a *Crummey* right of withdrawal to limit the amount which could be withdrawn to the amount which could "lapse" without constituting a "release." If this limitation is effectively imposed on the amount which can be withdrawn, a person's failure to exercise the right of withdrawal should have no gift tax consequences.

Similarly, a person's failure to exercise a right of withdrawal will have no estate tax consequences if the amount which could have been withdrawn does not exceed the lapse "exclusion amount." See § 2041(b)(2). (However, amounts which could have been withdrawn during the year in which death occurs are to be included in the holder's estate if the right of withdrawal has not lapsed at the date of death. See Reg. § 20.2041–3(d)(3).)

[¶ 19,556]

PRIVATE LETTER RULING 8901004

September 16, 1988.

In 1985, the Grantor created an irrevocable Trust for the benefit of his descendants.* * *

The Trust provides that, during the Grantor's life, the net income, if any, will be paid to the Grantor's descendants, in the trustee's discretion, to provide for the health, education, and support of the descendants.* * * At the Grantor's death, the trustee is to hold 50 percent of the Trust property for the exclusive use and benefit of the Grantor's Daughter and her descendants and 50 percent for the exclusive use and benefit of the Grantor's Son and his descendants. On the death of the Daughter, or the Grantor's death if the Daughter predeceases the Grantor, the property in the Daughter's fund will pass in fee simple, per stirpes to the Daughter's then living descendants. The Son's Trust is subject to identical provisions.

In addition, regarding subsequent additions to the Trust, each descendant and spouse has a noncumulative right, within 30 days after receiving notice that property has been added to the Trust, to withdraw a pro rata share of such addition. However, the Trust provides that, if upon the termination of any power of withdrawal the person holding the power will be deemed to have made a taxable gift for federal gift tax purposes, then such power of withdrawal will not lapse, but will continue to exist with respect to the amount that would have been a taxable gift and will terminate as soon as such termination will not result in a taxable gift. Finally, a donor of subsequent property to the

Trust may, in writing, exclude any person with a power of withdrawal from exercising that power as to any property subsequently added by the donor.

* * *

* * * Rev. Rul. 80–261, 1980–2 C.B. 279, provides that a gift of a right to demand and receive at least a pro rata portion of trust corpus conveyed to several donees is a gift of a present interest to the extent of each donee's pro rata portion, and the annual exclusion under § 2503 is allowable.

Accordingly, the transfer of property to the Trust over which the beneficiaries have a right of withdrawal are present interests that qualify for the annual gift tax exclusion under § 2503(b) of the Code, provided that there is no impediment to the appointment of a guardian under local law for any minors involved.

Issue 3:

Will the lapse of the right of withdrawal cause any beneficiary to be deemed to have made a gift and what will be the value of the gift?

* * *

In this case, the beneficiaries, through the power of withdrawal, have the power to appropriate or consume a pro rata portion of the corpus for their own benefit or for such other persons or entities as they may choose. Accordingly, each beneficiary's right of withdrawal is a general power of appointment for purposes of § 2514(b). Furthermore, in accordance with § 2514(e), a lapse of a general power of appointment is considered a transfer of property subject to the power to the extent of the excess of the greater of $5,000 or 5 percent of the aggregate value of the covered assets. Finally, during the Grantor's life and subsequently after the Trust has been divided into separate funds for the Grantor's two children and their descendants, payment of income to any beneficiary is subject to the trustee's discretion. Hence, no beneficiary has an exclusive lifetime benefit from the Trust or any part thereof. Accordingly, as no one beneficiary with the right of withdrawal retains an exclusive lifetime benefit from the trust and the power to control the disposition of the trust at death, each successive lapse of the right of withdrawal will be considered a completed gift for purposes of § 2511.

* * *

* * *[A] number of factors preclude valuation of the property reverting to the Trust on lapse of a power of withdrawal. Once the power to withdraw a pro rata portion of any contribution has lapsed for any beneficiary, no one other than the trustee can cause any beneficiary to receive a portion of that contribution. While distributions from the Trust are to be made to provide for the health, education and support of the current income beneficiaries, they are not to defray the Grantor's or the Spouse's legal obligations to their children. Also, unequal payments of income and principal will not be taken into consideration upon a subsequent division of the Trust. Finally, as the grantor has provided for a power of withdrawal for each of his living descendants and discretionary trust distributions for each descendant and upon termination of the trusts, distribution of the corpus will be made to all of the Son's and the Daughter's then living descendants, the number of beneficiaries is subject to change. Any attempt to value any one income beneficiary's interest in property reverting to the trust on lapse of a power of withdrawal would be no more than a guess. Accordingly, each time a beneficiary allows a power of withdrawal to lapse, each such beneficiary will be deemed to have made a gift to the Trust of their pro rata portion of the contribution to the extent such pro rata portion exceeds the greater of $5,000 or five percent of the contribution.

[¶ 19,557]

b.   Hanging Powers and Efforts to Coordinate the Use of "Five-and-Five" Powers with the Annual Gift Tax Exclusion

Suppose a donor takes full advantage of the per donee per annum gift tax exclusion under § 2503(b) and transfers $12,000 to a trust. However, the donor limits the *Crummey* right of withdrawal to $5,000, the nontaxable lapse amount. See § 2514(e); ¶ 19,555. To avoid the lapse of any withdrawal right exceeding $5,000, the donor creates a "hanging power" in the donee.

A hanging power allows the donee to withdraw an amount equal to the annual gift tax exclusion of $12,000, but a failure to withdraw will result only in a lapse equal to $5,000. The difference between the amount contributed to the trust and $5,000 will "hang," or carry over, as a continuing right of withdrawal until the next year. Then, provided no additional gifts are transferred to the trust, another $5,000 will lapse without tax consequences to the donee (assuming the donee does not exercise his or her continuing right of withdrawal). The right of withdrawal continues until the property available for withdrawal is: (1) exhausted through actual withdrawals or (2) fully lapsed (at a rate of $5,000 per annum). One minor drawback to this approach is that if the donee dies before the hanging power fully lapses, the unlapsed amount will be included in the donee's gross estate as property subject to a general power of appointment (inasmuch as the donee has a continuing right to withdraw the unlapsed amount). See Reg. § 20.2041–3(d)(3).

Significantly, the IRS claims, in Priv. Ltr. Rul. 8901004, that hanging powers are invalid under the *Procter* rule. Commissioner v. Procter is reprinted below at ¶ 19,559. Priv. Ltr. Rul. 8901004, reprinted at ¶ 19,556, provides, in pertinent part, as follows (citing *Procter* approvingly):

> Where a condition on a right of withdrawal provides that the right will not lapse until such lapse will not result in federal gift tax, is the condition valid?

* * *

In this case, the trust document provides, in part:

Notwithstanding the above, if upon the termination of any power of withdrawal, the person holding the power will be deemed to have made a taxable gift for federal gift tax purposes, then such power of withdrawal will not lapse, but will continue to exist with respect to the amount that

¶ 19,556

would have been a taxable gift and will terminate as soon as such termination will not result in a taxable gift.

Here the Trust provision will not be activated until after an addition to the Trust has been made; notice has been given to a beneficiary and the beneficiary's right of withdrawal has lapsed. At that time, the power of withdrawal will be recharacterized as not subject to a set time limit and hence an incomplete gift, so as to avoid federal gift tax consequences of the lapse. Accordingly, the provision is a condition subsequent and is deemed not valid as tending to discourage enforcement of federal gift tax provisions by either defeating the gift or rendering examination of the return ineffective.

[¶ 19,559]

c. *Savings Clauses*

COMMISSIONER v. PROCTER

United States Court of Appeals, Fourth Circuit, 1944.
142 F.2d 824, cert. denied, 323 U.S. 756 (1944).

PARKER, Circuit Judge.

* * *

[Frederick W. Procter made a transfer which he claimed to be free of federal gift tax if for no other reason than the instrument of transfer contained the following provision:]

Eleventh: The settlor is advised by counsel and satisfied that the present transfer is not subject to Federal gift tax. However, in the event it should be determined by final judgment or order of a competent federal court of last resort that any part of the transfer in trust hereunder is subject to gift tax, it is agreed by all the parties hereto that in that event the excess property hereby transferred which is decreed by such court to be subject to gift tax, shall automatically be deemed not to be included in the conveyance in trust hereunder and shall remain the sole property of Frederic W. Procter free from the trust hereby created.

We do not think that the gift tax can be avoided by any such device as this. Taxpayer has made a present gift of a future interest in property. He attempts to provide that, if a federal court of last resort shall hold the gift subject to gift tax, it shall be void as to such part of the property given as is subject to the tax. This is clearly a condition subsequent and void because contrary to public policy. A contrary holding would mean that upon a decision that the gift was subject to tax, the court making such decision must hold it not a gift and therefore not subject to tax. Such holding, however, being made in a tax suit to which the donees of the property are not parties, would not be binding upon them and they might later enforce the gift notwithstanding the decision of the Tax Court. It is manifest that a condition which involves this sort of trifling with the judicial process cannot be sustained.

The condition is contrary to public policy for three reasons: In the first place, it has a tendency to discourage the collection of the tax by the public officials charged with its collection, since the only effect of an attempt to enforce the tax would be to defeat the gift. In the second place, the effect of the condition would be to obstruct the administration of justice by requiring the courts to pass upon a moot case. If the condition were valid and the gift were held subject to tax, the only effect of the holding would be to defeat the gift so that it would not be subject to tax. The donor would thus secure the opinion of the court as to the taxability of the gift, when there would be before the court no controversy whatever with the taxing authorities which the court could decide, the only possible controversy being as to the validity of the gift and being between the donor and persons not before the court.* * *

* * *

In the third place the condition is to the effect that the final judgment of a court is to be held for naught because of the provision of an indenture necessarily before the court when the judgment is rendered. It should be remembered that it is not possible to obtain a declaratory judgment from a federal court as to whether the gift in question is subject to the gift tax.* * * The only way, therefore, in which it could be determined by "final judgment" of a federal court of last resort that any part of a transfer was subject to a gift tax would be for a tax to be assessed by the Commissioner and upheld by such court in the course of legal proceedings instituted for its enforcement or for its recovery after payment. This final judgment would fix the ability of the donor for the tax; and only then could the condition become operative. The condition, however, could not be given the effect of invalidating a judgment which had been rendered when the instrument containing the condition was before the court, since all matters are merged in the judgment. To state the matter differently, the condition is not to become operative until there has been a judgment; but after the judgment has been rendered it cannot become operative because the matter involved is concluded by the judgment.

[¶ 19,560]

Note

The Internal Revenue Service has continued to adamantly oppose savings clauses intended to adjust gifts to avoid gift taxes. Revenue Ruling 86–41, 1986–1 C.B. 300, unequivocally rejected the use of such post-gift adjustment clauses in two common situations in which a savings clause may be used. The first situation required a donee to transfer back to the taxpayer any interest in the transferred property that was determined by the IRS to exceed the annual gift tax exclusion. The second situation required the donee to convey consideration to the taxpayer equal to any interest in the property adjudged by the IRS to exceed the annual gift tax exclusion. The Ruling concluded that "if a donor transfers a specified portion of real property under terms that provide for a recharacterization of the transaction depending on the Service's valuation of the property for federal gift tax purposes, the adjustment clause will be disregarded for federal tax purposes." See also Priv. Ltr. Rul. 8531003 (savings clause disregarded where effect of clause was to adjust limited partnership interests received by taxpayer's descendant if the IRS valued the transfer in such a way as to create a gift tax payable). However, so-called formula defined benefit clauses were tested in McCord v. Commissioner, 461 F.3d 614 (5th Cir. 2006) and seemingly approved.

The Tenth Circuit, in King v. United States, 545 F.2d 700 (1976), upheld a savings clause in a situation where the taxpayer sold stock to a trust established for the benefit of his children. The transfer agreement contained a clause which adjusted the selling price of the shares if the IRS determined that the shares had a higher value. The court, in upholding the savings clause, emphasized the lack of donative intent on the part of the taxpayer and the intention to structure the transaction at arm's length and in the course of business. Id. at 706.

For other alternatives, see David R. Hodgman, Drafting Flexible Irrevocable Trusts—Whom Do You Trust? 23 Estate Planning 221 (1996) (describes use of a "trust protector" and empowering such person to modify irrevocable trusts); Neill G. McBryde & Frederick R. Keydel, Building Flexibility in Estate Planning Documents, 135 Trusts & Estates 56 (1996) (proposes that trustee be authorized to grant or eliminate general or special powers of appointment; conform marital deduction provisions to federal standards; and divide trusts into separate trusts).

Problem

[¶ 19,562]

Would the following language included in an irrevocable trust run afoul of the *Procter* rule?

Notwithstanding any other provision in this instrument to the contrary, at any time when someone other than a beneficiary of the trust is serving as trustee hereunder, such Trustee may terminate the trust, or any fund or share thereof, in the event such Trustee determines that the trust no longer serves a useful purpose or that the continuation of the trust will be unduly burdensome upon the trust estate or the beneficiaries thereof (whether by reason of tax considerations, size of the trust estate, or otherwise). In the event of such termination, the Trustee shall distribute to Settlor's spouse if such spouse is then living all of the assets then comprising the trust estate. If Settlor's spouse is not then living, such assets shall be distributed to Settlor's then living lineal descendants *per stirpes*. In lieu of such termination, the Trustee may alter, amend, or modify the trust in any manner whatsoever so as to accomplish the purpose of this trust which is to cause the exclusion from Settlor's estate and that of Settlor's spouse for federal estate tax purposes of other property constituting the trust estate. However, the Trustee may not exercise any of the authority given the Trustee in this paragraph at any time when a beneficiary of the trust has the right to remove the Trustee.

[¶ 19,563]

d. Income Tax Consequences

The income tax consequences to a person who has a right of withdrawal but does not exercise it in a particular year are the same as those experienced by a powerholder who exercises his or her right of withdrawal. See discussion at ¶ 19,539.

[¶ 19,571]

6. "OLD" TRUSTS

The increase in the annual gift tax exclusion from $3,000 to a then new $10,000 in 1981 ($12,000 in 2006) could have raised havoc with *Crummey* trusts which had been established prior to the increase in the exclusion. Many of these *Crummey* trusts provide that the amount which can be withdrawn in a single year is limited to the "annual gift tax exclusion." Some trusts make express reference to "$3,000" in limiting the amount which can be withdrawn.

Congress anticipated this problem by denying the then new $10,000 gift tax annual exclusion to trusts established before September 13, 1981. The $10,000 annual gift tax exclusion was denied to those trusts which contained a power of appointment "expressly defined in terms of, or by reference to, the amount of the gift tax exclusion." P.L. 97–34, § 441(a). With respect to these "old" trusts, the annual exclusion remains $3,000.

[¶ 19,579]

7. GIFT-SPLITTING

Where gift-splitting is contemplated, the drafter of the *Crummey* trust must be careful not to make the beneficiary's right to withdraw more than $12,000 contingent on whether the § 2513 election is made. Because the election is not made until the gift tax return is filed after the end of the calendar year, the amount available to the beneficiary is still uncertain at the close of the year. This means that the beneficiary has received a future, not a present, interest. See Priv. Ltr. Rul. 8022048.

For an additional discussion of rights of withdrawal, refer to ¶¶ 18,257–18,271.

Problem

[¶ 19,595]

From the discussion in text it should be clear that one objective to be accomplished in drafting every *Crummey* power is to limit the amount which can be withdrawn to that amount which will qualify for the gift tax exclusion.

The second objective is to limit the amount which can be withdrawn even further. The amount which can be withdrawn should be so limited that the failure to exercise the right of withdrawal will not constitute the taxable release of a general power of appointment. This means limiting the amount which could be withdrawn to the amount which could "lapse" without constituting a "release."

With those considerations in mind, review the excerpts (set out below) which are taken from a *Crummey* trust. Decide whether you would be comfortable including these provision in your *Crummey* trusts. You will note that paragraph 4.01 of the excerpts contains a "slop over" provision. Apparently the creator of the trust anticipated that contributors to the trust might want to take advantage of the $12,000 annual gift tax exclusion but would not want to put the *Crummey* powerholder in the position of making a taxable release if the powerholder does not exercise his or her right of withdrawal. (Go back and review the text material preceding this Problem if you do not understand this point.)

Refer to paragraphs 4.06 and 4.07 of the excerpts below and ask yourself why the creator of the trust established different distribution schemes upon termination of the trust depending upon whether the right of withdrawal was exercised. Do you think that was designed as a "penalty" provision to discourage the powerholder from exercising his or her right of withdrawal?

Do you think the person who created the *Crummey* trust below should be congratulated on a sophisticated scheme or be denounced for having constructed a monster which will lead only to litigation?

Can you explain each and every aspect of the provisions appearing in these excerpts? (Do you agree that you should strike each provision that you do not understand rather than risk a result that you could not anticipate? Or do you take the position that if someone was willing to publish a particular provision, it must be okay?)

DIVISION OF TRUST ESTATE AND DISTRIBUTION OF INCOME AND PRINCIPAL

4.01 *Division of Initial Trust Estate.* The Trustee shall divide the initial trust estate into two separate and distinct trust funds. One of such trust funds shall be referred to as the Crummey Trust Fund Account, and the other trust fund shall be referred to as the § 2503(c) Trust Fund Account.

    a. The Trustee shall allocate to the Crummey Trust Fund Account that fraction of the initial trust estate which does not exceed $5,000.

    b. The balance of the initial trust estate shall be allocated to the § 2503(c) Trust Fund Account.

4.02 *Additions to Trust Estate.* The donor of money or other property to the trust may designate the particular trust fund to which their addition shall be allocated. If the donor of money or other property fails to designate the particular trust fund to which his or her addition shall be allocated, the Trustee shall allocate each such donor's addition to the trust estate as follows:

    a. To the Crummey Trust Fund Account, an amount equal to the lesser of the value of the money or the property added to trust, or

¶ 19,595

the Annual Exclusion Amount, unless the donor is then married and the donor's spouse indicates, in writing to the Trustee, an intention to have the amount by which the addition exceeds the Annual Exclusion Amount attributed to such spouse for federal gift tax purposes. Notwithstanding the preceding sentence, the total value of the money or property allocated to the Crummey Trust Fund shall not exceed, in any one-year period, the Lapse Amount for that calendar year. For purposes of this paragraph, the Annual Exclusion Amount refers to the amount of property which a donor may exclude when computing the other taxable gifts for federal gift tax purposes for the year in which the addition to the trust estate is made. for purposes of this paragraph, the Lapse Amount shall be equal to the greater of $5,000 or 5 percent of the aggregate value of the Crummey Trust Fund Account determined on the last day of the calendar year in which an addition has been made to the Crummey Trust Fund Account. If, at any time during the continuance of the trust, the right to withdraw an amount of property in excess of the Lapse Amount from the Crummey Trust Fund Account will not constitute a taxable gift for federal gift tax purposes, the Lapse Amount shall be increased to equal the amount which could be so withdrawn.

b. To the § 2503(c) Trust Fund Account, that portion of each addition to the trust estate which is not allocated to the Crummey Trust Fund Account.

4.03 *Aggregation of Trust Fund Accounts.* The Trustee is authorized to aggregate the trust estates of the Crummey Trust Fund Account and the § 2503(c) Trust Fund Account for investment, management, and administrative purposes, but the Trustee shall maintain books and records accurately reflecting the principal and income comprising the two trusts created by this instrument.

4.04 *Distribution in General.* Until the beneficiary shall have attained 30 years of age, the Trustee may distribute to the beneficiary, or expend for the benefit of the beneficiary, from time to time, such amounts of the income or principal, or both, from the Crummey Trust Fund Account or the § 2503(c) Trust Fund Account, or both, as the Trustee, in the Trustee's sole discretion, may determine. To the extent that income from such accounts is not distributed or expended, it shall be accumulated by the Trustee and added to the trust fund account to which it is attributable at such time or times as the Trustee considers desirable. Distribution of all the principal and income is authorized if the Trustee shall determine, in the Trustee's sole discretion, that such distribution would be in the best interest of the beneficiary.

4.05 *Withdrawals from 2503(c) Trust Fund Account.* When the beneficiary attains 21 years of age, the beneficiary may withdraw all or part of the property then constituting the § 2503(c) Trust Fund Account. Such right of withdrawal shall be exercised in writing, signed and acknowledged by the beneficiary and delivered to the Trustee during the 60–day period commencing with the beneficiary's 21st birthday.

4.06 *Exercise of Withdrawal Rights.* If the beneficiary demands a distribution of the 2503(c) Trust Fund Account upon attaining the age of 21 years, as provided by paragraph 4.05, the Trustee shall distribute to the beneficiary, from the Crummey Trust Fund Account, the following:

a. An amount equal to one-third of the Crummey Trust Fund Account as soon as possible after the beneficiary attains 25 years of age; and

b. An amount equal to one-third of the Crummey Trust Fund Account as soon as possible after the beneficiary attains 30 years of age.

4.07 *Nonexercise of Withdrawal Rights.* If the beneficiary does not exercise his right to withdraw the § 2503(c) Trust Fund Account upon attaining 21 years of age, the Trustee shall distribute, to the beneficiary, from both the Crummey and the § 2503(c) Trust Fund Accounts, the following as soon as possible after the beneficiary attains the indicated ages:

a. An amount equal to one-third the property then constituting the trust estate, as soon as possible after the beneficiary attains 21 years of age; and

b. An amount equal to one-third of the property then constituting the trust estate, as soon as possible after the beneficiary attains 25 years of age.

4.08 *Computation.* For purpose of computing the amount to be distributed from the trust fund accounts on the indicated anniversary dates, the value of the trust fund accounts shall be determined as of the date on which the beneficiary attains the indicated age.

I. SELECTION OF TRUSTEE

[¶ 19,601]

1. ESTATE AND GIFT TAX CONSIDERATIONS

In considering the following materials, focus on the role of the ascertainable standard in structuring distribution provisions used in the trusts under consideration.

Recall that in ¶¶ 18,167–18,183 it was suggested that the distribution provisions used in trusts can generally be classified as "discretionary pay," "discretionary pay subject to an ascertainable standard," and "mandatory pay." Those materials focus on structuring the distribution provisions of the trust so as to allow the trust beneficiary to "control" the trust without having the trust property included in the estate of the powerholder for estate tax purposes and without having the trust income taxed to the beneficiary except to the extent it is distributed to the beneficiary. Central to this analysis is the § 2041(b)(1)(A) ascertainable standard exception to the rules applicable whenever a beneficiary is found to have a general power of appointment over trust property.

The following materials focus on the development of an ascertainable standard that will allow the person who has transferred property to an irrevocable trust to continue to control the enjoyment of that property. It is important to note that there is no statutorily created ascertainable standard that is available to shelter the transferor from estate taxation on the transferred property in cases where the transferor has retained until death (§ 2036(a)(2)) or enjoys at death (§ 2038) "control" over the trust property. The ascertainable standard exception to the inclusion rules of §§ 2036(a)(2) and 2038 is judge-made and is much broader than that provided in § 2041(b)(1)(A) as to general powers of appointment.

The importance of trustee selection relates to the conditions in which the transferor can be trustee of the irrevocable trust that he or she has created without having the trust property included in the transferor's gross estate for estate tax purposes. See Lober v. United States, 346 U.S. 335 (1953), reprinted at ¶ 19,299. Being able to enjoy such control after having transferred the property to the irrevocable trust means that the transferor can continue in his or her implementation of the unarticulated but presumably widely held view that "Who knows better than me what's good for thee." (Think about it. How many people want to make gifts of their hard-earned property so as to be able to vicariously enjoy the dissipation of that property by the donee?)

[¶ 19,603]

REVENUE RULING 73–143

1973–1 C.B. 401.

Advice has been requested whether the values of certain inter vivos trusts are includible in the gross estate of the settler under § 2038.* * *

The decedent, prior to his death on June 1, 1970, established inter vivos trusts in 1955 for the benefit of his son and daughter and named himself trustee of each trust. Under the terms of each instrument, the income is payable to the beneficiary for life and at the death of the beneficiary the remainder is to be distributed to the beneficiary's children then living or, if none, to designated noncharitable organizations.

The daughter's trust provides that:

In the event of special need on the part of the said income beneficiary, the Trustee, in his sole discretion, may pay to her or use for her benefit such amount or amounts of the principal of the Trust Estate as shall seem to him advisable for her support and education.

The son's trust provides that:

In the event of special need on the part of the said income beneficiary, the Trustee, in his sole discretion, may pay to said beneficiary or use for his benefit such amount or amounts of the principal of the Trust Estate as shall seem to him advisable.

Section 2038 provides that the value of the gross estate shall include the value of all property transferred by the decedent, in trust or otherwise, over which he holds at his death, either alone or in conjunction with any other person, the power to alter, amend, revoke, or terminate the enjoyment of the beneficial interest.

The question is whether the decedent-trustee's powers to invade the trust principals are powers to alter, amend, revoke or terminate within the scope of § 2038.

Nondiscretionary powers to vary the beneficial interests of a trust held by a settlor-trustee do not render the value of the property subject to the trust includible in his gross estate under § 2038. Nondiscretionary powers are those limited by an ascertainable standard.* * * A power to alter or amend, the exercise of which is not limited by definite external standards and which is, therefore, discretionary in nature renders the value of the property subject to the power includible in the decedent-settlor-trustee's gross estate.* * *

The invasion clause in the trust for the settlor's daughter indicates that the corpus of that trust may be invaded only for her support and education and then only in the event of special need. The power to distribute corpus for support and education is an ascertainable standard which can be objectively applied.

Under the terms of the trust for the decedent's son, the trustee may invade corpus in the event of special need. However, it is significant that there is no restriction upon the purpose for which the trust corpus may be invaded. "Special need" as used in this trust would cover any need that is out the ordinary or that arises from unexpected circumstances. In Michigan Trust Company v. Kavanagh, 284 F.2d 502 (1960), the court considered a power held by the decedent-trustee to invade corpus "should what the Trustee deems a *special emergency* arise." In holding that this power was discretionary in nature and not limited by an ascertainable standard, the court ruled that the value of the property subject to the power was includible in the decedent's gross estate under § 811(d)(2). [1986 Code § 2038(a)(2)]. The court noted that "Here, * * * the exercise of the power is left to the unbridled discretion of the settlor. The alleged limitation furnished no guide as to what constituted 'a special emergency.' " Similarly, the term "special need" where used without any restrictions or limitations is too broad and vague to constitute an ascertainable standard of invasion.

Accordingly, it is held that the value of the property held in trust for the decedent-trustee's daughter is not includible in his gross estate under § 2038 because his power to invade corpus was governed by a determinable standard. On the other hand, the value of the trust for the decedent-trustee's son is includible in his gross estate because the power to invade corpus was not so limited.

¶ 19,603

[¶ 19,605]

OLD COLONY TRUST CO. v. UNITED STATES

United States Court of Appeals, First Circuit, 1970.
423 F.2d 601.

ALDRICH, Chief Judge:

The sole question in this case is whether the estate of a settlor of an inter vivos trust, who was a trustee until the date of his death, is to be charged with the value of the principal he contributed by virtue of reserved powers in the trust.* * *

The initial life beneficiary of the trust was the settlor's adult son. Eighty per cent of the income was normally to be payable to him, and the balance added to principal. Subsequent beneficiaries were the son's widow and his issue. The powers upon which the government relies to cause the corpus to be includible in the settlor-trustee's estate are contained in two articles.* * *

Article 4 permitted the trustees to increase the percentage of income payable to the son beyond the eighty per cent,

> in their absolute discretion * * * when in their opinion such increase is needed in case of sickness, or desirable in view of changed circumstances.

In addition, under Article 4 the trustees were given the discretion to cease paying income to the son, and add it all to principal,

> during such period as the Trustees may decide that the stoppage of such payments is for his best interests.

Article 7 gave broad administrative or management powers to the trustees, with discretion to acquire investments not normally held by trustees, and the right to determine what was to be charged or credited to income or principal, including stock dividends or deductions for amortization. It further provided that all divisions and decisions made by the trustees in good faith should be conclusive on all parties, and in summary, stated that the trustees were empowered, "generally to do all things in relation to the Trust Fund which the Donor could do if living and this Trust had not been executed."

The government claims that each of these two articles meant that the settlor-trustee had "the right * * * to designate the persons who shall possess or enjoy the [trust] property or the income therefrom" within the meaning of § 2036(a)(2)* * *, and that the settlor-trustee at the date of his death possessed a power "to alter, amend, revoke, or terminate" within the meaning of § 2038(a)(1).* * *

If State Street Trust Co. v. United States 1 Cir., 1959, 263 F.2d 635, was correctly decided in this aspect, the government must prevail because of the Article 7 powers. There this court, Chief Judge Magruder dissenting, held against the taxpayer because broad powers similar to those in Article 7 meant that the trustees "could very substantially shift the economic benefits of the trusts between the life tenants and the remaindermen," so that the settlor "as long as he lived, in substance and effect and in a very real sense * * * 'retained for his life * * * the right * * * to designate the persons who shall possess or enjoy the property or the income therefrom.* * *'" 263 F.2d at 639–40, quoting § 2036(a)(2). We accept the taxpayer's invitation to reconsider this ruling.

It is common ground that a settlor will not find the corpus of the trust included in his estate merely because he named himself a trustee.* * * He must have reserved a power to himself that is inconsistent with the full termination of ownership. The government's brief defines this as "sufficient dominion and control until his death." Trustee powers given for the administration or management of the trust must be equitably exercised, however, for the benefit of the trust as a whole.* * * The court in *State Street* conceded that the powers at issue were all such powers, but reached the conclusion that, cumulatively, they gave the settlor dominion sufficiently unfettered to be in the nature of ownership. With all respect to the majority of the then court, we find it difficult to see how a power can be subject to control by the probate court, and exercisable only in what the trustee fairly concludes is in the interests of the trust and its beneficiaries as a whole, and at the same time be an ownership power.

The government's position, to be sound, must be that the trustee's powers are beyond the court's control. Under Massachusetts law, however, no amount of administrative discretion prevents judicial supervision of the trustee. Thus in Appeal of Davis, 1903, 183 Mass. 499, a trustee was given "full power to make purchases, investments and exchanges * * * in such manner as to them shall seem expedient; it being my intention to give my trustees * * * the same dominion and control over said trust property as I now have." In spite of this language, and in spite of their good faith, the court charged the trustees for failing sufficiently to diversify their investment portfolio.

The Massachusetts court has never varied from this broad rule of accountability, and has twice criticized *State Street* for its seeming departure.* * * We make a further observation, which the court in *State Street* failed to note, that the provision in that trust (as in the case at bar) that the trustees could "do all things in relation to the Trust Fund which I, the Donor, could do if * * * the Trust had not been executed," is almost precisely the provision which did not protect the trustees from accountability in *Appeal of Davis, supra.*

We do not believe that trustee powers are to be more broadly construed for tax purposes than the probate court would construe them for administrative purposes. More basically, we agree with Judge Magruder's observation that nothing is "gained by lumping them together." State Street Trust Co. v. United States, supra, at 642. We hold that no aggregation of purely administrative powers can meet the government's amorphous test of "sufficient dominion and control" so as to be equated with ownership.

This does not resolve taxpayer's difficulties under Article 4. Quite different considerations apply to distribution powers. Under them the trustee can, expressly, prefer one beneficiary over another. Furthermore, his freedom of choice may vary greatly, depending upon the terms of the individual trust. If there is an ascertainable standard, the trustee can be compelled to follow it. If there is not, even though he is a fiduciary, it is not unreasonable to say that his retention of an unmeasurable freedom of choice is equivalent to retaining some of the incidents of ownership. Hence, under the cases, if there is an ascertainable standard the settlor-trustee's estate is not taxed.* * *

The trust provision which is uniformly held to provide an ascertainable standard is one which, though variously expressed, authorizes such distributions as may be needed to continue the beneficiary's accustomed way of life.* * * On the other hand, if the trustee may go further, and has power to provide for the beneficiary's "happiness," * * * or "pleasure," * * * or "use and benefit," * * * or "reasonable requirement[s]," * * * the standard is so loose that the trustee is in effect uncontrolled* * *

In the case at bar the trustees could increase the life tenant's income "in case of sickness, or [if] desirable in view of changed circumstances." Alternatively, they could reduce it "for his best interests." "Sickness" presents no problem. Conceivably, providing for "changed circumstances" is roughly equivalent to maintaining the son's present standard of living.* * * The unavoidable stumbling block is the trustees' right to accumulate income and add it to capital (which the son would never receive) when it is to the "best interests" of the son to do so. Additional payments to a beneficiary whenever in his "best interests" might seem to be too broad a standard in any event. In * * * Estate of Yawkey, 1949, 12 T. C. 1164, * * * the court said, at p. 1170,

> We can not regard the language involved ["best interest"] as limiting the usual scope of a trustee's discretion. It must always be anticipated that trustees will act for the best interests of a trust beneficiary, and an exhortation to act "in the interests and for the welfare" of the beneficiary does not establish an external standard.

Power, however, to decrease or cut off a beneficiary's income when in his "best interests," is even more troublesome. When the beneficiary is the son, and the trustee the father, a particular purpose comes to mind, parental control through holding the purse strings. The father decides what conduct is to the "best interests" of the son, and if the son does not agree, he loses his allowance. Such a power has the plain indicia of ownership control. The alternative, that the son, because of other means, might not need this income, and would prefer to have it accumulate for his widow and children after his death, is no better. If the trustee has power to confer "happiness" on the son by generosity to someone else, this seems clearly an unascertainable standard.* * *

Problems

[¶ 19,618]

1. Five years before he died, Dad created an irrevocable trust of $2,000,000 for the benefit of Son, age 5. Would the trust be included in Dad's gross estate in the following cases (comparing Estate of Gokey v. Commissioner, 72 T.C. 721 (1979), reprinted at ¶ 19,383, with Old Colony Trust Co. v. United States, reprinted at ¶ 19,605):

    (a) The Accumulation National Bank was the trustee and distributions of income and principal to Son from the trust were to be only if the trustee determined such distributions to be "appropriate and desirable."

(b) Dad was the trustee. All of the income of the trust was to be distributed quarterly. Distributions of principal were not authorized.

(c) Dad was the trustee. Distributions of income and principal were to be made when such distributions were "necessary for the health, education, maintenance, and support" of Son.

(d) Same facts as in (c), except that the trust expressly prohibited distributions to discharge Dad's legal obligation to support Son.

2. Refer to the preceding problem and determine whether additions made to the respective trusts would qualify for the $12,000 per donee per annum gift tax exclusion under § 2503(c). See ¶ 19,365.

[¶ 19,640]

2. INCOME TAX CONSIDERATIONS

In a number of instances, the grantor trust rules imposed by §§ 671–677 cause the settlor to be taxed on trust income even if someone other than the settlor receives that income. See Chapter 22. Practically speaking, that means that the settlor cannot be trustee unless the trust is "mandatory pay," i.e., unless the trustee is obligated to distribute all of the trust income except during the beneficiary's minority. See § 674(b)(7). Where the settlor is trustee of a "discretionary pay" trust, the settlor will be taxed on the trust income even if someone else receives that income (or it is warehoused in the trust). § 674(a). Even if the settlor's discretion is limited by an ascertainable standard, the settlor will be taxed on the trust income if the settlor is trustee. § 674(d).

As a result, where trust distributions are discretionary with the trustee, an independent trustee is necessary (if the trust income is not to be taxed to the settlor). § 674(c). However, where distributions are subject to an ascertainable standard, the trustee can be anyone other than the settlor or the settlor's spouse. § 674(d). In such a case, the trustee need not qualify as "independent" as defined in § 674(c).

J. RIGHT TO REMOVE TRUSTEE

[¶ 19,651]

The ability to change trustees is an important feature. Its presence means that the trustee will have more incentive to be competitive in fees and, perhaps, more carefully tailor an investment strategy to the particular requirements of the trust beneficiaries. Its presence also provides a safety valve, an outlet for the frustrations that can develop during valleys in economic activity. That is, knowing that the trustee can be removed will sometimes be all that a disgruntled beneficiary needs to enable him or her to more honestly appraise the efforts of the trustee and enter into a more collaborative relationship.

¶ 19,651

Revenue Ruling 79–353, 1979–2 C.B. 325, was, for a time, one of those very few rulings known by its identifying number to every estate planning professional. It was the center of controversy upon publication, with most bar groups claiming that its conclusion was not well founded in precedent or policy.

In Revenue Ruling 79–353 the decedent created an irrevocable trust for the benefit of his adult children, appointed a corporate trustee, and retained the right to remove, without cause, the corporate trustee and appoint a successor corporate trustee. The trustee had discretion to distribute trust income and principal to the adult children "at such times and in such amounts as the trustee deems proper without limitation." Looking to §§ 2036(a)(2) and 2038, the ruling concluded that the trust property must be included in the estate of the person who transferred that property to the trust since the transferor has retained the power to remove the corporate trustee and appoint another corporate trustee. The ruling distinguished this trust with its discretionary pay feature from trusts in which the trustee's ability to make distributions is limited by an ascertainable standard.

On an identical set of facts, the Tax Court, in Estate of Wall v. Commissioner, 101 T.C. 300 (1993), rejected the conclusion reached in Revenue Ruling 79–353. The government had argued that the decedent, who had created the trust, effectively controlled the corporate trustee because of his ability to remove the trustee and appoint another corporate trustee (even though the decedent was not a beneficiary of the trust). The court rejected this argument, noting "the trustee's duty of sole fidelity to the beneficiary" and not to the settlor. 101 T.C. at 312. The court refused "to infer any kind of fraudulent side agreement" between the settlor and the corporate trustee. To suggest otherwise invites a widespread indictment of all trustees. In addition, in a supplemental opinion, the court added, "the conclusion reached in Revenue Ruling 79–353 was not supported by the case law cited therein" by the IRS. 102 T.C. 391, 394.

Ultimately, Revenue Ruling 95–58, 95–2 C.B. 191, revoked Revenue Ruling 79–353. As a result, a settlor may now retain the right to remove and replace a trustee holding discretionary authority with an independent trustee without adverse estate tax consequences under §§ 2036–38. Also rendered obsolete was Priv. Ltr. Rul. 8916032 which extended the rationale of Revenue Ruling 79–353 to beneficiaries holding the power to remove and replace a trustee with an independent trustee. The fact that it constituted the IRS position for 16 years is suggestive of the concerns that a draftsperson must have for the aspirations of the IRS when crafting these gifts.

Problems

[¶ 19,670]

1. Milt established an irrevocable trust for the benefit of his sister, Sue, for life with remainder to her then living descendants, *per stirpes*. The trustee was Accumulation National Bank. All distributions from the trust were at the discretion of the trustee. Although Milt reserved the right to remove the trustee and appoint another, he never exercised the right to remove

the trustee. At Milt's death, five years after the trust was established, the trust had a value of $200,000. Is any part of the $200,000 in Milt's gross estate?

2. On the facts in the preceding problem, Milt could appoint a successor trustee only if Accumulation National Bank ceased to serve. He did not have the right to remove the trustee. Is the estate tax result any different?

3. On the facts in the first problem, assume that the trustee could make distributions only for the health, education, maintenance, and support of Milt's sister. Is the estate tax result any different?

4. Do you think the decedent in Revenue Ruling 79–353 retained the right to remove the trustee in order to retain effective control over the trust? Or did he retain the right of removal merely as a safeguard in the event the trustee did not discharge his administrative responsibilities in a satisfactory manner?

5. Would the use of a Trust Committee as suggested by the following language avoid the result of Revenue Ruling 79–353?

> 3.02   *Removal of Trustee by Trust Committee.* The Trust Committee shall have the power, in its sole discretion and by majority vote of the members then serving, to remove the Trustee herein named and any Successor Trustee and to appoint as Successor Trustee any unincorporated person, or national bank in the United States, or any state bank provided that any such successor corporate Trustee shall have trust powers and a capital and surplus of Five Million Dollars ($5,000,000) or more. Such removal and appointment shall be by written instrument duly executed and acknowledged by a majority of the Trust Committee members then serving and by the Successor Trustee. A member of the Trust Committee or the Successor Trustee shall promptly deliver a copy of such instrument to the Trustee then serving, which shall immediately deprive such Trustee of all powers as Trustee hereunder. Notwithstanding the foregoing, at any time when a beneficiary of the trust has the right to remove the Trustee, the Trust Committee shall exercise its authority only after consulting such person if such person is readily accessible for such consultation even though the advice of that person shall not be binding upon the Trust Committee.

> 3.03   *Trust Committee.* As used herein, the term "Trust Committee" shall mean the following individuals:

> a.   I. M. Prudent

> b.   Harry Straight

> c.   A person to be appointed by the other members of the Trust Committee.

> If through any member's ceasing or failing to serve, the membership of said Trust Committee shall be reduced to less than three (3) persons, the remaining members shall appoint by a majority vote a

sufficient number of persons to bring the total membership to three (3) individuals. The Trust Committee members shall not be required to furnish bond. The members of the Trust Committee shall not be liable, either jointly or severally, for any losses suffered by the trust estate as a result of the Committee's failure or the failure of any one of them to exercise the power given them unless such failure shall be the result of gross negligence or willful misconduct in office. Members of the Trust Committee hereunder from time to time shall receive reasonable compensation from the trust estate for their services.

6. Chloe was the beneficiary of a $6 million trust established by her longtime companion, Chun. The trust instrument authorized Chloe to remove the corporate trustee at any time and appoint another *corporate* trustee. Should any part of the trust property be included in Chloe's estate at her death? See Reg. § 20.2041–1(b)(1). Would it make any difference if Chloe had or had not exercised the power to remove and appoint?

K. CHANGING BENEFICIARIES

[¶ 19,675]

REVENUE RULING 80–255

1980–2 C.B. 272.

ISSUE

For purposes of §§ 2036(a)(2) and 2038(a)(1), did a decedent-settlor retain a power to change the beneficial interests of a trust, requiring inclusion of the trust property in the settlor's gross estate, if under the trust instrument all of the decedent-settlor's after-born and after-adopted children were to become trust beneficiaries?

FACTS

In 1975, the decedent, D, created an irrevocable trust. The trust instrument provided that income was to be paid in equal shares to D's children. Principal was to be distributed twenty-one years after the creation of the trust in equal shares to each child (or the child's heirs). The trust instrument also provided that the children of D, born or adopted after the creation of the trust, were to be additional beneficiaries. When the trust was created, D had two children, A and B. In 1978, D's third child, C, was born.

D died in 1980. At that time, A, B, and C were beneficiaries of the trust.

LAW AND ANALYSIS

Rev. Rul. 72–307, 1972–1 C.B. 307, provided that the power to cancel a group-term life insurance policy solely terminating employment is not an incident of ownership, under Reg. § 20.2042–1(c), in the policy. The revenue ruling at 308, stated:

¶ 19,670

An insured's power to cancel his insurance coverage by terminating his employment is a collateral consequence of the power that every employee has to terminate his employment. The examples in Reg. § 20.2042–1(c), on the other hand, concern powers that directly affect the insurance policy or the payment of its proceeds without potentially costly related consequences. Where the power to cancel an insurance policy is exercisable only by terminating employment, it is not deemed to be an incident of ownership in the policy.

Accordingly, the revenue ruling held that the value of the proceeds of the group insurance was not includible in the decedent's gross estate under § 2042. In Estate of Whitworth, T.C.M. 1963–41, the Tax Court concluded that Congress did not intend to include the ability to terminate one's employment, thereby revoking a spouse's rights to pension benefits, as a power to revoke within the meaning of § 2038.

In Estate of Tully v. United States, 528 F.2d 1401 (Ct. Cl. 1976), the decedent-employee entered into an employment contract whereby the employer promised to pay death benefits to the decedent's widow. The court held that the decedent did not have a power to revoke under § 2038(a)(1) of the Code, even though the decedent could have divorced the spouse, thereby eliminating the spouse's possible status as widow. The court said: "In reality, a man might divorce his wife, but to assume that he would fight through an entire divorce process merely to alter employee death benefits approaches the absurd."

Likewise, the act of bearing or adopting children is an act of independent significance, the incidental and collateral consequence of which is to add the child as beneficiary to the trust. Although D's act of bearing or adopting children will automatically result in adding the child as beneficiary to the trust, such result is merely a collateral consequence of the bearing or adopting children.* * *

Thus, a trust provision automatically including the settlor's after-born and after-adopted children as beneficiaries is not equivalent to the settlor's retention of a power to designate or change beneficial interests within the meaning of §§ 2036(a) and 2038.

For the same reason, at the time of creation of the trust, D is not treated as having reserved a power to change beneficial interests under Reg. § 25.2511–2(c) as a result of providing in the trust instrument that D's after-born or after-adopted children are to be trust beneficiaries.* * * Therefore, D's establishment of the trust was a completed gift, because D did not retain dominion and control over the transferred property.

HOLDING

D did not retain a power to change the beneficial interests of the trust, for purposes of §§ 2036(a)(2) and 2038(a)(1), notwithstanding that all of D's after-born and after-adopted children were to become beneficiaries. Therefore, the trust property is not includible in D's gross estate.

¶ **19,675**

Problem

[¶ 19,685]

Bill is setting up an irrevocable trust for the benefit of his spouse, Heather, and his child, Charley. His relationship with his spouse "leaves much to be desired" and he wants to make certain that any new spouse can be substituted for Heather. In terms of eligibility to receive distributions from the trust, will the following pass the test of Revenue Ruling 80–255: "References to my spouse shall be to the person who is my spouse as of the date for which reference is required"?

L.   RECIPROCAL OR CROSSED TRUSTS

[¶ 19,690]

"Crossed trusts" should be avoided. Suppose Dad creates a discretionary trust for Jasper's benefit, naming Mom as trustee, and, on the same day, Mom creates a discretionary trust for Jasper's benefit, naming Dad as trustee. At Dad's death, for example, the trusts might well be be uncrossed for estate tax purposes, and Dad will be treated as settlor of the trust Mom created for Jasper. As a result, the trust Mom created for Jasper will be included in Dad's estate on the theory that Dad was the real transferor (or, at least, that transferor-like status is attributed to Dad by uncrossing the trusts) and that, at death, Dad had control over the transferred property. See Estate of Bischoff v. Commissioner, 69 T.C. 32 (1977). It is impossible to suggest how different the terms of the respective trusts must be to prevent the trusts from being uncrossed where they are obviously interrelated. Regarding the latter point, see ¶ 10,138.

Putting *Bischoff* in perspective, though, compare *Schuler*, which follows, with *Estate of Green* v. *United States*, 68 F.3d 151 (6th Cir.1995), a contentious 2–1 decision (in which the majority use strongly worded footnotes to contradict the dissent). The *Green* majority said that *Bischoff* had been "rejected by every circuit which has considered the application of the reciprocal trust doctrine." *Id.* At 153. The majority concluded that retained economic benefits are crucial to application of the reciprocal trust doctrine and that "retained fiduciary powers to reinvest income and time distribution of trust income and corpus until the beneficiaries reach 21 years of age do not constitute a retained economic benefit that satisfies the core mandate of *Grace* 'that the arrangement, to the extent of mutual value, leaves the settlors in approximately the same economic position as they would have been in had they created trusts naming themselves as life beneficiaries.'" *Id.* at 153–54. In *Green*, Jack created an irrevocable trust for the benefit of granddaughter Jennifer and designated wife Norma as trustee; Norma created a "substantially identical" trust for granddaughter Greer (Jennifer's sister) and designated husband Jack as trustee. For the *Green* majority, the *Grace* test would apply to uncross the trusts only if the Jack and Norma were themselves beneficiaries of the trust created by the other.

[¶ 19,692]

ESTATE OF SCHULER v. COMMISSIONER

United States Court of Appeals, Eighth Circuit, 2002.
282 F.3d 575.

RILEY, Circuit Judge:

During 1994 and 1995, the decedent, Robert Schuler, transferred stock in two family-owned businesses to members of his brother's family. The Internal Revenue Service (IRS) determined the stock transfers were reciprocal cross-gifts and assessed a deficiency of $215,758 against the estate. The United States Tax Court upheld the deficiencies. We affirm the tax court's judgment.

I. Background

A. *Factual Summary*

Two brothers, Robert Schuler (Robert) and George Schuler, Jr. (George), owned interests in two family operated companies—Minn–Kota Ag Products, Inc. (Minn-Kota) and Sigco Sunplant, Inc. (Sigco). Prior to the stock transfers at issue, George's son, Jody, owned all Minn–Kota Class A voting common stock, and Robert's son, Jay, George, and Jody owned all the restricted Class B common stock. Sigco was equally owned by Robert and George.

Before Robert's death, he and George had discussed with their insurance agent their desire to have their families succeed them in the businesses. The brothers told their insurance agent they wanted Robert's family to control Sigco and George's family to control Minn–Kota. Together, with assistance from the insurance agent, Robert and George devised two three-step plans to transfer divided ownership of Minn–Kota and Sigco to each other's family and to employ § 2503(b) to exclude the transfers from estate taxes.

The first step for gaining family control of Sigco required Robert and his wife to make joint gifts of Sigco stock equal to approximately $20,000 each to their children, their spouses and grandchildren and to Jody, his wife and son during December 1994 and January 1995. The second step required George and his wife to make joint transfers of stock equal to approximately $20,000 to each of Robert's children and their spouses. The third step required several of Robert's children to transfer their shares to four siblings, including Jay and his children.

Similarly, the first step for gaining family control of Minn–Kota required George and his wife to make joint gifts of Minn-Kota stock valued at approximately $20,000 to each of their children and grandchildren in December 1994 and January 1995. The second step required Robert and his wife to transfer approximately $20,000 of Minn–Kota stock each to George, his wife and their children. The third step required some of George's children and their spouses to transfer stock valued at approximately $10,000 each to Jody, his wife, and their children.

Between December 1994 and January 1995, Robert transferred stock valued at $440,467.20 to George's family, and George transferred stock valued at $382,140 to Robert's family. After these stock transfers, Robert's family owned nearly 80 percent of Sigco, George's family owned nearly 68 percent of Minn–Kota, and Jody retained ownership of all Minn-Kota voting common stock.

Robert and George separately filed Form 709s for the years 1994 and 1995. On both Form 709s Robert and his wife claimed twelve gift tax exclusions for gifts made to George's family along with additional exclusions for gifts made to their own family members. On both Form 709s George and his wife claimed nine gift tax exclusions for gifts made to Robert's family along with additional exclusions for gifts made to their own family members.

In October 1995, Robert died. His sons, Jay and Thomas Schuler, filed a Form 706 excluding gifts of Sigco and Minn-Kota stock made in 1994 and 1995 from their deceased father's taxable gifts. Thereafter, on December 18, 1996, January 2, 1997, and January 2, 1998, George and his wife made transfers of Minn–Kota stock, each valued at $19,926, to Robert's son, Jay. The aggregate value of these three subsequent stock transfers totaled $59,778, which, when added to the value of George's 1994–95 stock transfers, amounted to $441,918, or just $1,451 more than the value of stock Robert had transferred to George's family in 1994 and 1995.

B. Procedural Summary

In June 1999, the IRS issued to Robert's estate a notice of deficiency in the amount of $215,758. The IRS denied annual exclusions for gifts made by Robert in 1994 and 1995 to members of George's family on the basis that "[s]uch gifts are reciprocal or cross gifts designed to maximize gifts to the donor's family while sheltering such gifts through annual exclusions to other donees." In August 1999, the estate filed a petition in the tax court objecting to the deficiency. The sole issue before the tax court was whether Robert's transfers of stock in 1994 and 1995 to George's family were, in substance, indirect gifts of stock to members of his own family.

* * * Applying the reciprocal trust doctrine set forth in United States v. Estate of Grace, 395 U.S. 316, 321 (1969), the tax court found the stock transfers were inter-related, a quid pro quo, and the brothers' plans to exchange stock via transfers to each other's families on the exact days in 1994 and 1995 established reciprocal transfers. The tax court further found Robert's family members received gifts of stock of approximately the same economic value, via the circuitous route devised, as they would have received by direct transfers from Robert. The tax court also rejected as implausible the estate's claim that the reciprocal trust doctrine did not apply because Robert would have made the stock transfers to George's family regardless of whether George had made reciprocal transfers. The tax court explained that it is "well settled that the Federal estate tax does not hinge upon the subjective intent of the decedent."

Based on these findings, the tax court sustained the IRS's determination of a $215,758 deficiency. The estate now appeals, claiming the tax court erred in finding the gifts given to each family were substantially similar and in finding the brothers were in the same economic position as if they had made the transfers directly to their own children.

II. DISCUSSION

* * * We review the tax court's factual findings for clear error and its legal conclusions de novo. "Whether a transaction lacks economic substance, and whether several transactions should be considered integrated steps of a single transaction, are both fact questions which we review for clear error." Sather v. Commissioner, 251 F.3d 1168, 1173 (8th Cir. 2001) (citations omitted).

For purposes of this appeal, we must determine whether the gifts at issue, similar stock transfers made by Robert and George to each other's children, were reciprocal cross gifts, that is, indirect gifts to each donor's own children. In doing so, we are guided by our recent decision in *Sather*. Id. at 1173–76 (applying the reciprocal trust doctrine in a gift tax context to determine the economic substance of gift transfers).

We explained in *Sather* that the reciprocal trust doctrine is a variation of the substance over form concept which developed in the trust context "to prevent taxpayers from transferring similar property in trust to each other as life tenants, thus removing the property from the settlor's estate and avoiding estate taxes, while receiving identical property for their lifetime enjoyment that would likewise not be included in their estate." Id. at 1173 (citing *Estate of Grace*, 395 U.S. at 320). The application of the reciprocal trust doctrine is not limited only to identifying the true transferor or transferee, but also applies to determining the nature of the property transferred. *Sather*, 251 F.3d at 1174. The doctrine applies to multiple transactions which are interrelated and which, "to the extent of mutual value, leave . . . the settlors in approximately the same economic position as they would have been in had they created trusts naming themselves as life beneficiaries." Id. at 1173–74 (quoting *Estate of Grace*, 395 U.S. at 324).

Applying these trust principles to gifts in *Sather*, we ruled the gifts were part of a jointly designed and executed plan devised for the purpose of benefitting each brother's own children. Id. at 1174–75. The *Sather* case involved three brothers, each of whom had three children. The Sather brothers made identical gifts of stock in a family-owned corporation on the same date to each of their children and to each of their six nieces and nephews for a total of nine gifts. A fourth, unmarried brother also made identical gifts of stock on the same date to his nine nieces and nephews. Id. at 1170–71.

Subsequent to the stock transfers, each child (transferee) was left in the same economic position as if his father had given the stock directly to him. Id. at 1174–75. We deemed as immaterial the fact that the brothers circuitously routed the gifts to their own children through their nieces and nephews, and we upheld the tax court's ruling that each brother was entitled to only three annual exclusions. We also concluded that the result was not affected by the fact the fourth, unmarried brother had made gifts of stock to his nieces and nephews which resulted in a net decrease in his economic value. The effect of uncrossing the reciprocal transfers left each of the transferors (except the unmarried brother) with children in the same economic position as if he had made stock transfers only to his own children. Id. at 1175.

Applying the reciprocal trust doctrine to this case, we cannot say the tax court was clearly erroneous in finding the gifts of stocks were interrelated. Robert and George Schuler jointly sought the advice of their insurance agent on how to have their children succeed them in the family-owned businesses. With their insurance agent's assistance, they devised a plan whereby Robert's family would increase its interest in Sigco while George's family would increase its interest in Minn–Kota. The 1994 and 1995 reciprocal transfers of stock were identical in type and amount and occurred on the same days. Similar to the Sather brothers, the Schuler brothers received no direct economic benefit from the stock transfers, but they received an economic benefit indirectly by benefitting their children as successors to the family-controlled businesses.

The Schulers contend their case is distinguishable from *Estate of Grace* and *Sather*, inter alia, because those cases involved transfers of identical property. In contrast, Schulers argue this case involves transfers of stock in two distinct companies whose assets, businesses, and management are different. We find such distinctions immaterial. Certainly, the three-part plans jointly executed in this case were more complicated than the transfers in *Sather*. However, the net effect was the same—simultaneous cross transfers of stock amounting to transfers of each brother's stock to his own children.

Nor are we persuaded the tax court was clearly wrong in finding inter-relatedness when Robert and George had a business purpose in separating the ownership of the two businesses between the children of the two Schuler families. Intrafamily transfers demand close scrutiny "precisely because the genuineness of the transaction cannot reasonably be inferred" from assurances of business purpose. Kincaid v. United States, 682 F.2d 1220, 1225 (5th Cir. 1982) (quoting Fehrs v. United States, 620 F.2d 255, 260 (Ct. Cl. 1980)). In this case, the tax court flatly rejected the assertion that business purpose was the primary motivation for making the reciprocal stock transfers. Instead, the tax court reached the "inescapable conclusion that decedent and his brother made the circuitous transfers for the primary purpose of increasing the number of exclusions under § 2503 (b) that otherwise would have been available to them."

After uncrossing the gifts to discern the taxability of the transactions, the tax court found Robert's children received stock from George of approximately the same economic value as they would have received by direct transfers from Robert. The tax court rested its finding on the fact that the difference in the value of the 1994 and 1995 cross stock transfers, which amounted to $58,327.20, was all but eliminated by George's transfers of stock valued at $59,778 to Robert's son in the three years following Robert's death.

The Schulers contend the tax court ignored the substantial changes in ownership and control that resulted from the reciprocal transfers. After the stock transfers, the Schulers claim Robert's family interest in Sigco increased from 75 percent to 80 percent. In analyzing the effect of the stock transfers, the tax court recognized the stock transfers resulted in a small shift in Sigco ownership from 75 percent to almost 80 percent. Before the transfers, Robert owned 25 percent of Sigco shares outstanding and his son, Jay, owned 50 percent; together they owned a 75 percent majority. Before and after the transfers, George's son, Jody, owed 100 percent of the Minn–Kota voting stock. Thus, the tax court found that acquiring control of the family business was not the purpose of the transfers.

III. Conclusion

We cannot say the tax court clearly erred in finding that, following the 1994 and 1995 stock transfers, and also considering George's transfers of stock in the next three years to Robert's son, Robert's children were left in approximately the same economic position as if Robert had made direct transfers of his stock and estate to them.

M. INTEREST-FREE LOANS

[¶ 19,701]

1. INTRODUCTION

For a time, it had become almost commonplace for taxpayers to attempt to shift the income from money or property to a lower-bracket taxpayer by making an interest-free loan of the money or property to the lower-bracket taxpayer. The scheme had appeal because the lender's ability to "call" the loan meant that the lender had not lost control over the borrowed funds as would have occurred had the property been gifted to the borrower.

Interest-free loans became extremely popular as a result of the decision in Crown v. Commissioner, 585 F.2d 234 (7th Cir.1978), in which it was held that the lender had not made a taxable gift by virtue of giving the borrower the right to use the borrowed funds interest free. However, "Crown loans," as they were called, collapsed as a scheme for shifting income when the United States Supreme Court in Dickman v. Commissioner, 465 U.S. 330 (1984), rejected the rationale of Crown and held that the right to use the funds borrowed without interest constituted a taxable gift.

While Dickman did much to eliminate the attractiveness of interest-free loans of large amounts, Congress finished the task by adopting § 7872. Section 7872 is applicable to "below-market loans" outstanding on June 6, 1984.

[¶ 19,709]

2. BELOW-MARKET LOANS

a. General Rules

Section 7872 provides that the following general rules are applicable in the typical intra-family loan context:

a. The lender will be deemed to have made a gift–subject to gift tax–to the borrower to the extent the interest to be paid under the note is less than "the applicable federal rate." Hereinafter the difference between the "applicable federal rate" and the rate of interest provided for in the note is referred to as the "foregone interest." It should be noted, however, that the term "foregone interest" is otherwise defined in the nonfamily, nongift context and where the loan is a term loan. See § 7872(b)(1). Section 7872(f)(2)(B) states that "the applicable federal rate shall be the federal short-term rate in effect under § 1274(d) for the period for which the amount of the foregone interest is being determined."

b. The borrower will be deemed to have paid the lender interest on the amount of the loan equal to the amount of the foregone interest. However, inasmuch as personal interest is nondeductible, no income tax deduction is available to the borrower for the interest deemed paid. See § 163(f)(1).

c. The lender will be treated as having realized taxable income to the extent of the foregone interest (plus any interest actually paid by the borrower to the lender).

d. This rule may come to be referred to as the "transfer-and-retransfer" rule.

Section 7872 is not limited to the intra-family context. It also applies to all "below-market loans." While the term "below-market loan" should be self-explanatory, § 7872(e)(2) defines it as "any loan if—

(A) in the case of a demand loan, interest is payable on the loan at a rate less than the applicable federal rate, or

(B) in the case of a term loan, the amount loaned exceeds the present value of all payments under the loan."

Examples include a corporation that makes a below-market loan to one of its shareholders. In this instance, the corporation will be deemed to have paid a dividend to the shareholder who receives the loan to the extent of the foregone interest. This dividend, like other dividends, will not be tax deductible to the corporation but will constitute taxable income to the shareholder who receives the loan.

Similarly, in the case where an employer makes a below-market loan to an employee, the employer will be deemed to have paid tax deductible compensation to the employee to the extent of the foregone interest and the employee will be deemed to have received taxable income to the same extent.

[¶ 19,717]

b. *Kinds of Below–Market Loans*

There are two kinds of below-market loans, namely "gift loans" and "others." § 7872(a) applies to gift loans. Section 7872(b) applies to "others." However, nothing is that simple! For example, gift loans that are term loans—rather than demand loans—are governed by § 7872(b). § 7872(d)(2). "Ah ha," you say, "with that organizational chart in mind, we can easily turn to § 7872 and determine the tax consequences that follow from loans." Try it and, if you are not happy with your progress, return to this text and consider the following approach.

[¶ 19,725]

c. *Application of § 7872*

In an effort to make § 7872 more readily understandable, the following decisional tree may be useful. It does not purport to be exhaustive, but is designed to serve as a "crutch" as the reader "experiences" § 7872.

Step 1. Classify the loan.

(a) The loan may be:

(1) A gift loan which is payable on demand;

(2) A gift loan which is a term loan;

(3) A nongift loan which is payable on demand; or

(4) A nongift loan which is a term loan.

(b) "Gift loans" are below-market loans where the forgoing of interest is in the nature of a gift. § 7872(f)(3).

(c) "Demand loans" are, as might be expected, "loans which are payable in full at any time on the demand of the lender." § 7872(f)(5).

(d) "Term loans" are loans which are not demand loans. § 7872(f)(6).

Step 2. If the loan is a gift loan directly between individuals, GO TO STEP 5.

Step 3. If the loan is a gift loan but the loan is *not* between individuals, GO TO STEP 9.

Step 4. If the loan is a nongift loan, whether it be a term or demand loan, GO TO STEP 9.

Step 5. Determine the amount of the loan.

(a) All of the rules of § 7872 (the transfer and retransfer rules) are expressly inapplicable to "gift loans directly between individuals" for "any day on which the aggregate outstanding amount of loans between such individuals does not exceed $12,000." § 7872(c)(2)(A). However, the $12,000 de minimis exception does not apply if the "gift loan is directly attributable to the purchase or carrying of income-producing assets." § 7872(c)(2)(B).

(b) Thus, if the amount of the loan is less than $12,000, the loan will not produce any gift, estate, or income tax consequences, and no further investigation need be undertaken. QUIT!

(c) However, if the gift loan is not sheltered by the $12,000 de minimis exception (either because the amount of the loan exceeds $12,000 or because the loan was used to acquire income-producing assets), GO TO STEP 6.

Step 6. Determine the amount of the transfer from lender to borrower and from borrower to lender in the case of gift loans directly between individuals. Section 7872(a)(1) provides that the amount transferred shall be the foregone

¶ 19,725

interest. "Foregone interest" means, "with respect to any period during which the loan is outstanding, the excess of—

(A) the amount of interest which would have been payable on the loan for the period if interest accrued on the loan at the applicable federal rate and were paid annually * * * [on the last day of the calendar year], over

(B) any interest payable on the loan properly allocable to such period."

Step 7. If the loan between individuals is a term loan, GO TO STEP 9. If the gift loan between individuals is a demand loan, GO TO STEP 8.

Step 8. Determine whether the gift loan to individuals is entitled to be sheltered from income, estate, and gift tax consequences.

(a) § 7872(d)(1)(A) provides that the amount transferred by the borrower to the lender in the case of a gift loan between individuals is limited to the borrower's "net investment income" determined as provided in § 163(d)(4).

(1) § 163(d)(4) provides that net investment income means the excess of investment income over investment expenses.

(A) Investment income means gross income from the property held for investment, e.g., income from interest, dividends, rents from net lease property, royalties, etc. It also includes gains realized on the disposition of property held for investment. The gains to be taken into account are determined using a complex formula.

(B) Investment expenses are those deductible expenses directly connected with the production of investment income. Investment expense does *not* include interest inasmuch as the purpose of the net investment income rule is to prevent taxpayers from incurring large interest expense which they can offset against ordinary income while investing in property producing little or no current income, with the expectation that the eventual sale of the property will produce long-term capital gain.

(2) For purposes of determining the amount transferred by the borrower to the lender in the case of a gift loan between individuals, "if the net investment income of any borrower for any year does not exceed $1,000, the net investment income of such borrower for such year shall be treated as zero." § 7872(d)(1)(E)(ii).

(A) Suppose Daddy lends Junior $100,000, which Junior uses to purchase a personal residence. In such a case Junior will not have net investment income. If Junior has no investment income, Daddy will not be deemed to have realized any income from the loan.

(B) However, it appears that Daddy will be considered to have made a taxable gift to Junior of the amount of the foregone interest without regard to the "borrower's net investment income." Why? Because § 7872(d)(1)(A) provides that "in the case of a gift loan directly between individuals the amount treated as retransferred by the borrower * * * shall not exceed the borrower's net investment income." Nowhere does § 7872(d)(1)(A) speak of the amount "transferred," but only the amount "retransferred" in providing the net investment income limitation.

(C) Of course, transfers that are considered gifts can be sheltered by the $12,000 annual gift tax exclusion and Daddy's unified credit.

(3) Furthermore, the limitation to net investment income "shall not apply to any loan made from a lender to a borrower for any day on which the aggregate outstanding amount of loans between borrower and lender exceeds $100,000." § 7872(d)(1)(D).

(4) Furthermore, the limitation to net investment interest in § 7872(d)(1)(A) is not applicable if "1 of the principal purposes" of the "interest arrangements" with respect to the loan is the "avoidance of any federal tax." § 7872(d)(1)(B).

(5) Where the borrower has gift loans from more than one lender, the net investment income is to be allocated among such loans proportionally. § 7872(d)(1)(C).

(b) QUIT!

Step 9. Determine the amount of the transfer from lender to borrower and the amount borrower is deemed to have received where the loan is other than a gift loan directly between individuals.

(a) § 7872(b)(1) provides that "the lender shall be treated as having transferred on the date the loan was made * * * and the borrower shall be treated as having received on such date, cash in an amount equal to the excess of—

(A) the amount loaned, over

(B) the present value of all payments required to be made under the terms of the loan."

(1) The "present value" of the "payments required to be made under the terms of the loan" is to be "determined in the manner provided by the regulations* * *—

(A) as of the date of the loan, and

(B) by using the discount rate equal to the applicable federal rate."

(2) The "applicable federal rate," in the case of *term* loans, shall be the rate prescribed in § 1274(d), being variously, the federal short-term rate, the federal mid-term rate, and the federal long-term rate, depending upon the maturity of the loan. § 7872(e)(2)(A). The rate so determined shall be compounded semiannually.

(3) The "applicable federal rate," in the case of *demand* loans, shall be the federal short-term rate prescribed in § 1274(d) "for the period

for which the amount of foregone interest is being determined."
§ 7872(e)(2)(B).

(b) The foregone interest transferred by lender to borrower "shall be treated" as "original issue discount." § 7872(b)(2)(A).

    (1) § 1272(a)(1) specifies that "the holder of any debt instrument having original issue discount" shall include in his or her gross income "an amount equal to the sum of the daily portions of the original issue discount for each day during the taxable year on which the holder held such debt instrument."

    (2) The effect of § 7872(b)(2)(A) is to cause the lender to recognize income over the term of the loan. "As a result," in the words used in the House Committee Report, "the lender is treated as receiving interest income at a constant rate over the life of the loan."

(c) If the loan qualifies as both a term loan and a gift loan directly between individuals, GO TO STEP 8. Otherwise, read on.

(d) The effect of § 7872(b)(1) is to recognize that below-market loans may be made in a nondonative (nongift) context. In such a case, then the lender may be entitled to an income tax deduction for the value of the foregone interest and the borrower may have taxable income. Illustrations include:

    (1) Loans to shareholder where the foregone interest shall be deemed to constitute a nondeductible dividend to the corporation and taxable income to the shareholder.

    (2) Loans to employees where the foregone interest constitutes taxable compensation to the employee and entitles the employer to a tax deduction so long as the compensation is reasonable. See § 162(a)(1).

(e) QUIT!

Problems

[¶ 19,795]

1. What are the estate tax consequences of an interest-free loan? If the lender dies when the loan is outstanding, what, if anything, is included in the lender's estate? See Reg. § 20.2031–4.

2. Describe the circumstances, if any, in which an interest-free loan could be effectively utilized in (1) the intra-family context; (2) the corporation-shareholder context; and (3) the employer-employee context.

3. Mr. Sharpe has proposed the following plan. He will borrow $50,000 at 7 percent interest from Neighborhood Bank; establish a trust for his son, Horatio Sharpe, now age six months; make a demand loan of the $50,000 to the trustee; the trustee will deposit the $50,000 in an 8 percent certificate of deposit at Neighborhood Bank; the trustee will pledge to Mr. Sharpe the 8 percent CD as security for the loan from Mr. Sharpe; and Mr. Sharpe will, in turn, pledge the 8 percent CD to Neighborhood Bank to collateralize the bank's loan to him. Mr. Sharpe is in the top income tax

bracket. The trust may well be in a lower income tax bracket as its only income will be the interest earned on the CD.

(a) What is the advantage of the transaction to Mr. Sharpe?

(b) Would you recommend Mr. Sharpe's scheme to a client?

(c) Describe the tax consequences that result from Mr. Sharpe's scheme. How does it stand up against the "aroma" test?

4. Suppose Grandpa lends Sally $1,000,000 which Sally uses to purchase a personal residence. Sally has no net investment income. Will Grandpa be deemed to have realized taxable income to the extent of the foregone interest? Should Sally be able to claim an income tax deduction for the payment of the foregone interest to Grandpa as qualified residence interest under § 163(h)(3)? Will Grandpa be deemed to have made a taxable gift to Sally of the foregone interest?

N. INTENTIONALLY DEFECTIVE GRANTOR TRUSTS

[¶ 19,801]

One gifting technique involves the use of an intentionally defective grantor trust (IDGT). (Recall that §§ 671–678 specify the circumstances in which trust income will be taxed to someone other than the person or entity that receives that income. See Chapter 22.) This technique is successful because the federal income tax and the federal estate and gift taxes are not synchronized. The result is estate and gift tax savings without tax cost.

Suppose Helena created an irrevocable trust for Chelsea's benefit and deliberately structured the trust so that the income would be taxable to Helena—even though that income was either retained in the trust or distributed to Chelsea. In this way Helena can have made a completed taxable gift by her transfer of property to the trust, a taxable transfer which may be sheltered by the § 2503 $12,000 per donee per annum gift tax exclusion or even by use of the § 2505 $192,800 unified credit. In addition, when Helena pays the income tax on the trust income, the amount of income tax paid itself effects a reduction in the size of her estate for federal estate tax purposes. Moreover, the grantor's payment of the income taxes is not considered a further gift to the trust. Rev. Rul. 2004–64, 2004–2 C.B. 7. In the meantime, the trust income comes to Chelsea free of income tax.

Critical to the success of the transaction is including a provision in the trust which will cause Helena to be taxed on the trust income under the grantor trust rules set out in §§ 671–678 (even though Helena does not receive that income) while making certain that the tainting provision is not one which will cause the trust property to be included in Helena's estate for estate tax purposes under §§ 2036(a)(2) or 2038 (or some other provision of the estate tax). Among the provisions with the desired effect would be the following: (1) allowing a nonadverse party to use trust income to pay premiums on life insurance insuring the life of either Helena or William, her husband (inasmuch as § 677(a)(3) causes such income to be taxed to the grantor of the trust) or (2) giving a nonadverse party the discretion to distribute income and principal among a class of persons without being limited by an ascertainable standard, as provided in § 674(d).

Use of the intentionally defective grantor trust technique may not be for the faint of heart (notwithstanding its widespread implementation). It illustrates the aforementioned lack of synchronization between the income tax and the estate and gift taxes—and the possibility for exploiting that condition. That possibility alone raises issues of appropriateness of such behavior on the part of tax professionals and raises questions as to whether planning should be loophole driven or policy driven. Even if policy driven, however, does use of the defective trust technique offend tax policy? Or is it consistent with Judge Learned Hand's suggestion that a taxpayer is free to arrange his or her affairs as he or she pleases and that the taxpayer has no duty to arrange his or her affairs so as to generate the most tax revenue?

When considering the defective grantor trust possibility, the professional would be advised to keep in mind that, at a bottom-line minimum, clients want the answer to the following two questions: (1) "How do I get out of the transaction if I change my mind at some future time?" and (2) "What is the worst thing that can go wrong and how will it impact me?"

Problem

[¶ 19,840]

Refer to the situation described, above, and consider whether the trust would qualify under § 2503(b) for the $12,000 per donee per annum gift tax exclusion if Helena's husband, William, was given the right to borrow the income and principal of the trust without providing adequate interest or security. See § 675(2).

Chapter 20

LIFE INSURANCE CHOICES

A. OBJECTIVES

[¶ 20,001]

More than two-thirds of American families own some type of life insurance protection. American Council of Life Insurers, Life Insurers Fact Book 89 (2002). The growth in the amount of life insurance in force has been phenomenal. In 1991, approximately $10 trillion worth of life insurance was in force, compared with approximately $16.3 trillion in 2001. Id. at 101 (Table 7.8). The benefit proceeds paid out on these policies amounted to over $93 billion in 2001 alone. Id. at 66 (Table 5.1).

With so many policies being purchased and the substantial amount of money paid in premiums, the impact of life insurance on the client's estate cannot be ignored. Furthermore, life insurance can provide the estate planner and the client a number of advantages. If structured properly, the proceeds can be passed free of both federal estate and income tax. Additionally, life insurance payable to a designated beneficiary is considered a nontestamentary transfer and, as such, is not subject to probate. Finally, some states exempt life insurance policies, the cash value of such policies, and the death benefits received by the beneficiaries of such policies from creditors of the insured, creditors of the owner of the policy, and creditors of the beneficiaries. See, e.g., Tex. Ins. Code Ann. § 1108.051(b) (Vernon Supp. 2004).

The purpose of this chapter is to provide materials which enable the reader to begin the process of determining how the client can best maximize the benefits of life insurance, a valuable and important asset.

B. KINDS OF LIFE INSURANCE

[¶ 20,051]

1. THE WHOLE LIFE v. TERM INSURANCE DEBATE

a. *Differences Between Products*

In the minds of unsophisticated consumers, the difference between term and whole life insurance can probably be best expressed in terms of premium cost. For young persons, the annual premium for yearly renewable term insurance is significantly less than the annual premium for whole life insurance. For older persons, the annual premium for yearly renewable term insurance is significantly higher than the annual premium for whole life insurance. Does this difference suggest that term is for the young and whole life is for the aged? Or is the question more complex than first appears?

First, consider the economic characteristics of term and whole life insurance in the simplist and most general of terms. When buying yearly renewable term insurance, the insured is being grouped with others in similar health and of identical age. The insurance company knows from prior experience—mortality tables—that a certain number of its insureds of similar health and identical age will die in the first year after the policy is issued. Accordingly, the insurance company must collect sufficient premium income from this group in this first year to cover its contractual obligations to those in the group who are going to die that year. In addition, the premium collections must be sufficient to cover the company's overhead—including commission to the selling agent—as well as generate a reserve against the possibility that more of the company's insureds will die that year than is suggested by the company's previous experience with persons of this age and health.

Obviously, the number of persons aged 30 who will die in a particular year is significantly less than the number of persons aged 60 who will die in the same year. Accordingly, the insurance company must collect more premiums from 60-year-old insureds than from 30-year-old insureds if the company is to be able to meet its contractual obligations to the 60-year-olds that it has insured. For that reason, premiums for yearly renewable term insurance escalate over the lifetime of the insured. At some point, these premiums become prohibitive as the group of insureds age and the risk of death becomes fairly significant.

Whole life insurance—sometimes referred to as permanent insurance—uses a different economic principle. Typically, whole life insurance is characterized by level premiums over the life of the insured. How is this possible, since purchasers of whole life insurance will not necessarily have any greater life expectancy as a group than purchasers of term insurance?

The difference between term and whole life can be explained in terms of how premium dollars for these two kinds of insurance are allocated. Each premium dollar paid for whole life is, in principle, subject to four distinct claims. A portion must be allocated to death benefit claims made by persons in the insured group; a portion to overhead—including commission to the selling agent; a portion to the company's reserve against catastrophes and other unexpected losses; and, a portion of each whole life premium dollar is allocated to "cash surrender value." Conceptually speaking, the "cash surrender value" allocated to each insured is then invested for the insured by the company and the insured's account is credited with interest determined using, at least, a certain minimum rate stated in the policy. In addition, generally speaking, the cash surrender value is available to be borrowed by the insured—at an interest rate stated in the policy. In the event the policy is surrendered, the cash surrender value accumulated in the insured's account under the policy will be paid to the insured less any applicable surrender charges (except to the extent the cash surrender value has been depleted through loans to the insured).

When the insured dies, the amount paid to the beneficiary will consist *in part* of a death benefit which represents the contributions to the death benefit fund in the year of the insured's death by the surviving insureds in the insured's group. In addition, the remainder paid to the beneficiary will include the cash surrender value that has been accumulated in the insured's account.

If the insured is elderly at death, a large portion of the amount paid to the beneficiary will be accumulated cash surrender value. But, if the insured is young, the amount paid the beneficiary will be largely a death benefit and will include little cash surrender value.

Cash surrender value is often called "forced savings" and is the explanation for the company's ability to keep premiums for whole life insurance level through the term of the policy. The insured contributes more in the form of premiums in the early years of the policy than is required by the company to meet its death claims and overhead and, in the later years, when premiums collected do not meet death benefit claims, the company makes up the difference by returning cash surrender value to the insured's beneficiary at the death of the insured, along with some death benefit.

[¶ 20,059]

b. Which to Buy?

Which is better for the consumer: locking in level premiums over a lifetime—and acquiring significantly less insurance for the premium dollar expended—or planning for escalating premiums over a lifetime but being able to purchase more insurance while still young for the same premium dollars? As an illustration, it is useful to note that, generally speaking, a 30-year-old will be able to purchase at least four times as much yearly renewable term insurance as whole life insurance for the same premium dollars.

Term or whole life? This question is a continuing plague to consumers, for there appears to be no real answer. On the one hand, term insurance premiums rise sharply as you age. For example, in 1991, it was reported that the annual premium on a $100,000 term policy purchased from Prudential Insurance Company of America can range from $155 for a 30-year-old individual, to $710 for a 60-year-old individual, to $2,516 for a 70-year-old individual. See Karen Slater, Term Insurance or Cash-Value? No Easy Answer, WALL ST. J., June 28, 1991, at C1. However, the proponents of term insurance are adamant in urging consumers to "buy term and invest the difference." James A. Margolis Associates determined that if a 45-year-old man purchases a $250,000 whole life policy, he would have to own the policy for a minimum of 14 years before the cash surrender value was greater than if he had purchased an equivalent term policy and invested the difference. Id. Obviously this analysis depends upon the assumed price of permanent insurance and must take into account the taxes that will be imposed on the income generated by the savings realized by purchasing the cheaper term insurance.

¶ **20,059**

The argument against "buy term and invest the difference" is that most consumers will probably not "invest the difference." As a result, as they age and the term insurance premiums become greater, it is arguable that the tendency of most insureds will be to discontinue the premium payments for the term insurance, resulting in "no insurance and no savings." Thus, one argument for whole life insurance can be expressed in terms of forced savings. As the insured ages, the amount of insurance in the insured's contract—his or her death benefit—decreases, while the savings in the contract—the cash surrender value—increases. While it is clearly arguable that the earnings credited by the insurance company on the insured's cash surrender value would not be as great as could be earned through other investments, the reduced earnings could be looked upon as a premium to be paid by the insured for the security of knowing that his or her cash surrender value is available savings to be obtained at any time by borrowing or by surrender of the policy itself.

However, the argument against purchasing whole life because of the forced savings feature goes to the very nature of insurance. That argument is, "Why buy insurance if you don't need it?" For example, in the early adult years, most persons' obligations far outstrip their resources. School debts, housing requirements, and support obligations all contribute to create an enormous cash need among young adults. Insurance plays an enormous role in the financial planning of these young adults if they are concerned about the possibility of premature death. Given the needs of these young adults, is it not arguable that their limited cash resources could be best utilized by buying greater amounts of term insurance rather than smaller amounts of whole life insurance for the same premium dollar expenditure? Such a scheme is obviously dependent upon the belief that the insured will be satisfied to be without insurance in his or her later years because, as noted above, term insurance premiums will become prohibitively expensive and many insureds will discontinue making these payments.

Actually, that conclusion is not always compelled. An individual can, in his or her later years, purchase whole life insurance if he or she can "pass the physical." On this point, the insurance companies will vary as to the risks they are willing to assume. Some companies are even willing to insure an applicant who has been turned down by other insurance companies. Of course, rates can be and are adjusted by the insurance company depending upon the health of the insured. Therefore, depending upon the need for the insurance, insurance can often be obtained in later life even if the premium must be greater to compensate the insurance company for the "nonstandard" risk being assumed. Inasmuch as many persons will not need insurance later in life, perhaps the risk of ill health in later life, when an insurance need surfaces, is a risk that some persons may want to accept and "buy term." Alternatively, term buyers may purchase guaranteed renewable term insurance with a guaranteed right to convert to whole life insurance at some future date. These guarantee features will come at a premium, and it is likely that the premium for the whole life purchased through the guarantee will be higher than the policy that could be obtained if the applicant could establish insurability at "standard" rates at the time of the exercise of the guarantee.

¶ 20,059

Notwithstanding the foregoing argument, does the purchase of term make economic sense? That is, is term insurance actually cheaper than whole life insurance? Can the two forms of insurance be compared? "Interest adjusted cost indices" are published showing at various rates the true cost per $1,000 of life insurance over 10- and 20-year periods. However, it has been argued that these indices contemplate that the policies being compared will be surrendered at the end of either the 10- or 20-year period. And, as a practical matter, whole life insurance is purchased because it represents "permanent" insurance and surrender is not generally contemplated before the death of the insured. Thus, so the argument goes, it is only appropriate to compare the surrender cost indices of like kinds of insurance offered by different companies rather than term and whole life.

Many other considerations and product features impact the term-whole life analysis. However, further discussion of those ideas is beyond the scope of this undertaking. Moreover, the foregoing discussion is not complete. It is intended only to identify some of the issues associated with the term-whole life debate; it should not be read as suggesting any particular course of action since it is clear that there is no consensus as to the "best" alternative. Clearly, one or more insurance professionals must be consulted when an insurance need has been identified, and those professionals should be charged with the responsibility of suggesting products appropriate to the need identified. The number of different insurance products available is truly astonishing, and only a competent insurance professional could ever hope to know of all of those that might be helpful in meeting a particular need. Therefore, the following discussion can, at best, present only a brief description of some of the more popular plans available.

[¶ 20,067]

2. UNIVERSAL LIFE INSURANCE

a. In General

Universal life insurance is a hybrid form of insurance, which combines the variable mortality costs of a term policy with an investment aspect similar to the "cash surrender value" of whole life. The insured pays a single premium, which is allocated in a fashion similar to that of a whole life premium. After mortality costs and policy expenses are deducted from each payment, the remaining premium dollars are placed in a reserve fund. Like the "cash surrender value" of whole life, the reserve fund is invested and is credited with a guaranteed minimal interest rate; however, if the current rate of interest is higher than the guaranteed rate, the insured will be credited the higher rate. Therefore, like an investment, the earnings that exceed the guaranteed rate accrue to the benefit of the policy owner rather than the insurance company. Furthermore, universal life policies provide a tax shelter because the interest accumulations in the reserve fund are not taxable until withdrawn.

Universal life policies provide the insured a number of advantages. The insured can borrow some or all of the available cash value of the reserve account, and, in that sense, universal life resembles whole life policies. However, unlike whole life, the insured is given more flexibility in the premium payments. The insured can change either the amount or the frequency of the payments and the death benefits, under the same policy, without affecting coverage. The only requirement is that the insured pay sufficient premiums to cover the cost of the death benefit equivalent to a term policy. However, if the insured misses a payment, the payment can be withdrawn from the reserve fund without disrupting coverage. It is important to note that, like whole life, universal life is better suited for persons with long-term life insurance needs.

[¶ 20,075]

b. Variable Universal Life Insurance

Variable universal life insurance is a form of regular universal life, with a twist. The insured is given the option of determining the type of investments the reserve fund will be invested in, such as stocks, bonds, and mutual funds. Therefore, although the insured can benefit from stock market booms, he or she must be willing to accept the risk of loss. Because of the substantial risk involved in variable universal life policies, the insured should be a relatively sophisticated investor willing to forgo the insurance security provided by the other forms of insurance available.

[¶ 20,083]

3. "SECOND-TO-DIE" LIFE INSURANCE

a. In General

"Second-to-die" life insurance is a versatile form of insurance undoubtedly created in response to the unlimited estate tax marital deduction. This form of life insurance pays its death benefit after the death of the surviving spouse. It provides spouses with an estate planning tool to protect against the potentially sizable estate tax that may be due after the surviving spouse's death.

The primary difference between second-to-die life insurance and single insured policies is that the mortality component is based on two lives instead of one. However, because many of these policies will not pay death benefits for up to 40 years later, special care should be taken to choose a financially secure company from which to purchase a second-to-die policy. See Robert D. Stuchiner, Picking Survivorship Policies, 129 TR. & EST. 39 (1990).

Second-to-die whole life and universal life forms, which are similar to single insured policies, are available.

[¶ 20,091]

b. Second-to-Die Whole Life

Purchasers of second-to-die whole life pay a fixed premium and enjoy the benefits of a cash surrender value. The premium is generally payable until the younger spouse turns 100 years old or until the death of the second to die, whichever occurs last. Many of these policies pay the policy owner a dividend if the policy performs better than the guaranteed rate. An owner may be able to apply the dividend toward the premiums.

[¶ 20,099]

c. Second-to-Die Universal Life

Second-to-die universal life insurance involves the two basic aspects of regular universal life. First, the variable mortality costs are calculated similarly to those of a term policy, using the age of the younger spouse until he or she is approximately 100 years old. Second, the remaining portion of the annual premium is placed in a reserve fund to build the cash value. This policy provides the spouses with the flexibility to determine both the amount of necessary death benefits and the amount of any cash surrender value to be accumulated.

[¶ 20,107]

4. GUARANTEED INSURANCE PURCHASE RIDER

The guaranteed insurance purchase rider is not a form of life insurance but an option to purchase life insurance. These are generally attached to a spouse's regular single insured policy and serve as an option for the surviving spouse to purchase death benefit insurance without any other proof of insurability. This is especially beneficial to persons who may not be able to demonstrate that they represent a "standard" risk of premature death.

The purchase of a guaranteed insurance purchase rider allows the surviving spouse to defer the expense of purchasing life insurance until after the first spouse's death. Furthermore, if the surviving spouse is the beneficiary of the deceased spouse's policy, the death benefits may be used to pay the premiums for the surviving spouse's life insurance policy.

[¶ 20,115]

5. GROUP-TERM LIFE INSURANCE

Employers often provide life insurance coverage for their employees without cost to the employee. This is a valuable fringe benefit. It is valuable not only because of the benefit provided but because this is one fringe benefit that is tax deductible to the employer but does not constitute taxable income to the employee if the insurance is limited in amount. That is, the employer can deduct the premium paid to keep the policy in force whatever the amount. On the other hand, the employee will exclude from his or her income the portion of the premium attributable to the purchase of the first $50,000 of term life insurance. § 79(a). The portion of the premium paid by the employer to purchase insurance for the employee which is in excess of $50,000 constitutes taxable income to the employee in the year paid by the employer. Reg. § 1.79-3(d).

¶ 20,115

[¶ 20,123]

6. FINANCED LIFE INSURANCE

a. *Historical Significance*

"Financed life insurance" was a concept created in order to help policy owners reduce their cash outlays for premiums paid on *whole* life insurance policies. It did this by allowing the policy owner to "borrow" the policy's cash value each year in order to pay the premium. Furthermore, some policies, such as the "minimum deposit" plan, included a dividend option which could be used to lessen the cash outflow necessary to pay the yearly premiums. Pre-1986 tax law made these plans advantageous in a number of ways. First, the policy owner borrowed the necessary funds to pay the premium from the built-up cash value at a favorable interest rate. This reduced the amount of funds necessary to pay the premiums on a yearly basis. Second, for a time, § 163(a) allowed the policy owner an income tax deduction for the interest paid on the policy loan. Consequently, for a taxpayer in the then prevailing 50 percent tax bracket, the cost of the policy was cut in half.

[¶ 20,131]

b. *Current Status*

Personal interest is no longer deductible. § 163(h). As a result, not only has financed life insurance lost its appeal, but taxpayers who have borrowed a substantial amount from their policy, relying on the deductibility of personal interest, encounter special problems. First, these taxpayers find themselves with a large required payment equal to the annual premium, plus interest due on a yearly basis without an offsetting income tax deduction for the interest paid. Second, if the policy owner decides to discontinue the policy prior to death, he or she might incur a taxable gain for the excess of the policy's cash value over its cost basis.

What should persons who have "financed" the purchase of life insurance do now? Some companies allow policy owners to trade in the old policy for a new policy without the old loan and the related high interest costs. The policy owner is required to pay the new policy premium; the premium, however, can be reduced by policy dividends that become payable. The paramount dilemma for estate planners and policy owners alike is whether the trade-in will be deemed a taxable exchange by the IRS. See Sanford L. Jacobs, Insurance Sold As Tax Break Is Now a Burden, WALL ST. J., June 26, 1987, at B21, col. 3.

Because of this uncertainty, the safest course for a policy owner may be to keep the old policy but begin to pay the annual premiums without depending on a loan from the cash value of the policy and to use any available dividends to decrease the balance of the outstanding policy loan as soon as possible. Id.

[¶ 20,139]

7. SPLIT-DOLLAR ARRANGEMENTS

"Split dollar" life insurance is a method of purchasing life insurance whereby two parties can jointly acquire an interest in the policy for their shared benefit. The "split dollar" feature is a means of financing the policy premiums on a regular whole life policy. Because the two parties split the cost, they split the dollars spent on financing the life insurance policy. This arrangement is generally used by employers as part of compensation packages; however, it can also be used by two individuals, such as spouses, or between an individual and an Irrevocable Life Insurance Trust, for estate planning purposes. The split dollar plans are generally termed as "regular," "reverse," or "private" split-dollar arrangements.

[¶ 20,147]

a. *Regular Split-Dollar Insurance*

Generally, the beneficiary rights in a whole life policy are "split" between the insured-employee and the employer. Under a regular, or "non-equity," split-dollar arrangement, upon the employee's death, the employer will receive the cash value portion of the policy and the employee (or his designated beneficiary) will receive the "at-risk" portion. See ¶ 20,051. Under an "equity" split-dollar arrangement, the employer reserves the right to receive the lesser of either the cash value of the policy or the amount of the premiums paid by him. The employer may also "split" the premium costs with the employee.

In an effort to more effectively regulate "equity" split-dollar arrangements, the Internal Revenue Service revised the tax scheme governing all split-dollar arrangements in 2002. Now, the method of taxation is determined by the ownership of the policy. IRS Notice 2002–8, 2002–1 C.B. 398. In an employment setting, if the employer owns the policy it will be governed by the economic benefit analysis set forth in Reg. § 1.61–22. If the employee owns the policy, taxation will be analyzed under the loan framework spelled out in Reg. § 1.7872–15.

Under the economic benefit rules, in a regular split-dollar arrangement the employer is providing the employee with an economic benefit equal to the present value of the "at-risk" portion of the life insurance policy, less any cash value. This benefit is then taxed as income to the employee. Valuation of the policy is determined by using Table 2001, which is found in IRS Notice 2002–8.

> *Example.* B, the employer, owns a $1 million life insurance policy on his 55-year-old employee, K. The policy has a present cash value of $200,000. This year, K's economic benefit is $3520, and this amount is then added to his gross income.

Under an "equity" split-dollar arrangement, the employee is taxed not only on the value of the "at-risk" portion but also on his interest in the cash value of the policy. How to measure the "equity" interest in the policy has yet to be determined, but one possible scenario is to subtract the present value of the amount the owner of the policy is to receive from the current premium payments.

If ownership of the policy is transferred, to the employee's spouse or an irrevocable life insurance trust, for example, a transfer tax will be assessed.

¶ 20,147

The new owner will be deemed to have received from the previous owner an amount equal to the fair market value of the life insurance policy less any consideration paid to the previous owner, and less any economic benefits previously taxed. The relationship between the new and the previous owner will determine whether the income tax or gift tax statutes will govern the transaction.

Under the loan rules, the employee is the owner of the life insurance policy, and the employer (non-owner) is making the premium payments. These payments will be considered a loan if: the payments are made either directly or indirectly by the non-owner to the owner; the payment is either a loan under general tax law principles, or a reasonable person would expect the premium payment to be repaid; and repayment is to be made, or secured by, the life insurance policy's death benefit or cash value. Reg. § 1.7872-15(a)(2)(i). If the payments are considered a loan, and the interest assessed falls below the Applicable Federal Rate, the shortfall will be taxed to the employee/borrower as income.

Table 2001 effectively replaces the P.S. 58 cost table, which the Internal Revenue Service had been using for the previous forty years. The new table also applies to most current split-dollar arrangements. IRS Notice 2002–8, 2002–1 C.B. 398. However, in cases where the split-dollar arrangement is part of an employee's compensation package, and the rates found in the P.S. 58 table were contractually agreed upon, the parties may continue to rely upon them. Under the previous set of rules, if the insurance company issuing the life insurance policy provided a rate table for a similar term policy, and the cost was less than the P.S. 58 cost table, the employee was permitted to realize income equal to the lesser cost as determined by the insurance company. Rev. Rul. 67–154, 1967–1 C.B. 11. IRS Notice 2002–8 did not specifically revoke this ruling (it did revoke many others), but it did not specifically address it, either. The Notice states that split-dollar arrangements that have relied on Rev. Rul. 67–154 may continue to do so provided that the insurance company's rate table accurately reflects the cost of term insurance.

At the employee's death, the death benefit payable from a split-dollar policy is exempt from income taxes. § 101(a). The employee's beneficiary receives the balance of the policy's death benefits after the employer's portion is deducted.

[¶ 20,155]

b. *Reverse Split-Dollar Insurance*

A reverse split-dollar arrangement reverses the beneficiary rights in a regular split-dollar arrangement. The employer receives the at-risk portion of the policy and the employee receives the cash surrender value. This is an effective way to create "key person" insurance coverage in which the employer receives the at-risk portion in the event of an untimely death.

Under the "equity" split-dollar rules, any interest that the employee has in the cash value of a life insurance policy is considered to be an economic benefit.

An advantage of the reverse arrangement is that it can be structured so that the employee may receive all beneficiary rights upon retirement. The employer, however, should retain ownership of the policy in order to avoid the tax associated with a change in ownership. At retirement, the employee can continue to pay the whole annual premium if the policy is not yet paid up. The employee, therefore, will be able to benefit from the cash value during life (since he has already been taxed on it), and the employee's beneficiary will still be entitled to the death benefits at death without further income tax consequences.

[¶ 20,163]

c. *Private Split-Dollar Insurance*

A private split-dollar arrangement involves splitting a life insurance policy between two individuals or an individual and a trust. For example, the insured's spouse may receive the cash value and an irrevocable trust may own the policy and receive the at-risk portion of the death benefit. Under the new regulations, these arrangements will likely be governed by the economic benefit rules, since one of the goals of the insured is to reduce his estate (a loan would have to be repaid to the insured's estate). In the private setting, the economic benefits provided will be subject to gift tax rules, although the benefits are still calculated the same way.

Use of private split-dollar arrangements has diminished in recent years. One reason is the loss of the personal interest deduction. See § 163(h). In the past a spouse that owned the policy and was receiving the cash value could borrow against the policy to pay the annual premiums and then take a deduction for the interest paid on the loan. The benefit of this type of arrangement was that, if a trust received the at-risk portion and the spouse retained the cash value, the policy would be effectively excluded from the insured's estate but the insured would still benefit from the income tax deduction by filing a joint income tax return. The only current advantage of such a plan is that the cash value portion would be included in the spouse's estate and excluded from the insured's estate.

The primary drawback to a private split-dollar arrangement is that the insured can never receive the cash value portion of the policy. In Revenue Ruling 79–129, 1979–1 C.B. 306, the IRS ruled that, in a private split-dollar arrangement, if the insured could borrow against any of the cash value of the policy, the entire policy was includible in the insured's estate. The IRS determined that the right to borrow against the policy was equivalent to an incident of ownership. Therefore, the cash value portion would be included in the insured's gross estate under § 2042(1) and the at-risk portion under § 2042(2). See also Reg. § 20.2042-1(c)(2).

C. AMOUNT OF LIFE INSURANCE

[¶ 20,201]

The subject of how much, if any, life insurance should be purchased is as controversial as what kind of life insurance should be purchased. There are probably two reasons to purchase life insurance. One is estate creation. The other is estate conservation.

[¶ 20,209]

1. ESTATE CREATION

The role of life insurance in estate creation is to provide protection against not living long enough. An individual might acquire life insurance because of a need to share with fellow insureds some of the risk that the individual will not survive long enough to build sufficient capital to provide for those loved ones who are dependent upon the individual. If insurance is purchased with the hope that the proceeds will be collected by the insured's loved ones after a short pay-in period, the insured is not thinking of risk-sharing but is gambling. Insurance is not gambling; it is risk-sharing.

When speaking about the use of insurance in estate creation, first project fund *application*. Applications can oftentimes be expressed in terms of family income requirements, family educational requirements, and retirement needs. How much income is required to maintain the family in the lifestyle to which it has become accustomed? What will be the educational needs of the family in future years? What kind of retirement income will be needed? Clearly, expenses will diminish in the retirement years. (Although medical expenses often increase in the retirement years, other forms of insurance are often available to meet these needs.) Moreover, at some point in time, only the surviving spouse's needs will have to be met from the funds on hand. Finally, while insurance is a useful vehicle to establish a retirement fund for a dependent spouse in the event the other spouse dies prematurely, it is arguable that other investments are better vehicles through which to establish a retirement fund for *both* spouses.

In looking at *sources* of funds, consider first social security benefits that are available to surviving spouses while there are minor children and the benefits that are available to surviving spouses (without minor children) after such persons attain a specified age. Of course, there are benefits available for minor children (both for support and for education after minority) and for those who are permanently disabled. These benefits are presently tied to cost-of-living indices but that may change because of the enormous cost of sustaining these benefit packages as the population ages.

After social security, look to the property which the prospective insured has accumulated at the time the insurance purchase is being considered. What income does it produce to meet the identified applications?

What role does inflation play? Would you be comfortable with the suggestion that inflation plays no role in determining future needs and that it is appropriate to project future needs in terms of current dollars? By way of explanation, consider these two approaches. Do you agree that either approach confirms this conclusion?

1. Future needs could be discounted to their present worth.

2. Present resources could be inflated to predict their future worth and the income stream that would then be generated.

¶ 20,201

Whichever course is chosen, the value of the unfulfilled needs would appear to be the same.

Finally, it is not uncommon to see published recommendations that each person should have insurance equal to six times his annual salary.

Can you suggest other techniques of analyzing insurance needs?

[¶ 20,217]

2. ESTATE CONSERVATION

Estate conservation is really tax related. How much insurance is necessary to pay death costs so as to avoid forced liquidations? There may be property which the survivors wish to retain but, because of death costs, are forced to liquidate. Or there may be property which they are happy to sell but at another time when the market may be better. Of course, if these properties have value, it should be possible to borrow against them. But borrowing is no solution if the properties are fully "loaned" up, which is oftentimes the case when a small—but viable—business is involved.

Life insurance, then, has a role here. It has a particular role in providing liquidity to small businesses in anticipation of one of the key people dying prematurely. When that happens it is generally agreed that the decedent's interests must be closed out of the business to allow it to prosper under the survivors. Life insurance can provide that liquidity.

There are many other applications of life insurance.

How much life insurance, if any, a person should have is an individual decision that can only be made after careful analysis of *sources* and *applications*. Keep in mind, though, that life insurance is neither an investment nor a gamble. It is risk-sharing.

D. SURRENDER OPTIONS

[¶ 20,251]

Although the use of life insurance can be a handy estate planning tool, it is not necessarily for everybody. More importantly, as time passes, circumstances change and sometimes the need for life insurance diminishes or at least the owner of the life insurance policy perceives a diminished need. What happens if the owner decides to cancel the policy?

[¶ 20,259]

1. ORDINARY LIFE INSURANCE

A life insurance company's risk of having to pay out on a policy by reason of the insured's death increases as the insured grows older. Yet the amount of premiums paid annually on the typical *whole* life policy, as contrasted with those paid on a *term* life insurance policy, remains fairly constant throughout the duration of the insurance contract. In the early years of the contract, then, a smaller portion of each premium goes toward the actual risk taken by

¶ 20,259

the insurance company and a greater portion is attributable to "cash value"—a sort of savings account to prepare for later years when the amount of the premium will not cover the insurer's risk. At one time, an insured party who discontinued his or her insurance policy lost any interest the insured had in the cash value and only a few insurance companies refunded any portion of it to the insured. State nonforfeiture laws now require insurance companies to at least refund the cash value of the policy upon termination of the insurance contract.

Refund of the cash value is only one of the options available to the policy owner upon surrender of the policy. Other alternatives include "extended term insurance" and "reduced paid-up insurance."

Extended term insurance is insurance equal to the face amount of the policy less any loan unpaid on the due date of the unpaid premium, extended for such period as the cash surrender value will provide. Thus, it is term insurance. In most policies, the period for which the insurance will be provided is specified for each of the first 20 years.

In lieu of claiming a refund of the policy's cash value or extended term insurance, the policy owner who prefers to do so may elect to have the net cash-surrender value of a policy used to purchase fully paid-up insurance of the same duration and kind as the policy provides, in whatever amount the cash-surrender value will purchase.

[¶ 20,267]

2. TERM LIFE INSURANCE

Pure term life insurance does not build cash values. Generally, premiums increase each year to reflect the increased mortality of a particular group as it ages. Accordingly, there is nothing to refund when term insurance is cancelled.

E.   SETTLEMENT OPTIONS

[¶ 20,301]

Once a client has decided that he or she needs or wants life insurance and has chosen the appropriate type and amount, the client must determine which of several methods of payment of insurance proceeds will best suit the client's purposes. Because so many people will have life insurance in their estates, consider the effect, both tax and otherwise, of the insurance and its form of payment.

[¶ 20,309]

1. INSURANCE SETTLEMENT OPTIONS

Insurance settlement options need to be understood—and need to be compared with the alternative of creating an inter vivos trust to receive the insurance proceeds. The tax consequences of each option are important, as are the planning considerations to keep in mind when choosing how to receive the proceeds. Remember, that there is no "best" option; rather, the goals and circumstances of each particular client will determine which option is most appropriate for the client's estate plan.

There are four basic settlement options—in addition to the most popular, namely for the beneficiary to receive a check for the face amount of the insurance policy upon the death of the insured. The other four settlement options result in the insurance proceeds being left with the insurance company. See Howard J. Saks, Life Insurance Settlement Options as a Viable Financial Planning Tool, 4 Estate Planning 415, 415–416 (1977). First, there is the interest only option, meaning that the insurance company keeps the policy proceeds and pays interest to the beneficiary, the interest being taxable income when received. In the normal case, the beneficiary can withdraw the proceeds in their entirety at any time. Typically, the proceeds left with the company are free of creditor claims.

The second option is for the proceeds to be left with the company for a fixed period where both proceeds and interest on the unpaid balance are payable for a fixed period. The third option, the fixed amount option, results in the payment of a fixed amount at regular intervals until the fund is exhausted. Meantime, the unpaid balance earns interest.

The life annuity option, the last of the options, is what it purports to be, namely, an undertaking by the insurance company to provide the beneficiary a lifetime of payments. Sometimes there is a guaranteed minimum number of payments (in anticipation of the beneficiary's premature death and his or her fear that money will, as a result, be left on the table); sometimes the option may include life payments for the longer of two lives.

The advantage of these settlement options is certainty. In most cases, there is no opportunity for appreciation in value (although it is possible that the life annuity option might include some variability depending on the wishes of the beneficiary). For material comparing trusts with settlement options, see ¶ 20,381.

[¶ 20,317]

2. INCOME TAX CONSEQUENCES

a. *Lump-Sum Payment*

The general rule under § 101(a) is that proceeds of life insurance, payable because of the death of the insured, are not included in the beneficiary's gross income.

[¶ 20,325]

b. *Interest Option*

Again, the general rule under § 101(a) is that only the *proceeds* of life insurance are excludable from gross income. Interest earned on the proceeds is *not* excludable. See § 101(c). Therefore, the full amount received by the beneficiary under the "interest only" option will be includible in gross income.

[¶ 20,333]

c. Fixed-Period, Fixed-Amount, and Life Income Options

Fixed-period, fixed-amount, and life income options are available. Payments to the beneficiary under these forms of settlement options will consist of a combination of the actual life insurance proceeds and the interest thereon. Income taxation of such payments will be governed by § 101(d), which provides for proration of the payment between principal and interest. The methods of proration and of distinguishing between principal and interest will vary according to the option chosen and to various other provisions of the policy such as guaranteed minimum payment. See Reg. § 1.101A(c) through (f). In each case, part of each payment will be of principal (excluded from the beneficiary's gross income) and part will be of interest (fully taxable).

[¶ 20,335]

d. Transfer for Value

The transfer-for-value rule provides that if a policy is transferred for valuable consideration, the death proceeds will generally be tax-exempt only to the extent of the consideration and the net premiums paid by the transferee. § 101(a)(2). Any amount above such payments is taxed as ordinary income to the recipient. There are several exceptions. If the transfer comes within one of the exceptions of § 101(a)(2)(A) or (B), the death proceeds are not taxable to the recipient. The exceptions are: (1) transfer to the insured; (2) transfer to a partner of the insured, to a partnership in which the insured is a partner, or to a corporation in which the insured is an officer or member; and (3) transfer where the policy has a basis in the hands of the transferee determined in whole or in part by reference to such basis in the hands of the transferor, e.g., a gift.

[¶ 20,341]

3. ESTATE TAX CONSEQUENCES

Regardless of the option chosen, the proceeds of the policy will be included in the insured's taxable estate if (1) the proceeds are payable to his executor, administrator or (2) the insured possessed any one or more of the incidents of ownership. See § 2042. For additional discussion, see ¶ 20,451.

[¶ 20,349]

a. Marital Deduction

Care must be taken if the proceeds are includible in the decedent's estate and the decedent wants them to qualify for the marital deduction. Payments in a lump sum to the surviving spouse will, of course, qualify for the marital deduction, but there is a possibility that other settlement options will be nondeductible terminable interests. For example, if the surviving spouse must survive the decedent by more than six months in order to receive the proceeds, the nondeductible terminable interest rule applies and the transfer of the life insurance proceeds fails to qualify for the marital deduction. See § 2056(b)(3). For discussion, see ¶ 14,351.

[¶ 20,357]

b. Unwanted Powers of Appointment

If one of the installment options is chosen, any insurance payments remaining undistributed at the beneficiary's death may be taxed to the beneficiary's estate if the beneficiary had any rights to withdraw those amounts or had a general power of appointment over these amounts. See § 2041; ¶ 18,247.

[¶ 20,365]

c. Tax Allocation Clauses

Once the choice of settlement option is made, the estate tax, as a result of applicable state default rules, *may* well be apportioned among all the property included in the insured's estate absent a provision in the will to the contrary—a so-called "tax allocation clause".

Technically speaking, consider the following: (1) § 2002 imposes the burden of paying the estate tax on the decedent's executor; (2) § 2206 allows the executor to recover from the recipient of the life insurance proceeds, an allocable share of the estate taxes—absent a tax allocation clause in the decedent's will that imposes the estate tax on the decedent's probate estate, *i.e.,* the property passing under the decedent's will. Adding complexity are the default rules applicable in the decedent's state of domicile. The default rules, *i.e.,* those that will allocate the burden of the estate tax absent a tax allocation clause, are of two kind, (1) those that adopt the "burden-on-the-residue" approach, *i.e.,* those that impose the burden of estate taxes on the decedent' residuary estate; and (2) those that follow an apportionment theory. (Section 3–916 of the Uniform Probate Code is a typical apportionment statute. Estate taxes are apportioned proportionally among the takers of the decedent's property except that takers of property interests that qualify for the marital and charitable estate tax deductions (§§ 2055; 2056) bear none of the taxes unless there is insufficient other property.)

Nonetheless, despite the curative potential of an appropriate tax allocation clause, a peculiar practice has developed among practitioners, one that is probably adopted largely for reasons of convenience. That practice is to *expressly* impose—sometimes it would appear by inadvertence—the burden of the estate tax on the will's residuary takers and oftentimes expressly state "without right of reimbursement"! Why? Because § 2002 charges the decedent's executor with paying the estate tax and "it's just easier" if the executor does not need to seek reimbursement from the recipient of the life insurance proceeds—even though § 2206 expressly allows the executor to recover the allocable estate tax from the recipient of the life insurance proceeds (absent, of course, a provision in the decedent's will to the contrary)! Thus, in those situations—where the tax allocation clause expressly imposes the estate tax on the decedent's residuary takers—the recipient of the life insurance proceeds will enjoy a genuine, but perhaps an unnecessary and unexpected, windfall. For further discussion, see ¶ 14,767.

Problem

[¶ 20,370]

Should every lawyer's "boiler plate" include a provision preventing allocation of any estate tax to life insurance proceeds included in the decedent's estate? Are there circumstances when such a provision unnecessarily complicates estate administration?

[¶ 20,373]

4. GIFT TAX CONSIDERATIONS

A gift is made when ownership of a life insurance policy is assigned to another or when the designation of a third-party beneficiary becomes irrevocable. See Reg. § 25.2511–2(f).

If the insured owns the policy at death, there is no federal gift tax liability with respect to proceeds paid by reason of the insured's death. This is true because there has been no inter vivos transfer. Under the same reasoning, there is no federal gift tax liability where payment of the policy proceeds is made by reason of the death of the insured and where the beneficiary is the owner of the policy.

If someone other than the beneficiary or the insured owns the policy, however, the policy's owner may incur federal gift tax liability if the policy proceeds are paid to a third party upon the death of the insured. See Goodman v. Commissioner, 156 F.2d 218 (2d Cir.1946).

Problem

[¶ 20,379]

Is the gift made when the owner of the insurance designates a third party as beneficiary or is the gift made only upon the death of the insured at which time the proceeds become actually payable?

———

Thus, it is *how* one becomes the policy's beneficiary and not the choice of settlement option that determines the existence of federal gift tax liability. One exception to this general proposition applies when the beneficiary chooses a joint and survivorship annuity option. A beneficiary choosing to extend payment of the proceeds over the span of the beneficiary's life *and another's* may be lessening *his or her* interest in the insurance proceeds in favor of creating a contingent interest in the other person. Election of this option can thus result in a gift of a contingent interest to that other person.

¶ 20,365

[¶ 20,381]

5. CHOICE OF BENEFICIARY: TRUST, INSURANCE COMPANY, OR NATURAL PERSON

Normally, life insurance proceeds are paid to a beneficiary who is a natural person. However, with increasing frequency policy owners are electing to have the proceeds paid to a trust, be it testamentary or inter vivos.

Payment to a trust does *not* change the general rule of § 101 which excludes the proceeds of life insurance from the gross income of the recipient, be it a trust or a natural person. Of course, the *income* earned by the investment of the insurance proceeds by the trustee will be taxed to the trust (if retained by the trust) or taxed to the trust beneficiary (if distributed by the trustee). See discussion at ¶ 8101.

An additional option, detailed at ¶ 20,309, is to leave the proceeds with the insurance company under one of the settlement options specified in the policy, e.g., the company's promise to provide the beneficiary with either an annuity or interest on the proceeds while in the company's hands. Comparing settlement options with the trust alternative, the following may be noted: (1) no direct charge for the settlement option by the insurance company while a trustee will ordinarily need to be compensated (and, if the trustee takes no fee, more likely than not, it will be an example of "you get what you pay for."); (2) little risk of loss when the proceeds are left with the company (but no appreciation in the normal situation, either, because the insurance company will be paying interest only) as contrasted with the potential for gain *or loss* when investments are left to the trustee; (3) guardianship needed to receive the payments from the insurance company if the beneficiary is under legal disability for any reason, e.g., age or physical or mental impairment, as contrasted with a trust where one of the principal selling points is the utility of the trust as a management vehicle for those beneficiaries unable to or uninterested in managing their property; and (4) the lack of flexibility with the insurance settlement option—it is a contract—as contrasted with the discretion quite commonly given a trustee by the governing instrument whereby the trustee manages the trust taking into account the needs of the beneficiaries, both present and future, and may well have the ability to spray benefits among a group of beneficiaries taking into respective need. See William S. Huff, Insurance Trusts for Everyman, 39 U. Colo. L. Rev. 239, 242–245 (1967).

[¶ 20,389]

6. MECHANICS OF OPTION ELECTION

Once it is determined which settlement option fits most appropriately in the client's estate plan, the question remains: Who makes the election, and how?

In general, the policy itself will specify the answers to these questions. Most policies provide that the policy owner may make the election at any time during his or her life, and, failing that, the beneficiary may choose the form of payment. If, however, the insured's executor or administrator is made the beneficiary, there is some question as to whether election of a settlement option is within his or her authority. This is more the function of the trustee than of the executor, whose main job it is to marshal the decedent's assets and distribute them according to the decedent's will. Sometimes the decedent's will or the insurance policy will allow the executor to choose the interest option for a limited period during administration, until the estate's liability for debts and taxes is determined; such a limited election is roughly equivalent to having the executor receive a lump-sum distribution and put it in a savings bank.

If the trustee of an inter vivos or testamentary trust is named as recipient of the policy proceeds, the trustee must nevertheless be given authority to elect an option by the terms of the will or the trust instrument. Moreover, many policies limit the power of a fiduciary to elect an option, or allow election only if the beneficiary is a member of the insured's family.

F.   ESTATE TAX CONSEQUENCES OF LIFE INSURANCE: AN OVERVIEW

[¶ 20,451]

One of the first steps to be taken in planning a client's estate is to determine which assets are included in the client's estate and to value these assets. This is equally true when the estate contains life insurance. As a general rule, the estate tax consequences of life insurance will depend mainly on the identities of the owner of the policy and the beneficiary or beneficiaries.

[¶ 20,459]

1.   IN GENERAL

The proceeds of a life insurance policy will not be included in the gross estate of the insured unless (1) the insured possessed *one or more* of the incidents of *ownership* of the policy or (2) the insured's estate is the beneficiary of the policy. § 2042. If the insured does not own the policy and the insured's estate is not the beneficiary, then the insured's death, so far as the life insurance policy is concerned, is simply the event which causes the proceeds to become payable to the beneficiary. In such a case, the insured has not transferred property, nor is the insured deemed to have transferred anything. There are, thus, no estate tax consequences on the insured's death. The fact that the insured paid the premiums on the policy is irrelevant to whether the policy proceeds are included in the insured's estate under § 2042.

[¶ 20,467]

2.   INSURED'S ESTATE AS BENEFICIARY

Where the insured's estate is the beneficiary, § 2042 requires the inclusion of the proceeds in the insured's gross estate. The regulations make it clear that it makes no difference whether the estate is specifically named as beneficiary or whether the estate gets the benefit, under a legally binding obligation, of some or all of the proceeds of the insurance. For example, if the proceeds are payable to another beneficiary, subject, under a legally binding obligation, to the beneficiary's payment of the estate's debts, taxes, and the like, then the proceeds are includible in the insured's gross estate to the extent of the beneficiary's obligation. See Reg. § 20.2042-1(b)(1). If the proceeds of the policy are community property, then only half of the proceeds will be included in the insured's gross estate. See Reg. § 20.2042-1(b)(2).

[¶ 20,475]

3. INSURED HAS INCIDENTS OF OWNERSHIP

Where the proceeds are payable to another beneficiary, but the insured possesses one or more of the "incidents of ownership" of the policy, the proceeds will be included in the insured's gross estate. The theory behind this rule is that the insured never gave up complete dominion and control over the policy before death, so that at the death of the insured, the insured *did* make a transfer of property.

[¶ 20,483]

4. INCIDENTS OF OWNERSHIP DEFINED

a. *Introduction*

Section 2042(2) does not define what is meant by "incidents of ownership" except to say that the term includes a reversionary interest in the policy if the value of the reversionary interest exceeds 5 percent of the policy value immediately before the decedent's death.

[¶ 20,491]

b. *Economic Benefits*

The regulations make it clear that "incidents of ownership" is a term meant to embrace more than just those circumstances in which the decedent owned the policy in the technical legal sense. If the insured possesses some sort of right or power under the policy which can be said to give the insured the "economic benefits" of the policy, the insured may be found to have some incidents of ownership. "Thus, it includes the power to change the beneficiary, to surrender or cancel the policy, to assign the policy, to revoke an assignment, to pledge the policy for a loan, or to obtain from the insurer a loan against the surrender value of the policy, etc." Reg. § 20.2042-1(c)(2). However, an employee's right to convert a group-term life insurance policy provided by his employer to individual insurance upon cessation of employment has been ruled not to be equivalent to an incident of ownership in a life insurance policy. Estate of Smead v. Commissioner, 78 T.C. 43 (1982); Rev. Rul. 84–130, 1984–2 C.B. 194.

If the insurance policy is held in trust, the insured can be found to possess incidents of ownership even if the insured possesses no *beneficial* interest in the trust. The proceeds of the policy may be included in the insured's estate if, under the policy, the insured has the power to change beneficial ownership of the policy or its proceeds, or to alter the time or manner of enjoyment of the proceeds. Reg. § 20.2042-1(c)(4). By way of contrast, in Estate of Rockwell v. Commissioner, it was held that a decedent did not possess the requisite incidents of ownership, although he retained the power to "veto any designation of a person who did not have an insurable interest in his life as a beneficiary or an assignee." 779 F.2d 931, 932 (3d Cir.1985). The court found that the veto power did not give the decedent a "right to the economic benefits of the underlying policy" and therefore he did not have the requisite incidents of ownership. Id. at 934.

[¶ 20,499]

c. Fiduciary Capacity

ESTATE OF CONNELLY v. UNITED STATES

United States Court of Appeals, Third Circuit, 1977.
551 F.2d 545.

FORMAN, Circuit Judge.

* * *

Appellant contends that decedent's power to elect optional modes of settlement exercisable in conjunction with his employer and the insurer, and the right to assign this power, constituted incidents of ownership. We do not agree.

In 1937 the Board of Tax Appeals was confronted with this precise argument in Billings v. Commissioner, 35 B.T.A. 1147 (1937), acq. 1937–2 Cum. Bull. 3. Billings involved a large number of life insurance policies, three of which gave the decedent much wider options as to the modes of settlement than those involved here. The Board of Tax Appeals held that "[t]he mere right to say when the proceeds of the insurance policies should be paid to the beneficiary does not amount to a control of the proceeds. They irrevocably belonged to the beneficiary from the date the policies were taken out." (35 B.T.A. at 1152.)

The Commissioner acquiesced in the Billings decision and that acquiescence remained in effect until 1972 when it was "withdrawn and nonacquiescence [was] substituted therefore."

In 1970, the Sixth Circuit focused on the meaning of "incidents of ownership," in Estate of Fruehauf v. Commissioner, 427 F.2d 80 (6th Cir. 1970). There, decedent's wife paid all the premiums on several insurance policies written on the life of decedent. Mrs. Fruehauf predeceased her husband by fourteen months, leaving a will naming decedent co-executor of her estate, and co-trustee and life beneficiary of a trust to which the life insurance policies passed. Mr. Fruehauf was given broad powers in a fiduciary capacity over the insurance policies. The Tax Court held that Fruehauf possessed incidents of ownership in the policies, regardless of the capacity in which such incidents of ownership could be exercised, and included the proceeds in his grosos estate.

Although the Sixth Circuit affirmed, it rejected the "Tax Court's broad *per se* rule" that the capacity in which powers are held should not be considered in determining whether such powers constitute incidents of ownership. The court stated that where the requisite powers over policies on his life have been transferred to a decedent, with no beneficial interest therein, "such arrangement can hardly be construed as a substitute for testamentary disposition on decedent's part." 427 F.2d at 84. The court held that decedent's powers were sufficient to constitute incidents of ownership only because as lifetime beneficiary of the trust, he could exercise his powers in such a way as to receive economic benefit from the insurance.

In Estate of Skifter v. Commissioner, 468 F.2d 699 (2d Cir. 1972), decedent made an irrevocable assignment of nine insurance policies on his life to his wife, more than three years before his death. His wife predeceased him and under her will the policies became part of a testamentary trust with the insured as trustee. Although Skifter's powers to effect changes in the beneficial ownership of the policies or their proceeds were broad, he could not exercise any power for his own economic benefit.

The Second Circuit, affirming the Tax Court, held that where powers which may not be exercised so as to benefit the decedent are conferred upon him in his capacity as trustee, the "incidents of ownership" test of § 2042(2) is not met. The court concluded that while nonbeneficial powers *retained in connection with a transfer* of the beneficial interest in the policies might constitute incidents of ownership, it distinguished that situation from *Skifter,* where decedent *received a grant* on non-beneficial powers.

The only case since *Billings* in 1937 to directly consider the issue whether the right to select a settlement option is an "incident of ownership" is Estate of Lumpkin v. Commissioner, 474 F.2d 1092 (5th Cir. 1973). The *Lumpkin* court considered the same insurance policy involved here. However, the decedent in *Lumpkin* possessed certain powers which Mr. Connelly did not: in *Lumpkin,* the decedent was still employed when he died and thus could quit his job thereby cancelling the policy; Mr. Connelly was retired. The decedent in *Lumpkin* was survived by a widow and under the terms of the policy had the power to *unilaterally* exercise a settlement option; Mr. Connelly had no unilateral powers. In *Lumpkin,* the decedent was found to have the right to assign the power to exercise the settlement option; under the law of New Jersey, Mr. Connelly did not have that right.

Relying on *Billings* and the language of Treasury Regulation 20.2042-1(c)(2), the Tax Court held that the nonbeneficial power possessed by decedent was not an appropriate predicate for the estate tax. The Court of Appeals reversed, holding that Lumpkin possessed an incident of ownership in the insurance policy.

The Fifth Circuit inferred from the legislative history of § 2042 that Congress was attempting to tax the value of life insurance proceeds over which the insured at death still possessed a substantial degree of control. The court framed the question of incidents of ownership in terms of the "right to alter the time and manner of enjoyment." Relying on an analogy to two trust cases, Lober v. U.S., 346 U.S. 335 (1953) and United States v. O'Malley, 383 U.S. 627 (1966), the court concluded that elements leading to inclusion in the gross estate there were also indicators of incidents of ownership under § 2042. The court stated: "[i]n view of the Congressional intention to make the estate tax treatment of life insurance roughly analogous to that bestowed upon other types of property, somewhat of an anomaly would be created if power over the time and manner of enjoyment was said to impart enough control to activate § 2036 and 2038 yet not enough to make it an 'incident of ownership' within the context of § 2042." 474 F.2d at 1097.

Appellant argues that *Lumpkin* controls the instant appeal. We disagree for a number of reasons. First, in our opinion, *Lumpkin* does not accurately reflect the applicable law. Second, the rights possessed by the decedent in Lumpkin were greater than those possessed by Mr. O'Malley.

The courts in *Skifter* and in *Lumpkin* concluded that Congress intended to give life insurance policies estate tax treatment roughly equivalent to that accorded other types of property under related sections of the Code. Thus, both courts examined the treatment given other property under §§ 2036, 2037 and 2038, in defining "incidents of ownership."

The federal estate tax is imposed on the privilege of transferring property at death coupled with "taxes upon other types of transfers that have some of the aspects of a testamentary transfer and would otherwise be resorted to in order to escape a tax limited to strictly testamentary transfers." Therefore, whether the right to exercise a settlement option is an incident of ownership depends in part upon whether the retention of such right is a "substitute for testamentary disposition of property." * * * In the instant case, Mr. Connelly did not purchase the insurance. It was a group term life insurance policy provided solely by his employer. The power to select an alternative mode of settlement, here, is not a substitute for testamentary disposition of property.

The *Lumpkin* court strongly relied on what it viewed as the intent of Congress to tax life insurance and other types of property equivalently. However, *Lumpkin's* construction of § 2042 would make it the only § in the Code that could reach property in which the decedent had no beneficial interest and over which he had no power exercisable for his own benefit. It is clear that Congress does not consider life insurance to be inherently testamentary. Thus if *Lumpkin* is correct in concluding that Congress meant to have the tax consequences of life insurance conform to other types of property, it would certainly seem more logical that Congress intended to equate incidents of ownership with the right to economic benefits of the policy. * * *

Furthermore, Reg. § 2042-1(c)(2) specifically provides that "incidents of ownership" refers "to the right of the insured or his estate to the economic benefits of the policy." Mr. Connelly had no rights whatsoever to the economic benefits of the policy.

¶ 20,499

Lumpkin's reliance upon *Lober* and *O'Malley* in defining § 2042 is misplaced. The facts of *Lober* and *O'Malley* were specifically covered by other sections of the Code. Moreover, the powers involved in *Lober* and *O'Malley* are directly parallel to explicit provisions of the regulations for life insurance, Reg. § 20.2042-1(c). If the same powers which were involved in *Lober* and *O'Malley* were translated to the parallel provisions for life insurance, the explicit language of the regulations would require inclusion. Both decisions are controlled by explicit regulations. Such is not the case here. *Lumpkin* erroneously extended *Lober* and *O'Malley* to a fact situation foreign to both and controlled by different statutory provisions.

The decedents in both *Lober* and *O'Malley* possessed the power to alter the time of the payments, which could be exercised to change the beneficiary of the proceeds. In *Lober* the decedent retained the power to accelerate the remainder of the trust, thereby cutting off the remaindermen and ensuring that the income beneficiaries would receive the entire corpus of the trust. In *O'Malley* the decedent reserved the power to accumulate income and add it to the principal, thereby reducing the payments to the income beneficiaries and increasing the benefits of the remaindermen. Possession of the power to change the beneficiary has long been held to constitute an incident of ownership. In this case, however, the decedent could change neither the beneficiaries themselves, nor the amounts the designated beneficiaries would receive. Regardless of the time of the payments, the designated beneficiary or his estate would receive the same amount. Connelly, therefore, unlike the decedents in *Lober* and *O'Malley,* could not alter the amount that any beneficiary would receive; he possessed only the power to change the time at which the proceeds would be received.

Connelly could, by electing to prolong the time of the payments, attempt to ensure that a designated beneficiary's estate, rather than the beneficiary himself, would receive a percentage of the insurance proceeds. However, this speculative power is so insignificant as compared with the power to change the beneficiaries, retained by the decedents in *Lober* and *O'Malley,* that it should not be considered an incident of ownership.

Lumpkin cited *Skifter* as authority for the proposition that Congress intended estate taxation of all property to be analogous, yet it subverted the crux of the *Skifter* opinion. *Skifter* focused on whether the property would be taxed under other sections if it were not life insurance. *Lumpkin* focused on whether the power held by the decedent would have been sufficient under those §§ to result in inclusion. *Skifter* properly required that the nature and source of the power, the way in which it is held, and whether the retention of power is a substitute for testamentary disposition of the property, be examined. *Lumpkin* completely ignored the distinctions between the type of property involved.

Moreover, as discussed above, Mr. Connelly's rights were not as broad as those possessed by the decedent in *Lumpkin*. The *Lumpkin* court found it important that the decedent "could easily have assigned the right to elect optional settlements, thereby completely divesting himself of control over the insurance proceeds and avoiding inclusion of their value in his gross estate."

¶ 20,499

474 F.2d at 1097–98. Here, decedent had no power to assign his rights under the contract. It was forbidden by New Jersey law.

Mr. Connelly's sole power to select a settlement option with the mutual agreement of his employer and the insurer did not give him a substantial degree of control sufficient to constitute an incident of ownership. Landorf v. United States, 408 F.2d 461 (Ct. Cl. 1969); Old Point National Bank, Executor, 39 B.T.A. 343 (1939); Estate of Chester H. Bowers, 23 T.C. 911 (1955). The power gave him no rights to the economic benefits of the policy. He had no power which by itself has ever been held to constitute an incident of ownership. Notwithstanding withdrawal of acquiescence by the Commissioner, *Billings* remains viable and controls the instant case as held by the District Court. The proceeds of the insurance should not have been included in decedent's gross estate.

[¶ 20,507]

Note

For several years following the *Connelly* decision, the Internal Revenue Service refused to follow the *Fruehauf* and *Skifter* decisions (cited in *Connelly*). In Revenue Ruling 76–261, 1976–2 C.B. 276, the IRS had declared that it did not agree with these decisions. However, finally, in 1984, Revenue Ruling 76–261 was revoked in Revenue Ruling 84–179, 1984–2 C.B. 195. In Revenue Ruling 84–179, the insured purchased a life insurance policy and transferred all incidents of ownership to his spouse. The spouse named their child as beneficiary. The spouse predeceased the insured. The spouse's will created a residuary trust which named the insured as trustee and the child as beneficiary. The insured's management powers as trustee included the right to assign, pledge, borrow against the policy, and choose settlement options. However, these powers could not be exercised for the insured's benefit. As a result, the Internal Revenue Service determined that the insured did not possess incidents of ownership in the policy.

Revenue Ruling 84–179 was expressly limited. Care was taken to announce that where the insured had been the transferor of the policy to the trust or had provided the consideration for purchasing or maintaining the policy or where the insured could exercise the incidents of ownership for his or her benefit, the insured would be considered to have taxable § 2042(2) incidents of ownership in the trust.

[¶ 20,515]

5. NONINSURED OWNER DIES FIRST

a. *Tax Consequences*

There are transfer tax consequences even if the owner of the policy is not the insured. If the owner dies before the insured, the ownership of the policy is an asset of the owner's estate. The value of the asset, since the proceeds are not yet payable, should be determined as provided in Reg. § 20.2031-8(a)(2). That is, the "interpolated terminal reserve" on the date of the policy owner's death (determined by asking the insurance company for this information) should be added to that portion of the last premium paid attributable to the period beyond the owner's death.

> *Example 1.*   H is insured under a $100,000 life insurance policy. W is the owner, and as owner, W has designated D as beneficiary of the policy. W predeceases both H and D. W's estate will include the interpolated terminal reserve value (and not face value) of the policy.

> *Example 2.*   Same facts as in Example 1, except that D predeceases both H and W. Because the gift is not complete (and D has not been irrevocably named as the beneficiary), D will have nothing in her estate as a result of being named beneficiary.

[¶ 20,523]

b. *Will Planning*

When drafting the will of a person who owns insurance on the life of another person, special care must be taken to quiz the testator about the disposition of the life insurance in anticipation of the possibility that the owner will die before the insured. Does the owner want to give the insurance to the insured? If so, counsel the owner that the result will be to put the insurance back into the estate of the insured for federal estate tax purposes at the insured's later death. Suggest to the owner that the insurance be given to someone other than the insured so that the insurance remains permanently out of the insured's gross estate. Point out that it is likely that the insured initially caused the owner to be designated "owner" of the insurance so as to keep it out of the insured's estate for tax purposes.

With the advent of the unlimited marital deduction, it is hard to find any justification for spouse-owned life insurance.

Problem

[¶ 20,529]

In routine will drafting, little attention will be given (unfortunately) to the possible ownership of insurance by the testator on the life of another person. With that in mind, and considering the IRS's position on incidents of ownership held in a fiduciary capacity, see ¶ 20,499, should the draftsman routinely include language like the following in the wills and trusts that he or she drafts:

> No one shall be appointed as Executor or Trustee hereunder nor continue to serve in such capacity at any time when the estate includes policies of insurance on the life of such person if such person's presence in that office will cause the proceeds of that insurance to be included in the gross estate of such person for federal estate tax purposes and if the presence of someone else in that office would avoid that result.

¶ 20,529

[¶ 20,531]

6. PROCEEDS PAYABLE TO A THIRD-PARTY BENEFICIARY

If the insured dies *before* the owner of the policy, the owner is deemed to have made a taxable gift to the beneficiary of the policy at the time of the insured's death. If the owner is the beneficiary, of course, no tax consequences result; but if the owner has designated a third party as beneficiary, the designation will be a sort of incomplete gift until the owner loses the right to change his or her designation. The insured's death, then, completes the gift. Reg. § 25.2511–2(f).There are no estate tax consequences to the insured, and nothing is included in the owner's gross estate at the owner's subsequent death (unless it occurs within three years, see § 2035(a)(2)).

> *Example.* H is insured under a $100,000 life insurance policy. W is the owner and D is the designated beneficiary. H predeceases both W and D. When H dies, the gift to D is complete, and W will have made a taxable transfer of the insurance proceeds.

[¶ 20,539]

7. COMMUNITY PROPERTY

Special problems arise, of course, if the client lives or has lived in a community property jurisdiction. One of the major issues is that of ownership of the policy and the proceeds—to whom are the insurance proceeds taxed? What difference does it make, if any, whether premiums were paid with separate or community property?

[¶ 20,547]

a. *Consequences of Community Property Status*

If the insured and the insured's spouse hold a life insurance policy on the insured's life as community property, then, at the insured's death, only half the proceeds will be included in the insured's gross estate, even though the insured had incidents of ownership or even though the proceeds were payable to the insured's estate. This is because one-half belongs to the spouse and therefore will not be considered receivable by the insured's estate. Reg. § 20.2042-1(b)(2).

If the uninsured spouse dies before the insured, the uninsured spouse's gross estate must include half the value of the policy on the date of death (or alternate valuation date). Reg. § 20.2031-8(a).

If the insured dies first, but the insurance proceeds are payable to some third party, the other spouse has made a taxable gift to that third party of the uninsured spouse's half of the community proceeds. Reg. § 25.2511-1(h)(9).

[¶ 20,555]

b. *Determination of Community Property Status*

Given these special consequences of community property status, how does one know what property is community property? How can the nature of the property be changed to separate?

¶ 20,531

Generally speaking, life insurance policies will be classified either as separate or community property, depending upon the nature of the funds expended for the premium payments. However, the general presumption in favor of community status applies to life insurance policies. Without convincing evidence as to the separate nature of funds used for premium payments, a life insurance policy owned or acquired during marriage will be presumed a community asset. The fact that only one spouse is named as the owner of the policy in the contract is not, by itself, sufficient proof of separate ownership. The community property presumption is, however, rebuttable.

Most of the problems concerning the classification of life insurance policies as separate or community occur when premiums on policies are paid with both separate and community funds. Two different judicial approaches to this situation have developed in the community property states. One is described as "tracing" and the other as "inception of title."

Using the tracing approach, where the premiums used to purchase life insurance policies are paid from both separate and community funds, the life insurance is considered a hybrid with both community and separate elements.

Example 1. Ben's life insurance policy has a current value of $100,000. Ben paid premiums of $10,000 before marriage. After marriage, the remaining $40,000 of premiums were paid with community funds. Since 60 percent of the premiums ($10,000 plus 50 percent of the community premiums) are traceable to the original purchaser, $60,000 is considered the value of his property interest in the policy.

Using the inception of title approach, the life insurance policy will be either separate or community depending upon whether the first premium was paid with separate or community property.

Example 2. Bob purchased a $1,000,000 policy and paid the first $10,000 of premiums with separate funds. The separate nature of the asset is established by the first separate premium payment and is not altered by the subsequent payment of $40,000 of premiums from community funds.

Under inception of title, the nonowner-spouse who contributed a half interest in the $40,000 of community funds used to pay premiums has a right of reimbursement for $20,000 from the owner spouse.

Problems

[¶ 20,595]

1. H is insured under a $10,000 policy of life insurance. He also is the owner of the policy. W, however, is the beneficiary of the proceeds of the insurance on H's life. Will the proceeds be excluded from H's gross estate for federal estate tax purposes?

2. H is insured under a $15,000 policy of life insurance. W is the owner of the policy. H's estate is the designated beneficiary of the policy. Will the proceeds of the policy be excluded from H's estate at his death because W is the owner of the policy?

3. H is insured under a $20,000 policy of life insurance. W is the owner, and, as owner, W has designated D as beneficiary of the policy. D predeceases

both H and W. Will the interpolated terminal reserve value of the policy be included in D's gross estate?

4.   Refer to the facts given in Problem 3 and assume W predeceases both H and D. In that case, will W have included in her gross estate the face value of the life insurance?

5.   H is insured under a $25,000 policy of life insurance. W is the owner and D is the designated beneficiary. H predeceases both W and D. As a consequence, could W be deemed to have made a taxable gift to D? Of what?

6.   W is to be designated owner of a $30,000 policy of life insurance on H's life. It is important from an estate tax standpoint for W to include a provision in her will providing that in the event that W predeceases H, ownership of the policy will pass to someone other than H. Why?

7.   Do you agree that the person who pays the premiums on a policy of life insurance on his life will have the proceeds of that policy included in his gross estate at death?

8.   H is the insured under a $35,000 policy of life insurance. H's spouse, W, owned the policy (at all times) but she predeceased H. Her will directed that her entire residuary estate be held in trust by H for the benefit of W's daughter, D. The policy of life insurance was included in W's residuary estate. The trust provided that the trustee should pay out so much or all of the income to D for life as the trustee believed appropriate and upon D's death to distribute the trust estate *per stirpes* to D's then living lineal descendants. If H predeceases D and is serving as trustee at his death, will any amount need to be included in H's gross estate?

9.   Would the result be different in the immediately preceding question if all the income was required to be distributed annually to D for life?

10.   H is insured under a $40,000 policy of whole (or ordinary) life insurance owned by a trustee under an irrevocable trust agreement established by H. The trust was funded by H with an amount of property which should be adequate to generate on an annual basis income equal to the premiums on the life insurance policy. The trustee is obligated to use the income from the trust to pay the premiums on the life insurance policy. Upon H's death the trustee is obligated to collect the proceeds of the life insurance policy, add those proceeds to the property already in trust, and pay the income to W for life, remainder to H's lineals. In this case will there be estate tax consequences to H (assuming the trust was not established within three years of H's death)?

G. TRANSFERS WITHIN THREE YEARS OF DEATH

[¶ 20,601]

1. POST 1981 DEATHS FOLLOWING LIFE INSURANCE TRANSFERS

Suppose the client dies within three years after having divested himself of ownership of the policy. Will the proceeds be recaptured and included in the client's gross estate? Also, what happens if the insured divests himself of ownership of the policy more than three years before death but continues to pay the premiums until death?

For many years, property transferred within three years of death was "recaptured" for estate tax purposes and included in the gross estate of the transferor at death. That all changed in 1981 when Congress effectively repealed, with certain exceptions, the long-standing rules respecting transfers within three years of death. One of the exceptions relates to life insurance, the effect of which is that any transfer of ownership of a life insurance policy within three years of the death of the owner is "recaptured" for estate tax purposes and included in the gross estate of the transferor at death. § 2035(a)(2). The rule also applies to premiums paid on life insurance policies.

Thus, it is clear that transfer of an insurance policy for less than full and adequate consideration within three years of death will cause inclusion of the policy in the decedent's gross estate if the decedent was the owner of the policy. Moreover, because the policy is valued at the date of death (or alternate valuation date, as provided in § 2032) rather than at the time of the transfer, the included amount is the amount of the policy proceeds. However, if a policy is purchased by someone other than the decedent, such as a trustee, within three years of the decedent's death, the policy is generally not included in the decedent's gross estate.

[¶ 20,609]

TECHNICAL ADVICE MEMORANDUM 9323002

February 24, 1993.

Are the proceeds of a life insurance policy includible in a decedent's gross estate under § 2035?

FACTS

The decedent died on July 27, 1990, survived by her two sons, A and B. On June 1, 1989, the decedent signed an application for a life insurance policy with a face value of $500,000. The decedent signed the application as the "Proposed Insured," designated her estate as the beneficiary, and left blank a space for the designation of a policy owner other than the insured.

Several lines above the decedent's signature, the application contains the printed statement, "I agree that any policy(ies) issued on this application

¶ **20,609**

shall take effect only if the first full premium is paid and such policy(ies) is issued and delivered to the owner.''

Later in the summer of 1989, the decedent completed a printed form from the same insurance company, entitled ''Supplementary Application,'' signing the form but leaving it undated. On this form, the decedent requested that the policy be split into two $250,000 policies; she named A as the beneficiary and owner of one policy and B as the beneficiary and owner of the other policy. The insurance company routinely uses supplementary applications for revising initial applications. The insurance company's records indicate that when this ''Supplemental Application'' was executed, no policy or policies on the decedent's life had yet been issued or delivered, nor had any premiums been paid on such a policy.

On August 28, 1989, A wrote a check to the insurance company for $3,670 to cover the first two premium payments on the policies. On August 29, 1989, the check was delivered to the insurance company which issued the policies for which the decedent had applied. Each was a $250,000 policy naming one of the decedent's sons as both the beneficiary and the owner. Each policy also expressly named the decedent as successor owner if the designated owner died. Under the terms of the policies, as owner, each son could obtain, alone and in all events, the cash surrender value of his policy at any time before the decedent's death, as well as exercising all other ownership powers.

Between the time that the decedent made her original application and the time the ''Supplementary Application'' was signed, the insurance company raised its rates. The insurance company did not view supplementary applications as new applications. Therefore, the policies on the decedent's life remained subject to the rates in effect when she made the initial application. If A and B had initially applied for the policies on the decedent's life at the time that the decedent executed the Supplementary Application, A and B would have been able to obtain premiums based upon the same life expectancy applicable to the decedent's first application; however, the new higher rates would have been applied.

A and B paid all of the premiums on the policies. At the decedent's death, all of the proceeds from each policy were paid to A and B, respectively, as beneficiaries.

Law and Analysis

[With respect to post 1981 deaths, § 2035(a) provides that in the case of property transfers within three years of death, the value of the transferor's gross estate shall include the value of all such property if such property would have been included under § 2036, 2037, 2038, or 2042 if such transfer had not been made.]

Under § 2042(2) , the gross estate includes the proceeds of insurance on the decedent's life receivable by beneficiaries other than the decedent's estate under policies in which the decedent possessed at death any incidents of ownership that can be exercised either alone or in conjunction with any other person.

¶ 20,609

Section 20.2042-1(a)(2) of the Estate Tax Regulations provides that the term "incidents of ownership" is not limited to legal ownership but refers to the right to the "economic benefits" of the policy. The term includes the power to change the beneficiary, to surrender or cancel the policy, to assign the policy, to revoke an assignment, to pledge the policy for a loan, or to obtain a loan against the surrender value of the policy.

[Section 2035(a) operates] to include a life insurance policy transferred by a decedent only if the policy would have been includible under § 2042 had the decedent "retained" the policy or incidents of ownership in the policy. Generally, the courts have concluded that, based on the statutory language, in order for a life insurance policy to be subject to inclusion under § [2035(a)(2)], the decedent must have actually owned the policy (or have had incidents of ownership in the policy) and must have actually transferred the policy. Estate of Perry v. Commissioner, 927 F.2d 209 (5th Cir. 1991), aff'q., 59 T.C.M. 1990-123; Estate of Headrick v. Commissioner, 918 F.2d 1263 (6th Cir. 1990), aff'q., 93 T.C. 171 (1989); Estate of Leder v. Commissioner, 893 F.2d 237 (10th Cir. 1989), aff'q., 89 T.C. 235 (1987).

This is in contrast to cases involving decedents dying before 1982, subject to the provisions of § 2035 prior to amendment by ERTA. In those cases, the government has successfully argued that if the decedent procured the policy and paid the premiums, but had the policy titled in the name of a third party, the decedent in substance, if not in form, transferred the policy. This deemed transfer was sufficient to cause inclusion under § 2035, prior to amendment. See, e.g., Knisley v. United States, 901 F.2d 793 (9th Cir. 1990).

Accordingly, in situations involving decedents dying after 1981, in order for a transferred life insurance policy to be subject to inclusion under § [2035(a)(2)], it must be determined that the decedent actually held incidents of ownership in the policy and actually transferred those incidents of ownership. This is a question of state law as well as of federal tax law.

In the present case, within three years of her death, the decedent initially applied for an insurance policy, specifying in the application that she was to be designated as owner. Subsequently, on a supplementary application, the decedent revised the initial application and requested issuance of two policies to be owned by A and B. These policies were issued.

Under applicable state law, the policies issued did not become effective until the first full premium was paid and the policies were issued and delivered to the owners, as provided in the application for insurance completed by the decedent. An application for insurance, according to the state law, is an offer to the insurance company which does not become bound in an insurance contract until accepting the offer. * * *

In the present case, the decedent's June 1, 1989, application named the decedent as insured and owner and her estate as beneficiary. However, under state law, that application was a mere offer to the insurance company for an insurance contract. Under the terms of the application, any policies issued would not be effective until the first premium was paid and the policy was delivered to the owner. When the decedent signed the Supplementary Application, the insurer's conditions for accepting an offer had not yet occurred. The first premium had not been paid, and no policies had been delivered.

After the decedent submitted her Supplementary Application, the first premium payment was paid to the insurance company on August 29, 1989, and the insurance company issued and delivered the two policies designating A and B as owners and beneficiaries to A and B on that date. In so doing, the insurance company created a binding insurance contract between itself and the decedent's sons, based on the decedent's Supplementary Application. The policies issued on August 29, 1989, were the only policies issued on the decedent's life. Thus, A and B held all of the incidents of ownership in the policies from the date of issuance, and the decedent never actually held any economic, ownership, or contractual rights in the policies and, therefore, would not be subject to inclusion under § 2035. See Estate of Perry v. Commissioner, supra.

We recognize that, at the time the decedent filed the Supplementary Application designating A and B as policy owners, the insurance company agreed to use the same favorable premium rate applicable at the time of the decedent's first application. Thus, to this extent, the decedent succeeded in passing to A and B a benefit concerning the cost of the policies to be issued to A and B as the designated owners. If A and B had applied for initial policies on the decedent's life at the time when the decedent executed the Supplementary Application, A and B could have obtained premiums based upon the same life expectancy applicable to the decedent's first application but not the more favorable rate schedule.

However, we believe it is questionable whether the transfer of this favorable premium rate, which may have facilitated the acquisition of the policies by A and B, would constitute the transfer of an incident of ownership in a policy itself. Generally, the term "incidents of ownership" focuses on the right to control the economic benefits of the policy, and the mere right to apply for insurance coverage is not an incident of ownership. See, e.g., Rev. Rul. 76–421, 1976–2 C.B. 280. In any event, we do not believe the transfer of this favorable premium rate would take this case out of the purview of Estate of Perry.

CONCLUSION

The proceeds of the life insurance policies on the decedent's life are not includible in a decedent's gross estate under § 2035.

2. UNIQUE ASPECTS OF TERM INSURANCE IMPACTED BY § 2035

An automatic renewal option can be important in limiting the reach of § 2035(a) where inclusion of term insurance in the gross estate is at issue.

[¶ 20,625]

REVENUE RULING 82–13

1982–1 C.B. 132.

D, the decedent, was an employee of X company, which covered its employees with a renewable group term life insurance policy. All premiums were paid by the X company. The policy was renewable upon payment of the annual premium at standard rates. No evidence of insurability was necessary for renewal.

On February 1, 1975, D, gratuitously assigned all rights under the policy (including any conversion privilege) to A and each subsequent yearly premium was paid by D's employer, the X company. D died on May 1, 1980, possessing no incidents of ownership in the policy.

LAW AND ANALYSIS

Section 2035(a) generally provides that the gross estate shall include the value of all property interests transferred by a decedent within three years before death.

The initial purchase of a life insurance policy by a decedent who designates a third party as owner of the policy is a transfer of the policy for purposes of § 2035 and the entire proceeds will be includible in the decedent's gross estate if such purchase is within three years of death. Detroit Bank & Trust Co. v. United States, 467 F.2d 964 (6th Cir. 1972), cert. denied, 410 U.S. 929 (1973); First National Bank of Oregon v. United States, 352 F. Supp. 1157 (D.C. Ore 1972), aff'd, 488 F.2d 575 (9th Cir. 1973). The result is the same if the policy is initially purchased by the decedent as owner more than three years before death but is subsequently transferred by the decedent to a third party owner within three years of the decedent's death. The result is also the same where the decedent annually repurchases a policy that expires in its entirety each year and upon each repurchase designates a third party as owner. In such a case, each repurchase constitutes a new transfer for purposes of § 2035, and the proceeds will be includible in the decedent's gross estate at death. See Bel v. United States, 452 F.2d 683 (5th Cir. 1971), cert. denied, 406 U.S. 919 (1972).

A term life insurance policy furnishes life insurance protection for a specified term, the face value of which is payable only if death occurs during the stipulated term. At the end of the policy term all premiums are fully earned, and all rights of the policy owner terminate. S. Huebner and K. Black, Life Insurance 73 (8th Ed. 1972). If, however, the policy contains a provision granting a right of renewal, the contract must be renewed upon demand (and payment of the premium) by the policy owner, without regard to the insurable status of the insured at the time. D. Gregg, and V. Lucas, Life and Health Insurance Handbook, 57 (3d ed. 1973).

In the instant case, the premiums paid by X company are attributable to D, for estate tax and gift tax purposes. See Rev. Rul. 76–490, 1976–2 C.B. 300. Thus, if the premium payment was deemed to purchase a new insurance contract each year, then the policy proceeds would be subject to inclusion under § 2035.

Under the group term policy considered here, there was an option for automatic renewal upon payment of the premium. This renewal was accomplished without providing evidence of insurability. The rights and obligations of the parties continued without interruption from the policy's inception, as long as the policy was renewed on each anniversary date. Thus, the payment of the premium at the time of the policy's renewal did not create new rights, nor was such payment a repurchase of insurance. The payment merely effectuated the continuation of an existing agreement. Therefore, when D, through X company, paid each renewal premium, it was not a new transfer of insurance coverage under § 2035 and the proceeds from the insurance policy are not includible in D's gross estate.

Compare Bel v. United States, where payments of annual premiums after creation of the policy were each considered purchases of a new policy. In *Bel,* an accidental death policy was involved that did not provide a renewal privilege.

HOLDING

The value of the renewable group term life insurance policy is not includible in the decedent's gross estate under § 2035 when the decedent assigned the policy more than three years before death, but is considered to have made premium payments until death.

Problem

[¶ 20,629]

1. Consider whether the following statements are correct. Give reasons for your conclusions.

(a) H is the insured under a policy of life insurance. Five years before his death H assigned ownership of the policy to W and W immediately designated herself as beneficiary of the policy proceeds. At the time H assigned ownership of the policy to W he was under the impression that he was suffering from terminal cancer and did not expect to live out the year. The proceeds of the insurance policy are to be included in H's estate as a transfer in contemplation of death.

(b) H is the insured under a policy of life insurance. Two years before his death he transferred ownership of the policy to W. The proceeds of the life insurance will *not* be included in H's gross estate because H's transfer to W was subject to gift tax.

(c) H is the insured under a policy of whole (or ordinary) life insurance. H transferred ownership of the policy to W more than three years before his death but he continued to pay the premiums on the policy up until his death. For that reason the policy proceeds will be included in H's gross estate at his death.

(d) H is insured under a policy of life insurance. W owns the policy and as owner has designated her daughter, D, as beneficiary. H pays the premiums on the policy and, as a result, the premiums paid within three years of H's death will be included in his gross estate unless H's executor can establish that H's sole motivation in making the premium payments was his belief that the federal estate tax is oppressive.

(e) H is insured under a policy of life insurance. The policy was taken out by the Accumulation National Bank as Trustee under an irrevocable trust established by W. W has funded the trust with property which should generate an amount of income sufficient to pay the premiums on the life insurance. The trust agreement provides that upon the death of H the trustee shall collect the proceeds of the life insurance policies, add the proceeds to the property already in the trust, and pay the income from the trust estate to W for life. Upon W's death the trust shall terminate and the trust property will be distributed *per stirpes* to the "then living lineal descendants" of W. In this case the entire trust estate will be included in W's gross estate at her death on the theory that she has retained for her life a life estate in the trust property. The same result would be obtained if W had not funded the trust but had merely paid the premiums when due on the policy of life insurance. It's altogether probable, however, that the proceeds of the life insurance policy could be kept out of W's estate if the only payments the trustee was obligated to make to W during her lifetime were those necessary for her health, maintenance, and support.

H. THE IRREVOCABLE LIFE INSURANCE TRUST

[¶ 20,651]

1. USES AND TYPES OF IRREVOCABLE LIFE INSURANCE TRUSTS

An irrevocable life insurance trust is a trust created to either purchase or receive assignment of a life insurance policy on the life of the insured. The trust becomes the owner and beneficiary of the policy and at the death of the insured the trust generally receives the policy proceeds free of income tax.

[¶ 20,659]

a. *Uses*

The irrevocable trust can serve as the principal component in the insured's estate plan. As such, for example, it can be used as a receptacle for property poured over from a will. See ¶ 4551 for a discussion of pourover wills. Generally, however, the irrevocable life insurance trust is utilized exclusively as a means of preventing insurance proceeds from being included in the insured's estate. In this role, the trust's function is to own the life insurance policy and serve as the beneficiary of the proceeds. It is generally structured similar to the bypass trust discussed beginning at ¶ 18,001. It is with respect to this limited purpose that most of the discussion in these materials is focused.

[¶ 20,667]

b. *Funded v. Unfunded Trusts*

An irrevocable insurance trust may be funded or unfunded. A funded trust is a trust which is able to pay part or all of the premiums on life insurance owned by the trust by using property owned by the trust (or earned by property owned by the trust). Generally, the grantor of the trust transfers not only one or more life insurance policies to the trust but also other property. The trustee can use this other property or any income produced by that property to fund the annual policy premiums. On the other hand, if the trust does not own or possess the means to pay the policy premiums, the trust is deemed unfunded. Unfunded trusts require special attention because there can be gift and estate tax consequences when the premium payments are made. See additional discussion at ¶ 20,601.

[¶ 20,675]

2. IRREVOCABLE LIFE INSURANCE TRUST CONDITIONS

The life insurance trust must be irrevocable if it is to serve its intended purpose of freeing proceeds of insurance from the estate tax. Section 2038 stipulates a decedent's gross estate includes the value of property "subject at the date of his death to any change through the exercise of a power * * * to alter, amend, revoke or terminate." § 2038(a)(1). Therefore, any power to revoke the trust or redirect to whom the proceeds should be paid will cause the proceeds to be included in the insured's gross estate and subject to the estate tax if the insured has a § 2038 power relative to the trust.

Second, the insured may not possess any incidents of ownership in the life insurance policies within three years of death. §§ 2035(a)(2), 2042(2). The regulations accompanying § 2042 describe incidents of ownership as "the right of the insured or his estate to the economic benefits of the policy." Reg. § 20.2042-2(c)(2). As a result, the insured may not possess the "power to change the beneficiary, to surrender or cancel the policy, to assign the policy, to revoke an assignment, to pledge the policy for a loan, * * * [to] obtain from the insurer a loan against the surrender value [or] possess a reversionary interest in the policy." Reg. § 20.2042-2(c)(2) and (3).

Third, the life insurance proceeds cannot be payable to the estate of the insured. Section 2042 provides that any amount receivable by the insured's executor will be included in the insured's gross estate. This includes any legally binding obligation, such as taxes and debts, that the beneficiary of the policy proceeds is required to pay as a condition to receipt of the life insurance proceeds.

> *Example.* The Abbott Irrevocable Trust is the beneficiary of a life insurance policy on the life of Mr. Abbott. The terms of the trust require the trustee to pay any and all estate taxes imposed on Mr. Abbott's estate at his death. Because of the payment requirement, Mr. Abbott's gross estate will include the amount of proceeds necessary to satisfy the estate tax payable. Reg. § 20.2042-1(b)(1).

¶ 20,667

Finally, if the insured purchased the policy initially and then transferred the policy to the trust, the insured must be alive for three years following the transfer. If the insured dies during this three-year period, the policy proceeds will be included in the insured's estate for tax purposes. § 2035(a)(2). However, if a policy is newly purchased by the trust or someone other than the insured within three years of the insured's death, the three-year rule will not apply.

[¶ 20,683]

3. ADVANTAGES AND DISADVANTAGES OF THE IRREVOCABLE TRUST

An irrevocable life insurance trust is a useful tool in creating a tax-free pool of capital, the ultimate beneficiaries of which are typically the insured's children. It is this emphasis on permanent tax savings that distinguishes the irrevocable life insurance trust from other techniques that offer mere tax deferral, examples being spouse-owned life insurance and child-owned life insurance.

The primary disadvantage with a irrevocable trust is that the insured must relinquish control over the life insurance policy. For example, the insured cannot borrow against the cash value in the event of an unexpected cash shortage, nor can the insured change the beneficiary of the policy once the trust is established. While some flexibility can be built into the trust in anticipation of changed circumstances, the donor must come to appreciate the meaning of the term "irrevocable" as applied to the trust. Ratner, How to Undo an ILIT, If You Really Have To, 145 Tr. & Est., Sept. 2006, at 18.

An irrevocable trust, additionally, can be expensive both to establish and to continue. A complicated trust document can require many hours of careful drafting. Furthermore, a trustee must be expected to charge an annual fee to manage the trust (except in instances where the trust beneficiary is also the trustee.)

[¶ 20,691]

4. GIFT TAX CONSIDERATIONS

Both the assignment of a life insurance policy to an irrevocable trust and the payment of subsequent premiums can have gift tax consequences.

[¶ 20,699]

a. Initial Transfer of the Life Insurance Policy to the Trust

When the insured unequivocally transfers ownership of a life insurance policy, the transfer is generally considered a taxable gift. Reg. § 25.2511-1(h)(8). In such instances, the transfer is subject to the gift tax unless it qualifies for the per donee per annum exclusion ($12,000 in 2006). See § 2503(b). Section 2503 requires the gift to be a gift of the present interest in order to qualify for the annual exclusion. Where the gift is to a trust, the terms of the trust affect whether the transfer qualifies as a gift of a

¶ 20,699

present interest. That is, a future interest "may be created by the limitations contained in the trust." Reg. § 25.2503-3(a).

[¶ 20,707]

i. Individually Purchased Policies

With respect to conventional individually purchased life insurance policies, Reg. § 25.2512–6 provides a series of examples illustrating how to value various life insurance policies. As a general rule, the value of a life insurance contract for gift tax purposes is equal to the cost of acquiring a similar life insurance policy on the day of the gift. If the policy requires future premium payments to be made, the value of the gift will equal the interpolated terminal reserve value at the date of the gift (generally the cash value) and any unearned premium currently paid on the policy. Reg. § 25.2512-6(a), Example (4). However, if the health of the insured has drastically changed such that the insured is currently uninsurable, the interpolated terminal reserve value may not be an appropriate measure of the value of the gift. See United States v. Ryerson, 312 U.S. 260 (1941).

[¶ 20,715]

ii. Group-Term Policies

A group-term policy is valued differently than a conventional individually purchased policy. Generally, a group policy's value at the time of the gift is the cost of replacing the policy or the amount of the unearned premium if a policy is already in existence at the time of the gift. Reg. § 25.2512-6(a). In Revenue Ruling 76–490, 1976–2 C.B. 300, the Internal Revenue Service concluded that a policy that was transferred to an irrevocable trust on the final day of the premium period was not a taxable gift. It reasoned that the "interest assigned had no ascertainable value at the time it was transferred, since the employer could have simply failed to make further premium payments."

As with individual policies, an exception may exist which makes the general valuation rule inapplicable. If the insured's health declined, rendering the insured uninsurable, an alternative valuation method would be required. F. Berall & S. Tate, Life Insurance and Life Insurance Trusts, 4 Notre Dame Est. Plan. Inst. 593, 673 (R. Campfield, ed. 1980).

Annual premium payments are also subject to gift tax. Payment, by either the employer of the insured or by the insured, to a trust or the insurance company, is a gift. Revenue Ruling 76–490 states that "each premium payment made by the employer for group-term life insurance on the life of D, where D irrevocably assigned the policy to the trust, is deemed an indirect transfer by D to the assignee of the policy * * * and subject to the gift tax." The gift created by an employer's payment of group-term life insurance premiums can generally be determined by reference to Table I provided in Reg. § 1.79-3(d)(2). See Rev. Rul. 84–147, 1984–2 C.B. 201.

¶ 20,699

The gift must be a gift of a present interest in order for the per donee per annum gift tax exclusion ($12,000 in 2006) to apply. § 2503(b). As in the case of the initial transfer of ownership of the policy to the trust discussed in ¶ 20,699, the terms of the trust instrument affect whether the premium payments will qualify as a present interest. If the trust provides that the insurance proceeds are payable to the insured's estate at the death of the insured, the premiums paid will qualify as a gift of a present interest. Rev. Rul. 76–490, 1976–2 C.B. 300.

However, the premiums will be gifts of a future interest in the case, for example, where the policy proceeds are to be held in trust for the benefit of the insured's children for life. See Rev. Rul. 79–47, 1979–1 C.B. 312.

[¶ 20,723]

b. *Crummey Powers to Obtain the Annual Gift Tax Exclusion*

Giving a donee a *Crummey* right to withdraw from a trust—a so-called *Crummey* power—may transform a transfer of a future interest into a gift of a present interest inasmuch as the donor's right of withdrawal may constitute a present right to enjoyment. See Crummey v. Commissioner, 397 F.2d 82 (9th Cir.1968), reprinted at ¶ 19,459. Although a beneficiary is given a *Crummey* power, the need to use the *Crummey* gift to pay the premiums on the life insurance policy requires that the beneficiary not exercise his or her right of withdrawal. This decision, by the beneficiary, not to exercise the withdrawal right, will often have gift tax consequences for the beneficiary because the lapse of a withdrawal power (a general power of appointment) may constitute a taxable gift. See § 2514. However, by structuring the withdrawal right so that it qualifies for the "five-and-five" lapse exclusion provided for in § 2514(e), some part or all of the gift tax consequences can be eliminated. See discussion at ¶¶ 18,247 and 19,555.

[¶ 20,731]

c. *Funding the Withdrawal Right*

As noted in ¶ 19,483, the *Crummey* withdrawal right will be seen as lacking in substance unless it is possible for the donee to actually receive the property over which he or she has a demand right. At first glance, this may not seem like much of a problem. When an addition is made to the trust, the donee having the withdrawal right notifies the trustee of his or her intention to exercise his or her withdrawal right—or does nothing, as the donor hopes will happen. Suppose, however, that the trustee is without cash to fund the exercise of a withdrawal right. This could happen, for example, upon the transfer of an existing life insurance policy to the trust. One solution in the case where the policy has cash surrender value is for the trustee to borrow some or all of the cash surrender value to fund any withdrawal request that is received. And where there is no cash surrender value, as in the case of term insurance, the right of withdrawal, if exercised, can be satisfied by distributing the policy itself.

Another dimension to the funding issue is presented in the case where the policy is of the group-term variety issued by the insured's employer. Here there is no policy to distribute. Moreover, each premium payment is made directly to the insurance company by the insured's employer. As a result, there really is "no beef" for those who are asking where it is. The solution may be to fund the trust with a permanent cash fund so as to satisfy the *Crummey* requirement that property be available to actually satisfy any withdrawal request that is received. However, bank service charges can make the use of a permanent cash fund expensive to maintain.

Problem

[¶ 20,737]

Would you agree that the following trust provisions would address most of the issues identified in the preceding material? Or do you think that, while these provisions solve some problems, they create more than they solve? For example, do you think the "penalty" provision in paragraph 5.1, included below, i.e., the ability of the donor to alter the beneficial interests in the trust at the time each addition is made to the trust would be effective to discourage a beneficiary from exercising his or her right of withdrawal? Or do you think it would be *too* effective in the sense that it might cost the donor the annual exclusion because the penalty provision would be seen as restricting the beneficiary's right of withdrawal (inasmuch as the beneficiary's withdrawal right might meet with donor disapproval, leading to exclusion of the disfavored beneficiary from participation in future additions to the trust)?

Look at the "floating" Annual Exclusion Amount and the Lapse Amount provided for in paragraph 16.1.1 in the excerpt below. Would the provisions for the Annual Exclusion Amount allow a donor to take advantage of the per donee per annum gift tax exclusion available for gifts made after 1981 ($12,000 in 2006) *if* this provision had been included in an irrevocable life insurance trust executed before 1981? See discussion of "old" trusts at ¶ 19,571.

Try your hand at simplifying the *Crummey* power so as to make it understandable to the settlor of the trust.

5.1. The trust shall terminate upon the last to occur of the following events:

    a.   The death of the last to die of the Settlor and the Settlor's spouse; and

    b.   The thirty-fifth (35) birthday of Settlor's youngest child then living or the death of all of Settlor's children not yet thirty-five (35) years of age.

Upon termination of the trust, the Trustee shall divide the trust estate so that there is one share for each of the Settlor's then living children and one share for each of the Settlor's children who are deceased but who have then living lineal descendants; provided, however, that in the event the donor of an addition to the trust during the lifetime of either the

Settlor or Settlor's spouse has specifically excluded one or more of the Settlor's children living at the termination of the trust from sharing in that addition, the trust estate shall be divided so that the portion of the trust estate allocated to the share set aside for each such child will be a fraction of the trust estate. The numerator of the fraction shall be the aggregate value of the additions to the trust estate which were allocated to each such child during the lifetime of either the Settlor or the Settlor's spouse. The denominator of the fraction shall be the aggregate value of all of the additions to the trust estate during Settlor's lifetime. The values used for federal gift tax purposes at the time of such additions shall be used in determining the numerator and denominator. Premiums paid (other than by the Trustee) on policies of life insurance included in the trust during Settlor's lifetime shall not be considered in determining the numerator and denominator of the fraction. The balance of the trust estate shall be divided among the Settlor's then living children and lineal descendants of deceased children as if the child or children whose share was determined by the foregoing fraction had died prior to the termination of the trust leaving no lineal descendants.

* * *

16.1.   The persons identified in this paragraph shall have the right to make withdrawals from the trust estate, or a specific fund, portion or share thereof, in accordance with the following terms and conditions.

16.1.1.   Additions to the trust (including the initial trust estate) other than those by will or by distribution from other trusts, shall be divided by the trustee on its books of account so as to provide one share for each of the Settlor's then living children unless the donor stipulates that no allocation be made to a specific child, and provided that in no event shall the value of the property allocated to the share set aside for a child exceed the Annual Exclusion Amount unless the donor is then married and the donor's spouse indicates in writing to the Trustee an intention to have the amount by which the addition exceeds the Annual Exclusion Amount attributed to such spouse for federal gift tax purposes. [For discussion, see ¶ 19,579.] Notwithstanding the foregoing, in no event shall the value of the property allocated to the share set aside for a child exceed the Lapse Amount. For purposes of this paragraph, the Annual Exclusion Amount refers to [the] amount of property which a donor may exclude when computing his or her taxable gifts for federal gift tax purposes for the year in which the addition to the trust estate is made. During the thirty (30) day period following the addition to the trust each such child shall have the right to withdraw property equal in value to that portion of the addition allocated to his share. Such right of withdrawal shall be exercised by a writing delivered to the Trustee and received by him within the thirty (30) day period. In the event any right of withdrawal is not effectively exercised within the period of time and manner specified, the Trustee shall add such addition to the trust estate.

16.1.2.   In addition, during the continuance of the trust, whenever premiums are paid directly to the insurance company on policies of life insurance included in the trust, the Settlor's then living children shall have the right to make withdrawals from the trust. Such withdrawals shall be made only during the calendar year in which such premium payments occur. Such rights of withdrawal may be exercised whether these premiums are paid by Settlor or by others.

    a. Each of Settlor's children's rights of withdrawal shall be limited to the lesser of (a) a fraction of the aggregate value of the premiums paid or (b) the Lapse Amount in each calendar year in which such withdrawal is authorized. The numerator of the fraction shall always be one (1) and the denominator shall be equal to the number of children living on the date of the premium payment.

    b. This right of withdrawal provided for in this paragraph 16.1.2 shall be exercised by a writing delivered to and received by the Trustee by December 31 of the year in which such premiums are paid, provided, however, in the case where an addition is made to the trust after December 1 of a particular year, each beneficiary shall have the right to withdraw his allocated portion of such addition at any time during the thirty (30) day period following such addition.

16.1.3.　Notwithstanding anything to the contrary in this instrument, the total value of the property which a child of the Settlor may withdraw through the exercise of all of the rights of withdrawal given that child in this instrument shall not exceed in any calendar year the Lapse Amount. For purposes of determining the aggregate amount which may be withdrawn in each year, the Trustee shall use the values assigned for federal gift tax purposes to the additions made and premiums paid.

16.1.4.　The rights of withdrawal provided for in this article may be exercised by a legal guardian or the equivalent fiduciary on behalf of the person who lacks legal capacity but the Trustee shall have no duty to seek the appointment of such a fiduciary. The Trustee may, but shall not be under any duty to, give notice of an addition to the trust or the payment of premiums to any person, including those having a right of withdrawal.

16.1.5.　These rights of withdrawal shall not be cumulative from year to year, shall lapse in respect to the current year to the extent not exercised within the time and in the manner specified in paragraphs (a) and (b) respectively, of this Article 16, and must be exercised separately for each period in which the right of withdrawal is exercisable.

16.1.6.　The Trustee may, in the Trustee's discretion, satisfy the exercise of any right of withdrawal by making a distribution in cash or in kind, including insurance policies and fractional interests therein.

16.1.7.　For purposes of this Article 16, the Lapse Amount shall be equal to the greater of $5,000 or 5 percent of the aggregate value of the property out of which the respective rights of withdrawal could be satisfied, determined on the last day of the calendar year in which an addition has been made to the trust. If, at any time during the continuance of the trust, the right to withdraw an amount of property in excess of the Lapse Amount will not constitute a taxable gift for federal gift tax purposes, the Lapse Amount shall be increased to equal the amount which could be so withdrawn.

[¶ 20,739]

5. INCOME TAX CONSIDERATIONS

a. Grantor Trust Rules May Apply

i. In General

The grantor trust rules set out in §§ 671–678 can significantly impact an irrevocable life insurance trust. For example, under § 677(a)(3), trust income *used* to pay premiums on insurance policies on the life of the grantor, without the approval or consent of an adverse party, is taxable to the grantor. The same is true where income of a trust is *used* to insure the grantor's spouse's life. The rules apply regardless of whether the trust instrument requires the income to be so used or simply fails to forbid such use. Moreover it is immaterial who *owns* the policy.

The "grantor" is the person who *actually furnishes* the trust property. Thus, where the insured gave funds to his daughters, who then established a trust whose income was used to pay premiums on policies on the father's life, the income was taxable to the father. Iversen v. Commissioner, 3 T.C. 756 (1944).

The grantor will not be taxed if the trust income is distributed to the beneficiary, who then voluntarily applies the income to purchase insurance on the grantor's life. Booth v. Commissioner, 3 T.C. 605 (1944), acq., 1944 C.B. 3. If, however, this is done under an agreement with the grantor, or by his suggestion, the grantor will be taxed on that portion of the trust income. Rom v. Commissioner, 6 T.C. 614 (1946); Foster v. Commissioner, 8 T.C. 197 (1947), acq., 1947–1 C.B. 2.

[¶ 20,747]

ii. Income Which May Be (But Is Not) Used for Premiums

A second situation is presented where trust income *may* be, but is not, used to pay premiums on insurance procured for the benefit of trust beneficiaries.

If there are existing policies on the life of the grantor or his spouse on which the trustee is authorized to pay the premiums without the approval or consent of any adverse party, the trust income, to the extent that it *could* be so used, is taxable to the grantor. Rieck v. Commissioner, 118 F.2d 110 (3d Cir.1941). However, where there are policies on the life of the grantor not placed in the trust, the trustee must be clearly authorized to pay premiums thereon if trust income is to be taxed to the grantor.

In Weil v. Commissioner, 3 T.C. 579 (1944), acq., 1944 C.B. 9, the grantor had transferred to himself, as trustee for the benefit of his wife, six insurance policies on his life, together with certain securities. The trust required the income from the securities to be applied first to the payment of premiums on these policies and the remainder to be paid to the beneficiary. He owned one other policy which he did not transfer to the trust, but he reserved the right as grantor to add other policies at any time. In addition, he empowered himself, as trustee, to purchase additional policies from trust income. The grantor reported, as taxable income to himself, the amounts expended from trust income for the payment of premiums on the six existing policies held by the trust. A deficiency was assessed against him on the theory that the entire income of the trust could have been used to purchase insurance on his life; hence, he was taxed on all of the trust's income during the year. The court, however, held for the grantor, saying:

> [T]he grantor's liability for tax depends upon the existence in the tax year of policies upon which it would have been physically possible for the trustee to pay premiums. There was in existence during the taxable year no policy (other than the six original policies) that fell in the described category. The grantor, as an individual, owned and paid the premiums on one other policy, but the trust instrument gave the trustee no power to pay such premiums.

The same question has sometimes arisen in connection with funded life insurance trusts under which the trustee is given the power to purchase additional policies on the life of the grantor, but no insurance has been purchased. In this situation, the Commissioner has argued that because the trustee may add other policies upon which the premiums would be paid out of the trust income, the entire income of the trust *may* be applied to the payment of premiums on policies on the grantor's life. Hence, the entire trust income should be taxable to him. The courts, however, have consistently rejected that argument, holding that taxability depends upon the *existence* of policies upon which premiums could have been paid. Commissioner v. Mott, 85 F.2d 315 (6th Cir.1936); Rand v. Commissioner, 40 B.T.A. 233 (1939), acq., 1939–2 C.B. 30, aff'd, 116 F.2d 929 (8th Cir.1941), cert. denied, 313 U.S. 594 (1941).

[¶ 20,755]

iii.   Impact of Crummey Power

Because the *Crummey* withdrawal power transforms a future interest into a present interest, it has become a basic element in forming an irrevocable life insurance trust. See ¶ 20,723.

Consider the case where Heathcliffe has established an irrevocable life insurance trust for a $1,000,000 policy on his life. His son Leander has been given a *Crummey* right of withdrawal which he does not exercise. Leander's right of withdrawal is a § 678(a)(1) power and Leander's failure to exercise the power causes Leander to become a grantor of the trust. See ¶ 18,257 and 19,539.

¶ 20,747

Under § 678(a)(1), a person other than the grantor is deemed to be the owner of any portion of a trust over which such person has the power to vest all or part of the corpus or income in himself or herself. Because the donee has the ability to control a share of the trust by exercising a power of withdrawal, the IRS, in Pvt. Ltr. Rul. 8521060, concluded that § 678(a)(1) makes a donee a co-owner of the trust. The donee therefore would be considered the owner of the portion of the trust that the donee could withdraw by exercising the right of withdrawal.

The conclusion reached in Priv. Ltr. Rul. 8521060 could be questioned. Section 678(b) provides an exception to § 678(a)(1) by providing that a person other than the grantor holding a power over income will not be considered the owner of the trust if the grantor is considered a grantor under the other grantor trust provisions. Although the exception does not expressly include corpus in addition to income, it is questionable whether a person other than the grantor who does not exercise a *Crummey* power over all or part of the trust corpus will be considered an "owner" of the trust if the grantor is also treated as the "owner" under the grantor trust provisions.

[¶ 20,763]

b.   Taxability of Life Insurance Proceeds When Paid to a Trustee

Where the beneficiary of a life insurance policy is a trustee who *distributes* the proceeds to beneficiaries of the trust, the *proceeds* are exempt from income tax both in the hands of the trustee and when distributed. § 101(a). The term "proceeds" means *only* the capital value of the policy upon the insured's death. Thus, where proceeds of life insurance policies *remain* in a trust fund, earnings on the proceeds are taxable in the same manner as any other trust income.

[¶ 20,771]

6.   ESTATE TAX CONSEQUENCES

a.   Transfers Within Three Years of Death

If the insured transfers life insurance to an irrevocable trust and dies within three years of the transfer, the policy proceeds will be included in the estate of the insured. § 2035(a)(2); ¶ 20,601. For that reason, in the case of married persons, consider including a contingent gift to the insured's spouse that will qualify for the marital deduction, a provision operative only if the insured dies within three years of the transfer to the irrevocable trust.

[¶ 20,775]

BROWN v. UNITED STATES

United States Court of Appeals, Ninth Circuit, 2003.
329 F.3d 664.

BERZON, Circuit Judge:

The estate tax combines into one sad transaction the only two certainties in life. Upon death, a decedent's estate must pay a tax on property owned immediately prior to death.* * *

¶ 20,775

... First, we must determine whether the Internal Revenue Service ("IRS") properly increased the estate tax owed by the estate of Willet Brown ("the Estate") under § 2035(c), a provision which increases the estate tax to account for gift taxes paid in the three years immediately prior to death. To answer that question, we must consider whether the IRS was entitled to apply the "step transaction" doctrine, treating gift taxes paid by Betty Brown as if paid by Willet Brown. The district court determined that the IRS properly ascribed the payment of the gift taxes to Willet Brown, as do we.

* * *

Background

Willet Brown ("Willet") died in 1993, leaving behind a sizeable estate, worth approximately $180,000,000. Pursuant to a pre-nuptial agreement between Willett and wife Betty Brown ("Betty"), the entire estate was Willet's separate property, California community property laws notwithstanding.

(A) The Estate Tax Plan

Prior to his death, Willet sought the advice of an estate tax attorney. Together, the two developed a plan ...

As part of this plan Willet [Brown] * * * created an insurance trust to hold life insurance on [his wife] Betty's life, presumably so that the heirs receiving the estate property upon her death could use the life insurance proceeds to pay estate taxes. To fund the life insurance trust Willet gave Betty a gift of $3,100,000. Betty promptly wrote a check from her separate checking account for that amount in favor of the life insurance trust.

Whether the $3,100,000 was paid by Betty or Willet is immaterial to the current appeal. The parties agree that the $3,100,000 payment into the life insurance trust was a taxable event, incurring gift tax liability of $1,415,732. They further agree that Willet and Betty properly elected to be jointly and severally liable for the gift taxes under § 2513(a) & (d). At issue is whether Willet or Betty paid the gift taxes. If the spouse who paid the gift taxes died within three years of doing so, § 2035(c) would require that spouse's estate to pay estate taxes on the $1,415,732 in gift taxes. As Willet died within three years of the payment, it is preferable to the estate that Betty be considered the individual who paid the gift tax.

We here pause to explain why the IRS would require a decedent to pay estate taxes on gift taxes, a concept that, on its face, gives new meaning to the phrase "double taxation." Section 2035(c) is designed to recoup any advantage gained by so-called "death-bed" transfers in which a taxpayer, cognizant of impending mortality, transfers property out of her estate in order to reduce estate tax liability. Although these *inter vivos* transfers incur gift tax liability, opting to transfer assets prior to death still carries a tax advantage. Gift tax is calculated using a tax exclusive method (the applicable rate is applied to the *net* gift, exclusive of gift taxes), whereas estate taxes are calculated on a tax inclusive method (the applicable rate is applied to the *gross* estate, before taxes are deducted). Section 2035(c) presumes that gifts made within three years of death are made with tax-avoidance motives and eliminates the tax advantage for those death bed transactions.

[In a footnote, the court added:

A stylized example of this effect might proceed as follows: Suppose a taxpayer had a taxable estate of $1,400,000. If the taxpayer waits to transfer the money through a post-mortem transfer, the estate tax would be calculated by applying the applicable tax rate (assume 40% for ease of calculation) to the gross amount of the estate ($1,400,000), resulting in an estate tax liability of $560,000 and a net gift to the heirs of $840,000. In contrast, had the taxpayer made an *inter vivos* gift of $1,000,000, the gift tax would be calculated by applying the applicable tax rate to the $1,000,000 gift, resulting in a gift tax liability of $400,000 (40% x $1,000,000) (In most instances gift and estate taxes are imposed at the same rate. §§ 2001(b-c); 2501(a)(1); 2502). Paying gift rather than estate taxes thus puts $160,000 more of the $1,400,000 in total funds in the pockets of the estate beneficiaries. See Jeffrey G. Sherman, Hairsplitting Under Section 2035(d): The Cause and The Cure, 16 Va. Tax Review 111, 121 & n. 49 (1996) (providing similar calculations); Jeffery N. Pennell & Alan Newman, Wealth Transfer Tax Basics, SD85 ALIABA 1, 40 (1999) (same).

The tax code does not care for such manipulable results. If an *inter vivos* gift is made within three years of the decedent's death, Section 2035(c) requires that the taxable estate include the $400,000 in previously untaxed gift taxes. This mandate creates an estate tax liability of $160,000 (40% x $400,000), thereby eliminating the advantage of *inter vivos* gifts. (This example does not take account of the provisions, discussed infra, allowing small annual gifts (§ 2503(b)) or "split-gift" treatment between spouses (§ 2513), nor does it consider a variety of other factors which could alter the details of any particular example.)]

Back to our story: Willet and his attorney realized at the time of the life insurance trust transaction, that in light of § 2035(c), it was a better actuarial bet for Betty, rather than Willet, to pay the gift taxes. True, if Betty paid the gift taxes and then died within three years of doing so, her estate might owe estate taxes on the gift taxes through the operation of § 2035(c). But Betty, age 71, was more likely to outlive the 3-year reach of § 2035(c) than was Willet, age 87. A good plan, but the couple faced a practical problem: Betty had little money of her own and was therefore unable to make the necessary payments from her separate property.

So Willet, on the advice of his estate tax attorney, gave Betty two checks totaling $1,415,732, which she deposited in her own account. The next day she drew two checks from her personal account payable to the IRS for the identical amount, in satisfaction of the gift tax liability. (Because gifts between spouses are tax free, the gifts from Willet to Betty enabling this actuarial wager did not otherwise risk any gift or estate tax liability.) As the Brown estate admits, this money was given to Betty on the "understanding" that Betty would use it to satisfy the gift tax liability. Betty was, however, under no legally enforceable obligation to use the funds in that fashion.

(B) The Estate Tax Return & Litigation

Willet won the actuarial bet he might have preferred to lose. He died in 1993, within three years of the gift tax payment.

In 1995, the Estate prepared an estate tax return indicating zero tax liability. The zero balance reflected: (1) the absence of any tax payment on the above-described gift tax, based on the assumption that Betty made the payment; and (2) a marital trust comprising the remaining estate (after expected administration expenses), which passed to Betty and was therefore eligible for the marital deduction. [§ 2056]

The IRS—predictably—disagreed with the Estate's tax return. The IRS claimed that, in substance if not in form, Willet paid the gift taxes so the $1,415,732 should be included in the Estate. In addition, as those funds did not pass to the marital trust but rather were used to benefit the beneficiaries of the life insurance trust, those funds, maintained the IRS, were not eligible for the marital deduction. The IRS consequently assessed a tax deficiency on the $1,415,732 and interest thereon.

The Estate—predictably—did not accept the IRS analysis. The executor remitted the requested sums but filed for a claim of abatement. After the IRS took no action on the abatement request, the executor filed for a rebate in 1999, raising several claims.

The Estate claims, first, that the gift taxes paid by Betty should not be included in the Estate. On cross-motions for summary judgment the district court denied that contention. Applying the "step transaction" doctrine, the district court determined that the transactions leading up to Betty's satisfaction of the gift tax liability should be treated, for tax purposes, as one integrated transaction. Using that approach, Willet becomes the taxpayer, as the gift tax payment traces back to Willet's gift to Betty of the precise amount of the tax. We agree with the district court that the gift tax payment is properly attributed to Willet.

* * *

ANALYSIS

(A) The Step Transaction

The "step-transaction" doctrine collapses "formally distinct steps in an integrated transaction" in order to assess federal tax liability on the basis of a "realistic view of the entire transaction." * * * As such, the doctrine is part of the "broader tax concept that substance should prevail over form." * * * Under these principles, the IRS argues, the two transactions which resulted in the payment of gift taxes (gift from Willett to Betty, payment by Betty) should be collapsed into one (payment by Willet).

¶ 20,775

The substance-over-form doctrines are, however, bound by, and in some tension with, the principle, equally lauded in tax law, that "anyone may so arrange his affairs that his taxes shall be as low as possible; he is not bound to choose the pattern which will best pay the Treasury." * * * We look to two principles to reconcile these competing concerns.

First, we attempt to distinguish between legitimate "tax avoidance"— actions which, although motivated in part by tax considerations, also have an independent purpose or effect—and illegitimate "tax evasion"—actions which have no, or minimal, purpose or effect beyond tax liabilities.

Second, we scrutinize whether the facts presented "fall within the intended scope of the Internal Revenue provision at issue." *Stewart,* 714 F.2d at 988. This second step is crucial in areas, such as estate planning, in which it is common for Congress to create, and taxpayers to exploit, various tax planning incentives. For example § 2513 allowed Willet and Betty by exercising certain elections, to treat the underlying $3,100,000 gift from Willet to the life insurance trust as if made by both of them, when in reality Willet supplied the entirety of the funds. The IRS has never argued that the substance-over-form doctrine invalidated that election, for obvious reasons: That approach would deny taxpayers the tax benefits intentionally created by the plain language of the Code. [The court added in a footnote:

Section 2513 was enacted to equalize the ability of couples to utilize the gift tax deductions of both spouses whether the couple lived in a community property state or not. Doerr v. United States, 819 F.2d 162, 166 (7th Cir.1987). The equalization effect applies only to gift tax, not to estate tax calculations.]

* * *

1. Betty As A Mere Conduit of Funds

Navigating the murky distinction between "tax avoidance" and "tax evasion" requires careful stewardship. In the context of the step transaction doctrine, however, we have identified a class of cases in which the form of the transaction is particularly suspect. Where a party acts as a "mere conduit" of funds—a fleeting stop in a predetermined voyage toward a particular result— we have readily ignored the role of the intermediary in order appropriately to characterize the transaction. * * *

Viewing the historical facts in the light most favorable to the Estate, it is nonetheless clear that Betty was a "mere conduit" of Willet's funds. The Browns do not advance any argument that the payment to Betty had any purpose or effect other than as a step towards facilitating Willet's payment of the gift tax liability and Betty owned Willet's funds for exactly one day. * * *

True, Betty was under no binding commitment to complete the prearranged plan. "Despite intimations to the contrary in the early cases," however, "there is ample authority for linking several prearranged or contemplated steps, even in the absence of a contractual obligation or financial compulsion to follow through." Boris I. Bittker, Fed. Inc. Tax'n of Indiv. § 1.03[5] (2d. ed.). See, e.g., Kornfeld v. Commissioner, 137 F.3d 1231, 1235–1236 (10th

Cir.1998); * * * Where the two parties to the transaction were sufficiently related or commonly controlled, we have twice applied the step transaction analysis without any finding that the intermediary was legally bound to complete the prearranged plan. * * *

Particularly apt is the Tenth Circuit's analysis in *Kornfeld*, applying the step transaction doctrine where, as here, family members colluded to accomplish a prearranged plan. In *Kornfeld*, the taxpayer, an experienced tax attorney, gave cash payments to his daughters and secretary. 137 F.3d at 1232–33.

The gift recipients then immediately used those funds to purchase remainder interests in bonds. Id. The Tenth Circuit determined that the series of transactions should be treated as if the taxpayer had purchased the bonds in fee simple and given the remainder interests to his daughters and secretary (a determination which had negative tax consequences for the taxpayer). *Id.* In so determining, the Tenth Circuit applied a heightened level of skepticism to transactions between related parties. Id. at 1235. In addition, the court was swayed by the facts that the "taxpayer [had] stipulated that his intention in making gifts was to enable the donees to make the purchases," and that the donees would be unlikely to flout the taxpayer's intention. Id. at 1236. As the court noted, "one does not look a gift horse in the mouth." Id.

The same factors which applied in Kornfeld apply here: The parties are related, so heightened scrutiny is appropriate. Willet's admitted intention in giving the funds to Betty was to enable her to make the gift tax payments. Finally, Betty was unlikely to flout the desires of her husband because it was she, as the initial beneficiary of the Estate, who stood to gain if the gift tax wager was successful. The two transactions culminating in gift tax payments should therefore be treated as one integrated whole despite the lack of a legally binding commitment.

2. The End Run Around § 2035

Our conclusion is reinforced by a consideration of the statute here at issue, § 2035(c). We begin, in considering that statute, with the Eighth Circuit's analysis of a quite similar situation in Estate of Sachs v. Commissioner, 856 F.2d 1158 (8th Cir.1988). In *Sachs*, Samuel Sachs gave stock in trust to his grandchildren within three years of his death. Id. at 1159. The gift was structured as a "net gift," meaning that the donees were legally bound to pay the gift taxes otherwise chargeable to the donor. Id. Relying in part on the plain language of § 2035, and in part on the substance- over-form doctrine, the Eighth Circuit held that "the gift tax paid under this arrangement is a 'tax paid * * * by the decedent or his estate' under § 2035." Id. at 1164.

The instant case differs from *Sachs*, however, in that Betty was jointly liable under § 2513(d) to pay the gift tax liability. In comparison, no matter how the beneficiaries in *Sachs* received funds to pay the gift taxes, the gift tax payment was attributable to the donor, if for no other reason than because only the donor was liable for the debt owed to the IRS. Id. at 1163–64.

The question then is whether the Willet-Betty-IRS transaction, though on its face an end-run around § 2035(c), is nonetheless authorized by § 2513.

Had Betty truly paid the gift tax from her own funds, § 2035 would not apply to Betty's payments of the gift tax, because of § 2513. [FN11] *Id.* at 1165. The Estate argues that because § 2513 authorizes the very "actuarial bet" the couple made, the source of Betty's funds is irrelevant. [The court added, in a footnote: Section 2513 applies only for purposes of the gift tax, not for the estate tax. Estate of Flandreau v. Commissioner, 994 F.2d 91, 93 n. 1 (2d Cir.1993). As discussed in the text, therefore, the § 2035(c) liability is not altered by the split-gift election when the decedent in fact pays the gift taxes.]

The source of the funds *is* pertinent. *Sachs,* 856 F.2d at 1165 (because the gift tax was paid with funds from decedent's estate, fact that gift was split between decedent and his wife under § 2513 did not alter application of § 2035(c)). The language and the history of § 2035(c) emphasize that this section applies to actual gift tax payments, regardless of the relative gift tax liability among spouses.

First, § 2035(c) requires that the decedent include in his estate gift taxes *"paid * * *"* on any gift made by the decedent *or his spouse."* (Emphasis added). Second, the legislative history states:

> The amount of the gift tax subject to this rule would include tax paid by the decedent or his estate on any gift made by the donor * * * It would not, however, include any gift tax paid by the spouse on a gift made by the decedent within three years of death which is treated as made one-half by the spouse [*e.g.,* under § 2513], *since the spouse's payment of such tax would not reduce the decedent's estate at the time of death.*

H. Rep. No. 94–1380, 14, 94th Cong., 2d. Sess. (1976) (emphasis added).

The reason the source of funds matters is that § 2035(c) was designed to reverse the effect of funds transferred out of an estate within three years of death. If Willet pays the gift tax, it is his net worth that is reduced and therefore his estate that will escape estate tax liability on the funds if he outlives the three-year reach of § 2035(c)(1993). Accordingly, it is his estate that must reverse the effect of the transfer if he dies within the three-year period. Only if Betty pays the gift tax by using her own financial resources is her estate reduced, such that her estate should bear the risk that the payment be included in her estate via § 2035(c).

By channeling Willet's funds through Betty's estate, the Browns created a transaction sequence in which the tax risk diverged from the economics of the payment. Where one spouse has significantly fewer assets than the other spouse, shifting the risk of § 2035-inclusion onto the estate of the less wealthy spouse, while actually transferring the assets out of the estate of the more wealthy spouse, could have tax evasion advantages for the couple beyond the effect of divergent mortality probabilities: The smaller estate may be subject to lower tax rates, *see* § 2001(c), or to no tax at all, *see* § 2010, so that the inclusion risk does not adequately reverse the effect of the reduction in the larger estate. We do not know whether this was the case in the Brown estate. We note the effect, however, to demonstrate that requiring, as the text and legislative history plainly do, that the § 2035 inclusion risk follow the economics of the gift tax payment is not a pointless formality. Thus, the fact that the "actuarial bet" the Browns attempted may have been proper under § 2035 and § 2513 had Betty actually paid the gift taxes does not imply that the Browns' maneuvering here was similarly appropriate.

In Magneson v. Commissioner, 753 F.2d 1490, 1497 (9th Cir.1985), we distinguished between a taxpayer's right to choose "[b]etween two equally direct ways of achieving the same result" the method "which entailed the most tax advantages" and the inability to "secure by a series of contrived steps, different tax treatment than if he had carried out the transaction directly." That distinction is illuminating: Had Betty and Willet both had adequate funds with which to pay the gift tax, they would be entitled to choose the most advantageous method from among two equally direct ways of paying the tax (*check from Willet to IRS v. check from Betty to IRS*). Here however, Willet actually supplied the funds, and Betty's involvement was merely a "contrived step" to secure tax treatment different from that which would have resulted if Willet had paid the IRS directly. The contrived step did not alter the economic reality that Willet paid the tax, and Betty's transient ownership over the funds for one day had no independent purpose or effect beyond the attempt to alter tax liabilities.

3. Impact of Lack of Certainty of Tax Benefit

In a variant of its assertion that the actuarial bet was entirely proper, the Estate, noting that the end result of the machinations did not create a *certain* tax advantage, contends that the transaction sequence is therefore immune from the step transaction doctrine. That the tax advantages flowing from Willet's plan were uncertain does not, as the Estate contends, distinguish this case from other instances in which the step transaction or substance over form doctrine has been applied.

* * * [A] certain tax advantage is not a prerequisite to application of the step transaction doctrine.

Tax consequences aside, the nature of the Browns' transaction sequence (ultimately, a transfer of funds from Willet to the IRS) was fixed the moment Betty wrote out the check to the IRS. Focusing only on Betty's role within that predetermined result, it is clear that her participation had no significance beyond the attempt to alter tax liabilities. Unlike a situation in which Betty paid the gift taxes by reducing her own net worth, a decision with independent economic effect on Betty's estate, Betty's role as a conduit altered the economics of the transaction *only* by shifting the risk of § 2035 inclusion from Willet's estate to Betty's estate. Where, as here, that risk shift did not reflect the reality of the underlying transaction sequence, application of the step transaction is appropriate.

The final component of the Estate's uncertainty argument relates to its complaint that the step transaction doctrine can be, and often is, applied asymmetrically: Had Betty died within three years of the gift tax payments, it is quite unlikely that the IRS would adamantly advocate in favor of treating the funds as if paid by Willet, so as to relieve Betty of the estate tax liability. The IRS's lawyer so indicated at oral argument.

The possibility of a one-way rachet does give us pause. We are not alone: Both courts and commentators have struggled with whether the substance over form principle is a one or two-way street, and whether, even if a two-way street, it nonetheless "run[s] downhill for the Commissioner and uphill for the taxpayer." Bittker & McMahon, Fed. Inc. Tax'n of Indiv., § 1.03 (quoting Rogers' Estate v. CIR, 70,192 P-H Memo. TC (1970), aff'd 445 F.2d 1020 (2d Cir.1971)) but see *Clark*, 489 U.S. at 737 (invoking the doctrine in favor of the taxpayer). See generally, William S. Blatt, Lost On A One-Way Street: The Taxpayers's Ability to Disavow Form, 70 Or. L.Rev 381 (1991).

Had Betty indeed died first, we would be faced with the difficult question of whether symmetry required application of the step transaction doctrine, or whether the taxpayer, having complete control over the form of the transaction, must bear the consequences of the chosen form without recourse to the step transaction doctrine. Whether the doctrine must be applied symmetrically is not, however, the issue now before us, and we do not reach it.

4. Effect on Estate Planning

The Estate also maintains, somewhat grandiosely, that our holding vitiates the entire estate tax planning profession. For example, notes the Estate, a typical estate planning tool, employed by many parents, involves annual gifts of approximately $10,000 per parent in order to take advantage of the annual gift exclusion of § 2503(b). Because those transactions are also motivated by a desire to avoid estate taxes, the Estate suggests, applying the substance-over-form doctrine to the instant case would require that we apply the substance-over-form doctrine to such annual gift giving and treat the gifts as if they were instead taxable estate transfers.

Rather than supporting the result the Estate favors, the *inter vivos* gift example usefully illustrates the boundaries of the substance-over-form doctrine. When parents elect to make an *inter vivos* gift to their children rather than bequeathing those assets, that decision does have effects independent of the tax consequences: The children receive the funds earlier, and the parent loses control over the assets. In comparison, Betty's ownership over the funds from Willet was transitory. She was simply a conduit, and her role in the transaction was a temporary artifice rather than an event with independent economic significance.

The *inter vivos* gift example differs from the present situation for a second reason as well. The plain language of § 2503(b) reveals that Congress intended to allow, and perhaps to encourage, small annual gifts free of tax, when it enacted § 2503(b). Otherwise, there would not be an annual dollar exclusion from the gift tax. In stark contrast, § 2035(c) discourages manipulation of the tax code by large *inter vivos* transfers, by reversing the tax benefits of those transfers. It can hardly be argued that the purpose of § 2035 is advanced by Willet's maneuvering to create the appearance that Betty paid the gift tax when in all practical effect, Willet did so.

[¶ 20,777]

b. Retained Life Estate

Consider the case where the premiums necessary to keep the policy in force are paid by Wilhelmina, the trust beneficiary. The sole asset of the trust is a $250,000 life insurance policy on the life of Harry, Wilhelmina's husband. The trust itself is irrevocable, having been created by Harry. Could it be claimed that Wilhelmina has, by making the premium payments, made a transfer subject to a retained life estate with the effect being that the trust is includible in Wilhelmina's estate for federal estate tax purposes? Two cases, Estate of Goodnow v. United States, 302 F.2d 516, 62–1 USTC ¶ 12,077 (Ct.Cl.1962), and Estate of Pyle v. Commissioner, 63–1 USTC ¶ 12,132, 313 F.2d 328 (3d Cir.1963), are sometimes cited as bearing on this issue but neither of them are really on point. In *Goodnow*, while the beneficiary paid the premiums, the trust was at all times revocable by the insured and the insured retained ownership of the policy itself. Thus, as a practical matter, the beneficiary was making gifts to the insured by the payment of the policy premiums because the beneficiary had no enforceable retained interest in the policy kept in force by the premiums she paid. The Court of Claims agreed with the trust beneficiary and none of the trust was included in her estate. In *Pyle*, on the other hand, Ida Pyle was the owner of a policy of insurance on the life of husband, Wallace. During her life, Ida arranged with the insurance company for the company to retain the proceeds of insurance on Wallace's life at his death and pay her interest on the policy proceeds for life, with remainder to Ida's children. Here, clearly, Ida was the transferor and had retained a life estate in the transferred property—and it is surprising that Ida argued to the contrary. The policy proceeds were properly in Ida's estate for estate tax purposes.

[¶ 20,779]

7. THE GENERATION-SKIPPING TAX

Irrevocable life insurance trusts enjoy no special exemption from the generation-skipping tax. As a result, whenever a policy is transferred to an irrevocable life insurance trust, whenever property is placed in trust to be used for premium payments, and whenever premiums are paid directly to the insurance company, the generation-skipping tax consequences must be evaluated. Generally speaking, in the typical situation, none of these transfers are excluded from the reach of the generation-skipping tax. Moreover, absent special provisions, none of these transfers will qualify for the per donee per annum generation-skipping tax exclusion ($12,000 in 2006). Equally important are special provisions present in the trust that allow each of these transfers to qualify for the $12,000 per donee per annum gift tax exclusion. See §§ 2503(b), 2642(c)(2); ¶¶ 20,723, 23,201.

The issue to be resolved when transferring property to the irrevocable life insurance trust is whether the donor should allocate a part of his or her generation-skipping tax exemption ($2 million in 2006) to shelter the transfers to the life insurance trust. See § 2631; ¶ 23,101. Practically speaking, if the policy is one that will remain in effect until the death of the insured, allocation of a part of the generation-skipping tax exemption is an efficient use of the exemption. But the portion of the exemption allocated to transfers of life insurance or premium payments will be lost to the extent that the policy is discontinued before death (except to the extent of any surrender value that continues in trust after the surrender of the policy).

[¶ 20,787]

8. USE OF INSURANCE PROCEEDS TO PAY DEATH COSTS

Taxpayers who consider using irrevocable life insurance trusts often have conflicting objectives. On the one hand, these taxpayers want to exclude the proceeds of the insurance from their estates for estate and inheritance tax purposes. On the other hand, they want the proceeds to be available for the purposes for which the insurance is uniquely suited. Life insurance is often purchased in the early years of life as a means of providing for loved ones in the event of the insured's untimely death. In later years, the insurance is often maintained in force to provide liquidity to the insured's estate to meet the costs associated with the insured's death, such as estate and inheritance taxes.

Generally speaking, the taxpayer who causes his or her life insurance to be placed in an irrevocable trust is able to free the insurance proceeds from estate and inheritance taxes. The taxpayer can also realize his or her objective of providing for loved ones because these persons can be beneficiaries of the irrevocable life insurance trust.

The problem remaining is how to make the proceeds of the insurance available to meet the liquidity needs associated with the death of the taxpayer without causing the insurance proceeds to be included in the gross estate of the insured taxpayer pursuant to § 2042.

[¶ 20,795]

a. Purchase of Assets

Oftentimes liquidity problems can be solved by allowing the trustee of the irrevocable trust to purchase liquid assets from the insured taxpayer's estate after death. In that way, the proceeds are made available to the estate for its needs, but property that is not easily liquidated or that the survivors do not wish to liquidate is retained for the benefit of the survivors.

[¶ 20,803]

b. Loans to the Insured's Estate

An alternative to direct sales in solving the liquidity problem is to authorize the trustee of the irrevocable life insurance trust to make loans to the insured's estate.

[¶ 20,811]

c. Discretionary Distributions

The trustee of the irrevocable life insurance trust can be authorized to make distributions to the insured's gross estate if the trustee believes such distributions are, for example, "in the best interests of the insured's family."

¶ 20,811

Using this approach means that the insured's estate would be seen as simply another beneficiary of the trust to whom distributions are permitted. If this alternative is to avoid causing unwanted tax consequences, the draftsman must take special care to provide that the trustee is free from any obligation to make the distributions to the insured's estate.

While unlikely, there is always risk that such distributions could be claimed to be disguised asset purchases, resulting in gain or loss to the estate. Jeffrey N. Pennel in Life Insurance Owned by a Third Party: Estate Planning Considering Income, Gift and Generation–Skipping Taxes, 18 Houston L. Rev. 103, 131–132 (1980).

Problem

[¶ 20,840]

Is the following trust provision a workable device for inclusion in an irrevocable life insurance trust to get the trust to pay the insured's death costs? Would your conclusion change if the Trustee were a beneficiary of the decedent's estate? The Trust?

> *Payment of taxes and other expenses.* The Trustee, in the Trustee's sole discretion, may pay from the trust estate all or any portion of any legacy, succession, inheritance, transfer, estate and other death tax or duty or any one or more of them, levied or assessed against the estate of the Settlor or the Settlor's spouse (including any and all interest and penalties thereon). In addition, to the extent that the Trustee, in the Trustee's sole discretion, deems it advisable for the best interests of Settlor's family as a whole, the Trustee may pay all or a portion of the following expenses arising out of the death of the Settlor and the Settlor's spouse: funeral expenses, claims allowed against each such estate, and expenses of administering each such estate. However, the Trustee has no legal obligation to make any of the payments described in this paragraph. Payments permitted by this paragraph for the benefit of the respective estates of the Settlor and the Settlor's spouse may be made to the estate of each of them or directly to those to whom his or her estate is indebted and the Trustee may rely exclusively upon the written representations of his or her executor regarding the amounts due and the identity of those persons entitled to such payments. None of the payments made pursuant to this paragraph shall be charged against or apportioned to any beneficiary of the trust estate.

[¶ 20,843]

9. SELECTION OF TRUSTEE

Trustee selection is always important, no less so where the trust is irrevocable. Where the trust includes life insurance, consider Reg. § 20.2042-1(b)(4), which provides that an insured has a taxable incident of ownership in a life insurance policy if the insured, "as trustee or otherwise," can change the "time or manner of enjoyment" of the policy proceeds even though the insured does not have a beneficial interest in the trust. See Rev. Rul. 84–179, 1984–2 C.B. 195, discussed at ¶ 20,507.

Fee arrangements are also important. The burdens and liabilities associated with serving as Trustee are not insignificant, and it is unrealistic to expect (or hope) that these services can be (or should be) provided without charge for an extended period (despite, perhaps, an initial expression of willingness to do so by the proposed trustee). The burdens are such that (even during the lifetime of the insured) use of a professional fiduciary (or at least the regular monitoring of the trust administration by an attorney) should be a requirement.

[¶ 20,851]

10. COMMUNITY PROPERTY

Where community property insurance is involved, it is particularly difficult to prevent the noninsured spouse's one-half interest from being included in his or her gross estate as a retained life estate under § 2036(a) where it was transferred along with the insured spouse's interest in the insurance to a trust of which he or she is a life income beneficiary. In order to do so, the policy must be purged of its community character so as to prevent the surviving spouse as beneficiary of the trust from being treated as having made a transfer of 50 percent of the policy and retaining the right to the income from that 50 percent.

Several techniques have been employed in order to accomplish this purging. One of the most common is to have the noninsured spouse give his or her interest in the policy to the insured spouse as the insured spouse's separate property, wait a "decent" interval, and then have the insured spouse establish the irrevocable trust for the benefit of the noninsured spouse and fund it with the policy. The reason for allowing a "decent" interval to elapse between the gift to the insured spouse and the transfer to the trust is to avoid any appearance that the gift from the noninsured spouse followed by the transfer into the trust for the benefit of the noninsured spouse is part of one transaction. Is there doubt in your mind?

The other scheme is a variation on the first. This alternative calls for the noninsured spouse to "sell" his or her interest in the policy to the insured spouse. Thereafter, the insured spouse will be "moved"—in the exercise of his independent judgment—to transfer the policy to the irrevocable trust for the benefit of the noninsured spouse!

How the court's will look at transactions like the foregoing remains to be seen. In the meantime consider the approaches described in the following Problems and suggest whether you believe these approaches will be more successful.

Problem

[¶ 20,860]

Consider the case of Sherwin and his spouse, Jane, who owned as their community property a $300,000 policy of insurance on Sherwin's life.

¶ 20,860

(a) Sherwin proposes to create an irrevocable trust and assign the $300,000 policy to the trustee. Accumulation National Bank has agreed to serve as Trustee. Jane is to be the beneficiary of the trust for life. Distributions from the trust are to be made only when the "Trustee believes, in the exercise of his sole discretion, that such distributions would be in the best interests of Jane." Will any part of the trust property be included in Jane's gross estate (assuming she survives Sherwin and the Trustee makes occasional distributions to her to help her with her country club dues and her monthly payments on her new 12-cylinder Belchfire). See ¶ 10,117.

(b) Sherwin is committed to having the proceeds of the $300,000 life insurance policy escape taxation at the death of both him and Jane. If the foregoing proposal will not accomplish Sherwin's objective, Sherwin's lawyer, U. B. Crafty, proposes that Sherwin create the irrevocable trust for the insurance policy but provide in the trust that the trust is revocable as to the portion of the policy which is Jane's community property. The trust is to stipulate that Jane is to receive all of the income from the trust and, at her death, the trust is to terminate and the undistributed trust property is to be distributed to Sherwin's then living lineal descendants *per stirpes*. When Sherwin dies, Jane will be deemed to have made a taxable gift to the remaindermen, but the value of the gift will be reduced because it will be offset by the value of the "consideration received by Jane"! Sherwin reports that Mr. Crafty explained that the life estate Sherwin gives Jane in Sherwin's 50 percent of the policy will be consideration for Jane's gift to the remaindermen. See John R. Price, The Uses and Abuses of Irrevocable Life Insurance Trusts, 14 U. Miami Est. Plan. Inst. ¶ 1100, 1111.1–1111.3 (1980). At this point, Sherwin lapsed into incoherence, alternatively extolling the ingenuity of lawyers and babbling about the complexity of the tax laws. For additional discussion of the "consideration offset" concept, see ¶ 11,901.

¶ 20,860

Chapter 21

DISCOUNTS, CREDITORS
AND BENEFICIARIES

A. OBJECTIVES

[¶ 21,001]

This is the "hot topics" chapter, i.e., selected somewhat currently controversial material. Fundamentally, though, it is about protecting the beneficiary
from the predators of the world (albeit that sometimes the biggest predator of
them all is the beneficiary himself or herself.) In using these materials, this
chapter could well be the alpha and omega, everything else only supplemental.

FLPs. Included here are materials on "family limited partnerships"
(FLPs), the much talked about, the much litigated, and the *much used* device
to shift wealth to beneficiaries *at a discount* and *before the donor is ready to
part with control*, all with the goal of reducing estate taxes at the later death
of the donor. Sometimes referred to as "value freezing", the FLP can be
applied to both business and nonbusiness interests (and, in that sense, the
FLP complements the strategies described in Chapter 12, inter alia, GRATs
and QPRTs).

Asset protection and spendthrift issues. Included here, too, are materials
on creditor protection, commonly referred to as asset protection. The ancient
and well accepted rule that a debtor could not "beat creditors by laundering
money or other property through a trust" has given way to changing state
laws that alter this notion so as to render each such state an attractive
destination for the property of those fearing creditor claims. Conventional
wisdom traditionally had it that only by "parking" property offshore could
that property be insulated from creditor claims. The drawback, of course, to
such solutions was the absence of United States law, i.e., in the vernacular,
the owner of such funds could not always be sure that his or her government
would send in the Marines to rescue the property in the event of political
instability or a change of law. The states that have changed their rules to
provide creditor protection expect to welcome a surge of property flowing to
those jurisdictions. While many issues will be making their way through the
courts as the years go forward, remaining is the federal bankruptcy law and
its effects as well as issues of full, faith and credit.

Discretionary pay, dynastic impulses, and dead hand control. While one
could debate the social good or ill of allowing property to be warehoused in

trusts that seemingly "last forever"—a distinct possibility with abandonment or modification of the rule against perpetuities by an increasing number of states—the practical question is how to effectively and meaningfully provide for the beneficiaries of these "dynasty trusts"—all trusts, for that matter, for the issues are oftentimes the same. While fun to speak of "dead hand control", the worry is that litigation will be the result if the trust beneficiaries do not find the trust responsive to their circumstances. Donors think of protecting beneficiaries from themselves—the "biggest predator of them all"—or possibly "incentivizing" beneficiary behavior; beneficiaries, however, more often than not, simply want the money.

From a technical perspective, distribution and accumulation of funds earned by a trust will have both transfer and income tax implications for the trust and its beneficiaries. Chapter 18 considered some of the transfer tax implications associated with distributions, particularly the effect of giving a surviving spouse or other beneficiary the right to demand distributions or, as trustee, to make them on his or her own behalf. This chapter will focus on the income tax effects of distributions and accumulations made by a trustee and will consider methods by which income taxes resulting from those actions can be best managed.

Note, though, that the materials in this chapter relate to trusts where income distributions are purely discretionary with the trustee or where an ascertainable standard governs the trustee's exercise of discretion. See ¶ 18,175–18,183. By way of contrast, these materials do not relate to cases where income is required to be distributed to the trust beneficiaries. See ¶ 18,167. In the latter case, income distribution planning is largely impossible inasmuch as all of the trust income is required to be distributed. Moreover, as noted in ¶ 18,207 and 21,409, if trust property which has appreciated is distributed in kind to a beneficiary in satisfaction of the beneficiary's right to have the trust income distributed to him or her, the trust is considered to have realized taxable income to the extent of the property's appreciation. See Reg. § 1.661(a)–2(f)(3); Rev. Rul. 67–74, 1967–1 C.B. 194.

Clearly making distributions of income discretionary with the trustee makes tax and nontax sensitive distribution planning a possibility. However, there are a number of special rules that apply whenever the trustee has discretion to accumulate or distribute the trust's income—and some of these rules will be explored in this chapter.

There is one cautionary note. Because giving a trustee who is also a beneficiary of the trust too much discretion over distributions to himself or herself can result in having the trust property included in the estate of the beneficiary/trustee for federal estate tax purposes (thus defeating another of the typical trust's major purposes), the trust beneficiary should not be trustee when distribution planning is a major goal. See § 2041(a)(2); ¶ 18,159–18,223.

While reviewing the related materials in this chapter, consider these questions:

1. Are there sufficient (any?) benefits to be derived from accumulating income within a trust so as to offset the burdens associated with such accumulations?

¶ 21,001

2. Can multiple trusts be used profitably as income tax shelters?

3. What can be done, non-tax-planning-wise, to anticipate and diffuse family discord, litigation, "hurt feelings", as well as keep fiduciaries out of the court house in the course of administering the plan?

Skipping the beneficiary's estate for estate tax purposes is one advantage of accumulating trust income. This is a viable strategy where the beneficiary is not in need of the trust income. It means that the accumulated income can escape estate tax at the death of the beneficiary in those cases where the trust is to continue for the benefit of others after the death of the first beneficiary—so long as the current beneficiary does not have a general power of appointment over the trust property. See § 2041; ¶ 18,067.

Rate compression and accumulation trusts. Also, warehousing income in small trusts will result in an income tax advantage possibly totaling $956 in 2006, for example, as a result of a "run up the income tax brackets" to 35 percent. See § 1(e); ¶ 21,051. However, few beneficiaries will be in the top income tax bracket of 35 percent, meaning that it will be the rare case where the income tax imposed at the trust level will be less than that which would be imposed on the trust income if trust income is distributed to the beneficiary in the year in which it is earned.

Nonetheless—and despite the obvious income tax disadvantage to warehousing income in the trust—having accumulated trust income escape estate tax at the beneficiary's death (where the beneficiary does not have a general power of appointment) can be a strong argument for accumulating income in the trust. This is particularly true where the trust is sheltered from the generation-skipping tax. (Discussion of the GST tax appears in Chapters 9 and 23.)

Families, transparency and fiduciary liability. Not to be overlooked is the heightened scrutiny given fiduciary responsibility where "downstream" beneficiaries worry that the playing field is not level, that "Dad always favored" my siblings "and the trustee continues in the same vein." How is it that the draftsperson "protects" the fiduciary—so as to minimize the expensive and corrosive effects of litigation—where one of more beneficiaries has experienced years' of hurt during the lifetime of the settlor.

Trust drafting and what it means to be a fiduciary is at the heart of all this.

B. INCOME IN RESPECT OF A DECEDENT

[¶ 21,101]

The presence of uncollected income in respect of a decedent (IRD)—a term statutorily defined in § 691(a)—may well give the client an illusion that his or her estate has a greater value than will ultimately be realized, with obvious implications in the planning process. The best illustration of IRD is undistributed property held in a tax qualified retirement plan at death. Consider Dad. Prior to his death, he designated his child, SugarPlum, as

¶ 21,101

728 DISCOUNTS, CREDITORS AND BENEFICIARIES Ch. 21

beneficiary of any undistributed property remaining in his tax qualified retirement plan at his death. (The plan was tax qualified in the sense that, like most such plans, contributions of property to the plan—perhaps by Dad's employer—were tax deductible by the employer at the time of contribution with the proviso that as distributions are made to Dad—normally in retirement—those distributions would be fully taxable to Dad at ordinary income tax rates (in 2006, as much as 35 percent, rather than tax preferred capital gain rates which could be as low as 5 percent although 15 percent would be the rate most commonly mentioned as the "capital gains rate"). See Chapters 29 and 30.) At Dad's death, any undistributed property—in this case, assume $2 million—remaining in his account will be included in his estate for estate tax purposes, and subject to a tax rate as high as 46 percent in 2006. Furthermore, when the benefits are distributed to Sugar Plum, those benefits are subject to income taxation at ordinary income tax rates (again, in 2006, as much as 35 percent). While Sugar Plum may be heard to complain of "double taxation", her only relief is the commonly referred to "§ 691(c) deduction" for IRD. Section 691(c) allows the recipient of IRD to claim an income tax deduction for estate taxes paid on items of IRD when received. (Noteworthy is the prospect that estate tax will be paid at Dad's death but income tax will be deferred until actual receipt by Sugar Plan of the plan benefits. In certain cases, sometimes because of planning, distribution—and income taxation and the § 691(c) deduction—might well be spread over Sugar Plum's lifetime.)

Practically speaking, it means that while Sugar Plum may look upon the $2 million as a "princely sum", reality is that the value of the $2 million to Sugar Plum is substantially less, having been reduced possibly by a 45 percent estate tax and a 35 percent income tax. See ¶ 30,001.

Planning for IRD must be done "upstream", i.e., at the donor level rather than the donee level. All the Sugar Plum can do is make certain to take full advantage of the § 691(c) deduction for estate taxes paid, not an insignificant task because of the sometimes complexity of the computation and the fact that as each distribution is made to Sugar Plum—perhaps over her lifetime— she must remember to do the § 691(c) calculation.

Upstream planning, i.e., planning at the donor level, is indeed a complicated undertaking with few sure benefits. See Chapter 30.

Problem

[¶ 21,120]

Butch, now a partner at his law firm *and in the top income tax bracket*, sometimes muses about the his mom's decision to have Butch receive over his life expectancy—using the required IRS minimum distribution rules (RMD)— the undistributed retirement plan benefits remaining at her death. Could he have saved taxes, he muses, if his mother had named a trust as the beneficiary of the retirement plan benefits and designated him the trust beneficiary? For example, the estate tax applicable exclusion amount was $2 million (as it is in 2006) at his mother's death. Suppose, he muses, that his mother gave him "everything" free of trust except for the $2 million retirement plan benefits which she placed into an irrevocable dynasty trust for him and his lineal descendants, a trust to last for the maximum perpetuities period. "Think of it, generation after generation enjoying the plan benefits as trust beneficiaries", he says, without having to pay estate tax on that property so long as it remained in the trust. What's the flaw? ¶ 30,135.

C.   Family Limited Partnerships (FLPs)

[¶ 21,201]

1.   IN GENERAL

The family limited partnership (FLP) is a tool designed (more after than not) specifically to reduce federal estate taxes. Its effectiveness comes because principal family assets are held by the partnership rather than by individual family members. For a good discussion of the issues raised by family limited partnerships, see Kenneth P. Brier & Joseph B. Darby, III, Family Limited Partnerships: Decanting Family Investment Assets Into New Bottles, 49 Tax Lawyer 127 (1995).

[¶ 21,203]

2.   STRUCTURE OF THE FAMILY LIMITED PARTNERSHIP

The typical FLP is created in the following manner: Sam and Mary Smith contribute assets worth $999,000 to an FLP in return for limited partnership interests. Sam also contributes $1,000 to the FLP in return for a general partnership interest. (A person may be both a general and a limited partner in jurisdictions which have adopted the Uniform Limited Partnership Act. See Uniform Limited Partnership Act § 404, 6 Unif. Laws Ann. (Supp. 1994).) Sam and Mary give each of their two children, Don and Betty, a gift of limited partnership interests worth $22,000. The FLP must provide that compensation for personal services is separate and distinct from compensation for capital invested, as § 704(e) prohibits assignment of a capital partner's personal service income to partners who are not capital partners. The FLP's design separates Sam's compensation for services rendered to the FLP and by the FLP from his return on capital invested in the FLP. The partnership agreement will restrict transferability of ownership of both limited and general partnership interests, requiring consent of some percentage of the other interests, except in the case of estate planning transfers to relatives or transfers on death.

As a general partner, Sam is entitled to receive reasonable compensation for his services to the FLP. He may be removed and replaced as general partner by the limited partners (Mary, Don and Betty), as provided in the partnership agreement. He has management control of the FLP, but also has unlimited liability for the operating debts of the FLP, including claims against the partnership. Sam's management control, however, may be limited somewhat in the partnership agreement (e.g., the agreement may prevent Sam from selling all partnership assets without the consent of some percentage of the limited partners' interest).

As limited partners, Mary, Don, Betty, and Sam (to the extent of his limited partnership interest), have limited liability and are therefore shielded from liability for the operating debts of the FLP. Their limited partnership interests may be protected from some actions by judgment creditors. See Uniform Limited Partnership Act § 703, Unif. Laws Ann. (Supp. 1994). Mary, Don, and Betty are not responsible for management of the FLP and its investments.

[¶ 21,207]

3. VALUATION OF FAMILY LIMITED PARTNERSHIP INTERESTS

a. In General: Disappearing Value

The ownership of all the family's principal assets by the partnership and the restrictions on transferability of partnership interests will reduce the fair market value of limited partnership interests in the FLP offered to the general public. This is because few investors will be willing to buy into another family's FLP, since the investor will not be able to sell his or her interest without the consent of the other partners. Therefore, the fair market value of Sam's interest, in the example above, might be discounted from a value of approximately $500,000 to a value of $250,000 if it can be shown that investors would pay only 50 cents on the dollar for Sam's interest. This means that Sam's estate will be worth much less, since transfers must be valued at fair market value, and the fair market value of Sam's interest is now worth half of the amount at which his capital contribution was valued. The Tax Court recognized substantial valuation discounts of limited partnership interests where there was a valid business purpose for the restrictions on their transferability. See, e.g., Estate of Harrison v. Commissioner, 52 T.C.M. (CCH) 1306, T.C.M. (P–H) ¶ 87,008 (1987). The taxpayer prevailed in *Estate of McLendon* v. *Commissioner*, 77 F.3d 477 (5th Cir.1995), an unreported decision in which the court held that transferred partnership interests were to be valued as assignee interests in partnership interests rather than as partnership interests. Under the terms of the partnership agreement and applicable state law, an assignee or purchaser of a partnership interest had no right to be admitted as a partner without the consent of all partners—and such consent could not be implied. The court said that objective criteria should be applied to transactions of this kind regardless of family considerations and commented that the "Tax Court does not sit to create its own rules of business organization governance". Thus, the lack of free transferability reduced the value of the decedent's partnership interest for tax and other purposes.

However, valuation discounts in family transfers have been curtailed by §§ 2701–2704 and the zero valuation rule. Under § 2703(a), fair market value is determined "without regard to (1) any option, agreement, or other right to acquire or use property at a price less than the fair market value of the property (without regard to such option, agreement, or right) or (2) any restriction on the right to sell or use such property." § 2703(b) provides an exception to § 2703(a)'s prohibition if the option, agreement, right or restriction is one of the following: (1) it is a bona fide business arrangement (i.e., a business purpose for it exists); (2) it is not a device to transfer the property to the decedent's family members for less than full and adequate consideration in money or money's worth; or (3) its terms are the same or similar to those of an arrangement in which the parties deal at arm's length. A lapse of a voting or liquidation right is to be treated as a gift or transfer includible in the descendant's estate if members of the transferor's family hold control of the entity both before and after the lapse. § 2704(a). Suppose in the example above that Sam held the right to liquidate the Smith family limited partnership, and Don and Betty had an option to acquire Sam's general partnership interest, including the right to liquidate. If Sam's estate held the liquidation right, the value of Sam's interest would be the full value of his capital contribution, or approximately $500,000. The value of the lapsed right of liquidation is determined under a fair market value standard as the value of all Sam's partnership interests (both limited and general) before and after the lapse. § 2704(a)(2).

[¶ 21,209]

PRIVATE LETTER RULING 9415007

January 12, 1994.

This is in response to your * * * letter requesting rulings under §§ 2036, 2038, 2503, and 2701 with respect to proposed transfers of limited partnership interests by a general partner.

The Transferor and his wife created the limited partnership (Partnership) in 1993. The Transferor initially contributed cash to the Partnership in exchange for a 9.259 percent general partnership interest and a 90.278 percent limited partnership interest. The Transferor's wife initially contributed cash in exchange for a 0.463 percent limited partnership interest. Subsequently, the trustees of certain trusts for the benefit of the Transferor's family and a custodian under a uniform gifts to minors act account invested additional funds in the Partnership in exchange for limited partnership interests.

The Transferor as general partner has exclusive management control of the Partnership, including full discretion to determine the amount and timing of distributions to the partners; provided, however, that if the general partner directs the distribution of partnership funds to the partners, distributions must be made to all partners at the same time in accordance with each partner's percentage interest in the Partnership (based on each partner's capital account).

Under the terms of the partnership agreement and applicable state law, the Transferor as general partner has a fiduciary duty to the limited partners to manage and operate the Partnership in the best interests of the Partnership and its partners. In exercising the powers granted in the partnership agreement, the general partner is bound to act in accordance with this fiduciary duty.

The partnership agreement provides that all items of income and deductions are to be allocated in accordance with the principles of § 704(b) and the regulations thereunder.

During the term of the Partnership, no partner is entitled to demand a distribution or a return of his capital account. However, the partners have the right to sell their interests to third parties, subject to the right of first refusal granted to the other partners.

When the partnership is dissolved, its assets will be distributed to the partners on a pro rata basis in accordance with their respective partnership interests.

The transferor proposes to make gifts of limited partnership interests. If the transferor desires to have a particular gift qualify for the $10,000 annual exclusion under § 2503(b), he will make the transfer either outright or to a trustee of a trust that meets the requirements of § 2503(c).

You request that we rule as follows:

1. The Transferor's proposed transfers (outright or to trusts qualifying under § 2503(c)) of limited partnership interests will constitute gifts of present interests for purposes of § 2503(b).

2. The value of the limited partnership interests gratuitously transferred will not be subject to the special valuation rules under § 2701.

3. Upon the death of the Transferor, the value of the transferred partnership interests will not be includible in the Transferor's gross estate under §§ 2036 or 2038 as a result of the Transferor's retained powers as general partner.

Issue 1

* * *

In the subject case, the management powers possessed by the Transferor/general partner under the partnership agreement, including control over partnership distributions, are similar to the powers possessed by general partners in most limited partnerships. A general partner must exercise such powers in a fiduciary capacity and is held to a high standard of conduct toward the limited partners. * * * Thus, in the subject case, the general partner's powers are not the equivalent of a trustee's discretionary authority to distribute or withhold trust income or property (i.e., a power that generally results in the characterization of a gift to such a trust as a gift of a future interest).

In the subject case, the proposed gifts of limited partnership interests will constitute outright gifts of ownership interests in a business entity. Each donee will receive the immediate use, possession, and enjoyment of the subject matter of the proposed gifts, including the right to sell or assign the interest (subject to the right of first refusal).

Accordingly, we conclude that the proposed gifts of limited partnership interests by the Transferor will constitute gifts of present interests that will qualify for the annual exclusion under § 2503(b).

¶ 21,209

ISSUE 2

Section 2701 provides that special valuation rules are applicable to a transfer of an interest in a corporation or partnership to a member of the transferor's family if the transferor or an applicable family member retains an "applicable retained interest."

The term "applicable retained interest" is defined in § 25.2701–2(b)(1) to include (among other things) an equity interest that constitutes a "distribution right" (as defined in § 25.2701–2(b)(3)) in a "controlled entity" (as defined in § 25.2701–2(b)(5)).

Section § 25.2701–2(b)(5) provides in part that, for purposes of § 2701, a "controlled entity" includes a partnership controlled, immediately before a transfer, by the transferor, applicable family members, and any lineal descendants of the parents of the transferor or the transferor's spouse. Section 25.2701–2(b)(5)(iii) provides in part that, in the case of a limited partnership, "control" means the holding of any equity interest as a general partner. Thus, in the subject case, the Partnership is a "controlled entity" *vis a vis* the Transferor because of his status as a general partner.

Having concluded that the Partnership is a "controlled entity" *vis a vis* the Transferor/general partner, the question remains whether the right to distributions from the Partnership that the Transferor/general partner proposes to retain are "distribution rights" within the meaning of § 2701(c)(1) and § 25.2701–2(b)(3). If the retained rights are not "distribution rights," the requisite "applicable retained interest" will not exist and, as a consequence, § 2701 will not apply.

Section 25.2701–2(b)(3)(i) provides that a "distribution right" does not include any right to receive distributions with respect to an interest that is of the same class as the transferred interest. Under § 25.2701–1(c)(3), a retained interest is in the same class as the transferred interest if the rights in the retained interest are identical to the rights of the transferred interest except for, in the case of a partnership, non-lapsing differences with respect to management and limitations on liability. For this purpose, non-lapsing provisions necessary to comply with partnership allocation requirements of the Internal Revenue Code (e.g., § 704(b)) are non-lapsing differences with respect to limitations on liability.

In the subject case, the right to distributions that the Transferor/general partner proposes to retain are rights with respect to an interest that is of the same class as the interests that he proposes to transfer. Consequently, the rights to be retained by the Transferor will not constitute "distribution rights." Thus, an "applicable retained interest" will not exist after the proposed transfers, and § 2701 will not apply.

ISSUE 3

* * *

Section 2036(b) provides that, for purposes of § 2036(a)(1), the retention of the right to vote, directly or indirectly, shares of stock of a controlled

¶ **21,209**

corporation shall be considered a retention of the enjoyment of the transferred property.

In United States v. Byrum, 408 U.S. 125 (1972) 1972–1 C.B. 518, the decedent was a controlling shareholder and a member of the board of directors of a closely-held corporation. The Court held that stock in the corporation transferred by the decedent to an irrevocable trust was not included in his gross estate under § 2036 even though the decedent expressly retained the right to vote the transferred stock and to veto the sale or disposition of the stock by the trustee. The Court held that the decedent, as a controlling shareholder and a member of the board of directors, had a fiduciary duty to promote the interests of the corporation and not to exercise his voting power to promote his personal interests at the expense of the minority shareholders. Accordingly, the decedent's retained power to vote the stock did not constitute the retained enjoyment of the transferred stock or right to designate the income from the transferred stock for purposes of § 2036.

As indicated above, the Transferor in the subject case is the general partner of the Partnership and as such has management authority over the Partnership, including the authority to control partnership distributions. However, as in the case of the decedent in *Byrum,* the Transferor in the subject case occupies a fiduciary position with respect to the limited partners and cannot distribute or withhold distributions or otherwise manage the partnership for purposes unrelated to the conduct of the partnership business.

Section 2038 provides that the value of the gross estate shall include the value of all property of which the decedent has at any time made a transfer (except in case of a bona fide sale for an adequate and full consideration in money or money's worth) in trust or otherwise, where the enjoyment thereof was subject to a power in the decedent to alter, amend, revoke, or terminate such interest or where any such power was relinquished during the 3–year period ending on the date of the decedent's death. Based upon the foregoing analysis with respect to § 2036, the Transferor's fiduciary duty with respect to the management of the Partnership will also preclude an inclusion in his gross estate under § 2038.

Accordingly, we conclude that the value of the partnership interests proposed to be transferred by the Transferor will not be includible in his gross estate under §§ 2036 or 2038 by reason of his status as general partner.

[¶ 21,212]

b. PDPA Qualification Requires Substantial Present Economic Benefit

While the transfer of the partnership interest in Priv. Ltr. Rul. 9415007 (¶ 20,207) was concluded to have qualified as a transfer of a present interest for purposes of § 2503(b)'s per donee per annum gift tax exclusion ($12,000 in 2006), the IRS may well claim that the transfer was of a future interest and thus deny the gift tax exclusion. Whether the gift is of a future interest, Reg. § 25.2503–3 (or a present interest and thus eligible for the gift tax exclusion) depends on whether the gift represents a "substantial present economic benefit" to the transferee. That was the conclusion reached in *Hackl* which follows—where the annual exclusion was denied—and, at issue in Crummey v. Commissioner, 397 F.2d 82 (9th Cir. 1968) (¶ 19,459), where it was allowed. Obviously, as in all such cases, the results are fact driven.

HACKL v. COMMISSIONER

United States Courts of Appeals, Tenth Circuit, 2003.
335 F.3d. 664.

TERENCE T. EVANS, Circuit Judge.

* * * Albert J. (A.J.) and Christine M. Hackl began a tree-farming business after A.J.'s retirement and gave shares in the company to family members. The Hackls believed the transfers were excludable from the gift tax, but the IRS thought otherwise. * * *

* * *A.J. purchased two tree farms (worth around $4.5 million) and contributed them, as well as about $8 million in cash and securities, to Treeco, LLC, a limited liability company that he set up * * *.

* * *

Shortly after Treeco's creation, A.J. and Christine began annual transfers of Treeco voting and nonvoting shares to their children, their children's spouses, and a trust set up for the couple's grandchildren.

* * *

* * * Because the Hackls gave up all of their property rights to the shares, they think that the shares were excludable gifts within the plain meaning of § 2503(b)(1). The government * * * argues that any transfer without a substantial present economic benefit is a future interest and ineligible for the gift tax exclusion.

* * * The Hackls argue that their position reflects the plain—and only meaning of "future interest" as used in the statute * * *. We disagree. Calling any tax law "plain" is a hard row to hoe, and a number of cases (including our decision in Stinson Estate v. United States, 214 F.3d 846 (7th Cir.2000)) have looked beyond the language of § 2503(b)(1) for guidance. * * * The Hackls do not cite any cases that actually characterize § 2503(b)(1) as plain, and the term "future interest" is not defined in the statute itself. Furthermore, the fact that both the government and the Hackls have proposed different—yet reasonable—interpretations of the statute shows that it is ambiguous.* * *

Hedging their bet, the Hackls say that the applicable Treasury regulation supports the conclusion that giving up all legal rights to a gift automatically makes it a present interest. The applicable Treasury regulation states that a "future interest" is a legal term that applies to interests "which are limited to commence in use, possession, or enjoyment at some future date or time," Reg. § 25.2503–3. The regulation also provides that a present interest in property is "[a]n unrestricted right to the immediate use, possession, or enjoyment of

¶ 21,212

property or the income from property (such as a life estate or term certain)."
We don't think that this language automatically excludes all outright transfers from the gift tax.

We previously addressed the issue of future interests for purposes of the
gift tax exclusion in *Stinson Estate*. In that case, forgiveness of a corporation's
indebtedness was a future interest outside the gift tax exclusion because
shareholders could not individually realize the gift without liquidating the
corporation or declaring a dividend—events that could not occur upon the
actions of any one individual under the corporation's bylaws. *See* 214 F.3d at
848. We said that the "sole statutory distinction between present and future
interests lies in the question of whether there is postponement of enjoyment
of specific rights, powers or privileges which would be forthwith existent if the
interest were present." *Id.* at 848–49 (quoting *Howe v. United States,* 142
F.2d 310, 312 (7th Cir.1944)). In other words, the phrase "present interest"
connotes the right to substantial present economic benefit.

In this case, Treeco's operating agreement clearly foreclosed the donees'
ability to realize any substantial present economic benefit. Although the
voting shares that the Hackls gave away had the same legal rights as those
that they retained, Treeco's restrictions on the transferability of the shares
meant that they were essentially without immediate value to the donees.
Granted, Treeco's operating agreement did address the possibility that a
shareholder might violate the agreement and sell his or her shares without
the manager's approval. But * * * the possibility that a shareholder might
violate the operating agreement and sell his or her shares to a transferee who
would then not have any membership or voting rights can hardly be called a
substantial economic benefit. Thus, the Hackls' gifts—while outright—were
not gifts of present interests.

The Hackls protest that Treeco is set up like any other limited liability
corporation and that its restrictions on the alienability of its shares are
common in closely held companies. While that may be true, the fact that other
companies operate this way does not mean that shares in such companies
should automatically be considered present interests for purposes of the gift
tax exclusion.

[¶ 21,217]

c. *Terminable Illness Impact on Valuation*

The IRS is unrelenting in its efforts to strip off the partnership wrapper
when valuing interests in family limited partnerships. No less dogged are the
attorneys who implement these schemes. Clearly the family limited partnership has become enormously popular among taxpayers as well as many
professional planners. *Schauerhamer*, below, involve a person terminally ill
when the partnership was created. The IRS refused to allow a lack of
marketability discount, claiming that (1) the formation of the partnership was
a testamentary act and should be disregarded; (2) § 2703 requires that the
restrictions on transfer of the underlying assets be disregarded; and (3)
§ 2704 requires that restrictions on the transfer of partnership interests be
disregarded.

ESTATE OF SCHAUERHAMER v. COMMISSIONER

73 T.C.M. (CCH) 2855, T.C.M. (RIA) 97,242 (1997).

FOLEY, Judge:

* * *

* * * Whether, pursuant to section 2036(a)(1), the value of certain assets transferred to family partnerships is includable in the decedent's gross estate. We hold that it is.

* * *

FINDINGS OF FACT

* * * At the time of her death, on December 13, 1991, Dorothy Schauerhamer (decedent) resided in Salt Lake City, Utah.

Decedent and her husband Willard Schauerhamer had three adult children, David Schauerhamer, Diane Liddiard, and Sandra Bradshaw, and jointly managed Economy Builders Supply, Inc., a closely held corporation engaged in the sale of building materials. After Willard's death in 1983, decedent took control of the business. She also managed several rental properties.

In late November of 1990, decedent was diagnosed with colon cancer. In early December of that year, she retained an attorney, Travis Bowen, to set her business affairs in order. Mr. Bowen, in consultation with decedent, prepared an estate plan.

On December 31, 1990, decedent, along with her three children and their spouses, met with Mr. Bowen at his office. Mr. Bowen explained that three family limited partnerships would be formed and that David, Sandra, and Diane would each become a general partner in a partnership. He explained that after the limited partnerships were formed, decedent's business holdings would be transferred to the partnerships, with each partnership receiving an undivided one-third interest in the transferred assets. He further advised that, after the partnerships were formed and funded, decedent would transfer limited partnership interests to her children and their family members. On December 31, 1990, three substantially identical limited partnership agreements were executed. The certificates of limited partnership were filed with the Utah Department of Commerce on May 13, 1991.

The partnership agreements set forth numerous terms and covenants with respect to the partnerships. Pursuant to the partnership agreements, David and decedent were the general partners in the "DAVID M. SCHAUERHAMER FAMILY LIMITED PARTNERSHIP", Diane and decedent were the general partners in the "DIANE KAY LIDDIARD FAMILY LIMITED PARTNERSHIP", and Sandra and decedent were the general partners in the "SANDRA GAYLE BRADSHAW FAMILY LIMITED PARTNERSHIP". Each partnership agreement also named decedent as the limited partner. In addition, decedent was named the managing partner of each partnership. The partnership agreements provided that decedent, in her capacity as managing partner, had "full power to

¶ 21,217

manage and conduct the Partnership's business operation in its usual course." From the time the partnerships were formed until shortly before decedent's death, she managed the partnership assets.

The partnership agreements included provisions relating to: (1) Capital contributions; (2) allocation of profits and losses; (3) partnership records; (4) management responsibilities and powers; (5) admission of new partners; (6) partnership dissolution and liquidation; and (7) agency relationships among partners. The partnership agreements provided that decedent would contribute $1 for her 1–percent interest as a general partner and $95 for her 95–percent interest as a limited partner. Each of decedent's children was required to contribute $4 for a 4–percent general partner interest.

On December 31, 1990, and on November 5, 1991, decedent transferred some of her business assets, in undivided one-third shares, to the partnerships. The assets included real estate, partnership interests, and notes receivable.

Also on December 31, 1990, decedent executed 33 documents (i.e., 11 relating to each of the three partnerships) entitled "ASSIGNMENT OF INTEREST IN LIMITED PARTNERSHIP". Each assignment stated that a $10,000 interest in the partnership was being assigned. On January 1, 1991, decedent executed an additional 33 assignments of partnership interests (i.e., 11 relating to each of the three partnerships) in the amount of $10,000 each. All 66 assignments were made to family members.

The partnership agreements each required that all income from the partnership be deposited into a partnership account. Shortly after the partnerships were formed, each partnership's initial capital was deposited into partnership bank accounts. Decedent deposited, into an account jointly held by her and David, all partnership income and income from other sources. She did not maintain any records to account separately for partnership and nonpartnership funds. Decedent utilized the account as her personal checking account, and from this account she paid personal and partnership expenses.

Decedent's executor filed Form 706 (United States Estate (and Generation-Skipping Transfer) Tax Return) dated September 14, 1992. On that return, the estate did not include in the gross estate the value of the 66 $10,000 limited partnership interests decedent had assigned to family members. The estate did, however, include the value of the remaining partnership interests. * * *

OPINION

* * *

Respondent contends that the value of the assets transferred to the purported partnerships is includable in decedent's gross estate pursuant to section 2033, 2036(a)(1), or 2038. We conclude that the value of the assets is includable pursuant to section 2036(a)(1). As a result, we do not address §§ 2033 and 2038.

Section 2036(a)(1) provides that a decedent's gross estate includes the value of all property interests transferred (other than for full and adequate consideration in money or money's worth) by a decedent during her life where she has retained for life the possession or enjoyment of the property, or the right to the income from the property. The term "enjoyment" refers to the economic benefits from the property. Thus, "Enjoyment as used in the death tax statute is not a term of art, but is synonymous with substantial present economic benefit."

Retained enjoyment may exist where there is an express or implied understanding at the time of the transfer that the transferror will retain the economic benefits of the property. The understanding need not be legally enforceable to trigger section 2036(a)(1). The retention of a property's income stream after the property has been transferred is "very clear evidence that the decedent did indeed retain 'possession or enjoyment.'" Estate of Hendry v. Commissioner, 62 T.C. 861, 873 (1974). Whether there was an implied agreement is a question of fact to be determined with reference to the facts and circumstances of the transfer and the subsequent use of the property. Id. at 872.

The facts of this case establish that an implied agreement existed among the partners. Decedent owned the assets subsequently transferred to the partnerships and collected the income these assets generated. On December 31, 1990, decedent formed the partnerships and contributed some of her business holdings. The partnership agreements required that each partnership maintain a bank account, and that all income from the partnerships be deposited into these accounts. After the formation of the partnerships, a partnership bank account was opened in the name of each partnership, and each partnership's $100 of initial capital was deposited into the account. As the partnerships earned income, however, decedent, in violation of the partnership agreements, did not deposit the income into the partnership accounts. Instead, she deposited the income into the account she utilized as her personal checking account, where it was commingled with income from other sources. Such deposits of income from transferred property into a personal account are highly indicative of "possession or enjoyment". Id.

David, Diane, and Sandra testified at trial that they were aware that decedent was depositing the funds into her personal, rather than a partnership, account. Moreover, they acknowledged that the formation of the partnerships was merely a way to enable decedent to assign interests in the partnership assets to members of her family. The assets and income would be managed by decedent exactly as they had been managed in the past. Where a decedent's relationship to transferred assets remains the same after as it was before the transfer, section 2036(a)(1) requires that the value of the assets be included in the decedent's gross estate.

Petitioner contends that decedent did not spend any of the partnership funds for her personal benefit. Petitioner bases this contention on bank statements relating to the account and the testimony of Richard Haynie, decedent's accountant. Neither is adequate to support petitioner's contention. The bank statements indicate that, on the date of decedent's death, the balance in the account exceeded the partnership income that she had deposited. There is no evidence, however, to establish that she did not spend the partnership income and later deposit income from other sources. In addition, Mr. Haynie testified that decedent did not spend partnership funds for her personal benefit. His testimony, which was apparently based on his review of the bank statements and not any personal, independent knowledge, fails to establish petitioner's contention.

As a result, the value of the partnership assets is includable in decedent's gross estate pursuant to section 2036(a)(1).

[¶ 21,222]

d. Retained Life Estate

As was the case in *Schauerhamer*, above, the claim of choice in challenging the FLP at the death of the transferor is § 2036(a)(1), i.e., an assertion that, on the facts and circumstances, an implied agreement existed whereby the transferor could be said to have retained an estate for life in the transferred property. The lower court dockets are crowded with FLP cases. (Look and ye shall find a case with a set of facts just like yours!) Notable cases at the appellate court level include Strangi v. Commissioner, 417 F.3d 468 (5th Cir. 2005) and Estate of Thompson v. Commissioner, 382 F.3d 367 (3rd Cir. 2004). In both cases, more than 95 percent of the decedent's property had been transferred to the challenged FLP.

Challenges are most likely to be successful—resulting in the transferred FLP property being included in the transferor's gross estate as a transfer subject to a retained life estate—where (1) the formalities of the partnership were ignored after the supposed transfer of property and the transferor continued to use and enjoy the FLP property without regard for its new status; (2) the transferor was without, practically speaking, other property for his or her support after the transfer; (3) the FLP was created while the transferor was on the death bed; and (4) FLP property was regularly distributed to the transferor for his or her support and maintenance. There is an argument, too, that challenge is likely where the transfer had no business purpose. Estate of Rosen v. Commissioner, T.C. Memo. 2006–115, 91 T.C.M. (CCH) 1220, T.C.M. (RIA) 2006–115 (U.S. Tax Ct. 2006). (Arguably that might be the case where the FLP was funded exclusively with marketable securities. However, the counter argument is that the transferor wanted family members who came to hold limited partnership interests to join in the common enterprise as managers and share responsibility and gain experience as managers before the transferors death.) All in all, the final chapter has not been written as to FLPs. See Internal Revenue Service, Appeals Settlement Guidelines: Family Limited Partnerships and Family Limited Liability Corporations (Oct. 20, 2006) available at http://www.irs.gov/pub/irs-utl/asg penalties family limited pships finalredacted10 20 06.pdf.

[¶ 21,229]

4. DISADVANTAGES TO THE FAMILY LIMITED PARTNERSHIP

Despite the seeming attractiveness of the family limited partnership, there are disadvantages. Some of the disadvantages of using the FLP are obvious, such as the cost of its creation and maintenance, and the requirement that the FLP's records be accurately maintained. Some families may find it difficult to amass the initial capital to set up the FLP, and may find maintaining the necessary business structure burdensome. The transfer of property to the FLP may also prove difficult or burdensome to the family. Money deposited in a bank account will not be especially difficult to transfer, but the transfer of securities or real estate can lead to future difficulties if the family member attempting the transfer is not knowledgeable in the requirements of the securities or real estate markets.

Additionally, some states may attempt to impose an income tax on investment income for residents, or even for companies domiciled in the state, if the investing entity is a trade or business. This may be avoided by providing in the partnership agreement that the general partner takes title to the partnership property as trustee. The passive loss rules may also prove disadvantageous to an FLP, as § 469(i)(6)(A) provides that where property conveyed to the FLP is generated by rental real estate which produces passive losses, the partnership is not entitled to the $25,000 allowance for a 10 percent (or more) owner who actively participates in the rental real estate activity.

Problem

[¶ 21,250]

Professor Slovinski, a widow, inherited $3 million, all of which she has invested in marketable securities of New York Exchange companies. Would she be advantaged to create a limited partnership with her adult children, the ultimate beneficiaries of her property at her death?

D. ASSET PROTECTION

[¶ 21,300]

1. OVERVIEW

As a general rule, spendthrift trusts are ineffective against claims of creditors of the trust's beneficiary to the extent of the property transferred to the trust by that beneficiary. In other words, individuals cannot launder property through a trust, retain a beneficial interest in the trust, and avoid the claims of his or creditors as to that property. And the rule applies not only to existing creditors but also to creditors acquired after the property was placed in the trust.

[¶ 21,309]

2. OFFSHORE

The same rules, however, generally do not apply to offshore trusts—even though the transferor is a beneficiary of the trust—and, as a result, such trusts have become a relatively popular means of protecting property from future creditors. Offshore trusts can shield property the transferor adds to the trust from the reach of present creditors as well as long the transferor is not rendered insolvent by the transfer. As might be imagined, fraudulent transfer statutes under the Bankruptcy Code and under state statutes prevent the use of offshore trusts as a way to hide assets once the settlor is "in trouble" with his or her creditors.

[¶ 21,315]

3. SELF SETTLED DOMESTIC TRUSTS: ALASKA, DELAWARE— AND COPYCAT JURISDICTIONS

While offshore trusts have proved somewhat popular—certainly on the cocktail party circuit if not in practice—concerns about expense as well as the political stability of offshore locales are limiting factors. (While more than one offshore trust candidate has been heard to utter the belief, perhaps tongue-in-cheek, that the U.S. Marines could be counted on to rescue his or her property from its island refuge if "everything goes to Hell", shifting political currents in the United States may make such a rescue less likely.) Fortunately, at least for these timid souls, Alaska and Delaware—perhaps to benefit local trustees—have made statutory changes that are said to offer offshore benefits to domestic trusts established in those jurisdictions. Essentially, the statutes prevent creditors from reaching the income or principal of self-settled trusts even though the settlor is a permissible beneficiary. This allows the trust settler to shield the trust property from creditors subject, of course, to the fraudulent transfer statutes, while retaining the ability to receive distributions from the trustee or even to use the trust assets on a rent-free basis. Qualifying trusts must (1) be irrevocable; (2) specifically incorporate the relevant state law as the law governing trust; (3) contain a spendthrift clause stating that the trust shall not be used to satisfy the claims of creditors; (4) name a trustee who is either a naturalized resident in the state or a bank or trust company authorized to act as a trustee in the state; and (5) direct that a number of significant administrative activities take place in the state. Additionally, there are significant limitations on protecting the trust assets from child support claims. Also, unresolved are certain conflict of law issues. For example, it is unlikely that an Iowan's personal property physically transferred to the trustee of an asset protection trust in Alaska will continue to be subject to the Iowa courts (unless the transfer was fraudulent), but Iowa real property obviously cannot be removed to Alaska. It has been suggested that this drawback can be overcome by draining the equity from real property by taking out a second mortgage and adding the proceeds to the trust.

For related discussion, see ¶¶ 5600, 7478, 10,119, 10,209, and 21,870.

[¶ 21,325]

4. SPENDTHRIFTS

Another important consideration is the extent of the creditor protection provided by spendthrift clauses included in trusts. The traditional rule is to recognize a "public policy exception" to the protection provided by spendthrift trusts in the case where the transferor of the property is a beneficiary of the trust to which the property was transferred. The Mississippi Supreme Court, in Sligh v. First Nat'l Bank of Holmes County, 706 So.2d 251 (Miss.1997), extended the exception to involuntary tort creditors of the trust beneficiary even though the trusts had been established by the beneficiary's mother *and not the beneficiary.* The court held that a plaintiff, who was injured by the beneficiary driving drunk, could recover from two spendthrift trusts for the benefit of drunk driver. The reasoning behind the decision focused on the fact that the driver's mother set up the spendthrift trusts knowing he was a habitual drunkard. The court likened the situation to the one allowing creditors who are victims of gross negligence or intentional torts to succeed against the beneficiary of a spendthrift trust, extending the exception slightly to cover an action that is typically considered an involuntary tort. This case may be limited to its spectacular facts, or it may cause the state legislatures to follow the Mississippi example and extend the exceptions to spendthrift protection.

E. COMPRESSED TAX RATE SCHEDULE

[¶ 21,351]

The income tax rates applicable to undistributed trust income are steeply progressive when compared to those applicable to individuals. In 2006, the rates applicable to trusts reach 35 percent on income exceeding $10,050. (By way of comparison, in 2006, only when the taxable income of married persons filing jointly, unmarried persons, or heads of households exceeds $336,550 will the excess be taxed at 35 percent.) There is probably no greater deterrent to accumulating or warehousing income in a trust than these income tax rates. Of course, if the trust beneficiary is himself or herself in the top income tax brackets, the trust income tax rates are a neutral factor.

Oftentimes the ultimate incentive to warehouse income in the trust is the opportunity for the warehoused income to escape estate taxation at the death of the trust beneficiary at a flat rate of 46 percent (in 2006), taxation which is the inevitable result in cases where the beneficiary accumulates the property distributed from the trust (rather than expending it in consumption or as part of a gift program). Too, there is the possible application of the generation skipping tax to trust distributions (depending, of course, on the generation assignment of the distributee and whether GST exemption has been assigned to the trust to shield trust distributions from the GST tax.)

At the other end of the spectrum, it is sometimes useful to note that when planning small trusts—such as those for child's college fund—warehousing income in the trust and taxing it to the trust rather than to the child may well be tax advantageous. The maximum savings in 2006 was $956.50. It would be realized in cases where that income, if received by the child was subject to the kiddie tax and taxed to the child at 35 percent, the parent's highest marginal income tax rate. The savings comes about, using 2006 rates, when the first $10,050 of income had its "run up the brackets"

$10,050 income taxed to the child (perhaps at parent's rates):

	$10,050.00	35%		$3,517.50

$10,050 income taxed to the trust:

$2,050	$0	$2,050.00	15%	$307.50
$4,850	$2,050	$2,800.00	25%	$700.00
$7,400	$4,850	$2,550.00	28%	$714.00
$10,050	$7,400	$2,650.00	33%	$874.50

$2,596.00   − $2,596.00

$921.50   Savings

Available trust income tax exemption:

$100.00	35%	$35.00	$35.00

$956.50   Savings

The foregoing rate brackets are, each year, to be adjusted for inflation. § 1(f).

Capital gains realized by trusts and estates are given preferential tax treatment. In 2006, for example, those gains were taxed at a maximum rate of 15 percent (or, in the case of low income taxpayers, as low as 5 percent). § 1(h).

Nontax considerations often play a part in the decisional process. Take, for example, the case of the disabled person unable to personally mange property. The trust is the only alternative for the beneficiary's property other than a court-appointed guardian. But where warehousing of income in the trust is not virtually compelled—as it is where the alternative is making a distribution to a court appointed guardianship and all of the expenses associated with court supervision—it may be argued that any income tax advantage to accumulating income in a trust will be more than offset by the expenses of maintaining the trust. Finally, there is always the ancient justification for the trust: protecting the beneficiary from the predators of the world. (Sometimes the biggest predator of the them all is the trust beneficiary!)

F. DISTRIBUTIONS IN KIND FROM DISCRETIONARY TRUSTS— OPPORTUNITIES

[¶ 21,400]

1. GENERAL RULES

"Discretionary pay" is a feature relatively common to accumulation trusts—and sometimes, that feature results in a distribution planning opportunity tax wise. Certainly, the tax consequences associated with distributions in kind need to be taken into account by the trustee in making distribution decisions.

Generally speaking, if distributable net income (DNI) is available, after reduction for any cash distribution from the trust, sufficient in amount to cover some part or all of the fair market value of property distributed in kind to the trust beneficiaries, then the trustee is put to an election. At this point the trustee must elect whether to claim a distribution deduction for the fair market value of the property immediately prior to distribution or only for the *basis* of the property in the hands of the trust. If the trustee claims a distribution deduction for the fair market value of the property, then the trust must recognize gain or loss equal to the difference between the value of the property and the basis of the property in the hands of the trust.

Technically speaking, § 643(e) has the effect of giving taxpayers an election as to the basis of property distributed in kind from an estate or trust. Section 643(e) provides that the basis, in the hands of the recipient, of property distributed in kind will be "the adjusted basis of such property in the hands of the estate or trust immediately before the distribution, adjusted for * * * any gain or loss recognized to the estate or trust on the distribution." However, whether gain or loss is recognized by the estate or trust will be optional, with the election to be made by the estate or trust. As § 643(e)(3)(A)(ii) reads, the estate or trust has the option of treating a distribution in kind "as if such property had been sold to the distributee at its fair market value." This means that the estate or trust recognizes gain if the property has appreciated, or loss if the property has depreciated. If the estate or trust elects to recognize gain or loss when making a distribution in kind, the estate or trust is able to claim a deduction against its distributable net income (DNI) for the fair market value of the distributed property. See § 643(e)(3)(A)(iii). Otherwise—that is, if gain or loss is not recognized—the distribution deduction available to the estate or trust is limited to the lesser of the fair market value of the property immediately prior to distribution or the basis of the property in the hands of the trustee immediately before the distribution. See § 643(e)(2).

If the estate or trust does not choose to recognize gain or loss on the distribution in kind, the distributee assumes the basis of the property to the estate or trust—essentially "carryover" basis—even if the property has declined in value in the estate or trust.

[¶ 21,409]

2. SPECIAL RULES

Section 643(e) does not apply to property distributed in kind in satisfaction of a specific bequest which meets the requirements of § 663(a)(1). See § 643(e)(4). Nor does § 643(e) apply to distributions in kind that are made to satisfy a requirement that "all income be distributed." In this latter case, the distribution is viewed as a "sale or exchange" for income tax purposes on the theory that the trustee is discharging a legal obligation by distributing the appreciated property in satisfaction of that obligation. See Reg. § 1.661(a)–2(f)(3); Rev. Rul. 67–74, 1967–1 C.B. 194. That is, if the trust is mandatory pay and appreciated trust property is distributed in kind in satisfaction of the beneficiary's right to income, the trust is considered to have realized taxable income to the extent of the property's appreciation.

Section 643(e) does not apply in cases where there is no DNI or the cash distributed from the estate or trust "soaks up" the DNI.

Assume that a trust which held appreciated property also provided that all distributions shall be at the sole discretion of the trustee. More specifically, assume that the trust has $500 of distributable net income, that it has an asset with a fair market value of $500 and a basis of $100, and that the trustee plans to exercise his discretion to distribute $500 to the beneficiary. If the trustee distributes $500 in cash, the trust will enjoy a distribution deduction of $500 and the beneficiary will have ordinary income of $500. See §§ 661(a), 662(a).

If the trustee elects to distribute the appreciated asset to the beneficiary, the trustee will be put to an election. The trustee can elect to claim a distribution deduction of $500. If the trustee does claim a $500 distribution deduction, the beneficiary will have taxable income of $500 and the property will have a basis of $500 in the hands of the beneficiary. In addition, the trust will be required to recognize gain of $400 (fair market value of $500 less basis of $100) on the distribution. Depending on the holding period of the trust, this gain may qualify for capital gains treatment which would mean that, effectively, in 1999, the maximum tax on the gain would be 20 percent of the gain. See § 1(h).

In lieu of claiming the $500 distribution deduction, the trustee could be content with claiming only a $100 distribution deduction. In that case, the beneficiary will be deemed to have received taxable income of only $100 and the beneficiary's basis in the distributed property would only be $100. If the beneficiary then sells the distributed property for $500, he or she would experience a $400 taxable gain.

[¶ 21,417]

3. APPLICATIONS

What considerations should impact the trustee in deciding whether to elect gain or loss recognition in lieu of carryover basis? Before considering this question, first it should be noted that if the trust's DNI is zero or consists entirely of tax-exempt income, then no part of the value of the distributed property is includible in the beneficiary's gross income. The distribution is then treated as any other distribution in excess of DNI—a gift subject entirely to the exclusion of § 102(a). Moreover, the beneficiary's basis is determined entirely by reference to § 1015.

Second, before proceeding to consider the factors to be considered in choosing between gain or loss recognition and carryover basis, consider how the distribution in kind would be treated if both the basis and the fair market value of the distributed property were greater than the available DNI. In such a case the trust's distribution deduction is limited to the amount of DNI. §§ 661(a), 662. Accordingly, the beneficiary's basis in the distributed property is determined only in part by reference to the basis or value of the property distributed to him or her—that portion of the basis or value covered by the DNI. Reg. § 1.661(a)–2(f)(3). To the extent that both the basis and the value of the property distributed exceed DNI, the basis rule of § 1015 applies in determining the beneficiary's basis for that portion of the distributed property. Thus, for basis purposes, when DNI is inadequate, i.e., less than both the basis and the value of the property distributed in kind, the distributed property should be viewed as divisible (Reg. § 1.661(a)–2(f)(3)), i.e., received in part as a distribution having a ratable gross income basis and in part by inheritance. See §§ 102(a), 1014.

Example 1. Assume that a trust with DNI of $30,000 distributes property having a basis to it of $75,000 and a fair market value of $90,000.

(1) If the trustee does not elect to recognize gain or loss on the distribution of the appreciated property, B would have gross income of $30,000; the trust would have a distribution deduction of $30,000; and B would have a basis of $75,000 in the distributed property.

(2) If the trustee elects to recognize gain or loss on the distribution of the appreciated property, the trustee would have $15,000 of taxable income ($90,000—$75,000). In addition, but unrelated to the trustee's decision to recognize income on the distribution of the appreciated property, the trust would have a distribution deduction of $30,000 (the amount of the DNI); and B would have gross income of $30,000 (again, the amount of the DNI). B's basis in the distribution would be $90,000.

(3) Changing the facts in the example, if DNI were $90,000, B's gross income and basis would be $90,000 if the trustee elected to recognize $15,000 of gain as taxable income. On the other hand, if the trustee did not make the election to recognize the $15,000 of gain, then B's gross income would be $75,000; his basis in the distributed property would be $75,000; and the trust's deduction for the distribution would be limited to $75,000 even though the trust had DNI of $90,000.

(4) If DNI were zero, B would have no gross income, but his basis would be $75,000, the trust's basis. § 1015.

If property is to be sold, the trust beneficiaries could be advantaged if the trustee distributed the property to the beneficiaries and they accomplished the sale. However, such a scenario would only be advantageous in the case where the beneficiaries are in a higher income tax bracket than the trust. Consider whether you agree with this conclusion by considering the Hatfield trust and the McCoy trust.

Example 2. The Hatfield trust is in the bottom income tax bracket but the trust's sole beneficiary, Dud, is in the top bracket. The McCoy trust is in the top income tax bracket and Bub, its sole beneficiary, is in the bottom bracket. The trustee of each trust proposes to sell stock having a basis of $200 and a fair market value of $1,000. The Hatfield trustee also wants to distribute $1,000 to Dud and the McCoy trustee, $1,000 to Bub.

If the trust includes property which has depreciated in value, i.e., has a fair market value below its basis in the hands of the estate or trust, distribution of that loss property carries out DNI only to the extent of the property's fair market value. However, the distributee will assume the basis of the property in the hands of the estate or trust unless the estate or trust elects to recognize the loss. In the ordinary case, it would seem that loss recognition would be warranted because it has the effect of reducing DNI and providing income tax relief without any immediate tax cost. Of course, if the property is to be sold, determining whether the loss should be claimed by the estate or trust or the distributee will depend upon the relative tax brackets of the estate or trust and the distributee.

Example 3. The Jones Trust plans to distribute 100 shares of stock to Ted, the trust beneficiary. The shares had a value of $2,000 at the time of acquisition but have declined in value to $1,200. Both Ted and the trust are in the top income tax bracket. The trust can elect to recognize the loss on the stock when the stock is distributed to Ted. His basis in the distributed stock will then be $1,200. If the trust does not elect to recognize the loss, Ted's basis in the distributed stock will be $2,000.

Problem

[¶ 21,440]

As part of his estate plan, Buck was asked whether a trust for his bride Sweetie should be "mandatory pay, discretionary pay, or discretionary pay subject to a standard." The trust is to terminate at Sweetie's death and the trust property is to be distributed to Buck's children, "Little" Buck and Sweet Thing. Buck has already decided to name Colossus Bank as trustee. Buck says the trust for Sweetie is to be funded with § 2010(c)'s $2 million applicable exclusion allowance. He says that it is likely that the trust will be funded with shares of Bulldog Oil, his publicly traded company. Buck is currently hospitalized in grave condition and says that "time is of the essence but I got to understand this thang." Bulldog shares are selling for $10 but, according to Buck, it's "got no place to go but up." Buck, remembering a "Law for the Layman" course he took at the community college, says, "Give me one o' them hypos so that I kin know whether I'm on foot or horseback" when he chooses among the distribution options.

Assume the following facts. In a given year, the trust has $20,000 of DNI. Bulldog is a defendant in a major environmental damage suit, and the trustee, wanting to spread the risk, proposes to distribute $20,000 of Bulldog stock, rather than cash, to Sweetie. The stock has a market value of $50 per share. The stock has a basis of $10 in the hands of the trustee.

Which of the following is the best distribution option if a distribution in kind is a possibility?

Option 1. The trustee is required to distribute all trust income.

Option 2. The trustee is required to distribute so much or all of the trust income and principal as shall be required for the "health, education, maintenance, and support" of Sweetie.

Option 3. The trustee is permitted to make distributions of income and principal to Sweetie whenever the trustee determines a distribution is in the "best interests" of Sweetie.

G. TO WAREHOUSE OR NOT?—USING ACCUMULATION AND MULTIPLE TRUSTS

[¶ 21,500]

1. THROWBACK RULES

a. *Historical Perspective*

Worth noting if nothing more than as an virtual historical curiosity are the "throwback rules". Although of little current application, these rules appear as §§ 665–667.

The purpose of the throwback rules was to tax "warehoused" trust income as if it had been distributed to the trust beneficiary in the year it was initially received by the trust. Congress also developed a multiple trust penalty, designed to impose a special income tax burden on taxpayers who are the recipients of accumulated or "warehoused" income from more than two trusts. § 667(c). The penalty applied only to those tax years in which more than two trusts accumulated income for the same beneficiary. That having been said, beginning with tax year 1998, the throwback rules (and multiple trust penalty rules) only apply to foreign trusts, domestic trusts that were once treated as foreign trusts, and domestic trusts created before March 1, 1984, that would be treated as "multiple trusts" under § 643(f). § 665(c). (Section 643(f) treats multiple trusts created by the same grantor for the same beneficiaries for tax avoidance purposes as a single trust for income tax purposes.) Trusts to which the throwback rules no longer apply are described as "qualified trusts." § 665(c)(1). Effectively, thus, the throwback rules are history, eliminating one of the disadvantages of accumulating income in a trust. (The principal disadvantage to income accumulations is the relatively small amount of income that can be taxed at income tax rates less than the current maximum (35 percent in 2006, § 1(i)). See ¶ 21,351.)

[¶ 21,510]

b. *Rationale*

At inception, the throwback rules reflected Congressional concern about the potential for income distortion inherent in the use of trusts. As Congress understood it, income generated by trust property could be taxed to the trust and warehoused there if not needed by the trust's beneficiaries. By taxing the income to the trust, the ultimate recipients of that income would have the benefit of "riding up" the progressive income tax brackets applicable to the trust's income, thereby taking advantage of the opportunity to have more income taxed at lower rates than would have been the case had the ultimate recipients received the income in the year in which it was earned. Needless to say, this opportunity could discriminate against those with modest resources because their circumstances did not permit them the luxury of using a trust to shelter any of their income.

By 1997, however, Congress had come to believe that its "rate compression" strategy (¶ 21,351), adopted in 1986, had rendered the throwback rules an unnecessary, complicating burden placed on trusts.

"Rate compression" means that the tax brackets applied to estates and trusts are compressed, resulting in estate and trust income, when warehoused, being taxed to the estate or trust for the most part at the top income tax rate. § 1(e). Since only a relatively few beneficiaries are in the top income tax bracket, Congress apparently thinks that trustees will opt to minimize income taxes by distributing trust income to lower bracket beneficiaries rather than warehousing it in the estate or trust where it will be taxed at the maximum rate.

[¶ 21,515]

c. *Significant Planning Incentive*

In some instances, trustees, perhaps with the concurrence of the trust beneficiaries, will warehouse income in the trust for the reason that the warehoused income will escape the federal estate tax at the death of the beneficiaries. This strategy, of course, only has appeal in those instances where the income distributions are likely to go unconsumed by the trust beneficiaries and the trust itself bypasses the beneficiaries' estates for death tax purposes—a likely result where the trust beneficiaries have not been given a general power of appointment over the trust property. For discussion of powers of appointment, see ¶ 18,067.

[¶ 21,520]

2. CONSOLIDATION OF MULTIPLE TRUSTS

Section 643(f) was adopted in 1984 in an attempt by Congress to limit the use of multiple trusts as income tax shelters. Arguably, with the advent of rate compression in 1986, the trust consolidation rules, like the throwback rules, has little utility and should have been repealed. That has not happened but it is likely that the rule is applied to few, if any, trusts (because the abuse potential is so scant). Section 643(f) provides:

2 or more trusts shall be treated as 1 trust if—

(1) such trusts have substantially the same grantor or grantors and substantially the same primary beneficiary or beneficiaries, and

(2) a principal purpose of such trusts is the avoidance of the tax imposed by this chapter.

For purposes of the preceding sentence, a husband and wife shall be treated as 1 person.

The exact text of § 643(f) is important because Congress had the option of copying Reg. § 1.641(a)–0(c) but chose to use other, perhaps more far-reaching, language to accomplish its objective. Reg. § 1.641(a)–0(c) provides:

Multiple trusts that have—

   (1) No substantially independent purposes (such as independent dispositive purchases),

   (2) The same grantor and substantially the same beneficiary, and

   (3) The avoidance or mitigation of (a) the progressive rates of tax (including mitigation as a result of deferral of tax) or (b) the minimum tax for tax preferences imposed by § 56 as their principal purpose,

shall be consolidated and treated as one trust for the purposes of subchapter J.

The Service had been less than successful in using Reg. § 1.641(a)–0(c) to consolidate trusts for income tax purposes. The case law generally considered trusts with common grantors, terms and beneficiaries to be separate taxpayers if they were administered as separate trusts. See E. Morris Trusts v. Commissioner, 51 T.C. 20 (1968), aff'd per curiam, 427 F.2d 1361 (9th Cir.1970). Moreover, in E.L. Stephenson Trust v. Commissioner, 81 T.C. 283 (1983), the Tax Court held Reg. § 1.641(a)–0(c) unconstitutional.

Section 643(f) is obviously broader than Reg. § 1.641(a)–0(c) inasmuch as § 643(f) dispenses with the "no substantially independent purposes" test of the Regulation and provides that § 643(f) is applicable when "the trusts have substantially the same grantor or grantors." The Regulation spoke in the singular and was applicable only if the trusts had "the same grantor." As a result, the Service has a stronger tool to use in reaching multiple trusts.

One possible application of § 643(f) is to separate trusts established by husband and wife for the benefit of their lineal descendants. Clearly these trusts for the benefit of the same persons would be treated as separate trusts under the consolidation regulation but, according to § 643(f), "husband and wife shall be treated as one person."

However, one could argue that the IRS has been limited in one respect. The Regulation applied to trusts which had as "their principal purpose," the "avoidance or mitigation of * * * the progressive rates of tax (including mitigation as a result of deferral of tax)." § 643(f) applies to trusts which have as "a principal purpose" the avoidance of tax. Thus, the question is, must the IRS prove "more" under § 643(f) to bring about consolidation than under the Regulation inasmuch as proving that the grantor had "avoidance" in mind would seem harder to accomplish than merely proving that the grantor wanted to "mitigate" the "progressive rates of tax" as the Regulation contemplated?

H. TOTAL RETURN TRUSTS, UNITRUST AMOUNT, AND EQUITABLE ADJUSTMENTS

[¶ 21,701]

1. IN GENERAL

Over time widespread agreement has developed as to what generally constitutes "fiduciary accounting income". ¶ 8651. Recently though changes in the financial markets are forcing a reexamination of these notions. At one level, the situation can be illustrated by reference to the once common provision requiring "all trust income is to be distributed at least annually" to one or more named trust beneficiaries and that "no distributions from principle are to be made". This worked acceptably in an economy where corporations were inclined to distribute corporate profits in the form of dividends. That changed in recent years because of the disparity in the income tax rates applicable to dividends (so-called "ordinary income") and those applicable to appreciation realized when a stock is sold (so called "capital gains"). Until 2003, dividends were taxed as ordinary income at a maximum rate verging on 40 percent (or more, effectively, in some cases) while appreciation—capital gains—were taxed at a maximum rate of 20 percent and not taxed at all until the gain is realized when the property is disposed of. In 2006, however, a maximum income tax rate of 15 percent is applicable to both dividends and capital gains. Despite this seeming equality, the enterprise manager, deciding to distribute or not distribute earnings in the form of dividends, may well take into account the income taxation of those earnings first to the corporation at corporate tax rates of roughly 35 percent (§ 11(b)) followed by taxation to shareholders at 15 percent—and decide against an earnings distribution in the form of a dividend, choosing, instead to reinvest the corporate earnings in the enterprise. As the argument goes, shareholders needing or wanting cash, can sell shares, shares likely to have appreciated (reflecting the reinvested earnings)—and pay tax on the realized appreciation at a maximum capital gains rate of 15 percent. §§ 61(a)(3); 1001(a). And, to encourage share appreciation, corporations not infrequently maintain "stock buyback" programs, i.e., use corporate cash to buy company stock. These buybacks suck out cash that might otherwise go to shareholders in the form of dividends. "Everybody wins," so it might be claimed—except the trust beneficiary limited to receiving distributions of trust income! There does not appear to be an organized lobby of trust beneficiaries and, thus, it is not uncommon to see dividends reduced with the explanation that cash is being conserved to increase stock price.

Obviously restrictive dividend policies work a major hardship on shareholders looking only to distributions of trust income for support and to facilitate lifestyle choices. While one rarely hears of trust beneficiaries "living under a bridge" because of dividend cuts (that have lead to a reduction in trust income), it is not hard to imagine that trust income in many trusts is lagging trust valuation (or at least it was most profoundly during the bull market of the late 1990's). To address this situation, state legislatures and persons creating new trusts are turning to new concepts of trust income. Talk is of "total return trusts" and making distributions of a "unitrust" amount; trustees fulfilling their duty of impartiality between income and remainder beneficiaries by making "equitable adjustments between income and principal" in cases where the trustee invests and manages the trust property under the state's "prudent investor standard"; or capital gains being allocated to income in a consistent fashion by a trustee exercising discretionary authority pursuant to state law or the governing instrument. In Reg. § 1.643(b)-(1), the IRS said that it would "respect" allocations between income and principal based on these concepts to the extent applicable local law permitted their utilization. Examples are provided in Reg. § 1.643(a)–3.

The effect of the state law changes is to increase the amount distributable to so-called income beneficiaries of the trust. In turn, the effect of the IRS acceptance of these state law changes—sometimes referred to as "ordering" rules—is to cause the tax liability to follow the income to the beneficiary, thereby avoiding an anomalous situation where "income" flows to a beneficiary but tax liability for that income is stuck at the trust level because the IRS based its regulations on an antiquated definition of "fiduciary accounting income".

[¶ 21,705]

2. TWO UPIAs

The "Two UPIAs" refer to Uniform Prudent Investor Act of 1994, 7B U.L.A. 15 (2006) ("UPIA 1") and the Uniform Principal and Income Act of 1997 ("UPIA 2"), 7A U.L.A. 63 (2006) (http://www. nccusl.org). Typically, when adopted by a state, both acts apply to new as well as *all* existing trusts and estates. UPIA 1 and UPIA 2 represent both a liability and opportunity for attorneys. For the unwary the new laws will be a liability. Attorneys unaware of the laws' unique provisions draft wills and trusts at their peril. (For impact of the two UPIAs on retirement plan distribution options, see ¶ 30,143.)

[¶ 21,708]

a. Uniform Prudent Investor Act

Prior to adoption of UPIA 1, trustees and executors ("fiduciaries") were expected to follow the *prudent person standard*. That standard required a fiduciary to exercise that degree of care and skill that a person of ordinary prudence would exercise in dealing with his or her own property. This standard concentrated on three factors: (1) the safety of the investment, (2) the asset's appreciation potential, and (3) expected income from the investment.

UPIA 1 provides a new standard for fiduciaries based on modern portfolio theory (MPT) Returns are maximized and risk, minimized, through diversity. (Professional money managers (such as mutual funds and pension funds) use MPT as the fiduciary standard against which their asset management is judged.) While MPT is a well accepted practice for financial investing in capital markets, it is a relatively novel concept for fiduciaries. MPT is based

¶ 21,708

on the relationship between risk and return. MPT allows some investments in the portfolio to contain risk. Moreover, previous restrictions on fiduciaries investing in "safe" investments has been abrogated in favor of the achieving an appropriate risk/return objective for the total portfolio. The overall portfolio may consist of stocks, bonds, cash, closely held business interests and real estate, rather than one type of investment or "safe" investment. The prudent investor standard allows fiduciaries to focus on a total return for the portfolio, income and appreciation, rather than just income.

UPIA 1 requires fiduciaries to diversify their investments in order to meet the prudent investor standard. The exact make up of the entire portfolio under UPIA 1 will differ for each trust and estate. In determining the total portfolio's makeup, fiduciaries must consider a range of issues, such as, general economic conditions, inflation or deflation, tax consequences of each investment, the role the investment plays in the overall portfolio, total return from income *and* appreciation, and an assets special relationship to the trust or beneficiaries.

UPIA 1 contains "default rules," which may be overridden by careful drafting. Without proper drafting, a fiduciary must diversify the trust or estate assets in compliance with the UPIA 1. Additionally, the UPIA 1 repealed the fiduciary's ability to retain property that constituted the initial trust corpus. The changes provided in the UPIA 1 have potentially dramatic effects on clients. For example, if a client's largest asset is a block of publicly traded bank stock or a ranch, the default rules would require fiduciaries to liquidate the assets to provide diversity and a greater total return. This may not be in accordance with the client's wishes.

In order to comply with UPIA 1, fiduciaries should develop procedures for reviewing all assets within a reasonable time and establish guidelines for investing the assets according to the prudent investor standard. For those fiduciaries that lack the sophistication or ability to meet UPIA 1's standard, another option exists. UPIA 1 allows fiduciaries to delegate their investment and management functions. Under the prior law, fiduciaries could delegate their responsibility to an agent, but the fiduciary remained liable for the agent's decisions. Under UPIA 1, if a fiduciary properly delegates the investment and management decisions, the fiduciary is not liable to the beneficiaries for decisions made by the agent. This provision allows non professional fiduciaries the ability to relieve themselves of liability and delegate their duties to professional fiduciaries, such as a bank trust department.

Fiduciaries owe duties to all beneficiaries. However, many times trusts provide either multiple current beneficiaries or successive generations as beneficiaries. It is very unlikely that each beneficiary's specific needs will be the same. UPIA 1 requires fiduciaries to invest and manage assets impartially between all beneficiaries. A fiduciary may consider other resources beneficiaries have when constructing the overall portfolio. But, the "duty to remain impartial" is to guide fiduciaries when considering conflicts between beneficiaries wishing income and beneficiaries wishing capital appreciation.

¶ 21,708

[¶ 21,715]

b.   *Uniform Principal and Income Act*

The Uniform Principal and Income Act ("UPIA 2") applies to both new and existing trusts. Like UPIA 1, UPIA 2 contains "default rules", which can be overridden by specific terms of a trust.

UPIA 2 provides guidance as to the allocation of expenses. Certain fees and expenses are required to be allocated equally against income and principal rather than the old standard of "just and equitable." Trustee compensation is now apportioned one-half against principal and one-half against income. UPIA 2 provides that expenses from judicial proceedings, accountings, investment advisers, custodial services are also allocated equally against income and principal. Furthermore, ordinary expenses incurred for the administration, management, or preservation of trust property and the distribution of income apply to income. Expenses applied to principal include: principal payments on debt, title insurance premiums, environmental expenses; and transfer taxes; such as estate and inheritance.

In addition to guidance on allocation of expenses between income and principal, UPIA 2 provides trustees the "power to adjust" between income and principal. The power to adjust does not apply to probate estates. The power to adjust enlarges the trustee's ability to maximize a trust's <u>total</u> return through investing for growth as well as income. This increased power for fiduciaries facilitates the prudent investor standard in UPIA 1. As a result, a trustee can now allocate capital gain to income. For example, a fiduciary may invest in real estate, sell the real estate and allocate the proceeds to income. Therefore, UPIA 2 enhances a trustee's ability to meet the prudent investor standard in UPIA 1.

In order to adjust a trustee must meet three prerequisites:

1. Invest and manage trust assets pursuant to the prudent investor standard in UPIA 1;

2. The trust terms must describe the amount that may or must be distributed to a beneficiary by referring to the trust's income; and

3. After applying the rules of allocation of trust income and principal that control the trust, the trustee is not able act impartially among beneficiaries.

In addition to the prerequisites, a trustee must consider numerous other factors when adjusting, including: the nature and length of the trust; the settlor's intent; the beneficiaries' needs; the need for liquidity, income, appreciation, and preservation of assets; the relationship between the assets held in the trust and their relationship to the beneficiaries; the terms of the trust; economic conditions; and tax consequences.

The power to adjust may be extremely controversial between different beneficiaries. Later generational beneficiaries may wish proceeds from real estate sales applied to principal. Current income beneficiaries may have a totally different view. In order to meet the requirements of UPIA 2 and prepare for disgruntled beneficiaries fiduciaries should establish policies and

¶ 21,715

procedures to review trust assets and whether or not they can and should exercise the power to adjust. Clients need to be counseled on UPIA 2 and whether their trusts should or should not include specific language denying the power to adjust. If the trust instrument is silent, but the trustee believes one or more beneficiaries will object to the adjustment, UPIA 2 allows a trustee to petition the court for assistance.

I. INCENTIVE TRUSTS

[¶ 21,750]

For most will and trust makers, "distributive justice" is the norm, e.g., all children are treated alike. ¶ 3051. However, sometimes, behavior modification becomes an aspect of trust and will distribution planning. These instruments may well represent the donor's "last chance" to speak to the donee "one more time." More often that not it is about "I love you and only want what is best for you", something that "you too will appreciate if you only follow my advice" and "much as I regret having to do this, I am directing that trust distributions come to you only if you undertake the following [behavior modification, career path, education, etc.]." How effective do you think these last gasp efforts are in bringing about the requested course? See Joshua C. Tate, Conditional Love: Incentive Trusts and the Inflexibility Problem, 41 Real Prop. Prob. & T. J. 445 (2006).

J. FAMILIES, SITUS, TRANSPARENCY, AND FIDUCIARY LIABILITY

[¶ 21,800]

The casual observer, untrained as are most people, might be inclined to use the word "dysfunctional" in describing some of the families known to them. Appropriate or not, "everybody's got a story" and sometimes that story leads to litigation, particularly where both money and principle are important, a not uncommon situation when it comes to families. Resolution is easier when the only issue is money. In the meantime, the role of the fiduciary is made much more difficult and it is all too easy for the fiduciary to "forget" what it means to be a fiduciary. Obviously, in *McNeil*, the case that follows, family dynamics and values—a whole lifetime—were reflected in the judgments made by the parents about the children, rightly or wrongly, and the children took exception to those judgements. Wills and trusts are sometimes said to be the last opportunity for the parent to speak to the children, the last opportunity to say "you are not hearing me, let met try one more time, and this time I am going to speak to you through my property." It is a strong argument for family mediation. Family misunderstandings can come about solely because one or more members conclude that, "despite the fact that I love you, you are not hearing me." Mediation is likely successful when the parties have been able to tell their "story" to someone—the mediator—who listened and carried the message to the other parties. Barring that, the alternative is wills and trusts which provide unequal treatment of similarly situated loved ones all of which causes "hurt feelings", feelings redressed sometimes at the court house where all the parties can tell their story to the judge. How then does the fiduciary not be drawn in so as to "continue the hurt" by its administration of the will or trust? Transparency is key. Think in terms of the trust beneficiaries who do not know that they are trust beneficiaries, that have never seen the trust agreement, that are regularly "blown off" by the trustee. More importantly, should parents tell children the contents of wills and trusts? Or does "outing" the issue require more courage than most people possess?

Could some family controversy be avoided if professional advisors would counsel clients that speaking to children and other loved ones through wills and trusts and property dispositions might not have the desired effect? Or is the draftsperson's role simply one of writing down the client's wishes? Is there some obligation to test those expressions when a disposition is "unnatural"?

Finally, consider the relationship of a professional co-trustee to non professional family members who are also co-trustees. Shared liability? Greater burden, i.e, higher standard, on the professional co-trustee, meaning "the bank"?

Consider whether *McNeil*, might have been avoided by greater transparency? At the parent level? At the trust level? Consider what provisions, if any, could have given the trustee greater protection? What, if anything, could have been done by the parents who, after the trust became irrevocable, decided that one child was to be treated differently than his siblings? Is this all about saving the beneficiaries from themselves? Is it possible to put "discretion" back into "discretion" so as to protect the trustees and contemplate changed circumstances?

Several states, e.g., New York (N.Y. Est. Powers & Trusts Law § 10–6.6(b) (McKinney 2001)); Alaska (Alaska Stat. § 13.36.157 (2004)); Delaware (Del. Code Ann. tit. 12, § 3528 (Supp. 2004)); and Tennessee (Tenn. Code Ann. § 35–15–816(b)(27) (LexisNexis Supp. 2005)), will allow a trustee, who has absolute discretion, to make distributions of trust assets from one trust to a new trust—perhaps one with more provisions seen as more to the liking of some, if not all, of the beneficiaries. Alan Halperin & Michelle R. Wandler, Decanting Discretionary Trusts: State Law and Tax Considerations, 29 Tax Mgm't Est. Gifts & Tr. J. 219 (2004). This might well be a helpful solution to conflict—although it might well provoke more of it (as the disgruntled become even more disgruntled)!

[¶ 21,825]

McNEIL v. McNEIL
Supreme Court of Delaware, 2002.
798 A.2d 503.

WALSH, Justice.

This is an appeal from a decision of the Court of Chancery which determined that the trustees of a large *inter vivos* trust had breached their fiduciary duties by ignoring the interests of a beneficiary. By way of a remedy, the court ordered a make-up distribution to the petitioner, surcharged the trustees, and removed certain of the trustees. The court rejected the beneficiary's request to further divide the trust and prevent the adoption of a unitrust formula. Upon full review of the record, we conclude that the Vice Chancellor properly exercised his discretion under applicable trust law in granting relief to the beneficiary, except with respect to the replacement of a trustee. As to that latter ruling, we conclude that the trust instrument, in the first instance, controlled the process for replacement. Accordingly, we affirm in part and reverse in part.

I

* * *

The trust in dispute was one of five trusts established by Henry Slack McNeil, Sr. ("McNeil, Sr.") in 1959 from the proceeds of the sale of a pharmaceutical company owned by him to Johnson and Johnson. Four of the trusts, referred to as the "Sibling Trusts," were designated for the benefit of McNeil, Sr.'s four children: Henry, Jr. ("Hank"), Barbara, Marjorie, and Robert. The fifth trust, established by McNeil, Sr. for his wife, Lois, came to be known as the Lois Trust. Each of the separate children's trusts was intended to accommodate the needs of the respective beneficiary with authorization to the trustees to afford each the means to live an affluent lifestyle. The children were quite young at the time of the creation of the trusts, ranging in age from eight to fifteen. It was not until some years later that the trustees of the Sibling Trusts were called upon to provide the children an independent source of income.

Although the children were under the impression, an impression apparently fostered by their father, that their interests in the Lois Trust were that of remaindermen, the terms of the trust provided otherwise. The trust instrument gave its trustees considerable discretion to "distribute any part or all of the income and principal of the trust to or among my lineal descendants and their spouses, and Lois." Thus, all of McNeil, Sr.'s children, and their descendants, were not remaindermen but current beneficiaries. It was the lack of such knowledge and its unequal dissemination that is at the root of the litigation between Hank and the trustees, with Hank's siblings ("The Other Siblings") also joined as defendants.

The original trustees of the Lois Trust included three individuals, George Brodhead, Robert C. Fernley, and Henry W. Gadsden, as general trustees, and Wilmington Trust Company as the administrative trustee. Later, Gadsden and Fernley were replaced by Charles E. Mather, III, a close friend of McNeil, Sr., and Provident National Bank ("PNC"). There is little question that Brodhead, a close friend and attorney for McNeil, Sr., was the dominant trustee, to whom the other trustees, and all the siblings, deferred. There is also no doubt, however, that all trustees, including the administrative trustees, were aware that the McNeil siblings enjoyed the status of current beneficiaries of the Lois Trust.

At some point, Hank became estranged from his parents and his siblings. A direct result of this estrangement was that Hank received nothing under his father's will and, upon the later death of his mother, only two million dollars, a paltry sum in comparison to that received by his siblings. Hank was not without substantial wealth, however, since his own trust responded to many, but not all, of his requests for distribution. Eventually, Hank sued the trustees of his trust, who were essentially the same as the trustees of the Lois Trust, seeking a greater distribution. The trustees requested Hank's own children, Cameron and Justin, take a position on Hank's petition because, under a mirror image provision of the Lois Trust, Hank's children were also current beneficiaries. Thus, it could be argued that Hank's request for additional distributions was adverse to all of his living descendants. Prior to the trustees' notification, Cameron and Justin had been unaware of their status. The question of Hank's right to distribution under his trust, *vis-a-vis* the entitlement of his children to share a current distribution, ultimately resulted in separate litigation in the Court of Chancery.

Claiming to have been misled, if not deceived, by the trustees of the Lois Trust concerning his current beneficiary status, Hank filed a complaint in the Court of Chancery seeking, *inter alia,* a make-up distribution from the trust, removal of and a surcharge against the trustees, and a restructuring of the trust operation. In addition to the trustees, other interested parties joined, or were joined, in the litigation, including Hank's siblings, Cameron and Justin, and a guardian *ad litem* representing the unborn beneficiaries of the Lois Trust.

II

The Vice Chancellor ultimately concluded that Hank's "outsider" status, which began during his father's lifetime, was continued by the trustees of the Lois Trust. By contrast, however, The Other Siblings not only benefitted directly from their parents' estates, but were made privy to many aspects of the operation of all five trusts and, through their participation in a family holding company, Claneil Industries, were never "outside the loop." The Vice Chancellor further concluded that not only did the trustees rebuff Hank's efforts to learn the specifics of the Lois Trust, they acquiesced in Lois' wish, expressed strongly during her lifetime, not to invade principal. That principal consisted primarily of Johnson and Johnson stock and had appreciated substantially in value over the life of the trust [having a value of over $300 million]. The Other Siblings were content with Lois' direction to permit principal to grow but the matter came to a head upon Lois' death in 1998, when the trustees proposed to make distribution of the Lois Trust in four equal divisions. The trustees also sought to adopt a "unitrust" approach for distribution under which the beneficiaries would receive a percentage of the total value of the trust, both principal and income, each year.

After trial, the Vice Chancellor determined that the trustees had breached their fiduciary duties by failing to inform Hank of his current beneficiary

¶ **21,825**

status in a timely fashion, showing partiality to The Other Siblings, and allowing the trust to operate "on autopilot." Since the trustees had considerable distribution discretion, the court recognized that it was somewhat "speculative" to fashion a remedy for the failure of the trustees to respond to requests never made, particularly given Lois' strongly expressed desire to maintain the trust corpus. Nevertheless, the court concluded that any uncertainty with respect to the appropriateness of the remedy should be resolved against the trustees, who failed to fulfill their obligation to consider the interests of different generations of the McNeil Family. A make-up distribution equal to 7.5 percent of the value of Hank's resulting trust was ordered to be shared by Hank with Cameron and Justin under the unitrust formula.

The Vice Chancellor also determined that the trustees' failure to discharge their fiduciary duties warranted some penalty. In particular, he faulted the institutional trustees, PNC and Wilmington Trust, who "failed to bring their professional expertise to bear in assisting lay trustees." PNC was removed as a trustee and all Lois Trustees were surcharged one-fifth of commissions received for the years 1987 to 1996. The Vice Chancellor declined to remove certain other individual trustees but appointed Edward L. Bishop, one of Hank's trustees, as a replacement trustee for PNC for the resulting trusts.

III

The individual and corporate trustees of the Lois Trust, John C. Bennett, Jr., Charles E. Mather, III, PNC Bank, N.A. and Wilmington Trust Company (the "Lois Trustees") have appealed from that portion of the Vice Chancellor's decision imposing a surcharge on their trustees' commission and removing PNC as a trustee. While accepting the Vice Chancellor's factual findings, they nonetheless argue that those findings do not permit the conclusion that any breach of fiduciary duty owed to Hank occurred. They point to the language of the trust instrument, which confers on the trustees extraordinarily broad authority to manage the trusts, as indicative of McNeil, Sr.'s intention to protect the trustees from personal liability and "judicial second-guessing." The conduct of the Lois Trustees, it is contended, must be reviewed over the span of forty years, during which time they deferred to the wishes of McNeil, Sr. and his wife, and, as a consequence, the trust prospered and all beneficiaries, including Hank, ultimately benefitted.

* * *

The Lois Trustees rely upon the express terms of the trust instrument as defining their duties. Three provisions of the Lois Trust appear to bear on this issue. Article II(a) gives the trustees wide discretion to distribute income or principal to any, all, or none of the beneficiaries as they see fit. Statements of this type are generally viewed as a definition of the trustees' powers, not as exculpatory of the liability of a trustee. *See* George Gleason Bogert, The Law of Trusts and Trustees, § 542 (1993) ("The grant of absolute or uncontrolled discretion to the trustee in the administration of the trust, without an exculpatory clause, may not relieve the trustee of liability for imprudent exercises of his powers ..."). Further, Article III(e) of the Lois Trust

¶ 21,825

specifies, "Decisions by the committee [of trustees] . . . [are] not subject to review by any court." Courts, however, flatly refuse to enforce provisions relieving a trustee of all liability. *Id.* (noting that exculpatory clauses that "provide[ ] that the trustee is not to be accountable to anyone . . . [are] not upheld"). A trust in which there is no legally binding obligation on a trustee is a trust in name only and more in the nature of an absolute estate or fee simple grant of property.

Finally, Article IV(c) states, "Any action taken by the trustees in good faith shall be proper, and I relieve the trustees of all personal liability except for gross negligence or willful wrongdoing." Generally, a trustee must act as the reasonable and prudent person in managing the trust. Courts often permit the settlor of a trust to exculpate a trustee for failure to exercise due care, however, so long as such conduct does not rise to the level of gross negligence.

A reasonable construction of these provisions, read together, is that the Lois Trustees were exculpated for ordinary negligence, but not the duty to (i) inform beneficiaries or (ii) treat them impartially. The duties to furnish information and to act impartially are not subspecies of the duty of care, but separate duties. *See* Restatement (Second) of Trusts §§ 173, 174, and 183 (1959) (devoting separate sections to a trustee's duty of care, duty to furnish information, and duty to act impartially). Whatever may have been McNeil, Sr.'s intention in this regard, he did not expressly relieve the trustees of the duties which formed the basis for Hank's petition in the Court of Chancery.

There is ample record support for the Vice Chancellor's conclusion that the Lois Trustees violated their duty to provide information. It may be the case that McNeil, Sr. and Lois did not favor treating their offspring as current beneficiaries of the Lois Trust, and that it was defensible for some of the trustees who served later on to assume that notification had already been accomplished. Nevertheless, both PNC and Wilmington Trust, institutional trustees with policies of notification, should have known better. Moreover, Henry's repeated attempts to get information should have put the trustees on notice that he did not know he was a current beneficiary. A trustee has a duty to furnish information to a beneficiary upon reasonable request. Furthermore, even in the absence of a request for information, a trustee must communicate essential facts, such as the existence of the basic terms of the trust. That a person is a current beneficiary of a trust is indeed an essential fact.

The Lois Trustees, and Brodhead in particular, denied important information to Hank even after he made a reasonable request for information. PNC's representative rebuffed a similar request, and Wilmington Trust's representative even misled Henry by telling him he was a remainderman in the Lois Trust. The trustees each had a vested interest in the way they had been doing business, and giving Hank information would have forced them to re-examine that method. Although Brodhead obviously dominated the trustees and controlled their approach to Hank, each trustee was charged with an independent fiduciary obligation which did not permit them to defer to Brodhead's exclusionary views.

At the same time they were excluding Hank from knowledge of the terms of the trust and its operating results, the Lois Trustees shared that informa-

¶ 21,825

tion with The Other Siblings, albeit in an indirect fashion through their participation in Claneil. This partiality precluded Hank from making distribution demands under circumstances not shared by his siblings. The trustees' claim that they distributed tens of millions of dollars to Hank from his own trust is no defense to their blatant failure to inform him of his current beneficiary status in the Lois Trust. As the Vice Chancellor noted, Hank "was at an obvious informational disadvantage to his Siblings with regard to the Lois Trust." The record amply supports the Vice Chancellor's conclusion that the Lois Trustees failed to discharge the fiduciary duties owed to all beneficiaries of the trust. Accordingly, we affirm that ruling.

IV

A.   The Lois Trustees next contend that even if they were deficient in the discharge of their duties, the remedy ordered by the Court of Chancery was not proportionate to any harm done. In particular, they argue that in the absence of proof that the trust res has suffered a loss, there is no basis for an assessment of damages. In order to assess damages where none have been proved, the argument runs, a court must adopt a punitive rationale, an approach clearly not appropriate here where there has been no finding of malice or bad faith.

The Court of Chancery imposed a one-fifth surcharge against the trustees on commissions earned from 1987 to 1996, an amount which the court viewed as not "substantial." In view of our affirmance of the Vice Chancellor's findings of dereliction, we find no abuse of discretion in surcharging the trustees who had not "properly" rendered the service for which compensation was given. *See* Restatement (Second) of Trusts § 243, cmt. a (1959). The conduct in question was not isolated but resulted from a pattern of deception and neglect over a span of many years. Imposing a surcharge representing a mere fraction of the commission charged to the trust is not out of proportion and we affirm.

B.   The Lois Trustees, joined by The Other Siblings, also dispute the Court of Chancery's ordering a make-up distribution of 7.5 percent of the value of Hank's resulting trust, "as part of the equitable remedy for breaches of the Lois Trust." Although he did not file a cross appeal from this portion of the Court of Chancery decision, Hank questions the source of the make-up distribution, contending that the court should have assessed the entire Lois Trust, not merely his resulting trust.

The imposition of a make-up distribution as a partial remedy in this case is, to a certain degree, speculative because it assumes that (a) Hank would have requested distribution had he known his status as a current beneficiary and (b) the trustees would have granted his request, particularly in the absence of similar requests from his siblings. There is ample reason to believe that Hank would have satisfied the demand requirement since he was continually seeking additional distribution from his own trust. Whether the trustees would have honored Hank's request is open to question but any doubt in that regard must be resolved against the trustees whose conduct led to the litigation and ultimate resolution of Hank's entitlement. Given the

¶ 21,825

concerted efforts of the trustees over a long period of time to "wall-off" Hank from the operation of the trust they are ill-suited to complain about the discretionary remedy ordered here. In any event, the make-up distribution does not invade the resulting trusts of The Other Siblings and, in effect, simply provides for a partial distribution of funds to which Hank had, at least, an equitable claim in previous years. We find no abuse of discretion with respect to this aspect of the remedy. Finally, permitting Cameron and Justin to share in the make-up distribution is clearly consistent with the pattern approved in the companion litigation and was equally within the court's discretion.

V

We next address the contention of the guardian *ad litem* that the Vice Chancellor's approval of the plan to divide the Lois Trust into four resulting trusts should be reversed as contrary to the settlor's intent. The class for which the guardian *ad litem* appears consists of a projected 119 individuals, representing the anticipated descendants of McNeil, Sr. who will be living at the time the trust expires in 2060. The guardian *ad litem* complains that the Court of Chancery's approval of the plan of the trustees of the Lois Trust to divide that trust into four resulting trusts creates a "pour-over" effect for the benefit of the siblings and their living descendants to the possible detriment of future generations of lineal descendants for whom the Lois Trust would have been intact.

There is no dispute that the trustees have the power to divide the Lois Trust. Article II(a) of the trust confers on the trustees the authority to "distribute any part or all of the income and principal of the trust to or among [the settlor's] lineal descendants and their spouses, and Lois." Article II(b) allows the trustees to make such distribution either "outright to, or in trust for, any one or more of the class among which they may distribute." The trustees decision to pour-over the Lois Trust into four resulting trusts did not occur because the Court of Chancery ordered it done to remedy a perceived inequity in the trust operation. The division was the decision of the trustees, who, in effect, sought the approval of the Court of Chancery in the course of the litigation. Given the express authority conferred in the trust instrument, the Court of Chancery, or this Court on review, can disturb the trustees decision to divide the Lois Trust only if a division of the trust was unreasonable under the circumstances, *i.e.,* lacking a basis in prudence and care. 12 Del. C. § 3303 (stating provisions of trust instrument control absent wilful misconduct); Wilmington Trust Co. v. Coulter, 200 A.2d 441 (Del.1964).

The Vice Chancellor approved the division of the Lois Trust as a "rational reaction" to the differing needs and desires of four different families. We agree and further add that the division will also reduce the likelihood of dispute and litigation over claims of uneven distribution. The guardian *ad litem's* claim that the interests of future unborn beneficiaries might be at risk is not persuasive. His protest, though well intentioned, is premature. The trustees are vested with broad discretionary powers of distribution and should they exercise this power improperly in the future, redress is available, as this litigation attests. Finally, given the large size of the resulting trusts, and the unitrust distribution plan discussed hereafter, it does not appear likely that there will be a dissipation of the corpus to the detriment of unborn lineal descendants.

VI

Hank has cross-appealed from the Vice Chancellor's approval of the Lois Trustees' adoption of the Unitrust Policy, under which the trustees proposed to treat 5 percent of the trust principal as distributable on an annual basis. Hank argues that the unitrust approach is not a satisfactory substitute for the broad discretion enjoyed by the trustees to invade principal to meet the reasonable demands of the beneficiaries, himself included.

The unitrust approach is designed to preserve principal by establishing a fixed and ascertainable pay out while at the same time broadening the source of distribution in periods, as at present, when income, particularly dividends, are of minor significance in measuring the growth of an equities-based trust. The Vice Chancellor approved the unitrust policy as within the discretion of the trustees in order to place the beneficiaries on notice of what distributions were available (approximately $4 million dollars annually per branch) and to encourage them to plan for such an allowance. Moreover, as the Court noted, the unitrust approach is merely a policy for distribution. The trustees continue to have the authority to invade principal to accommodate any unusual needs. We agree and add that along with the adoption of the pour-over separate trusts, the unitrust policy may also serve to redress the uncertainty and potential for friction between beneficiaries which engenders litigation. We find no basis to disturb the Vice Chancellor's approval of the unitrust.

VII

A. Perhaps the most contentious issue in this appeal, and one which has placed the disputants in odd alignment, is the disagreement over the Vice Chancellor's removal and/or replacement of trustees charged with administering the separate resulting trusts. We review that ruling under an abuse of discretion standard but only to the extent the Court of Chancery had full authority to select new trustees. The Lois Trustees, joined by Cameron and Justin, argue that the court should not have removed PNC. Hank supports the removal of PNC and defends the appointment of Bishop but complains that the court should also have removed Mather who participated equally in the trustees' misconduct. Cameron and Justin separately argue that the court lacked the authority to appoint Bishop to replace PNC.

The Court of Chancery has the power to remove a trustee as "ancillary to its duty to see that the trust is administered properly." In Re Catell's Estate, 38 A.2d 466, 469 (Del.Ch.1944). While that authority should "be exercised sparingly," the court enjoys the discretion to remove a trustee who fails to perform his duties through more than mere negligence. Id. at 470.

The Vice Chancellor removed PNC because it had failed in its fiduciary duties to Hank, both in its handling of his trust and as a trustee of the Lois Trust. The court felt so strongly about PNC's conduct that it suggested it also resign from Hank's trust. PNC violated its own administrative policies in failing to inform Hank that he was a current beneficiary of the Lois Trust and, in view of its role in disputing Hank's request for distribution from his own trust, it surely knew that Hank was keenly interested in securing additional distributions from any trust source. Moreover, PNC pointedly rebuffed the efforts of Hank's lawyer to gain information about the Lois Trust. Apart from the question of whether the trust, itself, was damaged by its action, PNC's studied course of conduct cannot be condoned and we find no abuse of discretion in its removal.

While removal of PNC as a trustee was clearly within the court's discretionary power, a different question arises with respect to its replacement of PNC as trustee with Edward Bishop. Cameron and Justin argue that the court's appointment of Bishop as a trustee of the Lois Trust exceeded the court's authority to the extent it contravened the intent of the settlor under the terms of the trust. This claim poses a legal question subject to *de novo* review.

Under Article III(c) of the Lois Trust, each trustee was given authority to name his own successor, and, in the event a trustee failed, or was unable to so designate, the remaining general trustees could fill the vacancies or increase or decrease the number of general trustees. PNC became a general trustee in 1978 when it was selected to replace Robert Fernley, who resigned. Unlike Wilmington Trust who functioned as an administrative trustee, PNC exercised full authority as a general trustee. Despite the explicit provisions of the trust instrument setting forth the mechanism for replacement of a trustee who resigns, or, as in this case, leaves involuntarily, the Court of Chancery did not seek the input of the trustees left in place, Mather and O'Malley, nor did it explain why it gave no consideration to the terms of the trust.

The Court of Chancery possesses undoubted authority to appoint a trustee if the trust instrument fails to do so. Where the terms of the trust provide a method for filling vacancies by some method other than by appointment of the court, however, the designated method of replacement should be followed. Scott on Trusts (Fourth ed.) § 388. Even when a court seeks to exercise its residual authority of appointment, it should do so "only in rare circumstances," since the identity and number of the trustees is central to the structure of the trust and a key indicator of the intent of the settlor. Schildberg v. Schildberg, 461 N.W.2d 186, 191 (Iowa 1990). See also Matter of Guardianship of Brown, 436 N.E.2d 877, 889 (Ind.App.1982) (holding court should defer to procedure prescribed in trust instrument "absent a showing that to do so would frustrate the purpose of the trust or be detrimental to the interests of the beneficiaries").

In selecting Bishop as a successor to PNC in the Lois Trust, the Vice Chancellor was apparently motivated by Bishop's compatibility with Hank in the operation of Hank's trust and the prospect that joint trusteeship would have some advantages. While these are worthwhile considerations, and perhaps entitled to deference were the Court of Chancery writing on a clean slate, they do not excuse disregard of the settlor's plan for replacement of trustees. In permitting Mather and O'Malley to remain as trustees, the Vice Chancellor recognized their suitability to discharge their duties as trustees.

¶ 21,825

The selection of a replacement trustee is a stipulated duty under the terms of the trust. The designation of replacement trustees is a matter for the settlor's determination in the first instance and, where that intention is expressed, should not be disregarded in the absence of compelling circumstances such as the unsuitability of a designated replacement. Accordingly, we reverse that portion of the Vice Chancellor's decision designating Bishop as a replacement for PNC in the resulting trusts and remand for further consideration on this issue, taking into account the settlor's intention.

B.   With respect to the Vice Chancellor's refusal to remove Mather, of which Hank complains, we defer to the Vice Chancellor's discretion. It is true that Mather was a trustee at the time Hank was misled by PNC and Wilmington Trust, but apparently Mather did not join in that deception. Moreover, as the Vice Chancellor noted, Mather was a layperson who relied upon the institutional trustees and Brodhead, who was a lawyer. Having observed Mather in two trials, the Vice Chancellor concluded that Mather acted in good faith with "sincere concern for all Family members." Given the Vice Chancellor's advantage of personal observation we are not inclined to disturb his judgment.

VIII

Finally, we find no abuse of discretion in the refusal of the Court of Chancery to require the Lois Trustees to pay Hank's legal fees and in permitting the trustees to be reimbursed for their fees from the Lois Trust.

The American rule, which is of general application, requires each side to bear the cost of its attorney's fees. The Court of Chancery may exercise its discretion to award attorneys' fees as an exception to this rule where a fund is created or, as here, the distribution of a trust is in dispute. Appropriate factors may include: (i) whether the trustees' breach of duty was fraudulent or in bad faith; (ii) the nature and extent of the wrongful conduct; and (iii) whether the action resulted in a benefit to the trust. Here, Henry's suit did not benefit the trust, only him. Although the extent of the breach was serious (and extended), the Court of Chancery specifically concluded that the trustees' actions were ill considered and wrong, but not in bad faith. Finally, the Court of Chancery observed that Hank was not successful in a significant portion of the claims he asserted in the litigation.

Although the Court of Chancery imposed a surcharge on the trustees, that fact alone does not preclude the recovery of counsel fees incurred in defending the litigation since success is not the test. Restatement (Second) of Torts, § 188 cmt. b (1959). Here, the Vice Chancellor, in the exercise of his discretion, concluded that the conduct of the Lois Trustees, particularly the individuals, did not warrant departure from the usual rule that trustees who defend litigation against the trust are entitled to look to the trust for reimbursement of that expense. We find no basis for disturbing that discretionary ruling.

IX

In sum, we affirm all rulings of the Court of Chancery which are the subject of the appeals and cross-appeals in this matter save one: the replace-

¶ 21,825

ment of PNC with Bishop. As to that ruling, we reverse and remand to the Court of Chancery for further proceedings consistent with this opinion.

K. LOCATION, LOCATION, LOCATION

[¶ 21,870]

A most important—in some instances, the most important determinant—to the success of the trust is situs, i.e., which law governs. Asset protection, the two UPIAs, elimination of the Rule Against Perpetuities, are only the beginning. State income taxes are another important determinant. While state income considerations may be said to being with choice of domicile—Florida and Texas are among the few states that do not have a state income tax—choice of trust situs is equally important. (While Delaware has a state income tax, it is not imposed on non resident trust beneficiaries.) For related material see ¶¶ 5600, 7478, 10,119, 10,205, 11,089, 18,067 (Delaware Tax Trap), and 21,315.

Delaware—and, aspirationally, Alaska (and others)—want to be known as trust friendly, thereby attracting trust business. Proud of a judicial structure—the Court of Chancery—staffed by experienced trust jurists and favorable state law, Delaware beckons, saying you will be advantaged to be part of our judicial system favorable to trusts, particularly dynastic trusts.

With the $2 million GST exemption (in 2006) shielding trust property in perpetuity—coupled with repeal of the, or a lengthened, Rule Against Perpetuities—the dynasty trust takes on added life (and makes use of the crystal ball even more important as settlors attempt to divine the future, the future being in trust in perpetuity). *Query:* Does a trust in perpetuity contravene any social objectives? Suppose, for example, $1 million is placed in trust for 75 years and that it enjoys a 5 percent rate of return after taxes. At the end of the period, the trust would have a value of roughly $39 million. That same $1, if given free of trust to successive generations of beneficiaries—who consumed none of it—but paid estate taxes of 45 percent every 25 years would have a value of roughly $6.5 million after 75 years. Dare more be said!

L. MARRIAGE, FREEDOM OF TESTATION, AND THE PRENUPTIAL AGREEMENT

[¶ 21,900]

Marriage has property law consequences. Married persons are able to split their income, thus spreading it over two people, and enjoy, in some but not all instances (by any means) a lower total income tax bill. § 1(a). Both lifetime and deathtime transfers are free of gift and estate taxes if made in a qualifying way. §§ 2523, 2056. See Chapter 14. However, with these sometimes elusive benefits comes spousal protection statutes giving the other spouse veto power over disposition of part of all of the other spouse's property. Marry, drop dead in the euphoria surrounding the wedding, and

¶ 21,900

your newly acquired spouse—the "surviving spouse", if you will—may well get a minimum of half of your property even against a will whereby you give your property to your grandmother or your children. See ¶ 4651–4667; Terry L. Turnipseed, Why Shouldn't I Be Allowed To Leave My Property to Whomever I Choose At My Death? (Or How I Learned To Stop Worrying and Start Loving The French), 44 U. Louisville L.J. 737 (2006)). Marry, soon after drop dead, and federal law gives your surviving spouse a lifetime annuity in your tax qualified retirement plan. § 417(a)(2); ¶ 29,135. For related discussion as to community property, see ¶¶ 4675, 11,089–11,201.

There are many compelling advantages to marriage, including the traditional ones. But marriage has consequences and some forethought will suggest the use of prenuptial agreements (although such agreements may not frustrate a surviving spouse's claim to the spousal annuity in a tax qualified retirement plan such as a 401(k)). See ¶ 29,541. Key to any hopes of a successful prenuptial agreement is that both parties make full disclosure of their property—after all they stand in a relationship of trust and confidence to one another—and that the agreement is understandingly made by both parties (meaning that both parties have independent legal counsel). Unif. Premarital Agreement Act § 6(a), 9C U.L.A. 48–49 (2001). For related discussion, see ¶ 11,201.

Children? They can be disinherited effectively and easily. By will? That is, can a will be bullet proofed against a will contest? Not with certitude. What about a trust? More so, perhaps. Think of the game of baseball and a pitcher who throws a really fast "fast ball." It has been said that "You can't hit it if you can't see it." Perhaps the same is true of the inter vivos trust, i.e., a free standing trust in the sense that it is not part of the will and, thus, absent special circumstances, is not a public document (unless made so as part of a court proceeding). For related discussion, see ¶¶ 4601, 4651–4667.

M. SPECIAL NEEDS TRUSTS

[¶ 21,930]

FLEMING & CURTI, P.L.C., IN WHICH WE TACKLE A READER'S QUESTIONS ABOUT SPECIAL NEEDS TRUSTS

13 Elder Law Issues No. 9, www.elder-law.com/2005/1309/html (August 29, 2005).

Would you advise the formation of a special needs trust for a developmentally disabled son?

Absolutely. That is the exact circumstance in which a special needs trust is best used. When you leave your assets to such a trust for your son, daughter or other beneficiary with a disability, the particular kind of special needs trust you create is usually called a "third party" trust. That kind of trust usually can have very generous rules and still retain your child's eligibility for Medicaid, SSI and other benefits.

Leaving a portion of your estate outright to a child with disabilities can actually make things more difficult for them. In many communities the services available to public benefits recipients are more diverse, better coordinated and often more appropriate than similar services that could be purchased with your child's outright inheritance. In addition, failure to create a special needs trust can force your child into the legal system, where the courts will appoint a guardian and/or conservator, and insist on carefully monitoring the use of funds for his or her benefit. While that may sound like a good thing, it is almost always expensive, invasive and ultimately unsatisfactory—particularly if there is a suitable person to act as trustee of the special needs trust.

Is it safe to create a Special Needs Trust while we are still living, as laws seem to change?

Yes, for two reasons. First, though there have been changes to the law (and more are expected), none of the changes seriously discussed will make special needs trusts obsolete. Second, and more importantly for your circumstance, most of the changes we are likely to see will focus on trusts created from the money belonging to the person with disabilities. In other words, failure to create a special needs trust while you are still alive will likely subject your child to more changes in benefits and the law of trusts.

Besides, we routinely provide for amendment of special needs trusts to accommodate changes in the law. While the issue is complex, it is too important to shrug your shoulders and say "you can't fight city hall." In fact, special needs trusts can be very flexible and effective—and they are, every day, in every community.

Is there a simple way to create such a trust?

Yes, there is. But this kind of trust really should be established by someone who really knows how the benefits system works. You might check out the website of the Special Needs Alliance at www.specialneedsalliance. com; its members are committed to keeping abreast of changing benefits rules, and are experienced at establishing special needs trusts and advising trustees.

Should the special needs trust be funded by assets that we gift now, or should we leave the trust as a beneficiary of our estate?

Although opinions reasonably differ, at this point we recommend creating your special needs trust as a separate entity and "funding" it (that is, transferring at least some assets into its name) now. That gives you a chance to see how much trouble the trust administration will really be, so that you can determine whether your chosen trustee is up to the task. It will also give you a chance to submit the trust to Social Security, Medicaid and other service providers; it is better to find out if eligibility workers will need to be brought up to speed when there is $3,000 in the trust than later, when it has inherited a share of your estate and you are no longer around to make changes. The trust can then be named as beneficiary of a share of your estate, so that the bulk of its assets are received after your death.

¶ **21,930**

N. MEDICAID QUALIFICATION

[¶ 21,960]

While the picture might not be flattering, all too many clients ask about how Mom can qualify for government supported health care "because Mom does not want to spend all her money and not have anything left for the kids" or some such! Sometimes the question is asked about asset transfers so that "we can get Mom eligible." Is that ethical?

FLEMING & CURTI, P.L.C., LEGAL Q & A: *WHAT IS MEDICAID?*

www.elder-law.com (September 18, 2006).

Medicaid is a health care program for the poor. It is authorized and partially funded by federal law, but administered by each state. Federal regulations sometimes limit states and frequently require minimum standards, but much of the implementation of the program is left to each state.

What is AHCCCS?

Arizona was the last state to adopt a Medicaid program. Concern about rising health care costs and the perception of widespread waste and abuse in Medicaid led Arizona's legislature to create the first managed-care Medicaid program in the country. The Arizona program has been called the Arizona Health Care Cost Containment System (or AHCCCS) since its inception. A key element of the AHCCCS program can be understood from its name: Arizona's approach has focused on containing the cost of Medicaid at least as much as on providing complete or quality care. Although the AHCCCS program was unique when created, it now represents a mainstream approach to Medicaid administration. Most AHCCCS rules will be similar to the rules for Medicaid programs in other states, though the answers to these questions have not been modified to reflect the laws, rules or practices in states other than Arizona.

What is ALTCS?

The AHCCCS program initially did not provide for (among other groups) impoverished individuals in nursing homes. Beginning in 1989 the federal government required AHCCCS to provide care to those populations not previously covered. The administrative entity created to handle the long term care component of AHCCCS is called the Arizona Long Term Care System, or ALTCS. For most purposes, ALTCS, AHCCCS and Medicaid are interchangeable terms, at least when referring to institutionalized patients. As with AHCCCS itself, most of the regulations governing the ALTCS program are set by federal law, and so residents of other states will see similar issues. The difference between states, however, can be both subtle and profound; the questions and answers here are specifically tailored to Arizona law and practice, and the answer to any given question may not be the same in another state.

¶ 21,960

What is the difference between Medicaid and Medicare?

Medicare is a purely federal program of health insurance for the elderly, blind and disabled. In order to receive Medicare benefits an individual must meet one of those categories AND have sufficient work history to qualify for Medicare coverage. Medicaid, although it is designed to benefit the same groups (the elderly, blind and disabled), is a welfare program and is available only to those who have insufficient assets or income to pay for their own care. Though it is fairly uncommon, some individuals will qualify for both Medicare and Medicaid benefits simultaneously. Generally speaking, Medicare's benefits are much more generous in home care, hospice and outpatient care, while Medicaid covers prescription drugs (Medicare's "Part D" coverage requires co-payments and premiums) and long term care (Medicare's benefit is very limited).

What benefits does Medicaid provide?

Medicaid benefits can be divided into two broad categories: acute care and long term care (there are also separate program rules for the developmentally disabled and the seriously mentally ill, but they are beyond the scope of this FAQ). Eligibility for each kind of benefit is different, though they are similar. One key difference: in Arizona (this rule is not the same in most other states) acute care AHCCCS eligibility is based only on income—available resources will not prevent general AHCCCS coverage. Eligibility for ALTCS, the long term care benefit, is usually much more difficult to establish, and is the focus of most Medicaid planning and advocacy work by elder law attorneys.

Does ALTCS/Medicaid pay for nursing home care?

Yes, ALTCS pays for nursing home care. In fact, the Medicaid program nationwide pays for over half of all nursing home costs (the next largest share comes from the personal income and savings of the nursing home residents). ALTCS is simply the Arizona program which handles those payments.

Will ALTCS/Medicaid provide care at home or in other settings?

Yes. In fact, about half of all recipients of ALTCS services in Southern Arizona now receive their services in settings other than a nursing home. Home care, adult care homes (also known as adult foster care) and assisted living have all benefited from this increase in non-institutional care, but the total amount of care provided to each individual outside the nursing home is much less than that provided to comparable individuals in institutions.

Does Medicaid cover prescription medications?

Yes, the Medicaid program pays for all prescription drugs. AHCCCS/Medicaid beneficiaries may receive their drugs through Medicare's Part D program, but the premiums and co-payments are paid by Medicaid.

Does the ALTCS/Medicaid recipient have to pay for any portion of his or her care?

An acute care patient covered by AHCCCS will not be required to contribute to his or her medical care (though some items may not be covered,

¶ 21,960

requiring the patient to pay privately if he or she wants those particular items). The long term care component of AHCCCS, however, works differently. ALTCS does impose a "share of cost" calculation on long term care recipients. The patient's ability to contribute to care will be determined by a formula, and that amount must be turned over to the nursing home each month. ALTCS is a subsidized long term care benefit, rather than being provided outright.

Will ALTCS place a lien against a recipient's home or property?

Arizona has now adopted a legal mechanism for imposing liens against homes in most cases. Those liens may not be enforceable, and ALTCS may forego placing a lien or release the lien if provided with information indicating that the lien was not a legally available option. Perhaps more importantly (in most cases), on an ALTCS patient's death the state will have a claim for reimbursement which it can assert against the recipient's estate; if the ALTCS recipient owned a home which must go through the probate process to be transferred to successors, the ALTCS claim will need to be dealt with (and usually paid off) before heirs receive any portion of the home or estate. ALTCS may even pursue its claim against the patient's home if it was transferred outside the probate process, though the agency's recent practice in this area is inconsistent.

If the ALTCS recipient has (or is survived by) a spouse, a dependent minor child, or a disabled child, ALTCS is not permitted to enforce its lien or pursue any claim against the recipient's estate. This is true even though the home may not have been left to the spouse or disabled child. Unfortunately, it often requires legal counsel and intervention to secure protection of the home in such circumstances.

Must an applicant's home be sold to qualify for ALTCS/Medicaid?

No. An ALTCS recipient is entitled to retain his or her home, so long as he or she intends to return home. The intent to return home is established by simply checking the appropriate space on the ALTCS application, so only the uninformed are confronted with having to dispose of their homes in order to receive benefits. And if the ALTCS recipient has a spouse or disabled child living in the home, it is not even necessary to check the appropriate box on the application form. None of this guarantees the security of the home; the ALTCS beneficiary may not be permitted to retain enough income to pay for upkeep, repairs or even taxes on the home, and the state may have a claim for reimbursement after his or her death. Still, it can be of considerable comfort to an ALTCS applicant (and his or her spouse) to know that neither ALTCS nor the nursing home can compel the sale of the recipient's home in order to qualify for benefits.

Is there any limit on the value of the home excluded from calculation of eligibility?

Yes. A home with a net equity (after deducting mortgage and other encumbrances) over $500,000 (some states, but not Arizona, increase that

¶ 21,960

figure up to as high as $750,000) will not be an exempt resource. For these purposes, your home is valued at the County appraiser's assessed valuation.

What other assets can an ALTCS/Medicaid recipient retain?

In addition to the home, an ALTCS recipient is also permitted to retain an automobile (without any limitation on its value), household furniture and furnishings, prepaid funeral/burial benefits and a few other items. Other than those categories, an unmarried applicant's total assets must be reduced to $2,000 in value.

What assets can a married couple retain and still have one spouse qualify for ALTCS/Medicaid benefits?

The rules are much more complicated for a married couple where only one spouse will be institutionalized (they become simple again—and very unforgiving—if both spouses are institutionalized). All assets available to either spouse (for these purposes, community property and other ownership rules are not considered) are added up, and the total divided in half. Total assets must then be reduced to the one-half figure (plus the $2,000 exemption available to an unmarried ALTCS applicant) before either spouse can qualify for ALTCS. To further complicate the calculation, the one-half figure is limited to a maximum of about $100,000 (the precise figure changes each year). There is also a minimum amount which can be retained, regardless of the total of available resources (about $20,000). These concepts, incidentally, are among the most variable from state to state—the Arizona approach may not apply in another state.

What is the CSRA (or CSRD)?

The calculation of half of a married couple's available resources as described in the previous section is often referred to as the "snapshot" amount (since it is based on a "snapshot" of the assets as of the time of institutionalization). Its formal name is the Community Spouse Resource Allowance—the CSRA (or, in Arizona, the Community Spouse Resource Deduction or CSRD).

How much income can an ALTCS/Medicaid recipient have?

As with the calculation of the CSRA/CSRD, income rules are different in other states. Unlike the asset calculation method, however, there are really only two variations. Some states, like Arizona, apply an income limitation on Medicaid long term care eligibility. About half of the states have an "income cap." Arizona's, like that in most states with an income cap, is set at 300% of the maximum federal SSI benefit. That means that an individual with gross income over about $1800 per month will not qualify for ALTCS (though it turns out that it is usually easy to overcome this limitation—see below).

What can an ALTCS/Medicaid applicant do if he or she has too much income to qualify for benefits?

An ALTCS applicant who has income over the "income cap" figure can benefit from an Income Cap Trust—usually referred to as a *"Miller"* trust

¶ 21,960

after the name of the Colorado case establishing the concept. [Miller v. Ibarra, 746 F.Supp. 19 (D.Colo.1990—Ed.] The rules governing *Miller* trusts are unnecessarily complex, but the result is simple: the applicant can qualify for ALTCS after the trust is properly established. *Miller* trusts are almost always a complete solution to the income cap problem, and only the uninformed need worry about being denied ALTCS eligibility for excess income. This does not mean, incidentally, that anyone contemplating long term care expenses should go ahead and establish a *Miller* trust just in case—there is no need to create the *Miller* trust in advance, and no benefit to creating one at all for those who do not have income above the monthly threshold amount.

How much of his or her income can an ALTCS/Medicaid recipient retain?

As previously noted, ALTCS requires the recipient to contribute to his or her own cost of care. The amount contributed is called the "share of cost," and calculating it is usually simple for a single person on ALTCS. The recipient is entitled to retain a monthly "personal needs allowance" amount fixed at 15% of the maximum federal SSI benefit (that means he or she keeps a little more than $90 per month), and all remaining income must be paid to the facility. If a recipient remains at home, there is no share of cost unless a *Miller* Trust is in place. The share of cost calculation does not consider the ALTCS beneficiary's other bills, even including child support, spousal mainte-nance or other court-ordered amounts.

How much income can a married couple have and still qualify for ALTCS/Medicaid benefits?

As explained above, a single ALTCS applicant may have a little more than $1800 per month in income. If the applicant is married, the calculation is somewhat more complicated. The total gross income of the applicant is looked at first. If the applicant's income is below the income cap threshold then the applicant qualifies regardless of the amount of income the spouse receives. If the applicant's income exceeds that level ALTCS will look at the total income of both spouses. If the couple's combined income is less than twice the income cap figure, the applicant will qualify under the income standard. Once again, this calculation method varies somewhat from state to state; only Arizona's method is described here.

How much of a couple's income can be retained by the spouse who does not receive ALTCS/Medicaid benefits?

In addition to the personal needs allowance explained above, the ALTCS recipient's spouse may be entitled to keep some or all of the applicant's income to pay for his or her living expenses. The calculation of this amount, referred to as the Minimum Monthly Maintenance Needs Allowance, is complicated and will vary significantly in individual cases. One piece of simple (and good) news: the community spouse is not required to contribute any portion of the income in his or her name alone toward the "share of cost."

What is meant by the "lookback" period for ALTCS/Medicaid benefits?

When an ALTCS application is filed, eligibility workers will inquire about any gifts made by the applicant, the applicant's spouse or anyone acting on behalf of either of them within the preceding 60 months. This pre-application timeframe is known as the "lookback" period—gifts made before that period will not affect eligibility. Gifts made during the "lookback" period will result in a period of ineligibility, and that disqualifying period will not start to run until the applicant has already spent down all of his or her assets and applied for ALTCS.

Can someone receive ALTCS/Medicaid benefits even if they have made gifts during the preceding five years?

If gifts have been made during the "lookback" period, the applicant will be ineligible for a number of months calculated from the date of application (NOT from the date of the gift). The ineligibility period is determined by dividing the value of the gift by a number intended to approximate the monthly cost of long term care in the community. That figure in Arizona depends on the county of residence and changes each year. The actual application of this penalty period is further complicated by multiple gifts, return of some or all of a gift and other factors; this overview must be reviewed with caution. As with many of the other principles described in this FAQ, the precise application of this calculation varies from state to state, and only Arizona calculations are explained here.

Can an ALTCS/Medicaid applicant purchase a new home, car, home furnishings or prepaid burial arrangements?

Yes. Available resources can easily be made unavailable by purchasing exempt assets. Of course, the applicant may then have difficulty paying the upkeep on a larger home, for example. Furthermore, the estate recovery program will result in the larger home being sold and the proceeds repaid to the ALTCS program in many cases. In other words, though eligibility may be easy to establish there may be additional problems with this simple approach. In some cases, however, such purchases can be very effective in establishing ALTCS/Medicaid eligibility.

How can annuities benefit ALTCS/Medicaid recipients?

In some limited circumstances (usually involving married couples), purchase of a commercial single-premium, immediate annuity may allow an ALTCS applicant to qualify for benefits more quickly. The effect of annuity planning can be dramatically beneficial, but depends entirely on the specific facts of each situation. Arizona's ALTCS program does not permit the same favorable treatment for annuities created by private parties (children, for instance), annuities with lump-sum payouts, or annuities that can be converted to cash—even if a penalty is imposed. Annuity planning should be undertaken only with expert advice.

What other eligibility requirements are there for ALTCS/Medicaid benefits?

In addition to the financial eligibility rules described above, an ALTCS applicant must meet three other eligibility standards:

¶ 21,960

- He or she must be a U.S. citizen or a qualified alien
- He or she must be a resident of Arizona (this requirement is easy to meet, however, since it requires only that the applicant be physically present in Arizona and not have any intent to leave)
- He or she must need skilled nursing care (this is determined by evaluating the applicant's medical chart as part of the PAS—the Pre–Admission Screening)

Chapter 22

GRANTOR TRUSTS: TRAPS
AND OPPORTUNITIES

A. OBJECTIVES

[¶ 22,001]

Many taxpayers look for techniques that will shrink their estates for purposes of estate tax liability. These same taxpayers, as well as others who need not be concerned about estate tax liability, often look for methods of deflecting some of their income to others within the family unit. Many such persons are in relatively high income tax brackets, while other members of the family unit, such as elderly parents and minor offspring, are in relatively low brackets.

Long ago, the Supreme Court determined that income derived from the sale of labor will be income to the person whose labor is sold. Similarly, income from property will be taxed to the person whose property produced the income. Accordingly, income deflection schemes must involve a transfer of the tree if the fruit is to be taxed to another.

While many taxpayers will freely shift income to others within the family unit, many of these same taxpayers want to control not only the tree which produces that fruit but also the enjoyment of the income. Given these constraints, income deflection schemes are severely limited. Clearly, an outright gift of the income-producing property is unacceptable because such a transfer affords control of neither the tree nor the fruit. The alternative, then, is to use a trust. Obviously the transferor would be most comfortable if he or she were the trustee; distributions were to be made only with his or her approval; and the trust income was taxed to the trust beneficiary!

One purpose of this chapter is to consider how much control the transferor can retain over the transferred property, yet cause the income from the property to be taxed to someone else. Similarly, considered here in part (and in part in Chapter 18) are the rules applicable in determining the circumstances under which trust income will be taxed to a nongrantor, i.e., to a person who is neither the transferor of the property giving rise to the income nor the recipient of the trust income. The applicable income tax rules are set forth in §§ 671–678 of the Internal Revenue Code. These rules, referred to as the grantor trust rules, have particular bearing on the trust arrangements discussed in Chapters 18, 19, and 20.

The other purpose of this chapter would appear to be a contradiction. It is to consider how little control the transferor can retain over the transferred property, yet be taxed on the trust income! While the gift tax is said to have been made necessary to discourage arrangements whose primary purpose was income tax shifting within family units, there is a lack of coordination between the estate tax and the income tax. That lack of coordination results in an opportunity to lower total taxes by creating trusts that are free of estate tax at the

> "The repeated initiatives of the Service (and other protectors of the fisc) to prevent the use of trusts for tax avoidance have evolved so that those initiatives have been converted into a road map for tax avoidance. The key to understanding the current state of affairs is the lack of conformity between income tax and estate tax rules. Indeed, from the very beginnings of the estate tax, the income tax and the estate tax have been marching to the beat of different drummers." John B. Huffaker and Edward Kessel, How the Disconnect Between the Income and Estate Tax Rules Created Planning for Grantor Trusts, 100 J. TAX'N 206 (2004).

transferor's death but taxable to the transferor for income taxes during the transferor's life. Thus, the intentionally defective grantor trust! Surprise. As discussed at ¶ 19,801, the IDGT is seen as a planning opportunity.

B.   HISTORICAL PERSPECTIVE

[¶ 22,051]

1.   HELVERING v. CLIFFORD

The landmark Supreme Court decision of Helvering v. Clifford, 309 U.S. 331 (1940), taxed the income of a short-term (five-year) trust to the person who established the trust (the "grantor"), even though that person had not received the trust income. The Court reasoned that the settlor had retained so large a bundle of rights that he was held to be the owner of the trust. Besides being the trustee, he had sole discretion over the amount of income to be distributed and broad powers over corpus. While the Court set out general principles to be applied in determining when trust income would be taxed to the grantor of the trust, it invited the Treasury to supply more precise standards for taxing settlors in similar cases.

[¶ 22,059]

2.   THE *MALLINCKRODT* CASE AND § 678

In Mallinckrodt v. Nunan, 146 F.2d 1 (8th Cir.1945), cert. denied, 324 U.S. 871, the taxpayer was the beneficiary of a trust over which he was held to have rights and powers no less substantial than those possessed by the settlor in *Clifford*. The court held that the trust income was taxable to the beneficiary as the true owner on the theory that he had command of it even though that beneficiary did not receive the income.

[¶ 22,067]

3.   THE *CLIFFORD* AND *MALLINCKRODT* REGULATIONS

In 1946, the Treasury attempted to set definite standards in the grantor trust field, promulgating what became known as the *Clifford* and *Mallinck-*

rodt Regulations. Based on the cases of the same names, the regulations departed from the ordinary rules of taxing trusts on the theory that to apply them would probably permit the settlor or other person with substantial ownership of corpus or income to escape tax on income which should rightfully be taxed to him or her. They incorporated some of the judicial rules which had been evolved in applying the definition of gross income as income derived from property ownership where the grantor or other person was found to possess such a bundle of rights with respect to a trust as to make the grantor or other person in substance its owner. But the *Clifford* bundle-of-rights test was replaced by independent standards, since the use of combinations of factors of control to impose taxability would have led to very complicated provisions. If a trust failed to meet any one of the separate and independent tests, income was taxed to the settlor or other person who was deemed to have substantial ownership of it. Also, all trusts reverting to the settlor within 10 or (in some cases) 15 years were taxed to the settlor where the settlor retained certain controls.

When the 1954 Code was being drafted, Congress decided to codify the grantor trust rules, rather than leave them to regulations. In addition to incorporating the 1939 Code provisions dealing with revocable trusts and trusts whose income is for the grantor's benefit, Congress generally adopted the approach of the *Clifford* and *Mallinckrodt* Regulations, with certain modifications.

C. OPERATION OF THE GRANTOR TRUST RULES

[¶ 22,101]

The effect of the grantor trust rules is simple. If, under the rules, the grantor (settlor) of the trust is deemed to be the "owner" of the trust, the income from that trust will be taxed to the grantor of the trust rather than to the trust or to the beneficiary of the trust. Note that the income will be taxed to the grantor in such cases even though the grantor never received it! The question, then, is to determine when the grantor of the trust should be deemed to be the "owner" of the trust.

Similarly, in the case of nongrantors, the question is to determine when someone other than the grantor of the trust should be deemed to be the "owner" of the trust for purposes of taxing the income of the trust to this nongrantor even though the nongrantor never receives it!

Sections 671–679 deal with three different types of trusts under which settlors and other persons are treated as owners for income tax purposes.

[¶ 22,109]

1. GRANTOR TRUSTS

A grantor trust is a trust over which the settlor has retained certain powers or interests, as described in §§ 672–677. As a result of retaining one or more of these, the settlor is considered to have dominion and control over the trust and is treated as the owner of either all or a portion of it.

¶ 22,109

The consequences to the settlor of being treated as the owner is that the settlor is required by § 671 to include, in computing his or her taxable income and credits, those items of income, deductions and credits against the tax of the trust (which are attributable to that portion of the trust of which the settlor is treated as the owner) to the extent that these items would be taken into account in computing an individual's taxable income or credits. But this is to be done only as specified in §§ 671–677. Any portion of the trust not affected by §§ 671–677 is taxable under the usual rules of trust taxation. See Chapter 8.

[¶ 22,117]

2. NONGRANTOR TRUSTS

A nongrantor trust is the term used here for a trust, part or all of which is treated as being owned in substance by a person other than the settlor. The nongrantor is treated as the owner of the trust in the circumstances described by § 678, meaning that § 678 sets out the circumstances in which someone other than the grantor of the trust will be taxed on the trust income *even though the other person did not receive that income.* In other words, oftentimes the nongrantor who is deemed to be the owner of the trust under § 678 (and taxed on the trust income) is not a beneficiary of the trust. Practically speaking, this means that the trust income could be taxed to the beneficiary of an accumulating trust, the trustee (even though there were no distributions made from the trust), the nongrantor parent of a minor beneficiary, or the holder of a power to appoint corpus. For a detailed discussion, see ¶ 18,263, 19,539, 19,563, and 20,755.

One qualification should be noted. Section 678 does not apply if the settlor is treated as an owner under §§ 671–677, meaning that if the trust income is taxed to the grantor, it will not be taxed to the nongrantor no matter what power the nongrantor has over the trust.

[¶ 22,125]

3. FOREIGN TRUSTS

A United States citizen who transfers property to a foreign trust with a United States beneficiary is treated as the owner of that trust under § 679. This provision, in combination with other provisions changing the tax rules applicable to foreign trusts, their settlors and beneficiaries is aimed at discouraging (if not eliminating entirely) the use of these trusts as tax avoidance devices. Treatment of the esoteric subject of foreign trusts is beyond that scope of this volume.

D. RELATIONSHIP OF INCOME, GIFT, AND ESTATE TAX RULES

[¶ 22,151]

1. RESULTS OF INCOMPLETE TRANSFERS UNDER THE INCOME, GIFT, AND ESTATE TAXES

The retention of some of the powers or interests enumerated in §§ 672–677, or of other powers or interests, may cause the creation of a trust to be treated as an incomplete transfer from the standpoint of the imposition of the gift and estate tax on the settlor or his or her estate. See Chapter 10.

[¶ 22,159]

2. TIME FOR TESTING A POWER

Since the income, gift and estate tax consequences of the rules dealing with retained powers and interests in trusts are usually determined at different times, the result under each of these three taxes will depend upon the status of the power at the date it needs to be tested.

For income tax purposes, retained powers which give a settlor dominion and control over a trust must be *looked at each year* in the light of §§ 672–677. Similarly, powers granted to someone other than a settlor must be tested annually against § 678. Should any of these provisions apply to the trust, § 671 will cause the settlor (or nongrantor) to be taxable on trust income as the owner rather than as the beneficiary. Thus, the settlor will report each item of income, deduction, and credit on his or her individual tax return as though the trust did not exist. Reg. § 1.671–4(b). (In such cases, a fiduciary income tax return is filed, the fiduciary return reporting that the trust is a grantor trust and the items of income and expense experienced by the trust are reported on the settlor's (or nongrantor's) individual return.)

The estate and gift tax rules relating to incomplete transfers in trust, contained in §§ 2036–2038 and the regulations, rulings and case law interpreting them, were developed in response to landmark estate and gift tax cases decided in the 1920s and 1930s. In contrast to the annual test for income tax purposes, whether a power causes a transfer to be incomplete for gift tax purposes is determined at the time of the gift and whether a transfer is incomplete for estate tax purposes is determined at the time of death. See §§ 2033, 2036, 2037, 2038; Reg. § 25.2511–2; ¶ 10,201.

E. REVOCABLE TRUSTS

[¶ 22,201]

The popular revocable trust is an example of a grantor trust. Commonly the centerpiece of a wealth transmission scheme, the revocable trust is ordinarily treated as an incomplete transfer for income, gift and estate tax purposes. § 676(a); Reg. § 25.2511–2(c). Thus, the creation of a revocable living trust is generally neutral with respect to taxes insofar as the settlor is concerned.

¶ 22,201

[¶ 22,217]

1. GENERAL RULE

The grantor is taxable on the income of any portion of a trust, whether or not he or she is taxable under any other statutory provision, "where at any time the power to revest in the grantor title to such portion is exercisable by the grantor or a nonadverse party, or both." § 676(a) The effect of this provision is to treat the revocable portion of the trust as if it had not been created in the first instance. Cf. Rev. Rul. 57–51, 1957–1 C.B. 171. Thus, although the power to revoke is not exercised and the beneficiaries receive the income, such amounts would constitute income of the grantor and gifts to the beneficiaries.

[¶ 22,225]

2. POWER AFFECTING BENEFICIAL ENJOYMENT AFTER OCCURRENCE OF AN EVENT

A grantor retaining power to affect beneficial enjoyment of trust income is not taxable on trust income if the power can only be exercised after the occurrence of an event, so long as the occurrence of the event would not result in the grantor being treated as the owner under § 673 if the power were a reversionary interest.

[¶ 22,233]

3. POWER TO REVOKE WITH CONSENT OF TRUSTEE

A trustee is not an adverse party merely by virtue of his or her role as trustee. Reinecke v. Smith, 289 U.S. 172 (1933). Accordingly, trust income will be taxable to the grantor even though exercise of the grantor's power to revoke requires the consent of the trustee. § 676(a).

[¶ 22,241]

4. POWER TO REVOKE HELD BY TRUSTEE ALONE

Since a trustee is not an adverse party, the trust income will be taxable to the grantor even where a third-party trustee alone has the power to revoke the trust by virtue of a power to distribute the income and principal of the trust to the grantor. Frease v. Commissioner, 150 F.2d 403 (6th Cir.1945).

[¶ 22,249]

5. POWER TO REVOKE WITH CONSENT OF BENEFICIARY

A beneficiary is an adverse party. Thus, where the grantor can revoke the trust only by and with the consent of the trust beneficiary or beneficiaries, the trust income is *not* taxable to the grantor and will be taxed only to the trust or to the beneficiaries.

¶ 22,217

F. REVERSIONARY INTERESTS

[¶ 22,301]

1. INTRODUCTION

Generally speaking, a grantor will be taxed on the income from each trust in which the grantor retains a reversion. More specifically, reversionary trusts—trusts providing benefits to persons other than the grantor but followed by a reversion in the grantor at the death of the nongrantor beneficiary or after a term of years—are effective income-shifting devices only in cases where the value of the grantor's reversionary interest, at the inception of the trust, is valued at 5 percent or less of the value of that portion of the trust in which the grantor has the reversionary interest. § 673(a). Practically speaking, when interest rates are very low, the grantor will always be burdened by a tainted reversion even in cases where the trust beneficiary is very, very young, *e.g.*, age 1 at the time the trust is created.

Example 1. In January, 2004, Grandpa established an irrevocable trust with Accumulation National Bank. Grandpa funded the trust with $100,000 and provided that the trust was to continue until the 73rd anniversary of the creation of the trust. During the continuance of the trust, all trust income was to be paid to Grandson, age 1 at the time the trust was created. Upon termination of the trust, the property then constituting the trust was to be paid over to Grandpa. In this case, the trust income will be taxable to Grandson, and not to Grandpa, since the value of Grandpa's reversion (using Table B prescribed in Reg. § 20.2031–7(d)(6), and an interest rate of 4.2 percent) is only $4,962, well within the 5–percent limit. However, had the trust been created for only 72 years, the trust income would be taxable to Grandpa rather than Grandson even though Grandson received that income because the value of Grandpa's reversion would be $5,170, which is more than 5 percent of the value of the trust corpus at the inception of the trust. (*Comment.* Table B provides factors for terms of 1 to 60 years. The factor for 72 and 73 years was obtained using Stephan R. Leimberg & Robert T. Leclair, Estate Planning Tools) (same program as Leimberg & LeClair's Number Cruncher), listed in Appendix A (where additional sources are also provided, including the IRS website).

Example 2. In January, 2004, Uncle established an irrevocable trust with Rockhard Bank & Trust. Uncle funded the trust with $100,000 and provided that the trust was to continue until the first to occur of the following events: (a) the death of Nephew or (b) the 73rd anniversary of the creation of the trust. Under this scenario, the trust income would be taxed to Uncle, and not Nephew (even though it was paid to Nephew) since the value of Uncle's reversion (using Table S prescribed in Reg. § 20.2031–7(d)(6), and an interest rate of 4.2 percent), $6,137, is greater than 5 percent of the value of the trust corpus. Note that using Table B (from Reg. § 20.2031–7(d)(6)) would have provided a reversionary value of only $4,962, well within the 5–percent limit. However, Table S, relating to life expectancy, must be used since it causes a higher value to be placed on Uncle's reversionary interest.

It should be noted, too, that, in determining the value of any reversionary interest, it is assumed that any discretionary powers over the trust, by whomsoever possessed, will be exercised for the maximum benefit of the grantor. § 673(c).

[¶ 22,309]

2. INTERESTS TAKING EFFECT AT DEATH OF A MINOR

Oftentimes taxpayers make gifts in trust for the benefit of a child, the trust to last only until the child attains 21 years of age, at which time the trust is to terminate and the property then constituting the trust estate is to be distributed to the child. This can be a tax-favored arrangement in the sense that § 2503's $12,000 per donee per annum gift tax exclusion (adjusted for inflation) will be available to shelter such a gift if the trust otherwise satisfies the requirements of § 2503(c). See ¶ 19,339. Section 673(b) anticipates that the grantor of such a trust may wish to retain, in that trust, a reversion that will be triggered only in the case where the child dies before attaining age 21. If the grantor retains a reversion in such a case, that retention alone will not cause the trust income to be taxed to the grantor (rather than to the child or to the trust itself) even though the value of the retained reversion may be greater than 5 percent of the trust property in which the grantor has the reversion.

[¶ 22,317]

3. *"CLIFFORD"* OR 10–YEAR TRUSTS

Reversionary trusts created before March 2, 1986—sometimes referred to as short-term trusts or 10–year trusts or even *Clifford* trusts, after the case by the same name, Helvering v. Clifford (see ¶ 22,051), are subject to different rules. See Tax Reform Act of 1986, § 1402(c)(1). In the case of those trusts, the trust income is taxed to the trust or to the recipient of the trust income—rather than to the grantor—so long as the reversion in the grantor could not reasonably have been expected to take effect in possession and enjoyment in the grantor for more than 10 years after the transfer of the property to the trust. Thus, it was commonplace for taxpayers to establish trusts to last for 10 years and 1 day. These trusts called for the trust income to be paid to someone other than the grantor—such as the grantor's child or an elderly parent—with the result that the trust income would be taxed to the recipient of the income and not to the grantor. At the end of the trust term, the trust property reverts to the grantor. In cases where the child or elderly parent looked to the grantor for support, and the child or elderly parent was in a lower income tax bracket than the grantor, these so-called 10–year trusts were attractive income-shifting devices.

G. POWER TO CONTROL BENEFICIAL ENJOYMENT OF THE TRUST

[¶ 22,351]

Subject to important exceptions discussed below, the grantor is treated as the owner of a trust, regardless of its duration, where the beneficial enjoyment of the trust property or income is subject to a power of disposition exercisable by the grantor or by a nonadverse party.

[¶ 22,359]

1. GENERAL RULE

The general rule is that the grantor is taxable as trust owner on the income of any portion of a trust where he, or a nonadverse party, or both, has a power, without the consent of an adverse party, to determine the beneficial enjoyment of trust income or principal. § 674(a).

An "adverse party" means any person having a substantial beneficial interest in the trust which would be adversely affected by the exercise or nonexercise of a power that the grantor possesses with respect to the trust. § 672(a). Logically, a "nonadverse party" is any person who is not an adverse party. § 672(b). The fiduciary relationship of a trustee is not enough to make the trustee's interest adverse. And, as stated in the regulations, "[o]rdinarily, a beneficiary will be an adverse party, but if his right in the income or corpus of a trust is limited to only a part, he may be an adverse party only as to that part." Reg. § 1.672(a)–1(b).

[¶ 22,361]

LUMAN v. COMMISSIONER

United States Tax Court, 1982.
79 T.C. 846.

SIMPSON, Judge: * * *

On May 13, 1974, Robert Luman executed a declaration of trust creating the family trust. The original trustees of the family trust were Doris B. Luman and Hazel Werner, a person unrelated to the Lumans. The declaration of trust gave the trustees the power to distribute "proceeds and income" in the trustees' unlimited discretion. The trust instrument also provided that a majority of all trustees was needed to constitute a quorum and to take any affirmative action. The trust instrument gave the trustees extremely broad powers respecting the trust property and the carrying on of any business. The trustees could amend the trust instrument by resolution "covering contingencies as they arise," and the minutes of the trustees' resolution authorizing any action were to be considered evidence that such an action was within their power. Finally, the trust instrument expressly declared "neither The Trustees, officers, or certificate holders, present or future, have or possess any beneficial interest in the property or assets of Said Trust." The certificates

¶ 22,361

representing units of beneficial interest in the trust also expressly stated that "This certificate conveys no interest of any kind in The Trust assets, management, or control thereof."

At the first meeting of the board of trustees of the family trust, held on June 25, 1974, Robert Luman was appointed a trustee of the family trust for life. He received a certificate representing all 100 beneficial units of the family trust. By quitclaim deeds and other documents, the Lumans transferred virtually all of their property to the family trust. This property consisted of the ranch, such non-income-producing property as the family residence and its furniture and fixtures, and a number of stocks, bonds, and Treasury notes. However, the Lumans retained as their own property two automobiles, which they subsequently leased to the trust, but which they continued thereafter to use for both business and personal purposes. Both Robert Luman and the petitioner also transferred to the family trust the exclusive use of their lifetime services and any income therefrom. The Lumans had not received any such income in the recent past, and they did not anticipate receiving any in the future. Neither Robert Luman nor the petitioner received any income from personal services performed for anyone other than the trust in 1974, 1975, or 1976.

On June 26, 1974, the certificate evidencing Robert Luman's ownership of all 100 units of beneficial interest in the family trust was canceled. On the same day, Robert Luman and the petitioner each received a certificate representing 50 units of beneficial interest in the family trust. On the next day, Hazel Werner, an original trustee, resigned, and she was replaced by a daughter of the Lumans, Roberta Luman Bacheller (the daughter), in July 1974. In November 1974, Robert Luman and the petitioner had their certificates of beneficial interest canceled. Robert Luman then received a new certificate representing 20 units of beneficial interest; the petitioner received a certificate representing 35 units; and each of the Lumans' three children received a certificate representing 15 units of interest. These children were all adults and were not dependent on Mr. Luman and the petitioner.

After the creation of the family trust, the Lumans operated the ranch in generally the same manner as they had prior to the creation of the trust. The trustees passed resolutions authorizing Robert Luman to manage the ranch and to invest trust income in stocks using his best discretion. The Lumans, as the trustees, prepared and executed minutes of their meetings in which they meticulously recorded their consideration and approval of investments and capital expenditures for the ranch and recorded their other decisions relating to the investments of the trust and the management of the ranch. The minutes also reflect a decision by the trustees to purchase a new refrigerator for the residence, but it is not clear who paid for such refrigerator. Nevertheless, the Lumans continued to make decisions together as they had done prior to the creation of the trust. The daughter rarely attended the trustees' meetings, although she communicated with the petitioner weekly by letter and telephone regarding important ranch matters. The petitioner and the daughter occasionally overruled Mr. Luman regarding decisions to be made in managing the ranch.

The family trust filed fiduciary income tax returns for 1974, 1975, and 1976, and on such returns, it reported all income earned from assets transferred to the trust by the Lumans. It also deducted all expenses connected with the operation of the ranch, including the costs of leasing and maintaining the automobiles leased from the Lumans and the consulting fees paid to them.

* * *

The income of the family trust was distributed to the holders of the beneficial units in accordance with their interests in the trust. The petitioner and her husband reported their share of this distributed income on their Federal income tax returns for 1974, 1975, and 1976. In addition, for 1975 and 1976, they reported as income consulting fees of $3,000 received from the trust each year. These fees were paid for Mr. Luman s managing the ranch.* * *

In his notice of deficiency, the Commissioner determined that all the income reported by the trust in 1974, 1975, and 1976 was includable in the income of Robert Luman and the petitioner for those years. The Commissioner removed the consulting fees of $3,000 from their taxable income for 1975 and 1976 because he included in their taxable income all trust income for those years.* * * Finally, the Commissioner determined additions to tax for each year pursuant to § 6653(a) for negligence or intentional disregard of rules and regulations.

OPINION

This case represents another in along series of cases arising out of the sale of "canned" trusts by ESP and similar organizations. Although the Lumans created the family trust for legitimate estate planning reasons, the arrangement has raised several tax questions.* * *

The first issue for decision is whether the income generated by the trust property is taxable to the Lumans individually or to the trust they created. The petitioner maintains that the income from the trust property is taxable to the trust and to its beneficiaries as distributed, that the facts of this case are unique, and that because of such facts, this trust is distinguishable from the many family trusts which have been held ineffective to shift the burden of Federal income taxation. See, e.g., Schulz v. Commissioner, 686 F.2d 490 (7th Cir.1982), affg. a Memorandum Opinion of this Court. On the other hand, the Commissioner maintains that the income from the trust property is taxable to the petitioner individually for three alternative reasons: (1) Because the trust has no economic substance; (2) because the trust effects an anticipatory assignment of income; and (3) because of the applicability of the grantor trust provisions of §§ 671 through 677. We will first consider the Commissioner s argument under the grantor trust provisions.

When the grantor of a trust retains any of the powers described in §§ 673 through 677, he is treated, for income tax purposes, as the "owner" of that portion of the trust over which the power extends. Where the grantor is so treated, § 671 includes in his income "those items of income, deductions, and credits against tax of the trust which are attributable to that portion of the trust to the extent that such items would be taken into account * * * in computing taxable income or credits against the tax of an individual." §§ 1.671–2, 1.671.3, Income Tax Regs. These provisions apply if their conditions are met, regardless of the existence of a bona fide non-tax reason for creating the trust. One of the retained powers which will trigger the operation of the grantor trust provisions is contained in § 677.* * * The declaration of trust executed by Robert Luman gave the trustees of the family trust the power to distribute income in their discretion. Nothing in the trust declaration prevented the trustees from distributing income to Robert Luman or his spouse, the petitioner. Accordingly, if such discretion was exercisable without the approval or consent of an adverse party, § 677 operates to cause this income to be taxable to Robert Luman and, by virtue of the election by the Lumans to file a joint return, to the petitioner. § 6013(d)(3).

Section 672 defines an "adverse party" for the purposes of § 677 as "any person having a substantial beneficial interest in the trust which would be adversely affected by the exercise or nonexercise of the power which he possesses respecting the trust." The trust declaration provided that the trustees could make decisions by majority vote. During the years in issue (except for the first 2 months of the trust's existence), the trustees were Robert Luman, the petitioner, and the daughter. From November 1974 through 1976, each trustee also held units of beneficial interest in the trust. Thus, it might appear that each trustee was an adverse party regarding distributions to any other trustee. However, for the reasons set forth hereinafter, we conclude that the petitioner and Robert Luman were not adverse parties regarding distributions to each other.

Section 677 was expanded by the Tax Reform Act of 1969,* * * to provide that the grantor is to be treated as the owner of any portion of a trust whose income could, in the discretion of the grantor or a nonadverse party or both, be distributed to, or accumulated for, the grantor's spouse. In light of this statutory change, we found in Vercio v. Commissioner, 73 T.C. 1246, 1258 (1980), that "Congress effectively ruled out the possibility of a spouse being treated as an adverse party when a provision in the trust allows for the income to be used for that spouse's benefit." See § 1.677(a)–1(b)(2), Income Tax Regs. The petitioner can hardly be considered adverse regarding distributions for her benefit.* * * [S]ec. 1.672(a)–1(a), Income Tax Regs. In this case, the grantor, Robert Luman, and a nonadverse party, the petitioner, constituted two-thirds of the trustees and thus had the power to distribute income to either or both of them without the daughter's consent. Accordingly, by virtue of §§ 671 and 677, the income from the trust property is taxable to the grantor individually. * * *

Problem

[¶ 22,363]

What, if any, modification in the governing instrument or the taxpayer's practices would have produced the tax result desired by the taxpayers in *Luman?*

¶ 22,361

[¶ 22,367]

2. POWERS NOT SUBJECTING GRANTOR TO TAX

While the general rule is that trust income will be taxed to the settlor where the settlor has dominion and control over beneficial enjoyment of the trust, there are a number of exceptions which are particularly notable. See § 674(b)-(d).

[¶ 22,370]

a. *Power to Apply Income to Support of a Dependent*

A power to apply income to the support or maintenance of the grantor's dependents, exercisable by the grantor as trustee, or by another person as trustee or otherwise, will only cause the income of the trust to be taxed to the grantor to the extent that such income is so applied and distributed. §§ 674(b)(1), 677(b). In other words, the *presence* of this power alone will not attract tax to the grantor; it is the *exercise* of this power that is a taxable event for the grantor.

An important consideration in establishing a trust for the benefit of the grantor's dependents is a desire by many owners of income-producing property who are in high income tax brackets to transfer the liability for the payments of the income taxes on such property to a lower-bracket beneficiary. If the grantor must utilize the trust income for the support of his or her dependents, this important reason for creating the trust is no longer present. As a practical matter, if the grantor must utilize the income in such a manner, more than likely his or her tax bracket would not be much higher than that of the trust or its beneficiaries.

[¶ 22,373]

b. *Power Affecting Beneficial Enjoyment After Occurrence of an Event*

A power, the exercise of which can only affect the income of the trust for a period commencing after the occurrence of an event will not subject the grantor to tax during the period. If such a power is still in existence after the occurrence of an event, however, the grantor will then be taxable on the income. § 674(b)(2). Thus, for example, if in a trust created on January 1, 2004, the grantor provides for the payment of income to his son, reserving the power to substitute other beneficiaries of income or principal after January 1, 2004, the grantor will not be treated as the owner of the trust with respect to ordinary income received *before* January 1, 2014. However, the grantor will be subject to tax on trust income, as an owner, on and after that date, unless the power is relinquished. Reg. § 1.674(b)–1(b)(2).

[¶ 22,376]

c. *Power Exercisable Only by Will*

In general, the grantor is not taxable on trust income if the grantor's power to control disposition is exercisable only by will. However, this exception is not applicable where the grantor, or a nonadverse party, or both, also have the power to accumulate trust income for disposition by will, without the approval or consent of any adverse party. § 674(b)(3). For example, if the grantor provides in the trust that the income is to be accumulated during the grantor's life, and that the grantor may appoint the accumulated income by will, the grantor is subject to income tax on the trust income. Moreover, where income is distributed but the grantor may appoint the trust remainder by will, and under the trust and local law, capital gains are added to corpus, the grantor is taxed on such gains. Reg. § 1.674(b)–1(b)(3).

[¶ 22,379]

d. *Power to Allocate Corpus or Income Among Charitable Beneficiaries*

The grantor will not be subject to tax on trust income where the grantor has power to determine the beneficiaries of income or corpus, provided that payment can only be made for charitable purposes. § 674(b)(4).

[¶ 22,381]

e. *Power to Distribute Corpus*

A power to distribute corpus to a beneficiary will not subject the grantor to tax if the power is limited by a reasonably definite standard set forth in the trust instrument. § 674(b)(5). For instance, a power to distribute corpus for the health, education, maintenance, or support (HEMS) of the beneficiary would be limited by a reasonably definite standard. On the other hand, a power to distribute corpus for the pleasure, desire, or happiness of a beneficiary is not limited by a reasonably definite standard. Reg. § 1.674(b)–1(b)(5).

Even though no standard is provided, a power to invade the corpus for a current income beneficiary is an excepted power, insofar as the distribution is chargeable against the proportionate share of corpus held in trust for the particular beneficiary. A power to distribute corpus is never an excepted power, however, if any person has a power to add trust beneficiaries, except where the action is merely to provide for after-born or after-adopted children. § 674(b)(5); cf. Rev. Rul. 80–255, 1980–2 C.B. 272, set out at ¶ 19,675.

[¶ 22,384]

f. *Power to Withhold Income Temporarily*

A power to pay or apply income to or for a current income beneficiary, or to accumulate such income for that beneficiary, will not subject the grantor to tax, provided that any such accumulated income must ultimately be payable either:

> (a) To such beneficiary, the beneficiary's estate, or the beneficiary's appointee under a power of appointment given such beneficiary which does not exclude from the class of possible appointees any person other than the beneficiary, the beneficiary's estate, the beneficiary's creditors or the creditors of the beneficiary's estate or

¶ 22,376

(b) Upon termination of the trust or in conjunction with a disposition of corpus which contains the accumulated income, to the current income beneficiaries in shares irrevocably specified in the trust instrument. § 674(b)(6). It is sufficient that the beneficiary has a broad special power of appointment; it is not necessary that the beneficiary be given a general power. Accumulated income is considered to be ultimately payable in accordance with the foregoing rules, even though the trust provides for payment to contingent beneficiaries if the primary beneficiary fails to survive to the date fixed for distribution, if such date may reasonably be expected to occur within the lifetime of the primary beneficiary.

The power to withhold income is not an excepted power, however, if any person has a power to add trust beneficiaries, except where the action is merely to provide for after-born or after-adopted children. § 674(b)(6).

[¶ 22,387]

g. Power to Withhold Income During Minority of Beneficiary

A power to pay or apply income to or for such beneficiary or to accumulate and add it to the corpus, which is exercisable only while an income beneficiary is under age 21 or is under some other legal disability, will not subject the grantor to tax. § 674(b)(7). Such a power is excepted even though the accumulated income will not be paid to the beneficiary from whom withheld. Accumulated income may be added to corpus and ultimately distributed to others. Reg. § 1.674(b)–1(b)(7). Thus, the grantor will not be taxed on the trust income under § 674 where the income is payable to the grantor's child for life, remainder to the grantor's grandchildren, although the grantor reserves the power to accumulate income and add it to principal while the grantor's child is under 21.

This power is not an excepted power, however, if any person has a power to add trust beneficiaries, except where the action is to provide for after-born or after-adopted children.

[¶ 22,390]

h. Power to Allocate Between Corpus and Income

A power to allocate receipts and disbursements between principal and income will not subject the grantor to tax, even though expressed in broad language. § 674(b)(8).

[¶ 22,392]

i. Powers Exercisable by Independent Trustees

A broader exception is made for certain powers when exercisable solely by independent trustees. See § 674(c). Trustees are often given the power to distribute, apportion or accumulate income to or for one or more beneficiaries or within a class of beneficiaries, or to pay out corpus to or for them. Such power will not subject the grantor to tax if solely exercisable by a trustee or trustees (without the consent of any other person), none of whom is the grantor, and no more than half of whom are *related or subordinate parties* who are subservient to the wishes of the grantor. Thus, in the ordinary sprinkling or spray trust, the co-trustees may be a corporate fiduciary and a family member (even the grantor's spouse).

The power is not an excepted power, however, if any person has a power to add trust beneficiaries, except where the action is merely to provide for after-born or after-adopted children. Nor does it achieve excepted-power status if the grantor has an unrestricted power to remove the trustee, unless the grantor is under a duty to substitute another independent trustee. Reg. § 1.674(d)–2(a).

A "related or subordinate party" means any nonadverse party who is the grantor's spouse if they are living together; a parent, issue, brother or sister, or employee of the grantor; a corporation or any employee thereof in which the stock holdings of the grantor and the trust are significant from the viewpoint of voting control; or a subordinate employee of a corporation in which the grantor is an executive. There is a rebuttable presumption that a related or subordinate party is subservient to the grantor. § 672(c).

The fact that the grantor exercises influence with respect to an independent trustee who is amenable to the grantor's wishes does not cause trust income to be taxable to the grantor in the absence of a legally enforceable power reserved by instrument or contract. Estate of H.W. Goodwyn v. Commissioner, 35 T.C.M. (CCH) 1026, T.C.M. (P–H) ¶ 76,238 (1976).

Therefore, by process of elimination, an independent trustee could be a bank, attorney, accountant or investment counselor. It could even be someone who would normally be considered a related or subordinate party provided that person has a "substantial beneficial interest in the trust which would be adversely affected by the exercise or nonexercise of the power which he possesses respecting the trust." Such a person is considered an adverse party under § 672(a). However, if an adverse party who is an income beneficiary of the trust is appointed as trustee and possesses discretion to distribute or accumulate income, that person will likely be taxed on all income of the trust under § 678(a).

[¶ 22,395]

j. *Power to Allocate Income Limited by a Standard*

A common power given to trustees is the power to distribute, apportion, or accumulate income to or for one or more beneficiaries or within a class of beneficiaries, but limited to a standard such as the reasonable needs of the beneficiaries. Such a power will not subject the grantor to tax if solely exercisable by a trustee or trustees, none of whom is the grantor or a spouse living with the grantor, provided such power is exercisable without the consent of any other person and is limited by a reasonably definite external standard which is set forth in the trust instrument. The exception applies even though the power is held by a related or subordinate trustee (other than the grantor's spouse living with the grantor), who is subservient to the grantor.

This power is not an excepted power, however, if any person has a power to add trust beneficiaries, except where the power is to provide solely for after-born or after-adopted children. § 674(d).

H. CONTROL OF ADMINISTRATIVE POWERS BY GRANTOR

[¶ 22,401]

The grantor is treated as the owner of any portion of a trust if, under the terms of the trust or circumstances attendant upon its operation, administrative control is exercisable primarily for the grantor's benefit rather than for the benefit of the trust beneficiaries. Instances of such control follow.

[¶ 22,409]

1. POWER TO DEAL WITH TRUST FOR INADEQUATE CONSIDERATION

The trust income is taxable to the grantor where a power exercisable by him or a nonadverse party, or both, without the consent of an adverse party, enables the grantor or any other person to deal with trust property or income for inadequate consideration. § 675(1).

[¶ 22,417]

2. POWER TO BORROW WITHOUT ADEQUATE INTEREST OR SECURITY

The trust income is taxable to the grantor where a power exercisable by the grantor or a nonadverse party, or both, enables the grantor, directly or indirectly, to borrow the corpus or income without adequate security.

There is an exception, however, to this rule. The rule does not apply where a trustee other than the grantor is authorized under a general leading power to make loans to *any* person without regard to interest or security. § 675(2).

[¶ 22,425]

3. BORROWING TRUST PROPERTY

Trust income is taxable to the grantor where the grantor has directly or indirectly borrowed the corpus or income and has not completely repaid the loan and any interest before the beginning of the taxable year.

The foregoing rule does not apply, however, to a loan that provides for adequate interest and adequate security and is made by a trustee who is neither the grantor nor a related or subordinate trustee subservient to the grantor. § 675(3).

[¶ 22,433]

4. GENERAL POWERS OF ADMINISTRATION

The trust income is taxable to the grantor where a power of administration is exercisable in a *nonfiduciary* capacity by any person without the approval or consent of any person in a fiduciary capacity. § 675(4). A "power of administration" means any one or more of the following powers:

1. A power to vote, or direct the voting of, stock or other securities of a corporation in which the holdings of the grantor and the trust are significant from the viewpoint of voting control;

2. A power to control the investment of trust funds by direction or veto, to the extent that such funds consist of stock or securities of corporations in which the holdings of the grantor and the trust are significant from the viewpoint of voting control; and

3. A power to reacquire the trust corpus by substituting other property of an equivalent value.

Under the above provisions, the grantor will only be taxed by reason of a power over investments where the investments are those in which the grantor and the trustee have significant voting control, and then only if the power is exercisable in a nonfiduciary capacity—that is, in such manner as to benefit the grantor individually rather than the trust beneficiaries.

As regards the distinction between fiduciary and nonfiduciary powers, a power exercisable by a person as trustee is presumed to be exercisable in a fiduciary capacity primarily in the beneficiaries' interests. This presumption may be rebutted only by clear and convincing evidence that the best interests of the beneficiaries are not being served. If a power is not exercisable by a person as trustee, the terms of the trust, and the circumstances regarding its creation and administration, must be examined to determine whether such power is exercisable in a fiduciary or nonfiduciary capacity. Reg. § 1.675–1(b)(4)(iii). See Cushman v. Commissioner, 153 F.2d 510 (2d Cir. 1946).

I. TRUST INCOME FOR BENEFIT OF GRANTOR

[¶ 22,451]

With certain exceptions, the grantor is treated as the owner of a trust for the purpose of taxing its income to the grantor, even though the grantor has no power of control over the beneficial enjoyment of the trust or other taxable power, where the trust income may be used for the benefit of the grantor or the grantor's spouse, without the approval or consent of any adverse party. § 677(a).

[¶ 22,459]

1. GENERAL RULE

Trust income is taxable to the grantor where the income is, or in the discretion of the grantor and a nonadverse party (and without the consent of an adverse party) may be:

1. Distributed to the grantor or the grantor's spouse;

2. Held or accumulated for future distribution to the grantor or the grantor's spouse; or

3. Applied to payment of life insurance premiums covering the grantor or the grantor's spouse, except policies irrevocably payable to charities. § 677(a). For discussion, see ¶ 20,739.

[¶ 22,467]

2. INCOME USED TO DISCHARGE GRANTOR'S OBLIGATIONS

The regulations provide, generally, that if the income of the trust may be used in discharge of the grantor's obligations, the grantor will be taxable on the trust income. Thus, if the grantor creates a trust, the income of which may, in the discretion of a nonadverse party, be applied in the payment of the grantor's debts, including the payment of the grantor's rent or other household expenses, such income is taxable to the grantor regardless of whether it is actually so applied. Reg. § 1.677(b)–1(d).

The income of an irrevocable trust used to pay any obligation which the grantor would be bound to pay, irrespective of the trust (except alimony and similar payments), is taxable to the grantor. Thus, where a trust was created in favor of certain beneficiaries, but the trust instrument directed the trustee to apply trust income to the payment of a debt owed by the grantor, such income was held taxable to the grantor. Helvering v. Blumenthal, 296 U.S. 552 (1935), rev'g 76 F.2d 507 (2d Cir.1935).

The Eighth Circuit affirmed the Tax Court when it held that since payment of a gift tax is the primary obligation of the grantor-donor, trust income used to pay this tax, either directly or by discharging a loan incurred by the trustee for this purpose, is taxable to the grantor. Estate of Sheaffer v. Commissioner, 313 F.2d 738 (8th Cir.1963); accord Rev. Rul. 57–564, 1957–2 C.B. 328. But see Commissioner v. Estate of Morgan, 316 F.2d 238 (6th Cir.1963).

[¶ 22,475]

3. UNEXERCISED POWER TO USE INCOME TO DISCHARGE GRANTOR'S SUPPORT OBLIGATIONS

A power to use trust income to discharge the grantor's support obligations, exercisable by someone other than the grantor, or by the grantor himself acting as trustee or co-trustee, will *not* cause trust income to be taxable to the grantor unless such income is actually used for support purposes. § 677(b). For related discussion, see ¶ 10,115.

J.   TRUSTS FOR SUPPORT AND MAINTENANCE OF DEPENDENTS

[¶ 22,501]

1.   IN GENERAL

Trust income which is *used* for the support or maintenance of the grantor's minor children or other legal dependents is taxable to the grantor. § 677(b). This represents a liberalization of the harsh result reached in Helvering v. Stuart, 317 U.S. 154 (1942), wherein it was held that the grantor was taxable on any income *available* for support, whether or not it was used for that purpose.

The grantor will also be taxed on that trust income which is *required to be used* for the support of the grantor's dependents, even though all of the income distributed was not actually expended for support during the taxable year. Reg. § 1.677(b)–1(f). See also Peierls v. Commissioner, 12 T.C. 741 (1949). However, trust income paid to a beneficiary whom the grantor is legally obligated to support is not taxable to the grantor merely because that relationship exists. Thus, trust income *required* to be paid to a legal dependent of the grantor was held not to be taxable to the grantor unless the income was received by the dependent in discharge of the grantor's legal obligation of support. Fruehauf v. Commissioner, 12 T.C. 681 (1949), acq., 1949–2 C.B. 2.

The grantor will not be taxed on trust income that is used for the support and maintenance of a person whom he is not legally obligated to support, such as his wife's relatives. Commissioner v. Donahue, 128 F.2d 739 (2d Cir.1942), or his adult children. At one time, the mother of minor children had no obligation to support them if the father was living and capable of supporting them; hence, it was held that she was not taxable on the income from a trust created by her which was used for the children's support and maintenance. Sharp v. Commissioner, 42 B.T.A. 336 (1940), acq., 1940–2 C.B. 6.

[¶ 22,509]

2.   MEANING OF SUPPORT

Section 677(b) does not say that the support or maintenance provided for the beneficiary has to be support and maintenance the grantor is legally obligated to provide. This enables the IRS to argue that *support or maintenance not legally required* but *actually provided* could result in the trust's income being taxed to the grantor, if the beneficiary is one the grantor is legally obligated to support. This distinction led the District Court in Brooke v. United States, 292 F.Supp. 571 (D.Mont.1968) to hold that where income was used to support and maintain a minor, the entire amount of the expenditures was taxable to the grantor, even though some of the expenditures exceeded the legal obligation as a parent.

Professor Casner observed that if the words "support and maintain" are not to be limited to expenditures which are legal obligations of the grantor, "it is difficult to imagine any expenditure of trust income for a minor that would not be for his support or maintenance. If this is true, the only safe course of action to follow in relation to a minor's trust would be to expend no income for his benefit." A.J. Casner, Estate Planning, 186, note 73 (4th ed. 1979). Professor Casner's observation is supported by Revenue Ruling 56–484, 1956–2 C.B. 23, which states that "the amount of such income includible in the gross income of a person obligated to support or maintain a minor is limited by the extent of his legal obligation under local law." Similarly, Reg. § 1.662(a)–4 provides that "support and maintenance" consists of what local law says a person is legally obligated to furnish that person's dependents.

On the basis of Revenue Ruling 56–484, the original District Court decision in *Brooke* was amended and the court agreed that the ruling should be followed. 300 F.Supp. 465 (D.Mont.1969). In *Brooke,* expenditures were for private school tuition, musical instruments, music, swimming, and public speaking lessons, an automobile for one child, and travel expenses to New Mexico for another child who had asthma. The Ninth Circuit affirmed the District Court's conclusion that under Montana law these expenditures did not discharge a legal obligation. 468 F.2d 1155 (9th Cir.1972). Not only is there no uniform rule as to whether an item is required for support, but few jurisdictions have clear-cut decisions on whether private school and college tuition, special courses and training, and cars are required items of support. Whether a given item is considered support depends upon a person's financial status. The result is that standards vary widely.

While state statutes may specify who has an obligation to support a person, items of support are not listed and must be determined under case law, which is usually in the domestic relations area.

In Morrill v. United States, 228 F.Supp. 734 (D.Me.1964), the court taxed payments made from a short-term trust to the settlor. The trustee used them to pay tuition and room charges of the settlor's four minor children attending private schools and colleges. The settlor had expressly assumed responsibility for payment of these expenses. School bills were submitted to him and he sent them to the trustee. Thus, the court concluded he was either expressly or impliedly liable for the schools' bills, since he had made the arrangements with them and the bills came to him. Accordingly, the court held that it was unnecessary to consider whether state law imposed a support obligation on him to pay these bills, since trust income was being used to discharge his legal obligations to the schools.

In Wyche v. United States, 749 CCH ¶ 7911 (Ct.Cl. Trial Judge's Report 1974), the court held that income from a trust established for three minor children and used to pay private school tuition, music and dancing lessons for them was not taxable to the grantor. His wife was the trustee and he was financially able to make the payments out of his own funds. Based on South Carolina law, it was held that he had no legal obligation to send his children to private day school or to pay for music and dancing lessons for them. The *Wyche* court distinguished *Morrill* on the ground that the settlor in *Morrill* became initially liable for the charges paid by the trust.

The first *Brooke* case is also important for another point. The lower court, 292 F.Supp. 571 (D.Mont.1968), held that the parent, who was also legal guardian of his child, was to be treated in the same manner as the trustee for purposes of determining taxability to him of funds expended by him in his capacity as guardian, under § 677. In the Ninth Circuit's affirmance of this decision, the court noted that "[t]he Montana Probate Court administers a guardianship with the same requisite independence of any court administered trust.* * * While a guardianship does not possess all trust requisites, for the purposes of taxation under § 677, it must be considered a trust." 468 F.2d at 1158–1159. This is a somewhat astounding observation by the court, inasmuch as a guardianship is not a separate tax entity, unlike a trust. For a discussion of how trusts are taxed, see ¶ 8101.

For additional discussion of "legal obligations," see ¶ 19,381–19,383.

By way of contrast, in Stone v. Commissioner, T.C. Memo 1987–454, the court, looking to California divorce cases as precedent, concluded that a parent's affluence rendered "private" high school education furnished his child a part of his legal obligation of support—and, accordingly trust dollars expended for this purpose were taxable to the parent having the obligation rather than to the trust. Furthermore, in *Braun*, below at ¶ 22,525, the court looked at New Jersey divorce cases as precedent, and also concluded that parent's affluence rendered his child's college expenses a part of his legal obligation of support—and, again, trust dollars expended for this purpose were taxable to the parent having the obligation rather than to the trust.

Reconciling *Wyche* with *Stone* and *Braun* may well turn on the precedental value of legal obligation of support determinations made in the context of divorce. Despite the *Braun* court's statement, should support and maintenance be relative, i.e., one standard, perhaps taking into account parental affluence, applies when parents are divorcing, and another standard, perhaps one more modest in aspiration, when divorce and division of parental financial responsibility are not at issue? *Stone*, like *Braun*, relying on divorce precedents, did not recognize a different standard and, in a footnote, quickly differentiated *Brooke* (cited approvingly in *Wyche)*, saying "few facts were reported therein", those reported were "markedly different", and that the "similar" Montana statute "was not identical to the California statute" looked to in *Stone*.

[¶ 22,525]

BRAUN v. COMMISSIONER

United States Tax Court, 1984.
48 T.C.M. (CCH) 210, T.C.M. (P–H) ¶ 84,285.

WHITAKER, JUDGE:

* * * [Dr. Frederick Braun and his wife, Marjorie, jointly established one trust for the benefit of three of their children (Trust I) and another trust for the benefit of their other three children (Trust II). Dr. and Mrs. Braun and "a friend," Mr. Torres, were the trustees. The terms of each trust provided that "the entire net income is to be distributed to the three children for whom the trust was established."]

* * * All of the distributed income was used for educational purposes. In 1976, 1977 and 1978, from Trust I the disbursements were for college tuition, room and board for Cynthia and Fred, two of the three beneficiaries of that trust. Both children were over 18 years of age in 1976. In 1976 the income from Trust II was used for tuition at the private high school attended by two of that trust's beneficiaries, Stephen and Christopher. In 1977 and 1978, a portion of the Trust II income was used for tuition, room and board of Stephen at college and a portion for Christopher at the private high school. During these years, none of the income was used for one beneficiary of each trust. Stephen became 18 in December of 1976, whereas Christopher did not become 18 until 1979.

* * *

Under section 677(b), the income of a trust is taxable to the grantor to the extent that such income is applied or distributed for the support or maintenance of a beneficiary whom the grantor is legally obligated to support or maintain. Petitioners argue that under New Jersey law the petitioners had no obligation to pay college tuition and room and board expenses of an unmarried child over 18 or to pay private school expense for an unmarried child under 18. Petitioners further argue that this issue has come up in New Jersey only in controversies between divorced parents and that such cases are inapplicable to this situation. We do not agree.

The recent decision of Newburgh v. Arrigo, 88 N.J. 529, 443 A.2d 1031 (1982), fully reviews the obligation of parents to continue to provide educational expenses for unmarried children over the age of 18. The Supreme Court of New Jersey held that necessary education is a flexible concept that can vary in different circumstances.

> In general, financially capable parents should contribute to the higher education of children who are qualified students. In appropriate circumstances, parental responsibility includes the duty to assure children of a college and even of a post-graduate education such as law school. [Newburgh v. Arrigo, supra at 1038.]

In an adversarial situation, courts in New Jersey consider all relevant factors, which include 12 which were enumerated in Newburgh v. Arrigo, supra. It is obvious that many of these factors would have no bearing except in a controversy between divorced parents or between a child and a noncustodial parent. But the support rule is not limited to such divorced parent context. Sakovits v. Sakovits, 178 N.J.Super. 623, 429 A.2d 1091, 1095 (1981). While many of these factors described by the New Jersey Supreme Court are not directly applicable to the instant facts, the import to our facts is clearly that petitioners retained the obligation to provide their children with a college education. They were both able and willing to do so, a college education was imminently reasonable in the light of the background, values and goals of the parents as well as the children, and petitioners have brought forward no facts or arguments which would militate against the recognition of this obligation on the part of these particular parents. Newburgh v. Arrigo, supra. With respect to private high school education, the law of New Jersey is less clear. There is dictum in the case of Rosenthal v. Rosenthal, 19 N.J. Super, 521, 88 A.2d 655 (1952), to the effect that a father is not required to provide his son with private school, college or professional training, or with any education beyond public schools, but that dictum as to college and professional education is certainly obsolete. Khalaf v. Khalaf, 58 N.J. 63, 275 A.2d 132, 137 (1971), refers with approval to Annot. 56 A.L.R.2d 1207 (1956). While that court's reference to the annotation was with respect to college expenses, the annotation also recognizes the existence of a parental obligation in similar circumstances to provide for private or boarding school education. It would be an anomaly to find a support obligation for college tuition for an emancipated child but none for private high school expense for a younger child in the same family. In view of the recent New Jersey cases cited, we do not think the dictum in Rosenthal v. Rosenthal, supra, represents the current view of the New Jersey courts. We believe that private high school education in appropriate cases would be held by the New Jersey courts to be within the scope of parental obligation. Accordingly, we hold that the income of these two trusts, to the extent actually utilized for tuition, room and board for four of the six children of petitioners was used to discharge Dr. Braun's legal support obligations and is therefore taxable to him under section 677(b).

Problems

[¶ 22,545]

1. Refer to §§ 671–677 and prepare a list of powers that you think that the settlor of a trust would want to have so as to retain maximum control over the trust corpus and income while, at the same time, avoiding being taxed on the income.

2. Refer to §§ 671–677 and prepare a list of powers which the settlor is prohibited from enjoying if the settlor is to avoid being taxed on the trust income.

3. Economic considerations dictate that the draftsperson use forms rather than draft each dispositive instrument. With that in mind, should the trust instrument expressly prohibit the settlor from enjoying the powers proscribed by §§ 671–677 so as to avoid any possibility that the settlor would indirectly be given one or more proscribed powers by another provision of the trust instrument?

4. Current case law appears to support an argument that a child's private school and college tuition will not be considered part of the parent's support obligation, where the parent is not obligated either expressly or by implied contract to make the payments, unless applicable local law clearly imposes a legal obligation on the parent. Therefore, in planning to use income from a trust to pay tuition, can you suggest techniques to be followed to minimize the settlor's risk of being taxed on this income?

K. SELECTION OF TRUSTEE

[¶ 22,551]

Persons who make lifetime transfers in trust for the benefit of loved ones typically want to keep control over the trust to the extent possible without compromising the available tax benefit. Practically speaking, "control" typically means that the settlor wants to be trustee. Common scenarios include cases like that of David, who created a trust for his own benefit. See ¶ 10,151. Unless income distributions can only be made with the consent of an adverse party, David will be taxed on the trust income even if he does not receive that income. § 677(a).

Another common scenario is the case where the settlor is trustee for the benefit of another. The settlor can be trustee where income distributions are "mandatory." However, where income distributions are "discretionary" or "discretionary subject to a standard," the settlor will be taxed on the trust income if the settlor is trustee even though the trust income is distributed to the trust beneficiary or warehoused in the trust. See § 674(a); ¶ 19,640. Where the income distributions are "discretionary," the trustee must qualify as "independent" if the settlor is to avoid being taxed on income he or she did not receive. See § 674(c); ¶ 22,392. Alternatively, if income distributions are "discretionary subject to a standard," the trustee can be anyone other than the settlor or the settlor's spouse. See § 674(d); ¶ 22,395.

Problem

[¶ 22,565]

Refer to §§ 671–677 and classify the following powers as either "permitted" or "prohibited" to the settlor of a trust who is serving as trustee.

(a) A power exercisable by the settlor or a nonadverse party, or both, without approval or consent of any adverse party, to enable the settlor or any person to purchase, exchange or otherwise deal with or dispose of corpus or income for less than adequate consideration.

(b) A power exercisable by the settlor or a nonadverse party or both, enabling the settlor to borrow corpus or income, directly or indirectly, without adequate interest or adequate security.

(c) A power exercisable by the trustee (other than the settlor) to make loans under a general lending power to any person without regard to interest or security.

(d) A power that allows the settlor to directly or indirectly borrow corpus or income which is not completely repaid, including any interest, before the beginning of the taxable year, although the loan provides for adequate interest and adequate security and is made by a trustee other than the settlor or a related or subordinate trustee subservient to the settlor?

(e) A power to vote or direct the voting of stock or other securities of a corporation in which the holdings of the settlor and trust are significant from the viewpoint of voting control.

¶ 22,565

(f) A power to control trust investment by direction or veto, to the extent that the trust fund consists of stock or securities of corporations in which the holdings of the settlor and trust are significant from the viewpoint of voting control.

(g) A power to reacquire corpus by substituting other property of an equivalent value.

(h) A power to sprinkle income among several beneficiaries of the trust.

Chapter 23

GENERATION-SKIPPING
TAX ALTERNATIVES

A. OBJECTIVES

[¶ 23,001]

Listen in on Harry and Louise in the middle of an after-dinner conversation. Harry is looking over diagrams received that day from their lawyer. (The diagrams are reproduced in Chapter 1.)

> While the GST exemption and the estate tax exemption—both $2 million in 2006 through 2008—are each scheduled to increase to $3.5 million in 2009, expire in 2010, and return in 2011 fixed at $1 million. The $10,000 gift tax per donee per annum exclusion is adjusted by the IRS for inflation as warranted. For 2006, it is $12,000.

"This is crazy," says Harry to Louise. "All I ever wanted to do was give you everything when I die. To my mind it was up to you to take care of the kids when you go. Now that lawyer has given us more trusts than I can count."

"That's not true, Harry," says Louise. "The lawyer explained it all. We're getting a bypass trust for me after you're gone—and we've been making gifts to the kids in trust. You know yourself that Buster and Missy can't handle their money—and you thought it was so funny when the lawyer said the kids' trusts were *Crummey*."

"Yeah, yeah, but what's this stuff about generation-skipping? I think Buster and Missy should just have at it and if there is nothing left, so what."

Interrupting, Louise says, "Look. It's what everybody is doing. None of our friends talk about anything else. They all have GST exempt trusts and some kind of backward QTIP, whatever that is. Eduardo was kidding me the other evening as I was leaving work about how I had 'some nerve' to use the tollway to get home nights when I couldn't afford to provide the children with a decent estate plan. I don't want to hear that stuff any more."

More from Harry and Louise later. In the meantime, note that application of the generation-skipping transfer tax (GST) is considered in Chapter 9. As was apparent from those materials, the GST is a success in taxing most of the transfers it was intended to tax. The GST provisions are tightly drafted and, consequently, in many situations, very little planning can be done to avoid imposition of the GST if the client's objectives are to be realized. Moreover, having the generation-skipping tax apply may lead to a tax result no worse than that flowing from alternative transfers which trigger estate or gift tax liability. Thus, if there are compelling reasons to place property in trust, "just do it" (notwithsatnding the GST tax)). To the extent that a generation-skipping transfer may defer payment of a tax, the deferred tax liability could be viewed as an interest-free loan from the government. There is also the possibility—highly unlikely—that the entire generation-skipping tax scheme could be repealed during the period of deferral, given changing political climates.

This does not mean that the GST can be ignored. The GST may well trap more than it was intended to trap, and many innocuous-seeming arrangements suddenly turn out to give rise to GST liability. The pitfalls of inarticulate (or insensitive) drafting are illustrated in these materials and make a case for requiring estate planners to evaluate every instrument for potential generation-skipping tax consequences.

In a number of situations, a simple change in language can eliminate needless generation-skipping tax liability. This can often be done without defeating the nontax objectives that caused the original inclusion of the offensive language.

B. ALLOCATING THE GST EXEMPTION

[¶ 23,051]

The allocation of the GST exemption—$2 million in 2006–08, with scheduled increases—is perhaps the most important planning decision in dealing with generation-skipping transfers. For discussion, see ¶ 9309.

In considering whether to allocate the exemption during the transferor's lifetime, several factors need to be considered. First, it must be determined whether generation-skipping transfers will occur with respect to the transferred property after the allocation is made to that property. If non-skip persons will receive a distribution of the property, the exemption could be effectively wasted because distributions to non-skip persons are not subject to the tax and the exemptions allocated to those distributions are therefore unavailable for allocation to other generation-skipping transfers which are subject to the tax. Second, the appreciation potential of the property needs to be assessed. If the property is likely to appreciate in value, the allocation of the exemption to this property should be made while the value of the property is relatively low. On the other hand, if the property will likely depreciate in value, the allocation should be delayed and the election out of the deemed allocation for direct skips should be made. Third, married couples should determine whether to split their exemption or to allocate their individual exemptions to a specific transfer.

The use of separate trusts for exempt and nonexempt transfer property should be considered. Since the exemption may be allocated among several

¶ 23,001

different trusts, the use of several different trusts will allow those which are completely exempt to remain exempt even though they increase in value over the exempt amount. For example, if three trusts were created, two with $1 million that are each allocated one-half of the GST exemption ($2 million in 2006 through 2008) and one trust with $1.6 million, the $1 million trusts would remain exempt from the GST even though they each grew in value to more than $2 million. If, however, the exemption was allocated equally among the three trusts, each exempted for $666,667, distributions from each of the three trusts to skip persons will be partially subject to the GST. Separate exempt and nonexempt trusts have other advantages. Distributions free of the GST may be made to skip persons from a totally exempt trust and distributions free of the GST may be made to non-skip persons from nonexempt trusts. In contrast, distributions to skip persons from partially exempt trusts will be considered partially taxable distributions.

If the exemptions have not been utilized during the transferor's lifetime, a provision in the transferor's will or trust should provide for the allocation of any remaining available exemptions at death. This should be done even if the transferor intends to allocate the exemptions during his or her lifetime to avoid wasting any exemptions that were not previously allocated or available. The exemption may be allocated by the executor by the use of a formula (e.g., "the allocation may be expressed in terms of the amount necessary to produce an inclusion ratio of zero"). Reg. § 26.2632–1(b)(2). Consideration should also be given to whether the transferor wishes to give the executor or the trustee the authority to divide the property into separate trusts.

In planning the use of the exemption, remember that a deemed allocation of any unused portion of the exemption is made to direct and indirect skips to the extent necessary to reduce the inclusion ratio to zero, unless the transferor elects out of the deemed allocation under § 2632(b)(3) and (c)(5)(A). Outright direct skips not subject to gift tax have an inclusion ratio of zero under § 2642(c)(1), but if the direct skip is made to a trust, the trust's inclusion ratio increases, resulting in a deemed allocation if the trust allows distributions to others during the skip person's life or is not includible in the transferor's gross estate. § 2642(c)(2). Even if the trust does not allow distributions to others during the skip person's life or is includible in the transferor's gross estate, a deemed allocation may still result if the trust provisions allow use of income for the skip person's support.

Example. Under T's will, $100,000 is transferred to a previously existing trust for the benefit of GC, T's grandchild. The trust was created by GC's parent, C. Under the provisions of the trust, the trustee is instructed to pay income to GC during GC's life, remainder to T's lineal descendants per stirpes. Since no distributions to any person other than GC during GC's lifetime are provided for, and the $100,000 is included in T's gross estate, a deemed allocation will not be made.

¶ 23,051

C. "OLD WILLS": MARRIED PERSONS AND THE REVERSE QTIP ELECTION

[¶ 23,101]

Mention is made of the reverse QTIP election—the "backward QTIP", ¶ 23,001—in part for historical reasons and, part, for very practical reasons. ("QTIP" refers to the qualified terminable interest property election provided for by § 2056(b)(7) so as to allow the marital deduction for gifts to qualifying trusts which would otherwise not be allowed.) Practically speaking, though, the language of the reverse QTIP technique should be found only in GST sensitive wills and trusts prepared for married persons prior to 2004, for it came to pass in 2004 that the conditions for use of the reverse QTIP technique were eliminated.

Beginning only in 2004 were the GST exemption and the estate tax applicable exclusion amount—the estate tax exemption—the same, i.e., both taxes came to enjoy a $1.5 million exemption in 2004, an exemption scheduled to rise over time in lockstep with one another. §§ 2010(c); 2631(c). This congruence eliminates the need for the reverse QTIP election. However, as recently as 2001, the so-called estate tax exemption was $675,000 while the GST exemption was $1 million (§§ 2010(c); 2631(a)), and the problem was very real. Fortunately, how to effectively maximize use of both exemptions was a problem also recognized by Congressional tax writers who provided for the reverse QTIP election in § 2652(a)(3).

Think of the problem in these terms. In 2001, married persons had a combined GST exemption of $2 million, which could have been effectively—if not directly—allocated between them by utilizing one or more QTIP trusts (authorized by § 2056(b)(7)) and a "reverse" QTIP election (authorized by § 2652(a)(3)). For example, assume a married couple with $2 million of property, all of which belonged to the first of them to die. Assume further that the will of the first to die provided a gift in trust for life for the surviving spouse of "the smallest amount necessary to eliminate federal estate tax at my death," the gift to the spouse being followed by a provision causing the balance of the decedent's property to flow into what is typically referred to as the bypass trust, generally for the benefit of the surviving spouse and the decedent's children. If, as expected, the executor of the estate of the first spouse to die made a QTIP election as to the property passing in trust from the decedent to the surviving spouse, the executor's action caused the trust property to be included in the estate of the surviving spouse (and to escape tax at the death of the deceased spouse because it qualified for the estate tax marital deduction). §§ 2056(b)(7), 2044. The widely used scheme was calculated to cause $675,000 to flow into the bypass trust, $675,000 being the maximum amount that could then be tax sheltered free of the federal estate tax. § 2010.

Continuing the example, $675,000 of the decedent's $1 million GST exemption could also be allocated to the bypass trust. That left $325,000 of GST exemption unallocated. This unused $325,000 GST exemption could not be applied to the QTIP trust because the surviving spouse, rather than the deceased spouse, was deemed to be the "transferor" of the QTIP property since the property was included in the surviving spouse's gross estate for estate tax purposes. § 2652(a). Because only the surviving spouse's GST exemption could have applied to the QTIP property in such a case, Congress acted to allow the use of the deceased spouse's unused exemption. This was accomplished by § 2652(a)(3), which permits a reverse QTIP election to be made. If the reverse QTIP election was made for GST purposes, the following analysis applied: (1) for estate tax purposes the QTIP property will be included in the estate of the surviving spouse at the survivor's later death because the surviving spouse was be treated as the "transferor" of the QTIP property, and (2) for GST purposes, the deceased spouse was treated as the "transferor" of the QTIP trust property. Because the deceased spouse was treated as the transferor of the QTIP property for GST purposes, a portion or all of the deceased spouse's $1 million GST exemption could thus be allocated to the QTIP property.

> *Example.* Mort died in 2001, survived by Mindy. Mort's will called for the initial division of his $1.8 million estate into two distinct trusts, to wit, (1) the marital trust and (2) the bypass trust. The marital trust was to be funded with the "smallest amount" of his estate necessary to eliminate federal estate tax at Mort's death. The balance of Mort's estate was to be allocated to the bypass trust. That means that $675,000 was allocated to the bypass trust and $1,125,000 to the marital trust. Mort's will then went on to provide that the marital trust is to be further divided into an exempt QTIP trust and the nonexempt QTIP trust. The exempt QTIP trust was to be funded with any portion of Mort's $1 million GST exemption that remained unallocated at his death—and which was not allocated to the bypass trust. In Mort's case, the resulting allocation meant that $675,000 of Mort's GST exemption was allocated to the bypass trust, $325,000 was allocated to the exempt QTIP trust, and $800,000 was allocated to the nonexempt QTIP trust. At Mindy's death the property then constituting the exempt QTIP trust was to be held for the benefit of Mort's grandchildren—as will the property in the bypass trust (meaning that Mort fully utilized his $1million GST exemption). That is, distributions from the exempt QTIP trust and the bypass trust to Mort's grandchildren will be free of the GST.

Interestingly, while partial QTIP elections can be made for purposes of the estate tax marital deduction, Reg. § 20.2056(b)–7(b)(2), ¶ 14,613, the reverse QTIP election could have been made only as to the entire QTIP trust property. § 2652(a)(3). For that reason, trusts drawn in anticipation of the reverse QTIP might well have authorized the trustee to divide the QTIP into separate trusts and to make reverse QTIP elections for one or more of the separate trusts.

As noted above, the reverse QTIP election technique is not needed after 2003. Thereafter the the GST exemption and the estate tax exemption will be the same. However, remaining is the problem of wills and trusts with reverse QTIP provisions that were signed before 2004. The garden-variety instruments will produce the correct result both before and after 2003 but such instruments need to be revised to clear out the clutter of the reverse QTIP provisions (which will have the effect, at least of possibly making complicated instruments more understandable to the clients who created them).

D. SECURING THE $12,000 PER DONEE PER ANNUM EXCLUSION

[¶ 23,151]

As discussed in ¶ 9365, transfers in trust do not qualify for the § 2503(b) $10,000 per donee per annum GST exclusion—$12,000 in 2006, adjusted for inflation—unless the person identified as the donee when the exclusion is claimed is the sole beneficiary of the trust. The effect is to limit the opportunity for use of so-called *Crummey* trusts to frustrate the reach of the GST.

A taxpayer, employing the scheme popularized in the *Crummey* case, Crummey v. Commissioner, 397 F.2d 82 (9th Cir.1968) (¶ 19,459), places property in trust, giving one or more persons the right to withdraw up to $12,000 from the trust for a period of 30 days after the gift was made. Any amount not withdrawn within this period is added to the principal of the trust. The person (or persons) holding the right to withdraw is said to have a *"Crummey* power." The withdrawal feature allows the amount transferred in trust to qualify for the $10,000 annual gift tax exclusion—$12,000 in 2006, adjusted for inflation. Typically, the terms of the trust are such that distributions can be made from the trust to *Crummey* powerholders who are more than one generation below that of the person who made the transfer in trust.

A transfer of $12,000 to such a trust would constitute a direct skip—and GST would be immediately payable—unless (1) the trust had a nonskip beneficiary; or (2) the skip person is the sole beneficiary of the trust during the skip person's life and the trust is includible in the skip person's gross estate if he or she dies prior to the termination of the trust, § 2642(c)(2); Reg. § 26.2642–1(c)(3); or (3) some part or all of the donor's GST exemption ($2 million in 2006–08) is allocated to the trust, ¶ 9309.

Problems

[¶ 23,195]

1. Grantor establishes a trust with income payable to Grantor's child, C, for life. Grantor's grandchild, GC, holds a continuing right to withdraw trust principal during C's life. When GC reaches age 35, GC is to receive one-half of the trust principal free of trust. The remainder of the trust principal is to be distributed free of trust to GC on C's death. C dies 15 years after the trust is created. Five years after the creation of the trust, GC withdraws $10,000. Is GC's withdrawal a generation-skipping transfer? Reg. § 26.2612–1(f), Example 12.

2. This year, on November 1, Grantor transfers $100,000 to a trust for the benefit of his grandchild, GC. GC has a right to withdraw up to $10,000

¶ 23,101

from the trust until December 1. Any amount not withdrawn prior to December 1 is to be added to the principal of the trust. GC's parents are alive at the time of the transfer. What are the tax consequences of this transfer? What could Grantor do to avoid the GST? See Reg. § 26.2642–1(c)(3).

E. POWER OF APPOINTMENT SOLUTION

[¶ 23,201]

The GST can be avoided or deferred through the use of powers of appointment. A general power of appointment may be used to completely avoid the tax, since the powerholder's estate will therefore be liable for estate tax whether or not the power is ever exercised. See § 2041; Reg. § 26.2612–1(b)(1)(i); ¶ 9245. However, use of a general power may result in the unnecessary payment of estate tax where the property will go to a non-skip person in the absence of the exercise of the power, since there would then be no GST due in such a case.

Those considerations aside, one technique available with respect to property in trust is to give the trustee discretion to give to one or more beneficiaries a general power of appointment over the trust. Such a grant by the trustee would cause the grantee to be the "transferor" for GST purposes and, in cases where the grantee is in a younger generation, the GST may well be avoided (in as much as all trust beneficiaries will be reclassified as either skip or nonskip persons in relationship to the new transferor). In many instances, the most desirable result will be for the trustee to split off a fraction of the trust for the beneficiary with the unused GST exemption and give that beneficiary a general power of appointment over the split-off trust only.

F. LAYERING

[¶ 23,225]

The very wealthy can best take advantage of the structure of the GST to "layer" two or more trusts to avoid some of the GST. A transfer to a person more than one generation below the transferor is generally a generation-skipping transfer, whether or not a person one generation below the transferor has any interest in the transferred property. However, if the transfer skips more than two generations below the transferor (i.e., it skips both the child and grandchild's generations) and no persons higher than the third generation have an interest in the property, only one generation-skipping transfer has occurred and only one GST is payable. For example, if a trust provides for distributions of income to a child, grandchild and great-grandchild, with the trust property passing to the great-grandchild upon the termination of the child and grandchild's interests, two taxable terminations will occur: one upon the child's death and a second upon the grandchild's death. If, however, the transferor made a direct skip to the great-grandchild, a single generation-skipping transfer has occurred. Reg. § 26.2612–1(f), Example 2. Similarly, if the transferor created a trust to pay income to the child and great-grandchild during the child's life with the remainder to the great-grandchild, only a single generation-skipping transfer will occur upon a distribution to the great-grandchild (a taxable distribution) or upon the death of the child (a taxable termination); the passing over of the grandchild will generate no generation-skipping transfer. Therefore, by creating a trust which ignores grandchildren entirely, but provides income for the life of a child with the remainder to the great-grandchildren and their lineal descendants, and providing for grandchildren through a trust which gives only grandchildren an interest, the transferor can "layer" these two trusts and avoid multiple generation-skipping transfers and their taxes.

Most taxpayers, however, cannot afford to utilize "layering" because it results in each generation of the transferor's descendants having access to beneficial enjoyment of only part of the transferor's wealth. Since it is possible for the third or fourth generation to have a dozen or more members, only a very large estate could be divided into two portions and then distributed among a large number of beneficiaries in the third or fourth generation without the final shares being very small. For this reason, layering is an estate planning device for the very rich.

G. DISCLAIMERS

[¶ 23,240]

Generation skipping trusts may be particularly useful for clients with large estates because they save estate tax at their children's level and may be eligible for allocation of part or all of the $2 million exemption (available in 2006). But clients may be reluctant to engage in such complex transactions due to the varying needs and situations of their children. For example, some of the children may not have children of their own either presently or in the future. This may lead to the unpleasant prospect of one sibling seeing his inheritance tied up in a trust for the benefit of his nieces and nephews upon his death. Or some children may have an immediate need for their inheritance while others do not. The clients may not wish to pay the added cost of planning for future generations that may never exist, or they may simply prefer to avoid the headache of deciding how to allocate inheritance based on individual children's needs without creating resentment in the children.

Provision for a disclaimer-activated generation-skipping trust should always be considered. For example, the clients could leave each child's share of the estate in trust for that child. The trust could then provide that the child shall receive income for life and may invade corpus under an ascertainable standard such as for health, education, support or maintenance. The trust could separately give the child a general power of appointment exercisable during life or at death with a gift over to the grandchildren if the power is not exercised. The children then have the option of a "second-look". That is, at a later point in time—death of the parent—the children have the option of exercising the power if they need the money or of disclaiming the power if

¶ 23,225

they wish to avoid inclusion of the corpus in their estate for estate tax purposes. Reg. § 25.2518–3(a)(1)(i) allows a beneficiary to disclaim, separately, "all or an undivided portion [of] each interest in property that is separately created by the transferor." The beneficiary cannot disclaim portions of an outright bequest, so the general power must be created separately. Reg. § 25.2518–3(d), Example 21.

The disclaimer option has other applications. For example, a surviving spouse could disclaim her beneficial interest in a will or trust and, if the instrument is disclaimer-ready, i.e., contains alternative provisions perhaps providing for the disclaimed property to be retained by the trustee in a QTIP-eligible trust in the event of an effective disclaimer, the options are limited only by the creative impulses of the person preparing the disclaimer-ready trust. For different, although more aggressive, ways to split interests in a trust, *see* Natalie B. Choate, *The Disclaimer–Activated Generation–Skipping Trust: A Useful Strategy*, 23 ESTATE PLANNING 210 (1996).

Disclaimer requirements are considered in Chapter 16.

H.   OTHER PLANNING POSSIBILITIES

[¶ 23,251]

1.   PAY ESTATE AND GIFT TAXES AND AVOID THE GST!

Harry and Louise are still at it. Listen in.

"Dadgummit!" says Harry, raising his voice. "I looked at that diagram showing that 'reverse' stuff and how it is going to be in trust for Buster and Missy for the rest of their lives. I bet some banker is licking his chops now waiting for all those trustee fees he'll get while denying the kids their money."

"Calm down," insists Louise. "While the kids don't appreciate us now, they will. Missy will be grateful one day that you made her come into the septic tank cleaning business with you—and Buster will be happy that we arranged that marriage to that heiress despite his infatuation with that "wanna bee" Hollywood starlet. That would never have worked out. And they'll appreciate these trusts one day, too."

"I'm not gonna do it," asserts Harry. "I want something simple, that I can understand—that Buster, on a good day, can perhaps understand. I say let's forget the 'exempt reverse stuff' or whatever it is and give it to the kids outright after you're gone. When they die they can pay tax on whatever is left. Meanwhile their lives will be much simpler."

Clearly, the simplest method of avoiding payment of GST is by giving the property to the children free of trust and allowing them to pay tax on it at death—and for the children to do the same for the grandchildren and so on. Sometimes, however, giving the property to the children in trust accomplishes nontax objectives, such as property management and protection from the predators lurking about—particularly when the trust beneficiary may be the most feared predator!

¶ 23,251

Example. Lonnie's parents put his "inheritance" in trust for life but gave him a power of appointment over the trust property which could only be exercised by Lonnie by provision in his will which made reference to the parents' trust. Not knowing the future, the parents wanted Lonnie to have maximum control over the ultimate disposition of the trust property. For that reason, Lonnie was allowed to exercise the power of appointment in favor of any person, including his own estate. This last feature will cause the trust property to be included in Lonnie's estate for estate tax purposes under § 2041—and free the parents' trust from the generation-skipping tax, even though Lonnie never exercises the power and the trust property passes to the parents' lineal descendants per stirpes under the default terms of the parents' trust. For more on general powers of appointment, see chapter 18.

An outright gift or bequest of the property to a non-skip person with a precatory request that the property be given to a skip person will subject the property to the gift tax when the transfer is made to the skip person. Once the property has been subjected to either estate or gift tax it will be free of liability for the generation-skipping tax, at least with regard to that transfer and except for direct skips. Complete avoidance of the generation-skipping tax in this manner, however, obviously may have other undesirable consequences.

[¶ 23,267]

a. *Advantages of Paying Estate and Gift Taxes Instead of the GST*

There are several advantages to subjecting the transferred property to the estate tax in the transferee's estate if the transferor has no significant reasons for causing the property to be placed in trust. By careful planning and drafting, electing to pay estate tax rather than the GST will defer—or may even eliminate altogether—the payment of any tax on the transfer to future generations. First, the transferee's marital deduction may be used to shelter property from the estate tax on the transferee's estate. Second, the transferee's GST exemption ($2 million in 2006–08 may be used to shelter future transfers of property to younger generations. Third, use of the applicable estate tax exclusion by the transferee will shield at least $2 million of property from estate tax.) Fourth, if the fair market value of the property at the time of the transferee's death is greater than the basis of the property, the basis step-up that results through paying the estate tax will be advantageous to the ultimate recipients of the property. See § 1014(a). For discussion of basis adjustment as a result of the GST, see ¶ 9429. Fifth, certain special elections may be available, such as extended payment of estate tax (§ 6166) or stock redemption (§ 303). Sixth, if the property was previously taxed in the transferor's estate, the § 2013 credit for previously taxed property may be available. See ¶ 7493.

Similar to the advantages of electing to pay the estate tax, an election to pay the gift tax for lifetime transfers may prove more beneficial to the transferee than choosing to pay the GST. First, the transferee can utilize his and his spouse's annual $10,000 exclusions—$12,000 in 2006, adjusted for inflation. See §§ 2503(b), 2513. Second, due to the fact that the gift tax is tax exclusive, ¶ 7185, while the taxable amount in taxable terminations and taxable distributions includes the generation-skipping tax, the tax rate will be lower except in the case of direct skips. Third, the transferor may pay the gift tax without increasing the taxable amount of the gift. Fourth, the transferor may use his or her $1 million gift tax applicable exclusion amount (§ 2505(a)) to shield all or part of the transferred property from the gift tax.

[¶ 23,275]

b.   *Disadvantages of Paying Estate and Gift Taxes Instead of the GST*

Carefully consider all the consequences of attempting to avoid the generation-skipping tax by paying estate or gift taxes.

First, there are some situations where the GST will be applied only once to the transferred property but if that property were subject to the estate tax, the estate tax may well be applied to the same property multiple times. For example, two or more generations may be skipped while the transferred property is subject to the GST only once (e.g., a "layered" gift as described in ¶ 23,291, such as a gift of property to a great-grandchild, skipping both the child and grandchild). On the other hand, the total transfer taxes on the same property if subject to the estate tax in each generation will likely be greater.

Second, direct skips will have an effective lower GST rate than the estate tax. The taxable amount on a direct skip is exclusive of the amount of the GST, instead consisting solely of the value of the property received by the skip person. The estate tax, in contrast, is tax inclusive. See ¶ 7185.

Third, by holding the property in trust for the benefit of several generations, payment of the GST can generally be deferred until the death of the last to die in each generation. This results from the language of § 2612(a), which provides that a taxable termination does not occur until the last non-skip person holding an interest in the trust dies. It is important to note, however, that when a termination occurring because of the death of a lineal descendant of the transferor results in the distribution of a specified portion of the trust to skip persons, a taxable termination of the specified portion occurs at the time of death.

[¶ 23,283]

2.   TAXABLE DISTRIBUTION PREFERRED TO TAXABLE TERMI-NATION

Planning the type of generation-skipping transfer which will occur as to property may reduce GST liability. If property is distributed to a skip person by a taxable distribution (¶ 9229) rather than a taxable termination (¶ 9246), a single generation-skipping transfer may occur, while a transfer to the same skip person by means of a taxable termination could constitute multiple generation-skipping transfers, i.e., multiple taxable terminations, each one of which is a GST-triggering event. For example, if a trust was created to pay the income to the transferor's child, grandchild and great-grandchild until the

¶ 23,283

death of the first to die of the child and grandchild and thereafter to the great-grandchild if he is then living, any distribution to the grandchild or the great-grandchild prior to the death of any of the beneficiaries is a taxable distribution. If the grandchild or great-grandchild survive the child, the death of the child is a taxable termination. If the great-grandchild survives the child and grandchild, and the grandchild survived the child, another taxable termination occurs at the death of the grandchild. Structuring the trust so as to allow the property to pass to the great-grandchild by a taxable distribution prior to the death of the child will subject the property to only one generation-skipping transfer.

I. PROBLEMS TO WATCH FOR

[¶ 23,301]

1. COMMON SITUATIONS

a. *Tax Provisions*

Where a will or trust does not mention the GST, which is the case with most pre–1986 wills and trusts, the tax will be charged to the transferred property, rather than to the residue of the estate or another source. This will cause otherwise equal distributions to be unequal if all the transferees are not in the same generation. An example of a provision which will prevent this from occurring can be found in the discussion of apportionment in ¶ 9301.

[¶ 23,309]

b. *Specific Bequests*

If several specific bequests to different persons are planned, each such bequest should be carefully examined to determine whether or not it qualifies as a direct skip. It will be necessary to know the donee's date of birth and relationship to the client to make this determination. If the bequest is a direct skip, it should then be decided whether or not the bequest should directly bear the GST.

[¶ 23,317]

c. *Survivorship Provisions*

It is unclear what the effect on the GST will be from a survivorship provision in a will containing bequests for children, with contingent bequests to grandchildren. If the survivorship period is for less than six months after the transferor's death, the actual disposition will presumably be used in determining whether the transfer is a direct skip. According to the regulations, however, the bequest should be treated as a trust arrangement if the survivorship period ends more than six months after the transferor's death. Reg. § 26.2652–1(b)(1), in defining a "trust," states that "a transfer as to which the identity of the transferee is contingent upon the occurrence of an event is a transfer in trust; however, a testamentary transfer as to which the identity of the transferee is contingent upon an event that must occur within

6 months of the transferor's death is not considered a transfer in trust solely by reason of the existence of the contingency.''

For additional background material, see ¶ 9157.

Problem

[¶ 23,323]

Grantor wants to bequeath $100,000 to his son, but only if his son survives him for some period of time. If his son does not survive Grantor by that period of time, Grantor wants the money to go to his grandson. Grantor wants his estate to bear as little tax as possible. What period of time would you advise Grantor to require his son to survive him in order to obtain the most favorable GST? Would the predeceased child exemption apply here? What is the result if the son survives the survivorship period? See Reg. § 26.2652–1(b)(1), Examples 2 and 3.

[¶ 23,325]

2. REVERSE QTIP ELECTION

Special problems can arise where a QTIP trust has been used by the transferor, since the surviving spouse is treated as the transferor of the QTIP trust property unless the original transferor makes a reverse QTIP election. §§ 2044, 2056(b)(7), 2652(a)(3); ¶ 23,151. As an example, in the case where no reverse QTIP election is made, a QTIP trust passing on the surviving spouse's death to the settlor's children and the issue of deceased children per stirpes will avoid the GST for transfers to the issue of a deceased child. This results from the treatment of the surviving spouse as the transferor, making the predeceased child exemption available. If, however, the reverse QTIP election has been made in this instance, the predeceased child exemption will not be available to shield transfers to the issue of deceased children since the settlor is then treated as the transferor. (Of course, a reverse QTIP election made as to a trust which is completely exempt from the tax will make this possibility a nonproblem.)

> *Example.* T creates a QTIP trust, with income for life to S, T's spouse, remainder to T's children, C1 and C2, if living at the time of S's death, otherwise to C1's and C2's lineal descendants per stirpes. C1 dies before S, leaving two children, GC1 and GC2. If no reverse QTIP election has been made, S is treated as the transferor and GC1 and GC2 move up one generation under the predeceased child exception to the children's generation. Therefore, no generation-skipping transfers have occurred on S's death. If, however, the reverse QTIP election has been made, T is treated as the transferor and the predeceased child exception is not available to avoid the GST for the transfer to GC1 and GC2 because C1 was alive at the time T transferred the property to the trust. If T had created two QTIP trusts originally, one subject to the GST and one exempt from the tax through allocation of the $2 million exemption, no GST would result from a reverse QTIP election as to the exempt QTIP trust.

¶ 23,325

Suppose Grantor, G, establishes a trust under which the income is to be paid to his spouse, S, for life, remainder to grantor's grandchild, GC. If G, or his executor, elects to treat the transferred property as QTIP property and a reverse QTIP election has been made, G is treated as the transferor and a taxable termination occurs on S's death. Reg. § 26.2652–2(d), Example 1. If, however, no reverse QTIP election has been made, S is treated as the transferor and a direct skip occurs on S's death because the property is included in S's gross estate. Reg. § 26.2652–1(a)(5), Example 3. This result occurs despite the fact that the original transfer to the trust was not a direct skip since S, a non-skip person, held an interest in the trust.

Problem

[¶ 23,331]

Determine whether a direct skip has occurred in the following circumstances:

(a) Upon the death of grantor's surviving spouse, the remainder of a QTIP trust passes to the grantor's grandson. No reverse QTIP election was made. See § 2652(a)(3); Reg. § 26.2652–1(a)(5), Example 5.

(b) Same facts as in (a), but a reverse QTIP election was made as to the trust property. See § 2652(a)(3).

[¶ 23,333]

3. RULES AS TO SEPARATE TRUSTS

Section 2654(b) sets out two situations in which a single trust is treated as two or more trusts, namely (1) where different transferors have transferred property to a single trust, the portions of the trust attributable to each transferor will be treated as a separate trust; and (2) where there is more than one beneficiary of the trust, each beneficiary's "substantially separate and independent share" will be treated as a separate trust. The phrase "substantially separate and independent shares" basically means that distributions to the beneficiaries "are to be made in substantially the same manner as if separate trusts had been created." Reg. § 1.663(c)–3. However, a separate share consisting of a portion of the trust property will not be recognized for GST purposes unless that share was created at the time the trust was created and the share continues its existence at all times thereafter during the life of the trust. Reg. § 26.2654–1(a)(1).

An example of the first situation—multiple transferors to a single trust—would be the case in which A transfers $100,000 to an irrevocable GST trust and B simultaneously transfers $50,000 to the same trust. The single trust is treated as two trusts for GST purposes from the time of the transfers. Two-thirds of the trust principal is treated as a separate trust created by A, since he contributed two-thirds of the value of the original principal. One-third of the trust principal is treated as a separate trust created by B, since he contributed one-third of the value of the original trust principal. Reg. § 26.2654–1(a)(5), Example 5.

An example of the second situation—separate shares as separate trusts— would be the case in which T transfers $100,000 to a trust under which income is to be paid in equal shares for 10 years to T's child, C, and T's grandchild, GC. No distributions of principal may be made during the term of the trust. When the 10–year term ends, the principal is to be distributed in equal shares to C and GC. C and GC have "substantially separate and independent shares"; therefore, their shares are treated as separate trusts. Treatment of C's and CG's shares as separate trusts would not result if the trustee could make distributions of principal, unless those distributions could only be made from a one-half, separate share of the initial trust principal. Reg. § 26.2654–1(a)(5), Example 1. Additionally, if the trustee, in his discretion, could distribute the income in any proportion between C and GC during the last year of the trust, the shares of C and GC are not separate and independent shares throughout the life of the trust and are therefore not treated as separate trusts. Reg. § 26.2654–1(a)(5), Example 2.

Certain pecuniary amounts are also treated as separate and independent shares, and therefore as separate trusts. See Reg. § 26.2654–1(a)(5), Example 3. However, treatment of this issue is beyond the scope of these materials.

Where a single trust is treated as separate trusts for purposes of GST payment, computation and filing of any tax other than the GST requires treatment of the trust as a single trust. Reg. § 26.2654–1(a)(1). Unless the governing instrument expressly provides otherwise, any additions to the trust or distributions from the trust are allocated pro rata among the separate trusts. Id. Where a transferor allocates all or part of his or her exemption to such a trust, the exemption will be allocated on a pro rata basis among the separate trusts of which he or she is a transferor, unless the transferor clearly indicates otherwise. Id.

J. SUMMARY

[¶ 23,401]

Planning for the GST involves making gifts to skip persons that are sheltered by both the gift tax $10,000 ($12,000 in 2006, adjusted for inflation) per donee per annum gift tax exclusion and GST $10,000 ($12,000 in 2006, adjusted for inflation) per donee per annum exclusion. It also involves determining how to maximize the benefit of the GST exemption ($2 million in 2006 through 2008), e.g., with respect to gifts in trust of life insurance, ¶ 20,779, or upon creation of a charitable lead trust. ¶ 26,275. Finally, in the case of trusts which are not GST exempt, planning requires a provision authorizing an independent trustee to divide the trust into separate trusts and permitting that trustee to confer upon one or more beneficiaries of one or more of those separate trusts a general power of appointment (thus allowing a downward shift of the "transferor" generation for purposes of the GST in cases, particularly, where the recipient of the general power has unused GST exemption).

*

¶ 23,401

Part VI

SPECIAL SITUATIONS

Chapter 24

CLOSELY HELD BUSINESS INTERESTS: VALUE FREEZING AND OTHER ISSUES

A. OBJECTIVES

[¶ 24,001]

A closely held business may represent more than a successful businessperson's greatest achievement; it may also embody the bulk of his or her wealth and be the primary source of the businessperson's income. These factors—the special personal relationship between the client and his or her business, and the predominant role of the business as a source of his or her income and wealth—make careful planning for the client with the closely held business both essential and challenging.

During the client's lifetime, a closely held business offers special opportunities for taking care of the financial needs of the client and the client's family. In the absence of careful planning, however, what appeared to be the goose that laid the golden egg while the client was alive may become the family albatross after the client's death. To avoid this result, certain questions must be asked, and answered to the greatest possible extent, in advance of the time when death or retirement will remove the client from the business.

This chapter will touch briefly upon the essential planning considerations that should be involved whenever a client owns an interest in a closely held business. The client should consider whether the present form of the business is best for satisfying his or her short-and long-term needs and those of his or her family. Would incorporation serve any useful purpose? If incorporation is pursued, how should the capital structure of the company be constructed? Looking further down the road, the client should also evaluate the likelihood that some family member will want to succeed to an active role in the business. How should that family member be brought into the business? What are the nontax and tax consequences flowing from a gift of an interest in the company to such a person? Should there be a sale instead? How should those family members who do not receive an interest in the company be treated?

On the other hand, what if no one in the family is interested in taking an active role in the client's business? If there are others who hold an interest in the business, can arrangements be made to "buy out" the client on his or her death or retirement? What form should any buyout take, and how should it be financed?

Since a closely held business will often lack liquidity, a client should also consider means by which funds can be made available to the client and to his or her family while the client lives. If the business is going to continue after the client's death, arrangements for raising funds to pay death taxes and administration costs should also be made. The cash-flow problems that may occur when the bulk of a client's estate is tied up in a closely held business interest are those most likely to cause trouble for a client's family after the client's death. This chapter will consider some of the options available for alleviating those problems.

Given careful planning, the closely held business need not become the family albatross. Such planning is not possible, however, without familiarity with the landscape of corporate and partnership taxation. Accordingly, review of pertinent sections of the Internal Revenue Code is part of planning for the closely held business. While a thorough understanding of these sections usually requires a course in corporate or business taxation, a careful reading of the noted sections should result in the understanding needed to appreciate the planning alternatives.

Reg. § 301.7701–1(a)(1) implements a "check-the-box" approach to the classification of an unincorporated business entity. Some of the notions reflected in these regulations include: (1) organizations will be treated as a trust if there are neither associates nor an objective to carry on business for profit; (2) an organization that has a single owner can choose to be recognized or disregarded as an entity separate from its owner; and (3) a business entity that is not automatically classified as a corporation can elect its classification for federal tax purposes. One consequence of these regulations is that provisions viewed as mandatory in partnership agreements to achieve partnership classification—continuity of life, free transferability of interests, etc., for example—can be removed. Plain and simple, small businesses can choose whether to be treated as a corporation or partnership for federal tax purposes. By the same token, failure to file IRS Form 8832 and check the appropriate box will result in partnership tax treatment—and if a single member business, the business entity will be disregarded and the enterprise treated, for federal income tax purposes, as a sole proprietorship. This is the default position. See Littriello v. United States, 95 A.F.T.R.2d 2005–2581, 2005–1 U.S.T.C. ¶ 50,385 (W.D. Ky. 2005) (mem.) (IRS permitted to levy against taxpayer's personal property for nonpayment of taxes by single member LLC where LLC did not check the box).

Finally, not to be ignored is the possible role of the corporation (or partnership) in shifting partial interests to downstream loved ones while maintaining the corporation as the management vehicle (as contrasted with fractionalizing ownership of different items of property). See Chapter 21 for consideration of the family limited partnership (FLP) for these purposes particularly.

¶ 24,001

B. PLANNING FOR A CLOSELY HELD BUSINESS: A CASE STUDY

[¶ 24,051]

To help illustrate some of the problems, pitfalls, solutions and opportunities provided by the closely held business, consider the following example: Jim and Ahmed are two equal partners in Super Electronics Co., a general partnership. They started the business about two years ago, after successful careers with a giant corporation, where they were unhappy because the giant, rather than they, was receiving all the money.

Super's balance sheet and profit and loss statement are set forth in Table 24.1. Jim and Ahmed each own a term life insurance policy on the life of the other partner in the amount of $250,000, which is most inadequate. Their accountant has advised them to incorporate to avoid business interruption if one of them should die, to enable them to participate in a proposed employee profit-sharing plan, and to enable them to go public in five years should the business continue to grow geometrically.

Table 24.1. PARTNERSHIP BALANCE SHEET AND PROFIT & LOSS STATEMENT (SUPER ELECTRONICS CO.)		
BALANCE SHEET		
	Cost	*Fair Market Value*
Cash	$50,000	$50,000
Receivables	200,000	200,000
Land and Plant........................... $500,000		
Machinery & Equipment 250,000	750,000	850,000
Goodwill	–0–	200,000
	$1,000,000	$1,300,000
Accounts Payable	$100,000	$100,000
Mortgage on plant	350,000	350,000
	$450,000	$450,000
Partners' capital.........................	550,000	850,000
	$1,000,000	$1,300,000
PROFIT & LOSS STATEMENT		
Sales		$1,400,000
Less: Cost of Sales		600,000
		800,000
Research and development.................	$200,000	
Interest	50,000	
Administrative expense....................	75,000	325,000
Net profit before partners' compensation..........		$475,000

Jim is married to Mai and has one son, Junior, and one daughter, Sandy. Junior has received his MBA and is ready to show Jim and Ahmed how to really run a business. Jim hopes that his investment in Junior's tuition will pay off, so that Junior will someday take his place in the management of

¶ 24,051

Super Electronics. Sandy, an artist, is married to the principal of the local grammar school, has three children, and could use some financial help.

Ahmed is married to Pam and has two daughters, Judy and Debbie. Pam considers her separate property her little nest egg and would be reluctant to give it up. Judy, a prolific writer of children's books, recently married a socially prominent young dentist (who believes that he can earn a lot of money if the anti-fluoride movement is successful), while Debbie and her husband are social workers with a local social service agency. Ahmed will want to be bought out in the event of his death, and maybe earlier.

How should Jim plan for his family in the event of his death? How should Ahmed plan for his death? In each case, how could the children be helped during the parent's lifetimes if the business continues in partnership form or, alternatively, is incorporated? Jim and Ahmed have furnished statements of their assets which are set forth in Tables 24.2 and 24.3, respectively.

Table 24.2. JIM'S STATEMENT OF ASSETS	
Cash	$ 40,000
Furniture	20,000
Land held for long-term appreciation	50,000
Equity in home	80,000
Marketable securities	100,000
Speculation in Dry Hole Oil Corp.	10,000
Partnership at book	275,000
Cash value of life insurance (face $500,000)	100,000
Term life policy on Ahmed	–0–
	$675,000
Mai's net worth	–0–

Table 24.3. AHMED'S STATEMENT OF ASSETS	
Cash	$ 25,000
Furniture, furnishings, etc.	20,000
Interest in family business run by brother (cash yield 5%)	100,000
Marketable securities	65,000
Equity in home	100,000
Loan to Judy	35,000
Loan to Debbie	10,000
Partnership interest at book	275,000
Term life policy on Jim	–0–
	$630,000
Pam's net worth:	
Land subject to ground lease	$112,000

C.   RETAINING THE CLOSELY HELD BUSINESS

[¶ 24,101]

1.   UNDERSTANDING THE FACTS

a.   *The Starting Point*

Jim has expressed a desire to have his family retain his share of Super Electronics. What kind of death planning should he have? A will? A revocable trust? The starting point of the analysis should not be any specific program or planning technique but, rather, obtaining a clear understanding of both the facts and the client's objectives. For example, in this case Jim has provided a statement of his assets. Are the figures provided by him fair market value, historical costs or mere puffing? If cost was used, the raw land may have tripled in value and the speculative investment may be worthless. Has Jim included contingent liabilities, such as bank guarantees? It is important that these types of questions be answered at the outset, so that Jim's situation and his potential problems can be appreciated.

[¶ 24,109]

b. *Valuing the Closely Held Business*

i. *Valuation Methods*

Valuation experts use a number of methods when valuing closely held business interests. Each method is to be evaluated in light of the principles expressed in Revenue Ruling 59–60, reproduced at ¶ 24,111.

1. *Capitalized earnings.* This method is based on an average of corporate earnings from the previous five years. This "earnings average" should not include extraordinary or nonrecurring items from any year and, once determined, should be multiplied by a capitalization rate. The capitalization rate should approximate the investment rate that comparable investments are earning.

2. *Discounted cash flow* or *discounted earnings.* Valuation using this method is determined by projecting cash flow or earnings a number of years into the future (typically, 10) and then discounting the projected cash flows or earnings back to a present value.

3. *Fair market value.* Valuation is based on the current fair market value of assets. This approach focuses on the balance sheet of a company, but corporate earnings are indirectly considered in the computation of goodwill.

4. *Price/earnings.* Under this method, the stock price and earnings of other companies within the industry are analyzed, and an industry "multiple" is calculated. The current earnings of the target company are then divided by the industry multiple to arrive at stock price.

5. *Capitalized dividends.* This method attempts to project the future dividend-paying capacity of the company, multiplying the result by a desired rate of return over a future term certain.

6. *Capitalized excess earnings.* Valuation under this method is very similar to the capitalized dividends method, except this method considers the ability of a target corporation to earn profits above the norm.

Number Cruncher and Estate Planning Tools, both listed in Appendix A, provide electronic implementation of these factors expressed as valuation models (and are enormously helpful).

[¶ 24,110]

ii.   Illustration

What about Super Electronics? What is it worth? The balance sheet shows that the physical assets exceed book value by $100,000. But the value of the business cannot be ascertained without also examining its earnings. While the starting point is the bottom line figure shown on the financial statements, adjustments are often required in order to have a true picture of the earnings. For example, in the case of Super Electronics Co., it is necessary to know what the large research and development expenses represent. Are they regular or recurrent expenditures, or do they largely reflect start-up expenses, so that in the future they will decline? If the latter, they are not a proper charge to current earnings for valuation purposes. Also, some reasonable allowance for compensation to the owners for their personal effects must be deducted. In this case, assume that Jim and Ahmed's combined salary can reasonably be set at $200,000. Thus, Super's net income appears to be about $275,000.

Still, the analysis is not complete. What about taxes? As a corporation, the business would have to deduct a 34 percent tax (or possibly as much as 39 percent) to arrive at net profits. § 11(b). The earnings of the business cannot have doubled, merely because of the failure to incorporate. Thus, to value the partnership, a hypothetical corporate tax—in this case $93,500—should be deducted from the $275,000 net income, leaving earnings of $181,500.

Having determined earnings for valuation purposes, it is possible to test whether there is any goodwill. Goodwill is an example of an asset which normally does not appear on a balance sheet at all. Its existence can be tested by allowing a reasonable return on invested capital and multiplying any excess earnings by a factor. The appropriate return and multiplier differ widely, depending upon the nature and stability of the business and the prejudices of the evaluator. A reasonable return may range between 12 and 25 percent while a reasonable multiplier of excess earnings may be anywhere from one to six, or occasionally as high as eight. In Super's case, a 15 percent return on invested capital in this attractive industry with a multiplier of excess earnings of four yields goodwill of roughly $336,000 [$181,500 − 15 percent x ($550,000 book value + $100,000 net land and machinery appreciation), which equals roughly $84,000 x 4].

Problems

[¶ 24,111]

1.   It may be appropriate to use a 20 percent return on invested capital and a multiplier of two since Super Electronics is a new business. What "goodwill figure" would this yield? Can the wide disparity between this amount and that determined above be defended on some rational basis? Given the wide range of results that flow from seemingly arbitrary shifts in the rate of return and multiplier, do you consider this an adequate or accurate method for valuing goodwill?

¶ 24,111

2. Read Revenue Ruling 59–60, 1959–1 C.B. 237, reproduced below, and consider whether the valuation technique utilized for Super Electronics above is consistent with the principles expressed in Revenue Ruling 59–60.

[¶ 24,112]

REVENUE RULING 59–60

1959–1 C.B. 237.

§ 1. PURPOSE.

The purpose of this Revenue Ruling is to outline and review in general the approach, methods and factors to be considered in valuing shares of the capital stock of closely held corporations for estate tax and gift tax purposes. The methods discussed herein will apply likewise to the valuation of corporate stocks on which market quotations are either unavailable or are of such scarcity that they do not reflect the fair market value.

§ 2. BACKGROUND AND DEFINITIONS.

.01 * * * Sections 2031(a), 2032 and 2512(a) (§§ 811 and 1005 of the 1939 Code) require that the property to be included in the gross estate, or made the subject of a gift, shall be taxed on the basis of the value of the property at the time of death of the decedent, the alternate date if so elected, or the date of gift.

.02 Section 20.2031–1(b) of the Estate Tax Regulations (§ 81.10 of the Estate Tax Regulations 105) and Reg. § 25.2512–1 (§ 86.19 of Gift Tax Regulations 108) define fair market value, in effect, as the price at which the property would change hands between a willing buyer and a willing seller when the former is not under any compulsion to buy and the latter is not under any compulsion to sell, both parties having reasonable knowledge of relevant facts. Court decisions frequently state in addition that the hypothetical buyer and seller are assumed to be able, as well as willing, to trade and to be well informed about the property and concerning the market for such property.

.03 Closely held corporations are those corporations the shares of which are owned by a relatively limited number of stockholders. Often the entire stock issue is held by one family. The result of this situation is that little, if any, trading in the shares takes place. There is, therefore, no established market for the stock and such sales as occur at irregular intervals seldom reflect all of the elements of a representative transaction as defined by the term "fair market value."

§ 3. APPROACH TO VALUATION.

.01 A determination of fair market value, being a question of fact, will depend upon the circumstances in each case. No formula can be devised that will be generally applicable to the multitude of different valuation issues arising in estate and gift tax cases. Often, an appraiser will find wide differences of opinion as to the fair market value of a particular stock. In resolving such differences, he should maintain a reasonable attitude in recognition of the fact that valuation is not an exact science. A sound valuation will be based upon all the relevant facts, but the elements of common sense, informed judgment and reasonableness must enter into the process of weighing those facts and determining their aggregate significance.

.02 The fair market value of specific shares of stock will vary as general economic conditions change from "normal" to "boom" or "depression," that is, according to the degree of optimism or pessimism with which the investing public regards the future at the required date of appraisal. Uncertainty as to the stability or continuity of the future income from a property decreases its value by increasing the risk of loss of earnings and value in the future. The value of shares of stock of a company with very uncertain future prospects is highly speculative. The appraiser must exercise his judgment as to the degree of risk attaching to the business of the corporation which issued the stock, but that judgment must be related to all of the other factors affecting value.

.03 Valuation of securities is, in essence, a prophesy as to the future and must be based on facts available at the required date of appraisal. As a generalization, the prices of stocks which are traded in volume in a free and active market by informed persons best reflect the consensus of the investing public as to what the future holds for the corporations and industries represented. When a stock is closely held, is traded infrequently, or is traded in an erratic market, some other measure of value must be used. In many instances, the next best measure may be found in the prices at which the stocks of companies engaged in the same or a similar line of business are selling in a free and open market.

§ 4. FACTORS TO CONSIDER.

.01 It is advisable to emphasize that in the valuation of the stock of closely held corporations or the stock of corporations where market quotations are either lacking or too scarce to be recognized, all available financial data, as well as all relevant factors affecting the fair market value, should be considered. The following factors, although not all inclusive are fundamental and require careful analysis in each case:

(a) The nature of the business and the history of the enterprise from its inception.

(b) The economic outlook in general and the condition and outlook of the specific industry in particular.

(c) The book value of the stock and the financial condition of the business.

(d) The earning capacity of the company.

(e) The dividend-paying capacity.

(f) Whether or not the enterprise has goodwill or other intangible value.

(g) Sales of the stock and the size of the block of stock to be valued.

¶ **24,112**

(h) The market price of stocks of corporations engaged in the same or a similar line of business having their stocks actively traded in a free and open market, either on an exchange or over-the-counter.

* * *

[Omitted is an extensive analysis of the foregoing factors.—*Ed.*]

§ 5. WEIGHT TO BE ACCORDED VARIOUS FACTORS.

The valuation of closely held corporate stock entails the consideration of all relevant factors as stated in § 4. Depending upon the circumstances in each case, certain factors may carry more weight than others because of the nature of the company's business. To illustrate:

(a) Earnings may be the most important criterion of value in some cases whereas asset value will receive primary consideration in others. In general, the appraiser will accord primary consideration to earning when valuing stocks of companies which sell products or services to the public; conversely, in the investment or holding type of company, the appraiser may accord the greatest weight to the assets underlying the security to be valued.

(b) The value of the stock of a closely held investment or real estate holding company, whether or not family owned, is closely related to the value of the assets underlying the stock. For companies of this type the appraiser should determine the fair market values of the assets of the company. Operating expenses of such a company and the cost of liquidating it, if any, merit consideration when appraising the relative values of the stock and the underlying assets. The market values of the underlying assets give due weight to potential earnings and dividends of the particular items of property underlying the stock, capitalized at rates deemed proper by the investing public at the date of appraisal. A current appraisal by the investing public should be superior to the retrospective opinion of an individual. For these reasons, adjusted net worth should be accorded greater weight in valuing the stock of a closely held investment or real estate holding company, whether or not family owned, than any of the other customary yardsticks of appraisal, such as earnings and dividend paying capacity.

§ 6. CAPITALIZATION RATES.

In the application of certain fundamental valuation factors, such as earnings and dividends, it is necessary to capitalize the average or current results at some appropriate rate. A determination of the proper capitalization rate presents one of the most difficult problems in valuation. That there is no ready or simple solution will become apparent by a cursory check of the rates of return and dividend yields in terms of the selling prices of corporate shares listed on the major exchanges of the country. Wide variations will be found even for companies in the same industry. Moreover, the ratio will fluctuate from year to year depending upon economic conditions. Thus, no standard tables of capitalization rates applicable to closely held corporations can be formulated. Among the more important factors to be taken into consideration in deciding upon a capitalization rate in a particular case are: (1) the nature of the business; (2) the risk involved; and (3) the stability or irregularity of earnings.

§ 7. AVERAGE OF FACTORS.

Because valuations cannot be made on the basis of a prescribed formula, there is no means whereby the various applicable factors in a particular case can be assigned mathematical weights in deriving the fair market value. For this reason, no useful purpose is served by taking an average of several factors (for example, book value, capitalized earnings and capitalized dividends) and basing the valuation on the result. Such a process excludes active consideration of other pertinent factors, and the end result cannot be supported by a realistic application of the significant facts in the case except by mere chance.

§ 8. RESTRICTIVE AGREEMENTS.

Frequently, in the valuation of closely held stock for estate and gift tax purposes, it will be found that the stock is subject to an agreement restricting its sale or transfer. Where shares of stock were acquired by a decedent subject to an option reserved by the issuing corporation to repurchase at a certain price, the option price is usually accepted as the fair market value for estate tax purposes. See Rev. Rul. 54–76, C.B. 1954–1, 194. However, in such case the option price is not determinative of fair market value for gift tax purposes. Where the option, or buy and sell agreement is the result of voluntary action by the stockholders and is binding during the life as well as at the death of the stockholders, such agreement may or may not, depending upon the circumstances of each case, fix the value for estate tax purposes. However, such agreement is a factor to be considered, with other relevant factors, in determining fair market value. Where the stockholder is free to dispose of his shares during life and the option is to become effective only upon his death, the fair market value is not limited to the option price. It is always necessary to consider the relationship of the parties, the relative number of shares held by the decedent, and other material facts, to determine whether the agreement represents a bona fide business arrangement or is a device to pass the decedent's shares to the natural objects of his bounty for less than an adequate and full consideration in money or money's worth. In this connection see Rev. Rul. 157, C.B. 1953–2, 255, and Rev. Rul. 189, C.B. 1953–2, 294.

[¶ 24,117]

c. *Premiums, Discounts, and the Marital Deduction*

For estate and gift tax purposes, two factors arguably to be taken into account in valuation are "control premium" and "minority discount."

Reg. § 20.2031–2(f) provides that the determination of the fair market value of a block of stock will depend on several relevant factors, including "the degree of control of the business represented by the block of stock." See Estate of Salsbury v. Commissioner, 34 T.C.M. (CCH) 1441, T.C.M. (P–H) ¶ 75,333 (1975) (control premium applied to shares in closely held corporation); Estate of Murphy v. Commissioner, 60 T.C.M. (CCH) 645, T.C.M. (P–H) ¶ 90,472 (1990) (control premium applied despite immediate predeath transfer of 2 percent of shares which changed decedent's status from that of majority shareholder to minority shareholder).

The minority discount is supported by the concept of the "willing buyer/willing seller" standard provided in Reg. § 20.2031–1(b). Fair market value is defined as "the price at which the property would change hands between a willing buyer and a willing seller, neither being under any compulsion to buy or sell and both having reasonable knowledge of relevant facts." Id. A minority discount typically consists of two components: a discount for lack of control over corporate policy and a discount for lack of marketability. Although there is some overlap between these two concepts, they are conceptually distinct. See, e.g., Estate of Newhouse v. Commissioner, 94 T.C. 193 (1990) nonacq., 1991–2 C.B. 1. The discount for lack of control takes into account the inability to direct the payment of dividends, inability to compel liquidation of assets, inability to select managers, and a general inability to direct corporate policy. See, e.g., Moore v. Commissioner, 62 T.C.M. (CCH) 1128, T.C.M. (P–H) ¶ 91,546 (1991). The discount for lack of marketability takes into account limitations on assignments and lack of established markets for ownership interests. Id.

An interesting issue is whether different blocks of stock should be aggregated for purposes of applying control premiums and minority discounts. In Tech. Adv. Mem. 9403002, the Service stated that two blocks of stock, one includible pursuant to § 2033 and the other pursuant to § 2038, should be aggregated for purposes of applying a control premium.

The decision in Chenoweth v. Commissioner, 88 T.C. 1577 (1987), raises another point. At the death of the sole shareholder, 51 percent of the shares passed to the shareholder's surviving spouse. A 38.1 percent control premium was placed on the shares for federal estate tax purposes. In dispute was the value of the shares for purposes of the marital deduction claimed by the shareholder's estate. Over objections by the IRS, the Tax Court concluded that the value of the shares passing to the surviving spouse for purposes of the marital deduction allowed by § 2056 was equal to the value of the shares for estate tax purposes. Suppose, however, that the shares passing to the surviving spouse constituted only 49 percent of the shares. Would that mean that the shares have one value for estate tax purposes and another value for marital deduction purposes? Such a result could dramatically change how the decedent's wealth is distributed in cases where the share passing to the surviving spouse is the "smallest amount necessary to eliminate estate tax" at the death of the decedent.

Notwithstanding *Chenoweth*, in 1994 the IRS concluded that a decedent's gift to his surviving spouse was to be valued as a separate minority interest block—and discounted accordingly—for purposes of the marital deduction. Tech. Adv. Mem. 9403005. The surviving spouse received preferred stock, a minority interest. The IRS, having discounted the preferred for marital deduction purposes, turned around and aggregated the preferred and common (the common passing to a credit shelter trust) for purposes of imposing a control premium on the aggregated value.

¶ 24,117

Estee Lauder (Estee), the cosmetics entrepreneur, was involved in a precedent setting situation when her husband, Joseph Lauder (Joe), died. EJL Corporation (EJL), the family business, was owned entirely Estee and Joe and their children (as well as family trusts). Each shareholder was contractually obligated (by virtue of a buy-sell agreement (buy-sell)) to sell his or her shares to EJL at death. Joe's shares were sold to EJL for $29.1 million, the price established in the buy-sell. Nonetheless, the Tax Court determined that the fair market value of the shares was $50.5 million for estate tax purposes—and that while Joe's estate received only $29.1 million for the shares, the estate tax to be paid by Joe's estate was to be based on a value of $50.5 million. Estate of Lauder v. Commissioner, 68 T.C.M. (CCH) 985, T.C.M. (RIA) ¶ 94,527 (1994).

At this point Estee made a novel argument which the Tax Court accepted. While Estee was not a beneficiary under Joe's will, she, nonetheless, claimed that she was enriched by the $21.4 increase in the value of Joe's EJL stock—and that the value of the enrichment she experienced qualified for the marital deduction in computing Joe' estate tax liability. Estee owned 39.26 percent of the shares of EJL and it was her contention that the value of her shares was increased by $8.4 million (39.26 percent of $21.4 million) as a result of the Tax Court's determination that Joe's shares were valued at $50.5 million. Confusing? The IRS thought so. It sputtered that Estee was "attempting to extend the marital deduction provision beyond its intended scope." In allowing the marital deduction to Joe's estate for the value of the enrichment experienced by Estee, the Tax Court explained:

> Section 2056(a) provides that the taxable estate shall be determined by deducting from the value of the gross estate an amount equal to the value of any interest in property which passes or has passed from the decedent to his surviving spouse, but only to the extent that such interest is included in determining the value of the gross estate and excepting any terminable interest as described in § 2056(b). While we recognize that the marital deduction is strictly construed * * *, we nevertheless agree with petitioner that the estate is entitled to a marital deduction under the circumstances presented.

> To briefly recapitulate, we determined that the fair market value of decedent's EJL stock exceeded the value assigned to the stock by petitioner on its Federal estate tax return. Because the difference, $21,443,544, will be included in decedent's gross estate, it follows that the first element required for the deduction under § 2056(a) is satisfied.

> Additionally, we are persuaded by petitioner's argument that an interest in property passed (albeit indirectly) from decedent to his surviving spouse, Estee, as a result of the transfer of decedent's stock to EJL at the formula price. We first note that there is no requirement in § 2056 that an interest must pass directly to the surviving spouse in order to qualify for the marital deduction. * * * Further, we agree with petitioner that Federal gift tax cases such as Ketteman Trust v. Commissioner, [86 T.C. 91 (1986)], are sufficiently analogous to lend support to their argument that an interest in property passed to Estee and the remaining

¶ 24,117

shareholders. Respondent has not convinced us otherwise. We likewise find it significant that respondent has permitted a marital deduction for purposes of the Federal gift tax under comparable circumstances. See Estate of Higgins v. Commissioner, [61 T.C.M. (CCH) 1789, 1991 WL 11502 (1991)]; Rev.Rul. 71–443, [1971–2 C.B. 337].

Thus, we are left with respondent's argument that the estate should be denied the marital deduction on the ground that any property interest deemed to have passed to Estee constitutes a terminable interest under § 2056(b). Although Estee agreed to offer her EJL stock to the company under the shareholder agreement, the fact remains that Estee generally will be subject to a Federal transfer tax should she or her estate transfer the stock for less than an adequate and full consideration. We cannot agree that such an interest is a terminable interest.

In sum, we are convinced that the technical requirements of § 2056(a) are satisfied. We are also persuaded that allowing a marital deduction under the circumstances presented is compatible with the policies underlying the provision.

[¶ 24,121]

ESTATE OF BRIGHT v. COMMISSIONER

United States Court of Appeals, Fifth Circuit, 1981.
658 F.2d 999.

R. LANIER ANDERSON III, Circuit Judge:

This case presents to the en banc court an important question involving the principles of federal estate tax valuation. Mary Frances Smith Bright died on April 3, 1971. During her lifetime, she and her husband, Mr. Bright, owned 55% of the common stock of East Texas Motor Freight Lines, Inc., 55% of the common stock of twenty-seven affiliated corporations, and 55% of the common and preferred stock of Southern Trust and Mortgage Company (the stock of all such corporations is hereinafter referred to collectively as the "stock").

During her lifetime, Mr. and Mrs. Bright held the 55% block of stock as their community property under the laws of the State of Texas. The remaining forty-five percent is owned by parties unrelated to the Brights.* * * None of the stock was publicly traded and no market existed for any of the stock on the date of Mrs. Bright's death. Mr. Bright is executor under the will of his wife. The will devised Mrs. Bright's interest in the stock to Mr. Bright as trustee of a trust for the primary benefit of Mrs. Bright's four children.

* * * The sole issue before the district court was the value of the estate's stock. Before the bench trial on the fair market value issue, the district judge ruled as a matter of law that "no element of control can be attributed to the decedent in determining the value of the decedent's interest in the stock * * * for estate tax purposes. * * * " At the trial the district court found that the value of the stock was consistent with the testimony of the estate's expert witnesses, and entered judgment for the estate. * * * We now affirm the judgment of the district court.

The only issue facing the en banc court is whether the district court erred in entering the above-quoted pretrial order relating to the element of control. We reject the heart of the government's arguments. * * *

Two principal arguments constitute the heart of the government's case, the first based on its description of the property transferred as an undivided one-half interest in the control block of 55% of the stock, and the second based on family attribution between the estate's stock interest and the stock interest held individually by Mr. Bright.

[Control Block]

First, the government argues that the property to be valued for estate tax purposes is an undivided one-half interest in the control block of 55% of the stock, and that the proper method of valuation would be to value the 55% control block, including a control premium, and then take one-half thereof. Both parties agree that the estate tax is an excise tax on the transfer of property at death, and that the property to be valued is the property which is actually transferred, as contrasted with the interest held by the decedent before death or the interest held by the legatee after death. * * * Both also agree that state law, Texas in this case, determines precisely what property is transferred. * * * Both parties agree that, under Texas law, the stock at issue was the community property of Mr. and Mrs. Bright during her life, that Mrs. Bright's death dissolved the community, that upon death the community is divided equally, that each spouse can exercise testamentary disposition over only his or her own half of the community, and that "only the decedent's half is includable in his gross estate for federal tax purposes." * * * Under Texas law, upon the division of the community at death, each spouse owns an undivided one-half interest in each item of community property. * * *

In its brief the government argued that, because the interest to be valued was an undivided one-half interest in the full 55% control block, the proper method would be to value the whole, including its control premium, and then take one-half thereof to establish the value of the estate's undivided one-half interest. The estate points out that the government's argument overlooks the fact that the block of stock is subject to the right of partition under Texas law at the instance of either the surviving spouse or the estate of the deceased's spouse. Tex. Prob. Code Ann. § 385 (Vernon 1980). The government has not argued that partition would not be freely granted in a case involving fungible shares, such as this case. Thus, the estate has no means to prevent the conversion of its interest into shares representing a 27 1/2% block, and we conclude that the estate's interest is the equivalent of a 27 1/2% block of the stock. Accordingly, we reject the government's approach of valuing the 55% control block, with its control premium, and then taking one-half thereof. * * *

[Family Attribution]

Having determined that the property which is to be valued for estate tax purposes is the 27 1/2% block of stock owned by the estate, we turn to the government's second argument, which is based on the doctrine of family attribution between the successive holders of interest to be taxed, the decedent, the executor, and the legatee, on the one hand, and the related party, Mr. Bright, on the other. The government argues that the following facts are relevant and should have been considered by the district court in valuing the 27 1/2% block: the fact that Mr. and Mrs. Bright were husband and wife and held their stock during her lifetime as a control block of 55%; the fact that Mr. Bright held the estate's 27 1/2% block after her death as executor and subsequently as trustee of the testamentary trust for their children, while he simultaneously held another 27 1/2% block in his individual capacity, thus continuing the control block after death; and the fact that the government might be able to adduce evidence that Mr. Bright, as executor or trustee, would not be willing to sell the estate's 27 1/2% block as a minority interest, but would be willing to sell it only as part of the block of 55% including his individually-owned stock so that a substantial control premium could be realized. Such facts and evidence, the government argues, would have formed the basis of expert testimony that the value of the estate's stock includes some control premium. For several reasons, we reject the government's attempt to import into this area of the estate tax law this kind of family attribution, and we hold that the foregoing evidence proffered by the government is not admissible to prove the value of the stock at issue.

First, we reject any family attribution to the estate's stock because established case law requires this result. A recent case directly in point is Estate of Lee v. Commissioner [69 T.C. 860 (1978)]. There Mr. and Mrs. Lee held as community property 4,000 of the 5,000 outstanding shares of the common stock of a closely held corporation. They also held all 50,000 shares of the preferred stock. Upon the death of Mrs. Lee, the community was dissolved, leaving Mr. Lee and the estate of Mrs. Lee each with an undivided one-half interest in each item of the community property. 69 T.C. at 873. The Tax Court held that this was the equivalent of 2,000 shares of common stock and 25,000 shares of preferred stock, and that the estate's interest was a minority interest. 69 T.C. at 874.

In United States v. Land [303 F.2d 170 (5th Cir.1962)], this court held that a restrictive agreement, which depressed the value of a partnership interest but which by its terms expired at decedent's death, did not affect value for estate tax purposes because the estate tax is an excise tax on the transfer of property at death and accordingly valuation is to be made at the time of the transfer, i.e., at death, and the valuation is to be measured by the interest that actually passes. 303 F.2d at 172. It follows necessarily from our *Land* holding that the fact that Mr. and Mrs. Bright held their stock during her lifetime as a control block of 55% is an irrelevant fact. It is a fact which antedates her death, and no longer exists at the time of her death. Dictum in *Land* also suggests that the post-death fact—that the estate's 27 1/2% will pass to Mr. Bright as trustee of the testamentary trust—is also irrelevant:

> Brief as is the instant of death, the court must pinpoint its valuation at this instant—the moment of truth, when the ownership of the decedent ends and the ownership of the successors begins. It is a fallacy, there, therefore, to argue value before—or—after death on the notion that

valuation must be determined by the value either of the *interest that ceases or of the interest that begins.* Instead, the valuation is determined by the interest that passes, and the value of the interest before or after death is pertinent only as it serves to indicate the value at death.

303 F.2d at 172. (Emphasis added.)

Beginning at least as early as 1940, the Tax Court has uniformly valued a decedent's stock for estate tax purposes as a minority interest when the decedent himself owned less than 50%, and despite the fact that control of the corporation was within the decedent's family. * * * Our research has uncovered no cases, and the government has cited none, which have attributed family owned stock to the estate's stock in determining the value thereof for estate tax purposes. * * *

Our second reason for rejecting this kind of family attribution is our conclusion that the doctrine is logically inconsistent with the willing buyer-seller rule set out in the regulations. Reg. § 20.2031–1(b) provides in pertinent part:

> The fair market value is the price at which the property would change hands between a willing buyer and a willing seller, neither being under any compulsion to buy or to sell and both having reasonable knowledge of relevant facts.

This cardinal rule for determining value has been universally applied, both by the Internal Revenue Service and the courts.

It is apparent from the language of the regulation that the "willing seller" is not the estate itself, but is a hypothetical seller. In Revenue Ruling 59–60, the Internal Revenue Service has so held:

> Court decisions frequently state in addition that the *hypothetical* buyer and seller are assumed to be able, as well as willing, to trade and to be well informed about the property and concerning the market for such property.1959–1 C.B. at 237 (emphasis added). Courts also have so held. In United States v. Simmons, 346 F.2d 213, 217 (5th Cir.1965), this court said that "the 'willing buyer and seller' are a hypothetical buyer and seller having a reasonable knowledge of relevant facts." * * *

The notion of the "willing seller" as being hypothetical is also supported by the theory that the estate tax is an excise tax on the transfer of property at death and accordingly that the valuation is to be made as of the moment of death and is to be measured by the interest that passes, as contrasted with the interest held by the decedent before death or the interest held by the legatee after death. Earlier in this opinion, we noticed that our United States v. Land, supra, decision logically requires a holding that the relationship between Mr. and Mrs. Bright and their stock is an irrelevant, before death fact. Thus, it is clear that the "willing seller" cannot be identified with Mrs. Bright, and therefore there can be no family attribution with respect to those related to Mrs. Bright. Similarly, the dictum in *Land*—that valuation is not determined by the value of the interest in the hands of the legatee—means that the "willing seller" cannot be identified with Mr. Bright as executor or as trustee of the testamentary trust. Therefore, there can be no family attribution based on identity of the executor and trustee, Mr. Bright. The *Land* dictum is established law. Edwards v. Slocum, 264 U.S. at 62 (Holmes, J. saying, "It [the tax] comes into existence before, and is independent of, the receipt of the property by the legatee."); Ithaca Trust Co. v. United States, 279 U.S. at 155 (Holmes, J. saying, "The tax is on the act of the testator, not on the receipt of the property by the legatees."); Walter v. United States, 341 F.2d 182, 185 (6th Cir.1965) ("[T]he estate tax is imposed upon the *transfer* of property by a decedent, and not the *receipt* of property by a beneficiary * * * " (emphasis in original)); * * * Reg. § 20.2033–1(a) ("[S]uch tax is an excise tax on the transfer of property at death and is not a tax on the property transferred."). The *Land* dictum also comports with common sense. It would be strange indeed if the estate tax value of a block of stock would vary depending upon the legatee to whom it was devised.

Our final reason for rejecting family attribution is based upon the important policy that the law should be stable and predictable. This policy is especially important in the tax laws, because there is widespread reliance by taxpayers upon established tax principles in planning their affairs. Estate of Hattie L. McNary v. Commissioner of Internal Revenue, 47 T.C. 467 (1967). Accordingly, we decline the government's invitation to depart from *Estate of Lee v. Commissioner, supra,* and the numerous other cases cited and discussed above.

Accordingly, we affirm the district court's ruling to the extent that it defined the interest to be valued as equivalent to 27 1/2% of the stock, to the extent that it excluded as evidence of value the fact that the estate's stock had, prior to decedent's death, been held jointly with Mr. Bright's interest as community property, and the fact that, after death the particular executor (Mr. Bright) and legatee (Mr. Bright as trustee) was related to another stockholder (Mr. Bright individually), and to the extent that it excluded any evidence that Mr. Bright, as executor or trustee, would have refused to sell the estate's 27 1/2% block except in conjunction with his own stock and as part of a 55% control block. We hold that family attribution cannot be applied to lump the estate's stock to that of any related party, but rather that the stock is deemed to be held by a hypothetical seller who is related to no one. * * *

For the foregoing reasons, we AFFIRM.

[¶ 24,125]

d. Family Attribution No Bar to Minority Discounts

Family corporate control, i.e., family "attribution," can be ignored when valuing transferred minority interests in closely held companies for estate and gift tax purposes. Rev. Rul. 93–12, 1993–1 C.B. 202. Thus, a minority discount can be attributed to the value of each block of stock transferred to individual children, such as would be given to strangers who purchased minority interests in the company. (Minority discounts are usually given when unrelated parties, dealing at arm's length, transfer blocks of shares which give the transferee less than controlling interest in the company.) Therefore, even though the family as a whole owns a controlling interest in the company, or one individual member of the family holds as an individual and as trustee for other family members a controlling share (such as the situation in *Estate of Bright*, ¶ 24,121,) valuation of individual transferred interests will not be required to take into account the control premium which might otherwise be attributed to the family's interest as a whole. Care should be taken, however, to ensure that the interest transferred truly is a minority interest and that the minority discount taken in determining the value of the interest is fair and accurate, as the value placed on these transferred interests is often closely scrutinized by the IRS.

[¶ 24,127]

e. *Establishing Estate Tax Value with a Buy–Sell Agreement*

Section 2703(a) sets forth the general rule that the value of property for estate and gift tax purposes will be determined without regard to the purchase price established in a buy-sell agreement. However, § 2703(b) softens the general rule of § 2703(a) by excepting from its grasp agreements that (1) are bona fide business arrangements; (2) are not "devices" to transfer property to natural objects of a decedent's bounty for less than full and adequate consideration; and (3) have terms comparable to similar arrangements entered into by persons in arm's-length transactions. Each of these three requirements must be independently satisfied for a buy-sell agreement to meet the exception. Reg. § 25.2703–1(b)(2).

For additional discussion, see ¶ 24,701–24,731.

[¶ 24,131]

f. *Undervaluation Penalty*

Underpayment of estate or gift taxes that results from a "substantial valuation understatement" may result in a penalty. § 6662. A substantial valuation understatement for estate and gift tax purposes is deemed to occur whenever "the value of any property claimed * * * is 65 percent or less of the amount determined to be the correct amount of such valuation." § 6662(g)(1). The penalty for substantial valuation understatement is 20 percent of the estate or gift tax underpayment amount. § 6662(a). A stiffer penalty of 40 percent is imposed when the property is valued at 40 percent or less of the (so-called) correct valuation amount, i.e., in the case of a "gross valuation misstatement." § 6662(h). However, no penalty is to be imposed unless the underpayment of tax exceeds $5,000. § 6662(g)(2).

This undervaluation penalty makes professional valuations of interests in closely held businesses almost mandatory. However, choosing appraisers must be done carefully. Section 330 of Title 31 of the U.S. Code bars opinion evidence on the value of property by an individual who has been assessed a penalty under § 6701 for aiding in the understatement of a taxpayer's tax liability.

[¶ 24,139]

g. *Exploring the Client's Wishes*

Having analyzed the numbers, one still should not turn to specific techniques. Rather, the next step should be to explore the client's wishes

¶ 24,139

regarding the family business. For example, in the case of Super Electronics, the $400,000 excess of insurance proceeds over cash value will more than pay for death taxes, if any, and administration expenses should Jim die first. (Estate tax may also be payable on Mai's death, since we assume the marital deduction provided by § 2056 will be used at Jim's death.) Nevertheless, the business represents 25 percent of his family's net worth after Jim's death. Are the benefits of retaining the business worth the risk? To answer this, one must explore with Jim whether his desire to do so is an emotional desire to have his son follow in his footsteps and whether Junior is likely to be a good businessman as well as a scholar. Is Jim the brains of the business or could Ahmed carry on without him? Who has the know-how? Who do the customers know? How competitive is the business?

If after reviewing these questions, Jim still wants to see the business continued, he should consider purchasing life insurance, perhaps a substantial 10–year term life insurance policy, in which the death benefits decrease each year. If the business and Junior live up to expectations, Jim's net worth will increase and the premium cost will not be missed. If not, Jim's wife will be protected until Jim can revise his plans.

[¶ 24,147]

2.   ADMINISTERING THE FAMILY BUSINESS

a.   *Will or Trust?*

Retaining the family business will pose special administrative problems for the decedent's estate. In some states, such as Texas, it will make little difference whether a will or revocable trust is used. However, in some other states a revocable trust will probably provide much greater flexibility. The key factor to consider is whether under local law, the executor would be permitted to continue as a partner.

[¶ 24,155]

b.   *Post-death Management*

Regardless of the type of instrument used, the fiduciary should be expressly authorized to retain the family business. See, e.g., Tex. Prob. Code § 238 (Vernon 2003). In addition, the fiduciary will need specific power regarding the handling of the business. Normally, a fiduciary cannot delegate his duties. But Ahmed will not want Jim's widow or banker to tell him how to run the business. And at the moment, Junior is inexperienced.

This problem can be dealt with in several ways. The fiduciary can be authorized to delegate management of the business to the existing management, or a different management can be agreed upon and specified in the will. Alternatively, the parties can agree that at the fiduciary's option, the parties will form a limited partnership to protect the decedent's family against the risk inherent in conducting an unincorporated business. To keep Ahmed motivated, he can be given extra compensation for his management responsibilities. If Junior has amassed enough experience to help run the business and he gets along with Ahmed, the option need not be exercised, or the fiduciary can sell a portion of the partnership interest to Junior and exercise the option as to the balance.

[¶ 24,163]

c. Accountings

Another problem posed by retaining the family business is that accountings of the details of the business may be required under local law, or demanded by beneficiaries pursuant to local law. These can prove burdensome, and if they are part of the public record, they may reveal trade secrets of the business to its competitors. The fiduciary should be authorized to rely on financial statements furnished by management, audited if desired. The business should be deemed a separate entity from the trust or estate, and it should be specifically provided that no accountings as to its operations need to be rendered to a court or any beneficiary. For related discussion, see ¶ 3617.

[¶ 24,171]

d. Financing

The possible need for additional financing is a problem which should be considered. It should be specified in the will or trust whether the executor or trustee may invest more money in the business. If the executor is authorized to do so, it may be desirable to set a limit on the amount (in fixed dollars or as a percentage of assets outside the business) which the executor can invest, so as to protect the remaining assets of the family. Also, it should be stated whether and to what extent the fiduciary may guarantee loans to the business. Finally, keep in mind that opportunities to sell or merge the business may arise at any time, and that for various other reasons it may become desirable to change the form of doing business. The fiduciary should therefore be authorized to incorporate, join in corporate dissolutions, and participate in corporate reorganizations of the business.

Problem

[¶ 24,190]

Try your hand at drafting trust language that enables the executor or trustee (you make the choice) to retain the decedent's interest in a closely held business. Review carefully the various decisions that must be made. What impact will a particular decision have on the business? On the decedent's heirs and devisees? On the executor? To what extent will the types of duties and powers delegated to the executor/trustee affect a testator's choice of fiduciary? Would a corporate fiduciary be preferable if considerable powers were being delegated?

D. LIFETIME TRANSFERS OF THE BUSINESS: THE ESTATE FREEZE

[¶ 24,201]

1. ZERO VALUATION RULE

For many years, an older family member could reduce the gift tax liability that resulted from lifetime gifts by transferring a property interest to a younger family member and retaining an interest in the property. The value of the transferred interest was reduced by the value of the retained interest, thus reducing the gift tax liability on the transfer of the interest to the younger family member. In some instances, the transferor could inflate the value of the retained interest, reducing gift tax liability even further.

In an attempt to prevent this type of overvaluation scheme, Congress added §§ 2701–2704 and thereby changed the rules applicable to the valuation of gifts. To insure that transfers of property are subjected to the estate and gift taxes, Congress has decreed that, except in specified circumstances, the value of the interest retained by the donor shall be zero where the transfer is made to a member of the transferor's family. § 2701(a)(3). The term "member of the family" includes only the transferor's spouse, lineal descendants of the transferor or the transferor's spouse, and the spouse of any such descendant. § 2701(e)(1).

The effect of the zero valuation rules is to deny—or at least limit—the ability of a donor to shift property to loved ones for little or no estate and gift tax cost while keeping control or some beneficial interest in the transferred property. Before §§ 2701–2704 were adopted, the donor would claim to have given away an ownership interest having little or no value—resulting in the payment of little or no gift tax—while retaining a bundle of rights in the property to which all the value in the transferred property as of the date of gift was assigned. The "game" was to allow all of the appreciation experienced by the property in the future to accrue for the benefit of the donee—while the donor's interest had been "frozen." Currently, however, as a result of §§ 2701–2704, the donor is stuck with the gift tax bill when the transfer is made because Congress "solved the problem" by directing that the bundle of rights retained by the donor had a value of "zero" for gift tax purposes.

The specificity that characterizes §§ 2701–2704 was believed necessary to finding a "solution" to the "problem" of how to attach substance to estate taxes and gift taxes in spite of form. That is, the classic "estate freeze" contemplated that the owner of the closely held business would cause the business to be recapitalized with the owner receiving preferred stock with features (such as liquidation, put, call, and conversion rights) sufficient to warrant much, if not all, of the current value of the enterprise being assigned to the preferred stock and younger family members receiving all of the common stock, the common stock to enjoy all of the future appreciation in value experienced by the enterprise. Critical to the success of the recapitalization (from the donor's vantage point) was the avoidance of gift tax on the delivery of the common shares to the younger family members. Gift tax could only have been avoided if the retained preferred stock could be professionally valued as being equal to the current value of the enterprise. If the value of the retained preferred was less than the value of the enterprise itself, the transfer of the common shares to the younger family members would have been a latent gift or payment of compensation. See Rev. Rul. 74–269, 1974–1 C.B. 87. Achieving this equality of value was often difficult in a small business which could not pay a large cumulative dividend on its preferred. However, in these circumstances, the value of the preferred stock was often bolstered by giving it additional rights such as voting rights, or a combination of a cumulative and a noncumulative dividend, or other limited participation in future growth through additional dividends payable upon various contingencies or in accordance with various formula dependent upon earnings. (The gap, however, could not be bridged by giving the preferred a redemption price which exceeded its issue price by more than a reasonable call premium without creating the potential for constructive dividends under § 305. Reg. § 1.305–5.)

In sum, the increasingly common use of sophisticated financial structures caused Congress to respond in kind—and with necessary specificity, i.e., to target the problem rather than paint with a broad, easily understood brush. The result was the incredibly complicated statutory scheme set out in §§ 2701–2704, an important part of which is the zero valuation rule.

[¶ 24,209]

2. DEFINITIONS

The task is to walk the narrow path, to know which retained interests trigger the zero valuation rule and which do not. Thus for purposes of understanding §§ 2701–2704, the definitions of a number of key terms must be noted (although a full understanding of some of terms requires some background in how business ownership interests can be structured).

In addition to the definitions discussed at ¶ 24,201, the following definitions are necessary to understand § 2701. An "applicable retained interest" is an interest to which there is a distribution, liquidation, put, call, or conversion right. § 2701(b)(1). However, a distribution right is not considered an "applicable retained interest" unless the transferor and "applicable family members" have "control" of the entity. § 2701(b)(1)(A). The term "applicable family member" includes the transferor's spouse, ancestors of the transferor or transferor's spouse, and the spouse of any such ancestor. § 2701(e)(2). With a corporation, the term "control" means holding at least 50 percent of stock in the corporation. § 2701(b)(2)(A). With a partnership, "control" means at least a 50 percent interest in capital or profits of a general partnership and any interest as a general partner in a limited partnership. § 2701(b)(2)(B).

A "distribution right" is a right to a distribution from a corporation with respect to its stock or, in the case of a partner's interest in a partnership, a right to distribution from the partnership. § 2701(c)(1)(A). Simple as that definition may appear, it must be qualified. Thus, "distribution right" does not include a right to a distribution with respect to any junior equity interest; any liquidation, put, call or conversion right; or any right to receive a

¶ 24,209

guaranteed payment. § 2701(c)(1)(B). Opening the next door, we learn that in the case of a corporation, a "junior equity interest" refers to common stock (assuming that there is only one class of preferred and common stock), and in the case of a partnership, it refers to any partnership interest under which the rights to income and capital are junior to the rights of all other equity interests. § 2701(a)(4)(B)(i). Thus, § 2701 generally does not apply when a transferor transfers preferred stock and keeps common stock, or when a partner retains a right to guaranteed payments pursuant to § 707.

These are, at best, an illustration of the complexity inherent in determining how and when the zero valuation rule is to be applied. The statute is almost impossible without the aid of the regulations, and the regulations often are in need of interpretation by learned commentators.

[¶ 24,217]

3. APPLICATION OF § 2701 TO PREFERRED INTEREST FREEZES

Section 2701 will apply to a preferred "freeze" transaction only if two conditions are satisfied. First, there must be a "transfer" of corporate stock or partnership interests to, or for the benefit of, a member of the transferor's family. A "transfer" includes transactions such as contributions to capital, redemptions, recapitalizations, and other changes in capital structure. H.R. Rep. No. 101–964, 101st Cong., 2d Sess. at 1136. Second, the transferor or an "applicable family member" must retain an "applicable retained right." If both these conditions are met, § 2701 will impute a zero valuation to the transferor's retained interest.

[¶ 24,225]

4. EXCEPTIONS TO ZERO VALUATION RULE

While zero valuation is the general rule, there are several exceptions. For example, if market quotations are readily available for a right conferred by the retained interest or for the transferred interest, then these retained interests are exempt from § 2701. § 2701(a)(2)(A). Similarly—and this is important—§ 2701 does not apply when the retained interest is of the same class as the transferred interest. This includes, but is not limited to, situations where the transferor gives a gift of common stock and retains rights in the same class of stock, or where a partner gives a gift of a partnership interest and the same proportion of income and loss is shared by each partnership interest. § 2701(a)(2)(B).

These exceptions can be understood by considering (1) what kind of rights a donor might likely find important to retain to provide either or both enjoyment or control of the transferred property and (2) what valuation abuse potential is inherent, for estate and gift tax purposes, in allowing the donor to take into account these retained rights for purposes of valuing the property interest transferred and the property interest that is retained during the donor's life.

Furthermore, an exclusion from the zero valuation rule of § 2701 is available if the rights in the retained interest are proportionally the same as all the rights in the transferred interest, without regard to nonlapsing differences in voting power (or, for a partnership, nonlapsing differences with respect to management and limitations on liability), such as a transfer of nonvoting stock in an S corporation where the transferor retains voting stock in the corporation. § 2701(a)(2)(C). This exception includes situations where the retained and transferred interests consist of two classes of common stock which share in all distributions, liquidations and other rights in the same ratio. However, the exception does not include partnerships which have both a general and a limited partner with one partner possessing a preference in distributions.

Also, § 2701(c)(2)(C) provides that § 2701 does not apply if the right in the retained interest is:

1. a right to convert into a fixed number or percentage of the shares of the same class as the transferred stock;

2. nonlapsing;

3. subject to proportionate adjustments for splits, etc.; and

4. adjusted for accumulated dividends not paid on a timely basis.

The reason for this last exception is that eventually the full appreciated value of this retained right will be subject to transfer taxes, i.e., gift and/or estate taxes, and there is therefore no need to apply the zero valuation rule of § 2701 to the immediate transfer.

Example. Assume Jim and Ahmed have incorporated Super Electronics as a C Corporation. Assume further that Jim owns a 50 percent interest in Super Electronics worth $500,000. If Jim transfers all his common stock to Junior and retains newly issued preferred stock with preferred distribution rights, § 2701 will apply and Jim's retained interest in Super Electronics will be valued at zero. As a result, Jim must pay a substantial amount of gift tax on the transfer of common stock to Junior.

[¶ 24,227]

PRIVATE LETTER RULING 9414012

December 28, 1993.

The facts as submitted indicate that Article V of the articles of incorporation of A Inc. currently authorizes issuance of Y shares of class A voting common stock at a par value of $a per share. No other equity interests in the corporation are authorized. At present, all of this authorized stock is issued and outstanding. The shareholders are B, B's three adult children, and the trustee of a trust established by B's deceased spouse. B owns more than 50 percent of the outstanding class A stock, enabling him to elect two of the three directors and thus control the election of officers.

The shareholders and directors of A Inc. propose to adopt a plan under which Article V of the corporation's articles of incorporation would be amended to authorize two classes of common stock—class A voting shares and class B nonvoting shares—each with a par value of $a. No other equity interests in the corporation will be authorized. The total authorized stock will be Y shares of class A stock and Z shares of class B stock. In addition, as amended, Article V will provide:

The Class A and Class B stock shall have the same designations, preferences, limitations and rights, excluding voting rights, specifically including all redemption rights and rights to dividends and liquidation distributions, without regard to Class or voting right. All property and stock distributions, whether by dividend or liquidation, shall be distributed between the two classes of stock proportionate to the number of then outstanding shares of each Class. The two classes of Common Stock shall differ only with respect to voting rights. The common stock currently issued shall be Class A Common Stock.

Each shareholder will return all shares of voting common stock to the corporation for cancellation. For each share of voting common stock returned, each shareholder will receive from the corporation one share of class A stock and five shares of class B stock. Consequently, the exchanges of stock [hereinafter the "Exchanges"] will maintain the current proportionate voting power among the shareholders.

The purpose of the proposed Exchanges is to maintain the stability of A Inc. by retaining the voting power in B during his life while allowing B to shift the ownership of A Inc. to younger generations through gifts of class B stock. Immediately after the Exchanges, B will begin transferring shares of his nonvoting stock to his children and grandchildren but will retain all of his voting stock.

It is represented that there are no provisions in the by-laws, the proposed plan for the Exchanges, or any other document that would cause (nor is there an oral or written agreement that would cause) the voting or liquidation rights of class A or class B stock to lapse or be restricted in any way (except that class B stock does not involve voting rights).

You have requested a ruling that neither the proposed Exchanges nor B's proposed transfers to his children and grandchildren of his nonvoting common stock in A Inc. will be subject to the valuation rules of § 2701.

* * *

Section 2701(a) provides that, for purposes of determining whether a transfer of an interest in a corporation to the transferor's family member is a gift (and the value of such transfer), the value of specified rights (such as distribution rights, liquidation rights, puts or calls) held by the transferor or applicable family member immediately after the transfer shall be determined as if those rights were valued at zero.

However, § 2701(a)(2) provides that § 2701(a)(1) does not apply to any right with respect to an applicable retained interest if such interest is proportionally the same as the transferred interest, without regard to nonlapsing differences in voting power.

¶ 24,227

Under Reg. § 25.2701–1(c)(3) of the Gift Tax Regulations, § 2701 does not apply if the retained interest is of the same class of equity as the transferred interest or is of a class proportional to the class of the transferred interest. A class meets either requirement if the rights of the class are identical to those of the transferred interest, except for nonlapsing differences in voting rights.

Section 2701(b)(1) defines "applicable retained interest" as meaning any interest in an entity with respect to which there is (A) a distribution right, but only if, immediately before the transfer, the transferor and applicable family members hold control of the entity, or (B) a liquidation, put, call, or conversion right.

Section 25.2701–2(b)(1) of the regulations provides that an applicable retained interest is any equity interest in a corporation or partnership with respect to which there is either an extraordinary payment right or a distribution right. An extraordinary payment right is any put, call, or conversion right, any right to compel liquidation, or any similar right, the exercise or nonexercise of which affects the value of the transferred interest. A distribution right is the right to receive distributions with respect to an equity interest, but does not include (1) any right to receive distributions with respect to an interest that is of the same class as, or a class that is subordinate to, the transferred interest, (2) any extraordinary payment right, or (3) certain other rights as described in Reg. § 25.2701–2(b)(4).

Section 2701(b)(2)(A) provides that, in the case of a corporation, the term "control" means the holding of at least 50 percent (by vote or value) of the stock of the corporation.

Section 2701(e)(1) provides that a member of the family is, with respect to any transferor, the transferor's spouse, any lineal descendant of the transferor or the transferor's spouse, or the spouse of any such lineal descendant.

Section 2701(e)(2) provides that an applicable family member is, with respect to any transferor, the transferor's spouse, any ancestor of the transferor or the transferor's spouse, or the spouse of any such ancestor.

Section 2701(e)(5) provides in pertinent part that, except as provided in regulations, a contribution to capital or a redemption, recapitalization, or other change in the capital structure of a corporation will be treated as a transfer of an interest to which § 2701 applies if the taxpayer or an applicable family member (A) receives an applicable retained interest in the corporation pursuant to the change in the capital structure or (B) under regulations, otherwise holds, immediately after the transfer, an applicable retained interest in the corporation. However, § 2701 will not apply to a change in the capital structure if the interests in the entity held by the transferor, applicable family members, and members of the transferor's family before and after the transaction are substantially identical.

Section 25.2701–1(b)(2)(i)(B) of the regulations provides in pertinent part that a transfer includes a capital structure transaction if (1) the transferor or an applicable family member receives an applicable retained interest in the

¶ **24,227**

capital structure transaction, (2) the transferor or applicable family member holding an applicable retained interest before the capital structure transaction surrenders an equity interest that is junior to the applicable retained interest and receives property other than an applicable retained interest, or (3) the transferor or an applicable family member holding an applicable retained interest before the capital structure transaction surrenders an equity interest in the entity (other than a subordinate interest) and the fair market value of the applicable retained interest is increased.

However, Reg. § 25.2701–1(b)(3)(i) provides an exception to this rule stating that a transfer does not include a capital structure transaction if the transferor, each applicable family member, and each member of the transferor's family holds substantially the same interest after the transaction as that individual held before the transaction.

In the present case, each shareholder would hold the same percentage of the issued and outstanding voting common stock and the same overall percentage interest in the total equity of the corporation after the proposed Exchanges as the shareholder held before the proposed Exchanges. Thus, each shareholder of A Inc. would hold substantially the same interest in the corporation after the proposed transaction as the shareholder held before the proposed transaction.

The applicable State X Business Corporation Act does not permit discrimination between classes of stock unless the articles of incorporation specify a preference. The proposed amendment to the articles of incorporation of A Inc. will specify that there are no preferences between classes A and B, except for nonlapsing differences in voting rights. Thus, the rights of the class A common stock will be identical to those of the class B common stock that B proposes to transfer, except for nonlapsing differences in voting rights.

Accordingly, we rule as follows:

(a) Under § 2701(e)(5), the proposed Exchanges will not be treated as the transfer of an interest to which § 2701 applies, because the interests in the corporation held by B and members of B's family before and after the proposed Exchanges will be substantially identical.

(b) Under § 2701(a)(2), the subsequent transfers of class B common stock by B to younger members of his family while retaining his class A common stock will not be transfers subject to § 2701 because the rights retained by B in his class A stock (except for his nonlapsing right to vote his Class A stock) will be identical to the rights of the transferred class B stock.

[¶ 24,233]

a. Treatment of Cumulative but Unpaid Distributions

Having qualified for one of the exceptions to the zero valuation rules of §§ 2701–2704, Congress anticipated that a donor would try to increase the value of his or her retained interest (in order to reduce gift tax liability resulting from the transfer) by, for example, neglecting to make some of the required "qualified" payments. (A "qualified payment" is defined as either a dividend payable periodically and at a fixed rate under any cumulative preferred stock or a comparable payment under any partnership agreement. § 2701(c)(3)(A). For purposes of this provision, a fixed rate is defined as one bearing a fixed relationship to a specified market rate. § 2701(c)(3)(B).) § 2701(d) provides that the taxable estate or taxable gifts of the donor shall be increased at the happening of certain events (i.e., the death of the transferor or the transfer of the retained interest) if required qualified payments are not timely made. Section 2701(d)(2) provides the method of calculating this increase to the taxable estate or taxable gift as the excess of the value of the qualified payments payable during the period beginning on the date of transfer and ending on the date of the taxable event *over* the value of the payments paid during such period computed on the basis of the time when they were actually paid. For purposes of calculating this increase, the numerator is to be determined as if such payments were made when due and all such payments were reinvested by the transferor as of the date of payment at a yield equal to the discount rate used in determining the value of the retained interest. Id. However, no such increase is to be made to a transferor's taxable estate (or taxable gifts) if the transfer qualified for the estate or gift tax marital deduction. § 2701(d)(3)(B).

Section 2701(d)(2)(C) provides a four-year grace period by treating payments of required distributions within four years after the due date as payments that were actually made on the due date. However, if the payment is made more than four years after the due date, the taxpayer may elect to treat the late payment as a taxable gift.

To limit the amount of the increase in the transfer tax value, Congress put a cap on the unpaid accumulated distributions by limiting the increase in the transfer to the benefit received by the donee from the failure to make the required distributions. § 2701(d)(2)(B). In addition, to prevent double taxation of rights that were previously given a zero value, Treasury regulations are required to provide for appropriate transfer tax adjustments. § 2701(e)(6).

[¶ 24,241]

b. *Liquidation, Put, Call, or Conversion Rights in Conjunction with Distribution Rights*

If a retained interest confers a distribution right consisting of the right to receive a "qualified payment," and there are one or more liquidation, put, call or conversion rights with respect to such interest, these rights are to be valued under the assumption that each right is exercised in the manner that results in the lowest value for all such rights. § 2701(a)(3)(B).

Example. A father retains cumulative preferred stock in a transaction to which §§ 2701–2704 apply. The stock provides for a cumulative dividend of $200 per year, and the stock may be redeemed after three years for $3,000. In such a case, the value of the cumulative preferred stock is the lesser of (1) the present value of three years of $200 dividends plus the present value of $3,000 in the third year or (2) the present value of $200 paid every year in perpetuity.

If the discount rate was 10 percent, then a perpetuity of $200 would have a present value of $2,000 while a three-year annuity with a $3,000 payment at the end of the third year would have a present value of $2,751. Therefore, for purposes of § 2701(a)(3)(B), the present value of the cumulative preferred stock would be the value of the perpetuity of $200 per year. However, if the discount rate was 5 percent, then the perpetuity would not be used to value the cumulative preferred stock because a perpetuity of $200 would have a present value of $4,000, while the annuity and $3,000 payment would have a present value of only $3,136.

[¶ 24,249]

5. LAPSING RIGHTS

In a family-controlled corporation or partnership, the lapse of a voting or liquidation right created after October 8, 1990, is treated as a transfer for gift tax purposes or as a transfer includible in the gross estate of the transferor for estate tax purposes. § 2704(a)(1). The amount of the transfer for gift and estate tax purposes is the excess of the value of all interests in the entity held by the transferor immediately before the lapse over the value of the interests immediately after the lapse. § 2704(a)(2).

Section 2704(b)(1) provides that if two conditions are satisfied, any restriction effectively limiting the liquidation ability of the corporation or partnership is to be ignored in valuing a transfer among family members. These two conditions are that (1) the transferor and the family members must control the corporation or partnership and (2) the restriction must either lapse after the transfer or be removable by the transferor or members of the transferor's family, either alone or collectively. § 2704(b)(2).

Section 2701(b)(1), however, does not apply to a commercially reasonable restriction that arises as part of a financing agreement with an unrelated party or a restriction required under state or federal law. § 2701(b)(3). Furthermore, the Secretary of the Treasury is given the power to disregard other restrictions which reduce the value of the transferred interest for transfer tax purposes, but which do not ultimately reduce the value of the interest to the transferee. § 2704(b)(4).

[¶ 24,257]

6. STATUTE OF LIMITATIONS

Knowing the tendency of taxpayers to under report gifts (or to ignore them altogether), Congress provided that, in cases where gifts are valued under § 2701 or 2702, the statute of limitations is inapplicable for the assessment of gift taxes on undisclosed or inadequately disclosed transfers, regardless of whether a gift tax return was filed for other transfers in the year in which the subject transfer occurred. § 6501(c)(9).

E. PLANNING FOR FINANCIAL NEEDS OF FAMILY MEMBERS USING PARTNERSHIPS

[¶ 24,301]

If a family business is to be retained, how can it be used to help family members with current income needs? In some instances, it may be appropriate to employ family members in the business. What about family members who, for lack of time or skill, cannot be employed in the family business? In the case of Super Electronics, the answer may be to look to other assets, such as Pam's ground lease, which generate a fixed income and might be used either to fund trusts or for outright gifts. However, Jim and Mai have no such assets, and Pam is understandably reluctant to part with her only asset. Most businesspersons have few outside assets and are more interested in their own retirement program than in making gifts of outside assets.

[¶ 24,303]

1. FAMILY PARTNERSHIPS

a. *Section 704(e) Requirements*

One possibility is to give family members an interest in the business and thereby deflect some of the taxable income from the business to the donees. This not only will provide funds for the donees, but also will shift the income to those who are probably in a lower tax bracket. A gift of a partnership interest in a family business will be given effect for income tax purposes only if the family partnership rules of § 704(e) are satisfied.

Problem

[¶ 24,307]

Read over § 704(e) and think about the following questions: (1) Can § 704(e) be characterized as a "safe harbor" provision? (2) If so, what benefit will accrue to a taxpayer who places himself within § 704(e)'s safe harbor? (3) What "hoops" must be jumped through by the taxpayer to come within the safe harbor? (4) What are the consequences to the taxpayer of attempting to qualify for § 704(e) treatment, but getting it wrong? (5) How do these consequences compare to those of making no effort to qualify at all?

[¶ 24,309]

b. *Satisfying the § 704(e) Requirements—The First Steps*

Section 704(e) provides, first, that all state law requirements for a valid transfer must be satisfied. Second, capital must be a material income-producing factor. § 704(e)(1). A gift of an interest in a personal service partnership will not be recognized for income tax purposes even though some furniture and other minor assets may be used in the business. Third, the donor must be paid a reasonable salary for his services. See § 704(e)(2). If he is not, the

¶ 24,309

donee's share of profits will be appropriately reduced. Fourth, the donee's share of earnings, after taking into account salaries, cannot exceed the donee's percentage of the partnership capital. These last requirements reflect the policy that only the income attributable to the capital transferred to the donee may be taxed to the donee. The family partnership cannot be used to disguise an otherwise prohibited assignment of income.

[¶ 24,313]

c.   *Parting with Control*

A second policy reflected by the family partnership rules is that the transfer must be genuine. Control must actually pass to the donee. Thus, a fifth requirement is that the donee must receive his share of partnership income. If reinvestment is required, the entire arrangement may be disregarded, although there is some flexibility in this rule for business exigencies. If a trust is to be used, an independent trustee (i.e., a bank which may be made a limited partner) is desirable. Reversionary trusts are more likely to be challenged without an independent trustee particularly where the grantor remains a partner in his or her own right.

Problem

[¶ 24,315]

In each of the following situations, identify whether the transfer described will be recognized as a valid income-shifting transfer under the provisions of § 704(e).

(a) Smith, a lawyer, held a one-quarter interest in the capital and profits of the law firm in which he was a partner. On his son's 25th birthday, Smith made a gift to his son of one-half of his capital and distributive interest in the partnership. The son is not a lawyer.

(b) Same as (a), except that Smith's son is a lawyer, and he has just joined the firm.

(c) Same as (a), except that the partnership is not a law partnership, but operates a foundry instead.

(d) Same as (c), except Smith's son will receive a distributive interest of 15 percent of partnership profits, although his capital interest amounts to only 12.5 percent of the partnership.

(e) Same as (c), except all of the profits from the business have been committed, by written agreement, to reinvestment. The company is growing rapidly and has a strong need for capital.

(f) Same as (e), except the company is stable and has considerable cash reserves.

(g) Oskar Jones, President and 75 percent partner in Oskar Jones Computers, gives a 25 percent capital and distributive interest in the partnership to each of his two sons, Kermit and Hektor. Oskar, widely regarded as the "key man" behind the phenomenal success of Oskar

Jones Computers, draws a salary of $12,500 per annum. The company made a profit of $450,000, net of taxes paid by partners, in 2001. Kermit and Hektor are allowed to vote their partnership interests, but they do not do any work with the partnership.

(h) Same as (g), but Oskar draws a $150,000 per annum salary, which is taken out of partnership earnings before the distribution of partnership profit shares.

(i) Same as (h), except Kermit and Hektor are not allowed to vote their shares in the partnership (Oskar has retained voting control).

[¶ 24,317]

d. Would a Family Partnership Transfer Work for Super Electronics?

A transfer of an interest in Super Electronics Co. could qualify under § 704(e). Capital is a material income-producing factor. The net profit after salaries (and before taxes) is $275,000. Thus, a gift of a 10 percent interest by Jim to a trust for Sandy would shift $27,500 of income to her and, accordingly, to a lower tax bracket. To prevent disputes over the validity of the transfer, Sandy's share of earnings should be distributed to her trust, except to meet a reasonable need of the business concurred in by the trustee. The distributed earnings should, in turn, be distributed by the trust to Sandy or reinvested in unrelated assets. A bank may be best as trustee, and the trustee should be made a limited partner for the trust's protection. If Jim is unwilling to use a bank, explore whether his concern is the way the bank will invest the funds it receives from the partnership, or whether it reflects an unwillingness to distribute earnings to the trust and otherwise deal with the trust on an arm's-length basis. If it is the latter which is troubling Jim, it would be a disservice to him to implement the gift.

[¶ 24,323]

e. Zero Valuation Rule

The zero valuation rule of § 2701 must be taken into account when considering any gifts of partnership interests. For discussion, see ¶ 24,201.

[¶ 24,327]

2. GIFT AND LEASEBACK OF BUSINESS PROPERTY

A simple approach to providing income for family members is to make gifts of business assets, such as the plant and major equipment, which the business owns but could lease. A gift of these assets to a trust, coupled with a lease of the assets to the business, can be used to shift income to beneficiaries. This offers significant advantages. Where the business is a partnership, the gift-leaseback avoids the complex rules pertaining to family partnerships. See ¶ 24,301. Furthermore, a share of the business may produce an uncertain amount of income, whereas one can more readily determine the amount of the income being transferred when giving assets which are to be leased to the business.

Obviously, in the case of a partnership, assets would be distributed in kind and any gifts would be made by the individual partners to trusts for their respective beneficiaries.

New assets acquired by the partners individually can also be used. A distribution from the partnership will not be a taxable event if each asset is distributed to the partners in proportion to their respective partnership shares. § 731. If a disproportionate distribution is made, gain may be realized should the distribution reduce some partners' shares and increase other partners' shares of unrealized receivables or substantially appreciated inventory. § 751(b).

For consideration of gift-lease back, see ¶ 12,901.

[¶ 24,343]

3. SALE OF A PARTNERSHIP INTEREST

As is apparently the case with Junior, some members of the family may wish to become more actively involved in the business. At some point, it may be desirable to transfer an interest in the business to these persons, prior to the death of the principal owners. As noted earlier, a gift can be made of an interest in the business. Certainly the sooner this is done, the more likely it is to involve a smaller valuation of the interest in the business for gift tax purposes. On the other hand, during the early years, it is also easier to provide economic rewards for the new participants in the business through compensation. Indeed, it may be more desirable, insofar as the morale of other employees is concerned, not to endow Junior with an interest in the business at the outset. And later it may be better for Junior's self-respect, and for Jim's conscience regarding equal treatment of his children, that Junior buy an interest in the business, even if Junior has to borrow the funds from Jim to make the purchase.

[¶ 24,345]

a. Income Tax Effects on the Purchaser

If Junior were to buy a one-eighth (12.5 percent) interest in Super Electronics Co. from Jim for $106,250, what would the income tax consequences be? First, Jim may have both capital gain and ordinary income, as will be discussed later. Second, as for Junior, the basis of his interest in the partnership is determined by reference to § 742, which refers the reader to the basic rules for acquisition of property by individual taxpayers. See §§ 1011–1017, 1019–1022. This basis is $162,500, the cash price he pays ($106,250) plus his share of liabilities assumed (12.5% x $450,000).

The partnership's basis for its assets is unaffected unless a § 754 election is in effect. See § 743(a). Thus, Junior's share of the partnership basis for its assets would be $125,000 (12.5% x $1,000,000). The extra $37,500 reflects Junior's share of the net appreciation in land and equipment (12.5% of

$100,000 = $12,500) and of goodwill (12.5% of $200,000 = $25,000). But the partnership's basis for depreciation and for measuring gain or loss on the disposition of these assets remains unchanged. It is small consolation to Junior that this discrepancy will be rectified when he sells his partnership interest or when the partnership is dissolved. § 731(a)(2).

[¶ 24,349]

b. The § 754 Election

A § 754 election is irrevocable without the consent of the district director for the internal revenue district in which the partnership return is required to be filed. Reg. § 1.754–1(c). It is made by the partnership and applies to a sale or other disposition of a partnership interest, a transfer by reason of the death of a partner (§ 743), and a distribution from the partnership to a partner of more than his share of some assets, and less than his share of other assets. § 734. If not previously made, the partnership makes the election by filing the appropriate statement with its return for the year in which the event requiring an adjustment occurs. Reg. § 1.754–1(b).

The adjustment in the example is computed as the excess of Junior's basis for his partnership interest ($162,500) over his share of the partnership's basis for all of its assets ($125,000). § 743(b). The $37,500 adjustment to the partnership's basis for its assets is allocated only to Junior, and will affect only the computation of gain or loss for him, or his share of depreciation. Id. The adjustment is allocated first between two categories of assets ("baskets"): capital and depreciable assets on the one hand, and other assets. See § 755(b). In Super's case, all the appreciation is in assets in the first category, so the entire adjustment is allocated to them. Within the category of capital and depreciable assets, the adjustment is allocated among specific assets so as to minimize the difference between the fair market value and the basis of each asset. § 755(a). See also Bartolme v. Commissioner, 62 T.C. 821 (1974). For Super, that would mean $25,000 would be allocated to goodwill and $12,500 to plant and equipment. Frequently, the election produces accounting complexities which far outweigh the tax benefits achieved and thus make it inadvisable. This is true for Super Electronics since neither the land nor goodwill is likely to be sold except on liquidation, and neither may be depreciated.

[¶ 24,359]

4. PRIVATE ANNUITIES

Since at Jim's death, Junior may owe Jim part or all of the purchase price of the interest purchased, it may be suggested that the purchase price be payable in the form of a private annuity, rather than a lump sum payable at a fixed date or in installments. A private annuity is an unsecured promise to pay periodic (usually monthly) fixed payments for the life of the annuitant. Its advantages are that the payments stop at the seller's death, and thus, there is nothing to include in his estate except any savings out of the annuity. If the annuity represents fair market value as determined by the Internal Revenue

Service tables, there is no gift. But, because of a number of drawbacks, it is rarely used. No security for the promise is permitted. Although a portion of the payments will be treated as interest to the annuitant, the buyer usually does not receive interest deductions. There are basis problems for the buyer since the buyer's cost is tentative, and unexpected gain or loss may be realized many years after the buyer sells the property acquired from the annuitant. If the seller lives beyond his or her life expectancy, the purchaser will overpay, and more importantly, this can create psychological and emotional pressures on the parties because the payments are tied to the duration of the seller's life.

The subject of private annuities is discussed far more than such annuities are actually used. It would appear that the nontax and tax disadvantages associated with such annuities usually lead to a decision against their use. For additional discussion of the private annuity, see ¶ 12,501–12,517.

[¶ 24,369]

5.　FAMILY LIMITED PARTNERSHIPS

"Number one" in any "top ten" list of "hot" planning ideas is the family limited partnership (FLP)! Consideration of FLPs begins at ¶ 21,201. With so much attention given to the federal estate tax savings that may well result from the implementation of an FLP, it requires diligence and understanding to see the possibilities of the tool from a nontax planning perspective, particularly in the active family business context where it may well have a natural and appropriate fit.

F.　INCORPORATING THE FAMILY BUSINESS

[¶ 24,401]

1.　REASONS FOR INCORPORATING

a.　*Continuing the Business*

Before turning to the estate planning problems and opportunities of the partner desiring to dispose of his interest in the business, it is useful to consider the possibility of incorporating the business. Why should Ahmed and Jim consider incorporating? First, it permits easier continuation of the business after the death of one of the owners. Although a partnership can be continued if the parties so agree during their lifetimes, particularly if a revocable trust is used, the technical termination problems are avoided if the business is unincorporated. Second, incorporation facilitates going public or being acquired by a public company in a tax-free reorganization. Third, it provides the opportunity to obtain limited liability, although this advantage is reduced considerably by the availability of insurance and by the requirement of shareholder guarantees by larger creditors of corporate businesses. Fourth, there can be tax advantages (or disadvantages) to incorporation, depending on the circumstances. A drawback to incorporation is the need for the corporation to be operated in a formal manner (i.e., keeping adequate books and records and holding shareholder and board of directors meetings).

[¶ 24,409]

b. Tax Rates

The maximum income tax rates applicable to individuals, from time to time, have been slightly higher than those applicable to corporations. §§ 1, 11. However, any tax rate advantage enjoyed by corporations is often more than offset by the problem of double taxation when the earnings are extracted from the corporation in the form of dividends. § 301. Of course, the techniques for avoiding this problem (salaries, leasing plant and equipment to the corporation, debt as opposed to equity capitalization) result in income being taxed to the individuals rather than the corporation. However, if the corporation is liquidated or sold, earnings accumulated in the corporation will be treated effectively as tax favored capital gain when received by the shareholders either as liquidating distributions or sale proceeds. § 331. Note that any unrealized appreciation on property distributed in kind will be recognized by the corporation. § 311(b).

[¶ 24,417]

c. Tax Qualified Retirement Plans

For years, one compelling tax consideration for incorporating was the ability to establish tax qualified pension and profit-sharing plans. While self-employed persons could establish such plans—commonly referred to as 401(k)s, Keogh Plans, or H.R. 10 plans when applied to the self-employed—many restrictions applied, not the least of which were contribution limitations. Since 1984, the self-employed have enjoyed "parity" with corporate employees in terms of contribution limitations and many other aspects of qualified benefit plans. And today, among the alternatives are SEPS and SIMPLES, all of which are considered in Chapter 29. Suffice it to say, that the tax deferral (and creditor protection) benefits of tax qualified retirement plans must be a part of planning for the business owner. The dialogue goes something like this. "Don't have a plan?" "Get one.!" "Can't afford it!" "Make it happen!"

[¶ 24,425]

d. Medical Plans

It is often said that one benefit of incorporating is the possible implementation of a medical reimbursement plan. See § 105. Medical reimbursement plans permit corporate employers to pay and deduct the medical expenses of employees and their dependents without the payment being included in the income of the employee. § 105(b). As a result, the corporation is permitted the deduction even though the employee could not deduct the expenses because of the 7.5 percent and other limitations in § 213. However, reimbursements under such plans are taxable to the recipients unless the plans satisfy ERISA-type prohibitions against discrimination in favor of highly compensated individuals. § 105(h).

¶ 24,425

That having been said, it should be noted, by way of comparison, that a self-employed person can sometimes obtain benefits for family members, if the family members are bona fide employees of the business. § 105(g); Rev. Rul. 71–588, 1971–2 C.B. 91; Priv. Ltr. Rul. 9409006 (sole proprietor allowed to deduct under § 162(a) amounts paid to spouse, an employee, as reimbursement of medical expenses under a written employer-provided accident and health plan; such amounts are excluded from the employee's income under § 105(b) as employer-provided medical reimbursements).

In contrast, note that the § 105(b) exclusion (of employer-provided reimbursements) is not available to partners or to more-than-two-percent shareholders in S corporations—or to sole proprietors without employees. These taxpayers enjoy 100 percent deduction for medical insurance premiums they pay (in addition to the ability to deduct medical expenses in excess of 7.5 percent of adjusted gross income). §§ 162(l), 213.

[¶ 24,435]

2. S CORPORATIONS

a. S Corporations: In General

Generally, a corporation's income is taxed twice. The corporation itself is taxed on its income, and shareholders are taxed on the dividends that they receive. Certain corporations, however, can elect to be S corporations (§ 1362) and thereby have the income of the corporation taxed directly to the shareholders without having corporate income taxes imposed. § 1363(a). This permits the owners of a business, in limited circumstances, to enjoy the tax advantages of both corporations and partnerships, such as the ability to use losses at the corporate level to offset a shareholder's other income as well as the nontax advantages of incorporation. § 1366(a)(1)(B).

Only a domestic corporation may elect S corporation status. The election may be made by a corporation that has:

1. no more than one class of stock;

2. only individuals, estates and certain trusts as shareholders (See ¶ 24,439 and 24,609);

3. no more than 100 shareholders (for purposes of this requirement, spouses (and their estates) will be treated under § 1361(c)(1) as one shareholder and if an election is made, all the members of a family may be treated as one shareholder § 1361(b)(1)(A)); and

4. no shareholder who is a nonresident alien.

Both tax exempt charitable organizations (§ 501(c)(3) organizations) and qualified pension plan trusts may be shareholders of S corporations. § 1361(c)(6). However, tax exempt entities will generally prefer partnerships and LLCs to S corporation status because income or loss from the S corporation is to flow through to the tax-exempt shareholder as unrelated business taxable income.

In addition to meeting the shareholder requirements, any S corporation that has accumulated Subchapter C earnings and profits each year for three consecutive tax years must also conduct an active business. If more than 25 percent of a corporation's income for each of the three years comes from passive sources (such as rents, interest or dividends), the corporation's S corporation election will be terminated. § 1362(d)(3)(A).

The decision to elect S corporation status depends on the number of owners, the type and amount of income (for the corporation's shareholders, as well as for the corporation itself), local taxes and fees, and the likelihood of dividends. There are also nontax factors to consider,

> *Popular with professionals and celebrities, use of an S Corp allowed a former candidate for Vice President of the United States to avoid paying almost $600,000 in Medicare tax on earnings of more than $26 million from his law practice. Michael Moss & Kate Zermike, Campaign Releases Edward's Earnings, N.Y. Times, July 10, 2004, at A5.*

such as continuity of life, the extent of the owner's liability, the ability to transfer ownership, and management structure.

[¶ 24,439]

b. *Qualified Subchapter S Trust (QSST)*

Trusts that are eligible to be S corporation shareholders include: (1) grantor trusts, including those that distribute all income to a single beneficiary who is treated as the owner of the trust under § 678; (2) a Qualified Subchapter S Trust (QSST) § 1361(c)(2); (2) trusts with more than one beneficiary, so long as each beneficiary has a "substantially separate and independent share;" (3) testamentary trusts but only with respect to stock transferred to the trust under the terms of a will and then only for two-year period beginning with the day of the transfer § 1361(c)(2)(A)(iii); (4) voting trusts; and (5) electing small business trusts.

[¶ 24,441]

i. *QSST Requirements*

In order to qualify as a QSST, the beneficiary of the trust or his legal representative must elect to be taxed as the owner of the trust for purposes of the grantor trust rules of § 678. The trust must also satisfy the following requirements of § 1361(d):

1. The trust must own stock in one or more S corporations (see Priv. Ltr. Rul. 9042026 where trust converted debt owed to it by S corporation into stock of S corporation);

2. The trust must have only one income beneficiary at a time, and that beneficiary must be a U.S. citizen or resident;

3. The trust must distribute all of its income (as defined in § 643(b)) currently; see Priv. Ltr. Ruls. 9043030; 9030051; and 9026024; but

¶ 24,441

see Priv. Ltr. Rul. 9035048 (for discussion of when an S corporation's undistributed income is not required to be distributed currently);

4. Distributions of corpus, if made, must be made to the income beneficiary only, see Priv. Ltr. Rul. 9040019 (IRS ruled that a "five-and-five" power held by the beneficiary would not disqualify the trust as a QSST);

5. The trust beneficiary, or legal representative, must make a timely, irrevocable election to be treated as the owner of the S corporation stock (for what constitutes a timely QSST election, Reg. § 1.1361–1(j)(6));

6. Each income interest in the trust must terminate on the earlier of the death of the beneficiary or the termination of the trust; and

7. All of the trust assets must, upon termination of the trust, be distributed to the income beneficiary.

The IRS has privately ruled, however, that a trust agreement granting a beneficiary a testamentary power of appointment will not disqualify the trust as a QSST where the trust terminates upon the beneficiary's death. Priv. Ltr. Rul. 9035052.

The QSST requirements must continue to be met throughout the life of the trust or the trust will cease to be an eligible shareholder. Generally, a trust loses its QSST status as of the first day it fails to meet any of the above requirements. § 1361(d)(4). However, with respect to the income distribution requirements listed at (2) and (3) above, QSST status will be lost as of the first tax year in which the trust fails to comply. *Id.* The IRS has privately ruled, however, that even though a trust was allowed, under the terms of the governing instrument, to accumulate income if and when the trust no longer held stock in an S corporation, the trust would qualify for QSST status. Priv. Ltr. Rul. 9044045.

Under the third requirement above, the IRS has ruled that a separate and independent share of a trust cannot qualify for QSST status if there is even a remote chance that the corpus of the trust will be distributed to a person other than the income beneficiary during that beneficiary's lifetime. Rev. Rul. 93–31, 1993–1 C.B. 186. Section 1361(d)(3) states that an individual's share of a trust meeting the definition of a "substantially separate and independent share" under § 663(c) will be treated as a separate trust for purposes of provisions allowing a QSST to be a S corporation shareholder. A separate and independent share is defined in the regulations as a share in a trust having more than one beneficiary where the terms of the trust are such that distributions from the trust are to be made in "substantially the same manner as if separate trusts had been created." Reg. § 1.663(c)–3. If separate and independent shares exist, they are treated as separate trusts under § 663(c) for the purpose of determining the beneficiaries' distributable net income when calculating their taxable amount and the trust's deductible amount.

Separate shares are not treated as separate trusts where the trustee has the power to distribute corpus, unless such distributions to one beneficiary will not affect the other beneficiaries' proportionate shares of the corpus. Separate trusts may be deemed to exist, however, where the possibility of the trustee's exercise of the power to distribute corpus is remote, even though the trustee has the power to distribute to one beneficiary a disproportionate share of the corpus. Reg. § 1.663(c)–3(d).

[¶ 24,445]

ii.   QSST Election

The QSST election is made on Form 2553 (Election by a Small Business Corporation) and remains in effect for each subsequent beneficiary, unless that beneficiary affirmatively refuses to consent to the election. § 1361(d)(2)(B). A separate election must be made with respect to each corporation, the stock of which is held by the trust. Id.

The election must be made within two months and 15 days after:

1.   The date on which the S corporation stock is transferred to the trust (Temp. Reg. § 1.1361–1(i)(6)(iii)) or

2.   The first day for which the S corporation election is effective (§ 1361(d)(2)(D)).

The QSST election cannot be made before the corporation files its election for S corporation status. Once made, the QSST election is revocable only with the consent of the IRS.

[¶ 24,449]

iii.   Disclaimer by QSST Beneficiary

A QSST beneficiary may, by means of a qualified disclaimer, irrevocably refuse to accept any interest in the trust. The IRS has privately ruled that an effective disclaimer of a beneficiary's entire interest in a trust will result in the succeeding beneficiary being able to make the QSST election, provided that the trust satisfies all of the QSST requirements. Priv. Ltr. Rul. 9025086. In order to be treated as an effective qualified disclaimer, several statutory requirements must be met. § 2518(b). For a discussion of disclaimers generally, see Chapter 16.

[¶ 24,453]

iv.   Reformation

An irrevocable trust that does not meet the QSST requirements may be classified as a QSST if it is granted approval by a court to reform the trust terms. Priv. Ltr. Ruls. 9032007 and 9040031. It is within a court's power to grant or to deny a request for reformation. Whether reformation will be granted in a particular case depends upon local law.

[¶ 24,461]

c. Trusts Qualifying as QSSTs

Many forms of trusts commonly used in estate planning may satisfy the requirements for treatment as a QSST. Such trusts are discussed in the paragraphs that follow.

[¶ 24,463]

i. QTIP Trusts

The marital deduction qualified terminable interest property (QTIP) trust that is authorized by § 2056(b)(7) would qualify as a QSST because the surviving spouse will be the sole income beneficiary and distributions of principal cannot be made to any other person during the spouse's lifetime. The marital deduction need not actually be claimed (by the executor making the election) in order for the QTIP to qualify as a QSST. Similarly, QSST qualification is not affected by whether the surviving spouse has either a general or a limited power of appointment over the trust. When the marital deduction is elective rather than mandatory, however, and the marital deduction is not claimed, the QSST can continue as a shareholder of the S corporation only for 60 days following the death of the surviving spouse. § 1361(c)(2)(A). Where the QSST is included in the estate of the surviving spouse for federal estate tax purposes, the QSST may continue as a shareholder for two years after the death of the surviving spouse. § 1361(c)(2)(A)(ii). The post-death holding period for S corporation stock held by testamentary trusts is two years.

[¶ 24,467]

ii. Trusts for Minors

Trusts qualifying under § 2503(c) (relating to gifts to minors) may also qualify as QSSTs. Section 2503(c) was created to allow the annual federal gift tax exclusion (currently, $11,000 per donee) to be available to donors who want to make gifts in trust for persons under 21 years of age. The governing instrument of a § 2503(c) trust must provide that the trust will terminate when the beneficiary reaches age 21 or dies. Upon termination of the trust, the trustee must be obligated to distribute the trust corpus to the named beneficiary if that beneficiary is living. If the beneficiary is deceased, the trustee must be obligated to distribute the trust corpus to the person or institution that the beneficiary has chosen by the exercise of a power of appointment or, in default of the effective exercise of such a power, to those who would take under the will of the beneficiary or by intestacy if the beneficiary has no will. Although a trust may accumulate income and qualify under § 2503, qualification as a QSST requires that the trust income be distributed currently. § 1361(d)(3)(B).

[¶ 24,471]

iii.   *Other Trusts*

Obviously, many other trusts, such as a general power of appointment marital deduction trust (see § 2056(b)(5)) or a "sprinkle" bypass or credit shelter trust (for discussion of bypass trust, see Chapter 18), will qualify as QSSTs. A settlor can establish a QSST during his or her lifetime or by the terms of his or her will. Moreover, there are no special requirements for the disposition of the trust property upon termination of the trust. Thus, for example, the beneficiary need not have a general power of appointment.

That having been said, it is appropriate to note, by way of contrast, that a charitable remainder trust is not eligible for QSST status. See Priv. Ltr. Rul. 8922014, which follows.

[¶ 24,473]

PRIVATE LETTER RULING 8922014
February 28, 1989.

Section 664(c) provides that, generally, a trust meeting the definition of a charitable remainder trust is exempt from federal income tax. The unitrust amount required to be distributed is taxable to the beneficiary under the rules contained in § 664(b) and Reg. § 1.664–1(d). Section 664(a) and the regulations thereunder provide that these provisions apply notwithstanding the other provisions of subchapter J (§§ 641–692).

Section 1361(d) permits certain qualifying subchapter S trusts (QSSTs) to be S corporation shareholders. The beneficiary of a trust otherwise meeting the definition of a qualified subchapter S trust contained in § 1361(d)(3) must elect to be treated under § 678(a) as the owner of the portion of the trust consisting of S corporation stock. See § 1361(d)(1).

A beneficiary electing under § 1361(d) to be treated as owner of the portion of the trust consisting of stock agrees to be taxed on all items of income relating to that stock. See § 671. As a result of the QSST election, the beneficiary, rather than the trust, is treated as the taxable owner of the stock. This election ensures that the trust represents only one S corporation shareholder and guarantees that all income earned by the trust relating to the stock is taxed to the trust's beneficiary.

In contrast, under § 664(b), the beneficiary of an income interest in a charitable remainder unitrust is only taxable on the unitrust amount. Tax is imposed on the income beneficiary only to the extent of the unitrust amount received and only to the extent the amount represents taxable income. Any other income is taxed to the trust and thus is, in general, tax exempt under § 664(c), because the income is being held for the benefit of charity.

Thus, § 664 and § 1361 contemplate two distinct systems of taxation. Section 1361 allows a trust meeting certain detailed requirements to qualify as an S corporation shareholder if the trust beneficiary elects tax treatment

¶ 24,473

under the grantor trust provisions. Section 664 applies to an arrangement meeting equally detailed requirements and provides favorable tax treatment in lieu of the other provisions of subchapter J. Under § 664(a) the charitable remainder unitrust provisions would override the tax treatment attending a QSST election. Thus, if the § 1361 election were allowed, an essential element of § 1361(d), imposing § 678 tax consequences on the beneficiary, would be avoided. The trust would represent, in effect, two owners of the S corporation stock: the income beneficiary who is taxed on the income to the extent received, and the trust whose income is not taxed because it is earmarked for charity. This consequence is contrary to the operation of § 1361(d). Therefore, a charitable remainder unitrust cannot qualify as an S corporation shareholder.

The inconsistency between the two systems of taxation for the two different trust arrangements is further highlighted by postulating a different situation. If a QSST election were permitted, and grantor trust treatment applied so that the trust beneficiary were to be taxed on all trust income deriving from the stock, then the trust would not function exclusively as a charitable remainder unitrust. Accordingly, all charitable deductions for transfers to the trust would be disallowed and the trust would not be tax exempt. See Reg. § 1.664–1(a)(4), ex 2. It is apparent that imposing the grantor trust provisions on the § 664 scheme of taxation would severely frustrate the intent and effect of the charitable remainder trust provisions.

Accordingly, we conclude that the trust arrangements described in §§ 664 and 1361(d) are mutually exclusive. A charitable remainder unitrust cannot qualify as a qualified subchapter S trust under § 1361(d), and a qualified subchapter S trust cannot qualify under § 664.

[¶ 24,479]

d. Disqualification

QSST status allows trust fiduciaries to meet their objectives by offering tax advantages, such as income-splitting, while protecting the trust assets and the interests of the beneficiary. Failure to meet the QSST requirements, however, will result in termination of QSST status. The trust will no longer qualify as an S corporation shareholder, and the S corporation election will generally terminate.

[¶ 24,481]

i. Termination of S Corporation Status by Fiduciaries

Fiduciaries need to be aware that certain actions, such as the creation of a second class of stock or the addition of a 101st shareholder, may result in termination of the S corporation election. If the termination was inadvertent, however, the fiduciary might be able to take corrective action to prevent the loss of S corporation status (see ¶ 24,535).

[¶ 24,485]

ii.   Inadvertent Termination

If a trust loses its QSST status, and a corporation's S election is terminated, and if the termination was inadvertent, the IRS may permit the corporation's S status to continue. § 1362(f).

The following scenario—illustrated in many private letter rulings—traces the sequence of how an inadvertent termination of QSST status results in the termination of the corporation's Subchapter S election. First, a trust exists which contains some stock of a corporation. Then, all the shareholders consent to the Subchapter S election. At the same time, the trust beneficiary makes the QSST election. Next, it is later discovered that the trust is a defective QSST since one or more QSST requirements are not met. Therefore, the trust is no longer a qualifying shareholder for purposes of § 1361(b)(1)(B); consequently, the corporation fails to qualify as a small business corporation as defined under § 1361(b). Once the corporation ceases to be a small business corporation, § 1362(d)(2) provides that the S corporation election terminates.

A corporation's Subchapter S status will be treated as having never been terminated if the following events occur:

1.   The IRS determines that the termination was inadvertent;

2.   The corporation, within a reasonable period of time after discovering the terminating event, takes steps to return to S corporation status; and

3.   Both the corporation and its shareholders agree to any adjustments that the IRS requires with respect to the termination period.

[¶ 24,489]

iii.   Termination by Sale of S Corporation Stock

The sale of S corporation stock by a QSST terminates the trust's QSST status. When the QSST status is terminated, the trust's "grantor trust" status is also terminated. See Chapter 22 for a discussion of the grantor trust rules. This, in turn, is generally held to be a deemed disposition by the grantor which can generate income. See Rev. Rul. 77–402, 1977–2 C.B. 222; Madorin v. Commissioner, 84 T.C. 667 (1985).

The income beneficiary of a QSST, rather than the QSST itself, recognizes the gain or loss when the QSST sells part or all of its shares in an S corporation. This occurs even if the gain or loss can be allocated to the corpus of the trust, rather than the income, under local trust law. Rev. Rul. 92–84, 1992–2 C.B. 216. This can be problematic where the sale is made on an installment basis or the S corporation redeems its stock for a partial cash payment and an installment note. For example, a QSST holds S corporation stock which is redeemed in 1994 by the S corporation for $100,000 cash and a

$1,000,000 installment note, payable over 20 years. See Chapter 12 for a discussion of installment sales. The IRS has stated that the redemption of S corporation stock from a QSST or the sale of such stock by a QSST will not qualify for installment reporting; the total sales price would instead be reportable in the year the sale occurs. See Rev. Rul. 92–84, 1992–2 C.B. 216. Therefore, in the above example, the entire $1,100,000 would be reportable in 1994. This means that the beneficiary will be immediately subject to significant tax liability for any gain from the sale, even though the installment payments will not be received until some future date. The IRS's reasoning is that the moment QSST status terminates due to the disposal by the QSST of all its S corporation stock in an installment sale, the trust is deemed to dispose of the installment obligation. Under § 453B, tax is immediately due upon the disposition of an installment obligation despite the fact that the proceeds of the sale will not be received until a future date. The IRS reasons that the termination of QSST and "grantor trust" status results in a deemed disposition by the grantor of the installment obligations to a newly created nongrantor trust.

One suggested method for avoiding the installment sale trap is to provide in the trust instrument that the QSST is to convert to a grantor trust under § 678 if the S corporation stock is sold in an installment sale. The trust, however, must not be irrevocable. This would allow the trust to continue its grantor trust status and thereby avoid the deemed disposition by the grantor of its installment obligations.

Problems

[¶ 24,495]

1. Examine § 1361 and the sections following it. Do the various restrictions seem complicated? What purpose do the restrictions serve? Are they necessary, or do they strike you as traps for the unwary?

2. Which of the following corporations could elect S corporation treatment?

   (a) Ace Corporation has 36 shareholders, including Mr. and Mrs. Smart, Mr. and Mrs. Bright, Mr. and Mrs. Wily, and the Estate of Henry Borden. All shareholders are residents of the United States. Ace earns 90 percent of its income from the manufacture of toy airplanes.

   (b) Same as (a), except that Mrs. Bright is a British subject who has been residing in London since her separation from Mr. Bright two years ago.

   (c) Same as (a), except that shares are now held by a testamentary trust established under the will of Henry Borden. Six months have passed since the shares passed to the trust.

   (d) Same as (a), except that shares are now held by a trust established by Henry Borden during his lifetime. Trust ownership had been attributed to Mr. Borden under the grantor trust rules, and when he died the entire trust was included in his estate. Mr. Borden died seven months ago.

(e) Same as (a), except that Ace, which had $10,000 in accumulated earnings and profits from the past three consecutive taxable years in which it had not elected S corporation treatment, has derived for each such taxable years 45 percent of its income from rents on various parcels of real property that the company owns, which it plans to use as the business expands.

[¶ 24,497]

e. *Estates of S Corporation Shareholders*

An estate may also be a shareholder in an S corporation without jeopardizing the corporation's S corporation status. § 1361(b)(1)(B). Because the function of an estate (the gathering and distribution of assets) differs from that of a trust (the preservation of assets), the approach of an executor or administrator of an estate to the S corporation shareholder matter would generally differ from that of the trustee of a QSST. Often, the executor or administrator will find that it could be more desirable for tax purposes to terminate or revoke the corporation's S corporation status. See ¶ 24,499. The executor or administrator of the estate may wish to distribute shares of an S corporation to a trust. In such a case, the current income beneficiary of the trust must make a timely QSST election in order to avoid termination of S corporation status. Priv. Ltr. Rul. 9038019.

[¶ 24,499]

i. *Estate's Termination of S Corporation Status*

If an estate owns more than half of the shares of an S corporation, the executor may terminate the S corporation election. § 1362(d)(1)(B). The desirability of terminating the S corporation election after the decedent's death will depend upon several factors, including:

1. the amount of the corporation's income or loss;

2. the estate's income tax bracket;

3. the estate's ability to make the loss usable, if the corporation is operating at a loss; and

4. the effect of retroactive termination on the decedent's estate and the other shareholders.

Continuing the S corporation election may be a useful way to distribute money for the support of the decedent's family without an additional tax at the corporate level. Pvt. Ltr. Rul. 9218019 is illustrative of the tax consequences and consideration involved when an estate liquidates an S corporation. See ¶ 24,507.

¶ 24,499

[¶ 24,501]

ii. Estate's Revocation of S Corporation Election

An executor may revoke the S corporation election. § 1362(d)(1). Executors wishing to do so, however, should be aware of an avoidable pitfall that may arise if the decedent, shortly before death, received a tax-free distribution from the corporation that reduced its accumulated adjustment account (an account that is used in computing the tax effect of distributions made by an S corporation with accumulated earnings and profits). § 1362(d)(3).

If the revocation is made during the first two and one-half months of the corporation's tax year, it will be effective retroactively as of the first day of the tax year, unless the revocation specifies another date. § 1362(d)(1)(C) and (D). Thus, the tax-free distribution would be taxable to the decedent as a dividend. Any revocation of the election during the first two and one-half months of the corporation's tax year should, therefore, specify a later date on which the revocation is to become effective.

Problem

[¶ 24,503]

Quacx Corp., a S corporation, is a manufacturer of children's toys that has the calendar year as its tax year. On October 1 of the current tax year, the corporation made a distribution of $1,000 to each of its 12 shareholders.

On December 15, Oliver Tompkins, owner of 52 percent of Quacx stock, died. On December 30, the newly appointed executor of Tompkins' estate met with the other shareholders and reported his intent to terminate the S corporation election by revocation, with the revocation to be made and to be effective on December 31. What is the effect of the executor's decision? Does this change the October distribution into an ordinary dividend? Will S corporation treatment still be in effect for the taxable year ending December 31?

Suppose that it is December 29, and you are one of the other Quacx shareholders. You receive a phone call from a fellow shareholder informing you that the executor of Tompkins' estate is about to revoke consent for the S corporation treatment of Quacx income. What should you do? Would it be in your best interest to get together with the other shareholders and arrange a deal with the executor, in which you all paid something to the estate in exchange for his agreement not to revoke consent? Assuming that the $1,000 distribution was the only distribution received from the corporation during the current taxable year by your client, and he is in the 30 percent marginal tax bracket, how much should you be prepared to offer? Why does the executor want to revoke consent?

¶ 24,501

[¶ 24,505]

iii.　Estate's Liquidation of S Corporation

The following Private Letter Ruling is illustrative of the tax consequences when an estate liquidates an S corporation.

[¶ 24,507]

PRIVATE LETTER RULING 9218019

January 23, 1992.

We received your letter on July 30, 1991, requesting a ruling on behalf of A about the tax consequences to a shareholder on a sale by an S corporation of its assets followed by a liquidating distribution of the proceeds of the sale in the same taxable year as the sale. This letter is in reply to your request.

* * * X elected S corporation status under § 1362(a).

* * * Since 1969, X has owned, as its sole capital asset, a commercial building. On December 31, 1990, X's adjusted basis for the commercial building was about $100,000. Depreciation on X's commercial building has been calculated on the straight line method.

At the time of death, B owned all of X corporation's stock. On B's death, B's estate, A, became the owner of all X corporation's stock. C, who is B's only beneficiary, does not wish to operate the commercial building that is the sole asset of X. Thus, the executors of A's propose to sell the commercial building owned by X, and to distribute the cash proceeds to A in complete liquidation of X.

Section 1014(a) provides, generally, that the basis of property in the hands of a person acquiring the property from a decedent is the fair market value of the property at the date of the decedent's death. Section 1001(a) provides, generally, that the gain from the sale or other disposition of property is the excess of the amount realized from the sale or disposition over the adjusted basis of the property.

Section 1367(a) provides, generally, that the basis of each shareholder's stock in an S corporation is increased for any period by the sum of items of income described in § 1366(a)(1)(A) and (B).

Section 1374(a) provides, generally, that if an S corporation has a net recognized built-in gain for any taxable year beginning in an S corporation's recognition period, a tax is imposed on the income of such corporation for such taxable year.

Section 1371(a)(1) provides, generally, that except as otherwise provided in the Internal Revenue Code, and except to the extent inconsistent with subchapter S, subchapter C applies to S corporations and S corporation shareholders. Reg. § 1.1372–1(c) provides, generally, that to the extent the provisions of subchapter C are not inconsistent with the provisions and

¶ 24,507

regulations under subchapter S such provisions will apply to an S corporation and its shareholders.

Section 336(a) requires, generally, that a liquidating corporation recognize gain or loss on the distribution of property in complete liquidation as if the property were sold to a distributee at its fair market value.

Section 331(a) provides that amounts received by a shareholder in a distribution in complete liquidation of a corporation are treated as in full payment in exchange for stock.

Based on the information submitted and the above representations made by the taxpayer, we reach the following conclusions.

Under § 1014(a), A's basis in the stock of X will be stepped-up to the fair market value of the property as of the date of B's death. Under § 1001(a), X's gain from the sale of its commercial building will be measured by the difference between the amount realized on the sale of the building and X's adjusted basis in the building.

Section 1366 requires all items of an S corporation's income to pass through to the S corporation shareholders. Thus, we conclude that the gain realized by X on the sale of its commercial building will pass through to and be recognized by A, its sole shareholder. Further, we conclude that under § 1367(a)(1), A's stepped-up basis under § 1014(a) will be increased by the amount realized and passed-through to A on X's sale of its building.

Under § 336(a), a liquidating corporation recognizes gain or loss on the distribution of property in complete liquidation. However, X is not a taxable entity under § 1363(a)(1), and any gain or loss recognized would be recognized by X's shareholder. In addition, X is distributing cash not appreciated assets. Thus, we conclude that § 336(a) does not require recognition of gain or loss on the distribution of cash in complete liquidation of X.

In addition, assuming the liquidation of X qualifies as a complete liquidation under § 331(a), we conclude that the amounts received by A in the distribution in complete liquidation of X are treated as in full payment in exchange for A's stock in accordance with § 331(a). We further conclude that A's gain or loss, under § 1001, will be measured by the difference between the amount of cash received and A's adjusted basis in its X stock surrendered.

Finally, assuming X has been continuously an S corporation, within the meaning of § 1361(a)(1), as of the effective date of its above-described S corporation election, and further assuming that X's election is not subject to a terminating event, within the meaning of § 1362(d), prior to the date of the complete liquidation, we reach the following conclusion.

X will not be subject to the tax on net built-in gains imposed by § 1374.

[¶ 24,515]

f. When to Terminate Subchapter S Election

Due to changing federal tax rates, it may be advantageous for a corporation to terminate existing Subchapter S status. In 2006, the top nominal individual income tax rate and the top corporate rate are both 35 percent. As a result, the advantage of pass-through taxation of Subchapter S status to an individual has been lost, although other advantages of S corporation status may still exist. The main consideration, of course, is whether termination of S corporation status will result in a lower tax liability. There are several factors which should be taken into account before the client is advised to change from S to C status.

In order for a change to aid a client's tax situation, three conditions should generally be met prior to termination of S corporation status. First, it should be fairly certain that the shareholders of the corporation will be taxed in the higher individual bracket. If the individual's tax rate will be only marginally higher than the corporate rate, few rate savings will be gained by termination of S corporation status. Second, the corporation's earnings should be earmarked for reinvestment in the growth of the company. Payment of earnings as salary, after deduction of expenses, reduces the advantages of termination since the money will then be taxed at both the corporate and individual rates under the double taxation scheme for corporations. A balancing factor may exist in this situation, however, if the individuals wish to get fringe benefits they cannot obtain with S corporation status. Third, few appreciated assets subject to tax upon sale of a C corporation should be held by the company. If the assets of the corporation, including goodwill, are appreciated, the owners of a S corporation will be in a better position upon sale of the company since single taxation, as opposed to the double taxation of a C corporation, of those assets will generally occur. Note, however, that the tax on built-in gains may cause double taxation even if S corporation status exists. See § 1374. This generally arises when the corporation was created as a C corporation, then later elected S corporation status and sold appreciated assets within 10 years of the election.

Even if these three conditions exist, other factors may still weigh against termination of S corporation status. First, basis in an owner's stock in a S corporation is increased to the extent that the corporation's earnings are left in the company and the value of the company thereby increases, thus reducing the taxable gain to the owner if the stock is sold. Basis in a C corporation does not similarly increase, so that the sale of C corporation stock at the same price will produce a higher taxable gain. This can be a considerable advantage, despite the taxation of the S corporation's business income to the owner. Second, appreciated assets can usually be sold by a S corporation without payment of double taxes on the gain, with the important caveat noted above. Third, state tax may not be applicable to S corporations. Fourth, S corporations are not subject to the tax on unreasonable accumulations. Fifth, as noted above in ¶ 24,435, the IRS does not challenge salaries to owner-employees of S corporations as excessive, and therefore nondeductible. Sixth, the alternative minimum tax does not apply to S corporations.

Once all these factors are taken into account, it may be concluded that termination of S corporation election will not be advantageous. Careful consideration of each client's position should be made to determine what will produce the least tax liability before any steps toward termination are taken.

¶ 24,515

[¶ 24,520]

g. *Electing Small Business Trust (ESBT)*

An "electing small business trust" (ESBT) may be a shareholder in an S corporation. Among the conditions for qualification as an ESBT are the requirements that (1) all of the beneficial interests in the trust be acquired by gift, bequest, or inheritance; and (2) the portion of the trust holding S corporation stock will be treated as a separate trust and the income from the S corporation stock will be taxed to the trust at the highest marginal income tax rate without any deduction for trust distributions. The use of the ESBT allows for more flexibility in planning than a QSST, because the QSST may only have one income beneficiary and the income must be distributed to that beneficiary.

[¶ 24,525]

3. LIMITED LIABILITY COMPANIES

Another option for a business entity is to form a limited liability company (LLC), now available in most states. The LLC is a hybrid entity, combining the most advantageous features of both corporations and partnerships. Similar to partnerships, the LLC is a pass-through entity for federal tax purposes, allowing income and losses to be taxed solely to the individual owners. The liability of the owners, however, is similar to that of corporate shareholders: the owners have limited liability for debts of the LLC and for claims against the LLC. Due to the relatively recent development of LLCs, there is little precedent or certainty in the manner in which these entities will be treated by the IRS, especially in terms of their treatment as part of an estate.

LLCs were first created in 1988 in response to the IRS's rulings that, for federal taxation purposes, it would treat an entity as a partnership if the entity lacked two or more of the characteristics of a corporation. See, e.g., Rev. Rul. 88–76, 1988–2 C.B. 360. These characteristics are: limited liability, continuity of life, free transferability of interests, and centralization of management. Limited liability exists if no member may be held personally liable under local law for claims against the company or for the company's debts. Reg. § 301.7701–2(d). Continuity of life is lacking in a business entity if it dissolves upon the death, retirement, insanity, bankruptcy, expulsion or some other act of withdrawal of a member of the entity (Reg. § 301.7701–2(b)(1)) and the remaining members cannot continue the business without the unanimous consent of those members. See Rev. Rul. 88–76, 1988–2 C.B. 360; but see Priv. Ltr. Rul. 9010028 (consent to continue the business by 85 percent of remaining members sufficient). Rev. Rul. 93–91, 1993–2 C.B. 316 (majority consent sufficient). Free transferability of interests exists where each of the members of the entity, or the members owning substantially all of the entity's interests, have the power to confer upon nonmembers all the attributes of their interests in the entity without the consent of the other members. Reg. § 301.7701–2(e)(1). Centralization of management exists where a person or group of persons, which does not include the full membership of the entity, have the exclusive authority for making managerial decisions in conducting the entity's business. Reg. § 301.7701–2(c)(1).

Most LLCs lack the corporate characteristics of free transferability of interests and continuity of life. This is achieved in most current state LLC statutes by providing for (1) limited liability; (2) dissolution upon death, resignation, retirement, expulsion, bankruptcy, or dissolution of a member unless the remaining members decide by either a majority or unanimous vote to continue the LLC; (3) determination of the management structure by the operating agreement; and (4) a requirement of the unanimous or majority consent of the remaining members or managers prior to the transfer of membership or management rights (but not the transfer of the right to profits). A common misunderstanding is that the limited duration of an LLC imposed by state statutes or LLC regulations will defeat continuity of life. The regulations expressly provide to the contrary. See Reg. § 301.7701–2(b)(3).

LLCs have several advantages over the use of both S corporations and limited partnerships. An LLC is not subject to the requirements for existence as a S corporation, such as the limitation on the number of members who may hold interests in the company, and so forth. Also, the LLC can step up the basis of its assets when selling membership interests under § 754 since it is taxed as a partnership. Operating and liquidating distributions of appreciated assets may be made by the LLC without recognizing income, and no gain need be recognized by members who contribute appreciated assets to the LLC but are not in control of the LLC after the contribution. LLC members can, as in partnerships, also deduct losses in amounts up to the sum of their basis in the membership interest, their allocable share of LLC income, and their allocable share of LLC debt. S corporation shareholders, in contrast, can only deduct losses in the amount of the sum of the shareholder's basis in stock and loans made by the shareholder to the corporation. The main advantage of LLCs over limited partnerships is that all members of the LLC are shielded by limited liability, i.e., no general partner with unlimited liability is required as in a limited partnership. A limited partnership, however, is more attractive than an LLC in two respects: (1) limited partnerships are recognized in every state so that the liability of limited partners is certain and (2) limited partnerships do not dissolve upon the withdrawal of a limited partner, unlike the withdrawal of an LLC member.

When converting to an LLC from a limited or general partnership, the change may be accomplished tax free, since the LLC is classified as a partnership for federal tax purposes. See Priv. Ltr. Rul. 9226035. The change from a C or S corporation, however, will generally not be tax free.

There are some drawbacks to the use of LLCs. First, although members of an LLC have limited liability, it is not an absolute protection. For example, LLC members have limited liability in the state in which the LLC is formed; this limited liability may not protect the members in states in which there is no LLC statute. Additionally, there is no right to an accounting (as a partner has in a partnership) and no right to bring a derivative suit against the LLC (as a shareholder has in a corporation). Protection against liability for the member's own negligence is also not offered under current state LLC statutes.

¶ 24,525

According to one recent decision, a member's liability for the LLC's debts may continue even after the member transfers his or her interest in the LLC, despite the limited liability provisions. See Weiss v. Commissioner, 956 F.2d 242 (11th Cir.1992). Second, the uncertainty as to the treatment of LLCs due to their relatively recent advent in the law requires careful and continuing scrutiny of the current status afforded to these entities and their members.

Problems

[¶ 24,533]

1. Abel, Brad, Chuck and Diane form an LLC and plan to operate under the name Spencer Furniture, L.L.C. Spencer's regulations require it to dissolve upon the death, retirement, insanity, bankruptcy, expulsion, or any act of withdrawal of a member. However, the regulations provide that Spencer can continue, notwithstanding a dissolution event, if a majority of the remaining members consent to continue. Is continuity of life present?

2. Spencer's regulations provide that the company will cease to exist 30 years from the date of incorporation. Is continuity of life present?

3. Assume Abel incorporates a different LLC in the state of Texas—a state that allows a one-man LLC. Abel is the only member of the LLC but is one of three managers who manage the company. Does the LLC have centralized management?

4. Assume the same facts as Problem 1. Spencer decides to make corporate distributions to Chuck and Diane with respect to their ownership interest. What are the tax effects to Spencer? Chuck? Diane?

[¶ 24,535]

4. CAPITALIZATION

a. *Retaining Assets Outside the Corporation*

Assume that Ahmed and Jim decide to incorporate Super Electronics Co., but not to elect S corporation status or to create a limited liability company. How should the corporation be capitalized? As a general rule, it is preferable to retain assets outside of the corporation. Once assets are owned by the corporation, it is often difficult to remove them without adverse tax consequences. Holding assets out and leasing them to the corporation can serve several useful purposes. It can permit the distribution of business income without dividend taxation. It can provide assets with which to make gifts to generate income for other family members. Retained assets can provide support after death to the surviving spouse or other members of the family. Such assets may provide some tax shelter for shareholders, particularly where depreciation deductions produce losses not currently usable by the new corporation.

In addition to fixed assets, it is also desirable to retain accounts receivable outside the corporation. Transferring these to the corporation only puts additional monies into the corporation which may be difficult to extract. It is usually desirable to transfer only inventory, small equipment and furnishings and some cash to the corporation. But it must be kept in mind that unless the corporation is adequately capitalized, creditors may be able to pierce the corporate veil. Additionally, a business planner must be careful to avoid transfers from the corporation to a shareholder that the Internal Revenue Service could reclass as "constructive dividends," thereby subjecting them to double taxation.

Retaining substantial fixed assets outside the corporation also produces a desirable side effect. It reduces the value of the stock of the corporation and thereby makes it easier to sell that stock of modest value to key employees, if that is desired. Additionally, retaining fixed assets outside the corporation helps minimize corporate tax liabilities, such as franchise tax and business property tax. A buy-sell agreement is advisable to terminate the interest of an employee, if the employee quits, dies, or is fired. Where the stock is subject to restrictions on transferability and a substantial risk of forfeiture, other than those which by their terms will never lapse, the employee should consider making a § 83(b) election to treat the difference, if any, between the price paid and the fair market value at the time of the transfer as compensation taxable in the year the stock is acquired.

Problem

[¶ 24,538]

Section 83(a) states the general rule regarding when an employee must "take into income" property received for services rendered. Now read § 83(b). What effect does a § 83(b) election have? When would a § 83(b) election be *most* advisable? Would you suggest a § 83(b) election in the following case? Reread § 83(a) and (b) before answering.

Bill is a young engineer with Rocketron, a recently organized aerospace and defense concern. Rocketron has been a bit pressed for cash of late, and Bill recently accepted Rocketron stock in lieu of 25 percent of his salary. The stock has been given to him at an exchange rate less than its current market value, but Bill must sell it back to the company at the price at which it was issued to him if he leaves the company within five years. When the stock was issued to Bill on October 20, it was issued for $5 per share (market value was $7 at the time). Shares of Rocketron rocketed to $22 on November 14. It is likely that Rocketron will continue to rise. It is now November 15th.

A § 83(b) election will preclude post-acquisition appreciation from being treated as compensation, rather than capital gain, when the restrictions actually lapse, or, if earlier, when the stock is sold. The election can be made even if there has been no bargain purchase, so that no income is reportable when the election is made. Reg. § 1.83–2(a).

[¶ 24,539]

b.　Preferred Stock

Unless a Subchapter S election is contemplated, which creates limitations on issuing of a second class of stock (§ 1361(b)(1)(D) and (c)(4)), issuing some preferred stock may be useful. It can be redeemed to pay death taxes, without the redemption disturbing the distribution of either voting power or the stockholders' respective shares in the future growth of the business. It is also useful for shifting wealth to younger generations. Jim might give Junior his common stock, as Junior becomes more active in the business, and retain only the preferred for himself. Since common stock is a junior equity interest under § 2701(a)(4)(B)(i), it is not subject to the zero valuation scheme of § 2701. § 2701(c)(1)(B). If preferred stock is issued, the capital of the corporation can be structured so as to confine as much as ninety percent of the original equity in the business to the preferred stock. By reducing the value of the common stock, Jim can give all or part of his common stock to Junior without incurring substantial transfer taxes. This capital structure also facilitates sales of common stock to family members or key employees. Finally, preferred stock issued at the time of incorporation will not be § 306 stock subject to the ordinary income treatment upon a subsequent disposition. § 306(c); Reg. § 1.306–3. A subsequent issuance of preferred stock by way of a stock dividend or recapitalization may well produce § 306 stock with its attendant problems.

Problem

[¶ 24,541]

What is "§ 306 stock"? Not surprisingly, the answer is found in § 306(c). Scan § 306. What is the effect of having stock labelled § 306 stock? What purpose does this rule serve? Do you consider it yet another trap for the unwary? See ¶ 24,641.

––––––––

There are some drawbacks to issuing preferred stock which should be considered. First, if the preferred stock creates different distribution or liquidation rights, a Subchapter S election is not available. § 1361(b)(1)(D) and (c)(4). Second, if substantial assets are retained outside of the corporation, there may not be sufficient asset value within it to create a meaningful amount of preferred. Finally, there may be some uncertainties as to the basis of the preferred stock which would create future planning problems. Since the preferred is unlikely to have a cumulative or mandatory dividend because of the cash flow drain that it would create, it will probably not be worth its par value. But the basis of the stock issued on incorporation must be allocated between the common and preferred stock according to their respective fair market value. Reg. § 1.358–2(b)(2). Thus, any later redemption of the preferred at par would produce a gain. One can boost the value of the preferred by making its dividend cumulative.

> *Note:* Except in unusual circumstances, the portion of the redemption price, if any, attributable to arrearages will be treated as capital gain provided that the redemption qualifies as a sale or exchange rather than a dividend distribution. Compare Rev. Rul. 69–131, 1969–1 C.B. 94, with

¶ 24,539

Rev. Rul. 75–320, 1975–2 C.B. 105; see also Reg. § 1.305–5(c), Example (5).

Allocations of voting powers and dividend participation rights will also affect the value of the preferred. Estate of Salsbury v. Commissioner, 34 T.C.M. (CCH) 1441, T.C.M. (P–H) ¶ 75,333 (1975).

[¶ 24,543]

c. *Debt*

Of course, adequate consideration has not been given to the alternatives of capitalizing a corporation unless one pauses to consider debt. Issuing debt in return for money or property contributed to the corporation has the advantages of creating interest payments which are deductible under § 162(a), whereas dividends are not. Furthermore, the debt can be repaid out of future earnings without dividend treatment. The difficulty in a closely held business is determining the extent to which the debt will be treated as a debt rather than equity for tax purposes. The courts apply a judicially created multifactor test when making this determination. Some common factors considered by the courts include: an unconditional obligation to pay, a fixed maturity date, a fixed interest rate, the intent of the parties, the ability of the corporation to obtain funds from outside sources, debt to equity ratios, the formal indicia of the arrangement, the source of the interest payments, and whether the debt is subordinated. See, e.g., In re Lane, 742 F.2d 1311 (11th Cir.1984) (detailed application of 13–factor list to facts of case); Roth Steel Tube Co. v. Commissioner, 800 F.2d 625 (6th Cir.1986), cert. denied, 481 U.S. 1014 (1987) (application of 11–factor test); Hardman v. United States, 827 F.2d 1409 (9th Cir.1987) (11–factor test); Segel v. Commissioner, 89 T.C. 816 (1987) (multifactor test).

An important consideration is the commercial reasonableness of the purported debt. Thus, in structuring the debt, the debt to equity ratio is a particularly significant factor, as is whether the terms are consistent with commercial loans made by banks, insurance companies, and other institutional lenders. Some possibilities often overlooked include: interest rates tied to prime rates of commercial banks, loan fees or standby fees where additional advances are contemplated, adequate security, restrictive covenants, a reasonable term in relationship to the security including the right to call the loan upon certain conditions, and amortization of principal particularly when the term is long. Whatever the terms of the loan are, if and when the transaction is viewed with hindsight, one of the most significant factors will be whether the loan was actually repaid in accordance with those terms. Slappey Drive Industrial Park v. United States, 561 F.2d 572 (5th Cir.1977) (cash advances constitute equity rather than debt where there was consistent failure to make payments by due date, and where shareholders sought payment only when corporation had sufficient cash). (*Note:* § 1361(c)(5) provides that a straight debt instrument issued by a S corporation to its stockholders is not treated as a second class of stock which can lead to a termination of Subchapter S status.)

Problem

[¶ 24,551]

Tom Smith is in the process of organizing Smith Corporation. He comes to your office with his "capitalization" plan and asks whether his characterization of one part of the plan as "debt" will be accepted by the IRS. Tom plans to use $200,000 to start up the corporation. Fifty thousand will come from sale of common stock (Tom plans to buy 51 percent himself); $50,000 will come from sale of preferred stock, and the remaining $100,000 will take the form of a loan from Tom's father. The loan is to bear an interest rate which will equal and vary with the prime rate. Interest payments will receive first priority, but principal payments will *not* be made if any preferred dividends are in arrears. There is no deadline for repayment, but the executor of Tom's father's estate will have the right to demand a five-year fixed repayment schedule when the father dies. Tom's father is 64 and in good health. Is this debt really equity?

[¶ 24,553]

d.　§ 1244

Once the capital structure has been determined, the common stock should always be issued pursuant to a § 1244 plan. This takes little extra effort but will provide favorable tax treatment in the event the business fails and a loss is incurred on the stock. § 1244(a). Ordinarily, losses incurred upon a sale or exchange of stock in a corporation, or by reason of its worthlessness, are capital losses. § 1221. As such, they are deductible in any year to the extent of capital gains or, if they exceed the gains, against not more (and occasionally less) than $3,000 of ordinary income. § 1211(b). Any unused capital loss may be carried over to subsequent years, until exhausted. § 1212(b). There is an exception to these rules, however, for losses on § 1244 stock which may be treated by the taxpayer as ordinary losses to the extent of $50,000 ($100,000 in the case of married persons filing joint returns) in any taxable year. § 1244(a) and (b).

Problem

[¶ 24,590]

Read § 1244. How would you characterize this section; in other words, why do you think it was enacted? Does it help those it was meant to help? What are some of its unexpected traps?

———

To qualify as § 1244 stock: the stock may be common or preferred stock (§ 1244(c)(1)); at the time the stock is issued the corporation must be a "small business corporation" (§ 1244(c)(1)(A)); the stock must be issued for cash or other property which is neither stock nor securities (§ 1244(c)(1)(B)); and for the five most recent taxable years prior to the issuance of the stock, not more than 50 percent of the corporation's gross receipts must have been from passive sources (i.e., royalties, rents, dividends, annuities and capital gains) (§ 1244(c)(1)(C)).

> *Note:* A corporation is a "small business corporation" if at the time of the issuance of the stock in question the aggregate amount of money or property received for stock (including the stock in question), as a contribution to capital and as paid-in surplus, does not exceed $1,000,000. § 1244(c)(3).

> *Additional Note:* Even if the mechanical limitations on passive income are satisfied, the stock of the corporation may not be eligible for § 1244 treatment if the corporation was "not largely an operating company." Reg. § 1.1244(c)–1(e)(2); Davenport v. Commissioner, 70 T.C. 922 (1978) (taxpayer not entitled to ordinary loss despite meeting gross receipts test because purpose underlying § 1244 limits benefits to largely operating companies).

To claim the benefits of § 1244, the taxpayer must be an individual (trusts and estates are not eligible) who held the stock directly or as a partner, and who acquired the stock upon its issuance. § 1244(a) and (d)(4). Transferees cannot utilize the provision. Furthermore, the basis of the stock for purposes of § 1244 cannot be increased by subsequent capital contributions. Thus, to the extent possible, it is better to cast future capital contributions as purchases of additional stock. If high basis but low value property is transferred to the corporation in return for the stock, the excess of the adjusted basis of the property over its fair market value will likewise be treated as basis of stock other than § 1244 stock. § 1244(d)(1).

G. PLANNING FOR FINANCIAL NEEDS OF FAMILY MEMBERS IN THE CORPORATE SETTING

[¶ 24,601]

1. GIFT AND LEASEBACK OF BUSINESS ASSETS

One of the easiest methods of providing income for family members is a gift of assets which can then be leased to the corporation. In the corporate setting, however, it is important to use either newly purchased assets or assets held out of the corporation on its formation. The distribution of existing assets to the shareholders will be a taxable dividend if the corporation has earnings and profits. § 301(a). And in most circumstances, the distribution of appreciated property will cause the corporation to recognize gain. See, e.g., § 311(b).

Because a corporation is a separate entity, gifts by an individual grantor followed by leasebacks to his own corporation are even more likely to withstand challenge than leasebacks to the grantor himself or his partnership. See Lerner v. Commissioner, 71 T.C. 290 (1978) acq., 1984–1 C.B. 1 (the Commissioner failed in attempts to have the rental deductions by the corporation disallowed and to have the rental income taxed to the grantor).

¶ 24,601

For additional consideration of gift-leaseback, see ¶ 12,901.

[¶ 24,609]

2. GIFT OF CORPORATE STOCK

a. *Shifting Present Income*

Another approach is a gift of stock in the corporation. Ordinarily this is not a useful tool for providing income to the donee, since dividends paid by the corporation will subject the distribution of the corporate earnings to a second tax at the shareholder level. In S corporations, however, where the corporate income is taxed to the shareholders without corporate tax, this technique can be useful. In this context, there is an analogy to the rules regarding family partnerships discussed at ¶ 24,401. Section 1366(e) gives the Commissioner the discretion to allocate or apportion dividends from S corporations among family members, including amounts of undistributed taxable income (which is included in shareholders' income as though it had been distributed as a dividend), so as to reflect the value of services rendered to the corporation by other family members. Thus, the Commissioner has the authority to prevent income attributable to the services of the donor from being shifted to the donee.

Problem

[¶ 24,615]

Given the Commissioner's authority to reallocate S corporation income among shareholders within a family, what is the likely outcome in the following situation?

Kenneth Bottoms formed Kenbot Corporation in 1995, for the purpose of carrying on Ken's professional consulting business. The corporation has four equal shareholders: Ken, his wife, and his two minor sons.

Last year Kenbot netted $220,000 in pretax income. The great bulk of this income consisted of fees generated by Ken's consulting work. From this amount, Ken drew a salary of $20,000. The remaining $200,000 was allocated equally among the taxpayers, but only enough was distributed to each as was necessary to pay their income tax liability for the year. The remainder was retained in the business, where it was used to purchase a new computer and make a down payment on a small office building.

None of the shareholders besides Ken takes an active part in the business. Note that Ken's sons have no other income other than that attributed to them from Kenbot's operations.

[¶ 24,617]

b. *Shifting Future Appreciation—The Byrum Problem*

Suppose that Ahmed wishes to donate some stock to a single trust for his two daughters. He is willing to let the trustee decide how much each of the beneficiaries needs in the way of current distributions and he is willing to use

¶ 24,601

a trustee independent of family control, but he is unwilling to release all control of the stock. He wants to retain the power to vote the stock, the power to veto sales of the stock, the power to veto trust investments, and the power to change to another corporate trustee; in other words, Ahmed wants to emulate the taxpayer in United States v. Byrum, 408 U.S. 125 (1972). In *Byrum,* the Service argued that the power to elect directors was tantamount to the power to control dividends which, in turn, was the equivalent of the power to accumulate or distribute income. Therefore, under § 2036(a)(2), Byrum had retained a power which would cause the property to be included in his gross estate upon his death. In addition, the Service argued that the power to vote the shares guaranteed the donor a job which amounted to the retention of income from the stock and also gave him the power to control mergers. Therefore, a power described in § 2036(a)(1) was also retained, also causing the property to be included in the donor's gross estate.

The Supreme Court rejected both of these arguments. As to the first argument, the Court noted that the trustee had the power to decide how much the beneficiaries needed and that only the trustee could regulate the flow of income to the beneficiaries. The donor could not influence the flow out of the trust, although he might have some influence on the flow of dividends from the corporation to the trust. The power to elect directors was not the equivalent of directing dividends, and therefore, of controlling the flow of income to the trust, since the directors are fiduciaries with responsibility to minority shareholders and to the general welfare of the corporation. As to the second argument, that Byrum had retained the income from the shares, the Court reasoned that the tax law is concerned with the rights in the transferred property itself. A salary is a right independent of the property, and the majority shareholder has a fiduciary duty to the minority shareholders and cannot merely take whatever salary he wishes. In addition, the Court concluded that deciding the case for the government would permit taxpayers to make gifts of publicly traded stock but not closely held shares, a discrimination not intended by Congress when it enacted § 2036.

The Tax Reform Act of 1976 effectively overruled the *Byrum* decision— adopting the so-called anti-*Byrum* rule—to the limited extent that a retention of voting rights in shares that are transferred will be considered a retention of the enjoyment of those shares. § 2036(b)(1). Thus, vesting the voting power in the transferred shares in a third party should avoid this problem. See, e.g., Priv. Ltr. Rul. 8701003; S. Eastland and R. Weylandt, The Real Estate Partnership as an Estate Planning Device, 22 U. Miami Est. Plan. Inst. ¶ 310.3 (J. Gaubatz ed. 1988). Moreover, anti-*Byrum* only applies to stock of a "controlled corporation." A "controlled corporation," for these purposes, is defined as a corporation in which the decedent (alone or in conjunction with others) had the right to vote stock possessing at least 20 percent of the total combined voting power of all classes of stock.

Regulation § 20.2036–1 contains rules implementing anti-*Byrum*.

¶ 24,617

Problem

[¶ 24,623]

Will the following arrangement cause an inclusion in the taxpayer's estate when he dies? What will be included?

Sidney made a series of conveyances to his son, Robert. He gave 25 percent of the common stock in Schenck Enterprises (a closely held corporation). Prior to the gift, Sidney had owned 45 percent of Schenck. (Sidney's wife Lydia also owned 15 percent.) Sidney retained the right to vote the Schenck shares for 10 years (or until his death).

Sidney also conveyed 10,000 shares in General Motors to Robert, retaining the voting rights.

Finally, Sidney conveyed his entire 75 percent interest in Sidney Corp., a closely held business, to a trust for Robert's benefit. Voting rights were conveyed to the trustee, the First National Bank of Walla Walla, Washington. (*Query:* Would the result be different if the trustee were an employee of Sidney or his corporations?)

Sidney dies six years later. Read § 2036 and see if the answers to the questions posed here are present there.

[¶ 24,625]

3. RECAPITALIZATION

a. *Zero Valuation Rule*

The zero valuation rule of §§ 2701–2704, discussed beginning at ¶ 24,201, has had a chilling effect on the use of the tax-free recapitalization, long the favored technique for transferring interests in the family business to the younger generation. § 368(a)(1)(E). (The popularity of recapitalization was evidenced by the sheer volume of private letter ruling requests. See Rev. Proc. 2002–1, 2002–1 C.B. 1, for a detailed checklist of the information required in a ruling request.)

For example, prior to the adoption of §§ 2701–2704, Jim might have considered a recapitalization as a means to shift the growth of Super Electronics to Junior. This could have been done either by recapitalizing the company, and then giving Junior the newly issued common stock or by giving Junior some of the existing common stock and then recapitalizing the company, with Jim receiving preferred stock which does not share in the unlimited growth of the business and Junior receiving common stock. The result would have been an "estate freeze," in that the value of Jim's interest in the company would have been frozen and future appreciation would have been shifted to Junior.

The estate freeze, in its classic formulation, was effectively put to rest by the zero valuation rules of §§ 2701–2704. What's left of "freezes" is somewhat beyond the scope of these materials, given the intricacies of §§ 2701–2704. See ¶ 24,201 and 24,217. Suffice it to say that the zero valuation rules make the classic freeze unattractive where the transfer is to a member of the transferor's family.

[¶ 24,641]

b.   § 306 Problem

In cases where a recapitalization is deemed appropriate, care must be taken so that the preferred stock not be § 306 stock, which would be subject to ordinary income treatment upon a future sale or redemption. Most preferred stock issued in a recapitalization has an extremely low basis.

Although it would appear that preferred stock issued pursuant to a recapitalization is § 306 stock, see Reg. § 1.306–3(d), it appears that if Jim is willing to give up all of his stock in Super Electronics, he can avoid having § 306 stock. See, e.g., Priv. Ltr. Ruls. 200211035, 199946002, 9804039, and 200029040. To achieve this result, the recipient of the common stock in the recapitalization would have to have some interest in the corporation before the recapitalization takes place, which the recipient can exchange for the common stock. Cf. Priv. Ltr. Rul. 7804090. However, Jim may not want to part with all of his common stock, since if the business is later sold for a substantial profit, Junior might be many times richer than his father. A sale of the entire business to a stranger avoids the problems of § 306. See § 306(b)(1).

The § 306 taint is removed by the death of the shareholder and the stock takes as its basis the value assigned the shares for federal estate tax purposes in the shareholder's estate. See § 306(c)(1) (by implication). The basis of the shares after the death of the shareholders is determined by § 1014(b)(1).

Problem

[¶ 24,690]

Evaluate the tax consequences of the following recapitalization plan: In 1967, Tom Sheehan and Henry Mattingly formed Nexus Corporation, a manufacturer of glue. Tom received 55 percent of the capital stock and Henry received 45 percent. As the years passed, Tom took an increasingly active role in the business and Henry was content to accede to Tom's judgments and watch the value of the business mushroom.

In 1982, Tom brought his son Bill into the business. On January 1, 1983 and each January 1 thereafter, Tom transferred a one percent interest in Nexus Corporation in exchange for a payment equal to market value of the interest, less $3,000. By January 1, 1994, Bill held a 10 percent interest in Nexus.

Tom has decided that he wants to retire and put Bill in control of the business. Henry agreed that Bill would be the best person to succeed Tom, and indicated that he would agree to any plan, so long as he received "fair value" for his interest. Tom then submitted the following plan of recapitalization.

Tom and Henry would each exchange their 45 percent common stock interests ("Old Common") for a "package" consisting of 30 percent of the common stock issued under the recapitalization ("New Common") and 50 percent of the preferred shares issued under the plan ("Preferred"). Bill was to receive 40 percent of the New Common.

The preferred shares do not have voting rights, unless their cumulative dividends are more than two years in arrears. The Preferred shares pay a dividend that is 75 percent of the dividend paid on the Old Common. A diagram of the recapitalization is set out below:

	Old Common	New Common	Preferred
Tom	45%	30%	50%
Henry	45%	30%	50%
Bill	10%	40%	—

Transfer ratios: ....   1% of Old Common equals 4% of New Common
                                       % of Old Common equals 1.33% of Preferred

Tom and Henry each transferred 37.5 percent of their Old Common for their 50 percent chunks of Preferred. They transferred their remaining 7.5 percent of Old Common for a 30 percent hunk of New Common. Bill transferred his 10 percent of Old Common for 40 percent of New Common.

H.   BUYOUTS AT DEATH

[¶ 24,701]

1.   PARTNERSHIP BUY–SELL ARRANGEMENTS

The problem of planning for Ahmed's death needs to be considered. Unlike Jim, it is clear that Ahmed wishes to be bought out upon his death. No member of his family is interested in carrying on the business.

The basic concerns in planning a buyout at the death of a partner are: Will a price set in advance determine the value of the partnership interest sold for estate tax purposes? What is the best method for the buyout, from an income tax perspective? In particular, will the payments be ordinary income or capital gains?

Buy-sell agreements are relatively common. A buy-sell agreement is an agreement under which the owner's interest in a business is to be offered for sale, or sold, to either of the other owners of the business or directly to the business in accordance with the valuation method specified in the agreement and upon the occurrence of certain specified events, such as the owner's death, retirement, or attempt to transfer his interest. The valuation method utilized under these agreements will often produce a price lower than that which would have been produced without the agreement. This is generally due to the desire to reduce estate tax by reducing the value of the decedent's business interest, especially where the decedent's interest would pass to the receiving family members regardless of the agreement. The effectiveness of the valuation method provided by the agreement may, in certain circumstances, determine the business value for estate tax purposes. In fact, the existence of a buy-sell agreement is a factor taken into account by both the courts and the Internal Revenue Service in determining the value of a closely held business for estate tax purposes. See Reg. § 20.2031–2(h).

For valuation purposes, § 2703(a) provides that options, restrictive sale agreements or buy-sell arrangements are to be disregarded unless the taxpayer can establish under § 2703(b)(1) and (2) that they are bona fide arrangements and not a device to transfer property to a decedent's family members for less than full and adequate consideration. However, even in cases where this can be proven, § 2703(b)(3) requires that the terms of the option, restriction, or agreement be comparable to similar arrangements entered into by persons in an arm's-length transaction. Nevertheless, general business practices include more than one methodology for valuation; therefore, a difference in the valuation formula will not render a binding agreement invalid. In such a case, the Conference Committee Report says that any one of several generally accepted methodologies may be used for valuation purposes. H.R. Conf. Rep. No. 964, 101st Cong., 2d Sess. 1137 (1990), reprinted in 1990 U.S.C.C.A.N. 2842.

It should also be noted that for valuation purposes, § 2703 only disregards options, restrictive sale agreements, and buy-sell agreements created after October 8, 1990. Id. at 1133, 1990 U.S.C.C.A.N. 2838.

At issue, always, is whether the agreed price results in the agreement being a testamentary substitute. See ¶ 24,735.

Problems

[¶ 24,703]

1. Two brothers, Xeros and Yacko, enter into a partnership. As the business grows, Xeros brings his two daughters and Yacko brings his son into the partnership. As of 1995, each of the brothers holds a 10 percent managing share and a 25 percent nonmanaging share of the partnership. The children of Xeros and Yacko each hold a 10 percent managing share which carries one-fourth of the voting power held by Xeros and Yacko. The partnership agreement requires the younger generation partners to purchase for book value the managing interest of any managing partner who dies, withdraws, is disabled, or adjudicated as incompetent. In addition, when either Xeros or Yacko ceases to be a managing partner, both of their limited partnership interests (the 25 percent nonmanaging shares) cease to participate in profits, losses, and liquidation shares. At that time the limited interests become "fixed." The partnership will then pay $100,000 annually, adjusted for inflation, to each of the holders of the limited interest. At the end of 2001, Xeros wants to withdraw from the partnership. At this time, the book value of Xeros' 10 percent managing share is $840,000, the book value of his 25 percent nonmanaging interest is $2.1 million, and the fair market value of the partnership's assets is $24 million. Do §§ 2701 and 2703 apply? Would the required purchase of Xeros' managing share for book value (below fair market value in this case) by the younger generation partners be ruled a gift from Xeros to the younger generation partners?

2. In an attempt to insulate each asset from liabilities of other assets and to limit each partner's liability, a general partnership reorganizes into a group of limited partnerships and S corporations. Prior to the reorganization, the transfer of a partner's interest required approval by 90 percent of the partnership interest, and the new partner had to agree to comply with the partnership agreement. In addition, upon the death or withdrawal of a general partner, the partnership was required to purchase 49 percent of the withdrawing partner's interest, with the remaining 51 percent to be purchased at the election of the remaining partners within 10 years of withdrawal. The purchase price was to be paid in 10 equal annual installments with interest on the unpaid balance at 4 percent annually.

The purchase price was to be determined by referring to the partner's most recent certificate of value. If the certificate of value is more than five years old, then five percent of the value of the certificate is to be added to the purchase price for each five-year period between the date of the certificate and the date of withdrawal. However, there is no prorating for periods of less than five years.

The general partnership agreement was to be used for limited partnerships and S corporations with the exception that the 4 percent annual interest rate was to be changed to the long-term applicable federal rate compounded annually. Will § 2703 apply to:

(a) The execution of a new certificate of value increasing the value of the general partnership and the use of the AFR instead of the 4 percent rate of interest?

(b) The reorganization of the general partnership?

(c) The application of the general partnership's buy-sell agreement to the reorganized entities?

[¶ 24,705]

a. *Effect of Price on Estate Tax Valuation*

The price specified in a buy-sell agreement will be binding for estate tax valuation purposes, if there was a valid business purpose for its creation, the agreement is not a device to transfer property to members of a decedent's family for less than full and adequate consideration, and its terms are comparable to similar arrangements entered into by persons in an arm's-length transaction. § 2703(b); Estate of Bischoff v. Commissioner, 69 T.C. 32 (1977) (desire to maintain continuity of management and control held valid business purpose); Estate of Harrison v. Commissioner, 52 T.C.M. (CCH) 1306, T.C.M. (P–H) ¶ 87,008 (1987) (agreement will be ignored only if there is no business purpose for its creation or if it is merely a substitute for a testamentary disposition). The agreement must not be a disguised bequest. Thus, if the sale is made to the deceased partner's heirs, the price must be high enough to be realistic.

There are two methods for retiring a partner's interest, each with differing tax consequences: (1) The surviving partners can personally acquire the deceased partner's interest, a so-called cross-purchase arrangement or (2) the partnership itself can acquire the interest, usually referred to as an "entity purchase." In most instances, the entity approach will be preferable because of the greater flexibility and potential savings it affords.

[¶ 24,709]

b. The Cross–Purchase Plan

Assume that Jim and Junior will personally buy Ahmed's interest at his death for $450,000 plus an extra $50,000 representing Ahmed's one-half share of partnership profits to the date of his death. The $50,000 is income in respect of a decedent, just like the salary of an employee which has accrued at death. §§ 736(a)(1) and 753.

As for the remaining portion of the purchase price, the decedent's estate will have gain to the extent its basis for its partnership interest is less than the purchase price, but this will not necessarily be capital gain. § 741. A portion of the gain will be ordinary income if it is allocable either to unrealized receivables or to substantially appreciated inventory. § 751(a). Super clearly has no appreciated inventory, and it does not have an unrealized receivables since its balance sheet reveals that the receivables have already been taken into income. But the concept of unrealized receivables extends beyond amounts owing for goods delivered or services rendered to the extent not previously included in income; it also encompasses other potential ordinary income items, such as recapture of depreciation and depletion allowances. § 751(c). Thus, although the portion of the purchase price reflecting appreciation in Super's assets will be eligible for capital gain treatment, the portion of the gain attributable to the fact that the adjusted basis of the machinery is less than its fair market value because of depreciation is an unrealized receivable and, thus, ordinary income.

[¶ 24,713]

c. The Entity Approach

Assume now that the partnership will retire Ahmed's interest under the entity approach; the basic rules are the same. The earnings to date of death remain income in respect of a decedent. Gain, if any, attributable to depreciation recapture or other unrealized receivables or to substantially appreciated inventory is ordinary income. § 751(a). Other payments with respect to physical assets are capital gain or a return of capital depending upon Ahmed's estate's basis for his partnership interest. §§ 736(b), 731(a), 732(a). However, added flexibility is available in the treatment of goodwill.

Usually the estate of a deceased partner will receive payments in excess of the amounts enumerated in the last preceding paragraph. These excess payments should be referred to as retirement payments. If these payments are labeled goodwill, the decedent's estate will treat the gain attributable to them as ordinary income, and the partnership will amortize the payment over 15 years. § 736(b)(2)(B); Reg. § 1.736–1(b)(3); § 197(a) and (d). However, by characterizing the retirement payments as a distributive share of income (if dependent on partnership income) or a guaranteed payment (if determined without regard to partnership income) they can be made immediately deductible to the partnership. See Reg. § 1.736–1(a)(3) and (4). Since the deceased partner's estate and family are usually in a lower tax bracket than the surviving partners, this can produce significant tax savings.

For example, assume that Jim and Junior are in the 30 percent bracket, and Ahmed's one-half share of goodwill ($100,000) is paid out over five years. If labeled payments for goodwill, the payments will not be deductible by the partnership for the benefit of Jim and Junior, and at best will be tax free to the recipients. If labeled guaranteed payments, the payments can be increased to $130,000 so that, after taxes, the recipient receives $100,000, but the cost to Jim and Junior will be only $91,000 (.70 x $130,000) because the payments are deductible. The overall savings ($9,000) can be shared by increasing the amount of the retirement payments.

Because there are two different possible treatments for tax purposes, it is important to spell out which approach is to apply. If the agreement is silent, the tax laws will provide for the deduction to the partnership and ordinary income to the recipients. Reg. § 1.736–1(b)(2) and (3). It is wise to clarify the situation by stating in the partnership agreement which approach is to apply so as to avoid misunderstandings.

It is worth noting that an entity purchase is possible even if only one partner remains, since the partnership will be deemed to continue for tax purposes until the retiring or deceased partner has been fully paid. Reg. § 1.736–1(a)(6).

Problem

[¶ 24,715]

Bill Smith and Ed Jones are partners in Okie Oil Servicenter, a profitable service station. Bill is nearing 65 and wishes to retire. Ed, who is 48, wishes to buy Bill's share of the partnership. They agree on a price of $250,000.

Table 24.4. SERVICENTER'S BALANCE SHEET STATEMENT (SUPER ELECTRONICS CO.)	Book Value	Market Value
Cash	$40,000	$40,000
Inventory	16,000	25,000
Accounts receivable	20,000	20,000
Land and building		
Land		120,000
Building		
Purchase price	250,000	
Depreciation claimed	(75,000)	175,000
Other assets	100,000	100,000
Liabilities	50,000	(50,000)
Total		$430,000
Bill's share		$215,000
Ed's share		215,000
Total		$430,000

¶ 24,713

The difference between the $215,000 current asset value and the $250,000 sale price for Bill's partnership interest will be deemed a "retirement payment." Will Ed receive a deduction for the value of the retirement payment? How much of the settlement will Bill have to report as ordinary income? Would things be different using "entity" treatment? How?

[¶ 24,717]

d. Funding the Buyout

It is one thing to specify the mechanics of a buyout, but quite another to provide the necessary cash. Like any other growing business, Super Electronics needs all the cash it can generate and probably twice as much. It is possible to provide for a long-term buyout, such as over a 10–year period. This may still be difficult, since a large part of the payments will have to come from after tax earnings and a meaningful draw must be available for the surviving partners if they are to have enough incentive to continue the business. Moreover, the decedent's family will be at the risk of the business, and may find itself in a difficult position with regard to the payment of federal estate and state inheritance taxes unless deferment relief is available. See discussion at ¶ 24,849. If a long-term buyout is employed, the following should be considered: (1) an acceleration of the debt on the sale or liquidation of the business and (2) the need to pay the required minimum simple interest. (For the determination of the imputed rate of interest, see § 483; Reg. § 1.483–2. *Note:* In a step which appears to be a relief measure to aid in saving the family farm, § 483(e) places a 6 percent cap on imputed interest on any "sale or exchange of land by an individual to a member of such individual's family" to the extent that the sales price does not exceed $500,000.)

If the buyout is triggered by disability, there may be no alternative to a long-term buyout, since the proceeds from disability insurance are usually inadequate to fund a buyout.

[¶ 24,721]

e. Life Insurance

Many clients will find funding the buyout at death with life insurance the most practical alternative. It avoids strapping the business for cash and at the same time it eliminates the continuing interest in the business of the deceased partner's estate and family. The premiums on the life insurance are not deductible (§ 264; Rev. Rul. 70–117, 1970–1 C.B. 30; modified by Rev. Rul. 74–503, 1974–2 C.B. 117), but the proceeds will be tax free (§ 101) and can be used in part to make deductible guaranteed payments. Thus, in some instances, insurance in an amount less than the amount of the purchase price of the partnership interest may provide full funding. One problem that sometimes arises is that if the partners are of different ages, the premium costs for the policies on their lives will differ. This may be justified on the basis of the older partner's seniority and service; if the extra cost is considered the older partner's obligation, the partners can agree to a special allocation of the premium cost. See § 704(a) and (b).

Where there are multiple partners, an entity plan not only has the advantages noted earlier, but also requires fewer policies. Under an entity plan only one policy per partner is required, but under a cross-purchase plan multiple policies are required, expressed by the formula $N \times (N-1)$, where N is the number of partners. If a cross-purchase plan is used despite its relative inflexibility and the required number of policies, there is no transfer-for-value problem. See § 101(a)(2)(B), in connection with the purchase of the policies on the surviving partners' lives from the deceased partner's estate. § 101(a)(2)(B). The proceeds from the purchased policies will continue to be tax free. The designation of a trust as owner and beneficiary of the policies may also be desirable in order to make certain that the proceeds will be properly applied. In drafting such a trust, it should be made clear that the partnership, and not the partners, owns the policies to preserve the entity plan.

[¶ 24,731]

2. CORPORATE BUY–SELL ARRANGEMENTS

a. *Effect on Estate Tax Valuation*

In the context of a corporate business, the same two types of plans are available: cross-purchase and equity. Either plan, if properly structured, can fix the estate tax value. As mentioned earlier, in order to fix the estate tax value the buy-sell agreement must be a bona fide business arrangement that is not a device to transfer property to family members for less than full and adequate consideration, with terms similar to arrangements entered into by persons in an arm's-length transaction. § 2703(b). There might be a right or option in a third party to purchase the stock at a fixed or formula price. Reg. § 20.2031–2(h). The price must apply at death and upon attempted lifetime transfers. Compare Estate of Littick v. Commissioner, 31 T.C. 181 (1958), acq., 1959–2 C.B. 5, and Broderick v. Gore, 224 F.2d 892 (10th Cir.1955), with United States v. Land, 303 F.2d 170 (5th Cir.1962), cert. denied, 371 U.S. 862 (1962). See also Fiorito v. Commissioner, 33 T.C. 440 (1959), acq., 1960–1 C.B. 4. If the contract is with the decedent's heirs, extra care should be taken in setting the price so as to avoid the disguised bequest problem. See Reg. § 20.2031–2(h); Estate of Bischoff v. Commissioner, 69 T.C. 32 (1977). It is permissible and probably desirable to permit lifetime gifts outright or in trust, provided that each donee takes subject to the obligation to sell upon the donor's death, and subject to the restrictions on pre-death transfers.

[¶ 24,735]

b. *Setting the Price*

An important consideration is the manner in which the price is determined. A fixed price subject to revision is unrealistic. The parties often forget to revise it, and the Service has taken the position that a fixed price subject to revision does not create a determinable value for estate tax purposes. § 2703;

Estate of Blount v. Commissioner, 428 F.3d 1338 (11th Cir. 2005), aff'g in part, rev'g in part, T.C. Memo. 2004–116, 87 T.C.M. (CCH) 1303, T.C.M. (RIA) 2004–116 (U.S.Tax Ct. 2004) (buy-sell price not binding because evidence presented of "comparability" to similar arrangements at agreement's inception was limited to sale/purchase price of similarly situated businesses and did not include "non economic factors" even though sale was to ESOP (i.e., third party) and not to family members; court noted decedent's unilateral right to modify agreement without third party consent); Estate of True v. Commissioner, 390 F.3d 1210 (10th Cir. 2004) (price fixed as book value at agreement's inception indicative of testamentary substitute and thus is not controlling for estate tax value purposes); Priv. Ltr. Rul. 8710004. If a fixed price is used, one should provide a backup formula price in the event no revision is made to the fixed price within a specified period, such as two years before death or some other operative event.

Another measure often used is book value. It frequently is too low, and thus unfair, because it fails to reflect inflation and going concern value, and does reflect accelerated depreciation which often has no relation to realistic values. If book value is used, it should be defined. Ordinarily, goodwill and intangibles are excluded, except to the extent they appear on the books. In determining book value, it is best to specify the company's regular method of accounting. Generally accepted accounting principles may produce unanticipated surprises or be difficult to ascertain. Insurance should be considered only to the extent of its cash value. In some instances, book value can prove useful if coupled with a low multiplier of earnings or by specific adjustments such as the revelation of specific assets.

Another common method of valuation is multiples of earnings. Generally, it is better to take an average of several years' earnings, perhaps weighting the later years more heavily. The multiple should be applied to after-tax earnings, and the parties must agree in advance upon the multiplier. In some instances, there are other established guidelines peculiar to the particular industry, such as a multiple of gross revenues.

Finally, it is possible to specify that there will be an independent appraisal at the time of the buyout to determine the value of the business. Customarily each party selects an appraiser who in turn selects a third appraiser. Consider using the middle ("median") appraisal rather than an average of the three so as to avoid distortion by one prejudiced or erroneous appraiser.

Problem

[¶ 24,741]

Evaluate the following "buy-sell" agreement in terms of (1) its effectiveness in "fixing" the price at which the shares will be included in the shareholder's gross estate and (2) the "realism" of the price-determining mechanism.

1. On the death of any shareholder, the remaining shareholders shall have the right to purchase the decedent's shares, in a quantity proportionate to their holdings in the corporation, at $12 per share.

¶ 24,741

2. This purchase price shall be reconsidered once each year and shall be fixed by the Board of Directors of the company, which shall have complete discretion in making their determination of the price.

3. Should any shareholder decline to purchase his or her allotment of the decedent's shares, such shares shall be offered to the other shareholders in proportion to their shareholdings.

[¶ 24,743]

c. *Entity or Cross–Purchase Plan*

Once the method of valuation is determined, the question arises whether to use an entity plan or a cross-purchase plan. The advantages of an entity plan are that it uses corporate dollars rather than personal funds. All of the corporate assets are subject to the obligation and not just the shareholders' stock and their personal assets. If the plan is funded with life insurance, the corporation will pay the premium and fewer policies will be needed.

However, the entity plan also entails a number of disadvantages. It may be unenforceable because under state law purchases of a corporation's own stock are frequently limited to earned surplus. However, any insurance proceeds in excess of the value at which the insurance is carried on the company's books will add to earned surplus. For an uninsured long-term payout, one might prefer to have obligations of the individual shareholders backed by their stock and less risky personal assets rather than obligations backed solely by the business. In addition, with an entity buyout there is no increase in basis for the assets in the corporation or for the surviving shareholders' interests in the corporation; under a cross-purchase plan, the purchasing shareholders end up with a greater basis for the same percentage of the business.

A disadvantage of the entity plan is that any insurance proceeds are subject to the claims of corporate creditors. In addition, the continuous purchase by the corporation of the insurance may be used as evidence of unreasonable accumulation of surplus for accumulated earnings tax purposes. Accumulations of surplus in excess of reasonable present and anticipated business needs will trigger accumulated earnings tax problems. See § 531 et seq. If the insured is a majority shareholder, then a personal rather than business purpose may be inferred from the buyout, and conceivably from the purchase of insurance. Pelton Steel Casting Co. v. Commissioner, 251 F.2d 278 (7th Cir.), cert. denied, 356 U.S. 958 (1958). A corporate purpose is recognized for avoiding disputes with minority shareholders and between equal shareholders; thus, maintaining insurance on their lives should be a reasonable business need. Cf. Dill Mfg. Co. v. Commissioner, 39 B.T.A. 1023 (1939), nonacq., 1939–2 C.B. 47; Mountain State Steel Foundries, Inc. v. Commissioner, 284 F.2d 737 (4th Cir.1960). Section 303 redemption needs with respect to a deceased shareholder are recognized as reasonable needs for the taxable year in which the shareholder died and subsequent taxable years, but this narrow exception is too restrictive to encompass pre-death insurance premiums. § 537.

[¶ 24,747]

d. Redemptions—Avoiding Dividend Treatment

For the entity plan to be successful, the repurchase of the shares by the corporation must be treated as a sale or exchange to qualify for capital gain treatment, rather than a dividend-type distribution subject to the provisions of § 301. The disadvantage of dividend treatment will greatly outweigh any advantages offered by an equity buyout. To qualify for sale or exchange treatment, a repurchase must be considered a redemption and must satisfy one of the exceptions to the general rule that redemptions are dividend-type distributions. § 302(a).

Problem

[¶ 24,749]

Read § 302. What do you think is the purpose served by this rule? Why is capital gain treatment limited to "redemptions," and then only certain types of redemptions at that? Take a look at the definition of "redemption" in § 317(b). Does it shed any light on the question?

————

A redemption is a repurchase in which the shareholder receives property other than stock in the corporation purchasing his shares. § 317(a). Meeting this requirement is a problem only when there is a long-term payout, in which case the debt given in exchange for the stock could be viewed as equity. If the long-term obligation is treated as equity rather than true debt, the periodic payments and any distributions of cash in the form of a down payment would be treated as dividend distributions. The Internal Revenue Service will usually not give rulings where the payout period exceeds 15 years, see, e.g., Rev. Proc. 2002–3, 2002–1 I.R.B. 117, although the courts have sustained payouts of up to 20 years. Lisle v. Commissioner, 35 T.C.M. (CCH) 627, T.C.M. (P–H) ¶ 76,140 (1976) (redemption effected complete termination despite a price payable over 20 years). (*Note:* For an example of a ruling on an installment redemption, see Priv. Ltr. Rul. 7832099.) Among the relevant, but not necessarily determinative, factors will be whether repayment of the purported debt is subordinated to, or dependent upon earnings. Reg. § 1.302–4(d); Dunn v. Commissioner, 70 T.C. 715 (1978), aff'd, 615 F.2d 578 (2d Cir.1980) (subordination, while evidence of equity holdings, is only one of several factors to consider). Recall the discussion earlier regarding whether a contribution to capitalize would be deemed "debt" or "equity." See ¶ 24,543.

[¶ 24,751]

e. Complete Termination of Interest

Assuming the transaction is a redemption, one of the exceptions to dividend treatment must still apply in order to achieve a sale or exchange. A redemption will not be a dividend if it involves a complete termination of the distributee's interest in the corporation. See § 302(b)(3). But this test will not be satisfied if, under the attribution rules (constructive ownership rules) of § 318, the decedent's estate is deemed to own the stock owned by other family members or related corporations, partnerships, trusts or estates. § 302(c)(1). If Ahmed were to die and his estate were to be bought out, a complete termination could occur. No member of his family or any related entity would own any of Super Electronics Corporation's stock. On the other hand, assuming Jim had made a lifetime gift of the company's stock to Junior, or had sold some shares to him, a sale only by Jim's estate would not be a complete termination of interest for one of two reasons: Junior may be a beneficiary of Jim's estate, or Junior's stock would be attributed to his mother, Mai, whose indirect ownership would be attributed to the estate because she is a beneficiary under Jim's will (double attribution).

[¶ 24,755]

f. Substantially Disproportionate Redemptions

Another exception that might apply, however, is the exclusion from dividend treatment accorded substantially disproportionate redemptions. See § 302(b)(2). For the redemption to be considered substantially disproportionate, after the redemption, the estate must own less than 50 percent of the outstanding voting stock of the corporation, and its holdings of voting stock must have been reduced to less than 80 percent of what they were prior to the redemptions and its holdings of outstanding common stock (voting or nonvoting) must have been reduced to less than 80 percent of what they were prior to the redemption. The mechanical test applies to voting stock and cannot be availed of in the case of redemptions of nonvoting preferred. Again, the attribution rules apply. To illustrate, assume that after Junior has acquired one-eighth of the corporation's 1,000 common shares from Jim, the remaining three-eighths (375 shares) are purchased from Jim's estate. By reason of attribution from Junior, Jim's estate is deemed to own 500 shares or 50 percent of the outstanding common stock before the redemption. After the redemption, the estate is deemed to own Junior's 125 shares, or 20 percent of the outstanding 625 shares. Since 20 percent is less than 80 percent of 50 percent, the redemption qualifies as substantially disproportionate.

Problem

[¶ 24,758]

In which of the following situations would a redemption be deemed "substantially disproportionate"?

1. Decedent's estate owned 70 percent of X Corp. stock before redemption. After redemption it owned 49.5 percent.

2. Same as (1), except decedent's estate owned 60 percent prior to redemption.

3. Same as (1), except decedent's estate owned 50.5 percent after redemption.

¶ 24,751

[¶ 24,759]

g. Waiving Attributions—The 10–Year Rule

If, because of the attribution rules, the decedent's estate cannot satisfy either the complete termination of interest exception or the substantially disproportionate redemption exception, it may be able to qualify for sale or exchange treatment by obtaining a waiver of the attribution rules. § 302(c)(2). This provision is sometimes called the 10–year rule. The application of certain attribution rules can be waived in order to satisfy the complete termination of interest test. See §§ 302(c)(2) and 318.

To qualify for a waiver, several conditions must be met. First, within 10 years before the redemption there must have been no acquisition by the distributee of shares from persons whose stock would have been attributed to the distributee, and conversely, a similarly related person must not have acquired stock from the distributee unless such stock is also redeemed in the same transaction. § 302(c)(2)(B). This is usually not a problem for an estate since it was not in existence for a long time prior to the redemption. For 10 years after the redemption, the distributee may have no continuing interest in the corporation, either as a stockholder, director, officer, or employee, although the distributee may be a creditor, provided the obligation is debt and not recharacterizable as equity for tax purposes. § 302(c)(2)(A); Reg. § 1.302–4(d) and (c); Cerone v. Commissioner, 87 T.C. 1 (1986) (continued employment gave taxpayer financial stake in corporation); Duerr v. Commissioner, 30 T.C. 944 (1958) (debt reclassified as stock). Performing services as an independent contractor is permissible, Estate of Lennard v. Commissioner, 61 T.C. 554 (1974), nonacq., 1978–2 C.B. 3, acq. withdrawn, 1974–2 C.B. 3 (bona fide independent contractor status not fatal); Chertkof v. Commissioner, 72 T.C. 1113 (1979) (management contract not *per se* bad), but it would seem unwise to risk the sale or exchange treatment of the redemption by continuing an independent contractor relationship. Lynch v. Commissioner, 801 F.2d 1176 (9th Cir.1986) (both employer and independent contractor status prohibited). It is also possible to continue to be a lessor of equipment to the company provided that the rent is not subordinate to claims of general creditors and not dependent upon future earnings. Rev. Rul. 77–467, 1977–2 C.B. 92; see also Rev. Proc. 89–3, 1989–1 C.B. 761. During this 10–year post-redemption period, the statute of limitations on the tax treatment of the redemption must remain open; to achieve this, the distributee must consent to treat the transaction as a dividend if he reacquires an interest in the corporation during the 10 years following the redemption. § 302(c)(2)(A).

Partnerships, estates, trusts and corporations may waive the family attribution rules as applied to stock that the entity's beneficiary owns constructively by attribution from a member of the beneficiary's family. § 302(c)(2)(C). Waiver is permitted if the entity itself and each related person satisfy the normal waiver requirements discussed above, and each related person agrees to be jointly liable for any tax deficiency resulting from a prohibited acquisition during the 10–year period.

¶ 24,759

Problem

[¶ 24,761]

Will the taxpayer in the following situation have to report gain from the stock sale as ordinary income or capital gain? This can be determined by asking these questions: (1) Has there been a redemption? (2) Does the transaction fall within one of the "capital gain" exceptions to the general "ordinary income" rule? The first question is already answered, but what about the second?

Tom Hill formed Hill Corp. in 1979. At the time the corporation was formed, Tom received 40 percent of the capital stock and his wife, Betty, received 30 percent of the stock. The remainder was sold to friends.

In 1988, Tom purchased one-half of Betty's stock, giving him 55 percent of the stock. Two years later, he established a trust for the benefit of his son, Tom Jr. ("Junior"), funding it with 30 percent of the company's stock.

Tom has decided to retire. The company voted to redeem 15 percent from Tom's remaining shareholdings, reducing his holdings from 25 percent to 10 percent. The redemption will result in a substantial gain to Tom, and he hopes to qualify for capital gains treatment under the "substantially dispro-portionate redemption test." Tom has been told that Betty's 15 percent and the 30 percent in trust for Junior may be attributed to him, making capital gains treatment unavailable. He wishes to waive attribution. Is this possible? What must be done, in addition to what has been done already?

[¶ 24,763]

h. *Not Essentially a Dividend*

There is one final exception which, unlike the others, is not based on mechanical tests, but instead excludes from dividend treatment redemptions which are not essentially equivalent to a dividend. § 302(b)(1). Unfortunately, little comfort can be found in this vague standard. It will, however, apply to redemptions of preferred stock from shareholders owning no common stock whatsoever (by attribution or otherwise). Reg. § 1.302–2(a); Rev. Rul. 77–426, 1977–2 C.B. 87; Rev. Rul. 81–41, 1981–1 C.B. 121. This exception is not of much use after a family corporation's recapitalization, because the attribution rules will still cause the parents to own the common stock held by their children. It may be useful where a closely held business has been acquired through a merger and the former owners of the closely held business received only preferred stock.

[¶ 24,767]

i. *Cross–Purchase Plans—The Transfer for Value Problem*

Given all the problems with an entity plan, why not use a cross-purchase plan instead? It too has drawbacks. In a cross-purchase plan the individuals must fund the purchase or pay insurance premiums with their own after-tax dollars. The impact of this burden can be reduced somewhat through split-dollar policies, with respect to which the stockholders own the risk portion of the policies and the corporation owns the cash value. The corporation may pay all the premiums on such a policy, in which case the shareholder-beneficiaries would treat as income from the corporation the value of the risk portion as determined by Internal Revenue Service tables. Rev. Rul. 64–328, 1964–2 C.B. 11, amplified by Rev. Rul. 78–420, 1978–2 C.B. 67, and modified by Notice 2002–8, 2002–4 I.R.B. 398. Here too, however, the accumulated earnings problems noted in connection with the entity plan could conceivably arise. The cross-purchase plan also creates the problems of a multiplicity of policies and of policies subject to claims by the shareholders' creditors or divorcing spouses.

The most serious problem with the cross-purchase plan involves the policies owned by the decedent on the lives of the surviving shareholders. The transfer-for-value rule precludes a sale of these policies to other stockholders on a continuing cross ownership basis, since such a sale will cause the proceeds to be taxable. See § 101(a)(2).

Problem

[¶ 24,769]

Read § 101(a)(2) to see why this is so. Why is this § included in the Code? Do you think it was intended to snag "cross-purchase" plans in corporations, or is this an "accidental" consequence of the way the rule is written?

A decedent's policies may be sold to the corporation without invoking the transfer for value rule. Such a sale would produce a combination cross-purchase and entity plan. § 101(a)(2)(B). Another possibility is to use a partnership to hold the policies, to take advantage of the exception to the transfer-for-value rule for transfers by partners to other partners or to a partnership. Id. In this case the partnership must have economic reality and not merely be a device used to hold insurance policies, or it would most likely be disregarded for tax purposes. It would be best to use an existing partnership, such as one which retained the fixed assets of the business upon formation of the corporation.

[¶ 24,771]

j. Switching from Cross–Purchase to Entity Plan or Vice Versa

Because of the differing advantages and disadvantages of the two plans, it may turn out that it is desirable to switch from one plan to the other. Because of the transfer-for-value rules, it is far easier to switch from a cross-purchase plan to an entity plan than vice versa. One of the exceptions to the rule is a transfer to the corporation (but not to another shareholder). If a switch must be made to a cross-purchase arrangement, consider limiting the value of the stock to be purchased by the corporation, and then using a cross-purchase plan only for the excess funded with new policies. One additional trap must be avoided: if the corporation redeems stock which a shareholder is personally obligated to purchase, the transaction will be treated as a dividend to the shareholder whose obligation to purchase was satisfied. See, e.g., Schroeder v. Commissioner, 831 F.2d 856 (9th Cir.1987); Wall v. United States, 164 F.2d 462 (4th Cir.1947).

Problem

[¶ 24,790]

Consider whether the Blotto Distilleries' cross-purchase plan, described below, works. Is there a transfer-for-value problem with regard to the life insurance policies involved?

Blotto Distilleries was established in 1968 as a partnership. It was incorporated in 1977, with each of the four former partners receiving 25 percent of the new corporation's common stock. At the time of incorporation, the old partnership continued in existence and was used for several years to hold some land on which a future plant was to be constructed. Eventually, however, it was decided to sell the land, and the partnership held only nominal assets.

In 1987, the Blotto shareholders entered into a cross-purchase agreement. On the death of each shareholder, his shares were to be purchased by the remaining shareholders. Each purchase was to be financed by life insurance policies held by each on the life of the deceased shareholder.

When a shareholder died, any insurance policies held by him were sold, at cash value, to the partnership, which would then continue to make premium payments. Funding for these purchases was to come from the remaining shareholders, as would the payments made. When the policies "paid off," their proceeds would then be distributed among the surviving shareholders.

Shareholder Sam Adams died last week, and the remaining shareholders are in the process of reevaluating the wisdom of the cross-purchase plan. Should you reassure them? Or tell them to back out, after settling with all concerned parties?

I. RELIEF IN THE ABSENCE OF A BUYOUT

[¶ 24,801]

As we noted earlier, Jim wants his family to retain his interest in Super Electronics. Similarly, where a buy-sell agreement is used, the last surviving partner or shareholder will not benefit from an automatic purchase of his interest upon his death. In these cases, how can the burden of death taxes be met? In addition to insurance, there are several types of relief which may be available where the estate tax poses a special burden because of the concentration of the decedent's wealth in a closely held business. The relief falls into three basic categories: (1) limited redemptions of stock to help pay death taxes and funeral and administration expenses, (2) special valuation for real property used as a farm or in connection with a closely held business, and (3) the deferred payment of estate taxes. A fourth alternative, sale of the decedent's business to an Employee Stock Ownership Trust (ESOP), should also be considered.

[¶ 24,809]

1. § 303 REDEMPTIONS

Section 303 permits the withdrawal of corporate funds by stock redemptions in an amount sufficient to pay death taxes and funeral and administration expenses. It also applies to the generation-skipping tax. The redemptions are not treated as dividends (which would be subject to ordinary income treatment), despite the failure to satisfy one of the exceptions in § 302(b).

Because of appreciation in the value of redeemed stock in the post-death period, a redemption will sometimes result in capital gain. Nevertheless, § 303 does not permit the amount of stock redeemed to be increased to defray this income tax cost; as a result the redemption may not produce sufficient net proceeds to pay death taxes and funeral and administration expenses. Furthermore, it must be kept in mind that the gain on such redemption could be ordinary income, if the corporation is required to be treated as a "collapsible corporation" as defined in § 341(b)(1). The definition of a collapsible corporation is complex, but suffice it to say, for immediate purposes, that a corporation may be deemed "collapsible" if formed or availed of "with a view" to collapsing the corporation prior to the realization of corporate profits and thereby converting gain on property held by the corporation, which would otherwise be ordinary income, into capital gain. Collapsible treatment could apply to a stock redemption, although some comfort may be found in a number of cases that have held that the "requisite view" is not present where the sale is incidental to a sudden change of health. Reg. § 1.341–5(d), Example (3); Temkin v. Commissioner, 35 T.C. 906 (1961), acq., 1972–2 C.B. 3 (sudden illness of shareholder could not have been reasonably anticipated); Riley v. Commissioner, 35 T.C. 848 (1961), acq., 1972–2 C.B. 3; Shilowitz v. United States, 221 F.Supp. 179 (D.N.J.1963) (taxpayer did not contemplate selling stock until after heart attack).

[¶ 24,813]

a. *Redeeming Preferred Stock*

One technique for avoiding capital gain on a § 303 redemption is to redeem originally issued preferred stock, which is unlikely to be substantially appreciated. However, it is important not to overlook the basis allocation problems noted earlier, which might cause the preferred stock to have some built-in appreciation, albeit fixed in amount. See discussion at ¶ 24,461.

Preferred stock issued in a recapitalization can also be redeemed under § 303, but it is apt to have a low basis. Preferred stock issued by means of a stock dividend or recapitalization may create an additional problem of being § 306 stock, the gain on redemption of which may be ordinary income. See B. Bittker & J. Eustice, Federal Income Taxation of Corporations and Sharehold-

¶ 24,813

ers ¶ 8.62, at 8–127 to –135 (7th ed. 2004). However, the Revenue Act of 1978 cleanses preferred stock of the § 306 taint where § 303 applies. § 302(a). Moreover, if it is desirable to create preferred stock after incorporation for use in § 303 redemptions, one technique which has been suggested, see Lynch, New Look at Buy–Sell Agreements, 1978 S. Cal. Tax Inst. 775, 786–88 and Borini, The Personal Holding Company as an Estate Planning Tool, 1974 S. Cal. Tax Inst. 143, is to form a holding company which would issue the preferred stock upon its incorporation, for later redemption by the operating subsidiary. (*Note:* Such related corporate redemptions can qualify for § 303 for treatment. § 304(a)(2); cf. Webb v. Commissioner, 67 T.C. 293 (1976), aff'd, 572 F.2d 135 (5th Cir.1978). This technique runs the risk that it may preclude qualifying for the estate tax deferral provisions (discussed at ¶ 24,849) because of the absence of an active trade or business being carried on by the holding company.)

[¶ 24,817]

b. Eligibility

Section 303 is applicable only to shares included in the decedent's gross estate. To qualify for § 303, the value of all of the stock included in the decedent's estate must exceed 35 percent of the gross estate, reduced by the deductions for debts, funeral and administration expenses and losses. § 303(b)(2)(A). Two or more corporations may be aggregated if twenty percent or more of the value of the outstanding stock of each is included in the decedent's estate. § 303(b)(2)(B). To satisfy this test, the surviving spouse's interest in stock held in joint ownership can be counted. In addition to being included in the decedent's gross estate, the decedent's estate must also bear the burden of death taxes, administration and funeral expenses, or losses to the extent of the redemption. If the burden of those items is not borne by the shareholder from whom the stock is redeemed (e.g., the estate, trust or heir), the redemption will not be covered by § 303. The distribution in redemption under § 303 must be made within 90 days after the expiration of the statute of limitations on assessment of an estate tax deficiency, or within sixty days after a final Tax Court determination, except that the redemptions may be made later if the deferred payment provisions available under § 6166 are utilized. § 303(b)(1). For additional discussion, see ¶ 24,849.

Problem

[¶ 24,819]

In which of the following situations can a § 303 redemption be made?

1. Henry House, the founder of Columbia Cleaning Company (CCC), a manufacturer of detergents, died last year. At the date of his death, 75 percent of the value of his gross estate (net of debts, funeral and administration expenses, and losses) consisted of CCC stock. Under the terms of Henry's will, 70 percent of his CCC holdings passed to his widow, Myrtle House. Mrs. House was also responsible for paying all death taxes, estate and administration expenses associated with Henry's estate.On

Myrtle's request, the Board of CCC voted to redeem some of Myrtle's stock at current market value to help pay the estate expenses. This redemption took place two weeks after the IRS had assessed an estate tax deficiency against the estate.

2. Same as (1), except that the responsibility for paying all death taxes, estate and administrative expenses was placed upon the residuary legatee (Henry's "bypass trust,") but *Myrtle's* shares were redeemed.

3. Same as (1), except that the redeemed shares were not included in Henry's estate, having been part of a "bypass trust" created by Henry's father some years before. Henry's estate did not contain any CCC shares.

4. Same as (1), except the value of CCC stock included in Henry's gross estate was only 34.5 percent of the gross estate valued at date of death. (*Query:* What if it was 37 percent at a point six months after death?)

5. Same as (1), except that Henry lived in a community property state, and all of his CCC holdings were community property.

6. Willard Cross had owned substantial interests in two close corporations— Acme Donut and Cross Industries. He owned 30 percent of Acme and 27 percent of Cross, and all of those shares were included in his gross estate. Valued at the date of Willard's death, Acme made up 27 percent and Cross made up 25 percent of the "net" estate. Responsibility for paying death taxes, etc., rested with the residuary estate, which received half of Cross's holdings in the two corporations. Both companies voted to redeem shares held by the estate (residuary) to the extent necessary to pay death taxes. Only Cross shares were redeemed.

7. Same as (6), except Willard Cross owned 100 percent of Acme and 19 percent of Cross at the time of his death. What result if Mr. and Mrs. Cross jointly owned an additional 3 percent of Cross?

[¶ 24,821]

c. *Effects of Changes in Estate Tax Values*

In drafting § 303 redemption agreements, difficulties can arise because the first redemption usually takes place when the return is filed; that is when the executor needs money. Subsequently, the Internal Revenue Service may place a higher value on the redeemed shares. Therefore, it is desirable to provide that the price for the stock will be its value as finally determined for federal estate tax purposes and that an adjustment in the payments will be made, if necessary, when that value has been determined. It is also desirable to provide that if a deficiency is assessed, more shares will be redeemed.

As for funding § 303 redemptions, the shareholders may agree that the corporation will buy insurance. In fact, they may wish to limit the value of shares to be redeemed to the insurance proceeds, so as to avoid placing an unanticipated burden on the corporation. The burden can be especially severe when the plan is unfunded and the deceased shareholder has substantial assets included in his or her gross estate aside from his or her interest in the business.

¶ 24,821

[¶ 24,829]

2. SPECIAL VALUATION OF REAL PROPERTY

In 1976, Congress attempted to fashion limited estate tax relief for decedents whose estates were heavily invested in a farm or other closely held business. This relief took the form of § 2032A, which is an extremely complicated provision.

Section 2032A's provisions permit the valuation of such real property according to its special use value rather than its fair market value, which would be based upon its highest and best use. A number of technical numerical tests must be met in order to obtain the benefits of this relief.

[¶ 24,833]

a. Technical Requirements

First, to qualify for special use valuation under § 2032A, the property must be located in the United States, it must pass to a qualified heir, and the executor must make a proper election with a written agreement signed by all interested parties. Reg. § 20.2032A–8.

Second, the property must be employed in a qualified use. § 2032A(b). This includes farming, as well as any other trade or business. § 2032A(b)(2).

Third, the real property employed in the qualifying use must exceed 25 percent of the adjusted value of the estate. § 2032A(b)(1)(B). Moreover, for five of the eight years before the decedent's death, the real property is required to have been owned by the decedent or his family and employed in a qualified use. § 2032A(b)(1)(C).

Fourth, all of the property employed in a qualified use, whether real or personal (even though only the real property is eligible for the special valuation), must exceed 50 percent of the adjusted value of the decedent's estate, i.e., the gross estate less mortgages and debts in respect of the property. § 2032A(b)(1)(A). Thus, it is clear that the real property must be a substantial part of the decedent's estate and must not have been recently acquired.

Finally, the decedent or a member of the decedent's family must have participated materially in conducting the farm or business. § 2032A(b)(1)(C)(ii). Material participation is apparently intended to disqualify passive holdings and to limit the relief to situations where a highest and best use valuation might cause a farm or business actually conducted by the family to be sold. The quality of participation is to be determined in a manner similar to that used in § 1402(a) relating to self-employment earnings. § 2032A(e)(6). Family members include ancestors, lineal descendants, lineal descendants of a spouse, and lineal descendants of one's parents.

[¶ 24,837]

b. Substantial Compliance

An executor who timely elects special use valuation has a reasonable period of time to correct technical oversights in the form of the election.

¶ 24,829

§ 2032A(d)(3). The time for making the necessary corrections cannot exceed 90 days after notification of the technical "failures." Relief is available only if the election of special use is timely filed and the executor has "substantially" complied "with the regulations prescribed by the Secretary with respect to such elections."

[¶ 24,841]

c.   Methods of Valuation

In the case of farms, two alternative methods of valuation are specified: (1) the capitalization of the cash rentals for comparable local land used for farming purposes and (2) if there is no comparable land, or if the executor elects, then in the same manner as for real property used in other closely held businesses. § 2032A(e)(7)(A). Net share rentals may be substituted for cash rentals if actual comparable tracts rented for cash cannot be located. § 2032A(e)(7)(B).

Real property used in other closely held businesses is to be valued by considering the following factors: (1) the capitalization of income that can reasonably be expected from the property used as a farm or in the closely held business; (2) the capitalization of the fair rental value for such use; (3) assessed values in the state if the state provides for differential assessments based on farms or closely held businesses; and (4) comparable sales of land in the same are far enough away from metropolitan locations so as to eliminate the influence of nonagricultural uses, and any other fair factor. § 2032A(e)(8).

In the case where the property is disposed of by the decedent's heirs both before their deaths and before 10 years after decedent's death, there will be a recapture of the estate tax savings created by the lower valuation. § 2032A(c)(1). A qualified heir is personally liable for recapture of tax with respect to his or her interest in the business or farm, and there is a special lien on the property respecting the possible recapture. §§ 2032A(c)(5) and 6324B. Note that this lien subjects the property to a long-term liability. The Commissioner is authorized to adopt regulations providing for other security arrangements where the lien proves burdensome. § 6324B(d).

> *Example.* During one five-year period, the average annual gross cash rental value of the average farm with a fair market value of $2,000 per acre in a particular county was approximately $75 per acre. The average real estate taxes were about $9 per acre at the time. If 8.75 percent was the average effective Federal Land Bank loan rate, the net value per acre would be $754.

> On an 800–acre qualifying farm, his would result in a reduction of the value of the taxable estate by almost $1,000,000. After obtaining the § 2032A valuation, the special use valuation must be compared with the fair market value of the property based on its highest and best use. The reduction in value for special use is limited to $750,000 under § 2032A(a)(2).

In Estate of Hoover v. Commissioner, 69 F.3d 1044 (10th Cir.1995), the decedent owned her interest in a ranch through a limited partnership. Section

¶ 24,841

2032A applies to such interests. § 2032A(g). The case is important for several reasons the most notable of which is that a minority discount is available in conjunction with a claim of special use valuation. However, as to methodology, the decision affirms that special use value cannot be further reduced by applying a minority interest discount. Instead, the court concludes that any minority interest discount is to be taken in determining fair market value before applying special use valuation available under § 2032A—but that special use value is available in such circumstances.

Problems

[¶ 24,847]

1. Is the following estate eligible to take advantage of the § 2032A special use valuation? If so, how much can it save using such valuation?

   Fred Brown was a farmer. When he died last year, 40 percent of the adjusted value of his gross estate (gross estate *less* administration expenses, funeral expenses, claims against the estate and mortgages on farmland) consisted of farmland. During the last year of his life, Fred was unable to farm much of his property; up to that time, Fred had steadily farmed all his property since 1948. When the executor of Fred's estate added up the value of all *personal* and *real* property used by Fred in the business, it turned out to be 65 percent of Fred's adjusted gross estate value.

   Fred's entire farm passed to his son, William. William has continued to use the farmland for farming and intends to do so as long as possible. One problem facing continued operation of the farm relates to the changing nature of the farm community in which the land is located. Since the expressway from the city was extended out into the community, increasing amounts of farmland have been transformed into subdivisions. Shortly after Fred's death, a real estate agent offered Fred's executor $3,500 per acre for the farm, which is 100 acres in size.

   Farmland in Fred's community rents for $100/acre per year. Average local real estate taxes are about $20/acre per year. As of Fred's death, the interest rate for Federal Land Bank loans was eight percent.

2. What would happen if William sold the farm after five years? 10 years? 15 years? 20 years?

3. What would happen if the farm had passed to William but was farmed by William's son, Roger?

4. It would seem that an important part of any planning for the client with real estate used in a closely held business or farmland would be to consider restructuring the decedent's estate so as to qualify the land for special use valuation. Prepare a checklist of the minimum qualifications that must be present to enjoy the benefits of § 2032A.

5. As a matter of tax policy, does it make sense in your opinion to provide special treatment such as that provided in § 2032A (and §§ 6166 and 303)

for certain classes of taxpayers? Does such special treatment cause distortions in the decisions taxpayers make about the use of resources?

[¶ 24,849]

3. DEFERRED PAYMENT OF TAXES

If property cannot or should not be sold to pay death taxes and the taxes cannot be reduced through special valuation benefits, relief may still be available in the form of deferred payment of estate taxes. Two separate provisions—§§ 6161 and 6166—under varying circumstances and to different degrees, permit the deferral of estate tax. Estate tax deferred under § 6166 bears interest at only 2 percent, down from 4 percent (which, itself, was a rate preference).

[¶ 24,853]

a.   § 6166: 15–Year Deferral

Section 6166 applies to situations where any type of closely held business, whether sole proprietorship, corporation or partnership, is the source of illiquidity. It is intended to prevent forced bargain sales and to prevent sales of family businesses that the family wants to retain. By permitting the estate tax to be paid in installments, § 6166 essentially provides a government loan, available if certain mechanical tests are satisfied. The deferral applies only to the portion of the tax that bears the same ratio to the total tax that the value of the closely held business bears to the adjusted gross estate. Thus, the balance of the estate tax will be currently due and payable. Furthermore, it should be kept in mind that this deferral provision applies only to the estate tax imposed by § 2001. It does not apply to income or minimum taxes imposed on gain from sales or redemptions under § 303 or otherwise. And it does not apply to generation-skipping transfer taxes imposed by § 2601 except when a direct skip occurs at the same time and as the result of the decedent's death. See § 6166(i).

[¶ 24,857]

i.   Terms of Deferral

Assuming the qualifications can be met, § 6166 permits a 15–year deferral. The deferred tax may be paid in up to 10 equal annual installments, and the first installment can be deferred for five years. § 6166(a)(1) and (3). Interest is payable at only two percent per annum on the first $1 million of value of the closely held business; the usual rates are applicable to payments on the balance of the deferred tax. §§ 6166(f) and 6601(j). The interest is nondeductible as an administration expense for either estate tax or income tax purposes.

The election to take advantage of § 6166 must be made on or before the due date, including extensions, for filing the estate tax return. Reg. § 20.6166–1. The election applies also to deficiencies (other than those due to

¶ 24,857

negligence, fraud or intentional disregard of rules and regulations) that are prorated over remaining installments.

[¶ 24,861]

ii.   Mechanical Eligibility Tests

Section 6166 relief is available where the value of the business interest exceeds 35 percent of the adjusted gross estate. § 6166(a). Two or more businesses can be aggregated if 20 percent or more of the total value of each is included in the decedent's gross estate. § 6166(c).

Only businesses that are closely held may be counted. This includes any proprietorship, any partnership as to which 20 percent or more of the total capital interest is included in the decedent's gross estate or in which there are 45 or fewer partners, and any corporation as to which 20 percent or more of the value of the voting stock is included in the decedent's gross estate or in which there are 45 or fewer shareholders. § 6166(b)(1). These tests must have been met immediately before the decedent's death; post-death maneuvers do not help. Stock of a public corporation may qualify. A surviving spouse's jointly owned interest, whether the couple held it as community property, tenants in common, joint tenants with right of survivorship, or tenants by the entirety, counts toward the above percentages. Nevertheless, non-community property states have a substantial advantage since shares qualifying for the marital deduction will assist in meeting the 35 percent test as well.

Additional assistance in meeting the 20 percent test is provided by § 6166(b)(2)(D), which specifies that stock and partnership interests owned by family members (as defined in § 267(c)(4)) shall be treated as owned by the decedent. These interests shall also be included in determining the decedent's gross estate for purposes of meeting the 35 percent test, if the executor elects to forgo deferring the first installment beyond the date on which the estate tax return is due and to forgo the four percent interest rate and if, in the case of stock, there is no market for it on an exchange or over the counter. The estate can also recapture any gifts of interests in the business made within three years of the decedent's death for purposes of qualifying for § 6166 treatment. Although such gifts are not required to be included in the decedent's gross estate, they can still be used to determine the estate's qualification for deferral. See § 2035(c)(2).

[¶ 24,865]

iii.   Active Assets Only

The value of an interest eligible for § 6166 treatment may not include that portion of the interest which is attributable to "passive assets." § 6166(b)(9). A "passive asset" means "any asset other than an asset used in carrying on a trade or business." § 6166(b)(9)(B)(i). For example, "stock in another corporation" is a passive asset unless a "holding company" election is permitted by § 6166(b)(8). See § 6166(b)(9)(B). Similarly, owning raw land for appreciation does not qualify, but operating a motel probably does. See Rev. Rul. 75–365, 1975–2 C.B. 471 (income obtained through mere ownership of property not sufficient); Rev. Rul. 75–366, 1975–2 C.B. 472 (sharing in expenses and imported management decisions constitutes activity in a trade or business); Rev. Rul. 61–55, 1961–1 C.B. 713 (ownership, exploration, development and operation of oil and gas properties constitutes activity in a trade or business). Thus, whether it is a proprietorship, a partnership, or a corporation, assets unrelated to the business will be excluded.

[¶ 24,869]

iv.   Acceleration

Despite having originally qualified for the deferral of estate tax payment, the deferral will be accelerated upon the disposition or withdrawal of one-half of the value of the decedent's interest in the business. § 6166(g)(1)(A). For purposes of this provision, a distribution by the estate or by a revocable trust is not considered a disposition, nor is a subsequent transfer caused by the death of the transferor so long as the transferee is a member of the decedent's family. § 6166(g)(1)(D); Reg. § 20.6166A–3(e)(1). Section 303 redemptions will not trigger acceleration even though they cause a disposition of more than one-third of the business, provided that *all* of the redemption proceeds are actually used to pay federal estate tax (and not state inheritance taxes or funeral and administration expenses) on or before the due date of the next installment. All the proceeds of the redemption must be so used even though § 303 provides favorable sale or exchange treatment on a more liberal basis. Redemptions made more than four years after the decedent's death are eligible so long as they do not exceed the death taxes and funeral and administration expenses unpaid immediately prior to the distribution. § 303(b)(4). Although a properly applied § 303 redemption will not cause acceleration, the value of the business is reduced by the amount of the § 303 redemption for purposes of measuring whether other dispositions exceed the one-third limit. § 6166(g)(1)(B); see Rev. Rul. 72–188, 1972–1 C.B. 383; Rev. Rul. 86–54, 1986–1 C.B. 356. The value of the estate's interest in the business may be augmented, however, by the recapture of transfers made within three years of death. § 2035(d)(3). Acceleration also occurs upon a failure to pay any installment on time. Nevertheless, if the full amount of the delinquent payment is paid within six months, acceleration will not be triggered. The four percent interest rate will be lost, however, and a penalty is imposed, equal to five percent per month based on the amount of the payment. Finally, to prevent acceleration, it is necessary for the estate to apply the undistributed net income of the estate for any year after the due date of the first installment toward the unpaid balance of the estate tax.

In the event the § 6166 deferred payment provisions are elected, a special lien provision is available which permits the executor to be discharged from personal liability by substituting a lien on specified property in the estate designated in an agreement with the Internal Revenue Service. § 6324A. The maximum value of the property which the Commissioner can require to be subject to the lien is the aggregate amount of the deferred taxes and the total interest thereon. § 6324A(b)(2). The agreements must be signed by all persons having an interest in the property subject to the lien; the Internal Revenue Service may from time to time require additional security which, if not provided, will cause acceleration.

Problems

[¶ 24,871]

1. In each of the following situations, determine whether the decedent's estate is eligible for deferral of estate tax payment under § 6166. Assume, unless instructed otherwise, that these are active businesses.

    (a) As of Tom Smith's death, 75 percent of his adjusted gross estate (gross estate, *less* deductions allowable under §§ 2053 and 2054) consisted of shareholdings in Zpex Corp., a close corporation which had nine shareholders.

    (b) When Tom Smith died, 25 percent of his adjusted gross estate consisted of Zpex shares. Tom's wife owns stock in the corporation with an additional value equal to 35 percent of Tom's adjusted gross estate as her separate property.

    (c) When Abner Douglenight died, 5 percent of his adjusted gross estate consisted of stock in Brookwood Corporation, which had twelve shareholders. At the time of Abner's death, however, his children owned stock in Brookwood with a value equal to 75 percent of Abner's adjusted gross estate. (*Query:* If deferral is allowed under § 6166, what additional terms must Abner's estate agree to?)

    (d) Oscar Brant died owning 27 percent of Oakhurst Corp. and 34 percent of Allen Corp. Taken together, Oscar's holdings of Oakhurst and Allen made up 67 percent of Oscar's adjusted gross estate. Both Oakhurst and Allen had four shareholders apiece.

    (e) Same as (a), except that Zpex Corp. is a real estate holding company.

2. Assume the facts as stated in Problem 24–37(a). What will happen if Tom's wife, who received 70 percent of his Zpex shares, sells those shares two years after Tom's death?

[¶ 24,873]

b. § 6161—Deferral for Cause

Section 6161 provides for deferral of a somewhat different type. Qualification is based on cause rather than mechanical tests. It provides for the deferred payment of all types of taxes including estate and generation-skipping taxes. Relief for estate taxes is available for one year under § 6161(a)(1), which applies to all taxes (but has a shorter, six-month extension period for all taxes other than the estate tax). Relief is available for up to 10 years under § 6161(a)(2), which applies only to estate taxes (but not generation-skipping transfer taxes). Extensions may be granted for reasonable cause. Reasonable cause "is a much easier test to meet than the former test which required a showing of undue hardship. The reasonable cause test can be satisfied by showing that the executor needs time to collect liquid assets or to convert liquid assets to cash." H. Rept. 94–1380, 2d Sess., p. 28, 3 C.B. 762.

Relief under § 6161 must be requested on or before the due date of the tax. Reg. § 20.6161–1(b). Even when § 6166 relief is requested, it is advisable to always ask for relief under § 6161, since it may subsequently be determined that the mechanical tests of § 6166 have not been satisfied. However, the Service has ruled that a timely filed election under § 6166 will be treated as an application for extension under § 6161 if the taxpayer is mistaken in his or her belief that the § 6166 election is available. See Rev. Rul. 76–51, 1976–1 C.B. 382; Rev. Rul. 74–499, 1974–2 C.B. 397.

[¶ 24,877]

c. Security

The Internal Revenue Service may require a bond to secure all payments of the deferred tax (§ 6165), except that a bond may not be required where the executor has elected to have a special lien for deferred tax apply. § 6324A(d)(6). A bond is difficult to obtain as a practical matter, but the Service is supposedly flexible about working out other suitable security arrangements. Probate court approval of the arrangements is necessary if there is a court with jurisdiction. When pledged property is sold, the Service is cooperative in accepting substituted security. Some examples of security which has been accepted include mortgages on real property and pledges of closely held stock with the taxpayer's attorney acting as pledgeholder.

Although the deferral of estate tax can be an attractive possibility, the risk inherent in leveraging the closely held business should not be overlooked. While deferring the tax may avoid a sale of the business, if the business declines in value, the deferred liability can wipe out the decedent's estate. Indeed, it is this critical relationship between the closely held business and the financial well-being of the client's family that provides the touchstone for the challenging and rewarding task of planning for the closely held business. The best approach is not necessarily the one which saves the most taxes, but rather is the one which best balances that concern with the needs and desires of the client and members of his family.

[¶ 24,885]

4. EMPLOYEE STOCK OWNERSHIP PLANS (ESOPS)

An employee stock ownership plan (ESOP) is a form of pension plan that is "qualified" for special income tax treatment. (Qualified plans are the subject of Chapter 29.) Contributions to a qualified pension plan made by an employer on behalf of his or her employees are tax deductible when made subject to certain limitations. However, the employees will not be taxed on the benefits in the plan until the benefits are distributed to them. Moreover, the income earned by the plan assets escapes income taxation until distributed to the employees for whose account the income has accrued.

¶ 24,885

ESOPs are a special breed of qualified plan. Section 4975(e)(7) provides that an ESOP is a "defined contribution plan"—either a stock bonus plan or a stock bonus and a money purchase plan—which is "designed to invest primarily in qualifying employer securities." While defined contribution plans are discussed in Chapter 29, suffice it to say that, as a general proposition, tax deductible contributions to a defined contribution plan are limited to an amount determined annually by reference to § 415(c)(1). See ¶ 29,207. However, it is not the "defined contribution" feature that makes ESOPs special. They are special because they invest "primarily in employer securities."

ESOPs give employees an opportunity to become owners of those corporations by whom they are employed. Mechanically speaking, the employer funds the plan with tax deductible contributions—or loans—and the plan then purchases shares of stock issued by the employer corporation.

Chapter 25

TAX ASPECTS OF CHARITABLE GIFTS: AN OVERVIEW

A. OBJECTIVES

[¶ 25,001]

Charitable giving can provide solutions to many planning problems. For example, property which may not be readily saleable, such as closely held stock, or property which would be very time-consuming and troublesome to sell, such as used clothing, furniture and other household items, can be donated to charity and produce the equivalent of immediate cash in the form of a reduced tax bill for the year of donation.

On a larger scale, there have been a number of instances in the past where control of family corporations has been apparently perpetuated by donation of stock by the founder to a family controlled foundation. Obviously, other prospective donors of substantial means would welcome the opportunity to make substantial charitable contributions (for both tax and nontax reasons) if they could retain control of the transferred property. For that reason, these materials include discussions of the current limitations on the use of private foundations.

B. QUALIFIED CHARITIES FOR INCOME TAX PURPOSES

[¶ 25,051]

1. SECTION 170(c) ORGANIZATIONS

For a charitable donation to qualify as a deduction for federal *income* tax purposes, the donee must be a § 170(c) qualified domestic charitable organization or a federal, state or local governmental unit of the United States, and the contribution must be made "to or for the use of" the organization. § 170(c); see Davis v. United States, 495 U.S. 472 (1990). Corporate contributions to a trust, fund, or foundation are deductible only if they are to be used within the United States or any of its possessions exclusively for specified purposes. § 170(c)(2).

[¶ 25,059]

2. EXEMPT ORGANIZATIONS

It should be noted that while there are a number of organizations whose income is exempt from tax under §§ 501(a) or 401(a), these civic, social and business organizations, as well as employees' pension and profit-sharing plans, are not charities; therefore, contributions to them will not qualify for an income tax deduction. §§ 501(a), 401(a).

Comment: Contributions made to domestic fraternal societies, orders or associations operating under the lodge system are deductible if they are to be used exclusively for religious, charitable, literary or educational purposes, or for the prevention of cruelty to children or animals. § 170(c)(4).

[¶ 25,067]

3. PUBLISHED LIST OF QUALIFIED CHARITIES

Internal Revenue Service Publication No. 78, Cumulative List of Organizations Described in § 170(c), lists those organizations to which tax deductible contributions can be made. The publication and its updates are available on the IRS website and may be ordered from the Superintendent of Documents, United States Government Printing Office, Washington, D.C. 20402. The absence of an organization from Publication No. 78 does not necessarily mean that contributions to it are ineligible for a charitable deduction, however, since listing in this publication is not a condition for deductibility. Most churches, for example, are not listed, but contributions to them are deductible.

An updated Cumulative List is issued each year as of October 31, and additional updates are issued quarterly. Rev. Proc. 82–39, 1982–1 C.B. 759. Revocations in the tax-exempt status of organizations are published as Announcements in the Internal Revenue Bulletin, see, e.g., Ann. 2006–48, 2006–31 I.R.B. 135; Ann. 2006–37, 2006–23 I.R.B. 1039; Ann. 2006–33, 2006–20 I.R.B. 914; and the organizations are deleted from the updated Cumulative List. The Tax Court has denied a § 2055(a) estate tax deduction for funds distributed to an organization that had been deleted from the Cumulative List before the transfer. Estate of Clopton v. Commissioner, 93 T.C. 275 (1989).

When a client anticipates making a particularly large charitable gift, it is advisable to obtain from the charity a copy of the IRS determination letter declaring that the charity is an exempt organization to which deductible contributions may be made and to cross-check with the IRS to make sure that the organization still qualifies. Again, however, churches will not normally have determination letters or be listed in the IRS compilations.

[¶ 25,075]

4. GIFTS TO INDIVIDUALS

Despite a long tradition in the United States of people making charitable donations to help deserving poor people or other unfortunate individuals, no

¶ 25,059

charitable contribution deductions are allowed for gifts to such individuals or informal groups. See Bowles v. Commissioner, 1 B.T.A. 584 (1925); Mayo v. Commissioner, 30 T.C.M. (CCH) 505, T.C.M. (P–H) ¶ 71,118 (1971). Moreover, gifts to charity that are earmarked for one or more individuals are not deductible, i.e., where the donor names the person or persons who are the ultimate beneficiaries and the charity has no ability to depart from the donor's wishes.

C. GIFT TAX CHARITABLE DEDUCTION

[¶ 25,101]

The gift tax charitable deduction is *unlimited* and is available for a gift to a § 2522(a) qualified charitable organization. Section 2522 is similar to the § 170(c) income tax charitable deduction provision, and organizations recognized as qualified under § 170(c)(2) to receive income tax deductions generally qualify under § 2522(a) as well. However, a qualified charitable organization under § 2522(a) is not necessarily the same as an organization eligible for the income tax charitable deduction. For example, foreign charities qualify for the gift tax charitable deduction under § 2522(a)(2) but do not qualify for the income tax charitable deduction. § 170(c)(2)(A).

Note: The Service has ruled that although contributions and gifts to foreign governments for exclusively charitable purposes are deductible, an unrestricted bequest to a foreign government did not qualify as a bequest in trust for charitable purposes under § 2055(a)(3). Priv. Ltr. Rul. 8929001 (summarizes case law and Revenue Rulings regarding charitable bequests and outright gifts to foreign governments or entities).

D. ESTATE TAX CHARITABLE DEDUCTION

[¶ 25,151]

1. UNLIMITED DEDUCTION

A charitable disposition taking effect at death may be made in an *unlimited* amount (up to the entire value of the estate) to a domestic or foreign qualified charitable organization. § 2055(a). Thus, the estate tax may be eliminated if the entire estate passes to charity. The qualified charitable organizations described in § 2055(a) are similar, but not identical, to the organizations described in § 170(c)(2). See discussion in ¶ 25,101.

Example. Andrew, a widower with an adjusted gross estate of $2,000,000, bequeaths $200,000 to a charity and the balance of his estate to his children. The charitable gift results in Andrew's estate tax being reduced from $435,000 to $345,000. Thus, the $200,000 gift saves $90,000 of tax, and the economic cost of the gift is $110,000.

¶ 25,151

[¶ 25,159]

2. REQUIREMENTS FOR OBTAINING THE ESTATE TAX CHARI-TABLE DEDUCTION

The estate tax charitable deduction is available under § 2055(a) for gifts to qualified charitable organizations. For the most part, organizations qualified for the gift tax charitable deduction are also eligible recipients for purposes of the estate tax charitable deduction.

Although the estate tax charitable deduction is limited to the net value of the transferred property which is required to be included in the gross estate under § 2055(d), there are no distinctions among the types of property which qualify for the deduction. Furthermore, as in the case of the gift tax charitable deduction, the estate tax charitable deduction is *unlimited*. In this sense, the estate tax charitable deduction is unlike the income tax charitable deduction which, under § 170(b), is burdened by percentage limitations. See ¶ 25,151 for discussion of the percentage limitations on the income tax charitable deduction.

[¶ 25,162]

3. TAX ALLOCATION CLAUSE

Note that the estate tax charitable deduction will be reduced to the extent that the gifted property bears any of the estate or other death taxes imposed on the decedent's estate. This may well give rise to the interdependent variable problem, a problem that also burdens spousal gifts and is described in detail at ¶ 14,767. Suffice it to say, that the governing instrument should be blessed with a tax allocation clause and that clause should provide that none of the estate or other death taxes are to be paid from the property passing to charity and qualifying for the estate tax charitable deduction.

[¶ 25,167]

4. USE OF THE MARITAL DEDUCTION

A gift to a surviving spouse will qualify for the marital deduction even if the spouse's interest is followed by a remainder to a qualifying charity. Specifically, to qualify for the marital deduction, the gift must be in the form of: (1) a qualified terminal interest under § 2056(b)(7) or (2) a charitable remainder annuity trust or charitable remainder unitrust (as described in § 664) under § 2056(b)(8). A surviving spouse's income interest in a charitable remainder unitrust or annuity trust will qualify for the marital deduction only if the surviving spouse is the only noncharitable beneficiary of the trust. § 2056(b)(8). For example, in Priv. Ltr. Rul. 8730004, an interest in a unitrust to the decedent's surviving spouse that was followed by an interest to the decedent's brother if the brother survived the spouse did not qualify under § 2056(b)(8) because the surviving spouse was not the only noncharitable beneficiary. The letter ruling also disallowed the marital deduction because the surviving spouse was not entitled to all the income from the property as required by § 2056(b)(7).

¶ 25,159

In Roels v. United States, 928 F.Supp. 812 (E.D.Wis.1996), the marital deduction was denied. The surviving spouse had been given all the income from her dead husband's trust until her death or remarriage. The trust was then to terminate and all the remaining trust property was to be distributed to charity. The surviving spouse's interest was found to be terminable upon remarriage and, thus, did not qualify as QTIP as provided in § 2056(b)(7). Moreover, the trust did not qualify as a charitable remainder annuity or unitrust as provided in § 2056(b)(8) because the charitable remainder was not determinable at the dead husband's death. The charitable deduction, too, would be unavailable to the dead husband's estate (because the gift to charity was not in a form specified for split interest gifts with both noncharitable and charitable beneficiaries).

[¶ 25,175]

5. ELIGIBLE DISPOSITIONS: AN OVERVIEW

Dispositions eligible for the estate tax charitable deduction include, *inter alia,* outright devises and bequests made under a will; the exercise of a general power of appointment in favor of a charity; and the disclaimer by a private beneficiary which results in the disclaimed interest passing to a charitable beneficiary.

A charitable trust of the donor's *entire interest* in certain property will qualify for charitable income, gift and estate tax deductions. In addition, a deduction is available for certain *split-interest* gifts in trust. "Split-interest gifts in trust" mean trusts which have both private and charitable beneficial interests. In such cases, § 2055(e)(2) disallows the charitable deduction for the value of the interest passing to charity unless the trust qualifies under § 664 either as a charitable remainder annuity trust or as a charitable remainder unitrust (discussed at ¶ 26,101); or under § 642(c)(3) as a pooled income fund (discussed at ¶ 26,149); or a charitable lead trust (discussed at ¶ 26,251); or a charitable income trust (discussed at ¶ 26,301).

Also, gifts to charity of undivided fractional interests in property may qualify for the charitable deduction. See Reg. § 20.2055–2(e)(2)(i); ¶ 27,173, 27,189.

Note: Split-interest charitable trusts are subject to the limitations on self-dealing and other rules imposed on private foundations by § 4947. For discussion, see ¶ 25,309.

E. PERCENTAGE LIMITATIONS FOR INCOME TAX PURPOSES

[¶ 25,201]

1. CONTRIBUTION BASE

While no percentage restrictions exist on amounts which can be given to charity for *gift* and *estate* tax purposes, a somewhat complex set of rules limits *income tax* deductions for charitable donations in any one year to varying percentages of the donor's "contribution base." The contribution base is adjusted gross income without regard to operating losses (§ 170(b)(1)(F)), meaning that most people in most taxable years will have as a contribution base their adjusted gross income. Adjusted gross income is defined in § 62 as gross income reduced by the deductions described in § 62.

The maximum percent of the contribution base that a donor can give to charity depends on the nature of the property donated and, in some instances, the use to which it is to be put, the length of its holding period by the donor, the status of the donee charity under the tax laws (in essence, some donees are considered more worthy recipients of charitable contributions than others), and whether the donor is an individual or a corporation. There are also limits on the amounts some donees may receive from any single donor. Reg. § 1.170A–9(e).

[¶ 25,209]

2. FIFTY PERCENT PROPERTY

The annual income tax deduction for an individual is limited to 50 percent of his contribution base (§ 170(b)(1)(A)) for gifts of cash (see ¶ 27,051) and, under certain circumstances, appreciated capital assets (or § 1231 property) which the donor has held for more than a year. See ¶ 27,101. The 50 percent limit is available only if the contributions are made to a public charity such as a church, school, hospital, governmental unit, an organization normally receiving a substantial part of its support from the government or the general public (see ¶ 25,429), and certain private foundations with the status of "operating" foundations (because they have distributed substantially all of their income directly to accomplish the purposes for which they are organized and operated and meet one of three other alternative tests with respect to the use of their assets and source of their support). § 170(b)(1)(A). See discussion at ¶ 25,381. Since these organizations are sometimes referred to as "50 percent organizations," contributions to them are sometimes called "50 percent property" contributions.

> *Example.* Mr. and Mrs. Mohammed, with a contribution base and taxable income of $110,000 without regard to charitable contributions, contributed $40,000 in cash to public charities. The full amount is deductible. Their tax is reduced from $33,000 to $21,000 (a savings of $12,000 based on a 30% tax rate) by reason of the gift. The cost of the $40,000 gift is reduced to $28,000 ($40,000 less $12,000 tax savings).

[¶ 25,217]

3. THIRTY PERCENT PROPERTY

An individual's income tax charitable deduction may be limited to 30 percent of his contribution base if the taxpayer's contribution consists of appreciated long-term capital gain property which, although made to a public charity, has not been reduced on account of the appreciation. If the donor elects to reduce the deduction by 100 percent of the amount of the appreciation, then the contribution limit is raised to 50 percent of its contribution base. § 170(b)(1)(C)(iii). These contributions are sometimes referred to as "30 percent property" contributions. See discussion at ¶ 27,101.

The election to reduce the amount of the income tax deduction for a charitable contribution of appreciated capital gains property by 100 percent of the amount of appreciation may be useful when the property has a value greater than 30 percent of the donor's contribution base and when there is relatively little appreciation.

> *Example.* Mr. and Mrs. Benevides, with a contribution base and taxable income of $100,000, without regard to charitable contributions, contributed $100,000 worth of appreciated real estate held for more than one year. Their basis in the real estate is $80,000, since they inherited it only 18 months earlier. Without the special election, Mr. and Mrs. Benevides can deduct $30,000 of their gift this year. With the election, they can deduct $50,000 of their gift this year, and their carryover of unused deduction will be reduced from $70,000 (no election) to $30,000.

Problem

[¶ 25,223]

What is the policy basis for the special rule applicable to appreciated capital gain property?

[¶ 25,225]

4. GIFTS TO PRIVATE FOUNDATIONS

Section 170(b)(1)(B)(i) allows a deduction of up to 30 percent of an individual's contribution base for gifts of cash, unappreciated property and ordinary income property to private foundations. However, as to gifts of appreciated property to private foundations, the deduction is limited to 20 percent. § 170(b)(1)(D)(i). In addition, where the gifts are to certain special private foundations which, as a result of contractual arrangements, are considered component trusts within an association of privately endowed, independently trusteed funds, the gifts are treated as being made to a public charity. § 170(b)(1)(E). See ¶ 25,429. Note, however, that the value of contributions to private foundations of appreciated property other than publicly traded securities is limited to the donor's basis in the gifted property, making private foundations unsuitable recipients of gifts of highly appreciated land, for example.

[¶ 25,233]

5. GIFTS BY CORPORATIONS

There is a 10 percent of taxable income limit on charitable contributions by corporations, whether these are made to private foundations or public charities. § 170(b)(2).

[¶ 25,241]

6. EXCESS CONTRIBUTIONS

Contributions in excess of the limits described above may be carried forward and deducted during the next succeeding five years, if these amounts carried forward, together with contributions for the years to which they are carried forward, do not exceed the limits for those years. § 170(d)(1)(A) and § 170(b)(1)(C)(ii). Section 170(b)(1)(B) allows a five-year carryover for gifts to private foundations which are entitled to 30 percent treatment and § 170(b)(1)(D) allows the same carryover of gifts to private foundations entitled to 20 percent treatment.

Problem

[¶ 25,299]

In January, Cynthia, with a contribution base of $30,000, contributed $20,000 to a public charity. What is the maximum amount deductible? How much does she carry over to next year? If, in that year, Cynthia's contribution base is again $30,000, and she contributes an additional $12,000 in cash, how much of the carryover can she use next year? How much does Cynthia carry over to the following year?

F. PUBLIC CHARITY OR PRIVATE FOUNDATION?

[¶ 25,301]

1. DISTINCTION

The tax law generally favors public charities. It does so (1) by placing severe restrictions on the operations of private foundations (which are not applied to public charities) and (2) by limiting the percentage of an individual's contribution base which can be utilized in gifts to private foundations, as described in ¶ 25,225, when compared to the higher 50 percent limit available for gifts to public charities.

Understanding private foundations is important because taxpayers who are charitably motivated often want to retain control over the property they give to charity. Retention of control is not often possible when the gift is made to a "public charity" and, therefore, such donors will want to consider setting up "a charity" to be the receptacle for such gifts. Few such "charities" will enjoy classification as a public charity. Instead, they will be burdened by the regulations imposed on private foundations.

[¶ 25,309]

2. PRIVATE FOUNDATIONS

With the exception of charitable organizations which qualify as public charities under § 509(a), and with certain other very limited exceptions, § 508(b) provides that *all* eleemosynary organizations (those described in § 501(c)(3)) are *presumed* to be private foundations. As a private foundation, these organizations are restricted by a set of rules which were designed to eliminate abuses called to the attention of Congress during the hearings on the 1969 Tax Reform Act. These rules have forced most such organizations to liquidate themselves or convert to public charity status, if that was possible.

These restrictions include a 2 percent excise tax which is imposed annually on the net investment income of a private foundation. § 4940(a). Under § 4940(e), the excise tax may be reduced to 1 percent if certain requirements as to qualifying distributions for charitable purposes are met.

In addition, severe penalties are imposed on persons who engage in acts of self-dealing with, or on behalf of, private foundations. The self-dealing rules prohibit virtually any transactions between a person who has created a foundation (or members of his family) and the foundation itself. § 4941. The Internal Revenue Code broadly defines a class of persons designated as "disqualified persons" and specifically prohibits certain dealings between a private foundation and such persons (including, for example, a sale or lease transaction between the disqualified person and the private foundation). § 4941(d)(1). (There is an exception for payment of reasonable compensation to disqualified persons.)

Several of the anti-abuse rules (and sanctions) have been extended to public charities.

[¶ 25,317]

a. *Qualifying Distributions*

Private foundations are required to distribute annually for charitable purposes an amount equal to a 5 percent return on the market value of assets not used directly in carrying out their exempt purposes. See § 4942(a), (c), (d), (e), and (g). Private foundations must distribute principal in satisfaction of the minimum payout requirements, if insufficient income is earned, and thus the foundation may in time be liquidated through capital distributions. See § 4942(e).

If a foundation fails to meet the payout requirement, it is subject to an initial penalty tax of 15 percent per year of the amount which was not paid. § 4942(a). An additional tax of 100 percent of the amount which the foundation fails to distribute is imposed on a foundation if it fails to distribute the required amount during a so-called "correction period." § 4942(b).

[¶ 25,325]

b. *Excess Business Holdings*

There is a percentage limit on a private foundation's ability to own stock in a business enterprise which isn't functionally related to the charitable operations of the foundation. If a private foundation acquires stock in a corporation, it must be determined whether the aggregate of such holdings and the holdings of "disqualified persons" exceeds a 20 percent limit on permitted holdings. § 4943(c)(2)(A).

If that percentage limitation is exceeded, the foundation must divest itself of the excess holdings within designated time periods. A foundation that fails to comply with the divestiture requirements is subject to a first-level tax of 5 percent of the value of its excess business holdings (§ 4943(a)(1)) and to a second level tax of 200 percent of the excess business holdings not divested within the designated "correction period." § 4943(b). The effect of this provision is that a private foundation generally may not retain stock in a family corporation for more than five years. § 4943(c)(6). However, § 4943(c)(7) gives the Service limited discretion to extend the divestiture period for an additional five years.

The broad implication of these rules is that the value of a private foundation as the donee of gifts of closely held stock or partnership interests is severely limited.

[¶ 25,333]

c. *Jeopardizing Investments*

A 5 percent excise tax is imposed on private foundations and on certain foundation managers if a private foundation invests any amount in such a manner as to jeopardize the carrying out of any of its exempt purposes. § 4944(a). An investment will be considered to be in jeopardy if the foundation managers, in making the investment, failed to exercise ordinary business care and prudence under the facts and circumstances prevailing at the time, in providing for the long-and short-term financial needs of the foundation. A second-level tax of 25 percent is imposed against the foundation and a 5 percent tax against the foundation manager if the investment is not removed from jeopardy within a correction period. § 4944(b).

[¶ 25,341]

d. *Expenditure Responsibility*

Private foundations are restricted in respect to expenditures for certain kinds of activities, such as carrying on propaganda, attempting to influence legislation, making grants to individuals, and making distributions to other organizations. § 4945(d) and (e). In particular, they are required to exercise "expenditure responsibility" over grants which they make to organizations other than public charities. § 4945(h). A private foundation which makes an expenditure contrary to these rules is subject to a first-level tax of 10 percent of the amount improperly paid. § 4945(a)(1). Also, tax is imposed against a foundation manager who has willfully agreed to the improper expenditure. § 4945(a)(2). A second-level tax of 100 percent of the expenditure is imposed on a foundation which fails to correct the situation within the required time. § 4945(b)(1). Furthermore, a second-level tax is imposed on a foundation manager who refuses to agree to the correction of the improper expenditure. § 4945(b)(2).

Note that a direct gift to an economically disadvantaged person is excepted from these rules barring gifts to individuals. But gifts for travel, study, or similar purposes are barred.

¶ 25,325

[¶ 25,349]

e. Recordkeeping

The requirements regarding minimum distributions and prohibited expenditures call for a private foundation to determine the tax status of each donee organization and to enter into certain agreements and restrictions in connection with grants made. § 4942(a)(2)(B) and (g). Failure to comply will result in the tax penalties described above in connection with expenditure responsibility. § 4945(d)(4).

[¶ 25,357]

f. Penalties for Repeated Violations

If a private foundation has repeatedly and flagrantly violated the above-described provisions, the foundation may be subject to a third-level 100 percent penalty and also to the so-called "termination tax." § 507(a)(2)(A). This latter tax may equal the aggregate tax benefits which the foundation and its substantial contributors have enjoyed since the inception of the foundation (but not more than the total net assets of the foundation). § 507(c).

The governing instrument of a private foundation, whether it be a corporation or a trust, must contain provisions which incorporate a number of the restrictive rules described in the preceding paragraphs, unless these are prescribed by a generally applicable state statute. Reg. § 1.508–3(d). If such restrictive provisions are not adopted, the foundation may lose its tax-exempt status. Many states have adopted such statutes.

[¶ 25,365]

g. Disclosure and Publicity Requirements

Private foundations are subject to numerous reporting and publicity requirements. Typically, a tax-exempt private foundation will be required to file an annual report (Reg. § 1.6033–2) and make the report available to anyone who requests it. The preparation of these forms and reports, which contain detailed information regarding, among other things, the source of the foundation's funds and the nature of its grants, is costly and time consuming. In particular, advertisement of the availability of an annual report may generate numerous inquiries and requests for funds.

Problem

[¶ 25,370]

Refer to the example in ¶ 27,157 and describe the impact of the private foundation rules on the charitable trust established by Mr. Ichabod.

[¶ 25,373]

3. PERCENTAGE LIMITATIONS ON CONTRIBUTIONS

Deductions of charitable contributions to a private foundation are subject to more severe limits than are contributions made to a public charity. See

¶ 25,201. Contributions of cash, unappreciated property or ordinary income property may be deducted up to the lesser of (1) 30 percent of the donor's contribution base for the year, or (2) 50 percent of the contribution base reduced by gifts to public charities. Excess contributions may be carried over up to five additional years. § 170(b)(1)(B). Contributions of appreciated property to private foundations are deductible only up to the lesser of (1) 20 percent of the donor's contribution base for the year or (2) the excess of 30 percent of the donor's contribution base for the year *over* the amount of the contributions of appreciated property to public charities for the year. Again, a five-year carryover of excess contributions is allowed. § 170(b)(1)(D). (This is in contrast to the limits on deductions to a public charity which are 30 percent or 50 percent of the donor's contribution base, depending on whether an election is made, with a carryover of up to five years for excess contributions. § 170(b)(1)(A) and (C)(ii).) However, a donor may make contributions to certain private foundations described at ¶ 25,381 and obtain deductions up to the 30 percent or 50 percent limits. § 170(b)(1)(A)(vii) and (B).

[¶ 25,381]

4. TAX-FAVORED PRIVATE FOUNDATIONS

There are three types of private foundations which have been exempted from the lower deduction ceiling, as well as having been granted other benefits. These special private foundations—operating foundations, conduit foundations, and directed pooled income funds—were created to meet certain special factual situations and not only are they not of general utility but the organizations remain private foundations subject to most of the restrictions.

[¶ 25,389]

a. *Operating Foundations*

An "operating foundation" is distinguished from a private foundation in that it is required to use its income and its assets directly for the active conduct of activities which constitute its charitable purpose or function. § 4942(j)(3)(A). Generally, a privately supported foundation will satisfy the definition if it is actively engaged in the conduct of research for charitable or educational purposes or the operation of a facility for public use, such as a museum. Reg. § 53.4942(b)–1(b)(1). A privately supported foundation that makes grants only to other organizations or to individuals (such as scholarships) will not satisfy the definition. Reg. § 53.4942(b)–1(b)(2).

If an organization meets the definition of an "operating foundation," it is nevertheless treated as a "private foundation," subject to all the restrictions described above, with the following exceptions:

1. An operating foundation may retain its earnings in furtherance of its operating needs and is not as likely to be subject to the requirements applicable to other private foundations that may necessitate distributions out of principal. Thus, it may be used to create an endowment for future giving.

¶ 25,373

2. Distributions from a grant-making private foundation (such as described at ¶ 25,397) to an operating foundation will be treated as qualifying distributions by the grantor foundation, on the same basis as if its grants were made to a public charity. Thus, operating foundations are in a preferred class in the sense that grant-making private foundations are encouraged to make qualifying distributions to them.

3. Contributions by individual donors to an operating foundation generally have the same income tax benefits as contributions to a public charity. For example, a gift by an individual of appreciated property to an operating foundation is generally deductible up to 30 percent of the individual's contribution base (or 50 percent of his contribution base if the individual so elects). § 170(b)(1)(A) and (C)(ii).

These advantages of an operating foundation make it an attractive vehicle for certain applications such as research or community development, but the operating foundation is nevertheless a private foundation, subject to the restrictions previously described, and its definition substantially restricts the type of activity which may be conducted. Individuals primarily interested in establishing or maintaining an organization which may make grants to others for carrying out charitable purposes will find that operating foundation status is not a viable alternative to, nor does it offer substantial benefits over, typical private foundation status.

[¶ 25,397]

b. Conduit Foundations

An individual contributor may obtain the same income tax benefits for a contribution to a private foundation as would otherwise be available for a contribution to a public charity if the private foundation redistributes the gift to one or more public charities.

The gift to such a "conduit foundation" is treated as if it had been made directly to the ultimate charitable distributee. Precise rules must be observed if the contributor is to receive the intended deduction. In particular, the private foundation must, within two and one-half months after the close of the taxable year for which the gift was received, distribute the asset itself, or an amount equal to the donated value of the asset plus a "qualifying distribution" computed on an annual basis at the rate of 5 percent. §§ 170(b)(1)(E)(ii), 4942(g).

In order for a contributor to substantiate the full income tax benefits of a contribution to a conduit foundation, the contributor must obtain adequate records or other sufficient evidence from the donee showing that the foundation properly redistributed the contributor's gifts. § 170(b)(1)(E)(ii).

Example. Gladys contributes stock having in one year a fair market value of $1,000 to a conduit foundation. The stock depreciates in value to $500 by the time of redistribution in the following year. An amount equal to $1,050 must still be distributed. If the foundation fails to distribute that amount within two and one-half months after the year in which the

¶ **25,397**

contribution was made, by recourse its own principal, Gladys will lose the income tax benefit of the contribution.

While a gift to a conduit foundation may provide benefits in certain cases, the technical requirements are such that there is a substantial risk of a violation which may cause the loss of the anticipated deduction. Moreover, even with the above-noted exceptions, the burdens previously described as applicable to private foundations are not reduced.

[¶ 25,405]

c. *Directed Pooled Income Fund*

The principal advantage of a directed pooled fund is that the donor or the donor's spouse may annually designate the organizations to which distributions from their part of the fund may be made. While for this reason (i.e., the control of distributions by the donor) the fund is treated for tax purposes as a private foundation, the donor is afforded the same deduction limits as if the gift were made to a public charity. This type of fund is attractive for those donors who require the certainty of being able to direct the fund's distributions. However, a directed fund (or an organization consisting of such funds) is a private foundation, and hence the fund and managers are subject to all the taxes and restrictions applicable to private foundations. A directed pooled fund must be operated in accord with specified rules, among which are the following:

1. All contributions must be pooled in a common fund.
2. The fund must be organized and operated for the benefit or support of one or more public charities. It must (except for the right of the donor to make directions as to distributions) be controlled, supervised, or operated by or in connection with one or more of those charities.
3. Only the donor and/or the donor's spouse may designate the recipients of distributions from the fund, and a public charity or charities must be chosen.
4. All income of the fund (but not less than 5 percent of the fund's value) must be distributed annually to one or more such public charities not later than two and one-half months after the close of the taxable year.
5. The corpus attributable to any donor's contribution must be distributed to one or more such public charities not later than one year after the donor's death (or after the death of a surviving spouse if the spouse had the right to designate the recipients of such corpus). Reg. § 1.170A–9(h).

[¶ 25,413]

5. SUPPORTING ORGANIZATIONS

Classification as a public charity of the support type is available to certain charitable trusts and foundations which might otherwise be classified as private foundations due to their inability to meet the public support requirements of public charity status under § 509(a)(1) or (2). A supporting organization, as described in § 509(a)(3), includes charitable organizations which are organized and operated exclusively for the benefit of, to perform the function of, or to carry out the purposes of one or more public charities where all the net income of the trust is required to be paid to an institution named in a trust instrument, which institution depends upon such trust for a significant and substantial part of its support or which controls or supervises the trust.

In order to qualify as a public charity of the support type, a charitable organization must meet three tests:

1. *Purpose test.* The foundation must be organized and operated to support or benefit one or more public charities specified in § 509(a)(1) or (2).

2. *Relationship test.* The foundation must be operated, supervised or controlled by or in connection with one or more § 509(a)(1) or (2) public charities.

3. *Control test.* The foundation must not be controlled by "disqualified persons" (other than the foundation manager and public charities described in § 509(a)(1) or (2)).

Once a charitable organization meets these three tests and qualifies for treatment as a "supporting foundation" under § 509(a)(3), it enjoys the benefits of being treated as a public charity for tax purposes. Hence the supporting foundation will not be subject to the two percent excise tax on investment income, or to the five percent minimum payout requirements normally imposed on private foundations.

> *Example.* Huang establishes a charitable trust with a bank as trustee. Under the terms of the trust all of the income is to be paid annually to a charity. Such a trust may qualify as a public charity of the support type under § 509(a)(3), and, for that reason, contributions to such an organization would qualify for the 50 percent limitation for gifts to public charities.

Note that the Pension Protection Act of 2006, as part of its anti-abuse effort, treats some supporting foundations more like private foundations than public charities.

[¶ 25,421]

6. CONVERSION OF A PRIVATE FOUNDATION

Often it is possible to modify the administrative and distribution procedures of a private foundation to meet the requirements of one of the special categories outlined above. Alternatively, if the governing instrument must be revised, recourse may be had to various judicial procedures to effect the necessary amendment.

> *Example 1.* Isabel established a charitable foundation to promote exploration. The terms of the foundation provide that three of the five trustees shall each be a representative of, or designated by, an institution con-

cerned with exploration. The other two initial trustees are to be Isabel's descendants. The foundation as established is a private foundation; however, it may become a public charity of the support type by amending its governing instrument to specify, by name or by class, the institutions whose officials are to be represented on the board of trustees of the foundation.

Example 2. Jack established a charitable corporation many years ago for general charitable purposes. His son and daughter and their lawyer now constitute the board of directors of the corporation. If (1) the Articles of Organization of the corporation are amended so that its purposes are restated to provide that it shall be operated exclusively to make distributions for the benefit of a certain public charity in furtherance of the charity's exempt purposes and (2) the board of directors is expanded to seven members, four of whom (a majority) are selected by and are representatives of the public charity, the former family foundation will qualify as a public charity of the support type.

Continued donor interest—and the prospect of additional contributions— is often given as a reason for continuing as a private foundation. Absent those considerations, given the negative aspects of operating as a private foundation, conversion of private foundations should be considered. An additional reason to convert is the increased donation limits offered by such special private foundation or public charity status.

Among the possibilities is for the private foundation to make an outright transfer of its assets by a terminating distribution for the general purposes of a public charity. Alternatively, the foundation could make an outright transfer of its assets by a terminating distribution to a segregated fund within a public charity which may be advised by a committee representing the transferor foundation and which may be impressed with a fiduciary responsibility to carry out the donor's charitable objectives. Such fund may carry on the name of the transferor foundation. Treasury Regulations provide the procedure and various guidelines with respect to the transfer of assets by a terminating foundation into a public charity. Reg. §§ 1.507–1—1.507–3.

Example 3. The Kryptonite Foundation will successfully remove itself from the operational burdens of private foundation status by transfer of its assets to a public charity as a terminating distribution, subject to the agreement that the assets shall be designated as the Kryptonite Fund to be separately accounted for and administered consistent with the purposes for which the Kryptonite Foundation was established. The officers of the Kryptonite Foundation may be appointed as an advisory committee of the Kryptonite Fund and render specific suggestions as to its distributions.

It is also possible for a charitable organization to maintain an independent existence as a component fund within a public charity if the latter has adopted a procedure for the inclusion of component funds within its ruling exemption. The procedure requires no more than for both the custodian and the private charitable foundation to be contractually subjected to the charter and bylaws provisions of the public charity so long as those provisions include

¶ 25,421

the powers required by Revenue Ruling 77–333, 1977–2 C.B. 75 (to remove the trustees for cause or for failure to produce an adequate investment return over a reasonable period of time and to modify the purposes of the foundation if they become impossible or impractical to fulfill).

> *Example 4.* The Yucco Foundation fails to receive one-third of its support from the public over a five-year period and it thus is classified as a private foundation. By resolution of the trustees it agrees to be subject to the Articles of Organization and By–Laws of a public charity and, upon approval by the Board of Directors of the latter, the Yucco Foundation will be considered a component fund of the public charity and will enjoy the advantages of public charity status. It may continue to operate as before, if consistent with the purposes of the public charity.

[¶ 25,429]

7. PUBLIC CHARITIES

Practically speaking, public charities are private foundations except for the fact that they qualify for exemption from treatment as a private foundation. Technically speaking, therefore, "the term 'private foundation' means a domestic or foreign organization described in § 501(c)(3) other than" public charities. § 509(a).

Public charities include churches, nonprofit schools and hospitals, and any governmental unit. Additionally, organizations described in §§ 509(a)(2) or 170(b)(1)(A)(vi) which receive a substantial portion of their support from the general public are treated as public charities.

Chapter 26

SPLIT-INTEREST CHARITABLE GIFTS

A. OBJECTIVES

[¶ 26,001]

An understanding of the tax consequences of charitable giving is important for those engaged in estate planning and administration. Apart from the more conventional and relatively small lifetime charitable gifts and charitable bequests, there are opportunities for substantial income and estate tax saving through the use of imaginative planning involving charitable dispositions.

Properly planned and implemented charitable donations entitle the donor to current income tax deductions while removing the donated property from the donor's gross estate without attracting a gift tax. For most donors, inter vivos charitable gifts are preferred because the value of a current income tax deduction is worth far more than the later estate tax deduction for a gift taking effect at the donor's death.

Understandably, the tax deduction is the motivation—or at least the catalyst—for some gifts to charity. Split-interest gifts to charity are a favored technique. While tax deductions for gifts of partial interests are generally disallowed, if structured properly, a donor can claim the tax deduction for the gift while retaining partial enjoyment of the transferred property.

This chapter considers gifts to trusts having both charitable and private beneficial interests. Gifts of partial interests in tangibles (¶ 27,173) and in real property (¶ 27,189) are considered in Chapter 27.

B. ACTUARIAL TABLES

[¶ 26,051]

Actuarial tables provided by the Internal Revenue Service are used in valuing gifts of a fractional interest. Currently, split-interest gifts, i.e., gifts of any interest for life or a term of years, or any remainder or reversionary interest, are valued using tables that are based on an interest rate equal to 120 percent of the federal midterm rate under § 1274(d)(1) (rounded to the nearest 2/10th of 1 percent) in effect for the month in which the valuation date falls. § 7520(a). The federal midterm rate is based on the average market yield of obligations of the United States. Technically speaking, if an income, estate, or gift tax charitable deduction is allowable for part of the property transferred, the taxpayer may elect to use the federal midterm rate in effect for the month of the transfer or for either of the two months preceding the valuation date. § 7520(a).

It should be noted in the examples following the discussions of charitable remainder annuity trusts (¶ 26,101) and charitable remainder unitrusts (¶ 26,109) that the choice of which interest rate to elect can have a significant effect on the valuation of split-interest gifts. Use of a higher rate would give the highest value for a gift to charity of a remainder interest and use of a lower rate will give the highest value to a gift of a "lead" interest to charity.

The revised valuation tables have been published in Internal Revenue Service, Actuarial Tables Alpha Volume (Publication 1457, July 1999) (http://www.irs.gov/pub/irs-pdf/p1457.pdf), and Internal Revenue Service, Actuarial Values Beta Volume (Publication 1458, July 1999) (http://www.irs.gov/pub/irs-pdf/p1458.pdf). Some tables are set out in Regs. §§ 20.2031–7(d) and 1.664–4 and are incorporated by reference into Reg. § 25.2512–5A. For a detailed discussion of the required computations, see Donald McGee Etheridge, Charitable Income Trusts, 866 Tax Mgmt. (BNA) A–10 (2002). Most practitioners rely on computer programs for these computations, as detailed at Appendix A, notably: NumberCruncher (http://www.leimberg.com/products/software/numberCruncher.asp), Intuitive Estate Planner (Windows) (http://west.thomson.com/IEP/), and Tiger Tables (http://www.tigertables.com).

C. CHARITABLE REMAINDER TRUSTS

[¶ 26,101]

1. ANNUITY TRUSTS

A charitable remainder annuity trust is a trust from which a specified sum or percentage (not more than 50 percent of the initial net fair market value of all the assets actually placed in trust) is to be paid annually to one or more noncharitable income beneficiaries. Each one of these beneficiaries must be living at the creation of the trust, and payments to them must terminate not later than 20 years after creation or at their deaths. § 664(d)(1)(A); Reg. § 1.664–2(a). At the time the charitable remainder annuity trust is created, there must be no more than a 5 percent chance that the annuity amount will exhaust the trust corpus; otherwise the charitable deduction will be disallowed. Rev. Rul. 77–374, 1977–2 C.B. 329. Thereafter, the remainder interest must pass to or for the use of a charity. § 664(d)(1)(C). The value of such remainder interest (as determined by § 7520) must be at least 10% of the initial net fair market value of all property placed in trust. § 664(d)(1)(D).

Charitable remainder annuity trusts must specify that the payout rate is not more than 50 percent of the initial value of the trust. § 664(d)(1)(A). Also, the charitable remainder interest must have a value of at least 10 percent of the initial trust value. § 664(d)(1)(D).

¶ 26,101

Example. Chad transfers property with a fair market value of $100,000 to a trustee in February 2002. The trustee is to annually pay 5 percent of the initial fair market value of the assets transferred to the trust, first to Chad, and, after his death, to Chad's wife, if she survives him. Upon the death of the survivor of the two, the trustee is to distribute the principal to a charity.

Assuming the trust satisfies all requirements under the Internal Revenue Code, it will be a qualified charitable remainder annuity trust and will be exempt from federal income tax (unless it has unrelated business income, for example, debt-financed income). Reg. § 1.664–1(c). Chad obtains an immediate charitable contribution deduction for income tax purposes for the present value of the charitable remainder interest determined under the appropriate actuarial tables.

Chad is age 60 at the time of the transfer and his wife is age 50. Payments are to be made quarterly. Assume that 5.6 percent is the applicable § 7520(a) interest rate. (Because the annuity is for the longer of two lives, the factor to be used in valuing the charitable remainder interest is found in Table R(2), which appears in IRS Publication 1457. One-life, two-life, and term of years factors are built into the computer programs described in ¶ 26,051.) Chad would be entitled to a deduction of $26,950 for federal income tax purposes subject to the usual 30 percent and 50 percent contribution limits (and permitted carryover). See discussion at ¶ 25,201.

Chad and his wife will be taxable on their receipt of income or capital gains from the trust. Since Chad is an income beneficiary, the value of the trust property will be includible in his gross estate by reason of his retained right but if the gift satisfies the requirements of § 2056(b)(8), the marital deduction will be available for the value of the trust property. At the subsequent death of Chad's surviving spouse, her estate will get a charitable deduction for the value of the property passing to charity.

[¶ 26,109]

2. UNITRUSTS

a. *The Standard Unitrust Arrangement*

A unitrust differs from an annuity trust, practically speaking, only in the method used for determining the amount of the income payments that are to be made to the noncharitable income beneficiaries and by the annual valuation requirements. Payments to noncharitable income beneficiaries must be expressed in terms of a fixed percentage, not more than 50 percent (the "unitrust percentage"), of the net fair market value of the assets, valued annually, rather than a certain sum or a specified percentage of the trust's initial net fair market value as is the case with annuity trusts. § 664(d)(2)(A); Reg. § 1.664–1(a)(1). Alternatively, the donor may provide in the instrument that, in any year, the trustee may pay to the income beneficiary: (1) the net income from the trust, if that amount is less than the unitrust percentage described above or (2) the net income plus any trust income in excess of the unitrust percentage, if all net income payments made in all prior years to the beneficiary total in the aggregate less than what the aggregate payments to the noncharitable beneficiary would have been had they been based upon the unitrust percentage. § 664(d)(3); Reg. § 1.664–3(a)(1)(i)(b). The value of the remainder interest passing to charity (as determined by § 7520) must be at least 10 percent of the net fair market value of each contribution of property to the trust, as determined on the date such property is contributed to the trust. § 664(d)(2)(D).

Problems

[¶ 26,110]

1. On January 1, 2002, Daisy transferred property worth $100,000 to a trustee to pay to her husband, Doug, each year an amount equal to 5 percent of the net fair market value of the trust's assets, valued annually. Upon Doug's death, the principal was to be paid outright to a charity. In 2002, the trustee paid Doug $5,000 (regardless of the income earned by the trust). Assume that on December 31, 2003, the trust assets were worth $110,000 (a 10 percent increase in value). In 2003 Doug receives $5,500 (again regardless of the income earned by the trust). Upon Doug's death, the assets in trust were distributed to the charity. Did the trust qualify as a unitrust? Did Daisy also make a gift to Doug at the time the trust was established? Of what? Did the gift to Doug qualify for the gift tax marital deduction? See § 2523(g).

2. Assume the same facts as the preceding example, except that the instrument provides in addition (1) that if the net trust income in any year is less than 5 percent of the net value of the trust assets for that year, Doug shall receive only the net income and (2) that if in any subsequent year the net trust income is greater than 5 percent of the net value of the trust assets for that year, Doug shall receive so much of the income as is required to equal what he would have received for all the years in which the trust has been in existence had he been paid at the level 5 percent figure. Assume that for 2002 (the first year of the trust) the trust has a net income of $3,000, and the net value of its principal was $100,000; since $3,000 is less than 5 percent ($5,000) of such net value, Doug received only $3,000. (Thus, the trust "owed" him $2,000 against potential future income.) If, at the end of 2003, the trust assets had a net value of $110,000 and net income of the trust was $8,000, how much did Doug receive? How much would he have received if the net income for 2002 had been $7,000?

3. Why did Congress insist that 5 percent be the minimum specified payment in both an annuity trust and a unitrust?

————

Charitable remainder unitrusts must specify that the payout rate is not more than 50 percent of the net fair market value of the trust property, valued annually. § 664(d)(2)(A). Also, the charitable remainder interest must have a value of at least 10 percent of the net fair market value of the property on the date it is contributed to the trust. § 664(d)(2)(D). As an example, note that a charitable remainder unitrust for the life of a single individual with a payout rate of the 5 percent minimum will not produce a 10 percent remainder if the individual is younger than 23.

When the trust provides for the income beneficiary to receive only the net income from the trust if the trust earns less income than the unitrust percentage provided, this arrangement is referred to as a "net income charitable remainder unitrust" (NICRUT). When the income beneficiary is to receive the net income plus any trust income in excess of the unitrust percentage if all income payments made in prior years total less than what the beneficiary would have received had the payments been based on the unitrust percentage, this arrangement is referred to as a "net income plus makeup charitable remainder unitrust" (NIMCRUT). In a NIMCRUT, when the income earned by the trust and paid to the beneficiary is less than the stated unitrust percentage, this difference is "made up" in subsequent years if the income earned by the trust exceeds the stated unitrust percentage.

Because unitrust income payments are based each year upon a percentage of the value of the assets in the trust, it is necessary for the trustee to value the assets each year. In order to avoid charges of self-dealing if a grantor or beneficiary serves as trustee, that grantor trustee is required to have a special independent trustee value any unmarketable property held in the trust. Reg. § 1.664–1(a)(7). As an alternative, a trustee who is also a donor or beneficiary may obtain a qualified appraisal each year.

[¶ 26,115]

b. The "Flip Unitrust"

The charitable remainder trust can be a very useful planning tool for a donor who wishes to transfer a highly appreciated piece of property into trust. Because a qualifying charitable remainder trust is not subject to income tax, a highly appreciated piece of property that is transferred into a charitable remainder trust and then sold by the trustee will not trigger the recognition of the capital gains tax upon the sale. By contrast, if the donor held onto the property and disposed of it herself, a significant portion of the return could be lost as a result of capital gains tax. The charitable remainder trust allows the donor to effect in essence an installment sale, because the beneficiary will enjoy a return of a fixed percentage of the asset over time.

Historically, a donor wishing to achieve such a result would have to choose between placing the asset in a standard CRUT or a NIMCRUT. If the donor chose to use the CRUT, he or she would have to gamble on whether the trustee would decide to sell the asset immediately. If the asset were not sold immediately, the trust would have to satisfy its distribution requirement with a *piece* of the asset. On the other hand, if the donor chose to use a NIMCRUT, he or she would be forced to take the chance that the trust would never generate enough income to meet the stated distribution percentage. As a solution to this dilemma, many planners have suggested using a charitable remainder trust that begins as a NIMCRUT and then converts to a standard

CRUT upon the sale of the highly appreciated assets held by the trust. This combination is commonly referred to as a "flip unitrust." Because the trust starts off as a NIMCRUT, the trustee is not required to make any income distributions. (This is so because the trust assets are highly appreciated pieces of property that do not generate income until sold.) Once the property is sold, the trust converts to a standard CRUT and then pays the noncharitable beneficiary the stated unitrust percentage.

Due to perceived abuses, the IRS limits the use of the "flip unitrust". Reg. § 1.664–3(c).

[¶ 26,116]

c. The Application of § 2702

Section 2702 values the donor's income interest in a charitable remainder unitrust at zero when the CRUT has a successor noncharitable beneficiary who is someone other than the donor. The practical effect of the application of § 2702 is to cause the value of the gift to the successor beneficiary to reflect the entire noncharitable interest in the CRUT, in most instances significantly increasing the value of the gift for gift tax purposes. See Reg. § 25.2702–1(b) and (c)(3).

[¶ 26,117]

3. SELECTING THE FORM OF REMAINDER TRUST

When planning which form of remainder trust to use, it should be noted that because the income to be distributed to the beneficiaries of a charitable remainder unitrust is determined based on the valuation of trust assets each year (Reg. § 1.664–3(a)(1)(iv)), and because additional contributions are allowed, if the trust instrument specifically provides for such contributions (Reg. § 1.664–3(b)), a unitrust is more likely to provide a greater return for a beneficiary during an inflationary period since the fair market value of the trust assets ordinarily will increase, providing a correspondingly larger distribution. A charitable remainder annuity trust is more likely to provide the security of level payments to the individual beneficiary if the value of the trust assets declines, but because no additional donations to a charitable remainder trust may be made after the initial contribution (Reg. § 1.664–2(b)) and because the annuity payments to the noncharitable beneficiary are determined as a fixed percentage of the initial fair market value of the trust assets, there is no hedge against inflation.

[¶ 26,125]

4. MANDATORY PROVISIONS

Special provisions must be included in the governing instrument of a charitable remainder trust or no deduction will be allowed. The Service has issued sample forms that meet the requirements of § 664 and the regulations for use in drafting qualified charitable remainder annuity trusts (CRAT) and unitrusts (CRUT), as shown in Table 26.1.

¶ 26,125

Table 26.1. SAMPLE CRAT AND CRUT FORMS SUPPLIED BY THE IRS

1. An inter vivos CRAT providing for annuity payments for one measuring life (see Rev. Proc. 2003–53, 2003–2 C.B. 230);

2. An inter vivos CRAT providing for annuity payments for a term of years (see Rev. Proc. 2003–54, 2003–2 C.B. 236);

3. An inter vivos CRAT providing for annuity payments payable consecutively for two measuring lives (see Rev. Proc. 2003–55, 2003–2 C.B. 242);

4. An inter vivos CRAT providing for annuity payments payable concurrently and consecutively for two measuring lives (see Rev. Proc. 2003–56, 2003–2 C.B. 249);

5. A testamentary CRAT providing for annuity payments for one measuring life (see Rev. Proc. 2003–57, 2003–2 C.B. 257);

6. A testamentary CRAT providing for annuity payments for a term of years (see Rev. Proc. 2003–58, 2003–2 C.B. 262);

7. A testamentary CRAT providing for annuity payments payable consecutively for two measuring lives (see Rev. Proc. 2003–59, 2003–2 C.B. 268); and

8. A testamentary (CRAT) with concurrent and consecutive interests for two measuring lives (see Rev. Proc. 2003–60, 2003–2 C.B. 274).

1. An inter vivos CRUT for one measuring life followed by the distribution of trust-assets to a charitable remainderman (see Rev. Proc. 2005–52, 2005–34 LR.B. 326).

2. An inter vivos CRUT providing for unitrust payments for a term of years (see Rev. Proc. 2005–53, 2005–34 I.R.B. 339);

3. An inter vivos CRUT providing for unitrust payments payable consecutively for two measuring lives (see Rev. Proc. 2005–54, 2005–34 I.R.B. 353);

4. An inter vivos CRUT providing for unitrust payments payable concurrently and consecutively for two measuring lives (see Rev. Proc. 2005–55, 2005–34 I.R.B. 367);

5. A testamentary CRUT providing for unitrust payments for one measuring life (see Rev. Proc. 2005–56, 2005–34 I.R.B. 383);

6. A testamentary CRUT providing for unitrust payments for a term of years (see Rev. Proc. 2005–57, 2005–34 I.R.B. 392);

7. A testamentary CRUT providing for unitrust payments payable consecutively for two measuring lives (see Rev. Proc. 2005–58, 2005–34 I.R.B. 402); and

8. A testamentary CRUT providing for unitrust payments payable concurrently and consecutively for two measuring lives (see Rev. Proc. 2005–59, 2005–34 I.R.B. 412).

The revenue procedures provide that if a trust "substantially similar" to one of the sample forms of trust is established, the trust will be recognized as meeting the requirements of § 664(d) as a charitable remainder trust. Ordinarily, private rulings on the qualification of a charitable remainder trust or whether transfers to such a trust qualify for a charitable deduction under §§ 170, 2055, and 2522 are not issued. Rev. Proc. 90–33, 1990–1 C.B. 551. However, in the case of trusts which do not include the IRS suggested provisions, the IRS says, Rev. Proc. 2003–60, 2003–2 C.B. 274, that it "generally will issue letter rulings on the effect of substantive trust provisions."

[¶ 26,133]

5. ANNUITY TRUST ILLUSTRATED

Consider the case of the donor who transferred, to a qualified annuity trust, cash in the amount of $50,000. The donor reserved for life an annuity of $3,000, payable at year-end. The remainder is to be paid to a charitable organization at the donor's death. The donor's contribution base (as determined for income tax purposes, see ¶ 25,201) is sufficient to allow the utilization of the full amount of the deduction in the year of contribution. Using the prescribed annuity factors for a donor aged 60, the tax results to the donor are shown in Table 26.2.

Table 26.2 Tax Benefits of Annuity Trust

Assume the donor is 60 and the annuity factor to be 11.2273 (using highest rate based on month of transfer and two preceding months). Reg. § 20.2031–7(d)(2)(iv)(B), Example, and (6), Table S (5.6%). *Note:* All income tax calculations assume a 30 percent flat rate.

	Type of Return		
	Joint	*Joint*	*Unmarried*
Taxable income before contribution	$50,000	$100,000	$100,000
Cash transferred to trust.	$50,000	$50,000	$50,000
Less present value of $3,000 annual annuity ($3,000 x 11.2273).	33,682	33,682	33,682
Amount of contribution	$16,318	$16,318	$16,318
Tax on income before contribution	$15,000	$30,000	$30,000
Tax on income after contribution	10,105	25,105	25,105
Reduction in tax due to contribution	$4,895	$4,895	$4,895

[¶ 26,141]

6. UNITRUST ILLUSTRATED

Table 26.3, in conjunction with Table 26.4, illustrates the tax benefits derived from a unitrust arrangement. It is assumed that the donor transfers to a qualified charitable organization, by means of a unitrust, cash in the amount of $50,000. Under the terms of the trust instrument, the assets are to be valued annually on the anniversary date of the transfer, at which time the donor must be paid 6 percent of the fair market value of the assets. The payments are to continue for the donor's lifetime; at the donor's death the remainder will be paid to a charitable organization. The donor's contribution base is sufficient to allow the utilization of the full amount of the deduction in the year of contribution.

Table 26.3 Tax Benefits of Unitrust Arrangement

Assume the donor is 60 and the remainder interest factor, using a rate of 5.6% (using highest rate based on month of transfer and months preceding the transfer), is .35375. Reg. § 1.664–4(d) and (e)(5) and (6) (Table U(1)) (5.6%). However, this factor of .35375 must be adjusted for frequency of payment and the time elapsed between the valuation and the first payout. This adjustment is reflected in the computation shown in Table 26.3. *Note:* All income tax calculations assume a 30 percent flat rate.

	Type of Return		
	Joint	*Joint*	*Unmarried*
Taxable income before contribution	$50,000	$100,000	$100,000
Cash transferred to trust.	$50,000	$50,000	$50,000
Remainder interest factor	0.34918	0.34918	0.34918
Amount of contribution	$17,458	$17,458	$17,458
Tax on income before contribution	$15,000	$30,000	$30,000
Tax on income after contribution	9,763	24,763	24,763
Reduction in tax due to contribution	$5,237	$5,237	$5,237

Table 26.4   REMAINDER INTEREST COMPUTATION FOR ONE-LIFE CHARITABLE REMAINDER UNITRUST

1.	Specified payout rate	6.00%
2.	Adjustment factor (Table F)	0.94697
3.	Adjusted payout rate (Line 1 x Line 2)	5.6818%
4.	Nearest usable percentage rate less than Line 3	5.6%
5.	Difference (Line 3 − Line 4)	0.0818
6.	Line 5 ÷ by 0.2	0.409
7.	Factor for age 60 at Line 4 rate (Table U(1))	0.35375
8.	Factor for age 60 at next higher rate (Table U(1))	0.34257
9.	Difference (Line 7 − Line 8)	0.0118
10.	Line 9 x Line 6	0.00457
11.	Interpolated factor (Line 7 − Line 10)	0.34918
12.	Amount transferred to trust $50,000	$50,000
13.	Present value of remainder interest (Line 11 x Line 12)	$17,459

[¶ 26,149]

7.   POOLED INCOME FUND

The principal difference between a pooled income fund and a charitable remainder unitrust or annuity trust is that the donor or other beneficiary of a pooled income fund is entitled only to the income actually earned by the fund, rather than to a fixed amount or fixed percentage of its value. A pooled income fund can be described in these terms (§ 642(c)(5)):

1. Multiple unrelated donors will transfer assets (either cash or other property) to the trust, each contributing a remainder interest in the assets he or she transfers to the charitable beneficiary for which the pooled income fund is operated.

2. The income interest in the gifted assets is reserved for the life of one or more persons, all of whom must have been born by the date of the transfer (e.g., unborn children would not qualify).

3. The assets transferred by the various donors are commingled.

4. The fund cannot invest in tax-exempt securities or state or municipal bonds.

5. The fund can hold only assets derived from contributions from donors pursuant to the provisions of the pooled income fund.

6. No donor or beneficiary may be a trustee of the fund.

7. Each beneficiary receives income from year to year based on the rate of return of the fund, i.e., each beneficiary receives income at the same rate.

The Internal Revenue Service has issued sample forms of a declaration of trust and instruments of transfer for a pooled income fund. Remainder interests in trusts that substantially comply with the sample form ordinarily will qualify for a charitable deduction under §§ 170, 2055, and 2522. Rev. Proc. 88–53, 1988–2 C.B. 712. Rulings as to whether a pooled income fund qualifies under § 642(c)(5) or whether a transfer to such a fund qualifies for the charitable deduction ordinarily are not issued. Rev. Proc. 88–54, 1988–2 C.B. 715.

A transfer by a donor to a pooled income fund will qualify as a charitable contribution in an amount equal to the present value of the contributions's remainder interest on the date of the gift. Reg. § 1.642(c)–6(a)(1). See Robert J. Rosepink, Charitable Remainder Trusts and Pooled Income Funds, 865 Tax Mgmt. (BNA) A–97 (2000), for a discussion of the calculation of the value of a charitable remainder interest in property contributed to a pooled income fund.

> *Example.* Richard, age 74, transfers property worth $100,000 to a pooled income fund. The share of the income of the fund attributable to his gift is to be paid to Richard for life and upon his death to Richard's wife Rhonda, age 68, for life. In the first year the fund earns a 6.2 percent return on its investments. Richard receives income of $6,200 (6.2 percent of $100,000). If in the next year the fund earns a 5 1/2 percent return on its investments, Richard receives income of $5,500 that year. The amount of the federal income tax charitable deduction available to Richard for his gift is based on the highest annual rate of return earned by the fund for any one of the three taxable years preceding the taxable year of the gift. Although actual experience will differ depending upon market and other conditions, if Richard were age 60 his charitable deduction should be approximately the same deduction as would be available with a charitable remainder annuity trust which provided for annual payments to him of $6,000 (6 percent of his gift), or from a charitable remainder unitrust which provided for annual payments to him of $6,000.

Note: Pooled income funds are allowed to assume a 6 percent earnings history for funds in existence for less than three years in computing the charitable deduction for gifts to the fund, regardless of the actual earnings history for those years. See § 642(c).

Problems

[¶ 26,150]

1. How do the tax economics of a pooled income fund compare with those of a charitable remainder unitrust or an annuity trust? For comparison purposes, assume the unitrust and annuity trust provide for a 6 percent payout.

2. What factors would a donor consider in choosing between a pooled income fund and establishing his own charitable remainder annuity trust or unitrust?

¶ 26,150

D. CHARITABLE GIFT ANNUITIES

[¶ 26,151]

1. INTRODUCTION

A charitable gift annuity involves a transfer of either property or money to a charity in exchange for the latter's promise to pay the donor or another noncharitable beneficiary a fixed amount per year for one or more lives. The payments may either begin immediately or be deferred until the annuitant reaches a certain age, in which case the gift is referred to as a deferred payment annuity.

A donor may transfer cash to a charity in exchange for its promise to pay a fixed annual amount of annuity, beginning immediately, for the annuitant's life (in which case it is called a single life gift). The amount of the charitable contribution deduction for this type of transfer depends upon what is considered to be the donor's investment in the contract. The latter is roughly equivalent to the cost of purchasing an annuity of this nature from an insurance company and can be computed under appropriate tables. Reg. § 1.170A–1(d)(2), referring to Reg. § 1.101–2(e)(1)(iii)(b)(2). The total cash contributed less the investment in the contract as so computed will equal the value of the gift qualifying for the charitable deduction. Reg. § 1.170A–1(d)(1).

[¶ 26,159]

2. INCOME TAX CONSEQUENCES

The normal rules for taxation of annuities govern the income tax consequences to the annuitant as payments are made. § 72(a); Reg. § 1.1011–2(c), Example (8). The annuitant may exclude from gross income a part of each annuity payment determined by an exclusion ratio. The exclusion ratio equals the investment in the contract divided by the expected return from the annuity. § 72(b). The "investment in the contract" is the present value of the right of the annuitant to receive the annuity, and the "expected return" is essentially an amount equal to the annual annuity payment times the life expectancy of the annuitant, that is, the total amount that the annuitant can expect to receive under the contract. See Reg. §§ 1.1011–2(c), Example (8), 1.72–9. This exclusion ratio permits the annuitant or the annuitant's designated beneficiary to recover the annuitant's investment in the annuity contract tax free as a return of capital. Only the portion of each payment exceeding a ratable share of this capital return will be included in the annuitant's gross income.

The donor is allowed a current income tax charitable contribution deduction for a deferred payment annuity. The value of the annuity is determined under § 7520. The charitable deduction equals the fair market value of the property transferred less the present cost of the annuity to be received, computed under the applicable tables and formulas. See Reg. §§ 20.2031–7(d)(6), 25.2512–5. The use of the deferred payment annuity allows the donor, who might be in a high income bracket, to obtain a current charitable deduction while deferring the receipt of the income from the annuity until a later year, when he expects his income to be taxed at a lower rate. The amount of each annuity payment includible in the recipient's gross income is determined by application of the principles which apply to a currently payable annuity.

[¶ 26,167]

3. APPRECIATED PROPERTY

When appreciated property is transferred to a charity in exchange for an annuity, the donor will realize taxable gain under the § 1011(b) bargain sales rules. See ¶ 27,351 for additional discussion. The gain generally is recognized over the expected period of the annuity until the total gain has been recognized. Reg. § 1.1011–2(a)(4) and (c), Example (8). The term "bargain sale" is defined as a transfer of property which is in part a sale or exchange of the property and in part a charitable contribution of the property. Reg. § 1.170A–4(c)(2)(ii). The amount of the charitable deduction is the fair market value of the property less the present value of the annuity. Reg. §§ 1.170A–1(d)(1), 1.1011–2(c), Example (8). The donor's basis of the transferred property must be allocated proportionately between the portion of the transfer constituting a sale of the property for the annuity and the portion which constitutes the deductible gift to charity. Reg. §§ 1.170A–4(c)(2)(i), 1.1011–2(b).

[¶ 26,175]

4. ILLUSTRATIONS

Consider Ezra, born on February 1, 1942, active in his church, but of limited resources. In response to a proposal from church fund-raisers Ezra gave the church $18,750 on February 1, 2001, when he was 60 years old. In return, the church promised to pay Ezra $1,200 annually on a quarterly basis for the rest of his life, beginning March 1, representing a standard payout rate of 6.4%. In addition, Ezra received an income tax deduction of $4,997 that year based on a 5.6 percent interest rate. See Reg. § 20.2031–7(d)(2)(iv)(B), Example, and (6), Table S [((1.00 − .37127) ÷ .056) x 1.0208 adjustment factor]. Ezra's income tax savings in 2001 would have been $1,499, based on a 30 percent marginal income tax rate.

Looking at the transaction from the standpoint of the church, Ezra would be deemed to have made a gift to the church equal to the amount by which his payment to the church ($18,750) exceeded the cost of the annuity, determined actuarially ($13,753).

For purposes of determining the actuarial and gift values of the annuity, the church uses the tables provided by the Internal Revenue Service in Reg. § 20.2031–7(d)(6). The annuity rate was determined by reference to tables provided as of July 2001, by the American Council on Gift Annuities (ACGA) (http://www.acga-web.org/giftrates.html), an unofficial organization of charitable institutions that have come together to provide unisex single-life and gender-based two-life "uniform gift annuity rates." (The rates are revised periodically, commonly on an annual basis.) Continuing with the illustration, for a person age 60, the annuity rate under the July 2001 table was 6.4 percent under the ACGA's tables. Thus, as a result of Ezra's deposit of $18,750 with the church, the church's total payments annually would equal $1,200 ($18,750 x 6.4%). (If Ezra had said, in 2001, that he wanted an annuity of $1,200 annually and wanted to know the purchase price of the annuity, the church would have simply divided $1,200 by the 6.4 percent annuity rate suggested by the Committee's table to determine the amount Ezra had to pay the church.)

Having determined the cost of the annuity, the next inquiry relates to the income tax consequences to Ezra as he receives each annuity payment. Because Ezra paid for the annuity, a portion of each annuity payment is a tax-free return of capital. The amount of each payment that is tax free is determined by the exclusion ratio. The exclusion ratio is a fraction, the numerator of which is the cost of the annuity ($13,753) and the denominator of which is the return Ezra expects from the annuity. The expected return is based currently on Ezra's age. Using a factor of 24.2 (taken from the life expectancy table appearing in Reg. § 1.72–9, Table V), because the $1,200 is to be paid to Ezra quarterly, the total expected return is $28,920. This fraction produces an exclusion ratio of 47.6 percent. That is, 47.6 percent of each payment received by Ezra will be free of income tax. The balance will constitute taxable income to him in the year of receipt.

The tax benefits of Ezra's gift annuity are illustrated in Table 26.5; the gift annuity federal income tax calculation appears in Table 26.6.

Table 26.5 Tax Benefits of Gift Annuity Plan

If the donor is age 60, the net cost of the annuity can be illustrated as shown in this table. The computation is illustrated in Table 26.5. All income tax calculations are based on a flat 30% rate.

		Type of Return	
	Joint	Joint	Unmarried
Taxable income before contribution	$60,000	$120,000	$120,000
Cash transferred to charity	$18,750	$18,750	$18,750
Value of annuity	$13,753	$13,753	$13,753
Amount of contribution	$4,997	$4,997	$4,997
Tax on income before contribution	$18,000	$36,000	$36,000
Tax on income after contribution	16,501	34,501	34,501
Reduction in tax due to contribution	$1,499	$1,499	$1,499
Net cost of annuity to donor	$17,251	$17,251	$17,251

Table 26.6 Gift Annuity Federal Income Tax Calculation

1.	Amount contributed	$18,750
2.	Annuity rate (payout rate recommended by Committee on Gift Annuities)	6.4%
3.	Annual annuity (line 1 x line 2)	$1,200
4.	Value of $1.00 at 6.4% (Reg. § 20.2031–7(d)(2)(iv)(B)), Example, and (6), Table S (1.00-(34745 ÷ .64))	11.46080
5.	Actuarial value (line 3 x line 4)	$13,753
6.	Gift value (line 1 − line 5)	$4,997

7.   Unadjusted expected return multiple (Reg. § 1/72(9), Table V) 24.2%
8.   Adjustment if not monthly . . . .   −0.1
9.   Expected return per $1.00 annual annuity (7 adjusted by 8) 24.1
10. Expected return (line 3 x line 9) $28,920
11. Exclusion ration (line 5 ÷ line 10) 48%
12. Exclusion (line 3 x line 11) $571
13. Taxable income annually (line 3 − line 12) $629

E.   GIFT ANNUITY v. CHARITABLE REMAINDER TRUST

[¶ 26,201]

1.   RECOGNITION OF GAIN

A donor retaining an annuity interest in property is going to be treated differently if he or she uses a gift annuity as distinct from a charitable remainder annuity trust. If the gift annuity is used, the donor will have to recognize gain over his or her life expectancy when appreciated property is transferred. On the other hand, no gain is normally recognized on such a transfer to a charitable remainder annuity trust. § 170(f)(2)(B); Reg. § 1.170A–6(c).

[¶ 26,209]

2.   INCOME TAX CONSEQUENCES

The income tax treatment of the annuity recipient is also markedly different from that of an income beneficiary of a charitable remainder annuity trust. A gift annuity is taxed as if it were an ordinary commercial annuity; thus, the annuitant is considered to recover the cost of the annuity as a tax-free portion of each annually received annuity payment. § 72(a) and regulations thereunder; Reg. § 1.1011–2(c), Example (8). By contrast, the income beneficiary of a charitable remainder annuity trust is taxable on the receipt of annuity payments under special statutory rules which apply to such trusts. § 664(b); Reg. § 1.664–1(d)(1)(i).

Computation of the charitable deductions for these two types of gifts is also different. In the case of a charitable remainder annuity trust, a charitable deduction is allowed for the value of the charitable remainder interest. §§ 170(f)(3)(B), 2055(e)(2). The amount of a charitable deduction for a gift annuity is the amount by which the amount paid for the annuity (the fair market value of transferred assets) exceeds the value of the annuity contract. Reg. § 1.170A–1(d)(1).

However, the relative advantages and disadvantages of the two types of gifts may only be determined by reference to actual factual circumstances. For example, because of the method of taxing gift annuity payments, gift annuities are often preferable to an annuity trust, particularly when cash is donated. On the other hand, where an annuity trust is invested to produce tax-free income, it will be superior. (Both examples assume equivalent payout percentages.)

¶ 26,209

F. CHARITABLE LEAD TRUSTS

[¶ 26,251]

1. INTRODUCTION

A charitably inclined individual or a wealthy person who wishes to save taxes by benefiting both a charitable organization and one or more individuals who do not currently need the benefits may consider using a charitable lead trust. A charitable lead trust provides a lead income interest to a qualifying charitable organization for a fixed term. A charitable lead trust is a taxable entity, but the trust receives an income tax deduction for payments made to the charitable organization. The lead income interest must be established either as a guaranteed annuity or a fixed percentage, distributed yearly, of the fair market value of the trust property (as determined annually) in order to qualify for an income tax deduction for the amounts paid to the charity. See §§ 170(f)(2)(B), 2055(e)(2)(B), 2522(c)(2)(B). At the end of the term, the property either can be distributed outright to noncharitable beneficiaries or continued in trust for their benefit.

The arrangement is the converse of a charitable remainder trust, previously described, in that the annuity interest is charitable and the remainder noncharitable. Charitable remainder trusts are ordinarily more beneficial where the donor desires the noncharitable beneficiary to have an immediate income interest in the property, but the charitable lead trust can provide major tax savings if the private beneficiaries can forego income during the term of years the charity will be the beneficiary.

[¶ 26,259]

2. ESTATE AND GIFT TAX CONSEQUENCES

The donor of a charitable lead trust (or the decedent at whose death the trust is funded or created) receives an estate or gift tax deduction for the present value of the annuity interest. §§ 2055(e)(2)(B), 2522(c)(2)(B). See ¶ 26,051.

Example 1. Fanny is a widow with a gross estate of about $10 million. If Fanny dies this year, leaving the entire estate outright to her children, who are already well established, the estate taxes on Fanny's estate will be $5 million (assuming a flat 50 percent tax rate). As an alternative, suppose Fanny created a testamentary charitable lead trust to last for 12 years. Suppose, too, that the interest rate applicable on the valuation date was 8.2 percent and that a $1,340,554 annuity is to be paid annually to the university Fanny attended. After the 12–year term, the trust is to end and all remaining assets are to be paid to Fanny's three children, or their issue, in equal shares. Using the tables given in Reg. § 20.2031–7(d)(6), Table B (8.2%), Fanny's estate would receive a $10 million estate tax deduction for the value of the charitable lead interest. If the trust could invest Fanny's assets in high-grade corporate bonds, or other investments, yielding 13.41 percent, after the 12–year term, Fanny's children and their issue would receive at least the entire $10 million almost free of estate taxes. Of course, if the investment performance of the trust produces a yield of less than 13.41 percent, part of the $10 million corpus will have to be paid to the university and will not be available to be returned to Fanny's children at the end of the 12–year term.

Example 2. Suppose Fanny decides that she really likes the charitable lead trust idea, but her children need some property at her death. Fanny can set up a $5 million charitable lead trust paying a $670,367 annuity for 12 years to the university and avoid taxes on $5 million. The taxes on the rest of Fanny's estate will be $2.5 million if Fanny dies this year, leaving $2.5 million available to the children immediately after her death.

[¶ 26,267]

3. INCOME TAX CONSEQUENCES

The income tax consequences that result from the establishment of a charitable lead trust are, to a certain extent, under the control of the donor because the availability of income tax deductions to the donor depend on the trust's classification as a grantor or nongrantor lead trust. See § 170(f)(2)(B).

If the trust is so structured that the donor is treated as an owner of the income interest under the grantor trust rules set out in §§ 671 through 677, the grantor is entitled to an income tax deduction *in the year in which property is placed in the trust* for the full amount of the actuarial value of the charitable income interest in the trust property. See § 170(f)(2)(B); Reg. § 1.170A–6(c). All of the trust income is taxable to the grantor in the year earned by the trust, even though that income is paid to the charity by the trust. Thus, the grantor is taxed on income that he or she does not receive. In effect, the charitable deduction is "recaptured." It is the opportunity to claim the immediate income tax deduction—notwithstanding the onerous income tax consequences in later years—that makes charitable lead trusts particularly appealing to taxpayers who find themselves with particularly high income in a single year.

If the charitable lead trust is structured as a nongrantor lead trust so as to escape the reach of the grantor trust rules, the trust's income will not be included in the gross income of the grantor. Instead, the trust's income will be taxed to the charitable lead trust and the trust will be entitled to a deduction for the value of the payments made each year to the charity. § 642(c)(1).

Note: For a discussion of the grantor trust rules, see Chapter 22.

There are several advantages to structuring the charitable lead trust so as to escape the grantor trust rules. The obvious advantage is that, while the donor does not receive any income tax deduction for the value of the payments to the charity by the charitable lead trust, neither does the donor have to report the trust's income on his or her personal income tax return in the year in which it is earned by the trust. There also is another not-so-obvious advantage. If the trust is structured as a nonqualifying charitable lead trust, so that the grantor trust rules do not apply, the trust will not be subject to the private foundation rules. § 4947(a)(2). If the grantor trust rules apply, the income tax deduction in the year of the transfer to the trust is subject to the 20 or 30 percent ceiling on charitable contributions applicable to contributions to private foundations. See § 170(b)(1)(B) and (D) and the discussion at ¶ 25,225 and 25,301. The deduction is limited to a maximum of 20 percent of the donor's contribution base, that is, adjusted gross income without reduction for any net operating loss carryback, for gifts of long-term capital gain property, and the lesser of 30 percent of the donor's adjusted gross income, or the amount by which 50 percent of the donor's adjusted gross income exceeds the amount of charitable contributions allowable as deductions to organizations that are eligible recipients for gifts of cash. § 170(b)(1)(D) and (B); Reg. § 1.170A–8. A five-year carryover of unused deductions is allowed in both cases. § 170(b)(1)(B) and (D)(ii); Priv. Ltr. Rul. 8824039 (gift to a lead trust payable to a private foundation is not eligible for carryforward).

[¶ 26,275]

4. GENERATION–SKIPPING TRANSFER TAX CONSEQUENCES

Transfers to charity can have implications for purposes of the generation-skipping tax. (See Chapter 9 for materials on the generation-skipping tax.) At this juncture, suffice it to note that because the termination of a charitable lead trust to "skip" persons is a taxable termination for generation-skipping purposes (§ 2612), a gift to a charitable lead annuity trust may have generation-skipping tax consequences.

As a quick summary, note that a generation-skipping transfer occurs when income or corpus is transferred to a beneficiary who is assigned to a generation at least two generations below the transferor's generation (i.e., a "skip person"). The amount of a transfer subject to the generation-skipping transfer tax is computed by calculating the "applicable fraction," which represents the exempt amount of a generation-skipping transfer, and multiplying the fraction by the "inclusion ratio," which is the excess of one over the "applicable fraction." See § 2642(a)(1) and (2). For additional discussion, see ¶¶ 9309, 9381–9427.

Under § 2642(e), the numerator of the applicable fraction for a charitable lead annuity trust is the "adjusted generation-skipping transfer tax exemption," defined as an amount equal to the allocated portion of the generation-skipping transfer tax exemption multiplied by the interest rate used for valuing the charitable interest, compounded annually for the term of the charitable interest. The denominator of the applicable fraction is the value of the trust property *immediately after* the termination of the charitable interest.

> *Example.* In 2003, Orville transferred $1,600,000 to a charitable annuity lead trust terminating in favor of his grandchildren. The value of the charitable lead was $600,000 and Orville allocated all of his $1,000,000 GST exemption to the trust. Under prior law, the numerator of the applicable fraction was $1,000,000, and the denominator of the applicable fraction was $1,000,000 ($1,600,000, the value of the property transferred to the trust, less $600,000, the value of the charitable lead). This meant that any generation-skipping transfer from the trust would be exempt from generation-skipping transfer tax.

¶ 26,267

However, under § 2642(e), the grantor's GST exemption would have been increased above $1,000,000 prevailing in 2003, depending on the interest rate and term of the trust. If, for example, application of these factors increased the grantor's GST exemption to $1,700,000, and the value of the trust property on termination of the trust would be $1,800,000, on termination of the trust, the applicable fraction would be $1,700,000/ $1,800,000, or 17/18, the adjusted GST exemption over the value of the property on termination of the trust. § 2642(e)(1). The inclusion ratio would equal 1/18 (1 − 17/18 = 1/18). If, however, the value of the property on termination of the trust was $1,700,000 (that is, the trust assets performed exactly as the Treasury tables indicated they would), the inclusion ratio would be zero.

A grantor therefore may allocate his or her GST exemption against the present value of the remainder interest in a lead unitrust, but § 2642(e) requires allocation of any GST exemption in a special way for a lead annuity trust. Because the GST exemption allocated to the trust is adjusted at the interest rate applicable at the time of the gift, the exemption may be too much or too little at time of termination, depending upon the performance of the trust.

[¶ 26,283]

5. FORM OF THE GIFT

For a gift of a charitable lead trust to qualify for the estate or gift tax deduction and for the lump-sum charitable income tax deduction, the charity's interest must be in the form of a unitrust interest or an annual guaranteed annuity. Reg. §§ 1.170A–6(c)(2)(i) and (ii), 25.2522(c)–3(c)(2)(vi) and (vii), 20.2055–2(e)(2)(vi) and (vii). Although there is no minimum annuity or unitrust percentage requirement for the annual payments made to the charity (§ 170(f)(2)(B)), the amount of the annuity may not vary from year to year. Reg. § 1.170A–6(c)(2)(i)(A). The remainder interest either passes to designated private beneficiaries or reverts to the donor at the end of the trust's term.

[¶ 26,291]

6. USE OF CHARITABLE LEAD TRUSTS

A charitable lead trust is particularly useful to a donor who desires to reduce gift taxes (at death, estate taxes) which might otherwise be imposed on transfers of property to members of his family.

Example. Golda, a widow, age 60, wanted to fund payments to a charity for a 10–year period and also to transfer substantial property to her daughter thereafter. Golda's adjusted gross income is $75,000 a year, and it is expected to continue at that rate. Golda transferred $500,000 worth of property to an annuity trust with a provision to pay the charity $30,000 each year for 10 years, at the end of which time the property is to be distributed free of the trust to Golda's daughter.

For federal gift tax purposes, using the June 2000 tables, Golda treats the gift as being approximately 45 percent to charity (valued at $225,000 ($30,000 x 7.50)) and the balance to her daughter. Reg. § 20.2031–7(d)(6), Table B (5.6%). The gift to charity does not generate gift tax because it is in the form of an annuity trust. If Golda has made no other taxable gifts, the federal gift tax on the remainder interest given to the daughter (valued at $275,000) would be zero since it is within the exemption amount available to Golda. § 2505. If a growth rate of a constant 15 percent (compounded annually) is assumed for 10 years, the $500,000 which has been placed in trust will pass to the daughter at a value of $1,413,667 without additional gift tax. By way of contrast, if the transfer to the daughter were deferred for 10 years, assuming the same compounded rate of growth of 15 percent annually, the transfer tax would be $172,877 ($518,677 tax minus $345,800 exemption amount).

For federal income tax purposes, Golda will exclude all of the trust's income from her own income, even though it exceeds her 50 percent maximum income tax charitable deduction of $37,500 per year for gifts to public charities. See ¶ 25,201 for discussion of percentage limitations. In fact, Golda's annual deduction limit is fully available for other charitable gifts.

G. CHARITABLE INCOME TRUSTS

[¶ 26,301]

1. INTRODUCTION

A variation on the charitable lead trust is the charitable income trust in which the grantor retains a reversionary interest rather than giving away the remainder interest. As the trust assets remain in the grantor's gross estate under § 2037, and as no other noncharitable beneficiary receives an interest, it is obvious that the focus of these trusts is income tax planning instead of estate and gift tax planning.

There are two types of charitable income trusts: the grantor charitable income trust and the nongrantor charitable income trust. The grantor charitable income trust provides an accelerated income tax deduction, while the nongrantor charitable income trust converts the deduction into an exclusion.

[¶ 26,309]

2. GRANTOR CHARITABLE INCOME TRUST

The grantor charitable income trust is a trust which both complies with the requirements of § 170(f)(2)(B) (an annuity or unitrust interest, and complex rules to prevent diversion of the charitable interest away from the charity) and breaches the grantor trust rules of §§ 671–679. The trust is similar to a grantor retained income trust (GRIT), except that, unlike a GRIT, the grantor gives up enjoyment of the income. (For discussion of GRITs, see Chapter 12.) The grantor receives an income tax deduction in the year the trust is created for the entire value of the charitable income interest which, if the grantor is in a particularly high tax bracket that year, may be useful.

The drawback with the grantor charitable income trust is that the grantor remains taxable as the owner of the trust under the grantor trust rules. Thus, while all deductions are exhausted in the first year the trust is created, or within the five-year carryover period, the grantor continues to have taxable income from the trust in the following years—even though the grantor receives none of the trust's cash distributions, these cash distributions being paid to the charity. This problem may be ameliorated by having the trust invest in tax-exempt municipal bonds.

[¶ 26,317]

3. NONGRANTOR CHARITABLE INCOME TRUST

The other type of charitable income trust is the nongrantor trust, which can be described as one in which the grantor retains a reversionary interest and the charitable income interest is not a qualifying annuity or unitrust interest. Because this type of trust is not a grantor trust, income earned by the trust is not taxable to the grantor. Accordingly, the grantor receives no income tax charitable deduction at the creation of the trust. However, the charitable income trust is taxed as a complex trust and is allowed a charitable income tax deduction under § 642(c) for amounts paid to a qualified charity in the year in which paid. Because § 642(c) does not limit the charitable income tax deduction to a percentage of income, the purpose of this type of trust is to avoid the percentage limitations on charitable gifts by removing the base income being given away from the grantor's tax computation. Thus, it converts a limited charitable deduction into an unlimited charitable exclusion. Such trusts tend most often to be established by corporations, which are subject to a strict limitation of 10 percent of taxable income on their charitable gifts. § 172(b)(2).

Chapter 27

SELECTING PROPERTY FOR CHARITABLE GIFTS

A. OUTRIGHT GIFTS

[¶ 27,001]

A donor who makes outright charitable gifts saves income taxes by obtaining a charitable deduction for the year of the gift. The donation is exempt from gift taxes. Estate taxes are saved because the gifted property will not be included in the donor's gross estate.

This chapter considers the rules that apply to gifts of different kinds of property.

B. RECORD KEEPING REQUIREMENTS

[¶ 27,025]

For contributions of cash in any amount, the donor must maintain a cancelled check, bank record, or receipt from the donee showing the name of the donee organization, the date of the contribution, and the amount of the contribution. (A deduction cannot be taken for cash claimed to have been placed in the church plate. See ¶ 27,051.) In the case of non cash contributions, a written acknowledgment must be obtained from the charity for all donations of $250 or more. § 170(f)(8). (As to gifts of used clothing and household goods, see ¶ 27,075. No income tax charitable deduction is allowed without a written acknowledgment. The acknowledgment must be obtained by the due date for filing the income tax return on which the deduction is claimed. The charity must: (1) describe the property received, and (2) indicate whether the it provided any goods or services to the donor and provide a good faith estimate of the value of those goods or services.

C. GIFTS OF CASH

[¶ 27,051]

Charitable gifts in the form of cash or checks are the usual and most convenient way small contributions are made. However, they provide the donor with the least tax saving, although they are the most convenient kinds of gifts when time is of the essence in making the gift. A contribution of cash, check, or other monetary gift is disallowed as a tax deduction unless the donor maintains as a record of the contribution a bank record, or a written communication from the donee showing the name of the donee organization, the date of the contribution, and the amount of the contribution. (The days of cash-in-the-collection plate being allowed as an income tax deduction ended beginning with the 2007 tax year.) Unlike gift checks to noncharitable donees, checks issued in good faith to charitable donees that remain outstanding at the death of the donee are not included in the donee's estate for estate tax purposes. Compare Estate of Belcher v. Commissioner, 83 T.C. 227 (1984), with McCarthy v. United States, 806 F.2d 129 (7th Cir.1986).

Cash gifts, however, do not provide the avoidance of tax on long-term capital gain which can be obtained from gifts of appreciated long-term capital gains property. Rev. Rul. 55–138, 1955–1 C.B. 223, modified by Rev. Rul. 68–69, 1968–1 C.B. 80; Rev. Rul. 55–275, 1955–1 C.B. 295; Rev. Rul. 55–531, 1955–2 C.B. 520; White v. Brodrick, 104 F.Supp. 213 (D.Kan.1952); Campbell v. Prothro, 209 F.2d 331 (5th Cir.1954).

> *Comment:* A gift of appreciated property to satisfy a charitable pledge will not give rise to taxable gain, since the transfer is not both a contribution and the satisfaction of a debt. Rev. Rul. 55–410, 1955–1 C.B. 297.

However, a gift of cash is more desirable than one of any asset in which the donor has a loss. A sale of the property in which the donor has a loss with a subsequent donation of the proceeds in cash is better than a donation of the loss property, because this results in prescribing the donor's ability to use the capital loss, which loss would not be recognized under gift circumstances. Id. (The same is true of ordinary loss property.)

D. USED CLOTHING AND HOUSEHOLD ITEMS

[¶ 27,075]

No deduction is allowed for contributions of clothing and household items that are not in good used condition or better. Deductions may be denied for items of minimal value such as used undergarments. However, used clothing and household items not in good used condition or better may be deducted if such items each have a value of more than $500 and the taxpayer includes with his or her tax return a qualified appraisal with respect to the property.

E. APPRECIATED CAPITAL ASSETS

[¶ 27,101]

1. PERCENTAGE LIMITATIONS

The income tax deduction for a contribution of an appreciated capital asset to a public charity is limited to thirty percent of the donor's contribution base for the taxable year of the gift and each of his next five taxable years.

§ 170(b)(1)(C). But if the donor elects to reduce the value of his contribution by 100 percent of the amount of his long-term capital gain, then the usual 50 percent ceiling applies, provided the gift is to a public charity. § 170(b)(1)(C)(iii). If a contribution is made to a private foundation (other than a private foundation that qualifies as a 50 percent-type organization, discussed at ¶ 25,381), then only the amount of the donor's adjusted basis in the property will be deductible. § 170(e)(1)(B)(ii). This limits the income tax deduction to the donor's cost. Section 170(e)(5) provides an exception to this rule for gifts of "qualified appreciated stock," i.e., corporate stock for which, on the date of contribution, market quotations on an established securities market are readily available and which is "capital gain property" as defined in § 170(b)(1)(C)(iv). Such gifts qualify for a full fair market value deduction. However, this provision will not apply to donations by a donor to the extent that all contributions of that stock by a donor to all private nonoperating foundations cumulatively exceed 10 percent of all stock outstanding in the corporation.

> *Example.* Suppose Zephyr transfers closely held stock with an adjusted basis of $100 per share to her private foundation after she has held it for more than a year and it is worth $350 per share. Assume it to be the policy of her foundation to accumulate contributions to make a lump-sum gift to a public charity in a subsequent year so that it therefore does not qualify as a distributing foundation. The deduction is limited to $100 per share because the transfer was to a private foundation; therefore, the appreciation in the stock is not deductible. Zephyr is limited to the deduction of the value of her basis in the stock.

[¶ 27,109]

2. INTANGIBLES

a. *Capital Assets*

Stocks, bonds, and other intangible assets are generally considered capital assets in the hands of the owner (except in the case of securities held as inventory by a dealer). § 1221. If these are held over a year, gain on their sale will be long term. § 1222. The income tax deduction for a contribution of long-term capital gain property is the fair market value of the property at the time of the gift. Reg. § 1.170A–1(c)(1). There is no tax on the appreciation, even if the property is contributed to satisfy a pledge. Rev. Rul. 55–410, 1955–1 C.B. 297.

[¶ 27,117]

b. *Closely Held Stock*

Where a donor is unable to dispose of stock owned immediately (because of SEC Rule 144 prohibitions or because the shares are of a closely held corporation without a defined market), a donation (at a present value discount basis of 15 percent) is equivalent to a sale at double the value of the stock in five years. Even where the securities may be readily sold, the difference between the charitable gift and the net amount realized on a sale of substantially appreciated shares after the payment of commissions, fees, and capital gains tax (even disregarding the present value of the tax savings) may be an insignificant consideration.

Problem

[¶ 27,123]

Several years ago, Feng, a 30 percent taxpayer, acquired, without cost, shares in a company which now offers to redeem the shares for $10,000. What will be the after-tax value of the redemption payment? If Feng donates the shares to a public charity which tenders the shares for redemption, what will be his after-tax savings? What is the net cost to Feng of the gift?

[¶ 27,125]

c. Deduction Limited to Adjusted Basis

The income tax deduction for the gift of appreciated securities or other property held for a year or less is limited to its adjusted basis. This is also true for donations of other assets which, if sold at their fair market value on the date of their contribution, would give rise to ordinary income (such as inventory, stock in trade and depreciable property used in a trade or business, to the extent that any depreciation already deducted on that property would be recaptured upon its sale). The income tax deduction is also limited to cost basis for the donor's own art works, literary and musical compositions, letters and memoranda prepared by or for the donor. See § 170(e)(1)(A).

[¶ 27,133]

d. Value of Donated Securities

The value of a charitable gift of securities will be the mean of the high and low prices of the stock on the date of gift (Reg. § 25.2512–2(b)), not the price for which the stock may be sold by the charity nor its value (based on the mean of the high and low) on the subsequent date of sale. Reg. § 1.170A–1(c)(1). Unlisted securities or other property must be appraised (Rev. Proc. 66–49, 1966–2 C.B. 1257), with the appraiser's fee deductible by the donor as an expense in determining the donor's income tax (Rev. Rul. 67–461, 1967–2 C.B. 125), and not as a charitable contribution and therefore not subject to the charitable contribution limits imposed for income tax purposes.

The value of closely held securities requires an examination of all available financial data and other relevant facts. Rev. Rul. 59–60, 1959–1 C.B. 237, modified by Rev. Rul. 65–193, 1965–2 C.B. 370; amplified by Rev. Rul. 77–287, 1977–2 C.B. 319; Rev. Rul. 68–609, 1968–2 C.B. 327; Rev. Rul. 80–213, 1980–2 C.B. 101; Rev. Rul. 83–120, 1983–2 C.B. 170. When reporting property contributions on a tax return, taxpayers must furnish detailed information, particularly where deductions exceeding $500 are claimed. Id. The donee may also be required to supply certain additional data with respect to the gift. Reg. § 1.170A–13(a)(2)(iii).

¶ 27,133

[¶ 27,141]

e. *Redemption of Closely Held Stock*

Closely held stock redeemed by the issuing corporation will not be treated as if the stock had been redeemed from the donor, despite the existence of an understanding that the stock would be so redeemed, so long as the donee-charity was not legally bound and therefore could not be compelled to render the donated stock for redemption. Rev. Rul. 78–197, 1978–1 C.B. 83. On the other hand, as previously mentioned, where a charitable donee sells appreciated property and the donor had engaged in negotiations with the buyer before making the contribution, the gain may be attributable to him. See Martin v. Machiz, 251 F.Supp. 381 (D.Md.1966); Magnolia Development Corp. v. Commissioner, 19 T.C.M. (CCH) 934, T.C.M. (P–H) ¶ 60,177 (1960).

The value of the redemption technique is most apparent in the case of an individual who owns all the stock of a corporation. The donor may donate such amount of the stock as the corporation has retained earnings to redeem and may deduct the value of the stock as a donation notwithstanding that the donor's stock ownership before the gift and after the redemption remains 100 percent. The cost will be the reduction of retained earnings of the corporation (which earnings have already been taxed in the hands of the corporation).

It often happens that a corporation must distribute earnings in order to avoid the penalties associated with unreasonable accumulations of surplus imposed by § 531. If the sole shareholder is also an employee of the corporation, a certain portion of the surplus may be paid out in the form of compensation for personal services and the amount so paid will be the deductible if it is reasonable. Reg. § 1.162–7. However, in the last analysis, the only alternative to declaring a dividend to reduce the earned surplus may be to donate shares by the corporation to a public charity. The redemption of the shares by the corporation will reduce its retained earnings and at the same time may not significantly dilute the donor's percentage of ownership.

Problem

[¶ 27,145]

Hadmore owns all the share of his company. In his hands, these shares have zero basis. He cannot withdraw additional amounts from the company as salary and remain within the reasonableness test of § 162. Thus, he is faced with declaring a dividend to meet his present needs. He decides to donate 30 percent of the outstanding shares, valued at $100,000, to a charity. It is apparent that the share will be tendered to the company for redemption, but the charity is not obligated to tender. If Hadmore is in the 35 percent bracket, how much federal income tax does he save by his gift? The company subsequently redeems the shares from the charity for $100,000. Had Hadmore received a dividend of $100,000, how much would he have netted after tax? How much tax has Hadmore saved by making the gift to charity? Moreover, by the redemption procedure, the withdrawal of $100,000 has not affected the stock ownership of his company.

[¶ 27,149]

f. Sale of a Business

An opportunity to make a substantial charitable contribution may occur when a substantial stockholder of a business contemplates selling out.

Example. Jack and Jill own a substantial part of the stock of J & J Corporation. Their stock is valued at $5 million. The cost basis of the stock is zero; therefore, all the value represents potential gain with a built-in tax. Assume Jack and Jill have total taxable income of $500,000. Acquisition, Inc. desires to purchase all the stock of the business for $5 million in cash. Assuming an income tax rate of 35 percent and a capital gain rate of 15 percent, the tax result will be as shown in Column A of Table 27.1, but if prior to the sale, Jack and Jill donate 10 percent of the stock (value $500,000) to a public charity, the cash available to Jack and Jill after taxes will be $207,000 less if the gift is made than if it is not made (and the charity will have $500,000). This is reflected in Column B of Table 27.1.

Table 27.1 TAX BENEFITS FROM CONTRIBUTIONS OF STOCK

		A Sale of all stock		B Contribution of 10% of stock, sale of 90%
Taxable income without regard to gift or sale		$500,000		$500,000
Charitable contribution		–0–		$500,000
Tax on income (35%)	$175,000	$500,000	–0–	
Capital gain from sale		$5,000,000		$4,500,000
Tax on capital gain (15%)	$750,000		$675,000	
Total income		$5,500,000		$5,000,000
Total tax	$925,000	$925,000	$675,000	$675,000
Net available to Jack and Jill after tax		$4,575,000		$4,325,000

[¶ 27,157]

g. Transferring Control of a Business

Transfer of control of the family business to the owner's family (or to other persons of the owner's choosing) can be accomplished advantageously while effecting a substantial gift to charity. The procedure involves a sale of shares of the company to the intended beneficiaries either by the owner or as a new issue by the corporation followed by the donation of the remainder of the owner's shares to a public charity and the redemption of those shares by the corporation. If the owner desires to continue to receive income, the owner may recapitalize the corporation with preferred stock for a portion of his interest and donate only the common. The general proscription against preferred stock bailouts under § 306 is not applied to charitable transfers. Rev. Rul. 57–328, 1957–2 C.B. 229; Priv. Ltr. Rul. 8035014.

Example. Ichabod and his wife want to transfer their shares to their son and daughter. They could give to the son and daughter over a period of years $40,000 ($20,000 to each child) of the stock annually without gift tax, and at such time as is desirable could donate all the remaining shares of the corporation to the I Family Charitable Trust. The corporation could redeem the shares or leave the shares in the trust. If redeemed, the shares will be held by the corporation as treasury shares and all issued shares will be in the hands of the son and daughter. The redemption of the charity's interest could be effected through key man insurance proceeds so that the retained earnings of the company need not be disturbed to effect the recovery of the shares by the corporation.

If the son and daughter are the trustees of the charitable trust, their control position is assured without the need for the redemption.

If Ichabod and his wife want to retain an income "stream" for life, they may create an annuity trust or a unitrust. See discussion at ¶ 25,175. Alternatively, they may simply exchange certain of their shares prior to the transaction described above in a tax-free exchange for preferred shares bearing a fixed rate of distribution or a participation in the profits of the company.

A possible variation on this technique would permit the passage of control (following the death of the owner) to the employees if, instead of trying to retain control of the stock indefinitely in a family foundation, the owner of the closely held shares gave them to charity and then had the corporation fund an employee stock ownership plan (ESOP) with deductible cash contributions, so that the ESOP could purchase the closely held stock from the charity to which it had been donated. (For introduction to ESOPs, see ¶ 24,885.)

The consequences of this would be to leave the charity with cash, provide the stockholder with a current income tax deduction for the gift, and provide the corporation with a current business deduction for a contribution to a qualified employee retirement plan, while eliminating the stock and any future appreciation from the owner's estate, with the corporation retaining control of its own stock through the ESOP.

[¶ 27,165]

3. TANGIBLE PERSONAL PROPERTY

a. *Usable for Charity's Exempt Purposes*

A gift to a public charity of appreciated tangible long-term capital gain property which is usable for that charity's exempt purposes entitles the donor to an income tax deduction for up to 30 percent of his or her contribution base or else to elect to reduce the amount of the contribution by 100 percent of the amount which would have been taxed as long-term capital gain had the donor sold the property outright, giving the donor an income tax deduction for up to 50 percent of his or her contribution base (under these circumstances). § 170(b)(1)(C)(i) and (iii). However, if the property is not usable directly in furtherance of the charity's exempt purposes, the donation's value will be reduced by 100 percent of the amount of the gain which would have been long-term capital gain on the sale of the property. § 170(e)(1)(B)(i).

¶ 27,157

Example 1. Marie owns a yacht and a coin collection, each of which she purchased and each of which she has held for more than 12 months. In each case, her cost is $100,000 and the value of the property is $500,000. Marie would like to make two gifts of $500,000 each, one to a school and one to a museum. If she gives the yacht to the school for use related to its tax-exempt purposes and the coin collection to the museum for display, she will be entitled to deductions totaling $1 million without reduction for the appreciation in the value of the property given. To reverse the donees, the school and the museum, would require a reduction of each donation by 100 percent of the amount of the appreciation of $400,000. Marie would be entitled to deductions totaling $200,000.

Problems

[¶ 27,171]

1. Gwen has been in the top income tax bracket. She will retire next year, after which her bracket will undoubtedly decline. Her contribution base this year is $200,000. Thereafter her contribution base is projected to be $50,000. Gwen wishes to donate a patent, which she purchased some years ago for $105,000 and which is now valued at $160,000, in order to receive the maximum after-tax advantage. Suppose she elects to reduce her gift by 100 percent of its appreciation ($55,000) and to use the optimal limit of 50 percent of her contribution base ($100,000). What would be the tax consequences if Gwen carried over the excess $5,000 until next year? Suppose she elects to use the 30 percent deduction limitation. Will any part of the deduction be lost to her?

2. Ken contributes a painting valued at $50,000 which he acquired several years earlier for $10,000. The charity cannot use it as such and sells it for $50,000. What amount could Ken claim as a charitable deduction?

3. What policy considerations caused Congress to make these rules?

––––––––

How long the gifted property is used by the charity for its exempt purposes is important. While there is no minimum holding period, use by the charity for a period of less than a year or less than three years may limit the tax benefits from the gift—including in some instances recovery of the tax benefit of the charitable contribution. Incidental rental of the asset may be consistent with its use by the charity, but the total rental period will be weighed against the actual utilization period. The donor has an affirmative burden of reasonably inquiring as to the use to which the asset is to be put. If it later turns out that it was sold or otherwise not appropriately used, the donor may lose part or all of his or her deduction.

Example 2. In the preceding example involving the donation of the yacht by Marie, if, within the year, the charity enters into a long-term lease for the use of the yacht by a third person or if the charity sells the yacht, due to financial constraints or lack of suitability of the yacht for its purposes, the donor may be required to reduce the value of her gift by 100 percent of its appreciation ($400,000). If Marie is in the 35 percent bracket, the reduction will mean an out-of-pocket cost of $135,000. The position of the Internal Revenue Service may well be that it was unreasonable of Marie, who was familiar with the costs of operating a large yacht, not to have inquired into the suitability of the yacht for use by the school in furtherance of its tax-exempt educational mission, as well as the proposed sources for its maintenance.

To avoid the possibility that a charity (particularly if it is a relatively small one or a private foundation receiving a "white elephant" type of gift) may not be able to use the donation in furtherance of its purposes, the donor should have an understanding in advance of making the gift of its intended use by the charity (including a letter of intent from the donee). Even a relatively large public charity may not be able to use the "white elephant" type of gift and will be forced to sell it, resulting in a partial loss of the donor's charitable deduction.

Additional and most careful review of the rules imposed by the Pension Protection Act of 2006 on gifts of tangible personal property is required as the applicable rules are increasingly refined and targeted to specific kinds of gifts as Congress seeks to end certain abuses which it has identified. The specifics are beyond these materials.

[¶ 27,173]

b. *Partial Interests*

An outright gift of a right to the possession of an item of tangible personal property for a specified term is not deductible. § 170(f)(3)(A). If the gift is made of a remainder interest in the property, following the donor's life estate, the deduction for this contribution will not be available until the donor's death. § 170(a)(3).

The transfer of possession (actual physical delivery) of tangible personal property to the charity is essential, since the deduction for the fair market value of the property is not allowed until all intervening interests (including any written or oral understandings as to possession or enjoyment) of the donor or the donor's family have ended. However, a gift of an undivided fractional interest qualifies for an income tax deduction (Reg. § 1.170A–7(b)(1)) if the charity's initial period of possession commences within a year of the gift. Reg. § 1.170A–5(a)(2). Cf. Winokur v. Commissioner, 90 T.C. 733 (1988), acq. 1989–2 C.B. 1.

Examples given in the regulations of undivided interests which would qualify under this rule are: gifts of a one-half interest in a life estate in an office building in which the donor holds no other interest; a 20 percent interest in a trust remainder in which the donor holds no other interest; 50 out of 100 acres owned by the donor; an open space easement in gross, given in perpetuity; and property where the donee is given the right, as a tenant in common with the donor, to possession, dominion and control thereof for a portion of each year appropriate to its interest in the property. Reg. § 1.170A–7(b)(1). Thus, the owner of a valuable painting kept in his summer home in which he spends only about a third of the year could donate an undivided two-thirds interest in the painting to the local art museum. Provided that possession is in fact given to the museum for eight months out of the year, the donor may deduct two-thirds of the painting's fair market value. Id.

Where the donor retains substantial rights in property in which he is giving a partial interest to charity, the deduction will not be available. Examples of some nondeductible partial interests include: gifts to a charitable organization of "an interest in original historic motion picture films * * * where the donor retains the exclusive right to make reproductions of such films and to exploit such reproductions commercially," (Reg. § 1.170A–7(b)(1)); a remainder interest in the household furnishings of a personal residence (Rev. Rul. 76–165, 1976–1 C.B. 279); a remainder interest in a personal residence where the residence was placed in trust (Rev. Rul. 76–357, 1976–2 C.B. 285); proceeds of the sale of a personal residence which, according to the terms of the bequest, was to be sold upon the death of the life tenant (Rev. Rul. 77–169, 1977–1 C.B. 286); and a remainder interest in a personal residence to charity with the condition that, should the life tenants be unable to continue living in the residence, it was to be sold and the proceeds divided among the charity and the life tenants in accordance with their respective interests in the property (Rev. Rul. 77–305, 1977–2 C.B. 72).

No deduction is allowed for a contribution of the right to use property, since such transfers are considered gifts of a partial interest. § 170(f)(3)(A). This rule, however, applies only to the use of property owned by the donor. Examples of gifts for which deductions are not permitted include rent-free use of a portion of a building owned by the donor or interest-free loans to charitable organizations. Reg. § 1.170A–7(d). However, a taxpayer whose only interest in a building is a life estate would be allowed a deduction for a gift of that life estate or a fractional interest therein. Reg. § 1.170A–7(b)(1).

Understandably, given the abuse potential, the rules governing charitable deductions of fractional interests were tightened in 2006. A donor might give a 10 percent interest in a painting to a museum and the museum, for its part, would display the painting 36 days each year. The next year, an additional 10 percent interest might be given. The second gift would be valued as of the date of the second gift—leading to a larger deduction if the painting had appreciated. Under the new rules, the second gift must be valued according to the value assigned to the first gift. (New York's Museum of Modern Art was reported has having 650 works in its collections that began as partial gifts. Jan M. Rosen, The Ins and Outs of Charitable Deductions, N.Y. Times, November 13, 2006, at 41.)

[¶ 27,181]

4. REAL ESTATE

a. *In General*

The maximum charitable contributions deduction for income tax purposes which is available for gifts of appreciated long-term capital gain property is available for a gift of real estate held for more than one year, so long as the donor held it for his own use or for investment. If the donor held it as a dealer or for sale to customers in the ordinary course of the donor's trade or business, or if the gain on sale would be ordinary income under the recapture rules, the contribution would not be eligible for a full deduction. If the appreciation would be taxable as long-term capital gain on the sale of the asset, then the full deduction is available.

Problem

[¶ 27,187]

Several years ago Nelson purchased a summer home for $100,000. When it was worth $300,000, he donated it to a charity. Describe the tax consequences to Nelson.

[¶ 27,188]

b. Conservation Easement: Exclusion If Qualified

Subject to certain maximums, up to 40 percent of the value of land subject to a qualified conservation easement may be excluded from a decedent's gross estate for estate tax purposes. § 2031(c). (The conservation easement is not available as to land for which an estate tax charitable deduction has been taken.) When integrated with § 2010(c)'s applicable exclusion amount, a substantial tax shelter effect can be realized. The exclusion only applies to conservation easements located within 25 miles of a metropolitan area; or within 25 miles of certain national parks or wilderness areas; or within 20 miles of an "urban national forest". It must be land owned by the decedent or a member of his or her family at all times during the three year period prior to death. The easement may be created before or after death by the decedent, a member of the decedent's family, the executor, or the trustee of a trust holding the land. The land may be held in a corporation, trust, or partnership so long as at least 30 percent is owned directly or indirectly by the decedent.

[¶ 27,189]

5. PARTIAL INTERESTS IN REAL ESTATE

A gift of a partial interest, such as a remainder interest in a farm or a personal residence (including cooperative apartment stock), whether it is the donor's principal residence or the donor's vacation home (Reg. § 1.170A–7(b)(3), (4)), is deductible at its fair market value less the actuarial value of the retained interest (which may be reserved exclusively for the donor's life or shared with the charity).

Comment: § 170(f)(4) provides that in determining the value of a remainder interest in real property, depreciation (computed on the straight-line method) and depletion are to be considered, and the value discounted at an annual rate of 10 percent, except that a different rate may be prescribed. See Reg. § 1.170A–12 for the method of calculation.

¶ 27,181

Since the donor retained a life income interest, the remainder will be included in the donor's gross estate for federal estate tax purposes. § 2036(a)(1). However, the charitable deduction will be available in determining the donor's taxable estate.

Donating a remainder interest in real estate gives more tax benefit during a period of high interest rates, when the taxes saved may be safely reinvested by the donor at a relatively high return or used to pay off the donor's debts.

Example. Oliver, a 35 percent taxpayer, is 84 years of age. For many years he has owned a vacation estate in Florida, the fair market value of which, after depreciation, considering "its highest and best use," is $1 million. His basis is $100,000. Upon the death of Oliver the property will not be retained by his family due to the large cost of its maintenance. The property has been on the market for some time, but the only buyers forthcoming have been developers who place value exclusively on the unimproved land and consider the residence to be a liability. They have offered $500,000 for the property. If Oliver sells the property to a developer, he will realize $399,500 after payment of a 6 percent brokerage commission and 15 percent capital gains tax. If Oliver donates the property with a retained use for life, the actuarial value of his retained use is calculated at 28.14 percent of the value of the property (using the tables prescribed by Reg. § 25.2512–5). Thus, his donation is reduced by $281,430 to $718,570 and he will net after tax $467,070 (65 percent of $718,570) and continue to occupy the property for his life.

Moreover, his heirs may well be as well off as if he had not made the donation. If Oliver does not donate the land as described, it will pass through his estate where it will be subject to a 45 percent estate tax at a minimum. However, if Oliver survives, donates the land, and enjoys success in his investment of his income tax savings, he may pass on no less to his heirs than had he not donated the property, all the while retaining use of the property and perhaps acting as advisor to the charity as to the disposition of its assets, and perhaps even selecting the trustees of the fund.

A deduction is available for contributions of a partial interest in real property, amounting to its dedication in whole or in part for conservation (including historic) purposes (see § 170(f)(3)(B)(iii) and (h)), such as for open space or for a nature walk for the public, as well for the release of the right to develop the property. Determining the fair market value is quite difficult and may be subject to abuse. In theory, the value of this type of donation is based on the value of the property prior to conveyance of the easement as compared with its value thereafter. In one case involving farmland, the donor gave an enforceable easement to a governmental body that precluded use of the premises other than as farmland. Land in the area had a value of $2,000 per acre but land restricted to farm use had a value of $1,500 per acre. Accordingly, the donor was allowed a deduction for a value of $500 per acre. Rev. Rul. 73–339, 1973–2 C.B. 68.

The partial interest rule has particular application to gifts of timber rights and mineral interests. Specifically, a gift of a mineral interest with

¶ 27,189

retention of the surface or a gift of timber rights with a retention of the land, or the converse, will violate the partial interest rule. Rev. Rul. 76–331, 1976–2 C.B. 52. Furthermore, it may well be that a gift of a royalty interest with a retention of mineral ownership will violate the partial interest rule.

Problem

[¶ 27,195]

Rayna, age 68 and divorced, has investment income of $50,000 and derives $100,000 from the operation of a sheep ranch, which passed down from her great-grandfather. Rayna's basis in the ranch is $200,000. The ranch after depreciation is now worth $1 million and is expected to rise in value over the next 10 years to $3 million. If Rayna dies owning the ranch, it may have to be sold to speculators, as the estate tax—barring use of the relief provisions of §§ 2032A or 6166—cannot be obtained based solely on the earnings of the ranch. Rayna proposes to sell the ranch to a family conservation trust at her basis of $200,000, retaining a life interest in the ranch. What are the tax consequences of the transaction to Rayna? Would you suggest that Rayna complete the proposed transaction? You might wish to note that the monies for the $200,000 acquisition may be borrowed by the trust on the security of the ranch, as the income of the ranch in the hands of the charity trust is sufficient to service the debt and provide management fees, provided the use as a sheep farm is not inconsistent with the conservation purpose of the donation.

[¶ 27,197]

6. ENCUMBERED PROPERTY

Where encumbered property is given to charity, whether or not the donee becomes liable for the encumbrance, the donor will be treated as if the donee had paid for the property, to the extent of the encumbrance, triggering the bargain sale rules (see ¶ 27,351) which will have the effects of producing taxable gain and reducing the donor's charitable contribution by the amount of the encumbrance.

[¶ 27,205]

7. REQUIRED APPRAISALS

Stringent provisions for verifying the value of appreciated property gifts are in effect. "Qualified appraisals" must be obtained for all such gifts over $5,000 in claimed value or in the case of nonpublicly traded stock, gifts over $10,000 in claimed value. An "appraisal summary" (IRS Form 8283) must be attached to the donor's income tax return. An exception for publicly traded securities applies. Additionally, § 6050L requires a charity which is a donee of property subject to the appraisal requirements above to file an information return (IRS Form 8282) with the Internal Revenue Service if the charity sells or disposes of the property donated within two years of the gift date.

F. DEPRECIATED (UNAPPRECIATED) ASSETS

[¶ 27,251]

Losses are not recognized when a charitable gift is made. Therefore, an asset with a value less than the donor's basis should not be given to charity, but should be sold so that the taxable loss can be used by the donor, while the proceeds are then given to charity, thus enabling the donor to receive a deduction for both the loss and charitable donation. A gift of depreciated property will merely entitle the donor to an income tax deduction for the fair market value of the property. The donor will thus lose the benefit of the tax saving available from a sale of the property at a loss.

G. ORDINARY INCOME PROPERTY

[¶ 27,301]

Any property the sale of which results in ordinary income or short-term capital gain, instead of long-term capital gain, is usually called ordinary income property. See § 170(e)(1)(A). Included in this category are capital assets held for less than 12 months, those produced by the donor (such as the donor's works of art, patents, books, etc.), and most improved real estate or personalty subject to the recapture rules to the extent of the portion of appreciation subject to recapture, and most inventory. Agricultural products grown by a farmer and business inventory items are also ordinary income property.

Ordinary income property, whether contributed by an individual or a corporation, may be deducted for income tax purposes only to the extent of its basis, or in the case of recapture property, the fair market value less the amount subject to recapture. § 170(e)(1). Thus, there is hardly any income tax advantage to a donation of this type of property if it has substantially appreciated.

Example. Kirby contributes to a public charity stock which he has held for 10 months and for which he paid $10,000. The stock has a value of $20,000 on the date of contribution. The amount deductible is $10,000, the $10,000 nondeductible portion being equal to the amount of short-term capital gain which would have been taxed if the stock had been sold.

H. BARGAIN SALE

[¶ 27,351]

A donor of appreciated property who wishes to recover his or her cost (or some amount other than the entire value of the property) could make a bargain sale of it to charity. This is a sale for less than the fair market value of the property, with the difference between the sale price and the value being given to the charity. Coulter v. Commissioner, 9 T.C.M. (CCH) 248, T.C.M. (P–H) ¶ 50,077 (1950); Potter v. Commissioner, 38 T.C. 951 (1962), acq.,

¶ **27,351**

1964–2 C.B. 7; Waller v. Commissioner, 39 T.C. 665 (1963), acq., 1963–2 C.B. 5; Reg. § 1.1001–1(e)(1).

For tax purposes, there must be an allocation of the donor's basis between the value of what the donor sells and the value the donor contributes in accordance with their relative fair market values. §§ 170(e)(2) and 1011(b).

Comment: This allocation is required only when the bargain sale gives rise to the allowance of a charitable contribution deduction. Reg. § 1.170A–4(c)(2) and (d), Example (8). If the stock sold is short-term gain property, there is no charitable contribution deduction for the short-term appreciation, and thus, the donor is not required to allocate any of his or her tax basis from the sale to the gift portion of the transaction, when the consideration paid is equal to the donor's basis. Thus, the donor recognizes no taxable gain and is not entitled to a charitable deduction. Where gain is recognized, that gain will be taxed as capital gain.

The following is a typical example of a bargain sale to a public charity and the tax treatment to the donor:

Example. Uriah purchased stock for a cost of $3,000. He has held it for investment for over 12 months. When the stock is worth $9,000, he sells it to a charity for an amount equal to his cost, $3,000, thereby intending to contribute $6,000. Uriah is entitled to his contribution deduction of $6,000, but he will be considered as having sold $3,000 worth of stock for which his cost is $1,000 (1/3 of his aggregate cost) and hence will recognize a long-term capital gain of $2,000.

The "bargain sale" rule will automatically come into effect when property subject to a liability (such as a mortgage) is transferred as a contribution. Whether or not the donee charity assumes the liability, the amount of the liability to which the property is subject is treated as if it represented a payment by the charity to the donor upon receipt of the property. § 1011(b); Reg. § 1.1011–2(a).

Problem

[¶ 27,390]

Billye has held real property as a capital asset for more than 12 months. It is valued at $100,000, but is subject to a mortgage of $10,000. She contributes the encumbered property to a public charity. Assuming her basis was $30,000, describe the tax consequences to Billye of this gift. You may assume, further, that Billye's contribution base was $100,000 for the taxable year in which the donation was made.

––––––

An exchange of property can also give rise to a bargain sale. An example of this would be where certain property is exchanged for other property of a lesser value, perhaps in a situation where a collector wishes to make a charitable contribution while retaining similar, but less costly items. Reg.

§ 1.1011–2(a). Where an annuity is granted in return for a gift, the deduction equals the difference between the present value of the annuity and the market value of the gift (Reg. § 1.170A–1(d)), with capital gain recognized by the donor on the difference between the donor's basis in the property and the value of the annuity, spread out over the donor's life expectancy, and the basis reallocated between the annuity and the property donated. Rev. Rul. 69–74, 1969–1 C.B. 43. However, if the exchange qualifies as a like-kind exchange, no gain will be recognized by the donor and the donor will receive a charitable deduction for the excess value passing to charity. See Reg. § 1.170A–4(c)(2); cf. Rev. Rul. 78–163, 1978–1 C.B. 257; Rev. Rul. 76–253, 1976–2 C.B. 51; Rev. Rul. 72–515, 1972–2 C.B. 466 . .

I. LIFE INSURANCE

[¶ 27,401]

A contribution of a life insurance or endowment insurance policy will give rise to an income tax deduction for the value of the policy at the time of the gift as well as a similar annual deduction for each subsequent premium payment. The value of the insurance will be excluded from the donor's gross estate at the donor's death. Ordinarily, such a contribution is made by an irrevocable assignment of the policy to charity.

The deduction for a paid-up policy equals the latter's replacement value. United States v. Ryerson, 312 U.S. 260 (1941); Reg. § 25.2512–6(a), Example (3). But if the replacement value exceeds the donor's basis, the deduction is limited to the basis. § 170(e)(1)(A). Where premiums remain to be paid on the policy (the usual case), the deduction ordinarily equals the interpolated terminal reserve value (an amount somewhat in excess of the cash surrender value) of the policy. Rev. Rul. 59–195, 1959–1 C.B. 18. The charity must either own the policy or be named irrevocable beneficiary and the insured may not reserve the right to surrender the policy for cash, if a deduction is to be available for premium payments. A charitable contribution deduction for premium payments on a policy assigned to a charity is also available to a corporation. Rev. Rul. 58–372, 1958–2 C.B. 99.

> *Example.* Paul owns a $100,000 face amount life insurance policy. If Paul donates the policy to a public charity, the deductible amount would be the interpolated terminal reserve value plus the unearned premium less any indebtedness. For purposes of this illustration, the deductible amount is assumed to be $70,000. Paul is in the 35 percent income tax bracket and it is projected that, upon his death, the maximum death tax rate to which his estate would be subject would be 45 percent. As a consequence, his gift will mean that he is out of pocket $22,980—and the charity has benefited because it receives the entire $100,000 proceeds of the policy upon his death. That is, Paul gets an immediate income tax deduction of $24,500 (35 percent of $70,000), and the policy is not included in his estate for estate tax purposes. If the gift were not made, Paul's noncharitable beneficiaries would net only $50,000 ($100,000 − 50 percent of $100,000). The difference between the possible net of $50,000 Paul's

noncharitable beneficiaries and his income tax savings of $24,500 equals $22,980, which is Paul's actual cost of the $100,000 gift.

Problem

[¶ 27,450]

Refer to the preceding example, and assume that Paul assigned ownership of the $100,000 policy to the trustee of an irrevocable trust whose corpus is payable to a public charity. Assume further that Paul reserved the power to amend the trust in favor of other public charities. What are the gift, estate, and income tax consequences to Paul and his estate? Assume Paul dies within three years of the transfer. More than three years? Would it make any difference if Paul was survived by Prudence, his wife of 39 years, and that Paul's will provided that Prudence was to get "the smallest amount necessary to eliminate all federal and state death taxes" (to the extent possible) on Paul's estate? The balance of Paul's estate was to flow into a bypass trust. See ¶ 13,059 for discussion of the bypass trust concept.

J.   INDIVIDUAL RETIREMENT ACCOUNTS (IRAs)

[¶ 27,501]

Some donors are permitted to make tax advantaged direct transfers of Individual Retirement Accounts (but not Keogh's (401(k)'s), SEPs and SIMPLEs, ¶ 30,001) to charity in 2006 and 2007. For discussion, see ¶ 30,001.

Part VII

FINANCIAL AND RETIREMENT COMPENSATION PLANNING

Chapter 28

NONQUALIFIED DEFERRED COMPENSATION OPPORTUNITIES

A. OBJECTIVES

[¶ 28,001]

Supplemental forms of compensation are popular. Many such plans are generously provided by employers in an effort, perhaps, to foster a psychology of dependence upon or loyalty to the employer. Just as frequently, over the last decade, highly compensated employees, particularly those whose tax-qualified retirement plan contributions or benefits are limited by law or employer policies, have negotiated to have money over and above traditional forms of direct compensation put aside for their benefit under a variety of schemes.

Example. Molly's employer has a survivor's income plan in place. In the event of Molly's death, a monthly payment of $1,000 will be made to Molly's husband for life.

Currently the popular media focus is on stock options, the compensation engine of the "new economy" (and the "old" as well). The fabulous wealth of the "dot.com millionaires" may well be said to often trace to options given employees to purchase shares of stock in the enterprise at bargain prices relative to the market price when the option becomes exercisable. Of course, it is only when the newly acquired shares are sold that the optionee locks in his or her windfall. And thus, it is not at all surprising that vast numbers of the shares acquired through options are sold immediately upon receipt at the time the option is exercised. Sound to good to be true? You wonder, "What are the drawbacks?" In sum, hard as it is to believe, there are none. While the tax consequences are not necessarily intuitive, most optionees find them to be in the "acceptable" range. This is not to say, though, that considerable estate planning initiative is not given to options planning, particularly gifting. For more, see ¶ 28,400.

Example. Luigi, one of the original employees of Pizza.com, Inc., in lieu of a salary increase, was given the option to 1,000 purchase shares of Pizza.com at $2 per share, the option being exercisable in 3 years. Luigi immediately gifted the option to his son, Rocco. Three years later, with shares of Pizza.com selling for $100 each, Rocco exercised the option, acquired 1,000 shares for a total of $2,000, and immediately sold the 1,000 shares for $100,000, realizing a $98,000 gain.

Supplemental compensation plans—many of which involve income deferral (with resulting income tax benefit in the sense that a "tax postponed is a tax saved")—of the kind considered here are commonly referred to as "nonqualified deferred compensation plans" so as to distinguish them from plans that have been expressly sanctioned by Congress for preferential income tax treatment. The latter, commonly referred to as "tax-qualified retirement plans", are tax preferred in the sense that: (1) the employer gets an immediate income tax deduction for contributions to the plan and (2) the employee pays income tax on the plan benefits only when distributed to the employee, usually in retirement. However, deferred compensation plans which are "tax-qualified"—commonly referred to as pension or profit-sharing plans—suffer some limitations, to wit, (1) § 415(c)'s aggregate limit—in 2006, $44,000—on the amount that can be contributed to tax qualified plans in any one year for a single individual; (2) such plans may not discriminate in favor of highly paid employees or owner-managers; and (3) regulation such as the Employee Retirement Income Security Act of 1974 (ERISA) and the Pension Protection Act of 2006 that some might find onerous. (See Chapter 29 for a discussion of tax-qualified deferred compensation plans.) It is these latter factors, coupled with limited enterprise resources and the enterprise's need or desire to provide additional nontaxable or tax-deferred compensation to management personnel, that has led to the proliferation of nonqualified deferred compensation programs.

Naturally, the Internal Revenue Service, concerned as it is with protecting the federal revenues and developing a fairly administered tax system, is committed to subjecting all of a taxpayer's income to income taxation and to doing it in the year in which the income is earned. Therefore, the IRS, when given the opportunity, will carefully review nonqualified deferred compensation plans to determine the year in which plan benefits are taxable. Accordingly, rightly or wrongly, a premium is placed on plan design if the wanted income tax deferral is to be permitted. See ¶ 28,111.

Obviously, participation in a nonqualified deferred compensation plan is preferable to nonparticipation. But with participation secured, the participant's attention turns to making plan participation attractive taxwise—and to securing the plan itself. That is, one objective of the plan participant is to protect the plan benefits from claims of the employer's creditors in the event the employer suffers financial reverses. These are very real concerns in cases where the employer is a small, closely held business. Important, too, in these cases is not only securing the plan benefits against creditor claims but also making certain that the plan is funded—and that the plan benefits are not left to future funding by the employer. See ¶ 28,351–28,367.

And, to the extent that the benefits being provided are in lieu of current compensation or a supplement to current compensation, the participant wants the plan structured so that the income taxes on the plan benefits are deferred or eliminated. That is, some plans are designed to allow the employee to defer tax on what might otherwise be current compensation taxable as ordinary

¶ 28,001

income in the year in which the compensation is earned. In that sense these plans mimic tax-qualified plans—but at a price. Income tax deferral usually means that the plan benefits are subject to the employer's creditors and, thus, to a substantial risk of forfeiture as required by § 83 if current income taxation is to be avoided.

Some nonqualified deferred compensation arrangements are attractive particularly because they seem to afford an opportunity for certain benefits to escape one or more of the taxes that usually snag compensation arrangements. Thus, from a tax standpoint, nonqualified deferred compensation can sometimes be somewhat like fringe benefits which are tax favored. In that sense nonqualified deferred compensation is unlike so-called qualified plan benefits which offer income tax deferral but no estate or gift tax exclusion.

The estate and gift tax consequences of nonqualified deferred compensation arrangements have been the subject of much litigation. The initial hurdle for the taxpayer is to avoid § 2039(a), the provision styled "Annuities" but the one which is clearly understood to have within its reach deferred compensation arrangements. Taxpayers who have successfully avoided § 2039(a) have done so largely on technical grounds, thereby rendering § 2039(a) somewhat of a disappointment because real economic benefits have been made available to taxpayers free of estate and gift tax consequences.

The escape hatch in § 2039(a) is the decedent's right to an annuity or other payment during life or during a period not ascertainable without reference to the decedent's death. Deferred compensation arrangements which could be described as "death benefit only" plans escape § 2039(a) because the decedent has no right to the benefits during life—and, thus, escape § 2039(a) whenever courts literally interpret § 2039(a). See, e.g., Schelberg v. Commissioner, 612 F.2d 25 (2d Cir.1979), ¶ 28,055. Usually such plans are structured to provide a benefit to the decedent's survivors (rather than to the decedent).

B. ESTATE AND GIFT TAX CONSEQUENCES TO EMPLOYEE

[¶ 28,051]

1. § 2039(a): ANNUITY AND OTHER PAYMENTS

While the IRS has tried to reach nonqualified deferred compensation plans using almost all of the estate tax provisions at one time or another, its efforts have concentrated on § 2039(a). In Reg. § 20.2039–1(b)(2), Example (6), the Treasury utilizes an "aggregation" theory to pull nonqualified deferred compensation plans into the web of § 2039(a). Using an aggregation theory to snag plan benefits for the estate tax is necessary because the terms of some plans—death benefit only plans—fall outside § 2039. Example (6) provides as follows:

The employer made contributions to two different funds set up under two different plans. One plan was to provide the employee, upon his retirement at age 60, with an annuity for life, and the other plan was to

¶ 28,001

provide the employee's designated beneficiary, upon the employee's death, with a similar annuity for life. Each plan was established at a different time and each plan was administered separately in every respect. Neither plan at any time met the requirements of § 401(a) (relating to qualified plans). The value of the designated beneficiary's annuity is includible in the employee's gross estate. All rights and benefits accruing to an employee and to others by reason of the employment (except rights and benefits accruing under certain plans meeting the requirements of § 401(a) (see Reg. § 20.2039–2)) are considered together in determining whether or not § 2039(a) and (b) applies. The scope of § 2039(a) and (b) cannot be limited by indirection.

The technique, then, is to structure plans that fall outside § 2039 so as to prevent aggregation. However, consider *Bahen* and *Schelberg,* both reprinted below. *Bahen,* a Court of Claims decision, is universally cited as the best explanation of § 2039—but it is also criticized as an apostle for aggregation so as to allow § 2039 to apply. It provides a clear opportunity to observe the expansive interpretation that can be placed on § 2039 bearing, as it does, the rather confining label "Annuities." In so doing, the *Bahen* court expressed its sense that "the general objective of the federal estate tax" was "to include in the decedent's estate * * * the valuable interests belonging to, accumulated by, or created by or for him, which pass to others at his death."

On the other hand, *Schelberg,* a Second Circuit decision, is implicitly critical of *Bahen* as it rejects aggregation and allows a survivor's income plan to avoid estate and gift taxation upon the death of the employee. Thus, *Schelberg* is important as an illustration of the very real economic benefits that can be provided an employee estate tax free. However, a decision like *Schelberg* also invites considerations of tax policy in the sense of leading to such questions as, "Is this the kind of interest Congress wanted to be beyond the reach of the estate tax?" Or is it enough to say that, "While the plan in *Schelberg* is beyond the reach of § 2039(a), it can be reached by other provisions of the estate tax." Consider Levin v. Commissioner, 90 T.C. 723 (1988), reprinted at ¶ 28,063.

Note, too, in thinking about aggregation that both *Bahen* and *Schelberg* explain that tax-qualified plans are not to be aggregated with nonqualified plans for purposes of determining the applicability of § 2039(a).

[¶ 28,053]

ESTATE OF BAHEN v. UNITED STATES

Court of Claims of the United States, 1962.
305 F.2d 827.

DAVIS, Judge, delivered the opinion of the court:

The estate of a former high-ranking officer of The Chesapeake and Ohio Railway Company claims that sums paid by the C. & O. to his widow on his death in 1955, under benefit plans unilaterally adopted by the railroad in 1952 and 1953, were improperly included in his gross estate for tax purposes.

* * *

[Death Benefit Plan]

After Mr. Bahen's death, the C. & O. made payments to his widow under two plans which it had earlier established for its employees. The first was the Death Benefit Plan, adopted in January 1952, which provided that, if a covered employee with more than 10 years' service died while in the company's employ and before becoming eligible for retirement, the C. & O. would pay, "in recognition of the services rendered by him", a sum equal to three months' salary to his widow or (if she died prior to payment) to the guardian of any of his minor children.

[Deferred Compensation Plan]

The more significant arrangement was the Deferred Compensation Plan adopted by the company in February 1953 for forty of its officers and executives. For a designated officer who was under 60 at that time, like Mr. Bahen, the C. & O. would pay a stated maximum sum ($100,000 in Mr. Bahen's case), at his death either before or after retirement, to his widow and to those of his surviving children under 21 the officer might specify (and in the proportions he designated), in 60 equal monthly installments. These payments were to be made only if a wife or minor child survived the officer and would continue only so long as there was a surviving wife or child under 21. However, if prior to retirement the officer became totally incapacitated, mentally or physically, for further performance of duty, the payments would be made to him in 60 equal monthly installments so long as he survived, any unpaid installment going to his widow or minor children. * * * Mr. Bahen was * * * notified of this Deferred Compensation Plan and its irrevocability.

* * *

Section 2039 was a development of the earlier provisions of the estate tax which spoke of the decedent's "property" and of "transfers" by the decedent in contemplation of or taking effect at death. * * * The new § does not use that phraseology but frames its operative requirements more directly in terms of particular types of transactions or arrangements involving the decedent. This change is significant. We must pay heed to the precise new form in which Congress cast its net and not become entangled in the older meshes.

[Deferred Compensation Plan Taxable]

A. *The Deferred Compensation Plan:* We first consider the application of § 2039 (and the Regulations) to the C. & O.'s major plan, the Deferred Compensation Plan (of 1953) under which $100,000 was paid to Mrs. Bahen in a five-year span. As we read the § and the Regulations, they demand inclusion in the estate of the proceeds of this Plan. Every requirement is squarely met, not only in literal terms but in harmony with the legislative aim.

[Contract or Agreement]

1. There is, initially, no doubt that the Plan, though adopted by the company unilaterally and without negotiation with the officers and employees, was a "form of contract or agreement" under the statute. This phrase is

defined by § 20.2039–1(b)(1)(ii) of the Treasury Regulations on Estate Tax to include "any arrangement, understanding or plan, or any combination of arrangements, understandings, or plans arising by reason of the decedent's employment." A compensation plan unilaterally adopted by the employer, but made irrevocable and communicated to the employee, falls directly within this definition, at least where the employee continues in the company's service after the adoption of the plan.

[Annuity or Other Payment]

2.   There is likewise no doubt that Mrs. Bahen, the beneficiary, received "an annuity or other payment" under the statute when she was paid the $100,000 in sixty equal installments. The Regulations (§ 20.2039–1(b)(1)(ii)) appropriately say that this double term in § 2039, as used with respect to both the beneficiary and the decedent, "has reference to one or more payments extending over any period of time", and that the payments may "be equal or unequal, conditional or unconditional, periodic or sporadic."

[Other Payment]

3.   The next problem is whether at Mr. Bahen's death there was payable to him or he possessed the right to receive *"an annuity or other payment."* The Deferred Compensation Plan provided that, if Mr. Bahen became totally incapacitated for further performance of duty before retirement, the C. & O. would pay him the $100,000 in 60 equal monthly installments. Under both the normal understanding of the statutory words "annuity or other payment" and the broad definition given them by the Regulations (referred to above), these sums must be characterized as at least an "other payment." * * * [T]he history and pattern of § 2039 fail to indicate that it deals only with true lifetime annuities (in installment form or in a commuted lump sum). The statute covers—as an "other payment", at least—disability compensation benefits of the type involved here.

[Payable to the Decedent]

4.   Were these benefit payments—assuming, as we have just decided, that they constituted an "annuity or other payment" within § 2039—"payable to" Mr. Bahen at his death or did he "possess the right to receive such annuity or payment"? The Regulations (§ 20.2039–1(1)(ii)) establish that amounts are "payable" to a decedent "if, at the time of his death, the decedent was in fact receiving an annuity or other payments, whether or not he had an enforceable right to have payments continue." Since Mr. Bahen was not receiving disability benefits when he died, this term of the statute is not satisfied.

We hold, however, that at his death Mr. Bahen did "possess the right" to receive the disability payments in the future if certain conditions were fulfilled, and therefore that the alternative requirement of § 2039 is met. The intentional juxtaposition in the statute of amounts "payable" and those the decedent "possessed the right to receive" indicates that the former relates to the present (i.e. at time of death) and the latter to the future. The Regulations make clear that, in circumstances like these, the decedent's interest in future

¶ **28,053**

benefits, even if contingent, is sufficient. * * * The arrangement may have been unilateral in inception but it was also irrevocable, and its irrevocability was deliberately communicated to the individuals covered. It thus became an integral article of Mr. Bahen's terms of employment by the C. & O. There can be no doubt that he and the others relied upon the Plan, as they were expected to do. * * * The right they possessed may have been contingent but it was not at the whim of the employer. * * *

In answer, the plaintiff insists that the decedent cannot be considered to have "possessed the right to receive" these disability payments because they were contingent on his becoming totally disabled before retirement, and would never have been received had he lived healthily to retirement age. Only future payments which are sure to be paid if the decedent lives to a designated time are covered by § 2039, plaintiff says. However, as we have pointed out, in specifically covering amounts not payable to the decedent at the time of his death but which he then had merely the "right to receive", the statute and the Regulations obviously cover sums becoming due in the future; and there is no support in the statute's language for the distinction plaintiff makes between the different types of such future payments (at least if they are not forfeitable at the will of another). Both classes of payment are contingent and neither is sure. A benefit payable only if a man lives to a certain age is conditioned upon his living that long, just as a benefit payable only if he becomes disabled is conditional on his future disability. Any distinction between the types seems rejected by the Regulations which include "conditional" payments without qualification. Moreover, the comparable term "right to income" in related earlier provisions of the estate tax * * * [now § 2036] has been in effect read as including a contingent right to receive income. The legislative history of § 2039 suggests that the rules applicable under § 2036, in this connection, should likewise control under the new provision. S. Rept. No. 1622, 83d Cong., 2d Sess., at p. 472; H. Rept. No. 1337, 83d Cong., 2d Sess., at p. A316.

[Right Not to End Before Death]

5.   Another requirement of § 2039 is that the decedent's right to receive payments must be possessed "for his life or for any period not ascertainable without reference to his death or for any period which does not in fact end before his death." For the period from February 1953, when the Deferred Compensation Plan was adopted, to his death in November 1955, Mr. Bahen had the right to receive, under this Plan, $100,000 in 60 installments upon his total disability prior to retirement. He thus possessed the right to receive this "annuity or other payment" for a period which did not in fact end before his death—and, accordingly, this element of § 2039 is also present. * * *

[Source of Contribution]

6.   The last element necessary for coverage by § 2039 is that Mr. Bahen must have "contributed" the "purchase price" of the "annuity or other payment" received by Mrs. Bahen which is to be included in the taxable estate. * * *

* * *

¶ 28,053

The second sentence of this * * * [§ 2039(b)] automatically attributes the employer's contribution to the employee "if made by reason of his employment." This phrase is given broad scope by the Senate Committee Report (S. Rept. No. 1622, 83d Cong., 2d Sess., at p. 471) which holds that it applies "if, for example, the annuity or other payment is offered by the employer as an inducement to employment, or a continuance thereof, or if the contributions are made by the employer in lieu of additional compensation or other rights, if so understood by employer and employee, whether or not expressly stated in the contract of employment or otherwise." The Deferred Compensation Plan, we have already noted, plainly meets this standard; it was an inducement to continued service with the C. & O. It is immaterial, we think, that the company did not formally make "contributions" to a separate fund, or actually purchase annuity or like contracts. Section 2039(b) does not use the words "contribution", "contributed", or "purchase price" in a narrow literal sense, any more than sub§ (a) uses "contract or agreement" in that rigid fashion. The § deals, for the area it covers, with the substance of transactions, not with the mechanical way they happen to be formulated. * * *

[Not Restricted to Literal Language]

7. To all of this the plaintiff * * * protests that despite its literal language § 2039 is applicable only where there is a true lifetime annuity payable to the decedent for life. Plaintiff correctly points out that the main impetus for the new § was the doubt in 1954 that the former estate tax provisions covered conventional joint and survivor annuities purchased wholly or partly *by the decedent's employer* (as distinguished from those purchased by the decedent himself). S. Rept. No. 1622, 83d Cong., 2d Sess., at p. 123; H. Rept. No. 1337, 83d Cong., 2d Sess., at p. 90. But the Committee Reports do not indicate that Congress, although using language in § 2039 which goes well beyond the precise situation which initially impelled the change, restricted the scope of the new provision to those very circumstances alone. We find nothing to show that Congress desired the broader words it carefully used in § 2039 not to have their normal significance and application; indeed some of the examples and words Congress used in the Committee Reports show that wider coverage was plainly intended. And the Treasury Regulations, as our prior discussion explains, cover annuities and payments to a decedent other than a full lifetime annuity.

[General Objective of Estate Tax]

8. Finally, we note briefly that § 2039, as we construe it, is harmonious with the general objective of the federal estate tax to include in the decedent's estate (with designated exceptions) the valuable interests belonging to, accumulated by, or created by or for him, which pass to others at his death. Many such benefits promised, given, and paid for by an employer were specifically brought within this framework by the new § in 1954. In [§ 2039(b)] * * * Congress provides that contributions by the employer "shall be considered to be contributed by the decedent if made by reason of his employment." Phrased in terms of the earlier concepts of a decedent's "property" "trans-

¶ 28,053

ferred" at his death, § 2039 declares that annuities or other payments payable by an employer to his employee, and on his death to a beneficiary, constitute his property—created by him through his employer as part of the employment arrangement and in consideration of his continued services—which is transferred to another at his death. * * * A new provision of the estate tax which attempts to apply these fundamental concepts to a fairly well understood set of concrete situations should not be grudgingly read so as to chip away at the specific rule and to continue (as in the past) to leave as much as possible to the ambiguities of the general sections.

* * *

[Death Benefit Plan]

B. *The Death Benefit Plan:* It is a more difficult question whether the Death Benefit Plan—under which the C. & O. paid Mrs. Bahen a sum equal to Mr. Bahen's salary for three months—is covered by § 2039. Under that arrangement no benefits were payable to the decedent during his life, and if the Plan were to be judged by itself it would fall outside the ambit of the § for lack of "an annuity or other payment" to the decedent. The defendant contends that this factor is present because the words "or other payment" can include the decedent-employee's regular salary; the Death Benefit Plan must be taken, defendant says, together with Mr. Bahen's entire employment arrangement including his ordinary compensation. We cannot agree. Since employees normally receive salary or wages, defendant's interpretation would effectively obliterate, for almost all employees, the express requirement in § 2039 of "an annuity or other payment" to the decedent. If Congress had intended that strange result, it would certainly have mentioned or referred to it. The Government's argument also runs counter to the theory and examples of the Regulations (§ 20.2039–1) which impliedly exclude ordinary salary from consideration.

[Aggregation of Plans]

But the Government makes another point which we do accept as bringing the Death Benefit Plan under § 2039. The suggestion is that this Plan should not be viewed in isolation but must be considered together with the Deferred Compensation Plan—as if both arrangements were combined into one plan, providing two types of benefits for beneficiaries after the employee's death but only one type of benefit (disability compensation) to the employee himself. There is some factual support, if that be necessary, for looking at the two plans together, since the Death Benefit Plan was adopted in January 1952 and the Deferred Compensation Plan only a year later in February 1953. There appears to be a common genesis and a unifying thread.

The firmer legal basis is provided by the Regulations (§ 20.2039–1(b)(2), Example (6)) * * * [providing for aggregation of plans]. Effect must be given to this declaration, adopted pursuant to the Treasury's recognized power to issue regulations and not challenged by plaintiff, since it does not violate the terms or the spirit of § 2039. In view of the general purpose of the statute to cover a large share of employer-contributed payments to an employee's

¶ 28,053

survivors, it is not unreasonable to lump together all of the employer's various benefit plans taking account of the employee's death (except those qualified under § 401(a), which are excepted by the statute * * * in order to decide whether and to what extent § 2039 applies to his estate. There is no immutable requirement in the legislation that each plan separately adopted by a company must be considered alone. One good ground for rejecting that position is to prevent attempts to avoid the reach of the statute by a series of contrived plans none of which, in itself, would fall under the section.

[Death Benefits Plan Taxable]

This directive in the Regulations that all rights and benefits "are to be considered together"—read with another part of the same Regulation which defines "contract or agreement" under § 2039 to cover "any combination of arrangements, understandings, or plans arising by reason of the decedent's employment"—requires the two plans of the C. & O. to be deemed a coordinated whole for the purposes of § 2039. On that view the payments under the Death Benefit Plan were includable in the decedent's gross estate for the reasons given above with respect to the Deferred Compensation Plan. If the two Plans are integrated into one, each element required for coverage of all payments is present.

* * *

[¶ 28,055]

SCHELBERG v. COMMISSIONER

United States Court of Appeals, Second Circuit, 1979.
612 F.2d 25.

FRIENDLY, Circuit Judge: This appeal * * * raises a serious question with respect to the interpretation of § 2039, which was added to the Internal Revenue Code in 1954.

I.

[The Facts]

Decedent William V. Schelberg was born on March 14, 1914 and died on January 6, 1974 from lung cancer after a week's illness. He was survived by his wife, Sarah, and two daughters, one aged 23 and the other 19. He had been employed by International Business Machines Corp. (IBM) since 1952. At his death he was serving as assistant director of international patent operations at a salary of $4,250 per month.

[Available Plans]

IBM maintained a variety of employee benefit plans, each adopted at a different time and separately administered. Those here relevant are the Group Life Insurance Plan, the Retirement Plan, the Sickness and Accident Income Plan, and the Total and Permanent Disability Plan. Schelberg was entitled to participate in each.

The Group Life Insurance Plan provided two basic benefits—a group term life insurance, which is not here at issue, and an uninsured and unfunded survivors income benefit, which is. This benefit, determined on the basis of the employee's compensation at the time of death and the amount of the aforementioned life insurance, was payable to a decedent's "eligible" survivors in an order of preference stated in the plan. Payment was to be made monthly, * * * until the total benefit was exhausted. Payments continued only so long as at least one eligible survivor remained.

* * *

[The Dispute]

At the time of his death Schelberg was not receiving benefits under any of these plans. By virtue of his decease his widow became entitled under the Group Life Insurance Plan to a death benefit of $23,666.67 under the group life insurance policy, and to a survivors benefit of $1,062.50 per month. The value of the latter amount was not included in decedent's gross estate in his federal estate tax return, although its existence was reported. The Commissioner of Internal Revenue entered a notice of deficiency on the sole ground that the present value of the survivors annuity, which is stipulated to have been $94,708.83, was includible in the estate pursuant to § 2039. * * * The Tax Court upheld the Commissioner. * * *

II.

[Taxpayer's Argument]

The estate does not dispute that the survivors benefit constituted "an annuity or other payment receivable by any beneficiary by reason of surviving the decedent under any form of contract or agreement entered into after March 3, 1931 (other than as insurance under policies on the life of the decedent)" within the opening clause of § 2039(a). It is likewise indisputable that this alone would not suffice to make the survivors benefit includible in the gross estate. The Commissioner must also satisfy the condition that "under such contract or agreement, an annuity or other payment was payable to the decedent, or the decedent possessed the right to receive such annuity or payment, either alone or in conjunction with another for his life or for any period not ascertainable without reference to his death or for any period which does not in fact end before his death."

[Commissioner's Argument Rejected]

Not contending that he can satisfy this requirement within the four corners of the Group Life Insurance Plan, the Commissioner asserts that, as provided by * * * Regulations * * * [§ 20.2039–1(b)] he is entitled to consider "any arrangement, understanding or plan, or any combination of arrangements or plans arising by reason of the decedent's employment". Although this is a rather sharp departure from the letter of the statute, we accept it with the *caveat* that while the Commissioner is entitled to "consider" such arrangements, this does not mean that the mere possibility of an employee's receiving some benefit under an arrangement other than that giving rise to the survivors benefit necessarily satisfies the condition of § 2039(a). The Commissioner does not rely on either the Retirement Plan or the Sickness and Accident Plan to satisfy the condition that "an annutiy or other payment" was payable to Schelberg. Apart from other considerations, any such reliance is precluded by previous revenue rulings. Revenue Ruling 76–380, 1976–2 C.B. 270, concluded that qualified plans, like the Retirement Plan, and non-qualified plans, like the Survivors Income Benefit Plan, were not to be considered together in determining the applicability of § 2039(a) and (b) * * * Revenue Ruling 77–183, 1977–1 C.B. 274, held that benefits such as those Schelberg might have been entitled to under the Sickness and Accident Plan had he lived longer "were in the nature of compensation" and thus no more meet the test set out in the condition than would compensation payments themselves, * * *. This left as the Commissioner's sole need the fact that, at the time of his death, Schelberg possessed the right that after 52 weeks (or more if he qualified for "individual consideration") under the Sickness and Accident Plan, he might become entitled to payments under the Disability Plan. The estate contends that Schelberg's rights under the Disability Plan were too dissimilar in nature from an "annuity or other payment" and too contingent to meet the condition of § 2039(a). We agree.

It is worth repeating that the Commissioner's position here would apply to every IBM employee having more than five years' service who dies before attaining age 64 (or taking early retirement) although he neither received nor had any reasonable expectation of receiving anything under the Disability Plan. On the other hand, if he died after attaining age 64 but before taking retirement, the survivors benefit would not be includible since the first twelve months away from work would be covered by the Sickness and Accident Plan and he could never become eligible for the Disability Plan. And, of course, if he died after actually taking retirement, the most common case, the survivors benefit would not be includible by virtue of Revenue Ruling 7380, 1976–2 C.B. 270. We find nothing in the language of § 2039, in its legislative history, or in the Treasury Regulations sufficient to justify a conclusion that the action of an employer in creating a plan whereby a handful of employees can receive disability benefits because of a rare health or accident syndrome should bring the survivors of all within § 2039.

[Legislative History]

* * * [T]he statute was aimed at "annuity contracts under which the purchaser (alone or with a joint annuitant) was entitled to payments for his life, with payments to continue after his death, at either the same or a reduced rate, to a survivor." Bittker, Estate and Gift Taxation under the 1954 Code: The Principal Changes, 29 Tul.L.Rev. 453, 469 (1955). While inclusion of the survivor's rights in the estate had been generally sustained, courts had differed as to the reason. Some courts had proceeded on the theory that purchase of the contract was in effect a transfer of property with the reservation of a life estate and thus taxable under the predecessors of § 2036. Others had proceeded on the theory that the transfer was intended to take effect at death. *Id.* A fundamental purpose of § 2039 was to supply an

affirmative answer to the question of inclusion in such cases without further need to debate the theory.

A further purpose, * * * was to settle the question of includibility of a joint and survivor annuity where the annuity was purchased by the decedent's employer or both the decedent and the employer made contributions. Congress decided that such an annuity should be included except when the employer's contributions were made pursuant to "an approved trust, pension or retirement plan."

Both text and context show that § 2039 was conceived as dealing only with the problem of what in substance was a joint annuity, although to be sure in all its various ramifications, not with the whole gamut of arrangements under which an employee, his employer or both may create benefits for the employee's survivors. The new § applied only "if, under such contract or agreement, an annuity or other payment was payable to the decedent, or the decedent possessed the right to receive such annuity or payment, either alone or in conjunction with another for his life or for any period not ascertainable without reference to his death or for any period which does not in fact end before his death." If Congress had wished to legislate more broadly, it would have eliminated this clause or chosen more general language for it. The intended sphere of application is made quite clear by the illustrations given in the House and Senate reports "as examples of contracts, but * * * not necessarily the only forms of contracts to which this § applies." Under all of these the decedent was receiving or entitled to receive at death what anyone would consider an "annuity or other payment" for the duration of his life or for a stipulated term. Furthermore, in each case the beneficiary succeeded to the interest of the decedent, as in the classic instance of a joint and survivor annuity, quite unlike the present case. Although the term "other payment" is literally broad, Congress was clearly thinking of payments in the nature of annuities—the same types of payments which, if made to the survivor, would be includible in the estate. * * * None of the examples is even close to payments receivable only if the deceased employee might have become totally and permanently disabled had he lived.

[Treasury Regulations]

We do not consider the case to be altered in the Government's favor by the Treasury Regulations. While these contain some broad language, there is nothing to indicate that their framers addressed the problem here presented. The closest of the illustrations is example (6). While we have no quarrel with this, it is inapposite since the payments both to the employee and to the beneficiary were life annuities. Without endeavoring to be too precise, we deem it plain that, in framing the condition on § 2039(a), Congress was not going beyond benefits the employee was sure to get as a result of his prior employment if he lived long enough. Even more plainly Congress was not thinking of disability payments which an employee would have had only a remote chance of ever collecting had he lived. Not only are the disability payments in this case extremely hypothetical, they are also far from the "annuity or other payment" contemplated by Congress. Courts have, consistent with basic principles of statutory construction, recognized that "annuity

¶ 28,055

or other payment" does not mean "annuity or any payment," but that the phrase is qualitatively limited by the context in which it appears. * * * The Service itself has acquiesced in and furthered this view. * * * Thus, it seems clear to us that Congress did not intend the phrase to embrace wages, * * * possible sickness and accident payments, which were a substitute for wages, * * * or the disability payments involved in this case, which likewise were a partial continuation of wages when an employee's physical health deteriorated even further. The disability payments theoretically achievable here by the decedent in his lifetime are closer to the sickness benefits which he would have received at an early stage of his illness than they are to post-retirement benefits. The Tax Court's treatment of possible disability benefits as presupposing a post-retirement status linked to the widow's ultimate succession thereto seems to us to be unsupported in fact. * * *

III.

[All v. McCobb]

* * *

In All [v. McCobb, 321 F.2d 633 (2d Cir. 1963)] the decedent had been receiving annuities under a noncontributory non-qualified annuity plan and a partially contributory nonqualified supplemental annuity plan of the Standard Oil Company of New Jersey. His widow received twelve monthly payments under a death benefit plan for such annuitants. The case for application of § 2039 would seem almost too clear for argument. The sole claim advanced against this by the taxpayer was that the payments were within the exception for insurance—a claim to which this court gave the short shrift that it deserved. The case thus has simply no bearing on the issue here before us.

[Estate of Bahen]

The most influential decision on what the decedent must receive or be entitled to receive in order to trigger application of § 2039 is Estate of Bahen v. United States 305 F.2d 827, 158 Ct.Cl. 141 (1962) (Davis, J.). The opinion is indeed a virtuoso performance which has tended to dominate the field to the extent that * * * courts seem to look to the Bahen opinion rather than to the statute and the committee reports as indicative of the legislative intent. * * *

The case involved payments by the Chesapeake & Ohio Ry. to Mr. Bahen's widow under two benefit plans. Under the more significant, a non-qualified Deferred Compensation Plan * * * would pay $100,000 to his widow or surviving children in 60 equal monthly instalments; if, prior to retirement, he became totally incapacitated, the payments would be made to him so long as he survived, any amounts unpaid at the time of his death to go to his widow or minor children. Another plan [the Death Benefit Plan] * * * would pay a sum equal to three months salary to his widow or minor children. * * * Most relevantly for our purposes, the court held that the provision for payments to Mr. Bahen under the Deferred Compensation Plan in the event of his disability prior to retirement satisfied the condition of § 2039(a), for the

¶ 28,055

purposes of both payments to Mrs. Bahen, since at the time of his death he possessed the right to receive such payments.

While, as indicated, the case bears some resemblance to ours, there is a different flavor about it, at least so far as concerns the payments under the Deferred Compensation Plan. There was in fact a unitary right to receive deferred compensation of $100,000 in 60 equal monthly payments, this to be paid to Mrs. Bahen if Bahen died or to him if he became totally disabled prior to retirement. There was no question of grouping separate plans together, since both Mr. and Mrs. Bahen's rights were pursuant to the same Deferred Compensation Plan. Even more to the point, if payments were being made to Mr. Bahen due to his disability and he died prior to exhausting the fund, the remaining payments would be made to Mrs. Bahen. In this respect the Deferred Compensation Plan was much like the joint and survivor annuity at which § 2039 was aimed. Here, of course, Mrs. Schelberg had no rights to any payments under the Disability Plan. The possible payments to Mr. Bahen were not, as under IBM's Disability Plan, true disability payments intended to cover a portion of previous salary; they were deferred compensation, as the plan's title indicates, payable by the railway in any event, to be made available to Mr. Bahen at a date earlier than death if his needs so required. They thus met the test * * * as IBM's disability benefits do not, of being of the same nature as the payments to the beneficiary. We are not sure that the distinction is sufficient or—what is more or less the same thing—that we would have decided *Bahen* as the Court of Claims did. For the moment we shall leave the matter that way.

[Holding]

We here decide only that to consider a deceased employee's potential ability to have qualified at some future time for payments under a plan protecting against total and permanent disability—a disagreeable feat that had been accomplished as of January 1, 1974, by only a quarter of one percent of IBM's employees as meeting the condition in § 2039(a) that there must be a contract or agreement under which the decedent received or be entitled to receive "an annuity or other payment", is such a departure from the language used by Congress, read in the light of the problem with which it was intending to deal, as to be at war with common sense. * * * Of the other decisions cited to us, there are clear grounds of distinguishing all with the possible exception of the leading one, *Estate of Bahen*, * * * [and] we would not wish to be understood as necessarily agreeing with all of them or with the general approach taken in *Bahen*. * * * Some other case may require complete rethinking whether courts, under the influence of the *Bahen* opinion, have not unduly eroded the condition in § 2039(a)[;] * * * on the other hand, Congress might decide to cast its net more widely and eliminate or broaden the condition, as it could have done in 1954. We simply decline to carry the erosion of the condition to the extent here urged by the Commissioner.

The judgment is reversed and the cause remanded with instructions to annul the determination of a deficiency.

¶ 28,055

[¶ 28,063]

2. OTHER ESTATE AND GIFT TAXATION POSSIBILITIES

LEVIN v. COMMISSIONER

United States Tax Court, 1988.
90 T.C. 723.

JACOBS, Judge:

* * *

At the time of his death, and for a period of 34 years prior thereto, the decedent was employed by Marstan, a Pennsylvania corporation engaged in the wholesale distribution of paper products and janitorial supplies, and a predecessor partnership. He served as Marstan's president from the time of its incorporation in January of 1952 until March 14, 1980, when his son, Mark, was elected president, and he became chairman of the board. * * *

* * *

On November 5, 1980, Marstan's directors adopted a plan effective October 1, 1980, which provided for the payment of an annuity to the surviving spouses of the officers of Marstan who died while in the employ of Marstan and who met certain eligibility requirements. The plan was adopted after consultation with the company's attorneys and representatives of an employee benefits consulting organization.

* * *

No trust was established nor were any assets set aside or segregated for purposes of making payments under the plan.

* * *

Upon the death of the decedent, Marstan became obligated under the plan to pay the decedent's widow, who was then 63 years old, a lifetime annuity of $34,000 per year in monthly installments. Such payments were currently being made as of the date of trial. The parties determined the commuted value of the annuity to Mrs. Levin to be $344,343.16 at the date of the decedent's death.

* * *

The commuted value of the annuity to Mrs. Levin was not included in the decedent's gross estate, nor did the decedent pay gift tax on the value of the annuity. Respondent contends that the value of such annuity is subject to estate taxation under either § 2035 or § 2038. Alternatively, respondent contends that the value of the annuity is subject to gift taxation under § 2511.

OPINION

The dispute involved herein is whether a post mortem annuity payable by the decedent's employer to his surviving spouse is subject to either Federal estate or gift taxation. We will first address whether the annuity is subject to Federal estate taxation.

Section 2001(a) imposes a tax on the transfer of the taxable estate of every decedent who is a citizen or resident of the United States. The taxable estate is defined as the decedent's gross estate, less specified deductions. § 2051.The value of the gross estate of a decedent includes * * * the value at the time of his death of all property owned by decedent, whether real or personal, tangible or intangible, wherever situated. Reg. § 20.0–2. However, the gross estate also may include property in which the decedent did not have an interest at the time of his death. Reg. § 20.0–2(b)(2). Such is the case when the transfer fails within the purview of either of the estate tax §§ here at issue, i.e., §§ 2035(a) and 2038(a)(1). Both §§ 2035 and 2038 address interests in property transferred by the decedent during his life under such circumstances as to bring the interests within the decedent's gross estate. Reg. § 20.2031–1(a)(2).

* * *

In order for the post mortem annuity to be includable in the decedent's gross estate under § 2038: (1) The decedent must have had a property interest in the post mortem annuity; (2) he must have made a transfer of the annuity during his life; and (3) he must have retained the power to alter, amend, revoke, or terminate the transfer.

Petitioner contends that § 2038 is inapplicable because the post mortem annuity was not property in which the decedent had an interest, and hence, he could not have made the requisite inter vivos transfer to his spouse. Further, petitioner contends that even if the decedent had a property interest in the post mortem annuity and made the requisite inter vivos transfer, he did not retain the power to "alter, amend, revoke or terminate" the transfer of such annuity. Respondent takes an opposing viewpoint.

Since § 2038(a)(1) is applicable only to property which is transferred by a decedent during his lifetime, we first must decide whether the decedent had a property interest in the post mortem annuity, and if so, whether he made the requisite inter vivos transfer. In this regard, we note that "a transfer of property procured through expenditures by the decedent with the purpose, effected at his death, of having it pass to another" is a transfer by a decedent of property. * * *

In order for the post mortem annuity to be considered the decedent's property, Marstan must have been contractually obligated to make the annuity payments. * * * In our opinion, Marstan offered the decedent and other qualified corporate officers a surviving spouse's annuity if they remained in the employ of Marstan. The decedent's continued employment constituted his acceptance of the company's offer and served as the consideration for the benefits to be paid under the plan. In essence, the surviving spouse's annuity constituted deferred compensation payable upon the death of the qualified corporate officer. Thus, the surviving spouse's annuity was property procured as a result of the decedent's rendering services to Marstan.

Petitioner contends, however, that because the plan was revocable, it did not amount to a binding contract but was at most a "mere expectancy" that the decedent's spouse would receive a future benefit. We disagree.

Under Pennsylvania law, Marstan's obligation under the plan, unless terminated by the board of directors, was fixed and could be enforced by the decedent's widow at the time of death. * * *

It was highly unlikely that Marstan's obligation under the plan would be terminated unless the decedent consented to such termination. The decedent owned more than 80 percent of Marstan's voting stock, and in reality, the plan could not be terminated without his approval. Indeed, the plan provides that no amendment could be made which would have an adverse impact on the benefits to be received without the written consent of the eligible officer or his surviving spouse. * * * Thus, the decedent had more than a "mere expectancy" that his spouse would receive a lifetime annuity.

* * *

In conclusion, we believe that Marstan was contractually obligated to pay the post mortem annuity benefits to the decedent's widow, since the annuity was procured by consideration furnished by the decedent. Therefore, for purposes of § 2038, the annuity is property in which the decedent transferred an interest during his lifetime to his spouse. * * *

The fact that the right to receive the post mortem benefits was contingent (from the decedent's widow's viewpoint), in our opinion, is not relevant. Additionally, we deem not relevant the fact that the decedent could not have received any of such payments. The decedent's previous and continued employment with the company was the source of the post mortem payments to the widow, and the transfer of such payments was the potentially taxable event. * * *

[Retained Power]

Having determined that the decedent transferred a property interest in the annuity to his spouse, we now must determine whether the decedent retained the power to alter, amend, revoke, or terminate such transfer. Although the plan could not be amended or terminated by the decedent in his individual capacity, he was able to do so as a member of the board of directors in conjunction with the other members. Decedent's ability to amend or revoke the plan in conjunction with other Marstan board members is a sufficient "power," to compel inclusion of the value of the post mortem annuity in the decedent's estate.

Petitioner places great emphasis on the occasions that the other board members acted in contradiction of the decedent's wishes. However, it is the existence of the right to amend or terminate the plan, rather than the likelihood of its exercise, that is the controlling factor. * * * Moreover, in this case, we believe the ability of the other board members to go against decedent's wishes was largely illusory.

¶ 28,063

[DiMarco *Distinguished*]

Petitioner cites Estate of DiMarco v. Commissioner, 87 T.C. 653 (1986), to support its position. In *DiMarco,* we held that the decedent did not make a taxable gift of a survivor's income benefit pursuant to a plan established and maintained by his employer (IBM) within the meaning of § 2503. The facts in this case are clearly distinguishable from those in *DiMarco.* In *DiMarco,* the decedent was not a controlling shareholder of IBM nor was he an officer or director thereof. Unlike the decedent herein, the decedent in *DiMarco* was not able to alter, amend, revoke, or terminate the IBM plan by which the widow received a survivor's income benefit. In contrast, the decedent herein, by virtue of his control of Marstan, was able to structure and amend the plan to suit his needs. Thus, our holding herein that the commuted value of the post mortem annuity payable to Mrs. Levin is includable in the gross estate of the decedent pursuant to § 2038(a)(1) is not contrary to the holding in *DiMarco.*

[Possible Gift Tax]

A second basis for respondent's determination of the deficiencies is his contention that the annuity constitutes an inter vivos gift from the decedent to Mrs. Levin, such that either an estate tax should be imposed pursuant to § 2035(a) or a gift tax should be imposed pursuant to § 2511. However, neither of these §§ applies in the absence of a completed inter vivos gift, whether direct or indirect, from the decedent to Mrs. Levin.

It has long been recognized that a transfer of property is not complete for purposes of the gift tax provisions, and is therefore not subject to gift tax, if the donor retains control over the disposition of the property. §§ 25.2511–2(b) and 25.2511–2(e). * * * Here, the decedent retained control over his wife's right to the post mortem annuity because he could defeat the transfer by terminating his employment with Marstan prior to his death, by divorcing his spouse, or by agreeing to terminate the plan. Because the decedent retained such control over the property transferred, in our opinion, no gift occurred.

[¶ 28,071]

Note

The IRS acquiesced in the result reached in *DiMarco* (cited in *Levin),* 1990–2 C.B. 1, and, subsequently, it revoked Revenue Ruling 81–31, 1981–1 C.B. 475. Rev. Rul. 92–68, 1992–2 C.B. 257.

Revenue Ruling 81–31 is particularly interesting. Under the terms of an employment contract, the employee's spouse was to receive a death benefit equal to twice the employee's salary at death, the promise being made in consideration of the future services to be rendered by the employee. The ruling concluded that the transfer became a completed gift only when the employee died and, as a result, it was at that point that the gift tax (not estate tax) was to be imposed. The ruling expressed the opinion the transfer was not complete at the time of the contract because: (1) it was impossible to ascertain the amount of the death benefit to be paid and (2) payment was dependent upon the employee being both employed and married at death.

The Tax Court in both *Levin* and *DiMarco* (and now the IRS in Revenue Ruling 92–68) rejected the conclusion reached in Revenue Ruling 81–31, the Tax Court saying, in *Levin* (footnote 15):

> To the extent that this ruling can be read as holding either that a transfer of property can be come complete for gift tax purposes by reason of the death of the donor, or that it is permissible to treat a completed transfer of property as an open transaction and to value the transferred property and impose the gift tax at some time other then when the completed transfer occurs, we regard the ruling as being inconsistent with the gift tax statute and the regulations.

Nonetheless, the approach taken in Revenue Ruling 81–31 remains noteworthy for purposes of gift tax policy development.

Problems

[¶ 28,090]

1. Nothing in the *Levin* opinion suggests that the court even entertained the possibility that Marston's postmortem annuity was snagged by § 2039(a). Why not?

2. Caitlin is employed full time as technician at a retail computer shop, Gismo, Inc., which is wholly owned by her father, Bulldog. Caitlin has been diagnosed as terminally ill. As a means of providing for her children, her father has proposed that he set up a plan whereby Gismo continues Caitlin's salary until her youngest child attains 18 with all payments being made to the children. Bulldog believes that the payments made by Gismo under the plan will be income-tax deductible (and taxable to the children upon receipt). His concern, however, is with respect to estate taxes. Caitlin is in the top percent estate tax bracket. Under no circumstances does Bulldog want the amounts to be paid to Caitlin's children to be included in her estate. Please review *Bahen, Schelberg,* and *Levin* and provide Bulldog with a list of features to include in the plan and a list of features to exclude (so as to avoid estate taxation).

C. INCOME TAX CONSEQUENCES TO EMPLOYEE

[¶ 28,101]

When the employee considers the income tax consequences of nonqualified deferred compensation plans, the employee is concerned at two levels. There is immediate concern about the income tax consequences at the time the plan is established for it is at that time that there is risk that the plan benefits will be deemed to have tax consequences. The employee is also concerned—but somewhat peripherally—with the income tax consequences of benefits payable under the plan during retirement and after his death. These are issues of tax accounting.

Among the advantages of the nonqualified deferred compensation plan (NQDCP) is freedom from the restrictions imposed on tax-qualified plans.

Among these are freedom to discriminate between or among employees in participation and vesting rules. However, there are some disadvantages as well. For example, generally speaking:

1. An employer does not receive a tax deduction until the amounts due under the NQDCP are taxed to employees. See §§ 83(h), 404(a)(5); Reg. §§ 1.83–6; 1.404(a)–12(b)(1).

2. An NQDCP's trust fund is not tax exempt; therefore, the trust may be taxed on contributions it receives and can be taxed on investment gains. §§ 641, 671–679.

3. An employee may be taxed on NQDCP benefits before he or she receives any benefits. See §§ 402(b), 451(a).

By way of contrast, a tax-qualified plan offers three significant tax benefits to the employer and the employees. First, the employer receives an immediate deduction for their contributions to the plan, regardless of when the employees are taxed. See § 404(a)(1)–(4). Second, if a trust is a funding device for a qualified plan, then contribution and investment gains of the trust fund are tax exempt. See § 501(a). And third, the employee is not taxed until he receives the benefits. See §§ 83, 402(b), 451(a); Reg. § 1.451–2(a).

Revenue Ruling 60–31 and the *Goldsmith* case, which are reproduced below, detail schemes used by other taxpayers to structure nonqualified deferred compensation plans which are to have no immediate income tax consequences to the employee. *Goldsmith,* particularly, raises the tax accounting issues of constructive receipt, assignment of income, and economic benefit. Critical, too, is the notion of security, i.e., whether the employee assumes any risk of nonpayment. Could it be said, that while an employee may enter into contracts to defer part or all of his or her compensation, the test used to determine whether a benefit constitutes taxable income immediately or subsequently, when the employee is in actual, physical receipt of the payment, depends upon whether, borrowing the words from § 83(a), there is any "substantial risk of forfeiture" of the benefit? Thus, the employee has taxable income when payment of the benefit is secured.

Life insurance is often an important factor in the structuring of nonqualified deferred compensation plans. Many plans are funded with life insurance, thereby easing the burden on the employer who is obligated under the plan. The *Goldsmith* plan was funded with life insurance. Investigate the tax consequences of such funding.

[¶ 28,109]

1. WHEN PLAN ESTABLISHED

REVENUE RULING 60–31
1960–1 C.B. 174.

Advice has been requested regarding the taxable year of inclusion in gross income of a taxpayer, using the cash receipts and disbursements method of accounting, of compensation for services received under the circumstances described below.

[Employment Contract]

(1) On January 1, 1958, the taxpayer and corporation X executed an employment contract under which * * * the taxpayer is entitled to a stated annual salary and to additional compensation of $10x$ dollars for each year. The additional compensation will be * * * [paid upon retirement or death. The obligation is purely contractual and no trust is to be created.]

[Executive]

(2) The taxpayer is an officer and director of corporation A, which has a plan for making future payments of additional compensation. * * * This amount is not currently paid to the participants; but, the corporation has set up on its books a separate account for each participant * * * Each account is also credited with the net amount, if any, realized from investing any portion of the amount in the account.

Distributions are to be made from these accounts annually beginning when the employee * * * [retires, dies, or is disabled. The obligation is purely contractual; no trust is to be created.] However, the corporation's liability to make these distributions is contingent upon the employee's (1) refraining from engaging in any business competitive to that of the corporation, (2) making himself available * * * [as a consultant to the corporation].

[Author Royalties]

(3) On October 1, 1957, the taxpayer, an author, and corporation Y, a publisher, executed an agreement under which the taxpayer granted to the publisher the exclusive right to print, publish and sell a book he had written. This agreement provides that the publisher will [pay the author royalties. A supplemental agreement provided that payment of royalties was limited to $100,000 in any one year. Any excess was to be deferred to subsequent years.] * * *

[Football Player]

(4) In June 1957, the taxpayer, a football player, entered into a two-year standard player's contract with a football club in which he agreed to play football and engage in activities related to football during the two-year term only for the club. In addition to a specified salary for the two-year term, it was mutually agreed that as an inducement for signing the contract the taxpayer would be paid a bonus of $150x$ dollars. The taxpayer could have demanded and received payment of this bonus at the time of signing the contract, but at his suggestion there was added to the standard contract form a paragraph providing substantially as follows:

The player shall receive the sum of $150x$ dollars upon signing of this contract, contingent upon the payment of this $150x$ dollars to an escrow agent designated by him. * * *

Pursuant to this added provision * * * the escrow agent agreed to pay this amount, plus interest, to the taxpayer in installments over a period of five years. * * * [I]n the event of the taxpayer's death during the escrow period the balance due will become part of his estate.

¶ 28,109

[Prize Fighter]

(5) The taxpayer, a boxer, entered into an agreement with a boxing club to fight a particular opponent * * * providing for payment of the taxpayer's share of the receipts from the match as follows: 25 percent thereof not later than two weeks after the bout, and 25 percent thereof during each of the three years following the year of the bout in equal semiannual installments. Such deferments are not customary in prize fighting contracts, and the supplemental agreement was executed at the demand of the taxpayer. * * *

[Applicable Law]

Section 1.451–1(a) of the Income Tax Regulations provides in part as follows:

> Gains, profits, and income are to be included in gross income for the taxable year in which they are actually or constructively received by the taxpayer unless includible for a different year in accordance with the taxpayer's method of accounting. * * *

And, with respect to the cash receipts and disbursements method of accounting, Reg. § 1.446–1(c)(1)(i) provides in part—

> Generally, under the cash receipts and disbursements method in the computation of taxable income, all items which constitute gross income (whether in the form of cash, property, or services) are to be included for the taxable year in which actually or constructively received. * * *

As previously stated, the individual concerned in each of the situations described above employs the cash receipts and disbursements method of accounting. Under that method, as indicated by the above-quoted provisions of the regulations, he is required to include the compensation concerned in gross income only for the taxable year in which it is actually or constructively received. Consequently, the question for resolution is whether in each of the situations described the income in question was constructively received in a taxable year prior to the taxable year of actual receipt.

A mere promise to pay, not represented by notes or secured in any way, is not regarded as a receipt of income within the intendment of the cash receipts and disbursements method.

* * * "Taxpayers on a receipts and disbursements basis are required to report only income actually received no matter how binding any contracts they may have to receive more."

This should not be construed to mean that under the cash receipts and disbursements method income may be taxed only when realized in cash. For, under that method a taxpayer is required to include in income that which is received in cash or cash equivalent. * * * And, as stated in the above-quoted provisions of the regulations, the "receipt" contemplated by the cash method may be actual or constructive.

[Constructive Receipt]

With respect to the constructive receipt of income, Reg. § 1.451–2(a) (which accords with prior regulations extending back to, and including, Article

¶ 28,109

53 of Regulation 45 under the Revenue Act of 1918) provides, in part, as follows:

> Income although not actually reduced to a taxpayer's possession is constructively received by him in the taxable year during which it is credited to his account or set apart for him so that he may draw upon it at any time. However, income is not constructively received if the taxpayer's control of its receipt is subject to substantial limitations or restrictions. Thus, if a corporation credits its employees with bonus stock, but the stock is not available to such employees until some future date, the mere crediting on the books of the corporation does not constitute receipt.

Thus, under the doctrine of constructive receipt, a taxpayer may not deliberately turn his back upon income and thereby select the year for which he will report it. * * * Nor may a taxpayer, by a private agreement, postpone receipt of income from one taxable year to another. * * *

However, the statute cannot be administered by speculating whether the payor would have been willing to agree to an earlier payment.

* * *

It is clear that the doctrine of constructive receipt is to be sparingly used; that amounts due from a corporation but unpaid, are not to be included in the income of an individual reporting his income on a cash receipts basis unless it appears that the money was available to him, that the corporation was able and ready to pay him, that his right to receive was not restricted, and that his failure to receive resulted from exercise of his own choice.

Consequently, it seems clear that in each case involving a deferral of compensation a determination of whether the doctrine of constructive receipt is applicable must be made upon the basis of the specific factual situation involved.

Applying the foregoing criteria to the situations described above, the following conclusions have been reached:

[Employment Contract]

(1) The additional compensation to be received by the taxpayer under the employment contract concerned will be includible in his gross income only in the taxable years in which the taxpayer actually receives installment payments in cash or other property previously credited to his account. To hold otherwise would be contrary to the provisions of the regulations and the court decisions mentioned above.

[Executive]

(2) For the reasons in (1) above, it is held that the taxpayer here involved also will be required to include the deferred compensation concerned in his gross income only in the taxable years in which the taxpayer actually receives

¶ 28,109

installment payments in cash or other property previously credited to his account. * * *

[Author Royalties]

(3) Here the principal agreement provided that the royalties were payable substantially as earned, and this agreement was supplemented by a further concurrent agreement which made the royalties payable over a period of years. This supplemental agreement, however, was made before the royalties were earned; in fact, it was made on the same day as the principal agreement and the two agreements were a part of the same transaction. Thus, for all practical purposes, the arrangement from the beginning is similar to that in (1) above. Therefore, it is also held that the author concerned will he required to include the royalties in his gross income only in the taxable years in which they are actually received in cash or other property.

[Football Player]

(4) In Revenue Ruling 55–727, the taxpayer, a professional baseball player, entered into a contract in 1953 in which he agreed to render services for a baseball club and to refrain from playing baseball for any other club during the term of the contract. In addition to specified compensation, the contract provided for a bonus to the player or his estate, payable one-half in January 1954 and one-half in January 1955, whether or not he was able to render services. * * * [The bonus was] taxable for the year in which received by the player. However, under the facts set forth in Revenue Ruling 55–727 there was no arrangement, as here, for placing the amount of the bonus in escrow. Consequently, the instant situation is distinguishable from that considered in Revenue Ruling 55–727.

In E.T. Sproull v. Commissioner, 16 T.C. 244, affirmed, 194 Fed. (2d) 541, the petitioner's employer in 1945 transferred in trust for the petitioner the amount of $10,500. The trustee was directed to pay out of principal to the petitioner the sum of $5,250 in 1946 and the balance, including income, in 1947. In the event of the petitioner's prior death, the amounts were to be paid to his administrator, executor, or heirs. * * * In this connection the court stated:

> * * * it is undoubtedly true that the amount which the Commissioner has included in petitioner's income for 1945 was used in that year for his benefit * * * in setting up the trust of which petitioner, or, in the event of his death then his estate, was the sole beneficiary * * *

> The question then becomes * * * was "any economic or financial benefit conferred on the employee as compensation" in the taxable year. If so, it was taxable to him in that year. This question we must answer in the affirmative. The employer's part of the transaction terminated in 1945. It was then that the amount of the compensation was fixed at $10,500 and irrevocably paid out for petitioner's sole benefit. * * *

Applying the principles stated in the *Sproull* decision to the facts here, it is concluded that the 150*x*-dollar bonus is includible in the gross income of the

¶ 28,109

football player concerned in 1957, the year in which the club unconditionally paid such amount to the escrow agent.

[Prize Fighter]

(5) In this case, the taxpayer and the boxing club, as well as the opponent whom taxpayer had agreed to meet, are each acting in his or its own right, the proposed match is a joint venture by all of these participants, and the taxpayer is not an employee of the boxing club. The taxpayer's share of the gross receipts from the match belong to him and never belonged to the boxing club. Thus, the taxpayer acquired all of the benefits to his share of the receipts except the right of immediate physical possession; and, although the club retained physical possession, it was by virtue of an arrangement with the taxpayer who, in substance and effect, authorized the boxing club to take possession and hold for him. The receipts, therefore, were income to the taxpayer at the time they were paid to and retained by the boxing club by his agreement and, in substance, at his direction, and are includible in his gross income in the taxable year in which so paid to the club.

[¶ 28,111]

GOLDSMITH v. UNITED STATES

United States Court of Claims, 1978.
586 F.2d 810.

PER CURIAM:

[The court adopted the opinion of the trial judge.]

SCHWARTZ, Trial Judge: * * * [Taxpayers] been the fulltime anesthesiologist at the Youngstown Osteopathic Hospital in Youngstown, Ohio. The issue is whether sums withheld from his compensation in 1969 and 1970, under a deferred compensation agreement made in 1969, were nevertheless taxable as income to him in those years, either as constructively received or on the ground of economic benefit conferred. It is here held that the entire amount withheld was not constructively received, but that certain insurance features of the agreement are taxable as conferring on the taxpayer a present economic benefit able to be valued.

* * *

* * * [Dr. Goldsmith's employment agreement was for a period of one year, terminable upon 90 days' notice.]

The agreement with the hospital provides that Dr. Goldsmith is to procure his own professional liability insurance and that the hospital is not to control or direct his work. * * *

By the agreement the hospital undertook to furnish the space, secretarial, billing and other services necessary for the performance of Dr. Goldsmith's services, and to pay him a compensation of 90 percent of his billings, in monthly installments. * * *

¶ 28,111

In 1969, after discussions with the hospital's executive director and an agent of the Continental Assurance Company, * * * [a]n agreement entitled "Deferred Compensation and Income Continuation Agreement" was thereafter executed between the taxpayer and the hospital. * * *

The agreement opened with an undertaking by Dr. Goldsmith to continue his status as independent contractor with the hospital until retirement age of 65. In return the hospital agreed to provide these benefits: Retirement benefits were payable beginning June 6, 1996, 27 years distant, when Dr. Goldsmith would reach 65, if his association with the hospital continued until that time. He could then elect to receive either $19,484 yearly for 10 years, his beneficiary to replace him if he died before the expiration of the 10 years; or $13,724.76 yearly for life, his beneficiary nevertheless to replace him, on his death, for a total of 10 years following his retirement.

Severance benefits were to be payable, at retirement and for 10 years, if he left the hospital's employ for reasons other than retirement, death or total disability. * * *

The agreement further provided for a death benefit to Dr. Goldsmith's children should he die before retirement while still employed. * * *

Finally, it was provided that the hospital should have "no obligation to set aside, earmark or entrust any fund or money with which to pay its obligations" under the agreement. Dr. Goldsmith was to "be and remain simply a creditor of the Hospital"

Remarkably there is no statement in the deferred compensation agreement that these very substantial amounts are not additional compensation, or that they are in lieu of any particular amount of compensation hitherto payable. In fact, however, it was well understood by both Dr. Goldsmith and the hospital that the benefits under the agreement would be in lieu of $450 of the monthly sum—90 percent of billings—payable to Dr. Goldsmith under his basic employment agreement with the hospital, and henceforth to be deducted from his monthly 90 percent share of billings. * * *

The deferred compensation agreement was terminable by either party on 30 days' notice; the underlying 1966 employment agreement was terminable on 3 months' notice. * * *

* * * [The agreement was to be] funded by the purchase by the hospital from the Continental Assurance Company of a life insurance endowment policy offered to the taxpayer, on which the monthly premium would be $450.

* * * The policy, issued on the life of Dr. Goldsmith and attuned to his age and years until retirement, names the hospital as owner and beneficiary.

On Dr. Goldsmith's accidental death or total disability, the benefits to the hospital were precisely those due to Dr. Goldsmith under the deferred compensation agreement. * * *

* * *

The taxpayer stands on the deferred compensation agreement, contending that it amended the earlier employment agreement with the hospital so as to put the monthly sum of $450 beyond his reach according to its terms. The Government's primary response is based on the taxpayer's control over the establishment of the deferred compensation arrangement and its responsiveness to his desires, and his continuing control over it through his power to end the deferment of compensation on 30 days' notice. These features, it is said, amount to current availability and constructive receipt of the entire $450 deducted from compensation each month, under Reg. § 1.451–2(a). A secondary Government position is that income was realized to the extent of the economic benefit to the taxpayer represented by the promises of the hospital to pay benefits on his death and to continue the accrual of benefits should he become totally disabled.

[Constructive Receipt]

Constructive receipt is a doctrine which holds, in the words of the regulations under § 451, that income is "constructively received" by a cash-basis taxpayer when it is set apart for him or otherwise made available so that he may draw upon it any time, without "substantial limitations or restrictions." § 451, Reg. § 1.451–2(a). * * * Thus "under the doctrine of constructive receipt a taxpayer may not deliberately turn his back upon income and thereby select the year for which he will report it." * * *

* * *

The deferred compensation agreement here involved in large measure follows the common form of nonqualified deferred compensation agreements between corporate employers and their executives. The type of agreement often made provides, in addition to a currently paid compensation, for deferred compensation in stated amounts, payable after a term of years, or in the case of those employees expected to remain in the employ until retirement, payable upon retirement, as an annuity for life or for a fixed number of years. Almost the whole purpose of these agreements is to postpone—"defer"—income and taxation to a time when the employee is presumably in a lower tax bracket.

* * *

Once uncertain as to their success in deferring income and taxation, these agreements have at least since 1960 flourished under the aegis of Rev. Rul. 60–31, *supra.* * * *

* * *

The agreement in this case between the taxpayer and his hospital seems to have had the characteristics of those which have been held to defer the employee's taxation. It was no sham, no mere pretense in which the employee actually got or could have gotten the money or its equivalent pretendedly deferred. * * * There is no evidence, direct or from the surrounding circumstances, that the present agreement to defer could or would be disregarded at will. It is quite true that the making of the agreement was characterized by considerable informality. The taxpayer neither made a written request for a deferred compensation agreement nor expressly authorized an adjustment in the payment of his fees, as the hospital's resolution contemplated. This shows nothing going to substance. The agreement to defer was plain, if inferable, from the conduct of the parties in making the agreement, in cooperating in the application for the policy, in which beneficiaries were named, and in withholding the agreed [upon] sums. The parties meant to be bound, and once the agreement was made and deductions began, there were patently the "substantial limitations or restrictions" on plaintiff's access to the deducted sums which under the regulation negative constructive receipt.

It is immaterial that the agreement to defer compensation was made in 1969, after the original payments were set by the basic 1966 employment agreement. The amendment of an existing agreement to defer a payment date does not entail constructive receipt of the payment at the earlier date, so long as the amendment is prior to the time the taxpayer has a right to receive the deferred sums. * * *

[Constructive Receipt: Control]

What then does the Government say converts the monthly deductions by the hospital into constructively received income? A first claim is based on the "control" over the arrangement exercised by the taxpayer, evidenced by his choice of the insurance company and the very decision to fund. A variation of this argument is that the reason for the deferment must be "inherent" in the transaction and may not arise from the "personal requirements" of the taxpayer.

There is no authority for either variation. * * *

The related suggestion that the hospital received no benefit from the deferred compensation arrangement, also, is not entirely valid. The hospital retained title to the insurance policy, for the benefit of all its creditors, of whom the taxpayer was only one. It had the right, too, to cease paying premiums, upon which the sums withheld would remain with the hospital. * * *

But even assuming no benefit to the hospital, the argument from the taxpayer's control and his "personal requirements" is rejected; not, however, on its facts. All the facts point to the conclusion that the determination of the amounts to be deducted, the choice of benefits and decision to fund, were decisions by the taxpayer, according to his desires. Even the hospital's bare legal right to discontinue funding could promptly be neutralized by the taxpayer's cancellation of the entire agreement. There was only the limitation that the hospital could either fund or see the end of the agreement.

[Contractual Obligation]

These facts as to the origins and duration of the agreement have, however, little to do with constructive receipt, essentially a question of the product of the agreement when in force. Who brought the plan to the hospital's attention, whether the taxpayer persuaded the hospital to agree or vice versa, whose "personal requirements" are served by an agreement which is not a sham, and the like, are questions irrelevant to receipt, constructive or actual, under the binding agreement in fact reached. Objective matters such as the receipt of income from a bargain do not depend upon which party in the bargain dominated the other. If the employer's funding of the agreement does not work a constructive receipt, to defeat a deferment of tax, and the Internal Revenue Service has explicitly ruled that it does not (in Rev. Rul. 68–99, supra), then it is no further ground for taxation that the funding was agreed to by the parties at the suggestion or even the demand of the employee.

[Security Interest]

The funding by insurance here was merely a method of investment by the hospital to finance its undertakings. No trust, escrow or other such arrangement affecting the withheld sums was constituted such as would invalidate the deferment by giving the taxpayer a security interest in the sums deferred. In example 1 of Rev. Rul. 60–31 the deferred sum was held nontaxable in part because the employer's promise was "not represented by notes or secured in any way" (1960–1 Cum. Bull. at 177); in example 4, a bonus to a football player was held taxable because it was paid to an escrow agent who would pay it to the player in 5 years (1960–1 Cum. Bull. at 179–80).

The taxpayer in the instant case had no rights in the withheld sums either against his hospital or the insurance company. The hospital was the sole owner and beneficiary of the policy, and the taxpayer could rely only on the credit of the hospital and the strength of its promise. * * *

The Government particularly emphasizes, in its argument of control, the taxpayer's ability to cancel the agreement on one month's notice. It is argued that this provision gave him an option every month to take his next month's compensation in cash, by cancelling the agreement, or to take it partly in cash and, as to $450 thereof, partly in deferred compensation benefits. But this is essentially the same right as the executive has in a continuing employment contract in which each year he may elect to take a specified percentage of his next year's compensation in deferred benefits, an arrangement explicitly approved by the Internal Revenue Service in Rev. Rul. 69–650, supra.

[Willingness to Pay]

Basically opposed to the Government's contentions based on "control" and "option" are the authorities to the effect that it is no impediment to the success of a deferred compensation plan that, as was no doubt here the case, the employer is willing to pay presently and immediately the compensation agreed to be deferred. In such cases the predominant if not the sole motivation is the desire and tax advantage of the employee. The prize fighter, corporate executive, author and football player all bargained for deferment, in one form or another, of sums which could at their will have been paid to them in the first year of the agreements for their services. * * * The purpose of the typical deferred compensation agreement—to benefit the taxpayer-employee by postponing income to a time when he is in a lower tax bracket—makes it inevitable that in most cases the employer would have been willing to make the payment currently and that the agreement should have been entered into pursuant to the desire of the employee-taxpayer.

* * *

[Assignment of Income]

In a wholly different approach the Government has also attacked the 1966 compensation arrangement, contending that the 90 percent billing arrangement was an anticipatory assignment of income and thus that the collections from patients were the taxpayer's income from the time he authorized the hospital to collect the bills. In support there is cited * * * the classic cases of Lucas v. Earl, 281 U.S. 111 (1930); Corliss v. Bowers, 281 U.S. 376 (1930) and Helvering v. Horst, 311 U.S. 112 (1940) which stand for the proposition that a person is in constructive receipt of income which he is free to enjoy or dispose of, and taxation is not avoided by an anticipatory assignment. * * *

One difficulty with this argument is that all the billings, the rights to which were perhaps originally owned by the taxpayer, were exchanged in the 1966 employment agreement for an appointment to the hospital's staff, access to the hospital's patients, the hospital's services in collection, and 90 percent of the billings. Another difficulty is that the billings, whatever their ownership, were not taxable income to this cash-basis taxpayer until received, and actual receipt was pursuant to an agreement limited to 90 percent of their total. And, finally, that agreement was amended by a further agreement which deferred $450 monthly of the 90 percent. While that last agreement existed, the sums to be deducted and withheld were not within the power of the taxpayer to assign.

The deferred compensation agreement was therefore valid, not a sham, and effectively limited and restricted the taxpayer's right to the $450 deducted from what would otherwise have been his compensation. The taxpayer was not in constructive receipt of the withheld amounts, and the second issue in this case is reached—whether the deferred compensation agreement provided the taxpayer with a taxable economic benefit.

[Economic Benefit]

* * * On this branch of the case the Government contends that the value of several of the hospital's promises under the deferred compensation agreement was taxable in the years involved, under the economic benefit doctrine. "The economic benefit doctrine does not depend for its applicability on whether the employee could have received cash by stretching out his hand. It is based on the theory that the promise to pay deferred compensation in the future in and of itself under certain circumstances may constitute an economic benefit or the equivalent of cash to be taxed currently at present value, if it can be valued currently with some exactness." McDonald, Deferred Compensation: Conceptual Astigmatism, 24 Tax L.Rev. 201, 204 (1969). The question is therefore whether any of the promises by the hospital were such economic benefits to the taxpayer in the years in question, and were capable of valuation.

¶ 28,111

The hospital's promises to pay retirement benefits and severance benefits would come due 27 years in the future when the taxpayer reached 65. The promises were not secured in any way. No trust or escrow was established granting the taxpayer a current benefit or removing these deferred sums from the potential claims of the hospital's other creditors. * * * Nor were these promises by the hospital represented by a note or other writing delivered to the taxpayer, which he could sell or assign. * * *

[Death Benefits]

The payments due upon death were a different matter. They were payable if the taxpayer died before age 65, while still employed by the hospital. For example, should the taxpayer die during the first year of the agreement, the hospital promised to pay his beneficiaries—he named his children—a death benefit of $157,603 in 120 monthly installments, with interest, liquidated as $1,479.89 per month. The total of the 120 payments would be $177,586.80. If the death were accidental, the hospital additionally promised his beneficiary a death benefit of $1,307.64 per month for 120 months, or a total of $156,916.80.

The size of these payments is to be contrasted with the amounts due as a severance benefit for one year's service. If the taxpayer left the employ after one year of employment he would receive 10 annual payments of $633, a total of $6,330, beginning only when he reached 65. * * * The contrast emphasizes the deliberateness with which life was insured, effective currently, and not at all postponed until retirement. In case of total disability, there was a still further promise that rights under the deferred compensation agreement would continue to accrue, as if the taxpayer were actively at work, earning money, and $450 was by the agreement being remitted by the hospital each month towards the increase in benefits.

It becomes quite clear that the promises of payment on death or disability were the familiar undertakings of a life insurance company, albeit made by a hospital. To the extent of these promises, the deferred compensation agreement provided the taxpayer with a current economic benefit as valuable as comparable promises by a life insurance company. Taxability is as plain as the taxability of an insurance premium paid by an employer, in other than a qualified pension or group plan, on a policy of which the employee is beneficiary. * * *

Square authority is scant but current economic benefit is plain. Close to the facts of the present case is United States v. Drescher, 179 F.2d 863 (2d Cir.), cert. denied, 340 U.S. 821 (1950), which concerned the taxability of single premium annuity contracts containing insurance features, purchased by an employer for an employee aged 45, the annuity to be payable when he reached 65. In a decision holding both annuity and insurance features to be taxable, as conferring a present economic benefit, the court said this of the insurance features of the annuities (179 F.2d at 866):

Likewise, the assurance that any beneficiary named by him at the time the contract was executed, or substituted by him at a later date, would in the event of his death receive the cost of each contract, plus interest after a few years, conferred a present economic benefit on him. Whatever present value the life insurance feature had to him is clearly taxable.

* * *

Valuation of the economic benefits conferred by the insurance features of the hospital's promises is in principle easily accomplished with evidence of the cost of comparable commercial insurance, in this case the portion of the premium for the policy which is attributable to its life insurance and disability features. The record, however, discloses only that $12.90 and $8.78 were the respective portions of the $450 monthly premium attributable to the accidental death and disability features of the policy. The balance of the $450 premium, $428.32, was stated to be the cost of the "endowment insurance." Presumably, however the insurance company can supply a breakdown, and further proceedings should not be necessary for a complete valuation in the years 1969 and 1970 of the taxable economic benefit, by the measure of the premium portion paid for the value in those two years of the hospital's promises in the nature of life, accidental death and disability insurance here held to have conferred a current economic benefit on the taxpayer. If the parties cannot agree on the amounts involved, the case will be set down for further proceedings under Rule 131(c).

In conclusion, the sums deducted from the taxpayer's compensation in 1969 and 1970 were income taxable to him at the time only to the extent of the portion which was attributable to the value of the three mentioned insurance features of the compensation agreement, and not otherwise. Petitioner is entitled to a refund of taxes assessed on the remaining portions of the sums deducted.

* * *

[¶ 28,117]

2. WHERE LIFE INSURANCE PURCHASED

As to whether the purchase of the life insurance in *Goldsmith* was properly determined to constitute a present economic benefit, consider Revenue Ruling 72–25, 1972–1 C.B. 127, and Revenue Ruling 68–99, 1968–1 C.B. 193, in which it was concluded that an employee does not receive income as a result of an employer's purchase of life insurance to provide a source of funds for deferred compensation plans. The rulings focused on the life insurance contracts as the employer's property that was subject to the employer's creditors.

[¶ 28,125]

3. WHEN BENEFITS PAID

Distributions to plan beneficiaries are normally ordinary income. Moreover, as a general rule, whenever plans are funded by life insurance, the normal exclusion of life insurance proceeds for income tax purposes as provided in § 101 is lost to the plan beneficiaries. See Essenfeld v. Commissioner, 311 F.2d 208 (2d Cir.1962). Of course, the § 101 exclusion is available to the employer who receives the life insurance proceeds upon the death of the employee whose life was insured.

Example. At Watson's death, his employer collected $500,000 under a policy of insurance on Watson's life. The employer was contractually bound to pay Watson's widow 10 percent of the proceeds of the life insurance annually until the fund was exhausted. The $500,000 was collected income tax free by the employer, but each payment to Watson's widow constituted taxable income to the widow.

[¶ 28,175]

4. SECTION 409A IMPACT

Beginning in 2005, § 409A impacted "when" nonqualified deferred compensation plan benefits are income taxable to the plan beneficiary. Section 409A provides that plan benefits are taxed to the beneficiary in the first of the following years: (1) the year determined using the rules specified by § 409A; or (2) the year determined using the rules that traditionally apply, i.e., the rules introduced in ¶¶ 28,101–28,125, rules that are referred to by § 409A as "any other provision of this chapter [1 of the Internal Revenue Code] or any other rule of law". § 409A(c).

Section 409A(a)(1)(A)(i) provides that a plan beneficiary shall be in "constructive receipt", i.e., income taxed on plan benefits, if not previously taxed on those benefits, in year in which those benefits are "not subject to a substantial risk of forfeiture." However, even if plan benefits in question are not subject to a substantial risk of forfeiture, income taxes on those benefits can be deferred if, by the terms of the plan, those benefits satisfy certain safe harbor rules that, practically speaking, have the effect of denying the plan beneficiary the opportunity to time the enjoyment of his or her benefits. See § 409A(a)(2)–(4). That is, Congress was concerned about the abuse potential inherent in allowing plan beneficiaries unfettered control of the time when plan benefits were to be subject to income tax. Thus, assuming receipt of plan benefits is, in fact, deferred, income taxation can be also be deferred so long as actual receipt is not at the whim of the plan beneficiary.

In sum, technically, income tax deferral is only available by the terms of § 409A if the plan meets the conditions for deferral specified in § 409A. For example, prior to § 409A, nonqualified deferred compensation plans, aiming at providing maximum flexibility to the plan beneficiary while deferring income taxation until actual receipt of the plan benefits by the plan beneficiary, would contain so-called "haircut" provisions, provisions which allowed the participant, practically, to receive distributions upon request, subject to forfeiture of only a minimal amount—perhaps, as little as two percent, the two percent forfeiture provision being seen as preventing the plan beneficiary from being in constructive receipt of the plan benefits in an earlier year. As a result of § 409A, however, among other provisions, where there is "no substantial risk of forfeiture", the plan beneficiary is deemed to be in constructive receipt of the plan benefits unless distributions are limited to those made upon separation from service, death, at a fixed time or pursuant to a fixed schedule, change in control of the corporation, or occurrence of an unforeseeable emergency, or the beneficiary's disability. § 409A(a)(2).

Penalties for noncompliance with § 409A are stiff, the penalties being as much as 20 percent. § 409A(a)(1)(B).

Section 409A does not apply to *bona fide* vacation leave, sick leave, compensatory time, disability pay, and death benefits. § 409A(d)(1). And it does not apply to qualified employer plans. By way of contrast, § 409A applies, for example, to discounted stock options, i.e., where the "strike price" (price at which the option can be exercised) is less than the fair market value of the stock on the date the option is granted. H.R. Conf. Rep. No. 108–755, 108th Cong., 2nd Sess., pt 1, at 721 (2004). It does not apply if the strike price is equal to the fair market value of the stock on the date of the grant. And it does not apply to incentive stock options (ISOs).

D. INCOME TAX CONSEQUENCES TO EMPLOYER

[¶ 28,201]

Two popular ways for an employer to cover the financial liabilities of a deferred compensation plan are: (1) to self-fund out of current cash flow and (2) to use a keyman life insurance policy. The two funding techniques produce some common income tax consequences.

[¶ 28,209]

1. INCOME TAX DEDUCTION

The employer may claim an income tax deduction for payments made to an employee from a nonqualified deferred compensation plan. However, no deduction is available until the plan benefits are included in the employee's income. See § 404(a)(5).

[¶ 28,217]

2. WHERE LIFE INSURANCE PURCHASED

Informal funding of nonqualified deferred compensation plans is often provided using life insurance. Nonetheless, the premiums paid by the employer on employer-owned policies on the life of an employee are not income tax deductible by the employer in cases where the employer is the beneficiary of the policies. § 264(a)(1). Only when the plan benefits are taxable to the employee will the employer be able to claim an income tax deduction—and then only for the plan benefits taxable to the employee. See Lundy Packing Co. v. United States, 302 F.Supp. 182 (1969).

Of course, as noted in ¶ 28,125, the § 101 exclusion from income of life insurance proceeds is available to the employer who receives the life insurance proceeds upon the death of the employee whose life was insured.

¶ 28,175

E. ERISA REQUIREMENTS

[¶ 28,251]

Nonqualified deferred compensation plans are intended to be free from the requirements imposed on tax-qualified plans. For that reason, it is important in the design and implementation phase of such plans that care be taken to cause the plan to fit into one or more of the ERISA exemption categories. Generally speaking, it means, *inter alia,* that the plan must avoid being treated as "funded" for ERISA purposes. ERISA 3(3), 4(a), 4(b)(5), 201(2), 301(a)(3), 401(a)(1); DOL Reg. § 2510.3–3(b); see Y. Tauber, Funding Non–Qualified Deferred Compensation Benefits, 1 Erisa & Ben. L.J. 177 (1992). A detailed examination of the ERISA requirements and the safe harbors, however, is beyond the scope of these materials.

F. PLANNING

Problems

[¶ 28,301]

1. What social or tax policy reason can you suggest is the basis for this special tax planning opportunity, enjoyed alike by employees and owner-managers of corporations who are able to avail themselves of nonqualified deferred compensation? What justification is there for denying similar benefits to the self-employed? See ¶ 29,401.

2. Joe Baldwin, President of Tunnelco, Inc., wishes to provide his employee, Robert, with additional benefits as a means of "tying" Robert to Tunnelco. An insurance salesman has convinced Joe that the best thing to do for Robert is to provide Robert's wife and children with $3,000 per month for 10 years if Robert dies while in Joe's employ and a similar benefit if Robert stays to retirement at age 65. The insurance salesman suggested funding Joe's plan with $250,000 of term life insurance (or a "key executive" increasing whole life contract) payable to Tunnelco in the event of Robert's death. What are the income, estate, and gift tax consequences of the scheme? How would you structure the plan to avoid any of the tax consequences that you deem both adverse and voidable? If you were representing Robert, what kind of formality would you suggest that the plan should have? Do you see any disadvantages to Robert in that Tunnelco is a small and relatively new corporation?

3. Joe Baldwin, President of Tunnelco, Inc., wants to maximize the benefits he provides himself, his brother Doug, and his employee, Robert. Suggest for Joe some other benefits that might be made available to him and indicate which ones are tax deductible to his corporation and nontaxable to him. Indicate which of them will not be subject to estate tax at his death. Consider, for example, installation of a group life insurance plan (see § 79 and discussion at ¶ 20,115); a medical reimbursement plan (see § 105); and a salary continuation plan (particularly in the event of disability).

G. RABBI TRUSTS AND SECULAR TRUSTS

[¶ 28,351]

"Rabbi trusts" and "secular trusts" are the popular names of two commonly used nonqualified deferred compensation plans. A secular trust must be irrevocable, but the rabbi trust can be either revocable or irrevocable. See Rev. Proc. 92–64, 1992–2 C.B. 422. However, the principal difference between the two is in the ownership of the tax liability. (The first published ruling, Priv. Ltr. Rul. 8113107, appeared in 1980, and covered a rabbi, hence the name.)

[¶ 28,359]

1. RABBI TRUSTS

The rabbi trust will generally provide that it is subject to the claims of the employer's general creditors. As a result, the employer is deemed owner of the trust and the employee-beneficiary is not subject to income tax on the deferred amounts until distributed to the employee (usually in a subsequent year when it is hoped that the employee will be in lower income tax bracket). When the employer's contributions become includible in the employee's taxable income, the employer is then allowed to deduct the contributions made to the trust. In the meantime, as owner of the trust, the employer is required to include in its taxable income and credits computations the items of income, deductions, and credits of the trust under the grantor trust rules. See §§ 671–679.

Revenue Procedure 92–64, 1992–2 C.B. 422, includes a model rabbi trust. The IRS has stated that it will not rule on unfunded deferred compensation arrangements that use a trust other than this model. The model trust language requires that the trust provide that all assets of the trust are subject to the claims of the general creditors of the company in the event of the company's insolvency or bankruptcy. However, since the publication of the model trust language, in the words of the House Committee report accompanying § 409A (H.R. REP. NO. 108–548, 108th CONG., 2nd SESS., PT 1, at 707–08 (2004)), "arrangements have developed which attempt to protect the assets from creditors despite the terms of the trust." Congress responded with § 409A(b) in 2004, striking particularly at offshore arrangements designed to provide the tainting creditor protection to rabbi trusts that, on their face, appear compliant with the policies expressed in Revenue Procedure 92–64.

[¶ 28,361]

PRIVATE LETTER RULING 9138040
June 21, 1991.

This is in reply to a request for a ruling * * * on behalf of Corporation C concerning the federal income tax consequences of establishing a trust to provide supplemental nonqualified deferred compensation benefits to certain management and highly compensated employees pursuant to C's nonqualified Deferred Compensation Plan (the "Plan").

¶ 28,351

[Plan Provisions]

The Plan provides for the payment of benefits to the participant or his beneficiary in the time and the manner prescribed under such Plan upon the participant's death or other termination of employment, or a termination of the plan following a change in control. Pursuant to the Plan, C will create a special bookkeeping account on its books for each participant for the purpose of crediting deferred compensation and C's matching contribution under the Plan to him. The Plan permits the participants to elect to defer a portion of their compensation for the next year. Participants must file their deferral election with C before December 31 specifying the portion of the compensation to be earned in the succeeding year that is to be deferred.

[Creditor Rights]

In order to provide assets from which to pay the benefit obligations to the participants, C has established by a trust agreement with a third party ("Trustee") a trust to which C may, in its discretion, contribute funds to provide for accrued deferred benefit payments. The Trustee will have the duty to invest the trust assets and funds in accordance with the terms of the trust agreement. The trust agreement provides that in the event of C's insolvency (as defined therein) the Trustee shall hold the assets for the benefit of C's general creditors. The trust agreement also provides that C's president and its board of directors must promptly notify the Trustee if C becomes insolvent.

The participants and their beneficiaries have the status of unsecured general creditors of C, have only C's unsecured promise to pay benefits, and receive no rights or security interest in the assets of C or the trust. The Plan and the trust agreement also provide that the benefits payable pursuant to such plans may not be assigned, transferred, pledged, or encumbered.

[Applicable Law]

Section 83(a) provides that the excess (if any) of the fair market value of property transferred in connection with the performance of services over the amount paid (if any) for the property is includible in the gross income of the person who performed the services for the first taxable year in which the property becomes transferable or is not subject to a substantial risk of forfeiture.

Reg. § 1.83–3(e) provides that for purposes of § 83 the term "property" does not include an unfunded and unsecured promise to pay money or property in the future. However, the term "property" does include a beneficial interest in assets (including money) transferred or set aside from claims of the transferor's creditors, for example, in a trust or escrow account.

Section 451(a) and Reg. § 1.431–1(a) provide that an item of gross income is includible in gross income for the taxable year in which actually or constructively received by a taxpayer using the cash receipts and disbursements method of accounting.

Under Reg. § 1.451–2(a), income is constructively received in the taxable year during which it is credited to the taxpayer's account, set apart, or

¶ 28,361

otherwise made available so that the taxpayer may draw on it at any time. However, income is not constructively received if the taxpayer's control of its receipt is subject to substantial limitations or restrictions.

[Revenue Ruling 60–31]

Various revenue rulings have considered the tax consequences of non-qualified deferred compensation arrangements. Rev. Rul. 60–31, *Situations 1–3*, 1960–1 C.B. 174, holds that a mere promise to pay, not represented by notes or secured in any way, does not constitute receipt of income within the meaning of the cash receipts and disbursements method of accounting. See also, Rev. Rul. 69–650, 1969–2 C.B. 106, and Rev. Rul. 69–649, 1969–2 C.B. 106.

[Economic Benefit Doctrine]

Under the economic benefit doctrine, an employee has currently includible income from an economic or financial benefit received as compensation, though not in cash form. Economic benefit applies when assets are unconditionally and irrevocably paid into a fund or trust to be used for the employee's sole benefit. Sproull v. Commissioner, 16 T.C. 244 (1951), aff'd per curiam, 194 F.2d 541 (6th Cir. 1952), Rev. Rul. 60–31, *Situation 4*. In Rev. Rul. 72–25, 1972–1 C.B. 127, and Rev. Rul. 68–99, 1968–1 C.B. 193, an employee does not receive income as a result of the employer's purchase of an insurance contract to provide a source of funds for deferred compensation because the insurance contract is the employer's asset, subject to claims of the employer's creditors.

Under the terms of the trust agreement, assets may be placed in trust to provide deferred compensation benefits to the participants or their beneficiaries. However, the Trustee has the obligation to hold the trust assets and income for the benefit of C's general creditors in the event of C's insolvency. The trust agreement further provides that an employee receives no beneficial ownership in or preferred claim on the trust assets. Therefore, although the assets are held in trust, in the event of C's insolvency they are fully within reach of C's general creditors, as are any other assets of C.

Section 402(b) provides that contributions made by an employer to an employees' trust that is not exempt from tax under § 501(a) are included in the employee's gross income in accordance with § 83, except that the value of the employee's interest in the trust will be substituted for the property's fair market value in applying § 83. Section 1.402(b)–1(a)(1) of the regulations provides that employer contributions to a nonexempt employees' trust shall be included as compensation in the employee's gross income for the taxable year in which the contribution is made, but only to the extent that the employee's interest in such contribution is substantially vested as defined in § 1.83–3(b).

Section 404(a)(5) provides the general deduction timing rules applicable to any plan or arrangement for the deferral of compensation, regardless of the Code section under which the amounts might otherwise be deductible. Pursuant to § 404(a)(5) and Reg. § 1.404(a)–12(b)(2), and provided that they otherwise meet the requirements for deductibility, amounts of contributions or compensation deferred under a nonqualified plan or arrangement are deductible in the taxable year in which they are paid or made available, whichever is earlier.

Section 301.7701–4(a) of the Procedure and Administration Regulations provides that, generally, an arrangement will be treated as a trust if it can be shown that the purpose of the arrangement is to vest in trustees responsibility for the protection and conservation of property for beneficiaries who cannot share in the discharge of this responsibility and, therefore, are not associates in a joint enterprise for the conduct of business for profit.

Section 671 provides that where a grantor shall be treated as the owner of any portion of a trust under subpart E, part I subchapter J, chapter 1 of the Code, there shall then be included in computing the taxable income and credits of the grantor those items of income, deductions, and credits against tax of the trust which are attributable to that portion of the trust to the extent that such items would be taken into account under chapter 1 in computing taxable income or credits against tax of an individual.

Section 677(a)(2) provides that the grantor shall be treated as the owner of any portion of a trust whose income without the approval or consent of any adverse party is, or, in the discretion of the grantor or a nonadverse party, or both, may be held or accumulated for future distribution to the grantor.

Section 1.677(a)–1(d) of the regulations provides that under § 677, a grantor is, in general, treated as the owner of a portion of a trust whose income is, or in the discretion of the grantor or a nonadverse party, or both, may be applied in discharge of a legal obligation of the grantor.

[Conclusion: Not Taxable]

Provided (i) that creation of the trusts does not cause the arrangement established by the Plan to be other than "unfunded" for purposes of Title I of the Employee Retirement Income Security Act of 1974, and (ii) that the provisions of the trust agreement requiring use of trust assets to satisfy claims of C's general creditors in the event of C's insolvency [are] enforceable by such creditors under the federal and state law, and based on the information submitted and representations made, we conclude that:

1.   The trust will be classified as a trust within the meaning of the Procedure and Administration Regulations. Because the principal and income of the trust may be applied in discharge of legal obligations of C, C shall be treated as the owner of the entire trust under § 677 of the Code. Accordingly, there shall be included in computing the taxable income and credits of C, the grantor, all items of income, deductions, and credits against tax of the trust. Section 671.

2.   Neither the creation of the trust, nor the accumulation of earnings by the trust, nor the contribution of assets to the trust will constitute a contribution to a nonexempt employees' trust under § 402(b) of the Code.

3.   Neither the adoption of the Plan, nor the creation of the trust, nor the contribution of assets by C to the trust will constitute transfers of property for purposes of § 83 or Reg. § 1.83–3(e).

¶ 28,361

4.   Neither C's establishment of the trust nor its contribution of assets to the trust, nor the accumulation of earnings upon such assets, nor the deferral of compensation by a Plan participant will cause current recognition of income by the Plan's participants or their beneficiaries, who are on the cash receipts and disbursements method of accounting, under either the constructive receipt or economic benefit doctrines.

5.   Amounts distributed under the Plan and the trust agreement will be included in the gross income of the participant or his beneficiary under the cash receipts and disbursements method of accounting in the taxable year in which actually paid or otherwise made available to the recipient, whichever is earlier.

6.   Corporation C will be allowed a deduction for amounts paid or made available under the Plan in the taxable year in which the amounts distributed are includible in the gross income of the recipient, pursuant to § 404(a)(5) of the Code, provided such amounts otherwise meet the requirements for deductibility under § 162. However, § 280G may limit the amount that may be deducted.

[¶ 28,367]

2.   SECULAR TRUSTS

A secular trust is distinguished from a rabbi trust in the sense that *the employer's contributions are not subject to a substantial risk of forfeiture.* See §§ 83(a), 404(a)(5). As a result, the employee is taxed not only on the employer's contribution to the trust in the year the contribution is made to the trust but also on the trust income in the year in which it is earned by the trust. §§ 409A(a)(1), 402(b)(1) and (2); see Priv. Ltr. Ruls. 9206009, 9212019, 9212024, 9302017. Typically, the trustee will be authorized to make current distributions to the employee to pay the additional income tax. The employer generally receives an immediate deduction for the contributions made to the secular trust.

Another distinction is that, while the employer's creditors can reach the property held in a rabbi trust, property held in a secular trust cannot be reached by the employer's creditors. Instead, the employee-beneficiary has an immediate vested interest in the contributions.

Life insurance is often used to fund secular trusts. The tax-free "inside build-up" of cash value in the policy is appealing, particularly since the insurance proceeds are receivable by the employer tax free at the death of the insured.

Problem

[¶ 28,380]

Pinnacle, Inc., a closely held corporation, desires to create a deferred compensation plan for Alexandra, its most valued employee. Pinnacle decides to utilize an NQDCP to gain freedom from the many limitations and restrictions imposed on qualified plans. Evaluate the tax consequences to Pinnacle

¶ 28,361

and Alexandra resulting from the creation and funding of the following NQDCPs.

(a) On January 1, Pinnacle established an irrevocable trust for the benefit of Alexandra. The trust principal and earnings thereon are to be held separate and apart from other funds of Pinnacle. All assets held by the trust will be subject to the claims of Pinnacle's general creditors, and any rights created under the trust in Alexandra will be unsecured rights against Pinnacle. In 2006, Pinnacle contributed $10,000 to the trust. The trust earned $500 in interest in 2006.

(b) Same facts as in (a), except that the trust assets are not subject to the claims of Pinnacle's general creditors, and the rights created under the trust in Alexandra are secured. Assume that Alexandra's interest is transferable and not subject to a substantial risk of forfeiture.

H. NON–QUALIFIED STOCK OPTIONS

[¶ 28,400]

1. STOCK OPTION MECHANICS

The grant of a stock option affords the person receiving the grant (the "optionee") the right to purchase the stock at a specific price (the "exercise price" or the "strike price") on a specified future date. The difference in the exercise price and the market price of the stock at the time of exercise is commonly referred to as the "spread", the spread being the compensation benefit to the employee. Because stock options are typically granted at an exercise price equal to the market price of the stock at the time of the grant, the "spread", practically speaking, refers to any appreciation in the value of the underlying stock since the time of the grant. It is the spread (the compensation benefit of which is realized when the stock is sold)—and the tax consequences the follow—that make stock options such a favored compensation technique. (In 2006, news accounts of the widespread, but undisclosed, practice of back dating stock option grants (to secure favorable pricing) were common.)

Example. Ashley worked nights at minimum wage cleaning the offices of Employer.com, a Silicon Valley company whose stock was publicly traded and widely held. A year into her employment, Employer.com gave Ashley the option to purchase 10,000 shares of Employer.com's stock two years from the date of the grant at $9 per share. Employer.com explained to Ashley that the option grant was in lieu of a salary increase. Ashley, who was then living in her car, was overjoyed at the prospect of "being rich when I buy the stock for $9 and immediately sell it for say maybe $100 per share" and had difficulty feigning disappointment (as she thought was expected of her) at Employer.com's decision to give her the options rather than a salary increase. Unfortunately, two years later Employer.com's stock was selling for $6 per share, her options were effectively worthless (since her strike price was $9 and she could buy the same stock in the open market at $6), and the back seat of her car was showing wear

¶ 28,400

as a result of its use as her principal residence. All the time Ashley "was sure" that the Employer.com stock would go to $100 per share, she would exercise her option to purchase shares from Employer.com at $9 per share, immediately sell the shares purchased from Employer.com for $100 per share, and enjoy the $91 spread per share (for a grand total "windfall" benefit, before taxes, of $910,000 for her two years of sleeping in the car). Ashley's disappointment was palpable. It was then that she remembered then Vice President Al Gore saying that investing social security money in the stock market was "risky", maybe ever "reckless".

[¶ 28,410]

2. "NON–QUALIFIED STOCK OPTIONS" DISTINGUISHED FROM "INCENTIVE STOCK OPTIONS"

For tax purposes, there are two types of stock options: Incentive Stock Options (ISOs), which are governed by the rules under §§ 421 and 422; and Non–Qualified Stock Options (NSOs) which are subject to the rules set forth in § 83 as compensation for property transferred in connection with the performance of services. Simply put, the difference is that NSOs are options which do not qualify as ISOs, *i.e.*, do not meet all of the restrictive requirements of § 422. There are advantages and disadvantages to both ISOs and NSOs but, generally speaking, ISOs are more tax advantaged than NSOs. That said, it is still important to note that NSOs, too, are greatly prized for their tax advantages.

ISOs can only be granted to employees (and not, for example, to nonemployee members of the company's board of directors or independent contractors engaged by the enterprise) and the employee must wait at least one year after exercise of then ISOs to sell the acquired shares. In addition, there is a $100,000 per annum limit on the option grant and ISOs are not transferable during life. These are several of the disadvantages of ISO.

The income tax rules applied to ISOs are clearly advantageous. There is no income tax to the employee when he or she receives the option or when the option is exercised. § 421. However, the spread is taxable income to the employee when the shares are sold—but at currently preferential capital gain rates. However, application of the alternate minimum tax to ISOs is complicated and can produce surprising and unwanted income tax consequences. § 56(b)(3). As for estate taxes, while the ISO is subject to estate taxes if unexercised at the employee's death, Reg. § 1.421–8(c), the ISO gets a new basis equal to fair market value of the ISO at the employee's death, Reg. § 1.421–8(c)(3)(i), possibly an important benefit for purposes of determining the gain realized when the acquired stock is sold by the employee's beneficiaries after the employee's death. The corporation at no time receives an income tax deduction for the ISO granted the employee. § 422(a).

While ISOs are not transferable during life, they are transferable at death by will or intestacy.

[¶ 28,420]

3. WHY USE NON-QUALIFIED STOCK OPTIONS

Most of the media attention is given to non-qualified stock options (NSOs). Grants of such options to highly paid executives have become an increasingly popular method of compensation because stock options give executives the incentive to contribute to the growth in value of a company while simultaneously allowing the executive to share in that potential growth without placing any of his or her own personal assets at risk. Moreover, NSOs can be easily transferred during the life of the optionee, thereby enabling the optionee to transfer potentially substantial economic value at a relatively low gift tax cost while decreasing the optionee's gross estate for estate tax purposes.

[¶ 28,430]

4. TAX CONSEQUENCES OF NON-QUALIFIED STOCK OPTIONS

a. *Donor's Income Tax Consequences*

In general, the application of the income tax rules to non-qualified stock options will depend upon whether the options have a "readily ascertainable fair market value" on the date the options are granted. If an option has a "readily ascertainable fair market value" on the date granted, the "optionee" may elect under § 83(b) to recognize taxable income at that time. The Regulations provide that an option with a "readily ascertainable fair market value" is one which is actively traded on an established market or whose fair market value can otherwise be measured with reasonable accuracy. See Reg. §§ 1.83–7(b)(1) and (2).

More commonly, however, a non-qualified stock option will not have a "readily ascertainable fair market value" on the date granted. As a result, § 83 would not apply at the time of the grant, and the optionee would not be required to recognize taxable income upon receipt of the options. Instead, while § 83 would appear to apply at the time the option is exercised or otherwise disposed of in an arm's length transaction, see Reg. § 1.83–7(a), the alternate rule provided in § 409A would seem to control—and the grant of the option would appear to be immediately taxable, i.e., the optionee would be in constructive receipt of income unless the strike price "was not less than the fair market value of the underlying stock on the date of grant." H.R. Conf. Rep. No. 108–755, 108th Cong., 2nd Sess., pt 1, at 721 (2004).

In cases satisfying the § 409A test, i.e., where the strike price is not less that the fair market value of the underlying stock on the date of grant, a gift of options to a family member is not considered an arm's length transaction. For that reason, there are no income tax consequences when the optionee transfers the options to a family member by gift. See Priv. Ltr. Rul. 9722022. The income tax burden, however, under § 83 remains with the donor optionee even after he or she relinquishes the dominion and control that makes the gift "complete" for gift tax purposes. Accordingly, when the donee subsequently exercises the option, the donor will be required to recognize taxable income on the amount of the spread at the time exercised. See Priv. Ltr. Ruls. 9714012 and 9349004.

[¶ 28,432]

b. *Donee's Income Tax Consequences*

At the time of the gift from the donor optionee to the donee, there are no *income tax* consequences to either party. Because the income tax liability under § 83 remains the burden of the donor optionee, the donee is required to recognize any ordinary income upon the subsequent exercise of the option. However, once the donee disposes of the stock acquired through the exercise of the options, by sale or otherwise, the donee is required to recognize a capital gain on the disposition, assuming the underlying stock has appreciated in value since it was acquired by exercise of the option. The donee's basis in the underlying stock for purposes of calculating the amount of the taxable gain is the exercise price of the option plus any income § 83 requires the donor optionee to recognize at the time of the option's exercise by the donee. The difference in the sales price of the stock and the donee's basis in the stock will equal the amount of taxable gain, which will be taxed at the applicable capital gains rate. Thus the income tax cost to the donee is merely the capital gains tax on the appreciation, if any, in the value of the underling stock *after* its receipt by the donee.

[¶ 28,440]

c. *Donor's Gift Tax Consequences*

When an optionee gifts NSOs to a family member, the value of the gift is equal to the fair market value of the option on the date of the gift. Assuming the underlying value of the stock will appreciate over time, this value should be substantially less than the value of the stock option when exercised at a later date. When stock options are gifted to family members in close proximity to the date of grant, the gift tax cost is minimal because the underlying stock has not had time to appreciate in value. Thus the primary advantage to gifting options is in shifting any potential post gift appreciation in the option's value to the optionee's family members without having to pay any transfer tax on the appreciation.

It has long been the IRS position that a gift is complete when a donor has so parted with dominion and control over the property so as to leave the donor with no power to change its disposition, whether for the donor's own benefit or for the benefit of another. See Reg. § 25.2511–2(b). In the case of gifts of options, the IRS, in several private letter rulings, has taken the position that when an optionee gifts options to family members, the gift is "complete" for gift tax purposes upon transfer. See Priv. Ltr. Ruls. 9722022, 96106035, and 9514017. However, in Revenue Ruling 98–21, 1998–1 CB 975, the IRS took the position that until an optionee has performed all services required as a precondition to exercising the option, an NSO is not yet a binding and enforceable property right capable of being transferred for gift tax purposes. The practical effect of this ruling is to place taxpayers on notice that the IRS will treat a gift of a non-vested or partially vested NSO as occurring at the time the right to exercise the option has fully vested. In the case of an optionee who transferred non-vested option to a family member, this would cause the gift value to include any appreciation in value between the time of transfer and the time of full vesting. If the underlying stock appreciated significantly in value during that interim period, the optionee could be hit with a large gift tax bill when the options fully vest. (Possibly posing a conceptual conflict with the IRS view is the willingness of state courts to treat non-vested NSOs as marital property subject to division upon divorce.)

Contrary to the income tax treatment of NSOs, for transfer tax purposes NSOs may be valued at the time of transfer, even if they are not actively traded on an established market. Traditionally, donor optionees have valued stock options through the use of various mathematical appraisal models which take into account the numerous factors associated with the value of options. This value would then be reduced to reflect discounts taken due to such factors as a lack of transferability or the possibility that the option may terminate within a certain period of time. A recent development in the area of valuation is a "safe harbor" method of valuing non-publicly traded stock options provided by the IRS in Revenue Procedure 98–34, 1998–2 CB 118, which allows for the use of certain accepted valuation models such as the Black Scholes model or the binomial model. The disadvantage to using this "safe harbor" method is that the optionee is not allowed to take a discount to the value determined according to the model, resulting in higher appraisal values.

[¶ 28,445]

d. *Donee's Gift Tax Consequences*

Because the burden of paying the gift tax lies with the transferor, there are no gift tax consequences to the donee when an optionee transfers an NSO to the donee by means of gift. As discussed above, once the option is exercised by the donee, the basis of the underlying stock in the hands of the donee is the exercise price plus any taxable income the donor may have recognized upon the exercise of the options by the donee. This basis is then used to calculate the amount of taxable gain recognized by the donee upon subsequent disposition of the stock.

[¶ 28,450]

e. *Donor's Estate Tax Consequences*

When an optionee dies in possession of non-qualified stock options and the terms of the options extend beyond the optionee's death, the date of death fair market value of the options is included in the optionee's estate. Due to the integrated nature of the transfer tax system, the means for valuing stock options at the time of death are identical to those for valuing stock options at the time of gift. For estate tax purposes, the most important aspect to remember is that the value of the options at the date of death will reflect any appreciation that occurred between the grant of the options and the date of death.

[¶ 28,452]

f. Planning

There are significant advantages to making life time transfers by gift in order to reduce the optionee's gross estate. First, by transferring the options to a family member immediately after the date on which the options are granted, the optionee removes any possibility of appreciation in value from his or her gross estate. Second, due to the tax exclusive nature of the gift tax, any gift tax paid by the optionee also serves to further decrease the gross estate of the optionee, without triggering additional gift tax. And third, the donor optionee's payment of the income tax upon exercise of the options by the donee serves to further decrease the gross estate of the optionee, without triggering additional gift tax.

[¶ 28,455]

g. Donee's Estate Tax Consequences

As a general rule, once there has been a "completed" gift for tax gift tax purposes, there will be no estate tax consequences to the recipient of the gift when the donor optionee subsequently dies. However, it remains unclear who would be responsible for the income tax due under § 83 when the donee exercises options *after* the donor optionee has died. Most likely the donor optionee's estate would be liable for the § 83 income. However, Reg. § 1.83–1(d) provides that if property has been transferred in connection with the performance of services and such property is still substantially non-vested when the transferee dies, the rules under § 691 apply, resulting in the income flowing from the exercise of the options to be viewed as income in respect of a decedent (IRD). One might argue that this forces the *donee* of the options to recognize the § 83 income at the time of exercise, instead of the decedent's estate.

Problem

[¶ 28,470]

Upstart.com is a closely held corporation whose non-qualified stock options (NSOs) are not actively traded on an established market and the fair market value of which cannot be measured with reasonable accuracy. On January 1st, Upstart.com granted executive Heather options enabling her to purchase 10,000 shares of Upstart.com at an exercise price of $5 per share, the then fair market value of the sock.

    (a) Suppose on January 5th, executive Heather gifts the options to her son Spencer when the fair market value of the stock of Upstart.com is $7 per share. What are the gift tax consequences to Heather? What are the gift tax consequences to Spencer?

(b) Suppose on March 5th, when the value of the stock of Upstart.com has appreciated to $14 per share, Spencer exercises the options. What are the income tax consequences to executive Heather?

(c) Suppose further that Spencer sells the shares on March 10th, when the value of the stock is $16 per share. What are the income tax consequences to Spencer?

(d) Suppose that instead of gifting the options to Spencer, executive Heather decided to hold on to them, and later died while still in possession of the options. What are the estate tax consequences?

Chapter 29

UNDERSTANDING QUALIFIED RETIREMENT PLANS AND IRAs

A. OBJECTIVES

[¶ 29,001]

Employer-provided retirement plans are an important part of most employees' financial planning. Retirement plans are either "qualified" or "nonqualified." The difference is that qualified plans, generally speaking, provide the employer and employee with certain tax advantages not available to the employee in a nonqualified plan. For a discussion of nonqualified plans, see Chapter 28. From the employer's standpoint, a nonqualified plan is less expensive not only from the standpoint of the cost of the benefits provided but also from the standpoint of administrative expenses. On the other hand, contributions to qualified plans are normally tax deductible by the employer when made.

From the employee's standpoint, if the plan is qualified, the employer's contribution to the plan is not taxable to the employee in the year in which the contribution is made. More important, income earned on the funds accumulating in a qualified plan is generally not subject to income tax in the year in which the income is earned. It is only when the benefits are paid out of the plan to the employee that the employer's contribution and the income earned on that contribution through the years are subject to income tax. Moreover, sometimes, some or all of the benefits paid out of the plan may be eligible for preferential income tax treatment, including tax-free rollover to another qualified plan or Individual Retirement Account (IRA).

Thus, the employee has the advantage of income tax deferral on employer provided benefits and earnings on employee contributions. This deferral continues until the benefits are paid, which usually is at a time when the employee is in a lower income tax bracket—and plan participants can be permitted to borrow from the plan (¶ 29,501) and even use tax deductible employer contributions to purchase life insurance (although there are drawbacks to using plan dollars to purchase life insurance). See ¶ 29,401.

In the case of closely held corporations, where the owners are also employees, the qualified plan provides an excellent tax shelter. The owners get the benefit of an immediate tax deduction for amounts set aside to accumulate tax free.

The statutory scheme governing qualified plans is extremely complex. It includes, principally, § 2039 in the estate tax provisions and Subchapter D of the Internal Revenue Code beginning with § 401. It also includes the provisions of the Employee Retirement Income Security Act of 1974 (hereinafter referred to as ERISA), parts of which have been incorporated into Subchapter D, as amended by the Retirement Equity Act of 1984 (hereinafter referred to as REA). Refinements were added by the Pension Protection Act of 2006. This chapter is necessarily selective and attempts to identify only some of the important issues. Chapter 30 details some of the distribution planning for qualified plan benefits.

Lastly, so as not to be misleading, persons other than employees can enjoy many, if not all, of the benefits—and burdens—of participating in a qualified retirement plan. The self-employed, for example, may establish so-called Keogh plans, thereby giving themselves the advantages of plan participation. See ¶ 29,401. And individual taxpayers may be entitled to establish individual retirement accounts (IRAs). IRA eligibility varies but is clearly limited. Factors that affect eligibility include, depending on the kind of IRA (there are several kinds), age, availability of compensation income, and total income.

B. TYPES OF QUALIFIED PLANS

[¶ 29,051]

1. INTRODUCTION

a. *Who Is Responsible for the Plan?*

Selecting and implementing a qualified plan is the work of specialists. However, as it is important for the estate planner to understand corporate planning issues (see Chapter 24), so too must the estate planner have some familiarity with qualified employee benefits. One reason is that, ordinarily, the qualified plan specialist represents the employer and is not engaged in structuring benefit distribution schemes for individual employees at retirement or death. Another reason is that the work of the estate planner may actually involve suggesting the use of a qualified plan to clients in appropriate circumstances. The estate planner may also be in the best position to make suggestions for plan amendments subsequent to the plan's implementation to provide improved benefits and flexibility for the owner-employee. Sometimes, the estate planning specialist will also have become a specialist in the implementation of qualified plans and, in such circumstances, he or she can make suggestions at the implementation stage with more regard for the estate planning problems of the participants.

[¶ 29,059]

b. *Defined Benefit and Defined Contribution Plans*

There are two basic kinds of qualified plans: defined benefit plans and defined contribution plans. A defined benefit plan is one in which the amount of the benefit to the employee at retirement is specified in the plan. On the other hand, a defined contribution plan (or individual account plan) is a plan which provides for individual accounts for the participants, and benefits are based solely on contributions and gains, losses, and expenses related to the contributions. Defined contribution plans include profit-sharing plans, money-purchase pension plans, target benefit plans, thrift and savings plans, stock bonus plans and employee stock ownership plans. ERISA § 3(34). While different, not to be ignored are § 403(b) annuities and § 457 plans, both similar to defined contribution plans but available to persons employed by nonprofit enterprises.

[¶ 29,067]

c. *Individual Retirement Accounts (IRAs)*

Individual Retirement Accounts (IRAs) are also available for the self-employed, as well as for employees who wish to make deductible contributions in addition to employer contributions. Generally, IRA deductions are limited to the lesser of $4,000 or the amount of the individual's gross income includible as compensation for the taxable year. § 219(b)(1). However, the deduction phases out at relatively modest income thresholds if the individual, or the individual's spouse, is an active participant in a pension plan. § 219(g).

[¶ 29,075]

d. *Top-Heavy Plans*

Note should be taken of the fact that stricter rules apply to so-called top-heavy qualified retirement plans. While discussion of these rules is beyond the scope of these materials, it is appropriate to note that § 416(g)(1) defines a "top-heavy" plan as any plan which provides "key employees" with more than 60 percent of the present value of the cumulative accrued benefits in the plan. A "key employee," as defined in § 416(i)(1), is any plan participant who at any time during the plan year is an officer of the employer having an annual compensation from the employer, in 2006, of more than $140,000; a "5–percent owner of the employer"; or a one percent owner of the employer having an annual compensation from the employer of more than $175,000. No more than 50 employees shall be treated as officers for purposes of § 416(i) unless the number of employees is less than 50, in which case no more than the lesser of 3, or 10 percent, of the employees shall be treated as officers.

Stricter rules were imposed on top-heavy plans because of the abuse potential inherent in qualified retirement plans controlled by owner-employees. The intent of these rules is to make certain that employees other than the owners are provided with "real" benefits by these plans and that the plans are more than simply a means by which the owner-employees provide themselves with a capital accumulation fund (rather than a retirement fund).

[¶ 29,083]

e. *Plan Selection*

The selection of the type of qualified plan involves an analysis of five basic considerations: the amount of income available; the amount of "investable" cash available; the cost of covering other employees; the nature of the employer's business; and the characteristics of the various types of plans.

[¶ 29,091]

i. Economic Considerations

The amount of income available in the business entity must be considered (inasmuch as the adoption of a qualified plan in no way makes the business more profitable). Actually, additional expenses are generally incurred in connection with the adoption of a plan related to covering other participants, as well as administrative expenses and fees for the installation and maintenance of the plan. Accordingly, projections regarding the income of the business and these other expenses must be made in order to determine the amount of income available to compensate the owner-employee and to provide a plan contribution for him or her.

A second and related consideration is the amount of spendable cash the owner-employee needs and the resulting "investable cash" he or she has. Contributions to a qualified plan are nothing more than tax-sheltered investments. Accordingly, the owner-employee must have investable cash before he or she can consider any plan contribution. Tax savings are achieved by providing for pretax investments. Thus, a contribution of $10,000 will result in a $2,800 tax savings for an owner-employee at the 28 percent tax bracket. This $10,000 will, however, reduce the owner-employee's "spendable" income by $7,200. If the owner-employee needs that $7,200 to live on, to pay debt service, or for any other purpose, then the tax savings associated with the tax-sheltered contribution to the qualified plan are simply not available.

[¶ 29,099]

ii. Nondiscrimination in Plan Coverage

As indicated above, one of the considerations in determining the amount of income the business entity has is the possibility of increased costs that result from providing plan contributions for other employees. A qualified plan may only require, as a condition of participation, that an employee be 21 years of age and/or that the employee complete one year of employment with the employer. § 410(a)(1). Otherwise, coverage must be on a nondiscriminatory basis. Accordingly, the cost of providing coverage, particularly in a labor-intensive business, may be substantial and must be considered before any recommendations are made with respect to the adoption of a particular type of qualified plan.

[¶ 29,107]

iii. Form of Doing Business

The nature of the business must also be considered. That is, is the business being conducted as a regular corporation, an S corporation, a sole proprietorship or a partnership? There are a few differences in the rules that apply to the types of plans and the contributions that may be made for owner-employees under these various types of plans. See, e.g., § 416 (top-heavy plans). There are also substantial other considerations associated with a change in the form of doing business which must be considered as part of the overall recommendation to adopt a qualified plan or a specific type of qualified plan.

[¶ 29,115]

iv. Plan Characteristics

Plan characteristics include the benefit payable from the plan; the contribution to the plan; the employer's liability for service rendered prior to the adoption of the plan; vesting and accrued benefits; the right to withdraw funds from the plan; the rights and liabilities upon termination of the plan; and the benefits provided by and obligations imposed by the Pension Benefit Guaranty Corporation. Analysis of each of these characteristics is an interwoven tapestry; they cannot be evaluated separately. However, for ease of presentation, the seven basic characteristics are analyzed separately for defined benefit plans, profit-sharing plans, and target benefit and money-purchase plans.

As you read further, ask yourself whether the characteristics of each plan are more suitable to one kind of business rather than another. For example, would a defined benefit plan be suitable in a business which is cyclical in nature? Or would one of the defined contribution plans be more suitable?

[¶ 29,123]

2. DEFINED BENEFIT PLANS

A defined benefit plan is a pension plan other than a defined contribution plan. ERISA § 3(35).

[¶ 29,131]

a. Benefits Payable

i. Amount of Benefit

A defined benefit plan may provide a participant with a benefit of a straight life annuity, with no ancillary benefits, in an amount equal to the lesser of either: (1) a maximum dollar amount per year ($175,000 in 2006), which is determined by reference to increases in the cost of living, or (2) 100 percent of the participant's average compensation for his or her three high years, beginning at age 62 (or later). § 415(b).

The amount of the benefit must be reduced in one situation. The benefit is reduced proportionately if a participant has less than 10 years of service with the employer. § 415(b)(5).

¶ 29,107

There is an exception to the maximum lifetime annuity. A participant may receive a $10,000 per year annuity (even if it exceeds 100 percent of the participant's average compensation for his or her three high years) so long as the employer never maintained a defined contribution plan in which the individual participated. § 415(b)(4).

[¶ 29,135]

ii. Form of Benefit: QJSA/QPSA

Defined benefit plans are required to make benefits available in two types of survivorship annuities that are designed to protect the spouses of plan participants. In general, the participant can elect other benefit forms but the plan must require compliance with formal spousal consent procedures for the election to be effective. § 417(a)(2). These mandatory survivorship benefits create a form of joint property with a right of survivorship that can frustrate estate planning devices like the bypass trust (described in ¶ 13,051). E. Gamble, Planning for Distributions from Retirement Plans, 45 NYU Inst. On Fed. Tax'n § 27.07[5]–[10](1987).

If a vested participant reaches the annuity starting date provided for in the plan, the plan must pay benefits in the form of a Qualified Joint and Survivor Annuity (QJSA) unless the participant, with the consent of his or her spouse, elects a different form of benefit (if any) provided by the plan. §§ 401(a)(11)(A)(i), 417(a)(2)(A)(i). A QJSA must provide the surviving spouse at least 50 percent of the benefits that the couple would have received during their joint lives. § 417(b). If a vested participant dies before the annuity starting date, the surviving spouse must be able to select a Qualified Preretirement and Survivor Annuity (QPSA), which provides the spouse a life annuity with benefits comparable to what the spouse would have received if the participant had lived to the earliest retirement age and then died. §§ 401(a)(11)(A)(ii), 417(c)(1).

If the plan fully subsidizes the benefits of the QJSA or QPSA, the plan is not required to permit election of a different form of benefit. § 417(a)(5). If the plan permits an election, the permissible time period for election is limited. A spouse can waive a QJSA only during the 90 days prior to the annuity's starting date. § 417(a)(6). The QPSA can generally be waived only beginning with the plan year in which the participant becomes 35 years old. § 417(a)(6). The regulations permit an earlier election; a new election, however, must be made after the participant reaches age 35. Reg. § 1.401(a)–20, Q & A 33. Furthermore, the waiver must comply with formal procedures which include a writing, a plan representative or notary as witness, and either an irrevocable election or a revocable election if future beneficiary changes require the spouse's further consent. § 417(a)(2)(A). Thus, the estate planner must monitor the plan benefits and timing requirements to avoid mandatory survivorship benefits from frustrating other aspects of the estate plan. See generally E. Gamble, Planning for Distributions from Retirement Plans, 45 NYU Inst. On Fed. Tax'n § 27.07[5]–[10] (1987); L. Mezzullo, Planning for

¶ 29,135

Distributions from Qualified Retirement Plans, 1990:1 Notre Dame Tax & Est. Plan. Inst. 3–78.

[¶ 29,139]

b. Contributions to the Plan

While the amount of the benefit from a defined benefit plan is specified by the plan, the employer's annual contribution is determined actuarily using assumptions for the cost of the annuity, interest, mortality and turnover. Therefore, the employer's contribution will be affected by the difference between the anticipated investment experience and the actual investment experience of the plan. In cases where the actual investment experience is less than that anticipated, the employer's contribution will have to be increased in order to make it possible for the plan to accumulate sufficient funds within a reasonable period of time to pay benefits to a participant when the participant is entitled to receive the benefits of the plan.

Obviously, the participant's age is one of the most important considerations in analyzing the cost of a defined benefit plan. The cost of providing the same benefit for two participants of different ages will be substantially larger for the older participant because of the fewer number of years for contributions and income accumulations. For example, the cost of providing a $1,000 per month benefit payable at age 65 for a 55–year-old participant may well be four times larger than the cost of providing the same benefit for a 40–year-old participant.

There are elaborate rules governing the amount of the income tax deduction for a defined benefit plan. The maximum amount deductible in a year is the full funding limitation determined under § 412(a). § 404(j). If an excess contribution is made in a given year, such excess contribution is nondeductible, but it can be carried forward and may be deductible in succeeding years according to the same limits. § 404(a)(1)(E).

[¶ 29,147]

c. Employer's Past Service Credit

Past service credit permits an employer to give credit for service rendered prior to the establishment of the plan for purposes of computing and funding a pension benefit. Past service credit is used to provide a greater benefit for an employee who has been employed by the employer for a number of years prior to the establishment of the plan.

A defined benefit plan may fund a past service credit. § 412. Original participants in the plan generally must be treated the same. Moreover, a plan that contains a minimum age and service requirement for eligibility and gives past service credit to original participants must do the same for subsequent participants. Past service credit may be given for all, or a portion of, prior service, for service after the attainment of a specified age or completion of minimum service. Other methods are to give past service credit for compensation in excess of a specified amount or to use different rates for different levels of compensation. However, these techniques must not discriminate in

¶ 29,135

favor of highly compensated participants. (In 2006, a person earning $100,000 is deemed highly compensated. § 414(q)(1)(B).)

The contribution to a plan for past service liability may be made over a period not to exceed 30 years. § 412(b)(2)(B)(iii). However, the maximum income tax deduction for past service liability may be amortized in 10 equal annual installments. § 404(a)(1)(A)(iii).

[¶ 29,155]

d. *Vesting and Accrued Benefits*

The employer may require that the employee work a certain minimum time with the employer before becoming entitled to any benefits under the plan. In order to preclude employers from establishing unreasonable employment requirements, § 411 establishes certain minimum vesting schedules. In general, a participant must be 100 percent vested in his or her accrued benefit at the end of either five (if 100 percent vested) or seven years of service (graded vesting).

These vesting requirements relate to the accrued benefit. The accrued benefit under a defined benefit plan is an actuarial concept based on the present value of the benefit provided by the plan at normal retirement as specified in the plan, reduced to present value for purposes of a lump-sum distribution. Section 411(b)(1) provides certain alternate minimum accrued benefit requirements, including the requirement that the benefit accrue at the rate of 3 percent per year of participation and the requirement that the benefit accrue ratably with each year of participation.

Example. If a 40–year-old employee began participating in a 100 percent defined benefit pension plan with an age 65 normal retirement date and terminated employment at age 50, the employee's accrued benefit could be 30 percent (3 percent method, determined by multiplying 3 percent by 10 years of participation) or 40 percent (fractional method, determined by dividing the 10 years of actual participation by 25 years of potential participation if the employee reached normal retirement) of the normal retirement benefit payable at age 65. The vesting schedule would then be applied to determine the percentage of the accrued benefit to which the terminated participant would be entitled. This could then be the benefit paid at age 65. If the benefit were to be paid earlier, the benefit would be reduced to its present value using the actuarial assumptions included in the plan.

[¶ 29,163]

e. *Right of Withdrawal*

Benefits accrued from employer contributions may not be withdrawn from a defined benefit pension plan prior to retirement except in the event of death, disability, termination of employment, or attainment of age 62. However, generally speaking, bona fide loans may be made to participants provided adequate security is given. § 4975(d)(1). Notwithstanding the foregoing, plan loans will be deemed taxable distributions under § 72(p), except for loans that do not exceed the lesser of:

1. $50,000, reduced by the excess of highest outstanding balance during the one-year period ending on the day before the loan over the outstanding balance of loans from the plan on the date on which such loan was made, or

2.   The greater of 50 percent of the present value of his or her accrued nonforfeitable benefit, or $10,000. § 72(p)(2)(A).

Plan loans must require repayment within five years. § 72(p)(2)(B). Excepted from this requirement are loans to acquire the participant's residence. § 72(p)(2)(B)(ii). Plan loans must also comply with the spousal consent requirements expressed in § 417(a)(2)(A)(i).

[¶ 29,171]

f.   Required Distributions

Qualified plans must begin distributing benefits to a participant by a certain time and in minimum amounts if a participant does not request distribution earlier. § 401(a)(14). The required beginning date for plan distributions is April 1 of the calendar year following the year that the participant attains age 70 ½ (or, in some cases, following the year the participant retires, if later). § 401(a)(9)(C). A participant's entire interest can be distributed in a lump sum on or before the required beginning date. Alternatively, the participant's interest can be distributed in installment payments that begin on or before the required beginning date and extend over a period equal to the life or life expectancy of the participant or the combined lives or life expectancies of the participant and a designated beneficiary. § 401(a)(9)(A).

For other rules affecting the timing of distributions, see ¶ 30,561 (penalty taxes).

[¶ 29,179]

g.   Rights and Liabilities on Termination

Sometimes tax or nontax issues, or both, cause an employer to terminate a plan. (In recent years, United States airlines and United States based automobile manufacturers concluded that plan termination was essential to their continued viability. The same considerations may cause small employers to consider or terminate a plan.) If an employer terminates a defined benefit plan, all participants are 100 percent vested in their accrued benefits. § 411(d)(3). Plans typically exonerate the employer from being contractually obligated to maintain the plan and, in the absence of fraud, malfeasance, and failure to meet the minimum funding requirements, the employer will not be liable for any loss. However, there are specific requirements for the allocation of plan assets upon termination so as to limit benefits payable to owners, managers or highly compensated participants and to prevent reversion of plan assets to the employer until the accrued benefits due rank-and-file employees have been paid or for which provisions have been made. A ruling should be

¶ 29,163

obtained from the Internal Revenue Service on the effect of the termination on the plan's qualified status.

[¶ 29,187]

h. Benefits and Obligations Imposed by the PBGC

Defined benefit plans are generally subject to the requirements of the Pension Benefit Guaranty Corporation (PBGC). Plans maintained by professional corporations with less than 25 participants are exempt.

The PBGC provides minimal insurance against plan terminations. Employers pay insurance premiums for such coverage. A covered plan cannot be terminated without PBGC approval.

[¶ 29,195]

3. TARGET BENEFIT AND MONEY–PURCHASE PENSION PLANS

a. Benefits Payable

i. Amount of Benefit

Money-purchase and target benefit plans are considered defined contribution plans (individual account plans) for purposes of participation, vesting and accrual of benefits, and contributions but are considered defined benefit plans for other purposes. ERISA §§ 3(35), 1015(b); § 414(i). There is no limitation on the benefit payable from a target benefit or money-purchase pension plan although the amount of the annual additions are limited as set forth below. The amount of the benefit is equal to the vested amount in the participant's account when the participant ceases to be a participant in the plan. Moreover, there is no specification of any benefit by a target benefit or money-purchase pension plan.

From a planning perspective, the younger the age of the plan participant, the greater the advantage of a defined contribution plan (except a target benefit plan) over a defined benefit plan. On the other hand, when plan contributions begin at a later age, defined benefit and defined contribution plans are more comparable. A defined benefit plan is better for older employees but more expensive to fund.

[¶ 29,199]

ii. Form of Benefit: QJSA/QPSA

So far as the forms in which benefits can be made available to plan participants, the discussion of the requirements for defined benefit pension plans is equally applicable to target benefit and money-purchase benefit plans (¶ 28,135). However, Qualified Preretirement (QPSA) and Survivor Annuities (QJSA) are defined differently for these plans. See § 417(c)(2).

¶ 29,199

[¶ 29,207]

b. Contributions to the Plan

The difference between a target benefit plan and a money-purchase pension plan is the method of calculating the contribution for a participant. A money-purchase pension plan requires a contribution of a specified or level percentage of the employee's compensation. Therefore, all employees, regardless of age, are treated the same. The contributions under a target benefit pension plan are actuarially determined based on the participant's age, "targeted retirement benefit," cost of the "targeted retirement benefit," and an assumed interest rate. Thus, the target benefit pension plan provides substantially higher contributions for older participants, as previously illustrated in the discussion of the cost of a defined benefit plan.

Target benefit plans or money-purchase pension plans are defined contribution plans. Therefore, the amount contributed to the account of each participant in a target benefit plan or money-purchase plan is limited.

While the total added to all of the participant's defined contribution plans in a single year may not exceed the lesser of $44,000 (in 2006) or 100 percent of the participant's compensation in that year (§ 415(c)(1)), there is a $220,000 cap on the compensation that can be taken into account in determining the maximum contribution to a single plan. § 401(a)(7). For example, the maximum tax deductible contribution in 2006 would be $22,000 (10 percent of $220,000) for a participant in a 10 percent money purchase plan—even if the participant's compensation was $1 million. § 404(a)(3). Thus, the maximum amount deductible in a year is the full funding limitation determined under § 412. § 404(a)(1)(A).

The target benefit plan and money-purchase pension plan are subject to minimum funding rules. A nondeductible excise tax is imposed if the plan fails to comply with the funding requirement. The tax is equal to 10 percent of the initial accumulated funding deficiency determined as of the end of each plan year plus 100 percent if the deficiency is not timely corrected. § 4971.

[¶ 29,215]

c. Employer's Past Service Liability

A money-purchase pension plan may not give credit for past service. However, the allocation of contributions to the participants in a money-purchase pension plan may take years of service into account if the allocation does not result in discrimination. Reg. § 1.401–4(a)(2)(iii); Rev. Rul. 69–592, 1969–2 C.B. 193.

A target benefit plan may fund a past service liability. However, there is a $220,000 cap, in 2006, on the compensation that can be taken into account in determining the maximum contribution (§ 401(a)(17)), and the maximum contribution itself is limited to the lesser of 100 percent of the participant's compensation or $44,000. For these reasons, it may not be possible to fully fund such past service liability. § 415(c)(1). To satisfy the legal requirements, original participants in the plan and future participants in the plan generally

¶ 29,207

must be treated the same. Thus, a plan that contains a minimum age and service requirement for eligibility and gives past service credit for original participants must give past service credit to, and not have stricter age and service requirements for, subsequent participants. Past service credit may be given for all or a portion of prior service, for service after the attainment of a specified age or completion of minimum service. Other methods may give past service credit for compensation in excess of a specified amount or by using different rates for different levels of compensation.

The contribution to a plan for past service liability may be made at any time. However, the income tax deduction for past service liability may be amortized in 10 equal annual installments. § 404(a)(1)(A)(iii).

[¶ 29,223]

d. *Vesting and Accrued Benefits*

The minimum vesting requirements discussed for a defined benefit plan are equally applicable to the target benefit and money-purchase pension plan. The accrued benefit of a participant in a defined contribution plan is simply the participant's account balance under the plan.

[¶ 29,231]

e. *Right of Withdrawal*

Since a target benefit pension plan is a defined contribution plan for purposes of contributions and benefits, there is no reduction of benefits for "early" retirement, i.e., retirement before, say, age 55 or with less than 10 years of service (both sometimes conditions for retirement under defined benefit plans). ERISA §§ 3(35), 1016(b); § 414(i). Similarly, benefits from a money-purchase pension plan are not required to be reduced because of early retirement. The benefit is only affected by the vesting provision.

Benefits accrued from employer contributions may not be withdrawn from a target benefit plan or money-purchase pension plan prior to retirement except in the event of death, disability or termination of employment or, after 2006, attainment of age 62. § 401(a)(36). However, bona fide loans may be made to participants subject to the limitations described above as being applicable in the case of loans from defined benefit plans. See § 4975(d)(1).

[¶ 29,239]

f. *Required Distributions*

The discussion of required distributions for defined benefit pension plans is equally applicable to target benefit plans and money-purchase pension plans. See ¶ 28,171.

[¶ 29,247]

g. *Rights and Liabilities Upon Termination*

If a money-purchase pension plan or target benefit plan is terminated, the participants are 100 percent vested in the amounts credited to the participants' accounts as of the date of termination of the plan. § 411(d)(3). A ruling should possibly be obtained from the Internal Revenue Service on the effect of the termination on the plan's qualified status.

[¶ 29,255]

h. Benefits and Obligations Imposed by the PBGC

Neither the target benefit pension plan nor the money-purchase pension plan is subject to the provisions of the PBGC.

[¶ 29,263]

4. PROFIT-SHARING PLANS

a. Benefits Payable

i. Amount of Benefit

Profit-sharing plans are another kind of defined contribution plan. There is no limitation on the benefit payable from a profit-sharing plan, although the amount of the annual addition to the plan is limited. The amount of the benefit is controlled by the amount of the annual additions and the plan's investment results. The amount of the benefit is equal to the vested amount of the participant's account when the participant ceases to be a participant in the plan. Furthermore, there is no specification of any benefit by a profit-sharing plan.

[¶ 29,267]

ii. Form of Benefit: QJSA/QPSA

The form in which benefits can be made available to participants in profit-sharing plans is generally the same as defined benefit pension plans. See ¶ 28,135. There is an exception if the plan provides that 100 percent of the participant's nonforfeitable accrued benefit is payable at death to the surviving spouse and the participant does not elect to receive the benefits in the form of a life annuity. § 401(a)(11)(B)(iii). Most discretionary profit-sharing plans are drafted to meet this exception so that they do not have to offer the QJSA or QPSA.

[¶ 29,271]

b. Contributions to the Plan

The employer's income tax deduction is limited to 25 percent of compensation of all employees under the plan. § 404(a)(3)(A). If the amount paid into the plan exceeds the 25 percent limitation, the excess (subject to a 10 percent penalty under § 4972) may be carried forward to succeeding taxable years. The 25 percent limitation will continue to apply to the deductibility of the aggregate amount of the carryover and the amount of compensation of all employees under the plan in the succeeding year. § 404(a)(3)(A). These limitations are subject to an additional overall limitation. While the total added to all of the participant's defined contribution plans in a single year may not exceed, in 2006, the lesser of $44,000 or 100 percent of the participant's compensation in that year (§ 415(c)(1)), there is also a $220,000 cap on the compensation that can be taken into account in determining the maximum contribution to a single plan. Rev. Proc. 2005–70, 2005–47 IRB 979. For example, the maximum tax deductible contribution in 2006 would be $55,000 (25 percent of $220,000) for a participant in a profit-sharing plan— even if the participant's compensation is $1 million. § 404(a)(3). As with target benefit and money-purchase pension plans, the $44,000 limitation is subject to cost-of-living adjustments.

A profit-sharing plan is not required to have a definite formula for contributions. Therefore, the employer's contribution may vary from year to year, and a contribution is not required in any given year. Reg. § 1.401–1(b). However, the contributions must be recurring and substantial to qualify as a profit-sharing plan.

[¶ 29,279]

c. *Employer's Past Service Liability*

Generally, a profit-sharing plan may not give credit for past service. However, allocations to the accounts of participants in a profit-sharing plan may account for years of service if the allocation does not result in discrimination. Reg. § 1.401–4(a)(2)(iii).

[¶ 29,287]

d. *Vesting and Accrued Benefits*

The minimum vesting requirements discussed for a defined benefit pension plan are equally applicable to a profit-sharing plan. The accrued benefit of a participant is simply the participant's account balance under the plan.

[¶ 29,295]

e. *Right of Withdrawal*

A profit-sharing plan is the most flexible type of plan for withdrawing funds from a plan prior to retirement. It may distribute benefits in the event of termination of employment, death, disability, permanent partial disability, hardship or after the contributions have been in the plan for two years. In addition, bona fide loans may be made to participants subject to the limitations described as being applicable in the case of loans from defined benefit pension plans. See § 4975(d)(1).

The stated retirement age in a profit-sharing plan does not have the same meaning as the "normal retirement age" in a pension plan. The retirement age in a profit-sharing plan is merely one of many events that may be designated as the time to commence distribution from the plan. A profit sharing plan may specify any age for distribution of benefits and any age for normal retirement if it is less than the later of age 65 or the 10th anniversary of the time a plan participant commenced participation in the plan. Therefore, benefits from a profit-sharing plan are not required to be reduced because of early retirement except if the participant is not 100 percent vested. Rev. Rul. 80–276, 1980–2 C.B. 131.

[¶ 29,303]

f. Required Distributions

The discussion of required distributions for defined benefit pension plans is equally applicable to profit-sharing plans at ¶ 29,171.

[¶ 29,311]

g. Rights and Liabilities Upon Termination

If a profit-sharing plan is terminated, the participants are 100 percent vested in the amounts credited to the participants' accounts as of the date of termination of the plan. A ruling should be obtained from the IRS on the effect of termination on the plan's qualified status.

[¶ 29,319]

h. Benefits and Obligations Imposed by the PBGC

Profit-sharing plans are not subject to the provisions of the PBGC.

[¶ 29,325]

5. SECTION 403(b) ANNUITIES AND SECTION 457 QUALIFIED PLANS

Defined contribution plans, both, § 403(b) annuities and § 457 plans are available to employees of nonprofit entities. The biggest provider of such plans is widely known by its initials, TIAA–CREF. In significant ways, these arrangements differ from pension and profit sharing plans.

[¶ 29,335]

6. TWO OR MORE QUALIFIED PLANS

There is a limitation on both the employer's income tax deduction and a participant's contributions or benefits if the employer maintains two or more qualified plans that cover one or more of the same participants. First, if an employer maintains:

1. One or more defined contribution plans and one or more defined benefit plans or

2. A combination of any two or more pension trusts, employee annuities, profit-sharing plans, or stock bonus trusts,

then the total amount deductible under all of the plans is limited to 25 percent of covered compensation or the amount required to meet the minimum funding requirement for the defined benefit plan, if greater. § 404(a)(7). Second, the limitation on the participant's benefit is also controlled by the

¶ 29,295

type of plans. If the employer has two defined contribution plans (including a target benefit plan), the amount allocated to a participant by the plans cannot exceed the annual addition of 100 percent of the participant's compensation or, in 2006, $44,000 (as adjusted for inflation). § 415(c).

What happens when the employee has several employers, all of which maintain qualified retirement plans? Must the plans be aggregated by the employee for purposes of the $44,000 cap provided by § 415(c)?

C. CASE ANALYSIS: USE OF DEFINED BENEFIT PENSION PLAN

[¶ 29,340]

A defined benefit pension plan may be used as an excellent estate planning vehicle. To illustrate, Hank, the 55–year-old founder and sole shareholder of a family corporate business worth between $450,000 and $700,000, was diagnosed as having a terminal illness. Hank was employed by the corporation at a salary of $50,000 a year. The corporation was contributing 10 percent of covered compensation to a money-purchase pension plan. Moreover, the corporation had an accumulated earnings tax problem. See § 531. Hank had not accumulated any significant assets outside of the business. His wife Wilda had never been active in the business and was dependent on her husband for support. Their sons were in the business. The corporation adopted a 50 percent defined benefit pension plan with a past service liability and continued the existing plan. The new defined benefit pension plan provided a survivor's annuity equal to 100 percent of its employee's benefit, which was not to be reduced on the death of the employee. The tax consequences of adopting a defined benefit pension plan affect the corporation, the estate, and the surviving spouse.

First, the corporation created an unfunded past service liability of approximately $200,000. This liability was not paid until after Hank's death. The unfunded liability is a debt of the corporation. Therefore, it reduces the value of the business, the estate and the potential accumulated earnings tax liability. Moreover, the corporation's contribution to the defined benefit pension plan for Hank is approximately five times the contribution to the money-purchase pension plan. To gain flexibility, the past service liability could be amortized over a period of time from 10 to 30 years. In addition, the past service liability, when paid, will be income tax deductible to the corporation.

Second, the value of the annuity, while not excluded from Hank's estate, may qualify for the marital deduction. § 2056(b)(7)(B)(ii) (last sentence); ¶ 30,131.

Third, the surviving spouse will receive an annuity for life of approximately $2,000 per month plus social security. The annuity is taxed to the surviving spouse, Wilda, when received, at her then current income tax bracket. The annuity is paid for by the business on a tax deductible basis. Therefore, the sons provide income to their mother on a pretax basis.

Problems

[¶ 29,345]

1. Could an owner-employee of a corporation establish a qualified benefit plan just for himself, to the exclusion of all of his other employees? See § 416.

2. Assume T Corporation is in a cyclical industry, alternating feasts and famines. Should T Corporation be advised to employ a defined benefit plan or a defined contribution plan? Would a profit-sharing plan be even more suitable?

3. Assume April was co-owner-employee of Y Corporation. April would like to make an investment in an apartment building complex. Could she borrow from the qualified plan for her own benefit? § 72(p). Would your answer be different if April, as plan administrator, decided to invest the plan funds in the apartment complex for the benefit of the plan beneficiaries?

4. Zeke, a 33 percent taxpayer, and the owner-employee of Z Corporation, paid himself the maximum amount he thought the IRS would deem reasonable compensation for purposes of allowing the corporation a tax deduction under § 162 for the payment. Rather than distribute an additional amount to himself as a dividend (taxable to him at 30 percent and not deductible by the corporation), he accumulated earnings in the corporation. The accumulation is now substantially beyond the needs of the business and Zeke knows that ultimately, the corporation will attract the accumulated earnings penalty tax. See § 531. Zeke is 55 years old and has 20 employees. Z Corporation has never bothered to institute a qualified employee benefit plan. Could such a plan help Z Corporation avoid the accumulated earnings penalty tax?

D. SIMPLIFIED EMPLOYEE PENSIONS (SEPS)

[¶ 29,350]

Simplified Employee Pensions (SEPs) are a less expensive alternative to qualified plans. SEPs are essentially employer-sponsored Individual Retirement Accounts (IRAs) for employees (SEP–IRA). To qualify as a SEP, the employer must make contributions to IRAs for its employees under a written plan that contains a definite allocation formula and the employer must comply with nondiscrimination provisions. § 408(k)(5). In general, all employees who have attained age 21, worked for the employer for three of the past five years, and received at least $450 in compensation from the employer must be participants in the plan. § 408(k)(2). The normal deduction limitations for IRAs do not apply to SEPs, and contributions to SEPs can be excluded from the employee's gross income up to, in 2006, the lesser of $44,000 (indexed for inflation) or 25 percent of the employee's compensation that is included in gross income. §§ 402(h)(2), 219(b)(2). SEPs also gain some flexibility by not being subject to the spousal benefit requirements provided in § 417(a)(2). The

IRS has published Form 5305–SEP to assist employers to create SEPs. E. Gamble, Planning for Distributions from Retirement Plans, 45 NYU Inst. On Fed. Tax'n § 27.02[2] (1987).

E. SAVINGS INCENTIVE MATCH PLAN FOR EMPLOYEES (SIMPLE)

[¶ 29,360]

The Savings Incentive Match Plan for Employees (SIMPLE) plan replaced what are referred to as SAR–SEPs in 1997 (although contributions can continue to be made to existing SEPs and employers can continue to establish SEPs; SIMPLEs are required only where the plan is to include a salary reduction feature). A SIMPLE can either be an IRA for each employee or part of a qualified cash or deferred arrangement, in other words, like a "401(k) plan". Simplified reporting requirements apply and nondiscrimination rules generally applicable to qualified plans are not applicable to SIMPLEs. They can be used only where there are less than 100 employees. Eligible employees are those earning $5,000 or more annually. The maximum contribution in 2005 was $10,000. The IRS has published Form 5304–SIMPLE to assist employers.

F. SELF-EMPLOYED INDIVIDUALS

[¶ 29,401]

Self-employed individuals, including sole proprietorships, routinely establish qualified retirement plans (including SEPs and SIMPLES). Such plans, in terms of the self-employed, are commonly called Keogh plans or H.R. 10 plans. As a result, self-employed individuals can avail themselves of the full range of benefits available through a qualified plan. However, corporate plans continue to have more flexibility than Keogh plans in several ways. For example, loans to owner-employees are prohibited from Keogh plans, and there are differences concerning fringe benefits such as medical, dental, and life insurance. See Kroll and Feldman, Estate Planning for Executive Compensation and Employee Benefits After DEFRA, 19 U. Miami Est. Plan. Inst. ¶ 1012 (1985).

G. ALIENATION OF PLAN BENEFITS

[¶ 29,501]

1. IN GENERAL

In general, for a retirement plan to be qualified, the plan must provide that its benefits cannot be assigned or alienated. § 401(a)(13)(A). This general rule has two exceptions: (1) loans and (2) Qualified Domestic Relations Orders. §§ 4975(d)(1), 401(a)(13)(B).

¶ 29,501

[¶ 29,509]

a. Loans

Qualified plans can make reasonable loans to participants. The loan must bear a reasonable rate of interest, be adequately secured, and be available to all participating employees on a nondiscriminatory basis. § 4975(d)(1). See ¶ 29,163 (for other loan limitations), 29,231, 29,401 (limitation on loans from Keogh plans).

[¶ 29,517]

b. *Qualified Domestic Relations Orders*

Section 414(p) provides for Qualified Domestic Relations Orders (QDROs) as the means by which qualified plan benefits are to be divided between participant and spouse upon divorce, the effect being to settle any uncertainty concerning the power of state divorce courts to assign qualified plan benefits. A QDRO provides child support, alimony, or marital property rights to an alternate payee and the amount or percentage of benefits to be received. § 414(p)(1)(B).

[¶ 29,525]

2. BANKRUPTCY

The Bankruptcy Abuse and Consumer Protection Act of 2005 (BACPA) created a broad federal exemption for tax-qualified retirement benefits, including, inter alia, individual retirement accounts (IRAs). ERISA seemingly provided broad creditor protection (Patterson v. Shumate, 504 U.S. 753 (1992)) (anti-alienation clause required in ERISA-covered plans is an enforceable restriction that causes such plans to be free of creditor claims in bankruptcy), but creditors were sometimes effective in making distinctions that allowed them to succeed despite the ERISA shield. For example, IRAs are not employee benefit pension plans and, therefore, arguably did not enjoy ERISA creditor protection. While the Supreme Court could be said to have rejected that analysis in Rousey v. Jacoway, 544 U.S. 320 (2005), technically, the Court concluded IRA exemption from bankruptcy proceedings was permitted only to the extent that the debtors could prove that the IRA was needed for their support.

BACPA would seem to have eliminated many if not all of these exceptions. By its plain terms, BACPA protections explicitly apply to IRAs, Roth IRAs, 457 plans and 403(b) plans, not just "ERISA" plans. It eliminates the claimed distinction between "solo business owner" plans and other qualified plans, the latter clearly having always enjoyed ERISA protection. No showing of need by the debtor is required, meaning that tax qualified plans of the wealthy, the not so wealthy, those with ill gotten gains—everybody, all the time—are creditor protected in bankruptcy. Even more importantly, bankruptcy protection even applies to ostensibly tax qualified retirement plans which, for some technical reason, are not tax qualified, e.g., because of over contribution to the plan by plan participants.

¶ 29,509

Short of bankruptcy, though, state law protections continue to remain important. For example, Keogh plans or HR 10 plans are not subject to ERISA where the only plan participants are the proprietor and the proprietor's spouse. Such plans are not considered "employee benefit plans" for ERISA purposes. 29 CFR § 2510.3–3(b) (1996). As a result a participant in such a plan must look to state law exemptions if the plan assets are to enjoy protection from creditors of the participant (other than in a bankruptcy). This is an important point to many lawyers and accountants who practice alone. The problem is avoided if the plan includes persons as participants other than the proprietor and spouse.

Not to be ignored are state law protections of tax qualified retirement plans, including IRAs, from creditor claims. See, e.g., Tex. Prop. Code Ann. § 42.0021 (West 2002). While not available in every state, these protections continue to be useful to plan participants not in bankruptcy.

[¶ 29,533]

3. SPOUSAL COMMUNITY PROPERTY RIGHTS AT DEATH

An issue in community property states is whether a nonemployee-spouse may make a will giving his or her one-half community interest in a retirement plan to a beneficiary other than the spouse. A Ninth Circuit decision held that the anti-alienation provisions provided by § 401(a)(3)(A) preempt California property law and that, as a result, the nonemployee-spouse could not divest the participant spouse of his retirement interest. Ablamis v. Roper, 937 F.2d 1450 (9th Cir.1991). However, in another case, the Texas Supreme Court held that one-half of a husband's retirement benefits were part of the nonemployee-wife's estate and these benefits could pass to her daughter and grandchildren under her will. Allard v. Frech, 754 S.W.2d 111 (Tex.1988), cert. denied, 488 U.S. 1006 (1989). See also ¶ 11,169. The United States Supreme Court, in a 5–4 decision, has resolved this issue by ruling that ERISA preempts community property law. *Boggs* v. *Boggs*, 520 U.S. 833 (1997) (striking down a state statute authorizing the nonparticipant spouse to transfer by testamentary instrument an interest in undistributed pension benefits).

But what of IRAs? In as much as ERISA does not apply to IRAs, is that to say that state community property laws are applicable? The answer is "yes"! And if the IRA was community property but the owner relocates to a noncommunity property state, the IRA remains community as to property on hand at the time of the relocation.

For additional material, see ¶¶ 3075–3091 (migrant client), and 11,089–11,177 (community property).

[¶ 29,541]

4. PRE- AND POSTNUPTIAL AGREEMENTS

Spousal rights in qualified retirement plans make the drafting of an effective antenuptial agreement a troublesome area. See § 417(a)(2)(A)(i); ¶ 28,135. Recall that the plan must comply with formal consent procedures for the spouse to make a valid election not to receive a survivorship benefit, and the consent can occur only within limited time periods. § 417(a)(2). As a result, a antenuptial agreement cannot directly bring about waiver of the spousal survivorship benefit because the parties are not then spouses; only a "spouse" can effect a waiver! Reg. § 1.401(a)–20, A–28. If the prospective spouse attempts to waive the survivorship benefits in a prenuptial agreement by agreeing to later "deliver her waiver", i.e., after marriage, the participant's recourse is uncertain if the spouse later refuses to perform the consent procedures. Fearful of such an outcome—or that it may be subsequently determined that such a provision in a prenuptial agreement is not permitted (perhaps on grounds that it is against public policy) and, thus, that entire prenuptial agreement is tainted—attorneys report a reluctance to make any provision whatsoever in prenuptial agreements regarding tax qualified retirement plan benefits.

For somewhat related discussion of pre- and post-nuptial agreements, see ¶¶ 11,201 and 21,900.

Chapter 30

DISTRIBUTIONS FROM QUALIFIED RETIREMENT PLANS AND IRAs

A. OBJECTIVES

[¶ 30,001]

The complexity associated with tax qualified retirement plans (of whatever name) is explicable. On the one hand, Congress thinks of these plans—including Individual Retirement Accounts (IRAs) and the like) as providing for retirement. On the other hand, many highly compensated employees and owner-employees—and plain old plan participants of whatever stripe—think of these plans as tax-sheltered capital accumulation funds. Much of the complexity associated with these tax qualified arrangement follows from Congress's wish to limit their inherent abuse potential and to provide plan participants with funds for retirement rather than funds to be turned over to the next generation. One result is that, for plan participants in the top federal estate tax bracket, it is not unthinkable for the unpaid balance remaining in the qualified plan at the death of the plan participant to be taxed at an effective rate of 75 percent—leaving little for the decedent's beneficiaries. As illustrated in Table 30.1, this is the effect of subjecting plan benefits to the income tax with rates as high as 35 percent, and the federal estate tax at a flat rate of 45 percent, and the federal generation-skipping tax also with a flat rate of 45 percent.

Table 30.1. ESTATE, INCOME AND GENERATION TAXES POTENTIALLY APPLICABLE TO RETIREMENT BENEFITS

(This illustration was constructed using the following software which is available from Brentmark Software, 3505 Lake Lydia Drive, Ste 262, Orlando, FL (http://www.Brentmark.com): Stephen R. Leimberg and Robert T. LeClair, Estate Planning Tools (2006). See Appendix A.)

Start with this Much in your Retirement Plan: ... $1,000,000

Tax 1:   Assume that your Taxable Estate without the Retirement Plan is $2,000,000 and would be subject to Federal Estate Tax of $0 because of the $2,000,000 applicable exclusion amount provided by § 2010(c)

1033   ¶ 30,001

Adding your $1,000,000 Retirement Plan to your $2,000,000 Taxable Estate increases your Taxable Estate to $3,000,000, resulting in Federal Estate Tax of $450,000 .... ($450,000)

Amount Remaining after Increased Death Taxes: $550,000

Tax 2: The GST Tax, if any, is based on $1,000,000
Less: Death Taxes of $450,000
Less: GST Tax of $170,690
Less: GST Exemption of $0
45% Rate is applied against $379,310
The GST Tax is $170,690 .... ($170,690)

Amount Remaining after Generation Skipping Tax: $379,310

Tax 3: The Lump Sum Income Tax is based on $1,000,000
Less: Federal Estate Tax of $450,000
Less: GST Tax of $170,690
The Income Tax of 35% on a Lump Sum of $379,310 is $132,759 .... ($132,759)

Amount Remaining after Federal Income Tax: $246,551

You Started With: $1,000,000
Total Taxes: $753,449
Net Amount Available to Heirs: $246,551

Cents per Dollar Received by Beneficiaries: $ 0.25

The possible application of these three taxes—income, estate, and generation skipping (and, in some instances, state-imposed inheritance taxes)—makes distribution planning terribly important, particularly to a generation of taxpayers whose principal wealth is their qualified retirement plan. When thinking of alternatives that will provide more of the plan benefits to "the downstream beneficiaries" it is probably fair to say that options for eliminating the estate tax and generation-skipping tax bite are limited; the planning is in minimizing the income tax bite through income tax deferral! By tax deferral is meant postponing distribution as long as possible, thereby allowing the untaxed dollars in the plan to continue to grow taxfree. Balanced against that, of course, is "beneficiary need" for those dollars *immediately if not sooner.* Satisfying that need means paying those taxes *immediately.*

Tax deferral means learning about terms such as "required minimum distribution" (RMD), "required beginning date" (RBD), and "designated beneficiary" (DB) with long life expectancies. It means taking advantage of the marital deduction for transfers to a surviving spouse. (Don't have one? Get one! It can be tax advantageous. Contra, ¶ 21,900.) It means taking exceptional care when planning for distribution of plan benefits to a trust because tax deferral may be compromised.

Nowithstanding the obvious appeal of tax deferral, before climbing on that horse, remember to compare the tax deferral gained by use of a tax qualified plan to warehouse retirement dollars (and the resulting 35 percent income tax burden) with the opportunity to tax dividends earned on equities held outside the plan at preferential rates such as the maximum rate of 15 percent that applies in 2006. Could that mean that the tax deferral promise inherent in loading up the tax qualified retirement plan might be somewhat tarnished? Or is the answer that those receiving distributions from tax qualified retirement plans are more often than not in the lower income brackets and thus not burdened by the top income tax rates?

Notably, from the world of it-doesn't-get-any-better-than-this, 70–1/2 and older charitably inclined donors have a tax free holiday in 2006 and 2007 in cases where the donor makes a charitable gift of part or all (up to $100,000) of his or her Individual Retirement Account (IRA). § 408(d)(8). Such a transfer—it must be directly from the plan to the charity—has these advantages: (1) it will qualify (or count toward) the donor's required minimum distribution (RMD) in the year made; (2) it will be excluded from the donor's income that year; and (3) it will not count against the donor's other charitable contributions that year (in determining the donor's tax deduction limits for charitable contributions, ¶ 25,373). These features are significant for, *otherwise*, the tax accounting for such a transfer commonly means (1) withdrawal from the IRA; (2) inclusion of the amount withdrawn in the donor's income in that year as required by § 72; and (3) transfer to the charity—but the tax deduction may well be limited by the § 170(b) limits on tax deductible contributions for that year (or, practically, because the donor does not otherwise itemize his or her deductions for income tax purposes as permitted by § 63(e), choosing, instead, § 63(c)'s so-called "standard" deduction).

This is only the beginning of what you need to know. Much, if not all, of the rest appears in Natalie B. Choate, Life and Death Planning for Retirement Benefits (6th ed. 2006).

B. TAXATION OF DISTRIBUTIONS FROM QUALIFIED PLANS

[¶ 30,051]

1. INTRODUCTION

Distributions from tax qualified retirement arrangements may be myriad in nature. Among the more common forms of distribution are lump-sum payments; periodic payments, typically in the form of an annuity; purchase and distribution of annuity contracts; distribution of employer stock; maintenance of segregated accounts for the participant and his or her beneficiary; and installment-type payments. Alternatively, plan participants who view the plan benefits as a capital warehouse will elect to take the "required minimum distribution" (RMD) and only after the "required beginning date" (RBD) However, whatever else is said—and there is much that can and needs to be said about this very complicated process—it is important that the recipient of plan benefits "expect" that, when received, plan benefits will constitute taxable income. There well may be some exceptions, in part, to this generalization, but they are few.

¶ 30,051

The two basic categories of distribution options for plan benefits, as well as the tax consequences of these options, are summarized in Table 30.2. A discussion of the options and their tax consequences follows.

Table 30.2. SELECTED PAYMENT POSSIBILITIES		
Distribution	*Periodic Payments*	*Lump-Sum Distribution*
If distributed to the plan participant prior to his or her death:	Plan benefits will be taxable as ordinary income to the plan participant as each periodic payment received. § 72.	Plan benefits will be taxable as ordinary income if received in a lump sum. However, lump sum payments will be excluded from income in specified circumstances if rolled over to an IRA or other qualified plan. § 402(c)
If plan benefits are paid at the death of the plan participant:	Plan benefits will be taxable as ordinary income to the recipient as each periodic payment received. § 72.	Plan benefits will be taxable as ordinary income if received in a lump sum. However, where the surviving spouse receives a lump-sum distribution after the death of the plan participant and elects to roll it over into an IRA or other qualified plan, income tax is deferred until distributions to the spouse commence. § 402(c)(1) and (9)
	Plan benefits at death will be included in the plan participant's estate for estate tax purposes as income in respect of a decedent (IRD) under § 691 without regard to whether the distribution is periodic or in a lump sum. However, if the beneficiary is the surviving spouse and the plan benefits pass to the surviving spouse in a qualified way, those benefits will qualify for the estate tax marital deduction. § 2056. Moreover, in cases where inclusion of the plan benefits in the participant's estate results in the payment of estate tax, an amount equivalent to the estate tax attributable to the income in respect of a decedent (IRD) will be allowed as income tax deduction to the recipient of those benefits in the year the benefits are reportable for income tax purposes by the recipient. § 691(c).	
To whom can undistributed plan benefits be paid at the death of the employee?	To an individual or a trust. Under certain kinds of plans, if there is a surviving spouse, an annuity must be paid for the spouse unless formally waived by the spouse. § 417(a)(2).	
To whom should payment be made?	• While there is no universally preferred beneficiary, often tax considerations suggest that the recipient of plan benefits after the death of the employee should be a trust—a "bypass trust", if you will—which will allow the plan benefits to be available to the decedent's loved ones but which also will cause the plan benefits to be excluded from the estate of his spouse. • However, plan benefits constitute IRD. See § 691. The income taxes to be paid on the receipt of these benefits may defeat a part of the estate tax-shelter potential inherent in the use of the trust because the income taxes to be paid on the plan benefits will siphon resources from the trust. • More importantly, absent extraordinary care in preparing the bypass trust, the tax deferral opportunity available to a "designated beneficiary" with a long life expectancy may well be lost.	

¶ 30,051

[¶ 30,123]

2. ESTATE TAXES

a. In General

Section 2039(a) provides that a decedent's gross estate includes "the value of an annuity or other payment receivable by any beneficiary by reason of surviving the decedent." As a result, with very limited exceptions (the discussion of which is beyond the scope of these materials), the balance remaining in the participant's qualified plan account at the participant's death is fully taxable for estate tax purposes.

Before 1982, an unlimited exclusion from the gross estate was available if the plan benefits were not paid directly or indirectly to the estate and the recipients did not elect special income averaging. This exclusion was reduced to $100,000 in 1982 and then repealed for the estates of decedents dying after 1984. Either of these exclusions may yet be available to qualifying plan participants who were receiving benefits from their plans or had irrevocably elected the form of benefit before specified effective dates. For the great majority, however, retirement plan benefits are fully taxable for estate tax purposes.

[¶ 30,131]

b. Married Plan Participants: Saving the "First" and "Second" Tax

Chapter 13 sets forth the basic tax planning scheme employed between a husband and wife. As suggested in Chapter 13, the objective of many married taxpayers is to avoid any tax in the estate of the first spouse to die while taking full advantage of the amount of property which is sheltered from tax by the unified credit. Ideally, that means that: (1) the current $2,000,000 applicable exclusion (tax-free) amount, § 2010, would flow into a credit shelter trust (for the benefit, perhaps, of the surviving spouse, although others could also benefit) and (2) all property in excess of the tax-free amount would flow to the surviving spouse in a form which would qualify for the marital deduction. Use of the marital deduction saves the "first" tax, and use of the credit shelter trust makes the $2,000,000 tax-free amount available to loved ones while keeping it free from the "second" tax, i.e., the credit shelter trust is structured to be free from estate tax at the death of the trust beneficiaries.

Ordinarily, qualified plan benefits are paid either in the form of annuity-type payments or in a lump sum. See ¶ 30,051. In the hands of the recipient, these benefits are like any other property and, to the extent on hand at the death of the recipient, will be included in the recipient's estate.

[¶ 30,135]

i. Bypass Trust

Generally speaking, as noted in ¶ 30,123, plan benefits cannot be excluded from the participant's estate for estate tax purposes. However, plan benefits could be directed to the bypass trust to save the second tax. The disadvantage of such a scheme is that the plan benefits will constitute taxable income to the recipient, in this case, the bypass trust, thereby depleting the bypass trust by the amount of the income tax to be paid. Since the amount passing to the bypass trust in the typical plan will be limited to the $2,000,000 applicable exclusion amount, payment of the income tax on the plan benefits from the bypass trust will reduce the amount that will escape the second tax. Sometimes, though, the bypass trust is the vehicle of choice. In such circumstances, identifying one of the trust beneficiaries as a designated beneficiary is critical to tax deferral. (A 35 percent income tax on $2 million of plan benefits leaves only $1.3 million for the bypass trust, the effect being that only $1.3 million passes estate tax free of the possible full $2 million.) For this reason alone, consideration should be given to directing the plan benefits away from the bypass trust and to the surviving spouse—provided the benefits qualify for the estate tax marital deduction.

[¶ 30,138]

ii. QTIP Trust

Other factors complicate use of a bypass trust for plan benefits. Where there is a surviving spouse, the spousal benefit requirements imposed by § 417(a)(2) may very well limit use of the bypass trust as the receptacle for plan benefits. (The survivorship requirement imposed by § 417(a)(2) prevents the benefits from from flowing into the bypass trust without the spouse's consent. For discussion of the spousal requirements, see ¶ 29,135.) Moreover, if the spousal annuity is fully subsidized by the employer, the employer does not have to allow changes in the form of benefit. Furthermore, even if an election is allowed, the time period in which it can be made is limited. Finally, even if an election is accomplished, an issue may arise as to whether the spouse's relinquishment of the statutory benefit and the placement of a portion of the benefit in a bypass trust for the spouse's benefit would constitute a retained life estate. § 2503(f). (Although spousal relinquishment does not constitute a taxable gift—and the estate and gift tax are construed in pari materia—that is not to say that the relinquishment could not constitute a transfer subject to a retained life estate as contemplated by § 2036(a)(1).) Absent an election, the participant would have to withdraw the plan benefits before death or the surviving spouse would have to disclaim the benefits—§ 2518—after the participant's death for the bypass trust to be utilized.

Thus, with the limitations inherent in the use of the bypass trust for plan benefits, the marital deduction is the primary planning device. The estate planner should ensure that distributions to the spouse are free of trust or, if in trust, in a form that qualifies for the marital deduction as a qualified terminable property interest (QTIP). Revenue Ruling 2006–26 is the blueprint and it follows.

QTIP qualification is a perilous path. At issue is making certain that the surviving spouse receives all of the income earned by the QTIP property at least annually (and that no one else is eligible to receive a distribution from the trust so long as the surviving spouse is alive). § 2056(b)(7). On one level, this requirement is not especially difficult to satisfy so long as the governing instrument contains these requirements. The difficulty comes about when IRA distributions to the QTIP trust are deferred, a condition likely favored by the surviving spouse because it defers income tax on the IRA property until actual distribution. (When actual distribution must take place is a function of the age of the surviving spouse and the required minimum distribution rules (RMD).) Meantime, the surviving spouse must receive, through the QTIP trust, the income earned on the IRA while it remains undistributed. Mechanically, this is a vexatious problem and great care must be taken in its resolution to avoid compromising eligibility for the QTIP election and the entire marital deduction. The matter is further complicated by state law adoption of provisions of the Uniform Principal and Income Act (UPIA) permitting adjustments between income and principal (total return legislation). ¶¶ 21,701–21,715.

[¶ 30,143]

REVENUE RULING 2006–26

2006–__ CB __.

If a marital trust described in Situations 1, 2, or 3 is the named beneficiary of a decedent's individual retirement account (IRA) or other qualified retirement plan described in § 4974(c) that is a defined contribution plan, under what circumstances is the surviving spouse considered to have a qualifying income interest for life in the IRA (or qualified retirement plan) and in the trust for purposes of an election to treat both the IRA and the trust as qualified terminable interest property (QTIP) under § 2056(b)(7)?

FACTS

A dies in 2004, at age 68, survived by spouse, B. Prior to death, A established an IRA described in § 408(a). A's will creates a testamentary marital trust (Trust) that is funded with assets in A's probate estate. As of A's death, Trust is irrevocable and is valid under applicable local law. Prior to death, A named Trust as the beneficiary of all amounts payable from the IRA after A's death. The IRA is properly included in A's gross estate for federal estate tax purposes. The IRA is currently invested in productive assets and B has the right (directly or through the trustee of Trust) to compel the investment of the IRA in assets productive of a reasonable income. The IRA document does not prohibit the withdrawal from the IRA of amounts in excess of the annual required minimum distribution amount under § 408(a)(6). The executor of A's estate elects under § 2056(b)(7) to treat both the IRA and Trust as QTIP.

Under Trust's terms, all income is payable annually to B for B's life, and no person has the power to appoint any part of the Trust principal to any person other than B during B's lifetime. B has the right to compel the trustee to invest the Trust principal in assets productive of a reasonable income. On B's death, the Trust principal is to be distributed to A's children, who are younger than B. Under the trust instrument, no person other than B and A's children has a beneficial interest in Trust (including any contingent beneficial interest). Further ... under Trust's terms, B has the power, exercisable annually, to compel the trustee to withdraw from the IRA an amount equal to all the income of the IRA for the year and to distribute that income to B. If B exercises this power, the trustee is obligated under Trust's terms to withdraw the greater of all of the income of the IRA or the annual required minimum distribution amount under § 408(a)(6), and distribute currently to B at least the income of the IRA. The Trust instrument provides that any excess of the required minimum distribution amount over the income of the IRA for that year is to be added to Trust's principal. If B does not exercise the power to compel a withdrawal from the IRA for a particular year, the trustee must withdraw from the IRA only the required minimum distribution amount under § 408(a)(6) for that year.

The trustee of Trust provides to the IRA trustee a copy of A's will (Trust's governing instrument) before October 31, 2005, in accordance with A–6(b) of Reg. § 1.401(a)(9)–4 . Because the requirements of A–4 and A–5 of Reg. § 1.401(a)(9)–4 are satisfied and there are no beneficiaries or potential beneficiaries that are not individuals, the beneficiaries of the trust may be treated as designated beneficiaries of the IRA. In accordance with § 408(a)(6) and the terms of the IRA instrument, the trustee of Trust elects to receive annual required minimum distributions using the exception to the five year rule in § 401(a)(9)(B)(iii) for distributions over a distribution period equal to a designated beneficiary's life expectancy. Because amounts may be accumulated in Trust for the benefit of A's children, B is not treated as the sole beneficiary and, thus, the special rule for a surviving spouse in § 401(a)(9)(B)(iv) is not applicable. Accordingly, the trustee of Trust elects to have the annual required minimum distributions from the IRA to Trust begin in 2005, the year immediately following the year of A's death. The amount of the annual required minimum distribution from the IRA for each year is calculated by dividing the account balance of the IRA as of December 31 of the immediately preceding year by the remaining distribution period. Because B's life expectancy is the shortest of all of the potential beneficiaries of Trust's interest in the IRA (including remainder beneficiaries), the distribution period for purposes of § 401(a)(9)(B)(iii) is B's life expectancy, based on the Single Life Table in A–1 of Reg. § 1.401(a)(9)–9, using B's age as of B's birthday in 2005, reduced by one for each calendar year that elapses after 2005. On B's death, the required minimum distributions with respect to any undistributed balance of the IRA will continue to be calculated in the same manner and be distributed to Trust over the remaining distribution period.

Situation 1—Authorized Adjustments Between Income and Principal. The facts and the terms of Trust are as described above. Trust is governed by the laws of State X. State X has adopted a version of the Uniform Principal and Income Act (UPIA) including a provision similar to § 104(a) of the UPIA providing that, in certain circumstances, the trustee is authorized to make adjustments between income and principal to fulfill the trustee's duty of impartiality between the income and remainder beneficiaries. More specifically, State X has adopted a provision providing that adjustments between income and principal may be made, as under § 104(a) of the UPIA, when trust assets are invested under State X's prudent investor standard, the amount to be distributed to a beneficiary is described by reference to the trust's income, and the trust cannot be administered impartially after applying State X's statutory rules regarding the allocation of receipts and disbursements to income and principal. In addition, State X's statute incorporates a provision similar to § 409(c) of the UPIA providing that, when a payment is made from an IRA to a trust: (i) if no part of the payment is characterized as interest, a dividend, or an equivalent payment, and all or part of the payment is required to be distributed currently to the beneficiary, the trustee must allocate 10 percent of the required payment to income and the balance to principal; and (ii) if no part of the payment made is required to be distributed from the trust or if the payment received by the trust is the entire amount to which the trustee is contractually entitled, the trustee must allocate the entire payment to principal. State X's statute further provides that, similar to § 409(d) of the UPIA, if in order to obtain an estate tax marital deduction for a trust a trustee must allocate more of a payment to income, the trustee is required to allocate to income the additional amount necessary to obtain the marital deduction.

For each calendar year, the trustee determines the total return of the assets held directly in Trust, exclusive of the IRA, and then determines the respective portion of the total return that is to be allocated to principal and to income under State X's version of § 104(a) of the UPIA in a manner that fulfills the trustee's duty of impartiality between the income and remainder beneficiaries. The amount allocated to income is distributed to B as income beneficiary of Trust, in accordance with the terms of the Trust instrument. Similarly, for each calendar year the trustee of Trust determines the total return of the assets held in the IRA and then determines the respective portion of the total return that would be allocated to principal and to income under State X's version of § 104(a) of the UPIA in a manner that fulfills a fiduciary's duty of impartiality. This allocation is made without regard to, and independent of, the trustee's determination with respect to Trust income and principal. If B exercises the withdrawal power, Trustee withdraws from the IRA the amount allocated to income (or the required minimum distribution amount under § 408(a)(6), if greater), and distributes to B the amount allocated to income of the IRA.

Situation 2—Unitrust Income Determination. The facts, and the terms of Trust, are as described above. Trust is governed by the laws of State Y. Under State Y law, if the trust instrument specifically provides or the interested parties consent, the income of the trust means a unitrust amount of 4 percent of the fair market value of the trust assets valued annually. In accordance with procedures prescribed by the State Y statute, all interested parties authorize the trustee to administer Trust and to determine withdrawals from the IRA in accordance with this provision. The trustee determines an amount equal to 4 percent of the fair market value of the IRA assets and an amount equal to 4 percent of the fair market value of Trust's assets, exclusive of the IRA, as of the appropriate valuation date. In accordance with the terms of Trust, trustee distributes the amount equal to 4 percent of the Trust assets, exclusive of the IRA, to B, annually. In addition, if B exercises the withdrawal power, Trustee withdraws from the IRA the greater of the required minimum distribution amount under § 408(a)(6) or the amount equal to 4 percent of the value of the IRA assets, and distributes to B at least the amount equal to 4 percent of the value of the IRA assets.

Situation 3—"Traditional" Definition of Income. The facts, and the terms of Trust, are as described above. Trust is governed by the laws of State Z. State Z has not enacted the UPIA, and therefore does not have provisions comparable to §§ 104(a) and 409(c) and (d) of the UPIA. Thus, in determining the amount of IRA income B can compel the trustee to withdraw from the IRA, the trustee applies the law of State Z regarding the allocation of receipts and disbursements to income and principal, with no power to allocate between income and principal. As in Situations 1 and 2, the income of Trust is determined without regard to the IRA, and the income of the IRA is separately determined based on the assets of the IRA.

LAW AND ANALYSIS

Section 2056(a) provides that the value of the taxable estate is, except as limited by § 2056(b), determined by deducting from the value of the gross estate an amount equal to the value of any interest in property that passes from the decedent to the surviving spouse, to the extent that interest is included in the value of decedent's gross estate.

Under § 2056(b)(1), if an interest passing to the surviving spouse will terminate or fail, no deduction is allowed with respect to the interest if an interest in the property passes or has passed from the decedent to any person other than the surviving spouse (or the estate of the spouse), that may be possessed or enjoyed by such other person after termination of the spouse's interest.

Section 2056(b)(7) provides that QTIP, for purposes of § 2056(a), is treated as passing to the surviving spouse and no part of the property is treated as passing to any person other than the surviving spouse. Section 2056(b)(7)(B)(i) defines QTIP as property that passes from the decedent, in which the surviving spouse has a qualifying income interest for life, and to which an election under § 2056(b)(7) applies. Under § 2056(b)(7)(B)(ii), the surviving spouse has a qualifying income interest for life if, inter alia, the surviving spouse is entitled to all the income from the property, payable annually or at more frequent intervals.

Section 20.2056(b)–7(d)(2) provides that the principles of § 20.2056(b)–5(f), relating to whether the spouse is entitled for life to all of the income from the property, apply in determining whether the surviving spouse is entitled for life to all of the income from the property for purposes of § 2056(b)(7).

Section 20.2056(b)–5(f)(1) provides that, if an interest is transferred in trust, the surviving spouse is entitled for life to all of the income from the entire interest if the effect of the trust is to give the surviving spouse substantially that degree of beneficial enjoyment of the trust property during the surviving spouse's life that the principles of the law of trusts accord to a person who is unqualifiedly designated as the life beneficiary of a trust. In addition, the surviving spouse is entitled for life to all of the income from the property if the spouse is entitled to income as determined by applicable local law that provides for a reasonable apportionment between the income and remainder beneficiaries of the total return of the trust and that meets the requirements of Reg. § 1.643(b)–1.

Section 20.2056(b)–5(f)(8) provides that the terms "entitled for life" and "payable annually or at more frequent intervals" require that under the terms of the trust the income referred to must be currently (at least annually) distributable to the spouse or that the spouse must have such command over the income that it is virtually the spouse's. Thus, the surviving spouse will be entitled for life to all of the income from the trust, payable annually, if, under the terms of the trust instrument, the spouse has the right exercisable annually (or at more frequent intervals) to require distribution to the spouse of the trust income and, to the extent that right is not exercised, the trust income is to be accumulated and added to principal.

Generally, Reg. § 1.643(b)–1 provides that, for purposes of the income taxation of estates and trusts, the term "income" means the amount of income of the estate or trust for the taxable year determined under the terms of the governing instrument and applicable local law. Under Reg. § 1.643(b)–1, trust provisions that depart fundamentally from traditional principles of income and principal generally will not be recognized. Under these traditional principles, items such as dividends, interest, and rents are generally allocated to income and proceeds from the sale or exchange of trust assets are generally allocated to principal.

However, under Reg. § 1.643(b)–1, the allocation of an amount between income and principal pursuant to applicable local law will be respected if local law provides for a reasonable apportionment between the income and remainder beneficiaries of the total return of the trust for the year, including ordinary and tax-exempt income, capital gains, and appreciation. For example, a state statute providing that income is a unitrust amount of no less than 3 percent and no more than 5 percent of the fair market value of the trust assets, whether determined annually or averaged on a multiple year basis, is a reasonable apportionment of the total return of the trust. Similarly, under Reg. § 1.643(b)–1, a state statute that permits the trustee to make adjustments between income and principal to fulfill the trustee's duty of impartiality between the income and remainder beneficiaries is generally a reasonable apportionment of the total return of the trust.

[Rev. Rul. 2000–2]

Rev. Rul. 2000–2, 2000–1 C.B. 305, concludes that a surviving spouse has a qualifying income interest for life under § 2056(b)(7)(B)(ii) in an IRA and in a marital trust named as the beneficiary of that IRA if the spouse has the power, exercisable annually, to compel the trustee to withdraw the income earned on the IRA assets and to distribute that income (along with the income earned on the trust assets other than the IRA) to the spouse. Therefore, assuming all other requirements of § 2056(b)(7) are satisfied, and provided the executor makes the election for both the IRA and the trust, the IRA and the trust will qualify for the marital deduction under § 2056(b)(7). The revenue ruling also concludes that the result would be the same if the terms of the trust require the trustee to withdraw an amount equal to the income earned on the IRA assets and to distribute that amount (along with the income earned on the trust assets other than the IRA) to the spouse.

[Impact of UPIA]

In Situation 1, under § 104(a) of the UPIA as enacted by State X, the trustee of Trust allocates the total return of the assets held directly in Trust (i.e., assets other than those held in the IRA) between income and principal in a manner that fulfills the trustee's duty of impartiality between the income and remainder beneficiaries. The trustee of Trust makes a similar allocation with respect to the IRA. The allocation of the total return of the IRA and the total return of Trust in this manner constitutes a reasonable apportionment of the total return of the IRA and Trust between the income and remainder beneficiaries under § 20.2056(b)–5(f)(1) and Reg. § 1.643(b)–1. Under the terms of Trust, the income of the IRA so determined is subject to B's withdrawal power, and the income of Trust, so determined, is payable to B annually. Accordingly, the IRA and Trust meet the requirements of § 20.2056(b)(7)(B)(ii) and therefore B has a qualifying income interest for life in both the IRA and Trust because B has the power to unilaterally access all of the IRA income, and the income of Trust is payable to B annually.

Depending upon the terms of Trust, the impact of State X's version of §§ 409(c) and (d) of the UPIA may have to be considered. State X's version of § 409(c) of the UPIA provides in effect that a required minimum distribution from the IRA under Code § 408(a)(6) is to be allocated 10 percent to income and 90 percent to principal. This 10 percent allocation to income, standing alone, does not satisfy the requirements of §§ 20.2056(b)–5(f)(1) and 1.643(b)–1, because the amount of the required minimum distribution is not based on the total return of the IRA (and therefore the amount allocated to income does not reflect a reasonable apportionment of the total return between the income and remainder beneficiaries). The 10 percent allocation to income also does not represent the income of the IRA under applicable state law without regard to a power to adjust between principal and income. State X's version of § 409(d) of the UPIA, requiring an additional allocation to income if necessary to qualify for the marital deduction, may not qualify the arrangement under § 2056. Cf. Rev. Rul. 75–440, 1975–2 C.B. 372, using a savings clause to determine testator's intent in a situation where the will is ambiguous, but citing Rev. Rul. 65–144, 1965–1 C.B. 422, for the position that savings clauses are ineffective to reform an instrument for federal transfer tax purposes. Based on the facts in Situation 1, if B exercises the withdrawal power, the trustee is obligated under Trust's terms to withdraw the greater of all of the income of the IRA or the annual required minimum distribution amount under § 408(a)(6), and to distribute at least the income of the IRA to B. Thus, in this case, State X's version of § 409(c) or (d) of UPIA would only operate to determine the portion of the required minimum distribution amount that is allocated to Trust income, and (because Trust income is determined without regard to the IRA or distributions from the IRA) would not affect the determination of the amount distributable to B. Accordingly, in Situation 1, the requirements of § 2056(b)(7)(B)(ii) are satisfied. However, if the terms of a trust do not require the distribution to B of at least the income of the IRA in the event that B exercises the right to direct the withdrawal from the IRA, then the requirements of § 2056(b)(7)(B)(ii) may not be satisfied unless the Trust's terms provide that State X's version of § 409(c) of the UPIA is not to apply.

In Situation 2, the trustee determines the income of Trust (excluding the IRA) and the income of the IRA under a statutory unitrust regime pursuant to which "income" is defined as a unitrust amount of 4 percent of the fair market value of the assets determined annually. The determination of what constitutes Trust income and the income of the IRA in this manner satisfies the requirements of § 20.2056(b)–5(f)(1) and Reg. § 1.643(b)–1. The Trustee distributes the income of Trust, determined in this manner, to B annually, and B has the power to compel the trustee annually to withdraw and distribute to B the income of the IRA, determined in this manner. Accordingly, in Situation 2, because B has the power to unilaterally access all income of the IRA, and the income of Trust is payable to B annually, the IRA and Trust meet the requirements of § 20.2056(b)(7)(B)(ii). The result would be the same if State Y had enacted both the statutory unitrust regime and a version of § 104(a) of the UPIA and the income of Trust is determined under § 104(a) of the UPIA as enacted by State Y, and the income of the IRA is determined under the statutory unitrust regime (or vice versa). Under these circumstances, Trust income and IRA income are each determined under state statutory provisions applicable to Trust that satisfy the requirements of § 20.2056(b)–5(f)(1) and Reg. § 1.643(b)–1, and therefore B has a qualifying income interest for life in both the IRA and Trust.

In Situation 3, B has the power to compel the trustee to withdraw the income of the IRA as determined under the law (whether common or statutory) of a jurisdiction that has not enacted § 104(a) of UPIA. Under the terms of Trust, if B exercises this power, the trustee must withdraw the greater of the required minimum distribution amount or the income of the IRA, and at least the income of the IRA must be distributed to B. Accordingly, in Situation 3, the IRA and Trust meet the requirements of § 2056(b)(7)(B)(ii), and therefore B has a qualifying income interest for life in both the IRA and Trust, because B receives the income of Trust (excluding the IRA) at least annually and B has the power to unilaterally access all of the IRA income determined in accordance with § 20.2056(b)–5(f)(1). The result would be the same if State Z had enacted § 104(a) of the UPIA, but the trustee decided to make no adjustments pursuant to that provision.

In Situations 1, 2, and 3, the income of the IRA and the income of Trust (excluding the IRA) are determined separately and without taking into account that the IRA distribution is made to Trust. In order to avoid any duplication in determining the total income to be paid to B, the portion of the IRA distribution to Trust that is allocated to trust income is disregarded in determining the amount of trust income that must be distributed to B under § 2056(b)(7).

The result in Situations 1, 2, and 3 would be the same if the terms of Trust directed the trustee annually to withdraw all of the income from the IRA and to distribute to B at least the income of the IRA (instead of granting B the power, exercisable annually, to compel the trustee to do so). Furthermore, if, instead of Trust being the named beneficiary of a decedent's interest in the IRA, Trust is the named beneficiary of a decedent's interest in some other qualified retirement plan described in § 4974(c) that is a defined contribution plan, the same principles would apply regarding whether B is considered to have a qualifying income interest for life in the qualified retirement plan.

HOLDING

If a marital trust is the named beneficiary of a decedent's IRA (or other qualified retirement plan described in § 4974(c) that is a defined contribution plan), the surviving spouse, under the circumstances described in Situations 1, 2, and 3 in this revenue ruling, will be considered to have a qualifying income interest for life in the IRA (or qualified retirement plan) and in the trust for purposes of an election to treat both the IRA (or qualified retirement plan) and the trust as QTIP under § 2056(b)(7). If the marital deduction is sought, the QTIP election must be made for both the IRA and the trust.

Taxpayers should be aware, however, that in situations such as those described in this revenue ruling in which a portion of any distribution from the IRA to Trust may be held in Trust for future distribution rather than being distributed to B currently, B is not the sole designated beneficiary of A's IRA. As a result, both B and the remainder beneficiaries must be taken into account as designated beneficiaries in order to determine the shortest life expectancy and whether only individuals are designated beneficiaries. See A–7(c) of Reg. § 1.401(a)(9)–5.

[¶ 30,171]

c. *Unmarried Plan Participants*

None of the conventional planning techniques will reduce the estate tax for unmarried plan participants.

[¶ 30,190]

3. INCOME TAXES GENERALLY

Generally speaking, distributions from an IRA in the form of a lump sum will constitute taxable income to the recipient in the year of receipt. § 408(d)(1). These principles are applicable where the distribution is made to the individual who established the account or to the designated beneficiary of the account after the death of the person who established the account.

There are exceptions, some self evident. For example, annuity contracts distributed from an IRA do not constitute taxable income in the year of distribution. However, each distribution under the annuity contract constitutes taxable income to the recipient in the year each payment is received. More fundamentally, where the IRA includes after tax dollars, distributions will be nontaxable to the extent of the plan participant's investment in the contract, i.e., until return of the participant's basis.

[¶ 30,200]

4.   INCOME TAXES WHEN THE PLAN PARTICIPANT IS LIVING

a.   *Periodic Distributions*

Generally speaking, periodic distributions from a tax qualified retirement plan, be it a qualified plan, an individual retirement account, or other plan, are taxed as ordinary income.

[¶ 30,210]

b.   *Lump–Sum Distributions*

Lump-sum distributions are taxed as ordinary income to the recipient. § 408(d)(1). Participants in qualified plans—but not IRAs—who attained age 50 before 1986 may make a one-time capital gain election of either 10–year averaging, and possibly capital gains treatment. Tax Reform Act of 1986, § 1122(h)(3). Due to the complexity of the transition rule—and the diminishing number of living persons who have yet to make this decision—it is merely noted here.

A lump-sum distribution is one made within a single tax year "of the balance to the credit of an employee which becomes payable to the recipient." § 402(e)(4)(D). If a distribution had been received by the recipient in a prior tax year, a final distribution of the balance in a later year will not qualify for lump-sum distribution treatment. Rev. Rul. 69–495, 1962–2 C.B. 100.

[¶ 30,212]

i.   *In General*

All qualified plans of the same type (i.e., profit-sharing, pension, or stock bonus) maintained by an employer are treated as a single plan. § 402(e)(4)(D)(ii).

Example. If an employee participates in two different profit-sharing plans of the same employer, the employee cannot elect to receive a lump-sum distribution from one and installment payments from the other.

[¶ 30,220]

ii.   *Electing Lump–Sum Distribution*

A lump-sum distribution may be elected if the individual dies, is disabled, attains age 59 1/2, or separates from employment. § 402(e)(4)(D).

¶ 30,220

[¶ 30,239]

iii.   Annuity Contracts as Lump–Sum Distributions

Often periodic payments from a plan are referred to as annuity or annuity-type payments. Actually, periodic payments and annuity-type payments should be distinguished from the distribution of an annuity contract from the plan. The annuity contract may be deemed a lump-sum distribution. §§ 402(e)(4)(D). If an annuity contract is distributed, the taxable amount of such distribution will be the contract's current actuarial value, determined on the date of such distribution, not the value of the annuity contract. See § 402(b)(2).

[¶ 30,283]

iv.   Avoiding Lump–Sum Characterization

Arranging to have a distribution from a qualified plan treated as other than a lump sum is fairly easy to accomplish. For example, arranging for distribution of all of the plan benefits in 12 monthly installments extending over two tax years has been deemed to be a non-lump-sum distribution. Priv. Ltr. Rul. 7817012. See ¶ 30,123.

[¶ 30,311]

REVENUE RULING 92–47

1992–1 C.B. 198.

ISSUE

What are the federal income tax consequences to the non-spouse beneficiary of an individual retirement account (IRA) of a decedent on receipt of a lump sum distribution from the IRA?

FACTS

A died owning an IRA. As of A's death, the IRA held assets that had appreciated since they were acquired by the IRA. Some of the contributions by A to the IRA had been nondeductible contributions. The designated beneficiary of the IRA was A's child, B. The entire balance in the IRA, including appreciation and income accruing before and after A's death, was distributed to B in a lump sum shortly after A's death.

LAW AND ANALYSIS

* * *

Reg. § 1.691(a)–1(b) provides that the term "income in respect of a decedent" refers to those amounts to which a decedent was entitled as gross income but that were not properly includible in computing taxable income for the taxable year ending with the date of death or for a previous taxable year under the method of accounting employed by the decedent.

Section 408(d)(1) provides that, except as otherwise provided in § 408(d) (relating to rollover contributions), any amount paid or distributed out of an IRA is included in gross income by the payee or distributee in the manner provided under § 72. Under § 72, nondeductible contributions to an IRA are not included in the gross income of the payee or distributee.

Section 408(e)(1) provides that an IRA is exempt from income taxation.

Reg. § 1.408–4(a)(2) provides that notwithstanding § 1015(d) or any other provision of the Code, the basis (or investment in the contract) of any person in an IRA is zero. This regulation has been superseded by changes in the law to the extent that an individual does have basis in his IRA equal to his nondeductible contributions.

Section 691(c)(1)(A) provides that a person who includes an amount in gross income under § 691(a) is allowed, for the same taxable year, as an income tax deduction an amount determined by reference to the estate tax attributable to the amount included in gross income under § 691(a). Section 691(c) and Reg. § 1.691(c)–1(a) provide rules for determining the amount of the deduction.

In Rev. Rul. 69–297, 1969–1 C.B. 131, an employee died designating his estate the beneficiary of his interest in a qualified profit-sharing trust. His interest in the trust, which included appreciated securities of the employer corporation, was distributed to his estate within one taxable year of his death. Rev. Rul. 69–297 holds that for the taxable year in which the distribution was made, the estate is required by § 402(a) to include in its gross income an amount equal to the cost or other basis to the trust of the employer securities (thus excluding any net unrealized appreciation in the employer securities), plus an amount equal to the cash and the fair market value of any other property received as part of the distribution, minus the amount of the employee's contributions. Rev. Rul. 69–297 characterizes this income as income in respect of a decedent under § 691(a), and holds that the estate is allowed a deduction under § 691(c) for that portion of the estate tax attributable to the inclusion in the decedent's estate of the distribution from the employee's trust. Rev. Rul. 69–297 further holds that the net unrealized appreciation in the securities of the employer is includible in gross income as income in respect of a decedent in the taxable year of their disposition by either the executor or the residuary legatees in a taxable transaction and that the transferor will be allowed the deduction provided under § 691(c) for any estate tax paid attributable to the net unrealized appreciation.

In Rev. Rul. 75–125, 1975–1 C.B. 254, a retired employee received from a qualified trust a lump sum distribution consisting entirely of securities of his corporate employer. The securities had a basis to the qualified trust of 5x dollars and a fair market value on the date of distribution of 10x dollars. Under § 402(a)(2), as in effect at the time of the distribution, the 5x dollars net unrealized appreciation in the securities was not taxed to the employee upon distribution. Following the distribution, the employee died leaving the securities to his surviving spouse. Rev. Rul. 75–125 holds that the net unrealized appreciation of 5x dollars attributable to the employer securities constitutes income in respect of a decedent under § 691(a) to be included in gross income by the surviving spouse when she disposes of the securities. Rev. Rul. 75–125 also holds that the surviving spouse is entitled to a deduction under § 691(c) for that portion of the federal estate tax attributable to the amount of the net unrealized appreciation included in the decedent's estate.

Amounts in A's IRA that were not distributed to A prior to A's death are not includible on A's final income tax return. If distributions from the IRA had been made to A prior to A's death, the distributions would have been taxable to A to the extent required under § 72. Upon A's death, the value of the IRA was included in A's estate and the entire balance in the IRA was distributed to B as designated beneficiary.

Under the above facts, the amount of the distribution that equals the balance in the IRA at A's death less A's nondeductible contributions to the IRA constitutes income in respect of a decedent and is includible in B's gross income for the taxable year in which B receives the distribution. The balance of the distribution, which represents appreciation and income accruing between the date of death and the date of distribution, is taxable to B under §§ 408(d) and 72. In computing income tax for the taxable year of inclusion of the income in respect of a decedent, B may claim a deduction for any federal estate tax on A's estate attributable to that income in respect of a decedent.

Problems

[¶ 30,337]

Mrs. Caldron retired seven years ago, at which time she elected to have her qualified plan benefits paid to her for her lifetime and, upon her death, the unpaid benefits were to be paid to the trustee of the revocable trust she had established during her lifetime. Essentially the trust provided that the trust property would be divided at her death so that her spouse would receive "the smallest amount" of her property that was necessary to eliminate all federal estate tax from her estate at her death. For background, see Chapter 15 for discussion of "formula" clauses. The balance of the trust property was to be placed in a bypass trust for her husband so that it would be available for his support but would not be included in his estate. The trust contained the following provision:

> *Allocation to Bypass Trust.* The Trustee shall allocate to the Bypass Trust, in cash or other property, or both, the entire balance of the trust estate remaining after the allocation provided for in paragraph 4.3 (including, specifically, the proceeds of any pension plan or other employee benefit plan or program), or all of the trust estate if Settlor's spouse does not survive Settlor, or is not deemed to survive Settlor as provided in paragraph 1.3(d).

Would you recommend that the foregoing provision be eliminated from Mrs. Caldron's trust and her spouse be designated recipient of her plan benefits?

¶ 30,311

[¶ 30,441]

c. *Rollover Distributions During the Lifetime of the Plan Participant*

A distribution of a participant's benefits from a qualified plan during the participant's life will not be includible in income if, and to the extent that, it constitutes a qualifying rollover distribution and is transferred into an eligible retirement plan within 60 days of receipt. § 402(c)(3). The rollover must be made to an individual retirement account (IRA) or annuity, another qualified plan, an eligible § 457(b) deferred compensation plan, a § 403(a) annuity plan, or a § 403(b) annuity. § 402(c)(8)(B).

If a partial distribution rollover is elected, only the amount transferred to an eligible retirement plan is excluded from income. § 402(c)(1).

[¶ 30,449]

PRIVATE LETTER RULING 200343030
July 31, 2003.

Taxpayer A, whose date of birth was Date 1, 1931, died testate on Date 2, 2002, at age 71 having reached his "required beginning date" as that term is defined in § 401(a)(9)(C). Taxpayer A was survived by three children including Taxpayer B and Taxpayer C. Taxpayer B, Taxpayer A's daughter, was alive as of the date of this ruling request.

As of his date of death, Taxpayer A was the owner of an individual retirement arrangement, IRA X, maintained with Company M. IRA X has a value of approximately Sum 1.

Taxpayer A's Last Will and Testament, dated Date 3, 1999, was duly admitted to probate in County O, State N. Item Four of Taxpayer A's Last Will and Testament provides for the outright distribution of Taxpayer A's estate to his three children in equal shares. On Date 4, 2002, Taxpayer C, Taxpayer A's son, was appointed sole executor of Taxpayer A's estate.

Taxpayer A did not designate a beneficiary of his IRA X. Thus, Taxpayer A's estate is the beneficiary thereof.

Taxpayer B proposes to transfer, by means of a trustee to trustee transfer, her one third interest in Taxpayer A's IRA X into a separate IRA titled "Taxpayer A (Deceased) IRA f/b/o Taxpayer B, beneficiary thereof". Taxpayer B then proposes to receive § 401(a)(9) required minimum distributions from her beneficiary IRA beginning in calendar year 2003 over Taxpayer A's remaining life expectancy.

Based on the above facts and representations, you, through your authorized representative, request the following letter rulings:

1. That Taxpayer B's one-third interest of Taxpayer A's IRA X can be segregated and held in a separate IRA for purposes of determining Taxpayer B's § 401(a)(9) required minimum distributions;

¶ **30,449**

2.   That the IRA created by means of a trustee to trustee transfer, which will be titled "Taxpayer A (Deceased) f/b/o Taxpayer B, beneficiary thereof", constitutes an inherited IRA under § 408(d)(3)(C);

3.   That Taxpayer B may receive § 401(a)(9) required distributions from the IRA set up in the name of Taxpayer A for her benefit over Taxpayer A's remaining life expectancy using the age of Taxpayer A as of Taxpayer A's birthday in the calendar year of Taxpayer A's death reduced by one for each calendar year pursuant to § 1.401(a)(9)–5 of the "Final" Income Tax Regulations, Question and Answer 5(a)(2); and

4.   That the transfer of Taxpayer B's one third interest in Taxpayer A's IRA X to the above described beneficiary IRA will not constitute a taxable distribution within the meaning of § 408(d)(1) to Taxpayer B and does not constitute a rollover as that term is used in § 408(d)(3).

With respect to your ruling requests, § 408(a)(6) provides that, under regulations prescribed by the Secretary, rules similar to the rules of § 401(a)(9) and the incidental death benefit requirements of § 401(a) shall apply to the distribution of the entire interest of an individual for whose benefit an IRA trust is maintained.

Section 401(a)(9)(A) provides, in general, that a trust will not be considered qualified unless the plan provides that the entire interest of each employee-(i) will be distributed to such employee not later than the required beginning date, or (ii) will be distributed, beginning not later than the required beginning date, over the life of such employee or over the lives of such employee and a designated beneficiary or over a period not extending beyond the life expectancy of such employee or the life expectancy of such employee and a designated beneficiary.

Section 401(a)(9)(B)(i) provides, in general, that if a plan participant (IRA holder) dies after the distribution of his interest has begun in accordance with subparagraph (A)(ii) (after his required beginning date), the remaining portion of his interest must be distributed at least as rapidly as under the method of distribution being used under subparagraph (A)(ii) as of the date of death.

Section 401(a)(9)(C) provides, in relevant part, that, for purposes of this paragraph, the term "required beginning date" means April 1 of the calendar year following the calendar year in which the IRA holder attains age 70 ½.

* * *

Section 1.401(a)(9)–4 of the "Final" regulations, Q & A–4, provides, in relevant part, that in order to be a designated beneficiary, an individual must be a beneficiary as of the date of (the employee's or IRA holder's) death. Generally, an employee's designated beneficiary will be determined based on the beneficiaries designated as of the date of death who remain beneficiaries as of September 30 of the calendar year following the calendar year of death.

Section 1.401(a)(9)–4 of the "Final" regulations, Q & A–3, provides that only individuals may be designated beneficiaries for purposes of § 401(a)(9). A person who is not an individual, such as the employee's estate, may not be a designated beneficiary. However, Q & A–5 of § 1.401(a)(9)–4 provides that

¶ 30,449

beneficiaries of a trust with respect to the trust's interest in an employee's benefit may be treated as designated beneficiaries if the following requirements are met:

Section 1.401(a)(9)–5 of the "Final" regulations, Q & A–5(a)(2) provides, in summary, that if an employee dies on or after his required beginning date without having designated a beneficiary, then post-death distributions must be made over the remaining life expectancy of the employee determined in accordance with paragraph (c) (3) of this A–5.

Section 1.401(a)(9)–5 of the "Final" regulations, Q & A–5(c)(3), provides, in general, that, with respect to an employee who does not have a designated beneficiary, the applicable distribution period measured by the employee's remaining life expectancy is the life expectancy of the employee using the age of the employee as of the employee's birthday in the calendar year of the employee's death. In subsequent calendar years, the applicable distribution period is reduced by one for each calendar year that has elapsed after the calendar year of the employee's death.

Section 1.401(a)(9)–9 of the "Final" regulations, Q & A–1, provides the relevant Single Life Expectancy Table.

Section 1.401(a)(9)–8 of the "Final" regulations, Q & A–2(a), provides the "separate account" rules with respect to defined contribution plans. A "separate account" is an account under which the beneficiary or beneficiaries differ from the beneficiary or beneficiaries of the other accounts. In general, if separate accounts are set up, for years subsequent to the calendar year containing the date on which the separate accounts were established, or the date of death if later, a separate account under a plan is not aggregated with the other separate accounts under the plan in order to determine whether the distributions from such separate account satisfy the requirements of § 401(a)(9). Instead, the rules in § 401(a)(9) apply separately to each separate account under the plan.

Section 1.401(a)(9)–8 of the "Final" regulations, Q & A–3, provides that a separate account is a separate portion of an employee's benefit which reflects the separate interest of an employee's beneficiary under the plan as of the employee's death for which separate accounting is maintained. The separate accounting must allocate all post-death investment gains and losses, contributions and forfeitures, for the period prior to the establishment of the separate accounts on a pro-rata basis in a consistent and reasonable manner among the separate accounts.

Section 1.401(a)(9)–4 of the "Final" regulations, Q & A–5(c), provides, in relevant part, that the separate account rules are not available to beneficiaries of a trust with respect to the trust's interest in an employee's benefit. In like manner, the "separate account" rules are not available to beneficiaries of an estate with respect to the estate's interest in an employee's plan or IRA interest.

Section 408(d)(1) provides, generally, that, in accordance with the rules of § 72, amounts paid or distributed from an IRA are included in the gross income by the payee or distributee.

¶ 30,449

Section 408(d)(3)(C) provides, generally, that amounts from an "inherited" IRA cannot be rolled over into another IRA. In general, an "inherited" IRA is an IRA maintained by an individual who acquired said IRA by reason of the death of another if the acquiring individual is not the surviving spouse of said other individual. In this case, as noted above, Taxpayer B is Taxpayer A's daughter.

Revenue Ruling 78–406, 1978–2 C.B. 157, provides that the direct transfer of funds from one IRA trustee to another IRA trustee, even if at the behest of the IRA holder, does not constitute a payment or distribution to a participant, payee or distributee as those terms are used in § 408(d). Furthermore, such a transfer does not constitute a rollover distribution.

Finally, Rev. Rul. 78–406 is applicable if the trustee to trustee transfer is directed by the beneficiary of an IRA after the death of the IRA owner as long as the transferee IRA is set up and maintained in the name of the deceased IRA owner for the benefit of the beneficiary.

The issues raised in this ruling request are whether a beneficiary-daughter of an IRA holder may, after the death of the IRA holder, transfer her one-third interest in the deceased's IRA to an IRA set up to solely benefit her, and whether she may receive distributions from her beneficiary IRA over the deceased's remaining life expectancy without regard to the distribution decisions made by the other IRA beneficiaries.

Although neither the nor the "Final" regulations promulgated under § 401(a)(9) preclude the posthumous division of IRA X into more than one IRA, the "Final" regulations do preclude "separate account" treatment for § 401(a)(9) purposes where amounts pass through an estate.

In this case, absent Taxpayer B's decision to transfer, by means of a trustee-to-trustee transfer, her one-third interest in Taxpayer A's IRA X to her beneficiary IRA, as described above, distributions of the entire IRA X interest, including Taxpayer B's one-third, would have to be made over Taxpayer A's remaining life expectancy in accordance with § 1.401(a)(9)–5 of the "Final" regulations, Q & A–5(c)(3). After the trustee to trustee transfer, Taxpayer B will receive required distributions over Taxpayer A's remaining life expectancy. Thus, the trustee to trustee transfer will have no effect on the timing or amount of required minimum distributions.

Additionally, a trustee to trustee transfer, as described in Rev. Rul. 78–406, does not constitute a distribution or payment as those terms are defined for purposes of § 408(d).

Finally, since Taxpayer B is Taxpayer A's daughter, her 1/3 interest in Taxpayer A's IRA X constitutes an inherited IRA as that term is defined in § 408(d)(3)(C).

Thus, based on the specific facts and representations surrounding this ruling request, we conclude as follows:

1.   That Taxpayer B's one-third interest of Taxpayer A's IRA X can be segregated and held in a separate IRA for purposes of receiving distributions.

¶ 30,449

Furthermore, with respect to determining over what period of time Taxpayer B must receive § 401(a)(9) required minimum distributions see our response to your third letter ruling request (below);

2. That the IRA created by means of a trustee to trustee transfer, which will be titled "Taxpayer A (Deceased) f/b/o Taxpayer B, beneficiary thereof", constitutes an inherited IRA under § 408(d)(3)(C);

3. That Taxpayer B may receive § 401(a)(9) required distributions from the IRA set up in the name of Taxpayer A for her benefit over Taxpayer A's remaining life expectancy using the age of Taxpayer A as of Taxpayer A's birthday in the calendar year of Taxpayer A's death reduced by one for each subsequent calendar year pursuant to § 1.401(a)(9)–5 of the "Final" Income Tax Regulations, Question and Answer 5(a)(2); and

4. That the transfer of Taxpayer B's one third interest in Taxpayer A's IRA X will not constitute a taxable distribution within the meaning of § 408(d)(1) to Taxpayer B and does not constitute a rollover as that term is used in § 408(d)(3).

This ruling letter is based on the assumption that IRA X and the beneficiary IRA created after the trustee to trustee transfer either have met, are meeting, or will meet the requirements of § 408 at all times relevant thereto.

Problem

[¶ 30,457]

In 1999, Ms. Skovornik established an IRA with Deposit Security Bank for her own benefit. She hoped that by making annual deposits of $3,000 she would have over $1,000,000 in the account at the time of her death. Unfortunately, she died in 2006. The designated beneficiary of her IRA was her nephew, Eddie Fitz. Eddie proposes to roll over Ms. Skovornik's IRA into one for his benefit. Would such a rollover be income tax free?

Would such a rollover cause the IRA to be free of estate taxes at Ms. Skovornik's death?

[¶ 30,459]

5. INCOME IN RESPECT OF A DECEDENT (IRD)

It should be emphasized that benefits paid from a qualified plan at the death of the participant constitute income in respect of a decedent (IRD) to the recipient. § 691.

As a result of including qualified plan benefits in the employee's gross estate, any estate taxes attributable thereto qualify as an income tax deduction for the recipient of the distribution. This § 691(c) deduction will mitigate the burden of the estate tax imposed on a distribution. See ¶ 21,101.

¶ 30,459

6. PENALTY TAXES ON PREMATURE DISTRIBUTIONS AND DELAYED DISTRIBUTIONS

[¶ 30,561]

a. Premature Distributions

Section 72(t) imposes an additional 10 percent penalty income tax on distributions from IRAs or qualified plans to participants who have not attained the age of 59 1/2. There are numerous exceptions to this general rule, including distributions due to the death or disability of an employee and distributions in periodic payments that extend over certain life expectancies of the participant or beneficiary. § 72(t)(2).

[¶ 30,565]

b. Delayed Distributions

Failure to make a required distribution results in a 50 percent penalty imposed on the delayed distribution.

Example. Jasper had retired and reached the "required beginning date" (RBD) but had not withdrawn the "required required minimum distribution" (RMD) by April 1st of the following year. The amount that should have been withdrawn in this case was $2,000. As a result Jasper owes a tax penalty of $1,000.

[¶ 30,571]

7. NONTAX CONSIDERATIONS

When contemplating distributions from a qualified plan, familiarity with and responsiveness to the income and estate tax costs of any proposed distribution from a qualified plan is essential, but the principal consideration should be the desires and needs of the plan participant and, later, the participant's beneficiary. Paramount among these needs will be their respective projected cash requirements. Such cash requirements may dictate payments which do not maximize tax savings.

C. LIFE INSURANCE

[¶ 30,581]

1. INTRODUCTION

A qualified plan is permitted to provide death benefits for its employees funded through the use of life insurance so long as such death benefits are "incidental" and not the primary purpose of the plan. Reg. § 1.401–1(b)(1)(i); Rev. Rul. 54–51, 1954 C.B. 147; Rev. Rul. 60–84, 1960–1 C.B. 159. Life insurance protection under a defined *contribution* plan is considered incidental if less than 50 percent of the amounts allocated to the participant's account is used to purchase only ordinary life insurance. If accident and/or health insurance is also purchased, the amount expended for health and accident insurance plus one-half of the ordinary life expenditures cannot exceed 25 percent of the amount credited. Rev. Rul. 76–353, 1976–2 C.B. 112; Rev. Rul. 61–164, 1961–2 C.B. 99.

Life insurance protection under a defined *benefit* plan is considered incidental where the proceeds of life insurance policies provide a death benefit that is not greater than 100 times the anticipated monthly normal retirement benefit. The plan may also provide that the participant's beneficiary can receive the investment side fund if no more than 50 percent of the "theoretical reserve" for such participant has been used to purchase whole life insurance protection for such participant. Rev. Rul. 74–115, 1974–1 C.B. 100; Rev. Rul. 74–307, 1974–1 C.B. 126.

More importantly, life insurance can be purchased on a selective basis through the use of separate accounts. ERISA § 404(c). In this case the incidental test may be satisfied if either the "100 x" test or the "less than 50 percent (25 percent)" test is met.

[¶ 30,589]

2. TAX CONSEQUENCES OF PREMIUM PAYMENTS

a. To the Employer

Employer contributions to a qualified plan are fully deductible regardless of whether the plan purchases life insurance so long as the foregoing limitations are not exceeded. Moreover, the purchase of life insurance through a defined benefit pension plan generally increases the annual contribution required to provide the retirement benefit and thereby increases the annual deduction.

It should be noted that plan contributions on behalf of self-employed plan participants that are allocable to life insurance protection are nondeductible. § 404(e).

[¶ 30,597]

b. To the Employee

The cost of current life insurance coverage purchased by a qualified plan will constitute currently taxable income to the employee. Reg. § 1.72–16(b)(2); 1.402(a)–1(a)(3). Current life insurance coverage is the excess of the death benefit over the policy's cash surrender value. Revenue Ruling 2002–8, 2002–1 C.B. 564, provides a table to be used to determine the income tax consequences to the plan participant. The plan participant will need cash—outside the plan—to pay the resulting income tax. Moreover, the obligation to pay income tax continues on the current life insurance coverage continues even if the plan stops paying insurance premiums (perhaps because the policy becomes paid up).

[¶ 30,600]

3. RETIREMENT OF THE EMPLOYEE

The principal disadvantage of plan-owned insurance occurs at retirement. At that time, the plan administrator must convert the value of all life

¶ 30,600

insurance policies into cash or an annuity for the employee or it must distribute the insurance contract to the employee, the latter being referred to as a "rollout." Rev. Rul. 54–51, 1954–1 C.B. 147; Rev. Rul. 60–84, 1960–1 C.B. 159. Life insurance policies may not be "rolled over" to an Individual Retirement Account (because an IRA cannot own life insurance). § 408(a)(3). Accordingly, the cash value of each such policy, as a general rule, will constitute taxable income to the plan participant when the distribution is made to him or her. See Reg. §§ 1.72–1(b), 1.72–2(a)(3), Example 6.

[¶ 30,603]

4. DEATH OF THE EMPLOYEE BEFORE RETIREMENT

a. *Income Tax Consequences*

The portion of the proceeds paid upon the death of the insured employee, which is equal to the cash value immediately before death, is not excludable from gross income under § 101(a). § 72(m)(3)(c). However, the amount in excess of the cash value constitutes current insurance protection and is excludable under § 101(a). § 101(a)(1); Reg. §§ 1.72–16(c)(2)(ii) and 1.402(a)–1(a)(4). Such net cash surrender value will be taxed like any other plan distribution. Thus, if the taxable portion of the cash value is paid out in the form of periodic payments, the payments will be taxable income when received.

[¶ 30,621]

b. *Estate Tax Consequences*

If the plan participant dies before retirement, the insurance proceeds are included in the taxable estate like other plan benefits.

[¶ 30,625]

5. PLANNING

a. *Use of Insurance in Qualified Plans*

There are conflicting considerations associated with the use of life insurance in a qualified plan. Purchase of life insurance through the plan permits the employer to obtain an income tax deduction for the premiums.

1. If the insurance is purchased by a defined *contribution* plan, the dollars used to pay the premiums will not be available for investment and the advantage of tax-free accumulation will be reduced.

2. If the insurance is purchased by a defined *benefit* pension plan, the annual contribution will be increased by an amount sufficient to pay the administrative costs of the policy and the difference, if any, between the plan's assumed interest rate and the increase in the cash surrender value of the policy. Accordingly, insurance may be considered for use in a defined benefit pension plan if the objective is to maximize contributions.

¶ 30,600

The use of insurance in qualified plans should be contrasted with the adoption of a group-life insurance plan as authorized by § 79. A group-life insurance plan is generally better (no income to the employee, a deduction to the corporation, proceeds totally income tax free), but the income-tax-free amount of coverage is limited to a maximum of the sum of $50,000 of insurance and the amount paid by the employee toward the purchase of such insurance.

[¶ 30,630]

b. Spouse–Owned Insurance

Purchase of insurance by a qualified plan may be preferable to having the insured's spouse own life insurance on the insured. As a practical matter, spouse-owned life insurance offers little or no advantages—and potentially significant disadvantages. See ¶ ¶ 20,515 and 20,523. The availability of the marital deduction renders almost meaningless the estate tax exclusion inherent in spouse-owned life insurance. And, where divorce occurs, there are inherent and obvious disadvantages to spouse-owned life insurance. Where a qualified plan owns the life insurance, the insured will have control over the proceeds during his or her life under the provisions of the plan. However, the policy proceeds will be included in the owner's estate.

Problem

[¶ 30,635]

Would ownership of life insurance on an employee's life by a qualified plan be preferable to ownership by an irrevocable trust established by the employee? (For discussion of irrevocable life insurance trusts, see ¶ 20,651 *et seq.*). The income tax treatment of insurance owned by the irrevocable trust would be similar to that of insurance owned by the plan. However, there could be some current income tax benefit if the plan owned the insurance. Premiums when paid by the corporation would constitute taxable income to the employee, the amount of the taxable income would be determined using the table provided in Reg. § 1.79–3(d)(2). This table might well provide values that are less than actual term insurance premiums paid. If the employee paid the premiums directly, the premiums would be paid out of after-tax dollars. Moreover, for gift tax purposes, ownership by the qualified plan would seem preferable. Why?

Would you agree that the irrevocable trust is a better vehicle in which to own life insurance?

[¶ 30,640]

c. Corporate–Owned Life Insurance

There may be income tax advantages to plan ownership of the insurance rather than ownership by the corporation itself. Premium payments by the corporation are not an income-tax-deductible expense, whereas premium payments by the corporation on plan-owned insurance is deductible by the

¶ 30,640

corporation. For estate tax purposes, there are no advantages. Corporate-owned life insurance on the life of a controlling stockholder is included in the stockholder's estate even if the proceeds are not paid to the corporation. Reg. § 20.2042–1(c). Proceeds of corporate-owned life insurance, which are payable to the corporation or a third party for a purpose other than a valid business purpose, are also included in the estate of a controlling stockholder.

D. DISTRIBUTION PLANNING

1. SOME OF THE APPLICABLE RULES

[¶ 30,701]

In 2002, the IRS issued regulations governing statutorily required distributions from qualified plans and IRAs. Rev. Rul. 2002–19, 2002–1 C.B. 778; Priv. Ltr. Rul. 200343030, reprinted at ¶ 30,439. These regulations greatly simplified the rules previously in place.

Section 401(a)(9) sets forth requirements for distributions from qualified plans and IRAs. The required beginning date (RBD) for distributions is April 1st of the year following the year in which the participant reaches age 70 ½ or, where applicable, the year following the year in which the participant retires. § 401(a)(9)(C). On that date, a required minimum distribution (RMD) must be made to the participant. In subsequent years a statutorily prescribed minimum amount (RMD) must be distributed annually. Standardized life expectancy tables are used to calculate the life expectancy of the plan participant and a hypothetical beneficiary (other than a spouse) who is assumed to be 10 years younger than the plan owner. If a plan participant names a spouse as beneficiary who is more than 10 years younger than the plan participant, then the participant must use their joint life expectancies, recalculated annually, to determine the minimum distributions. The required distribution is calculated each year by dividing the applicable life expectancy into the fair market value of the plan assets. The result is that the plan participant consults the Uniform Life Tables each year and recalculates the RMD annually. Unlike the prior rules, it makes no difference whether or not the participant has designated a beneficiary except in the case where the participant's spouse is more than 10 years younger.

It is important, however, for the plan participant to designate a beneficiary before his or her death. As the table below illustrates, it is always better to name at least one beneficiary prior to the death of the plan participant.

Table 30.3. DISTRIBUTIONS AFTER THE PARTICIPANT'S DEATH

	"Designated Beneficiary" (DB)	*No "Designated Beneficiary"*
1.	Nonspouse Beneficiary. If a beneficiary or beneficiaries are named who are not the participant's spouse, distributions after the death of the participant are based on the age of the oldest beneficiary -or- on the participant's age without recalculation if a smaller payout results in cases where the participant died on or after the required beginning date (RBD).	Where the plan participant dies *before* the required beginning date (RBD), the entire balance must be distributed within five years after the participant's death. § 409(a)(9)(B)(ii).

2. Spouse Beneficiary. If the participant names his or her spouse as the only designated beneficiary, then distributions are based on the spouse's life expectancy, recalculated annually. After the participant's spouse dies,	
distributions *to the spouse's beneficiary* will be based on the spouse's remaining life expectancy, without recalculation unless both spouses died before the end of the year in which the participant reached or would have reached age 70 ½.	Where the plan participant dies *after* the required beginning date (RBD), the required minimum distributions (RMDs) are based on the participant's remaining life expectancy (rather than the beneficiary's).
3. Spousal IRA. A surviving spouse who is a sole designated beneficiary may defer distributions until the end of the year in which the participant would have attained age 70 ½. Also a spouse (regardless of whether the spouse is a sole beneficiary) may roll-over IRA proceeds into a spousal IRA (which will then calculate minimum distributions based on the surviving spouse's RBD and the surviving spouse's life expectancy with recalculation).	

Table 30.4. UNIFORM LIFE TABLES USED IN DETERMINING APPLICABLE DISTRIBUTION DIVISOR (REG § 1.409(A)(9)–9)

Age	Applicable divisor	Age	Applicable divisor	Age	Applicable divisor	Age	Applicable divisor	Age	Applicable divisor
70	26.2	80	17.6	90	10.5	95	7.8	106	3.8
71	25.3	81	16.8	91	9.9	96	7.3	106	3.6
72	24.4	82	16.0	92	9.4	97	6.9	108	3.3
73	23.5	83	15.3	93	8.8	98	6.5	109	3.1
74	22.7	84	14.5	95	8.3	99	6.1	110	2.8
75	21.8	85	13.8	95	7.8	100	5.7	111	2.6
76	21.8	85	13.1	96	7.3	101	5.3	112	2.4
77	20.1	87	12.4	97	6.9	102	5.0	113	2.2
78	19.2	88	11.8	98	6.5	103	4.7	114	2.0
79	18.4	89	11.1	99	6.1	104	4.4	115 over	1.8
						105	4.1		

[¶ 30,721]

2. TYPES OF IRAs

a. *In General*

Although, while technically speaking, there are several more, only five types of Individual Retirement Accounts (IRAs) will be noted here. First, there is the individual account described at ¶ 29,067, established by an individual as an independent retirement vehicle or as a receptacle for a deductible or nondeductible employee contribution under § 219.

[¶ 30,722]

b. *Rollover, Spousal and Inherited IRAs*

Second is an IRA established with funds received as a distribution from a qualified plan (a "rollover"). Section 408(d)(3) provides that distributions from a qualified plan which are rolled over into an IRA will not be subject to income tax at the time of distribution. Accordingly, taxation of qualified plan distributions made to a rollover IRA can be postponed until the funds are distributed from the IRA.

Third is an "inherited IRA," provided for in § 408(d)(3)(C). An inherited IRA is one that was acquired by the beneficiary of the IRA "by reason of the death of another individual." Such IRAs can not be rolled over income tax free but they are eligible to receive tax-free direct rollovers from another plan owned by the same deceased participant and payable to the same designated beneficiary.

A fourth kind of an IRA is a "spousal IRA". While a form of inherited IRA, the "inherited IRA" rules do not apply if the IRA beneficiary is the surviving spouse of the decedent from whom the IRA was acquired. Thus, qualified plan distributions can be rolled over income tax free to an IRA for the benefit of the plan participant during the lifetime of the plan participant and rolled over again income tax free at the death of the plan participant to the participant's surviving spouse.

[¶ 30,723]

c. *Roth IRAs*

A fifth type of IRA is the "Roth–IRA." Roth IRAs were named for William Roth, chairman of the United States Senate Finance Committee at the time the Roth IRAs were introduced. The distinguishing—and exciting— aspect of a Roth IRA is that while contributions to a Roth IRA are not tax deductible (i.e., contributions must be made from "after tax dollars"), earnings by a Roth IRA are not taxable—and withdrawals of those earnings can be made *taxfree* if the IRA has been funded for at least 5 years and the person making the withdrawal is over 59 ½ years of age. § 408A(d). Roth IRAs are not free of estate taxes, however.

Annual contributions to a Roth IRA are limited to $4,000 (adjusted for inflation) but is not to exceed taxable compensation for the year. § 219. The contribution limit increases to $5,000 for those over 50. However, eligibility is limited to those having adjusted gross income of $110,000 or less (and is reduced in amount for those with adjusted gross income of $95,000 and up). § 408A(c)(3)(B). For married persons, the respective adjusted gross income thresholds are $160,000 and $150,000.

[¶ 30,754]

3. DURING LIFETIME OF PLAN PARTICIPANT

In many cases, the plan participant is able to choose the form in which plan benefits are distributed (as well as choose the beneficiary of any plan benefits remaining at the participant's death). Typically, the participants can choose: (1) an annuity for life or for the life of the survivor of the participant and the participant's spouse; (2) to take, after the "required beginning date" (RBD), the "required minimum distribution" (RMD) as determined by reference to a table provided by the IRS (Reg. § 1.409(a)(9)–9); or (3) a lump sum (with the prospect of rolling the lump sum over into an IRA). Receipt of a lump sum, unless rolled over into an IRA, subjects the distributed amount to income tax in the year of receipt. The other options provide income tax deferral, with income tax imposed each year only on the plan benefits received that year. (Estate tax upon the death of the plan participant is not affected by the choice. In all instances, the plan benefits remaining undistributed at death are included in the gross estate of the plan participant for estate tax purposes. § 2039.)

Choosing an annuity means that the participant (and the participant's spouse where a two-life annuity is selected) will receive a stream of periodic payments while the annuity lasts. Sometimes the payments will vary in amount (where the plan proceeds are invested in a fund containing equities); in other cases, the payments will be identical in amount (where the periodic payments are merely a contractual obligation of the annuity vendor).

Choosing a lump sum followed by a rollover into an IRA means that withdrawals can be deferred until the plan participant attains age 70 ½—the "required beginning date" (RBD)—and that any undistributed balance remaining at the death of the plan participant can be disposed of by designation of a beneficiary or by provision in his or her will. The same is true where the RMD option is selected.

Choosing between an annuity or a lump sum depends on whether the plan participant wants to use the plan proceeds as (1) a retirement fund, (2) a tax-deferred capital accumulation fund; or (3) source of immediate cash to satisfy current needs and wants. If the plan participant needs a steady income for his or her retirement, an annuity is the best alternative. But if the plan participant does not need the annuity but views the plan proceeds as merely another investment in a larger portfolio, then the lump-sum alternative is preferable. The advantage of an annuity is that it provides protection against living too long, i.e., outliving the plan benefits. Plan participants with these concerns will elect the annuity even though: (1) the annuity is more expensive since an insurance premium will be collected to cover the additional payments that must be made where the plan participant ("the annuitant") lives beyond his or her life expectancy; (2) there is risk that the annuitant (and the annuitant's spouse in the case of a two-life annuity) will die prematurely, leading to the forfeiture of some part of the plan proceeds; and (3) fees charged to administer the annuity may well be higher than those typically incurred for investment management of a lump sum, where the owner is free to shop for the best price or to manage the lump sum without professional help. Because of the foregoing factors, the annuity option must be seen as more expensive. Nonetheless, it will be the alternative of choice for many plan participants.

What do the numbers tell us? Various methods can be used to compare the economic impact of lump-sum distributions with the periodic payments provided by annuities. These include the present value method and the "exact" method. However, these methods—and all others—involve so many assumptions that reliable conclusions are probably impossible. Among others, assumptions must be made as to investment rates of return and projected

¶ 30,754

income tax rates. Moreover, despite any economic analysis that is made, the choice ultimately depends on the needs of the plan participant, i.e., whether the plan participant needs the security of an annuity.

From an income tax management perspective, it would seem self evident that where the plan participant chooses not to annuitize, the tax deferral opportunity presented by the RMD option (including the rollover option) would seem compelling. That is, take only what you need over and above the required minimum distribution. Income tax defer as long as possible—unless you expect to be in a much higher income tax bracket in later years.

Incidentally, but noteworthy, participants who begin receiving benefits before 59 ½ will pay a ten percent tax on the benefits received prior to 59 ½ unless retired or having experienced a hardship. § 72(t).

[¶ 30,775]

4. AFTER DEATH OF PLAN PARTICIPANT

Generally speaking, where income tax management is a goal, planning for receipt of plan benefits, if any, following the death of the plan participant means having a "designated beneficiary" (DB) (and where there is a surviving spouse, having named the spouse the "designated beneficiary") for it is only with a qualifying "designated beneficiary" in place that income tax deferral is possible over the beneficiary's life expectancy. Otherwise, at best, income tax deferral is five years after the plan participant's death—and only in cases where the participant dies before the RBD.

Obviously some plan participants will die before beginning to receive benefits and others will die after having begun to receive benefits. (Participants must begin receiving benefits in the year following the year he or she attains 70 ½—the required beginning date (RBD) unless the participant has not retired.) Undistributed plan benefits are subject to estate tax and state death tax (if any) at the participant's death—whether death occurs before or after the participant has begun to receive benefits (unless, of course, all benefits cease at death—either because of plan specification or election by the plan participant—and nothing is available to the participant's survivors).

[¶ 30,781]

a. *Before the Participant's Required Beginning Date (RBD)*

Where the plan participant dies before the "required beginning date" (RBD), the possibilities include:

1. All benefits cease and there is nothing for survivors—and, of course, in such a case, there will be no federal estate tax and no state death tax on the plan benefits;

2. The remaining plan benefits are distributed to the participant's estate for distribution under his or her will or by intestacy—and, of course, in this case the remaining plan benefits will be subject to federal estate tax and state death tax (if any) as well as income tax in the year of receipt by the estate (although deferral of receipt by the estate over what would have been participant's remaining life expectancy is permissible);

¶ 30,754

3. The remaining plan benefits are distributed to the participant's "designated beneficiary"—and, of course, in this case the remaining plan benefits will be subject to federal estate tax and state death tax (if any) as well as income tax in the year of receipt by the designated beneficiary but the designated beneficiary can defer receipt over his or her lifetime (or over what would have been the participant's life expectancy if longer), taking annually only the required minimum distribution;

4. The remaining plan benefits are distributed to the participant's spouse as the result of being the participant's "designated beneficiary"—and, of course, in this case, while the remaining plan benefits will be subject to federal estate tax and state death tax (if any), the plan benefits will, quite frequently, either by design or luck, qualify for the unlimited estate tax marital deduction under § 2056; the plan benefits will be subject to income tax in the year of receipt by the spouse but the spouse can roll these benefits over to his or her own IRA and defer receipt of any benefits until the spouse's required beginning date, i.e., April 1st of the year following the year in which the spouse attains 70 ½ years of age, at which time the required minimum distribution is calculated using the spouse's age (and not that of the deceased plan participant); or

5. The remaining plan benefits are distributed to a trust at the direction of the plan participant—and, while these remaining plan benefits will be subject to federal estate tax and state death tax (if any), income tax deferral opportunities depend upon whether a trust beneficiary qualifies as a "designated beneficiary".

[¶ 30,801]

b. After the Participant's Required Beginning Date (RBD)

Where the plan participant dies after his or her required beginning date (RBD), the possibilities include, with one exception, those described in 30,781, above, as being available where the participant dies before his or her RBD. Where the deceased participant has reached the RBD and has no designated beneficiary, e.g., where the plan benefits are distributed to the participant's estate for distribution under his or her will or by intestacy, receipt of plan benefits cannot be deferred for five years as is permitted when the participant dies before attaining his or her RBD. Instead, a distribution must be taken in the year following death and in all subsequent years until the account is fully distributed, the minimum distribution each year being determined by the deceased plan participant's remaining life expectancy.

[¶ 30,821]

c. Using a Trust

Designating a trust as beneficiary of plan benefits is perilous, perilous in the sense that it is entirely possible that a misstep will result in all of the plan benefits becoming immediately income taxable, i.e., the risk is loss of the income tax deferral opportunity that otherwise may well be available. In the well executed situation, the trust beneficiary (beneficiaries) are the participant's "designated beneficiary" (DB), meaning that the trust must take required distributions in annual installments over a period not longer than the life expectancy of the oldest beneficiary (or the life expectancy of the plan participant if longer). Where the surviving spouse is the trust's beneficiary, as in the case of a trust which is a qualified terminable interest property (QTIP) trust, the trust must be specially configured, as discussed in ¶ 30,143, not only to qualify the plan benefits for the marital deduction but also to permit maximum income tax deferral for undistributed plan benefits.

[¶ 30,831]

d. *Estate Tax on Undistributed Plan Benefits*

The discussion has been and always is about deferring income taxes. Estate taxes are payable on plan benefits except in instances where the designated beneficiary of those benefits is the surviving spouse (in which case the benefits qualify for the marital deduction provided by § 2056). The problem is exacerbated where the designated beneficiary is the bypass or credit shelter trust. Said otherwise, in as much as plan benefits often constitute the largest asset in a decedent's estate—and having plan benefits pass to a designated beneficiary is income tax optimum—where does the plan participant find the property necessary to fund the bypass trust and take full advantage of the opportunity to tax shelter the applicable exclusion amount—$2 million in 2006—in the bypass? Should the bypass trust be funded with plan benefits? What are the consequences of so doing? Should the plan participant purchase life insurance as a source of cash? (Why? Proceeds of life insurance held in a properly structured irrevocable trust are already free of estate tax. ¶¶ 20,651–20,860.) In sum, the issue is how to reconcile the need for property to fund the bypass trust with the easily obtained benefits of having an individual (rather than a trust) qualify as the "designated beneficiary" of the plan benefits. Among the possibilities—there are no good solutions—the plan participant, during lifetime, could take a plan distribution sufficient to pay anticipated estate taxes as well as the income taxes on the distribution. At least, in this fashion, the $2 million applicable exclusion amount (§ 2010(c))—the tax shelter—would not be diminished by the income taxes payable on the amount required from the plan to pay the estate taxes on the value of the decedent's estate that exceeds the $2 million applicable exclusion amount.

[¶ 30,841]

e. *Some Generalizations*

Undoubtedly, for income tax deferral purposes, a plan participant should be certain to have named a qualifying "designated beneficiary" for the undistributed plan benefits at his or her death. And the greatest potential for deferral is normally found where the surviving spouse is the designated beneficiary because the spouse can roll the plan benefits to the spouse's own IRA which has the effect of postponing the RBD for distributions to the year following the year the surviving spouse attains 70 ½ and the RMD thereafter will be determined using the life expectancy of the surviving spouse.

¶ 30,821

Appendix A

ELECTRONIC SOURCES (INCLUDING ACTUARIAL FACTORS)

1. Estate Planning Tools (Brentmark Software, Inc., 3505 Lake Lynda Drive, Suite 212, Orlando, FL 32817 (407–306–6160) (same program as Leimberg, Number Cruncher)

2. Steve Leimberg's NumberCruncher (http://www.leimberg.com) (610–924–0515)

3. Steve Leimberg's Financial Calculator (http://www.leimberg.com or 610–924–0515)

4. Donald H. Kelley & Konrad Schmidt III, Intuitive Estate Planner (West Group, 620 Opperman Drive, P.O. Box 64605, St. Paul, MN 55164 (800–277–9378)); and

5. Lawrence Katzenstein, Tiger Tables Software, 4529 Pershing Place, St. Louis, MO 63108. (http://www.tigertables.com.) E-mail: info@tigertables.com.

The Internal Revenue Service website provides the following actuarial factors in .pdf format, all of which are more easily accessed using the above listed programs:

1. Actuarial Tables Alpha Volume (Publication 1457, July 1999) (http://www.irs.gov/pub/irs-pdf/p1457.pdf); and

2. Actuarial Values Beta Volume (Publication 1458, July 1999) (http://www.irs.gov/pub/irs-pdf/p1458.pdf)

Not to be overlooked are following excellent online sources:

1. Leimberg Information Services Newsletters/database (http://www.leimbergservices.com)

2. Robert Fleming, Elder Law Issues (http://www.elder-law.com) E-mail: robert@elder-law.com

Internal Revenue Service forms and publications are often an important aid to understanding and implementing planning and (needless to say) compliance. These are readily obtainable in .pdf format at: http://www.irs.gov. Of particular interest are Form 706 (Estate Tax Return); Form 709 (Gift Tax Return); and Form 1041 (Fiduciary Income Tax Return).

Wealth Transfer Planning, an important state-of-the-art estate planning system (will and trust drafting) powered by HotDocs and authored by Jonathan Blattmachr and Michael Graham is available from Interactive Legal Systems (888–315–0872) at: http://www.ilsdocs.com.

Appendix B

PROJECTS

How to Use These Projects

Assignments from the Projects material should be made selectively, with the students being instructed to prepare memoranda of law which will constitute the principal means of evaluation of their performance.

The Projects are of varying lengths with one notable exception. Project 3 is referred to as a long project and purports to require the preparation of a comprehensive estate plan. Projects 4 through 10 are based on the facts described in Project 3. It is thought that, if Project 3 is used, Projects 4 through 11 could be largely ignored. However, if these materials are used as the principal resource materials in the typical two credit hour seminar, Projects 2 and 3 could be utilized in the first several sessions, Projects 4–12, the remaining sessions, and Project 3 as a capstone problem to be utilized in the last class session.

A Few Words About Legal Research

In responding to the Projects set out in these materials, it is expected that the preparer will find it necessary to consult statutory authority, cases, rulings of the Internal Revenue Service, and the scholarship regularly published in law reviews and professional journals.

If memoranda of law are required, the preparer should keep in mind that a memorandum of law should set forth clearly not only recommended action but also the technical analysis which supports the recommendations. The memorandum should provide the reader with sufficient information about the legal issues that impact the conclusions reached so as to allow the reader to make an independent determination as to the validity of the conclusions without having to do any additional research and without having to read the authorities relied on for the conclusions reached. In a sense, then, a well-written memorandum is like an abstract of all of the applicable law. Reading the abstract is to be like experiencing the research firsthand.

To facilitate use of memoranda of law, preparers should grow accustomed to exclusively utilizing the Uniform System of Citation, commonly referred to as the "Blue Book."

Project 1

WILL DRAFTING (basic)

MEMORANDUM

To: Associates' Pool

From: Mr. Longhours

Mike Modest is a good client of mine. In a recent conversation we developed the facts set forth in this memorandum.

Please prepare a memorandum of law for me. Address the issues raised by the following facts. Also prepare a will for Mike.

Mike prides himself on being a simple person and so, naturally, his present will is quite simple. (He often says that "Modest is the name and simplicity is the game.") Mike's present will reads as follows:

"WILL

"1. My executor should first pay from my estate those of my debts that he believes should be paid.

"2. Pay my taxes.

"3. I give my stock in Fish Taco Cafe, Inc., to my nephew, Mortecai, who works with me in my business and has been a big success on the salads line.

"4. I give everything else to my daughter, Missy.

"5. Missy shall be my Executor and have the power to do all those things with my property that I could do if I were living.

/s/"Mike"

Mike's property consists of the following:

1. His Fish Taco Cafe stock. Mike claims that he is unable to place a value on the stock. He owns all of the outstanding 1,000 shares. In 2006, each share earned $120.

Mike is currently considering selling Fish Taco Cafe to Amalgamated Motors ("AM") (whose management is committed to diversification) in return for AM common stock. The sale may not be consummated, but if it is, Mike wants his nephew, Mortecai ("Mort"), to get the AM stock inasmuch as this is his only gift to Mort. (Mort was orphaned years ago, and he has been raised by Mike as his own child, even though he never formally adopted Mort.)

2. An arcade specializing in the electronic game known as Sack Man. This enterprise, started in 2001, is operated as a sole proprietorship. Mike has a two-year lease on the arcade premises. He leases the Sack Man units on a monthly basis. He is netting $10,000 per month from the arcade.

3. A 2002 Buick Century.

4. $300,000 in cash.

Missy's mother died ten years ago when Missy was only three years old.

Mike did not and does not want to make any provision for his son, Chip, from whom he has been estranged for years.

Mike is making no provision for his wife, Maud. Maud knows this and is somewhat disgruntled. However, Mike explains that, shortly before their marriage, he and Maud signed the following agreement:

"Agreement

"The undersigned, who are about to marry, agree that any property produced by the separate property of one of us or the labor of one of us shall be the separate property of the person whose separate property or labor produced that property and that the other shall have no claim on the property so produced.

"At the present time Maud has $9,800 in cash and household furnishings having an approximate value of $12,000. Mike has cash in the amount of $200,000 and all the stock in Fish Taco Cafe, Inc., which earned approximately $45 per share last year.

/s/ "Maud Moore"

/s/ "Mike Modest"

"November 30, 1991"

Reference: EP & D, Chapter 3 (Wills); ¶¶ 11,201 and 21,900 (prenuptial agreement).

Project 2

THE MIDDLE YEARS: NONESTATE PLANNING (basic)

MEMORANDUM

To: Associates Pool

From: Mr. Longhours

Please prepare a memorandum for me addressing the issues raised in this memorandum. Here are some background motions.

The middle years mean different things to different people. For some with property, the middle years begin in the middle forties when the children's educational needs are straining the family financial resources and the children's emotional development seems most precarious. Adding to these burdens, oftentimes, are aging parents who are also moving into a period of dependence, both physically and emotionally. Finally, for many, the middle years are a period when careers have plateaued, and both spouses find the need if not the desire to be in the work force outside the home. By the late fifties and early sixties, many of the problems common to the middle years will have passed and the presence of two wage earners in the household will produce a standard of living that these taxpayers consider acceptable, if not luxurious.

However, for some few others, the middle years come much earlier, usually in the thirties. For these people, the middle years are a way station—a transitional phase, if you will—through which people pass as careers grow increasingly successful and gracious living becomes a way of life. During this period children are born and parents wrestle with concerns about providing their children with the best educational opportunities and, oftentimes, accommodating two careers with successful parenting. It is almost a misnomer to describe this period in the lives of the upwardly mobile as the middle years. It is, however, the middle years economically. Like their counterparts who are in their forties when they experience the middle years, these upwardly mobile individuals have not accumulated substantial capital, but they have ever increasing incomes which are perceived as being burdened by high income tax rates. While the issues of capital accumulation and income shifting are for later, consider the planning that needs to be done for those in the middle years with nonestates.

Matt and Laura Ordinary are typical. They married, his career flourished, two children—Allison and Claire—were born, but, with the expenses associated with the perceived need for regularly improving their housing and building a medical practice, they have accumulated little capital. Matt says it is all because of "income taxes eating him alive." Whatever the cause, Matt and Laura have nonestates but a belief in the future.

Taxpayers with nonestates—a term popularized, if not coined by, Professor Thomas L. Shaffer—are those whose estates will be free of federal estate taxes when death occurs. While it may be convenient to describe these persons as being in their middle years, the federal estate tax is age neutral, and the greatest percentage of the American people will not be burdened by federal estate taxes. (In 2006, the exemption equivalent to the unified credit (applicable exclusion amount, § 2010(c)) was $2 million and scheduled to increase to $3.5 million in 2009 before ending in 2009—only to return to $1 million in 2011!) Accordingly, it is appropriate to think of the planning required for the middle years to also be the planning required for most people and all the planning that most people will require.

There is probably agreement that minimum planning means a will giving it "all to my spouse if my spouse survives me; otherwise per stirpes to my then living lineal descendants."

Remaining to be considered is provision for the care and feeding and lodging of children in the unlikely event they are orphaned during their minority.

1. What provisions does the state have for the care and protection of the person and property of minor children? Mentally handicapped persons?

2. What planning should be done to fill the "holes" in state law in providing for these developments?

3. In light of your investigation of state law, would you agree that, in the unlikely event that a child is orphaned during his or her minority, a trust is a vastly superior alternative to the property management scheme provided by your state law in such circumstances? Does it matter whether the trust is testamentary or inter vivos?

   a. Knowing the additional expense to be incurred if a trust is utilized, could you, in good conscience, recommend a trust to a client (instead of only a simple will) solely because of the unlikely possibility that the client's children will be orphaned while they are minors?

   b. Implicit in the foregoing comment is the assumption that "trusts are expensive". Is the assumption supported by the facts or, possibly, is the trust the least expensive alternative?

4. If a trust is to be utilized, could it not be done simply in a will which might take the following form?

"WILL

"I, Matt Ordinary, give all of my property to my wife, Laura, if she survives me for thirty days. If she does not survive me for this period of time, I give all of my property to my then living lineal descendants per stirpes; but if any one or more of my children has not attained _____ years of age at my death, each child's share of my estate shall be delivered to Accumulation National Bank as Trustee to be held, managed, and disposed of as provided below.

"During the continuance of each trust provided for in this will, the Trustee shall distribute so much or all of the income and principal of the trust as shall be necessary for the health, education, maintenance and support of the beneficiary of the trust.

"Each trust provided for in this instrument shall terminate when the trust beneficiary attains _____ years of age or dies. Upon termination, the Trustee shall distribute the property then comprising the trust to the beneficiary if he or she is then living; otherwise to the beneficiary's then living lineal descendants per stirpes; and, if none, to my then living lineal descendants per stirpes.

"I nominate my wife, Laura, to be executor of my estate, to serve without bond, and with full power to do anything and everything that I could do with my property if I were living.

[Include here the usual attestation clause and affidavit to cause the will to be self-proving.]

Would Matt and Laura be advantaged if their state of residence had adopted the Wisconsin Statutory Will, Wis. Stat.Ann. §§ 853.55–.56 (West 2002), (or that of another state such as California, Cal. Prob. Code § 6240 (West Supp. 2006), or Maine, Me. Rev. Stat. Ann. tit. 18–A, § 2–514 (1998), or Michigan, Mich. Comp. Laws Ann. § 700.2519 (West Supp. 2006), or New Mexico, N.M. Stat. Ann. § 45–2A–17 (LexisNexis 1995))? Or, do you think having the opportunity to consult with a lawyer—for a fee, of course— provides Matt and Laura a benefit over and above simply having professionally drafted wills? Identify some of those benefits. Also consider whether a lawyer has any conflicts of interest in representing the both of them.)

Consider, too, the possibility that either of both Matt and Laura may become legally (or practically) incompetent due to accident, illness, or advancing age.

1. What provisions does the state have for the care and protection of the person and property of those who are under legal disability?

2. What planning should be done to fill the "holes" in state law in providing for these developments?

3. Would a power of attorney be an appropriate addition to every estate plan? Who should be given the power? Should the powerholder have the authority to appoint a successor to him or her self? For how long should the power be given? Should it have a natural expiration? Should it be limited?

4. Would you recommend that Matt use a free standing—in lawyer speak, an inter vivos—trust (FST) rather than a testamentary trust (TT)? Can you give reasons for your recommendation?

5. In choosing between an inter vivos trust and a testamentary trust, consider using an inter vivos trust because of its utility as a vehicle for managing the settlor's property during a period of incompetency.

But, you say, "the settlor can provide for property management during periods of incompetency by giving someone a power of attorney". While the point is well taken, could it not also be argued that third parties might be reluctant to rely on an "old" power of attorney given the ever present possibility that the grantor of the power has revoked it? Also, consider whether the third party asked to rely on a power of attorney must familiarize himself or herself with local law to determine whether such powers survive periods of incompetence.

6.   A possible inter vivos trust appears below as Attachment 1 to Project 2.

Reference: EP & D, ¶ 2451 (joint representation), Chapter 4.

TRUST AGREEMENT

To: **Matt and Laura Ordinary,** Trustees (hereinafter referred to in the singular)

From: **Matt Ordinary** ("Matt")

Setting Up The Trust

1.   Please accept, as Trustees, the property listed on the attached Schedule A, to hold, manage, invest, and distribute according to the terms of this agreement for the benefit of me and the other persons identified in this agreement. If you sign this trust agreement, it will mean that you have accepted the trust (and the property described on Schedule A).

Name of the Trust

2. Please refer to this trust as the "Matt Ordinary Living Trust dated   (date signed by trustee)   ".

Identifications

3.   The term "Allison" refers to my child. The term "Claire" refers to my other child.

4.   No other children have been born to me and no other person shall be treated as a child of mine.

5.   The term "lineal descendants" (and like references) refers to Claire and Allison and to the lineal descendants of Claire and Allison, whether natural or adopted so long as any adoption occurs before the adopted child attains fourteen (14) years of age as well as to natural children of Claire or Allison that are adopted by another—but only those children adopted by another more than six (6) months after birth.

Adding To The Trust

6.   I may increase the principal of this trust by delivering additional property to you (during my lifetime or after my death by will or as a distribution from another trust).

Payments While I Am Living

7.   This trust is for my exclusive benefit during my lifetime.

8.   So long as I am living, you are to pay or apply for my benefit, so much of or all of the principal and income of the trust as I need for health, maintenance, support, comfort and happiness in my accustomed manner of living.

9.   You may use all or part of the principal in any way you believe will benefit me. Any decision you make in good faith will fully protect you and will bind everyone with an interest in this trust.

Payments After My Death

10. After my death, you may pay (but you are not required to pay), from the trust property that I may have placed in the trust during my lifetime, the expenses of administering my estate (including transfer taxes, penalties or interest imposed on my estate) but such payments are to be made only to the extent other property available to the executor of my will is not readily available for this purpose.

Withdrawals From the Trust While I Am Living

11. I can withdraw part or all of this trust at any time by notifying you in writing. Each withdrawal must be for at least $1,000. However, withdrawals may not be made more often than once each month. You may refuse a direction from me (but you are not required to) to withdraw from the trust unless that direction is signed in the presence of a Notary Public and two other witnesses, all of whom have signed the writing.

Ending The Trust

12. I may end this trust and withdraw all of the trust property by directing you to return the trust property. You may refuse a direction from me to end the trust (but you are not required to) unless that direction is signed in the presence of a Notary Public and two other witnesses, all of whom have signed the writing. This right to end the trust is personal to me and may not be exercised for me by anyone else including a court appointed guardian. However, the immediately preceding sentence shall not apply if its application means that I will be deemed to have made a taxable gift if a guardian is appointed for me (and such guardian is disabled from exercising my right of withdrawal by the foregoing sentence).

13. In addition, you, as Trustee, may end the trust during my lifetime at any time without cause by returning all of the trust property to me. You may act to end the trust in this way only if you act together if you are both then serving as trustee; if only one of you is then serving as trustee, the one so serving may act alone to end the trust by returning the trust property to me.

Division of Trust After My Death

14. After my death, the trustee shall distribute the trust property as then constituted to my spouse, Laura, if she is then living; otherwise the trustee shall divide the property constituting the trust estate so that there is one share for each child of mine who survives me and one share for each deceased child of mine who has lineal descendants living at my death.

   a. Each share set aside for a child of mine shall be distributed to that child.

   b. Each share set aside for a deceased child of mine shall be distributed *per stirpes* to the lineal descendants of the deceased child.

Distributions to Lineal Descendants of Deceased Children of Mine

15. Notwithstanding other provisions of this trust to the contrary, each share to be distributed to a lineal descendant of a deceased child of mine shall continue in trust for the benefit of the lineal descendant if that lineal descendant has not then attained 21 years of age.

   a. During the continuance of each trust set aside for a lineal descendant, the Trustee is to pay to or apply for the benefit of that person, so much of or all of the principal and income of the trust as that person needs for his or her health, education, maintenance and support in his or her accustomed manner of living taking into consideration any other resources readily available to that person for such purposes.

   b. Each trust set aside for a lineal descendant of mine shall terminate when that person attains 21 years of age or dies.

   c. Upon termination, each trust set aside for a lineal descendant of mine shall be distributed to that person free of trust; and if that person is not then living, the trust property shall be distributed *per stirpes* to that person's then living lineal descendants: and, if none, *per stirpes* to my then living lineal descendants.

Meaning of Words *"per stirpes"*

16. I recognize that the words *"per stirpes"* are technical terms but these words are used here because it is impossible to describe every possible situation that might exist at the time of my death.

Undistributed Property

17. Upon termination of each trust provided for in this agreement, any property in each such trust that remains undistributed (because no other provision of this trust agreement applies to that property) shall be distributed upon termination of such trust *per stirpes* to my then living lineal descendants.

Maximum Duration of Trust

18. Notwithstanding other provisions of this trust, all the trusts that I have provided for must terminate, at the latest, 21 years after the death of the last to die of me, you, and all of my lineal descendants who are living on the date of my death.

Changing Beneficiaries

19. I may change the beneficiaries of this trust by writing to you. You may either accept or reject the change—but if you reject the change you must notify me in writing. However, you must accept any instructions to change the trust beneficiaries if I give you the instruction in writing and the writing has been signed in the presence of a Notary Public and two other witnesses, all of whom have signed the writing in the presence of each other.

Payments to Incapable Persons

20. You need not pay principal or income to me or to anyone else (even after my death) who, in your good faith judgment or under the law (either because of age or disability), is incapable of managing his or her own affairs. Instead, you may pay the person having care or control of the incapable person, whether court appointed or not, or you may use it in any other way you believe will benefit the incapable person, including, in the case of persons under 21 years of age, by paying principal and income to a custodianship which you or another person establishes for such person under the Texas version of the Uniform Transfers to Minors Act (or any later legislation that is adopted for these purposes). Any decision you make in good faith will bind everyone with an interest in this trust and fully protect you.

Your Powers As Trustee

21. To the full extent permitted by applicable law, you are to administer this trust free from the supervision and jurisdiction of any court and you are to have all the powers, duties, discretions and immunities provided by the State of Alaska except to the extent the laws of Alaska are inconsistent with the provisions of this trust, in which case the provisions of this trust will prevail to the extent possible. Specifically, you may do all those things with the trust property that I could do with that property if it had not been placed in trust, including sell real estate or other property on such terms and conditions as you may deem appropriate and without court approval and without giving bond and without seeking the approval of anyone.

Undistributed Trust Income

22. You are to add to trust principal any trust income that you do not pay to me or to another beneficiary.

Your Investment Powers As Trustee

23. You may invest the funds from this trust in any assets you deem appropriate. However, until the value of the property held by you as trustee exceeds $5,000, you will not have any investment responsibilities, your duty being merely to keep the trust property separate from your own property and, if the property you hold is cash in an amount in excess of $100, deposit the cash in an account with a banking or similar institution authorized to accept deposits. Moreover, during my lifetime, you will be considered as having discharged your investment responsibilities if you hold all the trust property in interest bearing cash deposits or cash equivalents and make no effort to invest in equities. Securities may be held in the name of a nominee.

Accounting

24. You must account for your transactions as Trustee upon my request; upon the request of any person who is then eligible to get property from the trust; or upon the request of any court appointed guardian.

Bond Requirements

25. Neither you nor any other person serving as Trustee shall be required to post bond with any court nor register this trust with any court.

Transactions Between You And Other Persons.

26. Persons or organizations who deal with a co-trustee are not to suffer any loss because they relied upon that co-trustee's representation that he or she was acting within the scope of his or her authority as Trustee and such persons are not obligated to inquire into such person's power or authority or into the validity of such person's acts or be liable for the application of any money or other property paid or loaned to that person as Trustee.

Bank and Brokerage Accounts for Trust

27. I specifically authorize you to open bank accounts and brokerage accounts on behalf of the trust in your capacity as Trustee. The signature of only one co-trustee shall be required to open such accounts or to transact business on existing accounts. No bank nor brokerage institution shall be liable for relying on the signature of only one co-trustee.

Resigning

28. Any person may resign as Trustee anytime by notifying me in writing or, if I am not then living, by writing each of the persons who is then eligible to get property from the trust. A resignation will not be effective until the resigned person delivers the trust property to the new trustee and the new trustee accepts the trust property that is delivered to him or her (or them).

Changing Trustees

29. A person, including me, will be deemed to have resigned as trustee if two medical doctors certify in writing that that person is no longer capable of managing the trust, such certification is delivered to me, and I do not object in writing within 30 days (my written objection to be delivered to the other of you and to the successor trustees named in this trust to the extent such delivery can be reasonably accomplished but failure to effect delivery to all the persons named as successor trustees shall not prevent the notice from being effective).

New Trustee

30. In the event that only one of us is able or willing to serve, such one shall serve as sole successor trustee. Co-trustees are not required; a sole successor trustee may serve.

Powers of New Trustee

31. Persons serving as Successor Trustee, when serving as Trustee, are each to enjoy all of the powers, duties, discretions and immunities I am conferring on the initial or original Trustee.

No Other Changes

32. I understand that I can make only the changes to this trust that are described in this trust and that I cannot make any other changes in this trust by Will or otherwise.

33. No changes can be made in this trust agreement after my death.

Law That Governs

34. It is my intention that this trust shall be governed by _____ law, and to the extent that I have not made a different provision in this trust, the laws of _____ shall apply to this trust.

Meaning of "Property".

35. The term "property" as used in this trust agreement includes income.

Separate Property and Not Community Property

36. I intend to make a gift to the respective beneficiaries of each of the trusts that I have provided for of only that portion of the income and principal of the trust which is in fact distributed to them. Inasmuch as the amounts actually distributed to the respective beneficiaries constitute the gift I contemplated making, such distributions, whether they be income or principal, shall constitute the separate property of each such distributee and not the community property of such distributees. Furthermore, it is my intention that no beneficiary shall have any interest in any undistributed income and principal until the time for such distribution occurs and, accordingly, such undistributed income and principal shall not be deemed the community property (or marital property) of any such beneficiary.

Spendthrift.

37. No beneficiary of this trust shall have the right or power to anticipate, by assignment or otherwise, any income or principal given to such beneficiary by this trust, nor in advance of actually receiving the same have the right or power to sell, transfer, encumber or in anywise charge same; nor shall such income or principal, or any portion of the same, be subject to any execution, garnishment, attachment, insolvency, bankruptcy, or legal proceeding of any character, or legal sequestration, levy or sale, or in any event or manner be applicable or subject, voluntarily or involuntarily, to the payment of such beneficiary's debts.

Tax Elections

38. You are to have absolute discretion to make or not make any election, determination, or designation pursuant to any taxing statute, which you believe to be in the best interests of the trust and its beneficiaries.

Trustee Duties to Begin

39. Your duties as trustee shall begin on the date on which property is delivered to you as trustee by me or by someone acting on my behalf.

* * *

Project 3

THE LATER YEARS: TAX PLANNING FOR THE PROPERTIED CLIENT (comprehensive)

Even with the supposed reduction in the number of taxpayers who will be burdened by estate taxes, for many of these taxpayers, income taxes continue to be a source of concern. Also, as property values increase and accumulations grow, taxpayers become concerned about property management questions as they are faced with concerns about their own mortality, and they begin to look to the well-being of the next generation.

In many cases, it is "empty nesters" who are concerned about the burdens of the federal estate tax. But Greg and Chloe UpScalle, hardly "empty nesters", find themselves with these concerns, as is apparent from the memorandum which follows. While still relatively young, they have been fortunate enough to assemble substantial property. Consider yourself assigned to the "pool" at your law firm and respond to Mr. Longhours' memorandum.

MEMORANDUM

To: Associates' Pool

From: Mr. Longhours

Will one of you please prepare a comprehensive estate plan for my good client, Greg UpScalle, and his wife, Chloe. This plan should take the form of a memorandum to me reflecting both research and analysis. (You need not necessarily draft any instruments.)

I also ask that you prepare a letter for my signature transmitting your recommendations to Greg and Chloe.

To avoid prejudicing your work, I have not provided you with a complete or necessarily correct statement of the elements essential to a good estate plan for Greg and Chloe. Throughout this memorandum I have, however, given you direction and I rely on your own creativity and imagination (and research) to produce an acceptable product. Clearly a simple will giving everything to Chloe will not suffice!

Presentation is an essential ingredient of the estate plan (and of the young attorney's success or lack thereof). Your project will be judged in part on its effectiveness to communicate the plan to me. (See it as a self paced learning experience, the testing of approaches as you develop and become confident in your communication.)

You may make whatever assumptions are necessary.

PERSONAL DATA

1. Greg UpScalle, a child of illegal immigrants, was born in Hoynes Village, State of Nowhere, 47 years ago. He attended public schools in Hoynes Village, the University of Advanced Learning and its medical school. He interned in neurosurgery at the leading hospital in Nowhere.

2. Present residence: City of Ennyplace, State of Nowhere for the last 18 years.

> [Nowhere is a flexible jurisdiction. Its residents may elect the law which will govern their transactions. They may elect among the laws of any of the 50 states and they may treat the Uniform Probate Code as having been adopted by the jurisdiction they select. See EP & D ¶ 11,089 (Alaska).]

3. Married Chloe Hopeful on May 1st, 19 years ago in Hoynes Village. At the time Greg was finishing his residency and Chloe was in her first year of nurses' training. Neither Greg nor Chloe brought any property to their marriage. Chloe never completed nurses' training and has not been formally employed since she married Greg.

4. Children: Muffy and Chip UpScalle, ages 13 and 11, respectively. Chip is a popular happy boy but, apparently, of below average intelligence. Greg is fairly certain that Chip will not qualify for admission to a "good" college and, further, that Chip will not want to further his education. Chip has shown a keen interest in entrepreneurship by operating his own primitive computerized dating service for his 5th grade classmates.

Muffy is as intelligent as she is beautiful. She is the apple of her father's eye and he has every hope that she will follow in his footsteps and become a physician. She has proven to be a child prodigy of sorts and is deeply involved with the microcomputer she received on her birthday.

5. Parents: Greg and Chloe's parents are deceased. Neither Chloe nor Greg has brothers or sisters.

MEDICAL PRACTICE

Greg actively practices neurosurgery and has an excellent professional reputation. In order to keep his income under $250,000, he limits his practice to Tuesdays and Thursdays. In the early years of his practice, while working full time, his income averaged $500,000 per annum.

Greg rents office space, furniture, and equipment from another neurosurgeon. Greg has no financial interest in the building or the furniture and equipment. His lease is on a month-to-month basis. He accepts patients only on a cash-in-advance basis and has no accounts receivable. Most of his patients come to him on referral and usually with nonrecurring (frequently terminal) illnesses.

CLOSE CORPORATION

Greg, three other neurosurgeons, and a real estate developer each own a 20% stock interest in Touchright, Inc., an alternative keyboard to be used with a nationally marketed personal computer. The Touchright stock has not paid, and does not contemplate paying, any dividends. However, Computer Shanty, a major electronics distributor, recently offered $2,000,000 for all of the outstanding shares of Touchright. The offer was apparently based on capitalizing earnings at a return rate of 10 percent. Touchright had net earnings of $200,000 last year. Greg paid $25,000 for his 20% interest. (Although the stock is registered only in Greg's name, in fact, Chloe drew the $25,000 check on her personal checking account at Accumulation National.)

SHOE STORE

Greg is the sole proprietor of a retail shoe store. The store, known as "GoGo Shoes," has an excellent location and has begun to enjoy some success as its reputation builds. The average annual net income of the store has increased steadily from $5,000 in its first year of operation five years ago to $90,000 last year.

Greg has three employees at the shoe store, all of them are middle aged and none of them appear to have any interest in ever acquiring an ownership interest in the store. They are all good employees, but it doesn't appear that any of them will ever be in a position to or want to buy the store from Greg in the event that he should decide to sell it. At the present time, however, Greg contemplates continuing to actively manage and operate the shoe store. In fact, he would like to stay with it even after his retirement from medical practice. Chip works in the store on Saturdays and part time during vacations.

Chloe has had experience in all phases of the store's operation and, although she hasn't given too much thought to the matter, she feels that she has had enough experience in the business to take over and operate the store if something should happen to Greg.

The shoe store business has an estimated book value of $100,000, including inventory.

BANK ACCOUNTS

1. Greg: none.

2. Chloe:

Accumulation National Bank, checking account No. 1–46673–2 (avg. bal.)

$135,000.00

Accumulation National Bank, savings account No. 43–0061–3

$240,000.00

Greg has a fear of malpractice suits and, as a consequence, he gives all of the receipts from his medical practice and from the shoe store (except for spending money) to Chloe. Chloe faithfully deposits each dollar to her checking account, pays all of the family expenses, including Greg's office expenses, the premiums on his life insurance, and the expenses of the shoe store, and retains any excess in her savings account.

REAL ESTATE

1. Residential premises at 459 Old Prestige Court, Ennyplace, acquired 17 years ago for $40,000. Chloe advanced $10,000 from her bank account for the down payment and Accumulation National took a 20–year 7% mortgage for the balance of the purchase price. The mortgage was discharged four years later. All mortgage payments, including the final payment, came from Chloe's bank account. The present market value of the premises is approximately $525,000. The UpScalles have not made any capital improvements to the premises. Title was taken in the name of "Greg UpScalle and Chloe UpScalle, joint tenants with right of survivorship." The mortgage deed identified Greg and Chloe as the "Grantors".

2. Summer residence premises at RFD#2, Mountain Top Road, Ennyplace (30 miles north of the city in a rapidly developing luxury summer community). Acquired 11 years ago for $60,000. Chloe paid the full purchase price from her bank account and took title in her own name. Present market value: $190,000.

HOUSEHOLD GOODS

Value $200,000 approx. (acquired through disbursements from Chloe's checking account.)

PRESENT WILLS

None.

REVOCABLE LIFE INSURANCE TRUST

Greg wants to create a revocable trust with his wife, Chloe, as trustee. Always one to be concerned about the high cost of professional services, Greg (who describes himself as "always being one who knew a lot or was willing to learn a lot") began this process by "borrowing" a form from a med school friend now living where "they have community property" (and who apparently obtained it from a form book). Greg wanted us to use his borrowed form as a starting point. It is attached in pertinent part (Attachment 1 to Project 3—*Ed.*) He wants an explanation of the alternatives that you will find in the form; he says "they intrigue" him. (Incidently, he particularly likes the form because it is a two-grantor trust and he believes that he can save money having only one trust (in as much as the alternative may well be separate trusts for Greg and Chloe). The reference to community property may be a bonus. If Greg and Chloe have any community, the form takes it into account. Meanwhile, possibly, it is in its simplest form a joint trust.)

LIFE INSURANCE POLICIES

Greg has one life insurance policy in force. It is a term policy for $500,000 issued through the state medical association, annually renewable. Chloe is the designated beneficiary. Greg has been told by an insurance salesman that he doesn't have enough life insurance to give his estate "liquidity". He's not sure what the life insurance salesman meant but he is considering the purchase of additional life insurance while he remains insurable. Greg wants my counsel as to the options available to him. The agent has proposed an ordinary life policy, a term policy and a joint and survivor policy. Perhaps a comparison of the costs of the different policies might be in order. Different companies frequently have different experiences. Look to Best's Review, Life, Health Insurance Edition (A. M. Best Co.) for help here.

CLIENT'S WISHES

1. Greg and Chloe have both heard of the Uniform Gifts to Minors Act and are seriously considering giving each of their children a $50,000 cash gift. (All cash would come from Chloe's accounts). Greg would declare himself custodian for the gift to their son Chip, and Chloe would do the same for their daughter Muffy. They expect to continue these gifts of cash in future years. Their purpose for doing this is to avoid taxes, both estate, gift and income, and also to avoid probate at their respective deaths. Greg and Chloe have determined that they will not release the funds they hold as custodians until each child reaches the age of 30. (Is this permissible?) (It is important to note that many states have made significant modifications to the Uniform Gifts to Minors Act either upon initial adoption or after experience with the Uniform Act. Therefore, you must consult local law as to the exact form of the Act in the jurisdiction in which you are conducting your investigation.)

Please comment on the UpScalle's minority-giving program. What are the alternatives? A minority trust perhaps? What about income, estate and gift tax consequences? Compare and contrast the minority trust with the Uniform Gifts to Minors statute adopted by this jurisdiction or, alternatively, the Uniform Transfers to Minors Act. Prepare a suggested form of minority trust. How about life insurance as the basis for the gift? Who should be the trustee? Does it matter? Does it matter who the custodian is?

2. Sixteen years ago, Greg sired an illegitimate child, Oliver. The child's mother, Agnes Twist, was working as a nurse in the local hospital at the time. Greg has never acknowledged the child nor has paternity been judicially established. Chloe knows of Oliver and Agnes and, with her consent, Greg sends Agnes a personal check for $1,800 each month with the oral understanding that she "will make no trouble" for him. Greg would deny paternity if it were ever alleged.

Agnes has never married, is unemployed, and devotes herself to making a good home for her son. She has no property and relies on Greg's monthly check. Oliver is a tall, strapping boy with a keen mind. He's done exceptionally well in his school work, perhaps first in his class. He plans to attend college and, like many of his age, professes to "wants to be a doctor." Oliver knows of Greg's relationship to him, although they have never met. Greg wants to provide for Oliver's education and continue to maintain Oliver's mother.

3. Greg and Chloe have a tight-knit family unit and each of them has the other's welfare in mind. The primary beneficiaries of their love and devotion for each other are their children. With the exception of Greg's illegitimate son and the child's mother, there are no other persons who Greg and Chloe would want to benefit from their estate. Of course, it is expected that some of this affection for their children will transfer to grandchildren

and great-grandchildren in the years to come. Presently, the UpScalles' main concern is that their children receive a good education. After that, they want their two children to share equally in their property. This principle is very important to them. When applied in the context of the ultimate disposition of the shoe store, it raises certain problems. How can we accommodate the probable wishes of Chip to manage the shoe store (his parents think this a likely and wise career choice) and give Muffy (a probable "physician" (according to her dad) if, in her own words, she "can't make it as a computer programmer") an equal interest?

4.   It's clear that Greg wants Chloe as his trustee and executor and that Chloe wants Greg as her executor and trustee. Chloe is clearly competent, or at least she is at the moment. (Can we protect her and Greg against any future incompetency? Does Chloe serving as trustee and executor of Greg's estate create any special tax problems, particularly income tax problems? Is the same true of Greg's serving as executor and trustee of Chloe's estate?) Both Greg and Chloe have an unnatural distrust of banks even though neither of them seem to have any particular basis for this view. They wonder if they can give one another the power to designate successor trustees and executors unto themselves.

5.   Both Greg and Chloe are publicity shy and clearly want to avoid the so-called horrors of probate. They've read Dacey's How to Avoid Probate (and noticed Esperti & Peterson's Loving Trust and are wondering whether Dacey's forms may be "the solution for us." I would appreciate your analysis in order that I might effectively report back to the UpScalles. I understand that Dacey's book and his recommendations have come under heavy attack by the Bar.

6.   The UpScalles are committed to minimizing their current income and death tax burden.

SUGGESTED APPROACH

1.   It strikes me that Greg should proceed with his plan to establish a revocable trust; that Chloe should establish a revocable funded trust for her property providing for the collapse of that trust into Greg's trust upon the death of the survivor of her and Greg; and that each then should have "pou rover" wills.

2.   An essential part of this project is a detailed and thorough analysis of the marital deduction clauses which appears in Attachment 1 [to this Project 3—*Ed.*]. Please don't overlook it. (As you will see, Greg has already begun to mark up the document, personalizing it by adding his and Chloe's name. Don't let this distract you or cause you to assign more weight to the document than you might ordinarily to a "home brew" document.)

3.   Perhaps, too, Greg ought to consider an irrevocable trust for his illegitimate offspring and the boy's mother. What are the income, estate and gift tax consequences? What property would be suitable for funding such a trust.

4.   Keep in mind Greg and Chloe's proposed gifts to their children.

5. Neither Greg nor Chloe have ever filed any gift tax returns. Some attention should be given to all of the transfers Greg has made to Chloe. What gift tax returns should be filed, if any? If you propose any lifetime transfers which constitute taxable gifts, please prepare the necessary federal gift tax returns.

6. It's pretty clear that Greg and Chloe tend to disregard the legal niceties of "title" or "ownership" when dealing with the property they have accumulated. As you can see, the indiscriminate transfer of property from one to the other creates special problems. (Certainly, Greg feels he has transferred property "to Chloe", so far as his creditors are concerned. While you may disregard the creditors' rights issue, consider whether Greg's transfers have been effective for tax purposes.)

7. Some recommendations will have to be made with respect to the shoe store. Should it be incorporated?

8. What about the stock in closely held Touchright, Inc.? How shall it be valued for death tax purposes?

9. Don't overlook the assignability features of Greg's life insurance policy. (IRS position?) Perhaps life insurance would make a good gift.

10. If you wish, you may assume that Greg and Chloe are in a community property jurisdiction. That may radically change your analysis of the facts.

Reference: Virtually all EP & D chapters.

UPSCALLE LIVING TRUST (in pertinent part)

Created By: Greg and   **Trustees: Greg and Chloe**
Chloe Upscalle   **Upscalle**

* * *

ARTICLE 1

* * *

ARTICLE 2

DISTRIBUTIONS WHILE BOTH CHLOE AND GREG LIVE

2.1.   Distribution During Joint Lifetimes. While both **Chloe** and **Greg** are living, whenever the trust estate consists of property other than life insurance policies, the trust estate shall be held, managed and distributed as follows:

(a) Community Income and Principal. The Trustee shall pay to **Chloe** and **Greg** as community property, or apply for the benefit of either of them, the entire net income of the Community Estate, in monthly or other convenient installments. In addition to said net income, the Trustees shall also pay to or apply for the benefit of either **Chloe** and **Greg** as community property so much of the principal of the Community Estate as either of them shall request, from time to time, in one or more written instruments delivered to the Trustees during their joint lifetimes.

(b) Income and Principal from Separate Property. The Trustee shall pay to or apply for the benefit of each spouse for whom a Separate Estate exists the entire net income of such Separate Estate, in monthly or other convenient installments. The Trustee shall also pay to or apply for the benefit of such spouse so much of the principal of his or her Separate Property as he or she shall request from time to time. Such requests must be in writing and each such written request must be delivered to the Trustee during the lifetime of the spouse making the request.

(c) Additional Distributions. If, at any time or times, while both **Chloe** and **Greg** are living, either of them shall, in the discretion of the Trustee, be in need of additional moneys for his or her respective support, health, comfort or welfare, the Trustee shall distribute to each of them, or apply for his or her benefit, so much of the principal of the trust estate (up to and including the whole thereof) as the Trustee shall determine to be necessary or appropriate for said purposes. Distributions made pursuant to this paragraph 2.1.(c) shall be made first from the Community Estate until it is exhausted, and then equally from the Separate Estates, provided that if the Community Estate contains property that cannot be readily sold or can be sold only at a substantial sacrifice, the Trustee shall not be required to liquidate property in the Community Estate until the Trustee shall first exhaust the Separate Estates. If the Separate Estates also contain property which cannot be easily liquidated, the determination by the Trustee as to which property should be sold shall be binding on all interested parties.

(d) <u>Primary Beneficiary</u>. The provisions of subparagraph 2.1.(c) shall be construed in a liberal manner for the benefit of **Chloe** and **Greg** and the rights of other beneficiaries shall be considered of secondary significance.

2.2. <u>Lifetime Additions to Marital Trust</u>. Paragraph 2.1 shall not apply to property that has been made subject to Marital Trust when both **Greg** and **Chloe** are living.

ARTICLE 3

DIVISION OF TRUST AFTER DEATH OF
FIRST TO DIE OF CHLOE OR GREG

3.1. <u>Uncertainty as to Order of Deaths</u>. Where there is uncertainty as to the order in which **Greg** and **Chloe** died and no presumption as to survivorship is supplied elsewhere in this trust, the entire trust estate, including any additions to the trust estate (except those additions made to specific funds or shares of the trust estate) whether such additions be by will, as the result of the collection of the proceeds of life insurance or otherwise, shall be allocated to the Bypass Trust to be held, managed, and disposed of as provided in paragraph 6.1 (as if the Bypass Trust had terminated upon the death of the first to die of **Greg** or **Chloe**.)

3.2. <u>Death of One Spouse Survived by the Other</u>. Upon the death of one spouse (Deceased Spouse) survived by the other (Surviving Spouse), the Trustee shall divide the trust estate, including any additions to the trust estate (except those additions made to specific funds or shares of the trust estate) whether such additions be by will, as the result of the collection of the proceeds of life insurance or otherwise, into as many as <u>four</u> separate and distinct funds to be referred to, respectively, as Surviving Spouse's Share, Marital Share, Special Trust, and the Bypass Trust. In making this division the trust estate shall be considered as undiminished by transfer taxes paid or to be paid. The division shall be made in the manner specified in paragraphs 3.3, 3.4, 3.5 and 3.9.

(a) <u>Trustee's Determination Conclusive</u>. Except as otherwise herein specifically provided, the Trustee shall have full authority and discretion, in making a division of property provided for in paragraph 3.2 among Surviving Spouse's Share, Marital Share, Special Trust, and Bypass Trust, to select, designate and transfer cash, securities or other assets to each of said funds, and the exercise of said authority and discretion shall be final and binding upon all parties concerned.

(b) <u>Settlor's Intention as to When No Allocation to be Made</u>. Greg and Chloe both recognize that it is entirely possible that no property whatsoever may be allocated to the trusts provided for in paragraph 3.2, the determination being a function of a number of variables including, among other things, whether the first of them has made or makes gifts during life before or after this trust was created and whether gifts are made in the will of the first of them to die or in other provisions of this trust to persons other than the survivor of Greg and Chloe.

(c) <u>Distribution of Income Before Division of Trust</u>. Until such time as the Trustee can complete the allocation of property to Surviving Spouse's Share, Special Trust, Marital Share, and Bypass Trust in accordance with the provisions of paragraphs 3.3, 3.4, 3.5, 3.9, and 3.10, or until **Surviving Spouse's** death if such event shall sooner occur, the entire net income of the trust estate shall be paid to **Surviving Spouse** in quarter-annual or more frequent installments, provided, further, that if **Surviving Spouse's** death should occur before the allocation of property to Surviving Spouse's Share, Marital Share, Special Trust, and Bypass Trust has been completed, the Trustee shall pay to **Surviving Spouse's** estate any undistributed and accrued net income.

3.3. <u>Composition of Surviving Spouse's Share</u>. The property allocated to Surviving Spouse's Share, after the death of the first to die of **Greg** or **Chloe**, shall be the following:

(a) <u>Separate Estate</u>. The Separate Estate of the Surviving Spouse, if any, then included in the trust estate, including any proceeds of life insurance policies or employee benefit plans which were owned by the Surviving Spouse as his or her separate property prior to being placed in the trust;

(b) <u>One-Half Community Estate</u>. One-half (½) of the Community Estate included in the trust estate including, without limitation, the Surviving Spouse's community interest in employee benefit plans or in the proceeds of life insurance policies collected by the Trustee.

(c) <u>Additions by Surviving Spouse</u>. Any additions made to the trust estate by the Surviving Spouse which are not otherwise allocated by the terms of the instrument of transfer.

Surviving Spouse's Share, as finally constituted, shall be distributed as provided in paragraphs 4.1 and 4.2.

[ALTERNATIVE A]

3.4. <u>Composition of Marital Share</u>. The following shall govern the allocation of property to the Marital Share:

[ALTERNATE A-1]

(a) <u>Smallest Pecuniary Amount</u>. The property allocated to Marital Share, after the death of the first to die of **Greg** and **Chloe**, shall be equal to the smallest pecuniary amount which will result in the least possible federal estate tax being payable by reason of the death of the first to die of **Greg** and **Chloe**; provided further, that in the event **Greg** and **Chloe** die within six (6) months of each other, the amount allocated to the **Marital** Share shall not be greater than that amount necessary to equalize the estates of **Greg** and **Chloe** for federal estate tax purposes. In making the computations required by this paragraph 3.4.(a), the following shall be taken into account:

(1)   **Surviving Spouse's** estate shall be valued as of the date of **Deceased Spouse's** death (and not on the "alternate valuation date" as provided for in Section 2032 of the Internal Revenue Code of 1986);

(2)   All property which is included in **Deceased Spouse's** estate for federal estate tax purposes as well as all adjusted taxable gifts which are taken into account for federal estate tax purposes pursuant to section 2001 of the Internal Revenue Code of 1986;

(3)   All allowable deductions without regard to any tax elections which are made to claim deductions for administration expenses incurred by **Deceased Spouse's** estate as federal income tax deductions rather than federal estate tax deductions as is permitted by Section 642(g) of the Internal Revenue Code of 1986;

(4)   The federal credit for state death taxes paid allowed by Section 2011 of the Internal Revenue Code shall be taken into account only to the extent that, by so doing, the amount of state death taxes payable will <u>not</u> be increased;

(5)   The federal unified credit and the federal credit for gift taxes payable with respect to gifts made by the Settlor after December 31, 1976.

[ALTERNATE A-2]

(a) <u>Smallest Pecuniary Amount</u>. That pecuniary amount which, when added to any other property passing to the **Surviving Spouse**, whether under the provisions of the **Deceased Spouse's** will or otherwise and which is included in the **Deceased Spouse's** estate for federal estate purposes and which qualifies for the marital deduction, shall produce the maximum marital deduction allowed the **Deceased Spouse's** estate for federal estate tax purposes permitted by law as in effect at the date of the **Deceased Spouse's** death; provided, however, if after taking into consideration such maximum marital deduction, any charitable deductions, and all estate tax credits to which the **Deceased Spouse's** estate is entitled, the **Deceased Spouse's** estate would incur no federal estate tax, then such pecuniary amount shall be reduced by the Reduction Amount; provided further, however, that in the event the **Deceased Spouse** and the **Surviving Spouse** die within six (6) months of each other, and the **Surviving Spouse's** estate is greater, as of the date of her death, than that of the **Deceased Spouse**, then such pecuniary amount shall be zero. For purposes of this paragraph, the Reduction Amount shall be equal to the largest amount by which the maximum marital deduction could be reduced without the **Deceased Spouse's** estate incurring any federal estate tax, it being the intention of the **Deceased Spouse** to utilize fully the federal unified credit, any charitable deductions, and all other federal estate tax credits before utilizing the marital deduction. However, under no circumstances shall the federal credit for state death taxes paid be taken into account in computing the Reduction Amount if the effect is to increase the state death taxes payable as a result of the death of the **Deceased Spouse**.

(b)   <u>Reliance on Executor or Administrator</u>. For the purposes of paragraph 3.4.(a), the Trustee may rely upon the written representations of **Deceased Spouse's** executor or administrator or the executor or administrator of **Surviving Spouse's** estate as to all information the knowledge of which is necessary for the determination by the Trustee of the proper composition of the **Marital** Share and in the allocation of property thereto, and **Deceased Spouse** grants to the Trustee the right and authority to demand and receive from **Deceased Spouse's** executor or administrator and from the Internal Revenue Service copies of the federal estate tax return of **Deceased Spouse's** executor or administrator, any deficiency letter issued by the Internal Revenue Service, or any officer thereof, any final assessment of estate tax or any settlement agreement entered into by and between **Deceased Spouse's** executor or administrator and the Internal Revenue Service, or any officer thereof, and further to request and receive all other information or data the Trustee may require or consider helpful with respect to the final determination of the estate tax assessed by reason of **Deceased Spouse's** death.

(c)   Circumstances in Which No Allocation to be Made. **Greg** and **Chloe** both recognize that, despite the provisions of this instrument, it might not be possible to eliminate all federal estate taxes and other death taxes imposed at the first to die of **Greg** and **Chloe**. Such taxes may not be eliminated, for example, because property ownership arrangements and beneficiary designations made by either **Chloe** or **Greg** during life, both before and after execution of this instrument, may preclude the elimination of all such death taxes at the first of them to die. Furthermore, **Greg** and **Chloe** both recognize that if the survivor of them is not a citizen of the United States at the time of the death of the first of them to die, all such death taxes imposed on the estate of the first of them to die may not be eliminated.

(d)   Property Must Qualify for Marital Deduction. The property to be distributed to the Marital Share in satisfaction of the pecuniary amount shall be allocated either in money or in kind, or both, provided that any property so allocated shall be of the type which qualifies for the marital deduction; provided, however, that, to the extent practicable, there shall not be allocated to the Marital Share any property as to which a foreign death tax credit is available or any property that would constitute income in respect of a decedent (IRD) for federal or state income tax purposes.

(e)   Effect of Disclaimer and Partial QTIP Election. In determining the amount allocated to the Marital Share pursuant to paragraph 3.4.(a), the Trustee shall ignore any disclaimers or partial QTIP elections made pursuant to section 2056(b)(7) of the Internal Revenue Code of 1986 that result in the disqualification for the marital deduction of property that would qualify for the marital deduction but for the disclaimer or the partial QTIP election.

(f)   Valuation of Distribution in Kind. Notwithstanding any other provision of this instrument to the contrary, property distributed in kind in satisfaction of the pecuniary amount provided for in paragraph 3.4.(a) shall be valued for such purposes at the date of its distribution.

(g)   Settlor's Intention to Qualify for Marital Deduction. All provisions of this instrument shall be construed and applied so that the Marital Share qualifies for the marital deduction in **Deceased Spouse's** estate if **Surviving Spouse** survives or is presumed to survive **Deceased Spouse**. Any provision of this instrument that cannot be so construed shall not apply to Marital Share. The Trustee shall take such action and have such powers as are necessary to cause the Marital Share to qualify for the marital deduction and shall take no action and shall have no power that will impair the marital deduction. However, the foregoing sentence shall not be construed as requiring the executor of **Deceased Spouse's** estate to claim the marital deduction for the property held in the Marital Share if in the judgement of the executor such an election is inappropriate (or, if, because of provisions of this instrument, the marital deduction is not elective but is required).

(h)   <u>Distribution of Marital Share</u>. Marital Share, as finally constituted, shall be distributed as provided in paragraphs 4.1 and 4.2, to wit, the provisions of this instrument which, <u>inter alia</u>, cause all of the income generated from Marital Share to be distributed to Surviving Spouse.

3.5. <u>Composition of Bypass Trust</u>. The following property, which is to be allocated to the Bypass Trust, shall be held, managed, and disposed of as provided in paragraph 5.1:

(a)   <u>Unallocated Property</u>. Upon the death of the first to die of **Greg and Chloe**, the property which is then included in the trust estate (whether initially or as the result of additions to the trust which occur from time to time) which is not allocated to Surviving Spouse's Share, Marital Share, or Special Trust shall be allocated to the Bypass Trust and held, managed, and disposed of by the Trustee as provided herein for the Bypass Trust. Interests in property disclaimed by Surviving Spouse shall be distributed as provided in paragraph 3.10

(b)   <u>Property Added to Trust</u>. Any property added to the trust estate by persons other than **Greg** or **Chloe**, either by <u>inter vivos</u> transfer or by will, shall be allocated to the Bypass Trust unless otherwise allocated by the instrument of transfer.

_____ **[End of Alternative A]** _____

[ALTERNATIVE B]

3.7. <u>Composition of Bypass Trust</u>.

(a)   Upon the death of the first to die of **Greg** and **Chloe**, a portion or all of the property which is then included in the trust estate (whether initially or as a result of additions to the trust which occur from time to time) shall be allocated to the Bypass Trust. The property to be so allocated shall be the following:

(1) an amount, if any,

(A)   which is equal to the largest taxable estate for federal estate tax purposes that will produce a tax exactly equal to the unified credit available to the estate of the Deceased Spouse for federal estate tax purposes;

(2) reduced by:

(A)   the fair market value of all that property which is included in the gross estate of the Deceased Spouse for federal estate tax purposes but which does not qualify for the marital deduction allowed the estate of the Deceased Spouse for federal estate tax purposes; and

(B)   the amount of any gifts made by the Deceased Spouse during his or her lifetime which are deemed to be adjusted taxable gifts for federal estate tax purposes; and

(C)   the amount of any items which executor of the estate of the Deceased Spouse elects to deduct for federal income tax purposes; and

(D)   the amount of any state inheritance or estate taxes payable as a result of the death of the Deceased Spouse.

(b)   Property added to the trust estate by the will of the Surviving Spouse and property added to the trust estate by other persons, either by inter vivos transfer or by will, shall be allocated to the Bypass Trust unless otherwise allocated by the instrument of transfer.

The property which is allocated to the Bypass Trust shall be held, managed, and disposed of as provided in paragraph 5.1.

3.8. _Composition of Marital Share._

The property which is included in the trust estate at the death of first to die of **Greg** and Chloe, which is not allocated to either the Surviving Spouse's Share or to the Bypass Trust, shall be allocated to the Marital Share and held, managed, and disposed of by the Trustee as provided in paragraphs 4.1 and 4.2.

[End of Alternative B]

3.9.   Composition of Special Trust. In the event the marital deduction for federal estate tax purposes is not claimed for part or all of the property allocated to Marital Share as provided in paragraph 3.4 (assuming that the marital deduction is not mandatory), the portion or all of the property allocated to Marital Share for which the marital deduction is not claimed shall be allocated to the Special Trust. The Special Trust finally constituted shall be distributed as provided in paragraph 4.1.

3.10.   Disclaimer by Surviving Spouse.

(a) Disclaimer of Marital Share. In the event **Surviving Spouse** disclaims or refuses to accept a part or all of the interest provided **Surviving Spouse** in the Marital Share, such disclaimed interests shall be allocated to Bypass Trust to be held, managed, and disposed of as provided in paragraph 5.1.

(b) Disclaimer of Special Trust. In the event **Surviving Spouse** disclaims or refuses to accept a part or all of the interest provided **Surviving Spouse** in the Special Trust, such disclaimed interests shall be allocated to Bypass Trust to be held, managed, and disposed of as provided in paragraph 5.1.

(c) Disclaimer of Bypass Trust. In addition, in the event **Surviving Spouse** disclaims or refuses to accept a part or all of the Bypass

Trust such disclaimed interests shall be allocated to the Bypass Trust to be held, managed, and disposed of as provided in paragraph 6.1 (as if the Bypass Trust had terminated).

ARTICLE 4

DISTRIBUTIONS TO SURVIVING SPOUSE

4.1. Distributions from Surviving Spouse's Share, Marital Share, and Special Trust. Surviving Spouse's Share, Marital Share, and Special Trust, as finally constituted, shall be referred to as Surviving Spouse's Trust, Marital Trust, and Special Trust, respectively, and shall each be held, managed and disposed of by the Trustee as follows:

(a) Income. All of the net income from Surviving Spouse's Trust, Marital Trust, and Special Trust, respectively, trusts shall be paid to or applied for the benefit of Surviving Spouse at least annually or shall be distributed in such monthly or other periodic installments as the Trustee and **Surviving Spouse** agree upon.

(b) Principal. The Trustee shall also pay to or apply for the benefit of **Surviving Spouse** so much of the principal of any or all of Surviving Spouse's Trust, Marital Trust, and Special Trust, respectively, as shall be necessary for the health, education, maintenance, and support of **Surviving Spouse** in **Surviving Spouse's** accustomed manner of living; provided, however, that such distributions shall be first made from Surviving Spouse's Trust and Marital Share until both are exhausted.

(c) Termination. If not earlier terminated by distribution of the entire trust estate under the provisions of this instrument, Surviving Spouse's Trust, Marital Trust, and Special Trust, shall terminate upon **Surviving Spouse's** death. At that time, the Trustee shall pay over to **Surviving Spouse's** estate any accrued and undistributed income from both trusts and shall distribute the then remaining assets of both trusts to the Bypass Trust to be held, managed, and disposed of pursuant to the terms and conditions of the Bypass Trust as if such property had been part of the Bypass Trust immediately before the death of **Deceased Spouse**.

(d) NonIncome Producing Property. Any property transferred to Surviving Spouse's Trust, Marital Trust, and Special Trust, respectively, shall constitute a proper trust investment. The Trustee shall have no obligation to dispose of or convert to another form any such property; provided, however, that the Trustee shall make productive or convert into income-producing property any nonincome-producing property or underproductive property held in the Surviving Spouse's Trust, Marital Trust, and Special Trust, respectively.

(e) Mandatory Provisions. The following provisions shall apply to both the Marital Trust and the Special Trust notwithstanding any other provision in this instrument or applicable law to the contrary:

(1) All of the net income from both Marital Trust and Special Trust shall be distributed to Surviving Spouse at least annually and

(2) No distributions shall be made from either Marital Trust or Special Trust to any person other than Surviving Spouse during the lifetime of Surviving Spouse.

4.2. <u>Additional Distributions from the Surviving Spouse's Trust and from the Marital Trust.</u>

Alternative X	Alternative Y
<u>Withdrawals.</u> The Trustee shall pay to the Surviving Spouse so much or all of the principal of the Surviving Spouse's Trust and the Marital Trust as Surviving Spouse during his or her lifetime requests in writing. To be effective, each such request must be delivered to the Trustee during the lifetime of the Surviving Spouse.	<u>General Power of Appointment Created.</u> **Surviving Spouse** may, by provision in the Will of **Surviving Spouse** which makes specific reference to this paragraph 4.2.(b), appoint so much or all of the property constituting Marital Trust to such persons or institutions (including **Surviving Spouse's** estate) as **Surviving Spouse** shall determine, this power of appointment being exercisable in all events and in no way limited, **Surviving Spouse** to enjoy each every right or privilege necessary to qualify Marital Trust for the marital deduction available to **Deceased Spouse's** estate under section 2056(b)(5) of the Internal Revenue Code of 1986 and be freed from every restriction that would disqualify Marital Trust for the marital deduction.

ARTICLE 5

DISTRIBUTIONS FROM Bypass TRUST

5.1. <u>Distribution of Bypass Trust.</u> During the continuance of the Bypass Trust provided for in this instrument, after the death of **Deceased Spouse**, the Trustee shall pay to or expend for **Surviving Spouse's** benefit such part or all of the income and principal of the Bypass Trust as shall be necessary for **Surviving Spouse's** health, education, maintenance, and support in **Surviving Spouse's** accustomed manner of living.

5.2. <u>Primary Beneficiary.</u> While paragraph 5.1 limits distributions to the survivor of **Chloe** and **Greg**, whatever limited discretion is enjoyed by the Trustee shall be exercised in a liberal manner for the benefit of the survivor of **Chloe** and **Greg**, and the rights of other beneficiaries shall be considered of secondary significance.

ARTICLE 6

TERMINATION and DISTRIBUTION to LINEAL DESCENDANTS

6.1. <u>When Termination Occurs.</u> The Bypass Trust provided for in this instrument shall terminate upon the death of the last to die of **Greg** and **Chloe**.

6.2. <u>Distribution Upon Termination.</u> Upon termination of the Bypass Trust, the Trustee shall divide the trust estate so that there is one share for each of **Greg** and **Chloe**'s then living children and one share for each of

Greg and **Chloe**'s children who are deceased but who have then living lineal descendants.

(a) Each share set aside for a child who has attained thirty-five (35) years of age shall be distributed to that child forthwith.

(b) Each share set aside for a child who has not attained thirty-five (35) years of age shall be distributed as follows:

(1) If the child has attained thirty (30) years of age when the trust terminates, two-thirds (2/3) of that child's share shall be distributed to him or her forthwith. The balance of that child's share shall continue in trust, to be held, managed and disposed of as provided in paragraph 6.3.

(2) If the child has attained twenty-five (25) years of age when the trust terminates, one-third (1/3) of that child's share shall be distributed to him or her forthwith. The balance of that child's share shall continue in trust, to be held, managed and disposed of as provided in paragraph 6.3.

(3) If a child has not attained twenty-five (25) years of age when the trust terminates, that child's share shall continue in trust, to be held, managed and disposed of as provided in paragraph 6.3.

(c) Each share set aside for a deceased child shall be distributed to that child's then living lineal descendants per stirpes.

6.3. Distributions from Trusts for Children. During the continuance of each trust provided for in paragraph 6.2, the Trustee shall pay to or expend for the benefit of the indicated beneficiary, such sum or sums, from time to time, from the income and principal as the Trustee shall deem necessary or desirable for his or her health, education, maintenance, and support in his or her accustomed manner of living. In addition, the Trustee shall distribute from each trust to the beneficiary thereof:

(a) An amount equal to one-third (1/3) as soon as possible after each such beneficiary attains twenty-five (25) years of age (if the beneficiary had not attained twenty-five (25) years of age prior to the termination of the Bypass Trust);

(b) An amount equal to one-third (1/3) as soon as possible after each such beneficiary attains thirty (30) years of age (if the beneficiary had not attained thirty (30) years of age prior to the termination of the Bypass Trust).

For purposes of computing the amount to be distributed from each trust on the indicated anniversary dates, the value of each trust estate shall be determined as of the date on which the beneficiary of that trust attains the indicated age. Items of tangible personal property included in each child's trust shall be excluded from the base against which the indicated percentage is applied. In all cases the Trustee's good faith valuation of the trust estate shall be conclusive and binding.

6.4. Termination of Trusts for Children. Each trust referred to in paragraph 6.3 shall terminate when the indicated beneficiary attains thirty-five (35) years of age or dies, whichever shall first occur. Upon termination of the trust, the Trustee shall pay over and distribute the assets then comprising the trust estate to the child for whom the trust was maintained if he or she is living on the date the trust terminates; otherwise, to that child's then living lineal descendants <u>per stirpes</u>; otherwise, to Settlor's then living lineal descendants <u>per stirpes</u>.

6.5. <u>Distributions to Heirs-at-Law</u>. If all of the persons and classes designated as beneficiaries of any trust hereinabove created shall die prior to the termination of such trust, then upon the happening of such event, any portion of any such trust not otherwise distributable under the provisions of this agreement shall be distributed to such person or institution as **Greg** and **Chloe**'s last surviving child shall appoint by <u>inter vivos</u> or testamentary instrument but the child may not exercise such power of appointment in favor of himself, his creditors, his estate, or the creditors of his estate. In default of effective exercise of this power of appointment, the undistributable portion of each trust fund shall be distributed as follows:

(a) One-half (½) thereof to those persons who are **Greg**'s heirs determined under the intestate law of Nowhere as if **Greg** died on the date on which the trust terminated.

(b) One-half (½) thereof to those persons who are **Chloe**'s heirs determined under the intestate law of Nowhere as if **Chloe** died on the date on which the trust terminated.

* * *

Project 4

MARITAL DEDUCTION PLANNING (basic)

MEMORANDUM

To: Associates' Pool

From: Mr. Longhours

Greg and Chloe UpScalle are considering a revocable trust (Attachment 1 to Project 3). It contains contains three "alternative" marital deduction clauses. Clearly the trust adopted by Greg and Chloe UpScalle should contain only one such clause. Please give me a memorandum indicating which of these clauses, if any, should have been included in the UpScalles' trust. Also please indicate why you did not choose one of the other two clauses. Perhaps you will want to reject all three clauses and prepare a provision more to your liking. The reasons for your decisions are important to the successful completion of this project. It is also important to mention any other provisions which should be included in the trust to give effect to the clause you have chosen as particularly suitable for the UpScalles.

Background facts to be used in preparing your memorandum are set out in my previous memorandum. (Refer to Project 3.)

References: EP & D, Chapters 14 and 15.

Project 5

COMMUNITY PROPERTY AND THE WIDOW'S ELECTION (basic)

MEMORANDUM

To: Associates' Pool

From: Mr. Longhours

Assume that Greg and Chloe UpScalle have relocated to a community property jurisdiction. Will one of you please advise as to whether they should attempt to maintain the separate property status of their property or whether they should allow it to be commingled with their soon-to-be acquired community property.

In addition, advise as to how Greg and Chloe can take advantage of the widow's election tax planning device. Should they also attempt to utilize a widow's election—consideration offset scheme? Even if you don't think that Greg and Chloe should utilize the widow's election—consideration offset, please draft the dispositive provisions appropriate to implement such a scheme.

The facts to be used in preparing your memorandum are set out in my previous memorandum. (Refer to Project 3.)

Reference: EP & D, ¶¶ 11,901–11,977.

Project 6

POWERS OF APPOINTMENT (basic)

MEMORANDUM

To: Associates' Pool

From: Mr. Longhours

Greg UpScalle and his wife Chloe have expressed a great deal of mutual trust and affection for one another. It is clear that each of them wants their respective property to pass to the survivor of them and, if none, to their children. It is also clear that some tax planning should be in order for Greg and Chloe.

While it appears that the UpScalles are inclined to make modest gifts to their children, it does not appear that they are prepared to embark on a major gift-giving program. For that reason, it must be assumed that they want to retain effective control over their respective property interests. In that case, it would seem that minimum tax planning would consist of sheltering in a bypass trust that portion of their property which is equal to the exemption equivalent to the unified credit (applicable exclusion amount, § 2010(c))) available to the first of them to die. See EP & D, Chapters 13 and 18. As I see it, the problem is how to draft the trust for the survivor to insure that the trust property will be excused from the survivor's gross estate and, at the same time, give the survivor such control over the trust property that he or she will feel as little restriction as possible in the use of the trust property.

The UpScalles present what I feel will be an increasingly common fact pattern. Greg wants Chloe to have everything, but tax saving considerations may warrant the use of trusts. He is little concerned about professional management or protecting the property from a second spouse. In this kind of case, each spouse is happy to see the other spouse be the trustee of the bypass trust. Can this be done?

With these considerations in mind, will one of you please prepare all necessary dispositive provisions for a trust with Chloe as trustee and beneficiary. Chloe is to have every possible power over the trust short of causing the trust property to be included in her gross estate at her death. (The $5,000–5% withdrawal power has always held a special fascination for me and, given the UpScalles' interest in providing the survivor of them with maximum control over the bypass trust, consider whether such a provision should be offered to them for inclusion in the documents we prepare for them. See §§ 2514(e), 2041(b)(2). Also, see in general, EP & D ¶ 18,275 and 19,435.)

The survivor of Chloe and Greg is also to have power to dispose of the trust property at his or her death to the extent possible. (For example, if Chloe is the survivor, would it be possible to give her the power at her death to appoint the trust property to anyone in the world except herself, her estate, her creditors or the creditors of her estate and still keep the trust property out of her estate?)

The kind of provision(s) which would be appropriate here can be found as the dispositive provisions for the proposed Upscalle Bypass Trust [found in Article 6 that is a part of Attachment 1 to Project 3—*Ed.*]. (You will note that the Upscalle document is a two-grantor or joint trust; you may wish to create separate trusts for Greg and Chloe after considering the relative merits of both. Either way, the bypass trust should be largely the same.)

It would seem to me that you must draft the provision(s) and then describe the tax consequences of each aspect of the provision(s). Your analysis must be supported by references to statutes, cases and rulings. (Essentially, you are being asked to critique the proposed Upscalle Bypass Trust found in attachment 1 to Project 3.)

The facts to be used in preparing your memorandum are set out in my previous memorandum. (Refer to Project 3—*Ed.*)

Reference: EP & D, Chapter 18.

Project 7

GIFTS TO MINORS (basic)

MEMORANDUM

To: Associates' Pool

From: Mr. Longhours

1.   Will one of you prepare a memorandum (addressed to me as supervising attorney) recommending the form which Greg and Chloe UpScalle should use for making gifts to their minor children. You should also indicate which property should be the subject matter of the gift. Your memorandum should consider the respective advantages and disadvantages of the Uniform Gifts to Minors Act (UGMA), the Uniform Transfers to Minors Act (UTMA) and a minority trust. See, in general, EP & D, Chapter 19.

2.   Should the UpScalles consider making the children an interest-free loan? What kind of management device should they use? See EP & D ¶ 19,641.

3.   Wouldn't the best recommendation for the Greg and Chloe be for them to set up a so-called "529 plan"? Couldn't it tax advantageously take the place of gifts utilizing the Uniform Gifts to Minors Act or a minority trust under § 2503(c)? Detail the advantages and disadvantages of all options for me. In particular, look to the internet for a state-by-state comparison of the 529 plans. http://www.savingforcollege.com. See also Susan T. Bart, College planning Q & A, http://advisor. morningstar.com/ articles.

The facts to be used in preparing your memorandum are set out in my previous memorandum. (Refer to Project 3.)

Reference: EP & D, Chapter 19.

Project 8

LIFE INSURANCE (basic)

MEMORANDUM

To: Associates' Pool

From: Mr. Longhours

As I continue my review of the information provided by Greg and Chloe UpScalle, I note that Greg has life insurance. Given the present ownership of these policies, the proceeds will be included in Greg's gross estate at his death. Could one of you make some recommendations as to how we might avoid this result. I suppose we could recommend that Greg assign ownership of the policies to Chloe but that gets a bit untidy if Chloe dies first (particularly if her will gives everything to Greg and, as a result, he ends up with ownership of the policies). EP & D ¶ 20,523. However, I understand that it is becoming increasingly commonplace to recommend assignment of ownership of life insurance policies to a trustee under an irrevocable trust. EP & D ¶ 20,651 et. seq.

You should assume that Greg wants Chloe to be a beneficiary of any trust (that Greg may create) if she survives him and that he would like the proceeds to be available to pay death taxes. Your analysis must be supported by references to statutes, cases, and rulings.

The facts to be used in preparing your memorandum are set out in my previous memorandum. (Refer to Project 3.)

Reference: EP & D, Chapter 20.

Project 9

CLOSELY HELD BUSINESS INTERESTS (basic)

MEMORANDUM

To: Associates' Pool

From: Mr. Longhours

Greg UpScalle has interests in a shoe store and in a closely held corporation. Will one of you please value these interests for purposes of enabling me to estimate his federal estate tax obligation. EP & D ¶ 24,109 et seq. Give me a memorandum detailing your analysis and the basis for it, referring to applicable statutory, regulatory and judicial authority as well as scholarly writings.

I would also appreciate a short memorandum recommending an appropriate dispositive scheme for these business interests.

Background facts to be used in preparing your memorandum are developed in my previous memorandum. (Refer to Project 3.)

Reference: EP & D, Chapter 24.

Project 10

GIFTS TO CHARITY (basic)

MEMORANDUM

To: Associates' Pool

From: Mr. Longhours

I have just learned that Greg UpScalle was approached by a representative of the University of Advanced Learning with a request for a contribution. Apparently, Greg was quite impressed with the school's representation of the goals of the institution, and, without consulting us, he assigned ownership of some of his property to the school subject to an irrevocable trust under which Greg reserves an interest in the property for life. He has asked us to determine if he did the right thing.

I know little about charitable giving and would appreciate one of you giving me advice as to the income, estate, and gift tax consequences to Greg in this calendar year and the following years. EP & D ¶ 26,109 et seq. The trust agreement which appears as an attachment (Attachment 1 to Project 11—*Ed.*) seems to contain a lot of legalese. Can't this be simplified? Perhaps the more important question is: does it meet all the qualifications for the tax benefit that I would assume would be offered by this kind of gift to an educational institution. EP & D ¶ 26,125. What changes should we make in the document to give Greg maximum benefit from his gift? Can we make any changes?

At our meeting Greg UpScalle handed me the attached memorandum prepared by Santo (Sandy) Bisignano, Jr, an attorney in Dallas, Texas. Greg said that a fellow doctor had given him the copy. Apparently the memorandum was distributed at a continuing education seminar and found its way from doctor group to doctor group. The undated memorandum is entitled *Joint Spousal Charitable Remainder Trust (or "JSCRT")* (Attachment 2 to Project 10—*Ed.*) Greg says that he "wants to know if the memorandum has any application" to his situation—but what he really wants to know is whether there is a deal here (by which he can profit) that has not heretofore been suggested to him.

Background facts to be used in preparing your memorandum are developed in my previous memorandum. (Refer to Project 3—*Ed.*)

Reference: EP & D, Chapter 26.

Attachment 1 to PROJECT 10

CHARITABLE UNITRUST FOUNDATION

Created By: Greg Upscalle

Greg UpScalle, Donor, hereby gives and transfers the assets listed on Exhibit A, which is attached hereto and made a part hereof, to the University of Advanced Learning, as Trustee, for the uses and purposes hereinafter set forth.

The Trustee agrees to hold the corpus hereof and any reinvestment thereof pursuant to the terms of this instrument of trust in and as an irrevocable unitrust.

1.   The Trustee shall pay to the Donor, Greg UpScalle, for and during his natural life, in installments not less frequently than quarter annually, an amount equal to Five per cent (5%) of the net fair market value of the corpus of this trust, re-evaluated annually as hereinafter set forth. The annual amount of trust income so to be paid (as determined under Section 643(b) of the Internal Revenue Code, as amended and the regulations thereunder) shall be such trust income to the extent that the amount thereof is not more than the amount determined by applying the applicable percentage hereinabove set forth to the net fair market value of the trust assets as determined annually in each year; provided, however, that if the aggregate of the amounts of trust income paid in prior years is less than the aggregate of the amounts required to be paid hereunder, then the trust income shall be paid, if such trust income is in excess of the amount required to be paid for such year, but not in an amount greater than the aggregate of such deficiency in required payments for prior years.

2.   In the event that Chloe UpScalle, wife of the Donor, survives the Donor, the Trustee shall pay to Chloe UpScalle for and during her natural life, in installments not less frequently than quarter annually, an amount equal to Five per cent (5%) of the net fair market value of the corpus of this trust, reevaluated annually as hereinafter set forth. The annual amount of trust income so to be paid (as determined under Section 643(b) of the Internal Revenue Code, as amended and the regulations thereunder) shall be such trust income to the extent that the amount thereof is not more than the amount determined by applying the applicable percentage hereinabove set forth to the net fair market value of the trust assets as determined annually in each year; provided, however, that if the aggregate of the amounts of trust income paid in prior years is less than the aggregate of the amounts required to be paid hereunder, then the trust income shall be paid, if such trust income is in excess of the amount required to be paid for such year, but not in an amount greater than the aggregate of such deficiency in required payments for prior years.

3. In annually computing the net fair market value of the trust assets, there shall be taken into account all accrued assets and accrued liabilities of the trust. The net fair market value of trust assets shall be determined on any one date during the taxable year of the trust or by taking the average of the valuations made on more than one date during the taxable year of the trust, all as determined by the Trustee; provided, however, that the same valuation date or dates and methods shall be used each year. Except as provided in Paragraph (e) of I.R.S. Regulation Section 1.664–1 (relating to short taxable years), the amount of trust income payable under Paragraphs 1 and 2 hereof during each taxable year of the trust (including the first and the last taxable years regardless of whether those taxable years are for a period of less than twelve months) shall either be paid within each such taxable year of the trust or in any event within two and one-half months after the close of the taxable year of such trust. If in any year the net fair market value of trust assets is incorrectly determined, the Trustee shall pay to the recipient, in the case of an undervaluation, or be repaid by the recipient, in the case of an overvaluation, an amount equal to the difference in the amount which the Trustee should have paid if the correct value had been used, and the amount which the Trustee actually paid, such amount to be paid by the Trustee or by the recipient, as the case may be, within a reasonable period after the final determination of such value.

4. In the event of additional contributions to this trust, then for the purpose of the taxable year of the trust in which any such additional contribution is made, the following rules shall be followed by the Trustee:

(1) In the case where there is no valuation date after the time of the contribution, the additional property shall be valued at the time of contribution, and

(2) The amount of trust income payable for such year shall be computed by multiplying the fixed percentage referred to in Paragraphs 1 and 2 of this trust agreement by the sum of

(a) the net fair market value of the trust's assets (excluding the additional property as of the valuation date, including any income from and any appreciation of such property) and

(b) that proportion of the value of the additional property contributed (that was excluded under subdivision (a) hereof) which the number of days (excluding the day of transfer) remaining in the taxable year of the trust bears to the total number of days in that taxable year of the trust.

5. The terms of this Paragraph 5 shall be subject always to the restrictions and limitations imposed by Paragraph 6 hereof. The trust fund shall be invested and re-invested in the discretion of the Trustee in such assets as it deems appropriate and the Trustee is hereby expressly exempt from the provisions of all state property laws and regulations pertaining to the nature and character of investments by Trustees. Said Trustee, in its discretion, may invest in obligations the yield of which is exempt from federal income taxation or in any other form of securities, irrespective of whether evidencing a debtor-

creditor relationship to the issuer or a proprietary interest therein; provided, however, that no investment shall be made in mutual funds issued by regulated investment companies. Subject to the provisions of Section 643(b) of the Internal Revenue Code, as amended, and the regulations thereunder, the Trustee in determining distributable trust income hereunder shall be governed by the standards of applicable state property law pertaining thereto in like or similar circumstances; provided, however, that at no time shall principal, or any portion thereof, or any profit or loss resulting from any change in form of principal ever be considered as distributable net income.

6. The Trustee shall comply with and otherwise observe all of the pertinent rules imposed by Section 664 of the Internal Revenue Code of 1954, as amended, and all regulations and rulings pertaining thereto. The trust income for each taxable year of the trust shall be distributed at such time and in such manner as not to subject this trust to tax under Section 4942 of the Internal Revenue Code of 1954, as amended, and the applicable regulations thereunto pertaining. This trust is prohibited from engaging in any act of self-dealing as defined in Section 4941(d) of the Internal Revenue Code of 1954, as amended. In addition, this trust is prohibited from retaining any excess business holdings, if any there should be, as defined in Section 4943(c) of the Internal Revenue Code of 1954, as amended, and from making any investments in such manner as to subject this trust to tax under Section 4944 of the Internal Revenue Code of 1954, as amended, and also from making any taxable expenditures as defined in Section 4945(d) of the Internal Revenue Code of 1954, as amended. The Trustee shall not make any investments which jeopardize the charitable purpose as herein set forth as defined in Section 4944 of the Internal Revenue Code of 1954, as amended. As applicable, the Trustee shall comply with all of the mandates and interdictions imposed by the Internal Revenue Code of 1954, as amended, including, but not limited to, Sections 170, 508, 2055, 2106, 2622 and 4947, together with any and all supplements in respect thereof as may from time to time exist.

7. Unless from time to time required by the income beneficiary, said Trustee shall be exempt and excused from complying with the trust accounting requirements imposed by any law or regulation, state or federal, but the Trustee shall make reasonable periodic accountings, not more frequently than semi-annually, to the income beneficiary.

8. This trust shall terminate upon the demise of the last to die as between the Donor and his said spouse. Thereupon the principal and any then undistributed income shall be and become a part of the general funds of the University of Advanced Learning to be used as its appropriate governing body shall deem advisable in the best interests of the advancement of the educational aims and undertakings of the University of Advanced Learning. In the event that the University of Advanced Learning is not an organization described in Section 170(c) of the Internal Revenue Code of 1954, as amended, at the time when the distribution to the University of Advanced Learning is required pursuant to the terms of this paragraph 8, the distribution of corpus hereunder, as herein required, shall be distributed to the United States of America.

9. This trust shall be irrevocable from and after the moment when it becomes effective, and no person or party shall have any power whatsoever

and shall forever be without any power at any time to revoke, alter, amend or terminate this trust or any of the provisions thereof.

10. Reference is made to any prior charitable trust foundations created by the undersigned Donor and entered into by and between the Donor and the University of Advanced Learning.

The present writing, in addition to creating a trust under the terms herein set forth, shall constitute an amendment to such prior charitable trust foundations insofar as paragraph 6 of this instrument is concerned and said paragraph 6 shall be deemed a full and complete amendment in respect of such previously created trust foundations.

IN WITNESS WHEREOF, the parties respectively have hereunto caused to be subscribed their respective hands, effective December 31, 20__.

/s/Greg UpScalle

GREG UPSCALLE, Donor

UNIVERSITY OF ADVANCED LEARNING

AS TRUSTEE AFORESAID

By /s/ Learned Leeder, President

EXHIBIT A

December 31, 20__

20 Shs. Touchright, Inc.

100 Shs. AT&T

Attachment 2 to PROJECT 10

JOINT SPOUSAL CHARITABLE REMAINDER TRUST (or "JSCRT")
"A Great Technique for the Charitably Inclined Couple"

by

Santo (Sandy) Bisignano, Jr.

What is a Joint Spousal Charitable Remainder Trust? A joint spousal charitable remainder trust ("JSCRT") is an irrevocable trust that pays an "income interest" to the donor and the donor's spouse for their joint lifetime, and a remainder interest to a designated charity.

Example. George Generous (age 60) and Geraldine Generous (age 58) transfer 100,000 shares of X Corporation common stock (worth $10 per share) to a charitable remainder trust. X Corporation is publicly traded on the New York Stock Exchange and pays a very low dividend of 10¢ per share. George's and Geraldine's basis in the stock is zero. Under the terms of the trust, 7% of the net fair market value of the trust, as annually determined, is to be paid to George and Geraldine while they are both alive, and 100% of that amount is to be paid to the survivor for his or her lifetime. Upon the death of the last to die of George and Geraldine, the trust will terminate and the property shall be distributed to the University of Notre Dame. After the gift, the Trustee sells the stock and invests the proceeds in a manner that increases the trust by about 10% per year.

What are the Income Tax Consequences to the JSCRT if it Sells the X Corporation Common Stock? Charitable remainder trusts are exempt from income tax. Accordingly, if and when the trustee of the JSCRT sells the X Corporation common stock, no gain will be recognized by the trust.

What are the Income, Gift, and Estate Tax Consequences to George and Geraldine of Establishing the Joint Spousal Charitable Remainder Trust?

1. *Income Tax Consequences.* George and Geraldine will be entitled to a federal income tax charitable deduction equal to $186,721. This is equal to the present actuarial value of the remainder interest passing to Notre Dame.

In addition, when George and Geraldine receive each income payment, that amount will be taxable to them as income. The character of that income is based on a tier system. Thus, the distribution to George and Geraldine will be taxable as ordinary income to the extent of current and accumulated ordinary income in the trust, and then to the extent of current and accumulated capital gains. In short, while the trust is not taxable on any retained income, the distribution will "carry out" income to George and Geraldine based on this tier system.

2. *Gift Tax Consequences.* There are no adverse gift tax consequences to George and Geraldine upon the establishment of the trust. The entire amount transferred to the trust will qualify either for the federal gift tax charitable deduction or federal gift tax marital deduction.

3. *Estate Tax Consequences.* There are no adverse estate tax consequences to George and Geraldine upon the death of either of them.

Can George and/or Geraldine be the Sole Trustee(s) of the JSCRT? Yes.

What are the Costs Associated With the Establishment of a JSCRT? The following costs are associated with the establishment of a joint spousal charitable remainder trust:

a. The cost to draft and implement the trust document; and

b. Annual tax return preparation fee.

What Has Happened to George's and Geraldine's Income Stream? Assuming that the trustee makes prudent investments, George's and Geraldine's income stream from the stock has increased by seven-fold. Before the gift, they received $10,000 per year in dividends. After the gift, they receive $70,000 in the first year.

What Happens to the Income Stream if the Trust Increases or Decreases in Value? It will increase or decrease as well.

Project 11

PERSONAL RESIDENCE TRUSTS AND OTHER "GRAT" IDEAS (advanced)

MEMORANDUM

To: Associates' Pool

From: Mr. Longhours

Greg UpScalle is concerned about creditors and wants to be, as he says, "asset free". He also driven by his fear of taxes and wants to limit his death tax liability by giving his property to his children at the earliest opportunity.

The background facts are developed in my previous memorandum. (Refer to the facts in Project 3—*Ed.*)

Please look over Greg and Chloe's property picture and see if you have any suggestions. For example, could Greg and Chloe be tax advantaged by a gift of their personal residence and their vacation property to the children immediately? Of course, there would need to be an understanding that Greg and Chloe or the survivor of them could live there so long as they wished.

Alternatively, is there other property which could form the basis of a tax advantaged scheme. Consider, in this regard, particularly the attached undated memoranda (Attachments 1 and 2 to Project 11—Ed). Greg, I believe, will be "taken with" the idea of anything expressed in terms of "zero tax."

Please come up with a strategy—at least for discussion purposes and consideration by Greg and Chloe—and give me a memorandum which I will be able to use as a basis for my advice to Greg and Chloe when we meet. If a particular strategy seems workable, please prepare the appropriate instruments to accompany your memorandum.

What advantage, if any, is there in a two-life GRAT?

Reference: EP & D, Chapter 12.

ZERO GIFT TAX GRANTOR RETAINED ANNUITY TRUST
("Zero Tax GRAT")

By

Santo (Sandy) Bisignano, Jr.

What is a GRAT? A grantor-retained annuity trust (or "GRAT") is an irrevocable trust that pays a level amount to the grantor each year for a specified term of years. After that term of years expires, the assets of the trust are paid to the remainder beneficiaries who are usually the grantor's children (or trusts for their benefit).

> *Example.* George Generous (age 50) transfers 100,000 shares of X Corporation common stock, worth $10 per share, to a 15–year GRAT. The GRAT is required to pay $60,000 [of cash or property] to George each year over the 15–year term of the trust. When the trust terminates (15 years after its inception), whatever remains in the trust after the last payment, is paid to George's children, George, Jr., Gerald, Ginger and Ginny.

What are the Gift Tax Consequences to George of His Gift to the GRAT? When George gives the $1 million of X Corporation stock to the GRAT, he is deemed to have made a gift to the GRAT equal to $1 million minus the present actuarial value of the $60,000 per year income stream. The tax laws require that this $60,000 per year distribution be discounted by an IRS-approved discount rate in effect at the time of the transfer. If at the time of the transfer the IRS rate is 7%, the present value of the $60,000 per year income stream is $531,402. Therefore, the value of the gift is $468,598 ($1 million minus $531,402). This gift does not qualify for the $10,000 gift tax exclusion because it is a gift of a remainder interest.

What are the Income Tax Consequences to the Grantor of the $60,000 Annual Distributions? Under current tax laws, the GRAT would be taxed as a grantor trust. This means all of the income from the trust would be taxable to the grantor. Because of this fact, there are no further income tax consequences to the grantor when the $60,000 distribution is made to him. In fact, if in any year the GRAT earns less than $60,000, only that lesser amount shall be taxed to the grantor.

Must the $60,000 Distribution to the Grantor be a Cash Distribution? No. Any property, including $60,000 of X Corporation common stock, can be distributed to the grantor in satisfaction of the annual $60,000 distribution. Furthermore, there are no adverse tax consequences in distributing this stock back to the grantor.

What is a Zero Tax GRAT? A "Zero Tax GRAT" is just like the GRAT described above except the level annuity amount is set high enough so there are little or no gift tax consequences when the transfer is made.

> *Example.* George Generous transfers $1 million to a 15–year GRAT. Under the GRAT, George is to receive $110,000 [of cash and/or property]

each year. The present value of George's retained 15–year income stream (of $110,000 per year), using an assumed IRS prescribed rate of 7% is $974,237. Therefore, George is deemed to have made a gift to the GRAT equal to $25,763 (i.e., $1 million minus $974,237).

How Can a Zero Tax GRAT be Useful in Transferring Property to George's Children at Little or No Gift Tax Cost? If the assets in George's GRAT grow at a rate greater than 7% upon the termination of the GRAT, there will be assets in the trust that pass to George's children at little or no gift tax cost.

> *Example.* George Generous transfers $1,000,000 cash to a 15–year Zero Tax GRAT. George is to receive distributions equal to $110,000 per year. The cash is invested in securities and those securities grow at the rate of 15% per year. When the GRAT terminates (15 years later), and after the last annuity payment is made to George, there are $1,605,833 of securities remaining in the trust. This amount passes to George, Jr., Gerald, Ginger and Ginny for an adjusted taxable gift of $25,763.

What Happens if the Annual Return is Less Than or Equal to 7%? In the example immediately above, there will be very little in the trust when it terminates.

What Happens if George Dies During the Term of the Trust? Most, if not all, of the GRAT will be includable in George's estate for federal estate tax purposes. However, any unified credit used up by George will be fully restored. Therefore, the transaction would truly be a "heads I win, tails I break even" proposition.

Can George be the Sole Trustee of His GRAT? Yes.

What Costs are Associated With the Establishment of a GRAT? The following costs are associated with the establishment of a Zero Tax GRAT:

1. The cost to draft and implement the trust document;

2. Appraisal fees to value the property transferred to the GRAT and the value of the property transferred from the GRAT to the grantor (zero cost if readily marketable securities are owned by the GRAT);

3. Annual tax return preparation fee (nominal since GRAT is a grantor trust and all income tax to the grantor during the term of the GRAT);

4. One-time gift tax preparation fee.

What Procedures Should be Followed in Establishing the Zero Tax GRAT? The following simple steps should be followed with a Zero Tax GRAT that owns publicly traded securities:

1. Draft and fund GRAT;

2. Establish two brokerage accounts, one in the name of the GRAT and the other in the name of the grantor;

3. Once a year (on the same date each year) transfer the level annuity amount from the GRAT's brokerage account to the grantor's brokerage account; and

4. After the GRAT terminates, distribute the remaining property to the remainder beneficiaries.

QUALIFIED PERSONAL RESIDENCE TRUSTS

By

Santo (Sandy) Bisignano, Jr.

What is a QPRT? A qualified personal residence trust (or "QPRT") is an irrevocable and unamendable trust that generally owns the personal residence or vacation home of the grantor (i.e., the individual who created the trust and transferred the home to the trust). The QPRT lasts for a specified term of years. During that term, the grantor has the full use, benefit and enjoyment of the home. After the term of years expires, the home is typically transferred to the grantor's children or to trusts for their benefit.

> *Example.* George Generous (age 50) transfers his Santa Fe, New Mexico, vacation home to a 15–year QPRT. The vacation home is currently worth $1,000,000 and is located in a very desireable area of Santa Fe that is expected to have significant appreciation. During the term of the QPRT, George has the exclusive use and enjoyment of the home. If George outlives the 15–year term, the home will be distributed to George's children, George, Jr., Gerald, Ginger and Ginny.

What are the Gift Tax Consequences to George of His Gift to the QPRT? When George gives the $1,000,000 Santa Fe home to the QPRT, he has made a gift to the QPRT equal to $1,000,000 minus the present actuarial value of his right to continue to use and enjoy the home for 15 years. The IRS provides a table to use in calculating this value and the IRS further requires that in calculating this value, an IRS approved discount rate be used. If at the time of the transfer, the IRC Sec. 7520 rate is 5%, the present value of George's right to use the $1,000,000 home for 15 years is $585,900. Therefore, the value of George's gift is $414,100 ($1,000,000 minus $585,900). This gift does not qualify for the $12,000 gift tax exclusion because it is a gift of remainder interest.

What are the Gift Tax Advantages of the QRPT if George Outlives the Term of the Trust? The QPRT can have substantial gift tax advantages especially if the property grows in value.

> *Example.* Assume that under the earlier example, the Santa Fe home grows at a rate of 10% per year. At the end of the QPRT term, the value of the home is $4,177,248. This means that for a gift of $414,100 in value, George has transferred to his children property worth nearly $4,177,248. Had George retained the property, the home would have been subject to a 45% estate tax.

What Happens if George Dies During the Term of the Trust? The Santa Fe home will be includable in George's estate for federal estate tax purposes at the fair market value at the time of his death. However, any unified credit George used up will be fully restored. Therefore, the transaction would truly be a "heads I win, tails I break even" proposition.

Can George be the Sole Trustee of His QPRT? Yes.

Can George continue to use and enjoy the Santa Fe home after the trust term expires and his children own the property? Yes, if he pays his children fair rental for the property. The rent payments further reduce George's estate without the payment of any transfer taxes.

What is the Leverage Factor of the Above Example? Based on the above example, the "leverage factor" would be about "10 to 1" at a 10% growth rate, and about "5 to 1" at a 5% growth rate.

Project 12

FAMILY LIMITED PARTNERSHIPS (advanced)

MEMORANDUM

To: Associates' Pool

From: Mr. Longhours

Greg and Chloe UpScalle have attended a succession of "free" seminars on family limited partnerships. They even took a course on the subject offered at the community college. I suspect that they really don't understand the device but, as matters stand, they are some how of the opinion—admittedly somewhat tongue-in-cheek—that failure to create a family limited partnership is a form of child abuse for which they should be prosecuted. (Perhaps, more importantly, they think that any lawyer who fails to put each of his or her clients with taxable estates into a limited partnership is guilty of malpractice.) When I asked, "What is it that appeals to you about the limited partnership?", Greg and Chloe, almost in unison, said it is the "50% discount you get for estate tax purposes." (Their enthusiasm was so great that I almost expected them to begin chanting: "Discount! Discount! Discount!") Chloe tossed a undated memorandum (Attachment to Project 12—*Ed.*) at me, saying "Here. Look at this."

The UpScalles want to put "all their property", i.e., their stocks, bonds, shoe store, and shares of Touchright, Inc., into the partnership. All I could say was, "Wow!"

I need a memorandum from you detailing the availability, appropriateness, advantages, and disadvantages of a family limited partnership for the UpScalle family. Give me a draft of such an agreement—setting out, for the time being—only the principle provisions—for my consideration, detailing the income, gift, and estate consequences that flow from your draft.

Reference: EP & D, ¶¶ 21,201–21,250.

———

Attachment to PROJECT 12

DISCOUNTED GIFTS, ASSET MANAGEMENT AND ASSET PROTECTION WITH FAMILY LIMITED PARTNERSHIPS

By

Santo (Sandy) Bisignano, Jr.

WHAT IS A FAMILY LIMITED PARTNERSHIP?

A family limited partnership is a business and/or investment arrangement between grandparents, parents, children and/or grandchildren. Often the partnership owns investment assets. Typically, a member of the family's senior generation is the general partner and all others are limited partners.

> *Example.* George and Geraldine Generous own, as community property, oil and gas royalty interests having a total fair market value of $4,000,000. These royalties generate approximately $600,000 of annual royalty payments. George and Geraldine have sufficient funds from other resources to live comfortably for the rest of their lives. Accordingly, George and Geraldine would like to transfer all these royalty interests in equal shares to their four children. They would also like to create a business structure involving these royalties that would (1) facilitate the ongoing management of the royalties and any investments made with the royalty payments and (2) promote family interaction and family unity. George and Geraldine currently make all day-today decisions regarding the royalties and personally interface with the oil and gas operators. However, George and Geraldine would someday like to delegate part (or perhaps all) of that responsibility to one or more of their children.

STRUCTURE AND FUNDING OF THE PARTNERSHIP:

1. **Formation of Generous Reources, Ltd.** George and Geraldine form Generous Resources, Ltd. ("GRL"), a family limited partnership. George and Geraldine contribute the $4 million royalties to the partnership in return for two 49.5% limited partnership interests (one for George and one for Geraldine) and two 0.5% general partnership interests (one for George and one for Geraldine). George is also designated the Managing General Partner of GRL.

2. **Identity of Partners Immediately After Funding**. After the formation and capitalization of GRL, ownership is as follows:

Name of Partner	Type of Interest	% Interest
George	GP	0.5%
Geraldine	GP	0.5%
George	LP	49.5%
Geraldine	LP	49.5%

IMPORTANT TERMS OF PARTNERSHIP AND RELEVANT PARTNERSHIP LAW:

1. G & G, as general partner, controls and manages the partnership and is personally liable for partnership activities.

2. The limited partners have no personal liability for partnership activities, but in return for this limitation on liability, they have little or no say over how the partnership is managed or when distribution should be made.

3. The general partner can be removed with the approval of 80% in interest of the limited partners.

4. A partner cannot transfer his or her interest in the partnership outside the family without triggering a "fair market value" buy back right.

5. The partnership cannot be dissolved except by consent of all of the partners.

6. An assignee of a limited partnership interest will not be admitted as a substitute limited partner unless the consent of all partners is obtained.

THE GIFTS: Two months after GRL is formed and capitalized, George and Geraldine collectively give a 24.75% limited partnership interest to each child (99% total transfer). After the gifts, ownership of GPL is as follows:

Name of Partner	Type of Interest	% Interest
George	GP	0.5%
Geraldine	GP	0.5%
George, Jr.	LP	24.75%
Gerald	LP	24.75%
Ginger	LP	24.75%
Ginny	LP	24.75%
Total		100%

Each child is also admitted as a substitute limited partner.

WHAT HAS BEEN ACCOMPLISHED?

1 All income earned on the gifted partnership interests will be removed from George's and Geraldine's estates for federal estate tax purposes.

2. Ninety-nine percent of the appreciation in the royalties will be removed from George's and Geraldine's estates for federal estate tax purposes.

3. $1,386,000 in value of the partnership will immediately pass to the children gift tax free! In other words, 99% of a $4,000,000 partnership has been given away, but for gift tax purposes the gift is only worth $2,574,000.

Explanation: At first blush, when George and Geraldine transferred a 24.75% limited partnership interest to each child, for a total transfer of 99% of the partnership, it would appear that the total value of what was transferred was $3,960,000 (i.e., 99% of the $4,000,000 partnership). But that is not the way to look at it. The way you should look at it. Instead you should determine the "fair market value" of a gift of a 24.75% limited partnership interest and then multiply that result by four (because there are four gifts).

In determining the value of a 24.75% limited partnership interest in GRL, you should ask yourself what would a reasonable person pay for a 24.75% limited partnership interest in GRL? Would he or she pay $990,000 (i.e., 24.75% multiplied by the $4,000,000 of the partnership assets)? I believe that reasonable person would not pay any more than $643,500—i.e., you would discount the value by 35%. This is because the 24.75% interest is not marketable and represents a minority interest in GRL.

A $643,500 gift to each child totals $2,574,000. This amount utilizes all of George's and Geraldine's combined $2 million gift tax applicable exclusion amount. Gift tax must be paid on the excess—at a rate of 46 percent in 2006! (Of course, if the discount were greater than 35%.... (Or the value of the property transferred to the partnership were less....) Oh, well, you can't have everything.)

4. Control of the partnership rests with those who have an interest in and are capable of managing it.

5. If a partner has financial reversals and his partnership interest and stock are seized by a creditor, the creditor will find he has seized rather ugly and cumbersome assets.

Explanation: Ten years after formation and capitalization of GRL, it is now worth $10,000,000. Unfortunately, Ginny, a lawyer, is unjustly sued for malpractice and a "hometown outlaw jury" returns a $5,000,000 judgment against her that is upheld on appeal and not covered by malpractice insurance. The creditor seizes Ginny's partnership interest. So what does the creditor own? Answer: A 24½% assignee interest in a family owned and controlled partnership.

Here are some other questions you might have:

a. Can the creditor reach partnership assets? Answer: No.

b. Can the creditor vote on partnership matters: Answer: No, the creditor is not a partner. He is an assignee.

c. What can the creditor receive? Answer: A pro rata share of partnership distributions if and when made; and he can enforce this right in court through a charging order.

d. Do you think the creditor might be willing to sell his assignee interest and his stock for a substantial discount? Answer: What do you think?

e. Could the same results have been achieved if the partnership owned a portfolio of marketable securities rather than royalties? Answer: In my judgment, yes.

*

Topical Index

References are to paragraph (¶) numbers

†